OSW

OFFICIAL SCRABBLE® WORDS

OSW

OFFICIAL SCRABBLE® WORDS

Third edition

Managing editor

Catherine Schwarz

Chambers

Scrabble® is a registered trademark owned in the USA
and Canada by Milton Bradley Company, Massachusetts,
and elsewhere by J W Spear and Sons PLC,
Enfield, Middlesex EN3 7TB, UK.

CHAMBERS
An imprint of Larousse plc
43–45 Annandale Street
Edinburgh EH7 4AZ

This edition first published by Chambers 1994

First edition by W & R Chambers Ltd 1988
Second edition 1990

10 9 8 7 6 5 4 3 2

A CIP catalogue record for this book
is available from the British Library

ISBN 0 550 19043 0

The publishers wish to acknowledge the computing help
of Peter Schwarz in the compilation and revision of
Official Scrabble® Words.

Typeset by In Production Ltd, Edinburgh
Printed in England by Clays Ltd, St Ives plc

Preface to third edition

This new edition of *Official Scrabble® Words* (OSW) is the definitive work which will save family arguments in social games and enable challenges to be dealt with swiftly and effectively in Scrabble Clubs and tournaments. Publication in August 1993 of a major new edition of *The Chambers Dictionary*, the authority on which OSW is based, made it necessary to produce this, the third, edition of OSW.

J W Spear and Sons PLC and Chambers (now part of Larousse plc) have had a close relationship dating from Spear's decision to adopt Chambers Dictionary for their 1980 Championships. *Chambers* is loved by Scrabble players throughout most of the English-speaking world because of the rich fund of useful Scrabble words it contains. It is complementary to OSW, and should be consulted when you want to check the meaning of a word.

Because of the scale of changes in the 1993 edition of the Dictionary, a complete review of all the words in it was required for OSW. I should like to thank the Main Committee, many of whom have been involved in producing all three editions of OSW, and of course Catherine Schwarz and her colleagues at Chambers, for their painstaking work. Special thanks is also due to the Initial Adjudicating Committee, both in the UK and in Victoria, Australia, for their dedication in highlighting the areas of change.

I am sure that this latest edition of OSW, with the many new words it contains, will add to the enjoyment and satisfaction that you obtain from playing Scrabble.

Francis A Spear
Chairman
J W Spear and Sons PLC

Main committee

Darryl Francis, *London Scrabble League*
Philip Nelkon, *Manager, National Scrabble Clubs* and *Committee Chairman*
Terry Kirk, *London Scrabble League*
Ian Gucklhorn, *London Scrabble League*
Allan Simmons, *Association of Premier Scrabble Players*
Jim Warmington, *Australian Scrabble Players Association*

Initial adjudicating committee

UK

Steve Ablitt-Jones, *Croydon Scrabble Club*
Amy Byrne, *Edinburgh Scrabble Club*
Jackie Fallows, ——
John Grayson, *Newport Scrabble Club*
Raye Green, *Leicester Scrabble Club*
Mary Grylls, *Grantham Scrabble Club*
Ash Haji, *London Scrabble League*
Dorothy Harrison, *Plymouth Scrabble Club*
Josef Kollar, *Hythe Scrabble Club*
Hartley Moorhouse, *London Scrabble Club*
Roy Upton, *Derby Scrabble Club*

Victoria, Australia

Roger Blom, *Camberwell Scrabble Club*
June Ferndale, *Camberwell Scrabble Club*
Ruth Fewings, *Bendigo Scrabble Club*
Meg Henderson, *Camberwell Scrabble Club*
Alistair Kane, *Dandenong Scrabble Club*
Margaret Warmington, *Camberwell Scrabble Club*

Introduction

This third edition of *Official Scrabble® Words* is based on *The Chambers Dictionary* (1993), the latest in a long line of Chambers dictionaries. All words listed in that dictionary are permitted in Scrabble except:

> those only spelt with an initial capital letter;
> abbreviations and symbols;
> prefixes and suffixes;
> those requiring apostrophes and hyphens.

Official Scrabble Words (OSW) lists, and is the official authority for, all allowable words of up to 9 letters long and their inflections (plurals, etc). For longer words, *The Chambers Dictionary* is the authority. A number of words listed in *Chambers,* and hence in OSW, may be offensive to some people, or may not conform to 'political correctness'. These words are however part of the English language, which the Dictionary naturally reflects. We therefore have not followed the American Scrabble movement in disallowing such words for Scrabble.

Every relevant entry in *Chambers* has been thoroughly examined and considered for inclusion in OSW. Derivative forms have been carefully considered too, and appropriate inflections – plurals, verb forms, and comparatives and superlatives – have been included. Many new words have been added to the dictionary, and there have been other changes: some words have changed or augmented their labels (both part-of-speech and classification), some have changed their hyphenation or capitalization status, others have moved on from being abbreviations – all resulting in about 8000 new entries in this edition of OSW. Inevitably such changes, along with other Dictionary judgements, have resulted in deletions from the previous edition of OSW; there are about 900 of these.

In the compilation of this edition of OSW, a small number of errors were found in *The Chambers Dictionary*. Those confirmed by the publisher have not been perpetuated in OSW.

Allowable words

This edition of *Official Scrabble Words* is the final authority on allowed Scrabble words where the uninflected form of the word is up to 9 letters long. It is based on the 1993 edition of *The Chambers Dictionary*. All words listed in that dictionary are permitted in Scrabble except for those in the categories mentioned above.

It should be noted that entries which are labelled 'symbol' (for example AU, FF) are now, as well as abbreviations, barred from Scrabble use.

One particular entry in OSW worthy of special mention is PH. Since in the Dictionary the capitalized letter is not the initial letter, and since PH is deemed not to be an abbreviation or a symbol, it has been included here, along with its plural PHS.

The approaches that have been taken to various groups of words in this edition of OSW are explained below.

Accents

Accents have been dropped from this edition of *Official Scrabble Words*. As there are no accented letters in English-language Scrabble sets, it was felt unnecessary to retain accents in OSW. Where *The Chambers Dictionary* shows a word with an accent, the accent has been ignored in OSW.

Adverbs

Adverbs have been included in *Official Scrabble Words* if they are included in *Chambers*. No attempt has been made to include adverbial forms which are not explicitly shown in the Dictionary.

Comparatives and Superlatives

We have included a wide range of comparatives and superlatives in *Official Scrabble Words*. We have considered the possible comparative and superlative forms of all adjectives in OSW, and we have based our final selection on a range of criteria. These have included commonness or familiarity of the adjective, number of syllables, meaning, and whether the adjective is dialect, obsolete or foreign. We also took into account the euphony of the -ER and -EST forms, current usage, and listings in other dictionaries.

We cannot say that we have applied a mechanical formula in deciding which comparatives and superlatives to include. We have allowed the -IER and -IEST forms of most one- and two-syllable adjectives ending in -Y, and some of three syllables, but not all. We have excluded comparative and superlative forms of obsolete and archaic adjectives ending in -Y. We have not excluded the comparative and superlative forms of all adjectives of three syllables or more – some have been included. We have not excluded the comparatives and superlatives of all adjectives ending with certain specific groups of letters, such as -ATE, -ENT, -ETE and -ID. Again, some have been included.

Definitions

A feature of this new edition of *Official Scrabble Words* is a separate appendix containing the 2- and 3-letter words, with basic definitions, intended as aids in memorizing these important Scrabble words. For fuller treatment of these words, and to know the meaning of any other word in OSW, *The Chambers Dictionary* should be consulted.

Foreign Words

Foreign words appearing in *The Chambers Dictionary* have been included in *Official Scrabble Words*. Where a specific plural form appears in *Chambers,* we have included only that form. Where no plural is shown in the dictionary, we have used our judgement, and the appropriate plural form has been included. In some instances, this will be a foreign plural; in others, it will be an English plural (usually the addition of an -S). Occasionally, both types of plural will be included. Do be aware that not all plural forms in OSW are explicitly shown in *Chambers*. For example, as no plural form is shown in the dictionary for STERNUM, we have included both of the plural forms STERNA and STERNUMS.

Interjections

Interjections are treated not as nouns, but as parts of speech which do not permit plurals. In *Official Scrabble Words*, an interjection has no inflected forms, unless explicitly indicated in *Chambers*. A plural is only allowed if an interjection is also shown to be a noun; and verb forms are only allowed if an interjection is shown to be a verb. Some examples:

AW, QUOTHA and UM are interjections only, so no inflected forms are allowed;
EH is an interjection and a verb, so the inflected verb forms EHS, EHED and EHING are allowed;
OOH is an interjection, verb and noun, so the verb forms OOHS, OOHED and OOHING are allowed; OOHS is also the plural form of the noun.

If Chambers quite clearly lists a plural form of an interjection (for example, as at LO and OHO), then that is allowable.

Letters and letter sounds

Names of letters and letter sounds appearing in *The Chambers Dictionary* are included in *Official Scrabble Words*, as there is nothing in the rules of Scrabble to bar the use of such words. Accordingly, OSW lists familiar letter names (for example, AITCH, MU, NU and XI) as well as unfamiliar ones (for example, SAMPI, SAN, VAU and WYNN). Their plural forms are also included.

Obsolete words

Obsolete words are included in *Official Scrabble Words*, along with many of their relevant inflected forms (such as plurals and verb inflections). We have included plurals of obsolete nouns. We have included verb inflections of obsolete verbs. We have not included comparative and superlative forms of obsolete adjectives. We have not included derivatives of obsolete words, unless explicitly shown in *Chambers*. (For example, BROACH and BROACHER are both allowable words, and BROCH is in the dictionary as an obsolete spelling of BROACH – so BROACH, BROACHER and BROCH are all allowable, but we have not included BROCHER.)

Words marked in *Chambers* as being from the works of Shakespeare, Spenser and Milton have been treated in the same way as obsolete words.

Order of words

All the words in *Official Scrabble Words* are listed in strict alphabetical sequence, regardless of length. It is important to bear this in mind, particularly when checking the validity of plurals. For example:

the plural of FAD is not listed immediately after FAD but is shown at its correct alphabetical place between FADOS and FADY;

to determine whether FAB has a plural or not, it is necessary to check between the entries FABRICS and FABULAR. It is not listed there, so FABS is not allowed.

Plurals

With few exceptions, we have included in *Official Scrabble Words* the plurals of all nouns. Plural forms have been shown for all nouns ending in -ISM, -ITY and -NESS; while these plurals may be little used in regular English, all are available for use if needed in the English language. We have also included the plural forms of chemicals, chemical elements, minerals, man-made materials, natural materials, fibres, drugs, gases, rocks, oils, vitamins, enzymes, diseases, illnesses and the like.

This edition of OSW sees the inclusion of many more foreign plural forms than were in the previous edition. For many words, there are now two plural forms – an English plural and a foreign plural (for example, STERNUMS and STERNA). However, some words that previously only had an -S plural now only have a foreign plural. Where the compilers have found no evidence for these -S forms, only the foreign plurals are now included. For example, the plural of ANCILE is now only ANCILIA, although previously it was only ANCILES.

Word lengths

Official Scrabble Words users may well want to understand what criteria have been employed in considering word lengths. In compiling OSW we began by listing all the valid but uninflected words of length up to (and including) 9 letters. We then allowed the relevant inflections of these (namely plurals, verb forms, and comparatives and superlatives), resulting in words up to 13 letters long. (It is possible for a 9-letter verb to double a final consonant before adding -ING, giving 13 letters in all!) Here are some examples:

the 9-letter noun CACODEMON gives rise to the 10-letter plural CACODEMONS;

the 9-letter noun CACOPHONY gives rise to the 11-letter plural CACOPHONIES;

the 9-letter noun CANTHARIS gives rise to the 11-letter plural CANTHARIDES;

the 9-letter verb CALCULATE gives rise to these verb inflections: CALCULATED, CALCULATES and CALCULATING, having 10 or 11 letters;

the 8-letter verb CARBURET gives rise to these verb inflections: CARBURETS, CARBURETTED and CARBURETTING, having 9, 11 or 12 letters.

If any inflected form of a 9-letter word is also a singular noun in its own right, then a plural form of that noun is also included. For example:

the 9-letter verb CATERWAUL gives rise to these verb inflections: CATERWAULS, CATERWAULED and CATERWAULING; but since CATERWAULING is also shown in *Chambers* as a noun, the plural form of CATERWAULINGS has been included here;

the 8-letter verb CROSSCUT gives rise to these verb inflections: CROSSCUTS and CROSSCUTTING; but since CROSSCUTTING is also shown in *Chambers* as a noun, the plural form CROSSCUTTINGS has been included here.

There are a few instances of 9-letter adjectives which add an -S to become 10-letter nouns. For example, CANONICAL thus becomes CANONICALS, which is included. For convenience in adjudication, other similar cases are treated likewise: for example, the adverbs EARTHWARD and EARTHWARDS are both included.

There are instances of singular nouns having more than 9 letters, but with plurals of 9 letters or less. The singulars have not been included here, but the plurals have. For example, the singular AUDITORIUM has 10 letters, so hasn't been included, but its plural AUDITORIA has 9 letters, so is included.

Official Scrabble Words will not answer every possible query regarding the validity of words. Remember that for words longer than 9 letters, and their inflected forms, you will have to turn to *The Chambers Dictionary*. For example, AUDITORIUM, mentioned above, is perfectly valid for use in Scrabble; it's just that it isn't included here. There are plenty of other 10-15 letter words that could be played legitimately in Scrabble, and are in *Chambers*.

A

AA	ABATOR	ABEAR	ABILITY	ABNORMOUS
AARDVARK	ABATORS	ABEARING	ABIOSES	ABOARD
AARDVARKS	ABATTIS	ABEARS	ABIOSIS	ABODE
AARDWOLF	ABATTOIR	ABED	ABIOTIC	ABODED
AARDWOLVES	ABATTOIRS	ABEIGH	ABJECT	ABODEMENT
AAS	ABATTU	ABELE	ABJECTED	ABODEMENTS
AASVOGEL	ABATURE	ABELES	ABJECTING	ABODES
AASVOGELS	ABATURES	ABELIA	ABJECTION	ABODING
ABA	ABAXIAL	ABELIAS	ABJECTIONS	ABOIDEAU
ABAC	ABAYA	ABERRANCE	ABJECTLY	ABOIDEAUS
ABACA	ABAYAS	ABERRANCES	ABJECTS	ABOIL
ABACAS	ABB	ABERRANCIES	ABJOINT	ABOITEAU
ABACI	ABBA	ABERRANCY	ABJOINTED	ABOITEAUS
ABACK	ABBACIES	ABERRANT	ABJOINTING	ABOLISH
ABACS	ABBACY	ABERRATE	ABJOINTS	ABOLISHED
ABACTINAL	ABBAS	ABERRATED	ABJURE	ABOLISHES
ABACTOR	ABBATIAL	ABERRATES	ABJURED	ABOLISHING
ABACTORS	ABBE	ABERRATING	ABJURER	ABOLITION
ABACUS	ABBES	ABESSIVE	ABJURERS	ABOLITIONS
ABACUSES	ABBESS	ABESSIVES	ABJURES	ABOLLA
ABAFT	ABBESSES	ABET	ABJURING	ABOLLAE
ABALONE	ABBEY	ABETMENT	ABLATE	ABOLLAS
ABALONES	ABBEYS	ABETMENTS	ABLATED	ABOMASA
ABAMPERE	ABBOT	ABETS	ABLATES	ABOMASAL
ABAMPERES	ABBOTS	ABETTAL	ABLATING	ABOMASI
ABAND	ABBOTSHIP	ABETTALS	ABLATION	ABOMASUM
ABANDED	ABBOTSHIPS	ABETTED	ABLATIONS	ABOMASUS
ABANDING	ABBS	ABETTER	ABLATIVAL	ABOMASUSES
ABANDON	ABCEE	ABETTERS	ABLATIVE	ABOMINATE
ABANDONED	ABCEES	ABETTING	ABLATIVES	ABOMINATED
ABANDONEE	ABDABS	ABETTOR	ABLATOR	ABOMINATES
ABANDONEES	ABDICABLE	ABETTORS	ABLATORS	ABOMINATING
ABANDONING	ABDICANT	ABEYANCE	ABLAUT	ABONDANCE
ABANDONS	ABDICATE	ABEYANCES	ABLAUTS	ABONDANCES
ABANDS	ABDICATED	ABEYANCIES	ABLAZE	ABORAL
ABAS	ABDICATES	ABEYANCY	ABLE	ABORD
ABASE	ABDICATING	ABEYANT	ABLED	ABORDED
ABASED	ABDICATOR	ABHOR	ABLER	ABORDING
ABASEMENT	ABDICATORS	ABHORRED	ABLES	ABORDS
ABASEMENTS	ABDOMEN	ABHORRENT	ABLEST	ABORE
ABASES	ABDOMENS	ABHORRER	ABLET	ABORIGEN
ABASH	ABDOMINA	ABHORRERS	ABLETS	ABORIGENS
ABASHED	ABDOMINAL	ABHORRING	ABLING	ABORIGIN
ABASHEDLY	ABDUCE	ABHORRINGS	ABLINS	ABORIGINE
ABASHES	ABDUCED	ABHORS	ABLOOM	ABORIGINES
ABASHING	ABDUCENT	ABID	ABLOW	ABORIGINS
ABASHLESS	ABDUCES	ABIDANCE	ABLUSH	ABORNE
ABASHMENT	ABDUCING	ABIDANCES	ABLUTION	ABORNING
ABASHMENTS	ABDUCT	ABIDDEN	ABLUTIONS	ABORT
ABASING	ABDUCTED	ABIDE	ABLY	ABORTED
ABASK	ABDUCTEE	ABIDED	ABNEGATE	ABORTING
ABATABLE	ABDUCTEES	ABIDES	ABNEGATED	ABORTION
ABATE	ABDUCTING	ABIDING	ABNEGATES	ABORTIONS
ABATED	ABDUCTION	ABIDINGLY	ABNEGATING	ABORTIVE
ABATEMENT	ABDUCTIONS	ABIDINGS	ABNEGATOR	ABORTS
ABATEMENTS	ABDUCTOR	ABIES	ABNEGATORS	ABORTUARIES
ABATES	ABDUCTORS	ABIGAIL	ABNORMAL	ABORTUARY
ABATING	ABDUCTS	ABIGAILS	ABNORMITIES	ABOUGHT
ABATIS	ABEAM	ABILITIES	ABNORMITY	ABOULIA

The Chambers Dictionary is the authority for many longer words; see *OSW* Introduction, page xii.

ABOULIAS	ABRUPTLY	ABSORBERS	ABUTMENTS	ACARIDEAN
ABOUND	ABRUPTS	ABSORBING	ABUTS	ACARIDEANS
ABOUNDED	ABSCESS	ABSORBS	ABUTTAL	ACARIDIAN
ABOUNDING	ABSCESSED	ABSTAIN	ABUTTALS	ACARIDIANS
ABOUNDS	ABSCESSES	ABSTAINED	ABUTTED	ACARIDS
ABOUT	ABSCIND	ABSTAINER	ABUTTER	ACARINE
ABOUTS	ABSCINDED	ABSTAINERS	ABUTTERS	ACAROID
ABOVE	ABSCINDING	ABSTAINING	ABUTTING	ACAROLOGIES
ABRADANT	ABSCINDS	ABSTAINS	ABUZZ	ACAROLOGY
ABRADANTS	ABSCISE	ABSTERGE	ABVOLT	ACARPOUS
ABRADE	ABSCISED	ABSTERGED	ABVOLTS	ACARUS
ABRADED	ABSCISES	ABSTERGES	ABY	ACATER
ABRADES	ABSCISIN	ABSTERGING	ABYE	ACATERS
ABRADING	ABSCISING	ABSTINENT	ABYEING	ACATES
ABRAID	ABSCISINS	ABSTRACT	ABYES	ACATOUR
ABRAIDED	ABSCISS	ABSTRACTED	ABYING	ACATOURS
ABRAIDING	ABSCISSA	ABSTRACTER	ABYSM	ACAUDAL
ABRAIDS	ABSCISSAE	ABSTRACTERS	ABYSMAL	ACAUDATE
ABRAM	ABSCISSAS	ABSTRACTEST	ABYSMALLY	ACAULINE
ABRASION	ABSCISSE	ABSTRACTING	ABYSMS	ACAULOSE
ABRASIONS	ABSCISSES	ABSTRACTS	ABYSS	ACCABLE
ABRASIVE	ABSCISSIN	ABSTRICT	ABYSSAL	ACCEDE
ABRASIVES	ABSCISSINS	ABSTRICTED	ABYSSES	ACCEDED
ABRAXAS	ABSCOND	ABSTRICTING	ACACIA	ACCEDENCE
ABRAXASES	ABSCONDED	ABSTRICTS	ACACIAS	ACCEDENCES
ABRAY	ABSCONDER	ABSTRUSE	ACADEME	ACCEDER
ABRAYED	ABSCONDERS	ABSTRUSER	ACADEMES	ACCEDERS
ABRAYING	ABSCONDING	ABSTRUSEST	ACADEMIA	ACCEDES
ABRAYS	ABSCONDS	ABSURD	ACADEMIAS	ACCEDING
ABRAZO	ABSEIL	ABSURDER	ACADEMIC	ACCEND
ABRAZOS	ABSEILED	ABSURDEST	ACADEMICS	ACCENDED
ABREACT	ABSEILING	ABSURDISM	ACADEMIES	ACCENDING
ABREACTED	ABSEILINGS	ABSURDISMS	ACADEMISM	ACCENDS
ABREACTING	ABSEILS	ABSURDIST	ACADEMISMS	ACCENSION
ABREACTS	ABSENCE	ABSURDISTS	ACADEMIST	ACCENSIONS
ABREAST	ABSENCES	ABSURDITIES	ACADEMISTS	ACCENT
ABREGE	ABSENT	ABSURDITY	ACADEMY	ACCENTED
ABREGES	ABSENTED	ABSURDLY	ACAJOU	ACCENTING
ABRICOCK	ABSENTEE	ABTHANE	ACAJOUS	ACCENTOR
ABRICOCKS	ABSENTEES	ABTHANES	ACALEPH	ACCENTORS
ABRIDGE	ABSENTING	ABULIA	ACALEPHAN	ACCENTS
ABRIDGED	ABSENTLY	ABULIAS	ACALEPHANS	ACCENTUAL
ABRIDGER	ABSENTS	ABUNA	ACALEPHE	ACCEPT
ABRIDGERS	ABSEY	ABUNAS	ACALEPHES	ACCEPTANT
ABRIDGES	ABSEYS	ABUNDANCE	ACALEPHS	ACCEPTANTS
ABRIDGING	ABSINTH	ABUNDANCES	ACANTH	ACCEPTED
ABRIM	ABSINTHE	ABUNDANCIES	ACANTHA	ACCEPTER
ABRIN	ABSINTHES	ABUNDANCY	ACANTHAS	ACCEPTERS
ABRINS	ABSINTHS	ABUNDANT	ACANTHIN	ACCEPTING
ABROACH	ABSIT	ABUNE	ACANTHINE	ACCEPTIVE
ABROAD	ABSITS	ABURST	ACANTHINS	ACCEPTOR
ABROADS	ABSOLUTE	ABUSAGE	ACANTHOID	ACCEPTORS
ABROGATE	ABSOLUTES	ABUSAGES	ACANTHOUS	ACCEPTS
ABROGATED	ABSOLVE	ABUSE	ACANTHS	ACCESS
ABROGATES	ABSOLVED	ABUSED	ACANTHUS	ACCESSARIES
ABROGATING	ABSOLVER	ABUSER	ACANTHUSES	ACCESSARY
ABROGATOR	ABSOLVERS	ABUSERS	ACAPNIA	ACCESSED
ABROGATORS	ABSOLVES	ABUSES	ACAPNIAS	ACCESSES
ABROOKE	ABSOLVING	ABUSING	ACARI	ACCESSING
ABROOKED	ABSONANT	ABUSION	ACARIAN	ACCESSION
ABROOKES	ABSORB	ABUSIONS	ACARIASES	ACCESSIONED
ABROOKING	ABSORBATE	ABUSIVE	ACARIASIS	ACCESSIONING
ABRUPT	ABSORBATES	ABUSIVELY	ACARICIDE	ACCESSIONS
ABRUPTER	ABSORBED	ABUT	ACARICIDES	ACCESSORIES
ABRUPTEST	ABSORBENT	ABUTILON	ACARID	ACCESSORY
ABRUPTION	ABSORBENTS	ABUTILONS	ACARIDAN	ACCIDENCE
ABRUPTIONS	ABSORBER	ABUTMENT	ACARIDANS	ACCIDENCES

The Chambers Dictionary is the authority for many longer words; see *OSW* Introduction, page xii.

ACCIDENT	ACCOUNTS	ACEDIA	ACHIEVED	ACME
ACCIDENTS	ACCOURAGE	ACEDIAS	ACHIEVER	ACMES
ACCIDIE	ACCOURAGED	ACELLULAR	ACHIEVERS	ACMITE
ACCIDIES	ACCOURAGES	ACER	ACHIEVES	ACMITES
ACCINGE	ACCOURAGING	ACERATE	ACHIEVING	ACNE
ACCINGED	ACCOURT	ACERB	ACHILLEA	ACNES
ACCINGES	ACCOURTED	ACERBATE	ACHILLEAS	ACOCK
ACCINGING	ACCOURTING	ACERBATED	ACHIMENES	ACOEMETI
ACCIPITER	ACCOURTS	ACERBATES	ACHING	ACOLD
ACCIPITERS	ACCOUTER	ACERBATING	ACHINGLY	ACOLUTHIC
ACCITE	ACCOUTERED	ACERBER	ACHINGS	ACOLYTE
ACCITED	ACCOUTERING	ACERBEST	ACHKAN	ACOLYTES
ACCITES	ACCOUTERS	ACERBIC	ACHKANS	ACOLYTH
ACCITING	ACCOUTRE	ACERBITIES	ACHROMAT	ACOLYTHS
ACCLAIM	ACCOUTRED	ACERBITY	ACHROMATS	ACONITE
ACCLAIMED	ACCOUTRES	ACEROSE	ACHY	ACONITES
ACCLAIMING	ACCOUTRING	ACEROUS	ACICULAR	ACONITIC
ACCLAIMS	ACCOY	ACERS	ACICULATE	ACONITINE
ACCLIMATE	ACCOYED	ACERVATE	ACID	ACONITINES
ACCLIMATED	ACCOYING	ACES	ACIDER	ACONITUM
ACCLIMATES	ACCOYLD	ACESCENCE	ACIDEST	ACONITUMS
ACCLIMATING	ACCOYS	ACESCENCES	ACIDFREAK	ACORN
ACCLIVITIES	ACCREDIT	ACESCENCIES	ACIDFREAKS	ACORNED
ACCLIVITY	ACCREDITED	ACESCENCY	ACIDIC	ACORNS
ACCLIVOUS	ACCREDITING	ACESCENT	ACIDIFIED	ACOSMISM
ACCLOY	ACCREDITS	ACETABULA	ACIDIFIER	ACOSMISMS
ACCLOYED	ACCRETE	ACETAL	ACIDIFIERS	ACOSMIST
ACCLOYING	ACCRETED	ACETALS	ACIDIFIES	ACOSMISTS
ACCLOYS	ACCRETES	ACETAMIDE	ACIDIFY	ACOUCHI
ACCOAST	ACCRETING	ACETAMIDES	ACIDIFYING	ACOUCHIES
ACCOASTED	ACCRETION	ACETATE	ACIDITIES	ACOUCHIS
ACCOASTING	ACCRETIONS	ACETATES	ACIDITY	ACOUCHY
ACCOASTS	ACCRETIVE	ACETIC	ACIDLY	ACOUSTIC
ACCOIED	ACCREW	ACETIFIED	ACIDNESS	ACOUSTICS
ACCOIL	ACCREWED	ACETIFIES	ACIDNESSES	ACQUAINT
ACCOILS	ACCREWING	ACETIFY	ACIDOSES	ACQUAINTED
ACCOLADE	ACCREWS	ACETIFYING	ACIDOSIS	ACQUAINTING
ACCOLADES	ACCRUAL	ACETONE	ACIDS	ACQUAINTS
ACCOMPANIED	ACCRUALS	ACETONES	ACIDULATE	ACQUEST
ACCOMPANIES	ACCRUE	ACETOSE	ACIDULATED	ACQUESTS
ACCOMPANY	ACCRUED	ACETOUS	ACIDULATES	ACQUIESCE
ACCOMPANYING	ACCRUES	ACETYL	ACIDULATING	ACQUIESCED
ACCOMPT	ACCRUING	ACETYLENE	ACIDULENT	ACQUIESCES
ACCOMPTED	ACCUMBENT	ACETYLENES	ACIDULOUS	ACQUIESCING
ACCOMPTING	ACCURACIES	ACETYLS	ACIERAGE	ACQUIGHT
ACCOMPTS	ACCURACY	ACH	ACIERAGES	ACQUIGHTING
ACCORAGE	ACCURATE	ACHAENIA	ACIERATE	ACQUIGHTS
ACCORAGED	ACCURSE	ACHAENIUM	ACIERATED	ACQUIRAL
ACCORAGES	ACCURSED	ACHAENIUMS	ACIERATES	ACQUIRALS
ACCORAGING	ACCURSES	ACHAGE	ACIERATING	ACQUIRE
ACCORD	ACCURSING	ACHAGES	ACIFORM	ACQUIRED
ACCORDANT	ACCURST	ACHARNE	ACING	ACQUIRES
ACCORDED	ACCUSABLE	ACHARYA	ACINI	ACQUIRING
ACCORDER	ACCUSAL	ACHARYAS	ACINIFORM	ACQUIST
ACCORDERS	ACCUSALS	ACHATES	ACINOSE	ACQUISTS
ACCORDING	ACCUSE	ACHE	ACINOUS	ACQUIT
ACCORDION	ACCUSED	ACHED	ACINUS	ACQUITE
ACCORDIONS	ACCUSER	ACHENE	ACKEE	ACQUITES
ACCORDS	ACCUSERS	ACHENES	ACKEES	ACQUITING
ACCOST	ACCUSES	ACHENIA	ACKERS	ACQUITS
ACCOSTED	ACCUSING	ACHENIAL	ACKNEW	ACQUITTAL
ACCOSTING	ACCUSTOM	ACHENIUM	ACKNOW	ACQUITTALS
ACCOSTS	ACCUSTOMED	ACHENIUMS	ACKNOWING	ACQUITTED
ACCOUNT	ACCUSTOMING	ACHES	ACKNOWN	ACQUITTING
ACCOUNTED	ACCUSTOMS	ACHIER	ACKNOWNE	ACRAWL
ACCOUNTING	ACE	ACHIEST	ACKNOWS	ACRE
ACCOUNTINGS	ACED	ACHIEVE	ACLINIC	ACREAGE

The Chambers Dictionary is the authority for many longer words; see *OSW* Introduction, page xii.

ACREAGES

ACREAGES	ACTINIDE	ACULEATE	ADDERWORT	ADENOIDAL
ACRED	ACTINIDES	ACULEATED	ADDERWORTS	ADENOIDS
ACRES	ACTINISM	ACULEI	ADDICT	ADENOMA
ACRID	ACTINISMS	ACULEUS	ADDICTED	ADENOMAS
ACRIDER	ACTINIUM	ACUMEN	ADDICTING	ADENOMATA
ACRIDEST	ACTINIUMS	ACUMENS	ADDICTION	ADENOSINE
ACRIDIN	ACTINOID	ACUMINATE	ADDICTIONS	ADENOSINES
ACRIDINE	ACTINOIDS	ACUMINATED	ADDICTIVE	ADEPT
ACRIDINES	ACTINON	ACUMINATES	ADDICTS	ADEPTER
ACRIDINS	ACTINONS	ACUMINATING	ADDING	ADEPTEST
ACRIDITIES	ACTINS	ACUMINOUS	ADDIO	ADEPTLY
ACRIDITY	ACTION	ACUPOINTS	ADDIOS	ADEPTNESS
ACRIMONIES	ACTIONED	ACUSHLA	ADDITION	ADEPTNESSES
ACRIMONY	ACTIONING	ACUSHLAS	ADDITIONS	ADEPTS
ACROBAT	ACTIONIST	ACUTE	ADDITIVE	ADEQUACIES
ACROBATIC	ACTIONISTS	ACUTELY	ADDITIVES	ADEQUACY
ACROBATICS	ACTIONS	ACUTENESS	ADDLE	ADEQUATE
ACROBATS	ACTIVATE	ACUTENESSES	ADDLED	ADERMIN
ACROGEN	ACTIVATED	ACUTER	ADDLEMENT	ADERMINS
ACROGENIC	ACTIVATES	ACUTES	ADDLEMENTS	ADESPOTA
ACROGENS	ACTIVATING	ACUTEST	ADDLES	ADESSIVE
ACROLEIN	ACTIVATOR	ACYCLIC	ADDLING	ADESSIVES
ACROLEINS	ACTIVATORS	ACYCLOVIR	ADDOOM	ADHARMA
ACROLITH	ACTIVE	ACYCLOVIRS	ADDOOMED	ADHARMAS
ACROLITHS	ACTIVELY	ACYL	ADDOOMING	ADHERE
ACROMIA	ACTIVISM	ACYLS	ADDOOMS	ADHERED
ACROMIAL	ACTIVISMS	AD	ADDORSED	ADHERENCE
ACROMION	ACTIVIST	ADAGE	ADDRESS	ADHERENCES
ACRONICAL	ACTIVISTS	ADAGES	ADDRESSED	ADHERENT
ACRONYCAL	ACTIVITIES	ADAGIO	ADDRESSEE	ADHERENTS
ACRONYM	ACTIVITY	ADAGIOS	ADDRESSEES	ADHERER
ACRONYMIC	ACTON	ADAMANT	ADDRESSER	ADHERERS
ACRONYMS	ACTONS	ADAMANTLY	ADDRESSERS	ADHERES
ACROPETAL	ACTOR	ADAMANTS	ADDRESSES	ADHERING
ACROPHONIES	ACTORS	ADAPT	ADDRESSING	ADHESION
ACROPHONY	ACTRESS	ADAPTABLE	ADDRESSOR	ADHESIONS
ACROPOLIS	ACTRESSES	ADAPTED	ADDRESSORS	ADHESIVE
ACROPOLISES	ACTS	ADAPTER	ADDREST	ADHESIVES
ACROSOME	ACTUAL	ADAPTERS	ADDS	ADHIBIT
ACROSOMES	ACTUALISE	ADAPTING	ADDUCE	ADHIBITED
ACROSPIRE	ACTUALISED	ADAPTION	ADDUCED	ADHIBITING
ACROSPIRES	ACTUALISES	ADAPTIONS	ADDUCENT	ADHIBITS
ACROSS	ACTUALISING	ADAPTIVE	ADDUCER	ADIABATIC
ACROSTIC	ACTUALIST	ADAPTOR	ADDUCERS	ADIAPHORA
ACROSTICS	ACTUALISTS	ADAPTORS	ADDUCES	ADIEU
ACROTER	ACTUALITIES	ADAPTS	ADDUCIBLE	ADIEUS
ACROTERIA	ACTUALITY	ADAW	ADDUCING	ADIEUX
ACROTERS	ACTUALIZE	ADAWED	ADDUCT	ADIOS
ACROTISM	ACTUALIZED	ADAWING	ADDUCTED	ADIPOCERE
ACROTISMS	ACTUALIZES	ADAWS	ADDUCTING	ADIPOCERES
ACRYLIC	ACTUALIZING	ADAXIAL	ADDUCTION	ADIPOSE
ACRYLICS	ACTUALLY	ADAYS	ADDUCTIONS	ADIPOSITIES
ACT	ACTUARIAL	ADD	ADDUCTIVE	ADIPOSITY
ACTA	ACTUARIES	ADDAX	ADDUCTOR	ADIT
ACTABLE	ACTUARY	ADDAXES	ADDUCTORS	ADITS
ACTED	ACTUATE	ADDEBTED	ADDUCTS	ADJACENCIES
ACTIN	ACTUATED	ADDED	ADEEM	ADJACENCY
ACTINAL	ACTUATES	ADDEEM	ADEEMED	ADJACENT
ACTINALLY	ACTUATING	ADDEEMED	ADEEMING	ADJECTIVE
ACTING	ACTUATION	ADDEEMING	ADEEMS	ADJECTIVES
ACTINGS	ACTUATIONS	ADDEEMS	ADEMPTION	ADJOIN
ACTINIA	ACTUATOR	ADDEND	ADEMPTIONS	ADJOINED
ACTINIAE	ACTUATORS	ADDENDA	ADENINE	ADJOINING
ACTINIAN	ACTURE	ADDENDS	ADENINES	ADJOINS
ACTINIANS	ACTURES	ADDENDUM	ADENITIS	ADJOINT
ACTINIAS	ACUITIES	ADDER	ADENITISES	ADJOINTS
ACTINIC	ACUITY	ADDERS	ADENOID	ADJOURN

The Chambers Dictionary is the authority for many longer words; see *OSW* Introduction, page xii.

ADJOURNED ADMIXES ADRED ADVENED ADVOUTRERS
ADJOURNING ADMIXING ADRENAL ADVENES ADVOUTRIES
ADJOURNS ADMIXTURE ADRENALIN ADVENING ADVOUTRY
ADJUDGE ADMIXTURES ADRENALINS ADVENT ADVOWSON
ADJUDGED ADMONISH ADRENALS ADVENTIVE ADVOWSONS
ADJUDGES ADMONISHED ADRIFT ADVENTIVES ADWARD
ADJUDGING ADMONISHES ADROIT ADVENTS ADWARDED
ADJUNCT ADMONISHING ADROITER ADVENTURE ADWARDING
ADJUNCTLY ADMONITOR ADROITEST ADVENTURED ADWARDS
ADJUNCTS ADMONITORS ADROITLY ADVENTURES ADYNAMIA
ADJURE ADNASCENT ADRY ADVENTURING ADYNAMIAS
ADJURED ADNATE ADS ADVERB ADYNAMIC
ADJURES ADNATION ADSCRIPT ADVERBIAL ADYTA
ADJURING ADNATIONS ADSCRIPTS ADVERBS ADYTUM
ADJUST ADNOMINAL ADSORB ADVERSARIES ADZ
ADJUSTED ADNOUN ADSORBATE ADVERSARY ADZE
ADJUSTER ADNOUNS ADSORBATES ADVERSE ADZES
ADJUSTERS ADO ADSORBED ADVERSELY AE
ADJUSTING ADOBE ADSORBENT ADVERSER AECIA
ADJUSTOR ADOBES ADSORBENTS ADVERSEST AECIDIA
ADJUSTORS ADONISE ADSORBING ADVERSITIES AECIDIUM
ADJUSTS ADONISED ADSORBS ADVERSITY AECIUM
ADJUTAGE ADONISES ADSUM ADVERT AEDES
ADJUTAGES ADONISING ADULARIA ADVERTED AEDILE
ADJUTANCIES ADONIZE ADULARIAS ADVERTENT AEDILES
ADJUTANCY ADONIZED ADULATE ADVERTING AEFALD
ADJUTANT ADONIZES ADULATED ADVERTISE AEFAULD
ADJUTANTS ADONIZING ADULATES ADVERTISED AEGIRINE
ADJUVANCIES ADOORS ADULATING ADVERTISES AEGIRINES
ADJUVANCY ADOPT ADULATION ADVERTISING AEGIRITE
ADJUVANT ADOPTED ADULATIONS ADVERTISINGS AEGIRITES
ADJUVANTS ADOPTER ADULATOR ADVERTIZE AEGIS
ADLAND ADOPTERS ADULATORS ADVERTIZED AEGISES
ADLANDS ADOPTING ADULATORY ADVERTIZES AEGLOGUE
ADMAN ADOPTION ADULT ADVERTIZING AEGLOGUES
ADMASS ADOPTIONS ADULTERER ADVERTS AEGROTAT
ADMASSES ADOPTIOUS ADULTERERS ADVEW AEGROTATS
ADMEASURE ADOPTIVE ADULTERIES ADVEWED AEMULE
ADMEASURED ADOPTS ADULTERY ADVEWING AEMULED
ADMEASURES ADORABLE ADULTHOOD ADVEWS AEMULES
ADMEASURING ADORABLY ADULTHOODS ADVICE AEMULING
ADMEN ADORATION ADULTS ADVICEFUL AENEOUS
ADMIN ADORATIONS ADUMBRATE ADVICES AEOLIAN
ADMINICLE ADORE ADUMBRATED ADVISABLE AEOLIPILE
ADMINICLES ADORED ADUMBRATES ADVISABLY AEOLIPILES
ADMINS ADORER ADUMBRATING ADVISE AEOLIPYLE
ADMIRABLE ADORERS ADUNC ADVISED AEOLIPYLES
ADMIRABLY ADORES ADUNCATE ADVISEDLY AEON
ADMIRAL ADORING ADUNCATED ADVISER AEONIAN
ADMIRALS ADORINGLY ADUNCITIES ADVISERS AEONS
ADMIRANCE ADORN ADUNCITY ADVISES AERATE
ADMIRANCES ADORNED ADUNCOUS ADVISING AERATED
ADMIRE ADORNING ADUST ADVISINGS AERATES
ADMIRED ADORNMENT ADUSTED ADVISOR AERATING
ADMIRER ADORNMENTS ADUSTING ADVISORS AERATION
ADMIRERS ADORNS ADUSTS ADVISORY AERATIONS
ADMIRES ADOS ADVANCE ADVOCAAT AERATOR
ADMIRING ADOWN ADVANCED ADVOCAATS AERATORS
ADMISSION ADPRESS ADVANCES ADVOCACIES AERIAL
ADMISSIONS ADPRESSED ADVANCING ADVOCACY AERIALIST
ADMISSIVE ADPRESSES ADVANTAGE ADVOCATE AERIALISTS
ADMIT ADPRESSING ADVANTAGED ADVOCATED AERIALITIES
ADMITS ADRAD ADVANTAGES ADVOCATES AERIALITY
ADMITTED ADREAD ADVANTAGING ADVOCATING AERIALLY
ADMITTING ADREADED ADVECTION ADVOCATOR AERIALS
ADMIX ADREADING ADVECTIONS ADVOCATORS AERIE
ADMIXED ADREADS ADVENE ADVOUTRER AERIER

The Chambers Dictionary is the authority for many longer words; see *OSW* Introduction, page xii.

AERIES	AESC	AFFIDAVIT	AFFRENDED	AFTERNOON
AERIEST	AESCES	AFFIDAVITS	AFFRET	AFTERNOONS
AERIFORM	AESCULIN	AFFIED	AFFRETS	AFTERS
AERO	AESCULINS	AFFIES	AFFRICATE	AFTERTIME
AEROBE	AESIR	AFFILIATE	AFFRICATES	AFTERTIMES
AEROBES	AESTHESES	AFFILIATED	AFFRIGHT	AFTERWARD
AEROBIC	AESTHESIA	AFFILIATES	AFFRIGHTED	AFTERWARDS
AEROBICS	AESTHESIAS	AFFILIATING	AFFRIGHTING	AFTERWORD
AEROBIONT	AESTHESIS	AFFINE	AFFRIGHTS	AFTERWORDS
AEROBIONTS	AESTHETE	AFFINED	AFFRONT	AFTMOST
AEROBOMB	AESTHETES	AFFINES	AFFRONTE	AGA
AEROBOMBS	AESTHETIC	AFFINITIES	AFFRONTED	AGACANT
AEROBUS	AESTHETICS	AFFINITY	AFFRONTEE	AGACANTE
AEROBUSES	AESTIVAL	AFFIRM	AFFRONTING	AGACERIE
AERODART	AESTIVATE	AFFIRMANT	AFFRONTINGS	AGACERIES
AERODARTS	AESTIVATED	AFFIRMANTS	AFFRONTS	AGAIN
AERODROME	AESTIVATES	AFFIRMED	AFFUSION	AGAINST
AERODROMES	AESTIVATING	AFFIRMER	AFFUSIONS	AGALACTIA
AERODYNE	AETHER	AFFIRMERS	AFFY	AGALACTIAS
AERODYNES	AETHERS	AFFIRMING	AFFYDE	AGALLOCH
AEROFOIL	AETIOLOGIES	AFFIRMS	AFFYING	AGALLOCHS
AEROFOILS	AETIOLOGY	AFFIX	AFGHAN	AGAMI
AEROGRAM	AFALD	AFFIXED	AFGHANS	AGAMIC
AEROGRAMS	AFAR	AFFIXES	AFIELD	AGAMID
AEROGRAPH	AFARA	AFFIXING	AFIRE	AGAMIDS
AEROGRAPHS	AFARAS	AFFLATED	AFLAJ	AGAMIS
AEROLITE	AFAWLD	AFFLATION	AFLAME	AGAMOID
AEROLITES	AFEAR	AFFLATIONS	AFLATOXIN	AGAMOIDS
AEROLITH	AFEARD	AFFLATUS	AFLATOXINS	AGAMOUS
AEROLITHS	AFEARED	AFFLATUSES	AFLOAT	AGAPAE
AEROLITIC	AFEARING	AFFLICT	AFLUTTER	AGAPE
AEROLOGIES	AFEARS	AFFLICTED	AFOOT	AGAR
AEROLOGY	AFFABLE	AFFLICTING	AFORE	AGARIC
AEROMANCIES	AFFABLY	AFFLICTINGS	AFOREHAND	AGARICS
AEROMANCY	AFFAIR	AFFLICTS	AFORESAID	AGARS
AEROMETER	AFFAIRE	AFFLUENCE	AFORETIME	AGAS
AEROMETERS	AFFAIRES	AFFLUENCES	AFOUL	AGAST
AEROMETRIES	AFFAIRS	AFFLUENT	AFRAID	AGATE
AEROMETRY	AFFEAR	AFFLUENTS	AFREET	AGATES
AEROMOTOR	AFFEARD	AFFLUX	AFREETS	AGATEWARE
AEROMOTORS	AFFEARE	AFFLUXES	AFRESH	AGATEWARES
AERONAUT	AFFEARED	AFFLUXION	AFRIT	AGAVE
AERONAUTS	AFFEARES	AFFLUXIONS	AFRITS	AGAVES
AERONOMIES	AFFEARING	AFFOORD	AFRO	AGAZE
AERONOMY	AFFEARS	AFFOORDED	AFRONT	AGAZED
AEROPHOBE	AFFECT	AFFOORDING	AFROS	AGE
AEROPHOBES	AFFECTED	AFFOORDS	AFT	AGED
AEROPHONE	AFFECTER	AFFORCE	AFTER	AGEDNESS
AEROPHONES	AFFECTERS	AFFORCED	AFTERCARE	AGEDNESSES
AEROPHYTE	AFFECTING	AFFORCES	AFTERCARES	AGEE
AEROPHYTES	AFFECTION	AFFORCING	AFTERDECK	AGEING
AEROPLANE	AFFECTIONED	AFFORD	AFTERDECKS	AGEINGS
AEROPLANES	AFFECTIONING	AFFORDED	AFTEREYE	AGEISM
AEROS	AFFECTIONS	AFFORDING	AFTEREYED	AGEISMS
AEROSHELL	AFFECTIVE	AFFORDS	AFTEREYEING	AGEIST
AEROSHELLS	AFFECTS	AFFOREST	AFTEREYES	AGEISTS
AEROSOL	AFFEER	AFFORESTED	AFTEREYING	AGELAST
AEROSOLS	AFFEERED	AFFORESTING	AFTERGAME	AGELASTIC
AEROSPACE	AFFEERING	AFFORESTS	AFTERGAMES	AGELASTS
AEROSPACES	AFFEERS	AFFRAP	AFTERGLOW	AGELESS
AEROSTAT	AFFERENT	AFFRAPPED	AFTERGLOWS	AGELONG
AEROSTATS	AFFIANCE	AFFRAPPING	AFTERHEAT	AGEN
AEROTAXES	AFFIANCED	AFFRAPS	AFTERHEATS	AGENCIES
AEROTAXIS	AFFIANCES	AFFRAY	AFTERINGS	AGENCY
AEROTRAIN	AFFIANCING	AFFRAYED	AFTERMATH	AGENDA
AEROTRAINS	AFFICHE	AFFRAYING	AFTERMATHS	AGENDAS
AERY	AFFICHES	AFFRAYS	AFTERMOST	AGENE

The Chambers Dictionary is the authority for many longer words; see *OSW* Introduction, page xii.

AGENES
AGENT
AGENTED
AGENTIAL
AGENTING
AGENTIVE
AGENTIVES
AGENTS
AGERATUM
AGERATUMS
AGES
AGGER
AGGERS
AGGRACE
AGGRACED
AGGRACES
AGGRACING
AGGRADE
AGGRADED
AGGRADES
AGGRADING
AGGRATE
AGGRATED
AGGRATES
AGGRATING
AGGRAVATE
AGGRAVATED
AGGRAVATES
AGGRAVATING
AGGREGATE
AGGREGATED
AGGREGATES
AGGREGATING
AGGRESS
AGGRESSED
AGGRESSES
AGGRESSING
AGGRESSOR
AGGRESSORS
AGGRI
AGGRIEVE
AGGRIEVED
AGGRIEVES
AGGRIEVING
AGGRO
AGGROS
AGGRY
AGHA
AGHAS
AGHAST
AGILA
AGILAS
AGILE
AGILELY
AGILER
AGILEST
AGILITIES
AGILITY
AGIN
AGING
AGINGS
AGINNER
AGINNERS
AGIO
AGIOS
AGIOTAGE
AGIOTAGES

AGIST
AGISTED
AGISTER
AGISTERS
AGISTING
AGISTMENT
AGISTMENTS
AGISTOR
AGISTORS
AGISTS
AGITATE
AGITATED
AGITATES
AGITATING
AGITATION
AGITATIONS
AGITATIVE
AGITATO
AGITATOR
AGITATORS
AGITPROP
AGITPROPS
AGLEAM
AGLEE
AGLET
AGLETS
AGLEY
AGLIMMER
AGLITTER
AGLOW
AGMA
AGMAS
AGNAIL
AGNAILS
AGNAME
AGNAMED
AGNAMES
AGNATE
AGNATES
AGNATIC
AGNATICAL
AGNATION
AGNATIONS
AGNISE
AGNISED
AGNISES
AGNISING
AGNIZE
AGNIZED
AGNIZES
AGNIZING
AGNOMEN
AGNOMENS
AGNOMINA
AGNOMINAL
AGNOSIA
AGNOSIAS
AGNOSTIC
AGNOSTICS
AGO
AGOG
AGOGE
AGOGES
AGOGIC
AGOGICS
AGOING
AGON

AGONE
AGONIC
AGONIES
AGONISE
AGONISED
AGONISES
AGONISING
AGONIST
AGONISTES
AGONISTIC
AGONISTICS
AGONISTS
AGONIZE
AGONIZED
AGONIZES
AGONIZING
AGONS
AGONY
AGOOD
AGORA
AGORAS
AGOROT
AGOUTA
AGOUTAS
AGOUTI
AGOUTIES
AGOUTIS
AGOUTY
AGRAFFE
AGRAFFES
AGRAPHA
AGRAPHIA
AGRAPHIAS
AGRAPHIC
AGRAPHON
AGRARIAN
AGRASTE
AGRAVIC
AGREE
AGREEABLE
AGREEABLY
AGREED
AGREEING
AGREEMENT
AGREEMENTS
AGREES
AGREGE
AGREGES
AGREMENS
AGREMENT
AGREMENTS
AGRESTAL
AGRESTIAL
AGRESTIC
AGRIMONIES
AGRIMONY
AGRIN
AGRISE
AGRISED
AGRISES
AGRISING
AGRIZE
AGRIZED
AGRIZES
AGRIZING

AGROLOGIES
AGROLOGY
AGRONOMIC
AGRONOMICS
AGRONOMIES
AGRONOMY
AGROUND
AGRYZE
AGRYZED
AGRYZES
AGRYZING
AGUACATE
AGUACATES
AGUE
AGUED
AGUES
AGUISE
AGUISED
AGUISES
AGUISH
AGUISHLY
AGUISING
AGUIZE
AGUIZED
AGUIZES
AGUIZING
AGUTI
AGUTIS
AH
AHA
AHEAD
AHEAP
AHED
AHEIGHT
AHEM
AHENT
AHIGH
AHIMSA
AHIMSAS
AHIND
AHING
AHINT
AHOLD
AHORSE
AHOY
AHS
AHULL
AHUNGERED
AHUNGRY
AI
AIA
AIAS
AIBLINS
AID
AIDANCE
AIDANCES
AIDANT
AIDE
AIDED
AIDER
AIDERS
AIDES
AIDFUL
AIDING
AIDLESS
AIDOI
AIDOS

AIDS
AIERIES
AIERY
AIGLET
AIGLETS
AIGRETTE
AIGRETTES
AIGUILLE
AIGUILLES
AIKIDO
AIKIDOS
AIKONA
AIL
AILANTHUS
AILANTHUSES
AILANTO
AILANTOS
AILED
AILERON
AILERONS
AILETTE
AILETTES
AILING
AILMENT
AILMENTS
AILS
AIM
AIMED
AIMING
AIMLESS
AIMLESSLY
AIMS
AIN
AINE
AINEE
AIOLI
AIOLIS
AIR
AIRBASE
AIRBASES
AIRBORNE
AIRBURST
AIRBURSTS
AIRCRAFT
AIRDRAWN
AIRDROME
AIRDROMES
AIRED
AIRER
AIRERS
AIRFIELD
AIRFIELDS
AIRFLOW
AIRFLOWS
AIRFOIL
AIRFOILS
AIRFRAME
AIRFRAMES
AIRGAP
AIRGAPS
AIRGRAPH
AIRGRAPHS
AIRHEAD
AIRHEADS
AIRHOLE
AIRHOLES
AIRIER

The Chambers Dictionary is the authority for many longer words; see *OSW* Introduction, page xii.

AIRIEST	AIRY	ALAMODE	ALBINESSES	ALCOHOLS
AIRILY	AIS	ALAMODES	ALBINIC	ALCORZA
AIRINESS	AISLE	ALAMORT	ALBINISM	ALCORZAS
AIRINESSES	AISLED	ALAND	ALBINISMS	ALCOVE
AIRING	AISLES	ALANG	ALBINO	ALCOVES
AIRINGS	AISLING	ALANGS	ALBINOISM	ALDEA
AIRLESS	AISLINGS	ALANINE	ALBINOISMS	ALDEAS
AIRLIFT	AIT	ALANINES	ALBINOS	ALDEHYDE
AIRLIFTED	AITCH	ALANNAH	ALBINOTIC	ALDEHYDES
AIRLIFTING	AITCHBONE	ALANNAHS	ALBITE	ALDER
AIRLIFTS	AITCHBONES	ALAP	ALBITES	ALDERMAN
AIRLINE	AITCHES	ALAPA	ALBITIC	ALDERMEN
AIRLINER	AITS	ALAPAS	ALBITISE	ALDERN
AIRLINERS	AITU	ALAPS	ALBITISED	ALDERS
AIRLINES	AITUS	ALAR	ALBITISES	ALDOSE
AIRLOCK	AIZLE	ALARM	ALBITISING	ALDOSES
AIRLOCKS	AIZLES	ALARMED	ALBITIZE	ALDRIN
AIRMAIL	AJAR	ALARMEDLY	ALBITIZED	ALDRINS
AIRMAILED	AJEE	ALARMING	ALBITIZES	ALE
AIRMAILING	AJOWAN	ALARMISM	ALBITIZING	ALEATORIC
AIRMAILS	AJOWANS	ALARMISMS	ALBRICIAS	ALEATORIES
AIRMAN	AJUTAGE	ALARMIST	ALBS	ALEATORY
AIRMEN	AJUTAGES	ALARMISTS	ALBUGO	ALEBENCH
AIRN	AJWAN	ALARMS	ALBUGOS	ALEBENCHES
AIRNED	AJWANS	ALARUM	ALBUM	ALECOST
AIRNING	AKARYOTE	ALARUMED	ALBUMEN	ALECOSTS
AIRNS	AKARYOTES	ALARUMING	ALBUMENS	ALECTRYON
AIRPLANE	AKE	ALARUMS	ALBUMIN	ALECTRYONS
AIRPLANES	AKED	ALARY	ALBUMINS	ALEE
AIRPORT	AKEDAH	ALAS	ALBUMS	ALEFT
AIRPORTS	AKEDAHS	ALASTRIM	ALBURNOUS	ALEGAR
AIRS	AKEE	ALASTRIMS	ALBURNUM	ALEGARS
AIRSCREW	AKEES	ALATE	ALBURNUMS	ALEGGE
AIRSCREWS	AKENE	ALATED	ALCAHEST	ALEGGED
AIRSHAFT	AKENES	ALAY	ALCAHESTS	ALEGGES
AIRSHAFTS	AKES	ALAYED	ALCAIDE	ALEGGING
AIRSHIP	AKIMBO	ALAYING	ALCAIDES	ALEMBIC
AIRSHIPS	AKIN	ALAYS	ALCALDE	ALEMBICS
AIRSICK	AKINESES	ALB	ALCALDES	ALEMBROTH
AIRSIDE	AKINESIA	ALBACORE	ALCARRAZA	ALEMBROTHS
AIRSIDES	AKINESIAS	ALBACORES	ALCARRAZAS	ALENGTH
AIRSPACE	AKINESIS	ALBARELLI	ALCATRAS	ALEPH
AIRSPACES	AKING	ALBARELLO	ALCATRASES	ALEPHS
AIRSPEED	AKKAS	ALBARELLOS	ALCAYDE	ALEPINE
AIRSPEEDS	AKOLUTHOS	ALBATA	ALCAYDES	ALEPINES
AIRSTOP	AKOLUTHOSES	ALBATAS	ALCAZAR	ALERCE
AIRSTOPS	AKVAVIT	ALBATROSS	ALCAZARS	ALERCES
AIRSTREAM	AKVAVITS	ALBATROSSES	ALCHEMIC	ALERION
AIRSTREAMS	ALA	ALBE	ALCHEMIES	ALERIONS
AIRSTRIP	ALAAP	ALBEDO	ALCHEMISE	ALERT
AIRSTRIPS	ALAAPS	ALBEDOS	ALCHEMISED	ALERTED
AIRT	ALABAMINE	ALBEE	ALCHEMISES	ALERTER
AIRTED	ALABAMINES	ALBEIT	ALCHEMISING	ALERTEST
AIRTIGHT	ALABASTER	ALBERGHI	ALCHEMIST	ALERTING
AIRTIME	ALABASTERS	ALBERGO	ALCHEMISTS	ALERTLY
AIRTIMES	ALACK	ALBERT	ALCHEMIZE	ALERTNESS
AIRTING	ALACRITIES	ALBERTITE	ALCHEMIZED	ALERTNESSES
AIRTS	ALACRITY	ALBERTITES	ALCHEMIZES	ALERTS
AIRWARD	ALAE	ALBERTS	ALCHEMIZING	ALES
AIRWARDS	ALAIMENT	ALBESCENT	ALCHEMY	ALEURON
AIRWAVE	ALAIMENTS	ALBESPINE	ALCHERA	ALEURONE
AIRWAVES	ALALAGMOI	ALBESPINES	ALCHERAS	ALEURONES
AIRWAY	ALALAGMOS	ALBESPYNE	ALCHYMIES	ALEURONS
AIRWAYS	ALALIA	ALBESPYNES	ALCHYMY	ALEVIN
AIRWOMAN	ALALIAS	ALBICORE	ALCOHOL	ALEVINS
AIRWOMEN	ALAMEDA	ALBICORES	ALCOHOLIC	ALEW
AIRWORTHY	ALAMEDAS	ALBINESS	ALCOHOLICS	ALEWASHED

The Chambers Dictionary is the authority for many longer words; see *OSW* Introduction, page xii.

ALEWIFE	ALIASES	ALIT	ALLAYMENTS	ALLIES
ALEWIVES	ALIASING	ALIUNDE	ALLAYS	ALLIGARTA
ALEWS	ALIASINGS	ALIVE	ALLCOMERS	ALLIGARTAS
ALEXIA	ALIBI	ALIVENESS	ALLEDGE	ALLIGATE
ALEXIAS	ALIBIS	ALIVENESSES	ALLEDGED	ALLIGATED
ALEXIC	ALICANT	ALIYA	ALLEDGES	ALLIGATES
ALEXIN	ALICANTS	ALIYAH	ALLEDGING	ALLIGATING
ALEXINS	ALICYCLIC	ALIYAHS	ALLEE	ALLIGATOR
ALEYE	ALIDAD	ALIYAS	ALLEES	ALLIGATORS
ALEYED	ALIDADE	ALIZARI	ALLEGE	ALLIS
ALEYES	ALIDADES	ALIZARIN	ALLEGED	ALLISES
ALEYING	ALIDADS	ALIZARINE	ALLEGEDLY	ALLIUM
ALFA	ALIEN	ALIZARINES	ALLEGER	ALLIUMS
ALFALFA	ALIENABLE	ALIZARINS	ALLEGERS	ALLNESS
ALFALFAS	ALIENAGE	ALIZARIS	ALLEGES	ALLNESSES
ALFAQUI	ALIENAGES	ALKAHEST	ALLEGGE	ALLNIGHT
ALFAQUIS	ALIENATE	ALKAHESTS	ALLEGGED	ALLOCABLE
ALFAS	ALIENATED	ALKALI	ALLEGGES	ALLOCARPIES
ALFERECES	ALIENATES	ALKALIES	ALLEGGING	ALLOCARPY
ALFEREZ	ALIENATING	ALKALIFIED	ALLEGIANT	ALLOCATE
ALFORJA	ALIENATOR	ALKALIFIES	ALLEGING	ALLOCATED
ALFORJAS	ALIENATORS	ALKALIFY	ALLEGORIC	ALLOCATES
ALFRESCO	ALIENED	ALKALIFYING	ALLEGORIES	ALLOCATING
ALGA	ALIENEE	ALKALINE	ALLEGORY	ALLOD
ALGAE	ALIENEES	ALKALIS	ALLEGRO	ALLODIAL
ALGAL	ALIENING	ALKALISE	ALLEGROS	ALLODIUM
ALGAROBA	ALIENISM	ALKALISED	ALLEL	ALLODIUMS
ALGAROBAS	ALIENISMS	ALKALISES	ALLELE	ALLODS
ALGARROBA	ALIENIST	ALKALISING	ALLELES	ALLOGAMIES
ALGARROBAS	ALIENISTS	ALKALIZE	ALLELS	ALLOGAMY
ALGARROBO	ALIENOR	ALKALIZED	ALLELUIA	ALLOGRAFT
ALGARROBOS	ALIENORS	ALKALIZES	ALLELUIAH	ALLOGRAFTS
ALGATE	ALIENS	ALKALIZING	ALLELUIAHS	ALLOGRAPH
ALGATES	ALIFORM	ALKALOID	ALLELUIAS	ALLOGRAPHS
ALGEBRA	ALIGARTA	ALKALOIDS	ALLEMANDE	ALLOMETRIES
ALGEBRAIC	ALIGARTAS	ALKALOSES	ALLEMANDES	ALLOMETRY
ALGEBRAS	ALIGHT	ALKALOSIS	ALLENARLY	ALLOMORPH
ALGERINE	ALIGHTED	ALKANE	ALLERGEN	ALLOMORPHS
ALGERINES	ALIGHTING	ALKANES	ALLERGENS	ALLONGE
ALGESES	ALIGHTS	ALKANET	ALLERGIC	ALLONGES
ALGESIA	ALIGN	ALKANETS	ALLERGICS	ALLONS
ALGESIAS	ALIGNED	ALKENE	ALLERGIES	ALLONYM
ALGESIS	ALIGNING	ALKENES	ALLERGIST	ALLONYMS
ALGICIDE	ALIGNMENT	ALKIE	ALLERGISTS	ALLOPATH
ALGICIDES	ALIGNMENTS	ALKIES	ALLERGY	ALLOPATHIES
ALGID	ALIGNS	ALKY	ALLERION	ALLOPATHS
ALGIDITIES	ALIKE	ALKYD	ALLERIONS	ALLOPATHY
ALGIDITY	ALIMENT	ALKYDS	ALLEVIATE	ALLOPHONE
ALGIN	ALIMENTAL	ALKYL	ALLEVIATED	ALLOPHONES
ALGINATE	ALIMENTED	ALKYLS	ALLEVIATES	ALLOPLASM
ALGINATES	ALIMENTING	ALKYNE	ALLEVIATING	ALLOPLASMS
ALGINIC	ALIMENTS	ALKYNES	ALLEY	ALLOSAUR
ALGINS	ALIMONIES	ALL	ALLEYCAT	ALLOSAURS
ALGOID	ALIMONY	ALLANTOIC	ALLEYCATS	ALLOSTERIES
ALGOLOGIES	ALINE	ALLANTOID	ALLEYED	ALLOSTERY
ALGOLOGY	ALINED	ALLANTOIDS	ALLEYS	ALLOT
ALGORISM	ALINEMENT	ALLANTOIS	ALLEYWAY	ALLOTMENT
ALGORISMS	ALINEMENTS	ALLANTOISES	ALLEYWAYS	ALLOTMENTS
ALGORITHM	ALINES	ALLATIVE	ALLHEAL	ALLOTROPE
ALGORITHMS	ALINING	ALLATIVES	ALLHEALS	ALLOTROPES
ALGUACIL	ALIPED	ALLAY	ALLIANCE	ALLOTROPIES
ALGUACILS	ALIPEDS	ALLAYED	ALLIANCES	ALLOTROPY
ALGUAZIL	ALIPHATIC	ALLAYER	ALLICE	ALLOTS
ALGUAZILS	ALIQUANT	ALLAYERS	ALLICES	ALLOTTED
ALGUM	ALIQUOT	ALLAYING	ALLICHOLIES	ALLOTTEE
ALGUMS	ALISMA	ALLAYINGS	ALLICHOLY	ALLOTTEES
ALIAS	ALISMAS	ALLAYMENT	ALLIED	ALLOTTERIES

The Chambers Dictionary is the authority for many longer words; see *OSW* Introduction, page xii.

ALLOTTERY
ALLOTTING
ALLOW
ALLOWABLE
ALLOWABLY
ALLOWANCE
ALLOWANCED
ALLOWANCES
ALLOWANCING
ALLOWED
ALLOWEDLY
ALLOWING
ALLOWS
ALLOY
ALLOYED
ALLOYING
ALLOYS
ALLS
ALLSEED
ALLSEEDS
ALLSORTS
ALLSPICE
ALLSPICES
ALLUDE
ALLUDED
ALLUDES
ALLUDING
ALLURE
ALLURED
ALLURER
ALLURERS
ALLURES
ALLURING
ALLUSION
ALLUSIONS
ALLUSIVE
ALLUVIA
ALLUVIAL
ALLUVION
ALLUVIONS
ALLUVIUM
ALLY
ALLYING
ALLYL
ALLYLS
ALMA
ALMAH
ALMAHS
ALMAIN
ALMAINS
ALMANAC
ALMANACS
ALMANDINE
ALMANDINES
ALMAS
ALME
ALMEH
ALMEHS
ALMERIES
ALMERY
ALMES
ALMIGHTY
ALMIRAH
ALMIRAHS
ALMOND
ALMONDS
ALMONER

ALMONERS
ALMONRIES
ALMONRY
ALMOST
ALMOUS
ALMS
ALMUCE
ALMUCES
ALMUG
ALMUGS
ALNAGE
ALNAGER
ALNAGERS
ALNAGES
ALOD
ALODIAL
ALODIUM
ALODIUMS
ALODS
ALOE
ALOED
ALOES
ALOETIC
ALOETICS
ALOFT
ALOGIA
ALOGIAS
ALOGICAL
ALOHA
ALONE
ALONELY
ALONENESS
ALONENESSES
ALONG
ALONGSIDE
ALONGST
ALOOF
ALOOFLY
ALOOFNESS
ALOOFNESSES
ALOPECIA
ALOPECIAS
ALOPECOID
ALOUD
ALOW
ALOWE
ALP
ALPACA
ALPACAS
ALPARGATA
ALPARGATAS
ALPEEN
ALPEENS
ALPENHORN
ALPENHORNS
ALPHA
ALPHABET
ALPHABETED
ALPHABETING
ALPHABETS
ALPHAS
ALPHASORT
ALPHASORTED
ALPHASORTING
ALPHASORTS
ALPHORN
ALPHORNS

ALPINE
ALPINES
ALPINISM
ALPINISMS
ALPINIST
ALPINISTS
ALPS
ALREADY
ALRIGHT
ALS
ALSIKE
ALSIKES
ALSO
ALSOON
ALSOONE
ALT
ALTAR
ALTARAGE
ALTARAGES
ALTARS
ALTARWISE
ALTER
ALTERABLE
ALTERANT
ALTERANTS
ALTERCATE
ALTERCATED
ALTERCATES
ALTERCATING
ALTERED
ALTERING
ALTERITIES
ALTERITY
ALTERN
ALTERNANT
ALTERNANTS
ALTERNAT
ALTERNATE
ALTERNATED
ALTERNATES
ALTERNATING
ALTERNATS
ALTERNE
ALTERNES
ALTERS
ALTESSE
ALTESSES
ALTEZA
ALTEZAS
ALTEZZA
ALTEZZAS
ALTHAEA
ALTHAEAS
ALTHEA
ALTHEAS
ALTHORN
ALTHORNS
ALTHOUGH
ALTIMETER
ALTIMETERS
ALTIMETRIES
ALTIMETRY
ALTISSIMO
ALTITUDE
ALTITUDES
ALTO
ALTOS

ALTRICES
ALTRICIAL
ALTRUISM
ALTRUISMS
ALTRUIST
ALTRUISTS
ALTS
ALUDEL
ALUDELS
ALULA
ALULAE
ALUM
ALUMINA
ALUMINAS
ALUMINATE
ALUMINATES
ALUMINISE
ALUMINISED
ALUMINISES
ALUMINISING
ALUMINIUM
ALUMINIUMS
ALUMINIZE
ALUMINIZED
ALUMINIZES
ALUMINIZING
ALUMINOUS
ALUMINUM
ALUMINUMS
ALUMISH
ALUMIUM
ALUMIUMS
ALUMNA
ALUMNAE
ALUMNI
ALUMNUS
ALUMS
ALUNITE
ALUNITES
ALURE
ALURES
ALVEARIES
ALVEARY
ALVEATED
ALVEOLAR
ALVEOLATE
ALVEOLE
ALVEOLES
ALVEOLI
ALVEOLUS
ALVINE
ALWAY
ALWAYS
ALYSSUM
ALYSSUMS
AM
AMABILE
AMADAVAT
AMADAVATS
AMADOU
AMADOUS
AMAH
AMAHS
AMAIN
AMALGAM
AMALGAMS
AMANDINE

AMANDINES
AMANITA
AMANITAS
AMARACUS
AMARACUSES
AMARANT
AMARANTH
AMARANTHS
AMARANTIN
AMARANTS
AMARETTO
AMARETTOS
AMARYLLID
AMARYLLIDS
AMARYLLIS
AMARYLLISES
AMASS
AMASSABLE
AMASSED
AMASSES
AMASSING
AMASSMENT
AMASSMENTS
AMATE
AMATED
AMATES
AMATEUR
AMATEURS
AMATING
AMATION
AMATIONS
AMATIVE
AMATOL
AMATOLS
AMATORIAL
AMATORIAN
AMATORY
AMAUROSES
AMAUROSIS
AMAUROTIC
AMAZE
AMAZED
AMAZEDLY
AMAZEMENT
AMAZEMENTS
AMAZES
AMAZING
AMAZINGLY
AMAZON
AMAZONIAN
AMAZONITE
AMAZONITES
AMAZONS
AMBAGE
AMBAGES
AMBAGIOUS
AMBAN
AMBANS
AMBASSAGE
AMBASSAGES
AMBASSIES
AMBASSY
AMBATCH
AMBATCHES
AMBER
AMBERED
AMBERGRIS

The Chambers Dictionary is the authority for many longer words; see *OSW* Introduction, page xii.

AMBERGRISES	AMBUSH	AMICE	AMOEBA	AMOVED
AMBERITE	AMBUSHED	AMICES	AMOEBAE	AMOVES
AMBERITES	AMBUSHES	AMID	AMOEBAEAN	AMOVING
AMBERJACK	AMBUSHING	AMIDE	AMOEBAS	AMP
AMBERJACKS	AMEARST	AMIDES	AMOEBIC	AMPASSIES
AMBEROID	AMEBA	AMIDMOST	AMOEBOID	AMPASSY
AMBEROIDS	AMEBAE	AMIDSHIPS	AMOK	AMPERAGE
AMBEROUS	AMEBAS	AMIDST	AMOMUM	AMPERAGES
AMBERS	AMEBIC	AMIE	AMOMUMS	AMPERE
AMBERY	AMEER	AMIES	AMONG	AMPERES
AMBIANCE	AMEERS	AMIGO	AMONGST	AMPERSAND
AMBIANCES	AMEIOSES	AMIGOS	AMOOVE	AMPERSANDS
AMBIENCE	AMEIOSIS	AMILDAR	AMOOVED	AMPERZAND
AMBIENCES	AMELCORN	AMILDARS	AMOOVES	AMPERZANDS
AMBIENT	AMELCORNS	AMINE	AMOOVING	AMPHIBIAN
AMBIENTS	AMELIA	AMINES	AMORAL	AMPHIBIANS
AMBIGUITIES	AMELIAS	AMIR	AMORALISM	AMPHIBOLE
AMBIGUITY	AMEN	AMIRS	AMORALISMS	AMPHIBOLES
AMBIGUOUS	AMENABLE	AMIS	AMORALIST	AMPHIBOLIES
AMBIT	AMENABLY	AMISES	AMORALISTS	AMPHIBOLY
AMBITION	AMENAGE	AMISS	AMORANCE	AMPHIGORIES
AMBITIONS	AMENAGED	AMISSES	AMORANCES	AMPHIGORY
AMBITIOUS	AMENAGES	AMISSIBLE	AMORANT	AMPHIOXUS
AMBITS	AMENAGING	AMISSING	AMORCE	AMPHIOXUSES
AMBITTY	AMENAUNCE	AMITIES	AMORCES	AMPHIPOD
AMBIVERT	AMENAUNCES	AMITOSES	AMORET	AMPHIPODS
AMBIVERTS	AMEND	AMITOSIS	AMORETS	AMPHOLYTE
AMBLE	AMENDABLE	AMITOTIC	AMORETTI	AMPHOLYTES
AMBLED	AMENDE	AMITY	AMORETTO	AMPHORA
AMBLER	AMENDED	AMLA	AMORINI	AMPHORAE
AMBLERS	AMENDER	AMLAS	AMORINO	AMPHORIC
AMBLES	AMENDERS	AMMAN	AMORISM	AMPLE
AMBLING	AMENDES	AMMANS	AMORISMS	AMPLENESS
AMBLINGS	AMENDING	AMMETER	AMORIST	AMPLENESSES
AMBLYOPIA	AMENDMENT	AMMETERS	AMORISTS	AMPLER
AMBLYOPIAS	AMENDMENTS	AMMIRAL	AMORNINGS	AMPLEST
AMBO	AMENDS	AMMIRALS	AMOROSA	AMPLEXUS
AMBONES	AMENE	AMMO	AMOROSAS	AMPLIFIED
AMBOS	AMENED	AMMON	AMOROSITIES	AMPLIFIER
AMBRIES	AMENING	AMMONAL	AMOROSITY	AMPLIFIERS
AMBROID	AMENITIES	AMMONALS	AMOROSO	AMPLIFIES
AMBROIDS	AMENITY	AMMONIA	AMOROSOS	AMPLIFY
AMBROSIA	AMENS	AMMONIAC	AMOROUS	AMPLIFYING
AMBROSIAL	AMENT	AMMONIAS	AMOROUSLY	AMPLITUDE
AMBROSIAN	AMENTA	AMMONITE	AMORPHISM	AMPLITUDES
AMBROSIAS	AMENTAL	AMMONITES	AMORPHISMS	AMPLOSOME
AMBROTYPE	AMENTIA	AMMONIUM	AMORPHOUS	AMPLOSOMES
AMBROTYPES	AMENTIAS	AMMONIUMS	AMORT	AMPLY
AMBRY	AMENTS	AMMONOID	AMORTISE	AMPOULE
AMBULACRA	AMENTUM	AMMONOIDS	AMORTISED	AMPOULES
AMBULANCE	AMERCE	AMMONS	AMORTISES	AMPS
AMBULANCES	AMERCED	AMMOS	AMORTISING	AMPUL
AMBULANT	AMERCES	AMNESIA	AMORTIZE	AMPULE
AMBULANTS	AMERCING	AMNESIAC	AMORTIZED	AMPULES
AMBULATE	AMERICIUM	AMNESIACS	AMORTIZES	AMPULLA
AMBULATED	AMERICIUMS	AMNESIAS	AMORTIZING	AMPULLAE
AMBULATES	AMETHYST	AMNESIC	AMOSITE	AMPULS
AMBULATING	AMETHYSTS	AMNESICS	AMOSITES	AMPUTATE
AMBULATOR	AMI	AMNESTIED	AMOUNT	AMPUTATED
AMBULATORS	AMIABLE	AMNESTIES	AMOUNTED	AMPUTATES
AMBUSCADE	AMIABLY	AMNESTY	AMOUNTING	AMPUTATING
AMBUSCADED	AMIANTHUS	AMNESTYING	AMOUNTS	AMPUTATOR
AMBUSCADES	AMIANTHUSES	AMNIA	AMOUR	AMPUTATORS
AMBUSCADING	AMIANTUS	AMNION	AMOURETTE	AMPUTEE
AMBUSCADO	AMIANTUSES	AMNIOTIC	AMOURETTES	AMPUTEES
AMBUSCADOES	AMICABLE	AMNIOTOMIES	AMOURS	AMRIT
AMBUSCADOS	AMICABLY	AMNIOTOMY	AMOVE	AMRITA

The Chambers Dictionary is the authority for many longer words; see *OSW* Introduction, page xii.

AMRITAS
AMRITS
AMTMAN
AMTMANS
AMTRACK
AMTRACKS
AMUCK
AMULET
AMULETIC
AMULETS
AMUSABLE
AMUSE
AMUSED
AMUSEDLY
AMUSEMENT
AMUSEMENTS
AMUSER
AMUSERS
AMUSES
AMUSETTE
AMUSETTES
AMUSING
AMUSINGLY
AMUSIVE
AMYGDAL
AMYGDALA
AMYGDALAS
AMYGDALE
AMYGDALES
AMYGDALIN
AMYGDALINS
AMYGDALS
AMYGDULE
AMYGDULES
AMYL
AMYLASE
AMYLASES
AMYLENE
AMYLENES
AMYLOID
AMYLOIDAL
AMYLOIDS
AMYLOPSIN
AMYLOPSINS
AMYLS
AMYLUM
AMYLUMS
AMYTAL
AMYTALS
AN
ANA
ANABAS
ANABASES
ANABASIS
ANABATIC
ANABIOSES
ANABIOSIS
ANABIOTIC
ANABLEPS
ANABLEPSES
ANABOLIC
ANABOLISM
ANABOLISMS
ANABOLITE
ANABOLITES
ANABRANCH
ANABRANCHES

ANACHARIS
ANACHARISES
ANACONDA
ANACONDAS
ANACRUSES
ANACRUSIS
ANADEM
ANADEMS
ANAEMIA
ANAEMIAS
ANAEMIC
ANAEROBE
ANAEROBES
ANAEROBIC
ANAGLYPH
ANAGLYPHS
ANAGOGE
ANAGOGES
ANAGOGIC
ANAGOGIES
ANAGOGY
ANAGRAM
ANAGRAMMED
ANAGRAMMING
ANAGRAMS
ANAL
ANALCIME
ANALCIMES
ANALCITE
ANALCITES
ANALECTA
ANALECTIC
ANALECTS
ANALEMMA
ANALEMMAS
ANALEMMATA
ANALEPTIC
ANALEPTICS
ANALGESIA
ANALGESIAS
ANALGESIC
ANALGESICS
ANALLY
ANALOG
ANALOGA
ANALOGIC
ANALOGIES
ANALOGISE
ANALOGISED
ANALOGISES
ANALOGISING
ANALOGIST
ANALOGISTS
ANALOGIZE
ANALOGIZED
ANALOGIZES
ANALOGIZING
ANALOGON
ANALOGONS
ANALOGOUS
ANALOGS
ANALOGUE
ANALOGUES
ANALOGY
ANALYSAND
ANALYSANDS
ANALYSE

ANALYSED
ANALYSER
ANALYSERS
ANALYSES
ANALYSING
ANALYSIS
ANALYST
ANALYSTS
ANALYTIC
ANALYTICS
ANALYZE
ANALYZED
ANALYZER
ANALYZERS
ANALYZES
ANALYZING
ANAMNESES
ANAMNESIS
ANAN
ANANA
ANANAS
ANANASES
ANANDROUS
ANANKE
ANANKES
ANANTHOUS
ANAPAEST
ANAPAESTS
ANAPEST
ANAPESTS
ANAPHASE
ANAPHASES
ANAPHORA
ANAPHORAS
ANAPHORIC
ANAPLASTIES
ANAPLASTY
ANAPTYXES
ANAPTYXIS
ANARCH
ANARCHAL
ANARCHIAL
ANARCHIC
ANARCHIES
ANARCHISE
ANARCHISED
ANARCHISES
ANARCHISING
ANARCHISM
ANARCHISMS
ANARCHIST
ANARCHISTS
ANARCHIZE
ANARCHIZED
ANARCHIZES
ANARCHIZING
ANARCHS
ANARCHY
ANAS
ANASARCA
ANASARCAS
ANASTASES
ANASTASIS
ANASTATIC
ANATASE
ANATASES
ANATHEMA

ANATHEMAS
ANATOMIC
ANATOMIES
ANATOMISE
ANATOMISED
ANATOMISES
ANATOMISING
ANATOMIST
ANATOMISTS
ANATOMIZE
ANATOMIZED
ANATOMIZES
ANATOMIZING
ANATOMY
ANATROPIES
ANATROPY
ANATTA
ANATTAS
ANATTO
ANATTOS
ANAXIAL
ANBURIES
ANBURY
ANCE
ANCESTOR
ANCESTORS
ANCESTRAL
ANCESTRIES
ANCESTRY
ANCHOR
ANCHORAGE
ANCHORAGES
ANCHORED
ANCHORESS
ANCHORESSES
ANCHORET
ANCHORETS
ANCHORING
ANCHORITE
ANCHORITES
ANCHORS
ANCHOVETA
ANCHOVETAS
ANCHOVIES
ANCHOVY
ANCHYLOSE
ANCHYLOSED
ANCHYLOSES
ANCHYLOSING
ANCIENT
ANCIENTLY
ANCIENTRIES
ANCIENTRY
ANCIENTS
ANCILE
ANCILIA
ANCILLARIES
ANCILLARY
ANCIPITAL
ANCLE
ANCLES
ANCOME
ANCOMES
ANCON
ANCONES
ANCORA
ANCRESS

ANCRESSES
AND
ANDANTE
ANDANTES
ANDANTINO
ANDANTINOS
ANDESINE
ANDESINES
ANDESITE
ANDESITES
ANDESITIC
ANDIRON
ANDIRONS
ANDROECIA
ANDROGEN
ANDROGENS
ANDROGYNE
ANDROGYNES
ANDROGYNIES
ANDROGYNY
ANDROID
ANDROIDS
ANDROLOGIES
ANDROLOGY
ANDROMEDA
ANDROMEDAS
ANDS
ANDVILE
ANDVILES
ANE
ANEAR
ANEARED
ANEARING
ANEARS
ANEATH
ANECDOTAL
ANECDOTE
ANECDOTES
ANECHOIC
ANELACE
ANELACES
ANELE
ANELED
ANELES
ANELING
ANEMIA
ANEMIAS
ANEMIC
ANEMOGRAM
ANEMOGRAMS
ANEMOLOGIES
ANEMOLOGY
ANEMONE
ANEMONES
ANENT
ANERLY
ANEROID
ANEROIDS
ANES
ANESTRA
ANESTRI
ANESTRUM
ANESTRUS
ANETIC
ANEUPLOID
ANEUPLOIDS
ANEURIN

ANEURINS	ANGLING	ANIMALISM	ANKYLOSES	ANNOYANCE
ANEURISM	ANGLINGS	ANIMALISMS	ANKYLOSING	ANNOYANCES
ANEURISMS	ANGLIST	ANIMALIST	ANKYLOSIS	ANNOYED
ANEURYSM	ANGLISTS	ANIMALISTS	ANLACE	ANNOYER
ANEURYSMS	ANGLOPHIL	ANIMALITIES	ANLACES	ANNOYERS
ANEW	ANGLOPHILS	ANIMALITY	ANLAGE	ANNOYING
ANGARIES	ANGOLA	ANIMALIZE	ANLAGEN	ANNOYS
ANGARY	ANGOPHORA	ANIMALIZED	ANLAGES	ANNS
ANGEKKOK	ANGOPHORAS	ANIMALIZES	ANN	ANNUAL
ANGEKKOKS	ANGORA	ANIMALIZING	ANNA	ANNUALISE
ANGEKOK	ANGORAS	ANIMALLY	ANNAL	ANNUALISED
ANGEKOKS	ANGRIER	ANIMALS	ANNALISE	ANNUALISES
ANGEL	ANGRIES	ANIMAS	ANNALISED	ANNUALISING
ANGELHOOD	ANGRIEST	ANIMATE	ANNALISES	ANNUALIZE
ANGELHOODS	ANGRILY	ANIMATED	ANNALISING	ANNUALIZED
ANGELIC	ANGRINESS	ANIMATER	ANNALIST	ANNUALIZES
ANGELICA	ANGRINESSES	ANIMATERS	ANNALISTS	ANNUALIZING
ANGELICAL	ANGRY	ANIMATES	ANNALIZE	ANNUALLY
ANGELICAS	ANGST	ANIMATIC	ANNALIZED	ANNUALS
ANGELS	ANGSTROM	ANIMATICS	ANNALIZES	ANNUITANT
ANGELUS	ANGSTROMS	ANIMATING	ANNALIZING	ANNUITANTS
ANGELUSES	ANGSTS	ANIMATION	ANNALS	ANNUITIES
ANGER	ANGUIFORM	ANIMATIONS	ANNAS	ANNUITY
ANGERED	ANGUINE	ANIMATISM	ANNAT	ANNUL
ANGERING	ANGUIPED	ANIMATISMS	ANNATES	ANNULAR
ANGERLESS	ANGUIPEDE	ANIMATOR	ANNATS	ANNULARS
ANGERLY	ANGUISH	ANIMATORS	ANNATTA	ANNULATE
ANGERS	ANGUISHED	ANIME	ANNATTAS	ANNULATED
ANGICO	ANGUISHES	ANIMES	ANNATTO	ANNULATES
ANGICOS	ANGUISHING	ANIMISM	ANNATTOS	ANNULET
ANGINA	ANGULAR	ANIMISMS	ANNEAL	ANNULETS
ANGINAL	ANGULATE	ANIMIST	ANNEALED	ANNULI
ANGINAS	ANGULATED	ANIMISTIC	ANNEALER	ANNULLED
ANGIOGRAM	ANHEDONIA	ANIMISTS	ANNEALERS	ANNULLING
ANGIOGRAMS	ANHEDONIAS	ANIMOSITIES	ANNEALING	ANNULMENT
ANGIOMA	ANHEDONIC	ANIMOSITY	ANNEALINGS	ANNULMENTS
ANGIOMAS	ANHEDRAL	ANIMUS	ANNEALS	ANNULOSE
ANGIOMATA	ANHUNGRED	ANIMUSES	ANNECTENT	ANNULS
ANGKLUNG	ANHYDRIDE	ANION	ANNELID	ANNULUS
ANGKLUNGS	ANHYDRIDES	ANIONIC	ANNELIDS	ANOA
ANGLE	ANHYDRITE	ANIONS	ANNEX	ANOAS
ANGLED	ANHYDRITES	ANIS	ANNEXE	ANODAL
ANGLER	ANHYDROUS	ANISE	ANNEXED	ANODE
ANGLERS	ANI	ANISEED	ANNEXES	ANODES
ANGLES	ANICONIC	ANISEEDS	ANNEXING	ANODIC
ANGLESITE	ANICONISM	ANISES	ANNEXION	ANODISE
ANGLESITES	ANICONISMS	ANISETTE	ANNEXIONS	ANODISED
ANGLEWISE	ANICONIST	ANISETTES	ANNEXMENT	ANODISES
ANGLEWORM	ANICONISTS	ANKER	ANNEXMENTS	ANODISING
ANGLEWORMS	ANICUT	ANKERITE	ANNEXURE	ANODIZE
ANGLICE	ANICUTS	ANKERITES	ANNEXURES	ANODIZED
ANGLICISE	ANIGH	ANKERS	ANNICUT	ANODIZES
ANGLICISED	ANIGHT	ANKH	ANNICUTS	ANODIZING
ANGLICISES	ANIL	ANKHS	ANNO	ANODYNE
ANGLICISING	ANILE	ANKLE	ANNOTATE	ANODYNES
ANGLICISM	ANILINE	ANKLED	ANNOTATED	ANOESES
ANGLICISMS	ANILINES	ANKLES	ANNOTATES	ANOESIS
ANGLICIST	ANILITIES	ANKLET	ANNOTATING	ANOESTRA
ANGLICISTS	ANILITY	ANKLETS	ANNOTATOR	ANOESTRI
ANGLICIZE	ANILS	ANKLONG	ANNOTATORS	ANOESTRUM
ANGLICIZED	ANIMA	ANKLONGS	ANNOUNCE	ANOESTRUS
ANGLICIZES	ANIMAL	ANKLUNG	ANNOUNCED	ANOETIC
ANGLICIZING	ANIMALIC	ANKLUNGS	ANNOUNCER	ANOINT
ANGLIFIED	ANIMALISE	ANKUS	ANNOUNCERS	ANOINTED
ANGLIFIES	ANIMALISED	ANKUSES	ANNOUNCES	ANOINTER
ANGLIFY	ANIMALISES	ANKYLOSE	ANNOUNCING	ANOINTERS
ANGLIFYING	ANIMALISING	ANKYLOSED	ANNOY	ANOINTING

The Chambers Dictionary is the authority for many longer words; see *OSW* Introduction, page xii.

ANOINTS	ANTARS	ANTHOLOGY	ANTIPHONY	ANTONYMIES
ANOMALIES	ANTAS	ANTHRACIC	ANTIPODAL	ANTONYMS
ANOMALOUS	ANTBEAR	ANTHRAX	ANTIPODE	ANTONYMY
ANOMALY	ANTBEARS	ANTHRAXES	ANTIPODES	ANTRA
ANOMIC	ANTBIRD	ANTHROPIC	ANTIPOLE	ANTRE
ANOMIE	ANTBIRDS	ANTHURIUM	ANTIPOLES	ANTRES
ANOMIES	ANTE	ANTHURIUMS	ANTIPOPE	ANTRORSE
ANOMY	ANTEATER	ANTI	ANTIPOPES	ANTRUM
ANON	ANTEATERS	ANTIAR	ANTIQUARIES	ANTS
ANONYM	ANTECEDE	ANTIARS	ANTIQUARK	ANUCLEATE
ANONYMA	ANTECEDED	ANTIBODIES	ANTIQUARKS	ANURIA
ANONYMAS	ANTECEDES	ANTIBODY	ANTIQUARY	ANURIAS
ANONYMISE	ANTECEDING	ANTIC	ANTIQUATE	ANUROUS
ANONYMISED	ANTECHOIR	ANTICHLOR	ANTIQUATED	ANUS
ANONYMISES	ANTECHOIRS	ANTICHLORS	ANTIQUATES	ANUSES
ANONYMISING	ANTED	ANTICIVIC	ANTIQUATING	ANVIL
ANONYMITIES	ANTEDATE	ANTICIZE	ANTIQUE	ANVILS
ANONYMITY	ANTEDATED	ANTICIZED	ANTIQUED	ANXIETIES
ANONYMIZE	ANTEDATES	ANTICIZES	ANTIQUELY	ANXIETY
ANONYMIZED	ANTEDATING	ANTICIZING	ANTIQUES	ANXIOUS
ANONYMIZES	ANTEFIX	ANTICK	ANTIQUING	ANXIOUSLY
ANONYMIZING	ANTEFIXA	ANTICKE	ANTIQUITIES	ANY
ANONYMOUS	ANTEFIXAL	ANTICKED	ANTIQUITY	ANYBODIES
ANONYMS	ANTEFIXES	ANTICKING	ANTIRIOT	ANYBODY
ANOPHELES	ANTEING	ANTICLINE	ANTIRUST	ANYHOW
ANORAK	ANTELOPE	ANTICLINES	ANTIS	ANYONE
ANORAKS	ANTELOPES	ANTICOUS	ANTISCIAN	ANYONES
ANORECTAL	ANTELUCAN	ANTICS	ANTISCIANS	ANYROAD
ANORECTIC	ANTENATAL	ANTIDOTAL	ANTISERA	ANYTHING
ANORECTICS	ANTENATI	ANTIDOTE	ANTISERUM	ANYTHINGS
ANORETIC	ANTENNA	ANTIDOTES	ANTISERUMS	ANYTIME
ANORETICS	ANTENNAE	ANTIENT	ANTISHIP	ANYWAY
ANOREXIA	ANTENNAL	ANTIENTS	ANTISKID	ANYWAYS
ANOREXIAS	ANTENNARY	ANTIGAY	ANTISPAST	ANYWHEN
ANOREXIC	ANTENNAS	ANTIGEN	ANTISPASTS	ANYWHERE
ANOREXICS	ANTENNULE	ANTIGENIC	ANTISTAT	ANYWISE
ANOREXIES	ANTENNULES	ANTIGENS	ANTISTATS	ANZIANI
ANOREXY	ANTEPAST	ANTIHELICES	ANTITANK	AORIST
ANORTHIC	ANTEPASTS	ANTIHELIX	ANTITHEFT	AORISTIC
ANORTHITE	ANTERIOR	ANTIKNOCK	ANTITHET	AORISTS
ANORTHITES	ANTEROOM	ANTIKNOCKS	ANTITHETS	AORTA
ANOSMIA	ANTEROOMS	ANTILOG	ANTITOXIC	AORTAE
ANOSMIAS	ANTES	ANTILOGIES	ANTITOXIN	AORTAL
ANOTHER	ANTEVERT	ANTILOGS	ANTITOXINS	AORTAS
ANOUGH	ANTEVERTED	ANTILOGY	ANTITRADE	AORTIC
ANOUROUS	ANTEVERTING	ANTIMASK	ANTITRADES	AORTITIS
ANOW	ANTEVERTS	ANTIMASKS	ANTITRAGI	AORTITISES
ANOXIA	ANTHELIA	ANTIMONIC	ANTITRUST	AOUDAD
ANOXIAS	ANTHELICES	ANTIMONIES	ANTITYPAL	AOUDADS
ANOXIC	ANTHELION	ANTIMONY	ANTITYPE	APACE
ANSATE	ANTHELIX	ANTING	ANTITYPES	APACHE
ANSATED	ANTHEM	ANTINGS	ANTITYPIC	APACHES
ANSERINE	ANTHEMED	ANTINODAL	ANTIVENIN	APADANA
ANSWER	ANTHEMIA	ANTINODE	ANTIVENINS	APADANAS
ANSWERED	ANTHEMING	ANTINODES	ANTIVIRAL	APAGE
ANSWERER	ANTHEMION	ANTINOISE	ANTIVIRUS	APAGOGE
ANSWERERS	ANTHEMS	ANTINOMIC	ANTIWAR	APAGOGES
ANSWERING	ANTHER	ANTINOMIES	ANTLER	APAGOGIC
ANSWERS	ANTHERS	ANTINOMY	ANTLERED	APAID
ANT	ANTHESES	ANTIPAPAL	ANTLERS	APANAGE
ANTA	ANTHESIS	ANTIPASTO	ANTLIA	APANAGED
ANTACID	ANTHOCARP	ANTIPASTOS	ANTLIAE	APANAGES
ANTACIDS	ANTHOCARPS	ANTIPATHIES	ANTLIATE	APART
ANTAE	ANTHOCYAN	ANTIPATHY	ANTLION	APARTHEID
ANTAR	ANTHOCYANS	ANTIPHON	ANTLIONS	APARTHEIDS
ANTARA	ANTHOID	ANTIPHONIES	ANTONYM	APARTMENT
ANTARAS	ANTHOLOGIES	ANTIPHONS	ANTONYMIC	APARTMENTS

The Chambers Dictionary is the authority for many longer words; see *OSW* Introduction, page xii.

APARTNESS
APARTNESSES
APATETIC
APATHATON
APATHATONS
APATHETIC
APATHIES
APATHY
APATITE
APATITES
APAY
APAYD
APAYING
APAYS
APE
APEAK
APED
APEDOM
APEDOMS
APEEK
APEHOOD
APEHOODS
APEMAN
APEMEN
APEPSIA
APEPSIAS
APEPSIES
APEPSY
APERCU
APERCUS
APERIENT
APERIENTS
APERIES
APERIODIC
APERITIF
APERITIFS
APERITIVE
APERITIVES
APERT
APERTNESS
APERTNESSES
APERTURE
APERTURES
APERY
APES
APETALIES
APETALOUS
APETALY
APEX
APEXES
APHAGIA
APHAGIAS
APHANITE
APHANITES
APHASIA
APHASIAC
APHASIACS
APHASIAS
APHASIC
APHELIA
APHELIAN
APHELION
APHERESES
APHERESIS
APHESES
APHESIS
APHETIC

APHETISE
APHETISED
APHETISES
APHETISING
APHETIZE
APHETIZED
APHETIZES
APHETIZING
APHICIDE
APHICIDES
APHID
APHIDES
APHIDIAN
APHIDIANS
APHIDIOUS
APHIDS
APHIS
APHONIA
APHONIAS
APHONIC
APHONIES
APHONOUS
APHONY
APHORISE
APHORISED
APHORISER
APHORISERS
APHORISES
APHORISING
APHORISM
APHORISMS
APHORIST
APHORISTS
APHORIZE
APHORIZED
APHORIZER
APHORIZERS
APHORIZES
APHORIZING
APHOTIC
APHTHA
APHTHAE
APHTHOUS
APHYLLIES
APHYLLOUS
APHYLLY
APIAN
APIARIAN
APIARIES
APIARIST
APIARISTS
APIARY
APICAL
APICALLY
APICES
APICIAN
APICULATE
APIECE
APING
APIOL
APIOLS
APISH
APISHLY
APISHNESS
APISHNESSES
APISM
APISMS

APIVOROUS
APLANAT
APLANATIC
APLANATS
APLASIA
APLASIAS
APLASTIC
APLENTY
APLITE
APLITES
APLOMB
APLOMBS
APLUSTRE
APLUSTRES
APNEA
APNEAS
APNOEA
APNOEAS
APOCOPATE
APOCOPATED
APOCOPATES
APOCOPATING
APOCOPE
APOCOPES
APOCRINE
APOCRYPHA
APOD
APODAL
APODE
APODES
APODICTIC
APODOSES
APODOSIS
APODOUS
APODS
APOENZYME
APOENZYMES
APOGAEIC
APOGAMIC
APOGAMIES
APOGAMOUS
APOGAMY
APOGEAL
APOGEAN
APOGEE
APOGEES
APOGRAPH
APOGRAPHS
APOLLO
APOLLOS
APOLOGIA
APOLOGIAS
APOLOGIES
APOLOGISE
APOLOGISED
APOLOGISES
APOLOGISING
APOLOGIST
APOLOGISTS
APOLOGIZE
APOLOGIZED
APOLOGIZES
APOLOGIZING
APOLOGUE
APOLOGUES
APOLOGY
APOMICTIC

APOMIXES
APOMIXIS
APOOP
APOPHASES
APOPHASIS
APOPHATIC
APOPHYGE
APOPHYGES
APOPHYSES
APOPHYSIS
APOPLEX
APOPLEXED
APOPLEXES
APOPLEXIES
APOPLEXING
APOPLEXY
APORIA
APORIAS
APORT
APOSITIA
APOSITIAS
APOSITIC
APOSPORIES
APOSPORY
APOSTASIES
APOSTASY
APOSTATE
APOSTATES
APOSTATIC
APOSTIL
APOSTILLE
APOSTILLES
APOSTILS
APOSTLE
APOSTLES
APOSTOLIC
APOTHECIA
APOTHEGM
APOTHEGMS
APOTHEM
APOTHEMS
APOZEM
APOZEMS
APPAID
APPAIR
APPAIRED
APPAIRING
APPAIRS
APPAL
APPALLED
APPALLING
APPALS
APPALTI
APPALTO
APPANAGE
APPANAGED
APPANAGES
APPARAT
APPARATS
APPARATUS
APPARATUSES
APPAREL
APPARELLED
APPARELLING
APPARELS
APPARENCIES
APPARENCY

APPARENT
APPARENTS
APPARITOR
APPARITORS
APPAY
APPAYD
APPAYING
APPAYS
APPEACH
APPEACHED
APPEACHES
APPEACHING
APPEAL
APPEALED
APPEALING
APPEALS
APPEAR
APPEARED
APPEARER
APPEARERS
APPEARING
APPEARS
APPEASE
APPEASED
APPEASER
APPEASERS
APPEASES
APPEASING
APPEL
APPELLANT
APPELLANTS
APPELLATE
APPELS
APPEND
APPENDAGE
APPENDAGES
APPENDANT
APPENDANTS
APPENDED
APPENDICES
APPENDING
APPENDIX
APPENDIXES
APPENDS
APPERIL
APPERILL
APPERILLS
APPERILS
APPERTAIN
APPERTAINED
APPERTAINING
APPERTAINS
APPESTAT
APPESTATS
APPETENCE
APPETENCES
APPETENCIES
APPETENCY
APPETENT
APPETIBLE
APPETISE
APPETISED
APPETISER
APPETISERS
APPETISES
APPETISING
APPETITE

APPETITES	APPRESSING	APSARASES	AQUAROBIC	ARAPAIMA
APPETIZE	APPRISE	APSE	AQUAROBICS	ARAPAIMAS
APPETIZED	APPRISED	APSES	AQUAS	ARAPONGA
APPETIZER	APPRISER	APSIDAL	AQUATIC	ARAPONGAS
APPETIZERS	APPRISERS	APSIDES	AQUATICS	ARAPUNGA
APPETIZES	APPRISES	APSIDIOLE	AQUATINT	ARAPUNGAS
APPETIZING	APPRISING	APSIDIOLES	AQUATINTA	ARAR
APPLAUD	APPRISINGS	APSIS	AQUATINTAS	ARAROBA
APPLAUDED	APPRIZE	APT	AQUATINTED	ARAROBAS
APPLAUDER	APPRIZED	APTED	AQUATINTING	ARARS
APPLAUDERS	APPRIZER	APTER	AQUATINTS	ARAUCARIA
APPLAUDING	APPRIZERS	APTERAL	AQUAVIT	ARAUCARIAS
APPLAUDS	APPRIZES	APTERIA	AQUAVITS	ARAYSE
APPLAUSE	APPRIZING	APTERISM	AQUEDUCT	ARAYSED
APPLAUSES	APPRIZINGS	APTERISMS	AQUEDUCTS	ARAYSES
APPLE	APPROACH	APTERIUM	AQUEOUS	ARAYSING
APPLES	APPROACHED	APTEROUS	AQUIFER	ARB
APPLIABLE	APPROACHES	APTERYX	AQUIFERS	ARBA
APPLIANCE	APPROACHING	APTERYXES	AQUILEGIA	ARBALEST
APPLIANCES	APPROBATE	APTEST	AQUILEGIAS	ARBALESTS
APPLICANT	APPROBATED	APTING	AQUILINE	ARBALIST
APPLICANTS	APPROBATES	APTITUDE	AQUILON	ARBALISTS
APPLICATE	APPROBATING	APTITUDES	AQUILONS	ARBAS
APPLIED	APPROOF	APTLY	AQUIVER	ARBITER
APPLIER	APPROOFS	APTNESS	AR	ARBITERS
APPLIERS	APPROVAL	APTNESSES	ARABA	ARBITRAGE
APPLIES	APPROVALS	APTOTE	ARABAS	ARBITRAGED
APPLIQUE	APPROVE	APTOTES	ARABESQUE	ARBITRAGES
APPLIQUES	APPROVED	APTOTIC	ARABESQUES	ARBITRAGING
APPLY	APPROVER	APTS	ARABICA	ARBITRAL
APPLYING	APPROVERS	APYRETIC	ARABICAS	ARBITRARY
APPOINT	APPROVES	APYREXIA	ARABIN	ARBITRATE
APPOINTED	APPROVING	APYREXIAS	ARABINOSE	ARBITRATED
APPOINTEE	APPUI	AQUA	ARABINOSES	ARBITRATES
APPOINTEES	APPUIED	AQUABATIC	ARABINS	ARBITRATING
APPOINTING	APPUIS	AQUABATICS	ARABIS	ARBITRESS
APPOINTOR	APPULSE	AQUABOARD	ARABISE	ARBITRESSES
APPOINTORS	APPULSES	AQUABOARDS	ARABISED	ARBITRIUM
APPOINTS	APPUY	AQUACADE	ARABISES	ARBITRIUMS
APPORT	APPUYED	AQUACADES	ARABISING	ARBLAST
APPORTION	APPUYING	AQUADROME	ARABIZE	ARBLASTER
APPORTIONED	APPUYS	AQUADROMES	ARABIZED	ARBLASTERS
APPORTIONING	APRAXIA	AQUAE	ARABIZES	ARBLASTS
APPORTIONS	APRAXIAS	AQUAFER	ARABIZING	ARBOR
APPORTS	APRES	AQUAFERS	ARABLE	ARBOREAL
APPOSE	APRICATE	AQUALUNG	ARACEOUS	ARBOREOUS
APPOSED	APRICATED	AQUALUNGS	ARACHIS	ARBORES
APPOSER	APRICATES	AQUANAUT	ARACHISES	ARBORET
APPOSERS	APRICATING	AQUANAUTS	ARACHNID	ARBORETA
APPOSES	APRICOCK	AQUAPHOBE	ARACHNIDS	ARBORETS
APPOSING	APRICOCKS	AQUAPHOBES	ARACHNOID	ARBORETUM
APPOSITE	APRICOT	AQUAPLANE	ARACHNOIDS	ARBORIST
APPRAISAL	APRICOTS	AQUAPLANED	ARAGONITE	ARBORISTS
APPRAISALS	APRIORISM	AQUAPLANES	ARAGONITES	ARBOROUS
APPRAISE	APRIORISMS	AQUAPLANING	ARAISE	ARBORS
APPRAISED	APRIORIST	AQUAPLANINGS	ARAISED	ARBOUR
APPRAISER	APRIORISTS	AQUARELLE	ARAISES	ARBOURED
APPRAISERS	APRIORITIES	AQUARELLES	ARAISING	ARBOURS
APPRAISES	APRIORITY	AQUARIA	ARAK	ARBS
APPRAISING	APRON	AQUARIAN	ARAKS	ARBUTE
APPREHEND	APRONED	AQUARIANS	ARALIA	ARBUTES
APPREHENDED	APRONFUL	AQUARIIST	ARALIAS	ARBUTUS
APPREHENDING	APRONFULS	AQUARIISTS	ARAME	ARBUTUSES
APPREHENDS	APRONING	AQUARIST	ARAMES	ARC
APPRESS	APRONS	AQUARISTS	ARANEID	ARCADE
APPRESSED	APROPOS	AQUARIUM	ARANEIDS	ARCADED
APPRESSES	APSARAS	AQUARIUMS	ARANEOUS	ARCADES

The Chambers Dictionary is the authority for many longer words; see *OSW* Introduction, page xii.

ARCADING	ARCHIVES	AREACH	ARGHAN	ARIL
ARCADINGS	ARCHIVING	AREACHED	ARGHANS	ARILLARY
ARCANA	ARCHIVIST	AREACHES	ARGIL	ARILLATE
ARCANE	ARCHIVISTS	AREACHING	ARGILLITE	ARILLATED
ARCANELY	ARCHIVOLT	AREAD	ARGILLITES	ARILLI
ARCANIST	ARCHIVOLTS	AREADING	ARGILS	ARILLODE
ARCANISTS	ARCHLET	AREADS	ARGININE	ARILLODES
ARCANUM	ARCHLETS	AREAL	ARGININES	ARILLOID
ARCCOS	ARCHLUTE	AREAR	ARGOL	ARILLUS
ARCCOSES	ARCHLUTES	AREAS	ARGOLS	ARILS
ARCED	ARCHLY	AREAWAY	ARGON	ARIOSI
ARCH	ARCHNESS	AREAWAYS	ARGONAUT	ARIOSO
ARCHAEI	ARCHNESSES	ARECA	ARGONAUTS	ARIOSOS
ARCHAEUS	ARCHOLOGIES	ARECAS	ARGONS	ARIOT
ARCHAIC	ARCHOLOGY	ARED	ARGOSIES	ARIPPLE
ARCHAISE	ARCHON	AREDD	ARGOSY	ARIS
ARCHAISED	ARCHONS	AREDE	ARGOT	ARISE
ARCHAISER	ARCHONTIC	AREDES	ARGOTS	ARISEN
ARCHAISERS	ARCHWAY	AREDING	ARGUABLE	ARISES
ARCHAISES	ARCHWAYS	AREFIED	ARGUABLY	ARISH
ARCHAISING	ARCHWISE	AREFIES	ARGUE	ARISHES
ARCHAISM	ARCING	AREFY	ARGUED	ARISING
ARCHAISMS	ARCINGS	AREFYING	ARGUER	ARISTA
ARCHAIST	ARCKED	AREG	ARGUERS	ARISTAE
ARCHAISTS	ARCKING	ARENA	ARGUES	ARISTAS
ARCHAIZE	ARCKINGS	ARENAS	ARGUFIED	ARISTATE
ARCHAIZED	ARCO	ARENATION	ARGUFIER	ARISTO
ARCHAIZER	ARCS	ARENATIONS	ARGUFIERS	ARISTOS
ARCHAIZERS	ARCSECOND	AREOLA	ARGUFIES	ARK
ARCHAIZES	ARCSECONDS	AREOLAE	ARGUFY	ARKED
ARCHAIZING	ARCSIN	AREOLAR	ARGUFYING	ARKING
ARCHANGEL	ARCSINS	AREOLATE	ARGUING	ARKITE
ARCHANGELS	ARCTAN	AREOLATED	ARGULI	ARKITES
ARCHDUCAL	ARCTANS	AREOLE	ARGULUS	ARKOSE
ARCHDUCHIES	ARCTIC	AREOLES	ARGUMENT	ARKOSES
ARCHDUCHY	ARCTICS	AREOMETER	ARGUMENTA	ARKS
ARCHDUKE	ARCTIID	AREOMETERS	ARGUMENTS	ARLE
ARCHDUKES	ARCTIIDS	AREOSTYLE	ARGUS	ARLED
ARCHED	ARCTOID	AREOSTYLES	ARGUSES	ARLES
ARCHEI	ARCTOPHIL	ARERE	ARGUTE	ARLING
ARCHER	ARCTOPHILS	ARES	ARGUTELY	ARM
ARCHERESS	ARCUATE	ARET	ARGYLE	ARMADA
ARCHERESSES	ARCUATED	ARETE	ARGYLES	ARMADAS
ARCHERIES	ARCUATION	ARETES	ARGYRIA	ARMADILLO
ARCHERS	ARCUATIONS	ARETS	ARGYRIAS	ARMADILLOS
ARCHERY	ARCUS	ARETT	ARGYRITE	ARMAMENT
ARCHES	ARCUSES	ARETTED	ARGYRITES	ARMAMENTS
ARCHEST	ARD	ARETTING	ARHYTHMIA	ARMATURE
ARCHETYPE	ARDEB	ARETTS	ARHYTHMIAS	ARMATURES
ARCHETYPES	ARDEBS	AREW	ARHYTHMIC	ARMBAND
ARCHEUS	ARDENCIES	ARGAL	ARIA	ARMBANDS
ARCHIL	ARDENCY	ARGALA	ARIAS	ARMCHAIR
ARCHILOWE	ARDENT	ARGALAS	ARID	ARMCHAIRS
ARCHILOWES	ARDENTLY	ARGALI	ARIDER	ARMED
ARCHILS	ARDOR	ARGALIS	ARIDEST	ARMET
ARCHIMAGE	ARDORS	ARGAN	ARIDITIES	ARMETS
ARCHIMAGES	ARDOUR	ARGAND	ARIDITY	ARMFUL
ARCHING	ARDOURS	ARGANDS	ARIDLY	ARMFULS
ARCHITECT	ARDRI	ARGANS	ARIDNESS	ARMGAUNT
ARCHITECTED	ARDRIGH	ARGEMONE	ARIDNESSES	ARMHOLE
ARCHITECTING	ARDRIGHS	ARGEMONES	ARIEL	ARMHOLES
ARCHITECTS	ARDRIS	ARGENT	ARIELS	ARMIES
ARCHITYPE	ARDS	ARGENTINE	ARIETTA	ARMIGER
ARCHITYPES	ARDUOUS	ARGENTINES	ARIETTAS	ARMIGERAL
ARCHIVAL	ARDUOUSLY	ARGENTITE	ARIETTE	ARMIGERO
ARCHIVE	ARE	ARGENTITES	ARIETTES	ARMIGEROS
ARCHIVED	AREA	ARGENTS	ARIGHT	ARMIGERS

The Chambers Dictionary is the authority for many longer words; see *OSW* Introduction, page xii.

ARMIL	AROMATISES	ARREARAGES	ARSE	ARTICULAR
ARMILLA	AROMATISING	ARREARS	ARSEHOLE	ARTIER
ARMILLAE	AROMATIZE	ARRECT	ARSEHOLES	ARTIES
ARMILLARY	AROMATIZED	ARREEDE	ARSENAL	ARTIEST
ARMILLAS	AROMATIZES	ARREEDES	ARSENALS	ARTIFACT
ARMILS	AROMATIZING	ARREEDING	ARSENATE	ARTIFACTS
ARMING	AROSE	ARREST	ARSENATES	ARTIFICE
ARMISTICE	AROUND	ARRESTED	ARSENIATE	ARTIFICER
ARMISTICES	AROUSAL	ARRESTEE	ARSENIATES	ARTIFICERS
ARMLESS	AROUSALS	ARRESTEES	ARSENIC	ARTIFICES
ARMLET	AROUSE	ARRESTER	ARSENICAL	ARTILLERIES
ARMLETS	AROUSED	ARRESTERS	ARSENICS	ARTILLERY
ARMLOCK	AROUSER	ARRESTING	ARSENIDE	ARTINESS
ARMLOCKED	AROUSERS	ARRESTIVE	ARSENIDES	ARTINESSES
ARMLOCKING	AROUSES	ARRESTOR	ARSENIOUS	ARTISAN
ARMLOCKS	AROUSING	ARRESTORS	ARSENITE	ARTISANAL
ARMOIRE	AROW	ARRESTS	ARSENITES	ARTISANS
ARMOIRES	AROYNT	ARRET	ARSES	ARTIST
ARMOR	AROYNTED	ARRETS	ARSHEEN	ARTISTE
ARMORIAL	AROYNTING	ARRIAGE	ARSHEENS	ARTISTES
ARMORIALS	AROYNTS	ARRIAGES	ARSHIN	ARTISTIC
ARMORIES	ARPEGGIO	ARRIDE	ARSHINE	ARTISTRIES
ARMORIST	ARPEGGIOS	ARRIDED	ARSHINES	ARTISTRY
ARMORISTS	ARPENT	ARRIDES	ARSHINS	ARTISTS
ARMORS	ARPENTS	ARRIDING	ARSINE	ARTLESS
ARMORY	ARPILLERA	ARRIERE	ARSINES	ARTLESSLY
ARMOUR	ARPILLERAS	ARRIERO	ARSIS	ARTS
ARMOURED	ARQUEBUS	ARRIEROS	ARSON	ARTSIER
ARMOURER	ARQUEBUSES	ARRIS	ARSONIST	ARTSIES
ARMOURERS	ARRACACHA	ARRISES	ARSONISTS	ARTSIEST
ARMOURIES	ARRACACHAS	ARRISH	ARSONITE	ARTSMAN
ARMOURS	ARRACK	ARRISHES	ARSONITES	ARTSMEN
ARMOURY	ARRACKS	ARRIVAL	ARSONS	ARTSY
ARMOZEEN	ARRAH	ARRIVALS	ART	ARTWORK
ARMOZEENS	ARRAIGN	ARRIVANCE	ARTAL	ARTWORKS
ARMOZINE	ARRAIGNED	ARRIVANCES	ARTEFACT	ARTY
ARMOZINES	ARRAIGNER	ARRIVANCIES	ARTEFACTS	ARUGULA
ARMPIT	ARRAIGNERS	ARRIVANCY	ARTEL	ARUGULAS
ARMPITS	ARRAIGNING	ARRIVE	ARTELS	ARUM
ARMS	ARRAIGNINGS	ARRIVED	ARTEMISIA	ARUMS
ARMURE	ARRAIGNS	ARRIVES	ARTEMISIAS	ARVAL
ARMURES	ARRANGE	ARRIVING	ARTERIAL	ARVICOLE
ARMY	ARRANGED	ARRIVISME	ARTERIES	ARVICOLES
ARNA	ARRANGER	ARRIVISMES	ARTERIOLE	ARVO
ARNAS	ARRANGERS	ARRIVISTE	ARTERIOLES	ARVOS
ARNICA	ARRANGES	ARRIVISTES	ARTERITIS	ARY
ARNICAS	ARRANGING	ARROBA	ARTERITISES	ARYBALLOS
ARNOTTO	ARRANT	ARROBAS	ARTERY	ARYBALLOSES
ARNOTTOS	ARRANTLY	ARROGANCE	ARTESIAN	ARYL
ARNUT	ARRAS	ARROGANCES	ARTFUL	ARYLS
ARNUTS	ARRASED	ARROGANT	ARTFULLY	ARYTENOID
AROBA	ARRASENE	ARROGATE	ARTHRITIC	ARYTENOIDS
AROBAS	ARRASENES	ARROGATED	ARTHRITICS	AS
AROID	ARRASES	ARROGATES	ARTHRITIS	ASAFETIDA
AROIDS	ARRAUGHT	ARROGATING	ARTHRITISES	ASAFETIDAS
AROINT	ARRAY	ARROW	ARTHROPOD	ASANA
AROINTED	ARRAYAL	ARROWED	ARTHROPODS	ASANAS
AROINTING	ARRAYALS	ARROWING	ARTHROSES	ASAR
AROINTS	ARRAYED	ARROWROOT	ARTHROSIS	ASARUM
AROLLA	ARRAYER	ARROWROOTS	ARTIC	ASARUMS
AROLLAS	ARRAYERS	ARROWS	ARTICHOKE	ASBESTIC
AROMA	ARRAYING	ARROWWOOD	ARTICHOKES	ASBESTINE
AROMAS	ARRAYMENT	ARROWWOODS	ARTICLE	ASBESTOS
AROMATIC	ARRAYMENTS	ARROWY	ARTICLED	ASBESTOSES
AROMATICS	ARRAYS	ARROYO	ARTICLES	ASBESTOUS
AROMATISE	ARREAR	ARROYOS	ARTICLING	ASCARID
AROMATISED	ARREARAGE	ARS	ARTICS	ASCARIDES

ASCARIDS	ASHAMED	ASMOULDER	ASPINES	ASSEGAI
ASCARIS	ASHAMEDLY	ASOCIAL	ASPIRANT	ASSEGAIED
ASCAUNT	ASHAMES	ASP	ASPIRANTS	ASSEGAIING
ASCEND	ASHAMING	ASPARAGUS	ASPIRATE	ASSEGAIS
ASCENDANT	ASHEN	ASPARAGUSES	ASPIRATED	ASSEMBLE
ASCENDANTS	ASHERIES	ASPARTAME	ASPIRATES	ASSEMBLED
ASCENDED	ASHERY	ASPARTAMES	ASPIRATING	ASSEMBLER
ASCENDENT	ASHES	ASPECT	ASPIRATOR	ASSEMBLERS
ASCENDENTS	ASHET	ASPECTED	ASPIRATORS	ASSEMBLES
ASCENDER	ASHETS	ASPECTING	ASPIRE	ASSEMBLIES
ASCENDERS	ASHIER	ASPECTS	ASPIRED	ASSEMBLING
ASCENDING	ASHIEST	ASPECTUAL	ASPIRES	ASSEMBLY
ASCENDS	ASHINE	ASPEN	ASPIRIN	ASSENT
ASCENSION	ASHIVER	ASPENS	ASPIRING	ASSENTED
ASCENSIONS	ASHLAR	ASPER	ASPIRINS	ASSENTER
ASCENSIVE	ASHLARED	ASPERATE	ASPLENIUM	ASSENTERS
ASCENT	ASHLARING	ASPERATED	ASPLENIUMS	ASSENTING
ASCENTS	ASHLARINGS	ASPERATES	ASPORT	ASSENTIVE
ASCERTAIN	ASHLARS	ASPERATING	ASPORTED	ASSENTOR
ASCERTAINED	ASHLER	ASPERGE	ASPORTING	ASSENTORS
ASCERTAINING	ASHLERED	ASPERGED	ASPORTS	ASSENTS
ASCERTAINS	ASHLERING	ASPERGER	ASPOUT	ASSERT
ASCESES	ASHLERINGS	ASPERGERS	ASPRAWL	ASSERTED
ASCESIS	ASHLERS	ASPERGES	ASPREAD	ASSERTER
ASCETIC	ASHORE	ASPERGILL	ASPROUT	ASSERTERS
ASCETICAL	ASHRAM	ASPERGILLS	ASPS	ASSERTING
ASCETICS	ASHRAMA	ASPERGING	ASQUAT	ASSERTION
ASCI	ASHRAMAS	ASPERITIES	ASQUINT	ASSERTIONS
ASCIAN	ASHRAMITE	ASPERITY	ASS	ASSERTIVE
ASCIANS	ASHRAMITES	ASPEROUS	ASSAGAI	ASSERTOR
ASCIDIA	ASHRAMS	ASPERS	ASSAGAIED	ASSERTORS
ASCIDIAN	ASHY	ASPERSE	ASSAGAIING	ASSERTORY
ASCIDIANS	ASIDE	ASPERSED	ASSAGAIS	ASSERTS
ASCIDIUM	ASIDES	ASPERSES	ASSAI	ASSES
ASCITES	ASINICO	ASPERSING	ASSAIL	ASSESS
ASCITIC	ASINICOS	ASPERSION	ASSAILANT	ASSESSED
ASCITICAL	ASININE	ASPERSIONS	ASSAILANTS	ASSESSES
ASCLEPIAD	ASININITIES	ASPERSIVE	ASSAILED	ASSESSING
ASCLEPIADS	ASININITY	ASPERSOIR	ASSAILER	ASSESSOR
ASCLEPIAS	ASK	ASPERSOIRS	ASSAILERS	ASSESSORS
ASCLEPIASES	ASKANCE	ASPERSORIES	ASSAILING	ASSET
ASCONCE	ASKANCED	ASPERSORY	ASSAILS	ASSETS
ASCORBATE	ASKANCES	ASPHALT	ASSAIS	ASSEVER
ASCORBATES	ASKANCING	ASPHALTED	ASSART	ASSEVERED
ASCOSPORE	ASKANT	ASPHALTER	ASSARTED	ASSEVERING
ASCOSPORES	ASKANTED	ASPHALTERS	ASSARTING	ASSEVERS
ASCOT	ASKANTING	ASPHALTIC	ASSARTS	ASSHOLE
ASCOTS	ASKANTS	ASPHALTING	ASSASSIN	ASSHOLES
ASCRIBE	ASKARI	ASPHALTS	ASSASSINS	ASSIDUITIES
ASCRIBED	ASKARIS	ASPHALTUM	ASSAULT	ASSIDUITY
ASCRIBES	ASKED	ASPHALTUMS	ASSAULTED	ASSIDUOUS
ASCRIBING	ASKER	ASPHERIC	ASSAULTER	ASSIEGE
ASCUS	ASKERS	ASPHODEL	ASSAULTERS	ASSIEGED
ASEISMIC	ASKESES	ASPHODELS	ASSAULTING	ASSIEGES
ASEITIES	ASKESIS	ASPHYXIA	ASSAULTS	ASSIEGING
ASEITY	ASKEW	ASPHYXIAL	ASSAY	ASSIENTO
ASEPALOUS	ASKING	ASPHYXIAS	ASSAYABLE	ASSIENTOS
ASEPSES	ASKLENT	ASPHYXIES	ASSAYED	ASSIGN
ASEPSIS	ASKS	ASPHYXY	ASSAYER	ASSIGNAT
ASEPTATE	ASLAKE	ASPIC	ASSAYERS	ASSIGNATS
ASEPTIC	ASLAKED	ASPICK	ASSAYING	ASSIGNED
ASEPTICS	ASLAKES	ASPICKS	ASSAYINGS	ASSIGNEE
ASEXUAL	ASLAKING	ASPICS	ASSAYS	ASSIGNEES
ASEXUALLY	ASLANT	ASPIDIA	ASSEGAAI	ASSIGNING
ASH	ASLEEP	ASPIDIOID	ASSEGAAIED	ASSIGNOR
ASHAKE	ASLOPE	ASPIDIUM	ASSEGAAIING	ASSIGNORS
ASHAME	ASMEAR	ASPINE	ASSEGAAIS	ASSIGNS

The Chambers Dictionary is the authority for many longer words; see *OSW* Introduction, page xii.

ASSIST	ASSURER	ASTONISHED	ASWIM	ATHANORS
ASSISTANT	ASSURERS	ASTONISHES	ASWING	ATHEISE
ASSISTANTS	ASSURES	ASTONISHING	ASWIRL	ATHEISED
ASSISTED	ASSURGENT	ASTONY	ASWOON	ATHEISES
ASSISTING	ASSURING	ASTONYING	ASYLUM	ATHEISING
ASSISTS	ASSWAGE	ASTOOP	ASYLUMS	ATHEISM
ASSIZE	ASSWAGED	ASTOUND	ASYMMETRIES	ATHEISMS
ASSIZED	ASSWAGES	ASTOUNDED	ASYMMETRY	ATHEIST
ASSIZER	ASSWAGING	ASTOUNDING	ASYMPTOTE	ATHEISTIC
ASSIZERS	ASTABLE	ASTOUNDS	ASYMPTOTES	ATHEISTS
ASSIZES	ASTARE	ASTRADDLE	ASYNDETIC	ATHEIZE
ASSIZING	ASTART	ASTRAGAL	ASYNDETON	ATHEIZED
ASSOCIATE	ASTARTED	ASTRAGALI	ASYNDETONS	ATHEIZES
ASSOCIATED	ASTARTING	ASTRAGALS	ASYNERGIA	ATHEIZING
ASSOCIATES	ASTARTS	ASTRAKHAN	ASYNERGIAS	ATHELING
ASSOCIATING	ASTATIC	ASTRAKHANS	ASYNERGIES	ATHELINGS
ASSOIL	ASTATINE	ASTRAL	ASYNERGY	ATHEMATIC
ASSOILED	ASTATINES	ASTRAND	ASYSTOLE	ATHEOLOGIES
ASSOILING	ASTATKI	ASTRANTIA	ASYSTOLES	ATHEOLOGY
ASSOILS	ASTATKIS	ASTRANTIAS	AT	ATHEOUS
ASSOILZIE	ASTEISM	ASTRAY	ATABAL	ATHERINE
ASSOILZIED	ASTEISMS	ASTRICT	ATABALS	ATHERINES
ASSOILZIEING	ASTELIC	ASTRICTED	ATABEG	ATHEROMA
ASSOILZIES	ASTELIES	ASTRICTING	ATABEGS	ATHEROMAS
ASSONANCE	ASTELY	ASTRICTS	ATABEK	ATHEROMATA
ASSONANCES	ASTER	ASTRIDE	ATABEKS	ATHETESES
ASSONANT	ASTERIA	ASTRINGE	ATABRIN	ATHETESIS
ASSONATE	ASTERIAS	ASTRINGED	ATABRINS	ATHETISE
ASSONATED	ASTERID	ASTRINGER	ATACAMITE	ATHETISED
ASSONATES	ASTERIDS	ASTRINGERS	ATACAMITES	ATHETISES
ASSONATING	ASTERISK	ASTRINGES	ATACTIC	ATHETISING
ASSORT	ASTERISKED	ASTRINGING	ATAGHAN	ATHETIZE
ASSORTED	ASTERISKING	ASTROCYTE	ATAGHANS	ATHETIZED
ASSORTER	ASTERISKS	ASTROCYTES	ATALAYA	ATHETIZES
ASSORTERS	ASTERISM	ASTRODOME	ATALAYAS	ATHETIZING
ASSORTING	ASTERISMS	ASTRODOMES	ATAMAN	ATHETOID
ASSORTS	ASTERN	ASTROFELL	ATAMANS	ATHETOSES
ASSOT	ASTEROID	ASTROFELLS	ATAP	ATHETOSIC
ASSOTS	ASTEROIDS	ASTROID	ATAPS	ATHETOSIS
ASSOTT	ASTERS	ASTROIDS	ATARACTIC	ATHETOTIC
ASSOTTED	ASTERT	ASTROLABE	ATARACTICS	ATHIRST
ASSOTTING	ASTERTED	ASTROLABES	ATARAXIA	ATHLETA
ASSUAGE	ASTERTING	ASTROLOGIES	ATARAXIAS	ATHLETAS
ASSUAGED	ASTERTS	ASTROLOGY	ATARAXIC	ATHLETE
ASSUAGES	ASTHENIA	ASTRONAUT	ATARAXICS	ATHLETES
ASSUAGING	ASTHENIAS	ASTRONAUTS	ATARAXIES	ATHLETIC
ASSUAGINGS	ASTHENIC	ASTRONOMIES	ATARAXY	ATHLETICS
ASSUASIVE	ASTHENICS	ASTRONOMY	ATAVISM	ATHRILL
ASSUETUDE	ASTHMA	ASTROPHEL	ATAVISMS	ATHROB
ASSUETUDES	ASTHMAS	ASTROPHELS	ATAVISTIC	ATHROCYTE
ASSUMABLE	ASTHMATIC	ASTRUT	ATAXIA	ATHROCYTES
ASSUMABLY	ASTHORE	ASTUCIOUS	ATAXIAS	ATHWART
ASSUME	ASTHORES	ASTUCITIES	ATAXIC	ATILT
ASSUMED	ASTICHOUS	ASTUCITY	ATAXIES	ATIMIES
ASSUMEDLY	ASTIGMIA	ASTUN	ATAXY	ATIMY
ASSUMES	ASTIGMIAS	ASTUNNED	ATCHIEVE	ATINGLE
ASSUMING	ASTILBE	ASTUNNING	ATCHIEVED	ATISHOO
ASSUMINGS	ASTILBES	ASTUNS	ATCHIEVES	ATISHOOS
ASSUMPSIT	ASTIR	ASTUTE	ATCHIEVING	ATLAS
ASSUMPSITS	ASTOMOUS	ASTUTELY	ATE	ATLASES
ASSURABLE	ASTONE	ASTUTER	ATEBRIN	ATLATL
ASSURANCE	ASTONED	ASTUTEST	ATEBRINS	ATLATLS
ASSURANCES	ASTONES	ASTYLAR	ATELIER	ATMAN
ASSURE	ASTONIED	ASUDDEN	ATELIERS	ATMANS
ASSURED	ASTONIES	ASUNDER	ATHANASIES	ATMOLOGIES
ASSUREDLY	ASTONING	ASWARM	ATHANASY	ATMOLOGY
ASSUREDS	ASTONISH	ASWAY	ATHANOR	ATMOLYSE

The Chambers Dictionary is the authority for many longer words; see *OSW* Introduction, page xii.

ATMOLYSED
ATMOLYSES
ATMOLYSING
ATMOLYSIS
ATMOLYZE
ATMOLYZED
ATMOLYZES
ATMOLYZING
ATMOMETER
ATMOMETERS
ATOC
ATOCIA
ATOCIAS
ATOCS
ATOK
ATOKAL
ATOKE
ATOKES
ATOKOUS
ATOKS
ATOLL
ATOLLS
ATOM
ATOMIC
ATOMICAL
ATOMICITIES
ATOMICITY
ATOMIES
ATOMISE
ATOMISED
ATOMISER
ATOMISERS
ATOMISES
ATOMISING
ATOMISM
ATOMISMS
ATOMIST
ATOMISTIC
ATOMISTS
ATOMIZE
ATOMIZED
ATOMIZER
ATOMIZERS
ATOMIZES
ATOMIZING
ATOMS
ATOMY
ATONAL
ATONALISM
ATONALISMS
ATONALIST
ATONALISTS
ATONALITIES
ATONALITY
ATONE
ATONED
ATONEMENT
ATONEMENTS
ATONER
ATONERS
ATONES
ATONIC
ATONICITIES
ATONICITY
ATONIES
ATONING
ATONINGLY

ATONY
ATOP
ATOPIC
ATOPIES
ATOPY
ATRAMENT
ATRAMENTS
ATRAZINE
ATRAZINES
ATREMBLE
ATRESIA
ATRESIAS
ATRIA
ATRIAL
ATRIP
ATRIUM
ATRIUMS
ATROCIOUS
ATROCITIES
ATROCITY
ATROPHIED
ATROPHIES
ATROPHY
ATROPHYING
ATROPIA
ATROPIAS
ATROPIN
ATROPINE
ATROPINES
ATROPINS
ATROPISM
ATROPISMS
ATROPOUS
ATTABOY
ATTACH
ATTACHE
ATTACHED
ATTACHES
ATTACHING
ATTACK
ATTACKED
ATTACKER
ATTACKERS
ATTACKING
ATTACKS
ATTAIN
ATTAINDER
ATTAINDERS
ATTAINED
ATTAINING
ATTAINS
ATTAINT
ATTAINTED
ATTAINTING
ATTAINTS
ATTAP
ATTAPS
ATTAR
ATTARS
ATTASK
ATTASKED
ATTASKING
ATTASKS
ATTASKT
ATTEMPER
ATTEMPERED
ATTEMPERING

ATTEMPERS
ATTEMPT
ATTEMPTED
ATTEMPTER
ATTEMPTERS
ATTEMPTING
ATTEMPTS
ATTEND
ATTENDANT
ATTENDANTS
ATTENDED
ATTENDEE
ATTENDEES
ATTENDER
ATTENDERS
ATTENDING
ATTENDS
ATTENT
ATTENTAT
ATTENTATS
ATTENTION
ATTENTIONS
ATTENTIVE
ATTENTS
ATTENUANT
ATTENUANTS
ATTENUATE
ATTENUATED
ATTENUATES
ATTENUATING
ATTERCOP
ATTERCOPS
ATTEST
ATTESTED
ATTESTER
ATTESTERS
ATTESTING
ATTESTOR
ATTESTORS
ATTESTS
ATTIC
ATTICS
ATTIRE
ATTIRED
ATTIRES
ATTIRING
ATTIRINGS
ATTITUDE
ATTITUDES
ATTOLLENS
ATTOLLENT
ATTOLLENTS
ATTONCE
ATTONE
ATTONES
ATTORN
ATTORNED
ATTORNEY
ATTORNEYED
ATTORNEYING
ATTORNEYS
ATTORNING
ATTORNS
ATTRACT
ATTRACTED
ATTRACTING
ATTRACTOR

ATTRACTORS
ATTRACTS
ATTRAHENS
ATTRAHENT
ATTRAHENTS
ATTRAP
ATTRAPPED
ATTRAPPING
ATTRAPS
ATTRIBUTE
ATTRIBUTED
ATTRIBUTES
ATTRIBUTING
ATTRIST
ATTRISTED
ATTRISTING
ATTRISTS
ATTRIT
ATTRITE
ATTRITED
ATTRITES
ATTRITING
ATTRITION
ATTRITIONS
ATTRITS
ATTRITTED
ATTRITTING
ATTUENT
ATTUITE
ATTUITED
ATTUITES
ATTUITING
ATTUITION
ATTUITIONS
ATTUITIVE
ATTUNE
ATTUNED
ATTUNES
ATTUNING
ATWAIN
ATWEEL
ATWEEN
ATWITTER
ATWIXT
ATYPICAL
AUBADE
AUBADES
AUBERGE
AUBERGES
AUBERGINE
AUBERGINES
AUBRETIA
AUBRETIAS
AUBRIETA
AUBRIETAS
AUBRIETIA
AUBRIETIAS
AUBURN
AUCEPS
AUCEPSES
AUCTION
AUCTIONED
AUCTIONING
AUCTIONS
AUCTORIAL
AUCUBA
AUCUBAS

AUDACIOUS
AUDACITIES
AUDACITY
AUDIBLE
AUDIBLES
AUDIBLY
AUDIENCE
AUDIENCES
AUDIENCIA
AUDIENCIAS
AUDIENT
AUDIENTS
AUDILE
AUDILES
AUDIO
AUDIOGRAM
AUDIOGRAMS
AUDIOLOGIES
AUDIOLOGY
AUDIOPHIL
AUDIOPHILS
AUDIOS
AUDIOTAPE
AUDIOTAPES
AUDIPHONE
AUDIPHONES
AUDIT
AUDITED
AUDITING
AUDITION
AUDITIONED
AUDITIONING
AUDITIONS
AUDITIVE
AUDITOR
AUDITORIA
AUDITORIES
AUDITORS
AUDITORY
AUDITRESS
AUDITRESSES
AUDITS
AUF
AUFGABE
AUFGABES
AUFS
AUGER
AUGERS
AUGHT
AUGHTS
AUGITE
AUGITES
AUGITIC
AUGMENT
AUGMENTED
AUGMENTER
AUGMENTERS
AUGMENTING
AUGMENTOR
AUGMENTORS
AUGMENTS
AUGUR
AUGURAL
AUGURED
AUGURER
AUGURERS
AUGURIES

The Chambers Dictionary is the authority for many longer words; see *OSW* Introduction, page xii.

AUGURING	AUREOLAS	AUTHORISED	AUTOGUIDES	AUTOTOMY
AUGURS	AUREOLE	AUTHORISES	AUTOGYRO	AUTOTOXIN
AUGURSHIP	AUREOLED	AUTHORISH	AUTOGYROS	AUTOTOXINS
AUGURSHIPS	AUREOLES	AUTHORISING	AUTOHARP	AUTOTROPH
AUGURY	AUREUS	AUTHORISM	AUTOHARPS	AUTOTROPHS
AUGUST	AURIC	AUTHORISMS	AUTOLATRIES	AUTOTYPE
AUGUSTE	AURICLE	AUTHORITIES	AUTOLATRY	AUTOTYPED
AUGUSTER	AURICLED	AUTHORITY	AUTOLOGIES	AUTOTYPES
AUGUSTES	AURICLES	AUTHORIZE	AUTOLOGY	AUTOTYPING
AUGUSTEST	AURICULA	AUTHORIZED	AUTOLYSE	AUTOVAC
AUGUSTLY	AURICULAR	AUTHORIZES	AUTOLYSED	AUTOVACS
AUGUSTS	AURICULAS	AUTHORIZING	AUTOLYSES	AUTUMN
AUK	AURIFIED	AUTHORS	AUTOLYSING	AUTUMNAL
AUKLET	AURIFIES	AUTISM	AUTOLYSIS	AUTUMNS
AUKLETS	AURIFORM	AUTISMS	AUTOLYTIC	AUTUMNY
AUKS	AURIFY	AUTISTIC	AUTOLYZE	AUTUNITE
AULA	AURIFYING	AUTISTICS	AUTOLYZED	AUTUNITES
AULARIAN	AURISCOPE	AUTO	AUTOLYZES	AUXESES
AULARIANS	AURISCOPES	AUTOBAHN	AUTOLYZING	AUXESIS
AULAS	AURIST	AUTOBAHNS	AUTOMAT	AUXETIC
AULD	AURISTS	AUTOBUS	AUTOMATA	AUXETICS
AULDER	AUROCHS	AUTOBUSES	AUTOMATE	AUXILIAR
AULDEST	AUROCHSES	AUTOCADE	AUTOMATED	AUXILIARIES
AULIC	AURORA	AUTOCADES	AUTOMATES	AUXILIARS
AULNAGE	AURORAE	AUTOCAR	AUTOMATIC	AUXILIARY
AULNAGER	AURORAL	AUTOCARP	AUTOMATICS	AUXIN
AULNAGERS	AURORALLY	AUTOCARPS	AUTOMATING	AUXINS
AULNAGES	AURORAS	AUTOCARS	AUTOMATON	AUXOMETER
AULOI	AUROREAN	AUTOCLAVE	AUTOMATONS	AUXOMETERS
AULOS	AUROUS	AUTOCLAVED	AUTOMATS	AVA
AUMAIL	AUSPICATE	AUTOCLAVES	AUTONOMIC	AVADAVAT
AUMAILED	AUSPICATED	AUTOCLAVING	AUTONOMICS	AVADAVATS
AUMAILING	AUSPICATES	AUTOCRACIES	AUTONOMIES	AVAIL
AUMAILS	AUSPICATING	AUTOCRACY	AUTONOMY	AVAILABLE
AUMBRIES	AUSPICE	AUTOCRAT	AUTONYM	AVAILABLY
AUMBRY	AUSPICES	AUTOCRATS	AUTONYMS	AVAILE
AUMIL	AUSTENITE	AUTOCRIME	AUTOPHAGIES	AVAILED
AUMILS	AUSTENITES	AUTOCRIMES	AUTOPHAGY	AVAILES
AUNE	AUSTERE	AUTOCROSS	AUTOPHOBIES	AVAILFUL
AUNES	AUSTERELY	AUTOCROSSES	AUTOPHOBY	AVAILING
AUNT	AUSTERER	AUTOCUE	AUTOPHONIES	AVAILS
AUNTER	AUSTEREST	AUTOCUES	AUTOPHONY	AVAL
AUNTERS	AUSTERITIES	AUTOCYCLE	AUTOPILOT	AVALANCHE
AUNTIE	AUSTERITY	AUTOCYCLES	AUTOPILOTS	AVALANCHED
AUNTIES	AUSTRAL	AUTODYNE	AUTOPISTA	AVALANCHES
AUNTLIER	AUSTRALES	AUTOFLARE	AUTOPISTAS	AVALANCHING
AUNTLIEST	AUTACOID	AUTOFLARES	AUTOPOINT	AVALE
AUNTLY	AUTACOIDS	AUTOFOCUS	AUTOPOINTS	AVALED
AUNTS	AUTARCHIC	AUTOFOCUSES	AUTOPSIA	AVALES
AUNTY	AUTARCHIES	AUTOGAMIC	AUTOPSIAS	AVALING
AURA	AUTARCHY	AUTOGAMIES	AUTOPSIED	AVANT
AURAE	AUTARKIC	AUTOGAMY	AUTOPSIES	AVANTI
AURAL	AUTARKIES	AUTOGENIC	AUTOPSY	AVARICE
AURALLY	AUTARKIST	AUTOGENICS	AUTOPSYING	AVARICES
AURAS	AUTARKISTS	AUTOGENIES	AUTOPTIC	AVAS
AURATE	AUTARKY	AUTOGENY	AUTOROUTE	AVASCULAR
AURATED	AUTEUR	AUTOGIRO	AUTOROUTES	AVAST
AURATES	AUTEURS	AUTOGIROS	AUTOS	AVATAR
AUREATE	AUTHENTIC	AUTOGRAFT	AUTOSCOPIES	AVATARS
AUREI	AUTHOR	AUTOGRAFTED	AUTOSCOPY	AVAUNT
AUREITIES	AUTHORED	AUTOGRAFTING	AUTOSOMAL	AVAUNTED
AUREITY	AUTHORESS	AUTOGRAFTS	AUTOSOME	AVAUNTING
AURELIA	AUTHORESSES	AUTOGRAPH	AUTOSOMES	AVAUNTS
AURELIAN	AUTHORIAL	AUTOGRAPHED	AUTOTELIC	AVE
AURELIANS	AUTHORING	AUTOGRAPHING	AUTOTIMER	AVENGE
AURELIAS	AUTHORINGS	AUTOGRAPHS	AUTOTIMERS	AVENGED
AUREOLA	AUTHORISE	AUTOGUIDE	AUTOTOMIES	AVENGEFUL

The Chambers Dictionary is the authority for many longer words; see *OSW* Introduction, page xii.

AVENGER	AVIDINS	AVOWALS	AWES	AXILLA
AVENGERS	AVIDITIES	AVOWED	AWESOME	AXILLAE
AVENGES	AVIDITY	AVOWEDLY	AWESOMELY	AXILLAR
AVENGING	AVIDLY	AVOWER	AWESTRIKE	AXILLARY
AVENIR	AVIDNESS	AVOWERS	AWESTRIKES	AXILS
AVENIRS	AVIDNESSES	AVOWING	AWESTRIKING	AXING
AVENS	AVIETTE	AVOWRIES	AWESTRUCK	AXINITE
AVENSES	AVIETTES	AVOWRY	AWETO	AXINITES
AVENTAIL	AVIFAUNA	AVOWS	AWETOS	AXIOLOGIES
AVENTAILE	AVIFAUNAE	AVOYER	AWFUL	AXIOLOGY
AVENTAILES	AVIFAUNAS	AVOYERS	AWFULLER	AXIOM
AVENTAILS	AVIFORM	AVULSE	AWFULLEST	AXIOMATIC
AVENTRE	AVINE	AVULSED	AWFULLY	AXIOMATICS
AVENTRED	AVION	AVULSES	AWFULNESS	AXIOMS
AVENTRES	AVIONIC	AVULSING	AWFULNESSES	AXIS
AVENTRING	AVIONICS	AVULSION	AWHAPE	AXISES
AVENTURE	AVIONS	AVULSIONS	AWHAPED	AXLE
AVENTURES	AVISANDUM	AVUNCULAR	AWHAPES	AXLES
AVENUE	AVISANDUMS	AVYZE	AWHAPING	AXMAN
AVENUES	AVISE	AVYZED	AWHEEL	AXMEN
AVER	AVISED	AVYZES	AWHEELS	AXOID
AVERAGE	AVISEMENT	AVYZING	AWHILE	AXOIDS
AVERAGED	AVISEMENTS	AW	AWING	AXOLOTL
AVERAGES	AVISES	AWA	AWKWARD	AXOLOTLS
AVERAGING	AVISING	AWAIT	AWKWARDER	AXON
AVERMENT	AVISO	AWAITED	AWKWARDEST	AXONS
AVERMENTS	AVISOS	AWAITING	AWKWARDLY	AXOPLASM
AVERRED	AVITAL	AWAITS	AWL	AXOPLASMS
AVERRING	AVIZANDUM	AWAKE	AWLBIRD	AY
AVERS	AVIZANDUMS	AWAKED	AWLBIRDS	AYAH
AVERSE	AVIZE	AWAKEN	AWLS	AYAHS
AVERSELY	AVIZED	AWAKENED	AWMOUS	AYAHUASCO
AVERSION	AVIZEFULL	AWAKENING	AWMRIE	AYAHUASCOS
AVERSIONS	AVIZES	AWAKENINGS	AWMRIES	AYATOLLAH
AVERSIVE	AVIZING	AWAKENS	AWMRY	AYATOLLAHS
AVERT	AVOCADO	AWAKES	AWN	AYE
AVERTABLE	AVOCADOS	AWAKING	AWNED	AYELP
AVERTED	AVOCATION	AWAKINGS	AWNER	AYENBITE
AVERTEDLY	AVOCATIONS	AWANTING	AWNERS	AYENBITES
AVERTIBLE	AVOCET	AWARD	AWNIER	AYES
AVERTING	AVOCETS	AWARDED	AWNIEST	AYGRE
AVERTS	AVOID	AWARDING	AWNING	AYONT
AVES	AVOIDABLE	AWARDS	AWNINGS	AYRE
AVGAS	AVOIDANCE	AWARE	AWNLESS	AYRES
AVGASES	AVOIDANCES	AWARENESS	AWNS	AYRIE
AVIAN	AVOIDED	AWARENESSES	AWNY	AYRIES
AVIARIES	AVOIDING	AWARER	AWOKE	AYS
AVIARIST	AVOIDS	AWAREST	AWOKEN	AYU
AVIARISTS	AVOISION	AWARN	AWORK	AYURVEDIC
AVIARY	AVOISIONS	AWARNED	AWRACK	AYUS
AVIATE	AVOSET	AWARNING	AWRONG	AYWORD
AVIATED	AVOSETS	AWARNS	AWRY	AYWORDS
AVIATES	AVOUCH	AWASH	AWSOME	AZALEA
AVIATING	AVOUCHED	AWATCH	AX	AZALEAS
AVIATION	AVOUCHES	AWAVE	AXE	AZAN
AVIATIONS	AVOUCHING	AWAY	AXED	AZANS
AVIATOR	AVOURE	AWAYES	AXEL	AZEOTROPE
AVIATORS	AVOURES	AWAYS	AXELS	AZEOTROPES
AVIATRESS	AVOUTERER	AWDL	AXEMAN	AZIDE
AVIATRESSES	AVOUTERERS	AWDLS	AXEMEN	AZIDES
AVIATRICES	AVOUTRER	AWE	AXES	AZIMUTH
AVIATRIX	AVOUTRERS	AWEARIED	AXIAL	AZIMUTHAL
AVIATRIXES	AVOUTRIES	AWEARY	AXIALITIES	AZIMUTHS
AVID	AVOUTRY	AWED	AXIALITY	AZINE
AVIDER	AVOW	AWEEL	AXIALLY	AZINES
AVIDEST	AVOWABLE	AWEIGH	AXIL	AZIONE
AVIDIN	AVOWAL	AWELESS	AXILE	AZIONES

The Chambers Dictionary is the authority for many longer words; see *OSW* Introduction, page xii.

AZOIC	AZOTIC	AZOTOUS	AZURINES	AZYGY
AZOLLA	AZOTISE	AZOTURIA	AZURITE	AZYM
AZOLLAS	AZOTISED	AZOTURIAS	AZURITES	AZYME
AZONAL	AZOTISES	AZULEJO	AZURN	AZYMES
AZONIC	AZOTISING	AZULEJOS	AZURY	AZYMITE
AZOTE	AZOTIZE	AZURE	AZYGIES	AZYMITES
AZOTES	AZOTIZED	AZUREAN	AZYGOS	AZYMOUS
AZOTH	AZOTIZES	AZURES	AZYGOSES	AZYMS
AZOTHS	AZOTIZING	AZURINE	AZYGOUS	

B

BA	BABOOSH	BACILLARY	BACKINGS	BACKSPINS
BAA	BABOOSHES	BACILLI	BACKLAND	BACKSTAGE
BAAED	BABOUCHE	BACILLUS	BACKLANDS	BACKSTALL
BAAING	BABOUCHES	BACK	BACKLASH	BACKSTALLS
BAAINGS	BABU	BACKACHE	BACKLASHES	BACKSTAYS
BAAS	BABUCHE	BACKACHES	BACKLIFT	BACKSTOP
BAASES	BABUCHES	BACKARE	BACKLIFTS	BACKSTOPS
BAASSKAP	BABUDOM	BACKBAND	BACKLIST	BACKSWING
BAASSKAPS	BABUDOMS	BACKBANDS	BACKLISTS	BACKSWINGS
BABA	BABUISM	BACKBEAT	BACKLOG	BACKSWORD
BABACO	BABUISMS	BACKBEATS	BACKLOGS	BACKSWORDS
BABACOOTE	BABUL	BACKBIT	BACKLOT	BACKTRACK
BABACOOTES	BABULS	BACKBITE	BACKLOTS	BACKTRACKED
BABACOS	BABUS	BACKBITER	BACKMOST	BACKTRACKING
BABAS	BABUSHKA	BACKBITERS	BACKPACK	BACKTRACKINGS
BABASSU	BABUSHKAS	BACKBITES	BACKPACKED	BACKTRACKS
BABASSUS	BABY	BACKBITING	BACKPACKING	BACKVELD
BABBITT	BABYFOOD	BACKBITINGS	BACKPACKINGS	BACKVELDS
BABBITTED	BABYFOODS	BACKBITTEN	BACKPACKS	BACKWARD
BABBITTING	BABYHOOD	BACKBOND	BACKPAY	BACKWARDS
BABBITTS	BABYHOODS	BACKBONDS	BACKPAYS	BACKWASH
BABBLE	BABYING	BACKBONE	BACKPIECE	BACKWASHED
BABBLED	BABYISH	BACKBONED	BACKPIECES	BACKWASHES
BABBLER	BACCA	BACKBONES	BACKRA	BACKWASHING
BABBLERS	BACCAE	BACKCHAT	BACKRAS	BACKWATER
BABBLES	BACCARA	BACKCHATS	BACKROOM	BACKWATERS
BABBLIER	BACCARAS	BACKCHATTED	BACKS	BACKWOODS
BABBLIEST	BACCARAT	BACKCHATTING	BACKSAW	BACKWORD
BABBLING	BACCARATS	BACKCOURT	BACKSAWS	BACKWORDS
BABBLINGS	BACCARE	BACKCOURTS	BACKSET	BACKWORK
BABBLY	BACCAS	BACKDOWN	BACKSETS	BACKWORKS
BABE	BACCATE	BACKDOWNS	BACKSEY	BACKYARD
BABEL	BACCHANAL	BACKDROP	BACKSEYS	BACKYARDS
BABELDOM	BACCHANALS	BACKDROPS	BACKSHISH	BACLAVA
BABELDOMS	BACCHANT	BACKED	BACKSHISHED	BACLAVAS
BABELISH	BACCHANTE	BACKER	BACKSHISHES	BACON
BABELISM	BACCHANTES	BACKERS	BACKSHISHING	BACONER
BABELISMS	BACCHANTS	BACKET	BACKSIDE	BACONERS
BABELS	BACCHIAC	BACKETS	BACKSIDES	BACONS
BABES	BACCHIAN	BACKFALL	BACKSIGHT	BACTERIA
BABICHE	BACCHIC	BACKFALLS	BACKSIGHTS	BACTERIAL
BABICHES	BACCHII	BACKFIELD	BACKSLID	BACTERIAN
BABIED	BACCHIUS	BACKFILE	BACKSLIDE	BACTERIC
BABIER	BACCIES	BACKFILES	BACKSLIDES	BACTERISE
BABIES	BACCIFORM	BACKFILL	BACKSLIDING	BACTERISED
BABIEST	BACCO	BACKFILLED	BACKSLIDINGS	BACTERISES
BABIRUSA	BACCOES	BACKFILLING	BACKSPACE	BACTERISING
BABIRUSAS	BACCOS	BACKFILLS	BACKSPACED	BACTERIUM
BABIRUSSA	BACCY	BACKFIRE	BACKSPACES	BACTERIZE
BABIRUSSAS	BACH	BACKFIRED	BACKSPACING	BACTERIZED
BABLAH	BACHARACH	BACKFIRES	BACKSPEER	BACTERIZES
BABLAHS	BACHARACHS	BACKFIRING	BACKSPEERED	BACTERIZING
BABOO	BACHED	BACKFISCH	BACKSPEERING	BACTEROID
BABOON	BACHELOR	BACKFISCHES	BACKSPEERS	BACTEROIDS
BABOONERIES	BACHELORS	BACKHAND	BACKSPEIR	BACULA
BABOONERY	BACHES	BACKHANDS	BACKSPEIRED	BACULINE
BABOONISH	BACHING	BACKHOE	BACKSPEIRING	BACULITE
BABOONS	BACHS	BACKHOES	BACKSPEIRS	BACULITES
BABOOS	BACILLAR	BACKING	BACKSPIN	BACULUM

The Chambers Dictionary is the authority for many longer words; see *OSW* Introduction, page xii.

BACULUMS	BAGFULS	BAILLIES	BAKHSHISHING	BALEFUL
BAD	BAGGAGE	BAILLIS	BAKING	BALEFULLY
BADASS	BAGGAGES	BAILMENT	BAKINGS	BALER
BADASSED	BAGGED	BAILMENTS	BAKLAVA	BALERS
BADASSES	BAGGIER	BAILOR	BAKLAVAS	BALES
BADDIE	BAGGIES	BAILORS	BAKSHEESH	BALING
BADDIES	BAGGIEST	BAILS	BAKSHEESHED	BALISTA
BADDISH	BAGGILY	BAILSMAN	BAKSHEESHES	BALISTAE
BADDY	BAGGINESS	BAILSMEN	BAKSHEESHING	BALISTAS
BADE	BAGGINESSES	BAININ	BALACLAVA	BALK
BADGE	BAGGING	BAININS	BALACLAVAS	BALKANISE
BADGED	BAGGINGS	BAINITE	BALADIN	BALKANISED
BADGER	BAGGIT	BAINITES	BALADINE	BALKANISES
BADGERED	BAGGITS	BAIRN	BALADINES	BALKANISING
BADGERING	BAGGY	BAIRNLIKE	BALADINS	BALKANIZE
BADGERLY	BAGMAN	BAIRNLY	BALALAIKA	BALKANIZED
BADGERS	BAGMEN	BAIRNS	BALALAIKAS	BALKANIZES
BADGES	BAGNIO	BAISEMAIN	BALANCE	BALKANIZING
BADGING	BAGNIOS	BAISEMAINS	BALANCED	BALKED
BADINAGE	BAGPIPE	BAIT	BALANCER	BALKER
BADINAGES	BAGPIPER	BAITED	BALANCERS	BALKERS
BADIOUS	BAGPIPERS	BAITER	BALANCES	BALKIER
BADLANDS	BAGPIPES	BAITERS	BALANCING	BALKIEST
BADLY	BAGPIPING	BAITFISH	BALANITIS	BALKINESS
BADMAN	BAGPIPINGS	BAITFISHES	BALANITISES	BALKINESSES
BADMASH	BAGS	BAITING	BALAS	BALKING
BADMASHES	BAGUETTE	BAITINGS	BALASES	BALKINGLY
BADMEN	BAGUETTES	BAITS	BALATA	BALKINGS
BADMINTON	BAGUIO	BAIZE	BALATAS	BALKLINE
BADMINTONS	BAGUIOS	BAIZED	BALBOA	BALKLINES
BADMOUTH	BAGWASH	BAIZES	BALBOAS	BALKS
BADMOUTHED	BAGWASHES	BAIZING	BALCONET	BALKY
BADMOUTHING	BAGWIG	BAJADA	BALCONETS	BALL
BADMOUTHS	BAGWIGS	BAJADAS	BALCONIED	BALLABILE
BADNESS	BAH	BAJAN	BALCONIES	BALLABILES
BADNESSES	BAHADA	BAJANS	BALCONY	BALLABILI
BADS	BAHADAS	BAJRA	BALD	BALLAD
BAEL	BAHT	BAJRAS	BALDACHIN	BALLADE
BAELS	BAHTS	BAJREE	BALDACHINS	BALLADED
BAETYL	BAHUT	BAJREES	BALDAQUIN	BALLADEER
BAETYLS	BAHUTS	BAJRI	BALDAQUINS	BALLADEERED
BAFF	BAHUVRIHI	BAJRIS	BALDER	BALLADEERING
BAFFED	BAHUVRIHIS	BAJU	BALDEST	BALLADEERS
BAFFIES	BAIGNOIRE	BAJUS	BALDICOOT	BALLADES
BAFFING	BAIGNOIRES	BAKE	BALDICOOTS	BALLADIN
BAFFLE	BAIL	BAKEAPPLE	BALDIES	BALLADINE
BAFFLED	BAILABLE	BAKEAPPLES	BALDING	BALLADINES
BAFFLEGAB	BAILBOND	BAKEBOARD	BALDISH	BALLADING
BAFFLEGABS	BAILBONDS	BAKEBOARDS	BALDLY	BALLADINS
BAFFLER	BAILED	BAKED	BALDMONEY	BALLADIST
BAFFLERS	BAILEE	BAKEHOUSE	BALDMONEYS	BALLADISTS
BAFFLES	BAILEES	BAKEHOUSES	BALDNESS	BALLADRIES
BAFFLING	BAILER	BAKEMEAT	BALDNESSES	BALLADRY
BAFFS	BAILERS	BAKEMEATS	BALDPATE	BALLADS
BAFFY	BAILEY	BAKEN	BALDPATED	BALLAN
BAFT	BAILEYS	BAKER	BALDPATES	BALLANS
BAFTS	BAILIE	BAKERIES	BALDRIC	BALLANT
BAG	BAILIES	BAKERS	BALDRICK	BALLANTED
BAGARRE	BAILIFF	BAKERY	BALDRICKS	BALLANTING
BAGARRES	BAILIFFS	BAKES	BALDRICS	BALLANTS
BAGASSE	BAILING	BAKESTONE	BALDY	BALLAST
BAGASSES	BAILIWICK	BAKESTONES	BALE	BALLASTED
BAGATELLE	BAILIWICKS	BAKEWARE	BALECTION	BALLASTING
BAGATELLES	BAILLI	BAKEWARES	BALECTIONS	BALLASTS
BAGEL	BAILLIAGE	BAKHSHISH	BALED	BALLAT
BAGELS	BAILLIAGES	BAKHSHISHED	BALEEN	BALLATED
BAGFUL	BAILLIE	BAKHSHISHES	BALEENS	BALLATING

The Chambers Dictionary is the authority for many longer words; see *OSW* Introduction, page xii.

BALLATS	BALMED	BANALIZES	BANDOLINE	BANJAX
BALLCLAY	BALMIER	BANALIZING	BANDOLINED	BANJAXED
BALLCLAYS	BALMIEST	BANALLY	BANDOLINES	BANJAXES
BALLCOCK	BALMILY	BANANA	BANDOLINING	BANJAXING
BALLCOCKS	BALMINESS	BANANAS	BANDONEON	BANJO
BALLED	BALMINESSES	BANAUSIAN	BANDONEONS	BANJOES
BALLERINA	BALMING	BANAUSIC	BANDONION	BANJOIST
BALLERINAS	BALMORAL	BANC	BANDONIONS	BANJOISTS
BALLERINE	BALMORALS	BANCO	BANDOOK	BANJOS
BALLET	BALMS	BANCOS	BANDOOKS	BANJULELE
BALLETED	BALMY	BANCS	BANDORA	BANJULELES
BALLETIC	BALNEAL	BAND	BANDORAS	BANK
BALLETING	BALNEARIES	BANDA	BANDORE	BANKABLE
BALLETS	BALNEARY	BANDAGE	BANDORES	BANKED
BALLING	BALONEY	BANDAGED	BANDROL	BANKER
BALLINGS	BALONEYS	BANDAGES	BANDROLS	BANKERLY
BALLISTA	BALOO	BANDAGING	BANDS	BANKERS
BALLISTAE	BALOOS	BANDALORE	BANDSMAN	BANKET
BALLISTAS	BALSA	BANDALORES	BANDSMEN	BANKETS
BALLISTIC	BALSAM	BANDANA	BANDSTAND	BANKING
BALLISTICS	BALSAMED	BANDANAS	BANDSTANDS	BANKINGS
BALLIUM	BALSAMIC	BANDANNA	BANDSTER	BANKROLL
BALLIUMS	BALSAMING	BANDANNAS	BANDSTERS	BANKROLLED
BALLOCKS	BALSAMS	BANDAR	BANDURA	BANKROLLING
BALLOCKSED	BALSAMY	BANDARS	BANDURAS	BANKROLLS
BALLOCKSES	BALSAS	BANDAS	BANDWAGON	BANKRUPT
BALLOCKSING	BALSAWOOD	BANDBRAKE	BANDWAGONS	BANKRUPTED
BALLON	BALSAWOODS	BANDBRAKES	BANDWIDTH	BANKRUPTING
BALLONET	BALTHASAR	BANDEAU	BANDWIDTHS	BANKRUPTS
BALLONETS	BALTHASARS	BANDEAUX	BANDY	BANKS
BALLONS	BALTHAZAR	BANDED	BANDYING	BANKSIA
BALLOON	BALTHAZARS	BANDELET	BANDYINGS	BANKSIAS
BALLOONED	BALU	BANDELETS	BANDYMAN	BANKSMAN
BALLOONING	BALUS	BANDELIER	BANDYMEN	BANKSMEN
BALLOONINGS	BALUSTER	BANDELIERS	BANE	BANLIEUE
BALLOONS	BALUSTERS	BANDEROL	BANEBERRIES	BANLIEUES
BALLOT	BALZARINE	BANDEROLE	BANEBERRY	BANNED
BALLOTED	BALZARINES	BANDEROLES	BANED	BANNER
BALLOTEE	BAM	BANDEROLS	BANEFUL	BANNERALL
BALLOTEES	BAMBINI	BANDICOOT	BANEFULLY	BANNERALLS
BALLOTING	BAMBINO	BANDICOOTED	BANES	BANNERED
BALLOTS	BAMBINOS	BANDICOOTING	BANG	BANNERET
BALLOW	BAMBOO	BANDICOOTS	BANGED	BANNERETS
BALLOWS	BAMBOOS	BANDIED	BANGER	BANNEROL
BALLPARK	BAMBOOZLE	BANDIER	BANGERS	BANNEROLS
BALLPOINT	BAMBOOZLED	BANDIES	BANGING	BANNERS
BALLPOINTS	BAMBOOZLES	BANDIEST	BANGINGS	BANNING
BALLROOM	BAMBOOZLING	BANDING	BANGLE	BANNISTER
BALLROOMS	BAMMED	BANDINGS	BANGLED	BANNISTERS
BALLS	BAMMER	BANDIT	BANGLES	BANNOCK
BALLSIER	BAMMERS	BANDITRIES	BANGS	BANNOCKS
BALLSIEST	BAMMING	BANDITRY	BANGSRING	BANNS
BALLSY	BAMPOT	BANDITS	BANGSRINGS	BANQUET
BALLUP	BAMPOTS	BANDITTI	BANGSTER	BANQUETED
BALLUPS	BAMS	BANDITTIS	BANGSTERS	BANQUETER
BALLY	BAN	BANDOBAST	BANI	BANQUETERS
BALLYHOO	BANAL	BANDOBASTS	BANIA	BANQUETING
BALLYHOOED	BANALER	BANDOG	BANIAN	BANQUETINGS
BALLYHOOING	BANALEST	BANDOGS	BANIANS	BANQUETS
BALLYHOOS	BANALISE	BANDOLEER	BANIAS	BANQUETTE
BALLYRAG	BANALISED	BANDOLEERS	BANING	BANQUETTES
BALLYRAGGED	BANALISES	BANDOLEON	BANISH	BANS
BALLYRAGGING	BANALISING	BANDOLEONS	BANISHED	BANSHEE
BALLYRAGS	BANALITIES	BANDOLERO	BANISHES	BANSHEES
BALM	BANALITY	BANDOLEROS	BANISHING	BANT
BALMACAAN	BANALIZE	BANDOLIER	BANISTER	BANTAM
BALMACAANS	BANALIZED	BANDOLIERS	BANISTERS	BANTAMS

The Chambers Dictionary is the authority for many longer words; see *OSW* Introduction, page xii.

BANTED	BARBARITIES	BARDIER	BARILLA	BAROCK
BANTENG	BARBARITY	BARDIEST	BARILLAS	BAROCKS
BANTENGS	BARBARIZE	BARDING	BARING	BAROGRAM
BANTER	BARBARIZED	BARDLING	BARISH	BAROGRAMS
BANTERED	BARBARIZES	BARDLINGS	BARITE	BAROGRAPH
BANTERER	BARBARIZING	BARDO	BARITES	BAROGRAPHS
BANTERERS	BARBAROUS	BARDOS	BARITONE	BAROMETER
BANTERING	BARBASCO	BARDS	BARITONES	BAROMETERS
BANTERINGS	BARBASCOS	BARDSHIP	BARIUM	BAROMETRIES
BANTERS	BARBASTEL	BARDSHIPS	BARIUMS	BAROMETRY
BANTING	BARBASTELS	BARDY	BARK	BAROMETZ
BANTINGS	BARBATE	BARE	BARKAN	BAROMETZES
BANTLING	BARBATED	BAREBACK	BARKANS	BARON
BANTLINGS	BARBE	BAREBOAT	BARKED	BARONAGE
BANTS	BARBECUE	BAREBONE	BARKEEPER	BARONAGES
BANTU	BARBECUED	BAREBONES	BARKEEPERS	BARONESS
BANTUS	BARBECUES	BARED	BARKEN	BARONESSES
BANXRING	BARBECUING	BAREFACED	BARKENED	BARONET
BANXRINGS	BARBED	BAREFOOT	BARKENING	BARONETCIES
BANYAN	BARBEL	BAREGE	BARKENS	BARONETCY
BANYANS	BARBELS	BAREGES	BARKER	BARONETS
BANZAI	BARBEQUE	BAREGINE	BARKERS	BARONG
BANZAIS	BARBEQUED	BAREGINES	BARKHAN	BARONGS
BAOBAB	BARBEQUES	BARELY	BARKHANS	BARONIAL
BAOBABS	BARBEQUING	BARENESS	BARKIER	BARONIES
BAP	BARBER	BARENESSES	BARKIEST	BARONNE
BAPS	BARBERED	BARER	BARKING	BARONNES
BAPTISE	BARBERING	BARES	BARKLESS	BARONS
BAPTISED	BARBERRIES	BARESARK	BARKS	BARONY
BAPTISES	BARBERRY	BARESARKS	BARKY	BAROQUE
BAPTISING	BARBERS	BAREST	BARLEY	BAROQUES
BAPTISM	BARBES	BARF	BARLEYS	BAROSCOPE
BAPTISMAL	BARBET	BARFED	BARM	BAROSCOPES
BAPTISMS	BARBETS	BARFING	BARMAID	BAROSTAT
BAPTIST	BARBETTE	BARFLIES	BARMAIDS	BAROSTATS
BAPTISTRIES	BARBETTES	BARFLY	BARMAN	BAROUCHE
BAPTISTRY	BARBICAN	BARFS	BARMBRACK	BAROUCHES
BAPTISTS	BARBICANS	BARFUL	BARMBRACKS	BARP
BAPTIZE	BARBICEL	BARGAIN	BARMEN	BARPERSON
BAPTIZED	BARBICELS	BARGAINED	BARMIER	BARPERSONS
BAPTIZES	BARBIE	BARGAINER	BARMIEST	BARPS
BAPTIZING	BARBIES	BARGAINERS	BARMINESS	BARQUE
BAPU	BARBING	BARGAINING	BARMINESSES	BARQUES
BAPUS	BARBITAL	BARGAINS	BARMIZVAH	BARRACAN
BAR	BARBITALS	BARGANDER	BARMIZVAHS	BARRACANS
BARACAN	BARBITONE	BARGANDERS	BARMKIN	BARRACE
BARACANS	BARBITONES	BARGE	BARMKINS	BARRACES
BARAGOUIN	BARBOLA	BARGED	BARMS	BARRACK
BARAGOUINS	BARBOLAS	BARGEE	BARMY	BARRACKED
BARASINGA	BARBOTINE	BARGEES	BARN	BARRACKER
BARASINGAS	BARBOTINES	BARGEESE	BARNACLE	BARRACKERS
BARATHEA	BARBS	BARGELLO	BARNACLED	BARRACKING
BARATHEAS	BARBULE	BARGELLOS	BARNACLES	BARRACKINGS
BARATHRUM	BARBULES	BARGEMAN	BARNED	BARRACKS
BARATHRUMS	BARCA	BARGEMEN	BARNEY	BARRACOON
BARAZA	BARCAROLE	BARGEPOLE	BARNEYS	BARRACOONS
BARAZAS	BARCAROLES	BARGEPOLES	BARNING	BARRACUDA
BARB	BARCAS	BARGES	BARNS	BARRACUDAS
BARBARIAN	BARCHAN	BARGEST	BARNSTORM	BARRAGE
BARBARIANS	BARCHANE	BARGESTS	BARNSTORMED	BARRAGES
BARBARIC	BARCHANES	BARGHAIST	BARNSTORMING	BARRANCA
BARBARISE	BARCHANS	BARGHAISTS	BARNSTORMINGS	BARRANCAS
BARBARISED	BARD	BARGHEST	BARNSTORMS	BARRANCO
BARBARISES	BARDASH	BARGHESTS	BARNYARD	BARRANCOS
BARBARISING	BARDASHES	BARGING	BARNYARDS	BARRAT
BARBARISM	BARDED	BARGOOSE	BAROCCO	BARRATOR
BARBARISMS	BARDIC	BARIC	BAROCCOS	BARRATORS

The Chambers Dictionary is the authority for many longer words; see *OSW* Introduction, page xii.

BARRATRIES	BARYE	BASICALLY	BASSING	BATHCUBES
BARRATRY	BARYES	BASICITIES	BASSIST	BATHE
BARRATS	BARYON	BASICITY	BASSISTS	BATHED
BARRE	BARYONS	BASICS	BASSO	BATHER
BARRED	BARYTA	BASIDIA	BASSOON	BATHERS
BARREFULL	BARYTAS	BASIDIAL	BASSOONS	BATHES
BARREL	BARYTES	BASIDIUM	BASSOS	BATHETIC
BARRELAGE	BARYTIC	BASIFIXED	BASSWOOD	BATHHOUSE
BARRELAGES	BARYTON	BASIFUGAL	BASSWOODS	BATHHOUSES
BARRELFUL	BARYTONE	BASIL	BASSY	BATHING
BARRELFULS	BARYTONES	BASILAR	BAST	BATHMIC
BARRELLED	BARYTONS	BASILICA	BASTA	BATHMISM
BARRELLING	BAS	BASILICAL	BASTARD	BATHMISMS
BARRELS	BASAL	BASILICAN	BASTARDIES	BATHOLITE
BARREN	BASALT	BASILICAS	BASTARDLY	BATHOLITES
BARRENER	BASALTIC	BASILICON	BASTARDS	BATHOLITH
BARRENEST	BASALTS	BASILICONS	BASTARDY	BATHOLITHS
BARRES	BASAN	BASILISK	BASTE	BATHORSE
BARRET	BASANITE	BASILISKS	BASTED	BATHORSES
BARRETS	BASANITES	BASILS	BASTER	BATHOS
BARRETTE	BASANS	BASIN	BASTERS	BATHOSES
BARRETTER	BASCULE	BASINET	BASTES	BATHROBE
BARRETTERS	BASCULES	BASINETS	BASTIDE	BATHROBES
BARRETTES	BASE	BASINFUL	BASTIDES	BATHROOM
BARRICADE	BASEBALL	BASINFULS	BASTILLE	BATHROOMS
BARRICADED	BASEBALLS	BASING	BASTILLES	BATHS
BARRICADES	BASEBAND	BASINS	BASTINADE	BATHTUB
BARRICADING	BASEBOARD	BASIPETAL	BASTINADED	BATHTUBS
BARRICADO	BASEBOARDS	BASIS	BASTINADES	BATHYAL
BARRICADOED	BASED	BASK	BASTINADING	BATHYBIUS
BARRICADOES	BASELARD	BASKED	BASTINADO	BATHYBIUSES
BARRICADOING	BASELARDS	BASKET	BASTINADOED	BATHYLITE
BARRICADOS	BASELESS	BASKETFUL	BASTINADOES	BATHYLITES
BARRICO	BASELINER	BASKETFULS	BASTINADOING	BATHYLITH
BARRICOES	BASELINERS	BASKETRIES	BASTING	BATHYLITHS
BARRICOS	BASELY	BASKETRY	BASTINGS	BATIK
BARRIER	BASEMAN	BASKETS	BASTION	BATIKS
BARRIERED	BASEMEN	BASKING	BASTIONED	BATING
BARRIERING	BASEMENT	BASKS	BASTIONS	BATISTE
BARRIERS	BASEMENTS	BASNET	BASTLE	BATISTES
BARRING	BASENESS	BASNETS	BASTLES	BATLER
BARRINGS	BASENESSES	BASOCHE	BASTO	BATLERS
BARRIO	BASENJI	BASOCHES	BASTOS	BATLET
BARRIOS	BASENJIS	BASON	BASTS	BATLETS
BARRISTER	BASEPLATE	BASONS	BAT	BATMAN
BARRISTERS	BASEPLATES	BASOPHIL	BATABLE	BATMEN
BARROW	BASER	BASOPHILS	BATATA	BATOLOGIES
BARROWS	BASES	BASQUE	BATATAS	BATOLOGY
BARRULET	BASEST	BASQUED	BATCH	BATON
BARRULETS	BASH	BASQUES	BATCHED	BATONED
BARS	BASHAW	BASQUINE	BATCHES	BATONING
BARTENDER	BASHAWISM	BASQUINES	BATCHING	BATONS
BARTENDERS	BASHAWISMS	BASS	BATCHINGS	BATOON
BARTER	BASHAWS	BASSE	BATE	BATOONED
BARTERED	BASHED	BASSED	BATEAU	BATOONING
BARTERER	BASHER	BASSER	BATEAUX	BATOONS
BARTERERS	BASHERS	BASSES	BATED	BATRACHIA
BARTERING	BASHES	BASSEST	BATELESS	BATS
BARTERS	BASHFUL	BASSET	BATELEUR	BATSMAN
BARTISAN	BASHFULLY	BASSETED	BATELEURS	BATSMEN
BARTISANS	BASHING	BASSETING	BATEMENT	BATSWING
BARTIZAN	BASHINGS	BASSETS	BATEMENTS	BATSWOMAN
BARTIZANS	BASHLESS	BASSI	BATES	BATSWOMEN
BARTON	BASHLIK	BASSIER	BATFISH	BATT
BARTONS	BASHLIKS	BASSIEST	BATFISHES	BATTA
BARWOOD	BASHO	BASSINET	BATH	BATTALIA
BARWOODS	BASIC	BASSINETS	BATHCUBE	BATTALIAS

The Chambers Dictionary is the authority for many longer words; see *OSW* Introduction, page xii.

BATTALION	BAUDRICS	BAYE	BEAKED	BEARSKIN
BATTALIONS	BAUDRONS	BAYED	BEAKER	BEARSKINS
BATTAS	BAUDRONSES	BAYES	BEAKERS	BEARWARD
BATTED	BAUDS	BAYING	BEAKIER	BEARWARDS
BATTEL	BAUERA	BAYLE	BEAKIEST	BEAST
BATTELED	BAUERAS	BAYLES	BEAKS	BEASTHOOD
BATTELER	BAUHINIA	BAYONET	BEAKY	BEASTHOODS
BATTELERS	BAUHINIAS	BAYONETED	BEAM	BEASTIE
BATTELING	BAUK	BAYONETING	BEAMED	BEASTIES
BATTELLED	BAUKED	BAYONETS	BEAMER	BEASTILY
BATTELLING	BAUKING	BAYOU	BEAMERS	BEASTINGS
BATTELS	BAUKS	BAYOUS	BEAMIER	BEASTLIER
BATTEMENT	BAULK	BAYS	BEAMIEST	BEASTLIEST
BATTEMENTS	BAULKED	BAYT	BEAMILY	BEASTLIKE
BATTEN	BAULKING	BAYTED	BEAMINESS	BEASTLY
BATTENED	BAULKS	BAYTING	BEAMINESSES	BEASTS
BATTENING	BAUR	BAYTS	BEAMING	BEAT
BATTENINGS	BAURS	BAZAAR	BEAMINGLY	BEATABLE
BATTENS	BAUSOND	BAZAARS	BEAMINGS	BEATEN
BATTER	BAUXITE	BAZAR	BEAMISH	BEATER
BATTERED	BAUXITES	BAZARS	BEAMLESS	BEATERS
BATTERIE	BAUXITIC	BAZAZZ	BEAMLET	BEATH
BATTERIES	BAVARDAGE	BAZAZZES	BEAMLETS	BEATHED
BATTERING	BAVARDAGES	BAZOOKA	BEAMS	BEATHING
BATTERO	BAVIN	BAZOOKAS	BEAMY	BEATHS
BATTEROS	BAVINS	BAZOUKI	BEAN	BEATIFIC
BATTERS	BAWBEE	BAZOUKIS	BEANBAG	BEATIFIED
BATTERY	BAWBEES	BDELLIUM	BEANBAGS	BEATIFIES
BATTIER	BAWBLE	BDELLIUMS	BEANED	BEATIFY
BATTIEST	BAWBLES	BE	BEANERIES	BEATIFYING
BATTILL	BAWCOCK	BEACH	BEANERY	BEATING
BATTILLED	BAWCOCKS	BEACHED	BEANFEAST	BEATINGS
BATTILLING	BAWD	BEACHES	BEANFEASTS	BEATITUDE
BATTILLS	BAWDIER	BEACHHEAD	BEANIE	BEATITUDES
BATTING	BAWDIES	BEACHHEADS	BEANIES	BEATNIK
BATTINGS	BAWDIEST	BEACHIER	BEANING	BEATNIKS
BATTLE	BAWDILY	BEACHIEST	BEANO	BEATS
BATTLED	BAWDINESS	BEACHING	BEANOS	BEAU
BATTLER	BAWDINESSES	BEACHY	BEANPOLE	BEAUFET
BATTLERS	BAWDKIN	BEACON	BEANPOLES	BEAUFETS
BATTLES	BAWDKINS	BEACONED	BEANS	BEAUFFET
BATTLING	BAWDRIES	BEACONING	BEANSTALK	BEAUFFETS
BATTOLOGIES	BAWDRY	BEACONS	BEANSTALKS	BEAUFIN
BATTOLOGY	BAWDS	BEAD	BEAR	BEAUFINS
BATTS	BAWDY	BEADED	BEARABLE	BEAUISH
BATTUE	BAWL	BEADIER	BEARABLY	BEAUT
BATTUES	BAWLED	BEADIEST	BEARBINE	BEAUTEOUS
BATTUTA	BAWLER	BEADING	BEARBINES	BEAUTIED
BATTUTAS	BAWLERS	BEADINGS	BEARD	BEAUTIES
BATTY	BAWLEY	BEADLE	BEARDED	BEAUTIFIED
BATWOMAN	BAWLEYS	BEADLEDOM	BEARDIE	BEAUTIFIES
BATWOMEN	BAWLING	BEADLEDOMS	BEARDIES	BEAUTIFUL
BAUBLE	BAWLINGS	BEADLES	BEARDING	BEAUTIFY
BAUBLES	BAWLS	BEADMAN	BEARDLESS	BEAUTIFYING
BAUBLING	BAWN	BEADMEN	BEARDS	BEAUTS
BAUCHLE	BAWNS	BEADS	BEARE	BEAUTY
BAUCHLED	BAWR	BEADSMAN	BEARED	BEAUTYING
BAUCHLES	BAWRS	BEADSMEN	BEARER	BEAUX
BAUCHLING	BAXTER	BEADY	BEARERS	BEAUXITE
BAUD	BAXTERS	BEAGLE	BEARES	BEAUXITES
BAUDEKIN	BAY	BEAGLED	BEARING	BEAVER
BAUDEKINS	BAYADERE	BEAGLER	BEARINGS	BEAVERED
BAUDRIC	BAYADERES	BEAGLERS	BEARISH	BEAVERIES
BAUDRICK	BAYARD	BEAGLES	BEARISHLY	BEAVERS
BAUDRICKE	BAYARDS	BEAGLING	BEARNAISE	BEAVERY
BAUDRICKES	BAYBERRIES	BEAGLINGS	BEARNAISES	BEBEERINE
BAUDRICKS	BAYBERRY	BEAK	BEARS	BEBEERINES

The Chambers Dictionary is the authority for many longer words; see *OSW* Introduction, page xii.

BEBEERU	BEDAGGLES	BEDFELLOW	BEDTIMES	BEERHALLS
BEBEERUS	BEDAGGLING	BEDFELLOWS	BEDUCK	BEERIER
BEBOP	BEDARKEN	BEDIDE	BEDUCKED	BEERIEST
BEBOPPED	BEDARKENED	BEDIGHT	BEDUCKING	BEERINESS
BEBOPPING	BEDARKENING	BEDIGHTING	BEDUCKS	BEERINESSES
BEBOPS	BEDARKENS	BEDIGHTS	BEDUIN	BEERS
BEBUNG	BEDASH	BEDIM	BEDUINS	BEERY
BEBUNGS	BEDASHED	BEDIMMED	BEDUNG	BEES
BECALL	BEDASHES	BEDIMMING	BEDUNGED	BEESOME
BECALLED	BEDASHING	BEDIMMINGS	BEDUNGING	BEESTINGS
BECALLING	BEDAUB	BEDIMS	BEDUNGS	BEESWAX
BECALLS	BEDAUBED	BEDIZEN	BEDUST	BEESWAXED
BECALM	BEDAUBING	BEDIZENED	BEDUSTED	BEESWAXES
BECALMED	BEDAUBS	BEDIZENING	BEDUSTING	BEESWAXING
BECALMING	BEDAWIN	BEDIZENS	BEDUSTS	BEESWING
BECALMS	BEDAWINS	BEDLAM	BEDWARD	BEESWINGS
BECAME	BEDAZE	BEDLAMISM	BEDWARDS	BEET
BECASSE	BEDAZED	BEDLAMISMS	BEDWARF	BEETED
BECASSES	BEDAZES	BEDLAMITE	BEDWARFED	BEETING
BECAUSE	BEDAZING	BEDLAMITES	BEDWARFING	BEETLE
BECCACCIA	BEDAZZLE	BEDLAMS	BEDWARFS	BEETLED
BECCACCIAS	BEDAZZLED	BEDMAKER	BEDYDE	BEETLES
BECCAFICO	BEDAZZLES	BEDMAKERS	BEDYE	BEETLING
BECCAFICOS	BEDAZZLING	BEDOUIN	BEDYED	BEETROOT
BECHAMEL	BEDBUG	BEDOUINS	BEDYEING	BEETROOTS
BECHAMELS	BEDBUGS	BEDPAN	BEDYES	BEETS
BECHANCE	BEDCOVER	BEDPANS	BEE	BEEVES
BECHANCED	BEDCOVERS	BEDPOST	BEECH	BEFALL
BECHANCES	BEDDABLE	BEDPOSTS	BEECHEN	BEFALLEN
BECHANCING	BEDDED	BEDRAGGLE	BEECHES	BEFALLING
BECHARM	BEDDER	BEDRAGGLED	BEEF	BEFALLS
BECHARMED	BEDDERS	BEDRAGGLES	BEEFALO	BEFANA
BECHARMING	BEDDING	BEDRAGGLING	BEEFALOES	BEFANAS
BECHARMS	BEDDINGS	BEDRAL	BEEFALOS	BEFELD
BECK	BEDE	BEDRALS	BEEFCAKE	BEFELL
BECKE	BEDEAFEN	BEDRENCH	BEEFCAKES	BEFFANA
BECKED	BEDEAFENED	BEDRENCHED	BEEFEATER	BEFFANAS
BECKES	BEDEAFENING	BEDRENCHES	BEEFEATERS	BEFINNED
BECKET	BEDEAFENS	BEDRENCHING	BEEFED	BEFIT
BECKETS	BEDECK	BEDRID	BEEFIER	BEFITS
BECKING	BEDECKED	BEDRIDDEN	BEEFIEST	BEFITTED
BECKON	BEDECKING	BEDRIGHT	BEEFING	BEFITTING
BECKONED	BEDECKS	BEDRIGHTS	BEEFS	BEFLOWER
BECKONING	BEDEGUAR	BEDROCK	BEEFSTEAK	BEFLOWERED
BECKONS	BEDEGUARS	BEDROCKS	BEEFSTEAKS	BEFLOWERING
BECKS	BEDEL	BEDROOM	BEEFY	BEFLOWERS
BECLOUD	BEDELL	BEDROOMS	BEEGAH	BEFLUM
BECLOUDED	BEDELLS	BEDROP	BEEGAHS	BEFLUMMED
BECLOUDING	BEDELS	BEDROPPED	BEEHIVE	BEFLUMMING
BECLOUDS	BEDELSHIP	BEDROPPING	BEEHIVES	BEFLUMS
BECOME	BEDELSHIPS	BEDROPS	BEEKEEPER	BEFOAM
BECOMES	BEDEMAN	BEDROPT	BEEKEEPERS	BEFOAMED
BECOMING	BEDEMEN	BEDS	BEELINE	BEFOAMING
BECQUEREL	BEDERAL	BEDSIDE	BEELINES	BEFOAMS
BECQUERELS	BEDERALS	BEDSIDES	BEEN	BEFOG
BECURL	BEDES	BEDSOCKS	BEENAH	BEFOGGED
BECURLED	BEDESMAN	BEDSORE	BEENAHS	BEFOGGING
BECURLING	BEDESMEN	BEDSORES	BEEP	BEFOGS
BECURLS	BEDEVIL	BEDSPREAD	BEEPED	BEFOOL
BED	BEDEVILLED	BEDSPREADS	BEEPER	BEFOOLED
BEDABBLE	BEDEVILLING	BEDSTEAD	BEEPERS	BEFOOLING
BEDABBLED	BEDEVILS	BEDSTEADS	BEEPING	BEFOOLS
BEDABBLES	BEDEW	BEDSTRAW	BEEPS	BEFORE
BEDABBLING	BEDEWED	BEDSTRAWS	BEER	BEFORTUNE
BEDAD	BEDEWING	BEDTICK	BEERAGE	BEFORTUNED
BEDAGGLE	BEDEWS	BEDTICKS	BEERAGES	BEFORTUNES
BEDAGGLED	BEDFAST	BEDTIME	BEERHALL	BEFORTUNING

The Chambers Dictionary is the authority for many longer words; see *OSW* Introduction, page xii.

BEFOUL	BEGIRT	BEHAVIOUR	BEJESUIT	BELEEING
BEFOULED	BEGLAMOUR	BEHAVIOURS	BEJESUITED	BELEES
BEFOULING	BEGLAMOURED	BEHEAD	BEJESUITING	BELEMNITE
BEFOULS	BEGLAMOURING	BEHEADAL	BEJESUITS	BELEMNITES
BEFRIEND	BEGLAMOURS	BEHEADALS	BEJEWEL	BELFRIED
BEFRIENDED	BEGLERBEG	BEHEADED	BEJEWELLED	BELFRIES
BEFRIENDING	BEGLERBEGS	BEHEADING	BEJEWELLING	BELFRY
BEFRIENDS	BEGLOOM	BEHEADINGS	BEJEWELS	BELGA
BEFRINGE	BEGLOOMED	BEHEADS	BEKAH	BELGARD
BEFRINGED	BEGLOOMING	BEHELD	BEKAHS	BELGARDS
BEFRINGES	BEGLOOMS	BEHEMOTH	BEKISS	BELGAS
BEFRINGING	BEGNAW	BEHEMOTHS	BEKISSED	BELIE
BEFUDDLE	BEGNAWED	BEHEST	BEKISSES	BELIED
BEFUDDLED	BEGNAWING	BEHESTS	BEKISSING	BELIEF
BEFUDDLES	BEGNAWS	BEHIGHT	BEKNAVE	BELIEFS
BEFUDDLING	BEGO	BEHIGHTING	BEKNAVED	BELIER
BEG	BEGOES	BEHIGHTS	BEKNAVES	BELIERS
BEGAD	BEGOING	BEHIND	BEKNAVING	BELIES
BEGAN	BEGONE	BEHINDS	BEKNOWN	BELIEVE
BEGAR	BEGONIA	BEHOLD	BEL	BELIEVED
BEGARS	BEGONIAS	BEHOLDEN	BELABOR	BELIEVER
BEGAT	BEGORED	BEHOLDER	BELABORED	BELIEVERS
BEGEM	BEGORRA	BEHOLDERS	BELABORING	BELIEVES
BEGEMMED	BEGORRAH	BEHOLDING	BELABORS	BELIEVING
BEGEMMING	BEGOT	BEHOLDINGS	BELABOUR	BELIKE
BEGEMS	BEGOTTEN	BEHOLDS	BELABOURED	BELITTLE
BEGET	BEGRIME	BEHOOF	BELABOURING	BELITTLED
BEGETS	BEGRIMED	BEHOOFS	BELABOURS	BELITTLES
BEGETTER	BEGRIMES	BEHOOVE	BELACE	BELITTLING
BEGETTERS	BEGRIMING	BEHOOVED	BELACED	BELIVE
BEGETTING	BEGRUDGE	BEHOOVES	BELACES	BELL
BEGGAR	BEGRUDGED	BEHOOVING	BELACING	BELLBIND
BEGGARDOM	BEGRUDGES	BEHOTE	BELAH	BELLBINDS
BEGGARDOMS	BEGRUDGING	BEHOTES	BELAHS	BELLCOTE
BEGGARED	BEGS	BEHOTING	BELAMIES	BELLCOTES
BEGGARIES	BEGUILE	BEHOVE	BELAMOURE	BELLE
BEGGARING	BEGUILED	BEHOVED	BELAMOURES	BELLED
BEGGARLY	BEGUILER	BEHOVEFUL	BELAMY	BELLES
BEGGARS	BEGUILERS	BEHOVELY	BELATE	BELLETER
BEGGARY	BEGUILES	BEHOVES	BELATED	BELLETERS
BEGGED	BEGUILING	BEHOVING	BELATEDLY	BELLHOP
BEGGING	BEGUIN	BEHOWL	BELATES	BELLHOPS
BEGGINGLY	BEGUINAGE	BEHOWLED	BELATING	BELLIBONE
BEGGINGS	BEGUINAGES	BEHOWLING	BELAUD	BELLIBONES
BEGHARD	BEGUINE	BEHOWLS	BELAUDED	BELLICOSE
BEGHARDS	BEGUINES	BEIGE	BELAUDING	BELLIED
BEGIFT	BEGUINS	BEIGEL	BELAUDS	BELLIES
BEGIFTED	BEGUM	BEIGELS	BELAY	BELLING
BEGIFTING	BEGUMS	BEIGES	BELAYED	BELLMAN
BEGIFTS	BEGUN	BEIGNET	BELAYING	BELLMEN
BEGILD	BEGUNK	BEIGNETS	BELAYS	BELLOW
BEGILDED	BEGUNKED	BEIN	BELCH	BELLOWED
BEGILDING	BEGUNKING	BEING	BELCHED	BELLOWER
BEGILDS	BEGUNKS	BEINGLESS	BELCHER	BELLOWERS
BEGILT	BEHALF	BEINGNESS	BELCHERS	BELLOWING
BEGIN	BEHALVES	BEINGNESSES	BELCHES	BELLOWS
BEGINNE	BEHAPPEN	BEINGS	BELCHING	BELLPUSH
BEGINNER	BEHAPPENED	BEINKED	BELDAM	BELLPUSHES
BEGINNERS	BEHAPPENING	BEINNESS	BELDAME	BELLS
BEGINNES	BEHAPPENS	BEINNESSES	BELDAMES	BELLWORT
BEGINNING	BEHATTED	BEJABERS	BELDAMS	BELLWORTS
BEGINNINGS	BEHAVE	BEJADE	BELEAGUER	BELLY
BEGINS	BEHAVED	BEJADED	BELEAGUERED	BELLYFUL
BEGIRD	BEHAVES	BEJADES	BELEAGUERING	BELLYFULS
BEGIRDED	BEHAVING	BEJADING	BELEAGUERS	BELLYING
BEGIRDING	BEHAVIOR	BEJANT	BELEE	BELLYINGS
BEGIRDS	BEHAVIORS	BEJANTS	BELEED	BELOMANCIES

The Chambers Dictionary is the authority for many longer words; see *OSW* Introduction, page xii.

BELOMANCY	BEMOANERS	BENEDIGHT	BENTHOS	BEPITYING
BELONG	BEMOANING	BENEFACT	BENTHOSES	BEPLASTER
BELONGED	BEMOANINGS	BENEFACTED	BENTIER	BEPLASTERED
BELONGER	BEMOANS	BENEFACTING	BENTIEST	BEPLASTERING
BELONGERS	BEMOCK	BENEFACTS	BENTONITE	BEPLASTERS
BELONGING	BEMOCKED	BENEFIC	BENTONITES	BEPLUMED
BELONGINGS	BEMOCKING	BENEFICE	BENTS	BEPOMMEL
BELONGS	BEMOCKS	BENEFICED	BENTWOOD	BEPOMMELLED
BELOVE	BEMOIL	BENEFICES	BENTWOODS	BEPOMMELLING
BELOVED	BEMOILED	BENEFIT	BENTY	BEPOMMELS
BELOVEDS	BEMOILING	BENEFITED	BENUMB	BEPOWDER
BELOVES	BEMOILS	BENEFITING	BENUMBED	BEPOWDERED
BELOVING	BEMONSTER	BENEFITS	BENUMBING	BEPOWDERING
BELOW	BEMONSTERED	BENEFITTED	BENUMBS	BEPOWDERS
BELS	BEMONSTERING	BENEFITTING	BENZAL	BEPRAISE
BELT	BEMONSTERS	BENEMPT	BENZALS	BEPRAISED
BELTED	BEMOUTH	BENES	BENZENE	BEPRAISES
BELTER	BEMOUTHED	BENET	BENZENES	BEPRAISING
BELTERS	BEMOUTHING	BENETS	BENZIDINE	BEPROSE
BELTING	BEMOUTHS	BENETTED	BENZIDINES	BEPROSED
BELTINGS	BEMUD	BENETTING	BENZIL	BEPROSES
BELTMAN	BEMUDDED	BENGALINE	BENZILS	BEPROSING
BELTMEN	BEMUDDING	BENGALINES	BENZINE	BEPUFF
BELTS	BEMUDDLE	BENI	BENZINES	BEPUFFED
BELTWAY	BEMUDDLED	BENIGHT	BENZOATE	BEPUFFING
BELTWAYS	BEMUDDLES	BENIGHTED	BENZOATES	BEPUFFS
BELUGA	BEMUDDLING	BENIGHTEN	BENZOIC	BEQUEATH
BELUGAS	BEMUDS	BENIGHTENED	BENZOIN	BEQUEATHED
BELVEDERE	BEMUFFLE	BENIGHTENING	BENZOINS	BEQUEATHING
BELVEDERES	BEMUFFLED	BENIGHTENINGS	BENZOL	BEQUEATHS
BELYING	BEMUFFLES	BENIGHTENS	BENZOLE	BEQUEST
BEMA	BEMUFFLING	BENIGHTER	BENZOLES	BEQUESTS
BEMAD	BEMUSE	BENIGHTERS	BENZOLINE	BERATE
BEMADDED	BEMUSED	BENIGHTING	BENZOLINES	BERATED
BEMADDING	BEMUSES	BENIGHTINGS	BENZOLS	BERATES
BEMADS	BEMUSING	BENIGHTS	BENZOYL	BERATING
BEMAS	BEN	BENIGN	BENZOYLS	BERAY
BEMATA	BENAME	BENIGNANT	BENZYL	BERAYED
BEMAUL	BENAMED	BENIGNER	BENZYLS	BERAYING
BEMAULED	BENAMES	BENIGNEST	BEPAINT	BERAYS
BEMAULING	BENAMING	BENIGNITIES	BEPAINTED	BERBERINE
BEMAULS	BENCH	BENIGNITY	BEPAINTING	BERBERINES
BEMAZED	BENCHED	BENIGNLY	BEPAINTS	BERBERIS
BEMBEX	BENCHER	BENIS	BEPAT	BERBERISES
BEMBEXES	BENCHERS	BENISEED	BEPATCHED	BERCEAU
BEMBIX	BENCHES	BENISEEDS	BEPATS	BERCEAUX
BEMBIXES	BENCHING	BENISON	BEPATTED	BERCEUSE
BEMEAN	BENCHMARK	BENISONS	BEPATTING	BERCEUSES
BEMEANED	BENCHMARKS	BENITIER	BEPEARL	BERDACHE
BEMEANING	BEND	BENITIERS	BEPEARLED	BERDACHES
BEMEANS	BENDED	BENJ	BEPEARLING	BERDASH
BEMEANT	BENDEE	BENJAMIN	BEPEARLS	BERDASHES
BEMEDAL	BENDER	BENJAMINS	BEPELT	BERE
BEMEDALLED	BENDERS	BENJES	BEPELTED	BEREAVE
BEMEDALLING	BENDIER	BENNE	BEPELTING	BEREAVED
BEMEDALS	BENDIEST	BENNES	BEPELTS	BEREAVEN
BEMETE	BENDING	BENNET	BEPEPPER	BEREAVES
BEMETED	BENDINGLY	BENNETS	BEPEPPERED	BEREAVING
BEMETES	BENDINGS	BENNI	BEPEPPERING	BEREFT
BEMETING	BENDLET	BENNIES	BEPEPPERS	BERES
BEMIRE	BENDLETS	BENNIS	BEPESTER	BERET
BEMIRED	BENDS	BENNY	BEPESTERED	BERETS
BEMIRES	BENDWISE	BENS	BEPESTERING	BERG
BEMIRING	BENDY	BENT	BEPESTERS	BERGAMA
BEMOAN	BENE	BENTHIC	BEPITIED	BERGAMAS
BEMOANED	BENEATH	BENTHOAL	BEPITIES	BERGAMASK
BEMOANER	BENEDICT	BENTHONIC	BEPITY	BERGAMASKS

The Chambers Dictionary is the authority for many longer words; see *OSW* Introduction, page xii.

BERGAMOT
BERGAMOTS
BERGANDER
BERGANDERS
BERGENIA
BERGENIAS
BERGERE
BERGERES
BERGFALL
BERGFALLS
BERGHAAN
BERGHAANS
BERGMEHL
BERGMEHLS
BERGOMASK
BERGOMASKS
BERGS
BERGYLT
BERGYLTS
BERIBERI
BERIBERIS
BERK
BERKELIUM
BERKELIUMS
BERKS
BERLEY
BERLEYS
BERLIN
BERLINE
BERLINES
BERLINS
BERM
BERMS
BEROB
BEROBBED
BEROBBING
BEROBS
BERRET
BERRETS
BERRIED
BERRIES
BERRY
BERRYING
BERRYINGS
BERSERK
BERSERKER
BERSERKERS
BERSERKLY
BERSERKS
BERTH
BERTHA
BERTHAGE
BERTHAGES
BERTHAS
BERTHE
BERTHED
BERTHES
BERTHING
BERTHS
BERYL
BERYLLIA
BERYLLIAS
BERYLLIUM
BERYLLIUMS
BERYLS
BESAINT
BESAINTED

BESAINTING
BESAINTS
BESANG
BESAT
BESAW
BESCATTER
BESCATTERED
BESCATTERING
BESCATTERS
BESCRAWL
BESCRAWLED
BESCRAWLING
BESCRAWLS
BESCREEN
BESCREENED
BESCREENING
BESCREENS
BESEE
BESEECH
BESEECHED
BESEECHER
BESEECHERS
BESEECHES
BESEECHING
BESEECHINGS
BESEEING
BESEEKE
BESEEKES
BESEEKING
BESEEM
BESEEMED
BESEEMING
BESEEMINGS
BESEEMLY
BESEEMS
BESEEN
BESEES
BESET
BESETMENT
BESETMENTS
BESETS
BESETTER
BESETTERS
BESETTING
BESHADOW
BESHADOWED
BESHADOWING
BESHADOWS
BESHAME
BESHAMED
BESHAMES
BESHAMING
BESHINE
BESHINES
BESHINING
BESHONE
BESHREW
BESHREWED
BESHREWING
BESHREWS
BESIDE
BESIDES
BESIEGE
BESIEGED
BESIEGER
BESIEGERS
BESIEGES

BESIEGING
BESIEGINGS
BESIGH
BESIGHED
BESIGHING
BESIGHS
BESING
BESINGING
BESINGS
BESIT
BESITS
BESITTING
BESLAVE
BESLAVED
BESLAVER
BESLAVERED
BESLAVERING
BESLAVERS
BESLAVES
BESLAVING
BESLOBBER
BESLOBBERED
BESLOBBERING
BESLOBBERS
BESLUBBER
BESLUBBERED
BESLUBBERING
BESLUBBERS
BESMEAR
BESMEARED
BESMEARING
BESMEARS
BESMIRCH
BESMIRCHED
BESMIRCHES
BESMIRCHING
BESMUT
BESMUTCH
BESMUTCHED
BESMUTCHES
BESMUTCHING
BESMUTS
BESMUTTED
BESMUTTING
BESOGNIO
BESOGNIOS
BESOIN
BESOINS
BESOM
BESOMED
BESOMING
BESOMS
BESONIAN
BESONIANS
BESORT
BESORTED
BESORTING
BESORTS
BESOT
BESOTS
BESOTTED
BESOTTING
BESOUGHT
BESOULED
BESPAKE
BESPANGLE
BESPANGLED

BESPANGLES
BESPANGLING
BESPAT
BESPATE
BESPATTER
BESPATTERED
BESPATTERING
BESPATTERS
BESPEAK
BESPEAKING
BESPEAKS
BESPECKLE
BESPECKLED
BESPECKLES
BESPECKLING
BESPED
BESPEED
BESPEEDING
BESPEEDS
BESPICE
BESPICED
BESPICES
BESPICING
BESPIT
BESPITS
BESPITTING
BESPOKE
BESPOKEN
BESPORT
BESPORTED
BESPORTING
BESPORTS
BESPOT
BESPOTS
BESPOTTED
BESPOTTING
BESPOUT
BESPOUTED
BESPOUTING
BESPOUTS
BESPREAD
BESPREADING
BESPREADS
BESPRENT
BEST
BESTAD
BESTADDE
BESTAIN
BESTAINED
BESTAINING
BESTAINS
BESTAR
BESTARRED
BESTARRING
BESTARS
BESTEAD
BESTEADED
BESTEADING
BESTEADS
BESTED
BESTIAL
BESTIALS
BESTIARIES
BESTIARY
BESTICK
BESTICKING
BESTICKS

BESTILL
BESTILLED
BESTILLING
BESTILLS
BESTING
BESTIR
BESTIRRED
BESTIRRING
BESTIRS
BESTORM
BESTORMED
BESTORMING
BESTORMS
BESTOW
BESTOWAL
BESTOWALS
BESTOWED
BESTOWER
BESTOWERS
BESTOWING
BESTOWS
BESTREAK
BESTREAKED
BESTREAKING
BESTREAKS
BESTREW
BESTREWED
BESTREWING
BESTREWN
BESTREWS
BESTRID
BESTRIDDEN
BESTRIDE
BESTRIDES
BESTRIDING
BESTRODE
BESTROWN
BESTS
BESTUCK
BESTUD
BESTUDDED
BESTUDDING
BESTUDS
BESUITED
BESUNG
BET
BETA
BETACISM
BETACISMS
BETAINE
BETAINES
BETAKE
BETAKEN
BETAKES
BETAKING
BETAS
BETATRON
BETATRONS
BETE
BETED
BETEEM
BETEEME
BETEEMED
BETEEMES
BETEEMING
BETEEMS
BETEL

BETELS	BETRAYED	BEWARE	BHANGS	BICKERING
BETES	BETRAYER	BEWARED	BHARAL	BICKERS
BETH	BETRAYERS	BEWARES	BHARALS	BICONCAVE
BETHANKIT	BETRAYING	BEWARING	BHEESTIE	BICONVEX
BETHANKITS	BETRAYS	BEWEEP	BHEESTIES	BICORN
BETHEL	BETREAD	BEWEEPING	BHEESTY	BICORNE
BETHELS	BETREADING	BEWEEPS	BHEL	BICORNES
BETHESDA	BETREADS	BEWENT	BHELS	BICORNS
BETHESDAS	BETRIM	BEWEPT	BHINDI	BICUSPID
BETHINK	BETRIMMED	BEWET	BHINDIS	BICUSPIDS
BETHINKING	BETRIMMING	BEWETS	BHISTEE	BICYCLE
BETHINKS	BETRIMS	BEWETTED	BHISTEES	BICYCLED
BETHOUGHT	BETROD	BEWETTING	BHISTI	BICYCLES
BETHRALL	BETRODDEN	BEWHORE	BHISTIS	BICYCLING
BETHRALLED	BETROTH	BEWHORED	BI	BICYCLIST
BETHRALLING	BETROTHAL	BEWHORES	BIANNUAL	BICYCLISTS
BETHRALLS	BETROTHALS	BEWHORING	BIANNUALS	BID
BETHS	BETROTHED	BEWIG	BIAS	BIDARKA
BETHUMB	BETROTHEDS	BEWIGGED	BIASED	BIDARKAS
BETHUMBED	BETROTHING	BEWIGGING	BIASES	BIDDABLE
BETHUMBING	BETROTHS	BEWIGS	BIASING	BIDDEN
BETHUMBS	BETS	BEWILDER	BIASINGS	BIDDER
BETHUMP	BETTED	BEWILDERED	BIASSED	BIDDERS
BETHUMPED	BETTER	BEWILDERING	BIASSES	BIDDIES
BETHUMPING	BETTERED	BEWILDERS	BIASSING	BIDDING
BETHUMPS	BETTERING	BEWITCH	BIATHLETE	BIDDINGS
BETHWACK	BETTERINGS	BEWITCHED	BIATHLETES	BIDDY
BETHWACKED	BETTERS	BEWITCHES	BIATHLON	BIDE
BETHWACKING	BETTIES	BEWITCHING	BIATHLONS	BIDED
BETHWACKS	BETTING	BEWRAY	BIAXAL	BIDENT
BETID	BETTINGS	BEWRAYED	BIAXIAL	BIDENTAL
BETIDE	BETTOR	BEWRAYING	BIB	BIDENTALS
BETIDED	BETTORS	BEWRAYS	BIBACIOUS	BIDENTATE
BETIDES	BETTY	BEY	BIBATION	BIDENTS
BETIDING	BETUMBLED	BEYOND	BIBATIONS	BIDES
BETIGHT	BETWEEN	BEYONDS	BIBBED	BIDET
BETIME	BETWEENS	BEYS	BIBBER	BIDETS
BETIMED	BETWIXT	BEZ	BIBBERS	BIDING
BETIMES	BEURRE	BEZANT	BIBBING	BIDINGS
BETIMING	BEURRES	BEZANTS	BIBCOCK	BIDON
BETING	BEVATRON	BEZAZZ	BIBCOCKS	BIDONS
BETISE	BEVATRONS	BEZAZZES	BIBELOT	BIDS
BETISES	BEVEL	BEZEL	BIBELOTS	BIELD
BETITLE	BEVELLED	BEZELS	BIBLE	BIELDED
BETITLED	BEVELLER	BEZES	BIBLES	BIELDIER
BETITLES	BEVELLERS	BEZIQUE	BIBLICAL	BIELDIEST
BETITLING	BEVELLING	BEZIQUES	BIBLICISM	BIELDING
BETOIL	BEVELLINGS	BEZOAR	BIBLICISMS	BIELDS
BETOILED	BEVELMENT	BEZOARDIC	BIBLICIST	BIELDY
BETOILING	BEVELMENTS	BEZOARS	BIBLICISTS	BIEN
BETOILS	BEVELS	BEZONIAN	BIBLIST	BIENNIAL
BETOKEN	BEVER	BEZONIANS	BIBLISTS	BIENNIALS
BETOKENED	BEVERAGE	BEZZLE	BIBS	BIER
BETOKENING	BEVERAGES	BEZZLED	BIBULOUS	BIERS
BETOKENS	BEVERS	BEZZLES	BICAMERAL	BIESTINGS
BETON	BEVIES	BEZZLING	BICARB	BIFACIAL
BETONIES	BEVUE	BHAGEE	BICARBS	BIFARIOUS
BETONS	BEVUES	BHAGEES	BICCIES	BIFF
BETONY	BEVVIED	BHAJAN	BICCY	BIFFED
BETOOK	BEVVIES	BHAJANS	BICE	BIFFIN
BETOSS	BEVVY	BHAJEE	BICEPS	BIFFING
BETOSSED	BEVY	BHAJEES	BICEPSES	BIFFINS
BETOSSES	BEWAIL	BHAKTI	BICES	BIFFS
BETOSSING	BEWAILED	BHAKTIS	BICHORD	BIFID
BETRAY	BEWAILING	BHANG	BICIPITAL	BIFILAR
BETRAYAL	BEWAILINGS	BHANGRA	BICKER	BIFOCAL
BETRAYALS	BEWAILS	BHANGRAS	BICKERED	BIFOCALS

The Chambers Dictionary is the authority for many longer words; see *OSW* Introduction, page xii.

BIFOLD	BIKES	BILLHOOK	BINGED	BIOLOGISTS
BIFOLIATE	BIKEWAY	BILLHOOKS	BINGEING	BIOLOGY
BIFORM	BIKEWAYS	BILLIARD	BINGER	BIOLYSES
BIFURCATE	BIKIE	BILLIARDS	BINGERS	BIOLYSIS
BIFURCATED	BIKIES	BILLIE	BINGES	BIOMASS
BIFURCATES	BIKING	BILLIES	BINGHI	BIOMASSES
BIFURCATING	BIKINGS	BILLING	BINGHIS	BIOME
BIG	BIKINI	BILLINGS	BINGIES	BIOMES
BIGA	BIKINIS	BILLION	BINGING	BIOMETRIC
BIGAE	BILABIAL	BILLIONS	BINGLE	BIOMETRICS
BIGAMIES	BILABIALS	BILLIONTH	BINGLED	BIOMETRIES
BIGAMIST	BILABIATE	BILLIONTHS	BINGLES	BIOMETRY
BIGAMISTS	BILANDER	BILLMAN	BINGLING	BIOMINING
BIGAMOUS	BILANDERS	BILLMEN	BINGO	BIOMININGS
BIGAMY	BILATERAL	BILLON	BINGOS	BIOMORPH
BIGARADE	BILBERRIES	BILLONS	BINGS	BIOMORPHS
BIGARADES	BILBERRY	BILLOW	BINGY	BIONIC
BIGENER	BILBO	BILLOWED	BINK	BIONICS
BIGENERIC	BILBOES	BILLOWIER	BINKS	BIONOMIC
BIGENERS	BILBOS	BILLOWIEST	BINMAN	BIONOMICS
BIGFOOT	BILE	BILLOWING	BINMEN	BIONT
BIGFOOTS	BILES	BILLOWS	BINNACLE	BIONTIC
BIGG	BILGE	BILLOWY	BINNACLES	BIONTS
BIGGED	BILGED	BILLS	BINNED	BIOPARENT
BIGGER	BILGES	BILLY	BINNING	BIOPARENTS
BIGGEST	BILGIER	BILLYBOY	BINOCLE	BIOPHOR
BIGGIE	BILGIEST	BILLYBOYS	BINOCLES	BIOPHORE
BIGGIES	BILGING	BILLYCOCK	BINOCULAR	BIOPHORES
BIGGIN	BILGY	BILLYCOCKS	BINOCULARS	BIOPHORS
BIGGING	BILHARZIA	BILOBAR	BINOMIAL	BIOPIC
BIGGINS	BILHARZIAS	BILOBATE	BINOMIALS	BIOPICS
BIGGISH	BILIAN	BILOBED	BINOMINAL	BIOPLASM
BIGGS	BILIANS	BILOBULAR	BINS	BIOPLASMS
BIGGY	BILIARIES	BILOCULAR	BINT	BIOPLAST
BIGHA	BILIARY	BILTONG	BINTS	BIOPLASTS
BIGHAS	BILIMBI	BILTONGS	BINTURONG	BIOPSIES
BIGHEADED	BILIMBING	BIMANAL	BINTURONGS	BIOPSY
BIGHORN	BILIMBINGS	BIMANOUS	BIO	BIOS
BIGHORNS	BILIMBIS	BIMANUAL	BIOASSAY	BIOSCOPE
BIGHT	BILINGUAL	BIMBASHI	BIOASSAYS	BIOSCOPES
BIGHTS	BILIOUS	BIMBASHIS	BIOBLAST	BIOSPHERE
BIGMOUTH	BILIOUSLY	BIMBETTE	BIOBLASTS	BIOSPHERES
BIGMOUTHS	BILIRUBIN	BIMBETTES	BIOCIDAL	BIOSTABLE
BIGNESS	BILIRUBINS	BIMBO	BIOCIDE	BIOTA
BIGNESSES	BILITERAL	BIMBOS	BIOCIDES	BIOTAS
BIGNONIA	BILK	BIMODAL	BIODATA	BIOTIC
BIGNONIAS	BILKED	BIMONTHLY	BIOETHICS	BIOTIN
BIGOT	BILKER	BIN	BIOG	BIOTINS
BIGOTED	BILKERS	BINARIES	BIOGAS	BIOTITE
BIGOTRIES	BILKING	BINARY	BIOGASES	BIOTITES
BIGOTRY	BILKS	BINATE	BIOGEN	BIOTYPE
BIGOTS	BILL	BINAURAL	BIOGENIC	BIOTYPES
BIGS	BILLABONG	BIND	BIOGENIES	BIPAROUS
BIGUANIDE	BILLABONGS	BINDER	BIOGENOUS	BIPARTITE
BIGUANIDES	BILLBOARD	BINDERIES	BIOGENS	BIPED
BIGWIG	BILLBOARDS	BINDERS	BIOGENY	BIPEDAL
BIGWIGS	BILLBOOK	BINDERY	BIOGRAPH	BIPEDS
BIJECTION	BILLBOOKS	BINDING	BIOGRAPHED	BIPHASIC
BIJECTIONS	BILLED	BINDINGS	BIOGRAPHIES	BIPHENYL
BIJOU	BILLET	BINDS	BIOGRAPHING	BIPHENYLS
BIJOUX	BILLETED	BINDWEED	BIOGRAPHS	BIPINNATE
BIJWONER	BILLETING	BINDWEEDS	BIOGRAPHY	BIPLANE
BIJWONERS	BILLETS	BINE	BIOGS	BIPLANES
BIKE	BILLFOLD	BINERVATE	BIOHAZARD	BIPOD
BIKED	BILLFOLDS	BINES	BIOHAZARDS	BIPODS
BIKER	BILLHEAD	BING	BIOLOGIES	BIPOLAR
BIKERS	BILLHEADS	BINGE	BIOLOGIST	BIPYRAMID

The Chambers Dictionary is the authority for many longer words; see *OSW* Introduction, page xii.

BIPYRAMIDS	BIRSIER	BISTER	BITTY	BLACKER
BIRAMOUS	BIRSIEST	BISTERS	BITUMED	BLACKEST
BIRCH	BIRSLE	BISTORT	BITUMEN	BLACKFACE
BIRCHED	BIRSLED	BISTORTS	BITUMENS	BLACKFACES
BIRCHEN	BIRSLES	BISTOURIES	BIVALENCE	BLACKFISH
BIRCHES	BIRSLING	BISTOURY	BIVALENCES	BLACKFISHES
BIRCHING	BIRSY	BISTRE	BIVALENCIES	BLACKGAME
BIRD	BIRTH	BISTRED	BIVALENCY	BLACKGAMES
BIRDBATH	BIRTHDAY	BISTRES	BIVALENT	BLACKHEAD
BIRDBATHS	BIRTHDAYS	BISTRO	BIVALENTS	BLACKHEADS
BIRDCAGE	BIRTHDOM	BISTROS	BIVALVE	BLACKING
BIRDCAGES	BIRTHDOMS	BISULCATE	BIVALVES	BLACKINGS
BIRDCALL	BIRTHED	BIT	BIVARIANT	BLACKISH
BIRDCALLS	BIRTHING	BITCH	BIVARIANTS	BLACKJACK
BIRDED	BIRTHINGS	BITCHED	BIVARIATE	BLACKJACKED
BIRDER	BIRTHMARK	BITCHERIES	BIVARIATES	BLACKJACKING
BIRDERS	BIRTHMARKS	BITCHERY	BIVIA	BLACKJACKS
BIRDIE	BIRTHS	BITCHES	BIVIOUS	BLACKLEAD
BIRDIED	BIRTHWORT	BITCHIER	BIVIUM	BLACKLEADS
BIRDIEING	BIRTHWORTS	BITCHIEST	BIVOUAC	BLACKLEG
BIRDIES	BIRYANI	BITCHILY	BIVOUACKED	BLACKLEGGED
BIRDING	BIRYANIS	BITCHING	BIVOUACKING	BLACKLEGGING
BIRDINGS	BIS	BITCHY	BIVOUACS	BLACKLEGS
BIRDLIKE	BISCACHA	BITE	BIVVIED	BLACKLIST
BIRDMAN	BISCACHAS	BITER	BIVVIES	BLACKLISTED
BIRDMEN	BISCUIT	BITERS	BIVVY	BLACKLISTING
BIRDS	BISCUITS	BITES	BIVVYING	BLACKLISTINGS
BIRDSEED	BISCUITY	BITING	BIZ	BLACKLISTS
BIRDSEEDS	BISE	BITINGS	BIZARRE	BLACKLY
BIRDSHOT	BISECT	BITLESS	BIZAZZ	BLACKMAIL
BIRDSHOTS	BISECTED	BITMAP	BIZAZZES	BLACKMAILED
BIRDSONG	BISECTING	BITMAPS	BIZCACHA	BLACKMAILING
BIRDSONGS	BISECTION	BITO	BIZCACHAS	BLACKMAILS
BIRDWING	BISECTIONS	BITONAL	BIZONAL	BLACKNESS
BIRDWINGS	BISECTOR	BITOS	BIZONE	BLACKNESSES
BIREME	BISECTORS	BITS	BIZONES	BLACKOUT
BIREMES	BISECTS	BITSIER	BIZZES	BLACKOUTS
BIRETTA	BISERIAL	BITSIEST	BLAB	BLACKS
BIRETTAS	BISERRATE	BITSY	BLABBED	BLACKTOP
BIRIYANI	BISES	BITT	BLABBER	BLACKTOPS
BIRIYANIS	BISEXUAL	BITTACLE	BLABBERS	BLACKWASH
BIRK	BISEXUALS	BITTACLES	BLABBING	BLACKWASHES
BIRKEN	BISH	BITTE	BLABBINGS	BLACKWOOD
BIRKIE	BISHES	BITTED	BLABS	BLACKWOODS
BIRKIER	BISHOP	BITTEN	BLACK	BLAD
BIRKIES	BISHOPDOM	BITTER	BLACKBALL	BLADDED
BIRKIEST	BISHOPDOMS	BITTERER	BLACKBALLED	BLADDER
BIRKS	BISHOPED	BITTEREST	BLACKBALLING	BLADDERED
BIRL	BISHOPESS	BITTERISH	BLACKBALLINGS	BLADDERS
BIRLE	BISHOPESSES	BITTERLY	BLACKBALLS	BLADDERY
BIRLED	BISHOPING	BITTERN	BLACKBAND	BLADDING
BIRLER	BISHOPRIC	BITTERNS	BLACKBANDS	BLADE
BIRLERS	BISHOPRICS	BITTERS	BLACKBIRD	BLADED
BIRLES	BISHOPS	BITTIE	BLACKBIRDS	BLADES
BIRLIEMAN	BISK	BITTIER	BLACKBOY	BLADEWORK
BIRLIEMEN	BISKS	BITTIES	BLACKBOYS	BLADEWORKS
BIRLING	BISMAR	BITTIEST	BLACKBUCK	BLADS
BIRLINGS	BISMARS	BITTING	BLACKBUCKS	BLAE
BIRLINN	BISMILLAH	BITTOCK	BLACKCAP	BLAEBERRIES
BIRLINNS	BISMUTH	BITTOCKS	BLACKCAPS	BLAEBERRY
BIRLS	BISMUTHS	BITTOR	BLACKCOCK	BLAER
BIRR	BISON	BITTORS	BLACKCOCKS	BLAES
BIRRED	BISONS	BITTOUR	BLACKED	BLAEST
BIRRING	BISQUE	BITTOURS	BLACKEN	BLAG
BIRRS	BISQUES	BITTS	BLACKENED	BLAGGED
BIRSE	BISSON	BITTUR	BLACKENING	BLAGGER
BIRSES	BISTABLE	BITTURS	BLACKENS	BLAGGERS

The Chambers Dictionary is the authority for many longer words; see *OSW* Introduction, page xii.

BLAGGING	BLARING	BLAZE	BLEMISHED	BLINDAGE
BLAGS	BLARNEY	BLAZED	BLEMISHES	BLINDAGES
BLAGUE	BLARNEYED	BLAZER	BLEMISHING	BLINDED
BLAGUES	BLARNEYING	BLAZERED	BLENCH	BLINDER
BLAGUEUR	BLARNEYS	BLAZERS	BLENCHED	BLINDERS
BLAGUEURS	BLASE	BLAZES	BLENCHES	BLINDEST
BLAH	BLASH	BLAZING	BLENCHING	BLINDFISH
BLAHED	BLASHES	BLAZON	BLEND	BLINDFISHES
BLAHING	BLASHIER	BLAZONED	BLENDE	BLINDFOLD
BLAHS	BLASHIEST	BLAZONER	BLENDED	BLINDFOLDED
BLAIN	BLASHY	BLAZONERS	BLENDER	BLINDFOLDING
BLAINS	BLASPHEME	BLAZONING	BLENDERS	BLINDFOLDS
BLAISE	BLASPHEMED	BLAZONRIES	BLENDES	BLINDING
BLAIZE	BLASPHEMES	BLAZONRY	BLENDING	BLINDINGS
BLAMABLE	BLASPHEMIES	BLAZONS	BLENDINGS	BLINDLESS
BLAMABLY	BLASPHEMING	BLEACH	BLENDS	BLINDLY
BLAME	BLASPHEMY	BLEACHED	BLENNIES	BLINDNESS
BLAMEABLE	BLAST	BLEACHER	BLENNY	BLINDNESSES
BLAMEABLY	BLASTED	BLEACHERIES	BLENT	BLINDS
BLAMED	BLASTEMA	BLEACHERS	BLESBOK	BLINDWORM
BLAMEFUL	BLASTEMAS	BLEACHERY	BLESBOKS	BLINDWORMS
BLAMELESS	BLASTEMATA	BLEACHES	BLESS	BLINI
BLAMES	BLASTER	BLEACHING	BLESSED	BLINIS
BLAMING	BLASTERS	BLEACHINGS	BLESSEDER	BLINK
BLANCH	BLASTING	BLEAK	BLESSEDEST	BLINKARD
BLANCHED	BLASTINGS	BLEAKER	BLESSEDLY	BLINKARDS
BLANCHES	BLASTMENT	BLEAKEST	BLESSES	BLINKED
BLANCHING	BLASTMENTS	BLEAKLY	BLESSING	BLINKER
BLANCO	BLASTOID	BLEAKNESS	BLESSINGS	BLINKERED
BLANCOED	BLASTOIDS	BLEAKNESSES	BLEST	BLINKERING
BLANCOING	BLASTS	BLEAKS	BLET	BLINKERS
BLANCOS	BLASTULA	BLEAKY	BLETHER	BLINKING
BLAND	BLASTULAE	BLEAR	BLETHERED	BLINKS
BLANDER	BLASTULAR	BLEARED	BLETHERER	BLINNED
BLANDEST	BLASTULAS	BLEARER	BLETHERERS	BLINNING
BLANDISH	BLAT	BLEAREST	BLETHERING	BLINS
BLANDISHED	BLATANT	BLEAREYED	BLETHERINGS	BLINTZ
BLANDISHES	BLATANTLY	BLEARIER	BLETHERS	BLINTZE
BLANDISHING	BLATE	BLEARIEST	BLETS	BLINTZES
BLANDLY	BLATER	BLEARING	BLETTED	BLIP
BLANDNESS	BLATEST	BLEARS	BLETTING	BLIPPED
BLANDNESSES	BLATHER	BLEARY	BLEUATRE	BLIPPING
BLANDS	BLATHERED	BLEAT	BLEW	BLIPS
BLANK	BLATHERER	BLEATED	BLEWART	BLISS
BLANKED	BLATHERERS	BLEATER	BLEWARTS	BLISSES
BLANKER	BLATHERING	BLEATERS	BLEWITS	BLISSFUL
BLANKEST	BLATHERS	BLEATING	BLEWITSES	BLISSLESS
BLANKET	BLATS	BLEATINGS	BLEY	BLIST
BLANKETED	BLATT	BLEATS	BLEYS	BLISTER
BLANKETIES	BLATTANT	BLEB	BLIGHT	BLISTERED
BLANKETING	BLATTED	BLEBS	BLIGHTED	BLISTERING
BLANKETINGS	BLATTER	BLED	BLIGHTER	BLISTERS
BLANKETS	BLATTERED	BLEE	BLIGHTERS	BLISTERY
BLANKETY	BLATTERING	BLEED	BLIGHTIES	BLITE
BLANKIES	BLATTERS	BLEEDER	BLIGHTING	BLITES
BLANKING	BLATTING	BLEEDERS	BLIGHTINGS	BLITHE
BLANKINGS	BLATTS	BLEEDING	BLIGHTS	BLITHELY
BLANKLY	BLAUBOK	BLEEDINGS	BLIGHTY	BLITHER
BLANKNESS	BLAUBOKS	BLEEDS	BLIMBING	BLITHERED
BLANKNESSES	BLAUD	BLEEP	BLIMBINGS	BLITHERING
BLANKS	BLAUDED	BLEEPED	BLIMEY	BLITHERS
BLANKY	BLAUDING	BLEEPER	BLIMP	BLITHEST
BLANQUET	BLAUDS	BLEEPERS	BLIMPISH	BLITZ
BLANQUETS	BLAWORT	BLEEPING	BLIMPS	BLITZED
BLARE	BLAWORTS	BLEEPS	BLIMY	BLITZES
BLARED	BLAY	BLEES	BLIN	BLITZING
BLARES	BLAYS	BLEMISH	BLIND	BLIVE

BLIZZARD	BLOODSHOT	BLOWED	BLUE	BLUIER
BLIZZARDS	BLOODWOOD	BLOWER	BLUEBACK	BLUIEST
BLIZZARDY	BLOODWOODS	BLOWERS	BLUEBACKS	BLUING
BLOAT	BLOODY	BLOWFISH	BLUEBEARD	BLUINGS
BLOATED	BLOODYING	BLOWFISHES	BLUEBEARDS	BLUISH
BLOATER	BLOOM	BLOWFLIES	BLUEBELL	BLUNDER
BLOATERS	BLOOMED	BLOWFLY	BLUEBELLS	BLUNDERED
BLOATING	BLOOMER	BLOWGUN	BLUEBERRIES	BLUNDERER
BLOATINGS	BLOOMERIES	BLOWGUNS	BLUEBERRY	BLUNDERERS
BLOATS	BLOOMERS	BLOWHARD	BLUEBIRD	BLUNDERING
BLOB	BLOOMERY	BLOWHARDS	BLUEBIRDS	BLUNDERINGS
BLOBBED	BLOOMIER	BLOWHOLE	BLUEBUCK	BLUNDERS
BLOBBING	BLOOMIEST	BLOWHOLES	BLUEBUCKS	BLUNGE
BLOBS	BLOOMING	BLOWIE	BLUECAP	BLUNGED
BLOC	BLOOMLESS	BLOWIER	BLUECAPS	BLUNGER
BLOCK	BLOOMS	BLOWIES	BLUECOAT	BLUNGERS
BLOCKADE	BLOOMY	BLOWIEST	BLUECOATS	BLUNGES
BLOCKADED	BLOOP	BLOWING	BLUED	BLUNGING
BLOCKADES	BLOOPED	BLOWJOB	BLUEFISH	BLUNK
BLOCKADING	BLOOPER	BLOWJOBS	BLUEFISHES	BLUNKED
BLOCKAGE	BLOOPERS	BLOWLAMP	BLUEGOWN	BLUNKER
BLOCKAGES	BLOOPING	BLOWLAMPS	BLUEGOWNS	BLUNKERS
BLOCKED	BLOOPS	BLOWN	BLUEGRASS	BLUNKING
BLOCKER	BLOOSME	BLOWPIPE	BLUEGRASSES	BLUNKS
BLOCKERS	BLOOSMED	BLOWPIPES	BLUEING	BLUNT
BLOCKHEAD	BLOOSMES	BLOWS	BLUEINGS	BLUNTED
BLOCKHEADS	BLOOSMING	BLOWSE	BLUELY	BLUNTER
BLOCKHOLE	BLORE	BLOWSED	BLUENESS	BLUNTEST
BLOCKHOLES	BLORES	BLOWSES	BLUENESSES	BLUNTING
BLOCKIER	BLOSSOM	BLOWSIER	BLUENOSE	BLUNTISH
BLOCKIEST	BLOSSOMED	BLOWSIEST	BLUENOSES	BLUNTLY
BLOCKING	BLOSSOMING	BLOWSY	BLUEPRINT	BLUNTNESS
BLOCKINGS	BLOSSOMINGS	BLOWTORCH	BLUEPRINTED	BLUNTNESSES
BLOCKISH	BLOSSOMS	BLOWTORCHES	BLUEPRINTING	BLUNTS
BLOCKS	BLOSSOMY	BLOWY	BLUEPRINTS	BLUR
BLOCKWORK	BLOT	BLOWZE	BLUER	BLURB
BLOCKWORKS	BLOTCH	BLOWZED	BLUES	BLURBED
BLOCKY	BLOTCHED	BLOWZES	BLUESIER	BLURBING
BLOCS	BLOTCHES	BLOWZIER	BLUESIEST	BLURBS
BLOKE	BLOTCHIER	BLOWZIEST	BLUEST	BLURRED
BLOKEISH	BLOTCHIEST	BLOWZY	BLUESTONE	BLURRING
BLOKES	BLOTCHING	BLUB	BLUESTONES	BLURS
BLONCKET	BLOTCHINGS	BLUBBED	BLUESY	BLURT
BLOND	BLOTCHY	BLUBBER	BLUETTE	BLURTED
BLONDE	BLOTS	BLUBBERED	BLUETTES	BLURTING
BLONDER	BLOTTED	BLUBBERING	BLUEWEED	BLURTINGS
BLONDES	BLOTTER	BLUBBERS	BLUEWEEDS	BLURTS
BLONDEST	BLOTTERS	BLUBBING	BLUEWING	BLUSH
BLONDS	BLOTTIER	BLUBS	BLUEWINGS	BLUSHED
BLOOD	BLOTTIEST	BLUCHER	BLUEY	BLUSHER
BLOODED	BLOTTING	BLUCHERS	BLUEYS	BLUSHERS
BLOODHEAT	BLOTTINGS	BLUDE	BLUFF	BLUSHES
BLOODHEATS	BLOTTO	BLUDES	BLUFFED	BLUSHET
BLOODIED	BLOTTY	BLUDGE	BLUFFER	BLUSHETS
BLOODIER	BLOUBOK	BLUDGED	BLUFFERS	BLUSHFUL
BLOODIES	BLOUBOKS	BLUDGEON	BLUFFEST	BLUSHING
BLOODIEST	BLOUSE	BLUDGEONED	BLUFFING	BLUSHINGS
BLOODILY	BLOUSED	BLUDGEONING	BLUFFLY	BLUSHLESS
BLOODING	BLOUSES	BLUDGEONS	BLUFFNESS	BLUSTER
BLOODLESS	BLOUSING	BLUDGER	BLUFFNESSES	BLUSTERED
BLOODLUST	BLOUSON	BLUDGERS	BLUFFS	BLUSTERER
BLOODLUSTS	BLOUSONS	BLUDGES	BLUGGY	BLUSTERERS
BLOODROOT	BLOW	BLUDGING	BLUID	BLUSTERIER
BLOODROOTS	BLOWBALL	BLUDIE	BLUIDIER	BLUSTERIEST
BLOODS	BLOWBALLS	BLUDIER	BLUIDIEST	BLUSTERING
BLOODSHED	BLOWDOWN	BLUDIEST	BLUIDS	BLUSTERINGS
BLOODSHEDS	BLOWDOWNS	BLUDY	BLUIDY	BLUSTERS

The Chambers Dictionary is the authority for many longer words; see *OSW* Introduction, page xii.

BLUSTERY	BOBAS	BODGERS	BOGGLER	BOLERO
BLUSTROUS	BOBBED	BODGES	BOGGLERS	BOLEROS
BLUTWURST	BOBBERIES	BODGIE	BOGGLES	BOLES
BLUTWURSTS	BOBBERY	BODGIER	BOGGLING	BOLETI
BO	BOBBIES	BODGIES	BOGGY	BOLETUS
BOA	BOBBIN	BODGIEST	BOGIE	BOLETUSES
BOAK	BOBBINET	BODGING	BOGIES	BOLIDE
BOAKED	BOBBINETS	BODHRAN	BOGLAND	BOLIDES
BOAKING	BOBBING	BODHRANS	BOGLANDS	BOLIVAR
BOAKS	BOBBINS	BODICE	BOGLE	BOLIVARES
BOAR	BOBBISH	BODICES	BOGLES	BOLIVARS
BOARD	BOBBLE	BODIED	BOGOAK	BOLIVIANO
BOARDED	BOBBLED	BODIES	BOGOAKS	BOLIVIANOS
BOARDER	BOBBLES	BODIKIN	BOGONG	BOLIX
BOARDERS	BOBBLIER	BODIKINS	BOGONGS	BOLIXED
BOARDING	BOBBLIEST	BODILESS	BOGS	BOLIXES
BOARDINGS	BOBBLING	BODILY	BOGUS	BOLIXING
BOARDROOM	BOBBLY	BODING	BOGY	BOLL
BOARDROOMS	BOBBY	BODINGS	BOGYISM	BOLLARD
BOARDS	BOBBYSOCK	BODKIN	BOGYISMS	BOLLARDS
BOARDWALK	BOBBYSOCKS	BODKINS	BOH	BOLLED
BOARDWALKS	BOBCAT	BODLE	BOHEA	BOLLEN
BOARFISH	BOBCATS	BODLES	BOHEAS	BOLLETRIE
BOARFISHES	BOBOLINK	BODRAG	BOHS	BOLLETRIES
BOARISH	BOBOLINKS	BODRAGS	BOHUNK	BOLLING
BOARS	BOBS	BODS	BOHUNKS	BOLLIX
BOART	BOBSLED	BODY	BOIL	BOLLIXED
BOARTS	BOBSLEDS	BODYGUARD	BOILED	BOLLIXES
BOAS	BOBSLEIGH	BODYGUARDS	BOILER	BOLLIXING
BOAST	BOBSLEIGHS	BODYING	BOILERIES	BOLLOCK
BOASTED	BOBSTAYS	BODYLINE	BOILERS	BOLLOCKED
BOASTER	BOBTAIL	BODYLINES	BOILERY	BOLLOCKING
BOASTERS	BOBTAILED	BODYSHELL	BOILING	BOLLOCKINGS
BOASTFUL	BOBTAILING	BODYSHELLS	BOILINGS	BOLLOCKS
BOASTING	BOBTAILS	BODYSUIT	BOILS	BOLLOCKSED
BOASTINGS	BOBWHEEL	BODYSUITS	BOING	BOLLOCKSES
BOASTLESS	BOBWHEELS	BODYWORK	BOINGED	BOLLOCKSING
BOASTS	BOBWIG	BODYWORKS	BOINGING	BOLLS
BOAT	BOBWIGS	BOEREWORS	BOINGS	BOLO
BOATBILL	BOCAGE	BOEREWORSES	BOINK	BOLOMETER
BOATBILLS	BOCAGES	BOFF	BOINKED	BOLOMETERS
BOATED	BOCCA	BOFFED	BOINKING	BOLOMETRIES
BOATEL	BOCCAS	BOFFIN	BOINKS	BOLOMETRY
BOATELS	BOCHE	BOFFING	BOK	BOLONEY
BOATER	BOCHES	BOFFINS	BOKE	BOLONEYS
BOATERS	BOCK	BOFFS	BOKED	BOLOS
BOATHOUSE	BOCKED	BOG	BOKES	BOLSHEVIK
BOATHOUSES	BOCKING	BOGAN	BOKING	BOLSHEVIKS
BOATIE	BOCKS	BOGANS	BOKO	BOLSHIE
BOATIES	BOD	BOGBEAN	BOKOS	BOLSHIER
BOATING	BODACH	BOGBEANS	BOKS	BOLSHIES
BOATINGS	BODACHS	BOGEY	BOLAS	BOLSHIEST
BOATMAN	BODDLE	BOGEYISM	BOLASES	BOLSHY
BOATMEN	BODDLES	BOGEYISMS	BOLD	BOLSTER
BOATRACE	BODE	BOGEYS	BOLDEN	BOLSTERED
BOATRACES	BODED	BOGGARD	BOLDENED	BOLSTERING
BOATS	BODEFUL	BOGGARDS	BOLDENING	BOLSTERINGS
BOATSWAIN	BODEGA	BOGGART	BOLDENS	BOLSTERS
BOATSWAINS	BODEGAS	BOGGARTS	BOLDER	BOLT
BOATTAIL	BODEGUERO	BOGGED	BOLDEST	BOLTED
BOATTAILS	BODEGUEROS	BOGGIER	BOLDLY	BOLTER
BOB	BODEMENT	BOGGIEST	BOLDNESS	BOLTERS
BOBA	BODEMENTS	BOGGINESS	BOLDNESSES	BOLTHEAD
BOBAC	BODES	BOGGINESSES	BOLDS	BOLTHEADS
BOBACS	BODGE	BOGGING	BOLE	BOLTHOLE
BOBAK	BODGED	BOGGLE	BOLECTION	BOLTHOLES
BOBAKS	BODGER	BOGGLED	BOLECTIONS	BOLTING

The Chambers Dictionary is the authority for many longer words; see *OSW* Introduction, page xii.

BOLTINGS	BOND	BONITO	BOOGIES	BOOMERS
BOLTS	BONDAGE	BONITOS	BOOH	BOOMING
BOLUS	BONDAGER	BONJOUR	BOOHED	BOOMINGS
BOLUSES	BONDAGERS	BONK	BOOHING	BOOMLET
BOMA	BONDAGES	BONKED	BOOHS	BOOMLETS
BOMAS	BONDED	BONKERS	BOOING	BOOMS
BOMB	BONDER	BONKING	BOOK	BOOMSLANG
BOMBARD	BONDERS	BONKS	BOOKABLE	BOOMSLANGS
BOMBARDED	BONDING	BONNE	BOOKCASE	BOON
BOMBARDING	BONDINGS	BONNES	BOOKCASES	BOONDOCKS
BOMBARDON	BONDMAID	BONNET	BOOKED	BOONG
BOMBARDONS	BONDMAIDS	BONNETED	BOOKFUL	BOONGS
BOMBARDS	BONDMAN	BONNETING	BOOKIE	BOONS
BOMBASINE	BONDMEN	BONNETS	BOOKIER	BOOR
BOMBASINES	BONDS	BONNIBELL	BOOKIES	BOORD
BOMBAST	BONDSMAN	BONNIBELLS	BOOKIEST	BOORDE
BOMBASTED	BONDSMEN	BONNIE	BOOKING	BOORDES
BOMBASTIC	BONDSTONE	BONNIER	BOOKINGS	BOORDS
BOMBASTING	BONDSTONES	BONNIES	BOOKISH	BOORISH
BOMBASTS	BONDUC	BONNIEST	BOOKLAND	BOORISHLY
BOMBAX	BONDUCS	BONNILY	BOOKLANDS	BOORKA
BOMBAXES	BONDWOMAN	BONNINESS	BOOKLESS	BOORKAS
BOMBAZINE	BONDWOMEN	BONNINESSES	BOOKLET	BOORS
BOMBAZINES	BONE	BONNY	BOOKLETS	BOORTREE
BOMBE	BONED	BONSAI	BOOKLICE	BOORTREES
BOMBED	BONEHEAD	BONSAIS	BOOKLORE	BOOS
BOMBER	BONEHEADS	BONSELLA	BOOKLORES	BOOSE
BOMBERS	BONELESS	BONSELLAS	BOOKLOUSE	BOOSED
BOMBES	BONER	BONSOIR	BOOKMAKER	BOOSES
BOMBILATE	BONERS	BONSPIEL	BOOKMAKERS	BOOSING
BOMBILATED	BONES	BONSPIELS	BOOKMAN	BOOST
BOMBILATES	BONESET	BONTEBOK	BOOKMARK	BOOSTED
BOMBILATING	BONESETS	BONTEBOKS	BOOKMARKS	BOOSTER
BOMBINATE	BONEYARD	BONUS	BOOKMEN	BOOSTERS
BOMBINATED	BONEYARDS	BONUSES	BOOKPLATE	BOOSTING
BOMBINATES	BONFIRE	BONXIE	BOOKPLATES	BOOSTS
BOMBINATING	BONFIRES	BONXIES	BOOKREST	BOOT
BOMBING	BONG	BONY	BOOKRESTS	BOOTBLACK
BOMBLET	BONGED	BONZA	BOOKS	BOOTBLACKS
BOMBLETS	BONGING	BONZE	BOOKSHELF	BOOTED
BOMBO	BONGO	BONZER	BOOKSHELVES	BOOTEE
BOMBORA	BONGOS	BONZES	BOOKSHOP	BOOTEES
BOMBORAS	BONGRACE	BOO	BOOKSHOPS	BOOTH
BOMBOS	BONGRACES	BOOB	BOOKSIE	BOOTHOSE
BOMBS	BONGS	BOOBED	BOOKSIER	BOOTHS
BOMBSHELL	BONHOMIE	BOOBIES	BOOKSIEST	BOOTIES
BOMBSHELLS	BONHOMIES	BOOBING	BOOKSTALL	BOOTIKIN
BOMBSITE	BONHOMMIE	BOOBOO	BOOKSTALLS	BOOTIKINS
BOMBSITES	BONHOMMIES	BOOBOOK	BOOKSTAND	BOOTING
BOMBYCID	BONHOMOUS	BOOBOOKS	BOOKSTANDS	BOOTLACE
BOMBYCIDS	BONIBELL	BOOBOOS	BOOKSTORE	BOOTLACES
BON	BONIBELLS	BOOBS	BOOKSTORES	BOOTLAST
BONA	BONIE	BOOBY	BOOKSY	BOOTLASTS
BONAMANI	BONIER	BOOBYISH	BOOKWORK	BOOTLEG
BONAMANO	BONIEST	BOOBYISM	BOOKWORKS	BOOTLEGGED
BONAMIA	BONIFACE	BOOBYISMS	BOOKWORM	BOOTLEGGING
BONAMIAS	BONIFACES	BOODIE	BOOKWORMS	BOOTLEGGINGS
BONANZA	BONILASSE	BOODIED	BOOKY	BOOTLEGS
BONANZAS	BONILASSES	BOODIES	BOOL	BOOTLESS
BONASSUS	BONINESS	BOODLE	BOOLS	BOOTLICK
BONASSUSES	BONINESSES	BOODLES	BOOM	BOOTLICKED
BONASUS	BONING	BOODY	BOOMED	BOOTLICKING
BONASUSES	BONINGS	BOODYING	BOOMER	BOOTLICKINGS
BONBON	BONISM	BOOED	BOOMERANG	BOOTLICKS
BONBONS	BONISMS	BOOGIE	BOOMERANGED	BOOTMAKER
BONCE	BONIST	BOOGIED	BOOMERANGING	BOOTMAKERS
BONCES	BONISTS	BOOGIEING	BOOMERANGS	BOOTS

The Chambers Dictionary is the authority for many longer words; see *OSW* Introduction, page xii.

BOOTSTRAP	BORECOLES	BOSCHVELD	BOTCHED	BOUCLES
BOOTSTRAPPED	BORED	BOSCHVELDS	BOTCHER	BOUDERIE
BOOTSTRAPPING	BOREDOM	BOSH	BOTCHERIES	BOUDERIES
BOOTSTRAPS	BOREDOMS	BOSHES	BOTCHERS	BOUDOIR
BOOTY	BOREE	BOSHTA	BOTCHERY	BOUDOIRS
BOOZE	BOREEN	BOSHTER	BOTCHES	BOUFFANT
BOOZED	BOREENS	BOSK	BOTCHIER	BOUGE
BOOZER	BOREES	BOSKAGE	BOTCHIEST	BOUGED
BOOZERS	BOREHOLE	BOSKAGES	BOTCHING	BOUGES
BOOZES	BOREHOLES	BOSKER	BOTCHINGS	BOUGET
BOOZEY	BOREL	BOSKET	BOTCHY	BOUGETS
BOOZIER	BORER	BOSKETS	BOTEL	BOUGH
BOOZIEST	BORERS	BOSKIER	BOTELS	BOUGHPOT
BOOZILY	BORES	BOSKIEST	BOTFLIES	BOUGHPOTS
BOOZINESS	BORGHETTO	BOSKINESS	BOTFLY	BOUGHS
BOOZINESSES	BORGHETTOS	BOSKINESSES	BOTH	BOUGHT
BOOZING	BORGO	BOSKS	BOTHAN	BOUGHTEN
BOOZY	BORGOS	BOSKY	BOTHANS	BOUGHTS
BOP	BORIC	BOSOM	BOTHER	BOUGIE
BOPPED	BORIDE	BOSOMED	BOTHERED	BOUGIES
BOPPER	BORIDES	BOSOMING	BOTHERING	BOUGING
BOPPERS	BORING	BOSOMS	BOTHERS	BOUILLI
BOPPING	BORINGLY	BOSOMY	BOTHIE	BOUILLIS
BOPS	BORINGS	BOSON	BOTHIES	BOUILLON
BOR	BORN	BOSONS	BOTHOLE	BOUILLONS
BORA	BORNE	BOSQUET	BOTHOLES	BOUK
BORACHIO	BORNITE	BOSQUETS	BOTHY	BOUKS
BORACHIOS	BORNITES	BOSS	BOTHYMAN	BOULDER
BORACIC	BORON	BOSSED	BOTHYMEN	BOULDERS
BORACITE	BORONIA	BOSSER	BOTONE	BOULE
BORACITES	BORONIAS	BOSSES	BOTRYOID	BOULES
BORAGE	BORONS	BOSSEST	BOTRYOSE	BOULEVARD
BORAGES	BOROUGH	BOSSIER	BOTS	BOULEVARDS
BORAK	BOROUGHS	BOSSIEST	BOTT	BOULLE
BORAKS	BORREL	BOSSILY	BOTTE	BOULLES
BORANE	BORRELL	BOSSINESS	BOTTED	BOULT
BORANES	BORROW	BOSSINESSES	BOTTEGA	BOULTED
BORAS	BORROWED	BOSSING	BOTTEGAS	BOULTER
BORATE	BORROWER	BOSSY	BOTTES	BOULTERS
BORATES	BORROWERS	BOSTANGI	BOTTIES	BOULTING
BORAX	BORROWING	BOSTANGIS	BOTTINE	BOULTINGS
BORAXES	BORROWINGS	BOSTON	BOTTINES	BOULTS
BORAZON	BORROWS	BOSTONS	BOTTING	BOUN
BORAZONS	BORS	BOSTRYX	BOTTLE	BOUNCE
BORD	BORSCH	BOSTRYXES	BOTTLED	BOUNCED
BORDAR	BORSCHES	BOSUN	BOTTLEFUL	BOUNCER
BORDARS	BORSCHT	BOSUNS	BOTTLEFULS	BOUNCERS
BORDE	BORSCHTS	BOT	BOTTLER	BOUNCES
BORDEL	BORSTAL	BOTANIC	BOTTLERS	BOUNCIER
BORDELLO	BORSTALL	BOTANICAL	BOTTLES	BOUNCIEST
BORDELLOS	BORSTALLS	BOTANICALS	BOTTLING	BOUNCILY
BORDELS	BORSTALS	BOTANIES	BOTTOM	BOUNCING
BORDER	BORT	BOTANISE	BOTTOMED	BOUNCY
BORDEREAU	BORTS	BOTANISED	BOTTOMING	BOUND
BORDEREAUX	BORTSCH	BOTANISES	BOTTOMRIES	BOUNDARIES
BORDERED	BORTSCHES	BOTANISING	BOTTOMRY	BOUNDARY
BORDERER	BORZOI	BOTANIST	BOTTOMS	BOUNDED
BORDERERS	BORZOIS	BOTANISTS	BOTTONY	BOUNDEN
BORDERING	BOS	BOTANIZE	BOTTS	BOUNDER
BORDERS	BOSBOK	BOTANIZED	BOTTY	BOUNDERS
BORDES	BOSBOKS	BOTANIZES	BOTULISM	BOUNDING
BORDS	BOSCAGE	BOTANIZING	BOTULISMS	BOUNDLESS
BORDURE	BOSCAGES	BOTANY	BOUCHE	BOUNDS
BORDURES	BOSCHBOK	BOTARGO	BOUCHEE	BOUNED
BORE	BOSCHBOKS	BOTARGOES	BOUCHEES	BOUNING
BOREAL	BOSCHE	BOTARGOS	BOUCHES	BOUNS
BORECOLE	BOSCHES	BOTCH	BOUCLE	BOUNTEOUS

BOUNTIES	BOVINELY	BOWSTRINGED	BRABBLING	BRAILLERS
BOUNTIFUL	BOVINES	BOWSTRINGING	BRACCATE	BRAILS
BOUNTREE	BOVVER	BOWSTRINGS	BRACCIA	BRAIN
BOUNTREES	BOVVERS	BOWSTRUNG	BRACCIO	BRAINBOX
BOUNTY	BOW	BOWWOW	BRACE	BRAINBOXES
BOUNTYHED	BOWAT	BOWWOWS	BRACED	BRAINCASE
BOUNTYHEDS	BOWATS	BOWYANG	BRACELET	BRAINCASES
BOUQUET	BOWBENT	BOWYANGS	BRACELETS	BRAINED
BOUQUETS	BOWED	BOWYER	BRACER	BRAINIER
BOURASQUE	BOWEL	BOWYERS	BRACERS	BRAINIEST
BOURASQUES	BOWELLED	BOX	BRACES	BRAINING
BOURBON	BOWELLING	BOXCAR	BRACH	BRAINISH
BOURBONS	BOWELS	BOXCARS	BRACHES	BRAINLESS
BOURD	BOWER	BOXED	BRACHET	BRAINPAN
BOURDER	BOWERED	BOXEN	BRACHETS	BRAINPANS
BOURDERS	BOWERIES	BOXER	BRACHIA	BRAINS
BOURDON	BOWERING	BOXERS	BRACHIAL	BRAINSICK
BOURDONS	BOWERS	BOXES	BRACHIATE	BRAINWASH
BOURDS	BOWERY	BOXFUL	BRACHIATED	BRAINWASHED
BOURG	BOWES	BOXFULS	BRACHIATES	BRAINWASHES
BOURGEOIS	BOWET	BOXIER	BRACHIATING	BRAINWASHING
BOURGEOISES	BOWETS	BOXIEST	BRACHIUM	BRAINWASHINGS
BOURGEON	BOWFIN	BOXINESS	BRACING	BRAINY
BOURGEONED	BOWFINS	BOXINESSES	BRACK	BRAIRD
BOURGEONING	BOWGET	BOXING	BRACKEN	BRAIRDED
BOURGEONS	BOWGETS	BOXINGS	BRACKENS	BRAIRDING
BOURGS	BOWHEAD	BOXKEEPER	BRACKET	BRAIRDS
BOURKHA	BOWHEADS	BOXKEEPERS	BRACKETED	BRAISE
BOURKHAS	BOWING	BOXROOM	BRACKETING	BRAISED
BOURLAW	BOWINGS	BOXROOMS	BRACKETS	BRAISES
BOURLAWS	BOWKNOT	BOXWALLAH	BRACKISH	BRAISING
BOURN	BOWKNOTS	BOXWALLAHS	BRACKS	BRAIZE
BOURNE	BOWL	BOXWOOD	BRACT	BRAIZES
BOURNES	BOWLDER	BOXWOODS	BRACTEAL	BRAKE
BOURNS	BOWLDERS	BOXY	BRACTEATE	BRAKED
BOURREE	BOWLED	BOY	BRACTEATES	BRAKELESS
BOURREES	BOWLER	BOYAR	BRACTEOLE	BRAKEMAN
BOURSE	BOWLERS	BOYARS	BRACTEOLES	BRAKEMEN
BOURSES	BOWLFUL	BOYAU	BRACTLESS	BRAKES
BOURSIER	BOWLFULS	BOYAUX	BRACTLET	BRAKIER
BOURSIERS	BOWLINE	BOYCOTT	BRACTLETS	BRAKIEST
BOURTREE	BOWLINES	BOYCOTTED	BRACTS	BRAKING
BOURTREES	BOWLING	BOYCOTTER	BRAD	BRAKY
BOUSE	BOWLINGS	BOYCOTTERS	BRADAWL	BRALESS
BOUSED	BOWLS	BOYCOTTING	BRADAWLS	BRAMBLE
BOUSES	BOWMAN	BOYCOTTS	BRADS	BRAMBLED
BOUSIER	BOWMEN	BOYED	BRAE	BRAMBLES
BOUSIEST	BOWNE	BOYFRIEND	BRAES	BRAMBLIER
BOUSING	BOWNED	BOYFRIENDS	BRAG	BRAMBLIEST
BOUSY	BOWNES	BOYG	BRAGGART	BRAMBLING
BOUT	BOWNING	BOYGS	BRAGGARTS	BRAMBLINGS
BOUTADE	BOWPOT	BOYHOOD	BRAGGED	BRAMBLY
BOUTADES	BOWPOTS	BOYHOODS	BRAGGING	BRAME
BOUTIQUE	BOWR	BOYING	BRAGLY	BRAMES
BOUTIQUES	BOWRS	BOYISH	BRAGS	BRAN
BOUTON	BOWS	BOYISHLY	BRAID	BRANCARD
BOUTONNE	BOWSE	BOYO	BRAIDE	BRANCARDS
BOUTONNEE	BOWSED	BOYOS	BRAIDED	BRANCH
BOUTONS	BOWSER	BOYS	BRAIDER	BRANCHED
BOUTS	BOWSERS	BOZO	BRAIDEST	BRANCHER
BOUZOUKI	BOWSES	BOZOS	BRAIDING	BRANCHERIES
BOUZOUKIS	BOWSHOT	BOZZETTI	BRAIDINGS	BRANCHERS
BOVATE	BOWSHOTS	BOZZETTO	BRAIDS	BRANCHERY
BOVATES	BOWSING	BRA	BRAIL	BRANCHES
BOVID	BOWSPRIT	BRABBLE	BRAILED	BRANCHIA
BOVIDS	BOWSPRITS	BRABBLED	BRAILING	BRANCHIAE
BOVINE	BOWSTRING	BRABBLES	BRAILLER	BRANCHIAL

The Chambers Dictionary is the authority for many longer words; see *OSW* Introduction, page xii.

BRANCHIER	BRASS	BRAVERY	BREADLINE	BREDED
BRANCHIEST	BRASSARD	BRAVES	BREADLINES	BREDES
BRANCHING	BRASSARDS	BRAVEST	BREADNUT	BREDING
BRANCHINGS	BRASSART	BRAVI	BREADNUTS	BREE
BRANCHLET	BRASSARTS	BRAVING	BREADROOM	BREECH
BRANCHLETS	BRASSERIE	BRAVO	BREADROOMS	BREECHED
BRANCHY	BRASSERIES	BRAVOES	BREADROOT	BREECHES
BRAND	BRASSES	BRAVOS	BREADROOTS	BREECHING
BRANDADE	BRASSET	BRAVURA	BREADS	BREECHINGS
BRANDADES	BRASSETS	BRAVURAS	BREADTH	BREED
BRANDED	BRASSICA	BRAW	BREADTHS	BREEDER
BRANDER	BRASSICAS	BRAWER	BREAK	BREEDERS
BRANDERED	BRASSIE	BRAWEST	BREAKABLE	BREEDING
BRANDERING	BRASSIER	BRAWL	BREAKABLES	BREEDINGS
BRANDERS	BRASSIERE	BRAWLED	BREAKAGE	BREEDS
BRANDIED	BRASSIERES	BRAWLER	BREAKAGES	BREEKS
BRANDIES	BRASSIES	BRAWLERS	BREAKAWAY	BREEM
BRANDING	BRASSIEST	BRAWLIER	BREAKAWAYS	BREER
BRANDISE	BRASSILY	BRAWLIEST	BREAKBACK	BREERED
BRANDISES	BRASSY	BRAWLING	BREAKDOWN	BREERING
BRANDISH	BRAST	BRAWLINGS	BREAKDOWNS	BREERS
BRANDISHED	BRASTING	BRAWLS	BREAKER	BREES
BRANDISHES	BRASTS	BRAWLY	BREAKERS	BREESE
BRANDISHING	BRAT	BRAWN	BREAKFAST	BREESES
BRANDLING	BRATCHET	BRAWNED	BREAKFASTED	BREEZE
BRANDLINGS	BRATCHETS	BRAWNIER	BREAKFASTING	BREEZED
BRANDRETH	BRATLING	BRAWNIEST	BREAKFASTS	BREEZES
BRANDRETHS	BRATLINGS	BRAWNS	BREAKING	BREEZEWAY
BRANDS	BRATPACK	BRAWNY	BREAKINGS	BREEZEWAYS
BRANDY	BRATS	BRAWS	BREAKNECK	BREEZIER
BRANGLE	BRATTICE	BRAXIES	BREAKS	BREEZIEST
BRANGLED	BRATTICED	BRAXY	BREAKTIME	BREEZILY
BRANGLES	BRATTICES	BRAY	BREAKTIMES	BREEZING
BRANGLING	BRATTICING	BRAYED	BREAM	BREEZY
BRANGLINGS	BRATTICINGS	BRAYER	BREAMED	BREGMA
BRANK	BRATTIER	BRAYERS	BREAMING	BREGMATA
BRANKED	BRATTIEST	BRAYING	BREAMS	BREGMATIC
BRANKIER	BRATTISH	BRAYS	BREARE	BREHON
BRANKIEST	BRATTISHED	BRAZE	BREARES	BREHONS
BRANKING	BRATTISHES	BRAZED	BREASKIT	BRELOQUE
BRANKS	BRATTISHING	BRAZELESS	BREASKITS	BRELOQUES
BRANKY	BRATTISHINGS	BRAZEN	BREAST	BREME
BRANLE	BRATTLE	BRAZENED	BREASTED	BREN
BRANLES	BRATTLED	BRAZENING	BREASTING	BRENNE
BRANNIER	BRATTLES	BRAZENLY	BREASTPIN	BRENNES
BRANNIEST	BRATTLING	BRAZENRIES	BREASTPINS	BRENNING
BRANNY	BRATTLINGS	BRAZENRY	BREASTS	BRENS
BRANS	BRATTY	BRAZENS	BREATH	BRENT
BRANSLE	BRATWURST	BRAZES	BREATHE	BRENTER
BRANSLES	BRATWURSTS	BRAZIER	BREATHED	BRENTEST
BRANTLE	BRAUNCH	BRAZIERS	BREATHER	BRER
BRANTLES	BRAUNCHED	BRAZIL	BREATHERS	BRERE
BRAS	BRAUNCHES	BRAZILEIN	BREATHES	BRERES
BRASERO	BRAUNCHING	BRAZILEINS	BREATHFUL	BRERS
BRASEROS	BRAUNITE	BRAZILIN	BREATHIER	BRETASCHE
BRASES	BRAUNITES	BRAZILINS	BREATHIEST	BRETASCHES
BRASH	BRAVA	BRAZILS	BREATHILY	BRETESSE
BRASHED	BRAVADO	BRAZING	BREATHING	BRETESSES
BRASHER	BRAVADOED	BREACH	BREATHINGS	BRETHREN
BRASHES	BRAVADOES	BREACHED	BREATHS	BRETON
BRASHEST	BRAVADOING	BREACHES	BREATHY	BRETONS
BRASHIER	BRAVADOS	BREACHING	BRECCIA	BRETTICE
BRASHIEST	BRAVE	BREAD	BRECCIAS	BRETTICED
BRASHING	BRAVED	BREADED	BRECHAM	BRETTICES
BRASHY	BRAVELY	BREADHEAD	BRECHAMS	BRETTICING
BRASIER	BRAVER	BREADHEADS	BRED	BREVE
BRASIERS	BRAVERIES	BREADING	BREDE	BREVES

BREVET	BRICOLE	BRIGHTENING	BRIOS	BROADBILLS
BREVETE	BRICOLES	BRIGHTENS	BRIQUET	BROADCAST
BREVETED	BRIDAL	BRIGHTER	BRIQUETS	BROADCASTED
BREVETING	BRIDALS	BRIGHTEST	BRIQUETTE	BROADCASTING
BREVETS	BRIDE	BRIGHTLY	BRIQUETTED	BROADCASTINGS
BREVETTED	BRIDECAKE	BRIGS	BRIQUETTES	BROADCASTS
BREVETTING	BRIDECAKES	BRIGUE	BRIQUETTING	BROADEN
BREVIARIES	BRIDED	BRIGUED	BRISE	BROADENED
BREVIARY	BRIDEMAID	BRIGUES	BRISES	BROADENING
BREVIATE	BRIDEMAIDS	BRIGUING	BRISK	BROADENS
BREVIATES	BRIDEMAN	BRIGUINGS	BRISKED	BROADER
BREVIER	BRIDEMEN	BRILL	BRISKEN	BROADEST
BREVIERS	BRIDES	BRILLER	BRISKENED	BROADISH
BREVITIES	BRIDESMAN	BRILLEST	BRISKENING	BROADLOOM
BREVITY	BRIDESMEN	BRILLIANT	BRISKENS	BROADLY
BREW	BRIDEWELL	BRILLIANTED	BRISKER	BROADNESS
BREWAGE	BRIDEWELLS	BRILLIANTING	BRISKEST	BROADNESSES
BREWAGES	BRIDGABLE	BRILLIANTS	BRISKET	BROADS
BREWED	BRIDGE	BRILLS	BRISKETS	BROADSIDE
BREWER	BRIDGED	BRIM	BRISKING	BROADSIDES
BREWERIES	BRIDGES	BRIMFUL	BRISKISH	BROADTAIL
BREWERS	BRIDGING	BRIMING	BRISKLY	BROADTAILS
BREWERY	BRIDGINGS	BRIMINGS	BRISKNESS	BROADWAY
BREWING	BRIDIE	BRIMLESS	BRISKNESSES	BROADWAYS
BREWINGS	BRIDIES	BRIMMED	BRISKS	BROADWISE
BREWIS	BRIDING	BRIMMER	BRISKY	BROCADE
BREWISES	BRIDLE	BRIMMERS	BRISLING	BROCADED
BREWPUB	BRIDLED	BRIMMING	BRISLINGS	BROCADES
BREWPUBS	BRIDLER	BRIMS	BRISTLE	BROCAGE
BREWS	BRIDLERS	BRIMSTONE	BRISTLED	BROCAGES
BREWSTER	BRIDLES	BRIMSTONES	BRISTLES	BROCARD
BREWSTERS	BRIDLING	BRIMSTONY	BRISTLIER	BROCARDS
BRIAR	BRIDOON	BRINDED	BRISTLIEST	BROCATEL
BRIARED	BRIDOONS	BRINDISI	BRISTLING	BROCATELS
BRIARS	BRIEF	BRINDISIS	BRISTLY	BROCCOLI
BRIBE	BRIEFED	BRINDLE	BRISTOLS	BROCCOLIS
BRIBED	BRIEFER	BRINDLED	BRISURE	BROCH
BRIBER	BRIEFEST	BRINDLES	BRISURES	BROCHAN
BRIBERIES	BRIEFING	BRINE	BRIT	BROCHANS
BRIBERS	BRIEFINGS	BRINED	BRITCHES	BROCHE
BRIBERY	BRIEFLESS	BRINES	BRITS	BROCHED
BRIBES	BRIEFLY	BRING	BRITSCHKA	BROCHES
BRIBING	BRIEFNESS	BRINGER	BRITSCHKAS	BROCHETTE
BRICABRAC	BRIEFNESSES	BRINGERS	BRITSKA	BROCHETTES
BRICABRACS	BRIEFS	BRINGING	BRITSKAS	BROCHING
BRICK	BRIER	BRINGINGS	BRITTLE	BROCHS
BRICKBAT	BRIERED	BRINGS	BRITTLELY	BROCHURE
BRICKBATS	BRIERIER	BRINIER	BRITTLER	BROCHURES
BRICKCLAY	BRIERIEST	BRINIEST	BRITTLES	BROCK
BRICKCLAYS	BRIERS	BRININESS	BRITTLEST	BROCKAGE
BRICKED	BRIERY	BRININESSES	BRITTLY	BROCKAGES
BRICKEN	BRIG	BRINING	BRITZKA	BROCKED
BRICKIE	BRIGADE	BRINISH	BRITZKAS	BROCKET
BRICKIER	BRIGADED	BRINJAL	BRITZSKA	BROCKETS
BRICKIES	BRIGADES	BRINJALS	BRITZSKAS	BROCKIT
BRICKIEST	BRIGADIER	BRINJARRIES	BRIZE	BROCKRAM
BRICKING	BRIGADIERS	BRINJARRY	BRIZES	BROCKRAMS
BRICKINGS	BRIGADING	BRINK	BRO	BROCKS
BRICKLE	BRIGALOW	BRINKMAN	BROACH	BROD
BRICKS	BRIGALOWS	BRINKMEN	BROACHED	BRODDED
BRICKWALL	BRIGAND	BRINKS	BROACHER	BRODDING
BRICKWALLS	BRIGANDRIES	BRINY	BROACHERS	BRODEKIN
BRICKWORK	BRIGANDRY	BRIO	BROACHES	BRODEKINS
BRICKWORKS	BRIGANDS	BRIOCHE	BROACHING	BRODKIN
BRICKY	BRIGHT	BRIOCHES	BROAD	BRODKINS
BRICKYARD	BRIGHTEN	BRIONIES	BROADBAND	BRODS
BRICKYARDS	BRIGHTENED	BRIONY	BROADBILL	BROG

The Chambers Dictionary is the authority for many longer words; see *OSW* Introduction, page xii.

BROGAN	BROMMER	BROOMING	BRUCHID	BRUSTS
BROGANS	BROMMERS	BROOMRAPE	BRUCHIDS	BRUT
BROGGED	BROMOFORM	BROOMRAPES	BRUCINE	BRUTAL
BROGGING	BROMOFORMS	BROOMS	BRUCINES	BRUTALISE
BROGH	BRONCHI	BROOMY	BRUCITE	BRUTALISED
BROGHS	BRONCHIA	BROOS	BRUCITES	BRUTALISES
BROGS	BRONCHIAL	BROOSE	BRUCKLE	BRUTALISING
BROGUE	BRONCHO	BROOSES	BRUHAHA	BRUTALISM
BROGUEISH	BRONCHOS	BROS	BRUHAHAS	BRUTALISMS
BROGUES	BRONCHUS	BROSE	BRUILZIE	BRUTALIST
BROGUISH	BRONCO	BROSES	BRUILZIES	BRUTALISTS
BROIDER	BRONCOS	BROTH	BRUISE	BRUTALITIES
BROIDERED	BROND	BROTHEL	BRUISED	BRUTALITY
BROIDERER	BRONDS	BROTHELS	BRUISER	BRUTALIZE
BROIDERERS	BRONDYRON	BROTHER	BRUISERS	BRUTALIZED
BROIDERIES	BRONDYRONS	BROTHERLY	BRUISES	BRUTALIZES
BROIDERING	BRONZE	BROTHERS	BRUISING	BRUTALIZING
BROIDERINGS	BRONZED	BROTHS	BRUISINGS	BRUTALLY
BROIDERS	BRONZEN	BROUGH	BRUIT	BRUTE
BROIDERY	BRONZER	BROUGHAM	BRUITED	BRUTED
BROIL	BRONZERS	BROUGHAMS	BRUITING	BRUTELIKE
BROILED	BRONZES	BROUGHS	BRUITS	BRUTENESS
BROILER	BRONZIER	BROUGHT	BRULE	BRUTENESSES
BROILERS	BRONZIEST	BROUHAHA	BRULYIE	BRUTER
BROILING	BRONZIFIED	BROUHAHAS	BRULYIES	BRUTERS
BROILS	BRONZIFIES	BROUZE	BRULZIE	BRUTES
BROKAGE	BRONZIFY	BROUZES	BRULZIES	BRUTIFIED
BROKAGES	BRONZIFYING	BROW	BRUMAL	BRUTIFIES
BROKE	BRONZING	BROWBAND	BRUMBIES	BRUTIFY
BROKED	BRONZINGS	BROWBANDS	BRUMBY	BRUTIFYING
BROKEN	BRONZITE	BROWBEAT	BRUME	BRUTING
BROKENLY	BRONZITES	BROWBEATEN	BRUMES	BRUTINGS
BROKER	BRONZY	BROWBEATING	BRUMMAGEM	BRUTISH
BROKERAGE	BROO	BROWBEATINGS	BRUMMAGEMS	BRUTISHLY
BROKERAGES	BROOCH	BROWBEATS	BRUMMER	BRUXISM
BROKERED	BROOCHED	BROWLESS	BRUMMERS	BRUXISMS
BROKERIES	BROOCHES	BROWN	BRUMOUS	BRYOLOGIES
BROKERING	BROOCHING	BROWNED	BRUNCH	BRYOLOGY
BROKERS	BROOD	BROWNER	BRUNCHES	BRYONIES
BROKERY	BROODED	BROWNEST	BRUNET	BRYONY
BROKES	BROODER	BROWNIE	BRUNETS	BRYOPHYTE
BROKING	BROODERS	BROWNIER	BRUNETTE	BRYOPHYTES
BROKINGS	BROODIER	BROWNIES	BRUNETTES	BUAT
BROLGA	BROODIEST	BROWNIEST	BRUNT	BUATS
BROLGAS	BROODING	BROWNING	BRUNTED	BUAZE
BROLLIES	BROODS	BROWNINGS	BRUNTING	BUAZES
BROLLY	BROODY	BROWNISH	BRUNTS	BUB
BROMATE	BROOK	BROWNNESS	BRUSH	BUBA
BROMATES	BROOKED	BROWNNESSES	BRUSHED	BUBAL
BROMELAIN	BROOKING	BROWNOUT	BRUSHER	BUBALINE
BROMELAINS	BROOKITE	BROWNOUTS	BRUSHERS	BUBALIS
BROMELIA	BROOKITES	BROWNS	BRUSHES	BUBALISES
BROMELIAD	BROOKLET	BROWNY	BRUSHIER	BUBALS
BROMELIADS	BROOKLETS	BROWS	BRUSHIEST	BUBAS
BROMELIAS	BROOKLIME	BROWSE	BRUSHING	BUBBIES
BROMELIN	BROOKLIMES	BROWSED	BRUSHINGS	BUBBLE
BROMELINS	BROOKS	BROWSER	BRUSHWOOD	BUBBLED
BROMIC	BROOKWEED	BROWSERS	BRUSHWOODS	BUBBLES
BROMIDE	BROOKWEEDS	BROWSES	BRUSHWORK	BUBBLIER
BROMIDES	BROOL	BROWSIER	BRUSHWORKS	BUBBLIES
BROMIDIC	BROOLS	BROWSIEST	BRUSHY	BUBBLIEST
BROMINE	BROOM	BROWSING	BRUSQUE	BUBBLING
BROMINES	BROOMBALL	BROWSINGS	BRUSQUELY	BUBBLY
BROMINISM	BROOMBALLS	BROWST	BRUSQUER	BUBBY
BROMINISMS	BROOMED	BROWSTS	BRUSQUEST	BUBINGA
BROMISM	BROOMIER	BROWSY	BRUST	BUBINGAS
BROMISMS	BROOMIEST	BRRR	BRUSTING	BUBO

BUBOES	BUCKRAKES	BUDMASH	BUGLETS	BULGURS
BUBONIC	BUCKRAM	BUDMASHES	BUGLING	BULGY
BUBS	BUCKRAMED	BUDO	BUGLOSS	BULIMIA
BUBUKLE	BUCKRAMING	BUDOS	BUGLOSSES	BULIMIAS
BUBUKLES	BUCKRAMS	BUDS	BUGONG	BULIMIC
BUCCAL	BUCKRAS	BUDWORM	BUGONGS	BULIMICS
BUCCANEER	BUCKS	BUDWORMS	BUGS	BULIMIES
BUCCANEERED	BUCKSAW	BUFF	BUGWORT	BULIMUS
BUCCANEERING	BUCKSAWS	BUFFA	BUGWORTS	BULIMUSES
BUCCANEERINGS	BUCKSHEE	BUFFALO	BUHL	BULIMY
BUCCANEERS	BUCKSHISH	BUFFALOED	BUHLS	BULK
BUCCANIER	BUCKSHISHED	BUFFALOES	BUHRSTONE	BULKED
BUCCANIERED	BUCKSHISHES	BUFFALOING	BUHRSTONES	BULKER
BUCCANIERING	BUCKSHISHING	BUFFE	BUIK	BULKERS
BUCCANIERS	BUCKSHOT	BUFFED	BUIKS	BULKHEAD
BUCCINA	BUCKSHOTS	BUFFER	BUILD	BULKHEADS
BUCCINAS	BUCKSKIN	BUFFERED	BUILDED	BULKIER
BUCELLAS	BUCKSKINS	BUFFERING	BUILDER	BULKIEST
BUCELLASES	BUCKSOM	BUFFERS	BUILDERS	BULKILY
BUCHU	BUCKTEETH	BUFFET	BUILDING	BULKINESS
BUCHUS	BUCKTHORN	BUFFETED	BUILDINGS	BULKINESSES
BUCK	BUCKTHORNS	BUFFETING	BUILDS	BULKING
BUCKAROO	BUCKTOOTH	BUFFETINGS	BUILT	BULKS
BUCKAROOS	BUCKU	BUFFETS	BUIRDLIER	BULKY
BUCKAYRO	BUCKUS	BUFFI	BUIRDLIEST	BULL
BUCKAYROS	BUCKWHEAT	BUFFING	BUIRDLY	BULLA
BUCKBEAN	BUCKWHEATS	BUFFINGS	BUIST	BULLACE
BUCKBEANS	BUCKYBALL	BUFFO	BUISTED	BULLACES
BUCKBOARD	BUCKYBALLS	BUFFOON	BUISTING	BULLAE
BUCKBOARDS	BUCOLIC	BUFFOONS	BUISTS	BULLARIES
BUCKED	BUCOLICAL	BUFFS	BUKE	BULLARY
BUCKEEN	BUCOLICS	BUFO	BUKES	BULLATE
BUCKEENS	BUD	BUFOS	BUKSHEE	BULLBAR
BUCKER	BUDDED	BUG	BUKSHEES	BULLBARS
BUCKEROO	BUDDHA	BUGABOO	BUKSHI	BULLBAT
BUCKEROOS	BUDDHAS	BUGABOOS	BUKSHIS	BULLBATS
BUCKERS	BUDDIER	BUGBANE	BULB	BULLDOG
BUCKET	BUDDIES	BUGBANES	BULBAR	BULLDOGGED
BUCKETED	BUDDIEST	BUGBEAR	BULBED	BULLDOGGING
BUCKETFUL	BUDDING	BUGBEARS	BULBEL	BULLDOGS
BUCKETFULS	BUDDINGS	BUGGAN	BULBELS	BULLDOZE
BUCKETING	BUDDLE	BUGGANE	BULBIL	BULLDOZED
BUCKETINGS	BUDDLED	BUGGANES	BULBILS	BULLDOZER
BUCKETS	BUDDLEIA	BUGGANS	BULBING	BULLDOZERS
BUCKHORN	BUDDLEIAS	BUGGED	BULBOSITIES	BULLDOZES
BUCKHORNS	BUDDLES	BUGGER	BULBOSITY	BULLDOZING
BUCKHOUND	BUDDLING	BUGGERED	BULBOUS	BULLDUST
BUCKHOUNDS	BUDDY	BUGGERIES	BULBOUSLY	BULLDUSTS
BUCKIE	BUDGE	BUGGERING	BULBS	BULLED
BUCKIES	BUDGED	BUGGERS	BULBUL	BULLER
BUCKING	BUDGER	BUGGERY	BULBULS	BULLERED
BUCKINGS	BUDGEREE	BUGGIER	BULGE	BULLERING
BUCKISH	BUDGERO	BUGGIES	BULGED	BULLERS
BUCKISHLY	BUDGEROS	BUGGIEST	BULGER	BULLET
BUCKLE	BUDGEROW	BUGGIN	BULGERS	BULLETIN
BUCKLED	BUDGEROWS	BUGGING	BULGES	BULLETINS
BUCKLER	BUDGERS	BUGGINGS	BULGHUR	BULLETRIE
BUCKLERED	BUDGES	BUGGINS	BULGHURS	BULLETRIES
BUCKLERING	BUDGET	BUGGY	BULGIER	BULLETS
BUCKLERS	BUDGETARY	BUGHOUSE	BULGIEST	BULLFIGHT
BUCKLES	BUDGETED	BUGHOUSES	BULGINE	BULLFIGHTS
BUCKLING	BUDGETING	BUGLE	BULGINES	BULLFINCH
BUCKLINGS	BUDGETS	BUGLED	BULGINESS	BULLFINCHES
BUCKO	BUDGIE	BUGLER	BULGINESSES	BULLFROG
BUCKOES	BUDGIES	BUGLERS	BULGING	BULLFROGS
BUCKRA	BUDGING	BUGLES	BULGINGLY	BULLGINE
BUCKRAKE	BUDLESS	BUGLET	BULGUR	BULLGINES

The Chambers Dictionary is the authority for many longer words; see *OSW* Introduction, page xii.

BULLHEAD	BUMBLINGS	BUNCOMBE	BUNKUM	BURDENOUS
BULLHEADS	BUMBO	BUNCOMBES	BUNKUMS	BURDENS
BULLIED	BUMBOS	BUNCOS	BUNNIA	BURDIE
BULLIER	BUMF	BUND	BUNNIAS	BURDIES
BULLIES	BUMFS	BUNDED	BUNNIES	BURDOCK
BULLIEST	BUMKIN	BUNDING	BUNNY	BURDOCKS
BULLING	BUMKINS	BUNDLE	BUNODONT	BURDS
BULLINGS	BUMMALO	BUNDLED	BUNRAKU	BUREAU
BULLION	BUMMALOTI	BUNDLES	BUNRAKUS	BUREAUS
BULLIONS	BUMMALOTIS	BUNDLING	BUNS	BUREAUX
BULLISH	BUMMAREE	BUNDLINGS	BUNSEN	BURET
BULLISHLY	BUMMAREES	BUNDOBUST	BUNSENS	BURETS
BULLNOSE	BUMMED	BUNDOBUSTS	BUNT	BURETTE
BULLNOSES	BUMMEL	BUNDOOK	BUNTAL	BURETTES
BULLOCK	BUMMELS	BUNDOOKS	BUNTALS	BURG
BULLOCKED	BUMMER	BUNDS	BUNTED	BURGAGE
BULLOCKIES	BUMMERS	BUNDU	BUNTER	BURGAGES
BULLOCKING	BUMMING	BUNDUS	BUNTERS	BURGANET
BULLOCKS	BUMMLE	BUNG	BUNTIER	BURGANETS
BULLOCKY	BUMMLED	BUNGALOID	BUNTIEST	BURGEE
BULLS	BUMMLES	BUNGALOIDS	BUNTING	BURGEES
BULLSHIT	BUMMLING	BUNGALOW	BUNTINGS	BURGEON
BULLSHITS	BUMMOCK	BUNGALOWS	BUNTLINE	BURGEONED
BULLSHITTED	BUMMOCKS	BUNGED	BUNTLINES	BURGEONING
BULLSHITTING	BUMP	BUNGEE	BUNTS	BURGEONS
BULLSHITTINGS	BUMPED	BUNGEES	BUNTY	BURGER
BULLWHACK	BUMPER	BUNGEY	BUNYA	BURGERS
BULLWHACKED	BUMPERED	BUNGEYS	BUNYAS	BURGESS
BULLWHACKING	BUMPERING	BUNGHOLE	BUNYIP	BURGESSES
BULLWHACKS	BUMPERS	BUNGHOLES	BUNYIPS	BURGH
BULLWHIP	BUMPH	BUNGIE	BUONAMANI	BURGHAL
BULLWHIPPED	BUMPHS	BUNGIES	BUONAMANO	BURGHER
BULLWHIPPING	BUMPIER	BUNGING	BUOY	BURGHERS
BULLWHIPS	BUMPIEST	BUNGLE	BUOYAGE	BURGHS
BULLY	BUMPILY	BUNGLED	BUOYAGES	BURGHUL
BULLYING	BUMPINESS	BUNGLER	BUOYANCE	BURGHULS
BULLYISM	BUMPINESSES	BUNGLERS	BUOYANCES	BURGLAR
BULLYISMS	BUMPING	BUNGLES	BUOYANCIES	BURGLARED
BULLYRAG	BUMPINGS	BUNGLING	BUOYANCY	BURGLARIES
BULLYRAGGED	BUMPKIN	BUNGLINGS	BUOYANT	BURGLARING
BULLYRAGGING	BUMPKINS	BUNGS	BUOYED	BURGLARS
BULLYRAGS	BUMPOLOGIES	BUNGY	BUOYING	BURGLARY
BULRUSH	BUMPOLOGY	BUNIA	BUOYS	BURGLE
BULRUSHES	BUMPS	BUNIAS	BUPLEVER	BURGLED
BULRUSHY	BUMPTIOUS	BUNION	BUPLEVERS	BURGLES
BULSE	BUMPY	BUNIONS	BUPPIES	BURGLING
BULSES	BUMS	BUNJE	BUPPY	BURGONET
BULWARK	BUMSUCKER	BUNJEE	BUPRESTID	BURGONETS
BULWARKED	BUMSUCKERS	BUNJEES	BUPRESTIDS	BURGOO
BULWARKING	BUN	BUNJES	BUR	BURGOOS
BULWARKS	BUNA	BUNJIE	BURAN	BURGRAVE
BUM	BUNAS	BUNJIES	BURANS	BURGRAVES
BUMALO	BUNCE	BUNJY	BURBLE	BURGS
BUMALOTI	BUNCED	BUNK	BURBLED	BURGUNDIES
BUMALOTIS	BUNCES	BUNKED	BURBLER	BURGUNDY
BUMBAG	BUNCH	BUNKER	BURBLERS	BURHEL
BUMBAGS	BUNCHED	BUNKERED	BURBLES	BURHELS
BUMBAZE	BUNCHES	BUNKERING	BURBLING	BURIAL
BUMBAZED	BUNCHIER	BUNKERS	BURBLINGS	BURIALS
BUMBAZES	BUNCHIEST	BUNKHOUSE	BURBOT	BURIED
BUMBAZING	BUNCHING	BUNKHOUSES	BURBOTS	BURIES
BUMBLE	BUNCHINGS	BUNKING	BURD	BURIN
BUMBLED	BUNCHY	BUNKO	BURDASH	BURINIST
BUMBLER	BUNCING	BUNKOED	BURDASHES	BURINISTS
BUMBLERS	BUNCO	BUNKOING	BURDEN	BURINS
BUMBLES	BUNCOED	BUNKOS	BURDENED	BURITI
BUMBLING	BUNCOING	BUNKS	BURDENING	BURITIS

The Chambers Dictionary is the authority for many longer words; see *OSW* Introduction, page xii.

BURK	BURRELS	BUSHELLINGS	BUSTED	BUTTERCUP
BURKA	BURRHEL	BUSHELMAN	BUSTEE	BUTTERCUPS
BURKAS	BURRHELS	BUSHELMEN	BUSTEES	BUTTERED
BURKE	BURRIER	BUSHELS	BUSTER	BUTTERFLIES
BURKED	BURRIEST	BUSHES	BUSTERS	BUTTERFLY
BURKES	BURRING	BUSHFIRE	BUSTIER	BUTTERIER
BURKING	BURRITO	BUSHFIRES	BUSTIERS	BUTTERIES
BURKS	BURRITOS	BUSHIDO	BUSTIEST	BUTTERIEST
BURL	BURRO	BUSHIDOS	BUSTING	BUTTERINE
BURLAP	BURROS	BUSHIER	BUSTINGS	BUTTERINES
BURLAPS	BURROW	BUSHIES	BUSTLE	BUTTERING
BURLED	BURROWED	BUSHIEST	BUSTLED	BUTTERNUT
BURLER	BURROWING	BUSHINESS	BUSTLER	BUTTERNUTS
BURLERS	BURROWS	BUSHINESSES	BUSTLERS	BUTTERS
BURLESQUE	BURRS	BUSHING	BUSTLES	BUTTERY
BURLESQUED	BURRSTONE	BUSHINGS	BUSTLING	BUTTES
BURLESQUES	BURRSTONES	BUSHMAN	BUSTS	BUTTIES
BURLESQUING	BURRY	BUSHMEN	BUSTY	BUTTING
BURLETTA	BURS	BUSHVELD	BUSY	BUTTLE
BURLETTAS	BURSA	BUSHVELDS	BUSYBODIED	BUTTLED
BURLEY	BURSAE	BUSHWALK	BUSYBODIES	BUTTLES
BURLEYS	BURSAL	BUSHWALKED	BUSYBODY	BUTTLING
BURLIER	BURSAR	BUSHWALKING	BUSYBODYING	BUTTOCK
BURLIEST	BURSARIAL	BUSHWALKINGS	BUSYING	BUTTOCKED
BURLINESS	BURSARIES	BUSHWALKS	BUSYNESS	BUTTOCKING
BURLINESSES	BURSARS	BUSHWHACK	BUSYNESSES	BUTTOCKS
BURLING	BURSARY	BUSHWHACKED	BUT	BUTTON
BURLS	BURSE	BUSHWHACKING	BUTADIENE	BUTTONED
BURLY	BURSES	BUSHWHACKINGS	BUTADIENES	BUTTONING
BURN	BURSIFORM	BUSHWHACKS	BUTANE	BUTTONS
BURNED	BURSITIS	BUSHWOMAN	BUTANES	BUTTONY
BURNER	BURSITISES	BUSHWOMEN	BUTANOL	BUTTRESS
BURNERS	BURST	BUSHY	BUTANOLS	BUTTRESSED
BURNET	BURSTED	BUSIED	BUTCH	BUTTRESSES
BURNETS	BURSTEN	BUSIER	BUTCHER	BUTTRESSING
BURNING	BURSTER	BUSIES	BUTCHERED	BUTTS
BURNINGLY	BURSTERS	BUSIEST	BUTCHERIES	BUTTY
BURNINGS	BURSTING	BUSILY	BUTCHERING	BUTTYMAN
BURNISH	BURSTS	BUSINESS	BUTCHERINGS	BUTTYMEN
BURNISHED	BURTHEN	BUSINESSES	BUTCHERLY	BUTYL
BURNISHER	BURTHENED	BUSING	BUTCHERS	BUTYLENE
BURNISHERS	BURTHENING	BUSINGS	BUTCHERY	BUTYLENES
BURNISHES	BURTHENS	BUSK	BUTCHES	BUTYLS
BURNISHING	BURTON	BUSKED	BUTCHEST	BUTYRATE
BURNISHINGS	BURTONS	BUSKER	BUTCHING	BUTYRATES
BURNOUS	BURWEED	BUSKERS	BUTCHINGS	BUTYRIC
BURNOUSE	BURWEEDS	BUSKET	BUTE	BUVETTE
BURNOUSES	BURY	BUSKETS	BUTENE	BUVETTES
BURNS	BURYING	BUSKIN	BUTENES	BUXOM
BURNSIDE	BUS	BUSKINED	BUTES	BUXOMER
BURNSIDES	BUSBIES	BUSKING	BUTLER	BUXOMEST
BURNT	BUSBOY	BUSKINGS	BUTLERAGE	BUXOMNESS
BUROO	BUSBOYS	BUSKINS	BUTLERAGES	BUXOMNESSES
BUROOS	BUSBY	BUSKS	BUTLERED	BUY
BURP	BUSED	BUSKY	BUTLERIES	BUYABLE
BURPED	BUSES	BUSMAN	BUTLERING	BUYABLES
BURPING	BUSGIRL	BUSMEN	BUTLERS	BUYER
BURPS	BUSGIRLS	BUSS	BUTLERY	BUYERS
BURQA	BUSH	BUSSED	BUTMENT	BUYING
BURQAS	BUSHCRAFT	BUSSES	BUTMENTS	BUYS
BURR	BUSHCRAFTS	BUSSING	BUTS	BUZZ
BURRAWANG	BUSHED	BUSSINGS	BUTT	BUZZARD
BURRAWANGS	BUSHEL	BUSSU	BUTTE	BUZZARDS
BURRED	BUSHELLED	BUSSUS	BUTTED	BUZZED
BURREL	BUSHELLER	BUST	BUTTER	BUZZER
BURRELL	BUSHELLERS	BUSTARD	BUTTERBUR	BUZZERS
BURRELLS	BUSHELLING	BUSTARDS	BUTTERBURS	BUZZES

The Chambers Dictionary is the authority for many longer words; see *OSW* Introduction, page xii.

BUZZIER
BUZZIEST
BUZZING
BUZZINGLY
BUZZINGS
BUZZWORD
BUZZWORDS
BUZZY
BWANA
BWANAS
BWAZI
BWAZIS
BY
BYCATCH
BYCATCHES
BYCOKET

BYCOKETS
BYE
BYES
BYGONE
BYGONES
BYKE
BYKED
BYKES
BYKING
BYLANDER
BYLANDERS
BYLAW
BYLAWS
BYLINE
BYLINES
BYLIVE

BYNAME
BYNAMES
BYNEMPT
BYPASS
BYPASSED
BYPASSES
BYPASSING
BYPATH
BYPATHS
BYPLACE
BYPLACES
BYRE
BYREMAN
BYREMEN
BYRES
BYREWOMAN

BYREWOMEN
BYRLADY
BYRLAKIN
BYRLAW
BYRLAWS
BYRNIE
BYRNIES
BYROAD
BYROADS
BYROOM
BYROOMS
BYS
BYSSAL
BYSSI
BYSSINE
BYSSOID

BYSSUS
BYSSUSES
BYSTANDER
BYSTANDERS
BYTE
BYTES
BYTOWNITE
BYTOWNITES
BYWAY
BYWAYS
BYWONER
BYWONERS
BYWORD
BYWORDS
BYZANT
BYZANTS

C

CAATINGA	CABLEWAYS	CACHOLONG	CADDISES	CAECITIS
CAATINGAS	CABLING	CACHOLONGS	CADDISH	CAECITISES
CAB	CABLINGS	CACHOLOT	CADDY	CAECUM
CABA	CABMAN	CACHOLOTS	CADDYING	CAERULE
CABAL	CABMEN	CACHOU	CADDYSS	CAERULEAN
CABALA	CABOB	CACHOUS	CADDYSSES	CAESAR
CABALAS	CABOBBED	CACHUCHA	CADE	CAESARS
CABALETTA	CABOBBING	CACHUCHAS	CADEAU	CAESE
CABALETTAS	CABOBS	CACIQUE	CADEAUX	CAESIOUS
CABALETTE	CABOC	CACIQUES	CADEE	CAESIUM
CABALISM	CABOCEER	CACIQUISM	CADEES	CAESIUMS
CABALISMS	CABOCEERS	CACIQUISMS	CADELLE	CAESTUS
CABALIST	CABOCHED	CACKLE	CADELLES	CAESTUSES
CABALISTS	CABOCHON	CACKLED	CADENCE	CAESURA
CABALLED	CABOCHONS	CACKLER	CADENCED	CAESURAE
CABALLER	CABOCS	CACKLERS	CADENCES	CAESURAL
CABALLERO	CABOODLE	CACKLES	CADENCIES	CAESURAS
CABALLEROS	CABOODLES	CACKLING	CADENCY	CAFARD
CABALLERS	CABOOSE	CACODEMON	CADENT	CAFARDS
CABALLINE	CABOOSES	CACODEMONS	CADENTIAL	CAFF
CABALLING	CABOSHED	CACODOXIES	CADENZA	CAFES
CABALS	CABOTAGE	CACODOXY	CADENZAS	CAFETERIA
CABANA	CABOTAGES	CACODYL	CADES	CAFETERIAS
CABANAS	CABRE	CACODYLIC	CADET	CAFF
CABARET	CABRETTA	CACODYLS	CADETS	CAFFEIN
CABARETS	CABRETTAS	CACOEPIES	CADETSHIP	CAFFEINE
CABAS	CABRIE	CACOEPY	CADETSHIPS	CAFFEINES
CABBAGE	CABRIES	CACOETHES	CADGE	CAFFEINS
CABBAGED	CABRIOLE	CACOLET	CADGED	CAFFEISM
CABBAGES	CABRIOLES	CACOLETS	CADGER	CAFFEISMS
CABBAGING	CABRIOLET	CACOLOGIES	CADGERS	CAFFILA
CABBAGY	CABRIOLETS	CACOLOGY	CADGES	CAFFILAS
CABBALA	CABRIT	CACOMIXL	CADGIER	CAFFS
CABBALAS	CABRITS	CACOMIXLS	CADGIEST	CAFILA
CABBALISM	CABS	CACOON	CADGING	CAFILAS
CABBALISMS	CACAFOGO	CACOONS	CADGY	CAFTAN
CABBALIST	CACAFOGOS	CACOPHONIES	CADI	CAFTANS
CABBALISTS	CACAFUEGO	CACOPHONY	CADIE	CAGE
CABBIE	CACAFUEGOS	CACOTOPIA	CADIES	CAGEBIRD
CABBIES	CACAO	CACOTOPIAS	CADIS	CAGEBIRDS
CABBY	CACAOS	CACTI	CADMIUM	CAGED
CABER	CACHAEMIA	CACTIFORM	CADMIUMS	CAGELING
CABERNET	CACHAEMIAS	CACTUS	CADRANS	CAGELINGS
CABERNETS	CACHAEMIC	CACTUSES	CADRANSES	CAGES
CABERS	CACHALOT	CACUMINAL	CADRE	CAGEWORK
CABIN	CACHALOTS	CACUMINALS	CADRES	CAGEWORKS
CABINED	CACHE	CAD	CADS	CAGEY
CABINET	CACHECTIC	CADASTRAL	CADUAC	CAGEYNESS
CABINETS	CACHED	CADASTRE	CADUACS	CAGEYNESSES
CABINING	CACHEPOT	CADASTRES	CADUCEAN	CAGIER
CABINS	CACHEPOTS	CADAVER	CADUCEI	CAGIEST
CABLE	CACHES	CADAVERIC	CADUCEUS	CAGILY
CABLED	CACHET	CADAVERS	CADUCITIES	CAGINESS
CABLEGRAM	CACHETS	CADDICE	CADUCITY	CAGINESSES
CABLEGRAMS	CACHEXIA	CADDICES	CADUCOUS	CAGING
CABLES	CACHEXIAS	CADDIE	CAECA	CAGOT
CABLET	CACHEXIES	CADDIED	CAECAL	CAGOTS
CABLETS	CACHEXY	CADDIES	CAECILIAN	CAGOUL
CABLEWAY	CACHING	CADDIS	CAECILIANS	CAGOULE

The Chambers Dictionary is the authority for many longer words; see *OSW* Introduction, page xii.

CAGOULES	CALABOOSE	CALCINE	CALIBRATED	CALLING
CAGOULS	CALABOOSES	CALCINED	CALIBRATES	CALLINGS
CAGY	CALABRESE	CALCINES	CALIBRATING	CALLIOPE
CAGYNESS	CALABRESES	CALCINING	CALIBRE	CALLIOPES
CAGYNESSES	CALADIUM	CALCITE	CALIBRED	CALLIPER
CAHIER	CALADIUMS	CALCITES	CALIBRES	CALLIPERED
CAHIERS	CALAMANCO	CALCIUM	CALICES	CALLIPERING
CAHOOTS	CALAMANCOES	CALCIUMS	CALICHE	CALLIPERS
CAILLACH	CALAMANCOS	CALCRETE	CALICHES	CALLOSITIES
CAILLACHS	CALAMARI	CALCRETES	CALICLE	CALLOSITY
CAILLE	CALAMARIES	CALCSPAR	CALICLES	CALLOUS
CAILLEACH	CALAMARY	CALCSPARS	CALICO	CALLOUSLY
CAILLEACHS	CALAMI	CALCULAR	CALICOES	CALLOW
CAILLES	CALAMINE	CALCULARY	CALICOS	CALLOWER
CAILLIACH	CALAMINES	CALCULATE	CALID	CALLOWEST
CAILLIACHS	CALAMINT	CALCULATED	CALIDITIES	CALLOWS
CAIMAC	CALAMINTS	CALCULATES	CALIDITY	CALLS
CAIMACAM	CALAMITE	CALCULATING	CALIF	CALLUNA
CAIMACAMS	CALAMITES	CALCULI	CALIFS	CALLUNAS
CAIMACS	CALAMITIES	CALCULOSE	CALIGO	CALLUS
CAIMAN	CALAMITY	CALCULOUS	CALIGOES	CALLUSES
CAIMANS	CALAMUS	CALCULUS	CALIGOS	CALM
CAIN	CALANDO	CALCULUSES	CALIMA	CALMANT
CAINS	CALANDRIA	CALDARIA	CALIMAS	CALMANTS
CAIQUE	CALANDRIAS	CALDARIUM	CALIOLOGIES	CALMATIVE
CAIQUES	CALANTHE	CALDERA	CALIOLOGY	CALMATIVES
CAIRD	CALANTHES	CALDERAS	CALIPASH	CALMED
CAIRDS	CALASH	CALDRON	CALIPASHES	CALMER
CAIRN	CALASHES	CALDRONS	CALIPEE	CALMEST
CAIRNED	CALATHEA	CALEFIED	CALIPEES	CALMIER
CAIRNGORM	CALATHEAS	CALEFIES	CALIPER	CALMIEST
CAIRNGORMS	CALATHI	CALEFY	CALIPERS	CALMING
CAIRNS	CALATHUS	CALEFYING	CALIPH	CALMLY
CAISSON	CALAVANCE	CALEMBOUR	CALIPHAL	CALMNESS
CAISSONS	CALAVANCES	CALEMBOURS	CALIPHATE	CALMNESSES
CAITIFF	CALCANEA	CALENDAR	CALIPHATES	CALMS
CAITIFFS	CALCANEAL	CALENDARED	CALIPHS	CALMSTONE
CAITIVE	CALCANEAN	CALENDARING	CALISAYA	CALMSTONES
CAITIVES	CALCANEI	CALENDARS	CALISAYAS	CALMY
CAJEPUT	CALCANEUM	CALENDER	CALIVER	CALOMEL
CAJEPUTS	CALCANEUS	CALENDERED	CALIVERS	CALOMELS
CAJOLE	CALCAR	CALENDERING	CALIX	CALORIC
CAJOLED	CALCARIA	CALENDERINGS	CALK	CALORICS
CAJOLER	CALCARINE	CALENDERS	CALKED	CALORIE
CAJOLERIES	CALCARS	CALENDRER	CALKER	CALORIES
CAJOLERS	CALCEATE	CALENDRERS	CALKERS	CALORIFIC
CAJOLERY	CALCEATED	CALENDRIC	CALKIN	CALORIST
CAJOLES	CALCEATES	CALENDRIES	CALKING	CALORISTS
CAJOLING	CALCEATING	CALENDRY	CALKINS	CALORY
CAJUN	CALCED	CALENDS	CALKS	CALOTTE
CAJUPUT	CALCEDONIES	CALENDULA	CALL	CALOTTES
CAJUPUTS	CALCEDONY	CALENDULAS	CALLA	CALOTYPE
CAKE	CALCES	CALENTURE	CALLAN	CALOTYPES
CAKED	CALCIC	CALENTURES	CALLANS	CALOYER
CAKES	CALCICOLE	CALF	CALLANT	CALOYERS
CAKEWALK	CALCICOLES	CALFDOZER	CALLANTS	CALP
CAKEWALKED	CALCIFIC	CALFDOZERS	CALLAS	CALPA
CAKEWALKING	CALCIFIED	CALFLESS	CALLED	CALPAC
CAKEWALKS	CALCIFIES	CALFS	CALLER	CALPACK
CAKEY	CALCIFUGE	CALFSKIN	CALLERS	CALPACKS
CAKIER	CALCIFUGES	CALFSKINS	CALLET	CALPACS
CAKIEST	CALCIFY	CALIATOUR	CALLETS	CALPAS
CAKING	CALCIFYING	CALIATOURS	CALLID	CALPS
CAKINGS	CALCIMINE	CALIBER	CALLIDITIES	CALQUE
CAKY	CALCIMINED	CALIBERED	CALLIDITY	CALQUED
CALABASH	CALCIMINES	CALIBERS	CALLIGRAM	CALQUES
CALABASHES	CALCIMINING	CALIBRATE	CALLIGRAMS	CALQUING

The Chambers Dictionary is the authority for many longer words; see *OSW* Introduction, page xii.

CALTHA	CAMASHES	CAMISADOS	CAMPLY	CANCELEER
CALTHAS	CAMASS	CAMISE	CAMPNESS	CANCELEERED
CALTHROP	CAMASSES	CAMISES	CAMPNESSES	CANCELEERING
CALTHROPS	CAMBER	CAMISOLE	CAMPO	CANCELEERS
CALTRAP	CAMBERED	CAMISOLES	CAMPODEID	CANCELIER
CALTRAPS	CAMBERING	CAMLET	CAMPODEIDS	CANCELIERED
CALTROP	CAMBERINGS	CAMLETS	CAMPOREE	CANCELIERING
CALTROPS	CAMBERS	CAMMED	CAMPOREES	CANCELIERS
CALUMBA	CAMBIA	CAMMING	CAMPOS	CANCELLED
CALUMBAS	CAMBIAL	CAMOGIE	CAMPS	CANCELLI
CALUMET	CAMBIFORM	CAMOGIES	CAMPSITE	CANCELLING
CALUMETS	CAMBISM	CAMOMILE	CAMPSITES	CANCELS
CALUMNIES	CAMBISMS	CAMOMILES	CAMPUS	CANCER
CALUMNY	CAMBIST	CAMORRA	CAMPUSES	CANCERATE
CALUTRON	CAMBISTRIES	CAMORRAS	CAMPY	CANCERATED
CALUTRONS	CAMBISTRY	CAMOTE	CAMS	CANCERATES
CALVARIA	CAMBISTS	CAMOTES	CAMSHAFT	CANCERATING
CALVARIAS	CAMBIUM	CAMOUFLET	CAMSHAFTS	CANCEROUS
CALVARIES	CAMBIUMS	CAMOUFLETS	CAMSHEUGH	CANCERS
CALVARY	CAMBOGE	CAMP	CAMSHO	CANCRINE
CALVE	CAMBOGES	CAMPAGNA	CAMSHOCH	CANCROID
CALVED	CAMBREL	CAMPAGNAS	CAMSTAIRY	CANCROIDS
CALVER	CAMBRELS	CAMPAIGN	CAMSTANE	CANDELA
CALVERED	CAMBRIC	CAMPAIGNED	CAMSTANES	CANDELAS
CALVERING	CAMBRICS	CAMPAIGNING	CAMSTEARY	CANDENT
CALVERS	CAMCORDER	CAMPAIGNS	CAMSTONE	CANDID
CALVES	CAMCORDERS	CAMPANA	CAMSTONES	CANDIDA
CALVING	CAME	CAMPANAS	CAMUS	CANDIDACIES
CALVITIES	CAMEL	CAMPANERO	CAMUSES	CANDIDACY
CALX	CAMELBACK	CAMPANEROS	CAMWOOD	CANDIDAL
CALXES	CAMELBACKS	CAMPANILE	CAMWOODS	CANDIDAS
CALYCES	CAMELEER	CAMPANILES	CAN	CANDIDATE
CALYCINAL	CAMELEERS	CAMPANILI	CANADA	CANDIDATES
CALYCINE	CAMELEON	CAMPANIST	CANADAS	CANDIDER
CALYCLE	CAMELEONS	CAMPANISTS	CANAIGRE	CANDIDEST
CALYCLED	CAMELID	CAMPANULA	CANAIGRES	CANDIDLY
CALYCLES	CAMELIDS	CAMPANULAS	CANAILLE	CANDIE
CALYCOID	CAMELINE	CAMPEADOR	CANAILLES	CANDIED
CALYCULE	CAMELINES	CAMPEADORS	CANAKIN	CANDIES
CALYCULES	CAMELISH	CAMPED	CANAKINS	CANDLE
CALYCULI	CAMELLIA	CAMPER	CANAL	CANDLED
CALYCULUS	CAMELLIAS	CAMPERS	CANALISE	CANDLENUT
CALYPSO	CAMELOID	CAMPESINO	CANALISED	CANDLENUTS
CALYPSOS	CAMELOIDS	CAMPESINOS	CANALISES	CANDLES
CALYPTERA	CAMELOT	CAMPEST	CANALISING	CANDLING
CALYPTERAS	CAMELOTS	CAMPFIRE	CANALIZE	CANDOCK
CALYPTRA	CAMELRIES	CAMPFIRES	CANALIZED	CANDOCKS
CALYPTRAS	CAMELRY	CAMPHANE	CANALIZES	CANDOR
CALYX	CAMELS	CAMPHANES	CANALIZING	CANDORS
CALYXES	CAMEO	CAMPHENE	CANALS	CANDOUR
CALZONE	CAMEOS	CAMPHENES	CANAPE	CANDOURS
CALZONES	CAMERA	CAMPHINE	CANAPES	CANDY
CALZONI	CAMERAE	CAMPHINES	CANARD	CANDYING
CAM	CAMERAL	CAMPHIRE	CANARDS	CANDYTUFT
CAMAIEU	CAMERAMAN	CAMPHIRES	CANARIED	CANDYTUFTS
CAMAIEUX	CAMERAMEN	CAMPHOR	CANARIES	CANE
CAMAN	CAMERAS	CAMPHORIC	CANARY	CANEBRAKE
CAMANACHD	CAMERATED	CAMPHORS	CANARYING	CANEBRAKES
CAMANACHDS	CAMES	CAMPIER	CANASTA	CANED
CAMANS	CAMESE	CAMPIEST	CANASTAS	CANEFRUIT
CAMARILLA	CAMESES	CAMPING	CANASTER	CANEFRUITS
CAMARILLAS	CAMION	CAMPION	CANASTERS	CANEH
CAMARON	CAMIONS	CAMPIONS	CANBANK	CANEHS
CAMARONS	CAMIS	CAMPLE	CANBANKS	CANELLA
CAMAS	CAMISADE	CAMPLED	CANCAN	CANELLAS
CAMASES	CAMISADES	CAMPLES	CANCANS	CANELLINI
CAMASH	CAMISADO	CAMPLING	CANCEL	CANEPHOR

The Chambers Dictionary is the authority for many longer words; see *OSW* Introduction, page xii.

CANEPHORA	CANNIKIN	CANT	CANTONAL	CAPELIN
CANEPHORAS	CANNIKINS	CANTABANK	CANTONED	CAPELINE
CANEPHORE	CANNILY	CANTABANKS	CANTONING	CAPELINES
CANEPHORES	CANNINESS	CANTABILE	CANTONISE	CAPELINS
CANEPHORS	CANNINESSES	CANTABILES	CANTONISED	CAPELLET
CANES	CANNING	CANTALA	CANTONISES	CAPELLETS
CANESCENT	CANNON	CANTALAS	CANTONISING	CAPELLINE
CANFIELD	CANNONADE	CANTALOUP	CANTONIZE	CAPELLINES
CANFIELDS	CANNONADED	CANTALOUPS	CANTONIZED	CAPER
CANFUL	CANNONADES	CANTAR	CANTONIZES	CAPERED
CANFULS	CANNONADING	CANTARS	CANTONIZING	CAPERER
CANG	CANNONED	CANTATA	CANTONS	CAPERERS
CANGLE	CANNONEER	CANTATAS	CANTOR	CAPERING
CANGLED	CANNONEERS	CANTATE	CANTORIAL	CAPERS
CANGLES	CANNONIER	CANTATES	CANTORIS	CAPES
CANGLING	CANNONIERS	CANTDOG	CANTORS	CAPESKIN
CANGS	CANNONING	CANTDOGS	CANTOS	CAPESKINS
CANGUE	CANNONRIES	CANTED	CANTRED	CAPEWORK
CANGUES	CANNONRY	CANTEEN	CANTREDS	CAPEWORKS
CANICULAR	CANNONS	CANTEENS	CANTREF	CAPI
CANID	CANNOT	CANTER	CANTREFS	CAPIAS
CANIDS	CANNS	CANTERED	CANTRIP	CAPIASES
CANIER	CANNULA	CANTERING	CANTRIPS	CAPILLARIES
CANIEST	CANNULAE	CANTERS	CANTS	CAPILLARY
CANIKIN	CANNULAR	CANTEST	CANTUS	CAPING
CANIKINS	CANNULAS	CANTHARI	CANTY	CAPITA
CANINE	CANNULATE	CANTHARID	CANULA	CAPITAL
CANINES	CANNY	CANTHARIDES	CANULAE	CAPITALLY
CANING	CANOE	CANTHARIDS	CANULAS	CAPITALS
CANINGS	CANOED	CANTHARIS	CANVAS	CAPITAN
CANINITIES	CANOEING	CANTHARUS	CANVASED	CAPITANI
CANINITY	CANOEINGS	CANTHI	CANVASES	CAPITANO
CANISTER	CANOEIST	CANTHOOK	CANVASING	CAPITANOS
CANISTERED	CANOEISTS	CANTHOOKS	CANVASS	CAPITANS
CANISTERING	CANOES	CANTHUS	CANVASSED	CAPITATE
CANISTERS	CANON	CANTICLE	CANVASSER	CAPITAYN
CANITIES	CANONESS	CANTICLES	CANVASSERS	CAPITAYNS
CANKER	CANONESSES	CANTICO	CANVASSES	CAPITELLA
CANKERED	CANONIC	CANTICOED	CANVASSING	CAPITULA
CANKERING	CANONICAL	CANTICOING	CANY	CAPITULAR
CANKEROUS	CANONICALS	CANTICOS	CANYON	CAPITULARS
CANKERS	CANONISE	CANTICOY	CANYONS	CAPITULUM
CANKERY	CANONISED	CANTICOYED	CANZONA	CAPIZ
CANN	CANONISES	CANTICOYING	CANZONAS	CAPIZES
CANNA	CANONISING	CANTICOYS	CANZONE	CAPLE
CANNABIC	CANONIST	CANTICUM	CANZONET	CAPLES
CANNABIN	CANONISTS	CANTICUMS	CANZONETS	CAPLET
CANNABINS	CANONIZE	CANTIER	CANZONI	CAPLETS
CANNABIS	CANONIZED	CANTIEST	CAP	CAPLIN
CANNABISES	CANONIZES	CANTILENA	CAPA	CAPLINS
CANNACH	CANONIZING	CANTILENAS	CAPABLE	CAPO
CANNACHS	CANONRIES	CANTINA	CAPABLER	CAPOCCHIA
CANNAE	CANONRY	CANTINAS	CAPABLEST	CAPOCCHIAS
CANNAS	CANONS	CANTINESS	CAPACIOUS	CAPOEIRA
CANNED	CANOODLE	CANTINESSES	CAPACITIES	CAPOEIRAS
CANNEL	CANOODLED	CANTING	CAPACITOR	CAPON
CANNELS	CANOODLES	CANTINGS	CAPACITORS	CAPONIER
CANNELURE	CANOODLING	CANTION	CAPACITY	CAPONIERE
CANNELURES	CANOPIED	CANTIONS	CAPARISON	CAPONIERES
CANNER	CANOPIES	CANTLE	CAPARISONED	CAPONIERS
CANNERIES	CANOPY	CANTLED	CAPARISONING	CAPONISE
CANNERS	CANOPYING	CANTLES	CAPARISONS	CAPONISED
CANNERY	CANOROUS	CANTLET	CAPAS	CAPONISES
CANNIBAL	CANS	CANTLETS	CAPE	CAPONISING
CANNIBALS	CANST	CANTLING	CAPED	CAPONIZE
CANNIER	CANSTICK	CANTO	CAPELET	CAPONIZED
CANNIEST	CANSTICKS	CANTON	CAPELETS	CAPONIZES

The Chambers Dictionary is the authority for many longer words; see *OSW* Introduction, page xii.

CAPONIZING	CAPSTONE	CARABINERS	CARBAMIDE	CARCAJOU
CAPONS	CAPSTONES	CARABINES	CARBAMIDES	CARCAJOUS
CAPORAL	CAPSULAR	CARABINS	CARBANION	CARCAKE
CAPORALS	CAPSULARY	CARACAL	CARBANIONS	CARCAKES
CAPOS	CAPSULATE	CARACALS	CARBARYL	CARCANET
CAPOT	CAPSULE	CARACARA	CARBARYLS	CARCANETS
CAPOTASTO	CAPSULES	CARACARAS	CARBAZOLE	CARCASE
CAPOTASTOS	CAPSULISE	CARACK	CARBAZOLES	CARCASED
CAPOTE	CAPSULISED	CARACKS	CARBIDE	CARCASES
CAPOTES	CAPSULISES	CARACOL	CARBIDES	CARCASING
CAPOTS	CAPSULISING	CARACOLE	CARBIES	CARCASS
CAPOTTED	CAPSULIZE	CARACOLED	CARBINE	CARCASSED
CAPOTTING	CAPSULIZED	CARACOLES	CARBINEER	CARCASSES
CAPOUCH	CAPSULIZES	CARACOLING	CARBINEERS	CARCASSING
CAPOUCHES	CAPSULIZING	CARACOLLED	CARBINES	CARCERAL
CAPPED	CAPTAIN	CARACOLLING	CARBINIER	CARCINOMA
CAPPER	CAPTAINCIES	CARACOLS	CARBINIERS	CARCINOMAS
CAPPERS	CAPTAINCY	CARACT	CARBOLIC	CARCINOMATA
CAPPING	CAPTAINED	CARACTS	CARBOLICS	CARD
CAPPINGS	CAPTAINING	CARACUL	CARBON	CARDAMINE
CAPRATE	CAPTAINRIES	CARACULS	CARBONADE	CARDAMINES
CAPRATES	CAPTAINRY	CARAFE	CARBONADES	CARDAMOM
CAPRIC	CAPTAINS	CARAFES	CARBONADO	CARDAMOMS
CAPRICCI	CAPTAN	CARAMBA	CARBONADOED	CARDAMON
CAPRICCIO	CAPTANS	CARAMBOLA	CARBONADOES	CARDAMONS
CAPRICCIOS	CAPTION	CARAMBOLAS	CARBONADOING	CARDAMUM
CAPRICE	CAPTIONED	CARAMBOLE	CARBONADOS	CARDAMUMS
CAPRICES	CAPTIONING	CARAMBOLED	CARBONATE	CARDBOARD
CAPRID	CAPTIONS	CARAMBOLES	CARBONATED	CARDBOARDS
CAPRIDS	CAPTIOUS	CARAMBOLING	CARBONATES	CARDECU
CAPRIFIED	CAPTIVATE	CARAMEL	CARBONATING	CARDECUE
CAPRIFIES	CAPTIVATED	CARAMELLED	CARBONIC	CARDECUES
CAPRIFIG	CAPTIVATES	CARAMELLING	CARBONISE	CARDECUS
CAPRIFIGS	CAPTIVATING	CARAMELS	CARBONISED	CARDED
CAPRIFOIL	CAPTIVE	CARANGID	CARBONISES	CARDER
CAPRIFOILS	CAPTIVED	CARANGIDS	CARBONISING	CARDERS
CAPRIFOLE	CAPTIVES	CARANGOID	CARBONIZE	CARDI
CAPRIFOLES	CAPTIVING	CARANGOIDS	CARBONIZED	CARDIAC
CAPRIFORM	CAPTIVITIES	CARANNA	CARBONIZES	CARDIACAL
CAPRIFY	CAPTIVITY	CARANNAS	CARBONIZING	CARDIACS
CAPRIFYING	CAPTOR	CARAP	CARBONS	CARDIALGIES
CAPRINE	CAPTORS	CARAPACE	CARBONYL	CARDIALGY
CAPRIOLE	CAPTURE	CARAPACES	CARBONYLS	CARDIES
CAPRIOLED	CAPTURED	CARAPS	CARBOXYL	CARDIGAN
CAPRIOLES	CAPTURER	CARAT	CARBOXYLS	CARDIGANS
CAPRIOLING	CAPTURERS	CARATS	CARBOY	CARDINAL
CAPROATE	CAPTURES	CARAUNA	CARBOYS	CARDINALS
CAPROATES	CAPTURING	CARAUNAS	CARBS	CARDING
CAPROIC	CAPUCHE	CARAVAN	CARBUNCLE	CARDIOID
CAPRYLATE	CAPUCHES	CARAVANCE	CARBUNCLES	CARDIOIDS
CAPRYLATES	CAPUCHIN	CARAVANCES	CARBURATE	CARDIS
CAPRYLIC	CAPUCHINS	CARAVANED	CARBURATED	CARDITIS
CAPS	CAPUERA	CARAVANER	CARBURATES	CARDITISES
CAPSAICIN	CAPUERAS	CARAVANERS	CARBURATING	CARDOON
CAPSAICINS	CAPUL	CARAVANING	CARBURET	CARDOONS
CAPSICUM	CAPULS	CARAVANNED	CARBURETS	CARDPHONE
CAPSICUMS	CAPUT	CARAVANNING	CARBURETTED	CARDPHONES
CAPSID	CAPYBARA	CARAVANS	CARBURETTING	CARDPUNCH
CAPSIDS	CAPYBARAS	CARAVEL	CARBURISE	CARDPUNCHES
CAPSIZAL	CAR	CARAVELS	CARBURISED	CARDS
CAPSIZALS	CARABAO	CARAWAY	CARBURISES	CARDUUS
CAPSIZE	CARABAOS	CARAWAYS	CARBURISING	CARDUUSES
CAPSIZED	CARABID	CARB	CARBURIZE	CARDY
CAPSIZES	CARABIDS	CARBACHOL	CARBURIZED	CARE
CAPSIZING	CARABIN	CARBACHOLS	CARBURIZES	CARED
CAPSTAN	CARABINE	CARBAMATE	CARBURIZING	CAREEN
CAPSTANS	CARABINER	CARBAMATES	CARBY	CAREENAGE

The Chambers Dictionary is the authority for many longer words; see *OSW* Introduction, page xii.

CAREENAGES
CAREENED
CAREENING
CAREENS
CAREER
CAREERED
CAREERING
CAREERISM
CAREERISMS
CAREERIST
CAREERISTS
CAREERS
CAREFREE
CAREFUL
CAREFULLY
CARELESS
CAREME
CAREMES
CARER
CARERS
CARES
CARESS
CARESSED
CARESSES
CARESSING
CARESSINGS
CARESSIVE
CARET
CARETAKE
CARETAKEN
CARETAKER
CARETAKERS
CARETAKES
CARETAKING
CARETOOK
CARETS
CAREWORN
CAREX
CARFARE
CARFARES
CARFAX
CARFAXES
CARFOX
CARFOXES
CARFUFFLE
CARFUFFLED
CARFUFFLES
CARFUFFLING
CARGEESE
CARGO
CARGOED
CARGOES
CARGOING
CARGOOSE
CARIACOU
CARIACOUS
CARIAMA
CARIAMAS
CARIBE
CARIBES
CARIBOU
CARIBOUS
CARICES
CARIERE
CARIERES
CARIES
CARILLON

CARILLONED
CARILLONING
CARILLONS
CARINA
CARINAE
CARINAS
CARINATE
CARING
CARIOCA
CARIOCAS
CARIOLE
CARIOLES
CARIOUS
CARITAS
CARITATES
CARJACOU
CARJACOUS
CARK
CARKED
CARKING
CARKS
CARL
CARLINE
CARLINES
CARLING
CARLINGS
CARLISH
CARLOAD
CARLOADS
CARLOCK
CARLOCKS
CARLOT
CARLOTS
CARLS
CARMAN
CARMELITE
CARMELITES
CARMEN
CARMINE
CARMINES
CARNAGE
CARNAGES
CARNAHUBA
CARNAHUBAS
CARNAL
CARNALISE
CARNALISED
CARNALISES
CARNALISING
CARNALISM
CARNALISMS
CARNALIST
CARNALISTS
CARNALITIES
CARNALITY
CARNALIZE
CARNALIZED
CARNALIZES
CARNALIZING
CARNALLED
CARNALLING
CARNALLY
CARNALS
CARNATION
CARNATIONS
CARNAUBA
CARNAUBAS

CARNELIAN
CARNELIANS
CARNEOUS
CARNET
CARNETS
CARNEY
CARNEYED
CARNEYING
CARNEYS
CARNIED
CARNIER
CARNIES
CARNIEST
CARNIFEX
CARNIFEXES
CARNIFIED
CARNIFIES
CARNIFY
CARNIFYING
CARNIVAL
CARNIVALS
CARNIVORE
CARNIVORES
CARNOSE
CARNOSITIES
CARNOSITY
CARNOTITE
CARNOTITES
CARNY
CARNYING
CAROB
CAROBS
CAROCHE
CAROCHES
CAROL
CAROLI
CAROLLED
CAROLLER
CAROLLERS
CAROLLING
CAROLS
CAROLUS
CAROLUSES
CAROM
CAROMED
CAROMEL
CAROMELLED
CAROMELLING
CAROMELS
CAROMING
CAROMS
CAROTENE
CAROTENES
CAROTID
CAROTIN
CAROTINS
CAROUSAL
CAROUSALS
CAROUSE
CAROUSED
CAROUSEL
CAROUSELS
CAROUSER
CAROUSERS
CAROUSES
CAROUSING
CARP

CARPAL
CARPALS
CARPARK
CARPARKS
CARPED
CARPEL
CARPELS
CARPENTER
CARPENTERED
CARPENTERING
CARPENTERS
CARPENTRIES
CARPENTRY
CARPER
CARPERS
CARPET
CARPETBAG
CARPETBAGS
CARPETED
CARPETING
CARPETINGS
CARPETS
CARPI
CARPING
CARPINGLY
CARPINGS
CARPOLOGIES
CARPOLOGY
CARPORT
CARPORTS
CARPS
CARPUS
CARR
CARRACK
CARRACKS
CARRACT
CARRACTS
CARRAGEEN
CARRAGEENS
CARRAT
CARRATS
CARRAWAY
CARRAWAYS
CARRECT
CARRECTS
CARREL
CARRELL
CARRELLS
CARRELS
CARRIAGE
CARRIAGES
CARRIED
CARRIER
CARRIERS
CARRIES
CARRIOLE
CARRIOLES
CARRION
CARRIONS
CARRITCH
CARRITCHES
CARRONADE
CARRONADES
CARROT
CARROTS
CARROTY
CARROUSEL

CARROUSELS
CARRS
CARRY
CARRYALL
CARRYALLS
CARRYCOT
CARRYCOTS
CARRYING
CARRYTALE
CARRYTALES
CARS
CARSE
CARSES
CARSEY
CARSEYS
CART
CARTA
CARTAGE
CARTAGES
CARTAS
CARTE
CARTED
CARTEL
CARTELISE
CARTELISED
CARTELISES
CARTELISING
CARTELISM
CARTELISMS
CARTELIST
CARTELISTS
CARTELIZE
CARTELIZED
CARTELIZES
CARTELIZING
CARTELS
CARTER
CARTERS
CARTES
CARTILAGE
CARTILAGES
CARTING
CARTLOAD
CARTLOADS
CARTOGRAM
CARTOGRAMS
CARTOLOGIES
CARTOLOGY
CARTON
CARTONAGE
CARTONAGES
CARTONED
CARTONING
CARTONS
CARTOON
CARTOONED
CARTOONING
CARTOONS
CARTOUCH
CARTOUCHE
CARTOUCHES
CARTRIDGE
CARTRIDGES
CARTROAD
CARTROADS
CARTS
CARTULARIES

The Chambers Dictionary is the authority for many longer words; see *OSW* Introduction, page xii.

CARTULARY	CASEMATES	CASSINOS	CASUALLY	CATAPAN
CARTWAY	CASEMEN	CASSIS	CASUALS	CATAPANS
CARTWAYS	CASEMENT	CASSISES	CASUALTIES	CATAPHYLL
CARTWHEEL	CASEMENTS	CASSOCK	CASUALTY	CATAPHYLLS
CARTWHEELED	CASEOUS	CASSOCKED	CASUARINA	CATAPLASM
CARTWHEELING	CASERN	CASSOCKS	CASUARINAS	CATAPLASMS
CARTWHEELS	CASERNE	CASSONADE	CASUIST	CATAPLEXIES
CARUCAGE	CASERNES	CASSONADES	CASUISTIC	CATAPLEXY
CARUCAGES	CASERNS	CASSONE	CASUISTRIES	CATAPULT
CARUCATE	CASES	CASSONES	CASUISTRY	CATAPULTED
CARUCATES	CASEWORK	CASSOULET	CASUISTS	CATAPULTING
CARUNCLE	CASEWORKS	CASSOULETS	CAT	CATAPULTS
CARUNCLES	CASH	CASSOWARIES	CATABASES	CATARACT
CARVACROL	CASHAW	CASSOWARY	CATABASIS	CATARACTS
CARVACROLS	CASHAWS	CAST	CATABOLIC	CATARHINE
CARVE	CASHED	CASTANET	CATACLASM	CATARRH
CARVED	CASHES	CASTANETS	CATACLASMS	CATARRHAL
CARVEL	CASHEW	CASTAWAY	CATACLYSM	CATARRHS
CARVELS	CASHEWS	CASTAWAYS	CATACLYSMS	CATASTA
CARVEN	CASHIER	CASTE	CATACOMB	CATASTAS
CARVER	CASHIERED	CASTED	CATACOMBS	CATATONIA
CARVERIES	CASHIERER	CASTELESS	CATAFALCO	CATATONIAS
CARVERS	CASHIERERS	CASTELLA	CATAFALCOES	CATATONIC
CARVERY	CASHIERING	CASTELLAN	CATALASE	CATATONICS
CARVES	CASHIERINGS	CASTELLANS	CATALASES	CATAWBA
CARVIES	CASHIERS	CASTELLUM	CATALEPSIES	CATAWBAS
CARVING	CASHING	CASTELLUMS	CATALEPSY	CATBIRD
CARVINGS	CASHLESS	CASTER	CATALEXES	CATBIRDS
CARVY	CASHMERE	CASTERS	CATALEXIS	CATBOAT
CARYATIC	CASHMERES	CASTES	CATALO	CATBOATS
CARYATID	CASIMERE	CASTIGATE	CATALOES	CATCALL
CARYATIDES	CASIMERES	CASTIGATED	CATALOG	CATCALLED
CARYATIDS	CASING	CASTIGATES	CATALOGED	CATCALLING
CARYOPSES	CASINGS	CASTIGATING	CATALOGER	CATCALLS
CARYOPSIDES	CASINO	CASTING	CATALOGERS	CATCH
CARYOPSIS	CASINOS	CASTINGS	CATALOGING	CATCHABLE
CASA	CASK	CASTLE	CATALOGS	CATCHED
CASAS	CASKED	CASTLED	CATALOGUE	CATCHEN
CASBAH	CASKET	CASTLES	CATALOGUED	CATCHER
CASBAHS	CASKETS	CASTLING	CATALOGUES	CATCHERS
CASCABEL	CASKING	CASTOCK	CATALOGUING	CATCHES
CASCABELS	CASKS	CASTOCKS	CATALOS	CATCHFLIES
CASCADE	CASQUE	CASTOR	CATALPA	CATCHFLY
CASCADED	CASQUES	CASTOREUM	CATALPAS	CATCHIER
CASCADES	CASSAREEP	CASTOREUMS	CATALYSE	CATCHIEST
CASCADING	CASSAREEPS	CASTORIES	CATALYSED	CATCHING
CASCADURA	CASSARIPE	CASTORS	CATALYSER	CATCHINGS
CASCADURAS	CASSARIPES	CASTORY	CATALYSERS	CATCHMENT
CASCARA	CASSATA	CASTRAL	CATALYSES	CATCHMENTS
CASCARAS	CASSATAS	CASTRATE	CATALYSING	CATCHPOLE
CASCHROM	CASSATION	CASTRATED	CATALYSIS	CATCHPOLES
CASCHROMS	CASSATIONS	CASTRATES	CATALYST	CATCHPOLL
CASCO	CASSAVA	CASTRATI	CATALYSTS	CATCHPOLLS
CASCOS	CASSAVAS	CASTRATING	CATALYTIC	CATCHT
CASE	CASSEROLE	CASTRATO	CATALYZE	CATCHUP
CASEATION	CASSEROLED	CASTS	CATALYZED	CATCHUPS
CASEATIONS	CASSEROLES	CASUAL	CATALYZER	CATCHWEED
CASEBOOK	CASSEROLING	CASUALISE	CATALYZERS	CATCHWEEDS
CASEBOOKS	CASSETTE	CASUALISED	CATALYZES	CATCHWORD
CASED	CASSETTES	CASUALISES	CATALYZING	CATCHWORDS
CASEIN	CASSIA	CASUALISING	CATAMARAN	CATCHY
CASEINS	CASSIAS	CASUALISM	CATAMARANS	CATE
CASEMAKER	CASSIMERE	CASUALISMS	CATAMENIA	CATECHISE
CASEMAKERS	CASSIMERES	CASUALIZE	CATAMITE	CATECHISED
CASEMAN	CASSINGLE	CASUALIZED	CATAMITES	CATECHISES
CASEMATE	CASSINGLES	CASUALIZES	CATAMOUNT	CATECHISING
CASEMATED	CASSINO	CASUALIZING	CATAMOUNTS	CATECHISINGS

The Chambers Dictionary is the authority for many longer words; see *OSW* Introduction, page xii.

CATECHISM	CATHEDRALS	CATTY	CAUSA	CAVALLY
CATECHISMS	CATHEDRAS	CATWORKS	CAUSAE	CAVALRIES
CATECHIST	CATHETER	CATWORM	CAUSAL	CAVALRY
CATECHISTS	CATHETERS	CATWORMS	CAUSALITIES	CAVASS
CATECHIZE	CATHETUS	CAUCHEMAR	CAUSALITY	CAVASSES
CATECHIZED	CATHETUSES	CAUCHEMARS	CAUSALLY	CAVATINA
CATECHIZES	CATHEXES	CAUCUS	CAUSATION	CAVATINAS
CATECHIZING	CATHEXIS	CAUCUSED	CAUSATIONS	CAVE
CATECHIZINGS	CATHISMA	CAUCUSES	CAUSATIVE	CAVEAT
CATECHOL	CATHISMAS	CAUCUSING	CAUSATIVES	CAVEATS
CATECHOLS	CATHODAL	CAUDAD	CAUSE	CAVED
CATECHU	CATHODE	CAUDAL	CAUSED	CAVEL
CATECHUS	CATHODES	CAUDATE	CAUSELESS	CAVELS
CATEGORIC	CATHODIC	CAUDATED	CAUSEN	CAVEMAN
CATEGORIES	CATHOLE	CAUDEX	CAUSER	CAVEMEN
CATEGORY	CATHOLES	CAUDEXES	CAUSERIE	CAVENDISH
CATELOG	CATHOLIC	CAUDICES	CAUSERIES	CAVENDISHES
CATELOGS	CATHOOD	CAUDICLE	CAUSERS	CAVER
CATENA	CATHOODS	CAUDICLES	CAUSES	CAVERN
CATENAE	CATHOUSE	CAUDILLO	CAUSEWAY	CAVERNED
CATENANE	CATHOUSES	CAUDILLOS	CAUSEWAYED	CAVERNING
CATENANES	CATION	CAUDLE	CAUSEWAYS	CAVERNOUS
CATENARIES	CATIONS	CAUDLED	CAUSEY	CAVERNS
CATENARY	CATKIN	CAUDLES	CAUSEYS	CAVERS
CATENAS	CATKINS	CAUDLING	CAUSING	CAVES
CATENATE	CATLIKE	CAUDRON	CAUSTIC	CAVESSON
CATENATED	CATLING	CAUDRONS	CAUSTICS	CAVESSONS
CATENATES	CATLINGS	CAUF	CAUTEL	CAVETTI
CATENATING	CATMINT	CAUGHT	CAUTELOUS	CAVETTO
CATER	CATMINTS	CAUK	CAUTELS	CAVIAR
CATERAN	CATNAP	CAUKER	CAUTER	CAVIARE
CATERANS	CATNAPS	CAUKERS	CAUTERANT	CAVIARES
CATERED	CATNEP	CAUKS	CAUTERANTS	CAVIARS
CATERER	CATNEPS	CAUL	CAUTERIES	CAVICORN
CATERERS	CATNIP	CAULD	CAUTERISE	CAVICORNS
CATERESS	CATNIPS	CAULDER	CAUTERISED	CAVIE
CATERESSES	CATOPTRIC	CAULDEST	CAUTERISES	CAVIES
CATERING	CATOPTRICS	CAULDRIFE	CAUTERISING	CAVIL
CATERINGS	CATS	CAULDRON	CAUTERISM	CAVILLED
CATERS	CATSKIN	CAULDRONS	CAUTERISMS	CAVILLER
CATERWAUL	CATSKINS	CAULDS	CAUTERIZE	CAVILLERS
CATERWAULED	CATSUIT	CAULES	CAUTERIZED	CAVILLING
CATERWAULING	CATSUITS	CAULICLE	CAUTERIZES	CAVILLINGS
CATERWAULINGS	CATSUP	CAULICLES	CAUTERIZING	CAVILS
CATERWAULS	CATSUPS	CAULICULI	CAUTERS	CAVING
CATES	CATTABU	CAULIFORM	CAUTERY	CAVINGS
CATFISH	CATTABUS	CAULINARY	CAUTION	CAVITATE
CATFISHES	CATTALO	CAULINE	CAUTIONED	CAVITATED
CATGUT	CATTALOES	CAULIS	CAUTIONER	CAVITATES
CATGUTS	CATTALOS	CAULK	CAUTIONERS	CAVITATING
CATHARISE	CATTED	CAULKED	CAUTIONING	CAVITIED
CATHARISED	CATTERIES	CAULKER	CAUTIONRIES	CAVITIES
CATHARISES	CATTERY	CAULKERS	CAUTIONRY	CAVITY
CATHARISING	CATTIER	CAULKING	CAUTIONS	CAVORT
CATHARIZE	CATTIES	CAULKINGS	CAUTIOUS	CAVORTED
CATHARIZED	CATTIEST	CAULKS	CAUVES	CAVORTING
CATHARIZES	CATTILY	CAULOME	CAVALCADE	CAVORTS
CATHARIZING	CATTINESS	CAULOMES	CAVALCADED	CAVY
CATHARSES	CATTINESSES	CAULS	CAVALCADES	CAW
CATHARSIS	CATTING	CAUM	CAVALCADING	CAWED
CATHARTIC	CATTISH	CAUMED	CAVALIER	CAWING
CATHARTICS	CATTISHLY	CAUMING	CAVALIERED	CAWINGS
CATHEAD	CATTLE	CAUMS	CAVALIERING	CAWK
CATHEADS	CATTLEMAN	CAUMSTONE	CAVALIERS	CAWKER
CATHECTIC	CATTLEMEN	CAUMSTONES	CAVALLA	CAWKERS
CATHEDRA	CATTLEYA	CAUP	CAVALLAS	CAWKS
CATHEDRAL	CATTLEYAS	CAUPS	CAVALLIES	CAWS

The Chambers Dictionary is the authority for many longer words; see *OSW* Introduction, page xii.

CAXON	CEILIS	CELLULAR	CENSUSED	CENTRINGS
CAXONS	CEILS	CELLULASE	CENSUSES	CENTRIOLE
CAY	CEINTURE	CELLULASES	CENSUSING	CENTRIOLES
CAYENNE	CEINTURES	CELLULE	CENT	CENTRISM
CAYENNED	CEL	CELLULES	CENTAGE	CENTRISMS
CAYENNES	CELADON	CELLULITE	CENTAGES	CENTRIST
CAYMAN	CELADONS	CELLULITES	CENTAL	CENTRISTS
CAYMANS	CELANDINE	CELLULOID	CENTALS	CENTRODE
CAYS	CELANDINES	CELLULOIDS	CENTARE	CENTRODES
CAYUSE	CELEBRANT	CELLULOSE	CENTARES	CENTROID
CAYUSES	CELEBRANTS	CELLULOSES	CENTAUR	CENTROIDS
CAZIQUE	CELEBRATE	CELOM	CENTAUREA	CENTRUM
CAZIQUES	CELEBRATED	CELOMS	CENTAUREAS	CENTRUMS
CEANOTHUS	CELEBRATES	CELS	CENTAURIES	CENTRY
CEANOTHUSES	CELEBRATING	CELSITUDE	CENTAURS	CENTS
CEAS	CELEBRITIES	CELSITUDES	CENTAURY	CENTUM
CEASE	CELEBRITY	CELT	CENTAVO	CENTUMS
CEASED	CELERIAC	CELTS	CENTAVOS	CENTUMVIR
CEASELESS	CELERIACS	CEMBALI	CENTENARIES	CENTUMVIRI
CEASES	CELERIES	CEMBALIST	CENTENARY	CENTUPLE
CEASING	CELERITIES	CEMBALISTS	CENTENIER	CENTUPLED
CEASINGS	CELERITY	CEMBALO	CENTENIERS	CENTUPLES
CEAZE	CELERY	CEMBALOS	CENTER	CENTUPLING
CEAZED	CELESTA	CEMBRA	CENTERED	CENTURIAL
CEAZES	CELESTAS	CEMBRAS	CENTERING	CENTURIES
CEAZING	CELESTE	CEMENT	CENTERINGS	CENTURION
CEBADILLA	CELESTES	CEMENTA	CENTERS	CENTURIONS
CEBADILLAS	CELESTIAL	CEMENTED	CENTESES	CENTURY
CECA	CELESTIALS	CEMENTER	CENTESIMO	CEORL
CECAL	CELESTINE	CEMENTERS	CENTESIMOS	CEORLS
CECILS	CELESTINES	CEMENTING	CENTESIS	CEP
CECITIES	CELESTITE	CEMENTITE	CENTIARE	CEPACEOUS
CECITIS	CELESTITES	CEMENTITES	CENTIARES	CEPHALAD
CECITISES	CELIAC	CEMENTS	CENTIGRAM	CEPHALATE
CECITY	CELIACS	CEMENTUM	CENTIGRAMS	CEPHALIC
CECROPIA	CELIBACIES	CEMETERIES	CENTIME	CEPHALICS
CECROPIAS	CELIBACY	CEMETERY	CENTIMES	CEPHALIN
CECUM	CELIBATE	CEMITARE	CENTIMO	CEPHALINS
CEDAR	CELIBATES	CEMITARES	CENTIMOS	CEPHALOUS
CEDARED	CELL	CENACLE	CENTINEL	CEPS
CEDARN	CELLA	CENACLES	CENTINELL	CERACEOUS
CEDARS	CELLAE	CENDRE	CENTINELLS	CERAMAL
CEDARWOOD	CELLAR	CENOBITE	CENTINELS	CERAMALS
CEDARWOODS	CELLARAGE	CENOBITES	CENTIPEDE	CERAMIC
CEDE	CELLARAGES	CENOTAPH	CENTIPEDES	CERAMICS
CEDED	CELLARED	CENOTAPHS	CENTNER	CERAMIST
CEDES	CELLARER	CENOTE	CENTNERS	CERAMISTS
CEDI	CELLARERS	CENOTES	CENTO	CERASIN
CEDILLA	CELLARET	CENS	CENTOIST	CERASINS
CEDILLAS	CELLARETS	CENSE	CENTOISTS	CERASTES
CEDING	CELLARING	CENSED	CENTONATE	CERASTIUM
CEDIS	CELLARIST	CENSER	CENTONES	CERASTIUMS
CEDRATE	CELLARISTS	CENSERS	CENTONIST	CERATE
CEDRATES	CELLARMAN	CENSES	CENTONISTS	CERATED
CEDRINE	CELLARMEN	CENSING	CENTOS	CERATES
CEDULA	CELLAROUS	CENSOR	CENTRA	CERATITIS
CEDULAS	CELLARS	CENSORED	CENTRAL	CERATITISES
CEE	CELLED	CENSORIAL	CENTRALLY	CERATODUS
CEES	CELLIST	CENSORIAN	CENTRE	CERATODUSES
CEIL	CELLISTS	CENSORING	CENTRED	CERATOID
CEILED	CELLO	CENSORS	CENTREING	CERBEREAN
CEILI	CELLOS	CENSUAL	CENTREINGS	CERBERIAN
CEILIDH	CELLOSE	CENSURE	CENTRES	CERCAL
CEILIDHS	CELLOSES	CENSURED	CENTRIC	CERCARIA
CEILING	CELLPHONE	CENSURES	CENTRICAL	CERCARIAE
CEILINGED	CELLPHONES	CENSURING	CENTRIES	CERCARIAN
CEILINGS	CELLS	CENSUS	CENTRING	CERCI

The Chambers Dictionary is the authority for many longer words; see *OSW* Introduction, page xii.

CERCUS	CERTES	CESURES	CHAFF	CHALCID
CERE	CERTIFIED	CETACEAN	CHAFFED	CHALCIDS
CEREAL	CERTIFIER	CETACEANS	CHAFFER	CHALDAISM
CEREALS	CERTIFIERS	CETACEOUS	CHAFFERED	CHALDAISMS
CEREBELLA	CERTIFIES	CETANE	CHAFFERER	CHALDER
CEREBRA	CERTIFY	CETANES	CHAFFERERS	CHALDERS
CEREBRAL	CERTIFYING	CETE	CHAFFERIES	CHALDRON
CEREBRATE	CERTITUDE	CETERACH	CHAFFERING	CHALDRONS
CEREBRATED	CERTITUDES	CETERACHS	CHAFFERS	CHALET
CEREBRATES	CERTS	CETES	CHAFFERY	CHALETS
CEREBRATING	CERULE	CETOLOGIES	CHAFFINCH	CHALICE
CEREBRIC	CERULEAN	CETOLOGY	CHAFFINCHES	CHALICED
CEREBRUM	CERULEIN	CETYL	CHAFFING	CHALICES
CEREBRUMS	CERULEINS	CETYLS	CHAFFINGS	CHALK
CERECLOTH	CERULEOUS	CETYWALL	CHAFFRON	CHALKED
CERECLOTHS	CERUMEN	CETYWALLS	CHAFFRONS	CHALKFACE
CERED	CERUMENS	CEVADILLA	CHAFFS	CHALKFACES
CEREMENT	CERUSE	CEVADILLAS	CHAFING	CHALKIER
CEREMENTS	CERUSES	CEVAPCICI	CHAFT	CHALKIEST
CEREMONIES	CERUSITE	CEVICHE	CHAFTS	CHALKING
CEREMONY	CERUSITES	CEVICHES	CHAGAN	CHALKPIT
CEREOUS	CERUSSITE	CEYLANITE	CHAGANS	CHALKPITS
CERES	CERUSSITES	CEYLANITES	CHAGRIN	CHALKS
CERESIN	CERVELAT	CEYLONITE	CHAGRINED	CHALKY
CERESINE	CERVELATS	CEYLONITES	CHAGRINING	CHALLAH
CERESINES	CERVICAL	CH	CHAGRINS	CHALLAHS
CERESINS	CERVICES	CHA	CHAI	CHALLAN
CEREUS	CERVID	CHABAZITE	CHAIN	CHALLANED
CEREUSES	CERVIDS	CHABAZITES	CHAINE	CHALLANING
CERGE	CERVINE	CHABOUK	CHAINED	CHALLANS
CERGES	CERVIX	CHABOUKS	CHAINES	CHALLENGE
CERIA	CERVIXES	CHACE	CHAINING	CHALLENGED
CERIAS	CESAREVNA	CHACED	CHAINLESS	CHALLENGES
CERIC	CESAREVNAS	CHACES	CHAINLET	CHALLENGING
CERING	CESIUM	CHACING	CHAINLETS	CHALLIE
CERIPH	CESIUMS	CHACK	CHAINMAN	CHALLIES
CERIPHS	CESPITOSE	CHACKED	CHAINMEN	CHALLIS
CERISE	CESS	CHACKING	CHAINS	CHALLISES
CERISES	CESSATION	CHACKS	CHAINSAW	CHALONE
CERITE	CESSATIONS	CHACMA	CHAINSAWS	CHALONES
CERITES	CESSE	CHACMAS	CHAINSHOT	CHALONIC
CERIUM	CESSED	CHACO	CHAINSHOTS	CHALS
CERIUMS	CESSER	CHACOES	CHAINWORK	CHALUMEAU
CERMET	CESSERS	CHACONNE	CHAINWORKS	CHALUMEAUX
CERMETS	CESSES	CHACONNES	CHAIR	CHALUTZ
CERNE	CESSING	CHACOS	CHAIRED	CHALUTZES
CERNED	CESSION	CHAD	CHAIRING	CHALUTZIM
CERNES	CESSIONS	CHADAR	CHAIRLIFT	CHALYBEAN
CERNING	CESSPIT	CHADARS	CHAIRLIFTS	CHALYBITE
CERNUOUS	CESSPITS	CHADDAR	CHAIRMAN	CHALYBITES
CEROGRAPH	CESSPOOL	CHADDARS	CHAIRMEN	CHAM
CEROGRAPHS	CESSPOOLS	CHADDOR	CHAIRS	CHAMADE
CEROMANCIES	CESTI	CHADDORS	CHAIS	CHAMADES
CEROMANCY	CESTODE	CHADOR	CHAISE	CHAMBER
CEROON	CESTODES	CHADORS	CHAISES	CHAMBERED
CEROONS	CESTOID	CHADS	CHAKRA	CHAMBERER
CEROTYPE	CESTOIDS	CHAETA	CHAKRAS	CHAMBERERS
CEROTYPES	CESTOS	CHAETAE	CHAL	CHAMBERING
CEROUS	CESTOSES	CHAETODON	CHALAN	CHAMBERINGS
CERRIAL	CESTUI	CHAETODONS	CHALANED	CHAMBERS
CERRIS	CESTUIS	CHAETOPOD	CHALANING	CHAMBRAY
CERRISES	CESTUS	CHAETOPODS	CHALANS	CHAMBRAYS
CERT	CESURA	CHAFE	CHALAZA	CHAMBRE
CERTAIN	CESURAE	CHAFED	CHALAZAE	CHAMELEON
CERTAINLY	CESURAL	CHAFER	CHALAZAS	CHAMELEONS
CERTAINTIES	CESURAS	CHAFERS	CHALAZIA	CHAMELOT
CERTAINTY	CESURE	CHAFES	CHALAZION	CHAMELOTS

The Chambers Dictionary is the authority for many longer words; see *OSW* Introduction, page xii.

CHAMFER
CHAMFERED
CHAMFERING
CHAMFERS
CHAMFRAIN
CHAMFRAINS
CHAMFRON
CHAMFRONS
CHAMISAL
CHAMISALS
CHAMISE
CHAMISES
CHAMISO
CHAMISOS
CHAMLET
CHAMLETS
CHAMMIES
CHAMMY
CHAMOIS
CHAMOMILE
CHAMOMILES
CHAMP
CHAMPAC
CHAMPACS
CHAMPAGNE
CHAMPAGNES
CHAMPAIGN
CHAMPAIGNS
CHAMPAK
CHAMPAKS
CHAMPART
CHAMPARTS
CHAMPED
CHAMPERS
CHAMPERTIES
CHAMPERTY
CHAMPING
CHAMPION
CHAMPIONED
CHAMPIONING
CHAMPIONS
CHAMPLEVE
CHAMPLEVES
CHAMPS
CHAMS
CHANCE
CHANCED
CHANCEFUL
CHANCEL
CHANCELS
CHANCER
CHANCERIES
CHANCERS
CHANCERY
CHANCES
CHANCEY
CHANCIER
CHANCIEST
CHANCING
CHANCRE
CHANCRES
CHANCROID
CHANCROIDS
CHANCROUS
CHANCY
CHANDELLE
CHANDELLED

CHANDELLES
CHANDELLING
CHANDLER
CHANDLERIES
CHANDLERS
CHANDLERY
CHANGE
CHANGED
CHANGEFUL
CHANGER
CHANGERS
CHANGES
CHANGING
CHANK
CHANKS
CHANNEL
CHANNELER
CHANNELERS
CHANNELLED
CHANNELLING
CHANNELS
CHANNER
CHANNERS
CHANOYU
CHANOYUS
CHANSON
CHANSONS
CHANT
CHANTAGE
CHANTAGES
CHANTED
CHANTER
CHANTERS
CHANTEUSE
CHANTEUSES
CHANTEY
CHANTEYS
CHANTIE
CHANTIES
CHANTING
CHANTOR
CHANTORS
CHANTRESS
CHANTRESSES
CHANTRIES
CHANTRY
CHANTS
CHANTY
CHAOLOGIES
CHAOLOGY
CHAOS
CHAOSES
CHAOTIC
CHAP
CHAPARRAL
CHAPARRALS
CHAPATI
CHAPATIS
CHAPATTI
CHAPATTIS
CHAPBOOK
CHAPBOOKS
CHAPE
CHAPEAU
CHAPEAUX
CHAPEL
CHAPELESS

CHAPELRIES
CHAPELRY
CHAPELS
CHAPERON
CHAPERONE
CHAPERONED
CHAPERONES
CHAPERONING
CHAPERONS
CHAPES
CHAPESS
CHAPESSES
CHAPITER
CHAPITERS
CHAPKA
CHAPKAS
CHAPLAIN
CHAPLAINS
CHAPLESS
CHAPLET
CHAPLETED
CHAPLETS
CHAPMAN
CHAPMEN
CHAPPAL
CHAPPALS
CHAPPED
CHAPPESS
CHAPPESSES
CHAPPIE
CHAPPIER
CHAPPIES
CHAPPIEST
CHAPPING
CHAPPY
CHAPRASSI
CHAPRASSIES
CHAPRASSIS
CHAPRASSY
CHAPS
CHAPSTICK
CHAPSTICKS
CHAPTER
CHAPTERED
CHAPTERING
CHAPTERS
CHAPTREL
CHAPTRELS
CHAR
CHARA
CHARABANC
CHARABANCS
CHARACID
CHARACIDS
CHARACIN
CHARACINS
CHARACTER
CHARACTERED
CHARACTERING
CHARACTERS
CHARADE
CHARADES
CHARANGO
CHARANGOS
CHARAS
CHARASES
CHARCOAL

CHARCOALED
CHARCOALING
CHARCOALS
CHARD
CHARDS
CHARE
CHARED
CHARES
CHARET
CHARETS
CHARGE
CHARGED
CHARGEFUL
CHARGER
CHARGERS
CHARGES
CHARGING
CHARIER
CHARIEST
CHARILY
CHARINESS
CHARINESSES
CHARING
CHARIOT
CHARIOTED
CHARIOTING
CHARIOTS
CHARISM
CHARISMA
CHARISMAS
CHARISMS
CHARITIES
CHARITY
CHARIVARI
CHARIVARIS
CHARK
CHARKA
CHARKAS
CHARKED
CHARKHA
CHARKHAS
CHARKING
CHARKS
CHARLADIES
CHARLADY
CHARLATAN
CHARLATANS
CHARLEY
CHARLEYS
CHARLIE
CHARLIES
CHARLOCK
CHARLOCKS
CHARLOTTE
CHARLOTTES
CHARM
CHARMED
CHARMER
CHARMERS
CHARMEUSE
CHARMEUSES
CHARMFUL
CHARMING
CHARMLESS
CHARMS
CHARNECO
CHARNECOS

CHARNEL
CHARNELS
CHAROSET
CHAROSETH
CHAROSETHS
CHAROSETS
CHARPIE
CHARPIES
CHARPOY
CHARPOYS
CHARQUI
CHARQUIS
CHARR
CHARRED
CHARRING
CHARRS
CHARRY
CHARS
CHART
CHARTA
CHARTAS
CHARTED
CHARTER
CHARTERED
CHARTERER
CHARTERERS
CHARTERING
CHARTERS
CHARTING
CHARTISM
CHARTISMS
CHARTIST
CHARTISTS
CHARTLESS
CHARTS
CHARWOMAN
CHARWOMEN
CHARY
CHAS
CHASE
CHASED
CHASEPORT
CHASEPORTS
CHASER
CHASERS
CHASES
CHASING
CHASINGS
CHASM
CHASMAL
CHASMED
CHASMIC
CHASMIER
CHASMIEST
CHASMS
CHASMY
CHASSE
CHASSEED
CHASSEING
CHASSEPOT
CHASSEPOTS
CHASSES
CHASSEUR
CHASSEURS
CHASSIS
CHASTE
CHASTELY

The Chambers Dictionary is the authority for many longer words; see *OSW* Introduction, page xii.

CHASTEN
CHASTENED
CHASTENER
CHASTENERS
CHASTENING
CHASTENS
CHASTER
CHASTEST
CHASTISE
CHASTISED
CHASTISES
CHASTISING
CHASTITIES
CHASTITY
CHASUBLE
CHASUBLES
CHAT
CHATEAU
CHATEAUX
CHATELAIN
CHATELAINS
CHATLINE
CHATLINES
CHATON
CHATONS
CHATOYANT
CHATS
CHATTA
CHATTAS
CHATTED
CHATTEL
CHATTELS
CHATTER
CHATTERED
CHATTERER
CHATTERERS
CHATTERING
CHATTERINGS
CHATTERS
CHATTI
CHATTIER
CHATTIES
CHATTIEST
CHATTING
CHATTIS
CHATTY
CHAUFE
CHAUFED
CHAUFER
CHAUFERS
CHAUFES
CHAUFF
CHAUFFED
CHAUFFER
CHAUFFERS
CHAUFFEUR
CHAUFFEURED
CHAUFFEURING
CHAUFFEURS
CHAUFFING
CHAUFFS
CHAUFING
CHAUMER
CHAUMERS
CHAUNCE
CHAUNCED
CHAUNCES

CHAUNCING
CHAUNGE
CHAUNGED
CHAUNGES
CHAUNGING
CHAUNT
CHAUNTED
CHAUNTER
CHAUNTERS
CHAUNTING
CHAUNTRIES
CHAUNTRY
CHAUNTS
CHAUSSES
CHAUVIN
CHAUVINS
CHAVE
CHAVENDER
CHAVENDERS
CHAW
CHAWBACON
CHAWBACONS
CHAWDRON
CHAWDRONS
CHAWED
CHAWING
CHAWS
CHAY
CHAYA
CHAYAS
CHAYOTE
CHAYOTES
CHAYROOT
CHAYROOTS
CHAYS
CHAZAN
CHAZANS
CHE
CHEAP
CHEAPEN
CHEAPENED
CHEAPENER
CHEAPENERS
CHEAPENING
CHEAPENS
CHEAPER
CHEAPEST
CHEAPIE
CHEAPIES
CHEAPLY
CHEAPNESS
CHEAPNESSES
CHEAPO
CHEAPS
CHEAPY
CHEAT
CHEATED
CHEATER
CHEATERIES
CHEATERS
CHEATERY
CHEATING
CHEATINGS
CHEATS
CHECHAKO
CHECHAKOES
CHECHAKOS

CHECHAQUA
CHECHAQUAS
CHECHAQUO
CHECHAQUOS
CHECHIA
CHECHIAS
CHECK
CHECKBOOK
CHECKBOOKS
CHECKED
CHECKER
CHECKERED
CHECKERS
CHECKING
CHECKLIST
CHECKLISTS
CHECKMATE
CHECKMATED
CHECKMATES
CHECKMATING
CHECKOUT
CHECKOUTS
CHECKRAIL
CHECKRAILS
CHECKREIN
CHECKREINS
CHECKROOM
CHECKROOMS
CHECKS
CHECKY
CHEDDITE
CHEDDITES
CHEECHAKO
CHEECHAKOES
CHEECHAKOS
CHEEK
CHEEKBONE
CHEEKBONES
CHEEKED
CHEEKIER
CHEEKIEST
CHEEKILY
CHEEKING
CHEEKS
CHEEKY
CHEEP
CHEEPED
CHEEPER
CHEEPERS
CHEEPING
CHEEPS
CHEER
CHEERED
CHEERER
CHEERERS
CHEERFUL
CHEERFULLER
CHEERFULLEST
CHEERIER
CHEERIEST
CHEERILY
CHEERING
CHEERIO
CHEERIOS
CHEERLESS
CHEERLY
CHEERS

CHEERY
CHEESE
CHEESED
CHEESES
CHEESEVAT
CHEESEVATS
CHEESIER
CHEESIEST
CHEESING
CHEESY
CHEETAH
CHEETAHS
CHEEWINK
CHEEWINKS
CHEF
CHEFS
CHEILITIS
CHEILITISES
CHEKA
CHEKAS
CHEKIST
CHEKISTS
CHELA
CHELAE
CHELAS
CHELASHIP
CHELASHIPS
CHELATE
CHELATED
CHELATES
CHELATING
CHELATION
CHELATIONS
CHELATOR
CHELATORS
CHELICERA
CHELICERAE
CHELIFORM
CHELIPED
CHELIPEDS
CHELOID
CHELOIDAL
CHELOIDS
CHELONE
CHELONES
CHELONIAN
CHELONIANS
CHEMIC
CHEMICAL
CHEMICALS
CHEMICKED
CHEMICKING
CHEMICS
CHEMISE
CHEMISES
CHEMISM
CHEMISMS
CHEMIST
CHEMISTRIES
CHEMISTRY
CHEMISTS
CHEMITYPE
CHEMITYPES
CHEMITYPIES
CHEMITYPY
CHEMMIES
CHEMMY

CHEMOSTAT
CHEMOSTATS
CHEMURGIC
CHEMURGIES
CHEMURGY
CHENAR
CHENARS
CHENET
CHENETS
CHENILLE
CHENILLES
CHENIX
CHENIXES
CHENOPOD
CHENOPODS
CHEONGSAM
CHEONGSAMS
CHEQUE
CHEQUER
CHEQUERED
CHEQUERING
CHEQUERS
CHEQUES
CHEQUY
CHER
CHERALITE
CHERALITES
CHERE
CHERIMOYA
CHERIMOYAS
CHERISH
CHERISHED
CHERISHES
CHERISHING
CHERNOZEM
CHERNOZEMS
CHEROOT
CHEROOTS
CHERRIED
CHERRIER
CHERRIES
CHERRIEST
CHERRY
CHERRYING
CHERT
CHERTIER
CHERTIEST
CHERTS
CHERTY
CHERUB
CHERUBIC
CHERUBIM
CHERUBIMS
CHERUBIN
CHERUBINS
CHERUBS
CHERUP
CHERUPED
CHERUPING
CHERUPS
CHERVIL
CHERVILS
CHESIL
CHESILS
CHESNUT
CHESNUTS
CHESS

The Chambers Dictionary is the authority for many longer words; see *OSW* Introduction, page xii.

CHESSEL	CHEWINKS	CHICKLINGS	CHIKOR	CHIMER
CHESSELS	CHEWS	CHICKPEA	CHIKORS	CHIMERA
CHESSES	CHEWY	CHICKPEAS	CHIKS	CHIMERAS
CHESSMAN	CHEZ	CHICKS	CHILBLAIN	CHIMERE
CHESSMEN	CHI	CHICKWEED	CHILBLAINS	CHIMERES
CHEST	CHIACK	CHICKWEEDS	CHILD	CHIMERIC
CHESTED	CHIACKED	CHICLE	CHILDBED	CHIMERID
CHESTFUL	CHIACKING	CHICLES	CHILDBEDS	CHIMERIDS
CHESTFULS	CHIACKINGS	CHICLY	CHILDE	CHIMERISM
CHESTIER	CHIACKS	CHICO	CHILDED	CHIMERISMS
CHESTIEST	CHIAO	CHICON	CHILDER	CHIMERS
CHESTING	CHIAREZZA	CHICONS	CHILDHOOD	CHIMES
CHESTNUT	CHIAREZZE	CHICORIES	CHILDHOODS	CHIMING
CHESTNUTS	CHIASM	CHICORY	CHILDING	CHIMLEY
CHESTS	CHIASMA	CHICOS	CHILDISH	CHIMLEYS
CHESTY	CHIASMAS	CHICS	CHILDLESS	CHIMNEY
CHETAH	CHIASMATA	CHID	CHILDLIKE	CHIMNEYED
CHETAHS	CHIASMI	CHIDDEN	CHILDLY	CHIMNEYING
CHETNIK	CHIASMS	CHIDE	CHILDNESS	CHIMNEYS
CHETNIKS	CHIASMUS	CHIDED	CHILDNESSES	CHIMO
CHEVALET	CHIASTIC	CHIDER	CHILDREN	CHIMP
CHEVALETS	CHIAUS	CHIDERS	CHILDS	CHIMPS
CHEVALIER	CHIAUSED	CHIDES	CHILE	CHIN
CHEVALIERS	CHIAUSES	CHIDING	CHILES	CHINA
CHEVELURE	CHIAUSING	CHIDINGS	CHILI	CHINAMPA
CHEVELURES	CHIBOL	CHIDLINGS	CHILIAD	CHINAMPAS
CHEVEN	CHIBOLS	CHIEF	CHILIADS	CHINAR
CHEVENS	CHIBOUK	CHIEFDOM	CHILIAGON	CHINAROOT
CHEVEREL	CHIBOUKS	CHIEFDOMS	CHILIAGONS	CHINAROOTS
CHEVERELS	CHIBOUQUE	CHIEFER	CHILIARCH	CHINARS
CHEVERIL	CHIBOUQUES	CHIEFERIES	CHILIARCHS	CHINAS
CHEVERILS	CHIC	CHIEFERY	CHILIASM	CHINAWARE
CHEVERON	CHICA	CHIEFESS	CHILIASMS	CHINAWARES
CHEVERONS	CHICANA	CHIEFESSES	CHILIAST	CHINCAPIN
CHEVERYE	CHICANAS	CHIEFEST	CHILIASTS	CHINCAPINS
CHEVERYES	CHICANE	CHIEFLESS	CHILIOI	CHINCH
CHEVET	CHICANED	CHIEFLING	CHILIOIS	CHINCHES
CHEVETS	CHICANER	CHIEFLINGS	CHILIS	CHINCOUGH
CHEVIED	CHICANERIES	CHIEFLY	CHILL	CHINCOUGHS
CHEVIES	CHICANERS	CHIEFRIES	CHILLADA	CHINDIT
CHEVILLE	CHICANERY	CHIEFRY	CHILLADAS	CHINDITS
CHEVILLES	CHICANES	CHIEFS	CHILLED	CHINE
CHEVIN	CHICANING	CHIEFSHIP	CHILLER	CHINED
CHEVINS	CHICANINGS	CHIEFSHIPS	CHILLERS	CHINES
CHEVRE	CHICANO	CHIEFTAIN	CHILLEST	CHINESE
CHEVRES	CHICANOS	CHIEFTAINS	CHILLI	CHINING
CHEVRETTE	CHICAS	CHIEL	CHILLIER	CHINK
CHEVRETTES	CHICCORIES	CHIELD	CHILLIES	CHINKAPIN
CHEVRON	CHICCORY	CHIELDS	CHILLIEST	CHINKAPINS
CHEVRONED	CHICER	CHIELS	CHILLILY	CHINKARA
CHEVRONS	CHICEST	CHIFFON	CHILLING	CHINKARAS
CHEVRONY	CHICH	CHIFFONS	CHILLINGS	CHINKED
CHEVY	CHICHA	CHIGGER	CHILLIS	CHINKIE
CHEVYING	CHICHAS	CHIGGERS	CHILLNESS	CHINKIER
CHEW	CHICHES	CHIGNON	CHILLNESSES	CHINKIES
CHEWABLE	CHICHI	CHIGNONS	CHILLS	CHINKIEST
CHEWED	CHICHIS	CHIGOE	CHILLUM	CHINKING
CHEWER	CHICK	CHIGOES	CHILLUMS	CHINKS
CHEWERS	CHICKADEE	CHIGRE	CHILLY	CHINKY
CHEWET	CHICKADEES	CHIGRES	CHILOPOD	CHINLESS
CHEWETS	CHICKAREE	CHIHUAHUA	CHILOPODS	CHINNED
CHEWIE	CHICKAREES	CHIHUAHUAS	CHIMAERA	CHINNING
CHEWIER	CHICKEN	CHIK	CHIMAERAS	CHINO
CHEWIES	CHICKENED	CHIKARA	CHIMB	CHINOOK
CHEWIEST	CHICKENING	CHIKARAS	CHIMBS	CHINOOKS
CHEWING	CHICKENS	CHIKHOR	CHIME	CHINOS
CHEWINK	CHICKLING	CHIKHORS	CHIMED	CHINOVNIK

The Chambers Dictionary is the authority for many longer words; see *OSW* Introduction, page xii.

CHINOVNIKS	CHIRPILY	CHIVVIED	CHOCOLATES	CHOLIAMB
CHINS	CHIRPING	CHIVVIES	CHOCOLATY	CHOLIAMBS
CHINSTRAP	CHIRPS	CHIVVING	CHOCOS	CHOLIC
CHINSTRAPS	CHIRPY	CHIVVY	CHOCS	CHOLINE
CHINTZ	CHIRR	CHIVVYING	CHOCTAW	CHOLINES
CHINTZES	CHIRRE	CHIVY	CHOCTAWS	CHOLIS
CHINTZIER	CHIRRED	CHIVYING	CHODE	CHOLTRIES
CHINTZIEST	CHIRRES	CHIYOGAMI	CHOENIX	CHOLTRY
CHINTZY	CHIRRING	CHIYOGAMIS	CHOENIXES	CHOMP
CHINWAG	CHIRRS	CHIZ	CHOICE	CHOMPED
CHINWAGGED	CHIRRUP	CHIZZ	CHOICEFUL	CHOMPING
CHINWAGGING	CHIRRUPED	CHIZZED	CHOICELY	CHOMPS
CHINWAGS	CHIRRUPING	CHIZZES	CHOICER	CHON
CHIP	CHIRRUPS	CHIZZING	CHOICES	CHONDRAL
CHIPBOARD	CHIRRUPY	CHLAMYDES	CHOICEST	CHONDRE
CHIPBOARDS	CHIRT	CHLAMYDIA	CHOIR	CHONDRES
CHIPMUCK	CHIRTED	CHLAMYDIAS	CHOIRBOY	CHONDRI
CHIPMUCKS	CHIRTING	CHLAMYS	CHOIRBOYS	CHONDRIFIED
CHIPMUNK	CHIRTS	CHLAMYSES	CHOIRED	CHONDRIFIES
CHIPMUNKS	CHIS	CHLOASMA	CHOIRING	CHONDRIFY
CHIPOCHIA	CHISEL	CHLOASMATA	CHOIRMAN	CHONDRIFYING
CHIPOCHIAS	CHISELLED	CHLORACNE	CHOIRMEN	CHONDRIN
CHIPOLATA	CHISELLER	CHLORACNES	CHOIRS	CHONDRINS
CHIPOLATAS	CHISELLERS	CHLORAL	CHOKE	CHONDRITE
CHIPPED	CHISELLING	CHLORALS	CHOKEBORE	CHONDRITES
CHIPPER	CHISELLINGS	CHLORATE	CHOKEBORES	CHONDROID
CHIPPERS	CHISELS	CHLORATES	CHOKECOIL	CHONDRULE
CHIPPIE	CHIT	CHLORDAN	CHOKECOILS	CHONDRULES
CHIPPIER	CHITAL	CHLORDANE	CHOKED	CHONDRUS
CHIPPIES	CHITALS	CHLORDANES	CHOKEDAMP	CHONS
CHIPPIEST	CHITCHAT	CHLORDANS	CHOKEDAMPS	CHOOF
CHIPPING	CHITCHATS	CHLORELLA	CHOKER	CHOOFED
CHIPPINGS	CHITCHATTED	CHLORELLAS	CHOKERS	CHOOFING
CHIPPY	CHITCHATTING	CHLORIC	CHOKES	CHOOFS
CHIPS	CHITIN	CHLORIDE	CHOKEY	CHOOK
CHIRAGRA	CHITINOID	CHLORIDES	CHOKEYS	CHOOKIE
CHIRAGRAS	CHITINOUS	CHLORIN	CHOKIDAR	CHOOKIES
CHIRAGRIC	CHITINS	CHLORINE	CHOKIDARS	CHOOKS
CHIRAL	CHITLINGS	CHLORINES	CHOKIER	CHOOM
CHIRALITIES	CHITON	CHLORINS	CHOKIES	CHOOMS
CHIRALITY	CHITONS	CHLORITE	CHOKIEST	CHOOSE
CHIRIMOYA	CHITS	CHLORITES	CHOKING	CHOOSER
CHIRIMOYAS	CHITTED	CHLORITIC	CHOKO	CHOOSERS
CHIRK	CHITTER	CHLOROSES	CHOKOS	CHOOSES
CHIRKED	CHITTERED	CHLOROSIS	CHOKRA	CHOOSEY
CHIRKING	CHITTERING	CHLOROTIC	CHOKRAS	CHOOSIER
CHIRKS	CHITTERINGS	CHLOROUS	CHOKRI	CHOOSIEST
CHIRL	CHITTERS	CHOANA	CHOKRIS	CHOOSING
CHIRLED	CHITTIER	CHOANAE	CHOKY	CHOOSY
CHIRLING	CHITTIES	CHOBDAR	CHOLAEMIA	CHOP
CHIRLS	CHITTIEST	CHOBDARS	CHOLAEMIAS	CHOPHOUSE
CHIRM	CHITTING	CHOC	CHOLAEMIC	CHOPHOUSES
CHIRMED	CHITTY	CHOCCIER	CHOLECYST	CHOPIN
CHIRMING	CHIV	CHOCCIES	CHOLECYSTS	CHOPINE
CHIRMS	CHIVALRIC	CHOCCIEST	CHOLELITH	CHOPINES
CHIROLOGIES	CHIVALRIES	CHOCCY	CHOLELITHS	CHOPINS
CHIROLOGY	CHIVALRY	CHOCHO	CHOLEMIA	CHOPLOGIC
CHIRONOMIES	CHIVAREE	CHOCHOS	CHOLEMIAS	CHOPLOGICS
CHIRONOMY	CHIVAREES	CHOCK	CHOLENT	CHOPPED
CHIROPODIES	CHIVE	CHOCKED	CHOLENTS	CHOPPER
CHIROPODY	CHIVED	CHOCKER	CHOLER	CHOPPERS
CHIRP	CHIVES	CHOCKING	CHOLERA	CHOPPIER
CHIRPED	CHIVIED	CHOCKO	CHOLERAIC	CHOPPIEST
CHIRPER	CHIVIES	CHOCKOS	CHOLERAS	CHOPPING
CHIRPERS	CHIVING	CHOCKS	CHOLERIC	CHOPPINGS
CHIRPIER	CHIVS	CHOCO	CHOLERS	CHOPPY
CHIRPIEST	CHIVVED	CHOCOLATE	CHOLI	CHOPS

The Chambers Dictionary is the authority for many longer words; see *OSW* Introduction, page xii.

CHOPSTICK	CHORTLES	CHROMED	CHUFFING	CHURCHISM
CHOPSTICKS	CHORTLING	CHROMEL	CHUFFS	CHURCHISMS
CHORAGI	CHORUS	CHROMELS	CHUFFY	CHURCHLY
CHORAGIC	CHORUSED	CHROMENE	CHUG	CHURCHMAN
CHORAGUS	CHORUSES	CHROMENES	CHUGGED	CHURCHMEN
CHORAGUSES	CHORUSING	CHROMES	CHUGGING	CHURCHWAY
CHORAL	CHOSE	CHROMIC	CHUGS	CHURCHWAYS
CHORALE	CHOSEN	CHROMIDIA	CHUKAR	CHURCHY
CHORALES	CHOSES	CHROMING	CHUKARS	CHURIDARS
CHORALIST	CHOTA	CHROMITE	CHUKKA	CHURINGA
CHORALISTS	CHOTT	CHROMITES	CHUKKAS	CHURINGAS
CHORALLY	CHOTTS	CHROMIUM	CHUKKER	CHURL
CHORALS	CHOU	CHROMIUMS	CHUKKERS	CHURLISH
CHORD	CHOUGH	CHROMO	CHUKOR	CHURLS
CHORDA	CHOUGHS	CHROMOGEN	CHUKORS	CHURN
CHORDAE	CHOULTRIES	CHROMOGENS	CHUM	CHURNED
CHORDAL	CHOULTRY	CHROMOS	CHUMLEY	CHURNING
CHORDATE	CHOUNTER	CHRONAXIE	CHUMLEYS	CHURNINGS
CHORDATES	CHOUNTERED	CHRONAXIES	CHUMMAGE	CHURNMILK
CHORDEE	CHOUNTERING	CHRONIC	CHUMMAGES	CHURNMILKS
CHORDEES	CHOUNTERS	CHRONICAL	CHUMMED	CHURNS
CHORDING	CHOUSE	CHRONICLE	CHUMMIER	CHURR
CHORDINGS	CHOUSED	CHRONICLED	CHUMMIES	CHURRED
CHORDS	CHOUSES	CHRONICLES	CHUMMIEST	CHURRING
CHORE	CHOUSING	CHRONICLING	CHUMMING	CHURRS
CHOREA	CHOUT	CHRONICS	CHUMMY	CHURRUS
CHOREAS	CHOUTS	CHRONON	CHUMP	CHURRUSES
CHOREE	CHOUX	CHRONONS	CHUMPING	CHUSE
CHOREES	CHOW	CHRYSALID	CHUMPINGS	CHUSES
CHOREGI	CHOWDER	CHRYSALIDES	CHUMPS	CHUSING
CHOREGIC	CHOWDERS	CHRYSALIDS	CHUMS	CHUT
CHOREGUS	CHOWKIDAR	CHRYSALIS	CHUNDER	CHUTE
CHOREGUSES	CHOWKIDARS	CHRYSALISES	CHUNDERED	CHUTES
CHOREIC	CHOWRI	CHRYSANTH	CHUNDERING	CHUTIST
CHORES	CHOWRIES	CHRYSANTHS	CHUNDERS	CHUTISTS
CHOREUS	CHOWRIS	CHTHONIAN	CHUNK	CHUTNEY
CHOREUSES	CHOWRY	CHTHONIC	CHUNKIER	CHUTNEYS
CHORIA	CHOWS	CHUB	CHUNKIEST	CHUTZPAH
CHORIAL	CHRISM	CHUBBIER	CHUNKING	CHUTZPAHS
CHORIAMB	CHRISMAL	CHUBBIEST	CHUNKINGS	CHYACK
CHORIAMBI	CHRISMALS	CHUBBY	CHUNKS	CHYACKED
CHORIAMBS	CHRISMS	CHUBS	CHUNKY	CHYACKING
CHORIC	CHRISOM	CHUCK	CHUNNEL	CHYACKS
CHORINE	CHRISOMS	CHUCKED	CHUNNELS	CHYLDE
CHORINES	CHRISTEN	CHUCKHOLE	CHUNNER	CHYLE
CHORIOID	CHRISTENED	CHUCKHOLES	CHUNNERED	CHYLES
CHORIOIDS	CHRISTENING	CHUCKIE	CHUNNERING	CHYLIFIED
CHORION	CHRISTENINGS	CHUCKIES	CHUNNERS	CHYLIFIES
CHORIONIC	CHRISTENS	CHUCKING	CHUNTER	CHYLIFY
CHORISES	CHRISTIE	CHUCKLE	CHUNTERED	CHYLIFYING
CHORISIS	CHRISTIES	CHUCKLED	CHUNTERING	CHYLURIA
CHORISM	CHRISTOM	CHUCKLES	CHUNTERS	CHYLURIAS
CHORISMS	CHRISTOMS	CHUCKLING	CHUPATI	CHYME
CHORIST	CHRISTY	CHUCKLINGS	CHUPATIS	CHYMES
CHORISTER	CHROMA	CHUCKS	CHUPATTI	CHYMIFIED
CHORISTERS	CHROMAKEY	CHUDDAH	CHUPATTIS	CHYMIFIES
CHORISTS	CHROMAKEYS	CHUDDAHS	CHUPPAH	CHYMIFY
CHORIZO	CHROMAS	CHUDDAR	CHUPPAHS	CHYMIFYING
CHORIZONT	CHROMATE	CHUDDARS	CHUPRASSIES	CHYMISTRIES
CHORIZONTS	CHROMATES	CHUDDIES	CHUPRASSY	CHYMISTRY
CHORIZOS	CHROMATIC	CHUDDY	CHURCH	CHYMOUS
CHOROID	CHROMATICS	CHUFA	CHURCHED	CHYND
CHOROIDS	CHROMATID	CHUFAS	CHURCHES	CHYPRE
CHOROLOGIES	CHROMATIDS	CHUFF	CHURCHIER	CHYPRES
CHOROLOGY	CHROMATIN	CHUFFED	CHURCHIEST	CIAO
CHORTLE	CHROMATINS	CHUFFIER	CHURCHING	CIAOS
CHORTLED	CHROME	CHUFFIEST	CHURCHINGS	CIBATION

The Chambers Dictionary is the authority for many longer words; see *OSW* Introduction, page xii.

CIBATIONS	CIGGIES	CINEREAL	CIRES	CITER
CIBOL	CIGGY	CINEREAS	CIRL	CITERS
CIBOLS	CIGS	CINEREOUS	CIRLS	CITES
CIBORIA	CILIA	CINERIN	CIRQUE	CITESS
CIBORIUM	CILIARY	CINERINS	CIRQUES	CITESSES
CICADA	CILIATE	CINGULA	CIRRATE	CITHARA
CICADAS	CILIATES	CINGULUM	CIRRHOPOD	CITHARAS
CICALA	CILICE	CINNABAR	CIRRHOPODS	CITHARIST
CICALAS	CILICES	CINNABARS	CIRRHOSES	CITHARISTS
CICATRICE	CILICIOUS	CINNAMIC	CIRRHOSIS	CITHER
CICATRICES	CILIOLATE	CINNAMON	CIRRHOTIC	CITHERN
CICATRISE	CILIUM	CINNAMONS	CIRRI	CITHERNS
CICATRISED	CILL	CINQUAIN	CIRRIFORM	CITHERS
CICATRISES	CILLS	CINQUAINS	CIRRIPED	CITIES
CICATRISING	CIMAR	CINQUE	CIRRIPEDE	CITIFIED
CICATRIX	CIMARS	CINQUES	CIRRIPEDES	CITIFIES
CICATRIXES	CIMBALOM	CION	CIRRIPEDS	CITIFY
CICATRIZE	CIMBALOMS	CIONS	CIRROSE	CITIFYING
CICATRIZED	CIMELIA	CIPHER	CIRROUS	CITIGRADE
CICATRIZES	CIMEX	CIPHERED	CIRRUS	CITING
CICATRIZING	CIMICES	CIPHERING	CIRSOID	CITIZEN
CICELIES	CIMIER	CIPHERINGS	CISALPINE	CITIZENRIES
CICELY	CIMIERS	CIPHERS	CISCO	CITIZENRY
CICERO	CIMINITE	CIPOLIN	CISCOES	CITIZENS
CICERONE	CIMINITES	CIPOLINS	CISCOS	CITO
CICERONED	CIMOLITE	CIPOLLINO	CISELEUR	CITOLE
CICERONEING	CIMOLITES	CIPOLLINOS	CISELEURS	CITOLES
CICERONES	CINCH	CIPPI	CISELURE	CITRANGE
CICERONI	CINCHED	CIPPUS	CISELURES	CITRANGES
CICEROS	CINCHES	CIRCA	CISLUNAR	CITRATE
CICHLID	CINCHING	CIRCADIAN	CISPADANE	CITRATES
CICHLIDS	CINCHINGS	CIRCAR	CISPLATIN	CITREOUS
CICHLOID	CINCHONA	CIRCARS	CISPLATINS	CITRIC
CICINNUS	CINCHONAS	CIRCINATE	CISSIER	CITRIN
CICINNUSES	CINCHONIC	CIRCITER	CISSIES	CITRINE
CICISBEI	CINCINNUS	CIRCLE	CISSIEST	CITRINES
CICISBEO	CINCINNUSES	CIRCLED	CISSOID	CITRINS
CICLATON	CINCT	CIRCLER	CISSOIDS	CITRON
CICLATONS	CINCTURE	CIRCLERS	CISSUS	CITRONS
CICLATOUN	CINCTURED	CIRCLES	CISSUSES	CITROUS
CICLATOUNS	CINCTURES	CIRCLET	CISSY	CITRUS
CICUTA	CINCTURING	CIRCLETS	CIST	CITRUSES
CICUTAS	CINDER	CIRCLING	CISTED	CITS
CID	CINDERED	CIRCLINGS	CISTERN	CITTERN
CIDARIS	CINDERING	CIRCLIP	CISTERNA	CITTERNS
CIDARISES	CINDERS	CIRCLIPS	CISTERNAE	CITY
CIDER	CINDERY	CIRCS	CISTERNS	CITYFIED
CIDERKIN	CINEAST	CIRCUIT	CISTIC	CITYFIES
CIDERKINS	CINEASTE	CIRCUITED	CISTRON	CITYFY
CIDERS	CINEASTES	CIRCUITIES	CISTRONS	CITYFYING
CIDERY	CINEASTS	CIRCUITING	CISTS	CITYSCAPE
CIDS	CINEMA	CIRCUITRIES	CISTUS	CITYSCAPES
CIEL	CINEMAS	CIRCUITRY	CISTUSES	CIVE
CIELED	CINEMATIC	CIRCUITS	CISTVAEN	CIVES
CIELING	CINEOL	CIRCUITY	CISTVAENS	CIVET
CIELINGS	CINEOLE	CIRCULAR	CIT	CIVETS
CIELS	CINEOLES	CIRCULARS	CITABLE	CIVIC
CIERGE	CINEOLS	CIRCULATE	CITADEL	CIVICALLY
CIERGES	CINEPLEX	CIRCULATED	CITADELS	CIVICS
CIG	CINEPLEXES	CIRCULATES	CITAL	CIVIL
CIGAR	CINERAMIC	CIRCULATING	CITALS	CIVILIAN
CIGARETTE	CINERARIA	CIRCULATINGS	CITATION	CIVILIANS
CIGARETTES	CINERARIAS	CIRCUS	CITATIONS	CIVILISE
CIGARILLO	CINERARY	CIRCUSES	CITATORY	CIVILISED
CIGARILLOS	CINERATOR	CIRCUSSY	CITE	CIVILISER
CIGARS	CINERATORS	CIRCUSY	CITEABLE	CIVILISERS
CIGGIE	CINEREA	CIRE	CITED	CIVILISES

The Chambers Dictionary is the authority for many longer words; see *OSW* Introduction, page xii.

CIVILISING
CIVILIST
CIVILISTS
CIVILITIES
CIVILITY
CIVILIZE
CIVILIZED
CIVILIZER
CIVILIZERS
CIVILIZES
CIVILIZING
CIVILLY
CIVISM
CIVISMS
CIVVIES
CIVVY
CLABBER
CLABBERS
CLACHAN
CLACHANS
CLACK
CLACKBOX
CLACKBOXES
CLACKDISH
CLACKDISHES
CLACKED
CLACKER
CLACKERS
CLACKING
CLACKS
CLAD
CLADDED
CLADDER
CLADDERS
CLADDING
CLADDINGS
CLADE
CLADES
CLADISM
CLADISMS
CLADIST
CLADISTIC
CLADISTICS
CLADISTS
CLADODE
CLADODES
CLADOGRAM
CLADOGRAMS
CLADS
CLAES
CLAG
CLAGGED
CLAGGIER
CLAGGIEST
CLAGGING
CLAGGY
CLAGS
CLAIM
CLAIMABLE
CLAIMANT
CLAIMANTS
CLAIMED
CLAIMER
CLAIMERS
CLAIMING
CLAIMS
CLAM

CLAMANCIES
CLAMANCY
CLAMANT
CLAMANTLY
CLAMBAKE
CLAMBAKES
CLAMBER
CLAMBERED
CLAMBERING
CLAMBERS
CLAME
CLAMES
CLAMMED
CLAMMIER
CLAMMIEST
CLAMMILY
CLAMMING
CLAMMY
CLAMOR
CLAMORED
CLAMORING
CLAMOROUS
CLAMORS
CLAMOUR
CLAMOURED
CLAMOURER
CLAMOURERS
CLAMOURING
CLAMOURS
CLAMP
CLAMPDOWN
CLAMPDOWNS
CLAMPED
CLAMPER
CLAMPERED
CLAMPERING
CLAMPERS
CLAMPING
CLAMPS
CLAMS
CLAMSHELL
CLAMSHELLS
CLAN
CLANG
CLANGBOX
CLANGBOXES
CLANGED
CLANGER
CLANGERS
CLANGING
CLANGINGS
CLANGOR
CLANGORED
CLANGORING
CLANGORS
CLANGOUR
CLANGOURED
CLANGOURING
CLANGOURS
CLANGS
CLANK
CLANKED
CLANKING
CLANKINGS
CLANKS
CLANNISH
CLANS

CLANSHIP
CLANSHIPS
CLANSMAN
CLANSMEN
CLAP
CLAPBOARD
CLAPBOARDS
CLAPBREAD
CLAPBREADS
CLAPDISH
CLAPDISHES
CLAPNET
CLAPNETS
CLAPPED
CLAPPER
CLAPPERED
CLAPPERING
CLAPPERINGS
CLAPPERS
CLAPPING
CLAPPINGS
CLAPS
CLAPTRAP
CLAPTRAPS
CLAQUE
CLAQUES
CLAQUEUR
CLAQUEURS
CLARAIN
CLARAINS
CLARENCE
CLARENCES
CLARENDON
CLARENDONS
CLARET
CLARETED
CLARETING
CLARETS
CLARIES
CLARIFIED
CLARIFIER
CLARIFIERS
CLARIFIES
CLARIFY
CLARIFYING
CLARINET
CLARINETS
CLARINI
CLARINO
CLARINOS
CLARION
CLARIONET
CLARIONETS
CLARIONS
CLARITIES
CLARITY
CLARKIA
CLARKIAS
CLARO
CLAROES
CLAROS
CLARSACH
CLARSACHS
CLART
CLARTED
CLARTIER
CLARTIEST

CLARTING
CLARTS
CLARTY
CLARY
CLASH
CLASHED
CLASHER
CLASHERS
CLASHES
CLASHING
CLASHINGS
CLASP
CLASPED
CLASPER
CLASPERS
CLASPING
CLASPINGS
CLASPS
CLASS
CLASSABLE
CLASSED
CLASSES
CLASSIBLE
CLASSIC
CLASSICAL
CLASSICS
CLASSIER
CLASSIEST
CLASSIFIC
CLASSIFIED
CLASSIFIES
CLASSIFY
CLASSIFYING
CLASSING
CLASSIS
CLASSISM
CLASSISMS
CLASSIST
CLASSLESS
CLASSMAN
CLASSMATE
CLASSMATES
CLASSMEN
CLASSROOM
CLASSROOMS
CLASSY
CLASTIC
CLASTS
CLAT
CLATCH
CLATCHED
CLATCHES
CLATCHING
CLATHRATE
CLATS
CLATTED
CLATTER
CLATTERED
CLATTERER
CLATTERERS
CLATTERING
CLATTERS
CLATTERY
CLATTING
CLAUCHT
CLAUCHTED
CLAUCHTING

CLAUCHTS
CLAUGHT
CLAUGHTED
CLAUGHTING
CLAUGHTS
CLAUSAL
CLAUSE
CLAUSES
CLAUSTRA
CLAUSTRAL
CLAUSTRUM
CLAUSULA
CLAUSULAE
CLAUSULAR
CLAUT
CLAUTED
CLAUTING
CLAUTS
CLAVATE
CLAVATED
CLAVATION
CLAVATIONS
CLAVE
CLAVECIN
CLAVECINS
CLAVER
CLAVERED
CLAVERING
CLAVERS
CLAVES
CLAVICLE
CLAVICLES
CLAVICORN
CLAVICORNS
CLAVICULA
CLAVICULAE
CLAVIE
CLAVIER
CLAVIERS
CLAVIES
CLAVIFORM
CLAVIGER
CLAVIGERS
CLAVIS
CLAVULATE
CLAW
CLAWBACK
CLAWBACKS
CLAWED
CLAWING
CLAWLESS
CLAWS
CLAY
CLAYED
CLAYEY
CLAYIER
CLAYIEST
CLAYING
CLAYISH
CLAYMORE
CLAYMORES
CLAYPAN
CLAYPANS
CLAYS
CLAYTONIA
CLAYTONIAS
CLEAN

The Chambers Dictionary is the authority for many longer words; see *OSW* Introduction, page xii.

CLEANED	CLEEKIT	CLERUCHIA	CLIMATAL	CLINT
CLEANER	CLEEKS	CLERUCHIAS	CLIMATE	CLINTS
CLEANERS	CLEEP	CLERUCHIES	CLIMATED	CLIP
CLEANEST	CLEEPED	CLERUCHS	CLIMATES	CLIPBOARD
CLEANING	CLEEPING	CLERUCHY	CLIMATIC	CLIPBOARDS
CLEANINGS	CLEEPS	CLEUCH	CLIMATING	CLIPE
CLEANLIER	CLEEVE	CLEUCHS	CLIMATISE	CLIPED
CLEANLIEST	CLEEVES	CLEUGH	CLIMATISED	CLIPES
CLEANLY	CLEF	CLEUGHS	CLIMATISES	CLIPING
CLEANNESS	CLEFS	CLEVE	CLIMATISING	CLIPPED
CLEANNESSES	CLEFT	CLEVEITE	CLIMATIZE	CLIPPER
CLEANS	CLEFTS	CLEVEITES	CLIMATIZED	CLIPPERS
CLEANSE	CLEG	CLEVER	CLIMATIZES	CLIPPIE
CLEANSED	CLEGS	CLEVERER	CLIMATIZING	CLIPPIES
CLEANSER	CLEIDOIC	CLEVEREST	CLIMATURE	CLIPPING
CLEANSERS	CLEITHRAL	CLEVERISH	CLIMATURES	CLIPPINGS
CLEANSES	CLEM	CLEVERLY	CLIMAX	CLIPS
CLEANSING	CLEMATIS	CLEVES	CLIMAXED	CLIPT
CLEANSINGS	CLEMATISES	CLEVIS	CLIMAXES	CLIQUE
CLEANSKIN	CLEMENCIES	CLEVISES	CLIMAXING	CLIQUES
CLEANSKINS	CLEMENCY	CLEW	CLIMB	CLIQUEY
CLEAR	CLEMENT	CLEWED	CLIMBABLE	CLIQUIER
CLEARAGE	CLEMENTLY	CLEWING	CLIMBED	CLIQUIEST
CLEARAGES	CLEMMED	CLEWS	CLIMBER	CLIQUISH
CLEARANCE	CLEMMING	CLIANTHUS	CLIMBERS	CLIQUISM
CLEARANCES	CLEMS	CLIANTHUSES	CLIMBING	CLIQUISMS
CLEARCOLE	CLENCH	CLICHE	CLIMBINGS	CLIQUY
CLEARCOLES	CLENCHED	CLICHEED	CLIMBS	CLITELLA
CLEARED	CLENCHES	CLICHES	CLIME	CLITELLAR
CLEARER	CLENCHING	CLICK	CLIMES	CLITELLUM
CLEARERS	CLEPE	CLICKED	CLINAMEN	CLITHRAL
CLEAREST	CLEPED	CLICKER	CLINAMENS	CLITIC
CLEARING	CLEPES	CLICKERS	CLINCH	CLITICS
CLEARINGS	CLEPING	CLICKET	CLINCHED	CLITORAL
CLEARLY	CLEPSYDRA	CLICKETED	CLINCHER	CLITORIS
CLEARNESS	CLEPSYDRAS	CLICKETING	CLINCHERS	CLITORISES
CLEARNESSES	CLERECOLE	CLICKETS	CLINCHES	CLITTER
CLEARS	CLERECOLES	CLICKING	CLINCHING	CLITTERED
CLEARSKIN	CLERGIES	CLICKINGS	CLINE	CLITTERING
CLEARSKINS	CLERGY	CLICKS	CLINES	CLITTERS
CLEARWAY	CLERGYMAN	CLIED	CLING	CLIVERS
CLEARWAYS	CLERGYMEN	CLIENT	CLINGER	CLIVIA
CLEARWING	CLERIC	CLIENTAGE	CLINGERS	CLIVIAS
CLEARWINGS	CLERICAL	CLIENTAGES	CLINGFILM	CLOACA
CLEAT	CLERICALS	CLIENTAL	CLINGFILMS	CLOACAE
CLEATED	CLERICATE	CLIENTELE	CLINGIER	CLOACAL
CLEATING	CLERICATES	CLIENTELES	CLINGIEST	CLOACALIN
CLEATS	CLERICITIES	CLIENTS	CLINGING	CLOACINAL
CLEAVABLE	CLERICITY	CLIES	CLINGS	CLOAK
CLEAVAGE	CLERICS	CLIFF	CLINGY	CLOAKED
CLEAVAGES	CLERIHEW	CLIFFED	CLINIC	CLOAKING
CLEAVE	CLERIHEWS	CLIFFHANG	CLINICAL	CLOAKROOM
CLEAVED	CLERISIES	CLIFFHANGING	CLINICIAN	CLOAKROOMS
CLEAVER	CLERISY	CLIFFHANGINGS	CLINICIANS	CLOAKS
CLEAVERS	CLERK	CLIFFHANGS	CLINICS	CLOAM
CLEAVES	CLERKDOM	CLIFFHUNG	CLINIQUE	CLOAMS
CLEAVING	CLERKDOMS	CLIFFIER	CLINIQUES	CLOBBER
CLEAVINGS	CLERKED	CLIFFIEST	CLINK	CLOBBERED
CLECHE	CLERKESS	CLIFFS	CLINKED	CLOBBERING
CLECK	CLERKESSES	CLIFFY	CLINKER	CLOBBERS
CLECKED	CLERKING	CLIFT	CLINKERS	CLOCHARD
CLECKING	CLERKISH	CLIFTED	CLINKING	CLOCHARDS
CLECKINGS	CLERKLY	CLIFTIER	CLINKS	CLOCHE
CLECKS	CLERKS	CLIFTIEST	CLINOAXES	CLOCHES
CLEEK	CLERKSHIP	CLIFTS	CLINOAXIS	CLOCK
CLEEKED	CLERKSHIPS	CLIFTY	CLINQUANT	CLOCKED
CLEEKING	CLERUCH	CLIMACTIC	CLINQUANTS	CLOCKER

The Chambers Dictionary is the authority for many longer words; see *OSW* Introduction, page xii.

CLOCKERS
CLOCKING
CLOCKINGS
CLOCKS
CLOCKWISE
CLOCKWORK
CLOCKWORKS
CLOD
CLODDED
CLODDIER
CLODDIEST
CLODDING
CLODDISH
CLODDY
CLODLY
CLODPATE
CLODPATED
CLODPATES
CLODPOLE
CLODPOLES
CLODPOLL
CLODPOLLS
CLODS
CLOFF
CLOFFS
CLOG
CLOGDANCE
CLOGDANCES
CLOGGED
CLOGGER
CLOGGERS
CLOGGIER
CLOGGIEST
CLOGGING
CLOGGY
CLOGS
CLOISON
CLOISONNE
CLOISONNES
CLOISONS
CLOISTER
CLOISTERED
CLOISTERING
CLOISTERS
CLOISTRAL
CLOKE
CLOKED
CLOKES
CLOKING
CLOMB
CLOMP
CLOMPED
CLOMPING
CLOMPS
CLONAL
CLONALLY
CLONE
CLONED
CLONES
CLONIC
CLONICITIES
CLONICITY
CLONING
CLONK
CLONKED
CLONKING
CLONKS

CLONUS
CLONUSES
CLOOP
CLOOPS
CLOOT
CLOOTS
CLOP
CLOPPED
CLOPPING
CLOPS
CLOQUE
CLOQUES
CLOSE
CLOSED
CLOSEDOWN
CLOSEDOWNS
CLOSEHEAD
CLOSEHEADS
CLOSELY
CLOSENESS
CLOSENESSES
CLOSER
CLOSERS
CLOSES
CLOSEST
CLOSET
CLOSETED
CLOSETING
CLOSETS
CLOSING
CLOSINGS
CLOSURE
CLOSURED
CLOSURES
CLOSURING
CLOT
CLOTBUR
CLOTBURS
CLOTE
CLOTEBUR
CLOTEBURS
CLOTES
CLOTH
CLOTHE
CLOTHED
CLOTHES
CLOTHIER
CLOTHIERS
CLOTHING
CLOTHINGS
CLOTHS
CLOTS
CLOTTED
CLOTTER
CLOTTERED
CLOTTERING
CLOTTERS
CLOTTIER
CLOTTIEST
CLOTTING
CLOTTINGS
CLOTTY
CLOTURE
CLOTURED
CLOTURES
CLOTURING
CLOU

CLOUD
CLOUDAGE
CLOUDAGES
CLOUDED
CLOUDIER
CLOUDIEST
CLOUDILY
CLOUDING
CLOUDINGS
CLOUDLAND
CLOUDLANDS
CLOUDLESS
CLOUDLET
CLOUDLETS
CLOUDS
CLOUDY
CLOUGH
CLOUGHS
CLOUR
CLOURED
CLOURING
CLOURS
CLOUS
CLOUT
CLOUTED
CLOUTER
CLOUTERS
CLOUTING
CLOUTS
CLOVE
CLOVEN
CLOVEPINK
CLOVEPINKS
CLOVER
CLOVERED
CLOVERS
CLOVERY
CLOVES
CLOW
CLOWDER
CLOWDERS
CLOWN
CLOWNED
CLOWNERIES
CLOWNERY
CLOWNING
CLOWNINGS
CLOWNISH
CLOWNS
CLOY
CLOYED
CLOYING
CLOYLESS
CLOYMENT
CLOYMENTS
CLOYS
CLOYSOME
CLOZE
CLUB
CLUBABLE
CLUBBABLE
CLUBBED
CLUBBER
CLUBBERS
CLUBBIER
CLUBBIEST

CLUBBING
CLUBBINGS
CLUBBISH
CLUBBISM
CLUBBISMS
CLUBBIST
CLUBBISTS
CLUBBY
CLUBHOUSE
CLUBHOUSES
CLUBLAND
CLUBLANDS
CLUBMAN
CLUBMEN
CLUBROOM
CLUBROOMS
CLUBROOT
CLUBROOTS
CLUBRUSH
CLUBRUSHES
CLUBS
CLUBWOMAN
CLUBWOMEN
CLUCK
CLUCKED
CLUCKIER
CLUCKIEST
CLUCKING
CLUCKS
CLUCKY
CLUDGIE
CLUDGIES
CLUE
CLUED
CLUEING
CLUELESS
CLUES
CLUING
CLUMBER
CLUMBERS
CLUMP
CLUMPED
CLUMPER
CLUMPERS
CLUMPIER
CLUMPIEST
CLUMPING
CLUMPS
CLUMPY
CLUMSIER
CLUMSIEST
CLUMSILY
CLUMSY
CLUNCH
CLUNCHES
CLUNG
CLUNK
CLUNKED
CLUNKING
CLUNKS
CLUPEID
CLUPEIDS
CLUPEOID
CLUPEOIDS
CLUSIA
CLUSIAS
CLUSTER

CLUSTERED
CLUSTERING
CLUSTERS
CLUSTERY
CLUTCH
CLUTCHED
CLUTCHES
CLUTCHING
CLUTTER
CLUTTERED
CLUTTERING
CLUTTERS
CLY
CLYING
CLYPE
CLYPEAL
CLYPEATE
CLYPED
CLYPEI
CLYPES
CLYPEUS
CLYPING
CLYSTER
CLYSTERS
CNEMIAL
CNIDA
CNIDAE
CNIDARIAN
CNIDARIANS
COACH
COACHDOG
COACHDOGS
COACHED
COACHEE
COACHEES
COACHER
COACHERS
COACHES
COACHIES
COACHING
COACHINGS
COACHLINE
COACHLINES
COACHLOAD
COACHLOADS
COACHMAN
COACHMEN
COACHWHIP
COACHWHIPS
COACHWOOD
COACHWOODS
COACHWORK
COACHWORKS
COACHY
COACT
COACTED
COACTING
COACTION
COACTIONS
COACTIVE
COACTS
COADAPTED
COADJUTOR
COADJUTORS
COADUNATE
COADUNATED
COADUNATES

The Chambers Dictionary is the authority for many longer words; see *OSW* Introduction, page xii.

COADUNATING	COARSELY	COBBLERS	COCHLEA	COCKROACHES
COAGULA	COARSEN	COBBLERY	COCHLEAE	COCKS
COAGULANT	COARSENED	COBBLES	COCHLEAR	COCKSCOMB
COAGULANTS	COARSENING	COBBLING	COCHLEATE	COCKSCOMBS
COAGULASE	COARSENS	COBBLINGS	COCK	COCKSFOOT
COAGULASES	COARSER	COBBS	COCKADE	COCKSFOOTS
COAGULATE	COARSEST	COBBY	COCKADES	COCKSHIES
COAGULATED	COARSISH	COBIA	COCKATEEL	COCKSHOT
COAGULATES	COAST	COBIAS	COCKATEELS	COCKSHOTS
COAGULATING	COASTAL	COBLE	COCKATIEL	COCKSHUT
COAGULUM	COASTED	COBLES	COCKATIELS	COCKSHUTS
COAITA	COASTER	COBLOAF	COCKATOO	COCKSHY
COAITAS	COASTERS	COBLOAVES	COCKATOOS	COCKSIER
COAL	COASTING	COBNUT	COCKBIRD	COCKSIEST
COALBALL	COASTINGS	COBNUTS	COCKBIRDS	COCKSPUR
COALBALLS	COASTLINE	COBRA	COCKBOAT	COCKSPURS
COALED	COASTLINES	COBRAS	COCKBOATS	COCKSURE
COALER	COASTS	COBRIC	COCKED	COCKSWAIN
COALERS	COASTWARD	COBRIFORM	COCKER	COCKSWAINED
COALESCE	COASTWARDS	COBS	COCKERED	COCKSWAINING
COALESCED	COASTWISE	COBURG	COCKEREL	COCKSWAINS
COALESCES	COAT	COBURGS	COCKERELS	COCKSY
COALESCING	COATE	COBWEB	COCKERING	COCKTAIL
COALFACE	COATED	COBWEBBED	COCKERS	COCKTAILS
COALFACES	COATEE	COBWEBBIER	COCKET	COCKY
COALFIELD	COATEES	COBWEBBIEST	COCKETS	COCO
COALFIELDS	COATER	COBWEBBING	COCKEYE	COCOA
COALFISH	COATERS	COBWEBBY	COCKEYED	COCOANUT
COALFISHES	COATES	COBWEBS	COCKEYES	COCOANUTS
COALHOUSE	COATI	COBZA	COCKFIGHT	COCOAS
COALHOUSES	COATING	COBZAS	COCKFIGHTS	COCONUT
COALIER	COATINGS	COCA	COCKHORSE	COCONUTS
COALIEST	COATIS	COCAINE	COCKHORSES	COCOON
COALING	COATLESS	COCAINES	COCKIER	COCOONED
COALISE	COATRACK	COCAINISE	COCKIES	COCOONERIES
COALISED	COATRACKS	COCAINISED	COCKIEST	COCOONERY
COALISES	COATS	COCAINISES	COCKILY	COCOONING
COALISING	COATSTAND	COCAINISING	COCKINESS	COCOONINGS
COALITION	COATSTANDS	COCAINISM	COCKINESSES	COCOONS
COALITIONS	COAX	COCAINISMS	COCKING	COCOPAN
COALIZE	COAXED	COCAINIST	COCKLAIRD	COCOPANS
COALIZED	COAXER	COCAINISTS	COCKLAIRDS	COCOPLUM
COALIZES	COAXERS	COCAINIZE	COCKLE	COCOPLUMS
COALIZING	COAXES	COCAINIZED	COCKLEBUR	COCOS
COALMAN	COAXIAL	COCAINIZES	COCKLEBURS	COCOTTE
COALMEN	COAXIALLY	COCAINIZING	COCKLED	COCOTTES
COALMINE	COAXING	COCAS	COCKLEMAN	COCTILE
COALMINER	COAXINGLY	COCCAL	COCKLEMEN	COCTION
COALMINERS	COB	COCCI	COCKLES	COCTIONS
COALMINES	COBALAMIN	COCCID	COCKLING	COCULTURE
COALS	COBALAMINS	COCCIDIA	COCKLOFT	COCULTURED
COALTAR	COBALT	COCCIDIUM	COCKLOFTS	COCULTURES
COALTARS	COBALTIC	COCCIDS	COCKMATCH	COCULTURING
COALY	COBALTITE	COCCO	COCKMATCHES	COCUSWOOD
COAMING	COBALTITES	COCCOID	COCKNEY	COCUSWOODS
COAMINGS	COBALTS	COCCOLITE	COCKNEYFIED	COD
COAPT	COBB	COCCOLITES	COCKNEYFIES	CODA
COAPTED	COBBED	COCCOLITH	COCKNEYFY	CODAS
COAPTING	COBBER	COCCOLITHS	COCKNEYFYING	CODDED
COAPTS	COBBERS	COCCOS	COCKNEYS	CODDER
COARB	COBBIER	COCCUS	COCKNIFIED	CODDERS
COARBS	COBBIEST	COCCYGEAL	COCKNIFIES	CODDING
COARCTATE	COBBING	COCCYGES	COCKNIFY	CODDLE
COARCTATED	COBBLE	COCCYGIAN	COCKNIFYING	CODDLED
COARCTATES	COBBLED	COCCYX	COCKPIT	CODDLES
COARCTATING	COBBLER	COCHINEAL	COCKPITS	CODDLING
COARSE	COBBLERIES	COCHINEALS	COCKROACH	CODE

The Chambers Dictionary is the authority for many longer words; see *OSW* Introduction, page xii.

CODEBOOK	COEQUALLY	COGGLIEST	COHERITORS	COIRS
CODEBOOKS	COEQUALS	COGGLING	COHESIBLE	COISTREL
CODED	COERCE	COGGLY	COHESION	COISTRELS
CODEINE	COERCED	COGIE	COHESIONS	COISTRIL
CODEINES	COERCES	COGIES	COHESIVE	COISTRILS
CODES	COERCIBLE	COGITABLE	COHIBIT	COIT
CODETTA	COERCIBLY	COGITATE	COHIBITED	COITAL
CODETTAS	COERCING	COGITATED	COHIBITING	COITION
CODEX	COERCION	COGITATES	COHIBITS	COITIONS
CODFISH	COERCIONS	COGITATING	COHO	COITS
CODFISHES	COERCIVE	COGNATE	COHOBATE	COITUS
CODGER	COETERNAL	COGNATES	COHOBATED	COITUSES
CODGERS	COEVAL	COGNATION	COHOBATES	COJOIN
CODICES	COEVALS	COGNATIONS	COHOBATING	COJOINED
CODICIL	COEXIST	COGNISANT	COHOE	COJOINING
CODICILS	COEXISTED	COGNISE	COHOES	COJOINS
CODIFIED	COEXISTING	COGNISED	COHOG	COJONES
CODIFIER	COEXISTS	COGNISES	COHOGS	COKE
CODIFIERS	COEXTEND	COGNISING	COHORN	COKED
CODIFIES	COEXTENDED	COGNITION	COHORNS	COKERNUT
CODIFY	COEXTENDING	COGNITIONS	COHORT	COKERNUTS
CODIFYING	COEXTENDS	COGNITIVE	COHORTS	COKES
CODILLA	COFACTOR	COGNIZANT	COHOS	COKESES
CODILLAS	COFACTORS	COGNIZE	COHUNE	COKIER
CODILLE	COFF	COGNIZED	COHUNES	COKIEST
CODILLES	COFFED	COGNIZES	COHYPONYM	COKING
CODING	COFFEE	COGNIZING	COHYPONYMS	COKY
CODINGS	COFFEES	COGNOMEN	COIF	COL
CODIST	COFFER	COGNOMENS	COIFED	COLA
CODISTS	COFFERDAM	COGNOMINA	COIFFEUR	COLANDER
CODLIN	COFFERDAMS	COGNOSCE	COIFFEURS	COLANDERS
CODLING	COFFERED	COGNOSCED	COIFFEUSE	COLAS
CODLINGS	COFFERING	COGNOSCES	COIFFEUSES	COLCANNON
CODLINS	COFFERS	COGNOSCING	COIFFURE	COLCANNONS
CODON	COFFIN	COGNOVIT	COIFFURED	COLCHICA
CODONS	COFFINED	COGNOVITS	COIFFURES	COLCHICUM
CODPIECE	COFFING	COGS	COIFFURING	COLCHICUMS
CODPIECES	COFFINING	COGUE	COIFING	COLCOTHAR
CODS	COFFINITE	COGUES	COIFS	COLCOTHARS
COED	COFFINITES	COGWHEEL	COIGN	COLD
COEDS	COFFINS	COGWHEELS	COIGNE	COLDBLOOD
COEHORN	COFFLE	COHAB	COIGNED	COLDBLOODS
COEHORNS	COFFLES	COHABIT	COIGNES	COLDER
COELIAC	COFFRET	COHABITED	COIGNING	COLDEST
COELIACS	COFFRETS	COHABITEE	COIGNS	COLDISH
COELOM	COFFS	COHABITEES	COIL	COLDLY
COELOMATE	COFT	COHABITING	COILED	COLDNESS
COELOMATES	COG	COHABITOR	COILING	COLDNESSES
COELOMIC	COGENCE	COHABITORS	COILS	COLDS
COELOMS	COGENCES	COHABITS	COIN	COLE
COELOSTAT	COGENCIES	COHABS	COINAGE	COLECTOMIES
COELOSTATS	COGENCY	COHEIR	COINAGES	COLECTOMY
COEMPTION	COGENER	COHEIRESS	COINCIDE	COLES
COEMPTIONS	COGENERS	COHEIRESSES	COINCIDED	COLESEED
COENOBIA	COGENT	COHEIRS	COINCIDES	COLESEEDS
COENOBITE	COGENTLY	COHERE	COINCIDING	COLESLAW
COENOBITES	COGGED	COHERED	COINED	COLESLAWS
COENOBIUM	COGGER	COHERENCE	COINER	COLETIT
COENOCYTE	COGGERS	COHERENCES	COINERS	COLETITS
COENOCYTES	COGGIE	COHERENCIES	COINHERE	COLEUS
COENOSARC	COGGIES	COHERENCY	COINHERED	COLEUSES
COENOSARCS	COGGING	COHERENT	COINHERES	COLEWORT
COENURI	COGGINGS	COHERER	COINHERING	COLEWORTS
COENURUS	COGGLE	COHERERS	COINING	COLEY
COENZYME	COGGLED	COHERES	COININGS	COLEYS
COENZYMES	COGGLES	COHERING	COINS	COLIBRI
COEQUAL	COGGLIER	COHERITOR	COIR	COLIBRIS

The Chambers Dictionary is the authority for many longer words; see *OSW* Introduction, page xii.

COLIC	COLLIDED	COLLYRIUM	COLOUREDS	COMARBS
COLICKY	COLLIDER	COLLYRIUMS	COLOURER	COMART
COLICS	COLLIDERS	COLOBI	COLOURERS	COMARTS
COLIFORM	COLLIDES	COLOBID	COLOURFUL	COMAS
COLIFORMS	COLLIDING	COLOBOMA	COLOURING	COMATE
COLIN	COLLIE	COLOBOMATA	COLOURINGS	COMATES
COLINS	COLLIED	COLOBUS	COLOURISE	COMATOSE
COLISEUM	COLLIER	COLOBUSES	COLOURISED	COMATULID
COLISEUMS	COLLIERIES	COLOCYNTH	COLOURISES	COMATULIDS
COLITIS	COLLIERS	COLOCYNTHS	COLOURISING	COMB
COLITISES	COLLIERY	COLOGNE	COLOURIST	COMBAT
COLL	COLLIES	COLOGNES	COLOURISTS	COMBATANT
COLLAGE	COLLIGATE	COLON	COLOURIZE	COMBATANTS
COLLAGEN	COLLIGATED	COLONEL	COLOURIZED	COMBATED
COLLAGENS	COLLIGATES	COLONELCIES	COLOURIZES	COMBATING
COLLAGES	COLLIGATING	COLONELCY	COLOURIZING	COMBATIVE
COLLAGIST	COLLIMATE	COLONELS	COLOURMAN	COMBATS
COLLAGISTS	COLLIMATED	COLONES	COLOURMEN	COMBE
COLLAPSAR	COLLIMATES	COLONIAL	COLOURS	COMBED
COLLAPSARS	COLLIMATING	COLONIALS	COLOURWAY	COMBER
COLLAPSE	COLLINEAR	COLONIC	COLOURWAYS	COMBERS
COLLAPSED	COLLING	COLONICS	COLOURY	COMBES
COLLAPSES	COLLINGS	COLONIES	COLS	COMBIER
COLLAPSING	COLLINS	COLONISE	COLT	COMBIEST
COLLAR	COLLINSES	COLONISED	COLTED	COMBINATE
COLLARD	COLLISION	COLONISES	COLTER	COMBINE
COLLARDS	COLLISIONS	COLONISING	COLTERS	COMBINED
COLLARED	COLLOCATE	COLONIST	COLTING	COMBINES
COLLARING	COLLOCATED	COLONISTS	COLTISH	COMBING
COLLARS	COLLOCATES	COLONITIS	COLTS	COMBINGS
COLLATE	COLLOCATING	COLONITISES	COLTSFOOT	COMBINING
COLLATED	COLLODION	COLONIZE	COLTSFOOTS	COMBLE
COLLATES	COLLODIONS	COLONIZED	COLUBRID	COMBLES
COLLATING	COLLOGUE	COLONIZES	COLUBRIDS	COMBLESS
COLLATION	COLLOGUED	COLONIZING	COLUBRINE	COMBO
COLLATIONS	COLLOGUES	COLONNADE	COLUGO	COMBOS
COLLATIVE	COLLOGUING	COLONNADES	COLUGOS	COMBRETUM
COLLATOR	COLLOID	COLONS	COLUMBARIES	COMBRETUMS
COLLATORS	COLLOIDAL	COLONY	COLUMBARY	COMBS
COLLEAGUE	COLLOIDS	COLOPHON	COLUMBATE	COMBUST
COLLEAGUED	COLLOP	COLOPHONIES	COLUMBATES	COMBUSTED
COLLEAGUES	COLLOPS	COLOPHONS	COLUMBIC	COMBUSTING
COLLEAGUING	COLLOQUE	COLOPHONY	COLUMBINE	COMBUSTOR
COLLECT	COLLOQUED	COLOR	COLUMBINES	COMBUSTORS
COLLECTED	COLLOQUES	COLORANT	COLUMBITE	COMBUSTS
COLLECTING	COLLOQUIA	COLORANTS	COLUMBITES	COMBWISE
COLLECTINGS	COLLOQUIED	COLORED	COLUMBIUM	COMBY
COLLECTOR	COLLOQUIES	COLORIFIC	COLUMBIUMS	COME
COLLECTORS	COLLOQUING	COLORING	COLUMEL	COMEBACK
COLLECTS	COLLOQUY	COLORS	COLUMELLA	COMEBACKS
COLLED	COLLOQUYING	COLOSSAL	COLUMELLAE	COMEDDLE
COLLEEN	COLLOTYPE	COLOSSEUM	COLUMELS	COMEDDLED
COLLEENS	COLLOTYPES	COLOSSEUMS	COLUMN	COMEDDLES
COLLEGE	COLLS	COLOSSI	COLUMNAL	COMEDDLING
COLLEGER	COLLUDE	COLOSSUS	COLUMNAR	COMEDIAN
COLLEGERS	COLLUDED	COLOSSUSES	COLUMNED	COMEDIANS
COLLEGES	COLLUDER	COLOSTOMIES	COLUMNIST	COMEDIC
COLLEGIA	COLLUDERS	COLOSTOMY	COLUMNISTS	COMEDIES
COLLEGIAL	COLLUDES	COLOSTRIC	COLUMNS	COMEDO
COLLEGIAN	COLLUDING	COLOSTRUM	COLURE	COMEDOS
COLLEGIANS	COLLUSION	COLOSTRUMS	COLURES	COMEDOWN
COLLEGIUM	COLLUSIONS	COLOTOMIES	COLZA	COMEDOWNS
COLLEGIUMS	COLLUSIVE	COLOTOMY	COLZAS	COMEDY
COLLET	COLLUVIES	COLOUR	COMA	COMELIER
COLLETS	COLLY	COLOURANT	COMAE	COMELIEST
COLLICULI	COLLYING	COLOURANTS	COMAL	COMELY
COLLIDE	COLLYRIA	COLOURED	COMARB	COMER

The Chambers Dictionary is the authority for many longer words; see *OSW* Introduction, page xii.

COMERS
COMES
COMET
COMETARY
COMETHER
COMETHERS
COMETIC
COMETS
COMFIER
COMFIEST
COMFIT
COMFITS
COMFITURE
COMFITURES
COMFORT
COMFORTED
COMFORTER
COMFORTERS
COMFORTING
COMFORTS
COMFREY
COMFREYS
COMFY
COMIC
COMICAL
COMICALLY
COMICE
COMICES
COMICS
COMING
COMINGS
COMITADJI
COMITADJIS
COMITAL
COMITATUS
COMITATUSES
COMITIA
COMITIES
COMITY
COMMA
COMMAND
COMMANDED
COMMANDER
COMMANDERS
COMMANDING
COMMANDO
COMMANDOS
COMMANDS
COMMAS
COMMENCE
COMMENCED
COMMENCES
COMMENCING
COMMEND
COMMENDAM
COMMENDAMS
COMMENDED
COMMENDING
COMMENDS
COMMENSAL
COMMENSALS
COMMENT
COMMENTED
COMMENTER
COMMENTERS
COMMENTING
COMMENTOR

COMMENTORS
COMMENTS
COMMER
COMMERCE
COMMERCED
COMMERCES
COMMERCING
COMMERE
COMMERES
COMMERGE
COMMERGED
COMMERGES
COMMERGING
COMMERS
COMMIE
COMMIES
COMMINATE
COMMINATED
COMMINATES
COMMINATING
COMMINGLE
COMMINGLED
COMMINGLES
COMMINGLING
COMMINUTE
COMMINUTED
COMMINUTES
COMMINUTING
COMMIS
COMMISSAR
COMMISSARS
COMMIT
COMMITS
COMMITTAL
COMMITTALS
COMMITTED
COMMITTEE
COMMITTEES
COMMITTING
COMMIX
COMMIXED
COMMIXES
COMMIXING
COMMO
COMMODE
COMMODES
COMMODITIES
COMMODITY
COMMODO
COMMODORE
COMMODORES
COMMON
COMMONAGE
COMMONAGES
COMMONED
COMMONER
COMMONERS
COMMONEST
COMMONEY
COMMONEYS
COMMONING
COMMONINGS
COMMONLY
COMMONS
COMMORANT
COMMORANTS
COMMOS

COMMOT
COMMOTE
COMMOTES
COMMOTION
COMMOTIONS
COMMOTS
COMMOVE
COMMOVED
COMMOVES
COMMOVING
COMMUNAL
COMMUNARD
COMMUNARDS
COMMUNE
COMMUNED
COMMUNES
COMMUNING
COMMUNINGS
COMMUNION
COMMUNIONS
COMMUNISE
COMMUNISED
COMMUNISES
COMMUNISING
COMMUNISM
COMMUNISMS
COMMUNIST
COMMUNISTS
COMMUNITIES
COMMUNITY
COMMUNIZE
COMMUNIZED
COMMUNIZES
COMMUNIZING
COMMUTATE
COMMUTATED
COMMUTATES
COMMUTATING
COMMUTE
COMMUTED
COMMUTER
COMMUTERS
COMMUTES
COMMUTING
COMMUTUAL
COMMY
COMODO
COMOSE
COMOUS
COMP
COMPACT
COMPACTED
COMPACTER
COMPACTEST
COMPACTING
COMPACTLY
COMPACTOR
COMPACTORS
COMPACTS
COMPADRE
COMPADRES
COMPAGE
COMPAGES
COMPANDER
COMPANDERS
COMPANDOR
COMPANDORS

COMPANIED
COMPANIES
COMPANING
COMPANION
COMPANIONED
COMPANIONING
COMPANIONS
COMPANY
COMPANYING
COMPARE
COMPARED
COMPARES
COMPARING
COMPART
COMPARTED
COMPARTING
COMPARTS
COMPASS
COMPASSED
COMPASSES
COMPASSING
COMPASSINGS
COMPAST
COMPEAR
COMPEARED
COMPEARING
COMPEARS
COMPED
COMPEER
COMPEERED
COMPEERING
COMPEERS
COMPEL
COMPELLED
COMPELLER
COMPELLERS
COMPELLING
COMPELS
COMPENDIA
COMPER
COMPERE
COMPERED
COMPERES
COMPERING
COMPERS
COMPESCE
COMPESCED
COMPESCES
COMPESCING
COMPETE
COMPETED
COMPETENT
COMPETES
COMPETING
COMPILE
COMPILED
COMPILER
COMPILERS
COMPILES
COMPILING
COMPING
COMPINGS
COMPITAL
COMPLAIN
COMPLAINED
COMPLAINING
COMPLAININGS

COMPLAINS
COMPLAINT
COMPLAINTS
COMPLEAT
COMPLECT
COMPLECTED
COMPLECTING
COMPLECTS
COMPLETE
COMPLETED
COMPLETER
COMPLETES
COMPLETEST
COMPLETING
COMPLEX
COMPLEXED
COMPLEXER
COMPLEXES
COMPLEXEST
COMPLEXING
COMPLEXLY
COMPLEXUS
COMPLEXUSES
COMPLIANT
COMPLICE
COMPLICES
COMPLIED
COMPLIER
COMPLIERS
COMPLIES
COMPLIN
COMPLINE
COMPLINES
COMPLINS
COMPLISH
COMPLISHED
COMPLISHES
COMPLISHING
COMPLOT
COMPLOTS
COMPLOTTED
COMPLOTTING
COMPLUVIA
COMPLY
COMPLYING
COMPO
COMPONE
COMPONENT
COMPONENTS
COMPONY
COMPORT
COMPORTED
COMPORTING
COMPORTS
COMPOS
COMPOSE
COMPOSED
COMPOSER
COMPOSERS
COMPOSES
COMPOSING
COMPOSITE
COMPOSITED
COMPOSITES
COMPOSITING
COMPOST
COMPOSTED

The Chambers Dictionary is the authority for many longer words; see *OSW* Introduction, page xii.

COMPOSTER	CONACRED	CONCERTS	CONCUBINES	CONDUCTORS
COMPOSTERS	CONACRES	CONCETTI	CONCUPIES	CONDUCTS
COMPOSTING	CONACRING	CONCETTO	CONCUPY	CONDUCTUS
COMPOSTS	CONARIA	CONCH	CONCUR	CONDUIT
COMPOSURE	CONARIAL	CONCHA	CONCURRED	CONDUITS
COMPOSURES	CONARIUM	CONCHAE	CONCURRING	CONDYLAR
COMPOT	CONATION	CONCHAL	CONCURS	CONDYLE
COMPOTE	CONATIONS	CONCHATE	CONCUSS	CONDYLES
COMPOTES	CONATIVE	CONCHE	CONCUSSED	CONDYLOID
COMPOTIER	CONATUS	CONCHED	CONCUSSES	CONDYLOMA
COMPOTIERS	CONCAUSE	CONCHES	CONCUSSING	CONDYLOMAS
COMPOTS	CONCAUSES	CONCHIE	CONCYCLIC	CONDYLOMATA
COMPOUND	CONCAVE	CONCHIES	COND	CONE
COMPOUNDED	CONCAVED	CONCHING	CONDEMN	CONED
COMPOUNDING	CONCAVELY	CONCHITIS	CONDEMNED	CONES
COMPOUNDS	CONCAVES	CONCHITISES	CONDEMNING	CONEY
COMPRADOR	CONCAVING	CONCHOID	CONDEMNS	CONEYS
COMPRADORS	CONCAVITIES	CONCHOIDS	CONDENSE	CONFAB
COMPRESS	CONCAVITY	CONCHS	CONDENSED	CONFABBED
COMPRESSED	CONCEAL	CONCHY	CONDENSER	CONFABBING
COMPRESSES	CONCEALED	CONCIERGE	CONDENSERS	CONFABS
COMPRESSING	CONCEALER	CONCIERGES	CONDENSES	CONFECT
COMPRINT	CONCEALERS	CONCILIAR	CONDENSING	CONFECTED
COMPRINTED	CONCEALING	CONCISE	CONDER	CONFECTING
COMPRINTING	CONCEALS	CONCISED	CONDERS	CONFECTS
COMPRINTS	CONCEDE	CONCISELY	CONDIDDLE	CONFER
COMPRISAL	CONCEDED	CONCISER	CONDIDDLED	CONFEREE
COMPRISALS	CONCEDER	CONCISES	CONDIDDLES	CONFEREES
COMPRISE	CONCEDERS	CONCISEST	CONDIDDLING	CONFERRED
COMPRISED	CONCEDES	CONCISING	CONDIE	CONFERRER
COMPRISES	CONCEDING	CONCLAVE	CONDIES	CONFERRERS
COMPRISING	CONCEDO	CONCLAVES	CONDIGN	CONFERRING
COMPS	CONCEIT	CONCLUDE	CONDIGNLY	CONFERS
COMPT	CONCEITED	CONCLUDED	CONDIMENT	CONFERVA
COMPTABLE	CONCEITING	CONCLUDES	CONDIMENTED	CONFERVAE
COMPTED	CONCEITS	CONCLUDING	CONDIMENTING	CONFERVAS
COMPTER	CONCEITY	CONCOCT	CONDIMENTS	CONFESS
COMPTERS	CONCEIVE	CONCOCTED	CONDITION	CONFESSED
COMPTIBLE	CONCEIVED	CONCOCTER	CONDITIONED	CONFESSES
COMPTING	CONCEIVES	CONCOCTERS	CONDITIONING	CONFESSING
COMPTROLL	CONCEIVING	CONCOCTING	CONDITIONINGS	CONFESSOR
COMPTROLLED	CONCENT	CONCOCTOR	CONDITIONS	CONFESSORS
COMPTROLLING	CONCENTER	CONCOCTORS	CONDO	CONFEST
COMPTROLLS	CONCENTERED	CONCOCTS	CONDOLE	CONFESTLY
COMPTS	CONCENTERING	CONCOLOR	CONDOLED	CONFETTI
COMPULSE	CONCENTERS	CONCORD	CONDOLENT	CONFIDANT
COMPULSED	CONCENTRE	CONCORDAT	CONDOLES	CONFIDANTS
COMPULSES	CONCENTRED	CONCORDATS	CONDOLING	CONFIDE
COMPULSING	CONCENTRES	CONCORDED	CONDOM	CONFIDED
COMPUTANT	CONCENTRING	CONCORDING	CONDOMS	CONFIDENT
COMPUTANTS	CONCENTS	CONCORDS	CONDONE	CONFIDENTS
COMPUTE	CONCENTUS	CONCOURS	CONDONED	CONFIDER
COMPUTED	CONCEPT	CONCOURSE	CONDONES	CONFIDERS
COMPUTER	CONCEPTI	CONCOURSES	CONDONING	CONFIDES
COMPUTERS	CONCEPTS	CONCREATE	CONDOR	CONFIDING
COMPUTES	CONCEPTUS	CONCREATED	CONDORS	CONFIGURE
COMPUTING	CONCEPTUSES	CONCREATES	CONDOS	CONFIGURED
COMPUTIST	CONCERN	CONCREATING	CONDUCE	CONFIGURES
COMPUTISTS	CONCERNED	CONCRETE	CONDUCED	CONFIGURING
COMRADE	CONCERNING	CONCRETED	CONDUCES	CONFINE
COMRADELY	CONCERNS	CONCRETES	CONDUCING	CONFINED
COMRADES	CONCERT	CONCRETING	CONDUCIVE	CONFINER
COMS	CONCERTED	CONCREW	CONDUCT	CONFINERS
COMUS	CONCERTI	CONCREWED	CONDUCTED	CONFINES
COMUSES	CONCERTING	CONCREWING	CONDUCTI	CONFINING
CON	CONCERTO	CONCREWS	CONDUCTING	CONFIRM
CONACRE	CONCERTOS	CONCUBINE	CONDUCTOR	CONFIRMED

The Chambers Dictionary is the authority for many longer words; see *OSW* Introduction, page xii.

CONFIRMEE	CONGAS	CONIFER	CONNERS	CONSIDERS
CONFIRMEES	CONGE	CONIFERS	CONNES	CONSIGN
CONFIRMER	CONGEAL	CONIFORM	CONNEXION	CONSIGNED
CONFIRMERS	CONGEALED	CONIINE	CONNEXIONS	CONSIGNEE
CONFIRMING	CONGEALING	CONIINES	CONNING	CONSIGNEES
CONFIRMINGS	CONGEALS	CONIMA	CONNINGS	CONSIGNER
CONFIRMOR	CONGED	CONIMAS	CONNIVE	CONSIGNERS
CONFIRMORS	CONGEE	CONIN	CONNIVED	CONSIGNING
CONFIRMS	CONGEED	CONINE	CONNIVENT	CONSIGNOR
CONFISEUR	CONGEEING	CONINES	CONNIVER	CONSIGNORS
CONFISEURS	CONGEES	CONING	CONNIVERS	CONSIGNS
CONFIT	CONGEING	CONINS	CONNIVES	CONSIST
CONFITEOR	CONGENER	CONJECT	CONNIVING	CONSISTED
CONFITEORS	CONGENERS	CONJECTED	CONNOTATE	CONSISTING
CONFITS	CONGENIAL	CONJECTING	CONNOTATED	CONSISTS
CONFITURE	CONGENIC	CONJECTS	CONNOTATES	CONSOCIES
CONFITURES	CONGER	CONJEE	CONNOTATING	CONSOLE
CONFIX	CONGERIES	CONJEED	CONNOTE	CONSOLED
CONFIXED	CONGERS	CONJEEING	CONNOTED	CONSOLER
CONFIXES	CONGES	CONJEES	CONNOTES	CONSOLERS
CONFIXING	CONGEST	CONJOIN	CONNOTING	CONSOLES
CONFLATE	CONGESTED	CONJOINED	CONNOTIVE	CONSOLING
CONFLATED	CONGESTING	CONJOINING	CONNS	CONSOLS
CONFLATES	CONGESTS	CONJOINS	CONNUBIAL	CONSOLUTE
CONFLATING	CONGIARIES	CONJOINT	CONODONT	CONSOMME
CONFLICT	CONGIARY	CONJUGAL	CONODONTS	CONSOMMES
CONFLICTED	CONGII	CONJUGANT	CONOID	CONSONANT
CONFLICTING	CONGIUS	CONJUGANTS	CONOIDAL	CONSONANTS
CONFLICTS	CONGLOBE	CONJUGATE	CONOIDIC	CONSONOUS
CONFLUENT	CONGLOBED	CONJUGATED	CONOIDS	CONSORT
CONFLUENTS	CONGLOBES	CONJUGATES	CONQUER	CONSORTED
CONFLUX	CONGLOBING	CONJUGATING	CONQUERED	CONSORTER
CONFLUXES	CONGO	CONJUGATINGS	CONQUERING	CONSORTERS
CONFOCAL	CONGOS	CONJUNCT	CONQUEROR	CONSORTIA
CONFORM	CONGOU	CONJURE	CONQUERORS	CONSORTING
CONFORMAL	CONGOUS	CONJURED	CONQUERS	CONSORTS
CONFORMED	CONGRATS	CONJURER	CONQUEST	CONSPIRE
CONFORMER	CONGREE	CONJURERS	CONQUESTS	CONSPIRED
CONFORMERS	CONGREED	CONJURES	CONS	CONSPIRER
CONFORMING	CONGREEING	CONJURIES	CONSCIENT	CONSPIRERS
CONFORMS	CONGREES	CONJURING	CONSCIOUS	CONSPIRES
CONFOUND	CONGREET	CONJURINGS	CONSCIOUSES	CONSPIRING
CONFOUNDED	CONGREETED	CONJUROR	CONSCRIBE	CONSTABLE
CONFOUNDING	CONGREETING	CONJURORS	CONSCRIBED	CONSTABLES
CONFOUNDS	CONGREETS	CONJURY	CONSCRIBES	CONSTANCIES
CONFRERE	CONGRESS	CONK	CONSCRIBING	CONSTANCY
CONFRERES	CONGRESSED	CONKED	CONSCRIPT	CONSTANT
CONFRERIE	CONGRESSES	CONKER	CONSCRIPTED	CONSTANTS
CONFRERIES	CONGRESSING	CONKERS	CONSCRIPTING	CONSTATE
CONFRONT	CONGRUE	CONKING	CONSCRIPTS	CONSTATED
CONFRONTE	CONGRUED	CONKS	CONSEIL	CONSTATES
CONFRONTED	CONGRUENT	CONKY	CONSEILS	CONSTATING
CONFRONTING	CONGRUES	CONN	CONSENSUS	CONSTER
CONFRONTS	CONGRUING	CONNATE	CONSENSUSES	CONSTERED
CONFUSE	CONGRUITIES	CONNATION	CONSENT	CONSTERING
CONFUSED	CONGRUITY	CONNATIONS	CONSENTED	CONSTERS
CONFUSES	CONGRUOUS	CONNE	CONSENTING	CONSTRAIN
CONFUSING	CONIA	CONNECT	CONSENTS	CONSTRAINED
CONFUSION	CONIAS	CONNECTED	CONSERVE	CONSTRAINING
CONFUSIONS	CONIC	CONNECTER	CONSERVED	CONSTRAINS
CONFUTE	CONICAL	CONNECTERS	CONSERVER	CONSTRICT
CONFUTED	CONICALLY	CONNECTING	CONSERVERS	CONSTRICTED
CONFUTES	CONICS	CONNECTOR	CONSERVES	CONSTRICTING
CONFUTING	CONIDIA	CONNECTORS	CONSERVING	CONSTRICTS
CONGA	CONIDIAL	CONNECTS	CONSIDER	CONSTRUCT
CONGAED	CONIDIUM	CONNED	CONSIDERED	CONSTRUCTED
CONGAING	CONIES	CONNER	CONSIDERING	CONSTRUCTING

The Chambers Dictionary is the authority for many longer words; see *OSW* Introduction, page xii.

CONSTRUCTS	CONTEMNERS	CONTRAIL	CONVENES	CONVOS
CONSTRUE	CONTEMNING	CONTRAILS	CONVENING	CONVOY
CONSTRUED	CONTEMNOR	CONTRAIR	CONVENOR	CONVOYED
CONSTRUER	CONTEMNORS	CONTRALTI	CONVENORS	CONVOYING
CONSTRUERS	CONTEMNS	CONTRALTO	CONVENT	CONVOYS
CONSTRUES	CONTEMPER	CONTRALTOS	CONVENTED	CONVULSE
CONSTRUING	CONTEMPERED	CONTRARIED	CONVENTING	CONVULSED
CONSUL	CONTEMPERING	CONTRARIES	CONVENTS	CONVULSES
CONSULAGE	CONTEMPERS	CONTRARY	CONVERGE	CONVULSING
CONSULAGES	CONTEMPT	CONTRARYING	CONVERGED	CONY
CONSULAR	CONTEMPTS	CONTRAS	CONVERGES	COO
CONSULARS	CONTEND	CONTRAST	CONVERGING	COOED
CONSULATE	CONTENDED	CONTRASTED	CONVERSE	COOEE
CONSULATES	CONTENDER	CONTRASTING	CONVERSED	COOEED
CONSULS	CONTENDERS	CONTRASTS	CONVERSES	COOEEING
CONSULT	CONTENDING	CONTRASTY	CONVERSING	COOEES
CONSULTA	CONTENDINGS	CONTRAT	CONVERT	COOEY
CONSULTAS	CONTENDS	CONTRATE	CONVERTED	COOEYED
CONSULTED	CONTENT	CONTRATS	CONVERTER	COOEYING
CONSULTEE	CONTENTED	CONTRIST	CONVERTERS	COOEYS
CONSULTEES	CONTENTING	CONTRISTED	CONVERTING	COOF
CONSULTER	CONTENTS	CONTRISTING	CONVERTOR	COOFS
CONSULTERS	CONTES	CONTRISTS	CONVERTORS	COOING
CONSULTING	CONTESSA	CONTRITE	CONVERTS	COOINGLY
CONSULTOR	CONTESSAS	CONTRIVE	CONVEX	COOINGS
CONSULTORS	CONTEST	CONTRIVED	CONVEXED	COOK
CONSULTS	CONTESTED	CONTRIVER	CONVEXES	COOKABLE
CONSUME	CONTESTER	CONTRIVERS	CONVEXITIES	COOKBOOK
CONSUMED	CONTESTERS	CONTRIVES	CONVEXITY	COOKBOOKS
CONSUMER	CONTESTING	CONTRIVING	CONVEXLY	COOKED
CONSUMERS	CONTESTS	CONTROL	CONVEY	COOKER
CONSUMES	CONTEXT	CONTROLE	CONVEYAL	COOKERIES
CONSUMING	CONTEXTS	CONTROLLED	CONVEYALS	COOKERS
CONSUMINGS	CONTICENT	CONTROLLING	CONVEYED	COOKERY
CONSUMPT	CONTINENT	CONTROLS	CONVEYER	COOKHOUSE
CONSUMPTS	CONTINENTS	CONTROUL	CONVEYERS	COOKHOUSES
CONTACT	CONTINUA	CONTROULED	CONVEYING	COOKIE
CONTACTED	CONTINUAL	CONTROULING	CONVEYOR	COOKIES
CONTACTING	CONTINUE	CONTROULS	CONVEYORS	COOKING
CONTACTOR	CONTINUED	CONTUMACIES	CONVEYS	COOKMAID
CONTACTORS	CONTINUER	CONTUMACY	CONVICT	COOKMAIDS
CONTACTS	CONTINUERS	CONTUMELIES	CONVICTED	COOKOUT
CONTADINA	CONTINUES	CONTUMELY	CONVICTING	COOKOUTS
CONTADINAS	CONTINUING	CONTUND	CONVICTS	COOKROOM
CONTADINE	CONTINUO	CONTUNDED	CONVINCE	COOKROOMS
CONTADINI	CONTINUOS	CONTUNDING	CONVINCED	COOKS
CONTADINO	CONTINUUM	CONTUNDS	CONVINCES	COOKWARE
CONTAGIA	CONTINUUMS	CONTUSE	CONVINCING	COOKWARES
CONTAGION	CONTLINE	CONTUSED	CONVIVE	COOKY
CONTAGIONS	CONTLINES	CONTUSES	CONVIVED	COOL
CONTAGIUM	CONTO	CONTUSING	CONVIVES	COOLABAH
CONTAIN	CONTORNO	CONTUSION	CONVIVIAL	COOLABAHS
CONTAINED	CONTORNOS	CONTUSIONS	CONVIVING	COOLAMON
CONTAINER	CONTORT	CONTUSIVE	CONVO	COOLAMONS
CONTAINERS	CONTORTED	CONUNDRUM	CONVOCATE	COOLANT
CONTAINING	CONTORTING	CONUNDRUMS	CONVOCATED	COOLANTS
CONTAINS	CONTORTS	CONURBAN	CONVOCATES	COOLED
CONTANGO	CONTOS	CONURBIA	CONVOCATING	COOLER
CONTANGOED	CONTOUR	CONURBIAS	CONVOKE	COOLERS
CONTANGOING	CONTOURED	CONURE	CONVOKED	COOLEST
CONTANGOS	CONTOURING	CONURES	CONVOKES	COOLHOUSE
CONTE	CONTOURS	CONVECTOR	CONVOKING	COOLHOUSES
CONTECK	CONTRA	CONVECTORS	CONVOLUTE	COOLIBAH
CONTECKS	CONTRACT	CONVENE	CONVOLVE	COOLIBAHS
CONTEMN	CONTRACTED	CONVENED	CONVOLVED	COOLIBAR
CONTEMNED	CONTRACTING	CONVENER	CONVOLVES	COOLIBARS
CONTEMNER	CONTRACTS	CONVENERS	CONVOLVING	COOLIE

The Chambers Dictionary is the authority for many longer words; see *OSW* Introduction, page xii.

COOLIES	COPACETIC	COPROLITE	COQUITOS	CORDITES
COOLING	COPAIBA	COPROLITES	COR	CORDLESS
COOLISH	COPAIBAS	COPROLITH	CORACLE	CORDOBA
COOLLY	COPAIVA	COPROLITHS	CORACLES	CORDOBAS
COOLNESS	COPAIVAS	COPROLOGIES	CORACOID	CORDON
COOLNESSES	COPAL	COPROLOGY	CORACOIDS	CORDONED
COOLS	COPALS	COPROSMA	CORAGGIO	CORDONING
COOLTH	COPARTNER	COPROSMAS	CORAGGIOS	CORDONS
COOLTHS	COPARTNERS	COPROZOIC	CORAL	CORDOTOMIES
COOLY	COPATAINE	COPS	CORALLA	CORDOTOMY
COOM	COPATRIOT	COPSE	CORALLINE	CORDOVAN
COOMB	COPATRIOTS	COPSED	CORALLINES	CORDOVANS
COOMBE	COPE	COPSES	CORALLITE	CORDS
COOMBES	COPECK	COPSEWOOD	CORALLITES	CORDUROY
COOMBS	COPECKS	COPSEWOODS	CORALLOID	CORDUROYS
COOMED	COPED	COPSHOP	CORALLUM	CORDWAIN
COOMIER	COPEMATE	COPSHOPS	CORALROOT	CORDWAINS
COOMIEST	COPEMATES	COPSIER	CORALROOTS	CORDWOOD
COOMING	COPEPOD	COPSIEST	CORALS	CORDWOODS
COOMS	COPEPODS	COPSING	CORALWORT	CORDYLINE
COOMY	COPER	COPSY	CORALWORTS	CORDYLINES
COON	COPERED	COPTER	CORAM	CORE
COONCAN	COPERING	COPTERS	CORAMINE	CORED
COONCANS	COPERS	COPULA	CORAMINES	COREGENT
COONDOG	COPES	COPULAR	CORANACH	COREGENTS
COONDOGS	COPESTONE	COPULAS	CORANACHS	CORELESS
COONHOUND	COPESTONES	COPULATE	CORANTO	CORELLA
COONHOUNDS	COPIED	COPULATED	CORANTOES	CORELLAS
COONS	COPIER	COPULATES	CORANTOS	COREOPSIS
COONSKIN	COPIERS	COPULATING	CORBAN	COREOPSISES
COONSKINS	COPIES	COPY	CORBANS	CORER
COONTIE	COPILOT	COPYBOOK	CORBE	CORERS
COONTIES	COPILOTS	COPYBOOKS	CORBEAU	CORES
COONTY	COPING	COPYCAT	CORBEAUS	COREY
COOP	COPINGS	COPYCATS	CORBEIL	COREYS
COOPED	COPIOUS	COPYCATTED	CORBEILLE	CORF
COOPER	COPIOUSLY	COPYCATTING	CORBEILLES	CORFHOUSE
COOPERAGE	COPITA	COPYHOLD	CORBEILS	CORFHOUSES
COOPERAGES	COPITAS	COPYHOLDS	CORBEL	CORGI
COOPERATE	COPLANAR	COPYING	CORBELED	CORGIS
COOPERATED	COPOLYMER	COPYISM	CORBELING	CORIA
COOPERATES	COPOLYMERS	COPYISMS	CORBELINGS	CORIANDER
COOPERATING	COPPED	COPYIST	CORBELLED	CORIANDERS
COOPERED	COPPER	COPYISTS	CORBELLING	CORIES
COOPERIES	COPPERAS	COPYREAD	CORBELLINGS	CORING
COOPERING	COPPERASES	COPYREADING	CORBELS	CORIOUS
COOPERINGS	COPPERED	COPYREADINGS	CORBES	CORIUM
COOPERS	COPPERING	COPYREADS	CORBICULA	CORIUMS
COOPERY	COPPERINGS	COPYRIGHT	CORBICULAE	CORIVAL
COOPING	COPPERISH	COPYRIGHTED	CORBIE	CORIVALLED
COOPS	COPPERS	COPYRIGHTING	CORBIES	CORIVALLING
COOPT	COPPERY	COPYRIGHTS	CORCASS	CORIVALRIES
COOPTED	COPPICE	COQUET	CORCASSES	CORIVALRY
COOPTING	COPPICED	COQUETRIES	CORD	CORIVALS
COOPTS	COPPICES	COQUETRY	CORDAGE	CORK
COORDINAL	COPPICING	COQUETS	CORDAGES	CORKAGE
COOS	COPPICINGS	COQUETTE	CORDATE	CORKAGES
COOSER	COPPIES	COQUETTED	CORDED	CORKBOARD
COOSERS	COPPIN	COQUETTES	CORDIAL	CORKBOARDS
COOST	COPPING	COQUETTING	CORDIALLY	CORKBORER
COOT	COPPINS	COQUILLA	CORDIALS	CORKBORERS
COOTIE	COPPLE	COQUILLAS	CORDIFORM	CORKED
COOTIES	COPPLES	COQUILLE	CORDINER	CORKER
COOTIKIN	COPPY	COQUILLES	CORDINERS	CORKERS
COOTIKINS	COPRA	COQUINA	CORDING	CORKIER
COOTS	COPRAS	COQUINAS	CORDINGS	CORKIEST
COP	COPRESENT	COQUITO	CORDITE	CORKINESS

The Chambers Dictionary is the authority for many longer words; see *OSW* Introduction, page xii.

CORKINESSES	CORNFIELD	CORODIES	CORRECTLY	CORSLETS
CORKING	CORNFIELDS	CORODY	CORRECTOR	CORSNED
CORKIR	CORNFLAG	COROLLA	CORRECTORS	CORSNEDS
CORKIRS	CORNFLAGS	COROLLARIES	CORRECTS	CORSO
CORKS	CORNFLAKE	COROLLARY	CORRELATE	CORSOS
CORKSCREW	CORNFLAKES	COROLLAS	CORRELATED	CORTEGE
CORKSCREWED	CORNFLIES	COROLLINE	CORRELATES	CORTEGES
CORKSCREWING	CORNFLOUR	CORONA	CORRELATING	CORTEX
CORKSCREWS	CORNFLOURS	CORONACH	CORRIDA	CORTEXES
CORKTREE	CORNFLY	CORONACHS	CORRIDAS	CORTICAL
CORKTREES	CORNHUSK	CORONAE	CORRIDOR	CORTICATE
CORKWOOD	CORNHUSKS	CORONAL	CORRIDORS	CORTICES
CORKWOODS	CORNI	CORONALS	CORRIE	CORTICOID
CORKY	CORNICE	CORONARIES	CORRIES	CORTICOIDS
CORM	CORNICED	CORONARY	CORRIGENT	CORTILE
CORMEL	CORNICES	CORONAS	CORRIGENTS	CORTILI
CORMELS	CORNICHE	CORONATE	CORRIVAL	CORTISOL
CORMIDIA	CORNICHES	CORONATED	CORRIVALLED	CORTISOLS
CORMIDIUM	CORNICING	CORONER	CORRIVALLING	CORTISONE
CORMORANT	CORNICLE	CORONERS	CORRIVALS	CORTISONES
CORMORANTS	CORNICLES	CORONET	CORRODE	CORUNDUM
CORMOUS	CORNICULA	CORONETED	CORRODED	CORUNDUMS
CORMS	CORNIER	CORONETS	CORRODENT	CORUSCANT
CORMUS	CORNIEST	CORONIS	CORRODENTS	CORUSCATE
CORMUSES	CORNIFIC	CORONISES	CORRODES	CORUSCATED
CORN	CORNIFORM	CORONIUM	CORRODIES	CORUSCATES
CORNACRE	CORNING	CORONIUMS	CORRODING	CORUSCATING
CORNACRES	CORNIST	CORONOID	CORRODY	CORVEE
CORNAGE	CORNISTS	COROZO	CORROSION	CORVEES
CORNAGES	CORNLAND	COROZOS	CORROSIONS	CORVES
CORNBALL	CORNLANDS	CORPORA	CORROSIVE	CORVET
CORNBALLS	CORNLOFT	CORPORAL	CORROSIVES	CORVETED
CORNBORER	CORNLOFTS	CORPORALS	CORRUGATE	CORVETING
CORNBORERS	CORNMILL	CORPORAS	CORRUGATED	CORVETS
CORNBRAKE	CORNMILLS	CORPORASES	CORRUGATES	CORVETTE
CORNBRAKES	CORNMOTH	CORPORATE	CORRUGATING	CORVETTED
CORNBRASH	CORNMOTHS	CORPOREAL	CORRUPT	CORVETTES
CORNBRASHES	CORNO	CORPORIFIED	CORRUPTED	CORVETTING
CORNBREAD	CORNOPEAN	CORPORIFIES	CORRUPTER	CORVID
CORNBREADS	CORNOPEANS	CORPORIFY	CORRUPTERS	CORVIDS
CORNCRAKE	CORNPIPE	CORPORIFYING	CORRUPTEST	CORVINE
CORNCRAKES	CORNPIPES	CORPOSANT	CORRUPTING	CORVUS
CORNEA	CORNRENT	CORPOSANTS	CORRUPTLY	CORVUSES
CORNEAL	CORNRENTS	CORPS	CORRUPTS	CORY
CORNEAS	CORNROW	CORPSE	CORS	CORYBANT
CORNED	CORNROWS	CORPSED	CORSAC	CORYBANTES
CORNEL	CORNS	CORPSES	CORSACS	CORYBANTS
CORNELIAN	CORNSTALK	CORPSING	CORSAGE	CORYDALIS
CORNELIANS	CORNSTALKS	CORPULENT	CORSAGES	CORYDALISES
CORNELS	CORNSTONE	CORPUS	CORSAIR	CORYLUS
CORNEMUSE	CORNSTONES	CORPUSCLE	CORSAIRS	CORYLUSES
CORNEMUSES	CORNU	CORPUSCLES	CORSE	CORYMB
CORNEOUS	CORNUA	CORRADE	CORSELET	CORYMBOSE
CORNER	CORNUAL	CORRADED	CORSELETS	CORYMBS
CORNERED	CORNUTE	CORRADES	CORSES	CORYPHAEI
CORNERING	CORNUTED	CORRADING	CORSET	CORYPHE
CORNERS	CORNUTES	CORRAL	CORSETED	CORYPHEE
CORNET	CORNUTING	CORRALLED	CORSETIER	CORYPHEES
CORNETCIES	CORNUTO	CORRALLING	CORSETIERS	CORYPHENE
CORNETCY	CORNUTOS	CORRALS	CORSETING	CORYPHENES
CORNETIST	CORNWORM	CORRASION	CORSETRIES	CORYPHES
CORNETISTS	CORNWORMS	CORRASIONS	CORSETRY	CORYZA
CORNETS	CORNY	CORRECT	CORSETS	CORYZAS
CORNETT	COROCORE	CORRECTED	CORSIVE	COS
CORNETTI	COROCORES	CORRECTER	CORSIVES	COSE
CORNETTO	COROCORO	CORRECTEST	CORSLET	COSEC
CORNETTS	COROCOROS	CORRECTING	CORSLETED	COSECANT

The Chambers Dictionary is the authority for many longer words; see *OSW* Introduction, page xii.

COSECANTS
COSECH
COSECHS
COSECS
COSED
COSEISMAL
COSEISMIC
COSES
COSET
COSETS
COSH
COSHED
COSHER
COSHERED
COSHERER
COSHERERS
COSHERIES
COSHERING
COSHERINGS
COSHERS
COSHERY
COSHES
COSHING
COSIER
COSIERS
COSIES
COSIEST
COSILY
COSINE
COSINES
COSINESS
COSINESSES
COSING
COSMEA
COSMEAS
COSMESES
COSMESIS
COSMETIC
COSMETICS
COSMIC
COSMICAL
COSMISM
COSMISMS
COSMIST
COSMISTS
COSMOCRAT
COSMOCRATS
COSMOGENIES
COSMOGENY
COSMOGONIES
COSMOGONY
COSMOLOGIES
COSMOLOGY
COSMONAUT
COSMONAUTS
COSMORAMA
COSMORAMAS
COSMOS
COSMOSES
COSMOTRON
COSMOTRONS
COSPHERED
COSPONSOR
COSPONSORED
COSPONSORING
COSPONSORS
COSS

COSSES
COSSET
COSSETED
COSSETING
COSSETS
COSSIE
COSSIES
COST
COSTA
COSTAE
COSTAL
COSTALGIA
COSTALGIAS
COSTALS
COSTARD
COSTARDS
COSTATE
COSTATED
COSTE
COSTEAN
COSTEANED
COSTEANING
COSTEANINGS
COSTEANS
COSTED
COSTER
COSTERS
COSTES
COSTING
COSTIVE
COSTIVELY
COSTLIER
COSTLIEST
COSTLY
COSTMARIES
COSTMARY
COSTREL
COSTRELS
COSTS
COSTUME
COSTUMED
COSTUMER
COSTUMERS
COSTUMES
COSTUMIER
COSTUMIERS
COSTUMING
COSTUS
COSTUSES
COSY
COT
COTANGENT
COTANGENTS
COTE
COTEAU
COTEAUX
COTED
COTELETTE
COTELETTES
COTELINE
COTELINES
COTENANT
COTENANTS
COTERIE
COTERIES
COTES
COTH

COTHS
COTHURN
COTHURNI
COTHURNS
COTHURNUS
COTICULAR
COTIDAL
COTILLION
COTILLIONS
COTILLON
COTILLONS
COTING
COTINGA
COTINGAS
COTISE
COTISED
COTISES
COTISING
COTLAND
COTLANDS
COTQUEAN
COTQUEANS
COTS
COTT
COTTA
COTTABUS
COTTABUSES
COTTAGE
COTTAGED
COTTAGER
COTTAGERS
COTTAGES
COTTAGEY
COTTAGING
COTTAGINGS
COTTAR
COTTARS
COTTAS
COTTED
COTTER
COTTERS
COTTID
COTTIDS
COTTIER
COTTIERS
COTTISE
COTTISED
COTTISES
COTTISING
COTTOID
COTTON
COTTONADE
COTTONADES
COTTONED
COTTONING
COTTONS
COTTONY
COTTOWN
COTTOWNS
COTTS
COTTUS
COTTUSES
COTWAL
COTWALS
COTYLAE
COTYLE
COTYLEDON

COTYLEDONS
COTYLES
COTYLOID
COUCAL
COUCALS
COUCH
COUCHANT
COUCHE
COUCHED
COUCHEE
COUCHEES
COUCHES
COUCHETTE
COUCHETTES
COUCHING
COUCHINGS
COUDE
COUGAR
COUGARS
COUGH
COUGHED
COUGHER
COUGHERS
COUGHING
COUGHINGS
COUGHS
COUGUAR
COUGUARS
COULD
COULEE
COULEES
COULIS
COULISSE
COULISSES
COULOIR
COULOIRS
COULOMB
COULOMBS
COULTER
COULTERS
COUMARIC
COUMARIN
COUMARINS
COUNCIL
COUNCILOR
COUNCILORS
COUNCILS
COUNSEL
COUNSELLED
COUNSELLING
COUNSELLINGS
COUNSELOR
COUNSELORS
COUNSELS
COUNT
COUNTABLE
COUNTED
COUNTER
COUNTERED
COUNTERING
COUNTERS
COUNTESS
COUNTESSES
COUNTIES
COUNTING
COUNTLESS
COUNTLINE

COUNTRIES
COUNTROL
COUNTROLLED
COUNTROLLING
COUNTROLS
COUNTRY
COUNTS
COUNTSHIP
COUNTSHIPS
COUNTY
COUP
COUPE
COUPED
COUPEE
COUPEES
COUPER
COUPERS
COUPES
COUPING
COUPLE
COUPLED
COUPLEDOM
COUPLEDOMS
COUPLER
COUPLERS
COUPLES
COUPLET
COUPLETS
COUPLING
COUPLINGS
COUPON
COUPONS
COUPS
COUPURE
COUPURES
COUR
COURAGE
COURAGES
COURANT
COURANTE
COURANTES
COURANTS
COURB
COURBARIL
COURBARILS
COURBED
COURBETTE
COURBETTES
COURBING
COURBS
COURD
COURE
COURED
COURES
COURGETTE
COURGETTES
COURIER
COURIERS
COURING
COURLAN
COURLANS
COURS
COURSE
COURSED
COURSER
COURSERS
COURSES

The Chambers Dictionary is the authority for many longer words; see *OSW* Introduction, page xii.

COURSING
COURSINGS
COURT
COURTED
COURTEOUS
COURTESAN
COURTESANS
COURTESIED
COURTESIES
COURTESY
COURTESYING
COURTEZAN
COURTEZANS
COURTIER
COURTIERS
COURTING
COURTINGS
COURTLET
COURTLETS
COURTLIER
COURTLIEST
COURTLIKE
COURTLING
COURTLINGS
COURTLY
COURTROOM
COURTROOMS
COURTS
COURTSHIP
COURTSHIPS
COURTYARD
COURTYARDS
COUSCOUS
COUSCOUSES
COUSIN
COUSINAGE
COUSINAGES
COUSINLY
COUSINRIES
COUSINRY
COUSINS
COUTER
COUTERS
COUTH
COUTHER
COUTHEST
COUTHIE
COUTHIER
COUTHIEST
COUTHY
COUTIL
COUTILLE
COUTILLES
COUTILS
COUTURE
COUTURES
COUTURIER
COUTURIERS
COUVADE
COUVADES
COUVERT
COUVERTS
COVALENCIES
COVALENCY
COVALENT
COVARIANT
COVARIANTS

COVARIED
COVARIES
COVARY
COVARYING
COVE
COVED
COVELET
COVELETS
COVELLITE
COVELLITES
COVEN
COVENANT
COVENANTED
COVENANTING
COVENANTS
COVENS
COVENT
COVENTS
COVER
COVERAGE
COVERAGES·
COVERALL
COVERALLS
COVERED
COVERING
COVERINGS
COVERLET
COVERLETS
COVERLID
COVERLIDS
COVERS
COVERSLIP
COVERSLIPS
COVERT
COVERTLY
COVERTS
COVERTURE
COVERTURES
COVES
COVET
COVETABLE
COVETED
COVETING
COVETISE
COVETISES
COVETOUS
COVETS
COVEY
COVEYS
COVIN
COVING
COVINGS
COVINOUS
COVINS
COVYNE
COVYNES
COW
COWAGE
COWAGES
COWAL
COWALS
COWAN
COWANS
COWARD
COWARDED
COWARDICE
COWARDICES

COWARDING
COWARDLY
COWARDREE
COWARDREES
COWARDRIES
COWARDRY
COWARDS
COWBANE
COWBANES
COWBELL
COWBELLS
COWBERRIES
COWBERRY
COWBIRD
COWBIRDS
COWBOY
COWBOYS
COWED
COWER
COWERED
COWERING
COWERS
COWFEEDER
COWFEEDERS
COWFISH
COWFISHES
COWGIRL
COWGIRLS
COWGRASS
COWGRASSES
COWHAGE
COWHAGES
COWHAND
COWHANDS
COWHEARD
COWHEARDS
COWHEEL
COWHEELS
COWHERB
COWHERBS
COWHERD
COWHERDS
COWHIDE
COWHIDED
COWHIDES
COWHIDING
COWHOUSE
COWHOUSES
COWING
COWISH
COWITCH
COWITCHES
COWL
COWLED
COWLICK
COWLICKS
COWLING
COWLINGS
COWLS
COWMAN
COWMEN
COWP
COWPAT
COWPATS
COWPEA
COWPEAS
COWPED

COWPING
COWPOKE
COWPOKES
COWPOX
COWPOXES
COWPS
COWRIE
COWRIES
COWRY
COWS
COWSHED
COWSHEDS
COWSLIP
COWSLIPS
COWTREE
COWTREES
COX
COXA
COXAE
COXAL
COXALGIA
COXALGIAS
COXCOMB
COXCOMBIC
COXCOMBRIES
COXCOMBRY
COXCOMBS
COXED
COXES
COXIER
COXIEST
COXINESS
COXINESSES
COXING
COXSWAIN
COXSWAINED
COXSWAINING
COXSWAINS
COXY
COY
COYER
COYEST
COYLY
COYNESS
COYNESSES
COYOTE
COYOTES
COYOTILLO
COYOTILLOS
COYPU
COYPUS
COYSTREL
COYSTRELS
COYSTRIL
COYSTRILS
COZ
COZE
COZED
COZEN
COZENAGE
COZENAGES
COZENED
COZENER
COZENERS
COZENING
COZENS
COZES

COZIER
COZIERS
COZIES
COZIEST
COZING
COZY
COZZES
CRAB
CRABBED
CRABBEDLY
CRABBER
CRABBERS
CRABBIER
CRABBIEST
CRABBILY
CRABBING
CRABBY
CRABLIKE
CRABS
CRABSTICK
CRABSTICKS
CRABWISE
CRACK
CRACKDOWN
CRACKDOWNS
CRACKED
CRACKER
CRACKERS
CRACKHEAD
CRACKHEADS
CRACKING
CRACKJAW
CRACKLE
CRACKLED
CRACKLES
CRACKLIER
CRACKLIEST
CRACKLING
CRACKLINGS
CRACKLY
CRACKNEL
CRACKNELS
CRACKPOT
CRACKPOTS
CRACKS
CRACKSMAN
CRACKSMEN
CRADLE
CRADLED
CRADLES
CRADLING
CRADLINGS
CRAFT
CRAFTED
CRAFTIER
CRAFTIEST
CRAFTILY
CRAFTING
CRAFTLESS
CRAFTS
CRAFTSMAN
CRAFTSMEN
CRAFTWORK
CRAFTWORKS
CRAFTY
CRAG
CRAGFAST

The Chambers Dictionary is the authority for many longer words; see *OSW* Introduction, page xii.

CRAGGED
CRAGGIER
CRAGGIEST
CRAGGY
CRAGS
CRAGSMAN
CRAGSMEN
CRAIG
CRAIGS
CRAKE
CRAKED
CRAKES
CRAKING
CRAM
CRAMBO
CRAMBOES
CRAME
CRAMES
CRAMESIES
CRAMESY
CRAMMABLE
CRAMMED
CRAMMER
CRAMMERS
CRAMMING
CRAMOISIES
CRAMOISY
CRAMP
CRAMPBARK
CRAMPBARKS
CRAMPED
CRAMPET
CRAMPETS
CRAMPIER
CRAMPIEST
CRAMPING
CRAMPIT
CRAMPITS
CRAMPON
CRAMPONS
CRAMPS
CRAMPY
CRAMS
CRAN
CRANAGE
CRANAGES
CRANBERRIES
CRANBERRY
CRANCH
CRANCHED
CRANCHES
CRANCHING
CRANE
CRANED
CRANEFLIES
CRANEFLY
CRANES
CRANIA
CRANIAL
CRANING
CRANIUM
CRANIUMS
CRANK
CRANKCASE
CRANKCASES
CRANKED
CRANKIER

CRANKIEST
CRANKILY
CRANKING
CRANKLE
CRANKLED
CRANKLES
CRANKLING
CRANKNESS
CRANKNESSES
CRANKS
CRANKY
CRANNIED
CRANNIES
CRANNOG
CRANNOGS
CRANNY
CRANNYING
CRANREUCH
CRANREUCHS
CRANS
CRANTS
CRANTSES
CRAP
CRAPE
CRAPES
CRAPIER
CRAPIEST
CRAPLE
CRAPLES
CRAPPED
CRAPPIER
CRAPPIEST
CRAPPING
CRAPPY
CRAPS
CRAPULENT
CRAPULOUS
CRAPY
CRARE
CRARES
CRASES
CRASH
CRASHED
CRASHES
CRASHING
CRASHLAND
CRASHLANDED
CRASHLANDING
CRASHLANDS
CRASHPAD
CRASHPADS
CRASIS
CRASS
CRASSER
CRASSEST
CRASSLY
CRASSNESS
CRASSNESSES
CRATCH
CRATCHES
CRATE
CRATED
CRATER
CRATERED
CRATERING
CRATEROUS
CRATERS

CRATES
CRATING
CRATON
CRATONS
CRATUR
CRATURS
CRAUNCH
CRAUNCHED
CRAUNCHES
CRAUNCHING
CRAVAT
CRAVATS
CRAVATTED
CRAVATTING
CRAVE
CRAVED
CRAVEN
CRAVENED
CRAVENING
CRAVENLY
CRAVENS
CRAVER
CRAVERS
CRAVES
CRAVING
CRAVINGS
CRAW
CRAWFISH
CRAWFISHED
CRAWFISHES
CRAWFISHING
CRAWL
CRAWLED
CRAWLER
CRAWLERS
CRAWLIER
CRAWLIEST
CRAWLING
CRAWLINGS
CRAWLS
CRAWLY
CRAWS
CRAYER
CRAYERS
CRAYFISH
CRAYFISHES
CRAYON
CRAYONED
CRAYONING
CRAYONS
CRAZE
CRAZED
CRAZES
CRAZIER
CRAZIES
CRAZIEST
CRAZILY
CRAZINESS
CRAZINESSES
CRAZING
CRAZY
CREACH
CREACHS
CREAGH
CREAGHS
CREAK
CREAKED

CREAKIER
CREAKIEST
CREAKILY
CREAKING
CREAKS
CREAKY
CREAM
CREAMED
CREAMER
CREAMERIES
CREAMERS
CREAMERY
CREAMIER
CREAMIEST
CREAMING
CREAMLAID
CREAMS
CREAMWARE
CREAMWARES
CREAMWOVE
CREAMY
CREANCE
CREANCES
CREANT
CREASE
CREASED
CREASER
CREASERS
CREASES
CREASIER
CREASIEST
CREASING
CREASOTE
CREASOTED
CREASOTES
CREASOTING
CREASY
CREATE
CREATED
CREATES
CREATIC
CREATIN
CREATINE
CREATINES
CREATING
CREATINS
CREATION
CREATIONS
CREATIVE
CREATOR
CREATORS
CREATRESS
CREATRESSES
CREATRIX
CREATRIXES
CREATURAL
CREATURE
CREATURES
CRECHE
CRECHES
CRED
CREDAL
CREDENCE
CREDENCES
CREDENDA
CREDENDUM
CREDENT

CREDENZA
CREDENZAS
CREDIBLE
CREDIBLY
CREDIT
CREDITED
CREDITING
CREDITOR
CREDITORS
CREDITS
CREDO
CREDOS
CREDS
CREDULITIES
CREDULITY
CREDULOUS
CREE
CREED
CREEDAL
CREEDS
CREEING
CREEK
CREEKIER
CREEKIEST
CREEKS
CREEKY
CREEL
CREELS
CREEP
CREEPER
CREEPERED
CREEPERS
CREEPIE
CREEPIER
CREEPIES
CREEPIEST
CREEPING
CREEPS
CREEPY
CREES
CREESE
CREESED
CREESES
CREESH
CREESHED
CREESHES
CREESHING
CREESHY
CREESING
CREMASTER
CREMASTERS
CREMATE
CREMATED
CREMATES
CREMATING
CREMATION
CREMATIONS
CREMATOR
CREMATORIES
CREMATORS
CREMATORY
CREME
CREMES
CREMOCARP
CREMOCARPS
CREMONA
CREMONAS

The Chambers Dictionary is the authority for many longer words; see *OSW* Introduction, page xii.

CREMOR	CRESCENDOING	CRIBBING	CRIMPLING	CRISPS
CREMORNE	CRESCENDOS	CRIBBLE	CRIMPS	CRISPY
CREMORNES	CRESCENT	CRIBBLED	CRIMPY	CRISSA
CREMORS	CRESCENTS	CRIBBLES	CRIMS	CRISSUM
CREMOSIN	CRESCIVE	CRIBBLING	CRIMSON	CRISTA
CREMSIN	CRESOL	CRIBELLA	CRIMSONED	CRISTAE
CRENA	CRESOLS	CRIBELLAR	CRIMSONING	CRISTATE
CRENAS	CRESS	CRIBELLUM	CRIMSONS	CRIT
CRENATE	CRESSES	CRIBLE	CRINAL	CRITERIA
CRENATED	CRESSET	CRIBRATE	CRINATE	CRITERION
CRENATION	CRESSETS	CRIBROSE	CRINATED	CRITH
CRENATIONS	CREST	CRIBROUS	CRINE	CRITHS
CRENATURE	CRESTED	CRIBS	CRINED	CRITIC
CRENATURES	CRESTING	CRIBWORK	CRINES	CRITICAL
CRENEL	CRESTLESS	CRIBWORKS	CRINGE	CRITICISE
CRENELATE	CRESTON	CRICETID	CRINGED	CRITICISED
CRENELATED	CRESTONS	CRICETIDS	CRINGER	CRITICISES
CRENELATES	CRESTS	CRICK	CRINGERS	CRITICISING
CRENELATING	CRESYLIC	CRICKED	CRINGES	CRITICISM
CRENELLE	CRETIC	CRICKET	CRINGING	CRITICISMS
CRENELLED	CRETICS	CRICKETED	CRINGINGS	CRITICIZE
CRENELLES	CRETIN	CRICKETER	CRINGLE	CRITICIZED
CRENELLING	CRETINISE	CRICKETERS	CRINGLES	CRITICIZES
CRENELS	CRETINISED	CRICKETING	CRINING	CRITICIZING
CRENULATE	CRETINISES	CRICKETINGS	CRINITE	CRITICS
CREODONT	CRETINISING	CRICKETS	CRINITES	CRITIQUE
CREODONTS	CRETINISM	CRICKEY	CRINKLE	CRITIQUED
CREOLE	CRETINISMS	CRICKING	CRINKLED	CRITIQUES
CREOLES	CRETINIZE	CRICKS	CRINKLES	CRITIQUING
CREOLIAN	CRETINIZED	CRICKY	CRINKLIER	CRITS
CREOLIANS	CRETINIZES	CRICOID	CRINKLIES	CRITTER
CREOLIST	CRETINIZING	CRICOIDS	CRINKLIEST	CRITTERS
CREOLISTS	CRETINOID	CRIED	CRINKLING	CRITTUR
CREOSOL	CRETINOIDS	CRIER	CRINKLY	CRITTURS
CREOSOLS	CRETINOUS	CRIERS	CRINOID	CRIVENS
CREOSOTE	CRETINS	CRIES	CRINOIDAL	CRIVVENS
CREOSOTED	CRETISM	CRIKEY	CRINOIDS	CROAK
CREOSOTES	CRETISMS	CRIM	CRINOLINE	CROAKED
CREOSOTING	CRETONNE	CRIME	CRINOLINES	CROAKER
CREPANCE	CRETONNES	CRIMED	CRINOSE	CROAKERS
CREPANCES	CREUTZER	CRIMEFUL	CRINUM	CROAKIER
CREPE	CREUTZERS	CRIMELESS	CRINUMS	CROAKIEST
CREPERIE	CREVASSE	CRIMEN	CRIOLLO	CROAKILY
CREPERIES	CREVASSED	CRIMES	CRIOLLOS	CROAKING
CREPES	CREVASSES	CRIMINA	CRIPES	CROAKINGS
CREPEY	CREVASSING	CRIMINAL	CRIPPLE	CROAKS
CREPIER	CREVETTE	CRIMINALS	CRIPPLED	CROAKY
CREPIEST	CREVETTES	CRIMINATE	CRIPPLES	CROC
CREPINESS	CREVICE	CRIMINATED	CRIPPLING	CROCEATE
CREPINESSES	CREVICES	CRIMINATES	CRIPPLINGS	CROCEIN
CREPITANT	CREW	CRIMINATING	CRISE	CROCEINS
CREPITATE	CREWE	CRIMINE	CRISES	CROCEOUS
CREPITATED	CREWED	CRIMING	CRISIS	CROCHE
CREPITATES	CREWEL	CRIMINI	CRISP	CROCHES
CREPITATING	CREWELIST	CRIMINOUS	CRISPATE	CROCHET
CREPITUS	CREWELISTS	CRIMMER	CRISPED	CROCHETED
CREPITUSES	CREWELLED	CRIMMERS	CRISPER	CROCHETING
CREPOLINE	CREWELLING	CRIMP	CRISPERS	CROCHETINGS
CREPOLINES	CREWELS	CRIMPED	CRISPEST	CROCHETS
CREPON	CREWES	CRIMPER	CRISPIER	CROCK
CREPONS	CREWING	CRIMPERS	CRISPIEST	CROCKED
CREPT	CREWS	CRIMPIER	CRISPIN	CROCKERIES
CREPUSCLE	CRIANT	CRIMPIEST	CRISPING	CROCKERY
CREPUSCLES	CRIB	CRIMPING	CRISPINS	CROCKET
CREPY	CRIBBAGE	CRIMPLE	CRISPLY	CROCKETS
CRESCENDO	CRIBBAGES	CRIMPLED	CRISPNESS	CROCKING
CRESCENDOED	CRIBBED	CRIMPLES	CRISPNESSES	CROCKS

The Chambers Dictionary is the authority for many longer words; see *OSW* Introduction, page xii.

CROCODILE
CROCODILES
CROCOITE
CROCOITES
CROCOSMIA
CROCOSMIAS
CROCS
CROCUS
CROCUSES
CROFT
CROFTER
CROFTERS
CROFTING
CROFTINGS
CROFTS
CROISSANT
CROISSANTS
CROMACK
CROMACKS
CROMB
CROMBED
CROMBIE
CROMBIES
CROMBING
CROMBS
CROME
CROMED
CROMES
CROMING
CROMLECH
CROMLECHS
CROMORNA
CROMORNAS
CROMORNE
CROMORNES
CRONE
CRONES
CRONET
CRONETS
CRONIES
CRONK
CRONKER
CRONKEST
CRONY
CRONYISM
CRONYISMS
CROODLE
CROODLED
CROODLES
CROODLING
CROOK
CROOKBACK
CROOKBACKS
CROOKED
CROOKEDER
CROOKEDEST
CROOKEDLY
CROOKER
CROOKEST
CROOKING
CROOKS
CROON
CROONED
CROONER
CROONERS
CROONING
CROONINGS

CROONS
CROOVE
CROOVES
CROP
CROPBOUND
CROPFUL
CROPFULL
CROPFULS
CROPLAND
CROPLANDS
CROPPED
CROPPER
CROPPERS
CROPPIES
CROPPING
CROPPINGS
CROPPY
CROPS
CROQUANTE
CROQUANTES
CROQUET
CROQUETED
CROQUETING
CROQUETS
CROQUETTE
CROQUETTES
CROQUIS
CRORE
CRORES
CROSIER
CROSIERED
CROSIERS
CROSS
CROSSBAND
CROSSBANDS
CROSSBAR
CROSSBARS
CROSSBEAM
CROSSBEAMS
CROSSBILL
CROSSBILLS
CROSSBIT
CROSSBITE
CROSSBITES
CROSSBITING
CROSSBITTEN
CROSSBOW
CROSSBOWS
CROSSBRED
CROSSBUCK
CROSSBUCKS
CROSSCUT
CROSSCUTS
CROSSCUTTING
CROSSCUTTINGS
CROSSE
CROSSED
CROSSER
CROSSES
CROSSEST
CROSSETTE
CROSSETTES
CROSSFALL
CROSSFALLS
CROSSFIRE
CROSSFIRES
CROSSFISH

CROSSFISHES
CROSSHEAD
CROSSHEADS
CROSSING
CROSSINGS
CROSSISH
CROSSJACK
CROSSJACKS
CROSSLET
CROSSLETS
CROSSLY
CROSSNESS
CROSSNESSES
CROSSOVER
CROSSOVERS
CROSSROAD
CROSSROADS
CROSSTIE
CROSSTIES
CROSSTOWN
CROSSTREE
CROSSTREES
CROSSWALK
CROSSWALKS
CROSSWAY
CROSSWAYS
CROSSWIND
CROSSWINDS
CROSSWISE
CROSSWORD
CROSSWORDS
CROTAL
CROTALA
CROTALINE
CROTALISM
CROTALISMS
CROTALS
CROTALUM
CROTCH
CROTCHED
CROTCHES
CROTCHET
CROTCHETS
CROTCHETY
CROTON
CROTONS
CROTTLE
CROTTLES
CROUCH
CROUCHED
CROUCHES
CROUCHING
CROUP
CROUPADE
CROUPADES
CROUPE
CROUPED
CROUPER
CROUPERS
CROUPES
CROUPIER
CROUPIERS
CROUPIEST
CROUPING
CROUPON
CROUPONS
CROUPOUS

CROUPS
CROUPY
CROUSE
CROUSELY
CROUSTADE
CROUSTADES
CROUT
CROUTE
CROUTES
CROUTON
CROUTONS
CROUTS
CROW
CROWBAR
CROWBARS
CROWBERRIES
CROWBERRY
CROWD
CROWDED
CROWDER
CROWDERS
CROWDIE
CROWDIES
CROWDING
CROWDS
CROWED
CROWFOOT
CROWFOOTS
CROWING
CROWN
CROWNED
CROWNER
CROWNERS
CROWNET
CROWNETS
CROWNING
CROWNINGS
CROWNLESS
CROWNLET
CROWNLETS
CROWNS
CROWNWORK
CROWNWORKS
CROWS
CROZE
CROZES
CROZIER
CROZIERS
CRU
CRUBEEN
CRUBEENS
CRUCES
CRUCIAL
CRUCIAN
CRUCIANS
CRUCIATE
CRUCIBLE
CRUCIBLES
CRUCIFER
CRUCIFERS
CRUCIFIED
CRUCIFIER
CRUCIFIERS
CRUCIFIES
CRUCIFIX
CRUCIFIXES
CRUCIFORM

CRUCIFY
CRUCIFYING
CRUCK
CRUCKS
CRUD
CRUDDED
CRUDDIER
CRUDDIEST
CRUDDING
CRUDDLE
CRUDDLED
CRUDDLES
CRUDDLING
CRUDDY
CRUDE
CRUDELY
CRUDENESS
CRUDENESSES
CRUDER
CRUDES
CRUDEST
CRUDITES
CRUDITIES
CRUDITY
CRUDS
CRUEL
CRUELLER
CRUELLEST
CRUELLS
CRUELLY
CRUELNESS
CRUELNESSES
CRUELS
CRUELTIES
CRUELTY
CRUET
CRUETS
CRUISE
CRUISED
CRUISER
CRUISERS
CRUISES
CRUISEWAY
CRUISEWAYS
CRUISIE
CRUISIES
CRUISING
CRUIVE
CRUIVES
CRULLER
CRULLERS
CRUMB
CRUMBED
CRUMBIER
CRUMBIEST
CRUMBING
CRUMBLE
CRUMBLED
CRUMBLES
CRUMBLIER
CRUMBLIES
CRUMBLIEST
CRUMBLING
CRUMBLY
CRUMBS
CRUMBY
CRUMEN

CRUMENAL	CRUSIE	CRYPTON	CUCKOO	CUISINES
CRUMENALS	CRUSIES	CRYPTONS	CUCKOOS	CUISINIER
CRUMENS	CRUST	CRYPTONYM	CUCULLATE	CUISINIERS
CRUMHORN	CRUSTA	CRYPTONYMS	CUCUMBER	CUISSE
CRUMHORNS	CRUSTAE	CRYPTOS	CUCUMBERS	CUISSER
CRUMMACK	CRUSTAL	CRYPTS	CUCURBIT	CUISSERS
CRUMMACKS	CRUSTATE	CRYSTAL	CUCURBITS	CUISSES
CRUMMIER	CRUSTATED	CRYSTALS	CUD	CUIT
CRUMMIES	CRUSTED	CSARDAS	CUDBEAR	CUITER
CRUMMIEST	CRUSTIER	CSARDASES	CUDBEARS	CUITERED
CRUMMOCK	CRUSTIEST	CTENE	CUDDEEHIH	CUITERING
CRUMMOCKS	CRUSTILY	CTENES	CUDDEEHIHS	CUITERS
CRUMMY	CRUSTING	CTENIFORM	CUDDEN	CUITIKIN
CRUMP	CRUSTLESS	CTENOID	CUDDENS	CUITIKINS
CRUMPED	CRUSTS	CUADRILLA	CUDDIE	CUITS
CRUMPER	CRUSTY	CUADRILLAS	CUDDIES	CUITTLE
CRUMPEST	CRUSY	CUB	CUDDIN	CUITTLED
CRUMPET	CRUTCH	CUBAGE	CUDDINS	CUITTLES
CRUMPETS	CRUTCHED	CUBAGES	CUDDLE	CUITTLING
CRUMPIER	CRUTCHES	CUBATURE	CUDDLED	CULCH
CRUMPIEST	CRUTCHING	CUBATURES	CUDDLES	CULCHES
CRUMPING	CRUVE	CUBBED	CUDDLIER	CULCHIE
CRUMPLE	CRUVES	CUBBIES	CUDDLIEST	CULCHIES
CRUMPLED	CRUX	CUBBING	CUDDLING	CULET
CRUMPLES	CRUXES	CUBBINGS	CUDDLY	CULETS
CRUMPLING	CRUZADO	CUBBISH	CUDDY	CULEX
CRUMPLINGS	CRUZADOES	CUBBY	CUDGEL	CULICES
CRUMPS	CRUZADOS	CUBE	CUDGELLED	CULICID
CRUMPY	CRUZEIRO	CUBEB	CUDGELLER	CULICIDS
CRUNCH	CRUZEIROS	CUBEBS	CUDGELLERS	CULICINE
CRUNCHED	CRWTH	CUBED	CUDGELLING	CULICINES
CRUNCHES	CRWTHS	CUBES	CUDGELLINGS	CULINARY
CRUNCHIER	CRY	CUBHOOD	CUDGELS	CULL
CRUNCHIEST	CRYBABIES	CUBHOODS	CUDS	CULLED
CRUNCHING	CRYBABY	CUBIC	CUDWEED	CULLENDER
CRUNCHY	CRYING	CUBICA	CUDWEEDS	CULLENDERS
CRUNKLE	CRYINGS	CUBICAL	CUE	CULLER
CRUNKLED	CRYOGEN	CUBICALLY	CUED	CULLERS
CRUNKLES	CRYOGENIC	CUBICAS	CUEING	CULLET
CRUNKLING	CRYOGENICS	CUBICLE	CUEIST	CULLETS
CRUOR	CRYOGENIES	CUBICLES	CUEISTS	CULLIED
CRUORES	CRYOGENS	CUBICS	CUES	CULLIES
CRUPPER	CRYOGENY	CUBIFORM	CUESTA	CULLING
CRUPPERS	CRYOLITE	CUBING	CUESTAS	CULLINGS
CRURAL	CRYOLITES	CUBISM	CUFF	CULLION
CRUS	CRYOMETER	CUBISMS	CUFFED	CULLIONLY
CRUSADE	CRYOMETERS	CUBIST	CUFFIN	CULLIONS
CRUSADED	CRYONIC	CUBISTIC	CUFFING	CULLIS
CRUSADER	CRYONICS	CUBISTS	CUFFINS	CULLISES
CRUSADERS	CRYOPROBE	CUBIT	CUFFLE	CULLS
CRUSADES	CRYOPROBES	CUBITAL	CUFFLED	CULLY
CRUSADING	CRYOSCOPE	CUBITS	CUFFLES	CULLYING
CRUSADO	CRYOSCOPES	CUBITUS	CUFFLING	CULLYISM
CRUSADOS	CRYOSCOPIES	CUBITUSES	CUFFO	CULLYISMS
CRUSE	CRYOSCOPY	CUBLESS	CUFFS	CULM
CRUSES	CRYOSTAT	CUBOID	CUFFUFFLE	CULMED
CRUSET	CRYOSTATS	CUBOIDAL	CUFFUFFLES	CULMEN
CRUSETS	CRYOTRON	CUBOIDS	CUIF	CULMENS
CRUSH	CRYOTRONS	CUBS	CUIFS	CULMINANT
CRUSHABLE	CRYPT	CUCKOLD	CUING	CULMINATE
CRUSHED	CRYPTADIA	CUCKOLDED	CUIRASS	CULMINATED
CRUSHER	CRYPTAL	CUCKOLDING	CUIRASSED	CULMINATES
CRUSHERS	CRYPTIC	CUCKOLDOM	CUIRASSES	CULMINATING
CRUSHES	CRYPTICAL	CUCKOLDOMS	CUIRASSING	CULMING
CRUSHING	CRYPTO	CUCKOLDRIES	CUISH	CULMS
CRUSIAN	CRYPTOGAM	CUCKOLDRY	CUISHES	CULOTTES
CRUSIANS	CRYPTOGAMS	CUCKOLDS	CUISINE	CULPABLE

The Chambers Dictionary is the authority for many longer words; see *OSW* Introduction, page xii.

CULPABLY	CUMULATED	CUPREOUS	CURDED	CURLPAPERS
CULPATORY	CUMULATES	CUPRIC	CURDIER	CURLS
CULPRIT	CUMULATING	CUPRITE	CURDIEST	CURLY
CULPRITS	CUMULI	CUPRITES	CURDINESS	CURN
CULT	CUMULOSE	CUPROUS	CURDINESSES	CURNEY
CULTCH	CUMULUS	CUPS	CURDING	CURNIER
CULTCHES	CUNABULA	CUPULAR	CURDLE	CURNIEST
CULTER	CUNCTATOR	CUPULATE	CURDLED	CURNS
CULTERS	CUNCTATORS	CUPULE	CURDLES	CURNY
CULTIC	CUNDIES	CUPULES	CURDLING	CURPEL
CULTIGEN	CUNDY	CUR	CURDS	CURPELS
CULTIGENS	CUNEAL	CURABLE	CURDY	CURR
CULTISH	CUNEATE	CURACAO	CURE	CURRACH
CULTISM	CUNEATIC	CURACAOS	CURED	CURRACHS
CULTISMS	CUNEIFORM	CURACIES	CURELESS	CURRAGH
CULTIST	CUNEIFORMS	CURACOA	CURER	CURRAGHS
CULTISTS	CUNETTE	CURACOAS	CURERS	CURRAJONG
CULTIVAR	CUNETTES	CURACY	CURES	CURRAJONGS
CULTIVARS	CUNJEVOI	CURARA	CURETTAGE	CURRANT
CULTIVATE	CUNJEVOIS	CURARAS	CURETTAGES	CURRANTS
CULTIVATED	CUNNER	CURARE	CURETTE	CURRANTY
CULTIVATES	CUNNERS	CURARES	CURETTED	CURRAWONG
CULTIVATING	CUNNING	CURARI	CURETTES	CURRAWONGS
CULTRATE	CUNNINGLY	CURARINE	CURETTING	CURRED
CULTRATED	CUNNINGS	CURARINES	CURFEW	CURRENCIES
CULTS	CUNT	CURARIS	CURFEWS	CURRENCY
CULTURAL	CUNTS	CURARISE	CURFUFFLE	CURRENT
CULTURE	CUP	CURARISED	CURFUFFLED	CURRENTLY
CULTURED	CUPBEARER	CURARISES	CURFUFFLES	CURRENTS
CULTURES	CUPBEARERS	CURARISING	CURFUFFLING	CURRICLE
CULTURING	CUPBOARD	CURARIZE	CURIA	CURRICLES
CULTURIST	CUPBOARDED	CURARIZED	CURIAE	CURRICULA
CULTURISTS	CUPBOARDING	CURARIZES	CURIALISM	CURRIE
CULTUS	CUPBOARDS	CURARIZING	CURIALISMS	CURRIED
CULTUSES	CUPCAKE	CURASSOW	CURIALIST	CURRIER
CULVER	CUPCAKES	CURASSOWS	CURIALISTS	CURRIERS
CULVERIN	CUPEL	CURAT	CURIAS	CURRIES
CULVERINS	CUPELED	CURATE	CURIE	CURRING
CULVERS	CUPELING	CURATED	CURIES	CURRISH
CULVERT	CUPELLED	CURATES	CURIET	CURRISHLY
CULVERTS	CUPELLING	CURATING	CURIETS	CURRS
CUM	CUPELS	CURATIVE	CURING	CURRY
CUMARIN	CUPFUL	CURATOR	CURIO	CURRYCOMB
CUMARINS	CUPFULS	CURATORS	CURIOS	CURRYCOMBS
CUMBENT	CUPGALL	CURATORY	CURIOSA	CURRYING
CUMBER	CUPGALLS	CURATRIX	CURIOSITIES	CURRYINGS
CUMBERED	CUPHEAD	CURATRIXES	CURIOSITY	CURS
CUMBERER	CUPHEADS	CURATS	CURIOUS	CURSAL
CUMBERERS	CUPID	CURB	CURIOUSER	CURSE
CUMBERING	CUPIDITIES	CURBABLE	CURIOUSLY	CURSED
CUMBERS	CUPIDITY	CURBED	CURIUM	CURSEDLY
CUMBRANCE	CUPIDS	CURBING	CURIUMS	CURSENARY
CUMBRANCES	CUPMAN	CURBLESS	CURL	CURSER
CUMBROUS	CUPMEN	CURBS	CURLED	CURSERS
CUMEC	CUPOLA	CURBSTONE	CURLER	CURSES
CUMECS	CUPOLAED	CURBSTONES	CURLERS	CURSI
CUMIN	CUPOLAING	CURCH	CURLEW	CURSING
CUMINS	CUPOLAR	CURCHES	CURLEWS	CURSINGS
CUMMER	CUPOLAS	CURCULIO	CURLICUE	CURSITOR
CUMMERS	CUPOLATED	CURCULIOS	CURLICUES	CURSITORS
CUMMIN	CUPPA	CURCUMA	CURLIER	CURSITORY
CUMMINS	CUPPAS	CURCUMAS	CURLIEST	CURSIVE
CUMQUAT	CUPPED	CURCUMIN	CURLINESS	CURSIVELY
CUMQUATS	CUPPER	CURCUMINE	CURLINESSES	CURSOR
CUMSHAW	CUPPERS	CURCUMINES	CURLING	CURSORARY
CUMSHAWS	CUPPING	CURCUMINS	CURLINGS	CURSORIAL
CUMULATE	CUPPINGS	CURD	CURLPAPER	CURSORILY

The Chambers Dictionary is the authority for many longer words; see *OSW* Introduction, page xii.

CURSORS	CUSCUS	CUSTOMIZING	CUTTIER	CYBORG
CURSORY	CUSCUSES	CUSTOMS	CUTTIES	CYBORGS
CURST	CUSEC	CUSTOS	CUTTIEST	CYBRID
CURSTNESS	CUSECS	CUSTREL	CUTTING	CYBRIDS
CURSTNESSES	CUSH	CUSTRELS	CUTTINGS	CYCAD
CURSUS	CUSHAT	CUSTUMARIES	CUTTLE	CYCADS
CURT	CUSHATS	CUSTUMARY	CUTTLES	CYCLAMATE
CURTAIL	CUSHAW	CUT	CUTTO	CYCLAMATES
CURTAILED	CUSHAWS	CUTANEOUS	CUTTOE	CYCLAMEN
CURTAILING	CUSHES	CUTAWAY	CUTTOES	CYCLAMENS
CURTAILS	CUSHIER	CUTAWAYS	CUTTY	CYCLE
CURTAIN	CUSHIEST	CUTBACK	CUTWORK	CYCLED
CURTAINED	CUSHION	CUTBACKS	CUTWORKS	CYCLER
CURTAINING	CUSHIONED	CUTCH	CUTWORM	CYCLERS
CURTAINS	CUSHIONET	CUTCHA	CUTWORMS	CYCLES
CURTAL	CUSHIONETS	CUTCHERIES	CUVEE	CYCLEWAY
CURTALAXE	CUSHIONING	CUTCHERRIES	CUVEES	CYCLEWAYS
CURTALAXES	CUSHIONS	CUTCHERRY	CUVETTE	CYCLIC
CURTALS	CUSHIONY	CUTCHERY	CUVETTES	CYCLICAL
CURTANA	CUSHY	CUTCHES	CUZ	CYCLICISM
CURTANAS	CUSK	CUTE	CUZZES	CYCLICISMS
CURTATE	CUSKS	CUTELY	CWM	CYCLICITIES
CURTATION	CUSP	CUTENESS	CWMS	CYCLICITY
CURTATIONS	CUSPATE	CUTENESSES	CYAN	CYCLING
CURTER	CUSPED	CUTER	CYANAMIDE	CYCLINGS
CURTESIES	CUSPID	CUTES	CYANAMIDES	CYCLIST
CURTEST	CUSPIDAL	CUTESIER	CYANATE	CYCLISTS
CURTESY	CUSPIDATE	CUTESIEST	CYANATES	CYCLIZINE
CURTILAGE	CUSPIDOR	CUTEST	CYANIC	CYCLIZINES
CURTILAGES	CUSPIDORE	CUTESY	CYANIDE	CYCLO
CURTLY	CUSPIDORES	CUTEY	CYANIDED	CYCLOID
CURTNESS	CUSPIDORS	CUTEYS	CYANIDES	CYCLOIDAL
CURTNESSES	CUSPIDS	CUTGLASS	CYANIDING	CYCLOIDS
CURTSEY	CUSPS	CUTICLE	CYANIDINGS	CYCLOLITH
CURTSEYED	CUSS	CUTICLES	CYANIN	CYCLOLITHS
CURTSEYING	CUSSED	CUTICULAR	CYANINE	CYCLONE
CURTSEYS	CUSSER	CUTIE	CYANINES	CYCLONES
CURTSIED	CUSSERS	CUTIES	CYANINS	CYCLONIC
CURTSIES	CUSSES	CUTIKIN	CYANISE	CYCLONITE
CURTSY	CUSSING	CUTIKINS	CYANISED	CYCLONITES
CURTSYING	CUSSWORD	CUTIN	CYANISES	CYCLOPEAN
CURULE	CUSSWORDS	CUTINISE	CYANISING	CYCLOPES
CURVATE	CUSTARD	CUTINISED	CYANITE	CYCLOPIAN
CURVATED	CUSTARDS	CUTINISES	CYANITES	CYCLOPIC
CURVATION	CUSTOCK	CUTINISING	CYANIZE	CYCLOPS
CURVATIONS	CUSTOCKS	CUTINIZE	CYANIZED	CYCLORAMA
CURVATIVE	CUSTODES	CUTINIZED	CYANIZES	CYCLORAMAS
CURVATURE	CUSTODIAL	CUTINIZES	CYANIZING	CYCLOS
CURVATURES	CUSTODIAN	CUTINIZING	CYANOGEN	CYCLOSES
CURVE	CUSTODIANS	CUTINS	CYANOGENS	CYCLOSIS
CURVED	CUSTODIER	CUTIS	CYANOSED	CYCLOTRON
CURVES	CUSTODIERS	CUTISES	CYANOSES	CYCLOTRONS
CURVESOME	CUSTODIES	CUTLASS	CYANOSIS	CYCLUS
CURVET	CUSTODY	CUTLASSES	CYANOTIC	CYCLUSES
CURVETED	CUSTOM	CUTLER	CYANOTYPE	CYDER
CURVETING	CUSTOMARIES	CUTLERIES	CYANOTYPES	CYDERS
CURVETS	CUSTOMARY	CUTLERS	CYANS	CYESES
CURVETTED	CUSTOMED	CUTLERY	CYANURET	CYESIS
CURVETTING	CUSTOMER	CUTLET	CYANURETS	CYGNET
CURVIER	CUSTOMERS	CUTLETS	CYATHI	CYGNETS
CURVIEST	CUSTOMISE	CUTLINE	CYATHUS	CYLICES
CURVIFORM	CUSTOMISED	CUTLINES	CYBERNATE	CYLINDER
CURVING	CUSTOMISES	CUTPURSE	CYBERNATED	CYLINDERS
CURVITAL	CUSTOMISING	CUTPURSES	CYBERNATES	CYLINDRIC
CURVITIES	CUSTOMIZE	CUTS	CYBERNATING	CYLIX
CURVITY	CUSTOMIZED	CUTTER	CYBERPUNK	CYMA
CURVY	CUSTOMIZES	CUTTERS	CYBERPUNKS	CYMAGRAPH

The Chambers Dictionary is the authority for many longer words; see *OSW* Introduction, page xii.

CYMAGRAPHS	CYNANCHES	CYPRUSES	CYTASE	CYTOSINE
CYMAR	CYNEGETIC	CYPSELA	CYTASES	CYTOSINES
CYMARS	CYNIC	CYPSELAE	CYTISI	CYTOSOME
CYMAS	CYNICAL	CYST	CYTISINE	CYTOSOMES
CYMATIA	CYNICALLY	CYSTEINE	CYTISINES	CYTOTOXIC
CYMATIUM	CYNICISM	CYSTEINES	CYTISUS	CYTOTOXIN
CYMBAL	CYNICISMS	CYSTIC	CYTODE	CYTOTOXINS
CYMBALIST	CYNICS	CYSTID	CYTODES	CZAPKA
CYMBALISTS	CYNOSURE	CYSTIDEAN	CYTOID	CZAPKAS
CYMBALO	CYNOSURES	CYSTIDEANS	CYTOKINE	CZAR
CYMBALOES	CYPHER	CYSTIDS	CYTOKINES	CZARDAS
CYMBALOS	CYPHERED	CYSTIFORM	CYTOKININ	CZARDASES
CYMBALS	CYPHERING	CYSTINE	CYTOKININS	CZARDOM
CYMBIDIA	CYPHERS	CYSTINES	CYTOLOGIES	CZARDOMS
CYMBIDIUM	CYPRESS	CYSTITIS	CYTOLOGY	CZAREVICH
CYMBIDIUMS	CYPRESSES	CYSTITISES	CYTOLYSES	CZAREVICHES
CYMBIFORM	CYPRIAN	CYSTOCARP	CYTOLYSIS	CZAREVNA
CYME	CYPRIANS	CYSTOCARPS	CYTOMETER	CZAREVNAS
CYMES	CYPRID	CYSTOCELE	CYTOMETERS	CZARINA
CYMOGRAPH	CYPRIDES	CYSTOCELES	CYTOMETRIES	CZARINAS
CYMOGRAPHS	CYPRIDS	CYSTOID	CYTOMETRY	CZARISM
CYMOID	CYPRINE	CYSTOIDS	CYTON	CZARISMS
CYMOPHANE	CYPRINID	CYSTOLITH	CYTONS	CZARIST
CYMOPHANES	CYPRINIDS	CYSTOLITHS	CYTOPENIA	CZARISTS
CYMOSE	CYPRINOID	CYSTOTOMIES	CYTOPENIAS	CZARITSA
CYMOUS	CYPRIS	CYSTOTOMY	CYTOPLASM	CZARITSAS
CYNANCHE	CYPRUS	CYSTS	CYTOPLASMS	CZARS

The Chambers Dictionary is the authority for many longer words; see *OSW* Introduction, page xii.

D

DA	DADOS	DAH	DAKERED	DAMASKINED
DAB	DADS	DAHABEEAH	DAKERING	DAMASKING
DABBED	DAE	DAHABEEAHS	DAKERS	DAMASKINING
DABBER	DAEDAL	DAHABIEH	DAKOIT	DAMASKINS
DABBERS	DAEDALIAN	DAHABIEHS	DAKOITI	DAMASKS
DABBING	DAEDALIC	DAHABIYAH	DAKOITIS	DAMASQUIN
DABBITIES	DAEING	DAHABIYAHS	DAKOITS	DAMASQUINED
DABBITY	DAEMON	DAHABIYEH	DAKS	DAMASQUINING
DABBLE	DAEMONIC	DAHABIYEHS	DAL	DAMASQUINS
DABBLED	DAEMONS	DAHL	DALE	DAMASSIN
DABBLER	DAES	DAHLIA	DALES	DAMASSINS
DABBLERS	DAFF	DAHLIAS	DALESMAN	DAMBOARD
DABBLES	DAFFED	DAHLS	DALESMEN	DAMBOARDS
DABBLING	DAFFIER	DAHS	DALI	DAMBROD
DABBLINGS	DAFFIES	DAIDLE	DALIS	DAMBRODS
DABCHICK	DAFFIEST	DAIDLED	DALLE	DAME
DABCHICKS	DAFFING	DAIDLES	DALLES	DAMES
DABS	DAFFINGS	DAIDLING	DALLIANCE	DAMFOOL
DABSTER	DAFFODIL	DAIKER	DALLIANCES	DAMMAR
DABSTERS	DAFFODILS	DAIKERED	DALLIED	DAMMARS
DACE	DAFFS	DAIKERING	DALLIER	DAMME
DACES	DAFFY	DAIKERS	DALLIERS	DAMMED
DACHA	DAFT	DAIKON	DALLIES	DAMMER
DACHAS	DAFTAR	DAIKONS	DALLOP	DAMMERS
DACHSHUND	DAFTARS	DAILIES	DALLOPS	DAMMING
DACHSHUNDS	DAFTER	DAILY	DALLY	DAMMIT
DACITE	DAFTEST	DAIMEN	DALLYING	DAMN
DACITES	DAFTIE	DAIMIO	DALMAHOY	DAMNABLE
DACKER	DAFTIES	DAIMIOS	DALMAHOYS	DAMNABLY
DACKERED	DAFTLY	DAIMON	DALMATIC	DAMNATION
DACKERING	DAFTNESS	DAIMONIC	DALMATICS	DAMNATIONS
DACKERS	DAFTNESSES	DAIMONS	DALS	DAMNATORY
DACOIT	DAG	DAINE	DALT	DAMNED
DACOITAGE	DAGABA	DAINED	DALTON	DAMNEDER
DACOITAGES	DAGABAS	DAINES	DALTONISM	DAMNEDEST
DACOITIES	DAGGA	DAINING	DALTONISMS	DAMNIFIED
DACOITS	DAGGAS	DAINT	DALTONS	DAMNIFIES
DACOITY	DAGGED	DAINTIER	DALTS	DAMNIFY
DACTYL	DAGGER	DAINTIES	DAM	DAMNIFYING
DACTYLAR	DAGGERS	DAINTIEST	DAMAGE	DAMNING
DACTYLIC	DAGGIER	DAINTILY	DAMAGED	DAMNS
DACTYLIST	DAGGIEST	DAINTY	DAMAGES	DAMOISEL
DACTYLISTS	DAGGING	DAIQUIRI	DAMAGING	DAMOISELS
DACTYLS	DAGGINGS	DAIQUIRIS	DAMAN	DAMOSEL
DAD	DAGGLE	DAIRIES	DAMANS	DAMOSELS
DADDED	DAGGLED	DAIRY	DAMAR	DAMOZEL
DADDIES	DAGGLES	DAIRYING	DAMARS	DAMOZELS
DADDING	DAGGLING	DAIRYINGS	DAMASCENE	DAMP
DADDLE	DAGGY	DAIRYMAID	DAMASCENED	DAMPED
DADDLED	DAGLOCK	DAIRYMAIDS	DAMASCENES	DAMPEN
DADDLES	DAGLOCKS	DAIRYMAN	DAMASCENING	DAMPENED
DADDLING	DAGO	DAIRYMEN	DAMASCENINGS	DAMPENING
DADDOCK	DAGOBA	DAIS	DAMASK	DAMPENS
DADDOCKS	DAGOBAS	DAISES	DAMASKED	DAMPER
DADDY	DAGOES	DAISIED	DAMASKEEN	DAMPERS
DADO	DAGOS	DAISIES	DAMASKEENED	DAMPEST
DADOED	DAGS	DAISY	DAMASKEENING	DAMPIER
DADOES	DAGWOOD	DAK	DAMASKEENS	DAMPIEST
DADOING	DAGWOODS	DAKER	DAMASKIN	DAMPING

The Chambers Dictionary is the authority for many longer words; see *OSW* Introduction, page xii.

DAMPINGS	DANELAGHS	DARAF	DARRAIGNES	DATABASE
DAMPISH	DANELAW	DARAFS	DARRAIGNING	DATABASES
DAMPLY	DANELAWS	DARBIES	DARRAIGNS	DATABLE
DAMPNESS	DANG	DARCIES	DARRAIN	DATABUS
DAMPNESSES	DANGED	DARCY	DARRAINE	DATABUSES
DAMPS	DANGER	DARCYS	DARRAINED	DATAL
DAMPY	DANGERED	DARE	DARRAINES	DATALLER
DAMS	DANGERING	DARED	DARRAINING	DATALLERS
DAMSEL	DANGEROUS	DAREFUL	DARRAINS	DATALS
DAMSELFLIES	DANGERS	DARES	DARRAYN	DATARIA
DAMSELFLY	DANGING	DARG	DARRAYNED	DATARIAS
DAMSELS	DANGLE	DARGA	DARRAYNING	DATARIES
DAMSON	DANGLED	DARGAS	DARRAYNS	DATARY
DAMSONS	DANGLER	DARGLE	DARRE	DATE
DAN	DANGLERS	DARGLES	DARRED	DATEABLE
DANCE	DANGLES	DARGS	DARRES	DATED
DANCEABLE	DANGLIER	DARI	DARRING	DATELESS
DANCED	DANGLIEST	DARIC	DARSHAN	DATER
DANCER	DANGLING	DARICS	DARSHANS	DATERS
DANCERS	DANGLINGS	DARING	DART	DATES
DANCES	DANGLY	DARINGLY	DARTBOARD	DATING
DANCETTE	DANGS	DARINGS	DARTBOARDS	DATINGS
DANCETTEE	DANIO	DARIOLE	DARTED	DATIVAL
DANCETTES	DANIOS	DARIOLES	DARTER	DATIVE
DANCETTY	DANK	DARIS	DARTERS	DATIVES
DANCING	DANKER	DARK	DARTING	DATOLITE
DANCINGS	DANKEST	DARKEN –	DARTINGLY	DATOLITES
DANDELION	DANKISH	DARKENED	DARTLE	DATUM
DANDELIONS	DANKNESS	DARKENING	DARTLED	DATURA
DANDER	DANKNESSES	DARKENS	DARTLES	DATURAS
DANDERED	DANKS	DARKER	DARTLING	DATURINE
DANDERING	DANNEBROG	DARKEST	DARTRE	DATURINES
DANDERS	DANNEBROGS	DARKEY	DARTRES	DAUB
DANDIACAL	DANS	DARKEYS	DARTROUS	DAUBE
DANDIER	DANSEUR	DARKIE	DARTS	DAUBED
DANDIES	DANSEURS	DARKIES	DARZI	DAUBER
DANDIEST	DANSEUSE	DARKISH	DARZIS	DAUBERIES
DANDIFIED	DANSEUSES	DARKLE	DAS	DAUBERS
DANDIFIES	DANT	DARKLED	DASH	DAUBERY
DANDIFY	DANTED	DARKLES	DASHBOARD	DAUBES
DANDIFYING	DANTING	DARKLING	DASHBOARDS	DAUBIER
DANDILY	DANTON	DARKLINGS	DASHED	DAUBIEST
DANDIPRAT	DANTONED	DARKLY	DASHEEN	DAUBING
DANDIPRATS	DANTONING	DARKMANS	DASHEENS	DAUBINGS
DANDLE	DANTONS	DARKNESS	DASHEKI	DAUBS
DANDLED	DANTS	DARKNESSES	DASHEKIS	DAUBY
DANDLER	DAP	DARKROOM	DASHER	DAUD
DANDLERS	DAPHNE	DARKROOMS	DASHERS	DAUDED
DANDLES	DAPHNES	DARKS	DASHES	DAUDING
DANDLING	DAPHNID	DARKSOME	DASHIKI	DAUDS
DANDRIFF	DAPHNIDS	DARKY	DASHIKIS	DAUGHTER
DANDRIFFS	DAPPED	DARLING	DASHING	DAUGHTERS
DANDRUFF	DAPPER	DARLINGS	DASHINGLY	DAULT
DANDRUFFS	DAPPERER	DARN	DASSIE	DAULTS
DANDY	DAPPEREST	DARNED	DASSIES	DAUNDER
DANDYFUNK	DAPPERLY	DARNEDER	DASTARD	DAUNDERED
DANDYFUNKS	DAPPERS	DARNEDEST	DASTARDIES	DAUNDERING
DANDYISH	DAPPING	DARNEL	DASTARDLY	DAUNDERS
DANDYISM	DAPPLE	DARNELS	DASTARDS	DAUNER
DANDYISMS	DAPPLED	DARNER	DASTARDY	DAUNERED
DANDYPRAT	DAPPLES	DARNERS	DASYPOD	DAUNERING
DANDYPRATS	DAPPLING	DARNING	DASYPODS	DAUNERS
DANEGELD	DAPS	DARNINGS	DASYURE	DAUNT
DANEGELDS	DAPSONE	DARNS	DASYURES	DAUNTED
DANEGELT	DAPSONES	DARRAIGN	DATA	DAUNTER
DANEGELTS	DAQUIRI	DARRAIGNE	DATABANK	DAUNTERS
DANELAGH	DAQUIRIS	DARRAIGNED	DATABANKS	DAUNTING

The Chambers Dictionary is the authority for many longer words; see *OSW* Introduction, page xii.

DAUNTLESS	DAYBREAK	DEADLIEST	DEASILS	DEBAUCHEES
DAUNTON	DAYBREAKS	DEADLINE	DEASIUL	DEBAUCHER
DAUNTONED	DAYDREAM	DEADLINES	DEASIULS	DEBAUCHERS
DAUNTONING	DAYDREAMED	DEADLOCK	DEASOIL	DEBAUCHES
DAUNTONS	DAYDREAMING	DEADLOCKED	DEASOILS	DEBAUCHING
DAUNTS	DAYDREAMS	DEADLOCKING	DEATH	DEBBIER
DAUPHIN	DAYDREAMT	DEADLOCKS	DEATHFUL	DEBBIES
DAUPHINE	DAYGLO	DEADLY	DEATHIER	DEBBIEST
DAUPHINES	DAYLIGHT	DEADNESS	DEATHIEST	DEBBY
DAUPHINS	DAYLIGHTS	DEADNESSES	DEATHLESS	DEBEL
DAUR	DAYLONG	DEADPAN	DEATHLIER	DEBELLED
DAURED	DAYMARK	DEADPANS	DEATHLIEST	DEBELLING
DAURING	DAYMARKS	DEADS	DEATHLIKE	DEBELS
DAURS	DAYNT	DEADSTOCK	DEATHLY	DEBENTURE
DAUT	DAYS	DEADSTOCKS	DEATHS	DEBENTURES
DAUTED	DAYSMAN	DEAF	DEATHSMAN	DEBILE
DAUTIE	DAYSMEN	DEAFEN	DEATHSMEN	DEBILITIES
DAUTIES	DAYSPRING	DEAFENED	DEATHWARD	DEBILITY
DAUTING	DAYSPRINGS	DEAFENING	DEATHWARDS	DEBIT
DAUTS	DAYSTAR	DEAFENINGS	DEATHY	DEBITED
DAVEN	DAYSTARS	DEAFENS	DEAVE	DEBITING
DAVENED	DAYTALE	DEAFER	DEAVED	DEBITOR
DAVENING	DAYTALER	DEAFEST	DEAVES	DEBITORS
DAVENPORT	DAYTALERS	DEAFLY	DEAVING	DEBITS
DAVENPORTS	DAYTALES	DEAFNESS	DEAW	DEBONAIR
DAVENS	DAYTIME	DEAFNESSES	DEAWIE	DEBOSH
DAVIDIA	DAYTIMES	DEAL	DEAWS	DEBOSHED
DAVIDIAS	DAZE	DEALBATE	DEAWY	DEBOSHES
DAVIT	DAZED	DEALER	DEB	DEBOSHING
DAVITS	DAZEDLY	DEALERS	DEBACLE	DEBOSS
DAW	DAZER	DEALFISH	DEBACLES	DEBOSSED
DAWBRIES	DAZERS	DEALFISHES	DEBAG	DEBOSSES
DAWBRY	DAZES	DEALING	DEBAGGED	DEBOSSING
DAWCOCK	DAZING	DEALINGS	DEBAGGING	DEBOUCH
DAWCOCKS	DAZZLE	DEALS	DEBAGGINGS	DEBOUCHE
DAWD	DAZZLED	DEALT	DEBAGS	DEBOUCHED
DAWDED	DAZZLER	DEAN	DEBAR	DEBOUCHES
DAWDING	DAZZLERS	DEANER	DEBARK	DEBOUCHING
DAWDLE	DAZZLES	DEANERIES	DEBARKED	DEBRIDE
DAWDLED	DAZZLING	DEANERS	DEBARKING	DEBRIDED
DAWDLER	DAZZLINGS	DEANERY	DEBARKS	DEBRIDES
DAWDLERS	DEACON	DEANS	DEBARMENT	DEBRIDING
DAWDLES	DEACONESS	DEANSHIP	DEBARMENTS	DEBRIEF
DAWDLING	DEACONESSES	DEANSHIPS	DEBARRASS	DEBRIEFED
DAWDS	DEACONRIES	DEAR	DEBARRASSED	DEBRIEFING
DAWED	DEACONRY	DEARE	DEBARRASSES	DEBRIEFINGS
DAWING	DEACONS	DEARED	DEBARRASSING	DEBRIEFS
DAWISH	DEAD	DEARER	DEBARRED	DEBRIS
DAWK	DEADED	DEARES	DEBARRING	DEBRUISED
DAWKS	DEADEN	DEAREST	DEBARS	DEBS
DAWN	DEADENED	DEARIE	DEBASE	DEBT
DAWNED	DEADENER	DEARIES	DEBASED	DEBTED
DAWNER	DEADENERS	DEARING	DEBASER	DEBTEE
DAWNERED	DEADENING	DEARLING	DEBASERS	DEBTEES
DAWNERING	DEADENINGS	DEARLINGS	DEBASES	DEBTOR
DAWNERS	DEADENS	DEARLY	DEBASING	DEBTORS
DAWNING	DEADER	DEARN	DEBATABLE	DEBTS
DAWNINGS	DEADERS	DEARNESS	DEBATE	DEBUG
DAWNS	DEADEST	DEARNESSES	DEBATED	DEBUGGED
DAWS	DEADHEAD	DEARNFUL	DEBATEFUL	DEBUGGING
DAWT	DEADHEADED	DEARNLY	DEBATER	DEBUGS
DAWTED	DEADHEADING	DEARNS	DEBATERS	DEBUNK
DAWTIE	DEADHEADS	DEARS	DEBATES	DEBUNKED
DAWTIES	DEADHOUSE	DEARTH	DEBATING	DEBUNKING
DAWTING	DEADHOUSES	DEARTHS	DEBAUCH	DEBUNKS
DAWTS	DEADING	DEARY	DEBAUCHED	DEBUS
DAY	DEADLIER	DEASIL	DEBAUCHEE	DEBUSSED

The Chambers Dictionary is the authority for many longer words; see *OSW* Introduction, page xii.

DEBUSSES	DECARBING	DECIBELS	DECLAIMED	DECOLOURING
DEBUSSING	DECARBS	DECIDABLE	DECLAIMER	DECOLOURS
DEBUT	DECARE	DECIDE	DECLAIMERS	DECOMPLEX
DEBUTANT	DECARES	DECIDED	DECLAIMING	DECOMPOSE
DEBUTANTE	DECASTERE	DECIDEDLY	DECLAIMINGS	DECOMPOSED
DEBUTANTES	DECASTERES	DECIDER	DECLAIMS	DECOMPOSES
DEBUTANTS	DECASTICH	DECIDERS	DECLARANT	DECOMPOSING
DEBUTED	DECASTICHS	DECIDES	DECLARANTS	DECONGEST
DEBUTING	DECASTYLE	DECIDING	DECLARE	DECONGESTED
DEBUTS	DECASTYLES	DECIDUA	DECLARED	DECONGESTING
DECACHORD	DECATHLON	DECIDUAE	DECLARER	DECONGESTS
DECACHORDS	DECATHLONS	DECIDUAL	DECLARERS	DECONTROL
DECAD	DECAUDATE	DECIDUAS	DECLARES	DECONTROLLED
DECADAL	DECAUDATED	DECIDUATE	DECLARING	DECONTROLLING
DECADE	DECAUDATES	DECIDUOUS	DECLASS	DECONTROLS
DECADENCE	DECAUDATING	DECIGRAM	DECLASSE	DECOR
DECADENCES	DECAY	DECIGRAMS	DECLASSED	DECORATE
DECADENCIES	DECAYED	DECILITER	DECLASSEE	DECORATED
DECADENCY	DECAYING	DECILITERS	DECLASSES	DECORATES
DECADENT	DECAYS	DECILITRE	DECLASSING	DECORATING
DECADENTS	DECCIE	DECILITRES	DECLINAL	DECORATOR
DECADES	DECCIES	DECILLION	DECLINANT	DECORATORS
DECADS	DECEASE	DECILLIONS	DECLINATE	DECOROUS
DECAFF	DECEASED	DECIMAL	DECLINE	DECORS
DECAFFS	DECEASES	DECIMALLY	DECLINED	DECORUM
DECAGON	DECEASING	DECIMALS	DECLINES	DECORUMS
DECAGONAL	DECEDENT	DECIMATE	DECLINING	DECOUPAGE
DECAGONS	DECEDENTS	DECIMATED	DECLIVITIES	DECOUPAGES
DECAGRAM	DECEIT	DECIMATES	DECLIVITY	DECOUPLE
DECAGRAMS	DECEITFUL	DECIMATING	DECLIVOUS	DECOUPLED
DECAHEDRA	DECEITS	DECIMATOR	DECLUTCH	DECOUPLES
DECAL	DECEIVE	DECIMATORS	DECLUTCHED	DECOUPLING
DECALCIFIED	DECEIVED	DECIME	DECLUTCHES	DECOUPLINGS
DECALCIFIES	DECEIVER	DECIMES	DECLUTCHING	DECOY
DECALCIFY	DECEIVERS	DECIMETER	DECO	DECOYED
DECALCIFYING	DECEIVES	DECIMETERS	DECOCT	DECOYING
DECALITRE	DECEIVING	DECIMETRE	DECOCTED	DECOYS
DECALITRES	DECEMVIR	DECIMETRES	DECOCTING	DECREASE
DECALOGUE	DECEMVIRI	DECIPHER	DECOCTION	DECREASED
DECALOGUES	DECEMVIRS	DECIPHERED	DECOCTIONS	DECREASES
DECALS	DECENCIES	DECIPHERING	DECOCTIVE	DECREASING
DECAMETRE	DECENCY	DECIPHERS	DECOCTS	DECREE
DECAMETRES	DECENNARIES	DECISION	DECOCTURE	DECREED
DECAMP	DECENNARY	DECISIONS	DECOCTURES	DECREEING
DECAMPED	DECENNIA	DECISIVE	DECODE	DECREES
DECAMPING	DECENNIAL	DECISORY	DECODED	DECREET
DECAMPS	DECENNIUM	DECISTERE	DECODER	DECREETS
DECANAL	DECENNIUMS	DECISTERES	DECODERS	DECREMENT
DECANE	DECENT	DECK	DECODES	DECREMENTED
DECANES	DECENTER	DECKCHAIR	DECODING	DECREMENTING
DECANI	DECENTEST	DECKCHAIRS	DECOHERER	DECREMENTS
DECANT	DECENTLY	DECKED	DECOHERERS	DECREPIT
DECANTATE	DECEPTION	DECKER	DECOKE	DECRETAL
DECANTATED	DECEPTIONS	DECKERS	DECOKED	DECRETALS
DECANTATES	DECEPTIVE	DECKHOUSE	DECOKES	DECRETIST
DECANTATING	DECEPTORY	DECKHOUSES	DECOKING	DECRETISTS
DECANTED	DECERN	DECKING	DECOLLATE	DECRETIVE
DECANTER	DECERNED	DECKINGS	DECOLLATED	DECRETORY
DECANTERS	DECERNING	DECKLE	DECOLLATES	DECREW
DECANTING	DECERNS	DECKLED	DECOLLATING	DECREWED
DECANTS	DECESSION	DECKLES	DECOLLETE	DECREWING
DECAPOD	DECESSIONS	DECKO	DECOLOR	DECREWS
DECAPODAL	DECHEANCE	DECKOED	DECOLORED	DECRIAL
DECAPODAN	DECHEANCES	DECKOING	DECOLORING	DECRIALS
DECAPODS	DECIARE	DECKOS	DECOLORS	DECRIED
DECARB	DECIARES	DECKS	DECOLOUR	DECRIER
DECARBED	DECIBEL	DECLAIM	DECOLOURED	DECRIERS

The Chambers Dictionary is the authority for many longer words; see *OSW* Introduction, page xii.

DECRIES	DEE	DEFAECATED	DEFER	DEFLEX
DECROWN	DEED	DEFAECATES	DEFERABLE	DEFLEXED
DECROWNED	DEEDED	DEFAECATING	DEFERENCE	DEFLEXES
DECROWNING	DEEDER	DEFALCATE	DEFERENCES	DEFLEXING
DECROWNS	DEEDEST	DEFALCATED	DEFERENT	DEFLEXION
DECRY	DEEDFUL	DEFALCATES	DEFERENTS	DEFLEXIONS
DECRYING	DEEDIER	DEFALCATING	DEFERMENT	DEFLEXURE
DECRYPT	DEEDIEST	DEFAME	DEFERMENTS	DEFLEXURES
DECRYPTED	DEEDILY	DEFAMED	DEFERRAL	DEFLORATE
DECRYPTING	DEEDING	DEFAMES	DEFERRALS	DEFLORATED
DECRYPTS	DEEDLESS	DEFAMING	DEFERRED	DEFLORATES
DECTET	DEEDS	DEFAMINGS	DEFERRER	DEFLORATING
DECTETS	DEEDY	DEFAST	DEFERRERS	DEFLOWER
DECUBITI	DEEING	DEFASTE	DEFERRING	DEFLOWERED
DECUBITUS	DEEJAY	DEFAT	DEFERS	DEFLOWERING
DECUMAN	DEEJAYED	DEFATS	DEFFER	DEFLOWERS
DECUMANS	DEEJAYING	DEFATTED	DEFFEST	DEFLUENT
DECUMBENT	DEEJAYS	DEFATTING	DEFFLY	DEFLUXION
DECUPLE	DEEK	DEFAULT	DEFIANCE	DEFLUXIONS
DECUPLED	DEEM	DEFAULTED	DEFIANCES	DEFOLIANT
DECUPLES	DEEMED	DEFAULTER	DEFIANT	DEFOLIANTS
DECUPLING	DEEMING	DEFAULTERS	DEFIANTLY	DEFOLIATE
DECURIA	DEEMS	DEFAULTING	DEFICIENT	DEFOLIATED
DECURIAS	DEEMSTER	DEFAULTS	DEFICIENTS	DEFOLIATES
DECURIES	DEEMSTERS	DEFEAT	DEFICIT	DEFOLIATING
DECURION	DEEN	DEFEATED	DEFICITS	DEFORCE
DECURIONS	DEENS	DEFEATING	DEFIED	DEFORCED
DECURRENT	DEEP	DEFEATISM	DEFIER	DEFORCES
DECURSION	DEEPEN	DEFEATISMS	DEFIERS	DEFORCING
DECURSIONS	DEEPENED	DEFEATIST	DEFIES	DEFOREST
DECURSIVE	DEEPENING	DEFEATISTS	DEFILADE	DEFORESTED
DECURVE	DEEPENS	DEFEATS	DEFILADED	DEFORESTING
DECURVED	DEEPER	DEFEATURE	DEFILADES	DEFORESTS
DECURVES	DEEPEST	DEFEATURED	DEFILADING	DEFORM
DECURVING	DEEPFELT	DEFEATURES	DEFILE	DEFORMED
DECURY	DEEPIE	DEFEATURING	DEFILED	DEFORMER
DECUSSATE	DEEPIES	DEFECATE	DEFILER	DEFORMERS
DECUSSATED	DEEPLY	DEFECATED	DEFILERS	DEFORMING
DECUSSATES	DEEPMOST	DEFECATES	DEFILES	DEFORMITIES
DECUSSATING	DEEPNESS	DEFECATING	DEFILING	DEFORMITY
DEDAL	DEEPNESSES	DEFECATOR	DEFINABLE	DEFORMS
DEDALIAN	DEEPS	DEFECATORS	DEFINABLY	DEFOUL
DEDANS	DEER	DEFECT	DEFINE	DEFOULED
DEDICANT	DEERBERRIES	DEFECTED	DEFINED	DEFOULING
DEDICANTS	DEERBERRY	DEFECTING	DEFINER	DEFOULS
DEDICATE	DEERE	DEFECTION	DEFINERS	DEFRAUD
DEDICATED	DEERHORN	DEFECTIONS	DEFINES	DEFRAUDED
DEDICATEE	DEERHORNS	DEFECTIVE	DEFINIENS	DEFRAUDER
DEDICATEES	DEERLET	DEFECTIVES	DEFINIENTIA	DEFRAUDERS
DEDICATES	DEERLETS	DEFECTOR	DEFINING	DEFRAUDING
DEDICATING	DEERSKIN	DEFECTORS	DEFINITE	DEFRAUDS
DEDICATOR	DEERSKINS	DEFECTS	DEFLATE	DEFRAY
DEDICATORS	DEES	DEFENCE	DEFLATED	DEFRAYAL
DEDIMUS	DEEV	DEFENCED	DEFLATER	DEFRAYALS
DEDIMUSES	DEEVE	DEFENCES	DEFLATERS	DEFRAYED
DEDUCE	DEEVED	DEFEND	DEFLATES	DEFRAYER
DEDUCED	DEEVES	DEFENDANT	DEFLATING	DEFRAYERS
DEDUCES	DEEVING	DEFENDANTS	DEFLATION	DEFRAYING
DEDUCIBLE	DEEVS	DEFENDED	DEFLATIONS	DEFRAYS
DEDUCING	DEF	DEFENDER	DEFLATOR	DEFREEZE
DEDUCT	DEFACE	DEFENDERS	DEFLATORS	DEFREEZES
DEDUCTED	DEFACED	DEFENDING	DEFLECT	DEFREEZING
DEDUCTING	DEFACER	DEFENDS	DEFLECTED	DEFROCK
DEDUCTION	DEFACERS	DEFENSE	DEFLECTING	DEFROCKED
DEDUCTIONS	DEFACES	DEFENSES	DEFLECTOR	DEFROCKING
DEDUCTIVE	DEFACING	DEFENSIVE	DEFLECTORS	DEFROCKS
DEDUCTS	DEFAECATE	DEFENSIVES	DEFLECTS	DEFROST

The Chambers Dictionary is the authority for many longer words; see *OSW* Introduction, page xii.

DEFROSTED	DEHISCE	DEJECTION	DELIBLE	DELUDER
DEFROSTER	DEHISCED	DEJECTIONS	DELICACIES	DELUDERS
DEFROSTERS	DEHISCENT	DEJECTORY	DELICACY	DELUDES
DEFROSTING	DEHISCES	DEJECTS	DELICATE	DELUDING
DEFROSTS	DEHISCING	DEJEUNE	DELICATES	DELUGE
DEFROZE	DEHORN	DEJEUNER	DELICE	DELUGED
DEFROZEN	DEHORNED	DEJEUNERS	DELICES	DELUGES
DEFT	DEHORNER	DEJEUNES	DELICIOUS	DELUGING
DEFTER	DEHORNERS	DEKALOGIES	DELICT	DELUNDUNG
DEFTEST	DEHORNING	DEKALOGY	DELICTS	DELUNDUNGS
DEFTLY	DEHORNS	DEKKO	DELIGHT	DELUSION
DEFTNESS	DEHORT	DEKKOED	DELIGHTED	DELUSIONS
DEFTNESSES	DEHORTED	DEKKOING	DELIGHTING	DELUSIVE
DEFUNCT	DEHORTER	DEKKOS	DELIGHTS	DELUSORY
DEFUNCTS	DEHORTERS	DEL	DELIMIT	DELVE
DEFUSE	DEHORTING	DELAINE	DELIMITED	DELVED
DEFUSED	DEHORTS	DELAINES	DELIMITING	DELVER
DEFUSES	DEHYDRATE	DELAPSE	DELIMITS	DELVERS
DEFUSING	DEHYDRATED	DELAPSED	DELINEATE	DELVES
DEFUZE	DEHYDRATES	DELAPSES	DELINEATED	DELVING
DEFUZED	DEHYDRATING	DELAPSING	DELINEATES	DEMAGOGIC
DEFUZES	DEI	DELAPSION	DELINEATING	DEMAGOGIES
DEFUZING	DEICIDAL	DELAPSIONS	DELIQUIUM	DEMAGOGUE
DEFY	DEICIDE	DELATE	DELIQUIUMS	DEMAGOGUES
DEFYING	DEICIDES	DELATED	DELIRIA	DEMAGOGY
DEGAGE	DEICTIC	DELATES	DELIRIANT	DEMAIN
DEGARNISH	DEICTICS	DELATING	DELIRIOUS	DEMAINE
DEGARNISHED	DEID	DELATION	DELIRIUM	DEMAINES
DEGARNISHES	DEIDER	DELATIONS	DELIRIUMS	DEMAINS
DEGARNISHING	DEIDEST	DELATOR	DELIS	DEMAN
DEGAS	DEIDS	DELATORS	DELIVER	DEMAND
DEGASSED	DEIFIC	DELAY	DELIVERED	DEMANDANT
DEGASSES	DEIFICAL	DELAYED	DELIVERER	DEMANDANTS
DEGASSING	DEIFIED	DELAYER	DELIVERERS	DEMANDED
DEGAUSS	DEIFIER	DELAYERS	DELIVERIES	DEMANDER
DEGAUSSED	DEIFIERS	DELAYING	DELIVERING	DEMANDERS
DEGAUSSES	DEIFIES	DELAYS	DELIVERLY	DEMANDING
DEGAUSSING	DEIFORM	DELE	DELIVERS	DEMANDS
DEGENDER	DEIFY	DELEBLE	DELIVERY	DEMANNED
DEGENDERED	DEIFYING	DELED	DELL	DEMANNING
DEGENDERING	DEIGN	DELEGABLE	DELLS	DEMANNINGS
DEGENDERS	DEIGNED	DELEGACIES	DELOPE	DEMANS
DEGOUT	DEIGNING	DELEGACY	DELOPED	DEMARCATE
DEGOUTS	DEIGNS	DELEGATE	DELOPES	DEMARCATED
DEGRADE	DEIL	DELEGATED	DELOPING	DEMARCATES
DEGRADED	DEILS	DELEGATES	DELOUSE	DEMARCATING
DEGRADING	DEINOSAUR	DELEGATING	DELOUSED	DEMARCHE
DEGRAS	DEINOSAURS	DELEING	DELOUSES	DEMARCHES
DEGREASE	DEIPAROUS	DELENDA	DELOUSING	DEMARK
DEGREASED	DEISEAL	DELES	DELPH	DEMARKED
DEGREASES	DEISEALS	DELETE	DELPHIC	DEMARKING
DEGREASING	DEISHEAL	DELETED	DELPHIN	DEMARKS
DEGREE	DEISHEALS	DELETES	DELPHINIA	DEMAYNE
DEGREES	DEISM	DELETING	DELPHS	DEMAYNES
DEGUM	DEISMS	DELETION	DELS	DEME
DEGUMMED	DEIST	DELETIONS	DELT	DEMEAN
DEGUMMING	DEISTIC	DELETIVE	DELTA	DEMEANE
DEGUMS	DEISTICAL	DELETORY	DELTAIC	DEMEANED
DEGUST	DEISTS	DELF	DELTAS	DEMEANES
DEGUSTATE	DEITIES	DELFS	DELTOID	DEMEANING
DEGUSTATED	DEITY	DELFT	DELTOIDS	DEMEANOR
DEGUSTATES	DEIXES	DELFTS	DELTS	DEMEANORS
DEGUSTATING	DEIXIS	DELI	DELUBRUM	DEMEANOUR
DEGUSTED	DEJECT	DELIBATE	DELUBRUMS	DEMEANOURS
DEGUSTING	DEJECTA	DELIBATED	DELUDABLE	DEMEANS
DEGUSTS	DEJECTED	DELIBATES	DELUDE	DEMENT
	DEJECTING	DELIBATING	DELUDED	DEMENTATE

The Chambers Dictionary is the authority for many longer words; see *OSW* Introduction, page xii.

DEMENTATED	DEMO	DEMURED	DENITRIFIED	DENTILS
DEMENTATES	DEMOB	DEMURELY	DENITRIFIES	DENTIN
DEMENTATING	DEMOBBED	DEMURER	DENITRIFY	DENTINE
DEMENTED	DEMOBBING	DEMURES	DENITRIFYING	DENTINES
DEMENTI	DEMOBS	DEMUREST	DENIZEN	DENTING
DEMENTIA	DEMOCRACIES	DEMURING	DENIZENED	DENTINS
DEMENTIAS	DEMOCRACY	DEMURRAGE	DENIZENING	DENTIST
DEMENTING	DEMOCRAT	DEMURRAGES	DENIZENS	DENTISTRIES
DEMENTIS	DEMOCRATIES	DEMURRAL	DENNED	DENTISTRY
DEMENTS	DEMOCRATS	DEMURRALS	DENNET	DENTISTS
DEMERARA	DEMOCRATY	DEMURRED	DENNETS	DENTITION
DEMERARAS	DEMODE	DEMURRER	DENNING	DENTITIONS
DEMERGE	DEMODED	DEMURRERS	DENOTABLE	DENTOID
DEMERGED	DEMOLISH	DEMURRING	DENOTATE	DENTS
DEMERGER	DEMOLISHED	DEMURS	DENOTATED	DENTURE
DEMERGERS	DEMOLISHES	DEMY	DENOTATES	DENTURES
DEMERGES	DEMOLISHING	DEMYSHIP	DENOTATING	DENUDATE
DEMERGING	DEMOLOGIES	DEMYSHIPS	DENOTE	DENUDATED
DEMERIT	DEMOLOGY	DEMYSTIFIED	DENOTED	DENUDATES
DEMERITS	DEMON	DEMYSTIFIES	DENOTES	DENUDATING
DEMERSAL	DEMONESS	DEMYSTIFY	DENOTING	DENUDE
DEMERSE	DEMONESSES	DEMYSTIFYING	DENOUNCE	DENUDED
DEMERSED	DEMONIAC	DEN	DENOUNCED	DENUDES
DEMERSES	DEMONIACS	DENARIES	DENOUNCER	DENUDING
DEMERSING	DEMONIAN	DENARII	DENOUNCERS	DENY
DEMERSION	DEMONIC	DENARIUS	DENOUNCES	DENYING
DEMERSIONS	DEMONISE	DENARY	DENOUNCING	DENYINGLY
DEMES	DEMONISED	DENATURE	DENS	DEODAND
DEMESNE	DEMONISES	DENATURED	DENSE	DEODANDS
DEMESNES	DEMONISING	DENATURES	DENSELY	DEODAR
DEMIC	DEMONISM	DENATURING	DENSENESS	DEODARS
DEMIES	DEMONISMS	DENAY	DENSENESSES	DEODATE
DEMIGOD	DEMONIST	DENAYED	DENSER	DEODATES
DEMIGODS	DEMONISTS	DENAYING	DENSEST	DEODORANT
DEMIJOHN	DEMONIZE	DENAYS	DENSIFIED	DEODORANTS
DEMIJOHNS	DEMONIZED	DENAZIFIED	DENSIFIER	DEODORISE
DEMIPIQUE	DEMONIZES	DENAZIFIES	DENSIFIERS	DEODORISED
DEMIPIQUES	DEMONIZING	DENAZIFY	DENSIFIES	DEODORISES
DEMIREP	DEMONRIES	DENAZIFYING	DENSIFY	DEODORISING
DEMIREPS	DEMONRY	DENDRITE	DENSIFYING	DEODORIZE
DEMISABLE	DEMONS	DENDRITES	DENSITIES	DEODORIZED
DEMISE	DEMOS	DENDRITIC	DENSITY	DEODORIZES
DEMISED	DEMOSES	DENDROID	DENT	DEODORIZING
DEMISES	DEMOTE	DENDRON	DENTAL	DEONTIC
DEMISING	DEMOTED	DENDRONS	DENTALIA	DEONTICS
DEMISS	DEMOTES	DENE	DENTALIUM	DEOXIDATE
DEMISSION	DEMOTIC	DENES	DENTALIUMS	DEOXIDATED
DEMISSIONS	DEMOTING	DENGUE	DENTALS	DEOXIDATES
DEMISSIVE	DEMOTION	DENGUES	DENTARIA	DEOXIDATING
DEMISSLY	DEMOTIONS	DENIABLE	DENTARIAS	DEOXIDISE
DEMIST	DEMOTIST	DENIABLY	DENTARIES	DEOXIDISED
DEMISTED	DEMOTISTS	DENIAL	DENTARY	DEOXIDISES
DEMISTER	DEMOUNT	DENIALS	DENTATE	DEOXIDISING
DEMISTERS	DEMOUNTED	DENIED	DENTATED	DEOXIDIZE
DEMISTING	DEMOUNTING	DENIER	DENTATION	DEOXIDIZED
DEMISTS	DEMOUNTS	DENIERS	DENTATIONS	DEOXIDIZES
DEMIT	DEMPSTER	DENIES	DENTED	DEOXIDIZING
DEMITASSE	DEMPSTERS	DENIGRATE	DENTEL	DEPAINT
DEMITASSES	DEMPT	DENIGRATED	DENTELLE	DEPAINTED
DEMITS	DEMULCENT	DENIGRATES	DENTELLES	DEPAINTING
DEMITTED	DEMULCENTS	DENIGRATING	DENTELS	DEPAINTS
DEMITTING	DEMULSIFIED	DENIM	DENTEX	DEPART
DEMIURGE	DEMULSIFIES	DENIMS	DENTEXES	DEPARTED
DEMIURGES	DEMULSIFY	DENITRATE	DENTICLE	DEPARTER
DEMIURGIC	DEMULSIFYING	DENITRATED	DENTICLES	DEPARTERS
DEMIURGUS	DEMUR	DENITRATES	DENTIFORM	DEPARTING
DEMIURGUSES	DEMURE	DENITRATING	DENTIL	DEPARTINGS

The Chambers Dictionary is the authority for many longer words; see *OSW* Introduction, page xii.

DEPARTS	DEPONED	DEPURANT	DERIGGING	DESCANTED
DEPARTURE	DEPONENT	DEPURANTS	DERIGS	DESCANTING
DEPARTURES	DEPONENTS	DEPURATE	DERING	DESCANTS
DEPASTURE	DEPONES	DEPURATED	DERISIBLE	DESCEND
DEPASTURED	DEPONING	DEPURATES	DERISION	DESCENDED
DEPASTURES	DEPORT	DEPURATING	DERISIONS	DESCENDER
DEPASTURING	DEPORTED	DEPURATOR	DERISIVE	DESCENDERS
DEPECHE	DEPORTEE	DEPURATORS	DERISORY	DESCENDING
DEPECHES	DEPORTEES	DEPUTE	DERIVABLE	DESCENDINGS
DEPEINCT	DEPORTING	DEPUTED	DERIVABLY	DESCENDS
DEPEINCTED	DEPORTS	DEPUTES	DERIVATE	DESCENT
DEPEINCTING	DEPOSABLE	DEPUTIES	DERIVATES	DESCENTS
DEPEINCTS	DEPOSAL	DEPUTING	DERIVE	DESCHOOL
DEPEND	DEPOSALS	DEPUTISE	DERIVED	DESCHOOLED
DEPENDANT	DEPOSE	DEPUTISED	DERIVES	DESCHOOLING
DEPENDANTS	DEPOSED	DEPUTISES	DERIVING	DESCHOOLINGS
DEPENDED	DEPOSER	DEPUTISING	DERM	DESCHOOLS
DEPENDENT	DEPOSERS	DEPUTIZE	DERMA	DESCRIBE
DEPENDENTS	DEPOSES	DEPUTIZED	DERMAL	DESCRIBED
DEPENDING	DEPOSING	DEPUTIZES	DERMAS	DESCRIBER
DEPENDS	DEPOSIT	DEPUTIZING	DERMATIC	DESCRIBERS
DEPICT	DEPOSITED	DEPUTY	DERMATOID	DESCRIBES
DEPICTED	DEPOSITING	DERACINE	DERMATOME	DESCRIBING
DEPICTER	DEPOSITOR	DERAIGN	DERMATOMES	DESCRIED
DEPICTERS	DEPOSITORS	DERAIGNED	DERMIC	DESCRIES
DEPICTING	DEPOSITS	DERAIGNING	DERMIS	DESCRIVE
DEPICTION	DEPOT	DERAIGNS	DERMISES	DESCRIVED
DEPICTIONS	DEPOTS	DERAIL	DERMOID	DESCRIVES
DEPICTIVE	DEPRAVE	DERAILED	DERMOIDS	DESCRIVING
DEPICTOR	DEPRAVED	DERAILER	DERMS	DESCRY
DEPICTORS	DEPRAVES	DERAILERS	DERN	DESCRYING
DEPICTS	DEPRAVING	DERAILING	DERNFUL	DESECRATE
DEPICTURE	DEPRAVITIES	DERAILS	DERNIER	DESECRATED
DEPICTURED	DEPRAVITY	DERANGE	DERNLY	DESECRATES
DEPICTURES	DEPRECATE	DERANGED	DERNS	DESECRATING
DEPICTURING	DEPRECATED	DERANGES	DEROGATE	DESELECT
DEPILATE	DEPRECATES	DERANGING	DEROGATED	DESELECTED
DEPILATED	DEPRECATING	DERATE	DEROGATES	DESELECTING
DEPILATES	DEPREDATE	DERATED	DEROGATING	DESELECTS
DEPILATING	DEPREDATED	DERATES	DERRICK	DESERT
DEPILATOR	DEPREDATES	DERATING	DERRICKED	DESERTED
DEPILATORS	DEPREDATING	DERATINGS	DERRICKING	DESERTER
DEPLANE	DEPREHEND	DERATION	DERRICKS	DESERTERS
DEPLANED	DEPREHENDED	DERATIONED	DERRIERE	DESERTING
DEPLANES	DEPREHENDING	DERATIONING	DERRIERES	DESERTION
DEPLANING	DEPREHENDS	DERATIONS	DERRIES	DESERTIONS
DEPLETE	DEPRESS	DERAY	DERRINGER	DESERTS
DEPLETED	DEPRESSED	DERAYED	DERRINGERS	DESERVE
DEPLETES	DEPRESSES	DERAYING	DERRIS	DESERVED
DEPLETING	DEPRESSING	DERAYS	DERRISES	DESERVER
DEPLETION	DEPRESSOR	DERBIES	DERRY	DESERVERS
DEPLETIONS	DEPRESSORS	DERBY	DERTH	DESERVES
DEPLETIVE	DEPRIVAL	DERE	DERTHS	DESERVING
DEPLETORY	DEPRIVALS	DERED	DERV	DESEX
DEPLORE	DEPRIVE	DERELICT	DERVISH	DESEXED
DEPLORED	DEPRIVED	DERELICTS	DERVISHES	DESEXES
DEPLORES	DEPRIVES	DERES	DERVS	DESEXING
DEPLORING	DEPRIVING	DERHAM	DESALT	DESICCANT
DEPLOY	DEPROGRAM	DERHAMS	DESALTED	DESICCANTS
DEPLOYED	DEPROGRAMMED	DERIDE	DESALTING	DESICCATE
DEPLOYING	DEPROGRAMMING	DERIDED	DESALTINGS	DESICCATED
DEPLOYS	DEPROGRAMS	DERIDER	DESALTS	DESICCATES
DEPLUME	DEPSIDE	DERIDERS	DESCALE	DESICCATING
DEPLUMED	DEPSIDES	DERIDES	DESCALED	DESIGN
DEPLUMES	DEPTH	DERIDING	DESCALES	DESIGNATE
DEPLUMING	DEPTHLESS	DERIG	DESCALING	DESIGNATED
DEPONE	DEPTHS	DERIGGED	DESCANT	DESIGNATES

The Chambers Dictionary is the authority for many longer words; see *OSW* Introduction, page xii.

DESIGNATING	DESORBS	DESTITUTE	DETERGED	DETRAINED
DESIGNED	DESPAIR	DESTITUTED	DETERGENT	DETRAINING
DESIGNER	DESPAIRED	DESTITUTES	DETERGENTS	DETRAINS
DESIGNERS	DESPAIRING	DESTITUTING	DETERGES	DETRAQUE
DESIGNFUL	DESPAIRS	DESTRIER	DETERGING	DETRAQUEE
DESIGNING	DESPATCH	DESTRIERS	DETERMENT	DETRAQUEES
DESIGNINGS	DESPATCHED	DESTROY	DETERMENTS	DETRAQUES
DESIGNS	DESPATCHES	DESTROYED	DETERMINE	DETRIMENT
DESILVER	DESPATCHING	DESTROYER	DETERMINED	DETRIMENTS
DESILVERED	DESPERADO	DESTROYERS	DETERMINES	DETRITAL
DESILVERING	DESPERADOES	DESTROYING	DETERMINING	DETRITION
DESILVERS	DESPERADOS	DESTROYS	DETERRED	DETRITIONS
DESINE	DESPERATE	DESTRUCT	DETERRENT	DETRITUS
DESINED	DESPIGHT	DESTRUCTED	DETERRENTS	DETRUDE
DESINENCE	DESPIGHTS	DESTRUCTING	DETERRING	DETRUDED
DESINENCES	DESPISAL	DESTRUCTS	DETERS	DETRUDES
DESINENT	DESPISALS	DESUETUDE	DETERSION	DETRUDING
DESINES	DESPISE	DESUETUDES	DETERSIONS	DETRUSION
DESINING	DESPISED	DESULPHUR	DETERSIVE	DETRUSIONS
DESIPIENT	DESPISER	DESULPHURED	DETERSIVES	DETUNE
DESIRABLE	DESPISERS	DESULPHURING	DETEST	DETUNED
DESIRABLES	DESPISES	DESULPHURS	DETESTED	DETUNES
DESIRABLY	DESPISING	DESULTORY	DETESTING	DETUNING
DESIRE	DESPITE	DESYATIN	DETESTS	DEUCE
DESIRED	DESPITES	DESYATINS	DETHRONE	DEUCED
DESIRER	DESPOIL	DESYNE	DETHRONED	DEUCEDLY
DESIRERS	DESPOILED	DESYNED	DETHRONER	DEUCES
DESIRES	DESPOILER	DESYNES	DETHRONERS	DEUDDARN
DESIRING	DESPOILERS	DESYNING	DETHRONES	DEUDDARNS
DESIROUS	DESPOILING	DETACH	DETHRONING	DEUS
DESIST	DESPOILS	DETACHED	DETHRONINGS	DEUTERATE
DESISTED	DESPOND	DETACHES	DETINUE	DEUTERATED
DESISTING	DESPONDED	DETACHING	DETINUES	DEUTERATES
DESISTS	DESPONDING	DETAIL	DETONATE	DEUTERATING
DESK	DESPONDINGS	DETAILED	DETONATED	DEUTERIDE
DESKBOUND	DESPONDS	DETAILING	DETONATES	DEUTERIDES
DESKILL	DESPOT	DETAILS	DETONATING	DEUTERIUM
DESKILLED	DESPOTAT	DETAIN	DETONATOR	DEUTERIUMS
DESKILLING	DESPOTATE	DETAINED	DETONATORS	DEUTERON
DESKILLS	DESPOTATES	DETAINEE	DETORSION	DEUTERONS
DESKS	DESPOTATS	DETAINEES	DETORSIONS	DEUTON
DESKTOP	DESPOTIC	DETAINER	DETORT	DEUTONS
DESKTOPS	DESPOTISM	DETAINERS	DETORTED	DEVA
DESMAN	DESPOTISMS	DETAINING	DETORTING	DEVALL
DESMANS	DESPOTS	DETAINS	DETORTION	DEVALLED
DESMID	DESPUMATE	DETECT	DETORTIONS	DEVALLING
DESMIDS	DESPUMATED	DETECTED	DETORTS	DEVALLS
DESMINE	DESPUMATES	DETECTING	DETOUR	DEVALUATE
DESMINES	DESPUMATING	DETECTION	DETOURED	DEVALUATED
DESMODIUM	DESSE	DETECTIONS	DETOURING	DEVALUATES
DESMODIUMS	DESSERT	DETECTIVE	DETOURS	DEVALUATING
DESMOID	DESSERTS	DETECTIVES	DETOX	DEVALUE
DESMOIDS	DESSES	DETECTOR	DETOXED	DEVALUED
DESMOSOME	DESTEMPER	DETECTORS	DETOXES	DEVALUES
DESMOSOMES	DESTEMPERED	DETECT3	DETOXIFIED	DEVALUING
DESOEUVRE	DESTEMPERING	DETENT	DETOXIFIES	DEVAS
DESOLATE	DESTEMPERS	DETENTE	DETOXIFY	DEVASTATE
DESOLATED	DESTINATE	DETENTES	DETOXIFYING	DEVASTATED
DESOLATER	DESTINATED	DETENTION	DETOXING	DEVASTATES
DESOLATERS	DESTINATES	DETENTIONS	DETRACT	DEVASTATING
DESOLATES	DESTINATING	DETENTS	DETRACTED	DEVEL
DESOLATING	DESTINE	DETENU	DETRACTING	DEVELLED
DESOLATOR	DESTINED	DETENUE	DETRACTINGS	DEVELLING
DESOLATORS	DESTINES	DETENUES	DETRACTOR	DEVELOP
DESORB	DESTINIES	DETENUS	DETRACTORS	DEVELOPE
DESORBED	DESTINING	DETER	DETRACTS	DEVELOPED
DESORBING	DESTINY	DETERGE	DETRAIN	DEVELOPER

The Chambers Dictionary is the authority for many longer words; see *OSW* Introduction, page xii.

DEVELOPERS DEVISORS DEWITT DIABLERIE DIALECTS
DEVELOPES DEVITRIFIED DEWITTED DIABLERIES DIALED
DEVELOPING DEVITRIFIES DEWITTING DIABLERY DIALING
DEVELOPS DEVITRIFY DEWITTS DIABLES DIALIST
DEVELS DEVITRIFYING DEWLAP DIABOLIC DIALISTS
DEVEST DEVLING DEWLAPPED DIABOLISE DIALLAGE
DEVESTED DEVLINGS DEWLAPS DIABOLISED DIALLAGES
DEVESTING DEVOICE DEWLAPT DIABOLISES DIALLAGIC
DEVESTS DEVOICED DEWPOINT DIABOLISING DIALLED
DEVIANCE DEVOICES DEWPOINTS DIABOLISM DIALLER
DEVIANCES DEVOICING DEWS DIABOLISMS DIALLERS
DEVIANCIES DEVOID DEWY DIABOLIST DIALLING
DEVIANCY DEVOIR DEXTER DIABOLISTS DIALLINGS
DEVIANT DEVOIRS DEXTERITIES DIABOLIZE DIALOG
DEVIANTS DEVOLVE DEXTERITY DIABOLIZED DIALOGIC
DEVIATE DEVOLVED DEXTEROUS DIABOLIZES DIALOGISE
DEVIATED DEVOLVES DEXTERS DIABOLIZING DIALOGISED
DEVIATES DEVOLVING DEXTRAL DIABOLO DIALOGISES
DEVIATING DEVONPORT DEXTRALLY DIABOLOGIES DIALOGISING
DEVIATION DEVONPORTS DEXTRAN DIABOLOGY DIALOGIST
DEVIATIONS DEVOT DEXTRANS DIABOLOS DIALOGISTS
DEVIATOR DEVOTE DEXTRIN DIACHYLON DIALOGITE
DEVIATORS DEVOTED DEXTRINE DIACHYLONS DIALOGITES
DEVIATORY DEVOTEDLY DEXTRINES DIACHYLUM DIALOGIZE
DEVICE DEVOTEE DEXTRINS DIACHYLUMS DIALOGIZED
DEVICEFUL DEVOTEES DEXTRORSE DIACID DIALOGIZES
DEVICES DEVOTES DEXTROSE DIACODION DIALOGIZING
DEVIL DEVOTING DEXTROSES DIACODIONS DIALOGS
DEVILDOM DEVOTION DEXTROUS DIACODIUM DIALOGUE
DEVILDOMS DEVOTIONS DEY DIACODIUMS DIALOGUED
DEVILED DEVOTS DEYS DIACONAL DIALOGUES
DEVILESS DEVOUR DHAK DIACONATE DIALOGUING
DEVILESSES DEVOURED DHAKS DIACONATES DIALS
DEVILET DEVOURER DHAL DIACRITIC DIALYSE
DEVILETS DEVOURERS DHALS DIACRITICS DIALYSED
DEVILING DEVOURING DHARMA DIACT DIALYSER
DEVILINGS DEVOURS DHARMAS DIACTINAL DIALYSERS
DEVILISH DEVOUT DHARMSALA DIACTINE DIALYSES
DEVILISM DEVOUTER DHARMSALAS DIACTINIC DIALYSING
DEVILISMS DEVOUTEST DHARNA DIADEM DIALYSIS
DEVILKIN DEVOUTLY DHARNAS DIADEMED DIALYTIC
DEVILKINS DEVVEL DHOBI DIADEMS DIALYZE
DEVILLED DEVVELLED DHOBIS DIADOCHI DIALYZED
DEVILLING DEVVELLING DHOLE DIADROM DIALYZER
DEVILMENT DEVVELS DHOLES DIADROMS DIALYZERS
DEVILMENTS DEW DHOLL DIAERESES DIALYZES
DEVILRIES DEWAN DHOLLS DIAERESIS DIALYZING
DEVILRY DEWANI DHOOLIES DIAGLYPH DIAMAGNET
DEVILS DEWANIS DHOOLY DIAGLYPHS DIAMAGNETS
DEVILSHIP DEWANNIES DHOOTI DIAGNOSE DIAMANTE
DEVILSHIPS DEWANNY DHOOTIS DIAGNOSED DIAMANTES
DEVILTRIES DEWANS DHOTI DIAGNOSES DIAMETER
DEVILTRY DEWAR DHOTIS DIAGNOSING DIAMETERS
DEVIOUS DEWARS DHOW DIAGNOSIS DIAMETRAL
DEVIOUSLY DEWATER DHOWS DIAGONAL DIAMETRIC
DEVISABLE DEWATERED DHURRA DIAGONALS DIAMOND
DEVISAL DEWATERING DHURRAS DIAGRAM DIAMONDED
DEVISALS DEWATERINGS DHURRIE DIAGRAMS DIAMONDS
DEVISE DEWATERS DHURRIES DIAGRAPH DIAMYL
DEVISED DEWED DI DIAGRAPHS DIANDRIES
DEVISEE DEWFULL DIABASE DIAGRID DIANDROUS
DEVISEES DEWIER DIABASES DIAGRIDS DIANDRY
DEVISER DEWIEST DIABASIC DIAL DIANETICS®
DEVISERS DEWILY DIABETES DIALECT DIANODAL
DEVISES DEWINESS DIABETIC DIALECTAL DIANOETIC
DEVISING DEWINESSES DIABETICS DIALECTIC DIANTHUS
DEVISOR DEWING DIABLE DIALECTICS DIANTHUSES

The Chambers Dictionary is the authority for many longer words; see *OSW* Introduction, page xii.

DIAPASE	DIASTERS	DICHASIUM	DICTIER	DIEGESIS
DIAPASES	DIASTOLE	DICHOGAMIES	DICTIEST	DIELDRIN
DIAPASON	DIASTOLES	DICHOGAMY	DICTING	DIELDRINS
DIAPASONS	DIASTOLIC	DICHORD	DICTION	DIELYTRA
DIAPAUSE	DIASTYLE	DICHORDS	DICTIONS	DIELYTRAS
DIAPAUSES	DIASTYLES	DICHOTOMIES	DICTS	DIENE
DIAPENTE	DIATHERMIES	DICHOTOMY	DICTUM	DIENES
DIAPENTES	DIATHERMY	DICHROIC	DICTY	DIERESES
DIAPER	DIATHESES	DICHROISM	DICTYOGEN	DIERESIS
DIAPERED	DIATHESIS	DICHROISMS	DICTYOGENS	DIES
DIAPERING	DIATHETIC	DICHROITE	DICYCLIC	DIESEL
DIAPERINGS	DIATOM	DICHROITES	DID	DIESELISE
DIAPERS	DIATOMIC	DICHROMAT	DIDACTIC	DIESELISED
DIAPHONE	DIATOMIST	DICHROMATS	DIDACTICS	DIESELISES
DIAPHONES	DIATOMISTS	DICHROMIC	DIDACTYL	DIESELISING
DIAPHRAGM	DIATOMITE	DICHT	DIDACTYLS	DIESELIZE
DIAPHRAGMS	DIATOMITES	DICHTED	DIDAKAI	DIESELIZED
DIAPHYSES	DIATOMS	DICHTING	DIDAKAIS	DIESELIZES
DIAPHYSIS	DIATONIC	DICHTS	DIDAKEI	DIESELIZING
DIAPIR	DIATRETUM	DICIER	DIDAKEIS	DIESELS
DIAPIRIC	DIATRETUMS	DICIEST	DIDAPPER	DIESES
DIAPIRISM	DIATRIBE	DICING	DIDAPPERS	DIESIS
DIAPIRISMS	DIATRIBES	DICINGS	DIDDER	DIESTRUS
DIAPIRS	DIATROPIC	DICK	DIDDERED	DIESTRUSES
DIAPYESES	DIAXON	DICKENS	DIDDERING	DIET
DIAPYESIS	DIAXONS	DICKER	DIDDERS	DIETARIAN
DIAPYETIC	DIAZEPAM	DICKERED	DIDDICOY	DIETARIANS
DIAPYETICS	DIAZEPAMS	DICKERING	DIDDICOYS	DIETARIES
DIARCH	DIAZEUXES	DICKERS	DIDDIER	DIETARY
DIARCHAL	DIAZEUXIS	DICKEY	DIDDIES	DIETED
DIARCHIC	DIAZO	DICKEYS	DIDDIEST	DIETER
DIARCHIES	DIAZOES	DICKHEAD	DIDDLE	DIETERS
DIARCHY	DIAZOS	DICKHEADS	DIDDLED	DIETETIC
DIARIAL	DIB	DICKIE	DIDDLER	DIETETICS
DIARIAN	DIBASIC	DICKIER	DIDDLERS	DIETHYL
DIARIES	DIBBED	DICKIES	DIDDLES	DIETICIAN
DIARISE	DIBBER	DICKIEST	DIDDLING	DIETICIANS
DIARISED	DIBBERS	DICKS	DIDDY	DIETINE
DIARISES	DIBBING	DICKTIER	DIDELPHIC	DIETINES
DIARISING	DIBBLE	DICKTIEST	DIDELPHID	DIETING
DIARIST	DIBBLED	DICKTY	DIDELPHIDS	DIETIST
DIARISTS	DIBBLER	DICKY	DIDICOI	DIETISTS
DIARIZE	DIBBLERS	DICLINISM	DIDICOIS	DIETITIAN
DIARIZED	DIBBLES	DICLINISMS	DIDICOY	DIETITIANS
DIARIZES	DIBBLING	DICLINOUS	DIDICOYS	DIETS
DIARIZING	DIBBS	DICOT	DIDO	DIFFER
DIARRHEA	DIBS	DICOTS	DIDOES	DIFFERED
DIARRHEAL	DIBUTYL	DICROTIC	DIDOS	DIFFERENT
DIARRHEAS	DICACIOUS	DICROTISM	DIDRACHM	DIFFERING
DIARRHEIC	DICACITIES	DICROTISMS	DIDRACHMA	DIFFERS
DIARRHOEA	DICACITY	DICROTOUS	DIDRACHMAS	DIFFICILE
DIARRHOEAS	DICAST	DICT	DIDRACHMS	DIFFICULT
DIARY	DICASTERIES	DICTA	DIDST	DIFFIDENT
DIASCOPE	DICASTERY	DICTATE	DIDYMIUM	DIFFLUENT
DIASCOPES	DICASTIC	DICTATED	DIDYMIUMS	DIFFORM
DIASPORA	DICASTS	DICTATES	DIDYMOUS	DIFFRACT
DIASPORAS	DICE	DICTATING	DIE	DIFFRACTED
DIASPORE	DICED	DICTATION	DIEB	DIFFRACTING
DIASPORES	DICENTRA	DICTATIONS	DIEBACK	DIFFRACTS
DIASTASE	DICENTRAS	DICTATOR	DIEBACKS	DIFFUSE
DIASTASES	DICER	DICTATORS	DIEBS	DIFFUSED
DIASTASIC	DICERS	DICTATORY	DIED	DIFFUSELY
DIASTASIS	DICES	DICTATRIX	DIEDRAL	DIFFUSER
DIASTATIC	DICEY	DICTATRIXES	DIEDRALS	DIFFUSERS
DIASTEMA	DICH	DICTATURE	DIEDRE	DIFFUSES
DIASTEMATA	DICHASIA	DICTATURES	DIEDRES	DIFFUSING
DIASTER	DICHASIAL	DICTED	DIEGESES	DIFFUSION

The Chambers Dictionary is the authority for many longer words; see *OSW* Introduction, page xii.

DIFFUSIONS DIGRAPHS DILLIS DIMMED DINICS
DIFFUSIVE DIGRESS DILLS DIMMER DINING
DIG DIGRESSED DILLY DIMMERS DINK
DIGAMIES DIGRESSES DILUENT DIMMEST DINKED
DIGAMIST DIGRESSING DILUENTS DIMMING DINKER
DIGAMISTS DIGS DILUTABLE DIMMISH DINKEST
DIGAMMA DIGYNIAN DILUTABLES DIMNESS DINKIER
DIGAMMAS DIGYNOUS DILUTE DIMNESSES DINKIES
DIGAMOUS DIHEDRA DILUTED DIMORPH DINKIEST
DIGAMY DIHEDRAL DILUTEE DIMORPHIC DINKING
DIGASTRIC DIHEDRALS DILUTEES DIMORPHS DINKS
DIGEST DIHEDRON DILUTER DIMPLE DINKUM
DIGESTED DIHEDRONS DILUTERS DIMPLED DINKY
DIGESTER DIHYBRID DILUTES DIMPLES DINMONT
DIGESTERS DIHYBRIDS DILUTING DIMPLIER DINMONTS
DIGESTING DIHYDRIC DILUTION DIMPLIEST DINNED
DIGESTION DIKA DILUTIONS DIMPLING DINNER
DIGESTIONS DIKAS DILUTOR DIMPLY DINNERED
DIGESTIVE DIKAST DILUTORS DIMS DINNERING
DIGESTIVES DIKASTS DILUVIA DIMWIT DINNERS
DIGESTS DIKE DILUVIAL DIMWITS DINNING
DIGGABLE DIKED DILUVIAN DIMYARIAN DINNLE
DIGGED DIKER DILUVION DIN DINNLED
DIGGER DIKERS DILUVIONS DINAR DINNLES
DIGGERS DIKES DILUVIUM DINARCHIES DINNLING
DIGGING DIKEY DILUVIUMS DINARCHY DINOSAUR
DIGGINGS DIKIER DIM DINARS DINOSAURS
DIGHT DIKIEST DIMBLE DINDLE DINOTHERE
DIGHTED DIKING DIMBLES DINDLED DINOTHERES
DIGHTING DIKKOP DIME DINDLES DINS
DIGHTS DIKKOPS DIMENSION DINDLING DINT
DIGIT DIKTAT DIMENSIONED DINE DINTED
DIGITAL DIKTATS DIMENSIONING DINED DINTING
DIGITALIN DILATABLE DIMENSIONS DINER DINTS
DIGITALINS DILATANCIES DIMER DINERS DIOCESAN
DIGITALIS DILATANCY DIMERIC DINES DIOCESANS
DIGITALISES DILATANT DIMERISE DINETTE DIOCESE
DIGITALS DILATATOR DIMERISED DINETTES DIOCESES
DIGITATE DILATATORS DIMERISES DINFUL DIODE
DIGITATED DILATE DIMERISING DING DIODES
DIGITISE DILATED DIMERISM DINGBAT DIOECIOUS
DIGITISED DILATER DIMERISMS DINGBATS DIOECISM
DIGITISER DILATERS DIMERIZE DINGE DIOECISMS
DIGITISERS DILATES DIMERIZED DINGED DIOESTRUS
DIGITISES DILATING DIMERIZES DINGER DIOESTRUSES
DIGITISING DILATION DIMERIZING DINGERS DIOPSIDE
DIGITIZE DILATIONS DIMEROUS DINGES DIOPSIDES
DIGITIZED DILATIVE DIMERS DINGESES DIOPTASE
DIGITIZER DILATOR DIMES DINGEY DIOPTASES
DIGITIZERS DILATORS DIMETER DINGEYS DIOPTER
DIGITIZES DILATORY DIMETERS DINGHIES DIOPTERS
DIGITIZING DILDO DIMETHYL DINGHY DIOPTRATE
DIGITS DILDOE DIMETHYLS DINGIER DIOPTRE
DIGLOT DILDOES DIMETRIC DINGIES DIOPTRES
DIGLOTS DILDOS DIMIDIATE DINGIEST DIOPTRIC
DIGLYPH DILEMMA DIMIDIATED DINGINESS DIOPTRICS
DIGLYPHS DILEMMAS DIMIDIATES DINGINESSES DIORAMA
DIGNIFIED DILIGENCE DIMIDIATING DINGING DIORAMAS
DIGNIFIES DILIGENCES DIMINISH DINGLE DIORAMIC
DIGNIFY DILIGENT DIMINISHED DINGLES DIORISM
DIGNIFYING DILL DIMINISHES DINGO DIORISMS
DIGNITARIES DILLI DIMINISHING DINGOES DIORISTIC
DIGNITARY DILLIER DIMINISHINGS DINGS DIORITE
DIGNITIES DILLIES DIMISSORY DINGUS DIORITES
DIGNITY DILLIEST DIMITIES DINGUSES DIORITIC
DIGONAL DILLING DIMITY DINGY DIOSGENIN
DIGRAPH DILLINGS DIMLY DINIC DIOSGENINS

The Chambers Dictionary is the authority for many longer words; see *OSW* Introduction, page xii.

DIOTA	DIPPINGS	DIRIGISMS	DISANCHORING	DISBELIEFS
DIOTAS	DIPPY	DIRIGISTE	DISANCHORS	DISBENCH
DIOXAN	DIPS	DIRIMENT	DISANNEX	DISBENCHED
DIOXANE	DIPSADES	DIRK	DISANNEXED	DISBENCHES
DIOXANES	DIPSAS	DIRKE	DISANNEXES	DISBENCHING
DIOXANS	DIPSO	DIRKED	DISANNEXING	DISBODIED
DIOXIDE	DIPSOS	DIRKES	DISANNUL	DISBOSOM
DIOXIDES	DIPSTICK	DIRKING	DISANNULLED	DISBOSOMED
DIOXIN	DIPSTICKS	DIRKS	DISANNULLING	DISBOSOMING
DIOXINS	DIPTERA	DIRL	DISANNULLINGS	DISBOSOMS
DIP	DIPTERAL	DIRLED	DISANNULS	DISBOWEL
DIPCHICK	DIPTERAN	DIRLING	DISANOINT	DISBOWELLED
DIPCHICKS	DIPTERANS	DIRLS	DISANOINTED	DISBOWELLING
DIPEPTIDE	DIPTERAS	DIRNDL	DISANOINTING	DISBOWELS
DIPEPTIDES	DIPTERIST	DIRNDLS	DISANOINTS	DISBRANCH
DIPHENYL	DIPTERISTS	DIRT	DISAPPEAR	DISBRANCHED
DIPHENYLS	DIPTEROI	DIRTED	DISAPPEARED	DISBRANCHES
DIPHONE	DIPTEROS	DIRTIED	DISAPPEARING	DISBRANCHING
DIPHONES	DIPTEROSES	DIRTIER	DISAPPEARS	DISBUD
DIPHTHONG	DIPTEROUS	DIRTIES	DISAPPLIED	DISBUDDED
DIPHTHONGS	DIPTYCH	DIRTIEST	DISAPPLIES	DISBUDDING
DIPHYSITE	DIPTYCHS	DIRTILY	DISAPPLY	DISBUDS
DIPHYSITES	DIRDAM	DIRTINESS	DISAPPLYING	DISBURDEN
DIPLEGIA	DIRDAMS	DIRTINESSES	DISARM	DISBURDENED
DIPLEGIAS	DIRDUM	DIRTING	DISARMED	DISBURDENING
DIPLEX	DIRDUMS	DIRTS	DISARMER	DISBURDENS
DIPLOE	DIRE	DIRTY	DISARMERS	DISBURSAL
DIPLOES	DIRECT	DIRTYING	DISARMING	DISBURSALS
DIPLOGEN	DIRECTED	DISA	DISARMS	DISBURSE
DIPLOGENS	DIRECTER	DISABLE	DISARRAY	DISBURSED
DIPLOID	DIRECTEST	DISABLED	DISARRAYED	DISBURSES
DIPLOIDIES	DIRECTING	DISABLES	DISARRAYING	DISBURSING
DIPLOIDY	DIRECTION	DISABLING	DISARRAYS	DISC
DIPLOMA	DIRECTIONS	DISABUSE	DISAS	DISCAGE
DIPLOMACIES	DIRECTIVE	DISABUSED	DISASTER	DISCAGED
DIPLOMACY	DIRECTIVES	DISABUSES	DISASTERS	DISCAGES
DIPLOMAED	DIRECTLY	DISABUSING	DISATTIRE	DISCAGING
DIPLOMAING	DIRECTOR	DISACCORD	DISATTIRED	DISCAL
DIPLOMAS	DIRECTORIES	DISACCORDED	DISATTIRES	DISCALCED
DIPLOMAT	DIRECTORS	DISACCORDING	DISATTIRING	DISCANDIE
DIPLOMATE	DIRECTORY	DISACCORDS	DISATTUNE	DISCANDIED
DIPLOMATED	DIRECTRICES	DISADORN	DISATTUNED	DISCANDIES
DIPLOMATES	DIRECTRIX	DISADORNED	DISATTUNES	DISCANDY
DIPLOMATING	DIRECTRIXES	DISADORNING	DISATTUNING	DISCANDYING
DIPLOMATS	DIRECTS	DISADORNS	DISAVOUCH	DISCANDYINGS
DIPLON	DIREFUL	DISAFFECT	DISAVOUCHED	DISCANT
DIPLONS	DIREFULLY	DISAFFECTED	DISAVOUCHES	DISCANTED
DIPLONT	DIREMPT	DISAFFECTING	DISAVOUCHING	DISCANTING
DIPLONTS	DIREMPTED	DISAFFECTS	DISAVOW	DISCANTS
DIPLOPIA	DIREMPTING	DISAFFIRM	DISAVOWAL	DISCARD
DIPLOPIAS	DIREMPTS	DISAFFIRMED	DISAVOWALS	DISCARDED
DIPLOZOA	DIRER	DISAFFIRMING	DISAVOWED	DISCARDING
DIPLOZOON	DIREST	DISAFFIRMS	DISAVOWING	DISCARDS
DIPNOAN	DIRGE	DISAGREE	DISAVOWS	DISCASE
DIPNOANS	DIRGES	DISAGREED	DISBAND	DISCASED
DIPNOOUS	DIRHAM	DISAGREEING	DISBANDED	DISCASES
DIPODIES	DIRHAMS	DISAGREES	DISBANDING	DISCASING
DIPODY	DIRHEM	DISALLIED	DISBANDS	DISCED
DIPOLAR	DIRHEMS	DISALLIES	DISBAR	DISCEPT
DIPOLE	DIRIGE	DISALLOW	DISBARK	DISCEPTED
DIPOLES	DIRIGENT	DISALLOWED	DISBARKED	DISCEPTING
DIPPED	DIRIGES	DISALLOWING	DISBARKING	DISCEPTS
DIPPER	DIRIGIBLE	DISALLOWS	DISBARKS	DISCERN
DIPPERS	DIRIGIBLES	DISALLY	DISBARRED	DISCERNED
DIPPIER	DIRIGISM	DISALLYING	DISBARRING	DISCERNER
DIPPIEST	DIRIGISME	DISANCHOR	DISBARS	DISCERNERS
DIPPING	DIRIGISMES	DISANCHORED	DISBELIEF	DISCERNING

The Chambers Dictionary is the authority for many longer words; see *OSW* Introduction, page xii.

DISCERNS	DISCOURES	DISEMPLOYS	DISGAVELS	DISHINGS
DISCERP	DISCOURING	DISENABLE	DISGEST	DISHOME
DISCERPED	DISCOURSE	DISENABLED	DISGESTED	DISHOMED
DISCERPING	DISCOURSED	DISENABLES	DISGESTING	DISHOMES
DISCERPS	DISCOURSES	DISENABLING	DISGESTS	DISHOMING
DISCHARGE	DISCOURSING	DISENDOW	DISGODDED	DISHONEST
DISCHARGED	DISCOVER	DISENDOWED	DISGORGE	DISHONOR
DISCHARGES	DISCOVERED	DISENDOWING	DISGORGED	DISHONORED
DISCHARGING	DISCOVERIES	DISENDOWS	DISGORGES	DISHONORING
DISCHURCH	DISCOVERING	DISENGAGE	DISGORGING	DISHONORS
DISCHURCHED	DISCOVERS	DISENGAGED	DISGOWN	DISHONOUR
DISCHURCHES	DISCOVERT	DISENGAGES	DISGOWNED	DISHONOURED
DISCHURCHING	DISCOVERY	DISENGAGING	DISGOWNING	DISHONOURING
DISCIDE	DISCREDIT	DISENROL	DISGOWNS	DISHONOURS
DISCIDED	DISCREDITED	DISENROLLED	DISGRACE	DISHORN
DISCIDES	DISCREDITING	DISENROLLING	DISGRACED	DISHORNED
DISCIDING	DISCREDITS	DISENROLS	DISGRACER	DISHORNING
DISCINCT	DISCREET	DISENTAIL	DISGRACERS	DISHORNS
DISCING	DISCREETER	DISENTAILED	DISGRACES	DISHORSE
DISCIPLE	DISCREETEST	DISENTAILING	DISGRACING	DISHORSED
DISCIPLED	DISCRETE	DISENTAILS	DISGRADE	DISHORSES
DISCIPLES	DISCRETER	DISENTOMB	DISGRADED	DISHORSING
DISCIPLING	DISCRETEST	DISENTOMBED	DISGRADES	DISHOUSE
DISCLAIM	DISCROWN	DISENTOMBING	DISGRADING	DISHOUSED
DISCLAIMED	DISCROWNED	DISENTOMBS	DISGUISE	DISHOUSES
DISCLAIMING	DISCROWNING	DISESTEEM	DISGUISED	DISHOUSING
DISCLAIMS	DISCROWNS	DISESTEEMED	DISGUISER	DISHTOWEL
DISCLOSE	DISCS	DISESTEEMING	DISGUISERS	DISHTOWELS
DISCLOSED	DISCUMBER	DISESTEEMS	DISGUISES	DISHUMOUR
DISCLOSES	DISCUMBERED	DISEUR	DISGUISING	DISHUMOURED
DISCLOSING	DISCUMBERING	DISEURS	DISGUISINGS	DISHUMOURING
DISCLOST	DISCUMBERS	DISEUSE	DISGUST	DISHUMOURS
DISCO	DISCURE	DISEUSES	DISGUSTED	DISHWATER
DISCOBOLI	DISCURED	DISFAME	DISGUSTING	DISHWATERS
DISCOED	DISCURES	DISFAMES	DISGUSTS	DISHY
DISCOER	DISCURING	DISFAVOR	DISH	DISILLUDE
DISCOERS	DISCURSUS	DISFAVORED	DISHABIT	DISILLUDED
DISCOID	DISCURSUSES	DISFAVORING	DISHABITED	DISILLUDES
DISCOIDAL	DISCUS	DISFAVORS	DISHABITING	DISILLUDING
DISCOING	DISCUSES	DISFAVOUR	DISHABITS	DISIMMURE
DISCOLOR	DISCUSS	DISFAVOURED	DISHABLE	DISIMMURED
DISCOLORED	DISCUSSED	DISFAVOURING	DISHABLED	DISIMMURES
DISCOLORING	DISCUSSES	DISFAVOURS	DISHABLES	DISIMMURING
DISCOLORS	DISCUSSING	DISFIGURE	DISHABLING	DISINFECT
DISCOLOUR	DISDAIN	DISFIGURED	DISHALLOW	DISINFECTED
DISCOLOURED	DISDAINED	DISFIGURES	DISHALLOWED	DISINFECTING
DISCOLOURING	DISDAINING	DISFIGURING	DISHALLOWING	DISINFECTS
DISCOLOURS	DISDAINS	DISFLESH	DISHALLOWS	DISINFEST
DISCOMFIT	DISEASE	DISFLESHED	DISHED	DISINFESTED
DISCOMFITED	DISEASED	DISFLESHES	DISHELM	DISINFESTING
DISCOMFITING	DISEASES	DISFLESHING	DISHELMED	DISINFESTS
DISCOMFITS	DISEASING	DISFLUENT	DISHELMING	DISINHUME
DISCOMMON	DISEDGE	DISFOREST	DISHELMS	DISINHUMED
DISCOMMONED	DISEDGED	DISFORESTED	DISHERIT	DISINHUMES
DISCOMMONING	DISEDGES	DISFORESTING	DISHERITED	DISINHUMING
DISCOMMONS	DISEDGING	DISFORESTS	DISHERITING	DISINTER
DISCORD	DISEMBARK	DISFORM	DISHERITS	DISINTERRED
DISCORDED	DISEMBARKED	DISFORMED	DISHES	DISINTERRING
DISCORDING	DISEMBARKING	DISFORMING	DISHEVEL	DISINTERS
DISCORDS	DISEMBARKS	DISFORMS	DISHEVELLED	DISINURE
DISCOS	DISEMBODIED	DISFROCK	DISHEVELLING	DISINURED
DISCOUNT	DISEMBODIES	DISFROCKED	DISHEVELS	DISINURES
DISCOUNTED	DISEMBODY	DISFROCKING	DISHFUL	DISINURING
DISCOUNTING	DISEMBODYING	DISFROCKS	DISHFULS	DISINVEST
DISCOUNTS	DISEMPLOY	DISGAVEL	DISHIER	DISINVESTED
DISCOURE	DISEMPLOYED	DISGAVELLED	DISHIEST	DISINVESTING
DISCOURED	DISEMPLOYING	DISGAVELLING	DISHING	DISINVESTS

The Chambers Dictionary is the authority for many longer words; see *OSW* Introduction, page xii.

DISJASKIT
DISJECT
DISJECTED
DISJECTING
DISJECTS
DISJOIN
DISJOINED
DISJOINING
DISJOINS
DISJOINT
DISJOINTED
DISJOINTING
DISJOINTS
DISJUNCT
DISJUNCTS
DISJUNE
DISJUNES
DISK
DISKED
DISKETTE
DISKETTES
DISKING
DISKLESS
DISKS
DISLEAF
DISLEAFED
DISLEAFING
DISLEAFS
DISLEAL
DISLEAVE
DISLEAVED
DISLEAVES
DISLEAVING
DISLIKE
DISLIKED
DISLIKEN
DISLIKENED
DISLIKENING
DISLIKENS
DISLIKES
DISLIKING
DISLIMB
DISLIMBED
DISLIMBING
DISLIMBS
DISLIMN
DISLIMNED
DISLIMNING
DISLIMNS
DISLINK
DISLINKED
DISLINKING
DISLINKS
DISLOAD
DISLOADED
DISLOADING
DISLOADS
DISLOCATE
DISLOCATED
DISLOCATES
DISLOCATING
DISLODGE
DISLODGED
DISLODGES
DISLODGING
DISLOIGN
DISLOIGNED

DISLOIGNING
DISLOIGNS
DISLOYAL
DISLUSTRE
DISLUSTRED
DISLUSTRES
DISLUSTRING
DISMAL
DISMALITIES
DISMALITY
DISMALLER
DISMALLEST
DISMALLY
DISMALS
DISMAN
DISMANNED
DISMANNING
DISMANS
DISMANTLE
DISMANTLED
DISMANTLES
DISMANTLING
DISMASK
DISMASKED
DISMASKING
DISMASKS
DISMAST
DISMASTED
DISMASTING
DISMASTS
DISMAY
DISMAYD
DISMAYED
DISMAYFUL
DISMAYING
DISMAYL
DISMAYLED
DISMAYLING
DISMAYLS
DISMAYS
DISME
DISMEMBER
DISMEMBERED
DISMEMBERING
DISMEMBERS
DISMES
DISMISS
DISMISSAL
DISMISSALS
DISMISSED
DISMISSES
DISMISSING
DISMODED
DISMOUNT
DISMOUNTED
DISMOUNTING
DISMOUNTS
DISNEST
DISNESTED
DISNESTING
DISNESTS
DISOBEY
DISOBEYED
DISOBEYING
DISOBEYS
DISOBLIGE
DISOBLIGED

DISOBLIGES
DISOBLIGING
DISORBED
DISORDER
DISORDERED
DISORDERING
DISORDERS
DISORIENT
DISORIENTED
DISORIENTING
DISORIENTS
DISOWN
DISOWNED
DISOWNER
DISOWNERS
DISOWNING
DISOWNS
DISPACE
DISPACED
DISPACES
DISPACING
DISPARAGE
DISPARAGED
DISPARAGES
DISPARAGING
DISPARATE
DISPARATES
DISPARITIES
DISPARITY
DISPARK
DISPARKED
DISPARKING
DISPARKS
DISPART
DISPARTED
DISPARTING
DISPARTS
DISPATCH
DISPATCHED
DISPATCHES
DISPATCHING
DISPATHIES
DISPATHY
DISPAUPER
DISPAUPERED
DISPAUPERING
DISPAUPERS
DISPEACE
DISPEACES
DISPEL
DISPELLED
DISPELLING
DISPELS
DISPENCE
DISPENCED
DISPENCES
DISPENCING
DISPEND
DISPENDED
DISPENDING
DISPENDS
DISPENSE
DISPENSED
DISPENSER
DISPENSERS
DISPENSES
DISPENSING

DISPEOPLE
DISPEOPLED
DISPEOPLES
DISPEOPLING
DISPERSAL
DISPERSALS
DISPERSE
DISPERSED
DISPERSER
DISPERSERS
DISPERSES
DISPERSING
DISPIRIT
DISPIRITED
DISPIRITING
DISPIRITS
DISPLACE
DISPLACED
DISPLACES
DISPLACING
DISPLANT
DISPLANTED
DISPLANTING
DISPLANTS
DISPLAY
DISPLAYED
DISPLAYER
DISPLAYERS
DISPLAYING
DISPLAYS
DISPLE
DISPLEASE
DISPLEASED
DISPLEASES
DISPLEASING
DISPLED
DISPLES
DISPLING
DISPLODE
DISPLODED
DISPLODES
DISPLODING
DISPLUME
DISPLUMED
DISPLUMES
DISPLUMING
DISPONDEE
DISPONDEES
DISPONE
DISPONED
DISPONEE
DISPONEES
DISPONER
DISPONERS
DISPONES
DISPONGE
DISPONGED
DISPONGES
DISPONGING
DISPONING
DISPORT
DISPORTED
DISPORTING
DISPORTS
DISPOSAL
DISPOSALS
DISPOSE

DISPOSED
DISPOSER
DISPOSERS
DISPOSES
DISPOSING
DISPOSINGS
DISPOST
DISPOSTED
DISPOSTING
DISPOSTS
DISPOSURE
DISPOSURES
DISPRAD
DISPRAISE
DISPRAISED
DISPRAISES
DISPRAISING
DISPREAD
DISPREADING
DISPREADS
DISPRED
DISPREDDEN
DISPREDDING
DISPREDS
DISPRISON
DISPRISONED
DISPRISONING
DISPRISONS
DISPRIZE
DISPRIZED
DISPRIZES
DISPRIZING
DISPROFIT
DISPROFITS
DISPROOF
DISPROOFS
DISPROOVE
DISPROOVED
DISPROOVES
DISPROOVING
DISPROVAL
DISPROVALS
DISPROVE
DISPROVED
DISPROVEN
DISPROVES
DISPROVING
DISPUNGE
DISPUNGED
DISPUNGES
DISPUNGING
DISPURSE
DISPURSED
DISPURSES
DISPURSING
DISPURVEY
DISPURVEYED
DISPURVEYING
DISPURVEYS
DISPUTANT
DISPUTANTS
DISPUTE
DISPUTED
DISPUTER
DISPUTERS
DISPUTES
DISPUTING

The Chambers Dictionary is the authority for many longer words; see *OSW* Introduction, page xii.

DISQUIET	DISSEIZING	DISTAINED	DISTRESSING	DITHELETE
DISQUIETED	DISSEIZINS	DISTAINING	DISTRICT	DITHELETES
DISQUIETING	DISSEIZOR	DISTAINS	DISTRICTED	DITHELISM
DISQUIETS	DISSEIZORS	DISTAL	DISTRICTING	DITHELISMS
DISRANK	DISSEMBLE	DISTALLY	DISTRICTS	DITHER
DISRANKED	DISSEMBLED	DISTANCE	DISTRUST	DITHERED
DISRANKING	DISSEMBLES	DISTANCED	DISTRUSTED	DITHERER
DISRANKS	DISSEMBLIES	DISTANCES	DISTRUSTING	DITHERERS
DISRATE	DISSEMBLING	DISTANCING	DISTRUSTS	DITHERIER
DISRATED	DISSEMBLINGS	DISTANT	DISTUNE	DITHERIEST
DISRATES	DISSEMBLY	DISTANTLY	DISTUNED	DITHERING
DISRATING	DISSENT	DISTASTE	DISTUNES	DITHERS
DISREGARD	DISSENTED	DISTASTED	DISTUNING	DITHERY
DISREGARDED	DISSENTER	DISTASTES	DISTURB	DITHYRAMB
DISREGARDING	DISSENTERS	DISTASTING	DISTURBED	DITHYRAMBS
DISREGARDS	DISSENTING	DISTEMPER	DISTURBER	DITING
DISRELISH	DISSENTS	DISTEMPERED	DISTURBERS	DITOKOUS
DISRELISHED	DISSERT	DISTEMPERING	DISTURBING	DITONE
DISRELISHES	DISSERTED	DISTEMPERS	DISTURBS	DITONES
DISRELISHING	DISSERTING	DISTEND	DISTYLE	DITROCHEE
DISREPAIR	DISSERTS	DISTENDED	DISTYLES	DITROCHEES
DISREPAIRS	DISSERVE	DISTENDING	DISUNION	DITS
DISREPUTE	DISSERVED	DISTENDS	DISUNIONS	DITSIER
DISREPUTES	DISSERVES	DISTENT	DISUNITE	DITSIEST
DISROBE	DISSERVING	DISTHENE	DISUNITED	DITSY
DISROBED	DISSES	DISTHENES	DISUNITES	DITT
DISROBES	DISSEVER	DISTHRONE	DISUNITIES	DITTANDER
DISROBING	DISSEVERED	DISTHRONED	DISUNITING	DITTANDERS
DISROOT	DISSEVERING	DISTHRONES	DISUNITY	DITTANIES
DISROOTED	DISSEVERS	DISTHRONING	DISUSAGE	DITTANY
DISROOTING	DISSHIVER	DISTICH	DISUSAGES	DITTAY
DISROOTS	DISSHIVERED	DISTICHAL	DISUSE	DITTAYS
DISRUPT	DISSHIVERING	DISTICHS	DISUSED	DITTED
DISRUPTED	DISSHIVERS	DISTIL	DISUSES	DITTIED
DISRUPTER	DISSIDENT	DISTILL	DISUSING	DITTIES
DISRUPTERS	DISSIDENTS	DISTILLED	DISVALUE	DITTING
DISRUPTING	DISSIGHT	DISTILLER	DISVALUED	DITTIT
DISRUPTOR	DISSIGHTS	DISTILLERS	DISVALUES	DITTO
DISRUPTORS	DISSIMILE	DISTILLING	DISVALUING	DITTOED
DISRUPTS	DISSIMILES	DISTILLINGS	DISVOUCH	DITTOING
DISS	DISSING	DISTILLS	DISVOUCHED	DITTOLOGIES
DISSAVING	DISSIPATE	DISTILS	DISVOUCHES	DITTOLOGY
DISSAVINGS	DISSIPATED	DISTINCT	DISVOUCHING	DITTOS
DISSEAT	DISSIPATES	DISTINCTER	DISYOKE	DITTS
DISSEATED	DISSIPATING	DISTINCTEST	DISYOKED	DITTY
DISSEATING	DISSOCIAL	DISTINGUE	DISYOKES	DITTYING
DISSEATS	DISSOLUTE	DISTORT	DISYOKING	DITZIER
DISSECT	DISSOLUTES	DISTORTED	DIT	DITZIEST
DISSECTED	DISSOLVE	DISTORTING	DITA	DITZY
DISSECTING	DISSOLVED	DISTORTS	DITAL	DIURESES
DISSECTINGS	DISSOLVES	DISTRACT	DITALS	DIURESIS
DISSECTOR	DISSOLVING	DISTRACTED	DITAS	DIURETIC
DISSECTORS	DISSOLVINGS	DISTRACTING	DITCH	DIURETICS
DISSECTS	DISSONANT	DISTRACTS	DITCHED	DIURNAL
DISSED	DISSUADE	DISTRAIL	DITCHER	DIURNALLY
DISSEISE	DISSUADED	DISTRAILS	DITCHERS	DIURNALS
DISSEISED	DISSUADER	DISTRAIN	DITCHES	DIUTURNAL
DISSEISES	DISSUADERS	DISTRAINED	DITCHING	DIV
DISSEISIN	DISSUADES	DISTRAINING	DITE	DIVA
DISSEISING	DISSUADING	DISTRAINS	DITED	DIVAGATE
DISSEISINS	DISSUNDER	DISTRAINT	DITES	DIVAGATED
DISSEISOR	DISSUNDERED	DISTRAINTS	DITHECAL	DIVAGATES
DISSEISORS	DISSUNDERING	DISTRAIT	DITHECOUS	DIVAGATING
DISSEIZE	DISSUNDERS	DISTRAITE	DITHEISM	DIVALENCIES
DISSEIZED	DISTAFF	DISTRESS	DITHEISMS	DIVALENCY
DISSEIZES	DISTAFFS	DISTRESSED	DITHEIST	DIVALENT
DISSEIZIN	DISTAIN	DISTRESSES	DITHEISTS	DIVALENTS

The Chambers Dictionary is the authority for many longer words; see *OSW* Introduction, page xii.

DIVAN	DIVINIFIED	DIZZIEST	DOCKETED	DODDIPOLL
DIVANS	DIVINIFIES	DIZZILY	DOCKETING	DODDIPOLLS
DIVAS	DIVINIFY	DIZZINESS	DOCKETS	DODDLE
DIVE	DIVINIFYING	DIZZINESSES	DOCKING	DODDLES
DIVED	DIVINING	DIZZY	DOCKINGS	DODDY
DIVELLENT	DIVINISE	DIZZYING	DOCKISE	DODDYPOLL
DIVER	DIVINISED	DJEBEL	DOCKISED	DODDYPOLLS
DIVERGE	DIVINISES	DJEBELS	DOCKISES	DODECAGON
DIVERGED	DIVINISING	DJELLABA	DOCKISING	DODECAGONS
DIVERGENT	DIVINITIES	DJELLABAH	DOCKIZE	DODGE
DIVERGES	DIVINITY	DJELLABAHS	DOCKIZED	DODGED
DIVERGING	DIVINIZE	DJELLABAS	DOCKIZES	DODGEMS
DIVERS	DIVINIZED	DJIBBAH	DOCKIZING	DODGER
DIVERSE	DIVINIZES	DJIBBAHS	DOCKLAND	DODGERIES
DIVERSED	DIVINIZING	DJINN	DOCKLANDS	DODGERS
DIVERSELY	DIVIS	DJINNI	DOCKS	DODGERY
DIVERSES	DIVISIBLE	DO	DOCKSIDE	DODGES
DIVERSIFIED	DIVISIBLY	DOAB	DOCKSIDES	DODGIER
DIVERSIFIES	DIVISIM	DOABLE	DOCKYARD	DODGIEST
DIVERSIFY	DIVISION	DOABS	DOCKYARDS	DODGING
DIVERSIFYING	DIVISIONS	DOAT	DOCQUET	DODGINGS
DIVERSING	DIVISIVE	DOATED	DOCQUETED	DODGY
DIVERSION	DIVISOR	DOATER	DOCQUETING	DODKIN
DIVERSIONS	DIVISORS	DOATERS	DOCQUETS	DODKINS
DIVERSITIES	DIVORCE	DOATING	DOCS	DODMAN
DIVERSITY	DIVORCED	DOATINGS	DOCTOR	DODMANS
DIVERSLY	DIVORCEE	DOATS	DOCTORAL	DODO
DIVERT	DIVORCEES	DOB	DOCTORAND	DODOES
DIVERTED	DIVORCER	DOBBED	DOCTORANDS	DODOS
DIVERTING	DIVORCERS	DOBBER	DOCTORATE	DODS
DIVERTIVE	DIVORCES	DOBBERS	DOCTORATED	DOE
DIVERTS	DIVORCING	DOBBIE	DOCTORATES	DOEK
DIVES	DIVORCIVE	DOBBIES	DOCTORATING	DOEKS
DIVEST	DIVOT	DOBBIN	DOCTORED	DOEN
DIVESTED	DIVOTS	DOBBING	DOCTORESS	DOER
DIVESTING	DIVS	DOBBINS	DOCTORESSES	DOERS
DIVESTS	DIVULGATE	DOBBY	DOCTORIAL	DOES
DIVESTURE	DIVULGATED	DOBCHICK	DOCTORING	DOEST
DIVESTURES	DIVULGATES	DOBCHICKS	DOCTORLY	DOETH
DIVI	DIVULGATING	DOBHASH	DOCTORS	DOFF
DIVIDABLE	DIVULGE	DOBHASHES	DOCTRESS	DOFFED
DIVIDANT	DIVULGED	DOBS	DOCTRESSES	DOFFER
DIVIDE	DIVULGES	DOC	DOCTRINAL	DOFFERS
DIVIDED	DIVULGING	DOCENT	DOCTRINE	DOFFING
DIVIDEDLY	DIVULSION	DOCENTS	DOCTRINES	DOFFS
DIVIDEND	DIVULSIONS	DOCHMIAC	DOCUDRAMA	DOG
DIVIDENDS	DIVULSIVE	DOCHMII	DOCUDRAMAS	DOGARESSA
DIVIDER	DIVVIES	DOCHMIUS	DOCUMENT	DOGARESSAS
DIVIDERS	DIVVY	DOCHMIUSES	DOCUMENTED	DOGATE
DIVIDES	DIWAN	DOCHT	DOCUMENTING	DOGATES
DIVIDING	DIWANS	DOCIBLE	DOCUMENTS	DOGBANE
DIVIDINGS	DIXI	DOCILE	DOD	DOGBANES
DIVIDIVI	DIXIE	DOCILER	DODDARD	DOGBERRIES
DIVIDIVIS	DIXIES	DOCILEST	DODDED	DOGBERRY
DIVIDUAL	DIXY	DOCILITIES	DODDER	DOGBOLT
DIVIDUOUS	DIZAIN	DOCILITY	DODDERED	DOGBOLTS
DIVINATOR	DIZAINS	DOCIMASIES	DODDERER	DOGCART
DIVINATORS	DIZEN	DOCIMASY	DODDERERS	DOGCARTS
DIVINE	DIZENED	DOCK	DODDERIER	DOGDAYS
DIVINED	DIZENING	DOCKAGE	DODDERIEST	DOGE
DIVINELY	DIZENS	DOCKAGES	DODDERING	DOGEATE
DIVINER	DIZYGOTIC	DOCKED	DODDERS	DOGEATES
DIVINERS	DIZZARD	DOCKEN	DODDERY	DOGES
DIVINES	DIZZARDS	DOCKENS	DODDIER	DOGESHIP
DIVINEST	DIZZIED	DOCKER	DODDIES	DOGESHIPS
DIVING	DIZZIER	DOCKERS	DODDIEST	DOGFIGHT
DIVINGS	DIZZIES	DOCKET	DODDING	DOGFIGHTS

The Chambers Dictionary is the authority for many longer words; see *OSW* Introduction, page xii.

DOGFISH	DOGTEETH	DOLLINESS	DOMINATOR	DONNATS
DOGFISHES	DOGTOOTH	DOLLINESSES	DOMINATORS	DONNE
DOGFOX	DOGTOWN	DOLLING	DOMINEE	DONNED
DOGFOXES	DOGTOWNS	DOLLISH	DOMINEER	DONNEE
DOGGED	DOGTROT	DOLLOP	DOMINEERED	DONNEES
DOGGEDER	DOGTROTS	DOLLOPS	DOMINEERING	DONNERD
DOGGEDEST	DOGVANE	DOLLS	DOMINEERS	DONNERED
DOGGEDLY	DOGVANES	DOLLY	DOMINEES	DONNERT
DOGGER	DOGWOOD	DOLLYING	DOMING	DONNES
DOGGEREL	DOGWOODS	DOLMA	DOMINICAL	DONNING
DOGGERELS	DOGY	DOLMADES	DOMINIE	DONNISH
DOGGERIES	DOH	DOLMAN	DOMINIES	DONNISM
DOGGERMAN	DOHS	DOLMANS	DOMINION	DONNISMS
DOGGERMEN	DOHYO	DOLMAS	DOMINIONS	DONNOT
DOGGERS	DOHYOS	DOLMEN	DOMINO	DONNOTS
DOGGERY	DOILED	DOLMENS	DOMINOES	DONOR
DOGGESS	DOILIES	DOLOMITE	DOMINOS	DONORS
DOGGESSES	DOILT	DOLOMITES	DOMY	DONS
DOGGIE	DOILTER	DOLOMITIC	DON	DONSHIP
DOGGIER	DOILTEST	DOLOR	DONA	DONSHIPS
DOGGIES	DOILY	DOLORIFIC	DONAH	DONSIE
DOGGIEST	DOING	DOLOROSO	DONAHS	DONSIER
DOGGINESS	DOINGS	DOLOROUS	DONARIES	DONSIEST
DOGGINESSES	DOIT	DOLORS	DONARY	DONUT
DOGGING	DOITED	DOLOUR	DONAS	DONUTS
DOGGINGS	DOITIT	DOLOURS	DONATARIES	DONUTTED
DOGGISH	DOITKIN	DOLPHIN	DONATARY	DONUTTING
DOGGISHLY	DOITKINS	DOLPHINET	DONATE	DONZEL
DOGGO	DOITS	DOLPHINETS	DONATED	DONZELS
DOGGONE	DOJO	DOLPHINS	DONATES	DOO
DOGGONED	DOJOS	DOLT	DONATING	DOOB
DOGGREL	DOLCE	DOLTISH	DONATION	DOOBS
DOGGRELS	DOLCES	DOLTISHLY	DONATIONS	DOOCOT
DOGGY	DOLDRUMS	DOLTS	DONATISM	DOOCOTS
DOGHOLE	DOLE	DOMAIN	DONATISMS	DOODAD
DOGHOLES	DOLED	DOMAINAL	DONATIVE	DOODADS
DOGIE	DOLEFUL	DOMAINS	DONATIVES	DOODAH
DOGIES	DOLEFULLY	DOMAL	DONATOR	DOODAHS
DOGMA	DOLENT	DOMANIAL	DONATORIES	DOODLE
DOGMAS	DOLERITE	DOMATIA	DONATORS	DOODLEBUG
DOGMATIC	DOLERITES	DOMATIUM	DONATORY	DOODLEBUGS
DOGMATICS	DOLERITIC	DOME	DONDER	DOODLED
DOGMATISE	DOLES	DOMED	DONDERED	DOODLER
DOGMATISED	DOLESOME	DOMES	DONDERING	DOODLERS
DOGMATISES	DOLIA	DOMESTIC	DONDERS	DOODLES
DOGMATISING	DOLICHOS	DOMESTICS	DONE	DOODLING
DOGMATISM	DOLICHOSES	DOMETT	DONEE	DOOK
DOGMATISMS	DOLICHURI	DOMETTS	DONEES	DOOKED
DOGMATIST	DOLINA	DOMICAL	DONENESS	DOOKET
DOGMATISTS	DOLINAS	DOMICIL	DONENESSES	DOOKETS
DOGMATIZE	DOLINE	DOMICILE	DONG	DOOKING
DOGMATIZED	DOLINES	DOMICILED	DONGA	DOOKS
DOGMATIZES	DOLING	DOMICILES	DONGAS	DOOL
DOGMATIZING	DOLIUM	DOMICILING	DONGED	DOOLALLY
DOGMATORY	DOLL	DOMICILS	DONGING	DOOLE
DOGS	DOLLAR	DOMIER	DONGLE	DOOLES
DOGSBODIES	DOLLARED	DOMIEST	DONGLES	DOOLIE
DOGSBODY	DOLLARS	DOMINANCE	DONGS	DOOLIES
DOGSHIP	DOLLDOM	DOMINANCES	DONING	DOOLS
DOGSHIPS	DOLLDOMS	DOMINANCIES	DONINGS	DOOM
DOGSHORES	DOLLED	DOMINANCY	DONJON	DOOMED
DOGSKIN	DOLLHOOD	DOMINANT	DONJONS	DOOMFUL
DOGSKINS	DOLLHOODS	DOMINANTS	DONKEY	DOOMIER
DOGSLED	DOLLIED	DOMINATE	DONKEYS	DOOMIEST
DOGSLEDS	DOLLIER	DOMINATED	DONNARD	DOOMING
DOGSLEEP	DOLLIERS	DOMINATES	DONNART	DOOMS
DOGSLEEPS	DOLLIES	DOMINATING	DONNAT	DOOMSAYER

The Chambers Dictionary is the authority for many longer words; see *OSW* Introduction, page xii.

DOOMSAYERS
DOOMSDAY
DOOMSDAYS
DOOMSMAN
DOOMSMEN
DOOMSTER
DOOMSTERS
DOOMWATCH
DOOMWATCHED
DOOMWATCHES
DOOMWATCHING
DOOMWATCHINGS
DOOMY
DOONA
DOONAS
DOOR
DOORBELL
DOORBELLS
DOORKNOB
DOORKNOBS
DOORKNOCK
DOORKNOCKED
DOORKNOCKING
DOORKNOCKS
DOORMAT
DOORMATS
DOORN
DOORNAIL
DOORNAILS
DOORNS
DOORPOST
DOORPOSTS
DOORS
DOORSMAN
DOORSMEN
DOORSTEP
DOORSTEPPED
DOORSTEPPING
DOORSTEPPINGS
DOORSTEPS
DOORSTONE
DOORSTONES
DOORSTOP
DOORSTOPS
DOORWAY
DOORWAYS
DOOS
DOP
DOPA
DOPAMINE
DOPAMINES
DOPANT
DOPANTS
DOPAS
DOPATTA
DOPATTAS
DOPE
DOPED
DOPER
DOPERS
DOPES
DOPEY
DOPIER
DOPIEST
DOPINESS
DOPINESSES
DOPING

DOPINGS
DOPPED
DOPPER
DOPPERS
DOPPIE
DOPPIES
DOPPING
DOPPINGS
DOPS
DOPY
DOR
DORAD
DORADO
DORADOS
DORADS
DOREE
DOREES
DORHAWK
DORHAWKS
DORIDOID
DORIDOIDS
DORIES
DORISE
DORISED
DORISES
DORISING
DORIZE
DORIZED
DORIZES
DORIZING
DORK
DORKIER
DORKIEST
DORKS
DORKY
DORLACH
DORLACHS
DORM
DORMANCIES
DORMANCY
DORMANT
DORMANTS
DORMER
DORMERS
DORMICE
DORMIE
DORMIENT
DORMITION
DORMITIONS
DORMITIVE
DORMITIVES
DORMITORIES
DORMITORY
DORMOUSE
DORMS
DORMY
DORNICK
DORNICKS
DORONICUM
DORONICUMS
DORP
DORPS
DORR
DORRED
DORRING
DORRS
DORS

DORSA
DORSAL
DORSALLY
DORSALS
DORSE
DORSEL
DORSELS
DORSER
DORSERS
DORSES
DORSIFLEX
DORSUM
DORT
DORTED
DORTER
DORTERS
DORTIER
DORTIEST
DORTING
DORTOUR
DORTOURS
DORTS
DORTY
DORY
DOS
DOSAGE
DOSAGES
DOSE
DOSED
DOSEH
DOSEHS
DOSES
DOSH
DOSHES
DOSIMETER
DOSIMETERS
DOSIMETRIES
DOSIMETRY
DOSING
DOSIOLOGIES
DOSIOLOGY
DOSOLOGIES
DOSOLOGY
DOSS
DOSSAL
DOSSALS
DOSSED
DOSSEL
DOSSELS
DOSSER
DOSSERS
DOSSES
DOSSHOUSE
DOSSHOUSES
DOSSIER
DOSSIERS
DOSSIL
DOSSILS
DOSSING
DOST
DOT
DOTAGE
DOTAGES
DOTAL
DOTANT
DOTANTS
DOTARD

DOTARDS
DOTATION
DOTATIONS
DOTE
DOTED
DOTER
DOTERS
DOTES
DOTH
DOTIER
DOTIEST
DOTING
DOTINGLY
DOTINGS
DOTISH
DOTS
DOTTED
DOTTEREL
DOTTERELS
DOTTIER
DOTTIEST
DOTTINESS
DOTTINESSES
DOTTING
DOTTIPOLL
DOTTIPOLLS
DOTTLE
DOTTLED
DOTTLER
DOTTLES
DOTTLEST
DOTTREL
DOTTRELS
DOTTY
DOTY
DOUANE
DOUANES
DOUANIER
DOUANIERS
DOUAR
DOUARS
DOUBLE
DOUBLED
DOUBLER
DOUBLERS
DOUBLES
DOUBLET
DOUBLETON
DOUBLETONS
DOUBLETS
DOUBLING
DOUBLINGS
DOUBLOON
DOUBLOONS
DOUBLY
DOUBT
DOUBTABLE
DOUBTED
DOUBTER
DOUBTERS
DOUBTFUL
DOUBTFULS
DOUBTING
DOUBTINGS
DOUBTLESS
DOUBTS
DOUC

DOUCE
DOUCELY
DOUCENESS
DOUCENESSES
DOUCEPERE
DOUCEPERES
DOUCER
DOUCEST
DOUCET
DOUCETS
DOUCEUR
DOUCEURS
DOUCHE
DOUCHED
DOUCHES
DOUCHING
DOUCINE
DOUCINES
DOUCS
DOUGH
DOUGHIER
DOUGHIEST
DOUGHNUT
DOUGHNUTS
DOUGHNUTTED
DOUGHNUTTING
DOUGHNUTTINGS
DOUGHS
DOUGHT
DOUGHTIER
DOUGHTIEST
DOUGHTILY
DOUGHTY
DOUGHY
DOULEIA
DOULEIAS
DOUMA
DOUMAS
DOUP
DOUPS
DOUR
DOURA
DOURAS
DOURER
DOUREST
DOURINE
DOURINES
DOURNESS
DOURNESSES
DOUSE
DOUSED
DOUSER
DOUSERS
DOUSES
DOUSING
DOUT
DOUTED
DOUTER
DOUTERS
DOUTING
DOUTS
DOUZEPER
DOUZEPERS
DOVE
DOVECOT
DOVECOTS
DOVED

The Chambers Dictionary is the authority for many longer words; see *OSW* Introduction, page xii.

DOVEISH	DOWLS	DOWNTRENDS	DRABBLES	DRAGONESSES
DOVEKIE	DOWN	DOWNTURN	DRABBLING	DRAGONET
DOVEKIES	DOWNA	DOWNTURNS	DRABBLINGS	DRAGONETS
DOVELET	DOWNBEAT	DOWNWARD	DRABBY	DRAGONFLIES
DOVELETS	DOWNBEATS	DOWNWARDS	DRABETTE	DRAGONFLY
DOVELIKE	DOWNBOW	DOWNWIND	DRABETTES	DRAGONISE
DOVER	DOWNBOWS	DOWNY	DRABLER	DRAGONISED
DOVERED	DOWNBURST	DOWP	DRABLERS	DRAGONISES
DOVERING	DOWNBURSTS	DOWPS	DRABLY	DRAGONISH
DOVERS	DOWNCAST	DOWRIES	DRABNESS	DRAGONISING
DOVES	DOWNCASTS	DOWRY	DRABNESSES	DRAGONISM
DOVETAIL	DOWNED	DOWS	DRABS	DRAGONISMS
DOVETAILED	DOWNER	DOWSE	DRACHM	DRAGONIZE
DOVETAILING	DOWNERS	DOWSED	DRACHMA	DRAGONIZED
DOVETAILINGS	DOWNFALL	DOWSER	DRACHMAE	DRAGONIZES
DOVETAILS	DOWNFALLS	DOWSERS	DRACHMAI	DRAGONIZING
DOVIE	DOWNFLOW	DOWSES	DRACHMAS	DRAGONNE
DOVIER	DOWNFLOWS	DOWSET	DRACHMS	DRAGONS
DOVIEST	DOWNFORCE	DOWSETS	DRACONE	DRAGOON
DOVING	DOWNFORCES	DOWSING	DRACONES	DRAGOONED
DOVISH	DOWNGRADE	DOWT	DRACONIAN	DRAGOONING
DOW	DOWNGRADED	DOWTS	DRACONIC	DRAGOONS
DOWABLE	DOWNGRADES	DOXIES	DRACONISM	DRAGS
DOWAGER	DOWNGRADING	DOXOLOGIES	DRACONISMS	DRAGSMAN
DOWAGERS	DOWNHILL	DOXOLOGY	DRACONTIC	DRAGSMEN
DOWAR	DOWNHILLS	DOXY	DRAD	DRAGSTER
DOWARS	DOWNHOLE	DOYEN	DRAFF	DRAGSTERS
DOWD	DOWNIER	DOYENNE	DRAFFIER	DRAIL
DOWDIER	DOWNIEST	DOYENNES	DRAFFIEST	DRAILED
DOWDIES	DOWNINESS	DOYENS	DRAFFISH	DRAILING
DOWDIEST	DOWNINESSES	DOYLEY	DRAFFS	DRAILS
DOWDILY	DOWNING	DOYLEYS	DRAFFY	DRAIN
DOWDINESS	DOWNLAND	DOYLIES	DRAFT	DRAINABLE
DOWDINESSES	DOWNLANDS	DOYLY	DRAFTED	DRAINAGE
DOWDS	DOWNLOAD	DOZE	DRAFTEE	DRAINAGES
DOWDY	DOWNLOADED	DOZED	DRAFTEES	DRAINED
DOWDYISH	DOWNLOADING	DOZEN	DRAFTER	DRAINER
DOWDYISM	DOWNLOADS	DOZENED	DRAFTERS	DRAINERS
DOWDYISMS	DOWNMOST	DOZENING	DRAFTIER	DRAINING
DOWED	DOWNPIPE	DOZENS	DRAFTIEST	DRAINPIPE
DOWEL	DOWNPIPES	DOZENTH	DRAFTING	DRAINPIPES
DOWELLED	DOWNPLAY	DOZENTHS	DRAFTS	DRAINS
DOWELLING	DOWNPLAYED	DOZER	DRAFTSMAN	DRAISENE
DOWELLINGS	DOWNPLAYING	DOZERS	DRAFTSMEN	DRAISENES
DOWELS	DOWNPLAYS	DOZES	DRAFTY	DRAISINE
DOWER	DOWNPOUR	DOZIER	DRAG	DRAISINES
DOWERED	DOWNPOURS	DOZIEST	DRAGEE	DRAKE
DOWERING	DOWNRIGHT	DOZINESS	DRAGEES	DRAKES
DOWERLESS	DOWNRUSH	DOZINESSES	DRAGGED	DRAM
DOWERS	DOWNRUSHES	DOZING	DRAGGIER	DRAMA
DOWF	DOWNS	DOZINGS	DRAGGIEST	DRAMAS
DOWFNESS	DOWNSIDE	DOZY	DRAGGING	DRAMATIC
DOWFNESSES	DOWNSIDES	DRAB	DRAGGLE	DRAMATICS
DOWIE	DOWNSIZE	DRABBED	DRAGGLED	DRAMATISE
DOWIER	DOWNSIZED	DRABBER	DRAGGLES	DRAMATISED
DOWIEST	DOWNSIZES	DRABBERS	DRAGGLING	DRAMATISES
DOWING	DOWNSIZING	DRABBEST	DRAGGY	DRAMATISING
DOWITCHER	DOWNSPOUT	DRABBET	DRAGHOUND	DRAMATIST
DOWITCHERS	DOWNSPOUTS	DRABBETS	DRAGHOUNDS	DRAMATISTS
DOWL	DOWNSTAGE	DRABBIER	DRAGLINE	DRAMATIZE
DOWLAS	DOWNSTAIR	DRABBIEST	DRAGLINES	DRAMATIZED
DOWLASES	DOWNSTAIRS	DRABBING	DRAGNET	DRAMATIZES
DOWLE	DOWNSWING	DRABBISH	DRAGNETS	DRAMATIZING
DOWLES	DOWNSWINGS	DRABBLE	DRAGOMAN	DRAMATURG
DOWLNE	DOWNTIME	DRABBLED	DRAGOMANS	DRAMATURGS
DOWLNES	DOWNTIMES	DRABBLER	DRAGON	DRAMMACH
DOWLNEY	DOWNTREND	DRABBLERS	DRAGONESS	DRAMMACHS

The Chambers Dictionary is the authority for many longer words; see *OSW* Introduction, page xii.

DRAMMED	DRAWLING	DREED	DRIBS	DRIVING
DRAMMING	DRAWLS	DREEING	DRICKSIE	DRIZZLE
DRAMMOCK	DRAWN	DREES	DRICKSIER	DRIZZLED
DRAMMOCKS	DRAWS	DREG	DRICKSIEST	DRIZZLES
DRAMS	DRAY	DREGGIER	DRIED	DRIZZLIER
DRANK	DRAYAGE	DREGGIEST	DRIER	DRIZZLIEST
DRANT	DRAYAGES	DREGGY	DRIERS	DRIZZLING
DRANTED	DRAYMAN	DREGS	DRIES	DRIZZLY
DRANTING	DRAYMEN	DREICH	DRIEST	DROGER
DRANTS	DRAYS	DREICHER	DRIFT	DROGERS
DRAP	DRAZEL	DREICHEST	DRIFTAGE	DROGHER
DRAPE	DRAZELS	DREK	DRIFTAGES	DROGHERS
DRAPED	DREAD	DREKS	DRIFTED	DROGUE
DRAPER	DREADED	DRENCH	DRIFTER	DROGUES
DRAPERIED	DREADER	DRENCHED	DRIFTERS	DROGUET
DRAPERIES	DREADERS	DRENCHER	DRIFTIER	DROGUETS
DRAPERS	DREADFUL	DRENCHERS	DRIFTIEST	DROICH
DRAPERY	DREADING	DRENCHES	DRIFTING	DROICHIER
DRAPERYING	DREADLESS	DRENCHING	DRIFTLESS	DROICHIEST
DRAPES	DREADLY	DRENT	DRIFTPIN	DROICHS
DRAPET	DREADS	DREPANIUM	DRIFTPINS	DROICHY
DRAPETS	DREAM	DREPANIUMS	DRIFTS	DROIL
DRAPIER	DREAMBOAT	DRERE	DRIFTWOOD	DROILED
DRAPIERS	DREAMBOATS	DRERES	DRIFTWOODS	DROILING
DRAPING	DREAMED	DRERIHEAD	DRIFTY	DROILS
DRAPPED	DREAMER	DRERIHEADS	DRILL	DROIT
DRAPPIE	DREAMERIES	DRESS	DRILLED	DROITS
DRAPPIES	DREAMERS	DRESSAGE	DRILLER	DROLE
DRAPPING	DREAMERY	DRESSAGES	DRILLERS	DROLER
DRAPPY	DREAMFUL	DRESSED	DRILLING	DROLES
DRAPS	DREAMHOLE	DRESSER	DRILLINGS	DROLEST
DRASTIC	DREAMHOLES	DRESSERS	DRILLS	DROLL
DRASTICS	DREAMIER	DRESSES	DRILLSHIP	DROLLED
DRAT	DREAMIEST	DRESSIER	DRILLSHIPS	DROLLER
DRATCHELL	DREAMILY	DRESSIEST	DRILY	DROLLERIES
DRATCHELLS	DREAMING	DRESSING	DRINK	DROLLERY
DRATTED	DREAMINGS	DRESSINGS	DRINKABLE	DROLLEST
DRAUGHT	DREAMLESS	DRESSMADE	DRINKER	DROLLING
DRAUGHTED	DREAMS	DRESSMAKE	DRINKERS	DROLLINGS
DRAUGHTER	DREAMT	DRESSMAKES	DRINKING	DROLLISH
DRAUGHTERS	DREAMTIME	DRESSMAKING	DRINKINGS	DROLLNESS
DRAUGHTIER	DREAMTIMES	DRESSMAKINGS	DRINKS	DROLLNESSES
DRAUGHTIEST	DREAMY	DRESSY	DRIP	DROLLS
DRAUGHTING	DREAR	DREST	DRIPPED	DROLLY
DRAUGHTS	DREARE	DREVILL	DRIPPIER	DROME
DRAUGHTY	DREARER	DREVILLS	DRIPPIEST	DROMEDARE
DRAUNT	DREARES	DREW	DRIPPING	DROMEDARES
DRAUNTED	DREAREST	DREY	DRIPPINGS	DROMEDARIES
DRAUNTING	DREARIER	DREYS	DRIPPY	DROMEDARY
DRAUNTS	DREARIEST	DRIB	DRIPS	DROMES
DRAVE	DREARILY	DRIBBED	DRISHEEN	DROMIC
DRAW	DREARING	DRIBBER	DRISHEENS	DROMICAL
DRAWABLE	DREARINGS	DRIBBERS	DRIVABLE	DROMOI
DRAWBACK	DREARS	DRIBBING	DRIVE	DROMON
DRAWBACKS	DREARY	DRIBBLE	DRIVEABLE	DROMOND
DRAWBAR	DRECK	DRIBBLED	DRIVEL	DROMONDS
DRAWBARS	DRECKIER	DRIBBLER	DRIVELLED	DROMONS
DRAWEE	DRECKIEST	DRIBBLERS	DRIVELLER	DROMOS
DRAWEES	DRECKS	DRIBBLES	DRIVELLERS	DRONE
DRAWER	DRECKY	DRIBBLET	DRIVELLING	DRONED
DRAWERS	DREDGE	DRIBBLETS	DRIVELS	DRONES
DRAWING	DREDGED	DRIBBLIER	DRIVEN	DRONGO
DRAWINGS	DREDGER	DRIBBLIEST	DRIVER	DRONGOES
DRAWL	DREDGERS	DRIBBLING	DRIVERS	DRONGOS
DRAWLED	DREDGES	DRIBBLY	DRIVES	DRONIER
DRAWLER	DREDGING	DRIBLET	DRIVEWAY	DRONIEST
DRAWLERS	DREE	DRIBLETS	DRIVEWAYS	DRONING

The Chambers Dictionary is the authority for many longer words; see *OSW* Introduction, page xii.

DRONINGLY	DROUKED	DRUID	DRYERS	DUCE
DRONISH	DROUKING	DRUIDESS	DRYING	DUCES
DRONISHLY	DROUKINGS	DRUIDESSES	DRYINGS	DUCHESS
DRONY	DROUKIT	DRUIDIC	DRYISH	DUCHESSE
DROOG	DROUKS	DRUIDICAL	DRYLY	DUCHESSES
DROOGISH	DROUTH	DRUIDISM	DRYMOUTH	DUCHIES
DROOGS	DROUTHIER	DRUIDISMS	DRYMOUTHS	DUCHY
DROOK	DROUTHIEST	DRUIDS	DRYNESS	DUCK
DROOKED	DROUTHS	DRUM	DRYNESSES	DUCKBILL
DROOKING	DROUTHY	DRUMBEAT	DRYSALTER	DUCKBILLS
DROOKINGS	DROVE	DRUMBEATS	DRYSALTERS	DUCKED
DROOKIT	DROVER	DRUMBLE	DSO	DUCKER
DROOKS	DROVERS	DRUMBLED	DSOBO	DUCKERS
DROOL	DROVES	DRUMBLES	DSOBOS	DUCKIER
DROOLED	DROVING	DRUMBLING	DSOMO	DUCKIES
DROOLING	DROVINGS	DRUMFIRE	DSOMOS	DUCKIEST
DROOLS	DROW	DRUMFIRES	DSOS	DUCKING
DROOME	DROWN	DRUMFISH	DUAD	DUCKINGS
DROOMES	DROWNDED	DRUMFISHES	DUADS	DUCKLING
DROOP	DROWNED	DRUMHEAD	DUAL	DUCKLINGS
DROOPED	DROWNER	DRUMHEADS	DUALIN	DUCKMOLE
DROOPIER	DROWNERS	DRUMLIER	DUALINS	DUCKMOLES
DROOPIEST	DROWNING	DRUMLIEST	DUALISM	DUCKS
DROOPILY	DROWNINGS	DRUMLIN	DUALISMS	DUCKSHOVE
DROOPING	DROWNS	DRUMLINS	DUALIST	DUCKSHOVED
DROOPS	DROWS	DRUMLY	DUALISTIC	DUCKSHOVES
DROOPY	DROWSE	DRUMMED	DUALISTS	DUCKSHOVING
DROP	DROWSED	DRUMMER	DUALITIES	DUCKWEED
DROPFLIES	DROWSES	DRUMMERS	DUALITY	DUCKWEEDS
DROPFLY	DROWSIER	DRUMMING	DUALLED	DUCKY
DROPLET	DROWSIEST	DRUMMOCK	DUALLING	DUCT
DROPLETS	DROWSIHED	DRUMMOCKS	DUALLY	DUCTED
DROPPED	DROWSIHEDS	DRUMS	DUALS	DUCTILE
DROPPER	DROWSILY	DRUMSTICK	DUAN	DUCTILITIES
DROPPERS	DROWSING	DRUMSTICKS	DUANS	DUCTILITY
DROPPING	DROWSY	DRUNK	DUAR	DUCTING
DROPPINGS	DRUB	DRUNKARD	DUARCHIES	DUCTLESS
DROPPLE	DRUBBED	DRUNKARDS	DUARCHY	DUCTS
DROPPLES	DRUBBING	DRUNKEN	DUARS	DUD
DROPS	DRUBBINGS	DRUNKENLY	DUB	DUDDER
DROPSICAL	DRUBS	DRUNKER	DUBBED	DUDDERIES
DROPSIED	DRUCKEN	DRUNKEST	DUBBIN	DUDDERS
DROPSIES	DRUDGE	DRUNKS	DUBBING	DUDDERY
DROPSTONE	DRUDGED	DRUPE	DUBBINGS	DUDDIE
DROPSTONES	DRUDGER	DRUPEL	DUBBINS	DUDDIER
DROPSY	DRUDGERIES	DRUPELET	DUBIETIES	DUDDIEST
DROPWISE	DRUDGERS	DRUPELETS	DUBIETY	DUDDY
DROSERA	DRUDGERY	DRUPELS	DUBIOSITIES	DUDE
DROSERAS	DRUDGES	DRUPES	DUBIOSITY	DUDEEN
DROSHKIES	DRUDGING	DRUSE	DUBIOUS	DUDEENS
DROSHKY	DRUDGISM	DRUSES	DUBIOUSLY	DUDES
DROSKIES	DRUDGISMS	DRUSIER	DUBITABLE	DUDGEON
DROSKY	DRUG	DRUSIEST	DUBITABLY	DUDGEONS
DROSS	DRUGGED	DRUSY	DUBITANCIES	DUDHEEN
DROSSES	DRUGGER	DRUTHERS	DUBITANCY	DUDHEENS
DROSSIER	DRUGGERS	DRUXIER	DUBITATE	DUDISH
DROSSIEST	DRUGGET	DRUXIEST	DUBITATED	DUDISM
DROSSY	DRUGGETS	DRUXY	DUBITATES	DUDISMS
DROSTDIES	DRUGGIE	DRY	DUBITATING	DUDS
DROSTDY	DRUGGIER	DRYAD	DUBS	DUE
DROSTDYS	DRUGGIES	DRYADES	DUCAL	DUED
DROUGHT	DRUGGIEST	DRYADS	DUCALLY	DUEFUL
DROUGHTIER	DRUGGING	DRYBEAT	DUCAT	DUEL
DROUGHTIEST	DRUGGIST	DRYBEATEN	DUCATOON	DUELLED
DROUGHTS	DRUGGISTS	DRYBEATING	DUCATOONS	DUELLER
DROUGHTY	DRUGGY	DRYBEATS	DUCATS	DUELLERS
DROUK	DRUGS	DRYER	DUCDAME	DUELLING

The Chambers Dictionary is the authority for many longer words; see *OSW* Introduction, page xii.

DUELLINGS	DULCIANAS	DUMFOUNDING	DUNGMERE	DUPER
DUELLIST	DULCIANS	DUMFOUNDS	DUNGMERES	DUPERIES
DUELLISTS	DULCIFIED	DUMKA	DUNGS	DUPERS
DUELLO	DULCIFIES	DUMKY	DUNGY	DUPERY
DUELLOS	DULCIFY	DUMMERER	DUNITE	DUPES
DUELS	DULCIFYING	DUMMERERS	DUNITES	DUPING
DUELSOME	DULCIMER	DUMMIED	DUNK	DUPION
DUENDE	DULCIMERS	DUMMIER	DUNKED	DUPIONS
DUENDES	DULCITE	DUMMIES	DUNKER	DUPLE
DUENNA	DULCITES	DUMMIEST	DUNKERS	DUPLET
DUENNAS	DULCITOL	DUMMINESS	DUNKING	DUPLETS
DUES	DULCITOLS	DUMMINESSES	DUNKS	DUPLEX
DUET	DULCITUDE	DUMMY	DUNLIN	DUPLEXER
DUETS	DULCITUDES	DUMMYING	DUNLINS	DUPLEXERS
DUETT	DULCOSE	DUMOSE	DUNNAGE	DUPLEXES
DUETTED	DULCOSES	DUMOSITIES	DUNNAGES	DUPLICAND
DUETTI	DULE	DUMOSITY	DUNNAKIN	DUPLICANDS
DUETTING	DULES	DUMOUS	DUNNAKINS	DUPLICATE
DUETTINO	DULIA	DUMP	DUNNART	DUPLICATED
DUETTINOS	DULIAS	DUMPBIN	DUNNARTS	DUPLICATES
DUETTIST	DULL	DUMPBINS	DUNNED	DUPLICATING
DUETTISTS	DULLARD	DUMPED	DUNNER	DUPLICITIES
DUETTO	DULLARDS	DUMPER	DUNNEST	DUPLICITY
DUETTOS	DULLED	DUMPERS	DUNNIER	DUPLIED
DUETTS	DULLER	DUMPIER	DUNNIES	DUPLIES
DUFF	DULLEST	DUMPIES	DUNNIEST	DUPLY
DUFFED	DULLIER	DUMPIEST	DUNNING	DUPLYING
DUFFEL	DULLIEST	DUMPINESS	DUNNINGS	DUPONDII
DUFFELS	DULLING	DUMPINESSES	DUNNISH	DUPONDIUS
DUFFER	DULLISH	DUMPING	DUNNITE	DUPPED
DUFFERDOM	DULLNESS	DUMPISH	DUNNITES	DUPPIES
DUFFERDOMS	DULLNESSES	DUMPISHLY	DUNNO	DUPPING
DUFFERISM	DULLS	DUMPLE	DUNNOCK	DUPPY
DUFFERISMS	DULLY	DUMPLED	DUNNOCKS	DUPS
DUFFERS	DULNESS	DUMPLES	DUNNY	DURA
DUFFEST	DULNESSES	DUMPLING	DUNS	DURABLE
DUFFING	DULOCRACIES	DUMPLINGS	DUNSH	DURABLES
DUFFINGS	DULOCRACY	DUMPS	DUNSHED	DURABLY
DUFFLE	DULOSES	DUMPY	DUNSHES	DURAL
DUFFLES	DULOSIS	DUN	DUNSHING	DURALS
DUFFS	DULOTIC	DUNCE	DUNT	DURALUMIN
DUG	DULSE	DUNCEDOM	DUNTED	DURALUMINS
DUGONG	DULSES	DUNCEDOMS	DUNTING	DURAMEN
DUGONGS	DULY	DUNCERIES	DUNTS	DURAMENS
DUGOUT	DUMA	DUNCERY	DUO	DURANCE
DUGOUTS	DUMAIST	DUNCES	DUODECIMO	DURANCES
DUGS	DUMAISTS	DUNCH	DUODECIMOS	DURANT
DUIKER	DUMAS	DUNCHED	DUODENA	DURANTS
DUIKERS	DUMB	DUNCHES	DUODENAL	DURAS
DUING	DUMBED	DUNCHING	DUODENARY	DURATION
DUKE	DUMBER	DUNDER	DUODENUM	DURATIONS
DUKED	DUMBEST	DUNDERS	DUOLOGUE	DURBAR
DUKEDOM	DUMBFOUND	DUNE	DUOLOGUES	DURBARS
DUKEDOMS	DUMBFOUNDED	DUNES	DUOMI	DURDUM
DUKELING	DUMBFOUNDING	DUNG	DUOMO	DURDUMS
DUKELINGS	DUMBFOUNDS	DUNGAREE	DUOMOS	DURE
DUKERIES	DUMBING	DUNGAREES	DUOPOLIES	DURED
DUKERY	DUMBLY	DUNGED	DUOPOLY	DUREFUL
DUKES	DUMBNESS	DUNGEON	DUOS	DURES
DUKESHIP	DUMBNESSES	DUNGEONED	DUOTONE	DURESS
DUKESHIPS	DUMBO	DUNGEONER	DUOTONES	DURESSE
DUKING	DUMBOS	DUNGEONERS	DUP	DURESSES
DULCAMARA	DUMBS	DUNGEONING	DUPABLE	DURGAN
DULCAMARAS	DUMDUM	DUNGEONS	DUPATTA	DURGANS
DULCET	DUMDUMS	DUNGIER	DUPATTAS	DURGIER
DULCIAN	DUMFOUND	DUNGIEST	DUPE	DURGIEST
DULCIANA	DUMFOUNDED	DUNGING	DUPED	DURGY

DURIAN	DUSTMAN	DWEEB	DYNAMISMS	DYSPEPTICS
DURIANS	DUSTMEN	DWEEBS	DYNAMIST	DYSPHAGIA
DURING	DUSTPROOF	DWELL	DYNAMISTS	DYSPHAGIAS
DURION	DUSTS	DWELLED	DYNAMITE	DYSPHAGIC
DURIONS	DUSTSHEET	DWELLER	DYNAMITED	DYSPHAGIES
DURMAST	DUSTSHEETS	DWELLERS	DYNAMITER	DYSPHAGY
DURMASTS	DUSTY	DWELLING	DYNAMITERS	DYSPHASIA
DURN	DUTCH	DWELLINGS	DYNAMITES	DYSPHASIAS
DURNS	DUTCHES	DWELLS	DYNAMITING	DYSPHONIA
DURO	DUTEOUS	DWELT	DYNAMIZE	DYSPHONIAS
DUROS	DUTEOUSLY	DWILE	DYNAMIZED	DYSPHONIC
DUROY	DUTIABLE	DWILES	DYNAMIZES	DYSPHORIA
DUROYS	DUTIED	DWINDLE	DYNAMIZING	DYSPHORIAS
DURRA	DUTIES	DWINDLED	DYNAMO	DYSPHORIC
DURRAS	DUTIFUL	DWINDLES	DYNAMOS	DYSPLASIA
DURRIE	DUTIFULLY	DWINDLING	DYNAMOTOR	DYSPLASIAS
DURRIES	DUTY	DWINE	DYNAMOTORS	DYSPNEA
DURST	DUUMVIR	DWINED	DYNAST	DYSPNEAL
DURUKULI	DUUMVIRAL	DWINES	DYNASTIC	DYSPNEAS
DURUKULIS	DUUMVIRI	DWINING	DYNASTIES	DYSPNEIC
DURUM	DUUMVIRS	DYABLE	DYNASTS	DYSPNOEA
DURUMS	DUVET	DYAD	DYNASTY	DYSPNOEAL
DUSH	DUVETINE	DYADIC	DYNATRON	DYSPNOEAS
DUSHED	DUVETINES	DYADS	DYNATRONS	DYSPNOEIC
DUSHES	DUVETS	DYARCHIES	DYNE	DYSPRAXIA
DUSHING	DUVETYN	DYARCHY	DYNES	DYSPRAXIAS
DUSK	DUVETYNE	DYBBUK	DYNODE	DYSTECTIC
DUSKED	DUVETYNES	DYBBUKS	DYNODES	DYSTHESIA
DUSKEN	DUVETYNS	DYE	DYSCHROA	DYSTHESIAS
DUSKENED	DUX	DYEABLE	DYSCHROAS	DYSTHETIC
DUSKENING	DUXELLES	DYED	DYSCHROIA	DYSTHYMIA
DUSKENS	DUXES	DYEING	DYSCHROIAS	DYSTHYMIAS
DUSKER	DUYKER	DYEINGS	DYSCRASIA	DYSTHYMIC
DUSKEST	DUYKERS	DYELINE	DYSCRASIAS	DYSTOCIA
DUSKIER	DVANDVA	DYELINES	DYSENTERIES	DYSTOCIAS
DUSKIEST	DVANDVAS	DYER	DYSENTERY	DYSTONIA
DUSKILY	DVORNIK	DYERS	DYSGENIC	DYSTONIAS
DUSKINESS	DVORNIKS	DYES	DYSGENICS	DYSTONIC
DUSKINESSES	DWALE	DYESTER	DYSLECTIC	DYSTOPIA
DUSKING	DWALES	DYESTERS	DYSLECTICS	DYSTOPIAN
DUSKISH	DWALM	DYESTUFF	DYSLEXIA	DYSTOPIAS
DUSKISHLY	DWALMED	DYESTUFFS	DYSLEXIAS	DYSTROPHIES
DUSKLY	DWALMING	DYING	DYSLEXIC	DYSTROPHY
DUSKNESS	DWALMS	DYINGLY	DYSLEXICS	DYSURIA
DUSKNESSES	DWAM	DYINGNESS	DYSLOGIES	DYSURIAS
DUSKS	DWAMMED	DYINGNESSES	DYSLOGY	DYSURIC
DUSKY	DWAMMING	DYINGS	DYSMELIA	DYSURIES
DUST	DWAMS	DYKE	DYSMELIAS	DYSURY
DUSTBIN	DWANG	DYKED	DYSMELIC	DYTISCID
DUSTBINS	DWANGS	DYKES	DYSODIL	DYTISCIDS
DUSTCART	DWARF	DYKEY	DYSODILE	DYVOUR
DUSTCARTS	DWARFED	DYKIER	DYSODILES	DYVOURIES
DUSTED	DWARFING	DYKIEST	DYSODILS	DYVOURS
DUSTER	DWARFISH	DYKING	DYSODYLE	DYVOURY
DUSTERS	DWARFISM	DYNAMIC	DYSODYLES	DZEREN
DUSTIER	DWARFISMS	DYNAMICAL	DYSPATHIES	DZERENS
DUSTIEST	DWARFS	DYNAMICS	DYSPATHY	DZHO
DUSTILY	DWARVES	DYNAMISE	DYSPEPSIA	DZHOS
DUSTINESS	DWAUM	DYNAMISED	DYSPEPSIAS	DZIGGETAI
DUSTINESSES	DWAUMED	DYNAMISES	DYSPEPSIES	DZIGGETAIS
DUSTING	DWAUMING	DYNAMISING	DYSPEPSY	DZO
DUSTLESS	DWAUMS	DYNAMISM	DYSPEPTIC	DZOS

The Chambers Dictionary is the authority for many longer words; see *OSW* Introduction, page xii.

E

EA	EARLDOM	EARTHLINGS	EASTMOST	EBONIES
EACH	EARLDOMS	EARTHLY	EASTS	EBONISE
EACHWHERE	EARLESS	EARTHMAN	EASTWARD	EBONISED
EADISH	EARLIER	EARTHMEN	EASTWARDS	EBONISES
EADISHES	EARLIES	EARTHS	EASY	EBONISING
EAGER	EARLIEST	EARTHWARD	EAT	EBONIST
EAGERER	EARLINESS	EARTHWARDS	EATABLE	EBONISTS
EAGEREST	EARLINESSES	EARTHWAX	EATABLES	EBONITE
EAGERLY	EARLOBE	EARTHWAXES	EATAGE	EBONITES
EAGERNESS	EARLOBES	EARTHWOLF	EATAGES	EBONIZE
EAGERNESSES	EARLOCK	EARTHWOLVES	EATCHE	EBONIZED
EAGERS	EARLOCKS	EARTHWORK	EATCHES	EBONIZES
EAGLE	EARLS	EARTHWORKS	EATEN	EBONIZING
EAGLES	EARLY	EARTHWORM	EATER	EBONS
EAGLET	EARMARK	EARTHWORMS	EATERIES	EBONY
EAGLETS	EARMARKED	EARTHY	EATERS	EBRIATE
EAGLEWOOD	EARMARKING	EARWAX	EATERY	EBRIATED
EAGLEWOODS	EARMARKS	EARWAXES	EATH	EBRIETIES
EAGRE	EARMUFFS	EARWIG	EATHE	EBRIETY
EAGRES	EARN	EARWIGGED	EATHLY	EBRILLADE
EALDORMAN	EARNED	EARWIGGING	EATING	EBRILLADES
EALDORMEN	EARNER	EARWIGGY	EATINGS	EBRIOSE
EALE	EARNERS	EARWIGS	EATS	EBRIOSITIES
EALES	EARNEST	EAS	EAU	EBRIOSITY
EAN	EARNESTLY	EASE	EAUS	EBULLIENT
EANED	EARNESTS	EASED	EAUX	EBURNEAN
EANING	EARNING	EASEFUL	EAVES	EBURNEOUS
EANLING	EARNINGS	EASEL	EAVESDRIP	ECAD
EANLINGS	EARNS	EASELESS	EAVESDRIPS	ECADS
EANS	EARPHONE	EASELS	EAVESDROP	ECARTE
EAR	EARPHONES	EASEMENT	EAVESDROPPED	ECARTES
EARACHE	EARPICK	EASEMENTS	EAVESDROPPING	ECAUDATE
EARACHES	EARPICKS	EASES	EAVESDROPPINGS	ECBOLE
EARBASH	EARPIECE	EASIER	EAVESDROPS	ECBOLES
EARBASHED	EARPIECES	EASIEST	EBAUCHE	ECBOLIC
EARBASHES	EARPLUG	EASILY	EBAUCHES	ECBOLICS
EARBASHING	EARPLUGS	EASINESS	EBB	ECCE
EARBOB	EARRING	EASINESSES	EBBED	ECCENTRIC
EARBOBS	EARRINGS	EASING	EBBING	ECCENTRICS
EARCON	EARS	EASLE	EBBLESS	ECCLESIA
EARCONS	EARSHOT	EASLES	EBBS	ECCLESIAE
EARD	EARSHOTS	EASSEL	EBBTIDE	ECCLESIAL
EARDED	EARST	EASSIL	EBBTIDES	ECCO
EARDING	EARTH	EAST	EBENEZER	ECCRINE
EARDROP	EARTHBORN	EASTBOUND	EBENEZERS	ECCRISES
EARDROPS	EARTHED	EASTED	EBENISTE	ECCRISIS
EARDRUM	EARTHEN	EASTER	EBENISTES	ECCRITIC
EARDRUMS	EARTHFALL	EASTERLIES	EBIONISE	ECCRITICS
EARDS	EARTHFALLS	EASTERLY	EBIONISED	ECDYSES
EARED	EARTHFAST	EASTERN	EBIONISES	ECDYSIAST
EARFLAP	EARTHFLAX	EASTERNER	EBIONISING	ECDYSIASTS
EARFLAPS	EARTHFLAXES	EASTERNERS	EBIONISM	ECDYSIS
EARFUL	EARTHIER	EASTING	EBIONISMS	ECH
EARFULS	EARTHIEST	EASTINGS	EBIONITIC	ECHAPPE
EARING	EARTHING	EASTLAND	EBIONIZE	ECHAPPES
EARINGS	EARTHLIER	EASTLIN	EBIONIZED	ECHE
EARL	EARTHLIES	EASTLING	EBIONIZES	ECHED
EARLAP	EARTHLIEST	EASTLINGS	EBIONIZING	ECHELON
EARLAPS	EARTHLING	EASTLINS	EBON	ECHELONS

The Chambers Dictionary is the authority for many longer words; see *OSW* Introduction, page xii.

ECHES	ECO	ECTHYMA	EDEMATA	EDUCE
ECHEVERIA	ECOCIDE	ECTHYMAS	EDEMATOSE	EDUCED
ECHEVERIAS	ECOCIDES	ECTOBLAST	EDEMATOUS	EDUCEMENT
ECHIDNA	ECOD	ECTOBLASTS	EDENTAL	EDUCEMENTS
ECHIDNAS	ECOFREAK	ECTOCRINE	EDENTATE	EDUCES
ECHIDNINE	ECOFREAKS	ECTOCRINES	EDENTATES	EDUCIBLE
ECHIDNINES	ECOLOGIC	ECTODERM	EDGE	EDUCING
ECHINATE	ECOLOGIES	ECTODERMS	EDGEBONE	EDUCT
ECHINATED	ECOLOGIST	ECTOGENIC	EDGEBONES	EDUCTION
ECHING	ECOLOGISTS	ECTOGENIES	EDGED	EDUCTIONS
ECHINI	ECOLOGY	ECTOGENY	EDGELESS	EDUCTOR
ECHINOID	ECONOMIC	ECTOMORPH	EDGER	EDUCTORS
ECHINOIDS	ECONOMICS	ECTOMORPHS	EDGERS	EDUCTS
ECHINUS	ECONOMIES	ECTOPHYTE	EDGES	EDUSKUNTA
ECHINUSES	ECONOMISE	ECTOPHYTES	EDGEWAYS	EDUSKUNTAS
ECHO	ECONOMISED	ECTOPIA	EDGEWISE	EE
ECHOED	ECONOMISES	ECTOPIAS	EDGIER	EECH
ECHOER	ECONOMISING	ECTOPIC	EDGIEST	EECHED
ECHOERS	ECONOMISM	ECTOPIES	EDGINESS	EECHES
ECHOES	ECONOMISMS	ECTOPLASM	EDGINESSES	EECHING
ECHOGRAM	ECONOMIST	ECTOPLASMS	EDGING	EEK
ECHOGRAMS	ECONOMISTS	ECTOPY	EDGINGS	EEL
ECHOIC	ECONOMIZE	ECTOSARC	EDGY	EELFARE
ECHOING	ECONOMIZED	ECTOSARCS	EDH	EELFARES
ECHOISE	ECONOMIZES	ECTOTHERM	EDHS	EELGRASS
ECHOISED	ECONOMIZING	ECTOTHERMS	EDIBILITIES	EELGRASSES
ECHOISES	ECONOMY	ECTOZOA	EDIBILITY	EELIER
ECHOISING	ECONUT	ECTOZOAN	EDIBLE	EELIEST
ECHOISM	ECONUTS	ECTOZOANS	EDIBLES	EELPOUT
ECHOISMS	ECOPHOBIA	ECTOZOIC	EDICT	EELPOUTS
ECHOIST	ECOPHOBIAS	ECTOZOON	EDICTAL	EELS
ECHOISTS	ECORCHE	ECTROPIC	EDICTALLY	EELWORM
ECHOIZE	ECORCHES	ECTROPION	EDICTS	EELWORMS
ECHOIZED	ECOSPHERE	ECTROPIONS	EDIFICE	EELWRACK
ECHOIZES	ECOSPHERES	ECTROPIUM	EDIFICES	EELWRACKS
ECHOIZING	ECOSSAISE	ECTROPIUMS	EDIFICIAL	EELY
ECHOLALIA	ECOSSAISES	ECTYPAL	EDIFIED	EEN
ECHOLALIAS	ECOSTATE	ECTYPE	EDIFIER	EERIE
ECHOLESS	ECOSYSTEM	ECTYPES	EDIFIERS	EERIER
ECHT	ECOSYSTEMS	ECU	EDIFIES	EERIEST
ECLAIR	ECOTOXIC	ECUELLE	EDIFY	EERILY
ECLAIRS	ECOTYPE	ECUELLES	EDIFYING	EERINESS
ECLAMPSIA	ECOTYPES	ECUMENIC	EDILE	EERINESSES
ECLAMPSIAS	ECRASEUR	ECUMENICS	EDILES	EERY
ECLAMPSIES	ECRASEURS	ECUMENISM	EDIT	EEVEN
ECLAMPSY	ECRITOIRE	ECUMENISMS	EDITED	EEVENS
ECLAMPTIC	ECRITOIRES	ECURIE	EDITING	EEVN
ECLAT	ECRU	ECURIES	EDITION	EEVNING
ECLATS	ECRUS	ECUS	EDITIONS	EEVNINGS
ECLECTIC	ECSTASES	ECZEMA	EDITOR	EEVNS
ECLECTICS	ECSTASIED	ECZEMAS	EDITORIAL	EF
ECLIPSE	ECSTASIES	EDACIOUS	EDITORIALS	EFF
ECLIPSED	ECSTASIS	EDACITIES	EDITORS	EFFABLE
ECLIPSES	ECSTASISE	EDACITY	EDITRESS	EFFACE
ECLIPSING	ECSTASISED	EDAPHIC	EDITRESSES	EFFACED
ECLIPTIC	ECSTASISES	EDDIED	EDITS	EFFACES
ECLIPTICS	ECSTASISING	EDDIES	EDUCABLE	EFFACING
ECLOGITE	ECSTASIZE	EDDISH	EDUCATE	EFFECT
ECLOGITES	ECSTASIZED	EDDISHES	EDUCATED	EFFECTED
ECLOGUE	ECSTASIZES	EDDO	EDUCATES	EFFECTER
ECLOGUES	ECSTASIZING	EDDOES	EDUCATING	EFFECTERS
ECLOSE	ECSTASY	EDDY	EDUCATION	EFFECTING
ECLOSED	ECSTASYING	EDDYING	EDUCATIONS	EFFECTIVE
ECLOSES	ECSTATIC	EDELWEISS	EDUCATIVE	EFFECTIVES
ECLOSING	ECSTATICS	EDELWEISSES	EDUCATOR	EFFECTOR
ECLOSION	ECTASES	EDEMA	EDUCATORS	EFFECTORS
ECLOSIONS	ECTASIS	EDEMAS	EDUCATORY	EFFECTS

The Chambers Dictionary is the authority for many longer words; see *OSW* Introduction, page xii.

EFFECTUAL	EGAD	EGOMANIAS	EIKONS	ELAPSED
EFFED	EGAL	EGOS	EIKS	ELAPSES
EFFEIR	EGALITIES	EGOTHEISM	EILD	ELAPSING
EFFEIRED	EGALITY	EGOTHEISMS	EILDING	ELASTANCE
EFFEIRING	EGALLY	EGOTISE	EILDINGS	ELASTANCES
EFFEIRS	EGAREMENT	EGOTISED	EILDS	ELASTASE
EFFENDI	EGAREMENTS	EGOTISES	EINE	ELASTASES
EFFENDIS	EGENCE	EGOTISING	EIRACK	ELASTIC
EFFERE	EGENCES	EGOTISM	EIRACKS	ELASTICS
EFFERED	EGENCIES	EGOTISMS	EIRENIC	ELASTIN
EFFERENCE	EGENCY	EGOTIST	EIRENICON	ELASTINS
EFFERENCES	EGER	EGOTISTIC	EIRENICONS	ELASTOMER
EFFERENT	EGERS	EGOTISTS	EISEL	ELASTOMERS
EFFERES	EGEST	EGOTIZE	EISELL	ELATE
EFFERING	EGESTA	EGOTIZED	EISELLS	ELATED
EFFETE	EGESTED	EGOTIZES	EISELS	ELATEDLY
EFFETELY	EGESTING	EGOTIZING	EITHER	ELATER
EFFICACIES	EGESTION	EGREGIOUS	EJACULATE	ELATERIN
EFFICACY	EGESTIONS	EGRESS	EJACULATED	ELATERINS
EFFICIENT	EGESTIVE	EGRESSES	EJACULATES	ELATERITE
EFFICIENTS	EGESTS	EGRESSION	EJACULATING	ELATERITES
EFFIERCE	EGG	EGRESSIONS	EJECT	ELATERIUM
EFFIERCED	EGGAR	EGRET	EJECTA	ELATERIUMS
EFFIERCES	EGGARS	EGRETS	EJECTED	ELATERS
EFFIERCING	EGGCUP	EH	EJECTING	ELATES
EFFIGIES	EGGCUPS	EHED	EJECTION	ELATING
EFFIGY	EGGED	EHING	EJECTIONS	ELATION
EFFING	EGGER	EHS	EJECTIVE	ELATIONS
EFFLUENCE	EGGERIES	EIDENT	EJECTMENT	ELATIVE
EFFLUENCES	EGGERS	EIDER	EJECTMENTS	ELATIVES
EFFLUENT	EGGERY	EIDERDOWN	EJECTOR	ELBOW
EFFLUENTS	EGGHEAD	EIDERDOWNS	EJECTORS	ELBOWED
EFFLUVIA	EGGHEADS	EIDERS	EJECTS	ELBOWING
EFFLUVIAL	EGGIER	EIDETIC	EKE	ELBOWS
EFFLUVIUM	EGGIEST	EIDETICS	EKED	ELCHEE
EFFLUX	EGGING	EIDOGRAPH	EKES	ELCHEES
EFFLUXES	EGGLER	EIDOGRAPHS	EKING	ELCHI
EFFLUXION	EGGLERS	EIDOLA	EKISTIC	ELCHIS
EFFLUXIONS	EGGMASS	EIDOLON	EKISTICS	ELD
EFFORCE	EGGMASSES	EIGENTONE	EKKA	ELDER
EFFORCED	EGGNOG	EIGENTONES	EKKAS	ELDERLIES
EFFORCES	EGGNOGS	EIGHT	EKLOGITE	ELDERLY
EFFORCING	EGGS	EIGHTEEN	EKLOGITES	ELDERS
EFFORT	EGGSHELL	EIGHTEENS	EKPHRASES	ELDERSHIP
EFFORTFUL	EGGSHELLS	EIGHTFOIL	EKPHRASIS	ELDERSHIPS
EFFORTS	EGGWASH	EIGHTFOILS	EKPWELE	ELDEST
EFFRAIDE	EGGWASHES	EIGHTFOLD	EKPWELES	ELDIN
EFFRAY	EGGY	EIGHTFOOT	EKUELE	ELDING
EFFRAYS	EGIS	EIGHTH	EL	ELDINGS
EFFS	EGISES	EIGHTHLY	ELABORATE	ELDINS
EFFULGE	EGLANTINE	EIGHTHS	ELABORATED	ELDRITCH
EFFULGED	EGLANTINES	EIGHTIES	ELABORATES	ELDS
EFFULGENT	EGLATERE	EIGHTIETH	ELABORATING	ELECT
EFFULGES	EGLATERES	EIGHTIETHS	ELAEOLITE	ELECTABLE
EFFULGING	EGMA	EIGHTS	ELAEOLITES	ELECTED
EFFUSE	EGMAS	EIGHTSMAN	ELAN	ELECTING
EFFUSED	EGO	EIGHTSMEN	ELANCE	ELECTION
EFFUSES	EGOISM	EIGHTSOME	ELANCED	ELECTIONS
EFFUSING	EGOISMS	EIGHTSOMES	ELANCES	ELECTIVE
EFFUSION	EGOIST	EIGHTVO	ELANCING	ELECTIVES
EFFUSIONS	EGOISTIC	EIGHTVOS	ELAND	ELECTOR
EFFUSIVE	EGOISTS	EIGHTY	ELANDS	ELECTORAL
EFS	EGOITIES	EIGNE	ELANET	ELECTORS
EFT	EGOITY	EIK	ELANETS	ELECTRESS
EFTEST	EGOMANIA	EIKED	ELANS	ELECTRESSES
EFTS	EGOMANIAC	EIKING	ELAPHINE	ELECTRET
EFTSOONS	EGOMANIACS	EIKON	ELAPSE	ELECTRETS

The Chambers Dictionary is the authority for many longer words; see *OSW* Introduction, page xii.

ELECTRIC	ELEVATING	ELLIPTIC	ELSHINS	EMANATING
ELECTRICS	ELEVATION	ELLOPS	ELSIN	EMANATION
ELECTRIFIED	ELEVATIONS	ELLOPSES	ELSINS	EMANATIONS
ELECTRIFIES	ELEVATOR	ELLS	ELT	EMANATIST
ELECTRIFY	ELEVATORS	ELLWAND	ELTCHI	EMANATISTS
ELECTRIFYING	ELEVATORY	ELLWANDS	ELTCHIS	EMANATIVE
ELECTRISE	ELEVEN	ELM	ELTS	EMANATORY
ELECTRISED	ELEVENS	ELMEN	ELUANT	EMBACE
ELECTRISES	ELEVENSES	ELMIER	ELUANTS	EMBACES
ELECTRISING	ELEVENTH	ELMIEST	ELUATE	EMBACING
ELECTRIZE	ELEVENTHS	ELMS	ELUATES	EMBAIL
ELECTRIZED	ELEVON	ELMWOOD	ELUCIDATE	EMBAILED
ELECTRIZES	ELEVONS	ELMWOODS	ELUCIDATED	EMBAILING
ELECTRIZING	ELF	ELMY	ELUCIDATES	EMBAILS
ELECTRO	ELFED	ELOCUTE	ELUCIDATING	EMBALE
ELECTRODE	ELFHOOD	ELOCUTED	ELUDE	EMBALED
ELECTRODES	ELFHOODS	ELOCUTES	ELUDED	EMBALES
ELECTRON	ELFIN	ELOCUTING	ELUDER	EMBALING
ELECTRONS	ELFING	ELOCUTION	ELUDERS	EMBALL
ELECTROS	ELFINS	ELOCUTIONS	ELUDES	EMBALLED
ELECTRUM	ELFISH	ELOCUTORY	ELUDIBLE	EMBALLING
ELECTRUMS	ELFLAND	ELOGE	ELUDING	EMBALLINGS
ELECTS	ELFLANDS	ELOGES	ELUENT	EMBALLS
ELECTUARIES	ELFLOCKS	ELOGIES	ELUENTS	EMBALM
ELECTUARY	ELFS	ELOGIST	ELUSION	EMBALMED
ELEGANCE	ELIAD	ELOGISTS	ELUSIONS	EMBALMER
ELEGANCES	ELIADS	ELOGIUM	ELUSIVE	EMBALMERS
ELEGANCIES	ELICIT	ELOGIUMS	ELUSIVELY	EMBALMING
ELEGANCY	ELICITED	ELOGY	ELUSORY	EMBALMINGS
ELEGANT	ELICITING	ELOIGN	ELUTE	EMBALMS
ELEGANTLY	ELICITOR	ELOIGNED	ELUTED	EMBANK
ELEGIAC	ELICITORS	ELOIGNER	ELUTES	EMBANKED
ELEGIACAL	ELICITS	ELOIGNERS	ELUTING	EMBANKER
ELEGIACS	ELIDE	ELOIGNING	ELUTION	EMBANKERS
ELEGIAST	ELIDED	ELOIGNS	ELUTIONS	EMBANKING
ELEGIASTS	ELIDES	ELOIN	ELUTOR	EMBANKS
ELEGIES	ELIDING	ELOINED	ELUTORS	EMBAR
ELEGISE	ELIGIBLE	ELOINER	ELUTRIATE	EMBARGO
ELEGISED	ELIGIBLES	ELOINERS	ELUTRIATED	EMBARGOED
ELEGISES	ELIGIBLY	ELOINING	ELUTRIATES	EMBARGOES
ELEGISING	ELIMINANT	ELOINMENT	ELUTRIATING	EMBARGOING
ELEGIST	ELIMINANTS	ELOINMENTS	ELUVIA	EMBARK
ELEGISTS	ELIMINATE	ELOINS	ELUVIAL	EMBARKED
ELEGIT	ELIMINATED	ELONGATE	ELUVIUM	EMBARKING
ELEGITS	ELIMINATES	ELONGATED	ELUVIUMS	EMBARKS
ELEGIZE	ELIMINATING	ELONGATES	ELVAN	EMBARRASS
ELEGIZED	ELISION	ELONGATING	ELVANITE	EMBARRASSED
ELEGIZES	ELISIONS	ELOPE	ELVANITES	EMBARRASSES
ELEGIZING	ELITE	ELOPED	ELVANS	EMBARRASSING
ELEGY	ELITES	ELOPEMENT	ELVER	EMBARRED
ELEMENT	ELITISM	ELOPEMENTS	ELVERS	EMBARRING
ELEMENTAL	ELITISMS	ELOPER	ELVES	EMBARRINGS
ELEMENTALS	ELITIST	ELOPERS	ELVISH	EMBARS
ELEMENTS	ELITISTS	ELOPES	ELYTRA	EMBASE
ELEMI	ELIXIR	ELOPING	ELYTRAL	EMBASED
ELEMIS	ELIXIRS	ELOPS	ELYTRON	EMBASES
ELENCH	ELK	ELOPSES	ELYTRUM	EMBASING
ELENCHI	ELKHOUND	ELOQUENCE	EM	EMBASSADE
ELENCHS	ELKHOUNDS	ELOQUENCES	EMACIATE	EMBASSADES
ELENCHUS	ELKS	ELOQUENT	EMACIATED	EMBASSAGE
ELENCTIC	ELL	ELPEE	EMACIATES	EMBASSAGES
ELEPHANT	ELLAGIC	ELPEES	EMACIATING	EMBASSIES
ELEPHANTS	ELLIPSE	ELS	EMALANGENI	EMBASSY
ELEUTHERI	ELLIPSES	ELSE	EMANANT	EMBASTE
ELEVATE	ELLIPSIS	ELSEWHERE	EMANATE	EMBATHE
ELEVATED	ELLIPSOID	ELSEWISE	EMANATED	EMBATHED
ELEVATES	ELLIPSOIDS	ELSHIN	EMANATES	EMBATHES

The Chambers Dictionary is the authority for many longer words; see *OSW* Introduction, page xii.

EMBATHING	EMBLOSSOMS	EMBRACED	EMBRUTED	EMETIC
EMBATTLE	EMBODIED	EMBRACEOR	EMBRUTES	EMETICAL
EMBATTLED	EMBODIES	EMBRACEORS	EMBRUTING	EMETICS
EMBATTLES	EMBODY	EMBRACER	EMBRYO	EMETIN
EMBATTLING	EMBODYING	EMBRACERIES	EMBRYOID	EMETINE
EMBAY	EMBOG	EMBRACERS	EMBRYOIDS	EMETINES
EMBAYED	EMBOGGED	EMBRACERY	EMBRYON	EMETINS
EMBAYING	EMBOGGING	EMBRACES	EMBRYONAL	EMEU
EMBAYLD	EMBOGS	EMBRACING	EMBRYONIC	EMEUS
EMBAYMENT	EMBOGUE	EMBRACIVE	EMBRYONS	EMEUTE
EMBAYMENTS	EMBOGUED	EMBRAID	EMBRYOS	EMEUTES
EMBAYS	EMBOGUES	EMBRAIDED	EMBRYOTIC	EMICANT
EMBED	EMBOGUING	EMBRAIDING	EMBUS	EMICATE
EMBEDDED	EMBOIL	EMBRAIDS	EMBUSIED	EMICATED
EMBEDDING	EMBOILED	EMBRANGLE	EMBUSIES	EMICATES
EMBEDDINGS	EMBOILING	EMBRANGLED	EMBUSQUE	EMICATING
EMBEDMENT	EMBOILS	EMBRANGLES	EMBUSQUES	EMICATION
EMBEDMENTS	EMBOLDEN	EMBRANGLING	EMBUSSED	EMICATIONS
EMBEDS	EMBOLDENED	EMBRASOR	EMBUSSES	EMICTION
EMBELLISH	EMBOLDENING	EMBRASORS	EMBUSSING	EMICTIONS
EMBELLISHED	EMBOLDENS	EMBRASURE	EMBUSY	EMICTORY
EMBELLISHES	EMBOLI	EMBRASURES	EMBUSYING	EMIGRANT
EMBELLISHING	EMBOLIC	EMBRAVE	EMCEE	EMIGRANTS
EMBER	EMBOLIES	EMBRAVED	EMCEED	EMIGRATE
EMBERS	EMBOLISM	EMBRAVES	EMCEEING	EMIGRATED
EMBEZZLE	EMBOLISMS	EMBRAVING	EMCEES	EMIGRATES
EMBEZZLED	EMBOLUS	EMBRAZURE	EME	EMIGRATING
EMBEZZLER	EMBOLUSES	EMBRAZURES	EMEER	EMIGRE
EMBEZZLERS	EMBOLY	EMBREAD	EMEERS	EMIGRES
EMBEZZLES	EMBORDER	EMBREADED	EMEND	EMINENCE
EMBEZZLING	EMBORDERED	EMBREADING	EMENDABLE	EMINENCES
EMBITTER	EMBORDERING	EMBREADS	EMENDALS	EMINENCIES
EMBITTERED	EMBORDERS	EMBREATHE	EMENDATE	EMINENCY
EMBITTERING	EMBOSCATA	EMBREATHED	EMENDATED	EMINENT
EMBITTERINGS	EMBOSCATAS	EMBREATHES	EMENDATES	EMINENTLY
EMBITTERS	EMBOSOM	EMBREATHING	EMENDATING	EMIR
EMBLAZE	EMBOSOMED	EMBREWE	EMENDATOR	EMIRATE
EMBLAZED	EMBOSOMING	EMBREWED	EMENDATORS	EMIRATES
EMBLAZES	EMBOSOMS	EMBREWES	EMENDED	EMIRS
EMBLAZING	EMBOSS	EMBREWING	EMENDING	EMISSARIES
EMBLAZON	EMBOSSED	EMBRITTLE	EMENDS	EMISSARY
EMBLAZONED	EMBOSSER	EMBRITTLED	EMERALD	EMISSILE
EMBLAZONING	EMBOSSERS	EMBRITTLES	EMERALDS	EMISSION
EMBLAZONS	EMBOSSES	EMBRITTLING	EMERAUDE	EMISSIONS
EMBLEM	EMBOSSING	EMBROCATE	EMERAUDES	EMISSIVE
EMBLEMA	EMBOST	EMBROCATED	EMERGE	EMIT
EMBLEMATA	EMBOUND	EMBROCATES	EMERGED	EMITS
EMBLEMED	EMBOUNDED	EMBROCATING	EMERGENCE	EMITTED
EMBLEMING	EMBOUNDING	EMBROGLIO	EMERGENCES	EMITTER
EMBLEMISE	EMBOUNDS	EMBROGLIOS	EMERGENCIES	EMITTERS
EMBLEMISED	EMBOW	EMBROIDER	EMERGENCY	EMITTING
EMBLEMISES	EMBOWED	EMBROIDERED	EMERGENT	EMMA
EMBLEMISING	EMBOWEL	EMBROIDERING	EMERGES	EMMARBLE
EMBLEMIZE	EMBOWELLED	EMBROIDERS	EMERGING	EMMARBLED
EMBLEMIZED	EMBOWELLING	EMBROIL	EMERIED	EMMARBLES
EMBLEMIZES	EMBOWELS	EMBROILED	EMERIES	EMMARBLING
EMBLEMIZING	EMBOWER	EMBROILING	EMERITI	EMMAS
EMBLEMS	EMBOWERED	EMBROILS	EMERITUS	EMMER
EMBLIC	EMBOWERING	EMBROWN	EMERODS	EMMERS
EMBLICS	EMBOWERS	EMBROWNED	EMERSED	EMMESH
EMBLOOM	EMBOWING	EMBROWNING	EMERSION	EMMESHED
EMBLOOMED	EMBOWS	EMBROWNS	EMERSIONS	EMMESHES
EMBLOOMING	EMBOX	EMBRUE	EMERY	EMMESHING
EMBLOOMS	EMBOXED	EMBRUED	EMERYING	EMMET
EMBLOSSOM	EMBOXES	EMBRUES	EMES	EMMETROPE
EMBLOSSOMED	EMBOXING	EMBRUING	EMESES	EMMETROPES
EMBLOSSOMING	EMBRACE	EMBRUTE	EMESIS	EMMETS

The Chambers Dictionary is the authority for many longer words; see *OSW* Introduction, page xii.

EMMEW	EMPATHIC	EMPIRIC	EMPTINESS	EMUNCTIONS
EMMEWED	EMPATHIES	EMPIRICAL	EMPTINESSES	EMUNCTORIES
EMMEWING	EMPATHISE	EMPIRICS	EMPTION	EMUNCTORY
EMMEWS	EMPATHISED	EMPLACE	EMPTIONAL	EMUNGE
EMMOVE	EMPATHISES	EMPLACED	EMPTIONS	EMUNGED
EMMOVED	EMPATHISING	EMPLACES	EMPTY	EMUNGES
EMMOVES	EMPATHIZE	EMPLACING	EMPTYING	EMUNGING
EMMOVING	EMPATHIZED	EMPLANE	EMPTYINGS	EMURE
EMOLLIATE	EMPATHIZES	EMPLANED	EMPTYSES	EMURED
EMOLLIATED	EMPATHIZING	EMPLANES	EMPTYSIS	EMURES
EMOLLIATES	EMPATHY	EMPLANING	EMPURPLE	EMURING
EMOLLIATING	EMPATRON	EMPLASTER	EMPURPLED	EMUS
EMOLLIENT	EMPATRONED	EMPLASTERED	EMPURPLES	EMYDES
EMOLLIENTS	EMPATRONING	EMPLASTERING	EMPURPLING	EMYS
EMOLUMENT	EMPATRONS	EMPLASTERS	EMPUSA	EN
EMOLUMENTS	EMPEACH	EMPLASTIC	EMPUSAS	ENABLE
EMONG	EMPEACHED	EMPLASTICS	EMPUSE	ENABLED
EMONGES	EMPEACHES	EMPLEACH	EMPUSES	ENABLER
EMONGEST	EMPEACHING	EMPLEACHED	EMPYEMA	ENABLERS
EMONGST	EMPENNAGE	EMPLEACHES	EMPYEMAS	ENABLES
EMOTE	EMPENNAGES	EMPLEACHING	EMPYEMATA	ENABLING
EMOTED	EMPEOPLE	EMPLECTON	EMPYEMIC	ENACT
EMOTES	EMPEOPLED	EMPLECTONS	EMPYESES	ENACTED
EMOTING	EMPEOPLES	EMPLECTUM	EMPYESIS	ENACTING
EMOTION	EMPEOPLING	EMPLECTUMS	EMPYREAL	ENACTION
EMOTIONAL	EMPERCE	EMPLONGE	EMPYREAN	ENACTIONS
EMOTIONS	EMPERCED	EMPLONGED	EMPYREANS	ENACTIVE
EMOTIVE	EMPERCES	EMPLONGES	EMPYREUMA	ENACTMENT
EMOTIVISM	EMPERCING	EMPLONGING	EMPYREUMATA	ENACTMENTS
EMOTIVISMS	EMPERIES	EMPLOY	EMS	ENACTOR
EMOVE	EMPERISE	EMPLOYED	EMU	ENACTORS
EMOVED	EMPERISED	EMPLOYEE	EMULATE	ENACTS
EMOVES	EMPERISES	EMPLOYEES	EMULATED	ENACTURE
EMOVING	EMPERISH	EMPLOYER	EMULATES	ENACTURES
EMPACKET	EMPERISHED	EMPLOYERS	EMULATING	ENALLAGE
EMPACKETED	EMPERISHES	EMPLOYING	EMULATION	ENALLAGES
EMPACKETING	EMPERISHING	EMPLOYS	EMULATIONS	ENAMEL
EMPACKETS	EMPERISING	EMPLUME	EMULATIVE	ENAMELLED
EMPAESTIC	EMPERIZE	EMPLUMED	EMULATOR	ENAMELLER
EMPAIRE	EMPERIZED	EMPLUMES	EMULATORS	ENAMELLERS
EMPAIRED	EMPERIZES	EMPLUMING	EMULE	ENAMELLING
EMPAIRES	EMPERIZING	EMPOISON	EMULED	ENAMELLINGS
EMPAIRING	EMPEROR	EMPOISONED	EMULES	ENAMELS
EMPALE	EMPERORS	EMPOISONING	EMULGE	ENAMOR
EMPALED	EMPERY	EMPOISONS	EMULGED	ENAMORADO
EMPALES	EMPHASES	EMPOLDER	EMULGENCE	ENAMORADOS
EMPALING	EMPHASIS	EMPOLDERED	EMULGENCES	ENAMORED
EMPANEL	EMPHASISE	EMPOLDERING	EMULGENT	ENAMORING
EMPANELLED	EMPHASISED	EMPOLDERS	EMULGES	ENAMORS
EMPANELLING	EMPHASISES	EMPORIA	EMULGING	ENAMOUR
EMPANELS	EMPHASISING	EMPORIUM	EMULING	ENAMOURED
EMPANOPLIED	EMPHASIZE	EMPORIUMS	EMULOUS	ENAMOURING
EMPANOPLIES	EMPHASIZED	EMPOWER	EMULOUSLY	ENAMOURS
EMPANOPLY	EMPHASIZES	EMPOWERED	EMULSIFIED	ENARCH
EMPANOPLYING	EMPHASIZING	EMPOWERING	EMULSIFIES	ENARCHED
EMPARE	EMPHATIC	EMPOWERS	EMULSIFY	ENARCHES
EMPARED	EMPHLYSES	EMPRESS	EMULSIFYING	ENARCHING
EMPARES	EMPHLYSIS	EMPRESSE	EMULSIN	ENARM
EMPARING	EMPHYSEMA	EMPRESSES	EMULSINS	ENARMED
EMPARL	EMPHYSEMAS	EMPRISE	EMULSION	ENARMING
EMPARLED	EMPIERCE	EMPRISES	EMULSIONS	ENARMS
EMPARLING	EMPIERCED	EMPTIED	EMULSIVE	ENATE
EMPARLS	EMPIERCES	EMPTIER	EMULSOID	ENATION
EMPART	EMPIERCING	EMPTIERS	EMULSOIDS	ENATIONS
EMPARTED	EMPIGHT	EMPTIES	EMULSOR	ENAUNTER
EMPARTING	EMPIRE	EMPTIEST	EMULSORS	ENCAENIA
EMPARTS	EMPIRES	EMPTILY	EMUNCTION	ENCAENIAS

The Chambers Dictionary is the authority for many longer words; see *OSW* Introduction, page xii.

ENCAGE	ENCHORIC	ENCORING	ENDARTED	ENDOGAMY
ENCAGED	ENCIERRO	ENCOUNTER	ENDARTING	ENDOGEN
ENCAGES	ENCIERROS	ENCOUNTERED	ENDARTS	ENDOGENIC
ENCAGING	ENCIPHER	ENCOUNTERING	ENDEAR	ENDOGENIES
ENCALM	ENCIPHERED	ENCOUNTERS	ENDEARED	ENDOGENS
ENCALMED	ENCIPHERING	ENCOURAGE	ENDEARING	ENDOGENY
ENCALMING	ENCIPHERS	ENCOURAGED	ENDEARS	ENDOLYMPH
ENCALMS	ENCIRCLE	ENCOURAGES	ENDEAVOR	ENDOLYMPHS
ENCAMP	ENCIRCLED	ENCOURAGING	ENDEAVORED	ENDOMIXES
ENCAMPED	ENCIRCLES	ENCOURAGINGS	ENDEAVORING	ENDOMIXIS
ENCAMPING	ENCIRCLING	ENCRADLE	ENDEAVORS	ENDOMIXISES
ENCAMPS	ENCIRCLINGS	ENCRADLED	ENDEAVOUR	ENDOMORPH
ENCANTHIS	ENCLASP	ENCRADLES	ENDEAVOURED	ENDOMORPHS
ENCANTHISES	ENCLASPED	ENCRADLING	ENDEAVOURING	ENDOPHAGIES
ENCARPUS	ENCLASPING	ENCRATIES	ENDEAVOURS	ENDOPHAGY
ENCARPUSES	ENCLASPS	ENCRATY	ENDECAGON	ENDOPHYTE
ENCASE	ENCLAVE	ENCREASE	ENDECAGONS	ENDOPHYTES
ENCASED	ENCLAVED	ENCREASED	ENDED	ENDOPLASM
ENCASES	ENCLAVES	ENCREASES	ENDEICTIC	ENDOPLASMS
ENCASH	ENCLAVING	ENCREASING	ENDEIXES	ENDORPHIN
ENCASHED	ENCLISES	ENCRIMSON	ENDEIXIS	ENDORPHINS
ENCASHES	ENCLISIS	ENCRIMSONED	ENDEIXISES	ENDORSE
ENCASHING	ENCLITIC	ENCRIMSONING	ENDEMIAL	ENDORSED
ENCASING	ENCLITICS	ENCRIMSONS	ENDEMIC	ENDORSEE
ENCAUSTIC	ENCLOSE	ENCRINAL	ENDEMICAL	ENDORSEES
ENCAUSTICS	ENCLOSED	ENCRINIC	ENDEMICS	ENDORSER
ENCAVE	ENCLOSER	ENCRINITE	ENDEMISM	ENDORSERS
ENCAVED	ENCLOSERS	ENCRINITES	ENDEMISMS	ENDORSES
ENCAVES	ENCLOSES	ENCROACH	ENDENIZEN	ENDORSING
ENCAVING	ENCLOSING	ENCROACHED	ENDENIZENED	ENDOSARC
ENCEINTE	ENCLOSURE	ENCROACHES	ENDENIZENING	ENDOSARCS
ENCEINTES	ENCLOSURES	ENCROACHING	ENDENIZENS	ENDOSCOPE
ENCHAFE	ENCLOTHE	ENCRUST	ENDERMIC	ENDOSCOPES
ENCHAFED	ENCLOTHED	ENCRUSTED	ENDERON	ENDOSCOPIES
ENCHAFES	ENCLOTHES	ENCRUSTING	ENDERONS	ENDOSCOPY
ENCHAFING	ENCLOTHING	ENCRUSTS	ENDEW	ENDOSMOSE
ENCHAIN	ENCLOUD	ENCRYPT	ENDEWED	ENDOSMOSES
ENCHAINED	ENCLOUDED	ENCRYPTED	ENDEWING	ENDOSPERM
ENCHAINING	ENCLOUDING	ENCRYPTING	ENDEWS	ENDOSPERMS
ENCHAINS	ENCLOUDS	ENCRYPTS	ENDGAME	ENDOSPORE
ENCHANT	ENCODE	ENCUMBER	ENDGAMES	ENDOSPORES
ENCHANTED	ENCODED	ENCUMBERED	ENDING	ENDOSS
ENCHANTER	ENCODES	ENCUMBERING	ENDINGS	ENDOSSED
ENCHANTERS	ENCODING	ENCUMBERS	ENDIRON	ENDOSSES
ENCHANTING	ENCOLOUR	ENCURTAIN	ENDIRONS	ENDOSSING
ENCHANTS	ENCOLOURED	ENCURTAINED	ENDITE	ENDOSTEA
ENCHARGE	ENCOLOURING	ENCURTAINING	ENDITED	ENDOSTEAL
ENCHARGED	ENCOLOURS	ENCURTAINS	ENDITES	ENDOSTEUM
ENCHARGES	ENCOLPION	ENCYCLIC	ENDITING	ENDOW
ENCHARGING	ENCOLPIONS	ENCYST	ENDIVE	ENDOWED
ENCHARM	ENCOLPIUM	ENCYSTED	ENDIVES	ENDOWER
ENCHARMED	ENCOLPIUMS	ENCYSTING	ENDLANG	ENDOWERS
ENCHARMING	ENCOLURE	ENCYSTS	ENDLESS	ENDOWING
ENCHARMS	ENCOLURES	END	ENDLESSLY	ENDOWMENT
ENCHASE	ENCOMIA	ENDAMAGE	ENDLONG	ENDOWMENTS
ENCHASED	ENCOMIAST	ENDAMAGED	ENDMOST	ENDOWS
ENCHASES	ENCOMIASTS	ENDAMAGES	ENDOBLAST	ENDOZOA
ENCHASING	ENCOMION	ENDAMAGING	ENDOBLASTS	ENDOZOIC
ENCHEASON	ENCOMIUM	ENDAMOEBA	ENDOCARP	ENDOZOON
ENCHEASONS	ENCOMIUMS	ENDAMOEBAE	ENDOCARPS	ENDS
ENCHEER	ENCOMPASS	ENDAMOEBAS	ENDOCRINE	ENDSHIP
ENCHEERED	ENCOMPASSED	ENDANGER	ENDOCRINES	ENDSHIPS
ENCHEERING	ENCOMPASSES	ENDANGERED	ENDODERM	ENDUE
ENCHEERS	ENCOMPASSING	ENDANGERING	ENDODERMS	ENDUED
ENCHILADA	ENCORE	ENDANGERS	ENDODYNE	ENDUES
ENCHILADAS	ENCORED	ENDARCH	ENDOGAMIC	ENDUING
ENCHORIAL	ENCORES	ENDART	ENDOGAMIES	ENDUNGEON

The Chambers Dictionary is the authority for many longer words; see *OSW* Introduction, page xii.

ENDUNGEONED	ENFEOFFING	ENFREEZES	ENGOBES	ENGROSSING
ENDUNGEONING	ENFEOFFS	ENFREEZING	ENGORE	ENGS
ENDUNGEONS	ENFESTED	ENFROSEN	ENGORED	ENGUARD
ENDURABLE	ENFETTER	ENFROZE	ENGORES	ENGUARDED
ENDURABLY	ENFETTERED	ENFROZEN	ENGORGE	ENGUARDING
ENDURANCE	ENFETTERING	ENG	ENGORGED	ENGUARDS
ENDURANCES	ENFETTERS	ENGAGE	ENGORGES	ENGULF
ENDURE	ENFIERCE	ENGAGED	ENGORGING	ENGULFED
ENDURED	ENFIERCED	ENGAGER	ENGORING	ENGULFING
ENDURER	ENFIERCES	ENGAGERS	ENGOULED	ENGULFS
ENDURERS	ENFIERCING	ENGAGES	ENGOUMENT	ENGULPH
ENDURES	ENFILADE	ENGAGING	ENGOUMENTS	ENGULPHED
ENDURING	ENFILADED	ENGAOL	ENGRACE	ENGULPHING
ENDWAYS	ENFILADES	ENGAOLED	ENGRACED	ENGULPHS
ENDWISE	ENFILADING	ENGAOLING	ENGRACES	ENGYSCOPE
ENE	ENFILED	ENGAOLS	ENGRACING	ENGYSCOPES
ENEMA	ENFIRE	ENGARLAND	ENGRAFF	ENHALO
ENEMAS	ENFIRED	ENGARLANDED	ENGRAFFED	ENHALOED
ENEMATA	ENFIRES	ENGARLANDING	ENGRAFFING	ENHALOES
ENEMIES	ENFIRING	ENGARLANDS	ENGRAFFS	ENHALOING
ENEMY	ENFIX	ENGENDER	ENGRAFT	ENHALOS
ENERGETIC	ENFIXED	ENGENDERED	ENGRAFTED	ENHANCE
ENERGETICS	ENFIXES	ENGENDERING	ENGRAFTING	ENHANCED
ENERGIC	ENFIXING	ENGENDERS	ENGRAFTS	ENHANCER
ENERGID	ENFLAME	ENGENDURE	ENGRAIL	ENHANCERS
ENERGIDS	ENFLAMED	ENGENDURES	ENGRAILED	ENHANCES
ENERGIES	ENFLAMES	ENGILD	ENGRAILING	ENHANCING
ENERGISE	ENFLAMING	ENGILDED	ENGRAILS	ENHANCIVE
ENERGISED	ENFLESH	ENGILDING	ENGRAIN	ENHEARSE
ENERGISES	ENFLESHED	ENGILDS	ENGRAINED	ENHEARSED
ENERGISING	ENFLESHES	ENGILT	ENGRAINER	ENHEARSES
ENERGIZE	ENFLESHING	ENGINE	ENGRAINERS	ENHEARSING
ENERGIZED	ENFLOWER	ENGINED	ENGRAINING	ENHEARTEN
ENERGIZES	ENFLOWERED	ENGINEER	ENGRAINS	ENHEARTENED
ENERGIZING	ENFLOWERING	ENGINEERED	ENGRAM	ENHEARTENING
ENERGUMEN	ENFLOWERS	ENGINEERING	ENGRAMMA	ENHEARTENS
ENERGUMENS	ENFOLD	ENGINEERINGS	ENGRAMMAS	ENHUNGER
ENERGY	ENFOLDED	ENGINEERS	ENGRAMS	ENHUNGERED
ENERVATE	ENFOLDING	ENGINER	ENGRASP	ENHUNGERING
ENERVATED	ENFOLDS	ENGINERIES	ENGRASPED	ENHUNGERS
ENERVATES	ENFORCE	ENGINERS	ENGRASPING	ENHYDRITE
ENERVATING	ENFORCED	ENGINERY	ENGRASPS	ENHYDRITES
ENERVE	ENFORCER	ENGINES	ENGRAVE	ENHYDROS
ENERVED	ENFORCERS	ENGINING	ENGRAVED	ENHYDROSES
ENERVES	ENFORCES	ENGIRD	ENGRAVEN	ENHYDROUS
ENERVING	ENFORCING	ENGIRDING	ENGRAVER	ENIAC
ENES	ENFOREST	ENGIRDLE	ENGRAVERIES	ENIACS
ENEW	ENFORESTED	ENGIRDLED	ENGRAVERS	ENIGMA
ENEWED	ENFORESTING	ENGIRDLES	ENGRAVERY	ENIGMAS
ENEWING	ENFORESTS	ENGIRDLING	ENGRAVES	ENIGMATIC
ENEWS	ENFORM	ENGIRDS	ENGRAVING	ENISLE
ENFACE	ENFORMED	ENGIRT	ENGRAVINGS	ENISLED
ENFACED	ENFORMING	ENGISCOPE	ENGRENAGE	ENISLES
ENFACES	ENFORMS	ENGISCOPES	ENGRENAGES	ENISLING
ENFACING	ENFRAME	ENGLOBE	ENGRIEVE	ENJAMB
ENFANT	ENFRAMED	ENGLOBED	ENGRIEVED	ENJAMBED
ENFANTS	ENFRAMES	ENGLOBES	ENGRIEVES	ENJAMBING
ENFEEBLE	ENFRAMING	ENGLOBING	ENGRIEVING	ENJAMBS
ENFEEBLED	ENFREE	ENGLOOM	ENGROOVE	ENJOIN
ENFEEBLES	ENFREED	ENGLOOMED	ENGROOVED	ENJOINED
ENFEEBLING	ENFREEDOM	ENGLOOMING	ENGROOVES	ENJOINER
ENFELON	ENFREEDOMED	ENGLOOMS	ENGROOVING	ENJOINERS
ENFELONED	ENFREEDOMING	ENGLUT	ENGROSS	ENJOINING
ENFELONING	ENFREEDOMS	ENGLUTS	ENGROSSED	ENJOINS
ENFELONS	ENFREEING	ENGLUTTED	ENGROSSER	ENJOY
ENFEOFF	ENFREES	ENGLUTTING	ENGROSSERS	ENJOYABLE
ENFEOFFED	ENFREEZE	ENGOBE	ENGROSSES	ENJOYABLY

The Chambers Dictionary is the authority for many longer words; see *OSW* Introduction, page xii.

ENJOYED	ENMESHES	ENRAGED	ENROUNDS	ENSILE
ENJOYER	ENMESHING	ENRAGES	ENS	ENSILED
ENJOYERS	ENMEW	ENRAGING	ENSAMPLE	ENSILES
ENJOYING	ENMEWED	ENRANCKLE	ENSAMPLED	ENSILING
ENJOYMENT	ENMEWING	ENRANCKLED	ENSAMPLES	ENSKIED
ENJOYMENTS	ENMEWS	ENRANCKLES	ENSAMPLING	ENSKIES
ENJOYS	ENMITIES	ENRANCKLING	ENSATE	ENSKY
ENKERNEL	ENMITY	ENRANGE	ENSCONCE	ENSKYING
ENKERNELLED	ENMOSSED	ENRANGED	ENSCONCED	ENSLAVE
ENKERNELLING	ENMOVE	ENRANGES	ENSCONCES	ENSLAVED
ENKERNELS	ENMOVED	ENRANGING	ENSCONCING	ENSLAVER
ENKINDLE	ENMOVES	ENRANK	ENSEAL	ENSLAVERS
ENKINDLED	ENMOVING	ENRANKED	ENSEALED	ENSLAVES
ENKINDLES	ENNAGE	ENRANKING	ENSEALING	ENSLAVING
ENKINDLING	ENNAGES	ENRANKS	ENSEALS	ENSNARE
ENLACE	ENNEAD	ENRAPT	ENSEAM	ENSNARED
ENLACED	ENNEADIC	ENRAPTURE	ENSEAMED	ENSNARES
ENLACES	ENNEADS	ENRAPTURED	ENSEAMING	ENSNARING
ENLACING	ENNEAGON	ENRAPTURES	ENSEAMS	ENSNARL
ENLARD	ENNEAGONS	ENRAPTURING	ENSEAR	ENSNARLED
ENLARDED	ENNOBLE	ENRAUNGE	ENSEARED	ENSNARLING
ENLARDING	ENNOBLED	ENRAUNGED	ENSEARING	ENSNARLS
ENLARDS	ENNOBLES	ENRAUNGES	ENSEARS	ENSORCELL
ENLARGE	ENNOBLING	ENRAUNGING	ENSEMBLE	ENSORCELLED
ENLARGED	ENNUI	ENRAVISH	ENSEMBLES	ENSORCELLING
ENLARGEN	ENNUIED	ENRAVISHED	ENSEW	ENSORCELLS
ENLARGENED	ENNUIS	ENRAVISHES	ENSEWED	ENSOUL
ENLARGENING	ENNUYE	ENRAVISHING	ENSEWING	ENSOULED
ENLARGENS	ENNUYED	ENRHEUM	ENSEWS	ENSOULING
ENLARGER	ENNUYING	ENRHEUMED	ENSHEATH	ENSOULS
ENLARGERS	ENODAL	ENRHEUMING	ENSHEATHE	ENSPHERE
ENLARGES	ENOKI	ENRHEUMS	ENSHEATHED	ENSPHERED
ENLARGING	ENOKIS	ENRICH	ENSHEATHES	ENSPHERES
ENLEVE	ENOMOTIES	ENRICHED	ENSHEATHING	ENSPHERING
ENLIGHT	ENOMOTY	ENRICHES	ENSHEATHS	ENSTAMP
ENLIGHTED	ENORM	ENRICHING	ENSHELL	ENSTAMPED
ENLIGHTEN	ENORMITIES	ENRIDGED	ENSHELLED	ENSTAMPING
ENLIGHTENED	ENORMITY	ENRING	ENSHELLING	ENSTAMPS
ENLIGHTENING	ENORMOUS	ENRINGED	ENSHELLS	ENSTATITE
ENLIGHTENS	ENOSES	ENRINGING	ENSHELTER	ENSTATITES
ENLIGHTING	ENOSIS	ENRINGS	ENSHELTERED	ENSTEEP
ENLIGHTS	ENOUGH	ENRIVEN	ENSHELTERING	ENSTEEPED
ENLINK	ENOUGHS	ENROBE	ENSHELTERS	ENSTEEPING
ENLINKED	ENOUNCE	ENROBED	ENSHIELD	ENSTEEPS
ENLINKING	ENOUNCED	ENROBES	ENSHIELDED	ENSTYLE
ENLINKS	ENOUNCES	ENROBING	ENSHIELDING	ENSTYLED
ENLIST	ENOUNCING	ENROL	ENSHIELDS	ENSTYLES
ENLISTED	ENOW	ENROLL	ENSHRINE	ENSTYLING
ENLISTING	ENPLANE	ENROLLED	ENSHRINED	ENSUE
ENLISTS	ENPLANED	ENROLLER	ENSHRINES	ENSUED
ENLIT	ENPLANES	ENROLLERS	ENSHRINING	ENSUES
ENLIVEN	ENPLANING	ENROLLING	ENSHROUD	ENSUING
ENLIVENED	ENPRINT	ENROLLS	ENSHROUDED	ENSURE
ENLIVENER	ENPRINTS	ENROLMENT	ENSHROUDING	ENSURED
ENLIVENERS	ENQUIRE	ENROLMENTS	ENSHROUDS	ENSURER
ENLIVENING	ENQUIRED	ENROLS	ENSIFORM	ENSURERS
ENLIVENS	ENQUIRER	ENROOT	ENSIGN	ENSURES
ENLOCK	ENQUIRERS	ENROOTED	ENSIGNCIES	ENSURING
ENLOCKED	ENQUIRES	ENROOTING	ENSIGNCY	ENSWATHE
ENLOCKING	ENQUIRIES	ENROOTS	ENSIGNED	ENSWATHED
ENLOCKS	ENQUIRING	ENROUGH	ENSIGNING	ENSWATHES
ENLUMINE	ENQUIRY	ENROUGHED	ENSIGNS	ENSWATHING
ENLUMINED	ENRACE	ENROUGHING	ENSILAGE	ENSWEEP
ENLUMINES	ENRACED	ENROUGHS	ENSILAGED	ENSWEEPING
ENLUMINING	ENRACES	ENROUND	ENSILAGEING	ENSWEEPS
ENMESH	ENRACING	ENROUNDED	ENSILAGES	ENSWEPT
ENMESHED	ENRAGE	ENROUNDING	ENSILAGING	ENTAIL

The Chambers Dictionary is the authority for many longer words; see *OSW* Introduction, page xii.

ENTAILED	ENTHRALLS	ENTRAMMELLED	ENUCLEATE	ENVISIONS
ENTAILER	ENTHRALS	ENTRAMMELLING	ENUCLEATED	ENVOI
ENTAILERS	ENTHRONE	ENTRAMMELS	ENUCLEATES	ENVOIS
ENTAILING	ENTHRONED	ENTRANCE	ENUCLEATING	ENVOY
ENTAILS	ENTHRONES	ENTRANCED	ENUMERATE	ENVOYS
ENTAME	ENTHRONING	ENTRANCES	ENUMERATED	ENVOYSHIP
ENTAMED	ENTHUSE	ENTRANCING	ENUMERATES	ENVOYSHIPS
ENTAMES	ENTHUSED	ENTRANT	ENUMERATING	ENVY
ENTAMING	ENTHUSES	ENTRANTS	ENUNCIATE	ENVYING
ENTAMOEBA	ENTHUSING	ENTRAP	ENUNCIATED	ENVYINGS
ENTAMOEBAE	ENTHYMEME	ENTRAPPED	ENUNCIATES	ENWALL
ENTAMOEBAS	ENTHYMEMES	ENTRAPPER	ENUNCIATING	ENWALLED
ENTANGLE	ENTIA	ENTRAPPERS	ENURE	ENWALLING
ENTANGLED	ENTICE	ENTRAPPING	ENURED	ENWALLOW
ENTANGLES	ENTICED	ENTRAPS	ENUREMENT	ENWALLOWED
ENTANGLING	ENTICER	ENTREAT	ENUREMENTS	ENWALLOWING
ENTASES	ENTICERS	ENTREATED	ENURES	ENWALLOWS
ENTASIS	ENTICES	ENTREATIES	ENURESES	ENWALLS
ENTAYLE	ENTICING	ENTREATING	ENURESIS	ENWHEEL
ENTAYLED	ENTICINGS	ENTREATS	ENURETIC	ENWHEELED
ENTAYLES	ENTIRE	ENTREATY	ENURETICS	ENWHEELING
ENTAYLING	ENTIRELY	ENTRECHAT	ENURING	ENWHEELS
ENTELECHIES	ENTIRES	ENTRECHATS	ENVASSAL	ENWIND
ENTELECHY	ENTIRETIES	ENTRECOTE	ENVASSALLED	ENWINDING
ENTELLUS	ENTIRETY	ENTRECOTES	ENVASSALLING	ENWINDS
ENTELLUSES	ENTITIES	ENTREE	ENVASSALS	ENWOMB
ENTENDER	ENTITLE	ENTREES	ENVAULT	ENWOMBED
ENTENDERED	ENTITLED	ENTREMES	ENVAULTED	ENWOMBING
ENTENDERING	ENTITLES	ENTREMETS	ENVAULTING	ENWOMBS
ENTENDERS	ENTITLING	ENTRENCH	ENVAULTS	ENWOUND
ENTENTE	ENTITY	ENTRENCHED	ENVEIGLE	ENWRAP
ENTENTES	ENTOBLAST	ENTRENCHES	ENVEIGLED	ENWRAPPED
ENTER	ENTOBLASTS	ENTRENCHING	ENVEIGLES	ENWRAPPING
ENTERA	ENTODERM	ENTREPOT	ENVEIGLING	ENWRAPPINGS
ENTERABLE	ENTODERMS	ENTREPOTS	ENVELOP	ENWRAPS
ENTERAL	ENTOIL	ENTRESOL	ENVELOPE	ENWREATHE
ENTERATE	ENTOILED	ENTRESOLS	ENVELOPED	ENWREATHED
ENTERED	ENTOILING	ENTREZ	ENVELOPES	ENWREATHES
ENTERER	ENTOILS	ENTRIES	ENVELOPING	ENWREATHING
ENTERERS	ENTOMB	ENTRISM	ENVELOPS	ENZIAN
ENTERIC	ENTOMBED	ENTRISMS	ENVENOM	ENZIANS
ENTERICS	ENTOMBING	ENTRIST	ENVENOMED	ENZONE
ENTERING	ENTOMBS	ENTRISTS	ENVENOMING	ENZONED
ENTERINGS	ENTOMIC	ENTROLD	ENVENOMS	ENZONES
ENTERITIS	ENTOPHYTE	ENTROPIES	ENVERMEIL	ENZONING
ENTERITISES	ENTOPHYTES	ENTROPION	ENVERMEILED	ENZOOTIC
ENTERON	ENTOPIC	ENTROPIONS	ENVERMEILING	ENZOOTICS
ENTERS	ENTOPTIC	ENTROPIUM	ENVERMEILS	ENZYMATIC
ENTERTAIN	ENTOPTICS	ENTROPIUMS	ENVIABLE	ENZYME
ENTERTAINED	ENTOTIC	ENTROPY	ENVIABLY	ENZYMES
ENTERTAINING	ENTOURAGE	ENTRUST	ENVIED	ENZYMIC
ENTERTAININGS	ENTOURAGES	ENTRUSTED	ENVIER	EOAN
ENTERTAINS	ENTOZOA	ENTRUSTING	ENVIERS	EOLIENNE
ENTERTAKE	ENTOZOAL	ENTRUSTS	ENVIES	EOLIENNES
ENTERTAKEN	ENTOZOIC	ENTRY	ENVIOUS	EOLIPILE
ENTERTAKES	ENTOZOON	ENTRYISM	ENVIOUSLY	EOLIPILES
ENTERTAKING	ENTRAIL	ENTRYISMS	ENVIRON	EOLITH
ENTERTOOK	ENTRAILED	ENTRYIST	ENVIRONED	EOLITHIC
ENTETE	ENTRAILING	ENTRYISTS	ENVIRONING	EOLITHS
ENTETEE	ENTRAILS	ENTWINE	ENVIRONS	EON
ENTHALPIES	ENTRAIN	ENTWINED	ENVISAGE	EONISM
ENTHALPY	ENTRAINED	ENTWINES	ENVISAGED	EONISMS
ENTHETIC	ENTRAINING	ENTWINING	ENVISAGES	EONS
ENTHRAL	ENTRAINS	ENTWIST	ENVISAGING	EORL
ENTHRALL	ENTRALL	ENTWISTED	ENVISION	EORLS
ENTHRALLED	ENTRALLES	ENTWISTING	ENVISIONED	EOSIN
ENTHRALLING	ENTRAMMEL	ENTWISTS	ENVISIONING	EOSINS

The Chambers Dictionary is the authority for many longer words; see *OSW* Introduction, page xii.

EOTHEN	EPHIALTES	EPIDOTE	EPINICION	EPITAPHIC
EPACRID	EPHOD	EPIDOTES	EPINICIONS	EPITAPHING
EPACRIDS	EPHODS	EPIDOTIC	EPINIKIAN	EPITAPHS
EPACRIS	EPHOR	EPIDURAL	EPINIKION	EPITASES
EPACRISES	EPHORALTIES	EPIDURALS	EPINIKIONS	EPITASIS
EPACT	EPHORALTY	EPIFOCAL	EPINOSIC	EPITAXIAL
EPACTS	EPHORS	EPIGAEAL	EPIPHANIC	EPITAXIES
EPAENETIC	EPIBLAST	EPIGAEAN	EPIPHRAGM	EPITAXY
EPAGOGE	EPIBLASTS	EPIGAEOUS	EPIPHRAGMS	EPITHELIA
EPAGOGES	EPIC	EPIGAMIC	EPIPHYSES	EPITHEM
EPAGOGIC	EPICAL	EPIGEAL	EPIPHYSIS	EPITHEMA
EPAINETIC	EPICALLY	EPIGEAN	EPIPHYTAL	EPITHEMATA
EPANODOS	EPICALYCES	EPIGENE	EPIPHYTE	EPITHEMS
EPANODOSES	EPICALYX	EPIGEOUS	EPIPHYTES	EPITHESES
EPARCH	EPICALYXES	EPIGON	EPIPHYTIC	EPITHESIS
EPARCHATE	EPICANTHI	EPIGONE	EPIPLOIC	EPITHET
EPARCHATES	EPICARP	EPIGONES	EPIPLOON	EPITHETED
EPARCHIES	EPICARPS	EPIGONI	EPIPLOONS	EPITHETIC
EPARCHS	EPICEDE	EPIGONS	EPIPOLIC	EPITHETING
EPARCHY	EPICEDES	EPIGRAM	EPIPOLISM	EPITHETON
EPATANT	EPICEDIA	EPIGRAMS	EPIPOLISMS	EPITHETONS
EPAULE	EPICEDIAL	EPIGRAPH	EPIRRHEMA	EPITHETS
EPAULES	EPICEDIAN	EPIGRAPHED	EPIRRHEMAS	EPITOME
EPAULET	EPICEDIUM	EPIGRAPHIES	EPISCOPAL	EPITOMES
EPAULETS	EPICENE	EPIGRAPHING	EPISCOPE	EPITOMIC
EPAULETTE	EPICENES	EPIGRAPHS	EPISCOPES	EPITOMISE
EPAULETTES	EPICENTER	EPIGRAPHY	EPISCOPIES	EPITOMISED
EPAXIAL	EPICENTERS	EPIGYNIES	EPISCOPY	EPITOMISES
EPEDAPHIC	EPICENTRE	EPIGYNOUS	EPISEMON	EPITOMISING
EPEE	EPICENTRES	EPIGYNY	EPISEMONS	EPITOMIST
EPEES	EPICIER	EPILATE	EPISODAL	EPITOMISTS
EPEIRA	EPICIERS	EPILATED	EPISODE	EPITOMIZE
EPEIRAS	EPICISM	EPILATES	EPISODES	EPITOMIZED
EPEIRID	EPICISMS	EPILATING	EPISODIAL	EPITOMIZES
EPEIRIDS	EPICIST	EPILATION	EPISODIC	EPITOMIZING
EPEOLATRIES	EPICISTS	EPILATIONS	EPISOME	EPITONIC
EPEOLATRY	EPICLESES	EPILATOR	EPISOMES	EPITOPE
EPERDU	EPICLESIS	EPILATORS	EPISPERM	EPITOPES
EPERDUE	EPICOTYL	EPILEPSIES	EPISPERMS	EPITRITE
EPERGNE	EPICOTYLS	EPILEPSY	EPISPORE	EPITRITES
EPERGNES	EPICRITIC	EPILEPTIC	EPISPORES	EPIZEUXES
EPHA	EPICS	EPILEPTICS	EPISTASES	EPIZEUXIS
EPHAH	EPICURE	EPILOBIUM	EPISTASIS	EPIZEUXISES
EPHAHS	EPICUREAN	EPILOBIUMS	EPISTATIC	EPIZOA
EPHAS	EPICUREANS	EPILOG	EPISTAXES	EPIZOAN
EPHEBE	EPICURES	EPILOGIC	EPISTAXIS	EPIZOANS
EPHEBES	EPICURISE	EPILOGISE	EPISTAXISES	EPIZOIC
EPHEBI	EPICURISED	EPILOGISED	EPISTEMIC	EPIZOON
EPHEBIC	EPICURISES	EPILOGISES	EPISTEMICS	EPIZOOTIC
EPHEBOS	EPICURISING	EPILOGISING	EPISTERNA	EPIZOOTICS
EPHEBUS	EPICURISM	EPILOGIST	EPISTLE	EPOCH
EPHEDRA	EPICURISMS	EPILOGISTS	EPISTLED	EPOCHA
EPHEDRAS	EPICURIZE	EPILOGIZE	EPISTLER	EPOCHAL
EPHEDRINE	EPICURIZED	EPILOGIZED	EPISTLERS	EPOCHAS
EPHEDRINES	EPICURIZES	EPILOGIZES	EPISTLES	EPOCHS
EPHELIDES	EPICURIZING	EPILOGIZING	EPISTLING	EPODE
EPHELIS	EPICYCLE	EPILOGS	EPISTOLER	EPODES
EPHEMERA	EPICYCLES	EPILOGUE	EPISTOLERS	EPODIC
EPHEMERAE	EPICYCLIC	EPILOGUES	EPISTOLET	EPONYM
EPHEMERAL	EPIDEMIC	EPIMER	EPISTOLETS	EPONYMIC
EPHEMERALS	EPIDEMICS	EPIMERIC	EPISTOLIC	EPONYMOUS
EPHEMERAS	EPIDERMAL	EPIMERS	EPISTYLE	EPONYMS
EPHEMERID	EPIDERMIC	EPINASTIC	EPISTYLES	EPOPEE
EPHEMERIDES	EPIDERMIS	EPINASTIES	EPITAPH	EPOPEES
EPHEMERIDS	EPIDERMISES	EPINASTY	EPITAPHED	EPOPOEIA
EPHEMERIS	EPIDOSITE	EPINEURAL	EPITAPHER	EPOPOEIAS
EPHEMERON	EPIDOSITES	EPINICIAN	EPITAPHERS	EPOPT

The Chambers Dictionary is the authority for many longer words; see *OSW* Introduction, page xii.

EPOPTS	EQUERRY	ERATHEMS	ERGOTIZE	EROTICAL
EPOS	EQUID	ERBIA	ERGOTIZED	EROTICISE
EPOSES	EQUIDS	ERBIAS	ERGOTIZES	EROTICISED
EPOXIDE	EQUINAL	ERBIUM	ERGOTIZING	EROTICISES
EPOXIDES	EQUINE	ERBIUMS	ERGOTS	EROTICISING
EPOXIES	EQUINIA	ERE	ERGS	EROTICISM
EPOXY	EQUINIAS	ERECT	ERIACH	EROTICISMS
EPRIS	EQUINITIES	ERECTED	ERIACHS	EROTICIST
EPRISE	EQUINITY	ERECTER	ERIC	EROTICISTS
EPROM	EQUINOX	ERECTERS	ERICA	EROTICIZE
EPROMS	EQUINOXES	ERECTILE	ERICAS	EROTICIZED
EPSILON	EQUIP	ERECTING	ERICK	EROTICIZES
EPSILONS	EQUIPAGE	ERECTION	ERICKS	EROTICIZING
EPSOMITE	EQUIPAGED	ERECTIONS	ERICOID	EROTICS
EPSOMITES	EQUIPAGES	ERECTIVE	ERICS	EROTISM
EPUISE	EQUIPAGING	ERECTLY	ERIGERON	EROTISMS
EPUISEE	EQUIPE	ERECTNESS	ERIGERONS	ERR
EPULARY	EQUIPES	ERECTNESSES	ERING	ERRABLE
EPULATION	EQUIPMENT	ERECTOR	ERINGO	ERRAND
EPULATIONS	EQUIPMENTS	ERECTORS	ERINGOES	ERRANDS
EPULIDES	EQUIPOISE	ERECTS	ERINGOS	ERRANT
EPULIS	EQUIPOISED	ERED	ERINITE	ERRANTLY
EPULISES	EQUIPOISES	ERELONG	ERINITES	ERRANTRIES
EPULOTIC	EQUIPOISING	EREMIC	ERIOMETER	ERRANTRY
EPULOTICS	EQUIPPED	EREMITAL	ERIOMETERS	ERRANTS
EPURATE	EQUIPPING	EREMITE	ERIONITE	ERRATA
EPURATED	EQUIPS	EREMITES	ERIONITES	ERRATIC
EPURATES	EQUISETA	EREMITIC	ERISTIC	ERRATICAL
EPURATING	EQUISETIC	EREMITISM	ERISTICAL	ERRATICS
EPURATION	EQUISETUM	EREMITISMS	ERK	ERRATUM
EPURATIONS	EQUISETUMS	ERENOW	ERKS	ERRED
EPYLLION	EQUITABLE	EREPSIN	ERMELIN	ERRHINE
EPYLLIONS	EQUITABLY	EREPSINS	ERMELINS	ERRHINES
EQUABLE	EQUITANT	ERES	ERMINE	ERRING
EQUABLY	EQUITIES	ERETHISM	ERMINED	ERRINGLY
EQUAL	EQUITY	ERETHISMS	ERMINES	ERRINGS
EQUALISE	EQUIVALVE	ERETHITIC	ERN	ERRONEOUS
EQUALISED	EQUIVOCAL	EREWHILE	ERNE	ERROR
EQUALISER	EQUIVOKE	ERF	ERNED	ERRORIST
EQUALISERS	EQUIVOKES	ERG	ERNES	ERRORISTS
EQUALISES	EQUIVOQUE	ERGATANER	ERNING	ERRORS
EQUALISING	EQUIVOQUES	ERGATANERS	ERNS	ERRS
EQUALITIES	ER	ERGATE	ERODE	ERS
EQUALITY	ERA	ERGATES	ERODED	ERSATZ
EQUALIZE	ERADIATE	ERGATIVE	ERODENT	ERSATZES
EQUALIZED	ERADIATED	ERGATOID	ERODENTS	ERSES
EQUALIZER	ERADIATES	ERGO	ERODES	ERST
EQUALIZERS	ERADIATING	ERGODIC	ERODIBLE	ERSTWHILE
EQUALIZES	ERADICATE	ERGOGRAM	ERODING	ERUCIFORM
EQUALIZING	ERADICATED	ERGOGRAMS	ERODIUM	ERUCT
EQUALLED	ERADICATES	ERGOGRAPH	ERODIUMS	ERUCTATE
EQUALLING	ERADICATING	ERGOGRAPHS	EROGENIC	ERUCTATED
EQUALLY	ERAS	ERGOMANIA	EROGENOUS	ERUCTATES
EQUALNESS	ERASABLE	ERGOMANIAS	EROSE	ERUCTATING
EQUALNESSES	ERASE	ERGOMETER	EROSION	ERUCTED
EQUALS	ERASED	ERGOMETERS	EROSIONS	ERUCTING
EQUANT	ERASEMENT	ERGON	EROSIVE	ERUCTS
EQUANTS	ERASEMENTS	ERGONOMIC	EROSTRATE	ERUDITE
EQUATE	ERASER	ERGONOMICS	EROTEMA	ERUDITELY
EQUATED	ERASERS	ERGONS	EROTEMAS	ERUDITES
EQUATES	ERASES	ERGOT	EROTEME	ERUDITION
EQUATING	ERASING	ERGOTISE	EROTEMES	ERUDITIONS
EQUATION	ERASION	ERGOTISED	EROTESES	ERUMPENT
EQUATIONS	ERASIONS	ERGOTISES	EROTESIS	ERUPT
EQUATOR	ERASURE	ERGOTISING	EROTETIC	ERUPTED
EQUATORS	ERASURES	ERGOTISM	EROTIC	ERUPTING
EQUERRIES	ERATHEM	ERGOTISMS	EROTICA	ERUPTION

The Chambers Dictionary is the authority for many longer words; see *OSW* Introduction, page xii.

ERUPTIONS
ERUPTIVE
ERUPTS
ERVALENTA
ERVALENTAS
ERVEN
ERYNGIUM
ERYNGIUMS
ERYNGO
ERYNGOES
ERYNGOS
ERYTHEMA
ERYTHEMAL
ERYTHEMAS
ERYTHRINA
ERYTHRINAS
ERYTHRISM
ERYTHRISMS
ERYTHRITE
ERYTHRITES
ES
ESCALADE
ESCALADED
ESCALADES
ESCALADING
ESCALADO
ESCALADOES
ESCALATE
ESCALATED
ESCALATES
ESCALATING
ESCALATOR
ESCALATORS
ESCALIER
ESCALIERS
ESCALLOP
ESCALLOPS
ESCALOP
ESCALOPE
ESCALOPED
ESCALOPES
ESCALOPING
ESCALOPS
ESCAPABLE
ESCAPADE
ESCAPADES
ESCAPADO
ESCAPADOES
ESCAPE
ESCAPED
ESCAPEE
ESCAPEES
ESCAPER
ESCAPERS
ESCAPES
ESCAPING
ESCAPISM
ESCAPISMS
ESCAPIST
ESCAPISTS
ESCARGOT
ESCARGOTS
ESCAROLE
ESCAROLES
ESCARP
ESCARPED
ESCARPING

ESCARPS
ESCHALOT
ESCHALOTS
ESCHAR
ESCHARS
ESCHEAT
ESCHEATED
ESCHEATING
ESCHEATOR
ESCHEATORS
ESCHEATS
ESCHEW
ESCHEWAL
ESCHEWALS
ESCHEWED
ESCHEWER
ESCHEWERS
ESCHEWING
ESCHEWS
ESCLANDRE
ESCLANDRES
ESCOLAR
ESCOLARS
ESCOPETTE
ESCOPETTES
ESCORT
ESCORTAGE
ESCORTAGES
ESCORTED
ESCORTING
ESCORTS
ESCOT
ESCOTS
ESCOTTED
ESCOTTING
ESCRIBANO
ESCRIBANOS
ESCRIBE
ESCRIBED
ESCRIBES
ESCRIBING
ESCROC
ESCROCS
ESCROL
ESCROLL
ESCROLLS
ESCROLS
ESCROW
ESCROWS
ESCUAGE
ESCUAGES
ESCUDO
ESCUDOS
ESCULENT
ESCULENTS
ESEMPLASIES
ESEMPLASY
ESILE
ESILES
ESKAR
ESKARS
ESKER
ESKERS
ESKIES
ESKY®
ESLOIN
ESLOINED

ESLOINING
ESLOINS
ESLOYNE
ESLOYNED
ESLOYNES
ESLOYNING
ESNE
ESNECIES
ESNECY
ESNES
ESOPHAGI
ESOPHAGUS
ESOTERIC
ESOTERICA
ESOTERIES
ESOTERISM
ESOTERISMS
ESOTERY
ESPADA
ESPADAS
ESPAGNOLE
ESPAGNOLES
ESPALIER
ESPALIERED
ESPALIERING
ESPALIERS
ESPARTO
ESPARTOS
ESPECIAL
ESPERANCE
ESPERANCES
ESPIAL
ESPIALS
ESPIED
ESPIEGLE
ESPIES
ESPIONAGE
ESPIONAGES
ESPLANADE
ESPLANADES
ESPOUSAL
ESPOUSALS
ESPOUSE
ESPOUSED
ESPOUSER
ESPOUSERS
ESPOUSES
ESPOUSING
ESPRESSO
ESPRESSOS
ESPRIT
ESPRITS
ESPUMOSO
ESPUMOSOS
ESPY
ESPYING
ESQUIRE
ESQUIRES
ESQUIRESS
ESQUIRESSES
ESQUISSE
ESQUISSES
ESS
ESSAY
ESSAYED
ESSAYER
ESSAYERS

ESSAYETTE
ESSAYETTES
ESSAYING
ESSAYISH
ESSAYIST
ESSAYISTS
ESSAYS
ESSE
ESSENCE
ESSENCES
ESSENTIAL
ESSENTIALS
ESSES
ESSIVE
ESSIVES
ESSOIN
ESSOINER
ESSOINERS
ESSOINS
ESSONITE
ESSONITES
ESSOYNE
ESSOYNES
EST
ESTABLISH
ESTABLISHED
ESTABLISHES
ESTABLISHING
ESTACADE
ESTACADES
ESTAFETTE
ESTAFETTES
ESTAMINET
ESTAMINETS
ESTANCIA
ESTANCIAS
ESTATE
ESTATED
ESTATES
ESTATING
ESTEEM
ESTEEMED
ESTEEMING
ESTEEMS
ESTER
ESTERIFIED
ESTERIFIES
ESTERIFY
ESTERIFYING
ESTERS
ESTHESIA
ESTHESIAS
ESTHETE
ESTHETES
ESTIMABLE
ESTIMABLY
ESTIMATE
ESTIMATED
ESTIMATES
ESTIMATING
ESTIMATOR
ESTIMATORS
ESTIVAL
ESTIVATE
ESTIVATED
ESTIVATES
ESTIVATING

ESTOC
ESTOCS
ESTOILE
ESTOILES
ESTOP
ESTOPPAGE
ESTOPPAGES
ESTOPPED
ESTOPPEL
ESTOPPELS
ESTOPPING
ESTOPS
ESTOVER
ESTOVERS
ESTRADE
ESTRADES
ESTRADIOL
ESTRADIOLS
ESTRAL
ESTRANGE
ESTRANGED
ESTRANGER
ESTRANGERS
ESTRANGES
ESTRANGING
ESTRAPADE
ESTRAPADES
ESTRAY
ESTRAYED
ESTRAYING
ESTRAYS
ESTREAT
ESTREATED
ESTREATING
ESTREATS
ESTREPE
ESTREPED
ESTREPES
ESTREPING
ESTRICH
ESTRICHES
ESTRIDGE
ESTRIDGES
ESTRILDID
ESTRILDIDS
ESTRO
ESTROGEN
ESTROGENS
ESTROS
ESTROUS
ESTRUM
ESTRUMS
ESTRUS
ESTRUSES
ESTS
ESTUARIAL
ESTUARIAN
ESTUARIES
ESTUARINE
ESTUARY
ESURIENCE
ESURIENCES
ESURIENCIES
ESURIENCY
ESURIENT
ETA
ETACISM

The Chambers Dictionary is the authority for many longer words; see *OSW* Introduction, page xii.

ETACISMS	ETHERIFY	ETHYNE	EUCHRED	EUNUCHIZE
ETAERIO	ETHERIFYING	ETHYNES	EUCHRES	EUNUCHIZED
ETAERIOS	ETHERION	ETIOLATE	EUCHRING	EUNUCHIZES
ETAGE	ETHERIONS	ETIOLATED	EUCLASE	EUNUCHIZING
ETAGERE	ETHERISE	ETIOLATES	EUCLASES	EUNUCHOID
ETAGERES	ETHERISED	ETIOLATING	EUCRITE	EUNUCHOIDS
ETAGES	ETHERISES	ETIOLIN	EUCRITES	EUNUCHS
ETALAGE	ETHERISING	ETIOLINS	EUCRITIC	EUOI
ETALAGES	ETHERISM	ETIOLOGIES	EUCYCLIC	EUONYMIN
ETALON	ETHERISMS	ETIOLOGY	EUDAEMONIES	EUONYMINS
ETALONS	ETHERIST	ETIQUETTE	EUDAEMONY	EUONYMUS
ETAPE	ETHERISTS	ETIQUETTES	EUDIALYTE	EUONYMUSES
ETAPES	ETHERIZE	ETNA	EUDIALYTES	EUOUAE
ETAS	ETHERIZED	ETNAS	EUGE	EUOUAES
ETAT	ETHERIZES	ETOILE	EUGENIA	EUPAD
ETATISME	ETHERIZING	ETOILES	EUGENIAS	EUPADS
ETATISMES	ETHERS	ETOURDI	EUGENIC	EUPATRID
ETATISTE	ETHIC	ETOURDIE	EUGENICS	EUPATRIDAE
ETATISTES	ETHICAL	ETRANGER	EUGENISM	EUPATRIDS
ETATS	ETHICALLY	ETRANGERE	EUGENISMS	EUPEPSIA
ETCETERA	ETHICALS	ETRANGERES	EUGENIST	EUPEPSIAS
ETCETERAS	ETHICISE	ETRANGERS	EUGENISTS	EUPEPSIES
ETCH	ETHICISED	ETRENNE	EUGENOL	EUPEPSY
ETCHANT	ETHICISES	ETRENNES	EUGENOLS	EUPEPTIC
ETCHANTS	ETHICISING	ETRIER	EUGH	EUPHAUSID
ETCHED	ETHICISM	ETRIERS	EUGHEN	EUPHAUSIDS
ETCHER	ETHICISMS	ETTERCAP	EUGHS	EUPHEMISE
ETCHERS	ETHICIST	ETTERCAPS	EUK	EUPHEMISED
ETCHES	ETHICISTS	ETTIN	EUKARYON	EUPHEMISES
ETCHING	ETHICIZE	ETTINS	EUKARYONS	EUPHEMISING
ETCHINGS	ETHICIZED	ETTLE	EUKARYOT	EUPHEMISM
ETEN	ETHICIZES	ETTLED	EUKARYOTE	EUPHEMISMS
ETENS	ETHICIZING	ETTLES	EUKARYOTES	EUPHEMIZE
ETERNAL	ETHICS	ETTLING	EUKARYOTS	EUPHEMIZED
ETERNALLY	ETHIOPS	ETUDE	EUKED	EUPHEMIZES
ETERNE	ETHIOPSES	ETUDES	EUKING	EUPHEMIZING
ETERNISE	ETHMOID	ETUI	EUKS	EUPHENICS
ETERNISED	ETHMOIDAL	ETUIS	EULACHAN	EUPHOBIA
ETERNISES	ETHNARCH	ETWEE	EULACHANS	EUPHOBIAS
ETERNISING	ETHNARCHIES	ETWEES	EULACHON	EUPHON
ETERNITIES	ETHNARCHS	ETYMA	EULACHONS	EUPHONIA
ETERNITY	ETHNARCHY	ETYMIC	EULOGIA	EUPHONIAS
ETERNIZE	ETHNIC	ETYMOLOGIES	EULOGIES	EUPHONIC
ETERNIZED	ETHNICAL	ETYMOLOGY	EULOGISE	EUPHONIES
ETERNIZES	ETHNICISM	ETYMON	EULOGISED	EUPHONISE
ETERNIZING	ETHNICISMS	ETYMONS	EULOGISES	EUPHONISED
ETESIAN	ETHNICITIES	ETYPIC	EULOGISING	EUPHONISES
ETH	ETHNICITY	ETYPICAL	EULOGIST	EUPHONISING
ETHAL	ETHNICS	EUCAIN	EULOGISTS	EUPHONISM
ETHALS	ETHNOCIDE	EUCAINE	EULOGIUM	EUPHONISMS
ETHANE	ETHNOCIDES	EUCAINES	EULOGIUMS	EUPHONIUM
ETHANES	ETHNOLOGIES	EUCAINS	EULOGIZE	EUPHONIUMS
ETHANOL	ETHNOLOGY	EUCALYPT	EULOGIZED	EUPHONIZE
ETHANOLS	ETHOLOGIC	EUCALYPTI	EULOGIZES	EUPHONIZED
ETHE	ETHOLOGIES	EUCALYPTS	EULOGIZING	EUPHONIZES
ETHENE	ETHOLOGY	EUCARYON	EULOGY	EUPHONIZING
ETHENES	ETHOS	EUCARYONS	EUMELANIN	EUPHONS
ETHER	ETHOSES	EUCARYOT	EUMELANINS	EUPHONY
ETHERCAP	ETHS	EUCARYOTE	EUMERISM	EUPHORBIA
ETHERCAPS	ETHYL	EUCARYOTES	EUMERISMS	EUPHORBIAS
ETHEREAL	ETHYLATE	EUCARYOTS	EUNUCH	EUPHORIA
ETHEREOUS	ETHYLATED	EUCHARIS	EUNUCHISE	EUPHORIAS
ETHERIAL	ETHYLATES	EUCHARISES	EUNUCHISED	EUPHORIC
ETHERIC	ETHYLATING	EUCHLORIC	EUNUCHISES	EUPHORIES
ETHERICAL	ETHYLENE	EUCHOLOGIES	EUNUCHISING	EUPHORY
ETHERIFIED	ETHYLENES	EUCHOLOGY	EUNUCHISM	EUPHRASIES
ETHERIFIES	ETHYLS	EUCHRE	EUNUCHISMS	EUPHRASY

The Chambers Dictionary is the authority for many longer words; see *OSW* Introduction, page xii.

EUPHROE	EVACUANT	EVENING	EVIDENT	EVOLVES
EUPHROES	EVACUANTS	EVENINGS	EVIDENTLY	EVOLVING
EUPHUISE	EVACUATE	EVENLY	EVIDENTS	EVOVAE
EUPHUISED	EVACUATED	EVENNESS	EVIL	EVOVAES
EUPHUISES	EVACUATES	EVENNESSES	EVILLER	EVULGATE
EUPHUISING	EVACUATING	EVENS	EVILLEST	EVULGATED
EUPHUISM	EVACUATOR	EVENSONG	EVILLY	EVULGATES
EUPHUISMS	EVACUATORS	EVENSONGS	EVILNESS	EVULGATING
EUPHUIST	EVACUEE	EVENT	EVILNESSES	EVULSE
EUPHUISTS	EVACUEES	EVENTED	EVILS	EVULSED
EUPHUIZE	EVADABLE	EVENTER	EVINCE	EVULSES
EUPHUIZED	EVADE	EVENTERS	EVINCED	EVULSING
EUPHUIZES	EVADED	EVENTFUL	EVINCES	EVULSION
EUPHUIZING	EVADER	EVENTIDE	EVINCIBLE	EVULSIONS
EUREKA	EVADERS	EVENTIDES	EVINCIBLY	EVZONE
EUREKAS	EVADES	EVENTING	EVINCING	EVZONES
EURHYTHMIES	EVADING	EVENTINGS	EVINCIVE	EWE
EURHYTHMY	EVAGATION	EVENTRATE	EVIRATE	EWER
EURIPI	EVAGATIONS	EVENTRATED	EVIRATED	EWERS
EURIPUS	EVAGINATE	EVENTRATES	EVIRATES	EWES
EURIPUSES	EVAGINATED	EVENTRATING	EVIRATING	EWEST
EURO	EVAGINATES	EVENTS	EVITABLE	EWFTES
EUROPIUM	EVAGINATING	EVENTUAL	EVITATE	EWGHEN
EUROPIUMS	EVALUATE	EVENTUATE	EVITATED	EWHOW
EUROS	EVALUATED	EVENTUATED	EVITATES	EWK
EURYTHERM	EVALUATES	EVENTUATES	EVITATING	EWKED
EURYTHERMS	EVALUATING	EVENTUATING	EVITATION	EWKING
EURYTHMIES	EVANESCE	EVER	EVITATIONS	EWKS
EURYTHMY	EVANESCED	EVERGLADE	EVITE	EWT
EUSOL	EVANESCES	EVERGLADES	EVITED	EWTS
EUSOLS	EVANESCING	EVERGREEN	EVITERNAL	EX
EUSTACIES	EVANGEL	EVERGREENS	EVITES	EXACT
EUSTACY	EVANGELIC	EVERMORE	EVITING	EXACTABLE
EUSTASIES	EVANGELIES	EVERSIBLE	EVOCABLE	EXACTED
EUSTASY	EVANGELS	EVERSION	EVOCATE	EXACTER
EUSTATIC	EVANGELY	EVERSIONS	EVOCATED	EXACTERS
EUSTYLE	EVANISH	EVERT	EVOCATES	EXACTEST
EUSTYLES	EVANISHED	EVERTED	EVOCATING	EXACTING
EUTAXIES	EVANISHES	EVERTING	EVOCATION	EXACTION
EUTAXITE	EVANISHING	EVERTOR	EVOCATIONS	EXACTIONS
EUTAXITES	EVANITION	EVERTORS	EVOCATIVE	EXACTLY
EUTAXITIC	EVANITIONS	EVERTS	EVOCATOR	EXACTMENT
EUTAXY	EVAPORATE	EVERY	EVOCATORS	EXACTMENTS
EUTECTIC	EVAPORATED	EVERYBODY	EVOCATORY	EXACTNESS
EUTECTICS	EVAPORATES	EVERYDAY	EVOE	EXACTNESSES
EUTECTOID	EVAPORATING	EVERYDAYS	EVOHE	EXACTOR
EUTECTOIDS	EVAPORITE	EVERYMAN	EVOKE	EXACTORS
EUTEXIA	EVAPORITES	EVERYMEN	EVOKED	EXACTRESS
EUTEXIAS	EVASIBLE	EVERYONE	EVOKER	EXACTRESSES
EUTHANASIES	EVASION	EVERYWAY	EVOKERS	EXACTS
EUTHANASY	EVASIONS	EVERYWHEN	EVOKES	EXALT
EUTHENICS	EVASIVE	EVES	EVOKING	EXALTED
EUTHENIST	EVASIVELY	EVET	EVOLUE	EXALTEDLY
EUTHENISTS	EVE	EVETS	EVOLUES	EXALTING
EUTHERIAN	EVECTION	EVHOE	EVOLUTE	EXALTS
EUTHERIANS	EVECTIONS	EVICT	EVOLUTED	EXAM
EUTRAPELIES	EVEJAR	EVICTED	EVOLUTES	EXAMEN
EUTRAPELY	EVEJARS	EVICTING	EVOLUTING	EXAMENS
EUTROPHIC	EVEN	EVICTION	EVOLUTION	EXAMINANT
EUTROPHIES	EVENED	EVICTIONS	EVOLUTIONS	EXAMINANTS
EUTROPHY	EVENEMENT	EVICTOR	EVOLUTIVE	EXAMINATE
EUTROPIC	EVENEMENTS	EVICTORS	EVOLVABLE	EXAMINATES
EUTROPIES	EVENER	EVICTS	EVOLVE	EXAMINE
EUTROPOUS	EVENERS	EVIDENCE	EVOLVED	EXAMINED
EUTROPY	EVENEST	EVIDENCED	EVOLVENT	EXAMINEE
EUXENITE	EVENFALL	EVIDENCES	EVOLVER	EXAMINEES
EUXENITES	EVENFALLS	EVIDENCING	EVOLVERS	EXAMINER

The Chambers Dictionary is the authority for many longer words; see *OSW* Introduction, page xii.

EXAMINERS	EXCEPTOR	EXCLUDED	EXECRATING	EXERGONIC
EXAMINES	EXCEPTORS	EXCLUDEE	EXECUTANT	EXERGUAL
EXAMINING	EXCEPTS	EXCLUDEES	EXECUTANTS	EXERGUE
EXAMPLAR	EXCERPT	EXCLUDER	EXECUTE	EXERGUES
EXAMPLARS	EXCERPTA	EXCLUDERS	EXECUTED	EXERT
EXAMPLE	EXCERPTED	EXCLUDES	EXECUTER	EXERTED
EXAMPLED	EXCERPTING	EXCLUDING	EXECUTERS	EXERTING
EXAMPLES	EXCERPTINGS	EXCLUSION	EXECUTES	EXERTION
EXAMPLING	EXCERPTOR	EXCLUSIONS	EXECUTING	EXERTIONS
EXAMS	EXCERPTORS	EXCLUSIVE	EXECUTION	EXERTIVE
EXANIMATE	EXCERPTS	EXCLUSIVES	EXECUTIONS	EXERTS
EXANTHEM	EXCERPTUM	EXCLUSORY	EXECUTIVE	EXES
EXANTHEMA	EXCESS	EXCORIATE	EXECUTIVES	EXEUNT
EXANTHEMATA	EXCESSES	EXCORIATED	EXECUTOR	EXFOLIATE
EXANTHEMS	EXCESSIVE	EXCORIATES	EXECUTORS	EXFOLIATED
EXARATE	EXCHANGE	EXCORIATING	EXECUTORY	EXFOLIATES
EXARATION	EXCHANGED	EXCREMENT	EXECUTRICES	EXFOLIATING
EXARATIONS	EXCHANGER	EXCREMENTS	EXECUTRIES	EXHALABLE
EXARCH	EXCHANGERS	EXCRETA	EXECUTRIX	EXHALANT
EXARCHAL	EXCHANGES	EXCRETAL	EXECUTRIXES	EXHALANTS
EXARCHATE	EXCHANGING	EXCRETE	EXECUTRY	EXHALE
EXARCHATES	EXCHEAT	EXCRETED	EXEDRA	EXHALED
EXARCHIES	EXCHEATS	EXCRETER	EXEDRAE	EXHALES
EXARCHIST	EXCHEQUER	EXCRETERS	EXEEM	EXHALING
EXARCHISTS	EXCHEQUERED	EXCRETES	EXEEMED	EXHAUST
EXARCHS	EXCHEQUERING	EXCRETING	EXEEMING	EXHAUSTED
EXARCHY	EXCHEQUERS	EXCRETION	EXEEMS	EXHAUSTER
EXCAMB	EXCIDE	EXCRETIONS	EXEGESES	EXHAUSTERS
EXCAMBED	EXCIDED	EXCRETIVE	EXEGESIS	EXHAUSTING
EXCAMBING	EXCIDES	EXCRETORIES	EXEGETE	EXHAUSTS
EXCAMBION	EXCIDING	EXCRETORY	EXEGETES	EXHEDRA
EXCAMBIONS	EXCIPIENT	EXCUBANT	EXEGETIC	EXHEDRAE
EXCAMBIUM	EXCIPIENTS	EXCUDIT	EXEGETICS	EXHIBIT
EXCAMBIUMS	EXCISABLE	EXCULPATE	EXEGETIST	EXHIBITED
EXCAMBS	EXCISE	EXCULPATED	EXEGETISTS	EXHIBITER
EXCARNATE	EXCISED	EXCULPATES	EXEME	EXHIBITERS
EXCARNATED	EXCISEMAN	EXCULPATING	EXEMED	EXHIBITING
EXCARNATES	EXCISEMEN	EXCURRENT	EXEMES	EXHIBITOR
EXCARNATING	EXCISES	EXCURSE	EXEMING	EXHIBITORS
EXCAUDATE	EXCISING	EXCURSED	EXEMPLA	EXHIBITS
EXCAVATE	EXCISION	EXCURSES	EXEMPLAR	EXHORT
EXCAVATED	EXCISIONS	EXCURSING	EXEMPLARS	EXHORTED
EXCAVATES	EXCITABLE	EXCURSION	EXEMPLARY	EXHORTER
EXCAVATING	EXCITANCIES	EXCURSIONED	EXEMPLE	EXHORTERS
EXCAVATOR	EXCITANCY	EXCURSIONING	EXEMPLES	EXHORTING
EXCAVATORS	EXCITANT	EXCURSIONS	EXEMPLIFIED	EXHORTS
EXCEED	EXCITANTS	EXCURSIVE	EXEMPLIFIES	EXHUMATE
EXCEEDED	EXCITE	EXCURSUS	EXEMPLIFY	EXHUMATED
EXCEEDING	EXCITED	EXCURSUSES	EXEMPLIFYING	EXHUMATES
EXCEEDS	EXCITEDLY	EXCUSABLE	EXEMPLUM	EXHUMATING
EXCEL	EXCITER	EXCUSABLY	EXEMPT	EXHUME
EXCELLED	EXCITERS	EXCUSAL	EXEMPTED	EXHUMED
EXCELLENT	EXCITES	EXCUSALS	EXEMPTING	EXHUMER
EXCELLING	EXCITING	EXCUSE	EXEMPTION	EXHUMERS
EXCELS	EXCITON	EXCUSED	EXEMPTIONS	EXHUMES
EXCELSIOR	EXCITONS	EXCUSER	EXEMPTS	EXHUMING
EXCELSIORS	EXCITOR	EXCUSERS	EXEQUATUR	EXIES
EXCENTRIC	EXCITORS	EXCUSES	EXEQUATURS	EXIGEANT
EXCENTRICS	EXCLAIM	EXCUSING	EXEQUIAL	EXIGEANTE
EXCEPT	EXCLAIMED	EXCUSIVE	EXEQUIES	EXIGENCE
EXCEPTANT	EXCLAIMING	EXEAT	EXEQUY	EXIGENCES
EXCEPTANTS	EXCLAIMS	EXEATS	EXERCISE	EXIGENCIES
EXCEPTED	EXCLAVE	EXECRABLE	EXERCISED	EXIGENCY
EXCEPTING	EXCLAVES	EXECRABLY	EXERCISER	EXIGENT
EXCEPTION	EXCLOSURE	EXECRATE	EXERCISERS	EXIGENTLY
EXCEPTIONS	EXCLOSURES	EXECRATED	EXERCISES	EXIGENTS
EXCEPTIVE	EXCLUDE	EXECRATES	EXERCISING	EXIGIBLE

The Chambers Dictionary is the authority for many longer words; see *OSW* Introduction, page xii.

EXIGUITIES	EXONYMS	EXPATIATE	EXPIRANT	EXPOSE
EXIGUITY	EXOPHAGIES	EXPATIATED	EXPIRANTS	EXPOSED
EXIGUOUS	EXOPHAGY	EXPATIATES	EXPIRE	EXPOSER
EXILE	EXOPLASM	EXPATIATING	EXPIRED	EXPOSERS
EXILED	EXOPLASMS	EXPATS	EXPIRES	EXPOSES
EXILEMENT	EXOPOD	EXPECT	EXPIRIES	EXPOSING
EXILEMENTS	EXOPODITE	EXPECTANT	EXPIRING	EXPOSITOR
EXILES	EXOPODITES	EXPECTANTS	EXPIRY	EXPOSITORS
EXILIAN	EXOPODS	EXPECTED	EXPISCATE	EXPOSTURE
EXILIC	EXORABLE	EXPECTER	EXPISCATED	EXPOSTURES
EXILING	EXORATION	EXPECTERS	EXPISCATES	EXPOSURE
EXILITIES	EXORATIONS	EXPECTING	EXPISCATING	EXPOSURES
EXILITY	EXORCISE	EXPECTINGS	EXPLAIN	EXPOUND
EXIMIOUS	EXORCISED	EXPECTS	EXPLAINED	EXPOUNDED
EXINE	EXORCISER	EXPEDIENT	EXPLAINER	EXPOUNDER
EXINES	EXORCISERS	EXPEDIENTS	EXPLAINERS	EXPOUNDERS
EXIST	EXORCISES	EXPEDITE	EXPLAINING	EXPOUNDING
EXISTED	EXORCISING	EXPEDITED	EXPLAINS	EXPOUNDS
EXISTENCE	EXORCISM	EXPEDITER	EXPLANT	EXPRESS
EXISTENCES	EXORCISMS	EXPEDITERS	EXPLANTED	EXPRESSED
EXISTENT	EXORCIST	EXPEDITES	EXPLANTING	EXPRESSES
EXISTING	EXORCISTS	EXPEDITING	EXPLANTS	EXPRESSING
EXISTS	EXORCIZE	EXPEDITOR	EXPLETIVE	EXPRESSLY
EXIT	EXORCIZED	EXPEDITORS	EXPLETIVES	EXPRESSO
EXITANCE	EXORCIZER	EXPEL	EXPLETORY	EXPRESSOS
EXITANCES	EXORCIZERS	EXPELLANT	EXPLICATE	EXPUGN
EXITED	EXORCIZES	EXPELLANTS	EXPLICATED	EXPUGNED
EXITING	EXORCIZING	EXPELLED	EXPLICATES	EXPUGNING
EXITS	EXORDIA	EXPELLEE	EXPLICATING	EXPUGNS
EXOCARP	EXORDIAL	EXPELLEES	EXPLICIT	EXPULSE
EXOCARPS	EXORDIUM	EXPELLENT	EXPLICITS	EXPULSED
EXOCRINE	EXORDIUMS	EXPELLENTS	EXPLODE	EXPULSES
EXOCRINES	EXOSMOSE	EXPELLING	EXPLODED	EXPULSING
EXODE	EXOSMOSES	EXPELS	EXPLODER	EXPULSION
EXODERM	EXOSMOSIS	EXPEND	EXPLODERS	EXPULSIONS
EXODERMAL	EXOSMOTIC	EXPENDED	EXPLODES	EXPULSIVE
EXODERMIS	EXOSPHERE	EXPENDER	EXPLODING	EXPUNCT
EXODERMISES	EXOSPHERES	EXPENDERS	EXPLOIT	EXPUNCTED
EXODERMS	EXOSPORAL	EXPENDING	EXPLOITED	EXPUNCTING
EXODES	EXOSPORE	EXPENDS	EXPLOITER	EXPUNCTS
EXODIC	EXOSPORES	EXPENSE	EXPLOITERS	EXPUNGE
EXODIST	EXOSTOSES	EXPENSES	EXPLOITING	EXPUNGED
EXODISTS	EXOSTOSIS	EXPENSIVE	EXPLOITS	EXPUNGER
EXODUS	EXOTERIC	EXPERT	EXPLORE	EXPUNGERS
EXODUSES	EXOTIC	EXPERTED	EXPLORED	EXPUNGES
EXOENZYME	EXOTICA	EXPERTING	EXPLORER	EXPUNGING
EXOENZYMES	EXOTICISM	EXPERTISE	EXPLORERS	EXPURGATE
EXOERGIC	EXOTICISMS	EXPERTISED	EXPLORES	EXPURGATED
EXOGAMIC	EXOTICS	EXPERTISES	EXPLORING	EXPURGATES
EXOGAMIES	EXOTOXIC	EXPERTISING	EXPLOSION	EXPURGATING
EXOGAMOUS	EXOTOXIN	EXPERTIZE	EXPLOSIONS	EXPURGE
EXOGAMY	EXOTOXINS	EXPERTIZED	EXPLOSIVE	EXPURGED
EXOGEN	EXPAND	EXPERTIZES	EXPLOSIVES	EXPURGES
EXOGENOUS	EXPANDED	EXPERTIZING	EXPO	EXPURGING
EXOGENS	EXPANDER	EXPERTLY	EXPONENT	EXQUISITE
EXOMION	EXPANDERS	EXPERTS	EXPONENTS	EXQUISITES
EXOMIONS	EXPANDING	EXPIABLE	EXPONIBLE	EXSCIND
EXOMIS	EXPANDOR	EXPIATE	EXPORT	EXSCINDED
EXOMISES	EXPANDORS	EXPIATED	EXPORTED	EXSCINDING
EXON	EXPANDS	EXPIATES	EXPORTER	EXSCINDS
EXONERATE	EXPANSE	EXPIATING	EXPORTERS	EXSECT
EXONERATED	EXPANSES	EXPIATION	EXPORTING	EXSECTED
EXONERATES	EXPANSILE	EXPIATIONS	EXPORTS	EXSECTING
EXONERATING	EXPANSION	EXPIATOR	EXPOS	EXSECTION
EXONIC	EXPANSIONS	EXPIATORS	EXPOSABLE	EXSECTIONS
EXONS	EXPANSIVE	EXPIATORY	EXPOSAL	EXSECTS
EXONYM	EXPAT	EXPIRABLE	EXPOSALS	EXSERT

The Chambers Dictionary is the authority for many longer words; see *OSW* Introduction, page xii.

EXSERTED	EXTERNALS	EXTRAITS	EXUBERATING	EYED
EXSERTILE	EXTERNAT	EXTRAPOSE	EXUDATE	EYEFUL
EXSERTING	EXTERNATS	EXTRAPOSED	EXUDATES	EYEFULS
EXSERTION	EXTERNE	EXTRAPOSES	EXUDATION	EYEGLASS
EXSERTIONS	EXTERNES	EXTRAPOSING	EXUDATIONS	EYEGLASSES
EXSERTS	EXTERNS	EXTRAS	EXUDATIVE	EYEHOOK
EXSICCANT	EXTINCT	EXTRAUGHT	EXUDE	EYEHOOKS
EXSICCATE	EXTINCTED	EXTRAVERT	EXUDED	EYEING
EXSICCATED	EXTINE	EXTRAVERTED	EXUDES	EYELASH
EXSICCATES	EXTINES	EXTRAVERTING	EXUDING	EYELASHES
EXSICCATING	EXTIRP	EXTRAVERTS	EXUL	EYELESS
EXSUCCOUS	EXTIRPATE	EXTREAT	EXULS	EYELET
EXTANT	EXTIRPATED	EXTREATS	EXULT	EYELETED
EXTASIES	EXTIRPATES	EXTREME	EXULTANCE	EYELETEER
EXTASY	EXTIRPATING	EXTREMELY	EXULTANCES	EYELETEERS
EXTATIC	EXTIRPED	EXTREMER	EXULTANCIES	EYELETING
EXTEMPORE	EXTIRPING	EXTREMES	EXULTANCY	EYELETS
EXTEMPORES	EXTIRPS	EXTREMEST	EXULTANT	EYELIAD
EXTEND	EXTOL	EXTREMISM	EXULTED	EYELIADS
EXTENDANT	EXTOLD	EXTREMISMS	EXULTING	EYELID
EXTENDED	EXTOLLED	EXTREMIST	EXULTS	EYELIDS
EXTENDER	EXTOLLER	EXTREMISTS	EXURB	EYELINER
EXTENDERS	EXTOLLERS	EXTREMITIES	EXURBAN	EYELINERS
EXTENDING	EXTOLLING	EXTREMITY	EXURBIA	EYES
EXTENDS	EXTOLMENT	EXTRICATE	EXURBIAS	EYESHADE
EXTENSE	EXTOLMENTS	EXTRICATED	EXURBS	EYESHADES
EXTENSILE	EXTOLS	EXTRICATES	EXUVIAE	EYESHADOW
EXTENSION	EXTORSIVE	EXTRICATING	EXUVIAL	EYESHADOWS
EXTENSIONS	EXTORT	EXTRINSIC	EXUVIATE	EYESIGHT
EXTENSITIES	EXTORTED	EXTRORSAL	EXUVIATED	EYESIGHTS
EXTENSITY	EXTORTING	EXTRORSE	EXUVIATES	EYESORE
EXTENSIVE	EXTORTION	EXTROVERT	EXUVIATING	EYESORES
EXTENSOR	EXTORTIONS	EXTROVERTED	EYALET	EYESTALK
EXTENSORS	EXTORTIVE	EXTROVERTING	EYALETS	EYESTALKS
EXTENT	EXTORTS	EXTROVERTS	EYAS	EYESTRAIN
EXTENTS	EXTRA	EXTRUDE	EYASES	EYESTRAINS
EXTENUATE	EXTRACT	EXTRUDED	EYE	EYING
EXTENUATED	EXTRACTED	EXTRUDER	EYEBALL	EYLIAD
EXTENUATES	EXTRACTING	EXTRUDERS	EYEBALLED	EYLIADS
EXTENUATING	EXTRACTOR	EXTRUDES	EYEBALLING	EYNE
EXTENUATINGS	EXTRACTORS	EXTRUDING	EYEBALLS	EYOT
EXTERIOR	EXTRACTS	EXTRUSION	EYEBOLT	EYOTS
EXTERIORS	EXTRADITE	EXTRUSIONS	EYEBOLTS	EYRA
EXTERMINE	EXTRADITED	EXTRUSIVE	EYEBRIGHT	EYRAS
EXTERMINED	EXTRADITES	EXTRUSORY	EYEBRIGHTS	EYRE
EXTERMINES	EXTRADITING	EXUBERANT	EYEBROW	EYRES
EXTERMINING	EXTRADOS	EXUBERATE	EYEBROWED	EYRIE
EXTERN	EXTRADOSES	EXUBERATED	EYEBROWING	EYRIES
EXTERNAL	EXTRAIT	EXUBERATES	EYEBROWS	EYRY

The Chambers Dictionary is the authority for many longer words; see *OSW* Introduction, page xii.

F

FA	FACIAS	FACULTIES	FAGGING	FAINNESSES
FAB	FACIES	FACULTY	FAGGINGS	FAINS
FABACEOUS	FACILE	FACUNDITIES	FAGGOT	FAINT
FABBER	FACILELY	FACUNDITY	FAGGOTED	FAINTED
FABBEST	FACILITIES	FAD	FAGGOTING	FAINTER
FABLE	FACILITY	FADABLE	FAGGOTINGS	FAINTEST
FABLED	FACING	FADAISE	FAGGOTS	FAINTIER
FABLER	FACINGS	FADAISES	FAGOT	FAINTIEST
FABLERS	FACONNE	FADDIER	FAGOTED	FAINTING
FABLES	FACONNES	FADDIEST	FAGOTING	FAINTINGS
FABLIAU	FACSIMILE	FADDINESS	FAGOTINGS	FAINTISH
FABLIAUX	FACSIMILED	FADDINESSES	FAGOTS	FAINTLY
FABLING	FACSIMILEING	FADDISH	FAGOTTI	FAINTNESS
FABLINGS	FACSIMILES	FADDISM	FAGOTTIST	FAINTNESSES
FABRIC	FACT	FADDISMS	FAGOTTISTS	FAINTS
FABRICANT	FACTICE	FADDIST	FAGOTTO	FAINTY
FABRICANTS	FACTICES	FADDISTS	FAGS	FAIR
FABRICATE	FACTICITIES	FADDLE	FAH	FAIRED
FABRICATED	FACTICITY	FADDLED	FAHLBAND	FAIRER
FABRICATES	FACTION	FADDLES	FAHLBANDS	FAIREST
FABRICATING	FACTIONAL	FADDLING	FAHLERZ	FAIRIES
FABRICKED	FACTIONS	FADDY	FAHLERZES	FAIRILY
FABRICKING	FACTIOUS	FADE	FAHLORE	FAIRING
FABRICS	FACTIS	FADED	FAHLORES	FAIRINGS
FABULAR	FACTISES	FADEDLY	FAHS	FAIRISH
FABULISE	FACTITIVE	FADEDNESS	FAIBLE	FAIRLY
FABULISED	FACTIVE	FADEDNESSES	FAIBLES	FAIRNESS
FABULISES	FACTOID	FADELESS	FAIENCE	FAIRNESSES
FABULISING	FACTOIDS	FADER	FAIENCES	FAIRS
FABULIST	FACTOR	FADERS	FAIK	FAIRWAY
FABULISTS	FACTORAGE	FADES	FAIKED	FAIRWAYS
FABULIZE	FACTORAGES	FADEUR	FAIKES	FAIRY
FABULIZED	FACTORED	FADEURS	FAIKING	FAIRYDOM
FABULIZES	FACTORIAL	FADGE	FAIKS	FAIRYDOMS
FABULIZING	FACTORIALS	FADGED	FAIL	FAIRYHOOD
FABULOUS	FACTORIES	FADGES	FAILED	FAIRYHOODS
FABURDEN	FACTORING	FADGING	FAILING	FAIRYISM
FABURDENS	FACTORINGS	FADIER	FAILINGS	FAIRYISMS
FACADE	FACTORISE	FADIEST	FAILLE	FAIRYLAND
FACADES	FACTORISED	FADING	FAILLES	FAIRYLANDS
FACE	FACTORISES	FADINGS	FAILS	FAIRYLIKE
FACED	FACTORISING	FADO	FAILURE	FAIRYTALE
FACELESS	FACTORIZE	FADOS	FAILURES	FAIRYTALES
FACEMAN	FACTORIZED	FADS	FAIN	FAITH
FACEMEN	FACTORIZES	FADY	FAINE	FAITHCURE
FACER	FACTORIZING	FAECAL	FAINEANCE	FAITHCURES
FACERS	FACTORS	FAECES	FAINEANCES	FAITHED
FACES	FACTORY	FAERIE	FAINEANCIES	FAITHFUL
FACET	FACTOTUM	FAERIES	FAINEANCY	FAITHING
FACETE	FACTOTUMS	FAERY	FAINEANT	FAITHLESS
FACETED	FACTS	FAFF	FAINEANTS	FAITHS
FACETIAE	FACTUAL	FAFFED	FAINED	FAITOR
FACETING	FACTUM	FAFFING	FAINER	FAITORS
FACETIOUS	FACTUMS	FAFFS	FAINES	FAITOUR
FACETS	FACTURE	FAG	FAINEST	FAITOURS
FACIA	FACTURES	FAGACEOUS	FAINING	FAIX
FACIAL	FACULA	FAGGED	FAINITES	FAJITAS
FACIALLY	FACULAE	FAGGERIES	FAINLY	FAKE
FACIALS	FACULAR	FAGGERY	FAINNESS	FAKED

The Chambers Dictionary is the authority for many longer words; see *OSW* Introduction, page xii.

FAKEMENT	FALLOW	FAMULUS	FANNELLS	FARADIZE
FAKEMENTS	FALLOWED	FAMULUSES	FANNELS	FARADIZED
FAKER	FALLOWER	FAN	FANNER	FARADIZES
FAKERIES	FALLOWEST	FANAL	FANNERS	FARADIZING
FAKERS	FALLOWING	FANALS	FANNIES	FARADS
FAKERY	FALLOWS	FANATIC	FANNING	FARAND
FAKES	FALLS	FANATICAL	FANNINGS	FARANDINE
FAKING	FALSE	FANATICS	FANNY	FARANDINES
FAKIR	FALSED	FANCIABLE	FANON	FARANDOLE
FAKIRISM	FALSEHOOD	FANCIED	FANONS	FARANDOLES
FAKIRISMS	FALSEHOODS	FANCIER	FANS	FARAWAY
FAKIRS	FALSELY	FANCIERS	FANTAD	FARAWAYS
FALAFEL	FALSENESS	FANCIES	FANTADS	FARCE
FALAFELS	FALSENESSES	FANCIEST	FANTAIL	FARCED
FALAJ	FALSER	FANCIFUL	FANTAILED	FARCES
FALANGISM	FALSERS	FANCILESS	FANTAILS	FARCEUR
FALANGISMS	FALSES	FANCY	FANTASIA	FARCEURS
FALANGIST	FALSEST	FANCYING	FANTASIAS	FARCEUSE
FALANGISTS	FALSETTO	FANCYWORK	FANTASIED	FARCEUSES
FALBALA	FALSETTOS	FANCYWORKS	FANTASIES	FARCI
FALBALAS	FALSEWORK	FAND	FANTASISE	FARCICAL
FALCADE	FALSEWORKS	FANDANGLE	FANTASISED	FARCIED
FALCADES	FALSIE	FANDANGLES	FANTASISES	FARCIES
FALCATE	FALSIES	FANDANGO	FANTASISING	FARCIFIED
FALCATED	FALSIFIED	FANDANGOS	FANTASIST	FARCIFIES
FALCATION	FALSIFIER	FANDED	FANTASISTS	FARCIFY
FALCATIONS	FALSIFIERS	FANDING	FANTASIZE	FARCIFYING
FALCES	FALSIFIES	FANDOM	FANTASIZED	FARCIN
FALCHION	FALSIFY	FANDOMS	FANTASIZES	FARCING
FALCHIONS	FALSIFYING	FANDS	FANTASIZING	FARCINGS
FALCIFORM	FALSING	FANE	FANTASM	FARCINS
FALCON	FALSISH	FANES	FANTASMS	FARCY
FALCONER	FALSISM	FANFARADE	FANTASQUE	FARD
FALCONERS	FALSISMS	FANFARADES	FANTASQUES	FARDAGE
FALCONET	FALSITIES	FANFARE	FANTAST	FARDAGES
FALCONETS	FALSITY	FANFARED	FANTASTIC	FARDED
FALCONINE	FALTBOAT	FANFARES	FANTASTICS	FARDEL
FALCONRIES	FALTBOATS	FANFARING	FANTASTRIES	FARDELS
FALCONRY	FALTER	FANFARON	FANTASTRY	FARDEN
FALCONS	FALTERED	FANFARONA	FANTASTS	FARDENS
FALCULA	FALTERING	FANFARONAS	FANTASY	FARDING
FALCULAS	FALTERINGS	FANFARONS	FANTASYING	FARDINGS
FALCULATE	FALTERS	FANFOLD	FANTEEG	FARDS
FALDAGE	FALX	FANG	FANTEEGS	FARE
FALDAGES	FAME	FANGED	FANTIGUE	FARED
FALDERAL	FAMED	FANGING	FANTIGUES	FARES
FALDERALS	FAMELESS	FANGLE	FANTOD	FAREWELL
FALDETTA	FAMES	FANGLED	FANTODS	FAREWELLS
FALDETTAS	FAMILIAL	FANGLES	FANTOM	FARFET
FALDSTOOL	FAMILIAR	FANGLESS	FANTOMS	FARINA
FALDSTOOLS	FAMILIARS	FANGLING	FANTOOSH	FARINAS
FALL	FAMILIES	FANGO	FANZINE	FARING
FALLACIES	FAMILISM	FANGOS	FANZINES	FARINOSE
FALLACY	FAMILISMS	FANGS	FAP	FARL
FALLAL	FAMILY	FANION	FAQUIR	FARLE
FALLALERIES	FAMINE	FANIONS	FAQUIRS	FARLES
FALLALERY	FAMINES	FANK	FAR	FARLS
FALLALS	FAMING	FANKLE	FARAD	FARM
FALLEN	FAMISH	FANKLED	FARADAY	FARMED
FALLER	FAMISHED	FANKLES	FARADAYS	FARMER
FALLERS	FAMISHES	FANKLING	FARADIC	FARMERESS
FALLIBLE	FAMISHING	FANKS	FARADISE	FARMERESSES
FALLIBLY	FAMOUS	FANLIGHT	FARADISED	FARMERIES
FALLING	FAMOUSED	FANLIGHTS	FARADISES	FARMERS
FALLINGS	FAMOUSES	FANNED	FARADISING	FARMERY
FALLOUT	FAMOUSING	FANNEL	FARADISM	FARMHOUSE
FALLOUTS	FAMOUSLY	FANNELL	FARADISMS	FARMHOUSES

The Chambers Dictionary is the authority for many longer words; see *OSW* Introduction, page xii.

FARMING	FASCINATING	FATED	FATWAS	FAVOUR
FARMINGS	FASCINE	FATEFUL	FAUBOURG	FAVOURED
FARMOST	FASCINES	FATEFULLY	FAUBOURGS	FAVOURER
FARMS	FASCIO	FATES	FAUCAL	FAVOURERS
FARMSTEAD	FASCIOLA	FATHER	FAUCES	FAVOURING
FARMSTEADS	FASCIOLAS	FATHERED	FAUCET	FAVOURITE
FARMYARD	FASCIOLE	FATHERING	FAUCETS	FAVOURITES
FARMYARDS	FASCIOLES	FATHERLY	FAUCHION	FAVOURS
FARNESOL	FASCISM	FATHERS	FAUCHIONS	FAVOUS
FARNESOLS	FASCISMI	FATHOM	FAUCHON	FAVRILE
FARNESS	FASCISMO	FATHOMED	FAUCHONS	FAVRILES
FARNESSES	FASCISMS	FATHOMING	FAUCIAL	FAVUS
FARO	FASCIST	FATHOMS	FAUGH	FAVUSES
FAROS	FASCISTA	FATIDICAL	FAULCHIN	FAW
FAROUCHE	FASCISTI	FATIGABLE	FAULCHINS	FAWN
FARRAGO	FASCISTIC	FATIGATE	FAULCHION	FAWNED
FARRAGOES	FASCISTS	FATIGATED	FAULCHIONS	FAWNER
FARRAND	FASH	FATIGATES	FAULT	FAWNERS
FARRANT	FASHED	FATIGATING	FAULTED	FAWNING
FARRED	FASHERIES	FATIGUE	FAULTFUL	FAWNINGLY
FARREN	FASHERY	FATIGUED	FAULTIER	FAWNINGS
FARRENS	FASHES	FATIGUES	FAULTIEST	FAWNS
FARRIER	FASHING	FATIGUING	FAULTILY	FAWS
FARRIERIES	FASHION	FATISCENT	FAULTING	FAX
FARRIERS	FASHIONED	FATLING	FAULTLESS	FAXED
FARRIERY	FASHIONER	FATLINGS	FAULTS	FAXES
FARRING	FASHIONERS	FATLY	FAULTY	FAXING
FARROW	FASHIONING	FATNESS	FAUN	FAY
FARROWED	FASHIONS	FATNESSES	FAUNA	FAYALITE
FARROWING	FASHIOUS	FATS	FAUNAE	FAYALITES
FARROWS	FAST	FATSIA	FAUNAL	FAYED
FARRUCA	FASTBACK	FATSIAS	FAUNAS	FAYENCE
FARRUCAS	FASTBACKS	FATSO	FAUNIST	FAYENCES
FARS	FASTBALL	FATSOES	FAUNISTIC	FAYER
FARSE	FASTBALLS	FATSOS	FAUNISTS	FAYEST
FARSED	FASTED	FATSTOCK	FAUNS	FAYING
FARSES	FASTEN	FATSTOCKS	FAURD	FAYNE
FARSING	FASTENED	FATTED	FAUSTIAN	FAYNED
FART	FASTENER	FATTEN	FAUTEUIL	FAYNES
FARTED	FASTENERS	FATTENED	FAUTEUILS	FAYNING
FARTHEL	FASTENING	FATTENER	FAUTOR	FAYRE
FARTHELS	FASTENINGS	FATTENERS	FAUTORS	FAYRES
FARTHER	FASTENS	FATTENING	FAUVETTE	FAYS
FARTHEST	FASTER	FATTENINGS	FAUVETTES	FAZE
FARTHING	FASTERS	FATTENS	FAUX	FAZED
FARTHINGS	FASTEST	FATTER	FAVE	FAZENDA
FARTING	FASTI	FATTEST	FAVEL	FAZENDAS
FARTLEK	FASTIGIUM	FATTIER	FAVELA	FAZES
FARTLEKS	FASTIGIUMS	FATTIES	FAVELAS	FAZING
FARTS	FASTING	FATTIEST	FAVELL	FEAGUE
FAS	FASTINGS	FATTINESS	FAVEOLATE	FEAGUED
FASCES	FASTISH	FATTINESSES	FAVER	FEAGUES
FASCI	FASTLY	FATTING	FAVEST	FEAGUING
FASCIA	FASTNESS	FATTISH	FAVISM	FEAL
FASCIAL	FASTNESSES	FATTRELS	FAVISMS	FEALED
FASCIAS	FASTS	FATTY	FAVOR	FEALING
FASCIATE	FASTUOUS	FATUITIES	FAVORABLE	FEALS
FASCIATED	FAT	FATUITOUS	FAVORABLY	FEALTIES
FASCICLE	FATAL	FATUITY	FAVORED	FEALTY
FASCICLED	FATALISM	FATUOUS	FAVORER	FEAR
FASCICLES	FATALISMS	FATWA	FAVORERS	FEARE
FASCICULE	FATALIST	FATWAED	FAVORING	FEARED
FASCICULES	FATALISTS	FATWAH	FAVORITE	FEARES
FASCICULI	FATALITIES	FATWAHED	FAVORITES	FEARFUL
FASCINATE	FATALITY	FATWAHING	FAVORLESS	FEARFULLY
FASCINATED	FATALLY	FATWAHS	FAVORS	FEARING
FASCINATES	FATE	FATWAING	FAVOSE	FEARLESS

The Chambers Dictionary is the authority for many longer words; see *OSW* Introduction, page xii.

FEARS	FECUND	FEERINGS	FELLATE	FEMINAL
FEARSOME	FECUNDATE	FEERINS	FELLATED	FEMINEITIES
FEASIBLE	FECUNDATED	FEERS	FELLATES	FEMINEITY
FEASIBLY	FECUNDATES	FEES	FELLATING	FEMININE
FEAST	FECUNDATING	FEESE	FELLATIO	FEMININES
FEASTED	FECUNDITIES	FEESED	FELLATION	FEMINISE
FEASTER	FECUNDITY	FEESES	FELLATIONS	FEMINISED
FEASTERS	FED	FEESING	FELLATIOS	FEMINISES
FEASTFUL	FEDARIE	FEET	FELLED	FEMINISING
FEASTING	FEDARIES	FEETLESS	FELLER	FEMINISM
FEASTINGS	FEDAYEE	FEEZE	FELLERS	FEMINISMS
FEASTS	FEDAYEEN	FEEZED	FELLEST	FEMINIST
FEAT	FEDELINI	FEEZES	FELLIES	FEMINISTS
FEATED	FEDELINIS	FEEZING	FELLING	FEMINITIES
FEATEOUS	FEDERACIES	FEGARIES	FELLNESS	FEMINITY
FEATHER	FEDERACY	FEGARY	FELLNESSES	FEMINIZE
FEATHERED	FEDERAL	FEGS	FELLOE	FEMINIZED
FEATHERIER	FEDERALS	FEHM	FELLOES	FEMINIZES
FEATHERIEST	FEDERARIE	FEHME	FELLOW	FEMINIZING
FEATHERING	FEDERARIES	FEHMIC	FELLOWLY	FEMITER
FEATHERINGS	FEDERARY	FEIGN	FELLOWS	FEMITERS
FEATHERS	FEDERATE	FEIGNED	FELLS	FEMME
FEATHERY	FEDERATED	FEIGNEDLY	FELLY	FEMMES
FEATING	FEDERATES	FEIGNING	FELON	FEMORA
FEATLY	FEDERATING	FEIGNINGS	FELONIES	FEMORAL
FEATOUS	FEDORA	FEIGNS	FELONIOUS	FEMUR
FEATS	FEDORAS	FEIJOA	FELONOUS	FEMURS
FEATUOUS	FEDS	FEIJOAS	FELONRIES	FEN
FEATURE	FEE	FEINT	FELONRY	FENCE
FEATURED	FEEBLE	FEINTED	FELONS	FENCED
FEATURELY	FEEBLED	FEINTER	FELONY	FENCELESS
FEATURES	FEEBLER	FEINTEST	FELSIC	FENCER
FEATURING	FEEBLES	FEINTING	FELSITE	FENCERS
FEBLESSE	FEEBLEST	FEINTS	FELSITES	FENCES
FEBLESSES	FEEBLING	FEIS	FELSITIC	FENCIBLE
FEBRICITIES	FEEBLISH	FEISEANNA	FELSPAR	FENCIBLES
FEBRICITY	FEEBLY	FEISTIER	FELSPARS	FENCING
FEBRICULA	FEED	FEISTIEST	FELSTONE	FENCINGS
FEBRICULAS	FEEDBACK	FEISTY	FELSTONES	FEND
FEBRICULE	FEEDBACKS	FELAFEL	FELT	FENDED
FEBRICULES	FEEDER	FELAFELS	FELTED	FENDER
FEBRIFIC	FEEDERS	FELDGRAU	FELTER	FENDERS
FEBRIFUGE	FEEDING	FELDGRAUS	FELTERED	FENDIER
FEBRIFUGES	FEEDINGS	FELDSHER	FELTERING	FENDIEST
FEBRILE	FEEDLOT	FELDSHERS	FELTERS	FENDING
FEBRILITIES	FEEDLOTS	FELDSPAR	FELTIER	FENDS
FEBRILITY	FEEDS	FELDSPARS	FELTIEST	FENDY
FECAL	FEEDSTOCK	FELICIA	FELTING	FENESTRA
FECES	FEEDSTOCKS	FELICIAS	FELTINGS	FENESTRAL
FECHT	FEEDSTUFF	FELICIFIC	FELTS	FENESTRALS
FECHTER	FEEDSTUFFS	FELICITER	FELTY	FENESTRAS
FECHTERS	FEEING	FELICITIES	FELUCCA	FENI
FECHTING	FEEL	FELICITY	FELUCCAS	FENIS
FECHTS	FEELER	FELID	FELWORT	FENITAR
FECIAL	FEELERS	FELIDS	FELWORTS	FENITARS
FECIT	FEELGOOD	FELINE	FEMAL	FENKS
FECK	FEELGOODS	FELINES	FEMALE	FENLAND
FECKLESS	FEELING	FELINITIES	FEMALES	FENLANDS
FECKLY	FEELINGLY	FELINITY	FEMALITIES	FENMAN
FECKS	FEELINGS	FELL	FEMALITY	FENMEN
FECULA	FEELS	FELLA	FEMALS	FENNEC
FECULAS	FEER	FELLABLE	FEME	FENNECS
FECULENCE	FEERED	FELLAH	FEMERALL	FENNEL
FECULENCES	FEERIE	FELLAHEEN	FEMERALLS	FENNELS
FECULENCIES	FEERIES	FELLAHIN	FEMES	FENNIER
FECULENCY	FEERIN	FELLAHS	FEMETARIES	FENNIES
FECULENT	FEERING	FELLAS	FEMETARY	FENNIEST

The Chambers Dictionary is the authority for many longer words; see *OSW* Introduction, page xii.

FENNISH
FENNY
FENS
FENT
FENTS
FENUGREEK
FENUGREEKS
FEOD
FEODAL
FEODARIES
FEODARY
FEODS
FEOFF
FEOFFED
FEOFFEE
FEOFFEES
FEOFFER
FEOFFERS
FEOFFING
FEOFFMENT
FEOFFMENTS
FEOFFOR
FEOFFORS
FEOFFS
FERACIOUS
FERACITIES
FERACITY
FERAL
FERALISED
FERALIZED
FERE
FERER
FERES
FEREST
FERETORIES
FERETORY
FERIAL
FERINE
FERITIES
FERITY
FERLIED
FERLIER
FERLIES
FERLIEST
FERLY
FERLYING
FERM
FERMATA
FERMATAS
FERMATE
FERMENT
FERMENTED
FERMENTING
FERMENTS
FERMI
FERMION
FERMIONS
FERMIS
FERMIUM
FERMIUMS
FERMS
FERN
FERNBIRD
FERNBIRDS
FERNERIES
FERNERY
FERNIER

FERNIEST
FERNING
FERNINGS
FERNS
FERNSHAW
FERNSHAWS
FERNTICLE
FERNTICLES
FERNY
FEROCIOUS
FEROCITIES
FEROCITY
FERRATE
FERRATES
FERREL
FERRELS
FERREOUS
FERRET
FERRETED
FERRETER
FERRETERS
FERRETING
FERRETS
FERRETY
FERRIAGE
FERRIAGES
FERRIC
FERRIED
FERRIES
FERRITE
FERRITES
FERRITIC
FERRITIN
FERRITINS
FERROTYPE
FERROTYPES
FERROUS
FERRUGO
FERRUGOS
FERRULE
FERRULES
FERRY
FERRYING
FERRYMAN
FERRYMEN
FERTILE
FERTILELY
FERTILER
FERTILEST
FERTILISE
FERTILISED
FERTILISES
FERTILISING
FERTILITIES
FERTILITY
FERTILIZE
FERTILIZED
FERTILIZES
FERTILIZING
FERULA
FERULAS
FERULE
FERULES
FERVENCIES
FERVENCY
FERVENT
FERVENTER

FERVENTEST
FERVENTLY
FERVID
FERVIDER
FERVIDEST
FERVIDITIES
FERVIDITY
FERVIDLY
FERVOROUS
FERVOUR
FERVOURS
FESCUE
FESCUES
FESS
FESSE
FESSES
FEST
FESTA
FESTAL
FESTALLY
FESTALS
FESTAS
FESTER
FESTERED
FESTERING
FESTERS
FESTILOGIES
FESTILOGY
FESTINATE
FESTINATED
FESTINATES
FESTINATING
FESTIVAL
FESTIVALS
FESTIVE
FESTIVELY
FESTIVITIES
FESTIVITY
FESTIVOUS
FESTOLOGIES
FESTOLOGY
FESTOON
FESTOONED
FESTOONING
FESTOONS
FESTS
FET
FETA
FETAL
FETAS
FETCH
FETCHED
FETCHES
FETCHING
FETE
FETED
FETES
FETIAL
FETICH
FETICHE
FETICHES
FETICHISE
FETICHISED
FETICHISES
FETICHISING
FETICHISM
FETICHISMS

FETICHIST
FETICHISTS
FETICHIZE
FETICHIZED
FETICHIZES
FETICHIZING
FETICIDAL
FETICIDE
FETICIDES
FETID
FETIDER
FETIDEST
FETIDNESS
FETIDNESSES
FETING
FETISH
FETISHES
FETISHISE
FETISHISED
FETISHISES
FETISHISING
FETISHISM
FETISHISMS
FETISHIST
FETISHISTS
FETISHIZE
FETISHIZED
FETISHIZES
FETISHIZING
FETLOCK
FETLOCKED
FETLOCKS
FETOR
FETORS
FETOSCOPIES
FETOSCOPY
FETS
FETT
FETTA
FETTAS
FETTED
FETTER
FETTERED
FETTERING
FETTERS
FETTING
FETTLE
FETTLED
FETTLER
FETTLERS
FETTLES
FETTLING
FETTLINGS
FETTS
FETTUCINE
FETTUCINES
FETTUCINI
FETTUCINIS
FETUS
FETUSES
FETWA
FETWAS
FEU
FEUAR
FEUARS
FEUD
FEUDAL

FEUDALISE
FEUDALISED
FEUDALISES
FEUDALISING
FEUDALISM
FEUDALISMS
FEUDALIST
FEUDALISTS
FEUDALITIES
FEUDALITY
FEUDALIZE
FEUDALIZED
FEUDALIZES
FEUDALIZING
FEUDALLY
FEUDARIES
FEUDARY
FEUDATORIES
FEUDATORY
FEUDED
FEUDING
FEUDINGS
FEUDIST
FEUDISTS
FEUDS
FEUED
FEUILLETE
FEUILLETES
FEUING
FEUS
FEUTRE
FEUTRED
FEUTRES
FEUTRING
FEVER
FEVERED
FEVERFEW
FEVERFEWS
FEVERING
FEVERISH
FEVEROUS
FEVERS
FEW
FEWER
FEWEST
FEWMET
FEWMETS
FEWNESS
FEWNESSES
FEWTER
FEWTERED
FEWTERING
FEWTERS
FEWTRILS
FFY
FEYED
FEYER
FEYEST
FEYING
FEYS
FEZ
FEZES
FEZZED
FEZZES
FIACRE
FIACRES
FIANCE

The Chambers Dictionary is the authority for many longer words; see *OSW* Introduction, page xii.

FIANCEE	FIBULAR	FIELDED	FIGHTING	FILCHER
FIANCEES	FIBULAS	FIELDER	FIGHTINGS	FILCHERS
FIANCES	FICHE	FIELDERS	FIGHTS	FILCHES
FIAR	FICHES	FIELDFARE	FIGMENT	FILCHING
FIARS	FICHU	FIELDFARES	FIGMENTS	FILCHINGS
FIASCO	FICHUS	FIELDING	FIGO	FILE
FIASCOES	FICKLE	FIELDINGS	FIGOS	FILED
FIASCOS	FICKLED	FIELDMICE	FIGS	FILEMOT
FIAT	FICKLER	FIELDS	FIGULINE	FILEMOTS
FIATED	FICKLES	FIELDSMAN	FIGULINES	FILENAME
FIATING	FICKLEST	FIELDSMEN	FIGURABLE	FILENAMES
FIATS	FICKLING	FIELDVOLE	FIGURAL	FILER
FIAUNT	FICO	FIELDVOLES	FIGURANT	FILERS
FIAUNTS	FICOS	FIELDWARD	FIGURANTE	FILES
FIB	FICTILE	FIELDWARDS	FIGURANTES	FILET
FIBBED	FICTION	FIELDWORK	FIGURANTS	FILETS
FIBBER	FICTIONAL	FIELDWORKS	FIGURATE	FILFOT
FIBBERIES	FICTIONS	FIEND	FIGURE	FILFOTS
FIBBERS	FICTIVE	FIENDISH	FIGURED	FILIAL
FIBBERY	FICTOR	FIENDS	FIGURES	FILIALLY
FIBBING	FICTORS	FIENT	FIGURINE	FILIATE
FIBER	FICUS	FIENTS	FIGURINES	FILIATED
FIBERED	FICUSES	FIERCE	FIGURING	FILIATES
FIBERLESS	FID	FIERCELY	FIGURIST	FILIATING
FIBERS	FIDDIOUS	FIERCER	FIGURISTS	FILIATION
FIBRE	FIDDIOUSED	FIERCEST	FIGWORT	FILIATIONS
FIBRED	FIDDIOUSES	FIERE	FIGWORTS	FILIBEG
FIBRELESS	FIDDIOUSING	FIERES	FIKE	FILIBEGS
FIBRES	FIDDLE	FIERIER	FIKED	FILICIDE
FIBRIFORM	FIDDLED	FIERIEST	FIKERIES	FILICIDES
FIBRIL	FIDDLER	FIERILY	FIKERY	FILIFORM
FIBRILLA	FIDDLERS	FIERINESS	FIKES	FILIGRAIN
FIBRILLAE	FIDDLES	FIERINESSES	FIKIER	FILIGRAINS
FIBRILLAR	FIDDLEY	FIERY	FIKIEST	FILIGRANE
FIBRILLIN	FIDDLEYS	FIESTA	FIKING	FILIGRANES
FIBRILLINS	FIDDLIER	FIESTAS	FIKISH	FILIGREE
FIBRILS	FIDDLIEST	FIFE	FIKY	FILIGREED
FIBRIN	FIDDLING	FIFED	FIL	FILIGREES
FIBRINOUS	FIDDLY	FIFER	FILABEG	FILING
FIBRINS	FIDEISM	FIFERS	FILABEGS	FILINGS
FIBRO	FIDEISMS	FIFES	FILACEOUS	FILIOQUE
FIBROCYTE	FIDEIST	FIFING	FILACER	FILIOQUES
FIBROCYTES	FIDEISTIC	FIFTEEN	FILACERS	FILL
FIBROID	FIDEISTS	FIFTEENER	FILAGREE	FILLE
FIBROIDS	FIDELITIES	FIFTEENERS	FILAGREES	FILLED
FIBROIN	FIDELITY	FIFTEENS	FILAMENT	FILLER
FIBROINS	FIDGE	FIFTEENTH	FILAMENTS	FILLERS
FIBROLINE	FIDGED	FIFTEENTHS	FILANDER	FILLES
FIBROLINES	FIDGES	FIFTH	FILANDERS	FILLET
FIBROLITE	FIDGET	FIFTHLY	FILAR	FILLETED
FIBROLITES	FIDGETED	FIFTHS	FILARIA	FILLETING
FIBROMA	FIDGETING	FIFTIES	FILARIAL	FILLETS
FIBROMAS	FIDGETS	FIFTIETH	FILARIAS	FILLIBEG
FIBROMATA	FIDGETY	FIFTIETHS	FILASSE	FILLIBEGS
FIBROS	FIDGING	FIFTY	FILASSES	FILLIES
FIBROSE	FIDIBUS	FIFTYISH	FILATORIES	FILLING
FIBROSED	FIDIBUSES	FIG	FILATORY	FILLINGS
FIBROSES	FIDS	FIGGED	FILATURE	FILLIP
FIBROSING	FIDUCIAL	FIGGERIES	FILATURES	FILLIPED
FIBROSIS	FIDUCIARIES	FIGGERY	FILAZER	FILLIPEEN
FIBROTIC	FIDUCIARY	FIGGING	FILAZERS	FILLIPEENS
FIBROUS	FIE	FIGHT	FILBERD	FILLIPING
FIBS	FIEF	FIGHTABLE	FILBERDS	FILLIPS
FIBSTER	FIEFDOM	FIGHTBACK	FILBERT	FILLISTER
FIBSTERS	FIEFDOMS	FIGHTBACKS	FILBERTS	FILLISTERS
FIBULA	FIEFS	FIGHTER	FILCH	FILLS
FIBULAE	FIELD	FIGHTERS	FILCHED	FILLY

The Chambers Dictionary is the authority for many longer words; see *OSW* Introduction, page xii.

FILM	FINALISM	FINI	FIPPLE	FIREWOMEN
FILMABLE	FINALISMS	FINIAL	FIPPLES	FIREWOOD
FILMDOM	FINALIST	FINIALS	FIR	FIREWOODS
FILMDOMS	FINALISTS	FINICAL	FIRE	FIREWORK
FILMED	FINALITIES	FINICALLY	FIREARM	FIREWORKS
FILMGOER	FINALITY	FINICKETY	FIREARMS	FIREWORM
FILMGOERS	FINALIZE	FINICKIER	FIREBALL	FIREWORMS
FILMIC	FINALIZED	FINICKIEST	FIREBALLS	FIRING
FILMIER	FINALIZES	FINICKING	FIREBOX	FIRINGS
FILMIEST	FINALIZING	FINICKINGS	FIREBOXES	FIRK
FILMINESS	FINALLY	FINICKY	FIREBRAND	FIRKED
FILMINESSES	FINALS	FINIKIN	FIREBRANDS	FIRKIN
FILMING	FINANCE	FINING	FIREBRAT	FIRKING
FILMISH	FINANCED	FININGS	FIREBRATS	FIRKINS
FILMLAND	FINANCES	FINIS	FIREBRICK	FIRKS
FILMLANDS	FINANCIAL	FINISH	FIREBRICKS	FIRLOT
FILMS	FINANCIER	FINISHED	FIREBUG	FIRLOTS
FILMSET	FINANCIERED	FINISHER	FIREBUGS	FIRM
FILMSETS	FINANCIERING	FINISHERS	FIRECREST	FIRMAMENT
FILMSETTING	FINANCIERS	FINISHES	FIRECRESTS	FIRMAMENTS
FILMSETTINGS	FINANCING	FINISHING	FIRED	FIRMAN
FILMY	FINBACK	FINISHINGS	FIREDAMP	FIRMANS
FILO	FINBACKS	FINITE	FIREDAMPS	FIRMED
FILOPLUME	FINCH	FINITELY	FIREDOG	FIRMER
FILOPLUMES	FINCHED	FINITUDE	FIREDOGS	FIRMERS
FILOPODIA	FINCHES	FINITUDES	FIREFLIES	FIRMEST
FILOS	FIND	FINJAN	FIREFLOAT	FIRMING
FILOSE	FINDER	FINJANS	FIREFLOATS	FIRMLESS
FILOSELLE	FINDERS	FINK	FIREFLY	FIRMLY
FILOSELLES	FINDING	FINKED	FIREGUARD	FIRMNESS
FILS	FINDINGS	FINKING	FIREGUARDS	FIRMNESSES
FILTER	FINDRAM	FINKS	FIREHOUSE	FIRMS
FILTERED	FINDRAMS	FINLESS	FIREHOUSES	FIRMWARE
FILTERING	FINDS	FINNAC	FIRELESS	FIRMWARES
FILTERS	FINE	FINNACK	FIRELIGHT	FIRN
FILTH	FINED	FINNACKS	FIRELIGHTS	FIRNS
FILTHIER	FINEER	FINNACS	FIRELOCK	FIRRIER
FILTHIEST	FINEERED	FINNAN	FIRELOCKS	FIRRIEST
FILTHILY	FINEERING	FINNANS	FIREMAN	FIRRING
FILTHS	FINEERS	FINNED	FIREMARK	FIRRINGS
FILTHY	FINEISH	FINNER	FIREMARKS	FIRRY
FILTRABLE	FINELESS	FINNERS	FIREMEN	FIRS
FILTRATE	FINELY	FINNESKO	FIREPAN	FIRST
FILTRATED	FINENESS	FINNIER	FIREPANS	FIRSTLING
FILTRATES	FINENESSES	FINNIEST	FIREPLACE	FIRSTLINGS
FILTRATING	FINER	FINNOCHIO	FIREPLACES	FIRSTLY
FIMBLE	FINERIES	FINNOCHIOS	FIREPOT	FIRSTS
FIMBLES	FINERS	FINNOCK	FIREPOTS	FIRTH
FIMBRIA	FINERY	FINNOCKS	FIREPROOF	FIRTHS
FIMBRIAE	FINES	FINNSKO	FIREPROOFED	FISC
FIMBRIATE	FINESSE	FINNY	FIREPROOFING	FISCAL
FIMBRIATED	FINESSED	FINO	FIREPROOFINGS	FISCALLY
FIMBRIATES	FINESSER	FINOCCHIO	FIREPROOFS	FISCALS
FIMBRIATING	FINESSERS	FINOCCHIOS	FIRER	FISCS
FIN	FINESSES	FINOCHIO	FIRERS	FISGIG
FINABLE	FINESSING	FINOCHIOS	FIRES	FISGIGS
FINAGLE	FINESSINGS	FINOS	FIRESHIP	FISH
FINAGLED	FINEST	FINS	FIRESHIPS	FISHABLE
FINAGLES	FINGAN	FINSKO	FIRESIDE	FISHBALL
FINAGLING	FINGANS	FIORD	FIRESIDES	FISHBALLS
FINAL	FINGER	FIORDS	FIRESTONE	FISHED
FINALE	FINGERED	FIORIN	FIRESTONES	FISHER
FINALES	FINGERING	FIORINS	FIRETHORN	FISHERIES
FINALISE	FINGERINGS	FIORITURA	FIRETHORNS	FISHERMAN
FINALISED	FINGERS	FIORITURE	FIREWEED	FISHERMEN
FINALISES	FINGERTIP	FIPPENCE	FIREWEEDS	FISHERS
FINALISING	FINGERTIPS	FIPPENCES	FIREWOMAN	FISHERY

The Chambers Dictionary is the authority for many longer words; see *OSW* Introduction, page xii.

FISHES	FISTULOUS	FIXTURE	FLAGGINGS	FLAMINGOS
FISHEYE	FISTY	FIXTURES	FLAGGY	FLAMM
FISHEYES	FIT	FIXURE	FLAGITATE	FLAMMABLE
FISHFUL	FITCH	FIXURES	FLAGITATED	FLAMMED
FISHGIG	FITCHE	FIZ	FLAGITATES	FLAMMING
FISHGIGS	FITCHEE	FIZGIG	FLAGITATING	FLAMMS
FISHIER	FITCHES	FIZGIGS	FLAGON	FLAMMULE
FISHIEST	FITCHET	FIZZ	FLAGONS	FLAMMULES
FISHIFIED	FITCHETS	FIZZED	FLAGPOLE	FLAMS
FISHIFIES	FITCHEW	FIZZEN	FLAGPOLES	FLAMY
FISHIFY	FITCHEWS	FIZZENS	FLAGRANCE	FLAN
FISHIFYING	FITCHY	FIZZER	FLAGRANCES	FLANCH
FISHINESS	FITFUL	FIZZERS	FLAGRANCIES	FLANCHED
FISHINESSES	FITFULLY	FIZZES	FLAGRANCY	FLANCHES
FISHING	FITLIER	FIZZGIG	FLAGRANT	FLANCHING
FISHINGS	FITLIEST	FIZZGIGS	FLAGS	FLANCHINGS
FISHSKIN	FITLY	FIZZIER	FLAGSHIP	FLANERIE
FISHSKINS	FITMENT	FIZZIEST	FLAGSHIPS	FLANERIES
FISHWIFE	FITMENTS	FIZZING	FLAGSTAFF	FLANEUR
FISHWIVES	FITNESS	FIZZINGS	FLAGSTAFFS	FLANEURS
FISHY	FITNESSES	FIZZLE	FLAGSTICK	FLANGE
FISHYBACK	FITS	FIZZLED	FLAGSTICKS	FLANGED
FISHYBACKS	FITT	FIZZLES	FLAGSTONE	FLANGES
FISK	FITTE	FIZZLING	FLAGSTONES	FLANGING
FISKED	FITTED	FIZZY	FLAIL	FLANK
FISKING	FITTER	FJORD	FLAILED	FLANKED
FISKS	FITTERS	FJORDS	FLAILING	FLANKER
FISNOMIE	FITTES	FLAB	FLAILS	FLANKERED
FISNOMIES	FITTEST	FLABBIER	FLAIR	FLANKERING
FISSILE	FITTING	FLABBIEST	FLAIRS	FLANKERS
FISSILITIES	FITTINGLY	FLABBILY	FLAK	FLANKING
FISSILITY	FITTINGS	FLABBY	FLAKE	FLANKS
FISSION	FITTS	FLABELLA	FLAKED	FLANNEL
FISSIONS	FIVE	FLABELLUM	FLAKES	FLANNELLED
FISSIPED	FIVEFOLD	FLABELLUMS	FLAKIER	FLANNELLING
FISSIPEDE	FIVEPENCE	FLABS	FLAKIES	FLANNELLY
FISSIPEDES	FIVEPENCES	FLACCID	FLAKIEST	FLANNELS
FISSIPEDS	FIVEPENNY	FLACCIDER	FLAKINESS	FLANNEN
FISSIVE	FIVEPIN	FLACCIDEST	FLAKINESSES	FLANNENS
FISSLE	FIVEPINS	FLACCIDLY	FLAKING	FLANS
FISSLED	FIVER	FLACK	FLAKS	FLAP
FISSLES	FIVERS	FLACKER	FLAKY	FLAPJACK
FISSLING	FIVES	FLACKERED	FLAM	FLAPJACKS
FISSURE	FIX	FLACKERING	FLAMBE	FLAPPABLE
FISSURED	FIXABLE	FLACKERS	FLAMBEAU	FLAPPED
FISSURES	FIXATE	FLACKET	FLAMBEAUS	FLAPPER
FISSURING	FIXATED	FLACKETS	FLAMBEAUX	FLAPPERS
FIST	FIXATES	FLACKS	FLAMBEED	FLAPPIER
FISTED	FIXATING	FLACON	FLAME	FLAPPIEST
FISTFUL	FIXATION	FLACONS	FLAMED	FLAPPING
FISTFULS	FIXATIONS	FLAFF	FLAMELESS	FLAPPINGS
FISTIANA	FIXATIVE	FLAFFED	FLAMELET	FLAPPY
FISTIC	FIXATIVES	FLAFFER	FLAMELETS	FLAPS
FISTICAL	FIXATURE	FLAFFERED	FLAMEN	FLAPTRACK
FISTICUFF	FIXATURES	FLAFFERING	FLAMENCO	FLAPTRACKS
FISTICUFFS	FIXED	FLAFFERS	FLAMENCOS	FLARE
FISTIER	FIXEDLY	FLAFFING	FLAMENS	FLARED
FISTIEST	FIXEDNESS	FLAFFS	FLAMES	FLARES
FISTING	FIXEDNESSES	FLAG	FLAMFEW	FLARIER
FISTMELE	FIXER	FLAGELLA	FLAMFEWS	FLARIEST
FISTMELES	FIXERS	FLAGELLUM	FLAMIER	FLARING
FISTS	FIXES	FLAGEOLET	FLAMIEST	FLARINGLY
FISTULA	FIXING	FLAGEOLETS	FLAMINES	FLARY
FISTULAE	FIXINGS	FLAGGED	FLAMING	FLASER
FISTULAR	FIXITIES	FLAGGIER	FLAMINGLY	FLASERS
FISTULAS	FIXITY	FLAGGIEST	FLAMINGO	FLASH
FISTULOSE	FIXIVE	FLAGGING	FLAMINGOES	FLASHBACK

The Chambers Dictionary is the authority for many longer words; see *OSW* Introduction, page xii.

FLASHBACKED	FLATUS	FLAY	FLEETEST	FLEXED
FLASHBACKING	FLATUSES	FLAYED	FLEETING	FLEXES
FLASHBACKS	FLATWARE	FLAYER	FLEETLY	FLEXIBLE
FLASHBULB	FLATWARES	FLAYERS	FLEETNESS	FLEXIBLY
FLASHBULBS	FLATWAYS	FLAYING	FLEETNESSES	FLEXILE
FLASHCUBE	FLATWISE	FLAYS	FLEETS	FLEXING
FLASHCUBES	FLATWORM	FLEA	FLEG	FLEXION
FLASHED	FLATWORMS	FLEAM	FLEGGED	FLEXIONS
FLASHER	FLAUGHT	FLEAMS	FLEGGING	FLEXITIME
FLASHERS	FLAUGHTED	FLEAPIT	FLEGS	FLEXITIMES
FLASHES	FLAUGHTER	FLEAPITS	FLEME	FLEXOR
FLASHEST	FLAUGHTERED	FLEAS	FLEMES	FLEXORS
FLASHGUN	FLAUGHTERING	FLEASOME	FLEMING	FLEXUOSE
FLASHGUNS	FLAUGHTERS	FLEAWORT	FLEMISH	FLEXUOUS
FLASHIER	FLAUGHTING	FLEAWORTS	FLEMISHED	FLEXURAL
FLASHIEST	FLAUGHTS	FLECHE	FLEMISHES	FLEXURE
FLASHILY	FLAUNCH	FLECHES	FLEMISHING	FLEXURES
FLASHING	FLAUNCHED	FLECHETTE	FLEMIT	FLEY
FLASHINGS	FLAUNCHES	FLECHETTES	FLENCH	FLEYED
FLASHY	FLAUNCHING	FLECK	FLENCHED	FLEYING
FLASK	FLAUNCHINGS	FLECKED	FLENCHES	FLEYS
FLASKET	FLAUNE	FLECKER	FLENCHING	FLIC
FLASKETS	FLAUNES	FLECKERED	FLENSE	FLICHTER
FLASKS	FLAUNT	FLECKERING	FLENSED	FLICHTERED
FLAT	FLAUNTED	FLECKERS	FLENSES	FLICHTERING
FLATBACK	FLAUNTER	FLECKING	FLENSING	FLICHTERS
FLATBACKS	FLAUNTERS	FLECKLESS	FLESH	FLICK
FLATBED	FLAUNTIER	FLECKS	FLESHED	FLICKED
FLATBEDS	FLAUNTIEST	FLECTION	FLESHER	FLICKER
FLATBOAT	FLAUNTING	FLECTIONS	FLESHERS	FLICKERED
FLATBOATS	FLAUNTS	FLED	FLESHES	FLICKERING
FLATFISH	FLAUNTY	FLEDGE	FLESHHOOD	FLICKERS
FLATFISHES	FLAUTIST	FLEDGED	FLESHHOODS	FLICKING
FLATHEAD	FLAUTISTS	FLEDGES	FLESHIER	FLICKS
FLATHEADS	FLAVIN	FLEDGIER	FLESHIEST	FLICS
FLATIRON	FLAVINE	FLEDGIEST	FLESHING	FLIER
FLATIRONS	FLAVINES	FLEDGING	FLESHINGS	FLIERS
FLATLET	FLAVINS	FLEDGLING	FLESHLESS	FLIES
FLATLETS	FLAVONE	FLEDGLINGS	FLESHLIER	FLIEST
FLATLING	FLAVONES	FLEDGY	FLESHLIEST	FLIGHT
FLATLINGS	FLAVOR	FLEE	FLESHLING	FLIGHTED
FLATLONG	FLAVORED	FLEECE	FLESHLINGS	FLIGHTIER
FLATLY	FLAVORING	FLEECED	FLESHLY	FLIGHTIEST
FLATMATE	FLAVORINGS	FLEECER	FLESHMENT	FLIGHTILY
FLATMATES	FLAVOROUS	FLEECERS	FLESHMENTS	FLIGHTING
FLATNESS	FLAVORS	FLEECES	FLESHWORM	FLIGHTS
FLATNESSES	FLAVOUR	FLEECH	FLESHWORMS	FLIGHTY
FLATS	FLAVOURED	FLEECHED	FLESHY	FLIMP
FLATTED	FLAVOURING	FLEECHES	FLETCH	FLIMPED
FLATTEN	FLAVOURINGS	FLEECHING	FLETCHED	FLIMPING
FLATTENED	FLAVOURS	FLEECHINGS	FLETCHER	FLIMPS
FLATTENING	FLAW	FLEECIER	FLETCHERS	FLIMSIER
FLATTENS	FLAWED	FLEECIEST	FLETCHES	FLIMSIES
FLATTER	FLAWIER	FLEECING	FLETCHING	FLIMSIEST
FLATTERED	FLAWIEST	FLEECY	FLETTON	FLIMSILY
FLATTERER	FLAWING	FLEEING	FLETTONS	FLIMSY
FLATTERERS	FLAWLESS	FLEER	FLEURET	FLINCH
FLATTERIES	FLAWN	FLEERED	FLEURETS	FLINCHED
FLATTERING	FLAWNS	FLEERER	FLEURETTE	FLINCHER
FLATTERS	FLAWS	FLEERERS	FLEURETTES	FLINCHERS
FLATTERY	FLAWY	FLEERING	FLEURON	FLINCHES
FLATTEST	FLAX	FLEERINGS	FLEURONS	FLINCHING
FLATTING	FLAXEN	FLEERS	FLEURY	FLINCHINGS
FLATTINGS	FLAXES	FLEES	FLEW	FLINDER
FLATTISH	FLAXIER	FLEET	FLEWED	FLINDERS
FLATULENT	FLAXIEST	FLEETED	FLEWS	FLING
FLATUOUS	FLAXY	FLEETER	FLEX	FLINGER

The Chambers Dictionary is the authority for many longer words; see *OSW* Introduction, page xii.

FLINGERS
FLINGING
FLINGS
FLINT
FLINTIER
FLINTIEST
FLINTIFIED
FLINTIFIES
FLINTIFY
FLINTIFYING
FLINTILY
FLINTLOCK
FLINTLOCKS
FLINTS
FLINTY
FLIP
FLIPPANCIES
FLIPPANCY
FLIPPANT
FLIPPED
FLIPPER
FLIPPERS
FLIPPEST
FLIPPING
FLIPS
FLIRT
FLIRTED
FLIRTIER
FLIRTIEST
FLIRTING
FLIRTINGS
FLIRTISH
FLIRTS
FLIRTY
FLISK
FLISKED
FLISKIER
FLISKIEST
FLISKING
FLISKS
FLISKY
FLIT
FLITCH
FLITCHES
FLITE
FLITED
FLITES
FLITING
FLITS
FLITT
FLITTED
FLITTER
FLITTERED
FLITTERING
FLITTERN
FLITTERNS
FLITTERS
FLITTING
FLITTINGS
FLIVVER
FLIVVERS
FLIX
FLIXED
FLIXES
FLIXING
FLOAT
FLOATABLE

FLOATAGE
FLOATAGES
FLOATANT
FLOATANTS
FLOATED
FLOATEL
FLOATELS
FLOATER
FLOATERS
FLOATIER
FLOATIEST
FLOATING
FLOATINGS
FLOATS
FLOATY
FLOCCI
FLOCCOSE
FLOCCULAR
FLOCCULE
FLOCCULES
FLOCCULI
FLOCCULUS
FLOCCUS
FLOCK
FLOCKED
FLOCKING
FLOCKS
FLOE
FLOES
FLOG
FLOGGED
FLOGGING
FLOGGINGS
FLOGS
FLOKATI
FLOKATIS
FLONG
FLONGS
FLOOD
FLOODED
FLOODGATE
FLOODGATES
FLOODING
FLOODINGS
FLOODLIT
FLOODMARK
FLOODMARKS
FLOODS
FLOODTIDE
FLOODTIDES
FLOODWALL
FLOODWALLS
FLOODWAY
FLOODWAYS
FLOOR
FLOORED
FLOORER
FLOORERS
FLOORHEAD
FLOORHEADS
FLOORING
FLOORINGS
FLOORS
FLOOSIE
FLOOSIES
FLOOSY
FLOOZIE

FLOOZIES
FLOOZY
FLOP
FLOPHOUSE
FLOPHOUSES
FLOPPED
FLOPPIER
FLOPPIES
FLOPPIEST
FLOPPILY
FLOPPING
FLOPPY
FLOPS
FLOR
FLORA
FLORAE
FLORAL
FLORALLY
FLORAS
FLOREAT
FLOREATED
FLORENCE
FLORENCES
FLORET
FLORETS
FLORIATED
FLORID
FLORIDEAN
FLORIDEANS
FLORIDER
FLORIDEST
FLORIDITIES
FLORIDITY
FLORIDLY
FLORIER
FLORIEST
FLORIFORM
FLORIGEN
FLORIGENS
FLORIN
FLORINS
FLORIST
FLORISTIC
FLORISTICS
FLORISTRIES
FLORISTRY
FLORISTS
FLORS
FLORUIT
FLORUITED
FLORUITING
FLORUITS
FLORY
FLOSCULAR
FLOSCULE
FLOSCULES
FLOSH
FLOSHES
FLOSS
FLOSSED
FLOSSES
FLOSSIER
FLOSSIEST
FLOSSING
FLOSSINGS
FLOSSY
FLOTA

FLOTAGE
FLOTAGES
FLOTANT
FLOTAS
FLOTATION
FLOTATIONS
FLOTE
FLOTEL
FLOTELS
FLOTES
FLOTILLA
FLOTILLAS
FLOTSAM
FLOTSAMS
FLOUNCE
FLOUNCED
FLOUNCES
FLOUNCIER
FLOUNCIEST
FLOUNCING
FLOUNCINGS
FLOUNCY
FLOUNDER
FLOUNDERED
FLOUNDERING
FLOUNDERS
FLOUR
FLOURED
FLOURIER
FLOURIEST
FLOURING
FLOURISH
FLOURISHED
FLOURISHES
FLOURISHING
FLOURISHY
FLOURS
FLOURY
FLOUSE
FLOUSED
FLOUSES
FLOUSH
FLOUSHED
FLOUSHES
FLOUSHING
FLOUSING
FLOUT
FLOUTED
FLOUTING
FLOUTS
FLOW
FLOWAGE
FLOWAGES
FLOWED
FLOWER
FLOWERAGE
FLOWERAGES
FLOWERED
FLOWERER
FLOWERERS
FLOWERET
FLOWERETS
FLOWERIER
FLOWERIEST
FLOWERING
FLOWERINGS
FLOWERPOT

FLOWERPOTS
FLOWERS
FLOWERY
FLOWING
FLOWINGLY
FLOWMETER
FLOWMETERS
FLOWN
FLOWS
FLU
FLUATE
FLUATES
FLUB
FLUBBED
FLUBBING
FLUBS
FLUCTUANT
FLUCTUATE
FLUCTUATED
FLUCTUATES
FLUCTUATING
FLUE
FLUELLIN
FLUELLINS
FLUENCE
FLUENCES
FLUENCIES
FLUENCY
FLUENT
FLUENTLY
FLUENTS
FLUES
FLUEWORK
FLUEWORKS
FLUEY
FLUFF
FLUFFED
FLUFFIER
FLUFFIEST
FLUFFING
FLUFFS
FLUFFY
FLUGEL
FLUGELMAN
FLUGELMEN
FLUGELS
FLUID
FLUIDAL
FLUIDIC
FLUIDICS
FLUIDIFIED
FLUIDIFIES
FLUIDIFY
FLUIDIFYING
FLUIDISE
FLUIDISED
FLUIDISES
FLUIDISING
FLUIDITIES
FLUIDITY
FLUIDIZE
FLUIDIZED
FLUIDIZES
FLUIDIZING
FLUIDNESS
FLUIDNESSES
FLUIDS

The Chambers Dictionary is the authority for many longer words; see *OSW* Introduction, page xii.

FLUIER	FLUSHNESS	FLYPED	FODDERING	FOH
FLUIEST	FLUSHNESSES	FLYPES	FODDERINGS	FOHN
FLUKE	FLUSHY	FLYPING	FODDERS	FOHNS
FLUKED	FLUSTER	FLYPITCH	FOE	FOHS
FLUKES	FLUSTERED	FLYPITCHES	FOEDARIE	FOIBLE
FLUKEY	FLUSTERING	FLYSCH	FOEDARIES	FOIBLES
FLUKIER	FLUSTERS	FLYSCHES	FOEDERATI	FOID
FLUKIEST	FLUSTERY	FLYTE	FOEHN	FOIDS
FLUKING	FLUSTRATE	FLYTED	FOEHNS	FOIL
FLUKY	FLUSTRATED	FLYTES	FOEMAN	FOILBORNE
FLUME	FLUSTRATES	FLYTING	FOEMEN	FOILED
FLUMES	FLUSTRATING	FLYTINGS	FOEN	FOILING
FLUMMERIES	FLUTE	FLYTRAP	FOES	FOILINGS
FLUMMERY	FLUTED	FLYTRAPS	FOETAL	FOILS
FLUMMOX	FLUTER	FLYWAY	FOETICIDE	FOIN
FLUMMOXED	FLUTERS	FLYWAYS	FOETICIDES	FOINED
FLUMMOXES	FLUTES	FLYWEIGHT	FOETID	FOINING
FLUMMOXING	FLUTIER	FLYWEIGHTS	FOETIDER	FOININGLY
FLUMP	FLUTIEST	FLYWHEEL	FOETIDEST	FOINS
FLUMPED	FLUTINA	FLYWHEELS	FOETOR	FOISON
FLUMPING	FLUTINAS	FOAL	FOETORS	FOISONS
FLUMPS	FLUTING	FOALED	FOETUS	FOIST
FLUNG	FLUTINGS	FOALFOOT	FOETUSES	FOISTED
FLUNK	FLUTIST	FOALFOOTS	FOG	FOISTER
FLUNKED	FLUTISTS	FOALING	FOGASH	FOISTERS
FLUNKEY	FLUTTER	FOALS	FOGASHES	FOISTING
FLUNKEYS	FLUTTERED	FOAM	FOGBOUND	FOISTS
FLUNKIES	FLUTTERING	FOAMED	FOGEY	FOLACIN
FLUNKING	FLUTTERS	FOAMIER	FOGEYDOM	FOLACINS
FLUNKS	FLUTY	FOAMIEST	FOGEYDOMS	FOLATE
FLUNKY	FLUVIAL	FOAMILY	FOGEYISH	FOLATES
FLUOR	FLUVIATIC	FOAMINESS	FOGEYISM	FOLD
FLUORESCE	FLUX	FOAMINESSES	FOGEYISMS	FOLDABLE
FLUORESCED	FLUXED	FOAMING	FOGEYS	FOLDAWAY
FLUORESCES	FLUXES	FOAMINGLY	FOGGAGE	FOLDBOAT
FLUORESCING	FLUXING	FOAMINGS	FOGGAGES	FOLDBOATS
FLUORIC	FLUXION	FOAMLESS	FOGGED	FOLDED
FLUORIDE	FLUXIONAL	FOAMS	FOGGER	FOLDER
FLUORIDES	FLUXIONS	FOAMY	FOGGERS	FOLDEROL
FLUORINE	FLUXIVE	FOB	FOGGIER	FOLDEROLS
FLUORINES	FLY	FOBBED	FOGGIEST	FOLDERS
FLUORITE	FLYABLE	FOBBING	FOGGILY	FOLDING
FLUORITES	FLYAWAY	FOBS	FOGGINESS	FOLDINGS
FLUOROSES	FLYBANE	FOCAL	FOGGINESSES	FOLDS
FLUOROSIS	FLYBANES	FOCALISE	FOGGING	FOLIA
FLUORS	FLYBELT	FOCALISED	FOGGY	FOLIAGE
FLUORSPAR	FLYBELTS	FOCALISES	FOGHORN	FOLIAGED
FLUORSPARS	FLYBLOW	FOCALISING	FOGHORNS	FOLIAGES
FLURR	FLYBLOWS	FOCALIZE	FOGIES	FOLIAR
FLURRED	FLYBOAT	FOCALIZED	FOGLE	FOLIATE
FLURRIED	FLYBOATS	FOCALIZES	FOGLES	FOLIATED
FLURRIES	FLYBOOK	FOCALIZING	FOGLESS	FOLIATES
FLURRING	FLYBOOKS	FOCALLY	FOGMAN	FOLIATING
FLURRS	FLYER	FOCI	FOGMEN	FOLIATION
FLURRY	FLYERS	FOCIMETER	FOGRAM	FOLIATIONS
FLURRYING	FLYEST	FOCIMETERS	FOGRAMITE	FOLIATURE
FLUS	FLYING	FOCUS	FOGRAMITES	FOLIATURES
FLUSH	FLYINGS	FOCUSED	FOGRAMITIES	FOLIE
FLUSHED	FLYLEAF	FOCUSES	FOGRAMITY	FOLIES
FLUSHER	FLYLEAVES	FOCUSING	FOGRAMS	FOLIO
FLUSHERS	FLYMAKER	FOCUSSED	FOGS	FOLIOED
FLUSHES	FLYMAKERS	FOCUSSES	FOGY	FOLIOING
FLUSHEST	FLYOVER	FOCUSSING	FOGYDOM	FOLIOLATE
FLUSHIER	FLYOVERS	FODDER	FOGYDOMS	FOLIOLE
FLUSHIEST	FLYPAPER	FODDERED	FOGYISH	FOLIOLES
FLUSHING	FLYPAPERS	FODDERER	FOGYISM	FOLIOLOSE
FLUSHINGS	FLYPE	FODDERERS	FOGYISMS	FOLIOS

The Chambers Dictionary is the authority for many longer words; see *OSW* Introduction, page xii.

FOLIOSE
FOLIUM
FOLK
FOLKIE
FOLKIES
FOLKLAND
FOLKLANDS
FOLKLORE
FOLKLORES
FOLKLORIC
FOLKMOOT
FOLKMOOTS
FOLKS
FOLKSIER
FOLKSIEST
FOLKSY
FOLKWAY
FOLKWAYS
FOLLICLE
FOLLICLES
FOLLIED
FOLLIES
FOLLOW
FOLLOWED
FOLLOWER
FOLLOWERS
FOLLOWING
FOLLOWINGS
FOLLOWS
FOLLY
FOLLYING
FOMENT
FOMENTED
FOMENTER
FOMENTERS
FOMENTING
FOMENTS
FOMES
FOMITES
FON
FOND
FONDA
FONDANT
FONDANTS
FONDAS
FONDED
FONDER
FONDEST
FONDING
FONDLE
FONDLED
FONDLER
FONDLERS
FONDLES
FONDLING
FONDLINGS
FONDLY
FONDNESS
FONDNESSES
FONDS
FONDUE
FONDUES
FONE
FONLY
FONNED
FONNING
FONS

FONT
FONTAL
FONTANEL
FONTANELS
FONTANGE
FONTANGES
FONTICULI
FONTLET
FONTLETS
FONTS
FOOD
FOODFUL
FOODIE
FOODIES
FOODISM
FOODISMS
FOODLESS
FOODS
FOODSTUFF
FOODSTUFFS
FOODY
FOOL
FOOLED
FOOLERIES
FOOLERY
FOOLHARDY
FOOLING
FOOLINGS
FOOLISH
FOOLISHER
FOOLISHEST
FOOLISHLY
FOOLPROOF
FOOLS
FOOLSCAP
FOOLSCAPS
FOOT
FOOTAGE
FOOTAGES
FOOTBALL
FOOTBALLS
FOOTBAR
FOOTBARS
FOOTBOARD
FOOTBOARDS
FOOTBOY
FOOTBOYS
FOOTCLOTH
FOOTCLOTHS
FOOTED
FOOTER
FOOTERS
FOOTFALL
FOOTFALLS
FOOTFAULT
FOOTFAULTED
FOOTFAULTING
FOOTFAULTS
FOOTGEAR
FOOTGEARS
FOOTHILL
FOOTHILLS
FOOTHOLD
FOOTHOLDS
FOOTIE
FOOTIER
FOOTIES

FOOTIEST
FOOTING
FOOTINGS
FOOTLE
FOOTLED
FOOTLES
FOOTLESS
FOOTLIGHT
FOOTLIGHTS
FOOTLING
FOOTLINGS
FOOTLOOSE
FOOTMAN
FOOTMARK
FOOTMARKS
FOOTMEN
FOOTMUFF
FOOTMUFFS
FOOTNOTE
FOOTNOTES
FOOTPACE
FOOTPACES
FOOTPAD
FOOTPADS
FOOTPAGE
FOOTPAGES
FOOTPATH
FOOTPATHS
FOOTPLATE
FOOTPLATES
FOOTPOST
FOOTPOSTS
FOOTPRINT
FOOTPRINTS
FOOTRA
FOOTRAS
FOOTREST
FOOTRESTS
FOOTROT
FOOTROTS
FOOTRULE
FOOTRULES
FOOTS
FOOTSLOG
FOOTSLOGGED
FOOTSLOGGING
FOOTSLOGGINGS
FOOTSLOGS
FOOTSORE
FOOTSTALK
FOOTSTALKS
FOOTSTEP
FOOTSTEPS
FOOTSTOOL
FOOTSTOOLS
FOOTWAY
FOOTWAYS
FOOTWEAR
FOOTWEARS
FOOTWELL
FOOTWELLS
FOOTWORK
FOOTWORKS
FOOTWORN
FOOTY
FOOZLE
FOOZLED

FOOZLER
FOOZLERS
FOOZLES
FOOZLING
FOOZLINGS
FOP
FOPLING
FOPLINGS
FOPPERIES
FOPPERY
FOPPISH
FOPPISHLY
FOPS
FOR
FORA
FORAGE
FORAGED
FORAGER
FORAGERS
FORAGES
FORAGING
FORAMEN
FORAMINA
FORAMINAL
FORANE
FORASMUCH
FORAY
FORAYED
FORAYER
FORAYERS
FORAYING
FORAYS
FORB
FORBAD
FORBADE
FORBEAR
FORBEARING
FORBEARS
FORBID
FORBIDDAL
FORBIDDALS
FORBIDDEN
FORBIDDER
FORBIDDERS
FORBIDDING
FORBIDDINGS
FORBIDS
FORBODE
FORBODES
FORBORE
FORBORNE
FORBS
FORBY
FORBYE
FORCAT
FORCATS
FORCE
FORCED
FORCEDLY
FORCEFUL
FORCELESS
FORCEMEAT
FORCEMEATS
FORCEPS
FORCEPSES
FORCER
FORCERS

FORCES
FORCIBLE
FORCIBLY
FORCING
FORCIPATE
FORCIPES
FORD
FORDABLE
FORDED
FORDID
FORDING
FORDO
FORDOES
FORDOING
FORDONE
FORDS
FORE
FOREANENT
FOREARM
FOREARMED
FOREARMING
FOREARMS
FOREBEAR
FOREBEARS
FOREBITT
FOREBITTS
FOREBODE
FOREBODED
FOREBODER
FOREBODERS
FOREBODES
FOREBODING
FOREBODINGS
FOREBRAIN
FOREBRAINS
FOREBY
FORECABIN
FORECABINS
FORECAR
FORECARS
FORECAST
FORECASTED
FORECASTING
FORECASTS
FORECLOSE
FORECLOSED
FORECLOSES
FORECLOSING
FORECLOTH
FORECLOTHS
FORECOURT
FORECOURTS
FOREDATE
FOREDATED
FOREDATES
FOREDATING
FOREDECK
FOREDECKS
FOREDOOM
FOREDOOMED
FOREDOOMING
FOREDOOMS
FOREFEEL
FOREFEELING
FOREFEELS
FOREFEET
FOREFELT

The Chambers Dictionary is the authority for many longer words; see *OSW* Introduction, page xii.

FOREFOOT	FOREMEANT	FORESHOWN	FORETIMES	FORGERS
FOREFRONT	FOREMEN	FORESHOWS	FORETOKEN	FORGERY
FOREFRONTS	FOREMOST	FORESIDE	FORETOKENED	FORGES
FOREGLEAM	FORENAME	FORESIDES	FORETOKENING	FORGET
FOREGLEAMS	FORENAMED	FORESIGHT	FORETOKENINGS	FORGETFUL
FOREGO	FORENAMES	FORESIGHTS	FORETOKENS	FORGETIVE
FOREGOER	FORENIGHT	FORESKIN	FORETOLD	FORGETS
FOREGOERS	FORENIGHTS	FORESKINS	FORETOOTH	FORGETTER
FOREGOES	FORENOON	FORESKIRT	FORETOP	FORGETTERS
FOREGOING	FORENOONS	FORESKIRTS	FORETOPS	FORGETTING
FOREGOINGS	FORENSIC	FORESLACK	FOREVER	FORGETTINGS
FOREGONE	FORENSICS	FORESLACKED	FOREVERS	FORGING
FOREGUT	FOREPART	FORESLACKING	FOREWARD	FORGINGS
FOREGUTS	FOREPARTS	FORESLACKS	FOREWARDS	FORGIVE
FOREHAND	FOREPAST	FORESLOW	FOREWARN	FORGIVEN
FOREHANDS	FOREPAW	FORESLOWED	FOREWARNED	FORGIVES
FOREHEAD	FOREPAWS	FORESLOWING	FOREWARNING	FORGIVING
FOREHEADS	FOREPEAK	FORESLOWS	FOREWARNINGS	FORGO
FOREHENT	FOREPEAKS	FORESPEAK	FOREWARNS	FORGOES
FOREHENTING	FOREPLAN	FORESPEAKING	FOREWEIGH	FORGOING
FOREHENTS	FOREPLANNED	FORESPEAKS	FOREWEIGHED	FORGONE
FOREIGN	FOREPLANNING	FORESPEND	FOREWEIGHING	FORGOT
FOREIGNER	FOREPLANS	FORESPENDING	FOREWEIGHS	FORGOTTEN
FOREIGNERS	FOREPLAY	FORESPENDS	FOREWENT	FORHAILE
FOREJUDGE	FOREPLAYS	FORESPENT	FOREWIND	FORHAILED
FOREJUDGED	FOREPOINT	FORESPOKE	FOREWINDS	FORHAILES
FOREJUDGES	FOREPOINTED	FORESPOKEN	FOREWING	FORHAILING
FOREJUDGING	FOREPOINTING	FOREST	FOREWINGS	FORHENT
FOREKING	FOREPOINTS	FORESTAGE	FOREWOMAN	FORHENTING
FOREKINGS	FORERAN	FORESTAGES	FOREWOMEN	FORHENTS
FOREKNEW	FOREREACH	FORESTAIR	FOREWORD	FORHOO
FOREKNOW	FOREREACHED	FORESTAIRS	FOREWORDS	FORHOOED
FOREKNOWING	FOREREACHES	FORESTAL	FORFAIR	FORHOOIE
FOREKNOWN	FOREREACHING	FORESTALL	FORFAIRED	FORHOOIED
FOREKNOWS	FOREREAD	FORESTALLED	FORFAIRING	FORHOOIEING
FOREL	FOREREADING	FORESTALLING	FORFAIRN	FORHOOIES
FORELAID	FOREREADINGS	FORESTALLINGS	FORFAIRS	FORHOOING
FORELAIN	FOREREADS	FORESTALLS	FORFAITER	FORHOOS
FORELAND	FORERUN	FORESTAY	FORFAITERS	FORHOW
FORELANDS	FORERUNNING	FORESTAYS	FORFAULT	FORHOWED
FORELAY	FORERUNS	FORESTEAL	FORFAULTS	FORHOWING
FORELAYING	FORES	FORESTED	FORFEIT	FORHOWS
FORELAYS	FORESAID	FORESTER	FORFEITED	FORINSEC
FORELEG	FORESAIL	FORESTERS	FORFEITER	FORINT
FORELEGS	FORESAILS	FORESTINE	FORFEITERS	FORINTS
FORELEND	FORESAW	FORESTING	FORFEITING	FORJASKIT
FORELENDING	FORESAY	FORESTRIES	FORFEITS	FORJESKIT
FORELENDS	FORESAYING	FORESTRY	FORFEND	FORJUDGE
FORELENT	FORESAYS	FORESTS	FORFENDED	FORJUDGED
FORELIE	FORESEE	FORETASTE	FORFENDING	FORJUDGES
FORELIES	FORESEEING	FORETASTED	FORFENDS	FORJUDGING
FORELIFT	FORESEEN	FORETASTES	FORFEX	FORK
FORELIFTED	FORESEES	FORETASTING	FORFEXES	FORKED
FORELIFTING	FORESHEW	FORETAUGHT	FORFICATE	FORKEDLY
FORELIFTS	FORESHEWED	FORETEACH	FORGAT	FORKER
FORELIMB	FORESHEWING	FORETEACHES	FORGATHER	FORKERS
FORELIMBS	FORESHEWN	FORETEACHING	FORGATHERED	FORKFUL
FORELOCK	FORESHEWS	FORETEETH	FORGATHERING	FORKFULS
FORELOCKS	FORESHIP	FORETELL	FORGATHERS	FORKHEAD
FORELS	FORESHIPS	FORETELLING	FORGAVE	FORKHEADS
FORELYING	FORESHOCK	FORETELLS	FORGE	FORKIER
FOREMAN	FORESHOCKS	FORETHINK	FORGEABLE	FORKIEST
FOREMAST	FORESHORE	FORETHINKING	FORGED	FORKINESS
FOREMASTS	FORESHORES	FORETHINKS	FORGEMAN	FORKINESSES
FOREMEAN	FORESHOW	FORETHOUGHT	FORGEMEN	FORKING
FOREMEANING	FORESHOWED	FORETHOUGHTS	FORGER	FORKS
FOREMEANS	FORESHOWING	FORETIME	FORGERIES	FORKTAIL

The Chambers Dictionary is the authority for many longer words; see *OSW* Introduction, page xii.

FORKTAILS
FORKY
FORLANA
FORLANAS
FORLEND
FORLENDING
FORLENDS
FORLENT
FORLESE
FORLESES
FORLESING
FORLORE
FORLORN
FORLORNER
FORLORNEST
FORLORNLY
FORLORNS
FORM
FORMABLE
FORMAL
FORMALIN
FORMALINS
FORMALISE
FORMALISED
FORMALISES
FORMALISING
FORMALISM
FORMALISMS
FORMALIST
FORMALISTS
FORMALITIES
FORMALITY
FORMALIZE
FORMALIZED
FORMALIZES
FORMALIZING
FORMALLY
FORMANT
FORMANTS
FORMAT
FORMATE
FORMATED
FORMATES
FORMATING
FORMATION
FORMATIONS
FORMATIVE
FORMATIVES
FORMATS
FORMATTED
FORMATTER
FORMATTERS
FORMATTING
FORME
FORMED
FORMER
FORMERLY
FORMERS
FORMES
FORMIATE
FORMIATES
FORMIC
FORMICANT
FORMICARIES
FORMICARY
FORMICATE
FORMING

FORMINGS
FORMLESS
FORMOL
FORMOLS
FORMS
FORMULA
FORMULAE
FORMULAIC
FORMULAR
FORMULARIES
FORMULARY
FORMULAS
FORMULATE
FORMULATED
FORMULATES
FORMULATING
FORMULISE
FORMULISED
FORMULISES
FORMULISING
FORMULISM
FORMULISMS
FORMULIST
FORMULISTS
FORMULIZE
FORMULIZED
FORMULIZES
FORMULIZING
FORMWORK
FORMWORKS
FORNENST
FORNENT
FORNICAL
FORNICATE
FORNICATED
FORNICATES
FORNICATING
FORNICES
FORNIX
FORPET
FORPETS
FORPINE
FORPINED
FORPINES
FORPINING
FORPIT
FORPITS
FORRAD
FORRADER
FORRAY
FORRAYED
FORRAYING
FORRAYS
FORREN
FORRIT
FORSAID
FORSAKE
FORSAKEN
FORSAKES
FORSAKING
FORSAKINGS
FORSAY
FORSAYING
FORSAYS
FORSLACK
FORSLACKED
FORSLACKING

FORSLACKS
FORSLOE
FORSLOED
FORSLOEING
FORSLOES
FORSLOW
FORSLOWED
FORSLOWING
FORSLOWS
FORSOOK
FORSOOTH
FORSPEAK
FORSPEAKING
FORSPEAKS
FORSPEND
FORSPENDING
FORSPENDS
FORSPENT
FORSPOKE
FORSPOKEN
FORSWATT
FORSWEAR
FORSWEARING
FORSWEARS
FORSWINK
FORSWINKED
FORSWINKING
FORSWINKS
FORSWONCK
FORSWORE
FORSWORN
FORSWUNK
FORSYTHIA
FORSYTHIAS
FORT
FORTALICE
FORTALICES
FORTE
FORTED
FORTES
FORTH
FORTHCAME
FORTHCOME
FORTHCOMES
FORTHCOMING
FORTHINK
FORTHINKING
FORTHINKS
FORTHOUGHT
FORTHWITH
FORTHY
FORTIES
FORTIETH
FORTIETHS
FORTIFIED
FORTIFIER
FORTIFIERS
FORTIFIES
FORTIFY
FORTIFYING
FORTILAGE
FORTILAGES
FORTING
FORTIS
FORTITUDE
FORTITUDES
FORTLET

FORTLETS
FORTNIGHT
FORTNIGHTS
FORTRESS
FORTRESSED
FORTRESSES
FORTRESSING
FORTS
FORTUITIES
FORTUITY
FORTUNATE
FORTUNE
FORTUNED
FORTUNES
FORTUNING
FORTUNIZE
FORTUNIZED
FORTUNIZES
FORTUNIZING
FORTY
FORTYISH
FORUM
FORUMS
FORWANDER
FORWANDERED
FORWANDERING
FORWANDERS
FORWARD
FORWARDED
FORWARDER
FORWARDERS
FORWARDEST
FORWARDING
FORWARDINGS
FORWARDLY
FORWARDS
FORWARN
FORWARNED
FORWARNING
FORWARNS
FORWASTE
FORWASTED
FORWASTES
FORWASTING
FORWEARIED
FORWEARIES
FORWEARY
FORWEARYING
FORWENT
FORWHY
FORWORN
FORZANDI
FORZANDO
FORZANDOS
FORZATI
FORZATO
FORZATOS
FOSS
FOSSA
FOSSAE
FOSSAS
FOSSE
FOSSED
FOSSES
FOSSETTE
FOSSETTES
FOSSICK

FOSSICKED
FOSSICKER
FOSSICKERS
FOSSICKING
FOSSICKINGS
FOSSICKS
FOSSIL
FOSSILISE
FOSSILISED
FOSSILISES
FOSSILISING
FOSSILIZE
FOSSILIZED
FOSSILIZES
FOSSILIZING
FOSSILS
FOSSOR
FOSSORIAL
FOSSORS
FOSSULA
FOSSULAE
FOSSULATE
FOSTER
FOSTERAGE
FOSTERAGES
FOSTERED
FOSTERER
FOSTERERS
FOSTERING
FOSTERINGS
FOSTERS
FOSTRESS
FOSTRESSES
FOTHER
FOTHERED
FOTHERING
FOTHERS
FOU
FOUAT
FOUATS
FOUD
FOUDRIE
FOUDRIES
FOUDS
FOUER
FOUEST
FOUET
FOUETS
FOUETTE
FOUETTES
FOUGADE
FOUGADES
FOUGASSE
FOUGASSES
FOUGHT
FOUGHTEN
FOUGHTIER
FOUGHTIEST
FOUGHTY
FOUL
FOULARD
FOULARDS
FOULDER
FOULDERED
FOULDERING
FOULDERS
FOULE

The Chambers Dictionary is the authority for many longer words; see *OSW* Introduction, page xii.

FOULED	FOUTRE	FRABBED	FRAISING	FRATERY
FOULER	FOUTRED	FRABBING	FRAME	FRATI
FOULES	FOUTRES	FRABBIT	FRAMED	FRATRIES
FOULEST	FOUTRING	FRABJOUS	FRAMER	FRATRY
FOULING	FOVEA	FRABS	FRAMERS	FRAU
FOULLY	FOVEAE	FRACAS	FRAMES	FRAUD
FOULMART	FOVEAL	FRACK	FRAMEWORK	FRAUDFUL
FOULMARTS	FOVEATE	FRACKING	FRAMEWORKS	FRAUDS
FOULNESS	FOVEOLA	FRACKINGS	FRAMING	FRAUDSMAN
FOULNESSES	FOVEOLAE	FRACT	FRAMINGS	FRAUDSMEN
FOULS	FOVEOLAS	FRACTAL	FRAMPAL	FRAUDSTER
FOUMART	FOVEOLE	FRACTALS	FRAMPLER	FRAUDSTERS
FOUMARTS	FOVEOLES	FRACTED	FRAMPLERS	FRAUGHT
FOUND	FOWL	FRACTING	FRAMPOLD	FRAUGHTED
FOUNDED	FOWLED	FRACTION	FRANC	FRAUGHTER
FOUNDER	FOWLER	FRACTIONS	FRANCHISE	FRAUGHTEST
FOUNDERED	FOWLERS	FRACTIOUS	FRANCHISED	FRAUGHTING
FOUNDERING	FOWLING	FRACTS	FRANCHISES	FRAUGHTS
FOUNDERS	FOWLINGS	FRACTURE	FRANCHISING	FRAULEIN
FOUNDING	FOWLS	FRACTURED	FRANCIUM	FRAULEINS
FOUNDINGS	FOWTH	FRACTURES	FRANCIUMS	FRAUS
FOUNDLING	FOWTHS	FRACTURING	FRANCO	FRAUTAGE
FOUNDLINGS	FOX	FRAE	FRANCOLIN	FRAUTAGES
FOUNDRESS	FOXBERRIES	FRAENA	FRANCOLINS	FRAY
FOUNDRESSES	FOXBERRY	FRAENUM	FRANCS	FRAYED
FOUNDRIES	FOXED	FRAG	FRANGIBLE	FRAYING
FOUNDRY	FOXES	FRAGGED	FRANION	FRAYINGS
FOUNDS	FOXGLOVE	FRAGGING	FRANIONS	FRAYS
FOUNT	FOXGLOVES	FRAGILE	FRANK	FRAZIL
FOUNTAIN	FOXHOLE	FRAGILELY	FRANKED	FRAZILS
FOUNTAINED	FOXHOLES	FRAGILER	FRANKER	FRAZZLE
FOUNTAINING	FOXHOUND	FRAGILEST	FRANKEST	FRAZZLED
FOUNTAINS	FOXHOUNDS	FRAGILITIES	FRANKING	FRAZZLES
FOUNTFUL	FOXIER	FRAGILITY	FRANKLIN	FRAZZLING
FOUNTS	FOXIEST	FRAGMENT	FRANKLINS	FREAK
FOUR	FOXINESS	FRAGMENTED	FRANKLY	FREAKED
FOURFOLD	FOXINESSES	FRAGMENTING	FRANKNESS	FREAKFUL
FOURGON	FOXING	FRAGMENTS	FRANKNESSES	FREAKIER
FOURGONS	FOXINGS	FRAGOR	FRANKS	FREAKIEST
FOURPENCE	FOXSHARK	FRAGORS	FRANTIC	FREAKING
FOURPENCES	FOXSHARKS	FRAGRANCE	FRANTICLY	FREAKISH
FOURPENNIES	FOXSHIP	FRAGRANCED	FRANZIER	FREAKS
FOURPENNY	FOXSHIPS	FRAGRANCES	FRANZIEST	FREAKY
FOURS	FOXTROT	FRAGRANCIES	FRANZY	FRECKLE
FOURSCORE	FOXTROTS	FRAGRANCING	FRAP	FRECKLED
FOURSES	FOXTROTTED	FRAGRANCY	FRAPPANT	FRECKLES
FOURSOME	FOXTROTTING	FRAGRANT	FRAPPE	FRECKLIER
FOURSOMES	FOXY	FRAGS	FRAPPED	FRECKLIEST
FOURTEEN	FOY	FRAICHEUR	FRAPPEE	FRECKLING
FOURTEENS	FOYER	FRAICHEURS	FRAPPES	FRECKLINGS
FOURTH	FOYERS	FRAIL	FRAPPING	FRECKLY
FOURTHLY	FOYLE	FRAILER	FRAPS	FREDAINE
FOURTHS	FOYLED	FRAILEST	FRAS	FREDAINES
FOUS	FOYLES	FRAILISH	FRASS	FREE
FOUSSA	FOYLING	FRAILLY	FRASSES	FREEBASE
FOUSSAS	FOYNE	FRAILNESS	FRATCH	FREEBASED
FOUSTIER	FOYNED	FRAILNESSES	FRATCHES	FREEBASES
FOUSTIEST	FOYNES	FRAILS	FRATCHETY	FREEBASING
FOUSTY	FOYNING	FRAILTEE	FRATCHIER	FREEBEE
FOUTER	FOYS	FRAILTEES	FRATCHIEST	FREEBEES
FOUTERED	FOZIER	FRAILTIES	FRATCHING	FREEBIE
FOUTERING	FOZIEST	FRAILTY	FRATCHY	FREEBIES
FOUTERS	FOZINESS	FRAIM	FRATE	FREEBOOTIES
FOUTH	FOZINESSES	FRAIMS	FRATER	FREEBOOTY
FOUTHS	FOZY	FRAISE	FRATERIES	FREEBORN
FOUTRA	FRA	FRAISED	FRATERNAL	FREED
FOUTRAS	FRAB	FRAISES	FRATERS	FREEDMAN

The Chambers Dictionary is the authority for many longer words; see *OSW* Introduction, page xii.

FREEDMEN	FREITS	FRESHNESS	FRIER	FRISEES
FREEDOM	FREITY	FRESHNESSES	FRIERS	FRISES
FREEDOMS	FREMD	FRESNEL	FRIES	FRISETTE
FREEHAND	FREMDS	FRESNELS	FRIEZE	FRISETTES
FREEHOLD	FREMIT	FRET	FRIEZED	FRISEUR
FREEHOLDS	FREMITS	FRETFUL	FRIEZES	FRISEURS
FREEING	FREMITUS	FRETFULLY	FRIEZING	FRISK
FREELANCE	FREMITUSES	FRETS	FRIG	FRISKA
FREELANCED	FRENA	FRETSAW	FRIGATE	FRISKAS
FREELANCES	FRENCH	FRETSAWS	FRIGATES	FRISKED
FREELANCING	FRENETIC	FRETTED	FRIGATOON	FRISKER
FREELOAD	FRENETICS	FRETTIER	FRIGATOONS	FRISKERS
FREELOADED	FRENNE	FRETTIEST	FRIGES	FRISKET
FREELOADING	FRENULA	FRETTING	FRIGGED	FRISKETS
FREELOADINGS	FRENULUM	FRETTINGS	FRIGGER	FRISKFUL
FREELOADS	FRENUM	FRETTY	FRIGGERS	FRISKIER
FREELY	FRENZICAL	FRETWORK	FRIGGING	FRISKIEST
FREEMAN	FRENZIED	FRETWORKS	FRIGGINGS	FRISKILY
FREEMASON	FRENZIES	FRIABLE	FRIGHT	FRISKING
FREEMASONS	FRENZY	FRIAND	FRIGHTED	FRISKINGS
FREEMEN	FRENZYING	FRIANDE	FRIGHTEN	FRISKS
FREENESS	FREON	FRIANDES	FRIGHTENED	FRISKY
FREENESSES	FREONS	FRIANDS	FRIGHTENING	FRISSON
FREEPHONE	FREQUENCE	FRIAR	FRIGHTENS	FRISSONS
FREEPHONES	FREQUENCES	FRIARBIRD	FRIGHTFUL	FRIST
FREER	FREQUENCIES	FRIARBIRDS	FRIGHTING	FRISTED
FREERS	FREQUENCY	FRIARIES	FRIGHTS	FRISTING
FREES	FREQUENT	FRIARLY	FRIGID	FRISTS
FREESHEET	FREQUENTED	FRIARS	FRIGIDER	FRISURE
FREESHEETS	FREQUENTER	FRIARY	FRIGIDEST	FRISURES
FREESIA	FREQUENTERS	FRIBBLE	FRIGIDITIES	FRIT
FREESIAS	FREQUENTEST	FRIBBLED	FRIGIDITY	FRITFLIES
FREEST	FREQUENTING	FRIBBLER	FRIGIDLY	FRITFLY
FREESTONE	FREQUENTS	FRIBBLERS	FRIGOT	FRITH
FREESTONES	FRERE	FRIBBLES	FRIGOTS	FRITHBORH
FREESTYLE	FRERES	FRIBBLING	FRIGS	FRITHBORHS
FREESTYLES	FRESCADE	FRIBBLISH	FRIJOL	FRITHGILD
FREET	FRESCADES	FRICADEL	FRIJOLE	FRITHGILDS
FREETIER	FRESCO	FRICADELS	FRIJOLES	FRITHS
FREETIEST	FRESCOED	FRICASSEE	FRIKKADEL	FRITS
FREETS	FRESCOER	FRICASSEED	FRIKKADELS	FRITTED
FREETY	FRESCOERS	FRICASSEEING	FRILL	FRITTER
FREEWAY	FRESCOES	FRICASSEES	FRILLED	FRITTERED
FREEWAYS	FRESCOING	FRICATIVE	FRILLIER	FRITTERER
FREEWHEEL	FRESCOINGS	FRICATIVES	FRILLIES	FRITTERERS
FREEWHEELED	FRESCOIST	FRICHT	FRILLIEST	FRITTERING
FREEWHEELING	FRESCOISTS	FRICHTED	FRILLING	FRITTERS
FREEWHEELINGS	FRESCOS	FRICHTING	FRILLINGS	FRITTING
FREEWHEELS	FRESH	FRICHTS	FRILLS	FRITURE
FREEWOMAN	FRESHED	FRICTION	FRILLY	FRITURES
FREEWOMEN	FRESHEN	FRICTIONS	FRINGE	FRIVOL
FREEZABLE	FRESHENED	FRIDGE	FRINGED	FRIVOLITIES
FREEZE	FRESHENER	FRIDGED	FRINGES	FRIVOLITY
FREEZER	FRESHENERS	FRIDGES	FRINGIER	FRIVOLLED
FREEZERS	FRESHENING	FRIDGING	FRINGIEST	FRIVOLLING
FREEZES	FRESHENS	FRIED	FRINGING	FRIVOLOUS
FREEZING	FRESHER	FRIEDCAKE	FRINGY	FRIVOLS
FREEZINGS	FRESHERS	FRIEDCAKES	FRIPON	FRIZ
FREIGHT	FRESHES	FRIEND	FRIPONS	FRIZE
FREIGHTED	FRESHEST	FRIENDED	FRIPPER	FRIZES
FREIGHTER	FRESHET	FRIENDING	FRIPPERER	FRIZING
FREIGHTERS	FRESHETS	FRIENDINGS	FRIPPERERS	FRIZZ
FREIGHTING	FRESHING	FRIENDLIER	FRIPPERIES	FRIZZANTE
FREIGHTS	FRESHISH	FRIENDLIES	FRIPPERS	FRIZZED
FREIT	FRESHLY	FRIENDLIEST	FRIPPERY	FRIZZES
FREITIER	FRESHMAN	FRIENDLY	FRIS	FRIZZIER
FREITIEST	FRESHMEN	FRIENDS	FRISEE	FRIZZIEST

The Chambers Dictionary is the authority for many longer words; see *OSW* Introduction, page xii.

FRIZZING	FRONTIERED	FROWIE	FRUITION	FUCHSITE
FRIZZLE	FRONTIERING	FROWIER	FRUITIONS	FUCHSITES
FRIZZLED	FRONTIERS	FROWIEST	FRUITIVE	FUCI
FRIZZLES	FRONTING	FROWN	FRUITLESS	FUCK
FRIZZLIER	FRONTLESS	FROWNED	FRUITLET	FUCKED
FRIZZLIEST	FRONTLET	FROWNING	FRUITLETS	FUCKER
FRIZZLING	FRONTLETS	FROWNS	FRUITS	FUCKERS
FRIZZLY	FRONTMAN	FROWS	FRUITWOOD	FUCKING
FRIZZY	FRONTMEN	FROWSIER	FRUITWOODS	FUCKINGS
FRO	FRONTON	FROWSIEST	FRUITY	FUCKS
FROCK	FRONTONS	FROWST	FRUMENTIES	FUCOID
FROCKED	FRONTOON	FROWSTED	FRUMENTY	FUCOIDAL
FROCKING	FRONTOONS	FROWSTER	FRUMP	FUCOIDS
FROCKINGS	FRONTS	FROWSTERS	FRUMPED	FUCUS
FROCKLESS	FRONTWARD	FROWSTIER	FRUMPIER	FUCUSED
FROCKS	FRONTWARDS	FROWSTIEST	FRUMPIEST	FUCUSES
FROG	FRONTWAYS	FROWSTING	FRUMPING	FUD
FROGBIT	FRONTWISE	FROWSTS	FRUMPISH	FUDDLE
FROGBITS	FRORE	FROWSTY	FRUMPLE	FUDDLED
FROGGED	FROREN	FROWSY	FRUMPLED	FUDDLER
FROGGERIES	FRORN	FROWY	FRUMPLES	FUDDLERS
FROGGERY	FRORNE	FROWZIER	FRUMPLING	FUDDLES
FROGGIER	FRORY	FROWZIEST	FRUMPS	FUDDLING
FROGGIEST	FROST	FROWZY	FRUMPY	FUDDLINGS
FROGGING	FROSTBIT	FROZE	FRUSH	FUDGE
FROGGINGS	FROSTBITE	FROZEN	FRUSHED	FUDGED
FROGGY	FROSTBITES	FRUCTANS	FRUSHES	FUDGES
FROGLET	FROSTBITING	FRUCTED	FRUSHING	FUDGING
FROGLETS	FROSTBITTEN	FRUCTIFIED	FRUST	FUDS
FROGLING	FROSTED	FRUCTIFIES	FRUSTA	FUEL
FROGLINGS	FROSTIER	FRUCTIFY	FRUSTRATE	FUELLED
FROGMAN	FROSTIEST	FRUCTIFYING	FRUSTRATED	FUELLER
FROGMARCH	FROSTILY	FRUCTIVE	FRUSTRATES	FUELLERS
FROGMARCHED	FROSTING	FRUCTOSE	FRUSTRATING	FUELLING
FROGMARCHES	FROSTINGS	FRUCTOSES	FRUSTS	FUELS
FROGMARCHING	FROSTLESS	FRUCTUARIES	FRUSTULE	FUERO
FROGMEN	FROSTLIKE	FRUCTUARY	FRUSTULES	FUEROS
FROGMOUTH	FROSTS	FRUCTUATE	FRUSTUM	FUFF
FROGMOUTHS	FROSTWORK	FRUCTUATED	FRUSTUMS	FUFFED
FROGS	FROSTWORKS	FRUCTUATES	FRUTEX	FUFFIER
FROISE	FROSTY	FRUCTUATING	FRUTICES	FUFFIEST
FROISES	FROTH	FRUCTUOUS	FRUTICOSE	FUFFING
FROLIC	FROTHED	FRUGAL	FRUTIFIED	FUFFS
FROLICKED	FROTHERIES	FRUGALIST	FRUTIFIES	FUFFY
FROLICKING	FROTHERY	FRUGALISTS	FRUTIFY	FUG
FROLICS	FROTHIER	FRUGALITIES	FRUTIFYING	FUGACIOUS
FROM	FROTHIEST	FRUGALITY	FRY	FUGACITIES
FROMENTIES	FROTHILY	FRUGALLY	FRYER	FUGACITY
FROMENTY	FROTHING	FRUICT	FRYERS	FUGAL
FROND	FROTHLESS	FRUICTS	FRYING	FUGALLY
FRONDAGE	FROTHS	FRUIT	FRYINGS	FUGATO
FRONDAGES	FROTHY	FRUITAGE	FUB	FUGATOS
FRONDED	FROTTAGE	FRUITAGES	FUBBED	FUGGED
FRONDENT	FROTTAGES	FRUITCAKE	FUBBERIES	FUGGIER
FRONDEUR	FROTTEUR	FRUITCAKES	FUBBERY	FUGGIEST
FRONDEURS	FROTTEURS	FRUITED	FUBBIER	FUGGING
FRONDOSE	FROUGHIER	FRUITER	FUBBIEST	FUGGY
FRONDS	FROUGHIEST	FRUITERER	FUBBING	FUGHETTA
FRONT	FROUGHY	FRUITERERS	FUBBY	FUGHETTAS
FRONTAGE	FROUNCE	FRUITERIES	FUBS	FUGIE
FRONTAGER	FROUNCED	FRUITERS	FUBSIER	FUGIES
FRONTAGERS	FROUNCES	FRUITERY	FUBSIEST	FUGITIVE
FRONTAGES	FROUNCING	FRUITFUL	FUBSY	FUGITIVES
FRONTAL	FROW	FRUITIER	FUCHSIA	FUGLE
FRONTALS	FROWARD	FRUITIEST	FUCHSIAS	FUGLED
FRONTED	FROWARDLY	FRUITING	FUCHSINE	FUGLEMAN
FRONTIER	FROWARDS	FRUITINGS	FUCHSINES	FUGLEMEN

The Chambers Dictionary is the authority for many longer words; see *OSW* Introduction, page xii.

FUGLES	FULMINATED	FUNCTIONS	FUNNIES	FURLONG
FUGLING	FULMINATES	FUND	FUNNIEST	FURLONGS
FUGS	FULMINATING	FUNDABLE	FUNNILY	FURLOUGH
FUGUE	FULMINE	FUNDAMENT	FUNNINESS	FURLOUGHED
FUGUES	FULMINED	FUNDAMENTS	FUNNINESSES	FURLOUGHING
FUGUIST	FULMINES	FUNDED	FUNNING	FURLOUGHS
FUGUISTS	FULMINING	FUNDER	FUNNY	FURLS
FULCRA	FULMINOUS	FUNDERS	FUNS	FURMENTIES
FULCRATE	FULNESS	FUNDI	FUNSTER	FURMENTY
FULCRUM	FULNESSES	FUNDIE	FUNSTERS	FURMETIES
FULCRUMS	FULSOME	FUNDIES	FUR	FURMETY
FULFIL	FULSOMELY	FUNDING	FURACIOUS	FURMITIES
FULFILL	FULSOMER	FUNDINGS	FURACITIES	FURMITY
FULFILLED	FULSOMEST	FUNDIS	FURACITY	FURNACE
FULFILLER	FULVID	FUNDLESS	FURAL	FURNACED
FULFILLERS	FULVOUS	FUNDS	FURALS	FURNACES
FULFILLING	FUM	FUNDUS	FURAN	FURNACING
FULFILLINGS	FUMADO	FUNDY	FURANE	FURNIMENT
FULFILLS	FUMADOES	FUNEBRAL	FURANES	FURNIMENTS
FULFILS	FUMADOS	FUNEBRE	FURANS	FURNISH
FULGENCIES	FUMAGE	FUNEBRIAL	FURBELOW	FURNISHED
FULGENCY	FUMAGES	FUNERAL	FURBELOWED	FURNISHER
FULGENT	FUMAROLE	FUNERALS	FURBELOWING	FURNISHERS
FULGENTLY	FUMAROLES	FUNERARY	FURBELOWS	FURNISHES
FULGID	FUMAROLIC	FUNEREAL	FURBISH	FURNISHING
FULGOR	FUMATORIA	FUNEST	FURBISHED	FURNISHINGS
FULGOROUS	FUMATORIES	FUNFAIR	FURBISHER	FURNITURE
FULGORS	FUMATORY	FUNFAIRS	FURBISHERS	FURNITURES
FULGOUR	FUMBLE	FUNG	FURBISHES	FUROL
FULGOURS	FUMBLED	FUNGAL	FURBISHING	FUROLE
FULGURAL	FUMBLER	FUNGI	FURCAL	FUROLES
FULGURANT	FUMBLERS	FUNGIBLES	FURCATE	FUROLS
FULGURATE	FUMBLES	FUNGICIDE	FURCATED	FUROR
FULGURATED	FUMBLING	FUNGICIDES	FURCATION	FURORE
FULGURATES	FUME	FUNGIFORM	FURCATIONS	FURORES
FULGURATING	FUMED	FUNGOID	FURCULA	FURORS
FULGURITE	FUMEROLE	FUNGOIDAL	FURCULAE	FURPHIES
FULGURITES	FUMEROLES	FUNGOSITIES	FURCULAR	FURPHY
FULGUROUS	FUMES	FUNGOSITY	FURDER	FURR
FULHAM	FUMET	FUNGOUS	FUREUR	FURRED
FULHAMS	FUMETS	FUNGS	FUREURS	FURRIER
FULL	FUMETTE	FUNGUS	FURFAIR	FURRIERIES
FULLAGE	FUMETTES	FUNGUSES	FURFAIRS	FURRIERS
FULLAGES	FUMETTI	FUNICLE	FURFUR	FURRIERY
FULLAM	FUMETTO	FUNICLES	FURFURAL	FURRIEST
FULLAMS	FUMIER	FUNICULAR	FURFURALS	FURRINESS
FULLAN	FUMIEST	FUNICULI	FURFURAN	FURRINESSES
FULLANS	FUMIGANT	FUNICULUS	FURFURANS	FURRING
FULLBACK	FUMIGANTS	FUNK	FURFUROL	FURRINGS
FULLBACKS	FUMIGATE	FUNKED	FURFUROLE	FURROW
FULLED	FUMIGATED	FUNKHOLE	FURFUROLES	FURROWED
FULLER	FUMIGATES	FUNKHOLES	FURFUROLS	FURROWING
FULLERENE	FUMIGATING	FUNKIA	FURFUROUS	FURROWS
FULLERENES	FUMIGATOR	FUNKIAS	FURFURS	FURROWY
FULLERS	FUMIGATORS	FUNKIER	FURIBUND	FURRS
FULLEST	FUMING	FUNKIEST	FURIES	FURRY
FULLING	FUMITORIES	FUNKINESS	FURIOSITIES	FURS
FULLISH	FUMITORY	FUNKINESSES	FURIOSITY	FURTH
FULLNESS	FUMOSITIES	FUNKING	FURIOSO	FURTHER
FULLNESSES	FUMOSITY	FUNKS	FURIOSOS	FURTHERED
FULLS	FUMOUS	FUNKY	FURIOUS	FURTHERER
FULLY	FUMS	FUNNED	FURIOUSLY	FURTHERERS
FULMAR	FUMY	FUNNEL	FURL	FURTHERING
FULMARS	FUN	FUNNELLED	FURLANA	FURTHERS
FULMINANT	FUNCTION	FUNNELLING	FURLANAS	FURTHEST
FULMINANTS	FUNCTIONED	FUNNELS	FURLED	FURTIVE
FULMINATE	FUNCTIONING	FUNNIER	FURLING	FURTIVELY

The Chambers Dictionary is the authority for many longer words; see *OSW* Introduction, page xii.

FURTIVER	FUSIFORM	FUSSING	FUTHARKS	FUZZED
FURTIVEST	FUSIL	FUSSY	FUTHORC	FUZZES
FURUNCLE	FUSILE	FUST	FUTHORCS	FUZZIER
FURUNCLES	FUSILEER	FUSTED	FUTHORK	FUZZIEST
FURY	FUSILEERS	FUSTET	FUTHORKS	FUZZILY
FURZE	FUSILIER	FUSTETS	FUTILE	FUZZINESS
FURZES	FUSILIERS	FUSTIAN	FUTILELY	FUZZINESSES
FURZIER	FUSILLADE	FUSTIANS	FUTILER	FUZZING
FURZIEST	FUSILLADES	FUSTIC	FUTILEST	FUZZLE
FURZY	FUSILLI	FUSTICS	FUTILITIES	FUZZLED
FUSAIN	FUSILS	FUSTIER	FUTILITY	FUZZLES
FUSAINS	FUSING	FUSTIEST	FUTON	FUZZLING
FUSAROL	FUSION	FUSTIGATE	FUTONS	FUZZY
FUSAROLE	FUSIONISM	FUSTIGATED	FUTTOCK	FY
FUSAROLES	FUSIONISMS	FUSTIGATES	FUTTOCKS	FYKE
FUSAROLS	FUSIONIST	FUSTIGATING	FUTURE	FYKED
FUSC	FUSIONISTS	FUSTILUGS	FUTURES	FYKES
FUSCOUS	FUSIONS	FUSTILY	FUTURISM	FYKING
FUSE	FUSS	FUSTINESS	FUTURISMS	FYLE
FUSED	FUSSED	FUSTINESSES	FUTURIST	FYLES
FUSEE	FUSSER	FUSTING	FUTURISTS	FYLFOT
FUSEES	FUSSERS	FUSTOC	FUTURITIES	FYLFOTS
FUSELAGE	FUSSES	FUSTOCS	FUTURITY	FYNBOS
FUSELAGES	FUSSIER	FUSTS	FUZE	FYNBOSES
FUSES	FUSSIEST	FUSTY	FUZEE	FYRD
FUSHION	FUSSILY	FUTCHEL	FUZEES	FYRDS
FUSHIONS	FUSSINESS	FUTCHELS	FUZES	FYTTE
FUSIBLE	FUSSINESSES	FUTHARK	FUZZ	FYTTES

G

GAB	GADFLIES	GAGES	GAITTS	GALILEES
GABARDINE	GADFLY	GAGGED	GAJO	GALINGALE
GABARDINES	GADGE	GAGGER	GAJOS	GALINGALES
GABBARD	GADGES	GAGGERS	GAL	GALIONGEE
GABBARDS	GADGET	GAGGING	GALA	GALIONGEES
GABBART	GADGETEER	GAGGLE	GALABEA	GALIOT
GABBARTS	GADGETEERS	GAGGLED	GALABEAH	GALIOTS
GABBED	GADGETRIES	GAGGLES	GALABEAHS	GALIPOT
GABBER	GADGETRY	GAGGLING	GALABEAS	GALIPOTS
GABBERS	GADGETS	GAGGLINGS	GALABIA	GALL
GABBIER	GADGIE	GAGING	GALABIAH	GALLABEA
GABBIEST	GADGIES	GAGMAN	GALABIAHS	GALLABEAH
GABBING	GADI	GAGMEN	GALABIAS	GALLABEAHS
GABBLE	GADIS	GAGS	GALACTIC	GALLABEAS
GABBLED	GADJE	GAGSTER	GALACTOSE	GALLABIA
GABBLER	GADJES	GAGSTERS	GALACTOSES	GALLABIAH
GABBLERS	GADLING	GAHNITE	GALAGE	GALLABIAHS
GABBLES	GADLINGS	GAHNITES	GALAGES	GALLABIAS
GABBLING	GADOID	GAID	GALAGO	GALLABIEH
GABBLINGS	GADOIDS	GAIDS	GALAGOS	GALLABIEHS
GABBRO	GADROON	GAIETIES	GALAH	GALLABIYA
GABBROIC	GADROONED	GAIETY	GALAHS	GALLABIYAS
GABBROID	GADROONS	GAIJIN	GALANGA	GALLANT
GABBROS	GADS	GAILLARD	GALANGAL	GALLANTER
GABBY	GADSMAN	GAILLARDE	GALANGALS	GALLANTEST
GABELLE	GADSMEN	GAILY	GALANGAS	GALLANTLY
GABELLER	GADSO	GAIN	GALANT	GALLANTRIES
GABELLERS	GADSOS	GAINABLE	GALANTINE	GALLANTRY
GABELLES	GADWALL	GAINED	GALANTINES	GALLANTS
GABERDINE	GADWALLS	GAINER	GALAPAGO	GALLATE
GABERDINES	GADZOOKS	GAINERS	GALAPAGOS	GALLATES
GABFEST	GAE	GAINEST	GALAS	GALLEASS
GABFESTS	GAED	GAINFUL	GALATEA	GALLEASSES
GABIES	GAELICISE	GAINFULLY	GALATEAS	GALLED
GABION	GAELICISED	GAINING	GALAXIES	GALLEON
GABIONADE	GAELICISES	GAININGS	GALAXY	GALLEONS
GABIONADES	GAELICISING	GAINLESS	GALBANUM	GALLERIA
GABIONAGE	GAELICISM	GAINLIER	GALBANUMS	GALLERIAS
GABIONAGES	GAELICISMS	GAINLIEST	GALDRAGON	GALLERIED
GABIONED	GAELICIZE	GAINLY	GALDRAGONS	GALLERIES
GABIONS	GAELICIZED	GAINS	GALE	GALLERY
GABLE	GAELICIZES	GAINSAID	GALEA	GALLERYING
GABLED	GAELICIZING	GAINSAY	GALEAE	GALLET
GABLES	GAES	GAINSAYER	GALEAS	GALLETED
GABLET	GAFF	GAINSAYERS	GALEATE	GALLETING
GABLETS	GAFFE	GAINSAYING	GALEATED	GALLETS
GABNASH	GAFFED	GAINSAYINGS	GALENA	GALLEY
GABNASHES	GAFFER	GAINSAYS	GALENAS	GALLEYS
GABS	GAFFERS	GAIR	GALENGALE	GALLFLIES
GABY	GAFFES	GAIRFOWL	GALENGALES	GALLFLY
GAD	GAFFING	GAIRFOWLS	GALENITE	GALLIARD
GADABOUT	GAFFINGS	GAIRS	GALENITES	GALLIARDS
GADABOUTS	GAFFS	GAIT	GALENOID	GALLIASS
GADDED	GAG	GAITED	GALERE	GALLIASSES
GADDER	GAGA	GAITER	GALERES	GALLIC
GADDERS	GAGAKU	GAITERS	GALES	GALLICISE
GADDING	GAGAKUS	GAITING	GALETTE	GALLICISED
GADE	GAGE	GAITS	GALETTES	GALLICISES
GADES	GAGED	GAITT	GALILEE	GALLICISING

The Chambers Dictionary is the authority for many longer words; see *OSW* Introduction, page xii.

GALLICISM
GALLICISMS
GALLICIZE
GALLICIZED
GALLICIZES
GALLICIZING
GALLIED
GALLIES
GALLINAZO
GALLINAZOS
GALLING
GALLINGLY
GALLINULE
GALLINULES
GALLIOT
GALLIOTS
GALLIPOT
GALLIPOTS
GALLISE
GALLISED
GALLISES
GALLISING
GALLISISE
GALLISISED
GALLISISES
GALLISISING
GALLISIZE
GALLISIZED
GALLISIZES
GALLISIZING
GALLIUM
GALLIUMS
GALLIVANT
GALLIVANTED
GALLIVANTING
GALLIVANTS
GALLIVAT
GALLIVATS
GALLIWASP
GALLIWASPS
GALLIZE
GALLIZED
GALLIZES
GALLIZING
GALLNUT
GALLNUTS
GALLON
GALLONAGE
GALLONAGES
GALLONS
GALLOON
GALLOONED
GALLOONS
GALLOP
GALLOPADE
GALLOPADED
GALLOPADES
GALLOPADING
GALLOPED
GALLOPER
GALLOPERS
GALLOPING
GALLOPS
GALLOW
GALLOWED
GALLOWING
GALLOWS

GALLOWSES
GALLS
GALLSTONE
GALLSTONES
GALLUMPH
GALLUMPHED
GALLUMPHING
GALLUMPHS
GALLUS
GALLUSES
GALLY
GALLYING
GALOCHE
GALOCHED
GALOCHES
GALOCHING
GALOOT
GALOOTS
GALOP
GALOPED
GALOPIN
GALOPING
GALOPINS
GALOPPED
GALOPPING
GALOPS
GALORE
GALOSH
GALOSHED
GALOSHES
GALOSHING
GALOWSES
GALRAVAGE
GALRAVAGED
GALRAVAGES
GALRAVAGING
GALS
GALTONIA
GALTONIAS
GALUMPH
GALUMPHED
GALUMPHER
GALUMPHERS
GALUMPHING
GALUMPHS
GALUT
GALUTH
GALUTHS
GALUTS
GALVANIC
GALVANISE
GALVANISED
GALVANISES
GALVANISING
GALVANISM
GALVANISMS
GALVANIST
GALVANISTS
GALVANIZE
GALVANIZED
GALVANIZES
GALVANIZING
GAM
GAMASH
GAMASHES
GAMAY
GAMAYS

GAMB
GAMBA
GAMBADO
GAMBADOED
GAMBADOES
GAMBADOING
GAMBADOS
GAMBAS
GAMBESON
GAMBESONS
GAMBET
GAMBETS
GAMBETTA
GAMBETTAS
GAMBIER
GAMBIERS
GAMBIR
GAMBIRS
GAMBIST
GAMBISTS
GAMBIT
GAMBITED
GAMBITING
GAMBITS
GAMBLE
GAMBLED
GAMBLER
GAMBLERS
GAMBLES
GAMBLING
GAMBLINGS
GAMBO
GAMBOGE
GAMBOGES
GAMBOGIAN
GAMBOGIC
GAMBOL
GAMBOLLED
GAMBOLLING
GAMBOLS
GAMBOS
GAMBREL
GAMBRELS
GAMBROON
GAMBROONS
GAMBS
GAME
GAMECOCK
GAMECOCKS
GAMED
GAMELAN
GAMELANS
GAMELY
GAMENESS
GAMENESSES
GAMER
GAMES
GAMESIER
GAMESIEST
GAMESOME
GAMEST
GAMESTER
GAMESTERS
GAMESY
GAMETAL
GAMETE
GAMETES

GAMETIC
GAMEY
GAMIC
GAMIER
GAMIEST
GAMIN
GAMINE
GAMINERIE
GAMINERIES
GAMINES
GAMINESS
GAMINESSES
GAMING
GAMINGS
GAMINS
GAMMA
GAMMADIA
GAMMADION
GAMMAS
GAMMATIA
GAMMATION
GAMME
GAMMED
GAMMER
GAMMERS
GAMMES
GAMMIER
GAMMIEST
GAMMING
GAMMOCK
GAMMOCKED
GAMMOCKING
GAMMOCKS
GAMMON
GAMMONED
GAMMONER
GAMMONERS
GAMMONING
GAMMONINGS
GAMMONS
GAMMY
GAMP
GAMPISH
GAMPS
GAMS
GAMUT
GAMUTS
GAMY
GAMYNESS
GAMYNESSES
GAN
GANCH
GANCHED
GANCHES
GANCHING
GANDER
GANDERISM
GANDERISMS
GANDERS
GANE
GANG
GANGBOARD
GANGBOARDS
GANGED
GANGER
GANGERS
GANGING

GANGINGS
GANGLAND
GANGLANDS
GANGLIA
GANGLIAR
GANGLIATE
GANGLIER
GANGLIEST
GANGLING
GANGLION
GANGLIONS
GANGLY
GANGPLANK
GANGPLANKS
GANGREL
GANGRELS
GANGRENE
GANGRENED
GANGRENES
GANGRENING
GANGS
GANGSMAN
GANGSMEN
GANGSTER
GANGSTERS
GANGUE
GANGUES
GANGWAY
GANGWAYS
GANISTER
GANISTERS
GANJA
GANJAS
GANNET
GANNETRIES
GANNETRY
GANNETS
GANNISTER
GANNISTERS
GANOID
GANOIDS
GANOIN
GANOINE
GANOINES
GANOINS
GANSEY
GANSEYS
GANT
GANTED
GANTING
GANTLET
GANTLETS
GANTLINE
GANTLINES
GANTLOPE
GANTLOPES
GANTRIES
GANTRY
GANTS
GAOL
GAOLED
GAOLER
GAOLERESS
GAOLERESSES
GAOLERS
GAOLING
GAOLS

The Chambers Dictionary is the authority for many longer words; see *OSW* Introduction, page xii.

GAP	GARDENED	GARNERS	GARS	GASOLENE
GAPE	GARDENER	GARNET	GART	GASOLENES
GAPED	GARDENERS	GARNETS	GARTER	GASOLIER
GAPER	GARDENIA	GARNI	GARTERED	GASOLIERS
GAPERS	GARDENIAS	GARNISH	GARTERING	GASOLINE
GAPES	GARDENING	GARNISHED	GARTERS	GASOLINES
GAPESEED	GARDENINGS	GARNISHEE	GARTH	GASOMETER
GAPESEEDS	GARDENS	GARNISHEED	GARTHS	GASOMETERS
GAPEWORM	GARDEROBE	GARNISHEEING	GARUDA	GASOMETRIES
GAPEWORMS	GARDEROBES	GARNISHEES	GARUDAS	GASOMETRY
GAPING	GARDYLOO	GARNISHER	GARUM	GASP
GAPINGLY	GARDYLOOS	GARNISHERS	GARUMS	GASPED
GAPINGS	GARE	GARNISHES	GARVIE	GASPER
GAPO	GAREFOWL	GARNISHING	GARVIES	GASPEREAU
GAPOS	GAREFOWLS	GARNISHINGS	GARVOCK	GASPEREAUS
GAPPED	GARFISH	GARNISHRIES	GARVOCKS	GASPERS
GAPPIER	GARFISHES	GARNISHRY	GAS	GASPIER
GAPPIEST	GARGANEY	GARNITURE	GASAHOL	GASPIEST
GAPPING	GARGANEYS	GARNITURES	GASAHOLS	GASPINESS
GAPPY	GARGARISE	GAROTTE	GASALIER	GASPINESSES
GAPS	GARGARISED	GAROTTED	GASALIERS	GASPING
GAR	GARGARISES	GAROTTER	GASBAG	GASPINGLY
GARAGE	GARGARISING	GAROTTERS	GASBAGS	GASPINGS
GARAGED	GARGARISM	GAROTTES	GASCON	GASPS
GARAGES	GARGARISMS	GAROTTING	GASCONADE	GASPY
GARAGING	GARGARIZE	GAROTTINGS	GASCONADED	GASSED
GARAGINGS	GARGARIZED	GARPIKE	GASCONADES	GASSER
GARAGIST	GARGARIZES	GARPIKES	GASCONADING	GASSERS
GARAGISTE	GARGARIZING	GARRAN	GASCONISM	GASSES
GARAGISTES	GARGET	GARRANS	GASCONISMS	GASSIER
GARAGISTS	GARGETS	GARRE	GASCONS	GASSIEST
GARB	GARGETY	GARRED	GASEITIES	GASSINESS
GARBAGE	GARGLE	GARRES	GASEITY	GASSINESSES
GARBAGES	GARGLED	GARRET	GASELIER	GASSING
GARBANZO	GARGLES	GARRETED	GASELIERS	GASSINGS
GARBANZOS	GARGLING	GARRETEER	GASEOUS	GASSY
GARBE	GARGOYLE	GARRETEERS	GASES	GAST
GARBED	GARGOYLES	GARRETS	GASFIELD	GASTED
GARBES	GARIAL	GARRIGUE	GASFIELDS	GASTER
GARBING	GARIALS	GARRIGUES	GASH	GASTERS
GARBLE	GARIBALDI	GARRING	GASHED	GASTFULL
GARBLED	GARIBALDIS	GARRISON	GASHES	GASTING
GARBLER	GARIGUE	GARRISONED	GASHFUL	GASTNESS
GARBLERS	GARIGUES	GARRISONING	GASHING	GASTNESSE
GARBLES	GARISH	GARRISONS	GASHLY	GASTNESSES
GARBLING	GARISHED	GARRON	GASHOLDER	GASTRAEA
GARBLINGS	GARISHES	GARRONS	GASHOLDERS	GASTRAEAS
GARBO	GARISHING	GARROT	GASIFIED	GASTRAEUM
GARBOARD	GARISHLY	GARROTE	GASIFIER	GASTRAEUMS
GARBOARDS	GARJAN	GARROTED	GASIFIERS	GASTRIC
GARBOIL	GARJANS	GARROTES	GASIFIES	GASTRIN
GARBOILS	GARLAND	GARROTING	GASIFORM	GASTRINS
GARBOLOGIES	GARLANDED	GARROTS	GASIFY	GASTRITIS
GARBOLOGY	GARLANDING	GARROTTE	GASIFYING	GASTRITISES
GARBOS	GARLANDRIES	GARROTTED	GASKET	GASTROPOD
GARBS	GARLANDRY	GARROTTER	GASKETS	GASTROPODS
GARBURE	GARLANDS	GARROTTERS	GASKIN	GASTRULA
GARBURES	GARLIC	GARROTTES	GASKINS	GASTRULAE
GARCINIA	GARLICKY	GARROTTING	GASLIGHT	GASTRULAS
GARCINIAS	GARLICS	GARROTTINGS	GASLIGHTS	GASTS
GARCON	GARMENT	GARRULITIES	GASLIT	GAT
GARCONS	GARMENTED	GARRULITY	GASMAN	GATE
GARDA	GARMENTING	GARRULOUS	GASMEN	GATEAU
GARDAI	GARMENTS	GARRYA	GASOGENE	GATEAUS
GARDANT	GARNER	GARRYAS	GASOGENES	GATEAUX
GARDANTS	GARNERED	GARRYOWEN	GASOHOL	GATECRASH
GARDEN	GARNERING	GARRYOWENS	GASOHOLS	GATECRASHED

The Chambers Dictionary is the authority for many longer words; see *OSW* Introduction, page xii.

GATECRASHES	GAUGE	GAVE	GAZERS	GECKOS
GATECRASHING	GAUGEABLE	GAVEL	GAZES	GECKS
GATED	GAUGED	GAVELKIND	GAZETTE	GED
GATEFOLD	GAUGER	GAVELKINDS	GAZETTED	GEDDIT
GATEFOLDS	GAUGERS	GAVELMAN	GAZETTEER	GEDS
GATEHOUSE	GAUGES	GAVELMEN	GAZETTEERED	GEE
GATEHOUSES	GAUGING	GAVELOCK	GAZETTEERING	GEEBUNG
GATELEG	GAUGINGS	GAVELOCKS	GAZETTEERS	GEEBUNGS
GATELESS	GAUJE	GAVELS	GAZETTES	GEECHEE
GATEMAN	GAUJES	GAVIAL	GAZETTING	GEECHEES
GATEMEN	GAULEITER	GAVIALS	GAZIER	GEED
GATEPOST	GAULEITERS	GAVOTTE	GAZIEST	GEEGAW
GATEPOSTS	GAULT	GAVOTTES	GAZING	GEEGAWS
GATES	GAULTER	GAWCIER	GAZOGENE	GEEING
GATEWAY	GAULTERS	GAWCIEST	GAZOGENES	GEEK
GATEWAYS	GAULTS	GAWCY	GAZON	GEEKIER
GATH	GAUM	GAWD	GAZONS	GEEKIEST
GATHER	GAUMED	GAWDS	GAZOO	GEEKS
GATHERED	GAUMIER	GAWK	GAZOOKA	GEEKY
GATHERER	GAUMIEST	GAWKED	GAZOOKAS	GEEP
GATHERERS	GAUMING	GAWKER	GAZOON	GEEPS
GATHERING	GAUMLESS	GAWKERS	GAZOONS	GEES
GATHERINGS	GAUMS	GAWKIER	GAZOOS	GEESE
GATHERS	GAUMY	GAWKIES	GAZPACHO	GEEZER
GATHS	GAUN	GAWKIEST	GAZPACHOS	GEEZERS
GATING	GAUNCH	GAWKIHOOD	GAZUMP	GEFUFFLE
GATINGS	GAUNCHED	GAWKIHOODS	GAZUMPED	GEFUFFLED
GATS	GAUNCHES	GAWKINESS	GAZUMPING	GEFUFFLES
GAU	GAUNCHING	GAWKINESSES	GAZUMPS	GEFUFFLING
GAUCHE	GAUNT	GAWKING	GAZUNDER	GEISHA
GAUCHER	GAUNTED	GAWKS	GAZUNDERED	GEISHAS
GAUCHERIE	GAUNTER	GAWKY·	GAZUNDERING	GEIST
GAUCHERIES	GAUNTEST	GAWP	GAZUNDERS	GEISTS
GAUCHESCO	GAUNTING	GAWPED	GAZY	GEIT
GAUCHEST	GAUNTLET	GAWPER	GEAL	GEITS
GAUCHO	GAUNTLETS	GAWPERS	GEALED	GEL
GAUCHOS	GAUNTLY	GAWPING	GEALING	GELADA
GAUCIE	GAUNTNESS	GAWPS	GEALOUS	GELADAS
GAUCIER	GAUNTNESSES	GAWPUS	GEALOUSIES	GELASTIC
GAUCIEST	GAUNTREE	GAWPUSES	GEALOUSY	GELATI
GAUCY	GAUNTREES	GAWSIER	GEALS	GELATIN
GAUD	GAUNTRIES	GAWSIEST	GEAN	GELATINE
GAUDEAMUS	GAUNTRY	GAWSY	GEANS	GELATINES
GAUDEAMUSES	GAUNTS	GAY	GEAR	GELATINS
GAUDED	GAUP	GAYAL	GEARBOX	GELATION
GAUDERIES	GAUPED	GAYALS	GEARBOXES	GELATIONS
GAUDERY	GAUPER	GAYER	GEARE	GELATO
GAUDGIE	GAUPERS	GAYEST	GEARED	GELD
GAUDGIES	GAUPING	GAYNESS	GEARES	GELDED
GAUDIER	GAUPS	GAYNESSES	GEARING	GELDER
GAUDIES	GAUPUS	GAYS	GEARINGS	GELDERS
GAUDIEST	GAUPUSES	GAYSOME	GEARLESS	GELDING
GAUDILY	GAUR	GAZAL	GEARS	GELDINGS
GAUDINESS	GAURS	GAZALS	GEARSHIFT	GELDS
GAUDINESSES	GAUS	GAZANIA	GEARSHIFTS	GELID
GAUDING	GAUSS	GAZANIAS	GEARWHEEL	GELIDER
GAUDS	GAUSSES	GAZE	GEARWHEELS	GELIDEST
GAUDY	GAUSSIAN	GAZEBO	GEASON	GELIDITIES
GAUFER	GAUZE	GAZEBOES	GEAT	GELIDITY
GAUFERS	GAUZES	GAZEBOS	GEATS	GELIDLY
GAUFFER	GAUZIER	GAZED	GEBUR	GELIDNESS
GAUFFERED	GAUZIEST	GAZEFUL	GEBURS	GELIDNESSES
GAUFFERING	GAUZINESS	GAZELLE	GECK	GELIGNITE
GAUFFERINGS	GAUZINESSES	GAZELLES	GECKED	GELIGNITES
GAUFFERS	GAUZY	GAZEMENT	GECKING	GELLED
GAUFRE	GAVAGE	GAZEMENTS	GECKO	GELLIES
GAUFRES	GAVAGES	GAZER	GECKOES	GELLING

The Chambers Dictionary is the authority for many longer words; see *OSW* Introduction, page xii.

GELLY	GENDARME	GENITAL	GENTLED	GEOLOGIANS
GELOSIES	GENDARMES	GENITALIA	GENTLEMAN	GEOLOGIC
GELOSY	GENDER	GENITALIC	GENTLEMEN	GEOLOGIES
GELS	GENDERED	GENITALS	GENTLER	GEOLOGISE
GELSEMINE	GENDERING	GENITIVAL	GENTLES	GEOLOGISED
GELSEMINES	GENDERS	GENITIVE	GENTLEST	GEOLOGISES
GELSEMIUM	GENE	GENITIVES	GENTLING	GEOLOGISING
GELSEMIUMS	GENEALOGIES	GENITOR	GENTLY	GEOLOGIST
GELT	GENEALOGY	GENITORS	GENTOO	GEOLOGISTS
GELTS	GENERA	GENITRICES	GENTOOS	GEOLOGIZE
GEM	GENERABLE	GENITRIX	GENTRICE	GEOLOGIZED
GEMATRIA	GENERAL	GENITRIXES	GENTRICES	GEOLOGIZES
GEMATRIAS	GENERALE	GENITURE	GENTRIES	GEOLOGIZING
GEMEL	GENERALIA	GENITURES	GENTRIFIED	GEOLOGY
GEMELS	GENERALLED	GENIUS	GENTRIFIES	GEOMANCER
GEMFISH	GENERALLING	GENIUSES	GENTRIFY	GEOMANCERS
GEMFISHES	GENERALLY	GENIZAH	GENTRIFYING	GEOMANCIES
GEMINATE	GENERALS	GENIZAHS	GENTRY	GEOMANCY
GEMINATED	GENERANT	GENLOCK	GENTS	GEOMANT
GEMINATES	GENERANTS	GENLOCKS	GENTY	GEOMANTIC
GEMINATING	GENERATE	GENNEL	GENU	GEOMANTS
GEMINI	GENERATED	GENNELS	GENUFLECT	GEOMETER
GEMINIES	GENERATES	GENNET	GENUFLECTED	GEOMETERS
GEMINOUS	GENERATING	GENNETS	GENUFLECTING	GEOMETRIC
GEMINY	GENERATOR	GENOA	GENUFLECTS	GEOMETRID
GEMMA	GENERATORS	GENOAS	GENUINE	GEOMETRIDS
GEMMAE	GENERIC	GENOCIDAL	GENUINELY	GEOMETRIES
GEMMAN	GENERICAL	GENOCIDE	GENUS	GEOMETRY
GEMMATE	GENERICS	GENOCIDES	GENUSES	GEOMYOID
GEMMATED	GENEROUS	GENOM	GEO	GEOPHAGIES
GEMMATES	GENES	GENOME	GEOCARPIC	GEOPHAGY
GEMMATING	GENESES	GENOMES	GEOCARPIES	GEOPHILIC
GEMMATION	GENESIS	GENOMS	GEOCARPY	GEOPHONE
GEMMATIONS	GENET	GENOTYPE	GEODE	GEOPHONES
GEMMATIVE	GENETIC	GENOTYPES	GEODES	GEOPHYTE
GEMMED	GENETICAL	GENOTYPIC	GEODESIC	GEOPHYTES
GEMMEN	GENETICS	GENRE	GEODESICS	GEOPHYTIC
GEMMEOUS	GENETRICES	GENRES	GEODESIES	GEOPONIC
GEMMERIES	GENETRIX	GENS	GEODESIST	GEOPONICS
GEMMERY	GENETRIXES	GENSDARMES	GEODESISTS	GEORGETTE
GEMMIER	GENETS	GENT	GEODESY	GEORGETTES
GEMMIEST	GENETTE	GENTEEL	GEODETIC	GEORGIC
GEMMING	GENETTES	GENTEELER	GEODETICS	GEORGICS
GEMMOLOGIES	GENEVA	GENTEELEST	GEODIC	GEOS
GEMMOLOGY	GENEVAS	GENTEELLY	GEOFACT	GEOSPHERE
GEMMULE	GENIAL	GENTES	GEOFACTS	GEOSPHERES
GEMMULES	GENIALISE	GENTIAN	GEOGENIES	GEOSTATIC
GEMMY	GENIALISED	GENTIANS	GEOGENY	GEOSTATICS
GEMOLOGIES	GENIALISES	GENTIER	GEOGNOSES	GEOTACTIC
GEMOLOGY	GENIALISING	GENTIEST	GEOGNOSIES	GEOTAXES
GEMONY	GENIALITIES	GENTILE	GEOGNOSIS	GEOTAXIS
GEMOT	GENIALITY	GENTILES	GEOGNOST	GEOTROPIC
GEMOTS	GENIALIZE	GENTILIC	GEOGNOSTS	GERAH
GEMS	GENIALIZED	GENTILISE	GEOGNOSY	GERAHS
GEMSBOK	GENIALIZES	GENTILISED	GEOGONIC	GERANIOL
GEMSBOKS	GENIALIZING	GENTILISES	GEOGONIES	GERANIOLS
GEMSHORN	GENIALLY	GENTILISH	GEOGONY	GERANIUM
GEMSHORNS	GENIC	GENTILISING	GEOGRAPHIES	GERANIUMS
GEMSTONE	GENIE	GENTILISM	GEOGRAPHY	GERBE
GEMSTONES	GENIES	GENTILISMS	GEOID	GERBERA
GEMUTLICH	GENII	GENTILITIES	GEOIDAL	GERBERAS
GEN	GENIP	GENTILITY	GEOIDS	GERBES
GENA	GENIPAP	GENTILIZE	GEOLATRIES	GERBIL
GENAL	GENIPAPS	GENTILIZED	GEOLATRY	GERBILLE
GENAPPE	GENIPS	GENTILIZES	GEOLOGER	GERBILLES
GENAPPES	GENISTA	GENTILIZING	GEOLOGERS	GERBILS
GENAS	GENISTAS	GENTLE	GEOLOGIAN	GERE

GERENT	GESTAPOS	GHAZEL	GIANTS	GIFTING
GERENTS	GESTATE	GHAZELS	GIANTSHIP	GIFTS
GERENUK	GESTATED	GHAZI	GIANTSHIPS	GIFTSHOP
GERENUKS	GESTATES	GHAZIS	GIAOUR	GIFTSHOPS
GERES	GESTATING	GHEE	GIAOURS	GIG
GERFALCON	GESTATION	GHEES	GIB	GIGA
GERFALCONS	GESTATIONS	GHERAO	GIBBED	GIGAHERTZ
GERIATRIC	GESTATIVE	GHERAOED	GIBBER	GIGAHERTZES
GERIATRICS	GESTATORY	GHERAOING	GIBBERED	GIGANTEAN
GERLE	GESTE	GHERAOS	GIBBERING	GIGANTIC
GERLES	GESTES	GHERKIN	GIBBERISH	GIGANTISM
GERM	GESTIC	GHERKINS	GIBBERISHES	GIGANTISMS
GERMAIN	GESTS	GHESSE	GIBBERS	GIGAS
GERMAINE	GESTURAL	GHESSED	GIBBET	GIGAWATT
GERMAINES	GESTURE	GHESSES	GIBBETED	GIGAWATTS
GERMAINS	GESTURED	GHESSING	GIBBETING	GIGGED
GERMAN	GESTURES	GHEST	GIBBETS	GIGGING
GERMANDER	GESTURING	GHETTO	GIBBING	GIGGIT
GERMANDERS	GET	GHETTOES	GIBBON	GIGGITED
GERMANE	GETA	GHETTOISE	GIBBONS	GIGGITING
GERMANELY	GETAS	GHETTOISED	GIBBOSE	GIGGITS
GERMANIUM	GETAWAY	GHETTOISES	GIBBOSITIES	GIGGLE
GERMANIUMS	GETAWAYS	GHETTOISING	GIBBOSITY	GIGGLED
GERMANS	GETS	GHETTOIZE	GIBBOUS	GIGGLER
GERMED	GETTABLE	GHETTOIZED	GIBBOUSLY	GIGGLERS
GERMEN	GETTER	GHETTOIZES	GIBBSITE	GIGGLES
GERMENS	GETTERED	GHETTOIZING	GIBBSITES	GIGGLIER
GERMICIDE	GETTERING	GHETTOS	GIBE	GIGGLIEST
GERMICIDES	GETTERINGS	GHI	GIBED	GIGGLING
GERMIN	GETTERS	GHILGAI	GIBEL	GIGGLINGS
GERMINAL	GETTING	GHILGAIS	GIBELS	GIGGLY
GERMINANT	GETTINGS	GHILLIE	GIBER	GIGLET
GERMINATE	GEUM	GHILLIED	GIBERS	GIGLETS
GERMINATED	GEUMS	GHILLIES	GIBES	GIGLOT
GERMINATES	GEWGAW	GHILLYING	GIBING	GIGLOTS
GERMINATING	GEWGAWS	GHIS	GIBINGLY	GIGMAN
GERMING	GEY	GHOST	GIBLET	GIGMANITIES
GERMINS	GEYAN	GHOSTED	GIBLETS	GIGMANITY
GERMS	GEYER	GHOSTIER	GIBS	GIGMEN
GERNE	GEYEST	GHOSTIEST	GIBUS	GIGOLO
GERNED	GEYSER	GHOSTING	GIBUSES	GIGOLOS
GERNES	GEYSERITE	GHOSTINGS	GID	GIGOT
GERNING	GEYSERITES	GHOSTLIER	GIDDAP	GIGOTS
GERONTIC	GEYSERS	GHOSTLIEST	GIDDIED	GIGS
GEROPIGA	GHARIAL	GHOSTLIKE	GIDDIER	GIGUE
GEROPIGAS	GHARIALS	GHOSTLY	GIDDIES	GIGUES
GERTCHA	GHARRI	GHOSTS	GIDDIEST	GILA
GERUND	GHARRIES	GHOSTY	GIDDILY	GILAS
GERUNDIAL	GHARRIS	GHOUL	GIDDINESS	GILBERT
GERUNDIVE	GHARRY	GHOULISH	GIDDINESSES	GILBERTS
GERUNDIVES	GHAST	GHOULS	GIDDUP	GILCUP
GERUNDS	GHASTED	GHYLL	GIDDY	GILCUPS
GESNERIA	GHASTFUL	GHYLLS	GIDDYING	GILD
GESNERIAS	GHASTFULL	GI	GIDGEE	GILDED
GESSAMINE	GHASTING	GIAMBEUX	GIDGEES	GILDEN
GESSAMINES	GHASTLIER	GIANT	GIDJEE	GILDER
GESSE	GHASTLIEST	GIANTESS	GIDJEES	GILDERS
GESSED	GHASTLY	GIANTESSES	GIDS	GILDING
GESSES	GHASTNESS	GIANTHOOD	GIE	GILDINGS
GESSING	GHASTNESSES	GIANTHOODS	GIED	GILDS
GESSO	GHASTS	GIANTISM	GIEING	GILET
GESSOES	GHAT	GIANTISMS	GIEN	GILETS
GEST	GHATS	GIANTLIER	GIES	GILGAI
GESTALT	GHAUT	GIANTLIEST	GIF	GILGAIS
GESTALTS	GHAUTS	GIANTLY	GIFT	GILGIE
GESTANT	GHAZAL	GIANTRIES	GIFTED	GILGIES
GESTAPO	GHAZALS	GIANTRY	GIFTEDLY	GILL

The Chambers Dictionary is the authority for many longer words; see *OSW* Introduction, page xii.

GILLAROO	GING	GIRAFFE	GIRTING	GLACIAL
GILLAROOS	GINGAL	GIRAFFES	GIRTLINE	GLACIALS
GILLED	GINGALL	GIRAFFID	GIRTLINES	GLACIATE
GILLET	GINGALLS	GIRAFFINE	GIRTS	GLACIATED
GILLETS	GINGALS	GIRAFFOID	GIS	GLACIATES
GILLFLIRT	GINGELLIES	GIRANDOLA	GISARME	GLACIATING
GILLFLIRTS	GINGELLY	GIRANDOLAS	GISARMES	GLACIER
GILLIE	GINGER	GIRANDOLE	GISM	GLACIERS
GILLIED	GINGERADE	GIRANDOLES	GISMO	GLACIS
GILLIES	GINGERADES	GIRASOL	GISMOLOGIES	GLACISES
GILLING	GINGERED	GIRASOLE	GISMOLOGY	GLAD
GILLION	GINGERING	GIRASOLES	GISMOS	GLADDED
GILLIONS	GINGERLY	GIRASOLS	GISMS	GLADDEN
GILLS	GINGEROUS	GIRD	GIST	GLADDENED
GILLY	GINGERS	GIRDED	GISTS	GLADDENING
GILLYING	GINGERY	GIRDER	GIT	GLADDENS
GILLYVOR	GINGHAM	GIRDERS	GITANA	GLADDER
GILLYVORS	GINGHAMS	GIRDING	GITANAS	GLADDEST
GILPEY	GINGILI	GIRDINGS	GITANO	GLADDIE
GILPEYS	GINGILIS	GIRDLE	GITANOS	GLADDIES
GILPIES	GINGIVAL	GIRDLED	GITE	GLADDING
GILPY	GINGKO	GIRDLER	GITES	GLADDON
GILRAVAGE	GINGKOES	GIRDLERS	GITS	GLADDONS
GILRAVAGED	GINGLE	GIRDLES	GITTERN	GLADE
GILRAVAGES	GINGLES	GIRDLING	GITTERNED	GLADES
GILRAVAGING	GINGLYMI	GIRDS	GITTERNING	GLADFUL
GILSONITE	GINGLYMUS	GIRKIN	GITTERNS	GLADIATE
GILSONITES	GINGS	GIRKINS	GIUST	GLADIATOR
GILT	GINHOUSE	GIRL	GIUSTED	GLADIATORS
GILTCUP	GINHOUSES	GIRLHOOD	GIUSTING	GLADIER
GILTCUPS	GINK	GIRLHOODS	GIUSTO	GLADIEST
GILTS	GINKGO	GIRLIE	GIUSTS	GLADIOLE
GILTWOOD	GINKGOES	GIRLIES	GIVE	GLADIOLES
GIMBAL	GINKS	GIRLISH	GIVEAWAY	GLADIOLI
GIMBALS	GINN	GIRLISHLY	GIVEAWAYS	GLADIOLUS
GIMCRACK	GINNED	GIRLOND	GIVED	GLADIOLUSES
GIMCRACKS	GINNEL	GIRLONDS	GIVEN	GLADIUS
GIMLET	GINNELS	GIRLS	GIVENNESS	GLADIUSES
GIMLETED	GINNER	GIRLY	GIVENNESSES	GLADLY
GIMLETING	GINNERIES	GIRN	GIVER	GLADNESS
GIMLETS	GINNERS	GIRNED	GIVERS	GLADNESSES
GIMMAL	GINNERY	GIRNEL	GIVES	GLADS
GIMMALLED	GINNIER	GIRNELS	GIVING	GLADSOME
GIMMALS	GINNIEST	GIRNER	GIVINGS	GLADY
GIMME	GINNING	GIRNERS	GIZMO	GLAIK
GIMMER	GINNY	GIRNIE	GIZMOLOGIES	GLAIKET
GIMMERS	GINORMOUS	GIRNIER	GIZMOLOGY	GLAIKIT
GIMMES	GINS	GIRNIEST	GIZMOS	GLAIKS
GIMMICK	GINSENG	GIRNING	GIZZ	GLAIR
GIMMICKED	GINSENGS	GIRNS	GIZZARD	GLAIRED
GIMMICKIER	GINSHOP	GIRO	GIZZARDS	GLAIREOUS
GIMMICKIEST	GINSHOPS	GIRON	GIZZEN	GLAIRIER
GIMMICKING	GIO	GIRONIC	GIZZENED	GLAIRIEST
GIMMICKRIES	GIOCOSO	GIRONS	GIZZENING	GLAIRIN
GIMMICKRY	GIOS	GIROS	GIZZENS	GLAIRING
GIMMICKS	GIP	GIROSOL	GIZZES	GLAIRINS
GIMMICKY	GIPPIES	GIROSOLS	GJU	GLAIRS
GIMMOR	GIPPO	GIRR	GJUS	GLAIRY
GIMMORS	GIPPOS	GIRRS	GLABELLA	GLAIVE
GIMP	GIPPY	GIRT	GLABELLAE	GLAIVED
GIMPED	GIPS	GIRTED	GLABELLAR	GLAIVES
GIMPIER	GIPSEN	GIRTH	GLABRATE	GLAM
GIMPIEST	GIPSENS	GIRTHED	GLABROUS	GLAMOR
GIMPING	GIPSIED	GIRTHING	GLACE	GLAMORED
GIMPS	GIPSIES	GIRTHLINE	GLACEED	GLAMORING
GIMPY	GIPSY	GIRTHLINES	GLACEING	GLAMORISE
GIN	GIPSYING	GIRTHS	GLACES	GLAMORISED

The Chambers Dictionary is the authority for many longer words; see *OSW* Introduction, page xii.

GLAMORISES	GLAUCOUS	GLEETIEST	GLIMMERY	GLOBALIZING
GLAMORISING	GLAUM	GLEETING	GLIMPSE	GLOBALLY
GLAMORIZE	GLAUMED	GLEETS	GLIMPSED	GLOBATE
GLAMORIZED	GLAUMING	GLEETY	GLIMPSES	GLOBATED
GLAMORIZES	GLAUMS	GLEG	GLIMPSING	GLOBBIER
GLAMORIZING	GLAUR	GLEGGER	GLIMS	GLOBBIEST
GLAMOROUS	GLAURIER	GLEGGEST	GLINT	GLOBBY
GLAMORS	GLAURIEST	GLEI	GLINTED	GLOBE
GLAMOUR	GLAURS	GLEIS	GLINTING	GLOBED
GLAMOURED	GLAURY	GLEN	GLINTS	GLOBES
GLAMOURING	GLAZE	GLENGARRIES	GLIOMA	GLOBIN
GLAMOURS	GLAZED	GLENGARRY	GLIOMAS	GLOBING
GLAMS	GLAZEN	GLENOID	GLIOMATA	GLOBINS
GLANCE	GLAZER	GLENOIDAL	GLIOSES	GLOBOID
GLANCED	GLAZERS	GLENOIDS	GLIOSIS	GLOBOIDS
GLANCES	GLAZES	GLENS	GLISK	GLOBOSE
GLANCING	GLAZIER	GLENT	GLISKS	GLOBOSES
GLANCINGS	GLAZIERS	GLENTED	GLISSADE	GLOBOSITIES
GLAND	GLAZIEST	GLENTING	GLISSADED	GLOBOSITY
GLANDERED	GLAZING	GLENTS	GLISSADES	GLOBOUS
GLANDERS	GLAZINGS	GLEY	GLISSADING	GLOBS
GLANDES	GLAZY	GLEYED	GLISSANDI	GLOBULAR
GLANDS	GLEAM	GLEYING	GLISSANDO	GLOBULE
GLANDULAR	GLEAMED	GLEYS	GLISSANDOS	GLOBULES
GLANDULE	GLEAMIER	GLIA	GLISTEN	GLOBULET
GLANDULES	GLEAMIEST	GLIADIN	GLISTENED	GLOBULETS
GLANS	GLEAMING	GLIADINE	GLISTENING	GLOBULIN
GLARE	GLEAMINGS	GLIADINES	GLISTENS	GLOBULINS
GLAREAL	GLEAMS	GLIADINS	GLISTER	GLOBULITE
GLARED	GLEAMY	GLIAL	GLISTERED	GLOBULITES
GLAREOUS	GLEAN	GLIAS	GLISTERING	GLOBULOUS
GLARES	GLEANED	GLIB	GLISTERS	GLOBY
GLARIER	GLEANER	GLIBBED	GLIT	GLODE
GLARIEST	GLEANERS	GLIBBER	GLITCH	GLOGG
GLARING	GLEANING	GLIBBERY	GLITCHES	GLOGGS
GLARINGLY	GLEANINGS	GLIBBEST	GLITS	GLOIRE
GLARY	GLEANS	GLIBBING	GLITTER	GLOIRES
GLASNOST	GLEAVE	GLIBLY	GLITTERED	GLOM
GLASNOSTS	GLEAVES	GLIBNESS	GLITTERING	GLOMERATE
GLASS	GLEBE	GLIBNESSES	GLITTERINGS	GLOMERATED
GLASSED	GLEBES	GLIBS	GLITTERS	GLOMERATES
GLASSEN	GLEBOUS	GLID	GLITTERY	GLOMERATING
GLASSES	GLEBY	GLIDDER	GLITZ	GLOMERULE
GLASSFUL	GLED	GLIDDERY	GLITZES	GLOMERULES
GLASSFULS	GLEDE	GLIDDEST	GLITZIER	GLOMERULI
GLASSIER	GLEDES	GLIDE	GLITZIEST	GLOMMED
GLASSIEST	GLEDGE	GLIDED	GLITZILY	GLOMMING
GLASSIFIED	GLEDGED	GLIDER	GLITZY	GLOMS
GLASSIFIES	GLEDGES	GLIDERS	GLOAMING	GLONOIN
GLASSIFY	GLEDGING	GLIDES	GLOAMINGS	GLONOINS
GLASSIFYING	GLEDS	GLIDING	GLOAT	GLOOM
GLASSILY	GLEE	GLIDINGLY	GLOATED	GLOOMED
GLASSINE	GLEED	GLIDINGS	GLOATER	GLOOMFUL
GLASSINES	GLEEDS	GLIFF	GLOATERS	GLOOMIER
GLASSING	GLEEFUL	GLIFFING	GLOATING	GLOOMIEST
GLASSLIKE	GLEEING	GLIFFINGS	GLOATS	GLOOMILY
GLASSMAN	GLEEK	GLIFFS	GLOB	GLOOMING
GLASSMEN	GLEEKED	GLIFT	GLOBAL	GLOOMINGS
GLASSWARE	GLEEKING	GLIFTS	GLOBALISE	GLOOMS
GLASSWARES	GLEEKS	GLIKE	GLOBALISED	GLOOMY
GLASSWORK	GLEEMAN	GLIKES	GLOBALISES	GLOOP
GLASSWORKS	GLEEMEN	GLIM	GLOBALISING	GLOOPED
GLASSWORT	GLEES	GLIMMER	GLOBALISM	GLOOPIER
GLASSWORTS	GLEESOME	GLIMMERED	GLOBALISMS	GLOOPIEST
GLASSY	GLEET	GLIMMERING	GLOBALIZE	GLOOPING
GLAUCOMA	GLEETED	GLIMMERINGS	GLOBALIZED	GLOOPS
GLAUCOMAS	GLEETIER	GLIMMERS	GLOBALIZES	GLOOPY

The Chambers Dictionary is the authority for many longer words; see *OSW* Introduction, page xii.

GLOP	GLOWLAMPS	GLUTELIN	GNASH	GOALMOUTHS
GLOPS	GLOWS	GLUTELINS	GNASHED	GOALPOST
GLORIA	GLOXINIA	GLUTEN	GNASHER	GOALPOSTS
GLORIAS	GLOXINIAS	GLUTENOUS	GNASHERS	GOALS
GLORIED	GLOZE	GLUTENS	GNASHES	GOANNA
GLORIES	GLOZED	GLUTEUS	GNASHING	GOANNAS
GLORIFIED	GLOZES	GLUTINOUS	GNAT	GOARY
GLORIFIES	GLOZING	GLUTS	GNATHAL	GOAS
GLORIFY	GLOZINGS	GLUTTED	GNATHIC	GOAT
GLORIFYING	GLUCAGON	GLUTTING	GNATHITE	GOATEE
GLORIOLE	GLUCAGONS	GLUTTON	GNATHITES	GOATEED
GLORIOLES	GLUCINA	GLUTTONIES	GNATHONIC	GOATEES
GLORIOSA	GLUCINAS	GLUTTONS	GNATLING	GOATFISH
GLORIOSAS	GLUCINIUM	GLUTTONY	GNATLINGS	GOATFISHES
GLORIOUS	GLUCINIUMS	GLYCERIA	GNATS	GOATHERD
GLORY	GLUCINUM	GLYCERIAS	GNAW	GOATHERDS
GLORYING	GLUCINUMS	GLYCERIC	GNAWED	GOATIER
GLOSS	GLUCOSE	GLYCERIDE	GNAWER	GOATIEST
GLOSSA	GLUCOSES	GLYCERIDES	GNAWERS	GOATISH
GLOSSAE	GLUCOSIC	GLYCERIN	GNAWING	GOATLING
GLOSSAL	GLUCOSIDE	GLYCERINE	GNAWN	GOATLINGS
GLOSSARIES	GLUCOSIDES	GLYCERINES	GNAWS	GOATS
GLOSSARY	GLUE	GLYCERINS	GNEISS	GOATSKIN
GLOSSAS	GLUED	GLYCEROL	GNEISSES	GOATSKINS
GLOSSATOR	GLUER	GLYCEROLS	GNEISSIC	GOATWEED
GLOSSATORS	GLUERS	GLYCERYL	GNEISSOID	GOATWEEDS
GLOSSED	GLUES	GLYCERYLS	GNEISSOSE	GOATY
GLOSSEME	GLUEY	GLYCIN	GNOCCHI	GOB
GLOSSEMES	GLUEYNESS	GLYCINE	GNOCCHIS	GOBANG
GLOSSER	GLUEYNESSES	GLYCINES	GNOMAE	GOBANGS
GLOSSERS	GLUG	GLYCINS	GNOME	GOBBED
GLOSSES	GLUGGED	GLYCOCOLL	GNOMES	GOBBELINE
GLOSSIER	GLUGGING	GLYCOCOLLS	GNOMIC	GOBBELINES
GLOSSIES	GLUGS	GLYCOGEN	GNOMISH	GOBBET
GLOSSIEST	GLUHWEIN	GLYCOGENS	GNOMIST	GOBBETS
GLOSSILY	GLUHWEINS	GLYCOL	GNOMISTS	GOBBI
GLOSSINA	GLUIER	GLYCOLIC	GNOMON	GOBBING
GLOSSINAS	GLUIEST	GLYCOLLIC	GNOMONIC	GOBBLE
GLOSSING	GLUING	GLYCOLS	GNOMONICS	GOBBLED
GLOSSITIS	GLUISH	GLYCONIC	GNOMONS	GOBBLER
GLOSSITISES	GLUM	GLYCONICS	GNOSES	GOBBLERS
GLOSSY	GLUME	GLYCOSE	GNOSIS	GOBBLES
GLOTTAL	GLUMELLA	GLYCOSES	GNOSTIC	GOBBLING
GLOTTIC	GLUMELLAS	GLYCOSIDE	GNOSTICAL	GOBBO
GLOTTIDES	GLUMES	GLYCOSIDES	GNU	GOBIES
GLOTTIS	GLUMLY	GLYCOSYL	GNUS	GOBIID
GLOTTISES	GLUMMER	GLYCOSYLS	GO	GOBIIDS
GLOUT	GLUMMEST	GLYPH	GOA	GOBIOID
GLOUTED	GLUMNESS	GLYPHIC	GOAD	GOBLET
GLOUTING	GLUMNESSES	GLYPHS	GOADED	GOBLETS
GLOUTS	GLUMPIER	GLYPTIC	GOADING	GOBLIN
GLOVE	GLUMPIEST	GLYPTICS	GOADS	GOBLINS
GLOVED	GLUMPISH	GMELINITE	GOADSMAN	GOBO
GLOVER	GLUMPS	GMELINITES	GOADSMEN	GOBOES
GLOVERS	GLUMPY	GNAR	GOADSTER	GOBONY
GLOVES	GLUON	GNARL	GOADSTERS	GOBOS
GLOVING	GLUONS	GNARLED	GOAF	GOBS
GLOVINGS	GLUT	GNARLIER	GOAFS	GOBURRA
GLOW	GLUTAEAL	GNARLIEST	GOAL	GOBURRAS
GLOWED	GLUTAEI	GNARLING	GOALBALL	GOBY
GLOWER	GLUTAEUS	GNARLS	GOALBALLS	GOD
GLOWERED	GLUTAMATE	GNARLY	GOALED	GODCHILD
GLOWERING	GLUTAMATES	GNARR	GOALIE	GODCHILDREN
GLOWERS	GLUTAMINE	GNARRED	GOALIES	GODDAM
GLOWING	GLUTAMINES	GNARRING	GOALING	GODDAMN
GLOWINGLY	GLUTEAL	GNARRS	GOALLESS	GODDAMNED
GLOWLAMP	GLUTEI	GNARS	GOALMOUTH	GODDED

The Chambers Dictionary is the authority for many longer words; see *OSW* Introduction, page xii.

GODDEN	GOFFERED	GOLDSPINK	GOMBROS	GOOD
GODDENS	GOFFERING	GOLDSPINKS	GOMERAL	GOODFACED
GODDESS	GOFFERINGS	GOLDSTICK	GOMERALS	GOODIER
GODDESSES	GOFFERS	GOLDSTICKS	GOMERIL	GOODIES
GODDING	GOFFING	GOLDSTONE	GOMERILS	GOODIEST
GODET	GOFFS	GOLDSTONES	GOMOKU	GOODINESS
GODETIA	GOGGLE	GOLDY	GOMOKUS	GOODINESSES
GODETIAS	GOGGLED	GOLE	GOMPA	GOODISH
GODETS	GOGGLER	GOLEM	GOMPAS	GOODLIER
GODFATHER	GOGGLERS	GOLEMS	GOMPHOSES	GOODLIEST
GODFATHERS	GOGGLES	GOLES	GOMPHOSIS	GOODLY
GODHEAD	GOGGLIER	GOLF	GOMUTI	GOODMAN
GODHEADS	GOGGLIEST	GOLFED	GOMUTIS	GOODMEN
GODHOOD	GOGGLING	GOLFER	GOMUTO	GOODNESS
GODHOODS	GOGGLINGS	GOLFERS	GOMUTOS	GOODNESSES
GODLESS	GOGGLY	GOLFIANA	GON	GOODNIGHT
GODLESSLY	GOGLET	GOLFIANAS	GONAD	GOODNIGHTS
GODLIER	GOGLETS	GOLFING	GONADAL	GOODS
GODLIEST	GOGO	GOLFINGS	GONADIAL	GOODSIRE
GODLIKE	GOIER	GOLFS	GONADIC	GOODSIRES
GODLILY	GOIEST	GOLIARD	GONADS	GOODTIME
GODLINESS	GOING	GOLIARDIC	GONDELAY	GOODWIFE
GODLINESSES	GOINGS	GOLIARDIES	GONDELAYS	GOODWILL
GODLING	GOITER	GOLIARDS	GONDOLA	GOODWILLS
GODLINGS	GOITERS	GOLIARDY	GONDOLAS	GOODWIVES
GODLY	GOITRE	GOLIAS	GONDOLIER	GOODY
GODMOTHER	GOITRED	GOLIASED	GONDOLIERS	GOODYEAR
GODMOTHERS	GOITRES	GOLIASES	GONE	GOODYEARS
GODOWN	GOITROUS	GOLIASING	GONENESS	GOOEY
GODOWNS	GOLD	GOLLAN	GONENESSES	GOOF
GODPARENT	GOLDARN	GOLLAND	GONER	GOOFBALL
GODPARENTS	GOLDCREST	GOLLANDS	GONERS	GOOFBALLS
GODROON	GOLDCRESTS	GOLLANS	GONFALON	GOOFED
GODROONED	GOLDEN	GOLLAR	GONFALONS	GOOFIER
GODROONS	GOLDENED	GOLLARED	GONFANON	GOOFIEST
GODS	GOLDENER	GOLLARING	GONFANONS	GOOFILY
GODSEND	GOLDENEST	GOLLARS	GONG	GOOFINESS
GODSENDS	GOLDENING	GOLLER	GONGED	GOOFINESSES
GODSHIP	GOLDENLY	GOLLERED	GONGING	GOOFING
GODSHIPS	GOLDENROD	GOLLERING	GONGS	GOOFS
GODSO	GOLDENRODS	GOLLERS	GONGSTER	GOOFY
GODSON	GOLDENS	GOLLIES	GONGSTERS	GOOGLE
GODSONS	GOLDER	GOLLIWOG	GONIA	GOOGLED
GODSOS	GOLDEST	GOLLIWOGS	GONIATITE	GOOGLES
GODSPEED	GOLDEYE	GOLLOP	GONIATITES	GOOGLIES
GODSPEEDS	GOLDEYES	GOLLOPED	GONIDIA	GOOGLING
GODWARD	GOLDFIELD	GOLLOPING	GONIDIAL	GOOGLY
GODWARDS	GOLDFIELDS	GOLLOPS	GONIDIC	GOOGOL
GODWIT	GOLDFINCH	GOLLY	GONIDIUM	GOOGOLS
GODWITS	GOLDFINCHES	GOLLYWOG	GONION	GOOIER
GOE	GOLDFINNIES	GOLLYWOGS	GONK	GOOIEST
GOEL	GOLDFINNY	GOLOMYNKA	GONKS	GOOK
GOELS	GOLDFISH	GOLOMYNKAS	GONNA	GOOKS
GOER	GOLDFISHES	GOLOSH	GONOCOCCI	GOOL
GOERS	GOLDIER	GOLOSHED	GONOCYTE	GOOLD
GOES	GOLDIEST	GOLOSHES	GONOCYTES	GOOLDS
GOETHITE	GOLDISH	GOLOSHING	GONOPHORE	GOOLEY
GOETHITES	GOLDLESS	GOLOSHOES	GONOPHORES	GOOLEYS
GOETIC	GOLDMINER	GOLP	GONORRHEA	GOOLIE
GOETIES	GOLDMINERS	GOLPE	GONORRHEAS	GOOLIES
GOETY	GOLDS	GOLPES	GONS	GOOLS
GOEY	GOLDSINNIES	GOLPS	GONYS	GOOLY
GOFER	GOLDSINNY	GOMBEEN	GONYSES	GOON
GOFERS	GOLDSIZE	GOMBEENS	GONZO	GOONDA
GOFF	GOLDSIZES	GOMBO	GOO	GOONDAS
GOFFED	GOLDSMITH	GOMBOS	GOOBER	GOONEY
GOFFER	GOLDSMITHS	GOMBRO	GOOBERS	GOONEYS

The Chambers Dictionary is the authority for many longer words; see *OSW* Introduction, page xii.

GOONS	GORGIO	GOSPELISING	GOURDE	GOWLING
GOOP	GORGIOS	GOSPELIZE	GOURDES	GOWLS
GOOPIER	GORGON	GOSPELIZED	GOURDIER	GOWN
GOOPIEST	GORGONEIA	GOSPELIZES	GOURDIEST	GOWNBOY
GOOPS	GORGONIAN	GOSPELIZING	GOURDS	GOWNBOYS
GOOPY	GORGONIANS	GOSPELLED	GOURDY	GOWNED
GOOR	GORGONISE	GOSPELLER	GOURMAND	GOWNING
GOOROO	GORGONISED	GOSPELLERS	GOURMANDS	GOWNMAN
GOOROOS	GORGONISES	GOSPELLING	GOURMET	GOWNMEN
GOORS	GORGONISING	GOSPELS	GOURMETS	GOWNS
GOOS	GORGONIZE	GOSPODAR	GOUSTIER	GOWNSMAN
GOOSANDER	GORGONIZED	GOSPODARS	GOUSTIEST	GOWNSMEN
GOOSANDERS	GORGONIZES	GOSSAMER	GOUSTROUS	GOWPEN
GOOSE	GORGONIZING	GOSSAMERS	GOUSTY	GOWPENFUL
GOOSED	GORGONS	GOSSAMERY	GOUT	GOWPENFULS
GOOSEFOOT	GORIER	GOSSAN	GOUTFLIES	GOWPENS
GOOSEFOOTS	GORIEST	GOSSANS	GOUTFLY	GOY
GOOSEGOB	GORILLA	GOSSE	GOUTIER	GOYIM
GOOSEGOBS	GORILLAS	GOSSES	GOUTIEST	GOYISCH
GOOSEGOG	GORILLIAN	GOSSIB	GOUTINESS	GOYISH
GOOSEGOGS	GORILLINE	GOSSIBS	GOUTINESSES	GOYS
GOOSEHERD	GORILLOID	GOSSIP	GOUTS	GOZZAN
GOOSEHERDS	GORILY	GOSSIPED	GOUTTE	GOZZANS
GOOSERIES	GORINESS	GOSSIPING	GOUTTES	GRAAL
GOOSERY	GORINESSES	GOSSIPINGS	GOUTWEED	GRAALS
GOOSES	GORING	GOSSIPRIES	GOUTWEEDS	GRAB
GOOSEY	GORINGS	GOSSIPRY	GOUTWORT	GRABBED
GOOSEYS	GORM	GOSSIPS	GOUTWORTS	GRABBER
GOOSIER	GORMAND	GOSSIPY	GOUTY	GRABBERS
GOOSIES	GORMANDS	GOSSOON	GOV	GRABBING
GOOSIEST	GORMED	GOSSOONS	GOVERN	GRABBLE
GOOSING	GORMIER	GOSSYPINE	GOVERNALL	GRABBLED
GOOSY	GORMIEST	GOSSYPOL	GOVERNALLS	GRABBLER
GOPAK	GORMING	GOSSYPOLS	GOVERNED	GRABBLERS
GOPAKS	GORMLESS	GOT	GOVERNESS	GRABBLES
GOPHER	GORMS	GOTHIC	GOVERNESSED	GRABBLING
GOPHERED	GORMY	GOTHICISE	GOVERNESSES	GRABEN
GOPHERING	GORP	GOTHICISED	GOVERNESSING	GRABENS
GOPHERS	GORPED	GOTHICISES	GOVERNING	GRABS
GOPURA	GORPING	GOTHICISING	GOVERNOR	GRACE
GOPURAM	GORPS	GOTHICIZE	GOVERNORS	GRACED
GOPURAMS	GORSE	GOTHICIZED	GOVERNS	GRACEFUL
GOPURAS	GORSEDD	GOTHICIZES	GOVS	GRACELESS
GORAL	GORSEDDS	GOTHICIZING	GOWAN	GRACES
GORALS	GORSES	GOTHITE	GOWANED	GRACILE
GORAMIES	GORSIER	GOTHITES	GOWANS	GRACILITIES
GORAMY	GORSIEST	GOTTA	GOWANY	GRACILITY
GORBLIMEY	GORSOON	GOTTEN	GOWD	GRACING
GORBLIMY	GORSOONS	GOUACHE	GOWDER	GRACIOSO
GORCOCK	GORSY	GOUACHES	GOWDEST	GRACIOSOS
GORCOCKS	GORY	GOUGE	GOWDS	GRACIOUS
GORCROW	GOS	GOUGED	GOWDSPINK	GRACIOUSES
GORCROWS	GOSH	GOUGERE	GOWDSPINKS	GRACKLE
GORE	GOSHAWK	GOUGERES	GOWF	GRACKLES
GORED	GOSHAWKS	GOUGES	GOWFED	GRAD
GORES	GOSHT	GOUGING	GOWFER	GRADABLE
GORGE	GOSHTS	GOUJEERS	GOWFERS	GRADABLES
GORGED	GOSLARITE	GOUJONS	GOWFING	GRADATE
GORGEOUS	GOSLARITES	GOUK	GOWFS	GRADATED
GORGERIN	GOSLET	GOUKS	GOWK	GRADATES
GORGERINS	GOSLETS	GOULASH	GOWKS	GRADATIM
GORGES	GOSLING	GOULASHES	GOWL	GRADATING
GORGET	GOSLINGS	GOURA	GOWLAN	GRADATION
GORGETS	GOSPEL	GOURAMI	GOWLAND	GRADATIONS
GORGIA	GOSPELISE	GOURAMIS	GOWLANDS	GRADATORY
GORGIAS	GOSPELISED	GOURAS	GOWLANS	GRADDAN
GORGING	GOSPELISES	GOURD	GOWLED	GRADDANED

The Chambers Dictionary is the authority for many longer words; see *OSW* Introduction, page xii.

GRADDANING	GRAITHING	GRANDSIRES	GRAPERIES	GRASTE
GRADDANS	GRAITHLY	GRANDSON	GRAPERY	GRAT
GRADE	GRAITHS	GRANDSONS	GRAPES	GRATE
GRADED	GRAKLE	GRANFER	GRAPESEED	GRATED
GRADELY	GRAKLES	GRANFERS	GRAPESEEDS	GRATEFUL
GRADER	GRALLOCH	GRANGE	GRAPESHOT	GRATER
GRADERS	GRALLOCHED	GRANGER	GRAPESHOTS	GRATERS
GRADES	GRALLOCHING	GRANGERS	GRAPETREE	GRATES
GRADIENT	GRALLOCHS	GRANGES	GRAPETREES	GRATICULE
GRADIENTS	GRAM	GRANITA	GRAPEVINE	GRATICULES
GRADIN	GRAMA	GRANITAS	GRAPEVINES	GRATIFIED
GRADINE	GRAMARIES	GRANITE	GRAPEY	GRATIFIER
GRADINES	GRAMARY	GRANITES	GRAPH	GRATIFIERS
GRADING	GRAMARYE	GRANITIC	GRAPHED	GRATIFIES
GRADINI	GRAMARYES	GRANITISE	GRAPHEME	GRATIFY
GRADINO	GRAMAS	GRANITISED	GRAPHEMES	GRATIFYING
GRADINS	GRAMASH	GRANITISES	GRAPHEMIC	GRATIN
GRADS	GRAMASHES	GRANITISING	GRAPHEMICS	GRATINATE
GRADUAL	GRAME	GRANITITE	GRAPHIC	GRATINATED
GRADUALLY	GRAMERCIES	GRANITITES	GRAPHICAL	GRATINATES
GRADUALS	GRAMERCY	GRANITIZE	GRAPHICLY	GRATINATING
GRADUAND	GRAMES	GRANITIZED	GRAPHICS	GRATINE
GRADUANDS	GRAMMA	GRANITIZES	GRAPHING	GRATINEE
GRADUATE	GRAMMAR	GRANITIZING	GRAPHITE	GRATING
GRADUATED	GRAMMARS	GRANITOID	GRAPHITES	GRATINGLY
GRADUATES	GRAMMAS	GRANIVORE	GRAPHITIC	GRATINGS
GRADUATING	GRAMMATIC	GRANIVORES	GRAPHIUM	GRATINS
GRADUATOR	GRAMME	GRANNAM	GRAPHIUMS	GRATIS
GRADUATORS	GRAMMES	GRANNAMS	GRAPHS	GRATITUDE
GRADUS	GRAMOCHE	GRANNIE	GRAPIER	GRATITUDES
GRADUSES	GRAMOCHES	GRANNIED	GRAPIEST	GRATTOIR
GRAFF	GRAMPUS	GRANNIEING	GRAPING	GRATTOIRS
GRAFFED	GRAMPUSES	GRANNIES	GRAPLE	GRATUITIES
GRAFFING	GRAMS	GRANNY	GRAPLES	GRATUITY
GRAFFITI	GRAN	GRANNYING	GRAPNEL	GRATULANT
GRAFFITIS	GRANARIES	GRANOLA	GRAPNELS	GRATULATE
GRAFFITO	GRANARY	GRANOLAS	GRAPPA	GRATULATED
GRAFFS	GRAND	GRANS	GRAPPAS	GRATULATES
GRAFT	GRANDAD	GRANT	GRAPPLE	GRATULATING
GRAFTED	GRANDADDIES	GRANTABLE	GRAPPLED	GRAUNCH
GRAFTER	GRANDADDY	GRANTED	GRAPPLES	GRAUNCHED
GRAFTERS	GRANDADS	GRANTEE	GRAPPLING	GRAUNCHER
GRAFTING	GRANDAM	GRANTEES	GRAPY	GRAUNCHERS
GRAFTINGS	GRANDAMS	GRANTER	GRASP	GRAUNCHES
GRAFTS	GRANDDAD	GRANTERS	GRASPABLE	GRAUNCHING
GRAIL	GRANDDADS	GRANTING	GRASPED	GRAUPEL
GRAILE	GRANDE	GRANTOR	GRASPER	GRAUPELS
GRAILES	GRANDEE	GRANTORS	GRASPERS	GRAVADLAX
GRAILS	GRANDEES	GRANTS	GRASPING	GRAVADLAXES
GRAIN	GRANDER	GRANULAR	GRASPLESS	GRAVAMEN
GRAINAGE	GRANDEST	GRANULARY	GRASPS	GRAVAMINA
GRAINAGES	GRANDEUR	GRANULATE	GRASS	GRAVE
GRAINE	GRANDEURS	GRANULATED	GRASSED	GRAVED
GRAINED	GRANDIOSE	GRANULATES	GRASSER	GRAVEL
GRAINER	GRANDLY	GRANULATING	GRASSERS	GRAVELESS
GRAINERS	GRANDMA	GRANULE	GRASSES	GRAVELLED
GRAINES	GRANDMAMA	GRANULES	GRASSHOOK	GRAVELLING
GRAINIER	GRANDMAMAS	GRANULITE	GRASSHOOKS	GRAVELLY
GRAINIEST	GRANDMAS	GRANULITES	GRASSIER	GRAVELS
GRAINING	GRANDNESS	GRANULOMA	GRASSIEST	GRAVELY
GRAININGS	GRANDNESSES	GRANULOMAS	GRASSING	GRAVEN
GRAINS	GRANDPA	GRANULOMATA	GRASSINGS	GRAVENESS
GRAINY	GRANDPAPA	GRANULOSE	GRASSLAND	GRAVENESSES
GRAIP	GRANDPAPAS	GRANULOUS	GRASSLANDS	GRAVER
GRAIPS	GRANDPAS	GRAPE	GRASSUM	GRAVERS
GRAITH	GRANDS	GRAPED	GRASSUMS	GRAVES
GRAITHED	GRANDSIRE	GRAPELESS	GRASSY	GRAVEST

The Chambers Dictionary is the authority for many longer words; see *OSW* Introduction, page xii.

GRAVEYARD	GREATLY	GREENNESS	GRESE	GRIESLY
GRAVEYARDS	GREATNESS	GREENNESSES	GRESES	GRIESY
GRAVID	GREATNESSES	GREENROOM	GRESSING	GRIEVANCE
GRAVIDITIES	GREATS	GREENROOMS	GRESSINGS	GRIEVANCES
GRAVIDITY	GREAVE	GREENS	GREVE	GRIEVE
GRAVIES	GREAVED	GREENSAND	GREVES	GRIEVED
GRAVING	GREAVES	GREENSANDS	GREW	GRIEVER
GRAVINGS	GREAVING	GREENTH	GREWED	GRIEVERS
GRAVITAS	GREBE	GREENTHS	GREWHOUND	GRIEVES
GRAVITASES	GREBES	GREENWASH	GREWHOUNDS	GRIEVING
GRAVITATE	GRECE	GREENWASHED	GREWING	GRIEVOUS
GRAVITATED	GRECES	GREENWASHES	GREWS	GRIFF
GRAVITATES	GRECIAN	GREENWASHING	GREY	GRIFFE
GRAVITATING	GRECIANS	GREENWEED	GREYBEARD	GRIFFES
GRAVITIES	GRECISE	GREENWEEDS	GREYBEARDS	GRIFFIN
GRAVITON	GRECISED	GREENWOOD	GREYED	GRIFFINS
GRAVITONS	GRECISES	GREENWOODS	GREYER	GRIFFON
GRAVITY	GRECISING	GREENY	GREYEST	GRIFFONS
GRAVLAX	GRECIZE	GREES	GREYHEN	GRIFFS
GRAVLAXES	GRECIZED	GREESE	GREYHENS	GRIFT
GRAVURE	GRECIZES	GREESES	GREYHOUND	GRIFTED
GRAVURES	GRECIZING	GREESING	GREYHOUNDS	GRIFTER
GRAVY	GRECQUE	GREESINGS	GREYING	GRIFTERS
GRAY	GRECQUES	GREET	GREYINGS	GRIFTING
GRAYED	GREE	GREETE	GREYISH	GRIFTS
GRAYER	GREECE	GREETED	GREYLY	GRIG
GRAYEST	GREECES	GREETER	GREYNESS	GRIGGED
GRAYFLIES	GREED	GREETERS	GREYNESSES	GRIGGING
GRAYFLY	GREEDIER	GREETES	GREYS	GRIGRI
GRAYING	GREEDIEST	GREETING	GREYSTONE	GRIGRIS
GRAYLE	GREEDILY	GREETINGS	GREYSTONES	GRIGS
GRAYLES	GREEDS	GREETS	GREYWACKE	GRIKE
GRAYLING	GREEDY	GREFFIER	GREYWACKES	GRIKES
GRAYLINGS	GREEGREE	GREFFIERS	GRIBBLE	GRILL
GRAYS	GREEGREES	GREGALE	GRIBBLES	GRILLADE
GRAYWACKE	GREEING	GREGALES	GRICE	GRILLADES
GRAYWACKES	GREEKING	GREGARIAN	GRICER	GRILLAGE
GRAZE	GREEKINGS	GREGARINE	GRICERS	GRILLAGES
GRAZED	GREEN	GREGARINES	GRICES	GRILLE
GRAZER	GREENBACK	GREGATIM	GRICING	GRILLED
GRAZERS	GREENBACKS	GREGE	GRICINGS	GRILLES
GRAZES	GREENED	GREGO	GRID	GRILLING
GRAZIER	GREENER	GREGOS	GRIDDER	GRILLINGS
GRAZIERS	GREENERIES	GREIGE	GRIDDERS	GRILLS
GRAZING	GREENERS	GREIN	GRIDDLE	GRILLWORK
GRAZINGS	GREENERY	GREINED	GRIDDLES	GRILLWORKS
GRAZIOSO	GREENEST	GREINING	GRIDE	GRILSE
GREASE	GREENFLIES	GREINS	GRIDED	GRILSES
GREASED	GREENFLY	GREISEN	GRIDELIN	GRIM
GREASER	GREENGAGE	GREISENS	GRIDELINS	GRIMACE
GREASERS	GREENGAGES	GREISLY	GRIDES	GRIMACED
GREASES	GREENHAND	GREMIAL	GRIDING	GRIMACES
GREASIER	GREENHANDS	GREMIALS	GRIDIRON	GRIMACING
GREASIES	GREENHORN	GREMLIN	GRIDIRONED	GRIMALKIN
GREASIEST	GREENHORNS	GREMLINS	GRIDIRONING	GRIMALKINS
GREASILY	GREENIE	GREMOLATA	GRIDIRONS	GRIME
GREASING	GREENIER	GREMOLATAS	GRIDLOCK	GRIMED
GREASY	GREENIES	GREN	GRIDLOCKS	GRIMES
GREAT	GREENIEST	GRENADE	GRIDS	GRIMIER
GREATCOAT	GREENING	GRENADES	GRIECE	GRIMIEST
GREATCOATS	GREENINGS	GRENADIER	GRIECED	GRIMILY
GREATEN	GREENISH	GRENADIERS	GRIECES	GRIMINESS
GREATENED	GREENLET	GRENADINE	GRIEF	GRIMINESSES
GREATENING	GREENLETS	GRENADINES	GRIEFFUL	GRIMING
GREATENS	GREENLY	GRENNED	GRIEFLESS	GRIMLY
GREATER	GREENMAIL	GRENNING	GRIEFS	GRIMMER
GREATEST	GREENMAILS	GRENS	GRIESIE	GRIMMEST

The Chambers Dictionary is the authority for many longer words; see *OSW* Introduction, page xii.

GRIMNESS	GRISON	GROGS	GROSSNESS	GROUSES
GRIMNESSES	GRISONS	GROIN	GROSSNESSES	GROUSEST
GRIMOIRE	GRIST	GROINED	GROSSULAR	GROUSING
GRIMOIRES	GRISTLE	GROINING	GROSSULARS	GROUT
GRIMY	GRISTLES	GROININGS	GROT	GROUTED
GRIN	GRISTLIER	GROINS	GROTESQUE	GROUTER
GRIND	GRISTLIEST	GROMA	GROTESQUER	GROUTERS
GRINDED	GRISTLY	GROMAS	GROTESQUES	GROUTIER
GRINDER	GRISTS	GROMET	GROTESQUEST	GROUTIEST
GRINDERIES	GRISY	GROMETS	GROTS	GROUTING
GRINDERS	GRIT	GROMMET	GROTTIER	GROUTINGS
GRINDERY	GRITH	GROMMETS	GROTTIEST	GROUTS
GRINDING	GRITHS	GROMWELL	GROTTO	GROUTY
GRINDINGS	GRITS	GROMWELLS	GROTTOES	GROVE
GRINDS	GRITSTONE	GRONE	GROTTOS	GROVEL
GRINGO	GRITSTONES	GRONED	GROTTY	GROVELED
GRINGOS	GRITTED	GRONEFULL	GROUCH	GROVELER
GRINNED	GRITTER	GRONES	GROUCHED	GROVELERS
GRINNER	GRITTERS	GRONING	GROUCHES	GROVELING
GRINNERS	GRITTEST	GROOF	GROUCHIER	GROVELLED
GRINNING	GRITTIER	GROOFS	GROUCHIEST	GROVELLER
GRINS	GRITTIEST	GROOLIER	GROUCHILY	GROVELLERS
GRIOT	GRITTING	GROOLIEST	GROUCHING	GROVELLING
GRIOTS	GRITTY	GROOLY	GROUCHY	GROVELS
GRIP	GRIVET	GROOM	GROUF	GROVES
GRIPE	GRIVETS	GROOMED	GROUFS	GROVET
GRIPED	GRIZE	GROOMING	GROUGH	GROVETS
GRIPER	GRIZES	GROOMS	GROUGHS	GROW
GRIPERS	GRIZZLE	GROOMSMAN	GROUND	GROWABLE
GRIPES	GRIZZLED	GROOMSMEN	GROUNDAGE	GROWER
GRIPING	GRIZZLER	GROOVE	GROUNDAGES	GROWERS
GRIPINGLY	GRIZZLERS	GROOVED	GROUNDED	GROWING
GRIPLE	GRIZZLES	GROOVER	GROUNDEN	GROWINGS
GRIPPE	GRIZZLIER	GROOVERS	GROUNDER	GROWL
GRIPPED	GRIZZLIES	GROOVES	GROUNDERS	GROWLED
GRIPPER	GRIZZLIEST	GROOVIER	GROUNDHOG	GROWLER
GRIPPERS	GRIZZLING	GROOVIEST	GROUNDHOGS	GROWLERIES
GRIPPES	GRIZZLY	GROOVING	GROUNDING	GROWLERS
GRIPPIER	GROAN	GROOVY	GROUNDINGS	GROWLERY
GRIPPIEST	GROANED	GROPE	GROUNDMAN	GROWLIER
GRIPPING	GROANER	GROPED	GROUNDMEN	GROWLIEST
GRIPPLE	GROANERS	GROPER	GROUNDNUT	GROWLING
GRIPPLES	GROANFUL	GROPERS	GROUNDNUTS	GROWLINGS
GRIPPY	GROANING	GROPES	GROUNDS	GROWLS
GRIPS	GROANINGS	GROPING	GROUNDSEL	GROWLY
GRIPSACK	GROANS	GROPINGLY	GROUNDSELS	GROWN
GRIPSACKS	GROAT	GROSBEAK	GROUP	GROWS
GRIPTAPE	GROATS	GROSBEAKS	GROUPABLE	GROWTH
GRIPTAPES	GROCER	GROSCHEN	GROUPAGE	GROWTHIST
GRIS	GROCERIES	GROSCHENS	GROUPAGES	GROWTHISTS
GRISAILLE	GROCERS	GROSER	GROUPED	GROWTHS
GRISAILLES	GROCERY	GROSERS	GROUPER	GROYNE
GRISE	GROCKLE	GROSERT	GROUPERS	GROYNES
GRISED	GROCKLES	GROSERTS	GROUPIE	GRUB
GRISELY	GRODIER	GROSET	GROUPIES	GRUBBED
GRISEOUS	GRODIEST	GROSETS	GROUPING	GRUBBER
GRISES	GRODY	GROSGRAIN	GROUPINGS	GRUBBERS
GRISETTE	GROG	GROSGRAINS	GROUPIST	GRUBBIER
GRISETTES	GROGGED	GROSS	GROUPISTS	GRUBBIEST
GRISGRIS	GROGGERIES	GROSSART	GROUPLET	GRUBBING
GRISING	GROGGERY	GROSSARTS	GROUPLETS	GRUBBLE
GRISKIN	GROGGIER	GROSSED	GROUPS	GRUBBLED
GRISKINS	GROGGIEST	GROSSER	GROUPY	GRUBBLES
GRISLED	GROGGING	GROSSES	GROUSE	GRUBBLING
GRISLIER	GROGGY	GROSSEST	GROUSED	GRUBBY
GRISLIEST	GROGRAM	GROSSING	GROUSER	GRUBS
GRISLY	GROGRAMS	GROSSLY	GROUSERS	GRUBSTAKE

The Chambers Dictionary is the authority for many longer words; see *OSW* Introduction, page xii.

GRUBSTAKED	GRUMPING	GUANINE	GUDDLING	GUICHETS
GRUBSTAKES	GRUMPS	GUANINES	GUDE	GUID
GRUBSTAKING	GRUMPY	GUANO	GUDEMAN	GUIDABLE
GRUDGE	GRUNGE	GUANOS	GUDEMEN	GUIDAGE
GRUDGED	GRUNGES	GUANS	GUDES	GUIDAGES
GRUDGEFUL	GRUNGIER	GUAR	GUDESIRE	GUIDANCE
GRUDGES	GRUNGIEST	GUARANA	GUDESIRES	GUIDANCES
GRUDGING	GRUNGY	GUARANAS	GUDEWIFE	GUIDE
GRUDGINGS	GRUNION	GUARANI	GUDEWIVES	GUIDEBOOK
GRUE	GRUNIONS	GUARANIES	GUDGEON	GUIDEBOOKS
GRUED	GRUNT	GUARANIS	GUDGEONED	GUIDED
GRUEING	GRUNTED	GUARANTEE	GUDGEONING	GUIDELESS
GRUEL	GRUNTER	GUARANTEED	GUDGEONS	GUIDELINE
GRUELING	GRUNTERS	GUARANTEEING	GUE	GUIDELINES
GRUELINGS	GRUNTING	GUARANTEES	GUENON	GUIDEPOST
GRUELLED	GRUNTINGS	GUARANTIED	GUENONS	GUIDEPOSTS
GRUELLING	GRUNTLE	GUARANTIES	GUERDON	GUIDER
GRUELLINGS	GRUNTLED	GUARANTOR	GUERDONED	GUIDERS
GRUELS	GRUNTLES	GUARANTORS	GUERDONING	GUIDES
GRUES	GRUNTLING	GUARANTY	GUERDONS	GUIDESHIP
GRUESOME	GRUNTS	GUARANTYING	GUEREZA	GUIDESHIPS
GRUESOMER	GRUPPETTI	GUARD	GUEREZAS	GUIDING
GRUESOMEST	GRUPPETTO	GUARDABLE	GUERIDON	GUIDINGS
GRUFE	GRUTCH	GUARDAGE	GUERIDONS	GUIDON
GRUFES	GRUTCHED	GUARDAGES	GUERILLA	GUIDONS
GRUFF	GRUTCHES	GUARDANT	GUERILLAS	GUIDS
GRUFFER	GRUTCHING	GUARDANTS	GUERITE	GUILD
GRUFFEST	GRUTTEN	GUARDED	GUERITES	GUILDER
GRUFFISH	GRYCE	GUARDEDLY	GUERNSEY	GUILDERS
GRUFFLY	GRYCES	GUARDEE	GUERNSEYS	GUILDHALL
GRUFFNESS	GRYDE	GUARDEES	GUERRILLA	GUILDHALLS
GRUFFNESSES	GRYDED	GUARDIAN	GUERRILLAS	GUILDRIES
GRUFTED	GRYDES	GUARDIANS	GUES	GUILDRY
GRUING	GRYDING	GUARDING	GUESS	GUILDS
GRUM	GRYESLY	GUARDLESS	GUESSABLE	GUILDSMAN
GRUMBLE	GRYESY	GUARDRAIL	GUESSED	GUILDSMEN
GRUMBLED	GRYFON	GUARDRAILS	GUESSER	GUILE
GRUMBLER	GRYFONS	GUARDROOM	GUESSERS	GUILED
GRUMBLERS	GRYKE	GUARDROOMS	GUESSES	GUILEFUL
GRUMBLES	GRYKES	GUARDS	GUESSING	GUILELESS
GRUMBLIER	GRYPE	GUARDSHIP	GUESSINGS	GUILER
GRUMBLIEST	GRYPES	GUARDSHIPS	GUESSWORK	GUILERS
GRUMBLING	GRYPHON	GUARDSMAN	GUESSWORKS	GUILES
GRUMBLINGS	GRYPHONS	GUARDSMEN	GUEST	GUILING
GRUMBLY	GRYPT	GUARISH	GUESTED	GUILLEMOT
GRUME	GRYSBOK	GUARISHED	GUESTEN	GUILLEMOTS
GRUMES	GRYSBOKS	GUARISHES	GUESTENED	GUILLOCHE
GRUMLY	GRYSELY	GUARISHING	GUESTENING	GUILLOCHED
GRUMMER	GRYSIE	GUARS	GUESTENS	GUILLOCHES
GRUMMEST	GU	GUAVA	GUESTING	GUILLOCHING
GRUMMET	GUACAMOLE	GUAVAS	GUESTS	GUILT
GRUMMETS	GUACAMOLES	GUAYULE	GUESTWISE	GUILTIER
GRUMNESS	GUACHARO	GUAYULES	GUFF	GUILTIEST
GRUMNESSES	GUACHAROS	GUB	GUFFAW	GUILTILY
GRUMOSE	GUACO	GUBBAH	GUFFAWED	GUILTLESS
GRUMOUS	GUACOS	GUBBAHS	GUFFAWING	GUILTS
GRUMP	GUAIACUM	GUBBINS	GUFFAWS	GUILTY
GRUMPED	GUAIACUMS	GUBBINSES	GUFFIE	GUIMBARD
GRUMPH	GUAN	GUBS	GUFFIES	GUIMBARDS
GRUMPHED	GUANA	GUCK	GUFFS	GUIMP
GRUMPHIE	GUANACO	GUCKIER	GUGA	GUIMPED
GRUMPHIES	GUANACOS	GUCKIEST	GUGAS	GUIMPING
GRUMPHING	GUANAS	GUCKS	GUGGLE	GUIMPS
GRUMPHS	GUANAZOLO	GUCKY	GUGGLED	GUINEA
GRUMPIER	GUANAZOLOS	GUDDLE	GUGGLES	GUINEAS
GRUMPIEST	GUANGO	GUDDLED	GUGGLING	GUIPURE
GRUMPILY	GUANGOS	GUDDLES	GUICHET	GUIPURES

The Chambers Dictionary is the authority for many longer words; see *OSW* Introduction, page xii.

GUIRO	GULPHS	GUNGIEST	GUP	GUSLES
GUIROS	GULPING	GUNGY	GUPPIES	GUSLI
GUISARD	GULPS	GUNHOUSE	GUPPY	GUSLIS
GUISARDS	GULY	GUNHOUSES	GUPS	GUSSET
GUISE	GUM	GUNITE	GUR	GUSSETED
GUISED	GUMBO	GUNITES	GURAMI	GUSSETING
GUISER	GUMBOIL	GUNK	GURAMIS	GUSSETS
GUISERS	GUMBOILS	GUNKS	GURDWARA	GUSSIE
GUISES	GUMBOOT	GUNLAYER	GURDWARAS	GUSSIES
GUISING	GUMBOOTS	GUNLAYERS	GURGE	GUST
GUISINGS	GUMBOS	GUNLESS	GURGES	GUSTABLE
GUITAR	GUMDROP	GUNLOCK	GURGLE	GUSTABLES
GUITARIST	GUMDROPS	GUNLOCKS	GURGLED	GUSTATION
GUITARISTS	GUMMA	GUNMAKER	GURGLES	GUSTATIONS
GUITARS	GUMMATA	GUNMAKERS	GURGLING	GUSTATIVE
GUIZER	GUMMATOUS	GUNMAN	GURGOYLE	GUSTATORY
GUIZERS	GUMMED	GUNMEN	GURGOYLES	GUSTED
GULA	GUMMIER	GUNMETAL	GURJUN	GUSTFUL
GULAG	GUMMIEST	GUNMETALS	GURJUNS	GUSTIE
GULAGS	GUMMINESS	GUNNAGE	GURL	GUSTIER
GULAR	GUMMINESSES	GUNNAGES	GURLED	GUSTIEST
GULAS	GUMMING	GUNNED	GURLET	GUSTINESS
GULCH	GUMMINGS	GUNNEL	GURLETS	GUSTINESSES
GULCHED	GUMMITE	GUNNELS	GURLIER	GUSTING
GULCHES	GUMMITES	GUNNER	GURLIEST	GUSTO
GULCHING	GUMMOSES	GUNNERA	GURLING	GUSTOS
GULDEN	GUMMOSIS	GUNNERAS	GURLS	GUSTS
GULDENS	GUMMOSITIES	GUNNERIES	GURLY	GUSTY
GULE	GUMMOSITY	GUNNERS	GURN	GUT
GULES	GUMMOUS	GUNNERY	GURNARD	GUTBUCKET
GULF	GUMMY	GUNNIES	GURNARDS	GUTBUCKETS
GULFED	GUMNUT	GUNNING	GURNED	GUTCHER
GULFIER	GUMNUTS	GUNNINGS	GURNET	GUTCHERS
GULFIEST	GUMP	GUNNY	GURNETS	GUTFUL
GULFING	GUMPED	GUNPLAY	GURNEY	GUTFULS
GULFS	GUMPHION	GUNPLAYS	GURNEYS	GUTLESS
GULFWEED	GUMPHIONS	GUNPOINT	GURNING	GUTROT
GULFWEEDS	GUMPING	GUNPOINTS	GURNS	GUTROTS
GULFY	GUMPS	GUNPORT	GURRAH	GUTS
GULL	GUMPTION	GUNPORTS	GURRAHS	GUTSED
GULLABLE	GUMPTIONS	GUNPOWDER	GURRIES	GUTSER
GULLED	GUMPTIOUS	GUNPOWDERS	GURRY	GUTSERS
GULLER	GUMS	GUNROOM	GURS	GUTSES
GULLERIES	GUMSHIELD	GUNROOMS	GURU	GUTSFUL
GULLERS	GUMSHIELDS	GUNRUNNER	GURUDOM	GUTSFULS
GULLERY	GUMSHOE	GUNRUNNERS	GURUDOMS	GUTSIER
GULLET	GUMSHOED	GUNS	GURUISM	GUTSIEST
GULLETS	GUMSHOEING	GUNSEL	GURUISMS	GUTSINESS
GULLEY	GUMSHOES	GUNSELS	GURUS	GUTSINESSES
GULLEYED	GUN	GUNSHIP	GURUSHIP	GUTSING
GULLEYING	GUNBOAT	GUNSHIPS	GURUSHIPS	GUTSY
GULLEYS	GUNBOATS	GUNSHOT	GUS	GUTTA
GULLIBLE	GUNCOTTON	GUNSHOTS	GUSH	GUTTAE
GULLIED	GUNCOTTONS	GUNSMITH	GUSHED	GUTTAS
GULLIES	GUNDIES	GUNSMITHS	GUSHER	GUTTATE
GULLING	GUNDY	GUNSTICK	GUSHERS	GUTTATED
GULLISH	GUNFIGHT	GUNSTICKS	GUSHES	GUTTATES
GULLS	GUNFIGHTING	GUNSTOCK	GUSHIER	GUTTATING
GULLY	GUNFIGHTS	GUNSTOCKS	GUSHIEST	GUTTATION
GULLYING	GUNFIRE	GUNSTONE	GUSHING	GUTTATIONS
GULOSITIES	GUNFIRES	GUNSTONES	GUSHINGLY	GUTTED
GULOSITY	GUNFLINT	GUNTER	GUSHY	GUTTER
GULP	GUNFLINTS	GUNTERS	GUSLA	GUTTERED
GULPED	GUNFOUGHT	GUNWALE	GUSLAR	GUTTERING
GULPER	GUNGE	GUNWALES	GUSLARS	GUTTERINGS
GULPERS	GUNGES	GUNYAH	GUSLAS	GUTTERS
GULPH	GUNGIER	GUNYAHS	GUSLE	GUTTIER

The Chambers Dictionary is the authority for many longer words; see *OSW* Introduction, page xii.

GUTTIES	GWINIAD	GYMPED	GYPPOS	GYROCAR
GUTTIEST	GWINIADS	GYMPING	GYPPY	GYROCARS
GUTTING	GWYNIAD	GYMPS	GYPS	GYRODYNE
GUTTLE	GWYNIADS	GYMS	GYPSEOUS	GYRODYNES
GUTTLED	GYAL	GYNAE	GYPSIED	GYROIDAL
GUTTLES	GYALS	GYNAECEUM	GYPSIES	GYROLITE
GUTTLING	GYBE	GYNAECEUMS	GYPSUM	GYROLITES
GUTTURAL	GYBED	GYNAECIA	GYPSUMS	GYROMANCIES
GUTTURALS	GYBES	GYNAECIUM	GYPSY	GYROMANCY
GUTTY	GYBING	GYNAECOID	GYPSYDOM	GYRON
GUTZER	GYELD	GYNAES	GYPSYDOMS	GYRONIC
GUTZERS	GYELDS	GYNANDRIES	GYPSYING	GYRONNY
GUV	GYLDEN	GYNANDRY	GYPSYISM	GYRONS
GUVS	GYM	GYNECIA	GYPSYISMS	GYROPLANE
GUY	GYMBAL	GYNECIUM	GYPSYWORT	GYROPLANES
GUYED	GYMBALS	GYNIE	GYPSYWORTS	GYROS
GUYING	GYMKHANA	GYNIES	GYRAL	GYROSCOPE
GUYLE	GYMKHANAS	GYNNEY	GYRALLY	GYROSCOPES
GUYLED	GYMMAL	GYNNEYS	GYRANT	GYROSE
GUYLER	GYMMALS	GYNNIES	GYRATE	GYROSTAT
GUYLERS	GYMNASIA	GYNNY	GYRATED	GYROSTATS
GUYLES	GYMNASIAL	GYNOCRACIES	GYRATES	GYROUS
GUYLING	GYMNASIC	GYNOCRACY	GYRATING	GYROVAGUE
GUYOT	GYMNASIEN	GYNOECIA	GYRATION	GYROVAGUES
GUYOTS	GYMNASIUM	GYNOECIUM	GYRATIONS	GYRUS
GUYS	GYMNASIUMS	GYNOPHORE	GYRATORY	GYRUSES
GUYSE	GYMNAST	GYNOPHORES	GYRE	GYTE
GUYSES	GYMNASTIC	GYNY	GYRED	GYTES
GUZZLE	GYMNASTICS	GYP	GYRES	GYTRASH
GUZZLED	GYMNASTS	GYPPED	GYRFALCON	GYTRASHES
GUZZLER	GYMNIC	GYPPIE	GYRFALCONS	GYVE
GUZZLERS	GYMNOSOPH	GYPPIES	GYRI	GYVED
GUZZLES	GYMNOSOPHS	GYPPING	GYRING	GYVES
GUZZLING	GYMP	GYPPO	GYRO	GYVING

The Chambers Dictionary is the authority for many longer words; see *OSW* Introduction, page xii.

H

HA	HACKED	HAEMAL	HAGGIS	HAIRCLOTHS
HAAF	HACKEE	HAEMATIC	HAGGISES	HAIRCUT
HAAFS	HACKEES	HAEMATIN	HAGGISH	HAIRCUTS
HAANEPOOT	HACKER	HAEMATINS	HAGGISHLY	HAIRDO
HAANEPOOTS	HACKERIES	HAEMATITE	HAGGLE	HAIRDOS
HAAR	HACKERS	HAEMATITES	HAGGLED	HAIRDRIER
HAARS	HACKERY	HAEMATOID	HAGGLER	HAIRDRIERS
HABANERA	HACKETTE	HAEMATOMA	HAGGLERS	HAIRDRYER
HABANERAS	HACKETTES	HAEMATOMAS	HAGGLES	HAIRDRYERS
HABDABS	HACKING	HAEMIC	HAGGLING	HAIRED
HABERDINE	HACKINGS	HAEMIN	HAGGS	HAIRGRIP
HABERDINES	HACKLE	HAEMINS	HAGIARCHIES	HAIRGRIPS
HABERGEON	HACKLED	HAEMOCOEL	HAGIARCHY	HAIRIER
HABERGEONS	HACKLER	HAEMOCOELS	HAGIOLOGIES	HAIRIEST
HABILABLE	HACKLERS	HAEMOCYTE	HAGIOLOGY	HAIRINESS
HABILE	HACKLES	HAEMOCYTES	HAGLET	HAIRINESSES
HABIT	HACKLET	HAEMONIES	HAGLETS	HAIRING
HABITABLE	HACKLETS	HAEMONY	HAGS	HAIRLESS
HABITABLY	HACKLIER	HAEMOSTAT	HAH	HAIRLIKE
HABITANS	HACKLIEST	HAEMOSTATS	HAHNIUM	HAIRLINE
HABITANT	HACKLING	HAEMS	HAHNIUMS	HAIRLINES
HABITANTS	HACKLY	HAEREMAI	HAICK	HAIRNET
HABITAT	HACKNEY	HAET	HAICKS	HAIRNETS
HABITATS	HACKNEYED	HAETS	HAIDUK	HAIRPIECE
HABITED	HACKNEYING	HAFF	HAIDUKS	HAIRPIECES
HABITING	HACKNEYS	HAFFET	HAIK	HAIRPIN
HABITS	HACKS	HAFFETS	HAIKAI	HAIRPINS
HABITUAL	HACQUETON	HAFFIT	HAIKS	HAIRS
HABITUALS	HACQUETONS	HAFFITS	HAIKU	HAIRSPRAY
HABITUATE	HAD	HAFFLIN	HAIL	HAIRSPRAYS
HABITUATED	HADAL	HAFFLINS	HAILED	HAIRST
HABITUATES	HADDEN	HAFFS	HAILER	HAIRSTED
HABITUATING	HADDIE	HAFNIUM	HAILERS	HAIRSTING
HABITUDE	HADDIES	HAFNIUMS	HAILIER	HAIRSTS
HABITUDES	HADDING	HAFT	HAILIEST	HAIRSTYLE
HABITUE	HADDOCK	HAFTED	HAILING	HAIRSTYLES
HABITUES	HADDOCKS	HAFTING	HAILS	HAIRY
HABITUS	HADE	HAFTS	HAILSHOT	HAITH
HABLE	HADED	HAG	HAILSHOTS	HAJ
HABOOB	HADES	HAGBERRIES	HAILSTONE	HAJES
HABOOBS	HADING	HAGBERRY	HAILSTONES	HAJI
HACEK	HADJ	HAGBOLT	HAILY	HAJIS
HACEKS	HADJES	HAGBOLTS	HAIN	HAJJ
HACHIS	HADJI	HAGBUT	HAINCH	HAJJES
HACHURE	HADJIS	HAGBUTS	HAINCHED	HAJJI
HACHURED	HADROME	HAGDEN	HAINCHES	HAJJIS
HACHURES	HADROMES	HAGDENS	HAINCHING	HAKA
HACHURING	HADRON	HAGDON	HAINED	HAKAM
HACIENDA	HADRONIC	HAGDONS	HAINING	HAKAMS
HACIENDAS	HADRONS	HAGDOWN	HAININGS	HAKAS
HACK	HADROSAUR	HAGDOWNS	HAINS	HAKE
HACKAMORE	HADROSAURS	HAGFISH	HAIQUE	HAKES
HACKAMORES	HADS	HAGFISHES	HAIQUES	HAKIM
HACKBERRIES	HADST	HAGG	HAIR	HAKIMS
HACKBERRY	HAE	HAGGARD	HAIRBELL	HALAL
HACKBOLT	HAECCEITIES	HAGGARDLY	HAIRBELLS	HALALLED
HACKBOLTS	HAECCEITY	HAGGARDS	HAIRBRUSH	HALALLING
HACKBUT	HAEING	HAGGED	HAIRBRUSHES	HALALS
HACKBUTS	HAEM	HAGGING	HAIRCLOTH	HALATION

HALATIONS	HALLAN	HALOTHANES	HAMMERING	HANDCLAP
HALAVAH	HALLANS	HALSE	HAMMERINGS	HANDCLAPS
HALAVAHS	HALLIAN	HALSED	HAMMERKOP	HANDCLASP
HALBERD	HALLIANS	HALSER	HAMMERKOPS	HANDCLASPS
HALBERDS	HALLIARD	HALSERS	HAMMERMAN	HANDCRAFT
HALBERT	HALLIARDS	HALSES	HAMMERMEN	HANDCRAFTS
HALBERTS	HALLING	HALSING	HAMMERS	HANDCUFF
HALCYON	HALLINGS	HALT	HAMMIER	HANDCUFFED
HALCYONS	HALLION	HALTED	HAMMIEST	HANDCUFFING
HALE	HALLIONS	HALTER	HAMMILY	HANDCUFFS
HALED	HALLMARK	HALTERED	HAMMING	HANDED
HALENESS	HALLMARKED	HALTERES	HAMMOCK	HANDER
HALENESSES	HALLMARKING	HALTERING	HAMMOCKS	HANDERS
HALER	HALLMARKS	HALTERS	HAMMY	HANDFAST
HALERS	HALLO	HALTING	HAMOSE	HANDFASTED
HALES	HALLOA	HALTINGLY	HAMOUS	HANDFASTING
HALEST	HALLOAED	HALTINGS	HAMPER	HANDFASTINGS
HALF	HALLOAING	HALTS	HAMPERED	HANDFASTS
HALFA	HALLOAS	HALVA	HAMPERING	HANDFUL
HALFAS	HALLOED	HALVAH	HAMPERS	HANDFULS
HALFEN	HALLOING	HALVAHS	HAMPSTER	HANDGRIP
HALFLIN	HALLOO	HALVAS	HAMPSTERS	HANDGRIPS
HALFLING	HALLOOED	HALVE	HAMS	HANDGUN
HALFLINGS	HALLOOING	HALVED	HAMSTER	HANDGUNS
HALFLINS	HALLOOS	HALVER	HAMSTERS	HANDHOLD
HALFPACE	HALLOS	HALVERS	HAMSTRING	HANDHOLDS
HALFPACES	HALLOUMI	HALVES	HAMSTRINGED	HANDICAP
HALFPENCE	HALLOUMIS	HALVING	HAMSTRINGING	HANDICAPPED
HALFPENNIES	HALLOW	HALYARD	HAMSTRINGS	HANDICAPPING
HALFPENNY	HALLOWED	HALYARDS	HAMSTRUNG	HANDICAPS
HALFS	HALLOWING	HAM	HAMULAR	HANDIER
HALFWAY	HALLOWS	HAMADRYAD	HAMULATE	HANDIEST
HALFWIT	HALLS	HAMADRYADES	HAMULI	HANDILY
HALFWITS	HALLSTAND	HAMADRYADS	HAMULUS	HANDINESS
HALIBUT	HALLSTANDS	HAMAL	HAMZA	HANDINESSES
HALIBUTS	HALLUCES	HAMALS	HAMZAH	HANDING
HALICORE	HALLUX	HAMAMELIS	HAMZAHS	HANDIWORK
HALICORES	HALLWAY	HAMAMELISES	HAMZAS	HANDIWORKS
HALIDE	HALLWAYS	HAMARTIA	HAN	HANDJAR
HALIDES	HALLYON	HAMARTIAS	HANAP	HANDJARS
HALIDOM	HALLYONS	HAMATE	HANAPER	HANDLE
HALIDOMS	HALM	HAMBLE	HANAPERS	HANDLEBAR
HALIEUTIC	HALMA	HAMBLED	HANAPS	HANDLEBARS
HALIEUTICS	HALMAS	HAMBLES	HANCE	HANDLED
HALIMOT	HALMS	HAMBLING	HANCES	HANDLER
HALIMOTE	HALO	HAMBURGER	HANCH	HANDLERS
HALIMOTES	HALOBIONT	HAMBURGERS	HANCHED	HANDLES
HALIMOTS	HALOBIONTS	HAME	HANCHES	HANDLESS
HALING	HALOED	HAMED	HANCHING	HANDLING
HALIOTIS	HALOES	HAMES	HAND	HANDLINGS
HALITE	HALOGEN	HAMEWITH	HANDBAG	HANDLIST
HALITES	HALOGENS	HAMFATTER	HANDBAGGED	HANDLISTS
HALITOSES	HALOID	HAMFATTERED	HANDBAGGING	HANDMADE
HALITOSIS	HALOIDS	HAMFATTERING	HANDBAGGINGS	HANDMAID
HALITOTIC	HALOING	HAMFATTERS	HANDBAGS	HANDMAIDS
HALITOUS	HALON	HAMING	HANDBELL	HANDOUT
HALITUS	HALONS	HAMLET	HANDBELLS	HANDOUTS
HALITUSES	HALOPHILE	HAMLETS	HANDBILL	HANDOVER
HALL	HALOPHILES	HAMMAL	HANDBILLS	HANDOVERS
HALLAL	HALOPHILIES	HAMMALS	HANDBOOK	HANDPLAY
HALLALI	HALOPHILY	HAMMAM	HANDBOOKS	HANDPLAYS
HALLALIS	HALOPHOBE	HAMMAMS	HANDBRAKE	HANDRAIL
HALLALLED	HALOPHOBES	HAMMED	HANDBRAKES	HANDRAILS
HALLALLING	HALOPHYTE	HAMMER	HANDCAR	HANDS
HALLALOO	HALOPHYTES	HAMMERED	HANDCARS	HANDSAW
HALLALOOS	HALOS	HAMMERER	HANDCART	HANDSAWS
HALLALS	HALOTHANE	HAMMERERS	HANDCARTS	HANDSEL

The Chambers Dictionary is the authority for many longer words; see *OSW* Introduction, page xii.

HANDSELLED	HANKING	HARASSINGS	HARDOKES	HARMALINS
HANDSELLING	HANKS	HARBINGER	HARDPARTS	HARMAN
HANDSELS	HANKY	HARBINGERED	HARDS	HARMANS
HANDSET	HANSEL	HARBINGERING	HARDSHELL	HARMATTAN
HANDSETS	HANSELLED	HARBINGERS	HARDSHIP	HARMATTANS
HANDSHAKE	HANSELLING	HARBOR	HARDSHIPS	HARMDOING
HANDSHAKES	HANSELS	HARBORAGE	HARDTACK	HARMDOINGS
HANDSOME	HANSOM	HARBORAGES	HARDTACKS	HARMED
HANDSOMER	HANSOMS	HARBORED	HARDTOP	HARMEL
HANDSOMEST	HANTLE	HARBORER	HARDTOPS	HARMELS
HANDSPIKE	HANTLES	HARBORERS	HARDWARE	HARMFUL
HANDSPIKES	HANUMAN	HARBORING	HARDWARES	HARMFULLY
HANDSTAFF	HANUMANS	HARBORS	HARDWOOD	HARMIN
HANDSTAFFS	HAOMA	HARBOUR	HARDWOODS	HARMINE
HANDSTAND	HAOMAS	HARBOURED	HARDY	HARMINES
HANDSTANDS	HAP	HARBOURER	HARE	HARMING
HANDSTAVES	HAPHAZARD	HARBOURERS	HAREBELL	HARMINS
HANDSTURN	HAPHAZARDS	HARBOURING	HAREBELLS	HARMLESS
HANDSTURNS	HAPLESS	HARBOURS	HARED	HARMONIC
HANDTOWEL	HAPLESSLY	HARD	HAREEM	HARMONICA
HANDTOWELS	HAPLOID	HARDBACK	HAREEMS	HARMONICAS
HANDWORK	HAPLOIDIES	HARDBACKS	HARELD	HARMONICS
HANDWORKS	HAPLOIDY	HARDBAKE	HARELDS	HARMONIES
HANDY	HAPLOLOGIES	HARDBAKES	HAREM	HARMONISE
HANDYMAN	HAPLOLOGY	HARDBALL	HAREMS	HARMONISED
HANDYMEN	HAPLY	HARDBALLS	HARES	HARMONISES
HANDYWORK	HAPPED	HARDBEAM	HAREWOOD	HARMONISING
HANDYWORKS	HAPPEN	HARDBEAMS	HAREWOODS	HARMONIST
HANEPOOT	HAPPENED	HARDBOARD	HARICOT	HARMONISTS
HANEPOOTS	HAPPENING	HARDBOARDS	HARICOTS	HARMONIUM
HANG	HAPPENINGS	HARDEN	HARIGALDS	HARMONIUMS
HANGABLE	HAPPENS	HARDENED	HARIGALS	HARMONIZE
HANGAR	HAPPIED	HARDENER	HARIM	HARMONIZED
HANGARS	HAPPIER	HARDENERS	HARIMS	HARMONIZES
HANGBIRD	HAPPIES	HARDENING	HARING	HARMONIZING
HANGBIRDS	HAPPIEST	HARDENINGS	HARIOLATE	HARMONY
HANGDOG	HAPPILY	HARDENS	HARIOLATED	HARMOST
HANGDOGS	HAPPINESS	HARDER	HARIOLATES	HARMOSTIES
HANGED	HAPPINESSES	HARDEST	HARIOLATING	HARMOSTS
HANGER	HAPPING	HARDFACE	HARISH	HARMOSTY
HANGERS	HAPPY	HARDFACES	HARK	HARMOTOME
HANGFIRE	HAPPYING	HARDGRASS	HARKED	HARMOTOMES
HANGFIRES	HAPS	HARDGRASSES	HARKEN	HARMS
HANGING	HAPTEN	HARDHACK	HARKENED	HARN
HANGINGS	HAPTENS	HARDHACKS	HARKENING	HARNESS
HANGMAN	HAPTERON	HARDHEAD	HARKENS	HARNESSED
HANGMEN	HAPTERONS	HARDHEADS	HARKING	HARNESSES
HANGNAIL	HAPTIC	HARDIER	HARKS	HARNESSING
HANGNAILS	HAPTICS	HARDIEST	HARL	HARNS
HANGNEST	HAQUETON	HARDIHEAD	HARLED	HARO
HANGNESTS	HAQUETONS	HARDIHEADS	HARLEQUIN	HAROS
HANGOUT	HARAM	HARDIHOOD	HARLEQUINED	HAROSET
HANGOUTS	HARAMBEE	HARDIHOODS	HARLEQUINING	HAROSETH
HANGOVER	HARAMBEES	HARDILY	HARLEQUINS	HAROSETHS
HANGOVERS	HARAMS	HARDIMENT	HARLING	HAROSETS
HANGS	HARANGUE	HARDIMENTS	HARLINGS	HARP
HANJAR	HARANGUED	HARDINESS	HARLOT	HARPED
HANJARS	HARANGUER	HARDINESSES	HARLOTRIES	HARPER
HANK	HARANGUERS	HARDISH	HARLOTRY	HARPERS
HANKED	HARANGUES	HARDLINE	HARLOTS	HARPIES
HANKER	HARANGUING	HARDLINER	HARLS	HARPING
HANKERED	HARASS	HARDLINERS	HARM	HARPINGS
HANKERING	HARASSED	HARDLY	HARMALA	HARPIST
HANKERINGS	HARASSER	HARDNESS	HARMALAS	HARPISTS
HANKERS	HARASSERS	HARDNESSES	HARMALIN	HARPOON
HANKIE	HARASSES	HARDNOSED	HARMALINE	HARPOONED
HANKIES	HARASSING	HARDOKE	HARMALINES	HARPOONER

The Chambers Dictionary is the authority for many longer words; see *OSW* Introduction, page xii.

HARPOONERS	HASHING	HATCHETY	HAULIER	HAVOCKING
HARPOONING	HASHISH	HATCHING	HAULIERS	HAVOCS
HARPOONS	HASHISHES	HATCHINGS	HAULING	HAW
HARPS	HASHMARK	HATCHLING	HAULM	HAWBUCK
HARPY	HASHMARKS	HATCHLINGS	HAULMS	HAWBUCKS
HARQUEBUS	HASHY	HATCHMENT	HAULS	HAWED
HARQUEBUSES	HASK	HATCHMENTS	HAULST	HAWFINCH
HARRIDAN	HASKS	HATCHWAY	HAULT	HAWFINCHES
HARRIDANS	HASLET	HATCHWAYS	HAUNCH	HAWING
HARRIED	HASLETS	HATE	HAUNCHED	HAWK
HARRIER	HASP	HATEABLE	HAUNCHES	HAWKBELL
HARRIERS	HASPED	HATED	HAUNCHING	HAWKBELLS
HARRIES	HASPING	HATEFUL	HAUNT	HAWKBIT
HARROW	HASPS	HATEFULLY	HAUNTED	HAWKBITS
HARROWED	HASSAR	HATELESS	HAUNTER	HAWKED
HARROWING	HASSARS	HATER	HAUNTERS	HAWKER
HARROWS	HASSLE	HATERENT	HAUNTING	HAWKERS
HARRUMPH	HASSLED	HATERENTS	HAUNTINGS	HAWKEY
HARRUMPHED	HASSLES	HATERS	HAUNTS	HAWKEYS
HARRUMPHING	HASSLING	HATES	HAURIANT	HAWKIE
HARRUMPHS	HASSOCK	HATFUL	HAURIENT	HAWKIES
HARRY	HASSOCKS	HATFULS	HAUSE	HAWKING
HARRYING	HASSOCKY	HATGUARD	HAUSED	HAWKINGS
HARSH	HAST	HATGUARDS	HAUSES	HAWKISH
HARSHEN	HASTA	HATH	HAUSFRAU	HAWKISHLY
HARSHENED	HASTATE	HATING	HAUSFRAUS	HAWKIT
HARSHENING	HASTATED	HATLESS	HAUSING	HAWKLIKE
HARSHENS	HASTE	HATPEG	HAUSTELLA	HAWKS
HARSHER	HASTED	HATPEGS	HAUSTORIA	HAWKSBILL
HARSHEST	HASTEN	HATPIN	HAUT	HAWKSBILLS
HARSHLY	HASTENED	HATPINS	HAUTBOIS	HAWKWEED
HARSHNESS	HASTENER	HATRACK	HAUTBOY	HAWKWEEDS
HARSHNESSES	HASTENERS	HATRACKS	HAUTBOYS	HAWM
HARSLET	HASTENING	HATRED	HAUTE	HAWMED
HARSLETS	HASTENS	HATREDS	HAUTEUR	HAWMING
HART	HASTES	HATS	HAUTEURS	HAWMS
HARTAL	HASTIER	HATSTAND	HAUYNE	HAWS
HARTALS	HASTIEST	HATSTANDS	HAUYNES	HAWSE
HARTBEES	HASTILY	HATTED	HAVE	HAWSED
HARTBEESES	HASTINESS	HATTER	HAVELOCK	HAWSEHOLE
HARTELY	HASTINESSES	HATTERED	HAVELOCKS	HAWSEHOLES
HARTEN	HASTING	HATTERING	HAVEN	HAWSEPIPE
HARTENED	HASTINGS	HATTERS	HAVENED	HAWSEPIPES
HARTENING	HASTY	HATTING	HAVENING	HAWSER
HARTENS	HAT	HATTINGS	HAVENS	HAWSERS
HARTLESSE	HATABLE	HATTOCK	HAVEOUR	HAWSES
HARTS	HATBAND	HATTOCKS	HAVEOURS	HAWSING
HARTSHORN	HATBANDS	HAUBERK	HAVER	HAWTHORN
HARTSHORNS	HATBOX	HAUBERKS	HAVERED	HAWTHORNS
HARUSPEX	HATBOXES	HAUD	HAVEREL	HAY
HARUSPICES	HATBRUSH	HAUDING	HAVERELS	HAYBAND
HARUSPICIES	HATBRUSHES	HAUDS	HAVERING	HAYBANDS
HARUSPICY	HATCH	HAUGH	HAVERINGS	HAYBOX
HARVEST	HATCHBACK	HAUGHS	HAVERS	HAYBOXES
HARVESTED	HATCHBACKS	HAUGHT	HAVERSACK	HAYCOCK
HARVESTER	HATCHED	HAUGHTIER	HAVERSACKS	HAYCOCKS
HARVESTERS	HATCHEL	HAUGHTIEST	HAVERSINE	HAYED
HARVESTING	HATCHELLED	HAUGHTILY	HAVERSINES	HAYFIELD
HARVESTS	HATCHELLING	HAUGHTY	HAVES	HAYFIELDS
HAS	HATCHELS	HAUL	HAVILDAR	HAYFORK
HASH	HATCHER	HAULAGE	HAVILDARS	HAYFORKS
HASHED	HATCHERIES	HAULAGES	HAVING	HAYING
HASHEESH	HATCHERS	HAULD	HAVINGS	HAYINGS
HASHEESHES	HATCHERY	HAULDS	HAVIOUR	HAYLE
HASHES	HATCHES	HAULED	HAVIOURS	HAYLES
HASHIER	HATCHET	HAULER	HAVOC	HAYLOFT
HASHIEST	HATCHETS	HAULERS	HAVOCKED	HAYLOFTS

The Chambers Dictionary is the authority for many longer words; see *OSW* Introduction, page xii.

HAYMAKER	HEADDRESS	HEADRINGS	HEARE	HEATED
HAYMAKERS	HEADDRESSES	HEADROOM	HEARER	HEATER
HAYMAKING	HEADED	HEADROOMS	HEARERS	HEATERS
HAYMAKINGS	HEADER	HEADROPE	HEARES	HEATH
HAYMOW	HEADERS	HEADROPES	HEARIE	HEATHBIRD
HAYMOWS	HEADFAST	HEADS	HEARING	HEATHBIRDS
HAYRICK	HEADFASTS	HEADSCARF	HEARINGS	HEATHCOCK
HAYRICKS	HEADFRAME	HEADSCARVES	HEARKEN	HEATHCOCKS
HAYRIDE	HEADFRAMES	HEADSET	HEARKENED	HEATHEN
HAYRIDES	HEADGEAR	HEADSETS	HEARKENER	HEATHENRIES
HAYS	HEADGEARS	HEADSHAKE	HEARKENERS	HEATHENRY
HAYSEED	HEADHUNT	HEADSHAKES	HEARKENING	HEATHENS
HAYSEEDS	HEADHUNTED	HEADSHIP	HEARKENS	HEATHER
HAYSEL	HEADHUNTING	HEADSHIPS	HEARS	HEATHERS
HAYSELS	HEADHUNTINGS	HEADSHOT	HEARSAY	HEATHERY
HAYSTACK	HEADHUNTS	HEADSHOTS	HEARSAYS	HEATHIER
HAYSTACKS	HEADIER	HEADSMAN	HEARSE	HEATHIEST
HAYWARD	HEADIEST	HEADSMEN	HEARSED	HEATHS
HAYWARDS	HEADILY	HEADSTALL	HEARSES	HEATHY
HAYWIRE	HEADINESS	HEADSTALLS	HEARSIER	HEATING
HAYWIRES	HEADINESSES	HEADSTICK	HEARSIEST	HEATINGS
HAZARD	HEADING	HEADSTICKS	HEARSING	HEATS
HAZARDED	HEADINGS	HEADSTOCK	HEARSY	HEATSPOT
HAZARDING	HEADLAMP	HEADSTOCKS	HEART	HEATSPOTS
HAZARDIZE	HEADLAMPS	HEADSTONE	HEARTACHE	HEAUME
HAZARDIZES	HEADLAND	HEADSTONES	HEARTACHES	HEAUMES
HAZARDOUS	HEADLANDS	HEADWAY	HEARTBEAT	HEAVE
HAZARDRIES	HEADLEASE	HEADWAYS	HEARTBEATS	HEAVED
HAZARDRY	HEADLEASES	HEADWORD	HEARTBURN	HEAVEN
HAZARDS	HEADLESS	HEADWORDS	HEARTBURNS	HEAVENLIER
HAZE	HEADLIGHT	HEADWORK	HEARTED	HEAVENLIEST
HAZED	HEADLIGHTS	HEADWORKS	HEARTEN	HEAVENLY
HAZEL	HEADLINE	HEADY	HEARTENED	HEAVENS
HAZELLY	HEADLINED	HEAL	HEARTENING	HEAVER
HAZELNUT	HEADLINER	HEALABLE	HEARTENS	HEAVERS
HAZELNUTS	HEADLINERS	HEALD	HEARTFELT	HEAVES
HAZELS	HEADLINES	HEALDED	HEARTH	HEAVIER
HAZER	HEADLINING	HEALDING	HEARTHS	HEAVIES
HAZERS	HEADLOCK	HEALDS	HEARTIER	HEAVIEST
HAZES	HEADLOCKS	HEALED	HEARTIES	HEAVILY
HAZIER	HEADLONG	HEALER	HEARTIEST	HEAVINESS
HAZIEST	HEADMAN	HEALERS	HEARTIKIN	HEAVINESSES
HAZILY	HEADMARK	HEALING	HEARTIKINS	HEAVING
HAZINESS	HEADMARKS	HEALINGLY	HEARTILY	HEAVINGS
HAZINESSES	HEADMEN	HEALINGS	HEARTING	HEAVY
HAZING	HEADMOST	HEALS	HEARTLAND	HEBDOMAD
HAZINGS	HEADNOTE	HEALSOME	HEARTLANDS	HEBDOMADS
HAZY	HEADNOTES	HEALTH	HEARTLESS	HEBE
HE	HEADPEACE	HEALTHFUL	HEARTLET	HEBEN
HEAD	HEADPEACES	HEALTHIER	HEARTLETS	HEBENON
HEADACHE	HEADPHONE	HEALTHIEST	HEARTLING	HEBENONS
HEADACHES	HEADPHONES	HEALTHILY	HEARTLINGS	HEBENS
HEADACHIER	HEADPIECE	HEALTHS	HEARTLY	HEBES
HEADACHIEST	HEADPIECES	HEALTHY	HEARTPEA	HEBETANT
HEADACHY	HEADRACE	HEAME	HEARTPEAS	HEBETATE
HEADAGE	HEADRACES	HEAP	HEARTS	HEBETATED
HEADAGES	HEADRAIL	HEAPED	HEARTSEED	HEBETATES
HEADBAND	HEADRAILS	HEAPIER	HEARTSEEDS	HEBETATING
HEADBANDS	HEADREACH	HEAPIEST	HEARTSOME	HEBETUDE
HEADBOARD	HEADREACHED	HEAPING	HEARTWOOD	HEBETUDES
HEADBOARDS	HEADREACHES	HEAPS	HEARTWOODS	HEBONA
HEADCASE	HEADREACHING	HEAPSTEAD	HEARTY	HEBONAS
HEADCASES	HEADREST	HEAPSTEADS	HEAST	HECATOMB
HEADCHAIR	HEADRESTS	HEAPY	HEASTE	HECATOMBS
HEADCHAIRS	HEADRIG	HEAR	HEASTES	HECH
HEADCLOTH	HEADRIGS	HEARD	HEASTS	HECHT
HEADCLOTHS	HEADRING	HEARDS	HEAT	HECHTING

The Chambers Dictionary is the authority for many longer words; see *OSW* Introduction, page xii.

HECHTS	HEEDING	HEISTERS	HELLEBORES	HELPMEET
HECK	HEEDLESS	HEISTING	HELLED	HELPMEETS
HECKLE	HEEDS	HEISTS	HELLENISE	HELPS
HECKLED	HEEDY	HEJAB	HELLENISED	HELVE
HECKLER	HEEHAW	HEJABS	HELLENISES	HELVED
HECKLERS	HEEHAWED	HEJIRA	HELLENISING	HELVES
HECKLES	HEEHAWING	HEJIRAS	HELLENIZE	HELVETIUM
HECKLING	HEEHAWS	HEJRA	HELLENIZED	HELVETIUMS
HECKLINGS	HEEL	HEJRAS	HELLENIZES	HELVING
HECKS	HEELED	HELCOID	HELLENIZING	HEM
HECOGENIN	HEELER	HELD	HELLER	HEMAL
HECOGENINS	HEELERS	HELE	HELLERS	HEME
HECTARE	HEELING	HELED	HELLFIRE	HEMES
HECTARES	HEELINGS	HELENIUM	HELLFIRES	HEMIALGIA
HECTIC	HEELS	HELENIUMS	HELLHOUND	HEMIALGIAS
HECTICAL	HEEZE	HELES	HELLHOUNDS	HEMICYCLE
HECTICS	HEEZED	HELIAC	HELLICAT	HEMICYCLES
HECTOGRAM	HEEZES	HELIACAL	HELLICATS	HEMIHEDRIES
HECTOGRAMS	HEEZIE	HELIBORNE	HELLIER	HEMIHEDRY
HECTOR	HEEZIES	HELIBUS	HELLIERS	HEMINA
HECTORED	HEEZING	HELIBUSES	HELLING	HEMINAS
HECTORER	HEFT	HELICAL	HELLION	HEMIOLA
HECTORERS	HEFTE	HELICALLY	HELLIONS	HEMIOLAS
HECTORING	HEFTED	HELICES	HELLISH	HEMIOLIA
HECTORINGS	HEFTIER	HELICOID	HELLISHLY	HEMIOLIAS
HECTORISM	HEFTIEST	HELICON	HELLO	HEMIOLIC
HECTORISMS	HEFTILY	HELICONS	HELLOED	HEMIONE
HECTORLY	HEFTINESS	HELICTITE	HELLOING	HEMIONES
HECTORS	HEFTINESSES	HELICTITES	HELLOS	HEMIONUS
HEDDLE	HEFTING	HELIDECK	HELLOVA	HEMIONUSES
HEDDLED	HEFTS	HELIDECKS	HELLS	HEMIOPIA
HEDDLES	HEFTY	HELIDROME	HELLUVA	HEMIOPIAS
HEDDLING	HEGEMONIC	HELIDROMES	HELLWARD	HEMIOPIC
HEDERAL	HEGEMONIES	HELIMAN	HELLWARDS	HEMIOPSIA
HEDERATED	HEGEMONY	HELIMEN	HELM	HEMIOPSIAS
HEDGE	HEGIRA	HELING	HELMED	HEMISPACE
HEDGEBILL	HEGIRAS	HELIODOR	HELMET	HEMISPACES
HEDGEBILLS	HEID	HELIODORS	HELMETED	HEMISTICH
HEDGED	HEIDS	HELIOLOGIES	HELMETS	HEMISTICHS
HEDGEHOG	HEIFER	HELIOLOGY	HELMING	HEMITROPE
HEDGEHOGS	HEIFERS	HELIOSES	HELMINTH	HEMITROPES
HEDGEPIG	HEIGH	HELIOSIS	HELMINTHS	HEMLOCK
HEDGEPIGS	HEIGHT	HELIOSTAT	HELMLESS	HEMLOCKS
HEDGER	HEIGHTEN	HELIOSTATS	HELMS	HEMMED
HEDGEROW	HEIGHTENED	HELIOTYPE	HELMSMAN	HEMMING
HEDGEROWS	HEIGHTENING	HELIOTYPES	HELMSMEN	HEMP
HEDGERS	HEIGHTENS	HELIOTYPIES	HELOT	HEMPEN
HEDGES	HEIGHTS	HELIOTYPY	HELOTAGE	HEMPIER
HEDGIER	HEIL	HELIOZOAN	HELOTAGES	HEMPIES
HEDGIEST	HEINOUS	HELIOZOANS	HELOTISM	HEMPIEST
HEDGING	HEINOUSLY	HELIOZOIC	HELOTISMS	HEMPS
HEDGINGS	HEIR	HELIPAD	HELOTRIES	HEMPY
HEDGY	HEIRDOM	HELIPADS	HELOTRY	HEMS
HEDONIC	HEIRDOMS	HELIPILOT	HELOTS	HEN
HEDONICS	HEIRED	HELIPILOTS	HELP	HENBANE
HEDONISM	HEIRESS	HELIPORT	HELPABLE	HENBANES
HEDONISMS	HEIRESSES	HELIPORTS	HELPED	HENCE
HEDONIST	HEIRING	HELISCOOP	HELPER	HENCHMAN
HEDONISTS	HEIRLESS	HELISCOOPS	HELPERS	HENCHMEN
HEDYPHANE	HEIRLOOM	HELISTOP	HELPFUL	HEND
HEDYPHANES	HEIRLOOMS	HELISTOPS	HELPING	HENDED
HEED	HEIRS	HELIUM	HELPINGS	HENDIADYS
HEEDED	HEIRSHIP	HELIUMS	HELPLESS	HENDIADYSES
HEEDFUL	HEIRSHIPS	HELIX	HELPLINE	HENDING
HEEDFULLY	HEIST	HELIXES	HELPLINES	HENDS
HEEDINESS	HEISTED	HELL	HELPMATE	HENEQUEN
HEEDINESSES	HEISTER	HELLEBORE	HELPMATES	HENEQUENS

The Chambers Dictionary is the authority for many longer words; see *OSW* Introduction, page xii.

HENEQUIN	HEPTAPODIES	HERCYNITES	HERLINGS	HERRINGS
HENEQUINS	HEPTAPODY	HERD	HERLS	HERRY
HENGE	HEPTARCH	HERDBOY	HERM	HERRYING
HENGES	HEPTARCHIES	HERDBOYS	HERMA	HERRYMENT
HENIQUIN	HEPTARCHS	HERDED	HERMAE	HERRYMENTS
HENIQUINS	HEPTARCHY	HERDEN	HERMANDAD	HERS
HENNA	HER	HERDENS	HERMANDADS	HERSALL
HENNAED	HERALD	HERDESS	HERMETIC	HERSALLS
HENNAS	HERALDED	HERDESSES	HERMETICS	HERSE
HENNED	HERALDIC	HERDIC	HERMIT	HERSED
HENNER	HERALDING	HERDICS	HERMITAGE	HERSELF
HENNERIES	HERALDRIES	HERDING	HERMITAGES	HERSES
HENNERS	HERALDRY	HERDMAN	HERMITESS	HERSHIP
HENNERY	HERALDS	HERDMEN	HERMITESSES	HERSHIPS
HENNIER	HERB	HERDS	HERMITS	HERTZ
HENNIES	HERBAGE	HERDSMAN	HERMS	HERTZES
HENNIEST	HERBAGED	HERDSMEN	HERN	HERY
HENNIN	HERBAGES	HERDWICK	HERNIA	HERYE
HENNING	HERBAL	HERDWICKS	HERNIAL	HERYED
HENNINS	HERBALISM	HERE	HERNIAS	HERYES
HENNY	HERBALISMS	HEREABOUT	HERNIATED	HERYING
HENOTIC	HERBALIST	HEREABOUTS	HERNS	HES
HENPECK	HERBALISTS	HEREAFTER	HERNSHAW	HESITANCE
HENPECKED	HERBALS	HEREAFTERS	HERNSHAWS	HESITANCES
HENPECKING	HERBAR	HEREAT	HERO	HESITANCIES
HENPECKS	HERBARIA	HEREAWAY	HEROE	HESITANCY
HENRIES	HERBARIAN	HEREBY	HEROES	HESITANT
HENRY	HERBARIANS	HEREDITIES	HEROIC	HESITATE
HENRYS	HERBARIES	HEREDITY	HEROICAL	HESITATED
HENS	HERBARIUM	HEREFROM	HEROICLY	HESITATES
HENT	HERBARIUMS	HEREIN	HEROICS	HESITATING
HENTING	HERBARS	HERENESS	HEROIN	HESITATOR
HENTS	HERBARY	HERENESSES	HEROINE	HESITATORS
HEP	HERBELET	HEREOF	HEROINES	HESP
HEPAR	HERBELETS	HEREON	HEROINS	HESPED
HEPARIN	HERBICIDE	HERESIES	HEROISE	HESPERID
HEPARINS	HERBICIDES	HERESY	HEROISED	HESPERIDS
HEPARS	HERBIER	HERETIC	HEROISES	HESPING
HEPATIC	HERBIEST	HERETICAL	HEROISING	HESPS
HEPATICAL	HERBIST	HERETICS	HEROISM	HESSIAN
HEPATICS	HERBISTS	HERETO	HEROISMS	HESSIANS
HEPATISE	HERBIVORA	HEREUNDER	HEROIZE	HESSONITE
HEPATISED	HERBIVORE	HEREUNTO	HEROIZED	HESSONITES
HEPATISES	HERBIVORES	HEREUPON	HEROIZES	HEST
HEPATISING	HERBIVORIES	HEREWITH	HEROIZING	HESTERNAL
HEPATITE	HERBIVORY	HERIED	HERON	HESTS
HEPATITES	HERBLESS	HERIES	HERONRIES	HET
HEPATITIS	HERBLET	HERIOT	HERONRY	HETAERA
HEPATITISES	HERBLETS	HERIOTS	HERONS	HETAERAE
HEPATIZE	HERBORISE	HERISSE	HERONSEW	HETAERISM
HEPATIZED	HERBORISED	HERISSON	HERONSEWS	HETAERISMS
HEPATIZES	HERBORISES	HERISSONS	HERONSHAW	HETAIRA
HEPATIZING	HERBORISING	HERITABLE	HERONSHAWS	HETAIRAI
HEPPER	HERBORIST	HERITABLY	HEROON	HETAIRAS
HEPPEST	HERBORISTS	HERITAGE	HEROONS	HETAIRIA
HEPS	HERBORIZE	HERITAGES	HEROSHIP	HETAIRIAS
HEPSTER	HERBORIZED	HERITOR	HEROSHIPS	HETAIRISM
HEPSTERS	HERBORIZES	HERITORS	HERPES	HETAIRISMS
HEPT	HERBORIZING	HERITRESS	HERPETIC	HETAIRIST
HEPTAD	HERBOSE	HERITRESSES	HERPETOID	HETAIRISTS
HEPTADS	HERBOUS	HERITRICES	HERRIED	HETE
HEPTAGLOT	HERBS	HERITRIX	HERRIES	HETERO
HEPTAGLOTS	HERBY	HERITRIXES	HERRIMENT	HETERODOX
HEPTAGON	HERCOGAMIES	HERKOGAMIES	HERRIMENTS	HETERONYM
HEPTAGONS	HERCOGAMY	HERKOGAMY	HERRING	HETERONYMS
HEPTANE	HERCULEAN	HERL	HERRINGER	HETEROPOD
HEPTANES	HERCYNITE	HERLING	HERRINGERS	HETEROPODS

The Chambers Dictionary is the authority for many longer words; see *OSW* Introduction, page xii.

HETEROS	HEXASTICHS	HIDAGES	HIGHBALLED	HILAR
HETEROSES	HEXASTYLE	HIDALGA	HIGHBALLING	HILARIOUS
HETEROSIS	HEXASTYLES	HIDALGAS	HIGHBALLS	HILARITIES
HETEROTIC	HEXED	HIDALGO	HIGHBOY	HILARITY
HETES	HEXENE	HIDALGOS	HIGHBOYS	HILCH
HETHER	HEXENES	HIDDEN	HIGHBROW	HILCHED
HETING	HEXES	HIDDENITE	HIGHBROWS	HILCHES
HETMAN	HEXING	HIDDENITES	HIGHCHAIR	HILCHING
HETMANATE	HEXINGS	HIDDENLY	HIGHCHAIRS	HILD
HETMANATES	HEXOSE	HIDDER	HIGHED	HILDING
HETMANS	HEXOSES	HIDDERS	HIGHER	HILDINGS
HETS	HEXYLENE	HIDE	HIGHERED	HILI
HEUCH	HEXYLENES	HIDED	HIGHERING	HILL
HEUCHS	HEY	HIDEOSITIES	HIGHERS	HILLED
HEUGH	HEYDAY	HIDEOSITY	HIGHEST	HILLFOLK
HEUGHS	HEYDAYS	HIDEOUS	HIGHING	HILLIER
HEUREKA	HEYDUCK	HIDEOUSLY	HIGHISH	HILLIEST
HEUREKAS	HEYDUCKS	HIDEOUT	HIGHJACK	HILLINESS
HEURETIC	HEYED	HIDEOUTS	HIGHJACKED	HILLINESSES
HEURETICS	HEYING	HIDER	HIGHJACKING	HILLING
HEURISM	HEYS	HIDERS	HIGHJACKS	HILLMEN
HEURISMS	HI	HIDES	HIGHLAND	HILLO
HEURISTIC	HIANT	HIDING	HIGHLANDS	HILLOCK
HEURISTICS	HIATUS	HIDINGS	HIGHLIGHT	HILLOCKS
HEVEA	HIATUSES	HIDLING	HIGHLIGHTED	HILLOCKY
HEVEAS	HIBACHI	HIDLINGS	HIGHLIGHTING	HILLOED
HEW	HIBACHIS	HIDLINS	HIGHLIGHTS	HILLOING
HEWED	HIBAKUSHA	HIDROSES	HIGHLY	HILLOS
HEWER	HIBERNAL	HIDROSIS	HIGHMAN	HILLS
HEWERS	HIBERNATE	HIDROTIC	HIGHMEN	HILLSIDE
HEWGH	HIBERNATED	HIDROTICS	HIGHMOST	HILLSIDES
HEWING	HIBERNATES	HIE	HIGHNESS	HILLTOP
HEWINGS	HIBERNATING	HIED	HIGHNESSES	HILLTOPS
HEWN	HIBERNISE	HIEING	HIGHROAD	HILLY
HEWS	HIBERNISED	HIELAMAN	HIGHROADS	HILT
HEX	HIBERNISES	HIELAMANS	HIGHS	HILTED
HEXACHORD	HIBERNISING	HIEMAL	HIGHT	HILTING
HEXACHORDS	HIBERNIZE	HIEMS	HIGHTAIL	HILTS
HEXACT	HIBERNIZED	HIERACIUM	HIGHTAILED	HILUM
HEXACTS	HIBERNIZES	HIERACIUMS	HIGHTAILING	HILUS
HEXAD	HIBERNIZING	HIERARCH	HIGHTAILS	HIM
HEXADIC	HIBISCUS	HIERARCHIES	HIGHTH	HIMATIA
HEXADS	HIBISCUSES	HIERARCHS	HIGHTHS	HIMATION
HEXAFOIL	HIC	HIERARCHY	HIGHTING	HIMATIONS
HEXAFOILS	HICATEE	HIERATIC	HIGHTS	HIMSELF
HEXAGLOT	HICATEES	HIERATICA	HIGHWAY	HIN
HEXAGON	HICCATEE	HIERATICAS	HIGHWAYS	HIND
HEXAGONAL	HICCATEES	HIEROCRAT	HIJAB	HINDBERRIES
HEXAGONS	HICCOUGH	HIEROCRATS	HIJABS	HINDBERRY
HEXAGRAM	HICCOUGHED	HIERODULE	HIJACK	HINDBRAIN
HEXAGRAMS	HICCOUGHING	HIERODULES	HIJACKED	HINDBRAINS
HEXAHEDRA	HICCOUGHS	HIEROGRAM	HIJACKER	HINDER
HEXAMETER	HICCUP	HIEROGRAMS	HIJACKERS	HINDERED
HEXAMETERS	HICCUPED	HIEROLOGIES	HIJACKING	HINDERER
HEXANE	HICCUPING	HIEROLOGY	HIJACKS	HINDERERS
HEXANES	HICCUPS	HIERURGIES	HIJINKS	HINDERING
HEXAPLA	HICCUPY	HIERURGY	HIJRA	HINDERS
HEXAPLAR	HICK	HIES	HIJRAH	HINDFEET
HEXAPLAS	HICKEY	HIGGLE	HIJRAHS	HINDFOOT
HEXAPLOID	HICKEYS	HIGGLED	HIJRAS	HINDHEAD
HEXAPLOIDS	HICKORIES	HIGGLER	HIKE	HINDHEADS
HEXAPOD	HICKORY	HIGGLERS	HIKED	HINDLEG
HEXAPODIES	HICKS	HIGGLES	HIKER	HINDLEGS
HEXAPODS	HICKWALL	HIGGLING	HIKERS	HINDMOST
HEXAPODY	HICKWALLS	HIGGLINGS	HIKES	HINDRANCE
HEXARCH	HID	HIGH	HIKING	HINDRANCES
HEXASTICH	HIDAGE	HIGHBALL	HILA	HINDS

The Chambers Dictionary is the authority for many longer words; see *OSW* Introduction, page xii.

HINDSIGHT	HIRCOSITIES	HISTOID	HOAING	HOBDAYING
HINDSIGHTS	HIRCOSITY	HISTOLOGIES	HOAR	HOBDAYS
HINDWARD	HIRE	HISTOLOGY	HOARD	HOBGOBLIN
HINDWING	HIREABLE	HISTONE	HOARDED	HOBGOBLINS
HINDWINGS	HIREAGE	HISTONES	HOARDER	HOBJOB
HING	HIREAGES	HISTORIAN	HOARDERS	HOBJOBBED
HINGE	HIRED	HISTORIANS	HOARDING	HOBJOBBER
HINGED	HIRELING	HISTORIC	HOARDINGS	HOBJOBBERS
HINGES	HIRELINGS	HISTORIED	HOARDS	HOBJOBBING
HINGING	HIRER	HISTORIES	HOARED	HOBJOBBINGS
HINGS	HIRERS	HISTORIFIED	HOARHEAD	HOBJOBS
HINNIED	HIRES	HISTORIFIES	HOARHEADS	HOBNAIL
HINNIES	HIRING	HISTORIFY	HOARHOUND	HOBNAILED
HINNY	HIRINGS	HISTORIFYING	HOARHOUNDS	HOBNAILING
HINNYING	HIRLING	HISTORISM	HOARIER	HOBNAILS
HINS	HIRLINGS	HISTORISMS	HOARIEST	HOBNOB
HINT	HIRPLE	HISTORY	HOARILY	HOBNOBBED
HINTED	HIRPLED	HISTORYING	HOARINESS	HOBNOBBING
HINTING	HIRPLES	HISTRIO	HOARINESSES	HOBNOBBY
HINTINGLY	HIRPLING	HISTRION	HOARING	HOBNOBS
HINTS	HIRRIENT	HISTRIONS	HOARS	HOBO
HIP	HIRRIENTS	HISTRIOS	HOARSE	HOBODOM
HIPNESS	HIRSEL	HISTS	HOARSELY	HOBODOMS
HIPNESSES	HIRSELLED	HIT	HOARSEN	HOBOED
HIPPARCH	HIRSELLING	HITCH	HOARSENED	HOBOES
HIPPARCHS	HIRSELS	HITCHED	HOARSENING	HOBOING
HIPPED	HIRSLE	HITCHER	HOARSENS	HOBOISM
HIPPER	HIRSLED	HITCHERS	HOARSER	HOBOISMS
HIPPEST	HIRSLES	HITCHES	HOARSEST	HOBOS
HIPPIATRIES	HIRSLING	HITCHIER	HOARY	HOBS
HIPPIATRY	HIRSTIE	HITCHIEST	HOAS	HOC
HIPPIC	HIRSUTE	HITCHILY	HOAST	HOCK
HIPPIE	HIRSUTISM	HITCHING	HOASTED	HOCKED
HIPPIEDOM	HIRSUTISMS	HITCHY	HOASTING	HOCKER
HIPPIEDOMS	HIRUDIN	HITHE	HOASTMAN	HOCKERS
HIPPIER	HIRUDINS	HITHER	HOASTMEN	HOCKEY
HIPPIES	HIRUNDINE	HITHERED	HOASTS	HOCKEYS
HIPPIEST	HIS	HITHERING	HOATZIN	HOCKING
HIPPING	HISH	HITHERS	HOATZINS	HOCKS
HIPPINGS	HISHED	HITHERTO	HOAX	HOCUS
HIPPISH	HISHES	HITHES	HOAXED	HOCUSED
HIPPO	HISHING	HITS	HOAXER	HOCUSES
HIPPOCRAS	HISN	HITTER	HOAXERS	HOCUSING
HIPPOCRASES	HISPID	HITTERS	HOAXES	HOCUSSED
HIPPODAME	HISPIDITIES	HITTING	HOAXING	HOCUSSES
HIPPODAMES	HISPIDITY	HIVE	HOB	HOCUSSING
HIPPOLOGIES	HISS	HIVED	HOBBIES	HOD
HIPPOLOGY	HISSED	HIVELESS	HOBBISH	HODDED
HIPPOS	HISSES	HIVELIKE	HOBBIT	HODDEN
HIPPURIC	HISSING	HIVER	HOBBITRIES	HODDENS
HIPPURITE	HISSINGLY	HIVERS	HOBBITRY	HODDING
HIPPURITES	HISSINGS	HIVES	HOBBITS	HODDLE
HIPPUS	HIST	HIVEWARD	HOBBLE	HODDLED
HIPPUSES	HISTAMINE	HIVEWARDS	HOBBLED	HODDLES
HIPPY	HISTAMINES	HIVING	HOBBLER	HODDLING
HIPPYDOM	HISTED	HIYA	HOBBLERS	HODIERNAL
HIPPYDOMS	HISTIDINE	HIZEN	HOBBLES	HODJA
HIPS	HISTIDINES	HIZENS	HOBBLING	HODJAS
HIPSTER	HISTIE	HIZZ	HOBBLINGS	HODMAN
HIPSTERS	HISTING	HIZZED	HOBBY	HODMANDOD
HIPT	HISTIOID	HIZZES	HOBBYISM	HODMANDODS
HIRABLE	HISTOGEN	HIZZING	HOBBYISMS	HODMEN
HIRAGANA	HISTOGENIES	HO	HOBBYIST	HODOGRAPH
HIRAGANAS	HISTOGENS	HOA	HOBBYISTS	HODOGRAPHS
HIRAGE	HISTOGENY	HOACTZIN	HOBBYLESS	HODOMETER
HIRAGES	HISTOGRAM	HOACTZINS	HOBDAY	HODOMETERS
HIRCINE	HISTOGRAMS	HOAED	HOBDAYED	HODOMETRIES

The Chambers Dictionary is the authority for many longer words; see *OSW* Introduction, page xii.

HODOMETRY	HOIK	HOLISM	HOLSTERS	HOMICIDAL
HODOSCOPE	HOIKED	HOLISMS	HOLT	HOMICIDE
HODOSCOPES	HOIKING	HOLIST	HOLTS	HOMICIDES
HODS	HOIKS	HOLISTIC	HOLY	HOMIER
HOE	HOING	HOLISTS	HOLYDAM	HOMIEST
HOED	HOISE	HOLLA	HOLYDAME	HOMILETIC
HOEDOWN	HOISED	HOLLAND	HOLYDAMES	HOMILETICS
HOEDOWNS	HOISES	HOLLANDS	HOLYDAMS	HOMILIES
HOEING	HOISING	HOLLAS	HOLYSTONE	HOMILIST
HOER	HOIST	HOLLER	HOLYSTONED	HOMILISTS
HOERS	HOISTED	HOLLERED	HOLYSTONES	HOMILY
HOES	HOISTER	HOLLERING	HOLYSTONING	HOMING
HOG	HOISTERS	HOLLERS	HOMAGE	HOMINGS
HOGAN	HOISTING	HOLLIDAM	HOMAGED	HOMINID
HOGANS	HOISTINGS	HOLLIDAMS	HOMAGER	HOMINIDS
HOGBACK	HOISTMAN	HOLLIES	HOMAGERS	HOMINIES
HOGBACKS	HOISTMEN	HOLLO	HOMAGES	HOMINOID
HOGEN	HOISTS	HOLLOA	HOMAGING	HOMINOIDS
HOGENS	HOISTWAY	HOLLOAED	HOMALOID	HOMINY
HOGG	HOISTWAYS	HOLLOAING	HOMALOIDS	HOMME
HOGGED	HOKE	HOLLOAS	HOMBRE	HOMMES
HOGGER	HOKED	HOLLOED	HOMBRES	HOMMOCK
HOGGEREL	HOKES	HOLLOES	HOME	HOMMOCKS
HOGGERELS	HOKEY	HOLLOING	HOMEBOUND	HOMO
HOGGERIES	HOKI	HOLLOS	HOMEBUYER	HOMODONT
HOGGERS	HOKIER	HOLLOW	HOMEBUYERS	HOMODYNE
HOGGERY	HOKIEST	HOLLOWARE	HOMECRAFT	HOMOEOBOX
HOGGET	HOKING	HOLLOWARES	HOMECRAFTS	HOMOEOSES
HOGGETS	HOKIS	HOLLOWED	HOMED	HOMOEOSIS
HOGGIN	HOKKU	HOLLOWER	HOMEFELT	HOMOEOTIC
HOGGING	HOKUM	HOLLOWEST	HOMELAND	HOMOGAMIC
HOGGINGS	HOKUMS	HOLLOWING	HOMELANDS	HOMOGAMIES
HOGGINS	HOLD	HOLLOWLY	HOMELESS	HOMOGAMY
HOGGISH	HOLDBACK	HOLLOWS	HOMELIER	HOMOGENIES
HOGGISHLY	HOLDBACKS	HOLLY	HOMELIEST	HOMOGENY
HOGGS	HOLDEN	HOLLYHOCK	HOMELIKE	HOMOGRAFT
HOGH	HOLDER	HOLLYHOCKS	HOMELILY	HOMOGRAFTS
HOGHOOD	HOLDERBAT	HOLM	HOMELY	HOMOGRAPH
HOGHOODS	HOLDERBATS	HOLMIA	HOMELYN	HOMOGRAPHS
HOGHS	HOLDERS	HOLMIAS	HOMELYNS	HOMOLOG
HOGS	HOLDFAST	HOLMIC	HOMEMAKER	HOMOLOGIES
HOGSHEAD	HOLDFASTS	HOLMIUM	HOMEMAKERS	HOMOLOGS
HOGSHEADS	HOLDING	HOLMIUMS	HOMEOBOX	HOMOLOGUE
HOGTIE	HOLDINGS	HOLMS	HOMEOMERIES	HOMOLOGUES
HOGTIED	HOLDOVER	HOLOCAUST	HOMEOMERY	HOMOLOGY
HOGTIES	HOLDOVERS	HOLOCAUSTS	HOMEOPATH	HOMOMORPH
HOGTYING	HOLDS	HOLOCRINE	HOMEOPATHS	HOMOMORPHS
HOGWARD	HOLE	HOLOGRAM	HOMEOSES	HOMONYM
HOGWARDS	HOLED	HOLOGRAMS	HOMEOSIS	HOMONYMIC
HOGWASH	HOLES	HOLOGRAPH	HOMEOTIC	HOMONYMIES
HOGWASHES	HOLESOM	HOLOGRAPHED	HOMEOWNER	HOMONYMS
HOGWEED	HOLESOME	HOLOGRAPHING	HOMEOWNERS	HOMONYMY
HOGWEEDS	HOLEY	HOLOGRAPHS	HOMER	HOMOPHILE
HOH	HOLIBUT	HOLOPHOTE	HOMERS	HOMOPHILES
HOHED	HOLIBUTS	HOLOPHOTES	HOMES	HOMOPHOBE
HOHING	HOLIDAY	HOLOPHYTE	HOMESICK	HOMOPHOBES
HOHS	HOLIDAYED	HOLOPHYTES	HOMESPUN	HOMOPHONE
HOI	HOLIDAYING	HOLOPTIC	HOMESPUNS	HOMOPHONES
HOICK	HOLIDAYS	HOLOTYPE	HOMESTALL	HOMOPHONIES
HOICKED	HOLIER	HOLOTYPES	HOMESTALLS	HOMOPHONY
HOICKING	HOLIES	HOLOTYPIC	HOMESTEAD	HOMOPHYLIES
HOICKS	HOLIEST	HOLOZOIC	HOMESTEADS	HOMOPHYLY
HOICKSED	HOLILY	HOLP	HOMEWARD	HOMOPLASIES
HOICKSES	HOLINESS	HOLPEN	HOMEWARDS	HOMOPLASY
HOICKSING	HOLINESSES	HOLS	HOMEWORK	HOMOPOLAR
HOIDEN	HOLING	HOLSTER	HOMEWORKS	HOMOS
HOIDENS	HOLINGS	HOLSTERED	HOMEY	HOMOTAXES

The Chambers Dictionary is the authority for many longer words; see *OSW* Introduction, page xii.

HOMOTAXIC	HONKIES	HOOKEY	HOOVES	HORNBEAK
HOMOTAXIS	HONKING	HOOKEYS	HOOVING	HORNBEAKS
HOMOTONIC	HONKS	HOOKIER	HOP	HORNBEAM
HOMOTONIES	HONKY	HOOKIES	HOPBIND	HORNBEAMS
HOMOTONY	HONOR	HOOKIEST	HOPBINDS	HORNBILL
HOMOTYPAL	HONORAND	HOOKING	HOPBINE	HORNBILLS
HOMOTYPE	HONORANDS	HOOKS	HOPBINES	HORNBOOK
HOMOTYPES	HONORARIA	HOOKY	HOPDOG	HORNBOOKS
HOMOTYPIC	HONORARIES	HOOLACHAN	HOPDOGS	HORNBUG
HOMOTYPIES	HONORARY	HOOLACHANS	HOPE	HORNBUGS
HOMOTYPY	HONORED	HOOLEY	HOPED	HORNED
HOMOUSIAN	HONORIFIC	HOOLEYS	HOPEFUL	HORNER
HOMOUSIANS	HONORIFICS	HOOLICAN	HOPEFULLY	HORNERS
HOMUNCLE	HONORING	HOOLICANS	HOPEFULS	HORNET
HOMUNCLES	HONORS	HOOLIER	HOPELESS	HORNETS
HOMUNCULE	HONOUR	HOOLIEST	HOPER	HORNFELS
HOMUNCULES	HONOURED	HOOLIGAN	HOPERS	HORNFUL
HOMUNCULI	HONOURER	HOOLIGANS	HOPES	HORNFULS
HOMY	HONOURERS	HOOLOCK	HOPING	HORNGELD
HON	HONOURING	HOOLOCKS	HOPINGLY	HORNGELDS
HONCHO	HONOURS	HOOLY	HOPLITE	HORNIER
HONCHOS	HONS	HOON	HOPLITES	HORNIEST
HOND	HOO	HOONS	HOPLOLOGIES	HORNINESS
HONDS	HOOCH	HOOP	HOPLOLOGY	HORNINESSES
HONE	HOOCHES	HOOPED	HOPPED	HORNING
HONED	HOOD	HOOPER	HOPPER	HORNINGS
HONER	HOODED	HOOPERS	HOPPERS	HORNISH
HONERS	HOODIE	HOOPING	HOPPIER	HORNIST
HONES	HOODIES	HOOPOE	HOPPIEST	HORNISTS
HONEST	HOODING	HOOPOES	HOPPING	HORNITO
HONESTER	HOODLESS	HOOPS	HOPPINGS	HORNITOS
HONESTEST	HOODLUM	HOORAH	HOPPLE	HORNLESS
HONESTIES	HOODLUMS	HOORAHED	HOPPLED	HORNLET
HONESTLY	HOODMAN	HOORAHING	HOPPLES	HORNLETS
HONESTY	HOODMEN	HOORAHS	HOPPLING	HORNPIPE
HONEWORT	HOODOO	HOORAY	HOPPY	HORNPIPES
HONEWORTS	HOODOOED	HOORAYED	HOPS	HORNS
HONEY	HOODOOING	HOORAYING	HOPSACK	HORNSTONE
HONEYBUN	HOODOOS	HOORAYS	HOPSACKS	HORNSTONES
HONEYBUNS	HOODS	HOORD	HOPSCOTCH	HORNTAIL
HONEYCOMB	HOODWINK	HOORDS	HOPSCOTCHES	HORNTAILS
HONEYCOMBED	HOODWINKED	HOOROO	HORAL	HORNWORK
HONEYCOMBING	HOODWINKING	HOOSEGOW	HORARY	HORNWORKS
HONEYCOMBINGS	HOODWINKS	HOOSEGOWS	HORDE	HORNWORM
HONEYCOMBS	HOOEY	HOOSGOW	HORDED	HORNWORMS
HONEYED	HOOEYS	HOOSGOWS	HORDEIN	HORNWORT
HONEYING	HOOF	HOOSH	HORDEINS	HORNWORTS
HONEYLESS	HOOFBEAT	HOOSHED	HORDEOLUM	HORNWRACK
HONEYMOON	HOOFBEATS	HOOSHES	HORDEOLUMS	HORNWRACKS
HONEYMOONED	HOOFED	HOOSHING	HORDES	HORNY
HONEYMOONING	HOOFER	HOOT	HORDING	HORNYHEAD
HONEYMOONS	HOOFERS	HOOTCH	HORDOCK	HORNYHEADS
HONEYPOT	HOOFING	HOOTCHES	HORDOCKS	HOROLOGE
HONEYPOTS	HOOFLESS	HOOTED	HORE	HOROLOGER
HONEYS	HOOFPRINT	HOOTER	HOREHOUND	HOROLOGERS
HONG	HOOFPRINTS	HOOTERS	HOREHOUNDS	HOROLOGES
HONGI	HOOFROT	HOOTING	HORIZON	HOROLOGIC
HONGING	HOOFROTS	HOOTNANNIES	HORIZONS	HOROLOGIES
HONGIS	HOOFS	HOOTNANNY	HORKEY	HOROLOGY
HONGS	HOOK	HOOTS	HORKEYS	HOROMETRIES
HONIED	HOOKA	HOOVE	HORME	HOROMETRY
HONING	HOOKAH	HOOVED	HORMES	HOROSCOPE
HONK	HOOKAHS	HOOVEN	HORMONAL	HOROSCOPES
HONKED	HOOKAS	HOOVER	HORMONE	HOROSCOPIES
HONKER	HOOKED	HOOVERED	HORMONES	HOROSCOPY
HONKERS	HOOKER	HOOVERING	HORMONIC	HORRENT
HONKIE	HOOKERS	HOOVERS	HORN	HORRIBLE

The Chambers Dictionary is the authority for many longer words; see *OSW* Introduction, page xii.

HORRIBLY	HOSED	HOTELIER	HOUSEBOATS	HOWES
HORRID	HOSEMAN	HOTELIERS	HOUSEBOY	HOWEVER
HORRIDER	HOSEMEN	HOTELS	HOUSEBOYS	HOWF
HORRIDEST	HOSEN	HOTEN	HOUSECOAT	HOWFED
HORRIDLY	HOSEPIPE	HOTFOOT	HOUSECOATS	HOWFF
HORRIFIC	HOSEPIPES	HOTHEAD	HOUSED	HOWFFED
HORRIFIED	HOSES	HOTHEADED	HOUSEFLIES	HOWFFING
HORRIFIES	HOSIER	HOTHEADS	HOUSEFLY	HOWFFS
HORRIFY	HOSIERIES	HOTHOUSE	HOUSEFUL	HOWFING
HORRIFYING	HOSIERS	HOTHOUSES	HOUSEFULS	HOWFS
HORROR	HOSIERY	HOTLINE	HOUSEHOLD	HOWITZER
HORRORS	HOSING	HOTLINES	HOUSEHOLDS	HOWITZERS
HORS	HOSPICE	HOTLY	HOUSEL	HOWK
HORSE	HOSPICES	HOTNESS	HOUSELESS	HOWKED
HORSEBACK	HOSPITAGE	HOTNESSES	HOUSELLED	HOWKER
HORSEBACKS	HOSPITAGES	HOTPOT	HOUSELLING	HOWKERS
HORSECAR	HOSPITAL	HOTPOTS	HOUSELLINGS	HOWKING
HORSECARS	HOSPITALE	HOTS	HOUSELS	HOWKS
HORSED	HOSPITALES	HOTSHOT	HOUSEMAID	HOWL
HORSEFLIES	HOSPITALS	HOTSHOTS	HOUSEMAIDS	HOWLED
HORSEFLY	HOSPITIA	HOTTED	HOUSEMAN	HOWLER
HORSEHAIR	HOSPITIUM	HOTTENTOT	HOUSEMEN	HOWLERS
HORSEHAIRS	HOSPODAR	HOTTENTOTS	HOUSEROOM	HOWLET
HORSEHIDE	HOSPODARS	HOTTER	HOUSEROOMS	HOWLETS
HORSEHIDES	HOSS	HOTTERED	HOUSES	HOWLING
HORSELESS	HOSSES	HOTTERING	HOUSETOP	HOWLINGS
HORSEMAN	HOST	HOTTERS	HOUSETOPS	HOWLS
HORSEMEAT	HOSTA	HOTTEST	HOUSEWIFE	HOWRE
HORSEMEATS	HOSTAGE	HOTTIE	HOUSEWIVES	HOWRES
HORSEMEN	HOSTAGES	HOTTIES	HOUSEWORK	HOWS
HORSEMINT	HOSTAS	HOTTING	HOUSEWORKS	HOWSO
HORSEMINTS	HOSTED	HOTTINGS	HOUSING	HOWSOEVER
HORSEPLAY	HOSTEL	HOTTISH	HOUSINGS	HOWTOWDIE
HORSEPLAYS	HOSTELER	HOUDAH	HOUSLING	HOWTOWDIES
HORSEPOND	HOSTELERS	HOUDAHS	HOUT	HOWZAT
HORSEPONDS	HOSTELLER	HOUDAN	HOUTED	HOX
HORSES	HOSTELLERS	HOUDANS	HOUTING	HOXED
HORSESHOE	HOSTELRIES	HOUF	HOUTINGS	HOXES
HORSESHOES	HOSTELRY	HOUFED	HOUTS	HOXING
HORSETAIL	HOSTELS	HOUFF	HOVE	HOY
HORSETAILS	HOSTESS	HOUFFED	HOVED	HOYA
HORSEWAY	HOSTESSED	HOUFFING	HOVEL	HOYAS
HORSEWAYS	HOSTESSES	HOUFFS	HOVELED	HOYDEN
HORSEWHIP	HOSTESSING	HOUFING	HOVELING	HOYDENISH
HORSEWHIPPED	HOSTILE	HOUFS	HOVELLED	HOYDENISM
HORSEWHIPPING	HOSTILELY	HOUGH	HOVELLER	HOYDENISMS
HORSEWHIPS	HOSTILITIES	HOUGHED	HOVELLERS	HOYDENS
HORSEY	HOSTILITY	HOUGHING	HOVELLING	HOYED
HORSIER	HOSTING	HOUGHS	HOVELS	HOYING
HORSIEST	HOSTINGS	HOUMMOS	HOVEN	HOYS
HORSINESS	HOSTLER	HOUMMOSES	HOVER	HUANACO
HORSINESSES	HOSTLERS	HOUMUS	HOVERED	HUANACOS
HORSING	HOSTLESSE	HOUMUSES	HOVERING	HUAQUERO
HORSINGS	HOSTRIES	HOUND	HOVERPORT	HUAQUEROS
HORSON	HOSTRY	HOUNDED	HOVERPORTS	HUB
HORSONS	HOSTS	HOUNDING	HOVERS	HUBBIES
HORST	HOT	HOUNDS	HOVES	HUBBUB
HORSTS	HOTBED	HOUR	HOVING	HUBBUBOO
HORSY	HOTBEDS	HOURI	HOW	HUBBUBOOS
HORTATION	HOTCH	HOURIS	HOWBE	HUBBUBS
HORTATIONS	HOTCHED	HOURLONG	HOWBEIT	HUBBY
HORTATIVE	HOTCHES	HOURLY	HOWDAH	HUBRIS
HORTATORY	HOTCHING	HOURPLATE	HOWDAHS	HUBRISES
HOS	HOTCHPOT	HOURPLATES	HOWDIE	HUBRISTIC
HOSANNA	HOTCHPOTS	HOURS	HOWDIES	HUBS
HOSANNAS	HOTE	HOUSE	HOWDY	HUCK
HOSE	HOTEL	HOUSEBOAT	HOWE	HUCKABACK

The Chambers Dictionary is the authority for many longer words; see *OSW* Introduction, page xii.

HUCKABACKS	HULKS	HUMECTANT	HUMMING	HUNDREDORS
HUCKLE	HULKY	HUMECTANTS	HUMMINGS	HUNDREDS
HUCKLES	HULL	HUMECTATE	HUMMOCK	HUNDREDTH
HUCKS	HULLED	HUMECTATED	HUMMOCKED	HUNDREDTHS
HUCKSTER	HULLIER	HUMECTATES	HUMMOCKS	HUNG
HUCKSTERED	HULLIEST	HUMECTATING	HUMMOCKY	HUNGER
HUCKSTERIES	HULLING	HUMECTED	HUMMUM	HUNGERED
HUCKSTERING	HULLO	HUMECTING	HUMMUMS	HUNGERFUL
HUCKSTERS	HULLOED	HUMECTIVE	HUMMUS	HUNGERING
HUCKSTERY	HULLOING	HUMECTIVES	HUMMUSES	HUNGERLY
HUDDEN	HULLOS	HUMECTS	HUMOGEN	HUNGERS
HUDDLE	HULLS	HUMEFIED	HUMOGENS	HUNGRIER
HUDDLED	HULLY	HUMEFIES	HUMONGOUS	HUNGRIEST
HUDDLES	HUM	HUMEFY	HUMOR	HUNGRILY
HUDDLING	HUMA	HUMEFYING	HUMORAL	HUNGRY
HUDDUP	HUMAN	HUMERAL	HUMORALLY	HUNK
HUE	HUMANE	HUMERALS	HUMORED	HUNKER
HUED	HUMANELY	HUMERI	HUMORESK	HUNKERED
HUELESS	HUMANER	HUMERUS	HUMORESKS	HUNKERING
HUER	HUMANEST	HUMF	HUMORING	HUNKERS
HUERS	HUMANISE	HUMFED	HUMORIST	HUNKIER
HUES	HUMANISED	HUMFING	HUMORISTS	HUNKIES
HUFF	HUMANISES	HUMFS	HUMORLESS	HUNKIEST
HUFFED	HUMANISING	HUMHUM	HUMOROUS	HUNKS
HUFFIER	HUMANISM	HUMHUMS	HUMORS	HUNKSES
HUFFIEST	HUMANISMS	HUMIC	HUMOUR	HUNKY
HUFFILY	HUMANIST	HUMID	HUMOURED	HUNT
HUFFINESS	HUMANISTS	HUMIDER	HUMOURING	HUNTED
HUFFINESSES	HUMANITIES	HUMIDEST	HUMOURS	HUNTER
HUFFING	HUMANITY	HUMIDIFIED	HUMOUS	HUNTERS
HUFFISH	HUMANIZE	HUMIDIFIES	HUMP	HUNTING
HUFFISHLY	HUMANIZED	HUMIDIFY	HUMPBACK	HUNTINGS
HUFFKIN	HUMANIZES	HUMIDIFYING	HUMPBACKS	HUNTRESS
HUFFKINS	HUMANIZING	HUMIDITIES	HUMPED	HUNTRESSES
HUFFS	HUMANKIND	HUMIDITY	HUMPEN	HUNTS
HUFFY	HUMANKINDS	HUMIDLY	HUMPENS	HUNTSMAN
HUG	HUMANLIKE	HUMIDNESS	HUMPER	HUNTSMEN
HUGE	HUMANLY	HUMIDNESSES	HUMPERS	HUP
HUGELY	HUMANNESS	HUMIDOR	HUMPH	HUPPAH
HUGENESS	HUMANNESSES	HUMIDORS	HUMPHED	HUPPAHS
HUGENESSES	HUMANOID	HUMIFIED	HUMPHING	HUPPED
HUGEOUS	HUMANOIDS	HUMIFIES	HUMPHS	HUPPING
HUGEOUSLY	HUMANS	HUMIFY	HUMPIER	HUPS
HUGER	HUMAS	HUMIFYING	HUMPIES	HURCHEON
HUGEST	HUMBLE	HUMILIANT	HUMPIEST	HURCHEONS
HUGGABLE	HUMBLED	HUMILIATE	HUMPING	HURDEN
HUGGED	HUMBLER	HUMILIATED	HUMPS	HURDENS
HUGGING	HUMBLES	HUMILIATES	HUMPTIES	HURDIES
HUGS	HUMBLESSE	HUMILIATING	HUMPTY	HURDLE
HUGY	HUMBLESSES	HUMILITIES	HUMPY	HURDLED
HUH	HUMBLEST	HUMILITY	HUMS	HURDLER
HUI	HUMBLING	HUMITE	HUMSTRUM	HURDLERS
HUIA	HUMBLINGS	HUMITES	HUMSTRUMS	HURDLES
HUIAS	HUMBLY	HUMLIE	HUMUNGOUS	HURDLING
HUIS	HUMBUG	HUMLIES	HUMUS	HURDLINGS
HUISSIER	HUMBUGGED	HUMMABLE	HUMUSES	HURDS
HUISSIERS	HUMBUGGER	HUMMAUM	HUMUSY	HURL
HUITAIN	HUMBUGGERS	HUMMAUMS	HUNCH	HURLBAT
HUITAINS	HUMBUGGING	HUMMED	HUNCHBACK	HURLBATS
HULA	HUMBUGS	HUMMEL	HUNCHBACKS	HURLED
HULAS	HUMBUZZ	HUMMELLED	HUNCHED	HURLER
HULE	HUMBUZZES	HUMMELLER	HUNCHES	HURLERS
HULES	HUMDINGER	HUMMELLERS	HUNCHING	HURLEY
HULK	HUMDINGERS	HUMMELLING	HUNDRED	HURLEYS
HULKIER	HUMDRUM	HUMMELS	HUNDREDER	HURLIES
HULKIEST	HUMDRUMS	HUMMER	HUNDREDERS	HURLING
HULKING	HUMECT	HUMMERS	HUNDREDOR	HURLINGS

The Chambers Dictionary is the authority for many longer words; see *OSW* Introduction, page xii.

HURLS	HUSKILY	HYALINIZING	HYDROGENS	HYGRODEIK
HURLY	HUSKINESS	HYALITE	HYDROID	HYGRODEIKS
HURRA	HUSKINESSES	HYALITES	HYDROIDS	HYGROLOGIES
HURRAED	HUSKING	HYALOID	HYDROLOGIES	HYGROLOGY
HURRAH	HUSKINGS	HYALONEMA	HYDROLOGY	HYGROPHIL
HURRAHED	HUSKS	HYALONEMAS	HYDROLYSE	HYGROSTAT
HURRAHING	HUSKY	HYBRID	HYDROLYSED	HYGROSTATS
HURRAHS	HUSO	HYBRIDISE	HYDROLYSES	HYING
HURRAING	HUSOS	HYBRIDISED	HYDROLYSING	HYKE
HURRAS	HUSS	HYBRIDISES	HYDROLYTE	HYKES
HURRAY	HUSSAR	HYBRIDISING	HYDROLYTES	HYLDING
HURRAYED	HUSSARS	HYBRIDISM	HYDROLYZE	HYLDINGS
HURRAYING	HUSSES	HYBRIDISMS	HYDROLYZED	HYLE
HURRAYS	HUSSIES	HYBRIDITIES	HYDROLYZES	HYLEG
HURRICANE	HUSSIF	HYBRIDITY	HYDROLYZING	HYLEGS
HURRICANES	HUSSIFS	HYBRIDIZE	HYDROMEL	HYLES
HURRICANO	HUSSY	HYBRIDIZED	HYDROMELS	HYLIC
HURRICANOES	HUSTINGS	HYBRIDIZES	HYDRONAUT	HYLICISM
HURRIED	HUSTLE	HYBRIDIZING	HYDRONAUTS	HYLICISMS
HURRIEDLY	HUSTLED	HYBRIDOMA	HYDROPIC	HYLICIST
HURRIES	HUSTLER	HYBRIDOMAS	HYDROPSIES	HYLICISTS
HURRY	HUSTLERS	HYBRIDOUS	HYDROPSY	HYLISM
HURRYING	HUSTLES	HYBRIDS	HYDROPTIC	HYLISMS
HURRYINGS	HUSTLING	HYBRIS	HYDROPULT	HYLIST
HURST	HUSTLINGS	HYBRISES	HYDROPULTS	HYLISTS
HURSTS	HUSWIFE	HYDATHODE	HYDROS	HYLOBATE
HURT	HUSWIVES	HYDATHODES	HYDROSKI	HYLOBATES
HURTER	HUT	HYDATID	HYDROSKIS	HYLOIST
HURTERS	HUTCH	HYDATIDS	HYDROSOMA	HYLOISTS
HURTFUL	HUTCHED	HYDATOID	HYDROSOMATA	HYLOPHYTE
HURTFULLY	HUTCHES	HYDRA	HYDROSOME	HYLOPHYTES
HURTING	HUTCHING	HYDRAEMIA	HYDROSOMES	HYLOZOISM
HURTLE	HUTIA	HYDRAEMIAS	HYDROSTAT	HYLOZOISMS
HURTLED	HUTIAS	HYDRANGEA	HYDROSTATS	HYLOZOIST
HURTLES	HUTMENT	HYDRANGEAS	HYDROUS	HYLOZOISTS
HURTLESS	HUTMENTS	HYDRANT	HYDROVANE	HYMEN
HURTLING	HUTS	HYDRANTH	HYDROVANES	HYMENAEAL
HURTS	HUTTED	HYDRANTHS	HYDROXIDE	HYMENAEAN
HUSBAND	HUTTING	HYDRANTS	HYDROXIDES	HYMENAL
HUSBANDED	HUTTINGS	HYDRAS	HYDROXY	HYMENEAL
HUSBANDING	HUTZPAH	HYDRATE	HYDROXYL	HYMENEALS
HUSBANDLY	HUTZPAHS	HYDRATED	HYDROXYLS	HYMENEAN
HUSBANDRIES	HUZOOR	HYDRATES	HYDROZOA	HYMENIA
HUSBANDRY	HUZOORS	HYDRATING	HYDROZOAN	HYMENIAL
HUSBANDS	HUZZA	HYDRATION	HYDROZOANS	HYMENIUM
HUSH	HUZZAED	HYDRATIONS	HYDROZOON	HYMENIUMS
HUSHABIED	HUZZAING	HYDRAULIC	HYDYNE	HYMENS
HUSHABIES	HUZZAS	HYDRAULICKED	HYDYNES	HYMN
HUSHABY	HUZZIES	HYDRAULICKING	HYE	HYMNAL
HUSHABYING	HUZZY	HYDRAULICS	HYED	HYMNALS
HUSHED	HWYL	HYDRAZINE	HYEING	HYMNARIES
HUSHER	HWYLS	HYDRAZINES	HYEN	HYMNARY
HUSHERED	HYACINE	HYDREMIA	HYENA	HYMNED
HUSHERING	HYACINES	HYDREMIAS	HYENAS	HYMNIC
HUSHERS	HYACINTH	HYDRIA	HYENS	HYMNING
HUSHES	HYACINTHS	HYDRIAE	HYES	HYMNIST
HUSHIER	HYAENA	HYDRIAS	HYETAL	HYMNISTS
HUSHIEST	HYAENAS	HYDRIC	HYETOLOGIES	HYMNODIES
HUSHING	HYALINE	HYDRIDE	HYETOLOGY	HYMNODIST
HUSHY	HYALINES	HYDRIDES	HYGIENE	HYMNODISTS
HUSK	HYALINISE	HYDRIODIC	HYGIENES	HYMNODY
HUSKED	HYALINISED	HYDRO	HYGIENIC	HYMNOLOGIES
HUSKER	HYALINISES	HYDROCELE	HYGIENICS	HYMNOLOGY
HUSKERS	HYALINISING	HYDROCELES	HYGIENIST	HYMNS
HUSKIER	HYALINIZE	HYDROFOIL	HYGIENISTS	HYNDE
HUSKIES	HYALINIZED	HYDROFOILS	HYGRISTOR	HYNDES
HUSKIEST	HYALINIZES	HYDROGEN	HYGRISTORS	HYOID

The Chambers Dictionary is the authority for many longer words; see *OSW* Introduction, page xii.

HYOSCINE
HYOSCINES
HYP
HYPALGIA
HYPALGIAS
HYPALLAGE
HYPALLAGES
HYPANTHIA
HYPATE
HYPATES
HYPE
HYPED
HYPER
HYPERBOLA
HYPERBOLAS
HYPERBOLE
HYPERBOLES
HYPERCUBE
HYPERCUBES
HYPEREMIA
HYPEREMIAS
HYPEREMIC
HYPERGAMIES
HYPERGAMY
HYPERLINK
HYPERLINKS
HYPERMART
HYPERMARTS
HYPERNYM
HYPERNYMIES
HYPERNYMS
HYPERNYMY
HYPERON
HYPERONS
HYPEROPIA

HYPEROPIAS
HYPERS
HYPERTEXT
HYPERTEXTS
HYPES
HYPHA
HYPHAE
HYPHAL
HYPHEN
HYPHENATE
HYPHENATED
HYPHENATES
HYPHENATING
HYPHENED
HYPHENIC
HYPHENING
HYPHENISE
HYPHENISED
HYPHENISES
HYPHENISING
HYPHENISM
HYPHENISMS
HYPHENIZE
HYPHENIZED
HYPHENIZES
HYPHENIZING
HYPHENS
HYPING
HYPINOSES
HYPINOSIS
HYPNA
HYPNIC
HYPNICS
HYPNOGENIES
HYPNOGENY

HYPNOID
HYPNOIDAL
HYPNOLOGIES
HYPNOLOGY
HYPNONE
HYPNONES
HYPNOSES
HYPNOSIS
HYPNOTEE
HYPNOTEES
HYPNOTIC
HYPNOTICS
HYPNOTISE
HYPNOTISED
HYPNOTISES
HYPNOTISING
HYPNOTISM
HYPNOTISMS
HYPNOTIST
HYPNOTISTS
HYPNOTIZE
HYPNOTIZED
HYPNOTIZES
HYPNOTIZING
HYPNOTOID
HYPNUM
HYPNUMS
HYPO
HYPOBLAST
HYPOBLASTS
HYPOBOLE
HYPOBOLES
HYPOCAUST
HYPOCAUSTS
HYPOCIST

HYPOCISTS
HYPOCOTYL
HYPOCOTYLS
HYPOCRISIES
HYPOCRISY
HYPOCRITE
HYPOCRITES
HYPODERM
HYPODERMA
HYPODERMAS
HYPODERMS
HYPOGAEA
HYPOGAEAL
HYPOGAEAN
HYPOGAEUM
HYPOGEA
HYPOGEAL
HYPOGEAN
HYPOGENE
HYPOGEOUS
HYPOGEUM
HYPOGYNIES
HYPOGYNY
HYPOID
HYPOMANIA
HYPOMANIAS
HYPOMANIC
HYPONASTIES
HYPONASTY
HYPONYM
HYPONYMIES
HYPONYMS
HYPONYMY
HYPOS
HYPOSTYLE

HYPOSTYLES
HYPOTAXES
HYPOTAXIS
HYPOTHEC
HYPOTHECS
HYPOTONIA
HYPOTONIAS
HYPOTONIC
HYPOXEMIA
HYPOXEMIAS
HYPOXEMIC
HYPOXIA
HYPOXIAS
HYPOXIC
HYPPED
HYPPING
HYPS
HYPURAL
HYRACES
HYRACOID
HYRAX
HYRAXES
HYSON
HYSONS
HYSSOP
HYSSOPS
HYSTERIA
HYSTERIAS
HYSTERIC
HYSTERICS
HYSTEROID
HYTHE
HYTHES

I

IAMB	ICHOR	IDEAL	IDIOBLASTS	IDOLIZER
IAMBI	ICHOROUS	IDEALISE	IDIOCIES	IDOLIZERS
IAMBIC	ICHORS	IDEALISED	IDIOCY	IDOLIZES
IAMBICS	ICHTHIC	IDEALISER	IDIOGRAPH	IDOLIZING
IAMBIST	ICHTHYIC	IDEALISERS	IDIOGRAPHS	IDOLS
IAMBISTS	ICHTHYOID	IDEALISES	IDIOLECT	IDOLUM
IAMBS	ICHTHYOIDS	IDEALISING	IDIOLECTS	IDS
IAMBUS	ICHTHYS	IDEALISM	IDIOM	IDYL
IAMBUSES	ICHTHYSES	IDEALISMS	IDIOMATIC	IDYLL
IANTHINE	ICICLE	IDEALIST	IDIOMS	IDYLLIAN
IATROGENIES	ICICLES	IDEALISTS	IDIOPHONE	IDYLLIC
IATROGENY	ICIER	IDEALITIES	IDIOPHONES	IDYLLIST
IBERIS	ICIEST	IDEALITY	IDIOPLASM	IDYLLISTS
IBERISES	ICILY	IDEALIZE	IDIOPLASMS	IDYLLS
IBEX	ICINESS	IDEALIZED	IDIOT	IDYLS
IBEXES	ICINESSES	IDEALIZER	IDIOTCIES	IF
IBICES	ICING	IDEALIZERS	IDIOTCY	IFF
IBIDEM	ICINGS	IDEALIZES	IDIOTIC	IFFIER
IBIS	ICKER	IDEALIZING	IDIOTICAL	IFFIEST
IBISES	ICKERS	IDEALLESS	IDIOTICON	IFFINESS
IBUPROFEN	ICKIER	IDEALLY	IDIOTICONS	IFFINESSES
IBUPROFENS	ICKIEST	IDEALOGUE	IDIOTISH	IFFY
ICE	ICKY	IDEALOGUES	IDIOTISM	IFS
ICEBALL	ICON	IDEALS	IDIOTISMS	IGAD
ICEBALLS	ICONIC	IDEAS	IDIOTS	IGAPO
ICEBERG	ICONIFIED	IDEATE	IDLE	IGAPOS
ICEBERGS	ICONIFIES	IDEATED	IDLED	IGARAPE
ICEBLINK	ICONIFY	IDEATES	IDLEHOOD	IGARAPES
ICEBLINKS	ICONIFYING	IDEATING	IDLEHOODS	IGLOO
ICEBOAT	ICONISE	IDEATION	IDLENESS	IGLOOS
ICEBOATS	ICONISED	IDEATIONS	IDLENESSES	IGNARO
ICEBOUND	ICONISES	IDEATIVE	IDLER	IGNAROES
ICEBOX	ICONISING	IDEE	IDLERS	IGNAROS
ICEBOXES	ICONIZE	IDEES	IDLES	IGNEOUS
ICECAP	ICONIZED	IDEM	IDLESSE	IGNESCENT
ICECAPS	ICONIZES	IDENTIC	IDLESSES	IGNESCENTS
ICED	ICONIZING	IDENTICAL	IDLEST	IGNITABLE
ICEFIELD	ICONOLOGIES	IDENTIFIED	IDLING	IGNITE
ICEFIELDS	ICONOLOGY	IDENTIFIES	IDLY	IGNITED
ICEPACK	ICONOSTAS	IDENTIFY	IDOCRASE	IGNITER
ICEPACKS	ICONOSTASES	IDENTIFYING	IDOCRASES	IGNITERS
ICER	ICONS	IDENTIKIT	IDOL	IGNITES
ICERS	ICTAL	IDENTIKITS	IDOLA	IGNITIBLE
ICES	ICTERIC	IDENTITIES	IDOLATER	IGNITING
ICESTONE	ICTERICAL	IDENTITY	IDOLATERS	IGNITION
ICESTONES	ICTERICALS	IDEOGRAM	IDOLATRIES	IGNITIONS
ICH	ICTERICS	IDEOGRAMS	IDOLATRY	IGNITRON
ICHABOD	ICTERID	IDEOGRAPH	IDOLISE	IGNITRONS
ICHED	ICTERIDS	IDEOGRAPHS	IDOLISED	IGNOBLE
ICHES	ICTERINE	IDEOLOGIC	IDOLISER	IGNOBLER
ICHING	ICTERUS	IDEOLOGIES	IDOLISERS	IGNOBLEST
ICHNEUMON	ICTERUSES	IDEOLOGUE	IDOLISES	IGNOBLY
ICHNEUMONS	ICTIC	IDEOLOGUES	IDOLISING	IGNOMIES
ICHNITE	ICTUS	IDEOLOGY	IDOLISM	IGNOMINIES
ICHNITES	ICTUSES	IDEOMOTOR	IDOLISMS	IGNOMINY
ICHNOLITE	ICY	IDEOPHONE	IDOLIST	IGNOMY
ICHNOLITES	ID	IDEOPHONES	IDOLISTS	IGNORABLE
ICHNOLOGIES	IDE	IDES	IDOLIZE	IGNORAMUS
ICHNOLOGY	IDEA	IDIOBLAST	IDOLIZED	IGNORAMUSES

The Chambers Dictionary is the authority for many longer words; see *OSW* Introduction, page xii.

IGNORANCE
IGNORANCES
IGNORANT
IGNORANTS
IGNORE
IGNORED
IGNORER
IGNORERS
IGNORES
IGNORING
IGUANA
IGUANAS
IGUANID
IGUANIDS
IGUANODON
IGUANODONS
IHRAM
IHRAMS
IJTIHAD
IJTIHADS
IKAT
IKATS
IKEBANA
IKEBANAS
IKON
IKONS
ILEA
ILEAC
ILEITIS
ILEITISES
ILEOSTOMIES
ILEOSTOMY
ILEUM
ILEUS
ILEUSES
ILEX
ILEXES
ILIA
ILIAC
ILIACUS
ILIACUSES
ILICES
ILIUM
ILK
ILKA
ILKADAY
ILKADAYS
ILKS
ILL
ILLAPSE
ILLAPSED
ILLAPSES
ILLAPSING
ILLATION
ILLATIONS
ILLATIVE
ILLATIVES
ILLEGAL
ILLEGALLY
ILLEGIBLE
ILLEGIBLY
ILLIAD
ILLIADS
ILLIBERAL
ILLICIT
ILLICITLY
ILLIMITED

ILLINIUM
ILLINIUMS
ILLIPE
ILLIPES
ILLIQUID
ILLISION
ILLISIONS
ILLITE
ILLITES
ILLNESS
ILLNESSES
ILLOGIC
ILLOGICAL
ILLOGICS
ILLS
ILLTH
ILLTHS
ILLUDE
ILLUDED
ILLUDES
ILLUDING
ILLUME
ILLUMED
ILLUMES
ILLUMINE
ILLUMINED
ILLUMINER
ILLUMINERS
ILLUMINES
ILLUMING
ILLUMINING
ILLUPI
ILLUPIS
ILLUSION
ILLUSIONS
ILLUSIVE
ILLUSORY
ILLUVIA
ILLUVIAL
ILLUVIUM
ILLUVIUMS
ILLY
ILMENITE
ILMENITES
IMAGE
IMAGEABLE
IMAGED
IMAGELESS
IMAGERIES
IMAGERY
IMAGES
IMAGINAL
IMAGINARY
IMAGINE
IMAGINED
IMAGINER
IMAGINERS
IMAGINES
IMAGING
IMAGINGS
IMAGINING
IMAGININGS
IMAGINIST
IMAGINISTS
IMAGISM
IMAGISMS
IMAGIST

IMAGISTIC
IMAGISTS
IMAGO
IMAGOES
IMAGOS
IMAM
IMAMATE
IMAMATES
IMAMS
IMARET
IMARETS
IMARI
IMARIS
IMAUM
IMAUMS
IMBALANCE
IMBALANCES
IMBAR
IMBARK
IMBARKED
IMBARKING
IMBARKS
IMBARRED
IMBARRING
IMBARS
IMBASE
IMBASED
IMBASES
IMBASING
IMBATHE
IMBATHED
IMBATHES
IMBATHING
IMBECILE
IMBECILES
IMBECILIC
IMBED
IMBEDDED
IMBEDDING
IMBEDS
IMBIBE
IMBIBED
IMBIBER
IMBIBERS
IMBIBES
IMBIBING
IMBITTER
IMBITTERED
IMBITTERING
IMBITTERS
IMBODIED
IMBODIES
IMBODY
IMBODYING
IMBORDER
IMBORDERED
IMBORDERING
IMBORDERS
IMBOSK
IMBOSKED
IMBOSKING
IMBOSKS
IMBOSOM
IMBOSOMED
IMBOSOMING
IMBOSOMS
IMBOSS

IMBOSSED
IMBOSSES
IMBOSSING
IMBOWER
IMBOWERED
IMBOWERING
IMBOWERS
IMBRANGLE
IMBRANGLED
IMBRANGLES
IMBRANGLING
IMBRAST
IMBREX
IMBRICATE
IMBRICATED
IMBRICATES
IMBRICATING
IMBRICES
IMBROGLIO
IMBROGLIOS
IMBROWN
IMBROWNED
IMBROWNING
IMBROWNS
IMBRUE
IMBRUED
IMBRUES
IMBRUING
IMBRUTE
IMBRUTED
IMBRUTES
IMBRUTING
IMBUE
IMBUED
IMBUES
IMBUING
IMBURSE
IMBURSED
IMBURSES
IMBURSING
IMIDAZOLE
IMIDAZOLES
IMIDE
IMIDES
IMIDIC
IMINE
IMINES
IMITABLE
IMITANCIES
IMITANCY
IMITANT
IMITANTS
IMITATE
IMITATED
IMITATES
IMITATING
IMITATION
IMITATIONS
IMITATIVE
IMITATOR
IMITATORS
IMMANACLE
IMMANACLED
IMMANACLES
IMMANACLING
IMMANE
IMMANELY

IMMANENCE
IMMANENCES
IMMANENCIES
IMMANENCY
IMMANENT
IMMANITIES
IMMANITY
IMMASK
IMMASKED
IMMASKING
IMMASKS
IMMATURE
IMMEDIACIES
IMMEDIACY
IMMEDIATE
IMMENSE
IMMENSELY
IMMENSER
IMMENSEST
IMMENSITIES
IMMENSITY
IMMERGE
IMMERGED
IMMERGES
IMMERGING
IMMERSE
IMMERSED
IMMERSES
IMMERSING
IMMERSION
IMMERSIONS
IMMESH
IMMESHED
IMMESHES
IMMESHING
IMMEW
IMMEWED
IMMEWING
IMMEWS
IMMIGRANT
IMMIGRANTS
IMMIGRATE
IMMIGRATED
IMMIGRATES
IMMIGRATING
IMMINENCE
IMMINENCES
IMMINENCIES
IMMINENCY
IMMINENT
IMMINGLE
IMMINGLED
IMMINGLES
IMMINGLING
IMMINUTE
IMMISSION
IMMISSIONS
IMMIT
IMMITS
IMMITTED
IMMITTING
IMMIX
IMMIXED
IMMIXES
IMMIXING
IMMIXTURE
IMMIXTURES

The Chambers Dictionary is the authority for many longer words; see *OSW* Introduction, page xii.

IMMOBILE	IMPANEL	IMPEDES	IMPLEACHED	IMPOLICIES
IMMODEST	IMPANELLED	IMPEDING	IMPLEACHES	IMPOLICY
IMMODESTIES	IMPANELLING	IMPEL	IMPLEACHING	IMPOLITE
IMMODESTY	IMPANELS	IMPELLED	IMPLEAD	IMPOLITER
IMMOLATE	IMPANNEL	IMPELLENT	IMPLEADED	IMPOLITEST
IMMOLATED	IMPANNELLED	IMPELLENTS	IMPLEADER	IMPOLITIC
IMMOLATES	IMPANNELLING	IMPELLER	IMPLEADERS	IMPONE
IMMOLATING	IMPANNELS	IMPELLERS	IMPLEADING	IMPONED
IMMOLATOR	IMPARITIES	IMPELLING	IMPLEADS	IMPONENT
IMMOLATORS	IMPARITY	IMPELS	IMPLEDGE	IMPONENTS
IMMOMENT	IMPARK	IMPEND	IMPLEDGED	IMPONES
IMMORAL	IMPARKED	IMPENDED	IMPLEDGES	IMPONING
IMMORALLY	IMPARKING	IMPENDENT	IMPLEDGING	IMPORT
IMMORTAL	IMPARKS	IMPENDING	IMPLEMENT	IMPORTANT
IMMORTALS	IMPARL	IMPENDS	IMPLEMENTED	IMPORTED
IMMOVABLE	IMPARLED	IMPENNATE	IMPLEMENTING	IMPORTER
IMMOVABLES	IMPARLING	IMPERATOR	IMPLEMENTS	IMPORTERS
IMMOVABLY	IMPARLS	IMPERATORS	IMPLETE	IMPORTING
IMMUNE	IMPART	IMPERFECT	IMPLETED	IMPORTS
IMMUNES	IMPARTED	IMPERFECTS	IMPLETES	IMPORTUNE
IMMUNISE	IMPARTER	IMPERIA	IMPLETING	IMPORTUNED
IMMUNISED	IMPARTERS	IMPERIAL	IMPLETION	IMPORTUNES
IMMUNISES	IMPARTIAL	IMPERIALS	IMPLETIONS	IMPORTUNING
IMMUNISING	IMPARTING	IMPERIL	IMPLEX	IMPORTUNINGS
IMMUNITIES	IMPARTS	IMPERILLED	IMPLEXES	IMPOSABLE
IMMUNITY	IMPASSE	IMPERILLING	IMPLEXION	IMPOSE
IMMUNIZE	IMPASSES	IMPERILS	IMPLEXIONS	IMPOSED
IMMUNIZED	IMPASSION	IMPERIOUS	IMPLICATE	IMPOSER
IMMUNIZES	IMPASSIONED	IMPERIUM	IMPLICATED	IMPOSERS
IMMUNIZING	IMPASSIONING	IMPETICOS	IMPLICATES	IMPOSES
IMMUNOGEN	IMPASSIONS	IMPETICOSSED	IMPLICATING	IMPOSING
IMMUNOGENS	IMPASSIVE	IMPETICOSSES	IMPLICIT	IMPOST
IMMURE	IMPASTE	IMPETICOSSING	IMPLIED	IMPOSTER
IMMURED	IMPASTED	IMPETIGINES	IMPLIEDLY	IMPOSTERS
IMMURES	IMPASTES	IMPETIGO	IMPLIES	IMPOSTOR
IMMURING	IMPASTING	IMPETIGOS	IMPLODE	IMPOSTORS
IMMUTABLE	IMPASTO	IMPETRATE	IMPLODED	IMPOSTS
IMMUTABLY	IMPASTOED	IMPETRATED	IMPLODENT	IMPOSTUME
IMP	IMPASTOS	IMPETRATES	IMPLODENTS	IMPOSTUMES
IMPACABLE	IMPATIENS	IMPETRATING	IMPLODES	IMPOSTURE
IMPACT	IMPATIENT	IMPETUOUS	IMPLODING	IMPOSTURES
IMPACTED	IMPAVE	IMPETUS	IMPLORE	IMPOT
IMPACTING	IMPAVED	IMPETUSES	IMPLORED	IMPOTENCE
IMPACTION	IMPAVES	IMPI	IMPLORER	IMPOTENCES
IMPACTIONS	IMPAVID	IMPIES	IMPLORERS	IMPOTENCIES
IMPACTITE	IMPAVIDLY	IMPIETIES	IMPLORES	IMPOTENCY
IMPACTITES	IMPAVING	IMPIETY	IMPLORING	IMPOTENT
IMPACTIVE	IMPAWN	IMPING	IMPLOSION	IMPOTS
IMPACTS	IMPAWNED	IMPINGE	IMPLOSIONS	IMPOUND
IMPAINT	IMPAWNING	IMPINGED	IMPLOSIVE	IMPOUNDED
IMPAINTED	IMPAWNS	IMPINGENT	IMPLOSIVES	IMPOUNDER
IMPAINTING	IMPEACH	IMPINGES	IMPLUNGE	IMPOUNDERS
IMPAINTS	IMPEACHED	IMPINGING	IMPLUNGED	IMPOUNDING
IMPAIR	IMPEACHER	IMPIOUS	IMPLUNGES	IMPOUNDS
IMPAIRED	IMPEACHERS	IMPIOUSLY	IMPLUNGING	IMPRECATE
IMPAIRER	IMPEACHES	IMPIS	IMPLUVIA	IMPRECATED
IMPAIRERS	IMPEACHING	IMPISH	IMPLUVIUM	IMPRECATES
IMPAIRING	IMPEARL	IMPISHLY	IMPLY	IMPRECATING
IMPAIRINGS	IMPEARLED	IMPLANT	IMPLYING	IMPRECISE
IMPAIRS	IMPEARLING	IMPLANTED	IMPOCKET	IMPREGN
IMPALA	IMPEARLS	IMPLANTING	IMPOCKETED	IMPREGNED
IMPALAS	IMPECCANT	IMPLANTS	IMPOCKETING	IMPREGNING
IMPALE	IMPED	IMPLATE	IMPOCKETS	IMPREGNS
IMPALED	IMPEDANCE	IMPLATED	IMPOLDER	IMPRESA
IMPALES	IMPEDANCES	IMPLATES	IMPOLDERED	IMPRESARI
IMPALING	IMPEDE	IMPLATING	IMPOLDERING	IMPRESAS
IMPANATE	IMPEDED	IMPLEACH	IMPOLDERS	IMPRESE

The Chambers Dictionary is the authority for many longer words; see *OSW* Introduction, page xii.

IMPRESES	IMPURPLES	INBREEDINGS	INCH	INCLOSURES
IMPRESS	IMPURPLING	INBREEDS	INCHASE	INCLUDE
IMPRESSE	IMPUTABLE	INBRING	INCHASED	INCLUDED
IMPRESSED	IMPUTABLY	INBRINGING	INCHASES	INCLUDES
IMPRESSES	IMPUTE	INBRINGINGS	INCHASING	INCLUDING
IMPRESSING	IMPUTED	INBRINGS	INCHED	INCLUSION
IMPREST	IMPUTER	INBROUGHT	INCHES	INCLUSIONS
IMPRESTS	IMPUTERS	INBURNING	INCHING	INCLUSIVE
IMPRIMIS	IMPUTES	INBURST	INCHMEAL	INCOGNITO
IMPRINT	IMPUTING	INBURSTS	INCHOATE	INCOGNITOS
IMPRINTED	IMSHI	INBY	INCHOATED	INCOME
IMPRINTING	IMSHY	INBYE	INCHOATES	INCOMER
IMPRINTINGS	IN	INCAGE	INCHOATING	INCOMERS
IMPRINTS	INABILITIES	INCAGED	INCHPIN	INCOMES
IMPRISON	INABILITY	INCAGES	INCHPINS	INCOMING
IMPRISONED	INACTION	INCAGING	INCIDENCE	INCOMINGS
IMPRISONING	INACTIONS	INCAPABLE	INCIDENCES	INCOMMODE
IMPRISONS	INACTIVE	INCAPABLES	INCIDENT	INCOMMODED
IMPROBITIES	INAIDABLE	INCAPABLY	INCIDENTS	INCOMMODES
IMPROBITY	INAMORATA	INCARNATE	INCIPIENT	INCOMMODING
IMPROMPTU	INAMORATAS	INCARNATED	INCIPIT	INCONDITE
IMPROMPTUS	INAMORATO	INCARNATES	INCISE	INCONIE
IMPROPER	INAMORATOS	INCARNATING	INCISED	INCONNU
IMPROV	INANE	INCASE	INCISES	INCONNUE
IMPROVE	INANELY	INCASED	INCISING	INCONNUES
IMPROVED	INANENESS	INCASES	INCISION	INCONNUS
IMPROVER	INANENESSES	INCASING	INCISIONS	INCONY
IMPROVERS	INANER	INCAUTION	INCISIVE	INCORPSE
IMPROVES	INANEST	INCAUTIONS	INCISOR	INCORPSED
IMPROVING	INANIMATE	INCAVE	INCISORS	INCORPSES
IMPROVISE	INANITIES	INCAVED	INCISORY	INCORPSING
IMPROVISED	INANITION	INCAVES	INCISURE	INCORRECT
IMPROVISES	INANITIONS	INCAVI	INCISURES	INCORRUPT
IMPROVISING	INANITY	INCAVING	INCITANT	INCREASE
IMPROVS	INAPT	INCAVO	INCITANTS	INCREASED
IMPRUDENT	INAPTLY	INCEDE	INCITE	INCREASER
IMPS	INAPTNESS	INCEDED	INCITED	INCREASERS
IMPSONITE	INAPTNESSES	INCEDES	INCITER	INCREASES
IMPSONITES	INARABLE	INCEDING	INCITERS	INCREASING
IMPUDENCE	INARCH	INCENSE	INCITES	INCREASINGS
IMPUDENCES	INARCHED	INCENSED	INCITING	INCREATE
IMPUDENT	INARCHES	INCENSER	INCIVIL	INCREMATE
IMPUGN	INARCHING	INCENSERS	INCIVISM	INCREMATED
IMPUGNED	INARM	INCENSES	INCIVISMS	INCREMATES
IMPUGNER	INARMED	INCENSING	INCLASP	INCREMATING
IMPUGNERS	INARMING	INCENSOR	INCLASPED	INCREMENT
IMPUGNING	INARMS	INCENSORIES	INCLASPING	INCREMENTED
IMPUGNS	INAUDIBLE	INCENSORS	INCLASPS	INCREMENTING
IMPULSE	INAUDIBLY	INCENSORY	INCLE	INCREMENTS
IMPULSED	INAUGURAL	INCENTIVE	INCLEMENT	INCRETION
IMPULSES	INAUGURALS	INCENTIVES	INCLES	INCRETIONS
IMPULSING	INAURATE	INCENTRE	INCLINE	INCROSS
IMPULSION	INBEING	INCENTRES	INCLINED	INCROSSED
IMPULSIONS	INBEINGS	INCEPT	INCLINES	INCROSSES
IMPULSIVE	INBENT	INCEPTED	INCLINING	INCROSSING
IMPUNDULU	INBOARD	INCEPTING	INCLININGS	INCRUST
IMPUNDULUS	INBORN	INCEPTION	INCLIP	INCRUSTED
IMPUNITIES	INBOUND	INCEPTIONS	INCLIPPED	INCRUSTING
IMPUNITY	INBREAK	INCEPTIVE	INCLIPPING	INCRUSTS
IMPURE	INBREAKS	INCEPTIVES	INCLIPS	INCUBATE
IMPURELY	INBREATHE	INCEPTOR	INCLOSE	INCUBATED
IMPURER	INBREATHED	INCEPTORS	INCLOSED	INCUBATES
IMPUREST	INBREATHES	INCEPTS	INCLOSER	INCUBATING
IMPURITIES	INBREATHING	INCERTAIN	INCLOSERS	INCUBATOR
IMPURITY	INBRED	INCESSANT	INCLOSES	INCUBATORS
IMPURPLE	INBREED	INCEST	INCLOSING	INCUBI
IMPURPLED	INBREEDING	INCESTS	INCLOSURE	INCUBOUS

The Chambers Dictionary is the authority for many longer words; see *OSW* Introduction, page xii.

INCUBUS	INDEMNIFIED	INDIGESTS	INDUCIAE	INEBRIOUS
INCUBUSES	INDEMNIFIES	INDIGN	INDUCIBLE	INEDIBLE
INCUDES	INDEMNIFY	INDIGNANT	INDUCING	INEDITED
INCULCATE	INDEMNIFYING	INDIGNIFIED	INDUCT	INEFFABLE
INCULCATED	INDEMNITIES	INDIGNIFIES	INDUCTED	INEFFABLY
INCULCATES	INDEMNITY	INDIGNIFY	INDUCTEE	INELASTIC
INCULCATING	INDENE	INDIGNIFYING	INDUCTEES	INELEGANT
INCULPATE	INDENES	INDIGNITIES	INDUCTILE	INEPT
INCULPATED	INDENT	INDIGNITY	INDUCTING	INEPTER
INCULPATES	INDENTED	INDIGO	INDUCTION	INEPTEST
INCULPATING	INDENTER	INDIGOES	INDUCTIONS	INEPTLY
INCULT	INDENTERS	INDIGOS	INDUCTIVE	INEPTNESS
INCUMBENT	INDENTING	INDIGOTIN	INDUCTOR	INEPTNESSES
INCUMBENTS	INDENTION	INDIGOTINS	INDUCTORS	INEQUABLE
INCUNABLE	INDENTIONS	INDIRECT	INDUCTS	INEQUITIES
INCUNABLES	INDENTS	INDIRUBIN	INDUE	INEQUITY
INCUR	INDENTURE	INDIRUBINS	INDUED	INERM
INCURABLE	INDENTURED	INDISPOSE	INDUES	INERMOUS
INCURABLES .	INDENTURES	INDISPOSED	INDUING	INERRABLE
INCURABLY	INDENTURING	INDISPOSES	INDULGE	INERRABLY
INCURIOUS	INDEW	INDISPOSING	INDULGED	INERRANCIES
INCURRED	INDEWED	INDITE	INDULGENT	INERRANCY
INCURRENT	INDEWING	INDITED	INDULGER	INERRANT
INCURRING	INDEWS	INDITER	INDULGERS	INERT
INCURS	INDEX	INDITERS	INDULGES	INERTER
INCURSION	INDEXAL	INDITES	INDULGING	INERTEST
INCURSIONS	INDEXED	INDITING	INDULIN	INERTIA
INCURSIVE	INDEXER	INDIUM	INDULINE	INERTIAL
INCURVATE	INDEXERS	INDIUMS	INDULINES	INERTIAS
INCURVATED	INDEXES	INDIVIDUA	INDULINS	INERTLY
INCURVATES	INDEXICAL	INDOCIBLE	INDULT	INERTNESS
INCURVATING	INDEXING	INDOCILE	INDULTS	INERTNESSES
INCURVE	INDEXINGS	INDOL	INDUMENTA	INERUDITE
INCURVED	INDEXLESS	INDOLE	INDUNA	INESSIVE
INCURVES	INDICAN	INDOLENCE	INDUNAS	INESSIVES
INCURVING	INDICANS	INDOLENCES	INDURATE	INEXACT
INCURVITIES	INDICANT	INDOLENCIES	INDURATED	INEXACTLY
INCURVITY	INDICANTS	INDOLENCY	INDURATES	INEXPERT
INCUS	INDICATE	INDOLENT	INDURATING	INFALL
INCUSE	INDICATED	INDOLES	INDUSIA	INFALLS
INCUSED	INDICATES	INDOLS	INDUSIAL	INFAME
INCUSES	INDICATING	INDOOR	INDUSIATE	INFAMED
INCUSING	INDICATOR	INDOORS	INDUSIUM	INFAMES
INCUT	INDICATORS	INDORSE	INDUSTRIES	INFAMIES
INDABA	INDICES	INDORSED	INDUSTRY	INFAMING
INDABAS	INDICIA	INDORSES	INDUVIAE	INFAMISE
INDAGATE	INDICIAL	INDORSING	INDUVIAL	INFAMISED
INDAGATED	INDICIUM	INDOXYL	INDUVIATE	INFAMISES
INDAGATES	INDICT	INDOXYLS	INDWELL	INFAMISING
INDAGATING	INDICTED	INDRAFT	INDWELLER	INFAMIZE
INDAGATOR	INDICTEE	INDRAFTS	INDWELLERS	INFAMIZED
INDAGATORS	INDICTEES	INDRAUGHT	INDWELLING	INFAMIZES
INDAMINE	INDICTING	INDRAUGHTS	INDWELLINGS	INFAMIZING
INDAMINES	INDICTION	INDRAWN	INDWELLS	INFAMOUS
INDART	INDICTIONS	INDRENCH	INDWELT	INFAMY
INDARTED	INDICTS	INDRENCHED	INEARTH	INFANCIES
INDARTING	INDIE	INDRENCHES	INEARTHED	INFANCY
INDARTS	INDIES	INDRENCHING	INEARTHING	INFANT
INDEBTED	INDIGENCE	INDRI	INEARTHS	INFANTA
INDECENCIES	INDIGENCES	INDRIS	INEBRIANT	INFANTAS
INDECENCY	INDIGENCIES	INDRISES	INEBRIANTS	INFANTE
INDECENT	INDIGENCY	INDUBIOUS	INEBRIATE	INFANTES
INDECORUM	INDIGENE	INDUCE	INEBRIATED	INFANTILE
INDECORUMS	INDIGENES	INDUCED	INEBRIATES	INFANTINE
INDEED	INDIGENT	INDUCER	INEBRIATING	INFANTRIES
INDELIBLE	INDIGENTS	INDUCERS	INEBRIETIES	INFANTRY
INDELIBLY	INDIGEST	INDUCES	INEBRIETY	INFANTS

The Chambers Dictionary is the authority for many longer words; see *OSW* Introduction, page xii.

INFARCT	INFIRMITY	INFORMANT	INGESTION	INHABITS
INFARCTS	INFIRMLY	INFORMANTS	INGESTIONS	INHALANT
INFARE	INFIX	INFORMED	INGESTIVE	INHALANTS
INFARES	INFIXED	INFORMER	INGESTS	INHALATOR
INFATUATE	INFIXES	INFORMERS	INGINE	INHALATORS
INFATUATED	INFIXING	INFORMING	INGINES	INHALE
INFATUATES	INFLAME	INFORMS	INGLE	INHALED
INFATUATING	INFLAMED	INFORTUNE	INGLENEUK	INHALER
INFAUST	INFLAMER	INFORTUNES	INGLENEUKS	INHALERS
INFECT	INFLAMERS	INFOS	INGLENOOK	INHALES
INFECTED	INFLAMES	INFRA	INGLENOOKS	INHALING
INFECTING	INFLAMING	INFRACT	INGLES	INHARMONIES
INFECTION	INFLATE	INFRACTED	INGLOBE	INHARMONY
INFECTIONS	INFLATED	INFRACTING	INGLOBED	INHAUL
INFECTIVE	INFLATES	INFRACTOR	INGLOBES	INHAULER
INFECTOR	INFLATING	INFRACTORS	INGLOBING	INHAULERS
INFECTORS	INFLATION	INFRACTS	INGLUVIAL	INHAULS
INFECTS	INFLATIONS	INFRARED	INGLUVIES	INHAUST
INFECUND	INFLATIVE	INFRAREDS	INGO	INHAUSTED
INFEFT	INFLATOR	INFRINGE	INGOES	INHAUSTING
INFEFTED	INFLATORS	INFRINGED	INGOING	INHAUSTS
INFEFTING	INFLATUS	INFRINGES	INGOINGS	INHEARSE
INFEFTS	INFLATUSES	INFRINGING	INGOT	INHEARSED
INFELT	INFLECT	INFULA	INGOTS	INHEARSES
INFER	INFLECTED	INFULAE	INGRAFT	INHEARSING
INFERABLE	INFLECTING	INFURIATE	INGRAFTED	INHERCE
INFERE	INFLECTS	INFURIATED	INGRAFTING	INHERCED
INFERENCE	INFLEXED	INFURIATES	INGRAFTS	INHERCES
INFERENCES	INFLEXION	INFURIATING	INGRAIN	INHERCING
INFERIAE	INFLEXIONS	INFUSCATE	INGRAINED	INHERE
INFERIOR	INFLEXURE	INFUSE	INGRAINING	INHERED
INFERIORS	INFLEXURES	INFUSED	INGRAINS	INHERENCE
INFERNAL	INFLICT	INFUSER	INGRAM	INHERENCES
INFERNO	INFLICTED	INFUSERS	INGRATE	INHERENCIES
INFERNOS	INFLICTER	INFUSES	INGRATELY	INHERENCY
INFERRED	INFLICTERS	INFUSIBLE	INGRATES	INHERENT
INFERRING	INFLICTING	INFUSING	INGRESS	INHERES
INFERS	INFLICTOR	INFUSION	INGRESSES	INHERING
INFERTILE	INFLICTORS	INFUSIONS	INGROOVE	INHERIT
INFEST	INFLICTS	INFUSIVE	INGROOVED	INHERITED
INFESTED	INFLOW	INFUSORIA	INGROOVES	INHERITING
INFESTING	INFLOWING	INFUSORY	INGROOVING	INHERITOR
INFESTS	INFLOWINGS	INGAN	INGROSS	INHERITORS
INFICETE	INFLOWS	INGANS	INGROSSED	INHERITS
INFIDEL	INFLUENCE	INGATE	INGROSSES	INHESION
INFIDELS	INFLUENCED	INGATES	INGROSSING	INHESIONS
INFIELD	INFLUENCES	INGATHER	INGROUP	INHIBIT
INFIELDER	INFLUENCING	INGATHERED	INGROUPS	INHIBITED
INFIELDERS	INFLUENT	INGATHERING	INGROWING	INHIBITER
INFIELDS	INFLUENTS	INGATHERINGS	INGROWN	INHIBITERS
INFILL	INFLUENZA	INGATHERS	INGROWTH	INHIBITING
INFILLED	INFLUENZAS	INGENER	INGROWTHS	INHIBITOR
INFILLING	INFLUX	INGENERS	INGRUM	INHIBITORS
INFILLINGS	INFLUXES	INGENIOUS	INGUINAL	INHIBITS
INFILLS	INFLUXION	INGENIUM	INGULF	INHOLDER
INFIMUM	INFLUXIONS	INGENIUMS	INGULFED	INHOLDERS
INFIMUMS	INFO	INGENU	INGULFING	INHOOP
INFINITE	INFOLD	INGENUE	INGULFS	INHOOPED
INFINITES	INFOLDED	INGENUES	INGULPH	INHOOPING
INFINITIES	INFOLDING	INGENUITIES	INGULPHED	INHOOPS
INFINITY	INFOLDS	INGENUITY	INGULPHING	INHUMAN
INFIRM	INFORCE	INGENUOUS	INGULPHS	INHUMANE
INFIRMARIES	INFORCED	INGENUS	INHABIT	INHUMANLY
INFIRMARY	INFORCES	INGEST	INHABITED	INHUMATE
INFIRMER	INFORCING	INGESTA	INHABITER	INHUMATED
INFIRMEST	INFORM	INGESTED	INHABITERS	INHUMATES
INFIRMITIES	INFORMAL	INGESTING	INHABITING	INHUMATING

The Chambers Dictionary is the authority for many longer words; see *OSW* Introduction, page xii.

INHUME	INKHOLDER	INNERVATE	INQUERE	INSCULPS
INHUMED	INKHOLDERS	INNERVATED	INQUERED	INSCULPT
INHUMER	INKHORN	INNERVATES	INQUERES	INSEAM
INHUMERS	INKHORNS	INNERVATING	INQUERING	INSEAMED
INHUMES	INKIER	INNERVE	INQUEST	INSEAMING
INHUMING	INKIEST	INNERVED	INQUESTS	INSEAMS
INIA	INKINESS	INNERVES	INQUIET	INSECT
INIMICAL	INKINESSES	INNERVING	INQUIETED	INSECTARIES
INION	INKING	INNERWEAR	INQUIETING	INSECTARY
INIQUITIES	INKLE	INNERWEARS	INQUIETLY	INSECTILE
INIQUITY	INKLED	INNING	INQUIETS	INSECTION
INISLE	INKLES	INNINGS	INQUILINE	INSECTIONS
INISLED	INKLING	INNKEEPER	INQUILINES	INSECTS
INISLES	INKLINGS	INNKEEPERS	INQUINATE	INSECURE
INISLING	INKPOT	INNOCENCE	INQUINATED	INSEEM
INITIAL	INKPOTS	INNOCENCES	INQUINATES	INSEEMED
INITIALED	INKS	INNOCENCIES	INQUINATING	INSEEMING
INITIALING	INKSPOT	INNOCENCY	INQUIRE	INSEEMS
INITIALLED	INKSPOTS	INNOCENT	INQUIRED	INSELBERG
INITIALLING	INKSTAND	INNOCENTS	INQUIRER	INSELBERGE
INITIALLY	INKSTANDS	INNOCUITIES	INQUIRERS	INSENSATE
INITIALS	INKSTONE	INNOCUITY	INQUIRES	INSERT
INITIATE	INKSTONES	INNOCUOUS	INQUIRIES	INSERTED
INITIATED	INKWELL	INNOVATE	INQUIRING	INSERTER
INITIATES	INKWELLS	INNOVATED	INQUIRY	INSERTERS
INITIATING	INKY	INNOVATES	INQUORATE	INSERTING
INITIATOR	INLACE	INNOVATING	INRO	INSERTION
INITIATORS	INLACED	INNOVATOR	INROAD	INSERTIONS
INJECT	INLACES	INNOVATORS	INROADS	INSERTS
INJECTED	INLACING	INNOXIOUS	INRUSH	INSET
INJECTING	INLAID	INNS	INRUSHES	INSETS
INJECTION	INLAND	INNUENDO	INRUSHING	INSETTING
INJECTIONS	INLANDER	INNUENDOED	INRUSHINGS	INSHALLAH
INJECTOR	INLANDERS	INNUENDOES	INS	INSHEATHE
INJECTORS	INLANDS	INNUENDOING	INSANE	INSHEATHED
INJECTS	INLAY	INNUENDOS	INSANELY	INSHEATHES
INJELLIED	INLAYER	INNYARD	INSANER	INSHEATHING
INJELLIES	INLAYERS	INNYARDS	INSANEST	INSHELL
INJELLY	INLAYING	INOCULA	INSANIE	INSHELLED
INJELLYING	INLAYINGS	INOCULATE	INSANIES	INSHELLING
INJERA	INLAYS	INOCULATED	INSANITIES	INSHELLS
INJERAS	INLET	INOCULATES	INSANITY	INSHELTER
INJOINT	INLETS	INOCULATING	INSATIATE	INSHELTERED
INJOINTED	INLIER	INOCULUM	INSATIETIES	INSHELTERING
INJOINTING	INLIERS	INODOROUS	INSATIETY	INSHELTERS
INJOINTS	INLOCK	INOPINATE	INSCAPE	INSHIP
INJUNCT	INLOCKED	INORB	INSCAPES	INSHIPPED
INJUNCTED	INLOCKING	INORBED	INSCIENCE	INSHIPPING
INJUNCTING	INLOCKS	INORBING	INSCIENCES	INSHIPS
INJUNCTS	INLY	INORBS	INSCIENT	INSHORE
INJURE	INLYING	INORGANIC	INSCONCE	INSHRINE
INJURED	INMATE	INORNATE	INSCONCED	INSHRINED
INJURER	INMATES	INOSITOL	INSCONCES	INSHRINES
INJURERS	INMESH	INOSITOLS	INSCONCING	INSHRINING
INJURES	INMESHED	INOTROPIC	INSCRIBE	INSIDE
INJURIES	INMESHES	INPAYMENT	INSCRIBED	INSIDER
INJURING	INMESHING	INPAYMENTS	INSCRIBER	INSIDERS
INJURIOUS	INMOST	INPHASE	INSCRIBERS	INSIDES
INJURY	INN	INPOURING	INSCRIBES	INSIDIOUS
INJUSTICE	INNARDS	INPOURINGS	INSCRIBING	INSIGHT
INJUSTICES	INNATE	INPUT	INSCROLL	INSIGHTS
INK	INNATELY	INPUTS	INSCROLLED	INSIGNE
INKBERRIES	INNATIVE	INPUTTER	INSCROLLING	INSIGNES
INKBERRY	INNED	INPUTTERS	INSCROLLS	INSIGNIA
INKED	INNER	INPUTTING	INSCULP	INSIGNIAS
INKER	INNERMOST	INQILAB	INSCULPED	INSINCERE
INKERS	INNERS	INQILABS	INSCULPING	INSINEW

The Chambers Dictionary is the authority for many longer words; see *OSW* Introduction, page xii.

INSINEWED	INSTAL	INSULT	INTENSATED	INTERESSES
INSINEWING	INSTALL	INSULTANT	INTENSATES	INTERESSING
INSINEWS	INSTALLED	INSULTED	INTENSATING	INTEREST
INSINUATE	INSTALLING	INSULTER	INTENSE	INTERESTED
INSINUATED	INSTALLS	INSULTERS	INTENSELY	INTERESTING
INSINUATES	INSTALS	INSULTING	INTENSER	INTERESTS
INSINUATING	INSTANCE	INSULTS	INTENSEST	INTERFACE
INSIPID	INSTANCED	INSURABLE	INTENSIFIED	INTERFACED
INSIPIDLY	INSTANCES	INSURANCE	INTENSIFIES	INTERFACES
INSIPIENT	INSTANCIES	INSURANCES	INTENSIFY	INTERFACING
INSIST	INSTANCING	INSURANT	INTENSIFYING	INTERFACINGS
INSISTED	INSTANCY	INSURANTS	INTENSION	INTERFERE
INSISTENT	INSTANT	INSURE	INTENSIONS	INTERFERED
INSISTING	INSTANTLY	INSURED	INTENSITIES	INTERFERES
INSISTS	INSTANTS	INSUREDS	INTENSITY	INTERFERING
INSNARE	INSTAR	INSURER	INTENSIVE	INTERFLOW
INSNARED	INSTARRED	INSURERS	INTENSIVES	INTERFLOWED
INSNARES	INSTARRING	INSURES	INTENT	INTERFLOWING
INSNARING	INSTARS	INSURGENT	INTENTION	INTERFLOWS
INSOLATE	INSTATE	INSURGENTS	INTENTIONS	INTERFOLD
INSOLATED	INSTATED	INSURING	INTENTIVE	INTERFOLDED
INSOLATES	INSTATES	INSWATHE	INTENTLY	INTERFOLDING
INSOLATING	INSTATING	INSWATHED	INTENTS	INTERFOLDS
INSOLE	INSTEAD	INSWATHES	INTER	INTERFUSE
INSOLENCE	INSTEP	INSWATHING	INTERACT	INTERFUSED
INSOLENCES	INSTEPS	INSWING	INTERACTED	INTERFUSES
INSOLENT	INSTIGATE	INSWINGER	INTERACTING	INTERFUSING
INSOLES	INSTIGATED	INSWINGERS	INTERACTS	INTERGREW
INSOLUBLE	INSTIGATES	INSWINGS	INTERBANK	INTERGROW
INSOLUBLY	INSTIGATING	INTACT	INTERBRED	INTERGROWING
INSOLVENT	INSTIL	INTAGLIO	INTERCEDE	INTERGROWN
INSOLVENTS	INSTILL	INTAGLIOED	INTERCEDED	INTERGROWS
INSOMNIA	INSTILLED	INTAGLIOING	INTERCEDES	INTERIM
INSOMNIAC	INSTILLING	INTAGLIOS	INTERCEDING	INTERIMS
INSOMNIACS	INSTILLS	INTAKE	INTERCEPT	INTERIOR
INSOMNIAS	INSTILS	INTAKES	INTERCEPTED	INTERIORS
INSOMUCH	INSTINCT	INTARSIA	INTERCEPTING	INTERJECT
INSOOTH	INSTINCTS	INTARSIAS	INTERCEPTS	INTERJECTED
INSOUL	INSTITUTE	INTEGER	INTERCITY	INTERJECTING
INSOULED	INSTITUTED	INTEGERS	INTERCOM	INTERJECTS
INSOULING	INSTITUTES	INTEGRAL	INTERCOMS	INTERJOIN
INSOULS	INSTITUTING	INTEGRALS	INTERCROP	INTERJOINED
INSPAN	INSTRESS	INTEGRAND	INTERCROPPED	INTERJOINING
INSPANNED	INSTRESSED	INTEGRANDS	INTERCROPPING	INTERJOINS
INSPANNING	INSTRESSES	INTEGRANT	INTERCROPS	INTERKNIT
INSPANS	INSTRESSING	INTEGRATE	INTERCUT	INTERKNITS
INSPECT	INSTRUCT	INTEGRATED	INTERCUTS	INTERKNITTED
INSPECTED	INSTRUCTED	INTEGRATES	INTERCUTTING	INTERKNITTING
INSPECTING	INSTRUCTING	INTEGRATING	INTERDASH	INTERLACE
INSPECTOR	INSTRUCTS	INTEGRITIES	INTERDASHED	INTERLACED
INSPECTORS	INSUCKEN	INTEGRITY	INTERDASHES	INTERLACES
INSPECTS	INSULA	INTELLECT	INTERDASHING	INTERLACING
INSPHERE	INSULAE	INTELLECTS	INTERDEAL	INTERLAID
INSPHERED	INSULAR	INTENABLE	INTERDEALING	INTERLARD
INSPHERES	INSULARLY	INTEND	INTERDEALS	INTERLARDED
INSPHERING	INSULAS	INTENDANT	INTERDEALT	INTERLARDING
INSPIRE	INSULATE	INTENDANTS	INTERDICT	INTERLARDS
INSPIRED	INSULATED	INTENDED	INTERDICTED	INTERLAY
INSPIRER	INSULATES	INTENDEDS	INTERDICTING	INTERLAYING
INSPIRERS	INSULATING	INTENDER	INTERDICTS	INTERLAYS
INSPIRES	INSULATOR	INTENDERED	INTERDINE	INTERLEAF
INSPIRING	INSULATORS	INTENDERING	INTERDINED	INTERLEAVES
INSPIRIT	INSULIN	INTENDERS	INTERDINES	INTERLINE
INSPIRITED	INSULINS	INTENDING	INTERDINING	INTERLINED
INSPIRITING	INSULSE	INTENDS	INTERESS	INTERLINES
INSPIRITS	INSULSITIES	INTENIBLE	INTERESSE	INTERLINING
INSTABLE	INSULSITY	INTENSATE	INTERESSED	INTERLININGS

The Chambers Dictionary is the authority for many longer words; see *OSW* Introduction, page xii.

INTERLINK	INTERREX	INTIMATE	INTRIGANT	INTWINE
INTERLINKED	INTERRING	INTIMATED	INTRIGANTS	INTWINED
INTERLINKING	INTERRUPT	INTIMATES	INTRIGUE	INTWINES
INTERLINKS	INTERRUPTED	INTIMATING	INTRIGUED	INTWINING
INTERLOCK	INTERRUPTING	INTIME	INTRIGUER	INTWIST
INTERLOCKED	INTERRUPTS	INTIMISM	INTRIGUERS	INTWISTED
INTERLOCKING	INTERS	INTIMISMS	INTRIGUES	INTWISTING
INTERLOCKS	INTERSECT	INTIMIST	INTRIGUING	INTWISTS
INTERLOPE	INTERSECTED	INTIMISTE	INTRINCE	INULA
INTERLOPED	INTERSECTING	INTIMISTES	INTRINSIC	INULAS
INTERLOPES	INTERSECTS	INTIMISTS	INTRO	INULASE
INTERLOPING	INTERSERT	INTIMITIES	INTRODUCE	INULASES
INTERLUDE	INTERSERTED	INTIMITY	INTRODUCED	INULIN
INTERLUDED	INTERSERTING	INTINE	INTRODUCES	INULINS
INTERLUDES	INTERSERTS	INTINES	INTRODUCING	INUMBRATE
INTERLUDING	INTERSEX	INTIRE	INTROIT	INUMBRATED
INTERMENT	INTERSEXES	INTIS	INTROITS	INUMBRATES
INTERMENTS	INTERTIE	INTITULE	INTROITUS	INUMBRATING
INTERMIT	INTERTIES	INTITULED	INTROITUSES	INUNCTION
INTERMITS	INTERVAL	INTITULES	INTROJECT	INUNCTIONS
INTERMITTED	INTERVALE	INTITULING	INTROJECTED	INUNDANT
INTERMITTING	INTERVALES	INTO	INTROJECTING	INUNDATE
INTERMIX	INTERVALS	INTOED	INTROJECTS	INUNDATED
INTERMIXED	INTERVEIN	INTOMB	INTROLD	INUNDATES
INTERMIXES	INTERVEINED	INTOMBED	INTROMIT	INUNDATING
INTERMIXING	INTERVEINING	INTOMBING	INTROMITS	INURBANE
INTERMURE	INTERVEINS	INTOMBS	INTROMITTED	INURE
INTERMURED	INTERVENE	INTONACO	INTROMITTING	INURED
INTERMURES	INTERVENED	INTONACOS	INTRON	INUREMENT
INTERMURING	INTERVENES	INTONATE	INTRONS	INUREMENTS
INTERN	INTERVENING	INTONATED	INTRORSE	INURES
INTERNAL	INTERVIEW	INTONATES	INTROS	INURING
INTERNALS	INTERVIEWED	INTONATING	INTROVERT	INURN
INTERNE	INTERVIEWING	INTONATOR	INTROVERTED	INURNED
INTERNED	INTERVIEWS	INTONATORS	INTROVERTING	INURNING
INTERNEE	INTERWAR	INTONE	INTROVERTS	INURNS
INTERNEES	INTERWIND	INTONED	INTRUDE	INUSITATE
INTERNES	INTERWINDING	INTONER	INTRUDED	INUST
INTERNET	INTERWINDS	INTONERS	INTRUDER	INUSTION
INTERNETS	INTERWORK	INTONES	INTRUDERS	INUSTIONS
INTERNING	INTERWORKED	INTONING	INTRUDES	INUTILITIES
INTERNIST	INTERWORKING	INTONINGS	INTRUDING	INUTILITY
INTERNISTS	INTERWORKS	INTORSION	INTRUSION	INVADE
INTERNODE	INTERWOUND	INTORSIONS	INTRUSIONS	INVADED
INTERNODES	INTERWOVE	INTORTED	INTRUSIVE	INVADER
INTERNS	INTERZONE	INTORTION	INTRUSIVES	INVADERS
INTERPAGE	INTERZONES	INTORTIONS	INTRUST	INVADES
INTERPAGED	INTESTACIES	INTOWN	INTRUSTED	INVADING
INTERPAGES	INTESTACY	INTRA	INTRUSTING	INVALID
INTERPAGING	INTESTATE	INTRADA	INTRUSTS	INVALIDED
INTERPLAY	INTESTATES	INTRADAS	INTUBATE	INVALIDING
INTERPLAYS	INTESTINE	INTRADOS	INTUBATED	INVALIDINGS
INTERPLED	INTESTINES	INTRADOSES	INTUBATES	INVALIDLY
INTERPONE	INTHRAL	INTRANT	INTUBATING	INVALIDS
INTERPONED	INTHRALL	INTRANTS	INTUIT	INVARIANT
INTERPONES	INTHRALLED	INTREAT	INTUITED	INVARIANTS
INTERPONING	INTHRALLING	INTREATED	INTUITING	INVASION
INTERPOSE	INTHRALLS	INTREATING	INTUITION	INVASIONS
INTERPOSED	INTHRALS	INTREATS	INTUITIONS	INVASIVE
INTERPOSES	INTI	INTRENCH	INTUITIVE	INVEAGLE
INTERPOSING	INTIFADA	INTRENCHED	INTUITS	INVEAGLED
INTERPRET	INTIFADAS	INTRENCHES	INTUMESCE	INVEAGLES
INTERPRETED	INTIL	INTRENCHING	INTUMESCED	INVEAGLING
INTERPRETING	INTIMA	INTREPID	INTUMESCES	INVECKED
INTERPRETS	INTIMACIES	INTRICACIES	INTUMESCING	INVECTED
INTERRED	INTIMACY	INTRICACY	INTUSE	INVECTIVE
INTERREGES	INTIMAE	INTRICATE	INTUSES	INVECTIVES

The Chambers Dictionary is the authority for many longer words; see *OSW* Introduction, page xii.

INVEIGH	INVOICES	IODISE	IREFULLY	IRONISED
INVEIGHED	INVOICING	IODISED	IRENIC	IRONISES
INVEIGHING	INVOKE	IODISES	IRENICAL	IRONISING
INVEIGHS	INVOKED	IODISING	IRENICISM	IRONIST
INVEIGLE	INVOKES	IODISM	IRENICISMS	IRONISTS
INVEIGLED	INVOKING	IODISMS	IRENICON	IRONIZE
INVEIGLER	INVOLUCEL	IODIZE	IRENICONS	IRONIZED
INVEIGLERS	INVOLUCELS	IODIZED	IRENICS	IRONIZES
INVEIGLES	INVOLUCRA	IODIZES	IRENOLOGIES	IRONIZING
INVEIGLING	INVOLUCRE	IODIZING	IRENOLOGY	IRONS
INVENIT	INVOLUCRES	IODOFORM	IRES	IRONSMITH
INVENT	INVOLUTE	IODOFORMS	IRID	IRONSMITHS
INVENTED	INVOLUTED	IODOPHILE	IRIDAL	IRONSTONE
INVENTING	INVOLUTES	IODOUS	IRIDEAL	IRONSTONES
INVENTION	INVOLUTING	IODURET	IRIDES	IRONWARE
INVENTIONS	INVOLVE	IODURETS	IRIDIAL	IRONWARES
INVENTIVE	INVOLVED	IODYRITE	IRIDIAN	IRONWOOD
INVENTOR	INVOLVES	IODYRITES	IRIDIC	IRONWOODS
INVENTORIED	INVOLVING	IOLITE	IRIDISE	IRONWORK
INVENTORIES	INWALL	IOLITES	IRIDISED	IRONWORKS
INVENTORS	INWALLED	ION	IRIDISES	IRONY
INVENTORY	INWALLING	IONIC	IRIDISING	IRRADIANT
INVENTORYING	INWALLS	IONISE	IRIDIUM	IRRADIATE
INVENTS	INWARD	IONISED	IRIDIUMS	IRRADIATED
INVERSE	INWARDLY	IONISER	IRIDIZE	IRRADIATES
INVERSELY	INWARDS	IONISERS	IRIDIZED	IRRADIATING
INVERSES	INWEAVE	IONISES	IRIDIZES	IRREALITIES
INVERSION	INWEAVES	IONISING	IRIDIZING	IRREALITY
INVERSIONS	INWEAVING	IONIUM	IRIDOLOGIES	IRREGULAR
INVERSIVE	INWICK	IONIUMS	IRIDOLOGY	IRREGULARS
INVERT	INWICKED	IONIZE	IRIDOTOMIES	IRRELATED
INVERTASE	INWICKING	IONIZED	IRIDOTOMY	IRRIGABLE
INVERTASES	INWICKS	IONIZER	IRIDS	IRRIGATE
INVERTED	INWIND	IONIZERS	IRIS	IRRIGATED
INVERTER	INWINDING	IONIZES	IRISATE	IRRIGATES
INVERTERS	INWINDS	IONIZING	IRISATED	IRRIGATING
INVERTIN	INWIT	IONOMER	IRISATES	IRRIGATOR
INVERTING	INWITH	IONOMERS	IRISATING	IRRIGATORS
INVERTINS	INWITS	IONONE	IRISATION	IRRIGUOUS
INVERTOR	INWORK	IONONES	IRISATIONS	IRRISION
INVERTORS	INWORKED	IONOPAUSE	IRISCOPE	IRRISIONS
INVERTS	INWORKING	IONOPAUSES	IRISCOPES	IRRISORY
INVEST	INWORKINGS	IONOPHORE	IRISED	IRRITABLE
INVESTED	INWORKS	IONOPHORES	IRISES	IRRITABLY
INVESTING	INWORN	IONS	IRITIC	IRRITANCIES
INVESTOR	INWOUND	IOS	IRITIS	IRRITANCY
INVESTORS	INWOVE	IOTA	IRITISES	IRRITANT
INVESTS	INWOVEN	IOTAS	IRK	IRRITANTS
INVEXED	INWRAP	IPECAC	IRKED	IRRITATE
INVIABLE	INWRAPPED	IPECACS	IRKING	IRRITATED
INVIDIOUS	INWRAPPING	IPOMOEA	IRKS	IRRITATES
INVIOLATE	INWRAPS	IPOMOEAS	IRKSOME	IRRITATING
INVIOUS	INWREATHE	IPPON	IRKSOMELY	IRRITATOR
INVISIBLE	INWREATHED	IPPONS	IROKO	IRRITATORS
INVISIBLES	INWREATHES	IPRINDOLE	IROKOS	IRRUPT
INVISIBLY	INWREATHING	IPRINDOLES	IRON	IRRUPTED
INVITE	INWROUGHT	IRACUND	IRONBARK	IRRUPTING
INVITED	INYALA	IRADE	IRONBARKS	IRRUPTION
INVITEE	INYALAS	IRADES	IRONED	IRRUPTIONS
INVITEES	IO	IRASCIBLE	IRONER	IRRUPTIVE
INVITER	IODATE	IRASCIBLY	IRONERS	IRRUPTS
INVITERS	IODATES	IRATE	IRONIC	IS
INVITES	IODIC	IRATELY	IRONICAL	ISABEL
INVITING	IODIDE	IRATER	IRONIES	ISABELLA
INVITINGS	IODIDES	IRATEST	IRONING	ISABELLAS
INVOICE	IODINE	IRE	IRONINGS	ISABELS
INVOICED	IODINES	IREFUL	IRONISE	ISAGOGE

The Chambers Dictionary is the authority for many longer words; see *OSW* Introduction, page xii.

ISAGOGES	ISOCHIME	ISOLATED	ISOTHERAL	ITEM
ISAGOGIC	ISOCHIMES	ISOLATES	ISOTHERALS	ITEMED
ISAGOGICS	ISOCHOR	ISOLATING	ISOTHERE	ITEMING
ISALLOBAR	ISOCHORE	ISOLATION	ISOTHERES	ITEMISE
ISALLOBARS	ISOCHORES	ISOLATIONS	ISOTHERM	ITEMISED
ISATIN	ISOCHORIC	ISOLATIVE	ISOTHERMS	ITEMISES
ISATINE	ISOCHORS	ISOLATOR	ISOTONE	ITEMISING
ISATINES	ISOCHRONE	ISOLATORS	ISOTONES	ITEMIZE
ISATINS	ISOCHRONES	ISOLINE	ISOTONIC	ITEMIZED
ISCHAEMIA	ISOCLINAL	ISOLINES	ISOTOPE	ITEMIZES
ISCHAEMIAS	ISOCLINALS	ISOLOGOUS	ISOTOPES	ITEMIZING
ISCHAEMIC	ISOCLINE	ISOLOGUE	ISOTOPIC	ITEMS
ISCHEMIA	ISOCLINES	ISOLOGUES	ISOTOPIES	ITERANCE
ISCHEMIAS	ISOCLINIC	ISOMER	ISOTOPY	ITERANCES
ISCHEMIC	ISOCLINICS	ISOMERASE	ISOTRON	ITERANT
ISCHIA	ISOCRACIES	ISOMERASES	ISOTRONS	ITERATE
ISCHIADIC	ISOCRACY	ISOMERE	ISOTROPIC	ITERATED
ISCHIAL	ISOCRATIC	ISOMERES	ISOTROPIES	ITERATES
ISCHIATIC	ISOCRYMAL	ISOMERIC	ISOTROPY	ITERATING
ISCHIUM	ISOCRYMALS	ISOMERISE	ISOTYPE	ITERATION
ISCHURIA	ISOCRYME	ISOMERISED	ISOTYPES	ITERATIONS
ISCHURIAS	ISOCRYMES	ISOMERISES	ISSEI	ITERATIVE
ISENERGIC	ISOCYCLIC	ISOMERISING	ISSEIS	ITERUM
ISH	ISODICA	ISOMERISM	ISSUABLE	ITINERACIES
ISHES	ISODICON	ISOMERISMS	ISSUABLY	ITINERACY
ISINGLASS	ISODOMA	ISOMERIZE	ISSUANCE	ITINERANT
ISINGLASSES	ISODOMON	ISOMERIZED	ISSUANCES	ITINERANTS
ISLAND	ISODOMONS	ISOMERIZES	ISSUANT	ITINERARIES
ISLANDED	ISODOMOUS	ISOMERIZING	ISSUE	ITINERARY
ISLANDER	ISODOMUM	ISOMEROUS	ISSUED	ITINERATE
ISLANDERS	ISODONT	ISOMERS	ISSUELESS	ITINERATED
ISLANDING	ISODONTAL	ISOMETRIC	ISSUER	ITINERATES
ISLANDS	ISODONTALS	ISOMETRICS	ISSUERS	ITINERATING
ISLE	ISODONTS	ISOMETRIES	ISSUES	ITS
ISLED	ISOETES	ISOMETRY	ISSUING	ITSELF
ISLEMAN	ISOGAMETE	ISOMORPH	ISTHMIAN	IURE
ISLEMEN	ISOGAMETES	ISOMORPHS	ISTHMUS	IVIED
ISLES	ISOGAMIC	ISONIAZID	ISTHMUSES	IVIES
ISLESMAN	ISOGAMIES	ISONIAZIDS	ISTLE	IVORIED
ISLESMEN	ISOGAMOUS	ISONOMIC	ISTLES	IVORIES
ISLET	ISOGAMY	ISONOMIES	IT	IVORIST
ISLETS	ISOGENIES	ISONOMOUS	ITA	IVORISTS
ISLING	ISOGENOUS	ISONOMY	ITACISM	IVORY
ISM	ISOGENY	ISOPLETH	ITACISMS	IVRESSE
ISMATIC	ISOGLOSS	ISOPLETHS	ITALIC	IVRESSES
ISMATICAL	ISOGLOSSES	ISOPOD	ITALICISE	IVY
ISMS	ISOGON	ISOPODAN	ITALICISED	IWIS
ISO	ISOGONAL	ISOPODOUS	ITALICISES	IXIA
ISOBAR	ISOGONALS	ISOPODS	ITALICISING	IXIAS
ISOBARE	ISOGONIC	ISOPOLITIES	ITALICIZE	IXODIASES
ISOBARES	ISOGONICS	ISOPOLITY	ITALICIZED	IXODIASIS
ISOBARIC	ISOGONS	ISOPRENE	ITALICIZES	IXTLE
ISOBARS	ISOGRAM	ISOPRENES	ITALICIZING	IXTLES
ISOBASE	ISOGRAMS	ISOPROPYL	ITALICS	IZARD
ISOBASES	ISOHEL	ISOPROPYLS	ITAS	IZARDS
ISOBATH	ISOHELS	ISOS	ITCH	IZVESTIA
ISOBATHIC	ISOHYET	ISOSCELES	ITCHED	IZVESTIAS
ISOBATHS	ISOHYETAL	ISOSPIN	ITCHES	IZVESTIYA
ISOBRONT	ISOHYETALS	ISOSPINS	ITCHIER	IZVESTIYAS
ISOBRONTS	ISOHYETS	ISOSPORIES	ITCHIEST	IZZARD
ISOCHASM	ISOKONT	ISOSPORY	ITCHINESS	IZZARDS
ISOCHASMS	ISOKONTAN	ISOSTASIES	ITCHINESSES	IZZAT
ISOCHEIM	ISOKONTANS	ISOSTASY	ITCHING	IZZATS
ISOCHEIMS	ISOKONTS	ISOSTATIC	ITCHWEED	
ISOCHIMAL	ISOLABLE	ISOSTERIC	ITCHWEEDS	
ISOCHIMALS	ISOLATE	ISOTACTIC	ITCHY	

The Chambers Dictionary is the authority for many longer words; see *OSW* Introduction, page xii.

J

JAB	JACKETING	JAGGIER	JAMBEAU	JANE
JABBED	JACKETS	JAGGIEST	JAMBEAUX	JANES
JABBER	JACKING	JAGGING	JAMBEE	JANGLE
JABBERED	JACKKNIFE	JAGGY	JAMBEES	JANGLED
JABBERER	JACKKNIFED	JAGHIR	JAMBER	JANGLER
JABBERERS	JACKKNIFES	JAGHIRDAR	JAMBERS	JANGLERS
JABBERING	JACKKNIFING	JAGHIRDARS	JAMBES	JANGLES
JABBERINGS	JACKKNIVES	JAGHIRE	JAMBEUX	JANGLIER
JABBERS	JACKMAN	JAGHIRES	JAMBIER	JANGLIEST
JABBING	JACKMEN	JAGHIRS	JAMBIERS	JANGLING
JABBLE	JACKPOT	JAGIR	JAMBIYA	JANGLINGS
JABBLED	JACKPOTS	JAGIRS	JAMBIYAH	JANGLY
JABBLES	JACKS	JAGS	JAMBIYAHS	JANISSARIES
JABBLING	JACKSHAFT	JAGUAR	JAMBIYAS	JANISSARY
JABERS	JACKSHAFTS	JAGUARS	JAMBO	JANITOR
JABIRU	JACKSIE	JAIL	JAMBOK	JANITORS
JABIRUS	JACKSIES	JAILED	JAMBOKKED	JANITRESS
JABORANDI	JACKSMITH	JAILER	JAMBOKKING	JANITRESSES
JABORANDIS	JACKSMITHS	JAILERESS	JAMBOKS	JANITRIX
JABOT	JACKSY	JAILERESSES	JAMBOLAN	JANITRIXES
JABOTS	JACOBIN	JAILERS	JAMBOLANA	JANIZAR
JABS	JACOBINS	JAILHOUSE	JAMBOLANAS	JANIZARIES
JACAMAR	JACOBUS	JAILHOUSES	JAMBOLANS	JANIZARS
JACAMARS	JACOBUSES	JAILING	JAMBONE	JANIZARY
JACANA	JACONET	JAILOR	JAMBONES	JANKER
JACANAS	JACONETS	JAILORESS	JAMBOOL	JANKERS
JACARANDA	JACQUARD	JAILORESSES	JAMBOOLS	JANN
JACARANDAS	JACQUARDS	JAILORS	JAMBOREE	JANNOCK
JACCHUS	JACTATION	JAILS	JAMBOREES	JANNOCKS
JACCHUSES	JACTATIONS	JAK	JAMBOS	JANNS
JACENT	JACULATE	JAKE	JAMBS	JANSKY
JACINTH	JACULATED	JAKES	JAMBU	JANSKYS
JACINTHS	JACULATES	JAKESES	JAMBUL	JANTEE
JACK	JACULATING	JAKS	JAMBULS	JANTIER
JACKAL	JACULATOR	JALAP	JAMBUS	JANTIES
JACKALLED	JACULATORS	JALAPENO	JAMDANI	JANTIEST
JACKALLING	JACUZZI	JALAPENOS	JAMDANIS	JANTY
JACKALS	JACUZZIS	JALAPIC	JAMES	JAP
JACKAROO	JADE	JALAPIN	JAMESES	JAPAN
JACKAROOED	JADED	JALAPINS	JAMJAR	JAPANNED
JACKAROOING	JADEDLY	JALAPS	JAMJARS	JAPANNER
JACKAROOS	JADEITE	JALOPIES	JAMMED	JAPANNERS
JACKASS	JADEITES	JALOPPIES	JAMMER	JAPANNING
JACKASSES	JADERIES	JALOPPY	JAMMERS	JAPANS
JACKBOOT	JADERY	JALOPY	JAMMIER	JAPE
JACKBOOTED	JADES	JALOUSE	JAMMIEST	JAPED
JACKBOOTING	JADING	JALOUSED	JAMMING	JAPER
JACKBOOTS	JADISH	JALOUSES	JAMMY	JAPERS
JACKDAW	JAEGER	JALOUSIE	JAMPAN	JAPES
JACKDAWS	JAEGERS	JALOUSIED	JAMPANEE	JAPING
JACKED	JAG	JALOUSIES	JAMPANEES	JAPINGS
JACKEEN	JAGER	JALOUSING	JAMPANI	JAPONICA
JACKEENS	JAGERS	JAM	JAMPANIS	JAPONICAS
JACKEROO	JAGGED	JAMADAR	JAMPANS	JAPPED
JACKEROOED	JAGGEDLY	JAMADARS	JAMPOT	JAPPING
JACKEROOING	JAGGER	JAMB	JAMPOTS	JAPS
JACKEROOS	JAGGERIES	JAMBALAYA	JAMS	JAR
JACKET	JAGGERS	JAMBALAYAS	JANDAL	JARARACA
JACKETED	JAGGERY	JAMBE	JANDALS	JARARACAS

The Chambers Dictionary is the authority for many longer words; see *OSW* Introduction, page xii.

JARARAKA	JASPIDEAN	JAYWALKED	JEFFING	JEQUIRITIES
JARARAKAS	JASPIS	JAYWALKER	JEFFS	JEQUIRITY
JARFUL	JASPISES	JAYWALKERS	JEHAD	JERBIL
JARFULS	JASPS	JAYWALKING	JEHADS	JERBILS
JARGON	JASS	JAYWALKINGS	JEJUNA	JERBOA
JARGONED	JASSES	JAYWALKS	JEJUNE	JERBOAS
JARGONEER	JASY	JAZERANT	JEJUNELY	JEREED
JARGONEERS	JATAKA	JAZERANTS	JEJUNITIES	JEREEDS
JARGONING	JATAKAS	JAZIES	JEJUNITY	JEREMIAD
JARGONISE	JATO	JAZY	JEJUNUM	JEREMIADS
JARGONISED	JATOS	JAZZ	JELAB	JERFALCON
JARGONISES	JAUNCE	JAZZED	JELABS	JERFALCONS
JARGONISING	JAUNCED	JAZZER	JELL	JERID
JARGONIST	JAUNCES	JAZZERS	JELLABA	JERIDS
JARGONISTS	JAUNCING	JAZZES	JELLABAS	JERK
JARGONIZE	JAUNDICE	JAZZIER	JELLED	JERKED
JARGONIZED	JAUNDICED	JAZZIEST	JELLIED	JERKER
JARGONIZES	JAUNDICES	JAZZILY	JELLIES	JERKERS
JARGONIZING	JAUNDICING	JAZZINESS	JELLIFIED	JERKIER
JARGONS	JAUNSE	JAZZINESSES	JELLIFIES	JERKIES
JARGOON	JAUNSED	JAZZING	JELLIFORM	JERKIEST
JARGOONS	JAUNSES	JAZZMAN	JELLIFY	JERKIN
JARK	JAUNSING	JAZZMEN	JELLIFYING	JERKINESS
JARKMAN	JAUNT	JAZZY	JELLING	JERKINESSES
JARKMEN	JAUNTED	JEALOUS	JELLO	JERKING
JARKS	JAUNTEE	JEALOUSE	JELLOS	JERKINGS
JARL	JAUNTIE	JEALOUSED	JELLS	JERKINS
JARLS	JAUNTIER	JEALOUSES	JELLY	JERKS
JAROOL	JAUNTIES	JEALOUSIES	JELLYBEAN	JERKWATER
JAROOLS	JAUNTIEST	JEALOUSING	JELLYBEANS	JERKWATERS
JAROSITE	JAUNTILY	JEALOUSLY	JELLYFISH	JERKY
JAROSITES	JAUNTING	JEALOUSY	JELLYFISHES	JEROBOAM
JARRAH	JAUNTS	JEAN	JELLYING	JEROBOAMS
JARRAHS	JAUNTY	JEANETTE	JELUTONG	JERQUE
JARRED	JAUP	JEANETTES	JELUTONGS	JERQUED
JARRING	JAUPED	JEANS	JEMADAR	JERQUER
JARRINGLY	JAUPING	JEAT	JEMADARS	JERQUERS
JARRINGS	JAUPS	JEATS	JEMIDAR	JERQUES
JARS	JAVEL	JEBEL	JEMIDARS	JERQUING
JARTA	JAVELIN	JEBELS	JEMIMA	JERQUINGS
JARTAS	JAVELINS	JEE	JEMIMAS	JERRICAN
JARUL	JAVELS	JEED	JEMMIED	JERRICANS
JARULS	JAW	JEEING	JEMMIER	JERRIES
JARVEY	JAWAN	JEEL	JEMMIES	JERRY
JARVEYS	JAWANS	JEELED	JEMMIEST	JERRYCAN
JARVIE	JAWARI	JEELIE	JEMMINESS	JERRYCANS
JARVIES	JAWARIS	JEELIED	JEMMINESSES	JERSEY
JASEY	JAWBATION	JEELIEING	JEMMY	JERSEYS
JASEYS	JAWBATIONS	JEELIES	JEMMYING	JESS
JASIES	JAWBONE	JEELING	JENNET	JESSAMIES
JASMINE	JAWBONED	JEELS	JENNETING	JESSAMINE
JASMINES	JAWBONES	JEELY	JENNETINGS	JESSAMINES
JASP	JAWBONING	JEELYING	JENNETS	JESSAMY
JASPE	JAWBONINGS	JEEPERS	JENNIES	JESSANT
JASPER	JAWBOX	JEEPNEY	JENNY	JESSED
JASPERISE	JAWBOXES	JEEPNEYS	JEOFAIL	JESSERANT
JASPERISED	JAWED	JEER	JEOFAILS	JESSERANTS
JASPERISES	JAWFALL	JEERED	JEOPARD	JESSES
JASPERISING	JAWFALLS	JEERER	JEOPARDED	JESSIE
JASPERIZE	JAWHOLE	JEERERS	JEOPARDER	JESSIES
JASPERIZED	JAWHOLES	JEERING	JEOPARDERS	JEST
JASPERIZES	JAWING	JEERINGLY	JEOPARDIED	JESTBOOK
JASPERIZING	JAWINGS	JEERINGS	JEOPARDIES	JESTBOOKS
JASPEROUS	JAWS	JEERS	JEOPARDING	JESTED
JASPERS	JAY	JEES	JEOPARDS	JESTEE
JASPERY	JAYS	JEFF	JEOPARDY	JESTEES
JASPES	JAYWALK	JEFFED	JEOPARDYING	JESTER

The Chambers Dictionary is the authority for many longer words; see *OSW* Introduction, page xii.

JESTERS	JEZAILS	JIGSAWING	JINKS	JOBED
JESTFUL	JHALA	JIGSAWS	JINN	JOBERNOWL
JESTING	JHALAS	JIHAD	JINNEE	JOBERNOWLS
JESTINGLY	JIAO	JIHADS	JINNI	JOBES
JESTINGS	JIAOS	JILGIE	JINNS	JOBING
JESTS	JIB	JILGIES	JINX	JOBLESS
JESUS	JIBBAH	JILL	JINXED	JOBS
JET	JIBBAHS	JILLAROO	JINXES	JOBSHARE
JETE	JIBBED	JILLAROOS	JINXING	JOBSHARES
JETES	JIBBER	JILLET	JIPYAPA	JOBSWORTH
JETFOIL	JIBBERED	JILLETS	JIPYAPAS	JOBSWORTHS
JETFOILS	JIBBERING	JILLFLIRT	JIRBLE	JOCK
JETLINER	JIBBERS	JILLFLIRTS	JIRBLED	JOCKETTE
JETLINERS	JIBBING	JILLION	JIRBLES	JOCKETTES
JETON	JIBBINGS	JILLIONS	JIRBLING	JOCKEY
JETONS	JIBE	JILLS	JIRD	JOCKEYED
JETPLANE	JIBED	JILT	JIRDS	JOCKEYING
JETPLANES	JIBER	JILTED	JIRGA	JOCKEYISM
JETS	JIBERS	JILTING	JIRGAS	JOCKEYISMS
JETSAM	JIBES	JILTS	JIRKINET	JOCKEYS
JETSAMS	JIBING	JIMCRACK	JIRKINETS	JOCKO
JETSOM	JIBS	JIMCRACKS	JISM	JOCKOS
JETSOMS	JICKAJOG	JIMINY	JISMS	JOCKS
JETSON	JICKAJOGGED	JIMJAM	JISSOM	JOCKSTRAP
JETSONS	JICKAJOGGING	JIMJAMS	JISSOMS	JOCKSTRAPS
JETSTREAM	JICKAJOGS	JIMMIED	JITNEY	JOCKTELEG
JETSTREAMS	JIFF	JIMMIES	JITNEYS	JOCKTELEGS
JETTATURA	JIFFIES	JIMMY	JITTER	JOCO
JETTATURAS	JIFFS	JIMMYING	JITTERBUG	JOCOSE
JETTED	JIFFY	JIMP	JITTERBUGGED	JOCOSELY
JETTIED	JIG	JIMPER	JITTERBUGGING	JOCOSITIES
JETTIER	JIGAJIG	JIMPEST	JITTERBUGS	JOCOSITY
JETTIES	JIGAJIGGED	JIMPIER	JITTERED	JOCULAR
JETTIEST	JIGAJIGGING	JIMPIEST	JITTERING	JOCULARLY
JETTINESS	JIGAJIGS	JIMPLY	JITTERS	JOCULATOR
JETTINESSES	JIGAJOG	JIMPNESS	JITTERY	JOCULATORS
JETTING	JIGAJOGGED	JIMPNESSES	JIVE	JOCUND
JETTISON	JIGAJOGGING	JIMPY	JIVED	JOCUNDITIES
JETTISONED	JIGAJOGS	JINGAL	JIVER	JOCUNDITY
JETTISONING	JIGAMAREE	JINGALS	JIVERS	JOCUNDLY
JETTISONS	JIGAMAREES	JINGBANG	JIVES	JODEL
JETTON	JIGGED	JINGBANGS	JIVING	JODELLED
JETTONS	JIGGER	JINGLE	JIZ	JODELLING
JETTY	JIGGERED	JINGLED	JIZZ	JODELS
JETTYING	JIGGERING	JINGLER	JIZZES	JODHPURS
JEU	JIGGERS	JINGLERS	JNANA	JOE
JEUNE	JIGGING	JINGLES	JNANAS	JOES
JEUX	JIGGINGS	JINGLET	JO	JOEY
JEW	JIGGISH	JINGLETS	JOANNA	JOEYS
JEWED	JIGGLE	JINGLIER	JOANNAS	JOG
JEWEL	JIGGLED	JINGLIEST	JOANNES	JOGGED
JEWELFISH	JIGGLES	JINGLING	JOANNESES	JOGGER
JEWELFISHES	JIGGLIER	JINGLY	JOB	JOGGERS
JEWELLED	JIGGLIEST	JINGO	JOBATION	JOGGING
JEWELLER	JIGGLING	JINGOES	JOBATIONS	JOGGINGS
JEWELLERIES	JIGGLY	JINGOISH	JOBBED	JOGGLE
JEWELLERS	JIGGUMBOB	JINGOISM	JOBBER	JOGGLED
JEWELLERY	JIGGUMBOBS	JINGOISMS	JOBBERIES	JOGGLES
JEWELLING	JIGJIG	JINGOIST	JOBBERS	JOGGLING
JEWELRIES	JIGJIGGED	JINGOISTS	JOBBERY	JOGPANTS
JEWELRY	JIGJIGGING	JINJILI	JOBBIE	JOGS
JEWELS	JIGJIGS	JINJILIS	JOBBIES	JOGTROT
JEWFISH	JIGOT	JINK	JOBBING	JOGTROTS
JEWFISHES	JIGOTS	JINKED	JOBBINGS	JOHANNES
JEWING	JIGS	JINKER	JOBCENTRE	JOHANNESES
JEWS	JIGSAW	JINKERS	JOBCENTRES	JOHN
JEZAIL	JIGSAWED	JINKING	JOBE	JOHNNIE

The Chambers Dictionary is the authority for many longer words; see *OSW* Introduction, page xii.

JOHNNIES
JOHNNY
JOHNS
JOIN
JOINDER
JOINDERS
JOINED
JOINER
JOINERIES
JOINERS
JOINERY
JOINING
JOININGS
JOINS
JOINT
JOINTED
JOINTER
JOINTERS
JOINTING
JOINTLESS
JOINTLY
JOINTNESS
JOINTNESSES
JOINTRESS
JOINTRESSES
JOINTS
JOINTURE
JOINTURED
JOINTURES
JOINTURING
JOINTWORM
JOINTWORMS
JOIST
JOISTED
JOISTING
JOISTS
JOJOBA
JOJOBAS
JOKE
JOKED
JOKER
JOKERS
JOKES
JOKESMITH
JOKESMITHS
JOKESOME
JOKEY
JOKIER
JOKIEST
JOKING
JOKINGLY
JOKOL
JOKY
JOLE
JOLED
JOLES
JOLING
JOLL
JOLLED
JOLLEY
JOLLEYER
JOLLEYERS
JOLLEYING
JOLLEYINGS
JOLLEYS
JOLLIED
JOLLIER

JOLLIES
JOLLIEST
JOLLIFIED
JOLLIFIES
JOLLIFY
JOLLIFYING
JOLLILY
JOLLIMENT
JOLLIMENTS
JOLLINESS
JOLLINESSES
JOLLING
JOLLITIES
JOLLITY
JOLLS
JOLLY
JOLLYBOAT
JOLLYBOATS
JOLLYER
JOLLYERS
JOLLYHEAD
JOLLYHEADS
JOLLYING
JOLLYINGS
JOLT
JOLTED
JOLTER
JOLTERS
JOLTHEAD
JOLTHEADS
JOLTIER
JOLTIEST
JOLTING
JOLTINGLY
JOLTS
JOLTY
JOMO
JOMOS
JONCANOE
JONCANOES
JONGLEUR
JONGLEURS
JONQUIL
JONQUILS
JONTIES
JONTY
JOOK
JOOKED
JOOKERIES
JOOKERY
JOOKING
JOOKS
JOR
JORAM
JORAMS
JORDAN
JORDANS
JORDELOO
JORDELOOS
JORS
JORUM
JORUMS
JOSEPH
JOSEPHS
JOSH
JOSHED
JOSHER

JOSHERS
JOSHES
JOSHING
JOSKIN
JOSKINS
JOSS
JOSSER
JOSSERS
JOSSES
JOSTLE
JOSTLED
JOSTLES
JOSTLING
JOSTLINGS
JOT
JOTA
JOTAS
JOTS
JOTTED
JOTTER
JOTTERS
JOTTING
JOTTINGS
JOTUN
JOTUNN
JOTUNNS
JOTUNS
JOUAL
JOUALS
JOUGS
JOUISANCE
JOUISANCES
JOUK
JOUKED
JOUKERIES
JOUKERY
JOUKING
JOUKS
JOULE
JOULED
JOULES
JOULING
JOUNCE
JOUNCED
JOUNCES
JOUNCING
JOUR
JOURNAL
JOURNALLED
JOURNALLING
JOURNALS
JOURNEY
JOURNEYED
JOURNEYER
JOURNEYERS
JOURNEYING
JOURNEYS
JOURNO
JOURNOS
JOURS
JOUST
JOUSTED
JOUSTER
JOUSTERS
JOUSTING
JOUSTS
JOVIAL

JOVIALITIES
JOVIALITY
JOVIALLY
JOW
JOWAR
JOWARI
JOWARIS
JOWARS
JOWED
JOWING
JOWL
JOWLED
JOWLER
JOWLERS
JOWLIER
JOWLIEST
JOWLING
JOWLS
JOWLY
JOWS
JOY
JOYANCE
JOYANCES
JOYED
JOYFUL
JOYFULLER
JOYFULLEST
JOYFULLY
JOYING
JOYLESS
JOYLESSLY
JOYOUS
JOYOUSLY
JOYS
JUBA
JUBAS
JUBATE
JUBBAH
JUBBAHS
JUBE
JUBES
JUBILANCE
JUBILANCES
JUBILANCIES
JUBILANCY
JUBILANT
JUBILATE
JUBILATED
JUBILATES
JUBILATING
JUBILEE
JUBILEES
JUD
JUDAS
JUDASES
JUDDER
JUDDERED
JUDDERING
JUDDERS
JUDGE
JUDGED
JUDGEMENT
JUDGEMENTS
JUDGES
JUDGESHIP
JUDGESHIPS
JUDGING

JUDGMENT
JUDGMENTS
JUDICABLE
JUDICATOR
JUDICATORS
JUDICIAL
JUDICIARIES
JUDICIARY
JUDICIOUS
JUDIES
JUDO
JUDOGI
JUDOGIS
JUDOIST
JUDOISTS
JUDOKA
JUDOKAS
JUDOS
JUDS
JUDY
JUG
JUGA
JUGAL
JUGALS
JUGATE
JUGFUL
JUGFULS
JUGGED
JUGGING
JUGGINGS
JUGGINS
JUGGINSES
JUGGLE
JUGGLED
JUGGLER
JUGGLERIES
JUGGLERS
JUGGLERY
JUGGLES
JUGGLING
JUGGLINGS
JUGHEAD
JUGHEADS
JUGLET
JUGLETS
JUGS
JUGULAR
JUGULARS
JUGULATE
JUGULATED
JUGULATES
JUGULATING
JUGUM
JUICE
JUICED
JUICELESS
JUICER
JUICERS
JUICES
JUICIER
JUICIEST
JUICINESS
JUICINESSES
JUICING
JUICY
JUJU
JUJUBE

The Chambers Dictionary is the authority for many longer words; see *OSW* Introduction, page xii.

JUJUBES	JUMBOIZES	JUNGLY	JURAL	JUSTIFY
JUJUS	JUMBOIZING	JUNIOR	JURALLY	JUSTIFYING
JUKE	JUMBOS	JUNIORITIES	JURANT	JUSTING
JUKED	JUMBUCK	JUNIORITY	JURANTS	JUSTLE
JUKES	JUMBUCKS	JUNIORS	JURAT	JUSTLED
JUKING	JUMBY	JUNIPER	JURATORY	JUSTLES
JUKSKEI	JUMELLE	JUNIPERS	JURATS	JUSTLING
JUKSKEIS	JUMELLES	JUNK	JURE	JUSTLY
JULEP	JUMP	JUNKANOO	JURIDIC	JUSTNESS
JULEPS	JUMPABLE	JUNKANOOS	JURIDICAL	JUSTNESSES
JULIENNE	JUMPED	JUNKED	JURIES	JUSTS
JULIENNED	JUMPER	JUNKER	JURIST	JUT
JULIENNES	JUMPERS	JUNKERS	JURISTIC	JUTE
JULIENNING	JUMPIER	JUNKET	JURISTS	JUTES
JUMAR	JUMPIEST	JUNKETED	JUROR	JUTS
JUMARRED	JUMPILY	JUNKETEER	JURORS	JUTTED
JUMARRING	JUMPINESS	JUNKETEERS	JURY	JUTTIED
JUMARS	JUMPINESSES	JUNKETING	JURYMAN	JUTTIES
JUMART	JUMPING	JUNKETINGS	JURYMAST	JUTTING
JUMARTS	JUMPS	JUNKETS	JURYMASTS	JUTTINGLY
JUMBAL	JUMPY	JUNKIE	JURYMEN	JUTTY
JUMBALS	JUNCATE	JUNKIER	JURYWOMAN	JUTTYING
JUMBIE	JUNCATES	JUNKIES	JURYWOMEN	JUVE
JUMBIES	JUNCO	JUNKIEST	JUS	JUVENAL
JUMBLE	JUNCOES	JUNKINESS	JUSSIVE	JUVENALS
JUMBLED	JUNCOS	JUNKINESSES	JUSSIVES	JUVENILE
JUMBLER	JUNCTION	JUNKING	JUST	JUVENILES
JUMBLERS	JUNCTIONS	JUNKMAN	JUSTED	JUVENILIA
JUMBLES	JUNCTURE	JUNKMEN	JUSTER	JUVES
JUMBLIER	JUNCTURES	JUNKS	JUSTEST	JUXTAPOSE
JUMBLIEST	JUNCUS	JUNKY	JUSTICE	JUXTAPOSED
JUMBLING	JUNCUSES	JUNTA	JUSTICER	JUXTAPOSES
JUMBLY	JUNEATING	JUNTAS	JUSTICERS	JUXTAPOSING
JUMBO	JUNEATINGS	JUNTO	JUSTICES	JYMOLD
JUMBOISE	JUNGLE	JUNTOS	JUSTICIAR	JYNX
JUMBOISED	JUNGLES	JUPATI	JUSTICIARS	JYNXES
JUMBOISES	JUNGLI	JUPATIS	JUSTIFIED	
JUMBOISING	JUNGLIER	JUPON	JUSTIFIER	
JUMBOIZE	JUNGLIEST	JUPONS	JUSTIFIERS	
JUMBOIZED	JUNGLIS	JURA	JUSTIFIES	

K

KA	KAHAWAI	KALE	KAMICHI	KAOLIANG
KAAMA	KAHAWAIS	KALENDAR	KAMICHIS	KAOLIANGS
KAAMAS	KAI	KALENDARED	KAMIK	KAOLIN
KABAB	KAIAK	KALENDARING	KAMIKAZE	KAOLINE
KABABBED	KAIAKED	KALENDARS	KAMIKAZES	KAOLINES
KABABBING	KAIAKING	KALENDS	KAMIKS	KAOLINISE
KABABS	KAIAKS	KALES	KAMILA	KAOLINISED
KABADDI	KAID	KALI	KAMILAS	KAOLINISES
KABADDIS	KAIDS	KALIAN	KAMIS	KAOLINISING
KABALA	KAIE	KALIANS	KAMISES	KAOLINITE
KABALAS	KAIES	KALIF	KAMME	KAOLINITES
KABAYA	KAIF	KALIFS	KAMPONG	KAOLINIZE
KABAYAS	KAIFS	KALINITE	KAMPONGS	KAOLINIZED
KABBALA	KAIKAI	KALINITES	KAMSEEN	KAOLINIZES
KABBALAH	KAIKAIS	KALIS	KAMSEENS	KAOLINIZING
KABBALAHS	KAIL	KALIUM	KAMSIN	KAOLINS
KABBALAS	KAILS	KALIUMS	KAMSINS	KAON
KABELE	KAILYAIRD	KALLITYPE	KANA	KAONS
KABELES	KAILYAIRDS	KALLITYPES	KANAKA	KAPOK
KABELJOU	KAILYARD	KALMIA	KANAKAS	KAPOKS
KABELJOUS	KAILYARDS	KALMIAS	KANAS	KAPPA
KABELJOUW	KAIM	KALONG	KANDIES	KAPPAS
KABELJOUWS	KAIMAKAM	KALONGS	KANDY	KAPUT
KABOB	KAIMAKAMS	KALOTYPE	KANEH	KAPUTT
KABOBBED	KAIMS	KALOTYPES	KANEHS	KARA
KABOBBING	KAIN	KALPA	KANG	KARABINER
KABOBS	KAING	KALPAK	KANGA	KARABINERS
KABUKI	KAINITE	KALPAKS	KANGAROO	KARAISM
KABUKIS	KAINITES	KALPAS	KANGAROOED	KARAISMS
KACCHA	KAINS	KALPIS	KANGAROOING	KARAIT
KACCHAS	KAIS	KALPISES	KANGAROOS	KARAITS
KACHA	KAISER	KALSOMINE	KANGAS	KARAKA
KACHAHRI	KAISERDOM	KALSOMINED	KANGHA	KARAKAS
KACHAHRIS	KAISERDOMS	KALSOMINES	KANGHAS	KARAKUL
KACHCHA	KAISERIN	KALSOMINING	KANGS	KARAKULS
KACHERI	KAISERINS	KALUMPIT	KANJI	KARAOKE
KACHERIS	KAISERISM	KALUMPITS	KANJIS	KARAOKES
KACHINA	KAISERISMS	KALYPTRA	KANS	KARAS
KACHINAS	KAISERS	KALYPTRAS	KANSES	KARAT
KADE	KAJAWAH	KAM	KANT	KARATE
KADES	KAJAWAHS	KAMA	KANTAR	KARATEIST
KADI	KAKA	KAMACITE	KANTARS	KARATEISTS
KADIS	KAKAPO	KAMACITES	KANTED	KARATEKA
KAE	KAKAPOS	KAMALA	KANTELA	KARATEKAS
KAED	KAKAS	KAMALAS	KANTELAS	KARATES
KAEING	KAKEMONO	KAMAS	KANTELE	KARATS
KAES	KAKEMONOS	KAME	KANTELES	KARITE
KAFFIYEH	KAKI	KAMEES	KANTEN	KARITES
KAFFIYEHS	KAKIEMON	KAMEESES	KANTENS	KARMA
KAFILA	KAKIEMONS	KAMEEZ	KANTHA	KARMAS
KAFILAS	KAKIS	KAMEEZES	KANTHAS	KARMIC
KAFTAN	KAKODYL	KAMELA	KANTIKOY	KAROSS
KAFTANS	KAKODYLS	KAMELAS	KANTIKOYED	KAROSSES
KAGO	KALAMDAN	KAMERAD	KANTIKOYING	KARRI
KAGOS	KALAMDANS	KAMERADED	KANTIKOYS	KARRIS
KAGOULE	KALAMKARI	KAMERADING	KANTING	KARSEY
KAGOULES	KALAMKARIS	KAMERADS	KANTS	KARSEYS
KAHAL	KALANCHOE	KAMES	KANZU	KARSIES
KAHALS	KALANCHOES	KAMI	KANZUS	KARST

The Chambers Dictionary is the authority for many longer words; see *OSW* Introduction, page xii.

KARSTIC	KATORGAS	KECKED	KEENLY	KELTIES
KARSTIFIED	KATS	KECKING	KEENNESS	KELTS
KARSTIFIES	KATTI	KECKLE	KEENNESSES	KELTY
KARSTIFY	KATTIS	KECKLED	KEENS	KELVIN
KARSTIFYING	KATYDID	KECKLES	KEEP	KELVINS
KARSTS	KATYDIDS	KECKLING	KEEPER	KEMB
KARSY	KAUGH	KECKLINGS	KEEPERS	KEMBED
KART	KAUGHS	KECKS	KEEPING	KEMBING
KARTER	KAURI	KECKSES	KEEPINGS	KEMBO
KARTERS	KAURIS	KECKSIES	KEEPNET	KEMBOED
KARTING	KAVA	KECKSY	KEEPNETS	KEMBOING
KARTINGS	KAVAS	KED	KEEPS	KEMBOS
KARTS	KAVASS	KEDDAH	KEEPSAKE	KEMBS
KARYOGAMIES	KAVASSES	KEDDAHS	KEEPSAKES	KEMP
KARYOGAMY	KAW	KEDGE	KEEPSAKY	KEMPED
KARYOLOGIES	KAWED	KEDGED	KEESHOND	KEMPER
KARYOLOGY	KAWING	KEDGER	KEESHONDEN	KEMPERS
KARYON	KAWS	KEDGEREE	KEESHONDS	KEMPING
KARYONS	KAY	KEDGEREES	KEEVE	KEMPINGS
KARYOSOME	KAYAK	KEDGERS	KEEVES	KEMPLE
KARYOSOMES	KAYAKED	KEDGES	KEF	KEMPLES
KARYOTIN	KAYAKING	KEDGIER	KEFFEL	KEMPS
KARYOTINS	KAYAKS	KEDGIEST	KEFFELS	KEMPT
KARYOTYPE	KAYLE	KEDGING	KEFFIYEH	KEN
KARYOTYPED	KAYLES	KEDGY	KEFFIYEHS	KENAF
KARYOTYPES	KAYO	KEDS	KEFIR	KENAFS
KARYOTYPING	KAYOED	KEECH	KEFIRS	KENDO
KARZIES	KAYOES	KEECHES	KEFS	KENDOS
KARZY	KAYOING	KEEK	KEFUFFLE	KENNED
KAS	KAYOINGS	KEEKED	KEFUFFLED	KENNEL
KASBAH	KAYOS	KEEKER	KEFUFFLES	KENNELLED
KASBAHS	KAYS	KEEKERS	KEFUFFLING	KENNELLING
KASHA	KAZATZKA	KEEKING	KEG	KENNELS
KASHAS	KAZATZKAS	KEEKS	KEGS	KENNER
KASHMIR	KAZI	KEEL	KEIGHT	KENNERS
KASHMIRS	KAZIS	KEELAGE	KEIR	KENNET
KASHRUS	KAZOO	KEELAGES	KEIRS	KENNETS
KASHRUSES	KAZOOS	KEELBOAT	KEISTER	KENNING
KASHRUT	KEA	KEELBOATS	KEISTERS	KENNINGS
KASHRUTH	KEAS	KEELED	KEITLOA	KENO
KASHRUTHS	KEASAR	KEELER	KEITLOAS	KENOS
KASHRUTS	KEASARS	KEELERS	KEKSYE	KENOSES
KAT	KEAVIE	KEELHAUL	KEKSYES	KENOSIS
KATA	KEAVIES	KEELHAULED	KELIM	KENOTIC
KATABASES	KEB	KEELHAULING	KELIMS	KENS
KATABASIS	KEBAB	KEELHAULINGS	KELL	KENSPECK
KATABATIC	KEBABBED	KEELHAULS	KELLAUT	KENT
KATAKANA	KEBABBING	KEELIE	KELLAUTS	KENTED
KATAKANAS	KEBABS	KEELIES	KELLIES	KENTIA
KATANA	KEBBED	KEELING	KELLS	KENTIAS
KATANAS	KEBBIE	KEELINGS	KELLY	KENTING
KATAS	KEBBIES	KEELIVINE	KELOID	KENTLEDGE
KATHAK	KEBBING	KEELIVINES	KELOIDAL	KENTLEDGES
KATHAKALI	KEBBOCK	KEELMAN	KELOIDS	KENTS
KATHAKALIS	KEBBOCKS	KEELMEN	KELP	KEP
KATHAKS	KEBBUCK	KEELS	KELPER	KEPHALIC
KATHARSES	KEBBUCKS	KEELSON	KELPERS	KEPHALICS
KATHARSIS	KEBELE	KEELSONS	KELPIE	KEPHALIN
KATHODE	KEBELES	KEELYVINE	KELPIES	KEPHALINS
KATHODES	KEBLAH	KEELYVINES	KELPS	KEPHIR
KATI	KEBLAHS	KEEN	KELPY	KEPHIRS
KATION	KEBOB	KEENED	KELSON	KEPI
KATIONS	KEBOBBED	KEENER	KELSONS	KEPIS
KATIPO	KEBOBBING	KEENERS	KELT	KEPPING
KATIPOS	KEBOBS	KEENEST	KELTER	KEPPIT
KATIS	KEBS	KEENING	KELTERS	KEPS
KATORGA	KECK	KEENINGS	KELTIE	KEPT

The Chambers Dictionary is the authority for many longer words; see *OSW* Introduction, page xii.

KERATIN
KERATINS
KERATITIS
KERATITISES
KERATOID
KERATOSE
KERATOSES
KERATOSIS
KERB
KERBS
KERBSIDE
KERBSIDES
KERBSTONE
KERBSTONES
KERCHIEF
KERCHIEFED
KERCHIEFING
KERCHIEFS
KERF
KERFS
KERFUFFLE
KERFUFFLED
KERFUFFLES
KERFUFFLING
KERMES
KERMESITE
KERMESITES
KERMESSE
KERMESSES
KERMIS
KERMISES
KERN
KERNE
KERNED
KERNEL
KERNELLED
KERNELLING
KERNELLY
KERNELS
KERNES
KERNING
KERNINGS
KERNISH
KERNITE
KERNITES
KERNS
KEROGEN
KEROGENS
KEROSENE
KEROSENES
KEROSINE
KEROSINES
KERRIA
KERRIAS
KERSEY
KERSEYS
KERVE
KERVED
KERVES
KERVING
KERYGMA
KERYGMAS
KERYGMATA
KESAR
KESARS
KESH
KESHES

KEST
KESTING
KESTREL
KESTRELS
KESTS
KET
KETA
KETAMINE
KETAMINES
KETAS
KETCH
KETCHES
KETCHING
KETCHUP
KETCHUPS
KETONE
KETONES
KETOSE
KETOSES
KETOSIS
KETS
KETTLE
KETTLEFUL
KETTLEFULS
KETTLES
KEVEL
KEVELS
KEX
KEXES
KEY
KEYBOARD
KEYBOARDED
KEYBOARDING
KEYBOARDS
KEYBUGLE
KEYBUGLES
KEYED
KEYHOLE
KEYHOLES
KEYING
KEYLESS
KEYLINE
KEYLINES
KEYNOTE
KEYNOTED
KEYNOTES
KEYNOTING
KEYPAD
KEYPADS
KEYPUNCH
KEYPUNCHED
KEYPUNCHES
KEYPUNCHING
KEYS
KEYSTONE
KEYSTONED
KEYSTONES
KEYSTONING
KEYSTROKE
KEYSTROKES
KEYWORD
KEYWORDS
KGOTLA
KGOTLAS
KHADDAR
KHADDARS
KHADI

KHADIS
KHAKI
KHAKIS
KHALAT
KHALATS
KHALIF
KHALIFA
KHALIFAH
KHALIFAHS
KHALIFAS
KHALIFAT
KHALIFATE
KHALIFATES
KHALIFATS
KHALIFS
KHAMSIN
KHAMSINS
KHAN
KHANATE
KHANATES
KHANGA
KHANGAS
KHANJAR
KHANJARS
KHANS
KHANSAMA
KHANSAMAH
KHANSAMAHS
KHANSAMAS
KHANUM
KHANUMS
KHARIF
KHARIFS
KHAT
KHATS
KHAYA
KHAYAS
KHEDA
KHEDAS
KHEDIVA
KHEDIVAL
KHEDIVAS
KHEDIVATE
KHEDIVATES
KHEDIVE
KHEDIVES
KHEDIVIAL
KHILAFAT
KHILAFATS
KHILAT
KHILATS
KHILIM
KHILIMS
KHODJA
KHODJAS
KHOJA
KHOJAS
KHOR
KHORS
KHOTBAH
KHOTBAHS
KHOTBEH
KHOTBEHS
KHUD
KHUDS
KHURTA
KHURTAS

KHUSKHUS
KHUSKHUSES
KHUTBAH
KHUTBAHS
KIANG
KIANGS
KIAUGH
KIAUGHS
KIBBLE
KIBBLED
KIBBLES
KIBBLING
KIBBUTZ
KIBBUTZIM
KIBE
KIBES
KIBITKA
KIBITKAS
KIBITZ
KIBITZED
KIBITZER
KIBITZERS
KIBITZES
KIBITZING
KIBLAH
KIBLAHS
KIBOSH
KIBOSHED
KIBOSHES
KIBOSHING
KICK
KICKABLE
KICKBACK
KICKBACKS
KICKBALL
KICKBALLS
KICKDOWN
KICKDOWNS
KICKED
KICKER
KICKERS
KICKING
KICKS
KICKSHAW
KICKSHAWS
KICKSHAWSES
KICKSTAND
KICKSTANDS
KID
KIDDED
KIDDER
KIDDERS
KIDDIED
KIDDIER
KIDDIERS
KIDDIES
KIDDING
KIDDLE
KIDDLES
KIDDO
KIDDOS
KIDDUSH
KIDDUSHES
KIDDY
KIDDYING
KIDDYWINK
KIDDYWINKS

KIDEL
KIDELS
KIDGE
KIDGIE
KIDGIER
KIDGIEST
KIDLET
KIDLETS
KIDLING
KIDLINGS
KIDNAP
KIDNAPPED
KIDNAPPER
KIDNAPPERS
KIDNAPPING
KIDNAPS
KIDNEY
KIDNEYS
KIDOLOGIES
KIDOLOGY
KIDS
KIDSKIN
KIDSKINS
KIDSTAKES
KIER
KIERIE
KIERIES
KIERS
KIESERITE
KIESERITES
KIEVE
KIEVES
KIF
KIFS
KIGHT
KIGHTS
KIKE
KIKES
KIKOI
KIKOIS
KIKUMON
KIKUMONS
KIKUYU
KIKUYUS
KILD
KILDERKIN
KILDERKINS
KILERG
KILERGS
KILEY
KILEYS
KILIM
KILIMS
KILL
KILLADAR
KILLADARS
KILLAS
KILLASES
KILLCOW
KILLCOWS
KILLCROP
KILLCROPS
KILLDEE
KILLDEER
KILLDEERS
KILLDEES
KILLED

The Chambers Dictionary is the authority for many longer words; see *OSW* Introduction, page xii.

KILLER	KIMONOS	KINGKLIP	KIPPERING	KITCHENED
KILLERS	KIN	KINGKLIPS	KIPPERS	KITCHENER
KILLICK	KINA	KINGLE	KIPPING	KITCHENERS
KILLICKS	KINAKINA	KINGLES	KIPPS	KITCHENING
KILLIFISH	KINAKINAS	KINGLESS	KIPS	KITCHENS
KILLIFISHES	KINAS	KINGLET	KIR	KITE
KILLING	KINASE	KINGLETS	KIRBEH	KITED
KILLINGS	KINASES	KINGLIER	KIRBEHS	KITENGE
KILLJOY	KINCHIN	KINGLIEST	KIRBIGRIP	KITENGES
KILLJOYS	KINCHINS	KINGLING	KIRBIGRIPS	KITES
KILLOCK	KINCOB	KINGLINGS	KIRIMON	KITH
KILLOCKS	KINCOBS	KINGLY	KIRIMONS	KITHARA
KILLOGIE	KIND	KINGMAKER	KIRK	KITHARAS
KILLOGIES	KINDA	KINGMAKERS	KIRKED	KITHE
KILLS	KINDED	KINGPOST	KIRKING	KITHED
KILLUT	KINDER	KINGPOSTS	KIRKINGS	KITHES
KILLUTS	KINDERS	KINGS	KIRKS	KITHING
KILN	KINDEST	KINGSHIP	KIRKTON	KITHS
KILNED	KINDIES	KINGSHIPS	KIRKTONS	KITING
KILNING	KINDING	KINGWOOD	KIRKWARD	KITINGS
KILNS	KINDLE	KINGWOODS	KIRKYAIRD	KITLING
KILO	KINDLED	KININ	KIRKYAIRDS	KITLINGS
KILOBAR	KINDLER	KININS	KIRKYARD	KITS
KILOBARS	KINDLERS	KINK	KIRKYARDS	KITSCH
KILOBIT	KINDLES	KINKAJOU	KIRMESS	KITSCHES
KILOBITS	KINDLESS	KINKAJOUS	KIRMESSES	KITSCHIER
KILOBYTE	KINDLIER	KINKED	KIRN	KITSCHIEST
KILOBYTES	KINDLIEST	KINKIER	KIRNS	KITSCHILY
KILOCYCLE	KINDLILY	KINKIEST	KIRPAN	KITSCHY
KILOCYCLES	KINDLING	KINKING	KIRPANS	KITTED
KILOGRAM	KINDLINGS	KINKLE	KIRRI	KITTEN
KILOGRAMS	KINDLY	KINKLES	KIRRIS	KITTENED
KILOGRAY	KINDNESS	KINKS	KIRS	KITTENING
KILOGRAYS	KINDNESSES	KINKY	KIRSCH	KITTENISH
KILOHERTZ	KINDRED	KINLESS	KIRSCHES	KITTENS
KILOHERTZES	KINDREDS	KINO	KIRTLE	KITTENY
KILOJOULE	KINDS	KINONE	KIRTLED	KITTIES
KILOJOULES	KINDY	KINONES	KIRTLES	KITTING
KILOMETRE	KINE	KINOS	KISAN	KITTIWAKE
KILOMETRES	KINEMA	KINRED	KISANS	KITTIWAKES
KILOS	KINEMAS	KINREDS	KISH	KITTLE
KILOTON	KINEMATIC	KINS	KISHES	KITTLED
KILOTONS	KINEMATICS	KINSFOLK	KISHKE	KITTLER
KILOVOLT	KINESCOPE	KINSFOLKS	KISHKES	KITTLES
KILOVOLTS	KINESCOPES	KINSHIP	KISMET	KITTLEST
KILOWATT	KINESES	KINSHIPS	KISMETS	KITTLIER
KILOWATTS	KINESICS	KINSMAN	KISS	KITTLIEST
KILP	KINESIS	KINSMEN	KISSABLE	KITTLING
KILPS	KINETIC	KINSWOMAN	KISSAGRAM	KITTLY
KILT	KINETICAL	KINSWOMEN	KISSAGRAMS	KITTUL
KILTED	KINETICS	KINTLEDGE	KISSED	KITTULS
KILTER	KINFOLK	KINTLEDGES	KISSEL	KITTY
KILTERS	KINFOLKS	KIOSK	KISSELS	KIVA
KILTIE	KING	KIOSKS	KISSER	KIVAS
KILTIES	KINGCRAFT	KIP	KISSERS	KIWI
KILTING	KINGCRAFTS	KIPE	KISSES	KIWIS
KILTS	KINGCUP	KIPES	KISSING	KLANG
KILTY	KINGCUPS	KIPP	KISSOGRAM	KLANGS
KIMBO	KINGDOM	KIPPA	KISSOGRAMS	KLAVIER
KIMBOED	KINGDOMED	KIPPAGE	KIST	KLAVIERS
KIMBOING	KINGDOMS	KIPPAGES	KISTED	KLAXON
KIMBOS	KINGED	KIPPAS	KISTING	KLAXONED
KIMCHI	KINGFISH	KIPPED	KISTS	KLAXONING
KIMCHIS	KINGFISHES	KIPPER	KISTVAEN	KLAXONS
KIMMER	KINGHOOD	KIPPERED	KISTVAENS	KLENDUSIC
KIMMERS	KINGHOODS	KIPPERER	KIT	KLEPHT
KIMONO	KINGING	KIPPERERS	KITCHEN	KLEPHTIC

The Chambers Dictionary is the authority for many longer words; see *OSW* Introduction, page xii.

KLEPHTISM	KNAPSCAL	KNIFINGS	KNOTS	KO
KLEPHTISMS	KNAPSCALS	KNIGHT	KNOTTED	KOA
KLEPHTS	KNAPSCULL	KNIGHTAGE	KNOTTER	KOALA
KLINKER	KNAPSCULLS	KNIGHTAGES	KNOTTERS	KOALAS
KLINKERS	KNAPSKULL	KNIGHTED	KNOTTIER	KOAN
KLINOSTAT	KNAPSKULLS	KNIGHTING	KNOTTIEST	KOANS
KLINOSTATS	KNAPWEED	KNIGHTLIER	KNOTTING	KOAS
KLIPDAS	KNAPWEEDS	KNIGHTLIEST	KNOTTINGS	KOB
KLIPDASES	KNAR	KNIGHTLY	KNOTTY	KOBAN
KLONDIKE	KNARL	KNIGHTS	KNOTWEED	KOBANG
KLONDIKED	KNARLS	KNIPHOFIA	KNOTWEEDS	KOBANGS
KLONDIKER	KNARRED	KNIPHOFIAS	KNOTWORK	KOBANS
KLONDIKERS	KNARRING	KNISH	KNOTWORKS	KOBOLD
KLONDIKES	KNARS	KNISHES	KNOUT	KOBOLDS
KLONDIKING	KNAVE	KNIT	KNOUTED	KOBS
KLONDYKE	KNAVERIES	KNITCH	KNOUTING	KOFF
KLONDYKED	KNAVERY	KNITCHES	KNOUTS	KOFFS
KLONDYKER	KNAVES	KNITS	KNOW	KOFTA
KLONDYKERS	KNAVESHIP	KNITTED	KNOWABLE	KOFTAS
KLONDYKES	KNAVESHIPS	KNITTER	KNOWE	KOFTGAR
KLONDYKING	KNAVISH	KNITTERS	KNOWER	KOFTGARI
KLOOCH	KNAVISHLY	KNITTING	KNOWERS	KOFTGARIS
KLOOCHES	KNAWEL	KNITTINGS	KNOWES	KOFTGARS
KLOOCHMAN	KNAWELS	KNITTLE	KNOWHOW	KOFTWORK
KLOOCHMANS	KNEAD	KNITTLES	KNOWHOWS	KOFTWORKS
KLOOCHMEN	KNEADED	KNITWEAR	KNOWING	KOHL
KLOOF	KNEADER	KNITWEARS	KNOWINGLY	KOHLRABI
KLOOFS	KNEADERS	KNIVE	KNOWLEDGE	KOHLRABIS
KLOOTCH	KNEADING	KNIVED	KNOWLEDGED	KOHLS
KLOOTCHES	KNEADS	KNIVES	KNOWLEDGES	KOINE
KLUDGE	KNEE	KNIVING	KNOWLEDGING	KOINES
KLUDGES	KNEECAP	KNOB	KNOWN	KOKANEE
KLUTZ	KNEECAPPED	KNOBBED	KNOWNS	KOKANEES
KLUTZES	KNEECAPPING	KNOBBER	KNOWS	KOKER
KLYSTRON	KNEECAPPINGS	KNOBBERS	KNUB	KOKERS
KLYSTRONS	KNEECAPS	KNOBBIER	KNUBBIER	KOKRA
KNACK	KNEED	KNOBBIEST	KNUBBIEST	KOKRAS
KNACKER	KNEEHOLE	KNOBBLE	KNUBBLE	KOKUM
KNACKERED	KNEEHOLES	KNOBBLED	KNUBBLED	KOKUMS
KNACKERIES	KNEEING	KNOBBLES	KNUBBLES	KOLA
KNACKERING	KNEEL	KNOBBLIER	KNUBBLIER	KOLAS
KNACKERS	KNEELED	KNOBBLIEST	KNUBBLIEST	KOLINSKIES
KNACKERY	KNEELER	KNOBBLING	KNUBBLING	KOLINSKY
KNACKIER	KNEELERS	KNOBBLY	KNUBBLY	KOLKHOZ
KNACKIEST	KNEELING	KNOBBY	KNUBBY	KOLKHOZES
KNACKISH	KNEELS	KNOBS	KNUBS	KOLO
KNACKS	KNEES	KNOCK	KNUCKLE	KOLOS
KNACKY	KNEIDLACH	KNOCKED	KNUCKLED	KOMATIK
KNAG	KNELL	KNOCKER	KNUCKLES	KOMATIKS
KNAGGIER	KNELLED	KNOCKERS	KNUCKLIER	KOMBU
KNAGGIEST	KNELLING	KNOCKING	KNUCKLIEST	KOMBUS
KNAGGY	KNELLS	KNOCKINGS	KNUCKLING	KOMISSAR
KNAGS	KNELT	KNOCKOUT	KNUCKLY	KOMISSARS
KNAIDEL	KNEVELL	KNOCKOUTS	KNUR	KOMITAJI
KNAIDLOCH	KNEVELLED	KNOCKS	KNURL	KOMITAJIS
KNAP	KNEVELLING	KNOLL	KNURLED	KON
KNAPPED	KNEVELLS	KNOLLED	KNURLIER	KOND
KNAPPER	KNEW	KNOLLING	KNURLIEST	KONFYT
KNAPPERS	KNICKER	KNOLLS	KNURLING	KONFYTS
KNAPPING	KNICKERED	KNOP	KNURLINGS	KONIMETER
KNAPPLE	KNICKERS	KNOPS	KNURLS	KONIMETERS
KNAPPLED	KNICKS	KNOSP	KNURLY	KONIOLOGIES
KNAPPLES	KNIFE	KNOSPS	KNURR	KONIOLOGY
KNAPPLING	KNIFED	KNOT	KNURRS	KONISCOPE
KNAPS	KNIFELESS	KNOTGRASS	KNURS	KONISCOPES
KNAPSACK	KNIFES	KNOTGRASSES	KNUT	KONK
KNAPSACKS	KNIFING	KNOTLESS	KNUTS	KONKED

The Chambers Dictionary is the authority for many longer words; see OSW Introduction, page xii.

KONKING	KOTOWING	KREESED	KULAN	KY
KONKS	KOTOWS	KREESES	KULANS	KYANG
KONNING	KOTTABOS	KREESING	KUMARA	KYANGS
KONS	KOTTABOSES	KREMLIN	KUMARAS	KYANISE
KOODOO	KOTWAL	KREMLINS	KUMARI	KYANISED
KOODOOS	KOTWALS	KRENG	KUMARIS	KYANISES
KOOK	KOULAN	KRENGS	KUMISS	KYANISING
KOOKED	KOULANS	KREOSOTE	KUMISSES	KYANITE
KOOKIE	KOUMISS	KREOSOTED	KUMMEL	KYANITES
KOOKIER	KOUMISSES	KREOSOTES	KUMMELS	KYANIZE
KOOKIEST	KOUPREY	KREOSOTING	KUMQUAT	KYANIZED
KOOKING	KOUPREYS	KREPLACH	KUMQUATS	KYANIZES
KOOKS	KOURBASH	KREUTZER	KUNKAR	KYANIZING
KOOKY	KOURBASHED	KREUTZERS	KUNKARS	KYAT
KOOLAH	KOURBASHES	KRILL	KUNKUR	KYATS
KOOLAHS	KOURBASHING	KRILLS	KUNKURS	KYBOSH
KOORI	KOUROI	KRIMMER	KUNZITE	KYBOSHED
KOORIS	KOUROS	KRIMMERS	KUNZITES	KYBOSHES
KOP	KOUSKOUS	KRIS	KURBASH	KYBOSHING
KOPASETIC	KOUSKOUSES	KRISED	KURBASHED	KYDST
KOPECK	KOW	KRISES	KURBASHES	KYE
KOPECKS	KOWHAI	KRISING	KURBASHING	KYLE
KOPH	KOWHAIS	KROMESKIES	KURGAN	KYLES
KOPHS	KOWS	KROMESKY	KURGANS	KYLICES
KOPJE	KOWTOW	KRONA	KURI	KYLIE
KOPJES	KOWTOWED	KRONE	KURIS	KYLIES
KOPPA	KOWTOWING	KRONEN	KURRAJONG	KYLIN
KOPPAS	KOWTOWS	KRONER	KURRAJONGS	KYLINS
KOPPIE	KRAAL	KRONOR	KURRE	KYLIX
KOPPIES	KRAALED	KRONUR	KURRES	KYLLOSES
KOPS	KRAALING	KRULLER	KURSAAL	KYLLOSIS
KORA	KRAALS	KRULLERS	KURSAALS	KYLOE
KORAS	KRAB	KRUMHORN	KURTA	KYLOES
KORE	KRABS	KRUMHORNS	KURTAS	KYMOGRAM
KORERO	KRAFT	KRUMMHORN	KURTOSES	KYMOGRAMS
KOREROS	KRAFTS	KRUMMHORNS	KURTOSIS	KYMOGRAPH
KORES	KRAIT	KRYOMETER	KURU	KYMOGRAPHS
KORFBALL	KRAITS	KRYOMETERS	KURUS	KYND
KORFBALLS	KRAKEN	KRYPSES	KURVEY	KYNDE
KORKIR	KRAKENS	KRYPSIS	KURVEYED	KYNDED
KORKIRS	KRAMERIA	KRYPTON	KURVEYING	KYNDES
KORMA	KRAMERIAS	KRYPTONS	KURVEYOR	KYNDING
KORMAS	KRANG	KRYTRON	KURVEYORS	KYNDS
KORORA	KRANGS	KRYTRONS	KURVEYS	KYNE
KORORAS	KRANS	KSAR	KUTCH	KYOGEN
KORUNA	KRANSES	KSARS	KUTCHA	KYOGENS
KORUNAS	KRANTZ	KUCHCHA	KUTCHES	KYPHOSES
KOS	KRANTZES	KUDOS	KVASS	KYPHOSIS
KOSES	KRANZ	KUDOSES	KVASSES	KYPHOTIC
KOSHER	KRANZES	KUDU	KVETCH	KYRIELLE
KOSHERED	KRATER	KUDUS	KVETCHED	KYRIELLES
KOSHERING	KRATERS	KUDZU	KVETCHER	KYTE
KOSHERS	KRAUT	KUDZUS	KVETCHERS	KYTES
KOSMOS	KRAUTS	KUFIYAH	KVETCHES	KYTHE
KOSMOSES	KREASOTE	KUFIYAHS	KVETCHING	KYTHED
KOSS	KREASOTED	KUKRI	KWACHA	KYTHES
KOSSES	KREASOTES	KUKRIS	KWACHAS	KYTHING
KOTO	KREASOTING	KUKU	KWANZA	KYU
KOTOS	KREATINE	KUKUS	KWANZAS	KYUS
KOTOW	KREATINES	KULAK	KWELA	
KOTOWED	KREESE	KULAKS	KWELAS	

L

LA
LAAGER
LAAGERED
LAAGERING
LAAGERS
LAB
LABARA
LABARUM
LABARUMS
LABDA
LABDACISM
LABDACISMS
LABDANUM
LABDANUMS
LABDAS
LABEL
LABELLA
LABELLED
LABELLING
LABELLOID
LABELLUM
LABELS
LABIA
LABIAL
LABIALISE
LABIALISED
LABIALISES
LABIALISING
LABIALISM
LABIALISMS
LABIALIZE
LABIALIZED
LABIALIZES
LABIALIZING
LABIALLY
LABIALS
LABIATE
LABIATES
LABILE
LABILITIES
LABILITY
LABIS
LABISES
LABIUM
LABLAB
LABLABS
LABOR
LABORED
LABORING
LABORIOUS
LABORS
LABOUR
LABOURED
LABOURER
LABOURERS
LABOURING
LABOURISM
LABOURISMS
LABOURIST

LABOURISTS
LABOURS
LABRA
LABRET
LABRETS
LABRID
LABRIDS
LABROID
LABROIDS
LABROSE
LABRUM
LABRYS
LABRYSES
LABS
LABURNUM
LABURNUMS
LABYRINTH
LABYRINTHS
LAC
LACCOLITE
LACCOLITES
LACCOLITH
LACCOLITHS
LACE
LACEBARK
LACEBARKS
LACED
LACERABLE
LACERANT
LACERATE
LACERATED
LACERATES
LACERATING
LACERTIAN
LACERTINE
LACES
LACET
LACETS
LACEWING
LACEWINGS
LACEY
LACHES
LACHESES
LACHRYMAL
LACHRYMALS
LACIER
LACIEST
LACING
LACINGS
LACINIA
LACINIAE
LACINIATE
LACK
LACKADAY
LACKED
LACKER
LACKERED
LACKERING
LACKERS

LACKEY
LACKEYED
LACKEYING
LACKEYS
LACKING
LACKLAND
LACKLANDS
LACKS
LACMUS
LACMUSES
LACONIC
LACONICAL
LACONISM
LACONISMS
LACQUER
LACQUERED
LACQUERER
LACQUERERS
LACQUERING
LACQUERINGS
LACQUERS
LACQUEY
LACQUEYED
LACQUEYING
LACQUEYS
LACRIMAL
LACRIMALS
LACRIMOSO
LACROSSE
LACROSSES
LACRYMAL
LACRYMALS
LACS
LACTARIAN
LACTARIANS
LACTASE
LACTASES
LACTATE
LACTATED
LACTATES
LACTATING
LACTATION
LACTATIONS
LACTEAL
LACTEALS
LACTEOUS
LACTIC
LACTIFIC
LACTONE
LACTONES
LACTOSE
LACTOSES
LACUNA
LACUNAE
LACUNAL
LACUNAR
LACUNARIA
LACUNARS
LACUNARY

LACUNATE
LACUNOSE
LACY
LAD
LADANUM
LADANUMS
LADDER
LADDERED
LADDERING
LADDERS
LADDERY
LADDIE
LADDIES
LADE
LADED
LADEN
LADES
LADIES
LADIFIED
LADIFIES
LADIFY
LADIFYING
LADING
LADINGS
LADLE
LADLED
LADLEFUL
LADLEFULS
LADLES
LADLING
LADRONE
LADRONES
LADS
LADY
LADYBIRD
LADYBIRDS
LADYBUG
LADYBUGS
LADYCOW
LADYCOWS
LADYFIED
LADYFIES
LADYFLIES
LADYFLY
LADYFY
LADYFYING
LADYHOOD
LADYHOODS
LADYISH
LADYISM
LADYISMS
LADYKIN
LADYKINS
LADYLIKE
LADYSHIP
LADYSHIPS
LAER
LAERED
LAERING

LAERS
LAESIE
LAETARE
LAETARES
LAEVIGATE
LAEVIGATED
LAEVIGATES
LAEVIGATING
LAEVULOSE
LAEVULOSES
LAG
LAGAN
LAGANS
LAGENA
LAGENAS
LAGER
LAGERS
LAGGARD
LAGGARDS
LAGGED
LAGGEN
LAGGENS
LAGGER
LAGGERS
LAGGIN
LAGGING
LAGGINGLY
LAGGINGS
LAGGINS
LAGNAPPE
LAGNAPPES
LAGNIAPPE
LAGNIAPPES
LAGOMORPH
LAGOMORPHS
LAGOON
LAGOONAL
LAGOONS
LAGRIMOSO
LAGS
LAGUNE
LAGUNES
LAH
LAHAR
LAHARS
LAHS
LAIC
LAICAL
LAICISE
LAICISED
LAICISES
LAICISING
LAICITIES
LAICITY
LAICIZE
LAICIZED
LAICIZES
LAICIZING
LAICS

The Chambers Dictionary is the authority for many longer words; see *OSW* Introduction, page xii.

LAID	LALANGS	LAMENESS	LAMPIONS	LANDFALL
LAIDED	LALDIE	LAMENESSES	LAMPLIGHT	LANDFALLS
LAIDING	LALDIES	LAMENT	LAMPLIGHTS	LANDFILL
LAIDLY	LALDY	LAMENTED	LAMPOON	LANDFILLS
LAIDS	LALLAN	LAMENTING	LAMPOONED	LANDFORCE
LAIGH	LALLANS	LAMENTINGS	LAMPOONER	LANDFORCES
LAIGHER	LALLATION	LAMENTS	LAMPOONERS	LANDFORM
LAIGHEST	LALLATIONS	LAMER	LAMPOONING	LANDFORMS
LAIGHS	LALLING	LAMES	LAMPOONS	LANDGRAVE
LAIK	LALLINGS	LAMEST	LAMPPOST	LANDGRAVES
LAIKA	LALLYGAG	LAMETER	LAMPPOSTS	LANDING
LAIKAS	LALLYGAGGED	LAMETERS	LAMPREY	LANDINGS
LAIKED	LALLYGAGGING	LAMIA	LAMPREYS	LANDLADIES
LAIKER	LALLYGAGS	LAMIAE	LAMPS	LANDLADY
LAIKERS	LAM	LAMIAS	LAMPSHADE	LANDLER
LAIKING	LAMA	LAMIGER	LAMPSHADES	LANDLERS
LAIKS	LAMAISTIC	LAMIGERS	LAMPUKA	LANDLESS
LAIN	LAMANTIN	LAMINA	LAMPUKAS	LANDLOPER
LAIR	LAMANTINS	LAMINABLE	LAMPUKI	LANDLOPERS
LAIRAGE	LAMAS	LAMINAE	LAMPUKIS	LANDLORD
LAIRAGES	LAMASERAI	LAMINAR	LAMS	LANDLORDS
LAIRD	LAMASERAIS	LAMINARY	LANA	LANDMAN
LAIRDS	LAMASERIES	LAMINATE	LANAS	LANDMARK
LAIRDSHIP	LAMASERY	LAMINATED	LANATE	LANDMARKS
LAIRDSHIPS	LAMB	LAMINATES	LANCE	LANDMASS
LAIRED	LAMBADA	LAMINATING	LANCED	LANDMASSES
LAIRIER	LAMBADAS	LAMINATOR	LANCEGAY	LANDMEN
LAIRIEST	LAMBAST	LAMINATORS	LANCEGAYS	LANDOWNER
LAIRING	LAMBASTE	LAMING	LANCELET	LANDOWNERS
LAIRISE	LAMBASTED	LAMINGTON	LANCELETS	LANDRACE
LAIRISED	LAMBASTES	LAMINGTONS	LANCEOLAR	LANDRACES
LAIRISES	LAMBASTING	LAMINITIS	LANCER	LANDRAIL
LAIRISING	LAMBASTS	LAMINITISES	LANCERS	LANDRAILS
LAIRIZE	LAMBDA	LAMINOSE	LANCES	LANDS
LAIRIZED	LAMBDAS	LAMISH	LANCET	LANDSCAPE
LAIRIZES	LAMBDOID	LAMITER	LANCETED	LANDSCAPED
LAIRIZING	LAMBED	LAMITERS	LANCETS	LANDSCAPES
LAIRS	LAMBENCIES	LAMMED	LANCH	LANDSCAPING
LAIRY	LAMBENCY	LAMMER	LANCHED	LANDSCRIP
LAISSE	LAMBENT	LAMMERS	LANCHES	LANDSCRIPS
LAISSES	LAMBENTLY	LAMMIE	LANCHING	LANDSIDE
LAITANCE	LAMBER	LAMMIES	LANCIFORM	LANDSIDES
LAITANCES	LAMBERS	LAMMIGER	LANCINATE	LANDSKIP
LAITH	LAMBERT	LAMMIGERS	LANCINATED	LANDSKIPPED
LAITIES	LAMBERTS	LAMMING	LANCINATES	LANDSKIPPING
LAITY	LAMBIE	LAMMINGS	LANCINATING	LANDSKIPS
LAKE	LAMBIES	LAMMY	LANCING	LANDSLIDE
LAKED	LAMBING	LAMP	LAND	LANDSLIDES
LAKELAND	LAMBITIVE	LAMPAD	LANDAMMAN	LANDSLIP
LAKELANDS	LAMBITIVES	LAMPADARIES	LANDAMMANS	LANDSLIPS
LAKELET	LAMBKIN	LAMPADARY	LANDAU	LANDSMAN
LAKELETS	LAMBKINS	LAMPADIST	LANDAULET	LANDSMEN
LAKER	LAMBLING	LAMPADISTS	LANDAULETS	LANDWARD
LAKERS	LAMBLINGS	LAMPADS	LANDAUS	LANDWARDS
LAKES	LAMBOYS	LAMPAS	LANDDAMNE	LANDWIND
LAKESIDE	LAMBS	LAMPASES	LANDDAMNED	LANDWINDS
LAKESIDES	LAMBSKIN	LAMPASSE	LANDDAMNES	LANE
LAKH	LAMBSKINS	LAMPASSES	LANDDAMNING	LANES
LAKHS	LAME	LAMPED	LANDDROS	LANEWAY
LAKIER	LAMED	LAMPERN	LANDDROSES	LANEWAYS
LAKIEST	LAMELLA	LAMPERNS	LANDDROST	LANG
LAKIN	LAMELLAE	LAMPERS	LANDDROSTS	LANGAHA
LAKING	LAMELLAR	LAMPHOLE	LANDE	LANGAHAS
LAKINS	LAMELLATE	LAMPHOLES	LANDED	LANGER
LAKISH	LAMELLOID	LAMPING	LANDER	LANGEST
LAKY	LAMELLOSE	LAMPINGS	LANDERS	LANGLAUF
LALANG	LAMELY	LAMPION	LANDES	LANGLAUFS

The Chambers Dictionary is the authority for many longer words; see *OSW* Introduction, page xii.

LANGOUSTE	LANTERNED	LAPSTREAK	LARK	LASHING
LANGOUSTES	LANTERNING	LAPSTREAKS	LARKED	LASHINGS
LANGRAGE	LANTERNS	LAPSUS	LARKER	LASHKAR
LANGRAGES	LANTHANUM	LAPSUSES	LARKERS	LASHKARS
LANGREL	LANTHANUMS	LAPTOP	LARKIER	LASING
LANGRELS	LANTHORN	LAPTOPS	LARKIEST	LASINGS
LANGRIDGE	LANTHORNS	LAPWING	LARKINESS	LASKET
LANGRIDGES	LANTS	LAPWINGS	LARKINESSES	LASKETS
LANGSPEL	LANTSKIP	LAPWORK	LARKING	LASQUE
LANGSPELS	LANTSKIPS	LAPWORKS	LARKISH	LASQUES
LANGSPIEL	LANUGO	LAQUEARIA	LARKS	LASS
LANGSPIELS	LANUGOS	LAR	LARKSPUR	LASSES
LANGUAGE	LANX	LARBOARD	LARKSPURS	LASSI
LANGUAGED	LANYARD	LARBOARDS	LARKY	LASSIE
LANGUAGES	LANYARDS	LARCENER	LARMIER	LASSIES
LANGUAGING	LAP	LARCENERS	LARMIERS	LASSIS
LANGUE	LAPDOG	LARCENIES	LARN	LASSITUDE
LANGUED	LAPDOGS	LARCENIST	LARNAKES	LASSITUDES
LANGUES	LAPEL	LARCENISTS	LARNAX	LASSLORN
LANGUET	LAPELLED	LARCENOUS	LARNED	LASSO
LANGUETS	LAPELS	LARCENY	LARNING	LASSOCK
LANGUETTE	LAPFUL	LARCH	LARNS	LASSOCKS
LANGUETTES	LAPFULS	LARCHEN	LAROID	LASSOED
LANGUID	LAPHELD	LARCHES	LARRIGAN	LASSOES
LANGUIDLY	LAPIDARIES	LARD	LARRIGANS	LASSOING
LANGUISH	LAPIDARY	LARDALITE	LARRIKIN	LASSOS
LANGUISHED	LAPIDATE	LARDALITES	LARRIKINS	LASSU
LANGUISHES	LAPIDATED	LARDED	LARRUP	LASSUS
LANGUISHING	LAPIDATES	LARDER	LARRUPED	LAST
LANGUISHINGS	LAPIDATING	LARDERER	LARRUPING	LASTAGE
LANGUOR	LAPIDEOUS	LARDERERS	LARRUPS	LASTAGES
LANGUORS	LAPIDIFIC	LARDERS	LARUM	LASTED
LANGUR	LAPIDIFIED	LARDIER	LARUMS	LASTER
LANGURS	LAPIDIFIES	LARDIEST	LARVA	LASTERS
LANIARD	LAPIDIFY	LARDING	LARVAE	LASTING
LANIARDS	LAPIDIFYING	LARDON	LARVAL	LASTINGLY
LANIARY	LAPILLI	LARDONS	LARVATE	LASTINGS
LANK	LAPIS	LARDOON	LARVATED	LASTLY
LANKED	LAPISES	LARDOONS	LARVICIDE	LASTS
LANKER	LAPJE	LARDS	LARVICIDES	LAT
LANKEST	LAPJES	LARDY	LARVIFORM	LATCH
LANKIER	LAPPED	LARE	LARVIKITE	LATCHED
LANKIEST	LAPPEL	LARES	LARVIKITES	LATCHES
LANKILY	LAPPELS	LARGE	LARYNGAL	LATCHET
LANKINESS	LAPPER	LARGELY	LARYNGEAL	LATCHETS
LANKINESSES	LAPPERED	LARGEN	LARYNGES	LATCHING
LANKING	LAPPERING	LARGENED	LARYNX	LATCHKEY
LANKLY	LAPPERS	LARGENESS	LARYNXES	LATCHKEYS
LANKNESS	LAPPET	LARGENESSES	LAS	LATE
LANKNESSES	LAPPETED	LARGENING	LASAGNA	LATED
LANKS	LAPPETS	LARGENS	LASAGNAS	LATEEN
LANKY	LAPPIE	LARGER	LASAGNE	LATEENS
LANNER	LAPPIES	LARGES	LASAGNES	LATELY
LANNERET	LAPPING	LARGESS	LASCAR	LATEN
LANNERETS	LAPPINGS	LARGESSE	LASCARS	LATENCE
LANNERS	LAPS	LARGESSES	LASE	LATENCES
LANOLIN	LAPSABLE	LARGEST	LASED	LATENCIES
LANOLINE	LAPSANG	LARGHETTO	LASER	LATENCY
LANOLINES	LAPSANGS	LARGHETTOS	LASERS	LATENED
LANOLINS	LAPSE	LARGISH	LASERWORT	LATENESS
LANOSE	LAPSED	LARGITION	LASERWORTS	LATENESSES
LANT	LAPSES	LARGITIONS	LASES	LATENING
LANTANA	LAPSING	LARGO	LASH	LATENS
LANTANAS	LAPSTONE	LARGOS	LASHED	LATENT
LANTERLOO	LAPSTONES	LARIAT	LASHER	LATENTLY
LANTERLOOS	LAPSTRAKE	LARIATS	LASHERS	LATER
LANTERN	LAPSTRAKES	LARINE	LASHES	LATERAL

The Chambers Dictionary is the authority for many longer words; see *OSW* Introduction, page xii.

LATERALLY	LATTICE	LAUREATE	LAWEST	LAYMAN
LATERALS	LATTICED	LAUREATED	LAWFUL	LAYMEN
LATERITE	LATTICES	LAUREATES	LAWFULLY	LAYOUT
LATERITES	LATTICING	LAUREATING	LAWIN	LAYOUTS
LATERITIC	LATTICINI	LAUREL	LAWING	LAYPERSON
LATESCENT	LATTICINO	LAURELLED	LAWINGS	LAYPERSONS
LATEST	LAUCH	LAURELS	LAWINS	LAYS
LATESTS	LAUCHING	LAUWINE	LAWK	LAYSTALL
LATEWAKE	LAUCHS	LAUWINES	LAWKS	LAYSTALLS
LATEWAKES	LAUD	LAV	LAWLAND	LAYTIME
LATEX	LAUDABLE	LAVA	LAWLANDS	LAYTIMES
LATEXES	LAUDABLY	LAVABO	LAWLESS	LAYWOMAN
LATH	LAUDANUM	LAVABOES	LAWLESSLY	LAYWOMEN
LATHE	LAUDANUMS	LAVABOS	LAWMAN	LAZAR
LATHED	LAUDATION	LAVAFORM	LAWMEN	LAZARET
LATHEE	LAUDATIONS	LAVAGE	LAWMONGER	LAZARETS
LATHEES	LAUDATIVE	LAVAGES	LAWMONGERS	LAZARETTO
LATHEN	LAUDATIVES	LAVALIERE	LAWN	LAZARETTOS
LATHER	LAUDATORIES	LAVALIERES	LAWNIER	LAZARS
LATHERED	LAUDATORY	LAVAS	LAWNIEST	LAZE
LATHERING	LAUDED	LAVATERA	LAWNMOWER	LAZED
LATHERS	LAUDER	LAVATERAS	LAWNMOWERS	LAZES
LATHERY	LAUDERS	LAVATION	LAWNS	LAZIER
LATHES	LAUDING	LAVATIONS	LAWNY	LAZIEST
LATHI	LAUDS	LAVATORIES	LAWS	LAZILY
LATHIER	LAUF	LAVATORY	LAWSUIT	LAZINESS
LATHIEST	LAUFS	LAVE	LAWSUITS	LAZINESSES
LATHING	LAUGH	LAVED	LAWYER	LAZING
LATHINGS	LAUGHABLE	LAVEER	LAWYERLY	LAZO
LATHIS	LAUGHABLY	LAVEERED	LAWYERS	LAZOED
LATHLIKE	LAUGHED	LAVEERING	LAX	LAZOES
LATHS	LAUGHER	LAVEERS	LAXATIVE	LAZOING
LATHY	LAUGHERS	LAVEMENT	LAXATIVES	LAZOS
LATHYRISM	LAUGHFUL	LAVEMENTS	LAXATOR	LAZULITE
LATHYRISMS	LAUGHIER	LAVENDER	LAXATORS	LAZULITES
LATHYRUS	LAUGHIEST	LAVENDERED	LAXER	LAZURITE
LATHYRUSES	LAUGHING	LAVENDERING	LAXES	LAZURITES
LATICES	LAUGHINGS	LAVENDERS	LAXEST	LAZY
LATICLAVE	LAUGHS	LAVER	LAXISM	LAZZARONE
LATICLAVES	LAUGHSOME	LAVEROCK	LAXISMS	LAZZARONI
LATIFONDI	LAUGHTER	LAVEROCKED	LAXIST	LAZZI
LATISH	LAUGHTERS	LAVEROCKING	LAXISTS	LAZZO
LATITANCIES	LAUGHY	LAVEROCKS	LAXITIES	LEA
LATITANCY	LAUNCE	LAVERS	LAXITY	LEACH
LATITANT	LAUNCED	LAVES	LAXLY	LEACHATE
LATITAT	LAUNCES	LAVING	LAXNESS	LEACHATES
LATITATS	LAUNCH	LAVISH	LAXNESSES	LEACHED
LATITUDE	LAUNCHED	LAVISHED	LAY	LEACHES
LATITUDES	LAUNCHER	LAVISHER	LAYABOUT	LEACHIER
LATKE	LAUNCHERS	LAVISHES	LAYABOUTS	LEACHIEST
LATKES	LAUNCHES	LAVISHEST	LAYAWAY	LEACHING
LATRANT	LAUNCHING	LAVISHING	LAYAWAYS	LEACHINGS
LATRATION	LAUNCING	LAVISHLY	LAYBACK	LEACHOUR
LATRATIONS	LAUND	LAVOLT	LAYBACKED	LEACHOURS
LATRIA	LAUNDER	LAVOLTA	LAYBACKING	LEACHTUB
LATRIAS	LAUNDERED	LAVOLTAED	LAYBACKS	LEACHTUBS
LATRINE	LAUNDERER	LAVOLTAING	LAYER	LEACHY
LATRINES	LAUNDERERS	LAVOLTAS	LAYERED	LEAD
LATROCINIES	LAUNDERING	LAVOLTED	LAYERING	LEADED
LATROCINY	LAUNDERS	LAVOLTING	LAYERINGS	LEADEN
LATRON	LAUNDRESS	LAVOLTS	LAYERS	LEADENED
LATRONS	LAUNDRESSES	LAVRA	LAYETTE	LEADENING
LATS	LAUNDRIES	LAVRAS	LAYETTES	LEADENLY
LATTEN	LAUNDRY	LAVS	LAYING	LEADENS
LATTENS	LAUNDS	LAW	LAYINGS	LEADER
LATTER	LAURA	LAWED	LAYLOCK	LEADERS
LATTERLY	LAURAS	LAWER	LAYLOCKS	LEADIER

The Chambers Dictionary is the authority for many longer words; see *OSW* Introduction, page xii.

LEADIEST	LEANINGS	LEATHERED	LEDDEN	LEG
LEADING	LEANLY	LEATHERING	LEDDENS	LEGACIES
LEADINGS	LEANNESS	LEATHERINGS	LEDGE	LEGACY
LEADLESS	LEANNESSES	LEATHERN	LEDGER	LEGAL
LEADLINE	LEANS	LEATHERS	LEDGERED	LEGALESE
LEADLINES	LEANT	LEATHERY	LEDGERING	LEGALESES
LEADS	LEANY	LEATS	LEDGERS	LEGALISE
LEADSMAN	LEAP	LEAVE	LEDGES	LEGALISED
LEADSMEN	LEAPED	LEAVED	LEDGIER	LEGALISES
LEADY	LEAPER	LEAVEN	LEDGIEST	LEGALISING
LEAF	LEAPEROUS	LEAVENED	LEDGY	LEGALISM
LEAFAGE	LEAPERS	LEAVENING	LEDUM	LEGALISMS
LEAFAGES	LEAPING	LEAVENINGS	LEDUMS	LEGALIST
LEAFBUD	LEAPOROUS	LEAVENOUS	LEE	LEGALISTS
LEAFBUDS	LEAPROUS	LEAVENS	LEEAR	LEGALITIES
LEAFED	LEAPS	LEAVER	LEEARS	LEGALITY
LEAFERIES	LEAPT	LEAVERS	LEECH	LEGALIZE
LEAFERY	LEAR	LEAVES	LEECHDOM	LEGALIZED
LEAFIER	LEARE	LEAVIER	LEECHDOMS	LEGALIZES
LEAFIEST	LEARED	LEAVIEST	LEECHED	LEGALIZING
LEAFINESS	LEARES	LEAVING	LEECHEE	LEGALLY
LEAFINESSES	LEARIER	LEAVINGS	LEECHEES	LEGATARIES
LEAFING	LEARIEST	LEAVY	LEECHES	LEGATARY
LEAFLESS	LEARING	LEAZE	LEECHING	LEGATE
LEAFLET	LEARN	LEAZES	LEED	LEGATEE
LEAFLETED	LEARNABLE	LEBBEK	LEEING	LEGATEES
LEAFLETING	LEARNED	LEBBEKS	LEEK	LEGATES
LEAFLETS	LEARNEDLY	LECANORA	LEEKS	LEGATINE
LEAFLETTED	LEARNER	LECANORAS	LEEP	LEGATION
LEAFLETTING	LEARNERS	LECH	LEEPED	LEGATIONS
LEAFLIKE	LEARNING	LECHED	LEEPING	LEGATO
LEAFS	LEARNINGS	LECHER	LEEPS	LEGATOR
LEAFY	LEARNS	LECHERED	LEER	LEGATORS
LEAGUE	LEARNT	LECHERIES	LEERED	LEGATOS
LEAGUED	LEARS	LECHERING	LEERIER	LEGEND
LEAGUER	LEARY	LECHEROUS	LEERIEST	LEGENDARIES
LEAGUERED	LEAS	LECHERS	LEERING	LEGENDARY
LEAGUERING	LEASABLE	LECHERY	LEERINGLY	LEGENDIST
LEAGUERS	LEASE	LECHES	LEERINGS	LEGENDISTS
LEAGUES	LEASEBACK	LECHING	LEERS	LEGENDRIES
LEAGUING	LEASEBACKS	LECHWE	LEERY	LEGENDRY
LEAK	LEASED	LECHWES	LEES	LEGENDS
LEAKAGE	LEASEHOLD	LECITHIN	LEESE	LEGER
LEAKAGES	LEASEHOLDS	LECITHINS	LEESES	LEGERING
LEAKED	LEASER	LECTERN	LEESING	LEGERINGS
LEAKER	LEASERS	LECTERNS	LEET	LEGERITIES
LEAKERS	LEASES	LECTIN	LEETLE	LEGERITY
LEAKIER	LEASH	LECTINS	LEETS	LEGERS
LEAKIEST	LEASHED	LECTION	LEEWARD	LEGES
LEAKINESS	LEASHES	LECTIONS	LEEWARDS	LEGGE
LEAKINESSES	LEASHING	LECTOR	LEEWAY	LEGGED
LEAKING	LEASING	LECTORATE	LEEWAYS	LEGGER
LEAKS	LEASINGS	LECTORATES	LEFT	LEGGERS
LEAKY	LEASOW	LECTORS	LEFTE	LEGGES
LEAL	LEASOWE	LECTRESS	LEFTIE	LEGGIER
LEALLY	LEASOWED	LECTRESSES	LEFTIES	LEGGIEST
LEALTIES	LEASOWES	LECTURE	LEFTISH	LEGGINESS
LEALTY	LEASOWING	LECTURED	LEFTISM	LEGGINESSES
LEAM	LEASOWS	LECTURER	LEFTISMS	LEGGING
LEAMED	LEAST	LECTURERS	LEFTIST	LEGGINGS
LEAMING	LEASTS	LECTURES	LEFTISTS	LEGGISM
LEAMS	LEASTWAYS	LECTURING	LEFTOVER	LEGGISMS
LEAN	LEASTWISE	LECTURN	LEFTOVERS	LEGGY
LEANED	LEASURE	LECTURNS	LEFTS	LEGHORN
LEANER	LEASURES	LECYTHI	LEFTWARD	LEGHORNS
LEANEST	LEAT	LECYTHUS	LEFTWARDS	LEGIBLE
LEANING	LEATHER	LED	LEFTY	LEGIBLY

The Chambers Dictionary is the authority for many longer words; see *OSW* Introduction, page xii.

LEGION	LEK	LENGTHFUL	LEPPED	LETHALITIES
LEGIONARIES	LEKE	LENGTHIER	LEPPING	LETHALITY
LEGIONARY	LEKKED	LENGTHIEST	LEPRA	LETHALLY
LEGIONED	LEKKING	LENGTHILY	LEPRAS	LETHARGIC
LEGIONS	LEKKINGS	LENGTHS	LEPROSE	LETHARGIES
LEGISLATE	LEKS	LENGTHY	LEPROSERIES	LETHARGY
LEGISLATED	LEKYTHOI	LENIENCE	LEPROSERY	LETHEAN
LEGISLATES	LEKYTHOS	LENIENCES	LEPROSIES	LETHEE
LEGISLATING	LEMAN	LENIENCIES	LEPROSITIES	LETHEES
LEGIST	LEMANS	LENIENCY	LEPROSITY	LETHIED
LEGISTS	LEME	LENIENT	LEPROSY	LETS
LEGIT	LEMED	LENIENTLY	LEPROUS	LETTABLE
LEGITIM	LEMEL	LENIENTS	LEPS	LETTED
LEGITIMS	LEMELS	LENIFIED	LEPTA	LETTER
LEGLAN	LEMES	LENIFIES	LEPTOME	LETTERBOX
LEGLANS	LEMING	LENIFY	LEPTOMES	LETTERBOXES
LEGLEN	LEMMA	LENIFYING	LEPTON	LETTERED
LEGLENS	LEMMAS	LENIS	LEPTONIC	LETTERER
LEGLESS	LEMMATA	LENITIES	LEPTONS	LETTERERS
LEGLET	LEMMATISE	LENITION	LEPTOSOME	LETTERING
LEGLETS	LEMMATISED	LENITIONS	LEPTOSOMES	LETTERINGS
LEGLIN	LEMMATISES	LENITIVE	LEPTOTENE	LETTERN
LEGLINS	LEMMATISING	LENITIVES	LEPTOTENES	LETTERNS
LEGROOM	LEMMATIZE	LENITY	LERE	LETTERS
LEGROOMS	LEMMATIZED	LENO	LERED	LETTING
LEGS	LEMMATIZES	LENOS	LERES	LETTINGS
LEGUME	LEMMATIZING	LENS	LERING	LETTRE
LEGUMES	LEMMING	LENSES	LERNAEAN	LETTRES
LEGUMIN	LEMMINGS	LENSMAN	LERNEAN	LETTUCE
LEGUMINS	LEMON	LENSMEN	LERP	LETTUCES
LEGWEAR	LEMONADE	LENT	LERPS	LEU
LEGWEARS	LEMONADES	LENTANDO	LES	LEUCAEMIA
LEGWORK	LEMONED	LENTEN	LESBIAN	LEUCAEMIAS
LEGWORKS	LEMONFISH	LENTI	LESBIANS	LEUCAEMIC
LEHR	LEMONFISHES	LENTIC	LESBIC	LEUCH
LEHRJAHRE	LEMONING	LENTICEL	LESBO	LEUCHEN
LEHRS	LEMONS	LENTICELS	LESBOS	LEUCIN
LEI	LEMONY	LENTICLE	LESES	LEUCINE
LEIDGER	LEMPIRA	LENTICLES	LESION	LEUCINES
LEIDGERS	LEMPIRAS	LENTIFORM	LESIONS	LEUCINS
LEIGER	LEMUR	LENTIGINES	LESS	LEUCITE
LEIGERS	LEMURES	LENTIGO	LESSEE	LEUCITES
LEIPOA	LEMURIAN	LENTIL	LESSEES	LEUCITIC
LEIPOAS	LEMURIANS	LENTILS	LESSEN	LEUCOCYTE
LEIR	LEMURINE	LENTISK	LESSENED	LEUCOCYTES
LEIRED	LEMURINES	LENTISKS	LESSENING	LEUCOMA
LEIRING	LEMUROID	LENTO	LESSENS	LEUCOMAS
LEIRS	LEMUROIDS	LENTOID	LESSER	LEUCOTOME
LEIS	LEMURS	LENTOR	LESSES	LEUCOTOMES
LEISH	LEND	LENTORS	LESSON	LEUCOTOMIES
LEISHER	LENDER	LENTOS	LESSONED	LEUCOTOMY
LEISHEST	LENDERS	LENTOUS	LESSONING	LEUGH
LEISLER	LENDING	LENVOY	LESSONINGS	LEUGHEN
LEISLERS	LENDINGS	LENVOYS	LESSONS	LEUKAEMIA
LEISTER	LENDS	LEONE	LESSOR	LEUKAEMIAS
LEISTERED	LENES	LEONES	LESSORS	LEUKEMIA
LEISTERING	LENG	LEONINE	LEST	LEUKEMIAS
LEISTERS	LENGED	LEOPARD	LESTED	LEV
LEISURE	LENGER	LEOPARDS	LESTING	LEVA
LEISURED	LENGEST	LEOTARD	LESTS	LEVANT
LEISURELY	LENGING	LEOTARDS	LET	LEVANTED
LEISURES	LENGS	LEP	LETCH	LEVANTER
LEISURING	LENGTH	LEPER	LETCHED	LEVANTERS
LEITMOTIF	LENGTHEN	LEPERS	LETCHES	LEVANTINE
LEITMOTIFS	LENGTHENED	LEPID	LETCHING	LEVANTINES
LEITMOTIV	LENGTHENING	LEPIDOTE	LETCHINGS	LEVANTING
LEITMOTIVS	LENGTHENS	LEPORINE	LETHAL	LEVANTS

The Chambers Dictionary is the authority for many longer words; see *OSW* Introduction, page xii.

LEVATOR	LEWISIA	LIBEL	LICENCE	LICTORS
LEVATORS	LEWISIAS	LIBELANT	LICENCED	LID
LEVE	LEWISITE	LIBELANTS	LICENCES	LIDDED
LEVEE	LEWISITES	LIBELED	LICENCING	LIDGER
LEVEED	LEWISSON	LIBELEE	LICENSE	LIDGERS
LEVEEING	LEWISSONS	LIBELEES	LICENSED	LIDLESS
LEVEES	LEX	LIBELER	LICENSEE	LIDO
LEVEL	LEXEME	LIBELERS	LICENSEES	LIDOCAINE
LEVELLED	LEXEMES	LIBELING	LICENSER	LIDOCAINES
LEVELLER	LEXES	LIBELINGS	LICENSERS	LIDOS
LEVELLERS	LEXICAL	LIBELLANT	LICENSES	LIDS
LEVELLEST	LEXICALLY	LIBELLANTS	LICENSING	LIE
LEVELLING	LEXICON	LIBELLED	LICENSOR	LIED
LEVELLINGS	LEXICONS	LIBELLEE	LICENSORS	LIEDER
LEVELS	LEXIGRAM	LIBELLEES	LICENSURE	LIEF
LEVER	LEXIGRAMS	LIBELLER	LICENSURES	LIEFER
LEVERAGE	LEXIS	LIBELLERS	LICH	LIEFEST
LEVERAGED	LEXISES	LIBELLING	LICHANOS	LIEFS
LEVERAGES	LEY	LIBELLINGS	LICHANOSES	LIEGE
LEVERAGING	LEYS	LIBELLOUS	LICHEE	LIEGEDOM
LEVERED	LEZ	LIBELOUS	LICHEES	LIEGEDOMS
LEVERET	LEZES	LIBELS	LICHEN	LIEGELESS
LEVERETS	LEZZ	LIBER	LICHENED	LIEGEMAN
LEVERING	LEZZES	LIBERAL	LICHENIN	LIEGEMEN
LEVERS	LEZZIES	LIBERALLY	LICHENINS	LIEGER
LEVIABLE	LEZZY	LIBERALS	LICHENISM	LIEGERS
LEVIATHAN	LI	LIBERATE	LICHENISMS	LIEGES
LEVIATHANS	LIABILITIES	LIBERATED	LICHENIST	LIEN
LEVIED	LIABILITY	LIBERATES	LICHENISTS	LIENAL
LEVIES	LIABLE	LIBERATING	LICHENOID	LIENS
LEVIGABLE	LIAISE	LIBERATOR	LICHENOSE	LIENTERIC
LEVIGATE	LIAISED	LIBERATORS	LICHENOUS	LIENTERIES
LEVIGATED	LIAISES	LIBERO	LICHENS	LIENTERY
LEVIGATES	LIAISING	LIBEROS	LICHES	LIER
LEVIGATING	LIAISON	LIBERS	LICHGATE	LIERNE
LEVIN	LIAISONS	LIBERTIES	LICHGATES	LIERNES
LEVINS	LIANA	LIBERTINE	LICHI	LIERS
LEVIRATE	LIANAS	LIBERTINES	LICHIS	LIES
LEVIRATES	LIANE	LIBERTY	LICHT	LIEU
LEVIS	LIANES	LIBIDINAL	LICHTED	LIEUS
LEVITATE	LIANG	LIBIDO	LICHTER	LIEVE
LEVITATED	LIANGS	LIBIDOS	LICHTEST	LIEVER
LEVITATES	LIANOID	LIBKEN	LICHTING	LIEVEST
LEVITATING	LIAR	LIBKENS	LICHTLIED	LIFE
LEVITE	LIARD	LIBRA	LICHTLIES	LIFEBELT
LEVITES	LIARDS	LIBRAE	LICHTLY	LIFEBELTS
LEVITIC	LIARS	LIBRAIRE	LICHTLYING	LIFEBOAT
LEVITICAL	LIART	LIBRAIRES	LICHTS	LIFEBOATS
LEVITIES	LIB	LIBRAIRIE	LICHWAKE	LIFEBUOY
LEVITY	LIBANT	LIBRAIRIES	LICHWAKES	LIFEBUOYS
LEVULOSE	LIBATE	LIBRARIAN	LICHWAY	LIFEFUL
LEVULOSES	LIBATED	LIBRARIANS	LICHWAYS	LIFEGUARD
LEVY	LIBATES	LIBRARIES	LICIT	LIFEGUARDS
LEVYING	LIBATING	LIBRARY	LICITLY	LIFEHOLD
LEW	LIBATION	LIBRAS	LICK	LIFELESS
LEWD	LIBATIONS	LIBRATE	LICKED	LIFELIKE
LEWDER	LIBATORY	LIBRATED	LICKER	LIFELINE
LEWDEST	LIBBARD	LIBRATES	LICKERISH	LIFELINES
LEWDLY	LIBBARDS	LIBRATING	LICKERS	LIFELONG
LEWDNESS	LIBBED	LIBRATION	LICKING	LIFER
LEWDNESSES	LIBBER	LIBRATIONS	LICKINGS	LIFERS
LEWDSBIES	LIBBERS	LIBRATORY	LICKPENNIES	LIFESOME
LEWDSBY	LIBBING	LIBRETTI	LICKPENNY	LIFESPAN
LEWDSTER	LIBECCHIO	LIBRETTO	LICKS	LIFESPANS
LEWDSTERS	LIBECCHIOS	LIBRETTOS	LICORICE	LIFESTYLE
LEWIS	LIBECCIO	LIBS	LICORICES	LIFESTYLES
LEWISES	LIBECCIOS	LICE	LICTOR	LIFETIME

The Chambers Dictionary is the authority for many longer words; see *OSW* Introduction, page xii.

LIFETIMES
LIFT
LIFTABLE
LIFTBACK
LIFTBACKS
LIFTED
LIFTER
LIFTERS
LIFTING
LIFTS
LIFULL
LIG
LIGAMENT
LIGAMENTS
LIGAN
LIGAND
LIGANDS
LIGANS
LIGASE
LIGASES
LIGATE
LIGATED
LIGATES
LIGATING
LIGATION
LIGATIONS
LIGATURE
LIGATURED
LIGATURES
LIGATURING
LIGER
LIGERS
LIGGE
LIGGED
LIGGEN
LIGGER
LIGGERS
LIGGES
LIGGING
LIGGINGS
LIGHT
LIGHTED
LIGHTEN
LIGHTENED
LIGHTENING
LIGHTENINGS
LIGHTENS
LIGHTER
LIGHTERS
LIGHTEST
LIGHTFUL
LIGHTING
LIGHTINGS
LIGHTISH
LIGHTLESS
LIGHTLIED
LIGHTLIES
LIGHTLY
LIGHTLYING
LIGHTNESS
LIGHTNESSES
LIGHTNING
LIGHTNINGS
LIGHTS
LIGHTSHIP
LIGHTSHIPS
LIGHTSOME

LIGNAGE
LIGNAGES
LIGNALOES
LIGNE
LIGNEOUS
LIGNES
LIGNIFIED
LIGNIFIES
LIGNIFORM
LIGNIFY
LIGNIFYING
LIGNIN
LIGNINS
LIGNITE
LIGNITES
LIGNITIC
LIGNOSE
LIGNOSES
LIGNUM
LIGNUMS
LIGROIN
LIGROINS
LIGS
LIGULA
LIGULAE
LIGULAR
LIGULAS
LIGULATE
LIGULE
LIGULES
LIGULOID
LIGURE
LIGURES
LIKABLE
LIKE
LIKEABLE
LIKED
LIKELIER
LIKELIEST
LIKELY
LIKEN
LIKENED
LIKENESS
LIKENESSES
LIKENING
LIKENS
LIKER
LIKERS
LIKES
LIKEWAKE
LIKEWAKES
LIKEWALK
LIKEWALKS
LIKEWISE
LIKIN
LIKING
LIKINGS
LIKINS
LILAC
LILACS
LILANGENI
LILIED
LILIES
LILL
LILLED
LILLING
LILLS

LILO
LILOS
LILT
LILTED
LILTING
LILTS
LILY
LIMA
LIMACEL
LIMACELS
LIMACEOUS
LIMACES
LIMACINE
LIMACON
LIMACONS
LIMAIL
LIMAILS
LIMAS
LIMATION
LIMATIONS
LIMAX
LIMB
LIMBATE
LIMBEC
LIMBECK
LIMBECKS
LIMBECS
LIMBED
LIMBER
LIMBERED
LIMBERING
LIMBERS
LIMBIC
LIMBING
LIMBLESS
LIMBMEAL
LIMBO
LIMBOS
LIMBOUS
LIMBS
LIME
LIMEADE
LIMEADES
LIMED
LIMEKILN
LIMEKILNS
LIMELIGHT
LIMELIGHTED
LIMELIGHTING
LIMELIGHTS
LIMELIT
LIMEN
LIMENS
LIMEPIT
LIMEPITS
LIMERICK
LIMERICKS
LIMES
LIMESTONE
LIMESTONES
LIMEWASH
LIMEWASHES
LIMEWATER
LIMEWATERS
LIMEY
LIMEYS
LIMIER

LIMIEST
LIMINAL
LIMINESS
LIMINESSES
LIMING
LIMINGS
LIMIT
LIMITABLE
LIMITARY
LIMITED
LIMITEDLY
LIMITEDS
LIMITER
LIMITERS
LIMITES
LIMITING
LIMITINGS
LIMITLESS
LIMITS
LIMMA
LIMMAS
LIMMER
LIMMERS
LIMN
LIMNAEID
LIMNAEIDS
LIMNED
LIMNER
LIMNERS
LIMNETIC
LIMNING
LIMNOLOGIES
LIMNOLOGY
LIMNS
LIMO
LIMONITE
LIMONITES
LIMONITIC
LIMOS
LIMOSES
LIMOSIS
LIMOUS
LIMOUSINE
LIMOUSINES
LIMP
LIMPED
LIMPER
LIMPEST
LIMPET
LIMPETS
LIMPID
LIMPIDITIES
LIMPIDITY
LIMPIDLY
LIMPING
LIMPINGLY
LIMPINGS
LIMPKIN
LIMPKINS
LIMPLY
LIMPNESS
LIMPNESSES
LIMPS
LIMULI
LIMULUS
LIMULUSES
LIMY

LIN
LINAC
LINACS
LINAGE
LINAGES
LINALOOL
LINALOOLS
LINCH
LINCHES
LINCHET
LINCHETS
LINCHPIN
LINCHPINS
LINCRUSTA
LINCRUSTAS
LINCTURE
LINCTURES
LINCTUS
LINCTUSES
LIND
LINDANE
LINDANES
LINDEN
LINDENS
LINDS
LINDWORM
LINDWORMS
LINE
LINEAGE
LINEAGES
LINEAL
LINEALITIES
LINEALITY
LINEALLY
LINEAMENT
LINEAMENTS
LINEAR
LINEARITIES
LINEARITY
LINEARLY
LINEATE
LINEATED
LINEATION
LINEATIONS
LINED
LINEMAN
LINEMEN
LINEN
LINENS
LINEOLATE
LINER
LINERS
LINES
LINESMAN
LINESMEN
LINEY
LING
LINGA
LINGAM
LINGAMS
LINGAS
LINGEL
LINGELS
LINGER
LINGERED
LINGERER
LINGERERS

The Chambers Dictionary is the authority for many longer words; see *OSW* Introduction, page xii.

LINGERIE	LINNY	LIPIDE	LIQUIDIZING	LITANY
LINGERIES	LINO	LIPIDES	LIQUIDLY	LITCHI
LINGERING	LINOCUT	LIPIDS	LIQUIDS	LITCHIS
LINGERINGS	LINOCUTS	LIPLESS	LIQUIDUS	LITE
LINGERS	LINOLEUM	LIPLIKE	LIQUIDUSES	LITED
LINGIER	LINOLEUMS	LIPOGRAM	LIQUOR	LITER
LINGIEST	LINOS	LIPOGRAMS	LIQUORED	LITERACIES
LINGLE	LINS	LIPOID	LIQUORICE	LITERACY
LINGLES	LINSANG	LIPOIDS	LIQUORICES	LITERAL
LINGO	LINSANGS	LIPOMA	LIQUORING	LITERALLY
LINGOES	LINSEED	LIPOMATA	LIQUORISH	LITERALS
LINGOT	LINSEEDS	LIPOSOMAL	LIQUORS	LITERARY
LINGOTS	LINSEY	LIPOSOME	LIRA	LITERATE
LINGS	LINSEYS	LIPOSOMES	LIRAS	LITERATES
LINGSTER	LINSTOCK	LIPPED	LIRE	LITERATI
LINGSTERS	LINSTOCKS	LIPPEN	LIRIPIPE	LITERATIM
LINGUA	LINT	LIPPENED	LIRIPIPES	LITERATO
LINGUAE	LINTEL	LIPPENING	LIRIPOOP	LITERATOR
LINGUAL	LINTELLED	LIPPENS	LIRIPOOPS	LITERATORS
LINGUALLY	LINTELS	LIPPIE	LIRK	LITERATUS
LINGUAS	LINTER	LIPPIER	LIRKED	LITEROSE
LINGUINE	LINTERS	LIPPIES	LIRKING	LITERS
LINGUINI	LINTIE	LIPPIEST	LIRKS	LITES
LINGUIST	LINTIER	LIPPING	LIS	LITH
LINGUISTS	LINTIES	LIPPITUDE	LISK	LITHARGE
LINGULA	LINTIEST	LIPPITUDES	LISKS	LITHARGES
LINGULAE	LINTS	LIPPY	LISLE	LITHATE
LINGULAR	LINTSEED	LIPS	LISLES	LITHATES
LINGULAS	LINTSEEDS	LIPSTICK	LISP	LITHE
LINGULATE	LINTSTOCK	LIPSTICKED	LISPED	LITHED
LINGY	LINTSTOCKS	LIPSTICKING	LISPER	LITHELY
LINHAY	LINTWHITE	LIPSTICKS	LISPERS	LITHENESS
LINHAYS	LINTWHITES	LIQUABLE	LISPING	LITHENESSES
LINIER	LINTY	LIQUATE	LISPINGLY	LITHER
LINIEST	LINY	LIQUATED	LISPINGS	LITHERLY
LINIMENT	LION	LIQUATES	LISPOUND	LITHES
LINIMENTS	LIONCEL	LIQUATING	LISPOUNDS	LITHESOME
LININ	LIONCELLE	LIQUATION	LISPS	LITHEST
LINING	LIONCELLES	LIQUATIONS	LISPUND	LITHIA
LININGS	LIONCELS	LIQUEFIED	LISPUNDS	LITHIAS
LININS	LIONEL	LIQUEFIER	LISSES	LITHIASES
LINK	LIONELS	LIQUEFIERS	LISSOM	LITHIASIS
LINKABLE	LIONESS	LIQUEFIES	LISSOME	LITHIC
LINKAGE	LIONESSES	LIQUEFY	LISSOMELY	LITHING
LINKAGES	LIONET	LIQUEFYING	LISSOMLY	LITHISTID
LINKBOY	LIONETS	LIQUESCE	LIST	LITHISTIDS
LINKBOYS	LIONISE	LIQUESCED	LISTED	LITHITE
LINKED	LIONISED	LIQUESCES	LISTEL	LITHITES
LINKER	LIONISES	LIQUESCING	LISTELS	LITHIUM
LINKERS	LIONISING	LIQUEUR	LISTEN	LITHIUMS
LINKING	LIONISM	LIQUEURED	LISTENED	LITHO
LINKMAN	LIONISMS	LIQUEURING	LISTENER	LITHOCYST
LINKMEN	LIONIZE	LIQUEURS	LISTENERS	LITHOCYSTS
LINKS	LIONIZED	LIQUID	LISTENING	LITHOID
LINKSTER	LIONIZES	LIQUIDATE	LISTENS	LITHOIDAL
LINKSTERS	LIONIZING	LIQUIDATED	LISTER	LITHOLOGIES
LINKWORK	LIONLIKE	LIQUIDATES	LISTERIA	LITHOLOGY
LINKWORKS	LIONLY	LIQUIDATING	LISTERIAS	LITHOPONE
LINN	LIONS	LIQUIDISE	LISTERS	LITHOPONES
LINNED	LIP	LIQUIDISED	LISTETH	LITHOS
LINNET	LIPARITE	LIQUIDISES	LISTFUL	LITHOTOME
LINNETS	LIPARITES	LIQUIDISING	LISTING	LITHOTOMES
LINNEY	LIPASE	LIQUIDITIES	LISTINGS	LITHOTOMIES
LINNEYS	LIPASES	LIQUIDITY	LISTLESS	LITHOTOMY
LINNIES	LIPECTOMIES	LIQUIDIZE	LISTS	LITHS
LINNING	LIPECTOMY	LIQUIDIZED	LIT	LITIGABLE
LINNS	LIPID	LIQUIDIZES	LITANIES	LITIGANT

The Chambers Dictionary is the authority for many longer words; see *OSW* Introduction, page xii.

LITIGANTS	LIVERY	LOAM	LOBIPED	LOCKAWAY
LITIGATE	LIVERYMAN	LOAMED	LOBLOLLIES	LOCKAWAYS
LITIGATED	LIVERYMEN	LOAMIER	LOBLOLLY	LOCKED
LITIGATES	LIVES	LOAMIEST	LOBO	LOCKER
LITIGATING	LIVESTOCK	LOAMINESS	LOBOS	LOCKERS
LITIGIOUS	LIVESTOCKS	LOAMINESSES	LOBOSE	LOCKET
LITING	LIVEWARE	LOAMING	LOBOTOMIES	LOCKETS
LITMUS	LIVEWARES	LOAMS	LOBOTOMY	LOCKFAST
LITMUSES	LIVID	LOAMY	LOBS	LOCKFUL
LITOTES	LIVIDER	LOAN	LOBSCOUSE	LOCKFULS
LITRE	LIVIDEST	LOANABLE	LOBSCOUSES	LOCKHOUSE
LITRES	LIVIDITIES	LOANBACK	LOBSTER	LOCKHOUSES
LITTEN	LIVIDITY	LOANBACKS	LOBSTERS	LOCKING
LITTER	LIVIDLY	LOANED	LOBULAR	LOCKJAW
LITTERED	LIVIDNESS	LOANING	LOBULATE	LOCKJAWS
LITTERING	LIVIDNESSES	LOANINGS	LOBULATED	LOCKMAN
LITTERS	LIVING	LOANS	LOBULE	LOCKMEN
LITTERY	LIVINGS	LOAST	LOBULES	LOCKOUT
LITTLE	LIVOR	LOATH	LOBULI	LOCKOUTS
LITTLEANE	LIVORS	LOATHE	LOBULUS	LOCKPICK
LITTLEANES	LIVRAISON	LOATHED	LOBUS	LOCKPICKS
LITTLER	LIVRAISONS	LOATHER	LOBWORM	LOCKRAM
LITTLES	LIVRE	LOATHERS	LOBWORMS	LOCKRAMS
LITTLEST	LIVRES	LOATHES	LOCAL	LOCKS
LITTLIN	LIXIVIA	LOATHEST	LOCALE	LOCKSMAN
LITTLING	LIXIVIAL	LOATHFUL	LOCALES	LOCKSMEN
LITTLINGS	LIXIVIATE	LOATHIER	LOCALISE	LOCKSMITH
LITTLINS	LIXIVIATED	LOATHIEST	LOCALISED	LOCKSMITHS
LITTORAL	LIXIVIATES	LOATHING	LOCALISER	LOCKSTEP
LITTORALS	LIXIVIATING	LOATHINGS	LOCALISERS	LOCKSTEPS
LITURGIC	LIXIVIOUS	LOATHLY	LOCALISES	LOCO
LITURGICS	LIXIVIUM	LOATHSOME	LOCALISING	LOCOED
LITURGIES	LIXIVIUMS	LOATHY	LOCALISM	LOCOES
LITURGIST	LIZARD	LOAVE	LOCALISMS	LOCOFOCO
LITURGISTS	LIZARDS	LOAVED	LOCALIST	LOCOFOCOS
LITURGY	LLAMA	LOAVES	LOCALISTS	LOCOMAN
LITUUS	LLAMAS	LOAVING	LOCALITIES	LOCOMEN
LITUUSES	LLANERO	LOB	LOCALITY	LOCOMOTE
LIVABLE	LLANEROS	LOBAR	LOCALIZE	LOCOMOTED
LIVE	LLANO	LOBATE	LOCALIZED	LOCOMOTES
LIVEABLE	LLANOS	LOBATION	LOCALIZER	LOCOMOTING
LIVEAXLE	LO	LOBATIONS	LOCALIZERS	LOCOMOTOR
LIVEAXLES	LOACH	LOBBED	LOCALIZES	LOCOMOTORS
LIVED	LOACHES	LOBBIED	LOCALIZING	LOCOPLANT
LIVELIER	LOAD	LOBBIES	LOCALLY	LOCOPLANTS
LIVELIEST	LOADED	LOBBING	LOCALS	LOCOS
LIVELILY	LOADEN	LOBBY	LOCATABLE	LOCOWEED
LIVELOD	LOADENED	LOBBYER	LOCATE	LOCOWEEDS
LIVELODS	LOADENING	LOBBYERS	LOCATED	LOCULAR
LIVELONG	LOADENS	LOBBYING	LOCATES	LOCULATE
LIVELONGS	LOADER	LOBBYINGS	LOCATING	LOCULE
LIVELOOD	LOADERS	LOBBYIST	LOCATION	LOCULES
LIVELOODS	LOADING	LOBBYISTS	LOCATIONS	LOCULI
LIVELY	LOADINGS	LOBE	LOCATIVE	LOCULUS
LIVEN	LOADS	LOBECTOMIES	LOCATIVES	LOCUM
LIVENED	LOADSTAR	LOBECTOMY	LOCELLATE	LOCUMS
LIVENER	LOADSTARS	LOBED	LOCH	LOCUPLETE
LIVENERS	LOADSTONE	LOBELET	LOCHAN	LOCUS
LIVENING	LOADSTONES	LOBELETS	LOCHANS	LOCUST
LIVENS	LOAF	LOBELIA	LOCHIA	LOCUSTA
LIVER	LOAFED	LOBELIAS	LOCHIAL	LOCUSTAE
LIVERIED	LOAFER	LOBELINE	LOCHS	LOCUSTED
LIVERIES	LOAFERISH	LOBELINES	LOCI	LOCUSTING
LIVERISH	LOAFERS	LOBES	LOCK	LOCUSTS
LIVERS	LOAFING	LOBI	LOCKABLE	LOCUTION
LIVERWORT	LOAFINGS	LOBING	LOCKAGE	LOCUTIONS
LIVERWORTS	LOAFS	LOBINGS	LOCKAGES	LOCUTORIES

The Chambers Dictionary is the authority for many longer words; see *OSW* Introduction, page xii.

LOCUTORY	LOGIC	LOITERED	LONGE	LOOKS
LODE	LOGICAL	LOITERER	LONGED	LOOM
LODEN	LOGICALLY	LOITERERS	LONGEING	LOOMED
LODENS	LOGICIAN	LOITERING	LONGER	LOOMING
LODES	LOGICIANS	LOITERINGS	LONGERON	LOOMS
LODESMAN	LOGICISE	LOITERS	LONGERONS	LOON
LODESMEN	LOGICISED	LOKE	LONGES	LOONIE
LODESTAR	LOGICISES	LOKES	LONGEST	LOONIER
LODESTARS	LOGICISING	LOKSHEN	LONGEVAL	LOONIES
LODESTONE	LOGICISM	LOLIGO	LONGEVITIES	LOONIEST
LODESTONES	LOGICISMS	LOLIGOS	LONGEVITY	LOONINESS
LODGE	LOGICIST	LOLIUM	LONGEVOUS	LOONINESSES
LODGED	LOGICISTS	LOLIUMS	LONGHAND	LOONING
LODGEMENT	LOGICIZE	LOLL	LONGHANDS	LOONINGS
LODGEMENTS	LOGICIZED	LOLLED	LONGHORN	LOONS
LODGEPOLE	LOGICIZES	LOLLER	LONGHORNS	LOONY
LODGEPOLES	LOGICIZING	LOLLERS	LONGHOUSE	LOOP
LODGER	LOGICS	LOLLIES	LONGHOUSES	LOOPED
LODGERS	LOGIE	LOLLING	LONGICORN	LOOPER
LODGES	LOGIER	LOLLINGLY	LONGICORNS	LOOPERS
LODGING	LOGIES	LOLLIPOP	LONGING	LOOPHOLE
LODGINGS	LOGIEST	LOLLIPOPS	LONGINGLY	LOOPHOLED
LODGMENT	LOGION	LOLLOP	LONGINGS	LOOPHOLES
LODGMENTS	LOGISTIC	LOLLOPED	LONGISH	LOOPHOLING
LODICULA	LOGISTICS	LOLLOPING	LONGITUDE	LOOPIER
LODICULAE	LOGJUICE	LOLLOPS	LONGITUDES	LOOPIEST
LODICULE	LOGJUICES	LOLLS	LONGLY	LOOPING
LODICULES	LOGLINE	LOLLY	LONGNESS	LOOPINGS
LOESS	LOGLINES	LOLLYGAG	LONGNESSES	LOOPS
LOESSES	LOGLOG	LOLLYGAGGED	LONGS	LOOPY
LOFT	LOGLOGS	LOLLYGAGGING	LONGSHIP	LOOR
LOFTED	LOGO	LOLLYGAGS	LONGSHIPS	LOORD
LOFTER	LOGOGRAM	LOLOG	LONGSHORE	LOORDS
LOFTERS	LOGOGRAMS	LOLOGS	LONGSOME	LOOS
LOFTIER	LOGOGRAPH	LOMA	LONGUEUR	LOOSE
LOFTIEST	LOGOGRAPHS	LOMAS	LONGUEURS	LOOSED
LOFTILY	LOGOGRIPH	LOME	LONGWALL	LOOSELY
LOFTINESS	LOGOGRIPHS	LOMED	LONGWALLS	LOOSEN
LOFTINESSES	LOGOMACHIES	LOMENT	LONGWAYS	LOOSENED
LOFTING	LOGOMACHY	LOMENTA	LONGWISE	LOOSENER
LOFTS	LOGOPEDIC	LOMENTS	LONICERA	LOOSENERS
LOFTY	LOGOPHILE	LOMENTUM	LONICERAS	LOOSENESS
LOG	LOGOPHILES	LOMES	LOO	LOOSENESSES
LOGAN	LOGORRHEA	LOMING	LOOBIER	LOOSENING
LOGANIA	LOGORRHEAS	LOMPISH	LOOBIES	LOOSENS
LOGANIAS	LOGOS	LONE	LOOBIEST	LOOSER
LOGANS	LOGOTHETE	LONELIER	LOOBILY	LOOSES
LOGAOEDIC	LOGOTHETES	LONELIEST	LOOBY	LOOSEST
LOGARITHM	LOGOTYPE	LONELY	LOOED	LOOSING
LOGARITHMS	LOGOTYPES	LONENESS	LOOF	LOOT
LOGBOARD	LOGS	LONENESSES	LOOFA	LOOTED
LOGBOARDS	LOGWOOD	LONER	LOOFAH	LOOTEN
LOGBOOK	LOGWOODS	LONERS	LOOFAHS	LOOTER
LOGBOOKS	LOGY	LONESOME	LOOFAS	LOOTERS
LOGE	LOID	LONESOMES	LOOFFUL	LOOTING
LOGES	LOIDED	LONG	LOOFFULS	LOOTINGS
LOGGAT	LOIDING	LONGA	LOOFS	LOOTS
LOGGATS	LOIDS	LONGAEVAL	LOOING	LOOVES
LOGGED	LOIN	LONGAN	LOOK	LOP
LOGGER	LOINCLOTH	LONGANS	LOOKED	LOPE
LOGGERS	LOINCLOTHS	LONGAS	LOOKER	LOPED
LOGGIA	LOINS	LONGBOAT	LOOKERS	LOPER
LOGGIAS	LOIPE	LONGBOATS	LOOKING	LOPERS
LOGGIE	LOIPEN	LONGBOW	LOOKISM	LOPES
LOGGING	LOIR	LONGBOWS	LOOKISMS	LOPGRASS
LOGGINGS	LOIRS	LONGCLOTH	LOOKOUT	LOPGRASSES
LOGIA	LOITER	LONGCLOTHS	LOOKOUTS	LOPHODONT

The Chambers Dictionary is the authority for many longer words; see *OSW* Introduction, page xii.

LOPING	LORINERS	LOUDENING	LOUTS	LOWLANDERS
LOPPED	LORING	LOUDENS	LOUVER	LOWLANDS
LOPPER	LORINGS	LOUDER	LOUVERED	LOWLIER
LOPPERED	LORIOT	LOUDEST	LOUVERS	LOWLIEST
LOPPERING	LORIOTS	LOUDISH	LOUVRE	LOWLIGHT
LOPPERS	LORIS	LOUDLY	LOUVRED	LOWLIGHTED
LOPPING	LORISES	LOUDMOUTH	LOUVRES	LOWLIGHTING
LOPPINGS	LORN	LOUDMOUTHS	LOVABLE	LOWLIGHTS
LOPS	LORRELL	LOUDNESS	LOVAGE	LOWLIHEAD
LOPSIDED	LORRELLS	LOUDNESSES	LOVAGES	LOWLIHEADS
LOQUACITIES	LORRIES	LOUGH	LOVAT	LOWLILY
LOQUACITY	LORRY	LOUGHS	LOVATS	LOWLINESS
LOQUAT	LORY	LOUIS	LOVE	LOWLINESSES
LOQUATS	LOS	LOUN	LOVEABLE	LOWLY
LOQUITUR	LOSABLE	LOUND	LOVEBIRD	LOWN
LOR	LOSE	LOUNDED	LOVEBIRDS	LOWND
LORAL	LOSED	LOUNDER	LOVEBITE	LOWNDED
LORAN	LOSEL	LOUNDERED	LOVEBITES	LOWNDING
LORANS	LOSELS	LOUNDERING	LOVED	LOWNDS
LORATE	LOSEN	LOUNDERINGS	LOVELESS	LOWNE
LORAZEPAM	LOSER	LOUNDERS	LOVELIER	LOWNED
LORAZEPAMS	LOSERS	LOUNDING	LOVELIES	LOWNES
LORCHA	LOSES	LOUNDS	LOVELIEST	LOWNESS
LORCHAS	LOSH	LOUNED	LOVELIGHT	LOWNESSES
LORD	LOSING	LOUNGE	LOVELIGHTS	LOWNING
LORDED	LOSINGLY	LOUNGED	LOVELILY	LOWNS
LORDING	LOSINGS	LOUNGER	LOVELOCK	LOWS
LORDINGS	LOSS	LOUNGERS	LOVELOCKS	LOWSE
LORDKIN	LOSSES	LOUNGES	LOVELORN	LOWSER
LORDKINS	LOSSIER	LOUNGING	LOVELY	LOWSES
LORDLESS	LOSSIEST	LOUNGINGS	LOVEMAKER	LOWSEST
LORDLIER	LOSSMAKER	LOUNING	LOVEMAKERS	LOWSING
LORDLIEST	LOSSMAKERS	LOUNS	LOVER	LOWSIT
LORDLING	LOSSY	LOUP	LOVERED	LOWT
LORDLINGS	LOST	LOUPE	LOVERLESS	LOWTED
LORDLY	LOT	LOUPED	LOVERLY	LOWTING
LORDOSES	LOTA	LOUPEN	LOVERS	LOWTS
LORDOSIS	LOTAH	LOUPES	LOVES	LOWVELD
LORDOTIC	LOTAHS	LOUPING	LOVESICK	LOWVELDS
LORDS	LOTAS	LOUPIT	LOVESOME	LOX
LORDSHIP	LOTE	LOUPS	LOVEY	LOXES
LORDSHIPS	LOTES	LOUR	LOVEYS	LOXODROME
LORDY	LOTH	LOURE	LOVING	LOXODROMES
LORE	LOTHEFULL	LOURED	LOVINGLY	LOXODROMIES
LOREL	LOTHER	LOURES	LOVINGS	LOXODROMY
LORELS	LOTHEST	LOURIER	LOW	LOXYGEN
LORES	LOTHFULL	LOURIEST	LOWAN	LOXYGENS
LORETTE	LOTIC	LOURING	LOWANS	LOY
LORETTES	LOTION	LOURINGLY	LOWBOY	LOYAL
LORGNETTE	LOTIONS	LOURINGS	LOWBOYS	LOYALIST
LORGNETTES	LOTO	LOURS	LOWE	LOYALISTS
LORGNON	LOTOS	LOURY	LOWED	LOYALLER
LORGNONS	LOTOSES	LOUSE	LOWER	LOYALLEST
LORIC	LOTS	LOUSED	LOWERED	LOYALLY
LORICA	LOTTED	LOUSES	LOWERIER	LOYALTIES
LORICAE	LOTTERIES	LOUSIER	LOWERIEST	LOYALTY
LORICATE	LOTTERY	LOUSIEST	LOWERING	LOYS
LORICATED	LOTTING	LOUSILY	LOWERINGS	LOZELL
LORICATES	LOTTO	LOUSINESS	LOWERMOST	LOZELLS
LORICATING	LOTTOS	LOUSINESSES	LOWERS	LOZEN
LORICS	LOTUS	LOUSING	LOWERY	LOZENGE
LORIES	LOTUSES	LOUSY	LOWES	LOZENGED
LORIKEET	LOUCHE	LOUT	LOWEST	LOZENGES
LORIKEETS	LOUCHELY	LOUTED	LOWING	LOZENGY
LORIMER	LOUD	LOUTING	LOWINGS	LOZENS
LORIMERS	LOUDEN	LOUTISH	LOWLAND	LUAU
LORINER	LOUDENED	LOUTISHLY	LOWLANDER	LUAUS

The Chambers Dictionary is the authority for many longer words; see *OSW* Introduction, page xii.

LUBBARD	LUCUMA	LUMBAGOS	LUMPS	LUNULATE
LUBBARDS	LUCUMAS	LUMBANG	LUMPY	LUNULATED
LUBBER	LUCUMO	LUMBANGS	LUMS	LUNULE
LUBBERLY	LUCUMONES	LUMBAR	LUNA	LUNULES
LUBBERS	LUCUMOS	LUMBER	LUNACIES	LUNYIE
LUBFISH	LUD	LUMBERED	LUNACY	LUNYIES
LUBFISHES	LUDIC	LUMBERER	LUNANAUT	LUPIN
LUBRA	LUDICALLY	LUMBERERS	LUNANAUTS	LUPINE
LUBRAS	LUDICROUS	LUMBERING	LUNAR	LUPINES
LUBRIC	LUDO	LUMBERINGS	LUNARIAN	LUPINS
LUBRICAL	LUDOS	LUMBERLY	LUNARIANS	LUPPEN
LUBRICANT	LUDS	LUMBERMAN	LUNARIES	LUPULIN
LUBRICANTS	LUDSHIP	LUMBERMEN	LUNARIST	LUPULINE
LUBRICATE	LUDSHIPS	LUMBERS	LUNARISTS	LUPULINIC
LUBRICATED	LUES	LUMBRICAL	LUNARNAUT	LUPULINS
LUBRICATES	LUETIC	LUMBRICALS	LUNARNAUTS	LUPUS
LUBRICATING	LUFF	LUMBRICI	LUNARS	LUPUSES
LUBRICITIES	LUFFA	LUMBRICUS	LUNARY	LUR
LUBRICITY	LUFFAS	LUMBRICUSES	LUNAS	LURCH
LUBRICOUS	LUFFED	LUMEN	LUNATE	LURCHED
LUCARNE	LUFFING	LUMENAL	LUNATED	LURCHER
LUCARNES	LUFFS	LUMENS	LUNATIC	LURCHERS
LUCE	LUG	LUMINA	LUNATICS	LURCHES
LUCENCIES	LUGE	LUMINAIRE	LUNATION	LURCHING
LUCENCY	LUGED	LUMINAIRES	LUNATIONS	LURDAN
LUCENT	LUGEING	LUMINAL	LUNCH	LURDANE
LUCERN	LUGEINGS	LUMINANCE	LUNCHED	LURDANES
LUCERNE	LUGER	LUMINANCES	LUNCHEON	LURDANS
LUCERNES	LUGERS	LUMINANT	LUNCHEONED	LURDEN
LUCERNS	LUGES	LUMINANTS	LUNCHEONING	LURDENS
LUCES	LUGGABLE	LUMINARIES	LUNCHEONS	LURE
LUCID	LUGGABLES	LUMINARY	LUNCHER	LURED
LUCIDER	LUGGAGE	LUMINE	LUNCHERS	LURES
LUCIDEST	LUGGAGES	LUMINED	LUNCHES	LURGI
LUCIDITIES	LUGGED	LUMINES	LUNCHING	LURGIES
LUCIDITY	LUGGER	LUMINESCE	LUNE	LURGIS
LUCIDLY	LUGGERS	LUMINESCED	LUNES	LURGY
LUCIDNESS	LUGGIE	LUMINESCES	LUNETTE	LURID
LUCIDNESSES	LUGGIES	LUMINESCING	LUNETTES	LURIDER
LUCIFER	LUGGING	LUMINING	LUNG	LURIDEST
LUCIFERIN	LUGHOLE	LUMINIST	LUNGE	LURIDLY
LUCIFERINS	LUGHOLES	LUMINISTS	LUNGED	LURIDNESS
LUCIFERS	LUGING	LUMINOUS	LUNGEING	LURIDNESSES
LUCIGEN	LUGINGS	LUMME	LUNGES	LURING
LUCIGENS	LUGS	LUMMIER	LUNGFUL	LURK
LUCK	LUGSAIL	LUMMIEST	LUNGFULS	LURKED
LUCKEN	LUGSAILS	LUMMOX	LUNGI	LURKER
LUCKIE	LUGWORM	LUMMOXES	LUNGIE	LURKERS
LUCKIER	LUGWORMS	LUMMY	LUNGIES	LURKING
LUCKIES	LUIT	LUMP	LUNGING	LURKINGS
LUCKIEST	LUITEN	LUMPED	LUNGIS	LURKS
LUCKILY	LUKE	LUMPEN	LUNGS	LURRIES
LUCKINESS	LUKEWARM	LUMPENLY	LUNGWORT	LURRY
LUCKINESSES	LULIBUB	LUMPER	LUNGWORTS	LURS
LUCKLESS	LULIBUBS	LUMPERS	LUNISOLAR	LUSCIOUS
LUCKS	LULL	LUMPFISH	LUNITIDAL	LUSH
LUCKY	LULLABIED	LUMPFISHES	LUNKER	LUSHED
LUCRATIVE	LULLABIES	LUMPIER	LUNKERS	LUSHER
LUCRE	LULLABY	LUMPIEST	LUNKHEAD	LUSHERS
LUCRES	LULLABYING	LUMPILY	LUNKHEADS	LUSHES
LUCTATION	LULLED	LUMPINESS	LUNT	LUSHEST
LUCTATIONS	LULLING	LUMPINESSES	LUNTED	LUSHIER
LUCUBRATE	LULLS	LUMPING	LUNTING	LUSHIEST
LUCUBRATED	LULU	LUMPISH	LUNTS	LUSHING
LUCUBRATES	LULUS	LUMPISHLY	LUNULA	LUSHLY
LUCUBRATING	LUM	LUMPKIN	LUNULAE	LUSHNESS
LUCULENT	LUMBAGO	LUMPKINS	LUNULAR	LUSHNESSES

The Chambers Dictionary is the authority for many longer words; see *OSW* Introduction, page xii.

LUSHY	LUTANISTS	LUXATION	LYKEWALKS	LYRICISM
LUSK	LUTE	LUXATIONS	LYM	LYRICISMS
LUSKED	LUTEAL	LUXE	LYME	LYRICIST
LUSKING	LUTECIUM	LUXES	LYMES	LYRICISTS
LUSKISH	LUTECIUMS	LUXMETER	LYMITER	LYRICON
LUSKS	LUTED	LUXMETERS	LYMITERS	LYRICONS
LUST	LUTEIN	LUXURIANT	LYMPH	LYRICS
LUSTED	LUTEINISE	LUXURIATE	LYMPHAD	LYRIFORM
LUSTER	LUTEINISED	LUXURIATED	LYMPHADS	LYRISM
LUSTERED	LUTEINISES	LUXURIATES	LYMPHATIC	LYRISMS
LUSTERING	LUTEINISING	LUXURIATING	LYMPHATICS	LYRIST
LUSTERS	LUTEINIZE	LUXURIES	LYMPHOID	LYRISTS
LUSTFUL	LUTEINIZED	LUXURIOUS	LYMPHOMA	LYSE
LUSTFULLY	LUTEINIZES	LUXURIST	LYMPHOMAS	LYSED
LUSTICK	LUTEINIZING	LUXURISTS	LYMPHOMATA	LYSERGIDE
LUSTIER	LUTEINS	LUXURY	LYMPHS	LYSERGIDES
LUSTIEST	LUTENIST	LUZ	LYMS	LYSES
LUSTIHEAD	LUTENISTS	LUZERN	LYNAGE	LYSIGENIC
LUSTIHEADS	LUTEOLIN	LUZERNS	LYNAGES	LYSIMETER
LUSTIHOOD	LUTEOLINS	LUZZES	LYNCEAN	LYSIMETERS
LUSTIHOODS	LUTEOLOUS	LYAM	LYNCH	LYSIN
LUSTILY	LUTEOUS	LYAMS	LYNCHED	LYSINE
LUSTINESS	LUTER	LYART	LYNCHES	LYSINES
LUSTINESSES	LUTERS	LYCEE	LYNCHET	LYSING
LUSTING	LUTES	LYCEES	LYNCHETS	LYSINS
LUSTIQUE	LUTESCENT	LYCEUM	LYNCHING	LYSIS
LUSTLESS	LUTETIUM	LYCEUMS	LYNCHPIN	LYSOL
LUSTRA	LUTETIUMS	LYCHEE	LYNCHPINS	LYSOLS
LUSTRAL	LUTHERN	LYCHEES	LYNE	LYSOSOME
LUSTRATE	LUTHERNS	LYCHGATE	LYNES	LYSOSOMES
LUSTRATED	LUTHIER	LYCHGATES	LYNX	LYSOZYME
LUSTRATES	LUTHIERS	LYCHNIS	LYNXES	LYSOZYMES
LUSTRATING	LUTING	LYCHNISES	LYOMEROUS	LYSSA
LUSTRE	LUTINGS	LYCOPOD	LYONNAISE	LYSSAS
LUSTRED	LUTIST	LYCOPODS	LYOPHIL	LYTE
LUSTRES	LUTISTS	LYDDITE	LYOPHILE	LYTED
LUSTRINE	LUTTEN	LYDDITES	LYOPHILIC	LYTES
LUSTRINES	LUTZ	LYE	LYOPHOBE	LYTHE
LUSTRING	LUTZES	LYES	LYOPHOBIC	LYTHES
LUSTRINGS	LUV	LYFULL	LYRATE	LYTING
LUSTROUS	LUVS	LYING	LYRATED	LYTTA
LUSTRUM	LUX	LYINGLY	LYRE	LYTTAE
LUSTRUMS	LUXATE	LYINGS	LYRES	
LUSTS	LUXATED	LYKEWAKE	LYRIC	
LUSTY	LUXATES	LYKEWAKES	LYRICAL	
LUTANIST	LUXATING	LYKEWALK	LYRICALLY	

M

MA	MACHAN	MACROCYTES	MADERIZE	MAFFICK
MAA	MACHANS	MACRODOME	MADERIZED	MAFFICKED
MAAED	MACHETE	MACRODOMES	MADERIZES	MAFFICKER
MAAING	MACHETES	MACROLOGIES	MADERIZING	MAFFICKERS
MAAR	MACHINATE	MACROLOGY	MADGE	MAFFICKING
MAARS	MACHINATED	MACRON	MADGES	MAFFICKINGS
MAAS	MACHINATES	MACRONS	MADHOUSE	MAFFICKS
MAATJES	MACHINATING	MACROPOD	MADHOUSES	MAFFLED
MAC	MACHINE	MACROPODS	MADID	MAFFLIN
MACABRE	MACHINED	MACROS	MADLING	MAFFLING
MACACO	MACHINERIES	MACRURAL	MADLINGS	MAFFLINGS
MACACOS	MACHINERY	MACRUROUS	MADLY	MAFFLINS
MACADAM	MACHINES	MACS	MADMAN	MAFIA
MACADAMIA	MACHINING	MACTATION	MADMEN	MAFIAS
MACADAMIAS	MACHINIST	MACTATIONS	MADNESS	MAFIC
MACADAMS	MACHINISTS	MACULA	MADNESSES	MAFICS
MACAHUBA	MACHISMO	MACULAE	MADOQUA	MAFIOSI
MACAHUBAS	MACHISMOS	MACULAR	MADOQUAS	MAFIOSO
MACALLUM	MACHMETER	MACULATE	MADRAS	MAG
MACALLUMS	MACHMETERS	MACULATED	MADRASA	MAGALOG
MACAQUE	MACHO	MACULATES	MADRASAH	MAGALOGS
MACAQUES	MACHOS	MACULATING	MADRASAHS	MAGAZINE
MACARISE	MACHREE	MACULE	MADRASAS	MAGAZINES
MACARISED	MACHREES	MACULES	MADRASES	MAGDALEN
MACARISES	MACHZOR	MACULOSE	MADRASSA	MAGDALENE
MACARISING	MACHZORIM	MAD	MADRASSAH	MAGDALENES
MACARISM	MACING	MADAM	MADRASSAHS	MAGDALENS
MACARISMS	MACINTOSH	MADAME	MADRASSAS	MAGE
MACARIZE	MACINTOSHES	MADAMED	MADREPORE	MAGENTA
MACARIZED	MACK	MADAMING	MADREPORES	MAGENTAS
MACARIZES	MACKEREL	MADAMS	MADRIGAL	MAGES
MACARIZING	MACKERELS	MADAROSES	MADRIGALS	MAGESHIP
MACARONI	MACKINAW	MADAROSIS	MADRONA	MAGESHIPS
MACARONIC	MACKINAWS	MADBRAIN	MADRONAS	MAGG
MACARONICS	MACKLE	MADCAP	MADRONE	MAGGED
MACARONIES	MACKLED	MADCAPS	MADRONES	MAGGING
MACARONIS	MACKLES	MADDED	MADRONO	MAGGOT
MACAROON	MACKLING	MADDEN	MADRONOS	MAGGOTS
MACAROONS	MACKS	MADDENED	MADS	MAGGOTY
MACASSAR	MACLE	MADDENING	MADWOMAN	MAGGS
MACASSARS	MACLED	MADDENS	MADWOMEN	MAGI
MACAW	MACLES	MADDER	MADWORT	MAGIAN
MACAWS	MACON	MADDERS	MADWORTS	MAGIANISM
MACCHIE	MACONS	MADDEST	MADZOON	MAGIANISMS
MACE	MACOYA	MADDING	MADZOONS	MAGIANS
MACED	MACOYAS	MADDINGLY	MAE	MAGIC
MACEDOINE	MACRAME	MADDOCK	MAELID	MAGICAL
MACEDOINES	MACRAMES	MADDOCKS	MAELIDS	MAGICALLY
MACER	MACRAMI	MADE	MAELSTROM	MAGICIAN
MACERATE	MACRAMIS	MADEFIED	MAELSTROMS	MAGICIANS
MACERATED	MACRO	MADEFIES	MAENAD	MAGICKED
MACERATES	MACROBIAN	MADEFY	MAENADIC	MAGICKING
MACERATING	MACROCODE	MADEFYING	MAENADS	MAGICS
MACERATOR	MACROCODES	MADELEINE	MAESTOSO	MAGILP
MACERATORS	MACROCOPIES	MADELEINES	MAESTRI	MAGILPS
MACERS	MACROCOPY	MADERISE	MAESTRO	MAGISM
MACES	MACROCOSM	MADERISED	MAESTROS	MAGISMS
MACHAIR	MACROCOSMS	MADERISES	MAFFIA	MAGISTER
MACHAIRS	MACROCYTE	MADERISING	MAFFIAS	MAGISTERIES

The Chambers Dictionary is the authority for many longer words; see *OSW* Introduction, page xii.

MAGISTERS	MAGPIE	MAIL	MAINPRISES	MAKER
MAGISTERY	MAGPIES	MAILABLE	MAINS	MAKERS
MAGISTRAL	MAGS	MAILBAG	MAINSAIL	MAKES
MAGISTRALS	MAGSMAN	MAILBAGS	MAINSAILS	MAKESHIFT
MAGLEV	MAGSMEN	MAILBOX	MAINSHEET	MAKESHIFTS
MAGMA	MAGUEY	MAILBOXES	MAINSHEETS	MAKIMONO
MAGMAS	MAGUEYS	MAILE	MAINSTAY	MAKIMONOS
MAGMATA	MAGUS	MAILED	MAINSTAYS	MAKING
MAGMATIC	MAGYAR	MAILER	MAINTAIN	MAKINGS
MAGNALIUM	MAHARAJA	MAILERS	MAINTAINED	MAKO
MAGNALIUMS	MAHARAJAH	MAILES	MAINTAINING	MAKOS
MAGNATE	MAHARAJAHS	MAILGRAM	MAINTAINS	MAKS
MAGNATES	MAHARAJAS	MAILGRAMMED	MAINTOP	MAL
MAGNES	MAHARANEE	MAILGRAMMING	MAINTOPS	MALACHITE
MAGNESES	MAHARANEES	MAILGRAMS	MAINYARD	MALACHITES
MAGNESIA	MAHARANI	MAILING	MAINYARDS	MALACIA
MAGNESIAN	MAHARANIS	MAILINGS	MAIOLICA	MALACIAS
MAGNESIAS	MAHARISHI	MAILLOT	MAIOLICAS	MALADIES
MAGNESITE	MAHARISHIS	MAILLOTS	MAIR	MALADROIT
MAGNESITES	MAHATMA	MAILMAN	MAIRE	MALADY
MAGNESIUM	MAHATMAS	MAILMEN	MAIRES	MALAGUENA
MAGNESIUMS	MAHLSTICK	MAILMERGE	MAIRS	MALAGUENAS
MAGNET	MAHLSTICKS	MAILMERGED	MAISE	MALAISE
MAGNETIC	MAHMAL	MAILMERGES	MAISES	MALAISES
MAGNETICS	MAHMALS	MAILMERGING	MAIST	MALAMUTE
MAGNETISE	MAHOE	MAILROOM	MAISTER	MALAMUTES
MAGNETISED	MAHOES	MAILROOMS	MAISTERED	MALANDER
MAGNETISES	MAHOGANIES	MAILS	MAISTERING	MALANDERS
MAGNETISING	MAHOGANY	MAILSACK	MAISTERS	MALAPERT
MAGNETISM	MAHONIA	MAILSACKS	MAISTRIES	MALAR
MAGNETISMS	MAHONIAS	MAILVAN	MAISTRING	MALARIA
MAGNETIST	MAHOUT	MAILVANS	MAISTRINGS	MALARIAL
MAGNETISTS	MAHOUTS	MAIM	MAISTRY	MALARIAN
MAGNETITE	MAHSEER	MAIMED	MAIZE	MALARIAS
MAGNETITES	MAHSEERS	MAIMING	MAIZES	MALARIOUS
MAGNETIZE	MAHSIR	MAIMINGS	MAJESTIC	MALARKEY
MAGNETIZED	MAHSIRS	MAIMS	MAJESTIES	MALARKEYS
MAGNETIZES	MAHUA	MAIN	MAJESTY	MALARKIES
MAGNETIZING	MAHUAS	MAINBOOM	MAJLIS	MALARKY
MAGNETO	MAHWA	MAINBOOMS	MAJLISES	MALARS
MAGNETON	MAHWAS	MAINBRACE	MAJOLICA	MALATE
MAGNETONS	MAHZOR	MAINBRACES	MAJOLICAS	MALATES
MAGNETOS	MAHZORIM	MAINDOOR	MAJOR	MALAX
MAGNETRON	MAID	MAINDOORS	MAJORAT	MALAXAGE
MAGNETRONS	MAIDAN	MAINED	MAJORATS	MALAXAGES
MAGNETS	MAIDANS	MAINER	MAJORED	MALAXATE
MAGNIFIC	MAIDED	MAINEST	MAJORETTE	MALAXATED
MAGNIFICO	MAIDEN	MAINFRAME	MAJORETTES	MALAXATES
MAGNIFICOES	MAIDENISH	MAINFRAMES	MAJORING	MALAXATING
MAGNIFIED	MAIDENLY	MAINING	MAJORITIES	MALAXATOR
MAGNIFIER	MAIDENS	MAINLAND	MAJORITY	MALAXATORS
MAGNIFIERS	MAIDHOOD	MAINLANDS	MAJORS	MALAXED
MAGNIFIES	MAIDHOODS	MAINLINE	MAJORSHIP	MALAXES
MAGNIFY	MAIDING	MAINLINED	MAJORSHIPS	MALAXING
MAGNIFYING	MAIDISH	MAINLINER	MAJUSCULE	MALE
MAGNITUDE	MAIDISM	MAINLINERS	MAJUSCULES	MALEATE
MAGNITUDES	MAIDISMS	MAINLINES	MAK	MALEATES
MAGNOLIA	MAIDLESS	MAINLINING	MAKABLE	MALEDICT
MAGNOLIAS	MAIDS	MAINLININGS	MAKAR	MALEDICTED
MAGNON	MAIEUTIC	MAINLY	MAKARS	MALEDICTING
MAGNONS	MAIEUTICS	MAINMAST	MAKE	MALEDICTS
MAGNOX	MAIGRE	MAINMASTS	MAKEABLE	MALEFFECT
MAGNOXES	MAIGRES	MAINOR	MAKEBATE	MALEFFECTS
MAGNUM	MAIK	MAINORS	MAKEBATES	MALEFIC
MAGNUMS	MAIKO	MAINOUR	MAKELESS	MALEFICE
MAGOT	MAIKOS	MAINOURS	MAKEOVER	MALEFICES
MAGOTS	MAIKS	MAINPRISE	MAKEOVERS	MALEIC

The Chambers Dictionary is the authority for many longer words; see *OSW* Introduction, page xii.

MALEMUTE	MALLENDER	MAMBAS	MANA	MANDIRS
MALEMUTES	MALLENDERS	MAMBO	MANACLE	MANDOLA
MALENGINE	MALLEOLAR	MAMBOED	MANACLED	MANDOLAS
MALENGINES	MALLEOLI	MAMBOING	MANACLES	MANDOLIN
MALES	MALLEOLUS	MAMBOS	MANACLING	MANDOLINE
MALFORMED	MALLEOLUSES	MAMEE	MANAGE	MANDOLINES
MALGRADO	MALLET	MAMEES	MANAGED	MANDOLINS
MALGRE	MALLETS	MAMELON	MANAGER	MANDOM
MALGRED	MALLEUS	MAMELONS	MANAGERS	MANDOMS
MALGRES	MALLEUSES	MAMELUCO	MANAGES	MANDORA
MALGRING	MALLING	MAMELUCOS	MANAGING	MANDORAS
MALI	MALLOW	MAMILLA	MANAKIN	MANDORLA
MALIC	MALLOWS	MAMILLAE	MANAKINS	MANDORLAS
MALICE	MALLS	MAMILLAR	MANANA	MANDRAKE
MALICED	MALM	MAMILLARY	MANANAS	MANDRAKES
MALICES	MALMAG	MAMILLATE	MANAS	MANDREL
MALICHO	MALMAGS	MAMMA	MANATEE	MANDRELS
MALICHOS	MALMS	MAMMAE	MANATEES	MANDRIL
MALICING	MALMSEY	MAMMAL	MANATI	MANDRILL
MALICIOUS	MALMSEYS	MAMMALIAN	MANATIS	MANDRILLS
MALIGN	MALMSTONE	MAMMALOGIES	MANCALA	MANDRILS
MALIGNANT	MALMSTONES	MAMMALOGY	MANCALAS	MANDUCATE
MALIGNANTS	MALODOUR	MAMMALS	MANCANDO	MANDUCATED
MALIGNED	MALODOURS	MAMMARY	MANCHE	MANDUCATES
MALIGNER	MALONATE	MAMMAS	MANCHES	MANDUCATING
MALIGNERS	MALONATES	MAMMATE	MANCHET	MANDYLION
MALIGNING	MALS	MAMMEE	MANCHETS	MANDYLIONS
MALIGNITIES	MALSTICK	MAMMEES	MANCIPATE	MANE
MALIGNITY	MALSTICKS	MAMMER	MANCIPATED	MANED
MALIGNLY	MALT	MAMMERED	MANCIPATES	MANEGE
MALIGNS	MALTALENT	MAMMERING	MANCIPATING	MANEGED
MALIK	MALTALENTS	MAMMERS	MANCIPLE	MANEGES
MALIKS	MALTASE	MAMMET	MANCIPLES	MANEGING
MALINGER	MALTASES	MAMMETRIES	MANCUS	MANEH
MALINGERED	MALTED	MAMMETRY	MANCUSES	MANEHS
MALINGERIES	MALTHA	MAMMETS	MAND	MANELESS
MALINGERING	MALTHAS	MAMMIES	MANDALA	MANENT
MALINGERS	MALTIER	MAMMIFER	MANDALAS	MANES
MALINGERY	MALTIEST	MAMMIFERS	MANDAMUS	MANET
MALIS	MALTING	MAMMIFORM	MANDAMUSES	MANEUVER
MALISM	MALTINGS	MAMMILLA	MANDARIN	MANEUVERED
MALISMS	MALTMAN	MAMMILLAE	MANDARINE	MANEUVERING
MALISON	MALTMEN	MAMMOCK	MANDARINES	MANEUVERS
MALISONS	MALTOSE	MAMMOCKED	MANDARINS	MANFUL
MALIST	MALTOSES	MAMMOCKING	MANDATARIES	MANFULLY
MALKIN	MALTREAT	MAMMOCKS	MANDATARY	MANG
MALKINS	MALTREATED	MAMMOGRAM	MANDATE	MANGA
MALL	MALTREATING	MAMMOGRAMS	MANDATED	MANGABEY
MALLAM	MALTREATS	MAMMON	MANDATES	MANGABEYS
MALLAMS	MALTS	MAMMONISH	MANDATING	MANGAL
MALLANDER	MALTSTER	MAMMONISM	MANDATOR	MANGALS
MALLANDERS	MALTSTERS	MAMMONISMS	MANDATORIES	MANGANATE
MALLARD	MALTWORM	MAMMONIST	MANDATORS	MANGANATES
MALLARDS	MALTWORMS	MAMMONISTS	MANDATORY	MANGANESE
MALLEABLE	MALTY	MAMMONITE	MANDIBLE	MANGANESES
MALLEATE	MALVA	MAMMONITES	MANDIBLES	MANGANIC
MALLEATED	MALVAS	MAMMONS	MANDILION	MANGANITE
MALLEATES	MALVASIA	MAMMOTH	MANDILIONS	MANGANITES
MALLEATING	MALVASIAS	MAMMOTHS	MANDIOC	MANGANOUS
MALLECHO	MALVESIE	MAMMY	MANDIOCA	MANGAS
MALLECHOS	MALVESIES	MAMS	MANDIOCAS	MANGE
MALLED	MALVOISIE	MAMSELLE	MANDIOCCA	MANGED
MALLEE	MALVOISIES	MAMSELLES	MANDIOCCAS	MANGEL
MALLEES	MAM	MAMZER	MANDIOCS	MANGELS
MALLEI	MAMA	MAMZERIM	MANDIR	MANGER
MALLEMUCK	MAMAS	MAMZERS	MANDIRA	MANGERS
MALLEMUCKS	MAMBA	MAN	MANDIRAS	MANGES

The Chambers Dictionary is the authority for many longer words; see *OSW* Introduction, page xii.

MANGETOUT	MANIKIN	MANORIAL	MANTRAPS	MAQUISARD
MANGETOUTS	MANIKINS	MANORS	MANTRAS	MAQUISARDS
MANGEY	MANILA	MANOS	MANTUA	MAR
MANGIER	MANILAS	MANPACK	MANTUAS	MARA
MANGIEST	MANILLA	MANPACKS	MANTY	MARABOU
MANGINESS	MANILLAS	MANPOWER	MANUAL	MARABOUS
MANGINESSES	MANILLE	MANPOWERS	MANUALLY	MARABOUT
MANGING	MANILLES	MANQUE	MANUALS	MARABOUTS
MANGLE	MANIOC	MANRED	MANUBRIA	MARACA
MANGLED	MANIOCS	MANREDS	MANUBRIAL	MARACAS
MANGLER	MANIPLE	MANRENT	MANUBRIUM	MARAE
MANGLERS	MANIPLES	MANRENTS	MANUKA	MARAES
MANGLES	MANIPLIES	MANRIDER	MANUKAS	MARAGING
MANGLING	MANIPULAR	MANRIDERS	MANUL	MARAGINGS
MANGO	MANIPULARS	MANRIDING	MANULS	MARAH
MANGOES	MANIS	MANS	MANUMEA	MARAHS
MANGOLD	MANITO	MANSARD	MANUMEAS	MARAS
MANGOLDS	MANITOS	MANSARDS	MANUMIT	MARASMIC
MANGONEL	MANITOU	MANSE	MANUMITS	MARASMUS
MANGONELS	MANITOUS	MANSES	MANUMITTED	MARASMUSES
MANGOSTAN	MANJACK	MANSHIFT	MANUMITTING	MARATHON
MANGOSTANS	MANJACKS	MANSHIFTS	MANURANCE	MARATHONS
MANGOUSTE	MANKIER	MANSION	MANURANCES	MARAUD
MANGOUSTES	MANKIEST	MANSIONS	MANURE	MARAUDED
MANGROVE	MANKIND	MANSONRIES	MANURED	MARAUDER
MANGROVES	MANKINDS	MANSONRY	MANURER	MARAUDERS
MANGS	MANKY	MANSUETE	MANURERS	MARAUDING
MANGY	MANLIER	MANSWORN	MANURES	MARAUDS
MANHANDLE	MANLIEST	MANTA	MANURIAL	MARAVEDI
MANHANDLED	MANLINESS	MANTAS	MANURING	MARAVEDIS
MANHANDLES	MANLINESSES	MANTEAU	MANURINGS	MARBLE
MANHANDLING	MANLY	MANTEAUS	MANUS	MARBLED
MANHOLE	MANNA	MANTEAUX	MANY	MARBLER
MANHOLES	MANNAS	MANTEEL	MANYATA	MARBLERS
MANHOOD	MANNED	MANTEELS	MANYATAS	MARBLES
MANHOODS	MANNEQUIN	MANTEL	MANYATTA	MARBLIER
MANHUNT	MANNEQUINS	MANTELET	MANYATTAS	MARBLIEST
MANHUNTS	MANNER	MANTELETS	MANYFOLD	MARBLING
MANI	MANNERED	MANTELS	MANYPLIES	MARBLINGS
MANIA	MANNERISM	MANTIC	MANZANITA	MARBLY
MANIAC	MANNERISMS	MANTICORA	MANZANITAS	MARC
MANIACAL	MANNERIST	MANTICORAS	MANZELLO	MARCASITE
MANIACS	MANNERISTS	MANTICORE	MANZELLOS	MARCASITES
MANIAS	MANNERLY	MANTICORES	MAORMOR	MARCATO
MANIC	MANNERS	MANTID	MAORMORS	MARCEL
MANICALLY	MANNIKIN	MANTIDS	MAP	MARCELLA
MANICURE	MANNIKINS	MANTIES	MAPLE	MARCELLAS
MANICURED	MANNING	MANTILLA	MAPLES	MARCELLED
MANICURES	MANNISH	MANTILLAS	MAPPED	MARCELLING
MANICURING	MANNITE	MANTIS	MAPPEMOND	MARCELS
MANIES	MANNITES	MANTISES	MAPPEMONDS	MARCH
MANIFEST	MANNITOL	MANTISSA	MAPPER	MARCHED
MANIFESTED	MANNITOLS	MANTISSAS	MAPPERIES	MARCHER
MANIFESTING	MANNOSE	MANTLE	MAPPERS	MARCHERS
MANIFESTO	MANNOSES	MANTLED	MAPPERY	MARCHES
MANIFESTOED	MANO	MANTLES	MAPPING	MARCHESA
MANIFESTOES	MANOAO	MANTLET	MAPPINGS	MARCHESAS
MANIFESTOING	MANOAOS	MANTLETS	MAPPIST	MARCHESE
MANIFESTOS	MANOEUVRE	MANTLING	MAPPISTS	MARCHESES
MANIFESTS	MANOEUVRED	MANTLINGS	MAPS	MARCHESI
MANIFOLD	MANOEUVRES	MANTO	MAPSTICK	MARCHING
MANIFOLDED	MANOEUVRING	MANTOES	MAPSTICKS	MARCHMAN
MANIFOLDING	MANOMETER	MANTOS	MAPWISE	MARCHMEN
MANIFOLDS	MANOMETERS	MANTRA	MAQUETTE	MARCHPANE
MANIFORM	MANOMETRIES	MANTRAM	MAQUETTES	MARCHPANES
MANIHOC	MANOMETRY	MANTRAMS	MAQUI	MARCONI
MANIHOCS	MANOR	MANTRAP	MAQUIS	MARCONIED

The Chambers Dictionary is the authority for many longer words; see *OSW* Introduction, page xii.

MARCONIING	MARINADE	MARLINGS	MARRIAGE	MARTING
MARCONIS	MARINADED	MARLINS	MARRIAGES	MARTINI
MARCS	MARINADES	MARLS	MARRIED	MARTINIS
MARD	MARINADING	MARLSTONE	MARRIER	MARTINS
MARDIED	MARINAS	MARLSTONES	MARRIERS	MARTLET
MARDIER	MARINATE	MARLY	MARRIES	MARTLETS
MARDIES	MARINATED	MARM	MARRING	MARTS
MARDIEST	MARINATES	MARMALADE	MARROW	MARTYR
MARDY	MARINATING	MARMALADES	MARROWED	MARTYRDOM
MARDYING	MARINE	MARMARISE	MARROWFAT	MARTYRDOMS
MARE	MARINER	MARMARISED	MARROWFATS	MARTYRED
MAREMMA	MARINERA	MARMARISES	MARROWING	MARTYRIA
MAREMMAS	MARINERAS	MARMARISING	MARROWISH	MARTYRIES
MARES	MARINERS	MARMARIZE	MARROWS	MARTYRING
MARESCHAL	MARINES	MARMARIZED	MARROWSKIED	MARTYRISE
MARESCHALS	MARINIERE	MARMARIZES	MARROWSKIES	MARTYRISED
MARG	MARIPOSA	MARMARIZING	MARROWSKY	MARTYRISES
MARGARIC	MARIPOSAS	MARMELISE	MARROWSKYING	MARTYRISING
MARGARIN	MARISCHAL	MARMELISED	MARROWY	MARTYRIUM
MARGARINE	MARISCHALLED	MARMELISES	MARRUM	MARTYRIZE
MARGARINES	MARISCHALLING	MARMELISING	MARRUMS	MARTYRIZED
MARGARINS	MARISCHALS	MARMELIZE	MARRY	MARTYRIZES
MARGARITA	MARISH	MARMELIZED	MARRYING	MARTYRIZING
MARGARITAS	MARISHES	MARMELIZES	MARRYINGS	MARTYRS
MARGARITE	MARITAGE	MARMELIZING	MARS	MARTYRY
MARGARITES	MARITAGES	MARMITE	MARSH	MARVEL
MARGAY	MARITAL	MARMITES	MARSHAL	MARVELLED
MARGAYS	MARITALLY	MARMOREAL	MARSHALCIES	MARVELLING
MARGE	MARITIME	MARMOSE	MARSHALCY	MARVELS
MARGENT	MARJORAM	MARMOSES	MARSHALLED	MARVER
MARGENTED	MARJORAMS	MARMOSET	MARSHALLING	MARVERED
MARGENTING	MARK	MARMOSETS	MARSHALLINGS	MARVERING
MARGENTS	MARKED	MARMOT	MARSHALS	MARVERS
MARGES	MARKEDLY	MARMOTS	MARSHES	MARXISANT
MARGIN	MARKER	MARMS	MARSHIER	MARY
MARGINAL	MARKERS	MAROCAIN	MARSHIEST	MARYBUD
MARGINALS	MARKET	MAROCAINS	MARSHLAND	MARYBUDS
MARGINATE	MARKETED	MARON	MARSHLANDS	MARZIPAN
MARGINED	MARKETEER	MARONS	MARSHWORT	MARZIPANS
MARGINING	MARKETEERS	MAROON	MARSHWORTS	MAS
MARGINS	MARKETER	MAROONED	MARSHY	MASA
MARGOSA	MARKETERS	MAROONER	MARSPORT	MASAS
MARGOSAS	MARKETING	MAROONERS	MARSPORTS	MASCARA
MARGRAVE	MARKETINGS	MAROONING	MARSUPIA	MASCARAS
MARGRAVES	MARKETS	MAROONINGS	MARSUPIAL	MASCARON
MARGS	MARKHOR	MAROONS	MARSUPIALS	MASCARONS
MARIA	MARKHORS	MAROQUIN	MARSUPIUM	MASCLE
MARIACHI	MARKING	MAROQUINS	MARSUPIUMS	MASCLED
MARIACHIS	MARKINGS	MAROR	MART	MASCLES
MARIALITE	MARKKA	MARORS	MARTAGON	MASCON
MARIALITES	MARKKAA	MARPLOT	MARTAGONS	MASCONS
MARID	MARKKAS	MARPLOTS	MARTED	MASCOT
MARIDS	MARKMAN	MARQUE	MARTEL	MASCOTS
MARIES	MARKMEN	MARQUEE	MARTELLED	MASCULINE
MARIGOLD	MARKS	MARQUEES	MARTELLING	MASCULINES
MARIGOLDS	MARKSMAN	MARQUES	MARTELLO	MASCULY
MARIGRAM	MARKSMEN	MARQUESS	MARTELLOS	MASE
MARIGRAMS	MARL	MARQUESSES	MARTELS	MASED
MARIGRAPH	MARLE	MARQUETRIES	MARTEN	MASER
MARIGRAPHS	MARLED	MARQUETRY	MARTENS	MASERS
MARIHUANA	MARLES	MARQUIS	MARTEXT	MASES
MARIHUANAS	MARLIER	MARQUISE	MARTEXTS	MASH
MARIJUANA	MARLIEST	MARQUISES	MARTIAL	MASHALLAH
MARIJUANAS	MARLIN	MARRAM	MARTIALLY	MASHED
MARIMBA	MARLINE	MARRAMS	MARTIN	MASHER
MARIMBAS	MARLINES	MARRED	MARTINET	MASHERS
MARINA	MARLING	MARRELS	MARTINETS	MASHES

The Chambers Dictionary is the authority for many longer words; see *OSW* Introduction, page xii.

MASHIE	MASSETERS	MASTOIDS	MATHS	MATTERFUL
MASHIER	MASSEUR	MASTS	MATICO	MATTERING
MASHIES	MASSEURS	MASTY	MATICOS	MATTERS
MASHIEST	MASSEUSE	MASU	MATIER	MATTERY
MASHING	MASSEUSES	MASULA	MATIEST	MATTES
MASHINGS	MASSICOT	MASULAS	MATILY	MATTIE
MASHLAM	MASSICOTS	MASURIUM	MATIN	MATTIES
MASHLAMS	MASSIER	MASURIUMS	MATINAL	MATTING
MASHLIM	MASSIEST	MASUS	MATINEE	MATTINGS
MASHLIMS	MASSIF	MAT	MATINEES	MATTINS
MASHLIN	MASSIFS	MATACHIN	MATINESS	MATTOCK
MASHLINS	MASSINESS	MATACHINA	MATINESSES	MATTOCKS
MASHLOCH	MASSINESSES	MATACHINAS	MATING	MATTOID
MASHLOCHS	MASSING	MATACHINI	MATINS	MATTOIDS
MASHLUM	MASSIVE	MATADOR	MATJES	MATTRESS
MASHLUMS	MASSIVELY	MATADORA	MATLO	MATTRESSES
MASHMAN	MASSOOLA	MATADORAS	MATLOS	MATURABLE
MASHMEN	MASSOOLAS	MATADORE	MATLOW	MATURATE
MASHUA	MASSY	MATADORES	MATLOWS	MATURATED
MASHUAS	MASSYMORE	MATADORS	MATOKE	MATURATES
MASHY	MASSYMORES	MATAMATA	MATOKES	MATURATING
MASING	MAST	MATAMATAS	MATOOKE	MATURE
MASJID	MASTABA	MATCH	MATOOKES	MATURED
MASJIDS	MASTABAS	MATCHABLE	MATRASS	MATURELY
MASK	MASTED	MATCHBOX	MATRASSES	MATURER
MASKED	MASTER	MATCHBOXES	MATRIARCH	MATURES
MASKER	MASTERATE	MATCHED	MATRIARCHS	MATUREST
MASKERS	MASTERATES	MATCHER	MATRIC	MATURING
MASKING	MASTERDOM	MATCHERS	MATRICE	MATURITIES
MASKS	MASTERDOMS	MATCHES	MATRICES	MATURITY
MASLIN	MASTERED	MATCHING	MATRICIDE	MATUTINAL
MASLINS	MASTERFUL	MATCHLESS	MATRICIDES	MATUTINE
MASOCHISM	MASTERIES	MATCHLOCK	MATRICS	MATWEED
MASOCHISMS	MASTERING	MATCHLOCKS	MATRICULA	MATWEEDS
MASOCHIST	MASTERINGS	MATCHWOOD	MATRICULAS	MATY
MASOCHISTS	MASTERLY	MATCHWOODS	MATRILINIES	MATZA
MASON	MASTERS	MATE	MATRILINY	MATZAH
MASONED	MASTERY	MATED	MATRIMONIES	MATZAHS
MASONIC	MASTFUL	MATELASSE	MATRIMONY	MATZAS
MASONING	MASTHEAD	MATELASSES	MATRIX	MATZO
MASONRIED	MASTHEADED	MATELESS	MATRIXES	MATZOH
MASONRIES	MASTHEADING	MATELOT	MATRON	MATZOON
MASONRY	MASTHEADS	MATELOTE	MATRONAGE	MATZOONS
MASONS	MASTHOUSE	MATELOTES	MATRONAGES	MATZOS
MASOOLAH	MASTHOUSES	MATELOTS	MATRONAL	MATZOT
MASOOLAHS	MASTIC	MATER	MATRONISE	MATZOTH
MASQUE	MASTICATE	MATERIAL	MATRONISED	MAUD
MASQUER	MASTICATED	MATERIALS	MATRONISES	MAUDLIN
MASQUERS	MASTICATES	MATERIEL	MATRONISING	MAUDS
MASQUES	MASTICATING	MATERIELS	MATRONIZE	MAUGRE
MASS	MASTICH	MATERNAL	MATRONIZED	MAUGRED
MASSA	MASTICHS	MATERNITIES	MATRONIZES	MAUGRES
MASSACRE	MASTICOT	MATERNITY	MATRONIZING	MAUGRING
MASSACRED	MASTICOTS	MATERS	MATRONLY	MAUL
MASSACRES	MASTICS	MATES	MATRONS	MAULED
MASSACRING	MASTIER	MATESHIP	MATROSS	MAULERS
MASSAGE	MASTIEST	MATESHIPS	MATROSSES	MAULGRE
MASSAGED	MASTIFF	MATEY	MATS	MAULGRED
MASSAGES	MASTIFFS	MATEYNESS	MATSURI	MAULGRES
MASSAGING	MASTING	MATEYNESSES	MATSURIS	MAULGRING
MASSAGIST	MASTITIS	MATFELON	MATT	MAULING
MASSAGISTS	MASTITISES	MATFELONS	MATTAMORE	MAULS
MASSAS	MASTLESS	MATGRASS	MATTAMORES	MAULSTICK
MASSE	MASTODON	MATGRASSES	MATTE	MAULSTICKS
MASSED	MASTODONS	MATH	MATTED	MAULVI
MASSES	MASTOID	MATHESES	MATTER	MAULVIS
MASSETER	MASTOIDAL	MATHESIS	MATTERED	MAUMET

The Chambers Dictionary is the authority for many longer words; see *OSW* Introduction, page xii.

MAUMETRIES
MAUMETRY
MAUMETS
MAUN
MAUND
MAUNDED
MAUNDER
MAUNDERED
MAUNDERER
MAUNDERERS
MAUNDERING
MAUNDERINGS
MAUNDERS
MAUNDIES
MAUNDING
MAUNDS
MAUNDY
MAUNGIER
MAUNGIEST
MAUNGY
MAUNNA
MAUSOLEAN
MAUSOLEUM
MAUSOLEUMS
MAUTHER
MAUTHERS
MAUVAIS
MAUVAISE
MAUVE
MAUVEIN
MAUVEINE
MAUVEINES
MAUVEINS
MAUVER
MAUVES
MAUVEST
MAUVIN
MAUVINE
MAUVINES
MAUVINS
MAVEN
MAVENS
MAVERICK
MAVERICKED
MAVERICKING
MAVERICKS
MAVIN
MAVINS
MAVIS
MAVISES
MAW
MAWBOUND
MAWK
MAWKIER
MAWKIEST
MAWKIN
MAWKINS
MAWKISH
MAWKISHLY
MAWKS
MAWKY
MAWMET
MAWMETRIES
MAWMETRY
MAWMETS
MAWPUS
MAWPUSES

MAWR
MAWRS
MAWS
MAWSEED
MAWSEEDS
MAWTHER
MAWTHERS
MAX
MAXES
MAXI
MAXILLA
MAXILLAE
MAXILLARIES
MAXILLARY
MAXILLULA
MAXILLULAE
MAXIM
MAXIMA
MAXIMAL
MAXIMALLY
MAXIMIN
MAXIMINS
MAXIMISE
MAXIMISED
MAXIMISES
MAXIMISING
MAXIMIST
MAXIMISTS
MAXIMIZE
MAXIMIZED
MAXIMIZES
MAXIMIZING
MAXIMS
MAXIMUM
MAXIS
MAXIXE
MAXIXES
MAXWELL
MAXWELLS
MAY
MAYA
MAYAS
MAYBE
MAYBES
MAYDAY
MAYDAYS
MAYED
MAYEST
MAYFLIES
MAYFLOWER
MAYFLOWERS
MAYFLY
MAYHAP
MAYHEM
MAYHEMS
MAYING
MAYINGS
MAYOR
MAYORAL
MAYORALTIES
MAYORALTY
MAYORESS
MAYORESSES
MAYORS
MAYORSHIP
MAYORSHIPS
MAYPOLE

MAYPOLES
MAYS
MAYST
MAYSTER
MAYSTERS
MAYWEED
MAYWEEDS
MAZARD
MAZARDS
MAZARINE
MAZARINES
MAZE
MAZED
MAZEFUL
MAZELTOV
MAZEMENT
MAZEMENTS
MAZER
MAZERS
MAZES
MAZHBI
MAZHBIS
MAZIER
MAZIEST
MAZILY
MAZINESS
MAZINESSES
MAZING
MAZOUT
MAZOUTS
MAZUMA
MAZUMAS
MAZURKA
MAZURKAS
MAZUT
MAZUTS
MAZY
MAZZARD
MAZZARDS
MBAQANGA
MBAQANGAS
MBIRA
MBIRAS
ME
MEACOCK
MEACOCKS
MEAD
MEADOW
MEADOWS
MEADOWY
MEADS
MEAGRE
MEAGRELY
MEAGRER
MEAGRES
MEAGREST
MEAL
MEALED
MEALER
MEALERS
MEALIE
MEALIER
MEALIES
MEALIEST
MEALINESS
MEALINESSES
MEALING

MEALS
MEALTIME
MEALTIMES
MEALWORM
MEALWORMS
MEALY
MEAN
MEANDER
MEANDERED
MEANDERING
MEANDERS
MEANDRIAN
MEANDROUS
MEANE
MEANED
MEANER
MEANES
MEANEST
MEANIE
MEANIES
MEANING
MEANINGLY
MEANINGS
MEANLY
MEANNESS
MEANNESSES
MEANS
MEANT
MEANTIME
MEANTIMES
MEANWHILE
MEANWHILES
MEANY
MEARE
MEARES
MEARING
MEASE
MEASED
MEASES
MEASING
MEASLE
MEASLED
MEASLES
MEASLIER
MEASLIEST
MEASLING
MEASLY
MEASURE
MEASURED
MEASURER
MEASURERS
MEASURES
MEASURING
MEASURINGS
MEAT
MEATAL
MEATBALL
MEATBALLS
MEATH
MEATHE
MEATHEAD
MEATHEADS
MEATHES
MEATHS
MEATIER
MEATIEST
MEATILY

MEATINESS
MEATINESSES
MEATLESS
MEATS
MEATUS
MEATUSES
MEATY
MEAWES
MEAZEL
MEAZELS
MEBOS
MEBOSES
MECHANIC
MECHANICS
MECHANISE
MECHANISED
MECHANISES
MECHANISING
MECHANISM
MECHANISMS
MECHANIST
MECHANISTS
MECHANIZE
MECHANIZED
MECHANIZES
MECHANIZING
MECONATE
MECONATES
MECONIC
MECONIN
MECONINS
MECONIUM
MECONIUMS
MEDACCA
MEDACCAS
MEDAEWART
MEDAEWARTS
MEDAKA
MEDAKAS
MEDAL
MEDALED
MEDALET
MEDALETS
MEDALING
MEDALIST
MEDALISTS
MEDALLED
MEDALLIC
MEDALLING
MEDALLION
MEDALLIONED
MEDALLIONING
MEDALLIONS
MEDALLIST
MEDALLISTS
MEDALS
MEDDLE
MEDDLED
MEDDLER
MEDDLERS
MEDDLES
MEDDLING
MEDDLINGS
MEDFLIES
MEDFLY
MEDIA
MEDIACIES

The Chambers Dictionary is the authority for many longer words; see *OSW* Introduction, page xii.

MEDIACY	MEDIUS	MEGACITY	MEINEY	MELILITES
MEDIAE	MEDIUSES	MEGACURIE	MEINEYS	MELILOT
MEDIAEVAL	MEDLAR	MEGACURIES	MEINIE	MELILOTS
MEDIAL	MEDLARS	MEGACYCLE	MEINIES	MELINITE
MEDIALLY	MEDLE	MEGACYCLES	MEINING	MELINITES
MEDIALS	MEDLED	MEGADEATH	MEINS	MELIORATE
MEDIAN	MEDLES	MEGADEATHS	MEINT	MELIORATED
MEDIANS	MEDLEY	MEGADOSE	MEINY	MELIORATES
MEDIANT	MEDLEYS	MEGADOSES	MEIOFAUNA	MELIORATING
MEDIANTS	MEDLING	MEGADYNE	MEIONITE	MELIORISM
MEDIATE	MEDRESSEH	MEGADYNES	MEIONITES	MELIORISMS
MEDIATED	MEDRESSEHS	MEGAFARAD	MEIOSES	MELIORIST
MEDIATELY	MEDULLA	MEGAFARADS	MEIOSIS	MELIORISTS
MEDIATES	MEDULLAE	MEGAFAUNA	MEIOTIC	MELIORITIES
MEDIATING	MEDULLAR	MEGAFAUNAE	MEISHI	MELIORITY
MEDIATION	MEDULLARY	MEGAFAUNAS	MEISHIS	MELISMA
MEDIATIONS	MEDULLAS	MEGAFLORA	MEITH	MELISMAS
MEDIATISE	MEDULLATE	MEGAFLORAE	MEITHS	MELISMATA
MEDIATISED	MEDUSA	MEGAFLORAS	MEJLIS	MELL
MEDIATISES	MEDUSAE	MEGAFOG	MEJLISES	MELLAY
MEDIATISING	MEDUSAN	MEGAFOGS	MEKOMETER	MELLAYS
MEDIATIVE	MEDUSANS	MEGAGAUSS	MEKOMETERS	MELLED
MEDIATIZE	MEDUSAS	MEGAGAUSSES	MEL	MELLING
MEDIATIZED	MEDUSOID	MEGAHERTZ	MELA	MELLITE
MEDIATIZES	MEDUSOIDS	MEGAHERTZES	MELAMINE	MELLITES
MEDIATIZING	MEED	MEGAJOULE	MELAMINES	MELLITIC
MEDIATOR	MEEDS	MEGAJOULES	MELAMPODE	MELLOW
MEDIATORS	MEEK	MEGALITH	MELAMPODES	MELLOWED
MEDIATORY	MEEKEN	MEGALITHS	MELANGE	MELLOWER
MEDIATRICES	MEEKENED	MEGAPHONE	MELANGES	MELLOWEST
MEDIATRIX	MEEKENING	MEGAPHONED	MELANIC	MELLOWING
MEDIC	MEEKENS	MEGAPHONES	MELANIN	MELLOWLY
MEDICABLE	MEEKER	MEGAPHONING	MELANINS	MELLOWS
MEDICAID	MEEKEST	MEGAPODE	MELANISM	MELLOWY
MEDICAIDS	MEEKLY	MEGAPODES	MELANISMS	MELLS
MEDICAL	MEEKNESS	MEGARA	MELANITE	MELOCOTON
MEDICALLY	MEEKNESSES	MEGARAD	MELANITES	MELOCOTONS
MEDICALS	MEEMIE	MEGARADS	MELANO	MELODEON
MEDICARE	MEEMIES	MEGARON	MELANOMA	MELODEONS
MEDICARES	MEER	MEGARONS	MELANOMAS	MELODIC
MEDICATE	MEERCAT	MEGASCOPE	MELANOMATA	MELODICA
MEDICATED	MEERCATS	MEGASCOPES	MELANOS	MELODICAS
MEDICATES	MEERED	MEGASPORE	MELANOSES	MELODICS
MEDICATING	MEERING	MEGASPORES	MELANOSIS	MELODIES
MEDICINAL	MEERKAT	MEGASS	MELANOTIC	MELODION
MEDICINE	MEERKATS	MEGASSE	MELANOUS	MELODIONS
MEDICINED	MEERS	MEGASSES	MELANURIA	MELODIOUS
MEDICINER	MEET	MEGASTORE	MELANURIAS	MELODISE
MEDICINERS	MEETER	MEGASTORES	MELANURIC	MELODISED
MEDICINES	MEETEST	MEGATON	MELAPHYRE	MELODISES
MEDICINING	MEETING	MEGATONS	MELAPHYRES	MELODISING
MEDICK	MEETINGS	MEGAVOLT	MELAS	MELODIST
MEDICKS	MEETLY	MEGAVOLTS	MELATONIN	MELODISTS
MEDICO	MEETNESS	MEGAWATT	MELATONINS	MELODIZE
MEDICOS	MEETNESSES	MEGAWATTS	MELD	MELODIZED
MEDICS	MEETS	MEGILLAH	MELDED	MELODIZES
MEDIEVAL	MEG	MEGILLAHS	MELDER	MELODIZING
MEDII	MEGA	MEGILLOTH	MELDERS	MELODRAMA
MEDINA	MEGABAR	MEGILP	MELDING	MELODRAMAS
MEDINAS	MEGABARS	MEGILPS	MELDS	MELODRAME
MEDIOCRE	MEGABIT	MEGOHM	MELEE	MELODRAMES
MEDITATE	MEGABITS	MEGOHMS	MELEES	MELODY
MEDITATED	MEGABUCK	MEGRIM	MELIC	MELOMANIA
MEDITATES	MEGABUCKS	MEGRIMS	MELICS	MELOMANIAS
MEDITATING	MEGABYTE	MEGS	MELIK	MELOMANIC
MEDIUM	MEGABYTES	MEIN	MELIKS	MELON
MEDIUMS	MEGACITIES	MEINED	MELILITE	MELONS

The Chambers Dictionary is the authority for many longer words; see *OSW* Introduction, page xii.

MELS	MENDER	MENSUAL	MERCERIZING	MERGES
MELT	MENDERS	MENSURAL	MERCERS	MERGING
MELTDOWN	MENDICANT	MENSWEAR	MERCERY	MERI
MELTDOWNS	MENDICANTS	MENSWEARS	MERCHANT	MERICARP
MELTED	MENDICITIES	MENT	MERCHANTED	MERICARPS
MELTING	MENDICITY	MENTA	MERCHANTING	MERIDIAN
MELTINGLY	MENDING	MENTAL	MERCHANTINGS	MERIDIANS
MELTINGS	MENDINGS	MENTALISM	MERCHANTS	MERIL
MELTITH	MENDS	MENTALISMS	MERCHET	MERILS
MELTITHS	MENE	MENTALIST	MERCHETS	MERIMAKE
MELTON	MENED	MENTALISTS	MERCHILD	MERIMAKES
MELTONS	MENEER	MENTALITIES	MERCHILDREN	MERING
MELTS	MENEERS	MENTALITY	MERCIABLE	MERINGUE
MEMBER	MENES	MENTALLY	MERCIES	MERINGUES
MEMBERED	MENFOLK	MENTATION	MERCIFIDE	MERINO
MEMBERS	MENFOLKS	MENTATIONS	MERCIFIED	MERINOS
MEMBRAL	MENG	MENTEE	MERCIFIES	MERIS
MEMBRANE	MENGE	MENTEES	MERCIFUL	MERISM
MEMBRANES	MENGED	MENTHOL	MERCIFY	MERISMS
MEMENTO	MENGES	MENTHOLS	MERCIFYING	MERISTEM
MEMENTOES	MENGING	MENTICIDE	MERCILESS	MERISTEMS
MEMENTOS	MENGS	MENTICIDES	MERCS	MERISTIC
MEMO	MENHADEN	MENTION	MERCURATE	MERIT
MEMOIR	MENHADENS	MENTIONED	MERCURATED	MERITED
MEMOIRISM	MENHIR	MENTIONING	MERCURATES	MERITING
MEMOIRISMS	MENHIRS	MENTIONS	MERCURATING	MERITS
MEMOIRIST	MENIAL	MENTO	MERCURIAL	MERK
MEMOIRISTS	MENIALS	MENTOR	MERCURIALS	MERKIN
MEMOIRS	MENING	MENTORIAL	MERCURIC	MERKINS
MEMORABLE	MENINGEAL	MENTORING	MERCURIES	MERKS
MEMORABLY	MENINGES	MENTORINGS	MERCURISE	MERL
MEMORANDA	MENINX	MENTORS	MERCURISED	MERLE
MEMORIAL	MENISCI	MENTOS	MERCURISES	MERLES
MEMORIALS	MENISCOID	MENTUM	MERCURISING	MERLIN
MEMORIES	MENISCUS	MENU	MERCURIZE	MERLING
MEMORISE	MENISCUSES	MENUISIER	MERCURIZED	MERLINGS
MEMORISED	MENOLOGIES	MENUISIERS	MERCURIZES	MERLINS
MEMORISES	MENOLOGY	MENUS	MERCURIZING	MERLON
MEMORISING	MENOMINEE	MENYIE	MERCUROUS	MERLONS
MEMORITER	MENOMINEES	MENYIES	MERCURY	MERLS
MEMORIZE	MENOMINI	MEOW	MERCY	MERMAID
MEMORIZED	MENOMINIS	MEOWED	MERE	MERMAIDEN
MEMORIZES	MENOPAUSE	MEOWING	MERED	MERMAIDENS
MEMORIZING	MENOPAUSES	MEOWS	MEREL	MERMAIDS
MEMORY	MENOPOME	MEPACRINE	MERELL	MERMAN
MEMOS	MENOPOMES	MEPACRINES	MERELLS	MERMEN
MEN	MENORAH	MEPHITIC	MERELS	MEROGONIES
MENACE	MENORAHS	MEPHITIS	MERELY	MEROGONY
MENACED	MENORRHEA	MEPHITISES	MERENGUE	MEROISTIC
MENACER	MENORRHEAS	MEPHITISM	MERENGUES	MEROME
MENACERS	MENSAL	MEPHITISMS	MERER	MEROMES
MENACES	MENSCH	MERC	MERES	MERONYM
MENACING	MENSCHES	MERCAPTAN	MERESMAN	MERONYMIES
MENADIONE	MENSE	MERCAPTANS	MERESMEN	MERONYMS
MENADIONES	MENSED	MERCAT	MEREST	MERONYMY
MENAGE	MENSEFUL	MERCATS	MERESTONE	MEROPIDAN
MENAGED	MENSELESS	MERCENARIES	MERESTONES	MEROPIDANS
MENAGERIE	MENSES	MERCENARY	MERFOLK	MEROSOME
MENAGERIES	MENSH	MERCER	MERFOLKS	MEROSOMES
MENAGES	MENSHED	MERCERIES	MERGANSER	MEROZOITE
MENAGING	MENSHES	MERCERISE	MERGANSERS	MEROZOITES
MENARCHE	MENSHING	MERCERISED	MERGE	MERPEOPLE
MENARCHES	MENSING	MERCERISES	MERGED	MERPEOPLES
MEND	MENSTRUA	MERCERISING	MERGENCE	MERRIER
MENDACITIES	MENSTRUAL	MERCERIZE	MERGENCES	MERRIES
MENDACITY	MENSTRUUM	MERCERIZED	MERGER	MERRIEST
MENDED	MENSTRUUMS	MERCERIZES	MERGERS	MERRILY

The Chambers Dictionary is the authority for many longer words; see *OSW* Introduction, page xii.

MERRIMENT	MESMERISM	MESSUAGES	METAYAGE	METHYLATE
MERRIMENTS	MESMERISMS	MESSY	METAYAGES	METHYLATED
MERRINESS	MESMERIST	MESTEE	METAYER	METHYLATES
MERRINESSES	MESMERISTS	MESTEES	METAYERS	METHYLATING
MERRY	MESMERIZE	MESTIZA	METAZOA	METHYLENE
MERRYMAN	MESMERIZED	MESTIZAS	METAZOAN	METHYLENES
MERRYMEN	MESMERIZES	MESTIZO	METAZOANS	METHYLIC
MERSALYL	MESMERIZING	MESTIZOS	METAZOIC	METHYLS
MERSALYLS	MESNE	MESTO	METAZOON	METHYSES
MERSE	MESOBLAST	MET	METCAST	METHYSIS
MERSES	MESOBLASTS	METABASES	METCASTS	METHYSTIC
MERSION	MESOCARP	METABASIS	METE	METIC
MERSIONS	MESOCARPS	METABATIC	METED	METICAL
MERYCISM	MESODERM	METABOLIC	METEOR	METICALS
MERYCISMS	MESODERMS	METACARPI	METEORIC	METICS
MES	MESOGLOEA	METAGE	METEORISM	METIER
MESA	MESOGLOEAS	METAGES	METEORISMS	METIERS
MESAIL	MESOLITE	METAIRIE	METEORIST	METIF
MESAILS	MESOLITES	METAIRIES	METEORISTS	METIFS
MESAL	MESOMORPH	METAL	METEORITE	METING
MESALLY	MESOMORPHS	METALED	METEORITES	METIS
MESARAIC	MESON	METALING	METEOROID	METISSE
MESARCH	MESONIC	METALIST	METEOROIDS	METISSES
MESAS	MESONS	METALISTS	METEOROUS	METOL
MESCAL	MESOPHYLL	METALIZE	METEORS	METOLS
MESCALIN	MESOPHYLLS	METALIZED	METER	METONYM
MESCALINS	MESOPHYTE	METALIZES	METERED	METONYMIC
MESCALISM	MESOPHYTES	METALIZING	METERING	METONYMIES
MESCALISMS	MESOTRON	METALLED	METERS	METONYMS
MESCALS	MESOTRONS	METALLIC	METES	METONYMY
MESCLUM	MESPRISE	METALLINE	METESTICK	METOPAE
MESCLUMS	MESPRISES	METALLING	METESTICKS	METOPE
MESCLUN	MESPRIZE	METALLINGS	METEWAND	METOPES
MESCLUNS	MESPRIZES	METALLISE	METEWANDS	METOPIC
MESDAMES	MESQUIN	METALLISED	METEYARD	METOPISM
MESE	MESQUINE	METALLISES	METEYARDS	METOPISMS
MESEL	MESQUIT	METALLISING	METHADON	METOPON
MESELED	MESQUITE	METALLIST	METHADONE	METOPONS
MESELS	MESQUITES	METALLISTS	METHADONES	METOPRYL
MESENTERA	MESQUITS	METALLIZE	METHADONS	METOPRYLS
MESENTERIES	MESS	METALLIZED	METHANAL	METRE
MESENTERY	MESSAGE	METALLIZES	METHANALS	METRED
MESES	MESSAGED	METALLIZING	METHANE	METRES
MESETA	MESSAGES	METALLOID	METHANES	METRIC
MESETAS	MESSAGING	METALLOIDS	METHANOL	METRICAL
MESH	MESSAGINGS	METALLY	METHANOLS	METRICATE
MESHED	MESSAN	METALS	METHEGLIN	METRICATED
MESHES	MESSANS	METALWORK	METHEGLINS	METRICATES
MESHIER	MESSED	METALWORKS	METHINK	METRICATING
MESHIEST	MESSENGER	METAMER	METHINKETH	METRICIAN
MESHING	MESSENGERS	METAMERE	METHINKS	METRICIANS
MESHINGS	MESSES	METAMERES	METHOD	METRICISE
MESHUGA	MESSIAH	METAMERIC	METHODIC	METRICISED
MESHUGAAS	MESSIAHS	METAMERS	METHODISE	METRICISES
MESHUGAASEN	MESSIANIC	METANOIA	METHODISED	METRICISING
MESHUGGA	MESSIAS	METANOIAS	METHODISES	METRICIST
MESHUGGE	MESSIASES	METAPELET	METHODISING	METRICISTS
MESHY	MESSIER	METAPHASE	METHODIST	METRICIZE
MESIAL	MESSIEST	METAPHASES	METHODISTS	METRICIZED
MESIALLY	MESSIEURS	METAPHOR	METHODIZE	METRICIZES
MESIAN	MESSILY	METAPHORS	METHODIZED	METRICIZING
MESIC	MESSINESS	METAPLASM	METHODIZES	METRICS
MESMERIC	MESSINESSES	METAPLASMS	METHODIZING	METRIFIER
MESMERISE	MESSING	METAPLOT	METHODS	METRIFIERS
MESMERISED	MESSMATE	METATARSI	METHOUGHT	METRING
MESMERISES	MESSMATES	METATE	METHS	METRIST
MESMERISING	MESSUAGE	METATES	METHYL	METRISTS

The Chambers Dictionary is the authority for many longer words; see *OSW* Introduction, page xii.

METRITIS	MIAOWS	MICROCOPY	MIDDEST	MIFFIEST
METRITISES	MIASM	MICROCOPYING	MIDDIES	MIFFILY
METRO	MIASMA	MICROCOPYINGS	MIDDLE	MIFFINESS
METROLOGIES	MIASMAL	MICROCOSM	MIDDLED	MIFFINESSES
METROLOGY	MIASMAS	MICROCOSMS	MIDDLEMAN	MIFFING
METRONOME	MIASMATA	MICROCYTE	MIDDLEMEN	MIFFS
METRONOMES	MIASMATIC	MICROCYTES	MIDDLES	MIFFY
METROPLEX	MIASMIC	MICRODOT	MIDDLING	MIFTY
METROPLEXES	MIASMOUS	MICRODOTS	MIDDLINGS	MIGHT
METROS	MIASMS	MICROFILM	MIDDY	MIGHTEST
METS	MIAUL	MICROFILMED	MIDFIELD	MIGHTFUL
METTLE	MIAULED	MICROFILMING	MIDFIELDS	MIGHTIER
METTLED	MIAULING	MICROFILMS	MIDGE	MIGHTIEST
METTLES	MIAULS	MICROFORM	MIDGES	MIGHTILY
MEU	MICA	MICROFORMS	MIDGET	MIGHTS
MEUNIERE	MICACEOUS	MICROGRAM	MIDGETS	MIGHTST
MEUS	MICAS	MICROGRAMS	MIDI	MIGHTY
MEUSE	MICATE	MICROLITE	MIDINETTE	MIGNON
MEUSED	MICATED	MICROLITES	MIDINETTES	MIGNONNE
MEUSES	MICATES	MICROLITH	MIDIRON	MIGRAINE
MEUSING	MICATING	MICROLITHS	MIDIRONS	MIGRAINES
MEVE	MICE	MICROLOGIES	MIDIS	MIGRANT
MEVED	MICELLA	MICROLOGY	MIDLAND	MIGRANTS
MEVES	MICELLAE	MICROMESH	MIDLANDS	MIGRATE
MEVING	MICELLAR	MICROMESHES	MIDMOST	MIGRATED
MEW	MICELLE	MICRON	MIDMOSTS	MIGRATES
MEWED	MICELLES	MICRONS	MIDNIGHT	MIGRATING
MEWING	MICHE	MICROPORE	MIDNIGHTS	MIGRATION
MEWL	MICHED	MICROPORES	MIDNOON	MIGRATIONS
MEWLED	MICHER	MICROPSIA	MIDNOONS	MIGRATOR
MEWLING	MICHERS	MICROPSIAS	MIDRIB	MIGRATORS
MEWLS	MICHES	MICROPUMP	MIDRIBS	MIGRATORY
MEWS	MICHING	MICROPUMPS	MIDRIFF	MIHRAB
MEWSED	MICHINGS	MICROPYLE	MIDRIFFS	MIHRABS
MEWSES	MICK	MICROPYLES	MIDS	MIKADO
MEWSING	MICKEY	MICROS	MIDSHIP	MIKADOS
MEYNT	MICKEYED	MICROSOME	MIDSHIPS	MIKE
MEZAIL	MICKEYING	MICROSOMES	MIDSIZE	MIKES
MEZAILS	MICKEYS	MICROTOME	MIDST	MIKRA
MEZE	MICKIES	MICROTOMES	MIDSTREAM	MIKRON
MEZEREON	MICKLE	MICROTOMIES	MIDSTREAMS	MIKRONS
MEZEREONS	MICKLES	MICROTOMY	MIDSTS	MIL
MEZEREUM	MICKS	MICROTONE	MIDSUMMER	MILADI
MEZEREUMS	MICKY	MICROTONES	MIDSUMMERS	MILADIES
MEZES	MICO	MICROWAVE	MIDTERM	MILADIS
MEZUZA	MICOS	MICROWAVED	MIDTERMS	MILADY
MEZUZAH	MICRA	MICROWAVES	MIDWAY	MILAGE
MEZUZAHS	MICRO	MICROWAVING	MIDWAYS	MILAGES
MEZUZOTH	MICROBAR	MICROWIRE	MIDWIFE	MILCH
MEZZANINE	MICROBARS	MICROWIRES	MIDWIFED	MILD
MEZZANINES	MICROBE	MICRURGIES	MIDWIFERIES	MILDEN
MEZZE	MICROBES	MICRURGY	MIDWIFERY	MILDENED
MEZZES	MICROBIAL	MICTION	MIDWIFES	MILDENING
MEZZO	MICROBIAN	MICTIONS	MIDWIFING	MILDENS
MEZZOS	MICROBIC	MICTURATE	MIDWIVE	MILDER
MEZZOTINT	MICROBUS	MICTURATED	MIDWIVED	MILDEST
MEZZOTINTS	MICROBUSES	MICTURATES	MIDWIVES	MILDEW
MGANGA	MICROCAR	MICTURATING	MIDWIVING	MILDEWED
MGANGAS	MICROCARD	MID	MIEN	MILDEWING
MHO	MICROCARDS	MIDAIR	MIENS	MILDEWS
MHORR	MICROCARS	MIDAIRS	MIEVE	MILDEWY
MHORRS	MICROCHIP	MIDBRAIN	MIEVED	MILDLY
MHOS	MICROCHIPS	MIDBRAINS	MIEVES	MILDNESS
MI	MICROCODE	MIDDAY	MIEVING	MILDNESSES
MIAOW	MICROCODES	MIDDAYS	MIFF	MILDS
MIAOWED	MICROCOPIED	MIDDEN	MIFFED	MILE
MIAOWING	MICROCOPIES	MIDDENS	MIFFIER	MILEAGE

The Chambers Dictionary is the authority for many longer words; see *OSW* Introduction, page xii.

MILEAGES	MILLEPEDE	MILREIS	MINBARS	MINIATION
MILER	MILLEPEDES	MILS	MINCE	MINIATIONS
MILERS	MILLEPEDS	MILSEY	MINCED	MINIATURE
MILES	MILLEPORE	MILSEYS	MINCEMEAT	MINIATURED
MILESTONE	MILLEPORES	MILT	MINCEMEATS	MINIATURES
MILESTONES	MILLER	MILTED	MINCER	MINIATURING
MILFOIL	MILLERITE	MILTER	MINCERS	MINIBIKE
MILFOILS	MILLERITES	MILTERS	MINCES	MINIBIKES
MILIARIA	MILLERS	MILTING	MINCEUR	MINIBREAK
MILIARIAS	MILLES	MILTONIA	MINCING	MINIBREAKS
MILIARY	MILLET	MILTONIAS	MINCINGLY	MINIBUS
MILIEU	MILLETS	MILTS	MINCINGS	MINIBUSES
MILIEUS	MILLIARD	MILTZ	MIND	MINICAB
MILIEUX	MILLIARDS	MILTZES	MINDED	MINICABS
MILITANCIES	MILLIARE	MILVINE	MINDER	MINICAM
MILITANCY	MILLIARES	MIM	MINDERS	MINICAMS
MILITANT	MILLIARIES	MIMBAR	MINDFUCK	MINIDISK
MILITANTS	MILLIARY	MIMBARS	MINDFUCKS	MINIDISKS
MILITAR	MILLIBAR	MIME	MINDFUL	MINIER
MILITARIA	MILLIBARS	MIMED	MINDFULLY	MINIEST
MILITARIES	MILLIEME	MIMER	MINDING	MINIFIED
MILITARY	MILLIEMES	MIMERS	MINDINGS	MINIFIES
MILITATE	MILLIME	MIMES	MINDLESS	MINIFY
MILITATED	MILLIMES	MIMESES	MINDS	MINIFYING
MILITATES	MILLIMOLE	MIMESIS	MINDSET	MINIKIN
MILITATING	MILLIMOLES	MIMESTER	MINDSETS	MINIKINS
MILITIA	MILLINER	MIMESTERS	MINE	MINIM
MILITIAS	MILLINERIES	MIMETIC	MINED	MINIMA
MILK	MILLINERS	MIMETICAL	MINEFIELD	MINIMAL
MILKED	MILLINERY	MIMETITE	MINEFIELDS	MINIMAX
MILKEN	MILLING	MIMETITES	MINEOLA	MINIMAXED
MILKER	MILLINGS	MIMIC	MINEOLAS	MINIMAXES
MILKERS	MILLION	MIMICAL	MINER	MINIMAXING
MILKFISH	MILLIONS	MIMICKED	MINERAL	MINIMENT
MILKFISHES	MILLIONTH	MIMICKER	MINERALS	MINIMENTS
MILKIER	MILLIONTHS	MIMICKERS	MINERS	MINIMISE
MILKIEST	MILLIPED	MIMICKING	MINES	MINIMISED
MILKILY	MILLIPEDE	MIMICRIES	MINESTONE	MINIMISES
MILKINESS	MILLIPEDES	MIMICRY	MINESTONES	MINIMISING
MILKINESSES	MILLIPEDS	MIMICS	MINETTE	MINIMISM
MILKING	MILLIREM	MIMING	MINETTES	MINIMISMS
MILKINGS	MILLIREMS	MIMMER	MINEVER	MINIMIST
MILKLESS	MILLOCRAT	MIMMEST	MINEVERS	MINIMISTS
MILKLIKE	MILLOCRATS	MIMMICK	MING	MINIMIZE
MILKMAID	MILLPOND	MIMMICKED	MINGE	MINIMIZED
MILKMAIDS	MILLPONDS	MIMMICKING	MINGED	MINIMIZES
MILKMAN	MILLRACE	MIMMICKS	MINGES	MINIMIZING
MILKMEN	MILLRACES	MIMOSA	MINGIER	MINIMS
MILKO	MILLRIND	MIMOSAS	MINGIEST	MINIMUM
MILKOS	MILLRINDS	MIMSEY	MINGIN	MINIMUS
MILKS	MILLRUN	MIMSIER	MINGINESS	MINIMUSES
MILKWOOD	MILLRUNS	MIMSIEST	MINGINESSES	MINING
MILKWOODS	MILLS	MIMSY	MINGING	MININGS
MILKWORT	MILLSCALE	MIMULUS	MINGLE	MINION
MILKWORTS	MILLSCALES	MIMULUSES	MINGLED	MINIONS
MILKY	MILLSTONE	MINA	MINGLER	MINIPILL
MILL	MILLSTONES	MINACIOUS	MINGLERS	MINIPILLS
MILLBOARD	MILLTAIL	MINACITIES	MINGLES	MINIRUGBIES
MILLBOARDS	MILLTAILS	MINACITY	MINGLING	MINIRUGBY
MILLDAM	MILO	MINAE	MINGLINGS	MINIS
MILLDAMS	MILOMETER	MINAR	MINGS	MINISCULE
MILLE	MILOMETERS	MINARET	MINGY	MINISCULES
MILLED	MILOR	MINARETS	MINI	MINISH
MILLENARIES	MILORD	MINARS	MINIATE	MINISHED
MILLENARY	MILORDS	MINAS	MINIATED	MINISHES
MILLENNIA	MILORS	MINATORY	MINIATES	MINISHING
MILLEPED	MILOS	MINBAR	MINIATING	MINISKIRT

MINISKIRTS	MINUTED	MIRRORING	MISBESTOW	MISCUING
MINISTER	MINUTELY	MIRRORS	MISBESTOWED	MISDATE
MINISTERED	MINUTEMAN	MIRS	MISBESTOWING	MISDATED
MINISTERING	MINUTEMEN	MIRTH	MISBESTOWS	MISDATES
MINISTERS	MINUTER	MIRTHFUL	MISBIRTH	MISDATING
MINISTRIES	MINUTES	MIRTHLESS	MISBIRTHS	MISDEAL
MINISTRY	MINUTEST	MIRTHS	MISBORN	MISDEALING
MINIUM	MINUTIA	MIRV	MISCALL	MISDEALS
MINIUMS	MINUTIAE	MIRVED	MISCALLED	MISDEALT
MINIVER	MINUTING	MIRVING	MISCALLING	MISDEED
MINIVERS	MINUTIOSE	MIRVS	MISCALLS	MISDEEDS
MINIVET	MINX	MIRY	MISCARRIED	MISDEEM
MINIVETS	MINXES	MIS	MISCARRIES	MISDEEMED
MINK	MINY	MISADVISE	MISCARRY	MISDEEMING
MINKE	MINYAN	MISADVISED	MISCARRYING	MISDEEMINGS
MINKES	MINYANIM	MISADVISES	MISCAST	MISDEEMS
MINKS	MINYANS	MISADVISING	MISCASTING	MISDEMEAN
MINNEOLA	MIOMBO	MISAIM	MISCASTS	MISDEMEANED
MINNEOLAS	MIOMBOS	MISAIMED	MISCEGEN	MISDEMEANING
MINNICK	MIOSES	MISAIMING	MISCEGENE	MISDEMEANS
MINNICKED	MIOSIS	MISAIMS	MISCEGENES	MISDEMPT
MINNICKING	MIOTIC	MISALIGN	MISCEGENS	MISDESERT
MINNICKS	MIOTICS	MISALIGNED	MISCEGINE	MISDESERTS
MINNIE	MIR	MISALIGNING	MISCEGINES	MISDIAL
MINNIES	MIRABELLE	MISALIGNS	MISCHANCE	MISDIALED
MINNOCK	MIRABELLES	MISALLEGE	MISCHANCED	MISDIALING
MINNOCKED	MIRABILIA	MISALLEGED	MISCHANCES	MISDIALLED
MINNOCKING	MIRABILIS	MISALLEGES	MISCHANCING	MISDIALLING
MINNOCKS	MIRABILISES	MISALLEGING	MISCHANCY	MISDIALS
MINNOW	MIRABLE	MISALLIED	MISCHARGE	MISDID
MINNOWS	MIRACIDIA	MISALLIES	MISCHARGED	MISDIET
MINO	MIRACLE	MISALLOT	MISCHARGES	MISDIETS
MINOR	MIRACLES	MISALLOTS	MISCHARGING	MISDIGHT
MINORED	MIRADOR	MISALLOTTED	MISCHIEF	MISDIRECT
MINORING	MIRADORS	MISALLOTTING	MISCHIEFED	MISDIRECTED
MINORITIES	MIRAGE	MISALLY	MISCHIEFING	MISDIRECTING
MINORITY	MIRAGES	MISALLYING	MISCHIEFS	MISDIRECTS
MINORS	MIRBANE	MISANDRIES	MISCIBLE	MISDO
MINORSHIP	MIRBANES	MISANDRY	MISCOLOR	MISDOER
MINORSHIPS	MIRE	MISAPPLIED	MISCOLORED	MISDOERS
MINOS	MIRED	MISAPPLIES	MISCOLORING	MISDOES
MINSHUKU	MIREPOIX	MISAPPLY	MISCOLORS	MISDOING
MINSHUKUS	MIRES	MISAPPLYING	MISCOLOUR	MISDOINGS
MINSTER	MIRI	MISARRAY	MISCOLOURED	MISDONE
MINSTERS	MIRIER	MISARRAYS	MISCOLOURING	MISDONNE
MINSTREL	MIRIEST	MISASSIGN	MISCOLOURS	MISDOUBT
MINSTRELS	MIRIFIC	MISASSIGNED	MISCOPIED	MISDOUBTED
MINT	MIRIFICAL	MISASSIGNING	MISCOPIES	MISDOUBTING
MINTAGE	MIRIN	MISASSIGNS	MISCOPY	MISDOUBTS
MINTAGES	MIRINESS	MISAUNTER	MISCOPYING	MISDRAW
MINTED	MIRINESSES	MISAUNTERS	MISCOUNT	MISDRAWING
MINTER	MIRING	MISAVISED	MISCOUNTED	MISDRAWINGS
MINTERS	MIRINS	MISBECAME	MISCOUNTING	MISDRAWN
MINTIER	MIRITI	MISBECOME	MISCOUNTS	MISDRAWS
MINTIEST	MIRITIS	MISBECOMES	MISCREANT	MISDREAD
MINTING	MIRK	MISBECOMING	MISCREANTS	MISDREADS
MINTS	MIRKER	MISBEGOT	MISCREATE	MISDREW
MINTY	MIRKEST	MISBEHAVE	MISCREDIT	MISE
MINUEND	MIRKS	MISBEHAVED	MISCREDITED	MISEASE
MINUENDS	MIRLIER	MISBEHAVES	MISCREDITING	MISEASES
MINUET	MIRLIEST	MISBEHAVING	MISCREDITS	MISEMPLOY
MINUETS	MIRLIGOES	MISBELIEF	MISCREED	MISEMPLOYED
MINUS	MIRLITON	MISBELIEFS	MISCREEDS	MISEMPLOYING
MINUSCULE	MIRLITONS	MISBESEEM	MISCUE	MISEMPLOYS
MINUSCULES	MIRLY	MISBESEEMED	MISCUED	MISENTRIES
MINUSES	MIRROR	MISBESEEMING	MISCUEING	MISENTRY
MINUTE	MIRRORED	MISBESEEMS	MISCUES	MISER

The Chambers Dictionary is the authority for many longer words; see *OSW* Introduction, page xii.

MISERABLE	MISGOING	MISJUDGED	MISMARRIES	MISPRINT
MISERABLES	MISGONE	MISJUDGES	MISMARRY	MISPRINTED
MISERABLY	MISGOTTEN	MISJUDGING	MISMARRYING	MISPRINTING
MISERE	MISGOVERN	MISKEN	MISMATCH	MISPRINTS
MISERERE	MISGOVERNED	MISKENNED	MISMATCHED	MISPRISE
MISERERES	MISGOVERNING	MISKENNING	MISMATCHES	MISPRISED
MISERES	MISGOVERNS	MISKENS	MISMATCHING	MISPRISES
MISERIES	MISGRAFF	MISKENT	MISMATE	MISPRISING
MISERLY	MISGRAFT	MISKEY	MISMATED	MISPRIZE
MISERS	MISGRAFTED	MISKEYED	MISMATES	MISPRIZED
MISERY	MISGRAFTING	MISKEYING	MISMATING	MISPRIZES
MISES	MISGRAFTS	MISKEYS	MISMETRE	MISPRIZING
MISESTEEM	MISGROWTH	MISKNEW	MISMETRED	MISPROUD
MISESTEEMED	MISGROWTHS	MISKNOW	MISMETRES	MISQUOTE
MISESTEEMING	MISGUGGLE	MISKNOWING	MISMETRING	MISQUOTED
MISESTEEMS	MISGUGGLED	MISKNOWN	MISNAME	MISQUOTES
MISFAITH	MISGUGGLES	MISKNOWS	MISNAMED	MISQUOTING
MISFAITHS	MISGUGGLING	MISLAID	MISNAMES	MISRATE
MISFALL	MISGUIDE	MISLAY	MISNAMING	MISRATED
MISFALLEN	MISGUIDED	MISLAYING	MISNOMER	MISRATES
MISFALLING	MISGUIDER	MISLAYS	MISNOMERED	MISRATING
MISFALLS	MISGUIDERS	MISLEAD	MISNOMERING	MISREAD
MISFALNE	MISGUIDES	MISLEADER	MISNOMERS	MISREADING
MISFARE	MISGUIDING	MISLEADERS	MISO	MISREADINGS
MISFARED	MISHANDLE	MISLEADING	MISOCLERE	MISREADS
MISFARES	MISHANDLED	MISLEADS	MISOGAMIES	MISRECKON
MISFARING	MISHANDLES	MISLEARED	MISOGAMY	MISRECKONED
MISFARINGS	MISHANDLING	MISLED	MISOGYNIES	MISRECKONING
MISFEASOR	MISHANTER	MISLEEKE	MISOGYNY	MISRECKONINGS
MISFEASORS	MISHANTERS	MISLEEKED	MISOLOGIES	MISRECKONS
MISFED	MISHAP	MISLEEKES	MISOLOGY	MISREGARD
MISFEED	MISHAPPED	MISLEEKING	MISONEISM	MISREGARDS
MISFEEDING	MISHAPPEN	MISLETOE	MISONEISMS	MISRELATE
MISFEEDS	MISHAPPENED	MISLETOES	MISONEIST	MISRELATED
MISFEIGN	MISHAPPENING	MISLIGHT	MISONEISTS	MISRELATES
MISFEIGNED	MISHAPPENS	MISLIGHTED	MISORDER	MISRELATING
MISFEIGNING	MISHAPPING	MISLIGHTING	MISORDERED	MISREPORT
MISFEIGNS	MISHAPS	MISLIGHTS	MISORDERING	MISREPORTED
MISFELL	MISHAPT	MISLIKE	MISORDERS	MISREPORTING
MISFIELD	MISHEAR	MISLIKED	MISOS	MISREPORTS
MISFIELDED	MISHEARD	MISLIKER	MISPICKEL	MISROUTE
MISFIELDING	MISHEARING	MISLIKERS	MISPICKELS	MISROUTED
MISFIELDS	MISHEARS	MISLIKES	MISPLACE	MISROUTEING
MISFILE	MISHEGAAS	MISLIKING	MISPLACED	MISROUTES
MISFILED	MISHEGAASEN	MISLIKINGS	MISPLACES	MISROUTING
MISFILES	MISHIT	MISLIPPEN	MISPLACING	MISRULE
MISFILING	MISHITS	MISLIPPENED	MISPLAY	MISRULED
MISFIRE	MISHITTING	MISLIPPENING	MISPLAYED	MISRULES
MISFIRED	MISHMASH	MISLIPPENS	MISPLAYING	MISRULING
MISFIRES	MISHMASHES	MISLIT	MISPLAYS	MISS
MISFIRING	MISHMEE	MISLIVE	MISPLEAD	MISSA
MISFIT	MISHMEES	MISLIVED	MISPLEADED	MISSABLE
MISFITS	MISHMI	MISLIVES	MISPLEADING	MISSAE
MISFITTED	MISHMIS	MISLIVING	MISPLEADINGS	MISSAID
MISFITTING	MISINFORM	MISLUCK	MISPLEADS	MISSAL
MISFORM	MISINFORMED	MISLUCKED	MISPLEASE	MISSALS
MISFORMED	MISINFORMING	MISLUCKING	MISPLEASED	MISSAW
MISFORMING	MISINFORMS	MISLUCKS	MISPLEASES	MISSAY
MISFORMS	MISINTEND	MISMADE	MISPLEASING	MISSAYING
MISGAVE	MISINTENDED	MISMAKE	MISPOINT	MISSAYINGS
MISGIVE	MISINTENDING	MISMAKES	MISPOINTED	MISSAYS
MISGIVEN	MISINTENDS	MISMAKING	MISPOINTING	MISSED
MISGIVES	MISJOIN	MISMANAGE	MISPOINTS	MISSEE
MISGIVING	MISJOINED	MISMANAGED	MISPRAISE	MISSEEING
MISGIVINGS	MISJOINING	MISMANAGES	MISPRAISED	MISSEEM
MISGO	MISJOINS	MISMANAGING	MISPRAISES	MISSEEMED
MISGOES	MISJUDGE	MISMARRIED	MISPRAISING	MISSEEMING

The Chambers Dictionary is the authority for many longer words; see *OSW* Introduction, page xii.

MISSEEMINGS	MISSUITED	MISTRAL	MITHER	MIZMAZE
MISSEEMS	MISSUITING	MISTRALS	MITHERED	MIZMAZES
MISSEEN	MISSUITS	MISTREAT	MITHERING	MIZZ
MISSEES	MISSUS	MISTREATED	MITHERS	MIZZEN
MISSEL	MISSUSES	MISTREATING	MITICIDAL	MIZZENS
MISSELS	MISSY	MISTREATS	MITICIDE	MIZZES
MISSEND	MIST	MISTRESS	MITICIDES	MIZZLE
MISSENDING	MISTAKE	MISTRESSED	MITIER	MIZZLED
MISSENDS	MISTAKEN	MISTRESSES	MITIEST	MIZZLES
MISSENT	MISTAKES	MISTRESSING	MITIGABLE	MIZZLIER
MISSES	MISTAKING	MISTRIAL	MITIGANT	MIZZLIEST
MISSET	MISTAKINGS	MISTRIALS	MITIGATE	MIZZLING
MISSETS	MISTAUGHT	MISTRUST	MITIGATED	MIZZLINGS
MISSETTING	MISTEACH	MISTRUSTED	MITIGATES	MIZZLY
MISSHAPE	MISTEACHES	MISTRUSTING	MITIGATING	MIZZONITE
MISSHAPED	MISTEACHING	MISTRUSTS	MITIGATOR	MIZZONITES
MISSHAPEN	MISTED	MISTRYST	MITIGATORS	MNA
MISSHAPES	MISTELL	MISTRYSTED	MITOGEN	MNAS
MISSHAPING	MISTELLING	MISTRYSTING	MITOGENIC	MNEME
MISSHOOD	MISTELLS	MISTRYSTS	MITOGENS	MNEMES
MISSHOODS	MISTEMPER	MISTS	MITOSES	MNEMIC
MISSIER	MISTEMPERED	MISTUNE	MITOSIS	MNEMON
MISSIES	MISTEMPERING	MISTUNED	MITOTIC	MNEMONIC
MISSIEST	MISTEMPERS	MISTUNES	MITRAILLE	MNEMONICS
MISSILE	MISTER	MISTUNING	MITRAILLES	MNEMONIST
MISSILERIES	MISTERED	MISTY	MITRAL	MNEMONISTS
MISSILERY	MISTERIES	MISUSAGE	MITRE	MNEMONS
MISSILES	MISTERING	MISUSAGES	MITRED	MO
MISSILRIES	MISTERM	MISUSE	MITRES	MOA
MISSILRY	MISTERMED	MISUSED	MITRIFORM	MOAN
MISSING	MISTERMING	MISUSER	MITRING	MOANED
MISSINGLY	MISTERMS	MISUSERS	MITT	MOANER
MISSION	MISTERS	MISUSES	MITTEN	MOANERS
MISSIONED	MISTERY	MISUSING	MITTENED	MOANFUL
MISSIONER	MISTFUL	MISUST	MITTENS	MOANFULLY
MISSIONERS	MISTHINK	MISWEEN	MITTIMUS	MOANING
MISSIONING	MISTHINKING	MISWEENED	MITTIMUSES	MOANS
MISSIONS	MISTHINKS	MISWEENING	MITTS	MOAS
MISSIS	MISTHOUGHT	MISWEENS	MITY	MOAT
MISSISES	MISTHOUGHTS	MISWEND	MITZVAH	MOATED
MISSISH	MISTICO	MISWENDING	MITZVAHS	MOATING
MISSIVE	MISTICOS	MISWENDS	MITZVOTH	MOATS
MISSIVES	MISTIER	MISWENT	MIURUS	MOB
MISSPEAK	MISTIEST	MISWORD	MIURUSES	MOBBED
MISSPEAKING	MISTIGRIS	MISWORDED	MIX	MOBBIE
MISSPEAKS	MISTIGRISES	MISWORDING	MIXABLE	MOBBIES
MISSPELL	MISTILY	MISWORDINGS	MIXED	MOBBING
MISSPELLED	MISTIME	MISWORDS	MIXEDLY	MOBBINGS
MISSPELLING	MISTIMED	MISWRITE	MIXEDNESS	MOBBISH
MISSPELLINGS	MISTIMES	MISWRITES	MIXEDNESSES	MOBBLE
MISSPELLS	MISTIMING	MISWRITING	MIXEN	MOBBLED
MISSPELT	MISTINESS	MISWRITTEN	MIXENS	MOBBLES
MISSPEND	MISTINESSES	MISWROTE	MIXER	MOBBLING
MISSPENDING	MISTING	MISYOKE	MIXERS	MOBBY
MISSPENDS	MISTINGS	MISYOKED	MIXES	MOBILE
MISSPENT	MISTITLE	MISYOKES	MIXIER	MOBILES
MISSPOKE	MISTITLED	MISYOKING	MIXIEST	MOBILISE
MISSPOKEN	MISTITLES	MITCH	MIXING	MOBILISED
MISSTATE	MISTITLING	MITCHED	MIXT	MOBILISER
MISSTATED	MISTLE	MITCHES	MIXTION	MOBILISERS
MISSTATES	MISTLED	MITCHING	MIXTIONS	MOBILISES
MISSTATING	MISTLES	MITE	MIXTURE	MOBILISING
MISSTEP	MISTLETOE	MITER	MIXTURES	MOBILITIES
MISSTEPPED	MISTLETOES	MITERED	MIXY	MOBILITY
MISSTEPPING	MISTLING	MITERING	MIZ	MOBILIZE
MISSTEPS	MISTOLD	MITERS	MIZEN	MOBILIZED
MISSUIT	MISTOOK	MITES	MIZENS	MOBILIZER

The Chambers Dictionary is the authority for many longer words; see *OSW* Introduction, page xii.

MOBILIZERS	MODELED	MODILLIONS	MOILER	MOLECULES
MOBILIZES	MODELER	MODIOLAR	MOILERS	MOLEHILL
MOBILIZING	MODELERS	MODIOLI	MOILING	MOLEHILLS
MOBLE	MODELING	MODIOLUS	MOILS	MOLEHUNT
MOBLED	MODELINGS	MODIOLUSES	MOINEAU	MOLEHUNTS
MOBLES	MODELLED	MODISH	MOINEAUS	MOLERAT
MOBLING	MODELLER	MODISHLY	MOIRE	MOLERATS
MOBOCRACIES	MODELLERS	MODIST	MOIRES	MOLES
MOBOCRACY	MODELLI	MODISTE	MOISER	MOLESKIN
MOBOCRAT	MODELLING	MODISTES	MOISERS	MOLESKINS
MOBOCRATS	MODELLINGS	MODISTS	MOIST	MOLEST
MOBS	MODELLO	MODIUS	MOISTED	MOLESTED
MOBSMAN	MODELLOS	MODIWORT	MOISTEN	MOLESTER
MOBSMEN	MODELS	MODIWORTS	MOISTENED	MOLESTERS
MOBSTER	MODEM	MODS	MOISTENING	MOLESTFUL
MOBSTERS	MODEMED	MODULAR	MOISTENS	MOLESTING
MOCASSIN	MODEMING	MODULATE	MOISTER	MOLESTS
MOCASSINS	MODEMS	MODULATED	MOISTEST	MOLIES
MOCCASIN	MODENA	MODULATES	MOISTIFIED	MOLIMEN
MOCCASINS	MODENAS	MODULATING	MOISTIFIES	MOLIMENS
MOCH	MODER	MODULATOR	MOISTIFY	MOLINE
MOCHA	MODERATE	MODULATORS	MOISTIFYING	MOLINES
MOCHAS	MODERATED	MODULE	MOISTING	MOLINET
MOCHELL	MODERATES	MODULES	MOISTLY	MOLINETS
MOCHELLS	MODERATING	MODULI	MOISTNESS	MOLL
MOCHIE	MODERATO	MODULO	MOISTNESSES	MOLLA
MOCHIER	MODERATOR	MODULUS	MOISTS	MOLLAH
MOCHIEST	MODERATORS	MODUS	MOISTURE	MOLLAHS
MOCHINESS	MODERATOS	MOE	MOISTURES	MOLLAS
MOCHINESSES	MODERN	MOELLON	MOIT	MOLLIE
MOCHS	MODERNER	MOELLONS	MOITHER	MOLLIES
MOCHY	MODERNEST	MOES	MOITHERED	MOLLIFIED
MOCK	MODERNISE	MOFETTE	MOITHERING	MOLLIFIER
MOCKABLE	MODERNISED	MOFETTES	MOITHERS	MOLLIFIERS
MOCKADO	MODERNISES	MOFUSSIL	MOITS	MOLLIFIES
MOCKADOES	MODERNISING	MOFUSSILS	MOJO	MOLLIFY
MOCKAGE	MODERNISM	MOG	MOJOES	MOLLIFYING
MOCKAGES	MODERNISMS	MOGGAN	MOJOS	MOLLITIES
MOCKED	MODERNIST	MOGGANS	MOKADDAM	MOLLS
MOCKER	MODERNISTS	MOGGIE	MOKADDAMS	MOLLUSC
MOCKERIES	MODERNITIES	MOGGIES	MOKE	MOLLUSCAN
MOCKERNUT	MODERNITY	MOGGY	MOKES	MOLLUSCS
MOCKERNUTS	MODERNIZE	MOGS	MOKI	MOLLUSK
MOCKERS	MODERNIZED	MOGUL	MOKIS	MOLLUSKAN
MOCKERY	MODERNIZES	MOGULED	MOKO	MOLLUSKS
MOCKING	MODERNIZING	MOGULS	MOKOS	MOLLY
MOCKINGLY	MODERNLY	MOHAIR	MOLA	MOLLYMAWK
MOCKINGS	MODERNS	MOHAIRS	MOLAL	MOLLYMAWKS
MOCKS	MODERS	MOHAWK	MOLALITIES	MOLOCH
MOCOCK	MODES	MOHAWKS	MOLALITY	MOLOCHISE
MOCOCKS	MODEST	MOHEL	MOLAR	MOLOCHISED
MOCUCK	MODESTER	MOHELS	MOLARITIES	MOLOCHISES
MOCUCKS	MODESTEST	MOHR	MOLARITY	MOLOCHISING
MOCUDDUM	MODESTIES	MOHRS	MOLARS	MOLOCHIZE
MOCUDDUMS	MODESTLY	MOHUR	MOLAS	MOLOCHIZED
MOD	MODESTY	MOHURS	MOLASSES	MOLOCHIZES
MODAL	MODI	MOI	MOLD	MOLOCHIZING
MODALISM	MODICUM	MOIDER	MOLDED	MOLOCHS
MODALISMS	MODICUMS	MOIDERED	MOLDING	MOLOSSI
MODALIST	MODIFIED	MOIDERING	MOLDS	MOLOSSUS
MODALISTS	MODIFIER	MOIDERS	MOLDWARP	MOLT
MODALITIES	MODIFIERS	MOIDORE	MOLDWARPS	MOLTED
MODALITY	MODIFIES	MOIDORES	MOLE	MOLTEN
MODALLY	MODIFY	MOIETIES	MOLECAST	MOLTENLY
MODALS	MODIFYING	MOIETY	MOLECASTS	MOLTING
MODE	MODII	MOIL	MOLECULAR	MOLTO
MODEL	MODILLION	MOILED	MOLECULE	MOLTS

The Chambers Dictionary is the authority for many longer words; see *OSW* Introduction, page xii.

MOLY
MOLYBDATE
MOLYBDATES
MOLYBDIC
MOLYBDOUS
MOM
MOME
MOMENT
MOMENTA
MOMENTANY
MOMENTARY
MOMENTLY
MOMENTOUS
MOMENTS
MOMENTUM
MOMES
MOMMA
MOMMAS
MOMMET
MOMMETS
MOMMIES
MOMMY
MOMS
MOMZER
MOMZERIM
MOMZERS
MON
MONA
MONACHAL
MONACHISM
MONACHISMS
MONACHIST
MONACID
MONACT
MONACTINE
MONAD
MONADES
MONADIC
MONADICAL
MONADISM
MONADISMS
MONADNOCK
MONADNOCKS
MONADS
MONAL
MONALS
MONANDRIES
MONANDRY
MONARCH
MONARCHAL
MONARCHIC
MONARCHIES
MONARCHS
MONARCHY
MONARDA
MONARDAS
MONAS
MONASES
MONASTERIES
MONASTERY
MONASTIC
MONASTICS
MONATOMIC
MONAUL
MONAULS
MONAURAL
MONAXIAL

MONAXON
MONAXONIC
MONAXONS
MONAZITE
MONAZITES
MONDAIN
MONDAINE
MONDAINES
MONDAINS
MONDIAL
MONDO
MONECIOUS
MONER
MONERA
MONERGISM
MONERGISMS
MONERON
MONERS
MONETARY
MONETH
MONETHS
MONETISE
MONETISED
MONETISES
MONETISING
MONETIZE
MONETIZED
MONETIZES
MONETIZING
MONEY
MONEYBAGS
MONEYED
MONEYER
MONEYERS
MONEYLESS
MONEYMAN
MONEYMEN
MONEYS
MONEYWORT
MONEYWORTS
MONG
MONGCORN
MONGCORNS
MONGER
MONGERIES
MONGERING
MONGERINGS
MONGERS
MONGERY
MONGOL
MONGOLISM
MONGOLISMS
MONGOLOID
MONGOLOIDS
MONGOLS
MONGOOSE
MONGOOSES
MONGREL
MONGRELLY
MONGRELS
MONGS
MONIAL
MONIALS
MONICKER
MONICKERS
MONIED
MONIES

MONIKER
MONIKERS
MONILIA
MONILIAS
MONIMENT
MONIMENTS
MONIPLIES
MONISM
MONISMS
MONIST
MONISTIC
MONISTS
MONITION
MONITIONS
MONITIVE
MONITOR
MONITORED
MONITORING
MONITORS
MONITORY
MONITRESS
MONITRESSES
MONK
MONKERIES
MONKERY
MONKEY
MONKEYED
MONKEYING
MONKEYISH
MONKEYISM
MONKEYISMS
MONKEYS
MONKFISH
MONKFISHES
MONKHOOD
MONKHOODS
MONKISH
MONKS
MONKSHOOD
MONKSHOODS
MONO
MONOACID
MONOAMINE
MONOAMINES
MONOBASIC
MONOCARP
MONOCARPS
MONOCEROS
MONOCEROSES
MONOCHORD
MONOCHORDS
MONOCLE
MONOCLED
MONOCLES
MONOCLINE
MONOCLINES
MONOCOQUE
MONOCOQUES
MONOCOT
MONOCOTS
MONOCRACIES
MONOCRACY
MONOCRAT
MONOCRATS
MONOCULAR
MONOCYTE
MONOCYTES

MONODIC
MONODICAL
MONODIES
MONODIST
MONODISTS
MONODONT
MONODRAMA
MONODRAMAS
MONODY
MONOECISM
MONOECISMS
MONOFIL
MONOFILS
MONOGAMIC
MONOGAMIES
MONOGAMY
MONOGENIC
MONOGENIES
MONOGENY
MONOGLOT
MONOGLOTS
MONOGONIES
MONOGONY
MONOGRAM
MONOGRAMS
MONOGRAPH
MONOGRAPHED
MONOGRAPHING
MONOGRAPHS
MONOGYNIES
MONOGYNY
MONOHULL
MONOHULLS
MONOLATER
MONOLATERS
MONOLATRIES
MONOLATRY
MONOLAYER
MONOLAYERS
MONOLITH
MONOLITHS
MONOLOGIC
MONOLOGIES
MONOLOGUE
MONOLOGUES
MONOLOGY
MONOMACHIES
MONOMACHY
MONOMANIA
MONOMANIAS
MONOMARK
MONOMARKS
MONOMER
MONOMERIC
MONOMERS
MONOMETER
MONOMETERS
MONOMIAL
MONOMIALS
MONOMODE
MONOPHAGIES
MONOPHAGY
MONOPHASE
MONOPHONIES
MONOPHONY
MONOPITCH
MONOPLANE

MONOPLANES
MONOPOD
MONOPODE
MONOPODES
MONOPODIA
MONOPODS
MONOPOLE
MONOPOLES
MONOPOLIES
MONOPOLY
MONOPSONIES
MONOPSONY
MONOPTERA
MONOPTOTE
MONOPTOTES
MONOPULSE
MONOPULSES
MONORAIL
MONORAILS
MONORCHID
MONORHINE
MONORHYME
MONORHYMES
MONOS
MONOSES
MONOSIES
MONOSIS
MONOSTICH
MONOSTICHS
MONOSTYLE
MONOSY
MONOTINT
MONOTINTS
MONOTONE
MONOTONED
MONOTONES
MONOTONIC
MONOTONIES
MONOTONING
MONOTONY
MONOTREME
MONOTREMES
MONOTROCH
MONOTROCHS
MONOTYPE
MONOTYPES
MONOTYPIC
MONOXIDE
MONOXIDES
MONOXYLON
MONOXYLONS
MONSIEUR
MONSOON
MONSOONAL
MONSOONS
MONSTER
MONSTERA
MONSTERAS
MONSTERS
MONSTROUS
MONTAGE
MONTAGED
MONTAGES
MONTAGING
MONTANE
MONTANT
MONTANTO

The Chambers Dictionary is the authority for many longer words; see *OSW* Introduction, page xii.

MONTANTOS	MOOLING	MOONY	MOPHEAD	MORASSES
MONTANTS	MOOLIS	MOOP	MOPHEADS	MORASSY
MONTARIA	MOOLS	MOOPED	MOPIER	MORAT
MONTARIAS	MOOLY	MOOPING	MOPIEST	MORATORIA
MONTE	MOON	MOOPS	MOPING	MORATORY
MONTEITH	MOONBEAM	MOOR	MOPINGLY	MORATS
MONTEITHS	MOONBEAMS	MOORAGE	MOPISH	MORAY
MONTEM	MOONBLIND	MOORAGES	MOPISHLY	MORAYS
MONTEMS	MOONCALF	MOORCOCK	MOPOKE	MORBID
MONTERO	MOONCALVES	MOORCOCKS	MOPOKES	MORBIDITIES
MONTEROS	MOONED	MOORED	MOPPED	MORBIDITY
MONTES	MOONER	MOORFOWL	MOPPER	MORBIDLY
MONTH	MOONERS	MOORFOWLS	MOPPERS	MORBIFIC
MONTHLIES	MOONEYE	MOORHEN	MOPPET	MORBILLI
MONTHLING	MOONEYES	MOORHENS	MOPPETS	MORBUS
MONTHLINGS	MOONFACE	MOORIER	MOPPIER	MORBUSES
MONTHLY	MOONFACES	MOORIEST	MOPPIEST	MORCEAU
MONTHS	MOONIER	MOORILL	MOPPING	MORCEAUX
MONTICLE	MOONIES	MOORILLS	MOPPY	MORDACITIES
MONTICLES	MOONIEST	MOORING	MOPS	MORDACITY
MONTICULE	MOONING	MOORINGS	MOPSIES	MORDANCIES
MONTICULES	MOONISH	MOORISH	MOPSTICK	MORDANCY
MONTRE	MOONLESS	MOORLAND	MOPSTICKS	MORDANT
MONTRES	MOONLET	MOORLANDS	MOPSY	MORDANTED
MONTURE	MOONLETS	MOORLOG	MOPUS	MORDANTING
MONTURES	MOONLIGHT	MOORLOGS	MOPUSES	MORDANTLY
MONUMENT	MOONLIGHTED	MOORMAN	MOPY	MORDANTS
MONUMENTED	MOONLIGHTING	MOORMEN	MOQUETTE	MORDENT
MONUMENTING	MOONLIGHTINGS	MOORS	MOQUETTES	MORDENTS
MONUMENTS	MOONLIGHTS	MOORVA	MOR	MORE
MONY	MOONLIT	MOORVAS	MORA	MOREEN
MONYPLIES	MOONPHASE	MOORY	MORACEOUS	MOREENS
MONZONITE	MOONPHASES	MOOS	MORAINAL	MOREISH
MONZONITES	MOONQUAKE	MOOSE	MORAINE	MOREL
MOO	MOONQUAKES	MOOSEYARD	MORAINES	MORELLO
MOOCH	MOONRAKER	MOOSEYARDS	MORAINIC	MORELLOS
MOOCHED	MOONRAKERS	MOOT	MORAL	MORELS
MOOCHER	MOONRISE	MOOTABLE	MORALE	MORENDO
MOOCHERS	MOONRISES	MOOTED	MORALES	MOREOVER
MOOCHES	MOONROCK	MOOTER	MORALISE	MOREPORK
MOOCHING	MOONROCKS	MOOTERS	MORALISED	MOREPORKS
MOOD	MOONROOF	MOOTEST	MORALISER	MORES
MOODIED	MOONROOFS	MOOTING	MORALISERS	MORGANITE
MOODIER	MOONS	MOOTINGS	MORALISES	MORGANITES
MOODIES	MOONSAIL	MOOTMAN	MORALISING	MORGAY
MOODIEST	MOONSAILS	MOOTMEN	MORALISM	MORGAYS
MOODILY	MOONSCAPE	MOOTS	MORALISMS	MORGEN
MOODINESS	MOONSCAPES	MOOVE	MORALIST	MORGENS
MOODINESSES	MOONSEED	MOOVED	MORALISTS	MORGUE
MOODS	MOONSEEDS	MOOVES	MORALITIES	MORGUES
MOODY	MOONSET	MOOVING	MORALITY	MORIA
MOODYING	MOONSETS	MOP	MORALIZE	MORIAS
MOOED	MOONSHEE	MOPANE	MORALIZED	MORIBUND
MOOI	MOONSHEES	MOPANES	MORALIZER	MORICHE
MOOING	MOONSHINE	MOPANI	MORALIZERS	MORICHES
MOOK	MOONSHINES	MOPANIS	MORALIZES	MORION
MOOKS	MOONSHINY	MOPBOARD	MORALIZING	MORIONS
MOOKTAR	MOONSHOT	MOPBOARDS	MORALL	MORISCO
MOOKTARS	MOONSHOTS	MOPE	MORALLED	MORISCOES
MOOL	MOONSTONE	MOPED	MORALLER	MORISCOS
MOOLA	MOONSTONES	MOPEDS	MORALLERS	MORISH
MOOLAH	MOONWALK	MOPEHAWK	MORALLING	MORKIN
MOOLAHS	MOONWALKED	MOPEHAWKS	MORALLS	MORKINS
MOOLAS	MOONWALKING	MOPER	MORALLY	MORLING
MOOLED	MOONWALKS	MOPERS	MORALS	MORLINGS
MOOLI	MOONWORT	MOPES	MORAS	MORMAOR
MOOLIES	MOONWORTS	MOPEY	MORASS	MORMAORS

The Chambers Dictionary is the authority for many longer words; see *OSW* Introduction, page xii.

MORN	MORSURES	MOSAIC	MOTHBALLED	MOTORISED
MORNAY	MORT	MOSAICISM	MOTHBALLING	MOTORISES
MORNAYS	MORTAL	MOSAICISMS	MOTHBALLS	MOTORISING
MORNE	MORTALISE	MOSAICIST	MOTHED	MOTORIST
MORNED	MORTALISED	MOSAICISTS	MOTHER	MOTORISTS
MORNES	MORTALISES	MOSAICS	MOTHERED	MOTORIUM
MORNING	MORTALISING	MOSCHATEL	MOTHERING	MOTORIUMS
MORNINGS	MORTALITIES	MOSCHATELS	MOTHERINGS	MOTORIZE
MORNS	MORTALITY	MOSE	MOTHERLY	MOTORIZED
MOROCCO	MORTALIZE	MOSED	MOTHERS	MOTORIZES
MOROCCOS	MORTALIZED	MOSES	MOTHERY	MOTORIZING
MORON	MORTALIZES	MOSEY	MOTHIER	MOTORMAN
MORONIC	MORTALIZING	MOSEYED	MOTHIEST	MOTORMEN
MORONS	MORTALLY	MOSEYING	MOTHPROOF	MOTORS
MOROSE	MORTALS	MOSEYS	MOTHPROOFED	MOTORWAY
MOROSELY	MORTAR	MOSHAV	MOTHPROOFING	MOTORWAYS
MOROSER	MORTARED	MOSHAVIM	MOTHPROOFS	MOTORY
MOROSEST	MORTARING	MOSHING	MOTHS	MOTOSCAFI
MOROSITIES	MORTARS	MOSHINGS	MOTHY	MOTOSCAFO
MOROSITY	MORTBELL	MOSING	MOTIER	MOTS
MORPH	MORTBELLS	MOSKONFYT	MOTIEST	MOTSER
MORPHEAN	MORTCLOTH	MOSKONFYTS	MOTIF	MOTSERS
MORPHEME	MORTCLOTHS	MOSLINGS	MOTIFS	MOTT
MORPHEMES	MORTGAGE	MOSQUE	MOTILE	MOTTE
MORPHEMIC	MORTGAGED	MOSQUES	MOTILES	MOTTES
MORPHEMICS	MORTGAGEE	MOSQUITO	MOTILITIES	MOTTIER
MORPHETIC	MORTGAGEES	MOSQUITOES	MOTILITY	MOTTIEST
MORPHEW	MORTGAGER	MOSQUITOS	MOTION	MOTTLE
MORPHEWS	MORTGAGERS	MOSS	MOTIONAL	MOTTLED
MORPHIA	MORTGAGES	MOSSBACK	MOTIONED	MOTTLES
MORPHIAS	MORTGAGING	MOSSBACKS	MOTIONING	MOTTLING
MORPHIC	MORTGAGOR	MOSSED	MOTIONIST	MOTTLINGS
MORPHINE	MORTGAGORS	MOSSES	MOTIONISTS	MOTTO
MORPHINES	MORTICE	MOSSIE	MOTIONS	MOTTOED
MORPHING	MORTICED	MOSSIER	MOTIVATE	MOTTOES
MORPHINGS	MORTICER	MOSSIES	MOTIVATED	MOTTS
MORPHO	MORTICERS	MOSSIEST	MOTIVATES	MOTTY
MORPHOS	MORTICES	MOSSINESS	MOTIVATING	MOTU
MORPHOSES	MORTICIAN	MOSSINESSES	MOTIVATOR	MOTUCA
MORPHOSIS	MORTICIANS	MOSSING	MOTIVATORS	MOTUCAS
MORPHOTIC	MORTICING	MOSSLAND	MOTIVE	MOTUS
MORPHS	MORTIFIC	MOSSLANDS	MOTIVED	MOTZA
MORRA	MORTIFIED	MOSSPLANT	MOTIVES	MOTZAS
MORRAS	MORTIFIER	MOSSPLANTS	MOTIVIC	MOU
MORRHUA	MORTIFIERS	MOSSY	MOTIVING	MOUCH
MORRHUAS	MORTIFIES	MOST	MOTIVITIES	MOUCHARD
MORRICE	MORTIFY	MOSTLY	MOTIVITY	MOUCHARDS
MORRICES	MORTIFYING	MOSTS	MOTLEY	MOUCHED
MORRION	MORTIFYINGS	MOSTWHAT	MOTLEYER	MOUCHER
MORRIONS	MORTISE	MOT	MOTLEYEST	MOUCHERS
MORRIS	MORTISED	MOTE	MOTLEYS	MOUCHES
MORRISED	MORTISER	MOTED	MOTLIER	MOUCHING
MORRISES	MORTISERS	MOTEL	MOTLIEST	MOUCHOIR
MORRISING	MORTISES	MOTELIER	MOTMOT	MOUCHOIRS
MORRO	MORTISING	MOTELIERS	MOTMOTS	MOUDIWART
MORROS	MORTLING	MOTELS	MOTOCROSS	MOUDIWARTS
MORROW	MORTLINGS	MOTEN	MOTOCROSSES	MOUDIWORT
MORROWS	MORTMAIN	MOTES	MOTOR	MOUDIWORTS
MORS	MORTMAINS	MOTET	MOTORABLE	MOUE
MORSAL	MORTS	MOTETS	MOTORAIL	MOUES
MORSE	MORTUARIES	MOTETT	MOTORAILS	MOUFFLON
MORSEL	MORTUARY	MOTETTIST	MOTORCADE	MOUFFLONS
MORSELLED	MORULA	MOTETTISTS	MOTORCADES	MOUFLON
MORSELLING	MORULAE	MOTETTS	MOTORED	MOUFLONS
MORSELS	MORULAR	MOTEY	MOTORIAL	MOUGHT
MORSES	MORWONG	MOTH	MOTORING	MOUILLE
MORSURE	MORWONGS	MOTHBALL	MOTORISE	MOUJIK

The Chambers Dictionary is the authority for many longer words; see *OSW* Introduction, page xii.

MOUJIKS	MOUSER	MOVEMENT	MPRET	MUCUS
MOULAGE	MOUSERIES	MOVEMENTS	MPRETS	MUCUSES
MOULAGES	MOUSERS	MOVER	MRIDAMGAM	MUD
MOULD	MOUSERY	MOVERS	MRIDAMGAMS	MUDBATH
MOULDABLE	MOUSES	MOVES	MRIDANG	MUDBATHS
MOULDED	MOUSEY	MOVIE	MRIDANGA	MUDCAT
MOULDER	MOUSIE	MOVIEGOER	MRIDANGAM	MUDCATS
MOULDERED	MOUSIER	MOVIEGOERS	MRIDANGAMS	MUDDED
MOULDERING	MOUSIES	MOVIELAND	MRIDANGAS	MUDDER
MOULDERS	MOUSIEST	MOVIELANDS	MRIDANGS	MUDDERS
MOULDIER	MOUSING	MOVIES	MU	MUDDIED
MOULDIEST	MOUSINGS	MOVING	MUCATE	MUDDIER
MOULDING	MOUSLE	MOVINGLY	MUCATES	MUDDIES
MOULDINGS	MOUSLED	MOW	MUCH	MUDDIEST
MOULDS	MOUSLES	MOWA	MUCHEL	MUDDILY
MOULDWARP	MOUSLING	MOWAS	MUCHELL	MUDDINESS
MOULDWARPS	MOUSME	MOWBURN	MUCHELLS	MUDDINESSES
MOULDY	MOUSMEE	MOWBURNED	MUCHELS	MUDDING
MOULIN	MOUSMEES	MOWBURNING	MUCHES	MUDDLE
MOULINET	MOUSMES	MOWBURNS	MUCHLY	MUDDLED
MOULINETS	MOUSSAKA	MOWBURNT	MUCHNESS	MUDDLER
MOULINS	MOUSSAKAS	MOWDIWART	MUCHNESSES	MUDDLERS
MOULS	MOUSSE	MOWDIWARTS	MUCID	MUDDLES
MOULT	MOUSSES	MOWDIWORT	MUCIGEN	MUDDLING
MOULTED	MOUST	MOWDIWORTS	MUCIGENS	MUDDY
MOULTEN	MOUSTACHE	MOWED	MUCILAGE	MUDDYING
MOULTING	MOUSTACHES	MOWER	MUCILAGES	MUDEJAR
MOULTINGS	MOUSTED	MOWERS	MUCIN	MUDEJARES
MOULTS	MOUSTING	MOWING	MUCINS	MUDFISH
MOUND	MOUSTS	MOWINGS	MUCK	MUDFISHES
MOUNDED	MOUSY	MOWN	MUCKED	MUDFLAP
MOUNDING	MOUTAN	MOWRA	MUCKENDER	MUDFLAPS
MOUNDS	MOUTANS	MOWRAS	MUCKENDERS	MUDFLAT
MOUNSEER	MOUTER	MOWS	MUCKER	MUDFLATS
MOUNSEERS	MOUTERED	MOXA	MUCKERED	MUDGE
MOUNT	MOUTERER	MOXAS	MUCKERING	MUDGED
MOUNTAIN	MOUTERERS	MOXIE	MUCKERS	MUDGER
MOUNTAINS	MOUTERING	MOXIES	MUCKHEAP	MUDGERS
MOUNTANT	MOUTERS	MOY	MUCKHEAPS	MUDGES
MOUNTANTS	MOUTH	MOYA	MUCKIER	MUDGING
MOUNTED	MOUTHABLE	MOYAS	MUCKIEST	MUDGUARD
MOUNTER	MOUTHED	MOYGASHEL	MUCKINESS	MUDGUARDS
MOUNTERS	MOUTHER	MOYGASHELS	MUCKINESSES	MUDHOLE
MOUNTING	MOUTHERS	MOYITIES	MUCKING	MUDHOLES
MOUNTINGS	MOUTHFEEL	MOYITY	MUCKLE	MUDHOOK
MOUNTS	MOUTHFEELS	MOYL	MUCKLES	MUDHOOKS
MOUP	MOUTHFUL	MOYLE	MUCKLUCK	MUDIR
MOUPED	MOUTHFULS	MOYLED	MUCKLUCKS	MUDIRIA
MOUPING	MOUTHIER	MOYLES	MUCKS	MUDIRIAS
MOUPS	MOUTHIEST	MOYLING	MUCKSWEAT	MUDIRIEH
MOURN	MOUTHING	MOYLS	MUCKSWEATS	MUDIRIEHS
MOURNED	MOUTHLESS	MOYS	MUCKY	MUDIRS
MOURNER	MOUTHS	MOZ	MUCLUC	MUDLARK
MOURNERS	MOUTHWASH	MOZE	MUCLUCS	MUDLARKED
MOURNFUL	MOUTHWASHES	MOZED	MUCOID	MUDLARKING
MOURNING	MOUTHY	MOZES	MUCOR	MUDLARKS
MOURNINGS	MOUTON	MOZETTA	MUCORS	MUDLOGGER
MOURNIVAL	MOUTONS	MOZETTAS	MUCOSA	MUDLOGGERS
MOURNIVALS	MOVABLE	MOZING	MUCOSAE	MUDPACK
MOURNS	MOVABLES	MOZZ	MUCOSITIES	MUDPACKS
MOUS	MOVABLY	MOZZES	MUCOSITY	MUDPUPPIES
MOUSAKA	MOVE	MOZZETTA	MUCOUS	MUDPUPPY
MOUSAKAS	MOVEABLE	MOZZETTAS	MUCRO	MUDRA
MOUSE	MOVEABLES	MOZZIE	MUCRONATE	MUDRAS
MOUSED	MOVEABLY	MOZZIES	MUCRONES	MUDS
MOUSEKIN	MOVED	MOZZLE	MUCROS	MUDSCOW
MOUSEKINS	MOVELESS	MOZZLES	MUCULENT	MUDSCOWS

The Chambers Dictionary is the authority for many longer words; see *OSW* Introduction, page xii.

MUDSLIDE
MUDSLIDES
MUDSTONE
MUDSTONES
MUDWORT
MUDWORTS
MUEDDIN
MUEDDINS
MUENSTER
MUENSTERS
MUESLI
MUESLIS
MUEZZIN
MUEZZINS
MUFF
MUFFED
MUFFETTEE
MUFFETTEES
MUFFIN
MUFFINEER
MUFFINEERS
MUFFING
MUFFINS
MUFFISH
MUFFLE
MUFFLED
MUFFLER
MUFFLERS
MUFFLES
MUFFLING
MUFFS
MUFLON
MUFLONS
MUFTI
MUFTIS
MUG
MUGEARITE
MUGEARITES
MUGFUL
MUGFULS
MUGGED
MUGGEE
MUGGEES
MUGGER
MUGGERS
MUGGIER
MUGGIEST
MUGGINESS
MUGGINESSES
MUGGING
MUGGINGS
MUGGINS
MUGGINSES
MUGGISH
MUGGY
MUGS
MUGSHOT
MUGSHOTS
MUGWORT
MUGWORTS
MUGWUMP
MUGWUMPS
MUID
MUIDS
MUIL
MUILS
MUIR

MUIRBURN
MUIRBURNS
MUIRS
MUIST
MUISTED
MUISTING
MUISTS
MUJAHEDIN
MUJAHIDIN
MUJIK
MUJIKS
MUKHTAR
MUKHTARS
MUKLUK
MUKLUKS
MULATTA
MULATTAS
MULATTO
MULATTOES
MULATTOS
MULBERRIES
MULBERRY
MULCH
MULCHED
MULCHES
MULCHING
MULCT
MULCTED
MULCTING
MULCTS
MULE
MULES
MULETEER
MULETEERS
MULEY
MULEYS
MULGA
MULGAS
MULISH
MULISHLY
MULL
MULLAH
MULLAHS
MULLARKIES
MULLARKY
MULLED
MULLEIN
MULLEINS
MULLER
MULLERS
MULLET
MULLETS
MULLEY
MULLEYS
MULLIGAN
MULLIGANS
MULLING
MULLION
MULLIONED
MULLIONS
MULLOCK
MULLOCKS
MULLOWAY
MULLOWAYS
MULLS
MULMUL
MULMULL

MULMULLS
MULMULS
MULSE
MULSES
MULSH
MULSHED
MULSHES
MULSHING
MULTEITIES
MULTEITY
MULTIFID
MULTIFIL
MULTIFILS
MULTIFOIL
MULTIFOILS
MULTIFORM
MULTIFORMS
MULTIGYM
MULTIGYMS
MULTIHULL
MULTIHULLS
MULTIMODE
MULTIPARA
MULTIPARAE
MULTIPARAS
MULTIPED
MULTIPEDE
MULTIPEDES
MULTIPEDS
MULTIPLE
MULTIPLES
MULTIPLET
MULTIPLETS
MULTIPLEX
MULTIPLEXED
MULTIPLEXES
MULTIPLEXING
MULTIPLIED
MULTIPLIES
MULTIPLY
MULTIPLYING
MULTITUDE
MULTITUDES
MULTIUSER
MULTUM
MULTUMS
MULTURE
MULTURED
MULTURER
MULTURERS
MULTURES
MULTURING
MUM
MUMBLE
MUMBLED
MUMBLER
MUMBLERS
MUMBLES
MUMBLING
MUMBLINGS
MUMCHANCE
MUMCHANCES
MUMM
MUMMED
MUMMER
MUMMERIES
MUMMERS

MUMMERY
MUMMIA
MUMMIAS
MUMMIED
MUMMIES
MUMMIFIED
MUMMIFIES
MUMMIFORM
MUMMIFY
MUMMIFYING
MUMMING
MUMMINGS
MUMMOCK
MUMMOCKS
MUMMS
MUMMY
MUMMYING
MUMP
MUMPED
MUMPER
MUMPERS
MUMPING
MUMPISH
MUMPISHLY
MUMPS
MUMPSIMUS
MUMPSIMUSES
MUMS
MUMSIER
MUMSIEST
MUMSY
MUN
MUNCH
MUNCHED
MUNCHER
MUNCHERS
MUNCHES
MUNCHING
MUNCHKIN
MUNCHKINS
MUNDANE
MUNDANELY
MUNDANER
MUNDANEST
MUNDANITIES
MUNDANITY
MUNDIC
MUNDICS
MUNDIFIED
MUNDIFIES
MUNDIFY
MUNDIFYING
MUNDUNGUS
MUNDUNGUSES
MUNGCORN
MUNGCORNS
MUNGO
MUNGOOSE
MUNGOOSES
MUNGOS
MUNICIPAL
MUNIFIED
MUNIFIES
MUNIFY
MUNIFYING
MUNIMENT
MUNIMENTS

MUNITE
MUNITED
MUNITES
MUNITING
MUNITION
MUNITIONED
MUNITIONING
MUNITIONS
MUNNION
MUNNIONS
MUNSHI
MUNSHIS
MUNSTER
MUNSTERS
MUNT
MUNTIN
MUNTING
MUNTINGS
MUNTINS
MUNTJAC
MUNTJACS
MUNTJAK
MUNTJAKS
MUNTS
MUNTU
MUNTUS
MUON
MUONIC
MUONIUM
MUONIUMS
MUONS
MUQADDAM
MUQADDAMS
MURAENA
MURAENAS
MURAGE
MURAGES
MURAL
MURALIST
MURALISTS
MURALS
MURDER
MURDERED
MURDEREE
MURDEREES
MURDERER
MURDERERS
MURDERESS
MURDERESSES
MURDERING
MURDEROUS
MURDERS
MURE
MURED
MURENA
MURENAS
MURES
MUREX
MUREXES
MURGEON
MURGEONED
MURGEONING
MURGEONS
MURIATE
MURIATED
MURIATES
MURIATIC

The Chambers Dictionary is the authority for many longer words; see *OSW* Introduction, page xii.

MURICATE	MURRIONS	MUSHED	MUSLINETS	MUTATED
MURICATED	MURRY	MUSHER	MUSLINS	MUTATES
MURICES	MURTHER	MUSHERS	MUSMON	MUTATING
MURIFORM	MURTHERED	MUSHES	MUSMONS	MUTATION
MURINE	MURTHERER	MUSHIER	MUSO	MUTATIONS
MURINES	MURTHERERS	MUSHIEST	MUSOS	MUTATIVE
MURING	MURTHERING	MUSHILY	MUSQUASH	MUTATORY
MURK	MURTHERS	MUSHINESS	MUSQUASHES	MUTCH
MURKER	MURVA	MUSHINESSES	MUSROL	MUTCHES
MURKEST	MURVAS	MUSHING	MUSROLS	MUTCHKIN
MURKIER	MUS	MUSHMOUTH	MUSS	MUTCHKINS
MURKIEST	MUSACEOUS	MUSHMOUTHS	MUSSE	MUTE
MURKILY	MUSANG	MUSHROOM	MUSSED	MUTED
MURKINESS	MUSANGS	MUSHROOMED	MUSSEL	MUTELY
MURKINESSES	MUSCADEL	MUSHROOMING	MUSSELLED	MUTENESS
MURKISH	MUSCADELS	MUSHROOMS	MUSSELS	MUTENESSES
MURKS	MUSCADIN	MUSHY	MUSSES	MUTER
MURKSOME	MUSCADINE	MUSIC	MUSSIER	MUTES
MURKY	MUSCADINES	MUSICAL	MUSSIEST	MUTEST
MURL	MUSCADINS	MUSICALE	MUSSINESS	MUTI
MURLAIN	MUSCARINE	MUSICALES	MUSSINESSES	MUTICOUS
MURLAINS	MUSCARINES	MUSICALLY	MUSSING	MUTILATE
MURLAN	MUSCAT	MUSICALS	MUSSITATE	MUTILATED
MURLANS	MUSCATEL	MUSICIAN	MUSSITATED	MUTILATES
MURLED	MUSCATELS	MUSICIANS	MUSSITATES	MUTILATING
MURLIER	MUSCATS	MUSICKED	MUSSITATING	MUTILATOR
MURLIEST	MUSCID	MUSICKER	MUSSY	MUTILATORS
MURLIN	MUSCIDS	MUSICKERS	MUST	MUTINE
MURLING	MUSCLE	MUSICKING	MUSTACHE	MUTINED
MURLINS	MUSCLED	MUSICS	MUSTACHES	MUTINEER
MURLS	MUSCLEMAN	MUSIMON	MUSTACHIO	MUTINEERED
MURLY	MUSCLEMEN	MUSIMONS	MUSTACHIOS	MUTINEERING
MURMUR	MUSCLES	MUSING	MUSTANG	MUTINEERS
MURMURED	MUSCLIER	MUSINGLY	MUSTANGS	MUTINES
MURMURER	MUSCLIEST	MUSINGS	MUSTARD	MUTING
MURMURERS	MUSCLING	MUSIT	MUSTARDS	MUTINIED
MURMURING	MUSCLINGS	MUSITS	MUSTED	MUTINIES
MURMURINGS	MUSCLY	MUSIVE	MUSTEE	MUTINING
MURMUROUS	MUSCOID	MUSK	MUSTEES	MUTINOUS
MURMURS	MUSCOLOGIES	MUSKED	MUSTELINE	MUTINY
MURPHIES	MUSCOLOGY	MUSKEG	MUSTELINES	MUTINYING
MURPHY	MUSCONE	MUSKEGS	MUSTER	MUTIS
MURRA	MUSCONES	MUSKET	MUSTERED	MUTISM
MURRAIN	MUSCOSE	MUSKETEER	MUSTERER	MUTISMS
MURRAINED	MUSCOVADO	MUSKETEERS	MUSTERERS	MUTON
MURRAINS	MUSCOVADOS	MUSKETOON	MUSTERING	MUTONS
MURRAM	MUSCOVITE	MUSKETOONS	MUSTERS	MUTOSCOPE
MURRAMS	MUSCOVITES	MUSKETRIES	MUSTH	MUTOSCOPES
MURRAS	MUSCULAR	MUSKETRY	MUSTHS	MUTT
MURRAY	MUSCULOUS	MUSKETS	MUSTIER	MUTTER
MURRAYS	MUSE	MUSKIER	MUSTIEST	MUTTERED
MURRE	MUSED	MUSKIEST	MUSTILY	MUTTERER
MURRELET	MUSEFUL	MUSKILY	MUSTINESS	MUTTERERS
MURRELETS	MUSEFULLY	MUSKINESS	MUSTINESSES	MUTTERING
MURREN	MUSEOLOGIES	MUSKINESSES	MUSTING	MUTTERINGS
MURRENS	MUSEOLOGY	MUSKING	MUSTS	MUTTERS
MURRES	MUSER	MUSKLE	MUSTY	MUTTON
MURREY	MUSERS	MUSKLES	MUTABLE	MUTTONS
MURREYS	MUSES	MUSKONE	MUTABLY	MUTTONY
MURRHA	MUSET	MUSKONES	MUTAGEN	MUTTS
MURRHAS	MUSETS	MUSKRAT	MUTAGENIC	MUTUAL
MURRHINE	MUSETTE	MUSKRATS	MUTAGENS	MUTUALISE
MURRIES	MUSETTES	MUSKS	MUTANDA	MUTUALISED
MURRIN	MUSEUM	MUSKY	MUTANDUM	MUTUALISES
MURRINE	MUSEUMS	MUSLIN	MUTANT	MUTUALISING
MURRINS	MUSH	MUSLINED	MUTANTS	MUTUALISM
MURRION	MUSHA	MUSLINET	MUTATE	MUTUALISMS

The Chambers Dictionary is the authority for many longer words; see *OSW* Introduction, page xii.

MUTUALITIES	MYCETOMAS	MYOFIBRIL	MYRIAD	MYTHICISE
MUTUALITY	MYCOLOGIC	MYOFIBRILS	MYRIADS	MYTHICISED
MUTUALIZE	MYCOLOGIES	MYOGEN	MYRIADTH	MYTHICISES
MUTUALIZED	MYCOLOGY	MYOGENIC	MYRIADTHS	MYTHICISING
MUTUALIZES	MYCOPHAGIES	MYOGENS	MYRIAPOD	MYTHICISM
MUTUALIZING	MYCOPHAGY	MYOGLOBIN	MYRIAPODS	MYTHICISMS
MUTUALLY	MYCORHIZA	MYOGLOBINS	MYRINGA	MYTHICIST
MUTUCA	MYCORHIZAS	MYOGRAM	MYRINGAS	MYTHICISTS
MUTUCAS	MYCOSES	MYOGRAMS	MYRIOPOD	MYTHICIZE
MUTULE	MYCOSIS	MYOGRAPH	MYRIOPODS	MYTHICIZED
MUTULES	MYCOTIC	MYOGRAPHIES	MYRIORAMA	MYTHICIZES
MUTUUM	MYCOTOXIN	MYOGRAPHS	MYRIORAMAS	MYTHICIZING
MUTUUMS	MYCOTOXINS	MYOGRAPHY	MYRISTIC	MYTHISE
MUX	MYDRIASES	MYOID	MYRMECOID	MYTHISED
MUXED	MYDRIASIS	MYOLOGIES	MYRMIDON	MYTHISES
MUXES	MYDRIATIC	MYOLOGIST	MYRMIDONS	MYTHISING
MUXING	MYDRIATICS	MYOLOGISTS	MYROBALAN	MYTHISM
MUZAKY	MYELIN	MYOLOGY	MYROBALANS	MYTHISMS
MUZHIK	MYELINS	MYOMA	MYRRH	MYTHIST
MUZHIKS	MYELITIS	MYOMANCIES	MYRRHIC	MYTHISTS
MUZZIER	MYELITISES	MYOMANCY	MYRRHINE	MYTHIZE
MUZZIEST	MYELOID	MYOMANTIC	MYRRHOL	MYTHIZED
MUZZILY	MYELOMA	MYOMAS	MYRRHOLS	MYTHIZES
MUZZINESS	MYELOMAS	MYOMATA	MYRRHS	MYTHIZING
MUZZINESSES	MYELOMATA	MYOPE	MYRTLE	MYTHOI
MUZZLE	MYELON	MYOPES	MYRTLES	MYTHOLOGIES
MUZZLED	MYELONS	MYOPIA	MYSELF	MYTHOLOGY
MUZZLER	MYGALE	MYOPIAS	MYSTAGOGIES	MYTHOMANE
MUZZLERS	MYGALES	MYOPIC	MYSTAGOGY	MYTHOMANES
MUZZLES	MYIASES	MYOPICS	MYSTERIES	MYTHOPOET
MUZZLING	MYIASIS	MYOPS	MYSTERY	MYTHOPOETS
MUZZY	MYLODON	MYOPSES	MYSTIC	MYTHOS
MVULE	MYLODONS	MYOSES	MYSTICAL	MYTHS
MVULES	MYLODONT	MYOSIN	MYSTICISM	MYTHUS
MY	MYLODONTS	MYOSINS	MYSTICISMS	MYTILOID
MYAL	MYLOHYOID	MYOSIS	MYSTICS	MYXEDEMA
MYALGIA	MYLOHYOIDS	MYOSITIS	MYSTIFIED	MYXEDEMAS
MYALGIAS	MYLONITE	MYOSITISES	MYSTIFIER	MYXEDEMIC
MYALGIC	MYLONITES	MYOSOTE	MYSTIFIERS	MYXOEDEMA
MYALISM	MYLONITIC	MYOSOTES	MYSTIFIES	MYXOEDEMAS
MYALISMS	MYNA	MYOSOTIS	MYSTIFY	MYXOMA
MYALL	MYNAH	MYOSOTISES	MYSTIFYING	MYXOMATA
MYALLS	MYNAHS	MYOTONIA	MYSTIQUE	MYXOVIRUS
MYCELIA	MYNAS	MYOTONIAS	MYSTIQUES	MYXOVIRUSES
MYCELIAL	MYNHEER	MYOTUBE	MYTH	MZEE
MYCELIUM	MYNHEERS	MYOTUBES	MYTHI	MZEES
MYCETES	MYOBLAST	MYRBANE	MYTHIC	MZUNGU
MYCETOMA	MYOBLASTS	MYRBANES	MYTHICAL	MZUNGUS

The Chambers Dictionary is the authority for many longer words; see *OSW* Introduction, page xii.

N

NA	NAG	NAIVETY	NANNAS	NAPRON
NAAM	NAGA	NAIVIST	NANNIED	NAPRONS
NAAMS	NAGANA	NAKED	NANNIES	NAPS
NAAN	NAGANAS	NAKEDER	NANNY	NARAS
NAANS	NAGAPIE	NAKEDEST	NANNYGAI	NARASES
NAARTJE	NAGAPIES	NAKEDLY	NANNYGAIS	NARC
NAARTJES	NAGARI	NAKEDNESS	NANNYGHAI	NARCEEN
NAB	NAGARIS	NAKEDNESSES	NANNYGHAIS	NARCEENS
NABBED	NAGAS	NAKER	NANNYING	NARCEINE
NABBER	NAGGED	NAKERS	NANNYISH	NARCEINES
NABBERS	NAGGER	NALA	NANOGRAM	NARCISSI
NABBING	NAGGERS	NALAS	NANOGRAMS	NARCISSUS
NABK	NAGGIER	NALLA	NANOMETRE	NARCISSUSES
NABKS	NAGGIEST	NALLAH	NANOMETRES	NARCO
NABLA	NAGGING	NALLAHS	NANS	NARCOS
NABLAS	NAGGY	NALLAS	NAOI	NARCOSES
NABOB	NAGMAAL	NALOXONE	NAOS	NARCOSIS
NABOBS	NAGMAALS	NALOXONES	NAOSES	NARCOTIC
NABS	NAGOR	NAM	NAP	NARCOTICS
NACARAT	NAGORS	NAMABLE	NAPA	NARCOTINE
NACARATS	NAGS	NAMASKAR	NAPALM	NARCOTINES
NACELLE	NAHAL	NAMASKARS	NAPALMED	NARCOTISE
NACELLES	NAHALS	NAMASTE	NAPALMING	NARCOTISED
NACH	NAIAD	NAMASTES	NAPALMS	NARCOTISES
NACHE	NAIADES	NAME	NAPAS	NARCOTISING
NACHES	NAIADS	NAMEABLE	NAPE	NARCOTISM
NACHO	NAIANT	NAMED	NAPERIES	NARCOTISMS
NACHOS	NAIF	NAMELESS	NAPERY	NARCOTIST
NACHTMAAL	NAIFER	NAMELY	NAPES	NARCOTISTS
NACHTMAALS	NAIFEST	NAMER	NAPHTHA	NARCOTIZE
NACKET	NAIK	NAMERS	NAPHTHAS	NARCOTIZED
NACKETS	NAIKS	NAMES	NAPHTHENE	NARCOTIZES
NACRE	NAIL	NAMESAKE	NAPHTHENES	NARCOTIZING
NACRED	NAILED	NAMESAKES	NAPHTHOL	NARCS
NACREOUS	NAILER	NAMETAPE	NAPHTHOLS	NARD
NACRES	NAILERIES	NAMETAPES	NAPIFORM	NARDED
NACRITE	NAILERS	NAMING	NAPKIN	NARDING
NACRITES	NAILERY	NAMINGS	NAPKINS	NARDOO
NACROUS	NAILING	NAMS	NAPLESS	NARDOOS
NADA	NAILINGS	NAN	NAPOLEON	NARDS
NADAS	NAILLESS	NANA	NAPOLEONS	NARE
NADIR	NAILS	NANAS	NAPOO	NARES
NADIRS	NAIN	NANCE	NAPOOED	NARGHILE
NAE	NAINSELL	NANCES	NAPOOING	NARGHILES
NAEBODIES	NAINSELLS	NANCIES	NAPOOS	NARGHILIES
NAEBODY	NAINSOOK	NANCY	NAPPA	NARGHILLIES
NAETHING	NAINSOOKS	NANDINE	NAPPAS	NARGHILLY
NAETHINGS	NAIRA	NANDINES	NAPPE	NARGHILY
NAEVE	NAIRAS	NANDOO	NAPPED	NARGILE
NAEVES	NAISSANT	NANDOOS	NAPPER	NARGILEH
NAEVI	NAIVE	NANDU	NAPPERS	NARGILEHS
NAEVOID	NAIVELY	NANDUS	NAPPES	NARGILES
NAEVUS	NAIVENESS	NANISM	NAPPIER	NARGILIES
NAFF	NAIVENESSES	NANISMS	NAPPIES	NARGILLIES
NAFFING	NAIVER	NANKEEN	NAPPIEST	NARGILLY
NAFFLY	NAIVEST	NANKEENS	NAPPINESS	NARGILY
NAFFNESS	NAIVETE	NANKIN	NAPPINESSES	NARIAL
NAFFNESSES	NAIVETES	NANKINS	NAPPING	NARICORN
NAFFS	NAIVETIES	NANNA	NAPPY	NARICORNS

NARINE
NARK
NARKED
NARKIER
NARKIEST
NARKING
NARKS
NARKY
NARQUOIS
NARRAS
NARRASES
NARRATE
NARRATED
NARRATES
NARRATING
NARRATION
NARRATIONS
NARRATIVE
NARRATIVES
NARRATOR
NARRATORS
NARRATORY
NARRE
NARROW
NARROWED
NARROWER
NARROWEST
NARROWING
NARROWINGS
NARROWLY
NARROWS
NARTHEX
NARTHEXES
NARTJIE
NARTJIES
NARWHAL
NARWHALS
NARY
NAS
NASAL
NASALISE
NASALISED
NASALISES
NASALISING
NASALITIES
NASALITY
NASALIZE
NASALIZED
NASALIZES
NASALIZING
NASALLY
NASALS
NASARD
NASARDS
NASCENCE
NASCENCES
NASCENCIES
NASCENCY
NASCENT
NASEBERRIES
NASEBERRY
NASHGAB
NASHGABS
NASION
NASIONS
NASTALIK
NASTALIKS

NASTIC
NASTIER
NASTIES
NASTIEST
NASTILY
NASTINESS
NASTINESSES
NASTY
NASUTE
NASUTES
NAT
NATAL
NATALITIES
NATALITY
NATANT
NATATION
NATATIONS
NATATORIA
NATATORY
NATCH
NATCHES
NATES
NATHELESS
NATHEMO
NATHEMORE
NATHLESS
NATIFORM
NATION
NATIONAL
NATIONALS
NATIONS
NATIVE
NATIVELY
NATIVES
NATIVISM
NATIVISMS
NATIVIST
NATIVISTS
NATIVITIES
NATIVITY
NATRIUM
NATRIUMS
NATROLITE
NATROLITES
NATRON
NATRONS
NATS
NATTER
NATTERED
NATTERER
NATTERERS
NATTERING
NATTERS
NATTERY
NATTIER
NATTIEST
NATTILY
NATTINESS
NATTINESSES
NATTY
NATURA
NATURAE
NATURAL
NATURALLY
NATURALS
NATURE
NATURED

NATURES
NATURING
NATURISM
NATURISMS
NATURIST
NATURISTS
NAUGHT
NAUGHTIER
NAUGHTIES
NAUGHTIEST
NAUGHTILY
NAUGHTS
NAUGHTY
NAUMACHIA
NAUMACHIAE
NAUMACHIAS
NAUMACHIES
NAUMACHY
NAUNT
NAUNTS
NAUPLII
NAUPLIOID
NAUPLIUS
NAUSEA
NAUSEANT
NAUSEANTS
NAUSEAS
NAUSEATE
NAUSEATED
NAUSEATES
NAUSEATING
NAUSEOUS
NAUTCH
NAUTCHES
NAUTIC
NAUTICAL
NAUTICS
NAUTILI
NAUTILUS
NAUTILUSES
NAVAID
NAVAIDS
NAVAL
NAVALISM
NAVALISMS
NAVARCH
NAVARCHIES
NAVARCHS
NAVARCHY
NAVARHO
NAVARHOS
NAVARIN
NAVARINS
NAVE
NAVEL
NAVELS
NAVELWORT
NAVELWORTS
NAVES
NAVETTE
NAVETTES
NAVEW
NAVEWS
NAVICERT
NAVICERTS
NAVICULA
NAVICULAR

NAVICULARS
NAVICULAS
NAVIES
NAVIGABLE
NAVIGABLY
NAVIGATE
NAVIGATED
NAVIGATES
NAVIGATING
NAVIGATOR
NAVIGATORS
NAVVIED
NAVVIES
NAVVY
NAVVYING
NAVY
NAWAB
NAWABS
NAY
NAYS
NAYTHLES
NAYWARD
NAYWARDS
NAYWORD
NAYWORDS
NAZE
NAZES
NAZIR
NAZIRS
NE
NEAFE
NEAFES
NEAFFE
NEAFFES
NEAL
NEALED
NEALING
NEALS
NEANIC
NEAP
NEAPED
NEAPING
NEAPS
NEAR
NEARED
NEARER
NEAREST
NEARING
NEARLY
NEARNESS
NEARNESSES
NEARS
NEARSIDE
NEARSIDES
NEAT
NEATEN
NEATENED
NEATENING
NEATENS
NEATER
NEATEST
NEATH
NEATLY
NEATNESS
NEATNESSES
NEB
NEBBED

NEBBICH
NEBBICHS
NEBBING
NEBBISH
NEBBISHE
NEBBISHER
NEBBISHERS
NEBBISHES
NEBBUK
NEBBUKS
NEBECK
NEBECKS
NEBEK
NEBEKS
NEBEL
NEBELS
NEBISH
NEBISHES
NEBRIS
NEBRISES
NEBS
NEBULA
NEBULAE
NEBULAR
NEBULAS
NEBULE
NEBULES
NEBULISE
NEBULISED
NEBULISER
NEBULISERS
NEBULISES
NEBULISING
NEBULIUM
NEBULIUMS
NEBULIZE
NEBULIZED
NEBULIZER
NEBULIZERS
NEBULIZES
NEBULIZING
NEBULOUS
NEBULY
NECESSARIES
NECESSARY
NECESSITIES
NECESSITY
NECK
NECKATEE
NECKATEES
NECKBAND
NECKBANDS
NECKBEEF
NECKBEEFS
NECKCLOTH
NECKCLOTHS
NECKED
NECKGEAR
NECKGEARS
NECKING
NECKINGS
NECKLACE
NECKLACED
NECKLACES
NECKLACING
NECKLACINGS
NECKLET

The Chambers Dictionary is the authority for many longer words; see *OSW* Introduction, page xii.

NECKLETS	NEEDLED	NEGOTIANTS	NEMESIS	NEOPRENES
NECKLINE	NEEDLEFUL	NEGOTIATE	NEMN	NEOTEINIA
NECKLINES	NEEDLEFULS	NEGOTIATED	NEMNED	NEOTEINIAS
NECKPIECE	NEEDLER	NEGOTIATES	NEMNING	NEOTENIC
NECKPIECES	NEEDLERS	NEGOTIATING	NEMNS	NEOTENIES
NECKS	NEEDLES	NEGRESS	NEMOPHILA	NEOTENOUS
NECKTIE	NEEDLESS	NEGRESSES	NEMOPHILAS	NEOTENY
NECKTIES	NEEDLIER	NEGRITUDE	NEMORAL	NEOTERIC
NECKVERSE	NEEDLIEST	NEGRITUDES	NEMOROUS	NEOTERICS
NECKVERSES	NEEDLING	NEGRO	NEMPT	NEOTERISE
NECKWEAR	NEEDLY	NEGROES	NENE	NEOTERISED
NECKWEARS	NEEDMENT	NEGROHEAD	NENES	NEOTERISES
NECKWEED	NEEDMENTS	NEGROHEADS	NENNIGAI	NEOTERISING
NECKWEEDS	NEEDS	NEGROID	NENNIGAIS	NEOTERISM
NECROLOGIES	NEEDY	NEGROIDAL	NENUPHAR	NEOTERISMS
NECROLOGY	NEELD	NEGROIDS	NENUPHARS	NEOTERIST
NECROPHIL	NEELDS	NEGROISM	NEOBLAST	NEOTERISTS
NECROPHILS	NEELE	NEGROISMS	NEOBLASTS	NEOTERIZE
NECROPSIES	NEELES	NEGROPHIL	NEODYMIUM	NEOTERIZED
NECROPSY	NEEM	NEGROPHILS	NEODYMIUMS	NEOTERIZES
NECROSE	NEEMB	NEGUS	NEOLITH	NEOTERIZING
NECROSED	NEEMBS	NEGUSES	NEOLITHS	NEOTOXIN
NECROSES	NEEMS	NEIF	NEOLOGIAN	NEOTOXINS
NECROSING	NEEP	NEIFS	NEOLOGIANS	NEP
NECROSIS	NEEPS	NEIGH	NEOLOGIC	NEPENTHE
NECROTIC	NEESBERRIES	NEIGHBOR	NEOLOGIES	NEPENTHES
NECROTISE	NEESBERRY	NEIGHBORED	NEOLOGISE	NEPER
NECROTISED	NEESE	NEIGHBORING	NEOLOGISED	NEPERS
NECROTISES	NEESED	NEIGHBORS	NEOLOGISES	NEPETA
NECROTISING	NEESES	NEIGHBOUR	NEOLOGISING	NEPETAS
NECROTIZE	NEESING	NEIGHBOURED	NEOLOGISM	NEPHALISM
NECROTIZED	NEEZE	NEIGHBOURING	NEOLOGISMS	NEPHALISMS
NECROTIZES	NEEZED	NEIGHBOURS	NEOLOGIST	NEPHALIST
NECROTIZING	NEEZES	NEIGHED	NEOLOGISTS	NEPHALISTS
NECROTOMIES	NEEZING	NEIGHING	NEOLOGIZE	NEPHELINE
NECROTOMY	NEF	NEIGHS	NEOLOGIZED	NEPHELINES
NECTAR	NEFANDOUS	NEIST	NEOLOGIZES	NEPHELITE
NECTAREAL	NEFARIOUS	NEITHER	NEOLOGIZING	NEPHELITES
NECTAREAN	NEFAST	NEIVE	NEOLOGY	NEPHEW
NECTARED	NEFS	NEIVES	NEOMYCIN	NEPHEWS
NECTARIAL	NEGATE	NEK	NEOMYCINS	NEPHOGRAM
NECTARIES	NEGATED	NEKS	NEON	NEPHOGRAMS
NECTARINE	NEGATES	NEKTON	NEONATAL	NEPHOLOGIES
NECTARINES	NEGATING	NEKTONS	NEONATE	NEPHOLOGY
NECTAROUS	NEGATION	NELIES	NEONATES	NEPHRALGIES
NECTARS	NEGATIONS	NELIS	NEONOMIAN	NEPHRALGY
NECTARY	NEGATIVE	NELLIES	NEONOMIANS	NEPHRIC
NED	NEGATIVED	NELLY	NEONS	NEPHRIDIA
NEDDIES	NEGATIVES	NELSON	NEOPAGAN	NEPHRITE
NEDDY	NEGATIVING	NELSONS	NEOPAGANS	NEPHRITES
NEDS	NEGATORY	NELUMBIUM	NEOPHILE	NEPHRITIC
NEE	NEGATRON	NELUMBIUMS	NEOPHILES	NEPHRITICS
NEED	NEGATRONS	NELUMBO	NEOPHILIA	NEPHRITIS
NEEDED	NEGLECT	NELUMBOS	NEOPHILIAS	NEPHRITISES
NEEDER	NEGLECTED	NEMATIC	NEOPHOBE	NEPHROID
NEEDERS	NEGLECTER	NEMATODE	NEOPHOBES	NEPHRON
NEEDFIRE	NEGLECTERS	NEMATODES	NEOPHOBIA	NEPHRONS
NEEDFIRES	NEGLECTING	NEMATOID	NEOPHOBIAS	NEPHROSES
NEEDFUL	NEGLECTS	NEMERTEAN	NEOPHOBIC	NEPHROSIS
NEEDFULLY	NEGLIGE	NEMERTEANS	NEOPHYTE	NEPHROTIC
NEEDIER	NEGLIGEE	NEMERTIAN	NEOPHYTES	NEPIONIC
NEEDIEST	NEGLIGEES	NEMERTIANS	NEOPHYTIC	NEPIT
NEEDILY	NEGLIGENT	NEMERTINE	NEOPILINA	NEPITS
NEEDINESS	NEGLIGES	NEMERTINES	NEOPILINAS	NEPOTIC
NEEDINESSES	NEGOCIANT	NEMESES	NEOPLASM	NEPOTISM
NEEDING	NEGOCIANTS	NEMESIA	NEOPLASMS	NEPOTISMS
NEEDLE	NEGOTIANT	NEMESIAS	NEOPRENE	NEPOTIST

The Chambers Dictionary is the authority for many longer words; see *OSW* Introduction, page xii.

NEPOTISTS	NESTFUL	NEURITICS	NEWEST	NGULTRUM
NEPS	NESTFULS	NEURITIS	NEWFANGLE	NGULTRUMS
NEPTUNIUM	NESTING	NEURITISES	NEWING	NGWEE
NEPTUNIUMS	NESTINGS	NEUROCHIP	NEWISH	NHANDU
NERD	NESTLE	NEUROCHIPS	NEWISHLY	NHANDUS
NERDIER	NESTLED	NEUROGLIA	NEWLY	NIACIN
NERDIEST	NESTLES	NEUROGLIAS	NEWMARKET	NIACINS
NERDS	NESTLIKE	NEUROGRAM	NEWMARKETS	NIAISERIE
NERDY	NESTLING	NEUROGRAMS	NEWNESS	NIAISERIES
NEREID	NESTLINGS	NEUROLOGIES	NEWNESSES	NIB
NEREIDES	NESTS	NEUROLOGY	NEWS	NIBBED
NEREIDS	NET	NEUROMA	NEWSAGENT	NIBBING
NERINE	NETBALL	NEUROMAS	NEWSAGENTS	NIBBLE
NERINES	NETBALLS	NEUROMATA	NEWSBOY	NIBBLED
NERITE	NETE	NEURON	NEWSBOYS	NIBBLER
NERITES	NETES	NEURONAL	NEWSCAST	NIBBLERS
NERITIC	NETFUL	NEURONE	NEWSCASTS	NIBBLES
NERK	NETFULS	NEURONES	NEWSED	NIBBLING
NERKA	NETHELESS	NEURONIC	NEWSES	NIBBLINGS
NERKAS	NETHER	NEURONS	NEWSFLASH	NIBLICK
NERKS	NETS	NEUROPATH	NEWSFLASHES	NIBLICKS
NEROLI	NETSUKE	NEUROPATHS	NEWSGIRL	NIBS
NEROLIS	NETSUKES	NEUROPIL	NEWSGIRLS	NICAD
NERVAL	NETT	NEUROPILS	NEWSHAWK	NICADS
NERVATE	NETTED	NEUROSES	NEWSHAWKS	NICCOLITE
NERVATION	NETTIER	NEUROSIS	NEWSHOUND	NICCOLITES
NERVATIONS	NETTIEST	NEUROTIC	NEWSHOUNDS	NICE
NERVATURE	NETTING	NEUROTICS	NEWSIER	NICEISH
NERVATURES	NETTINGS	NEUROTOMIES	NEWSIES	NICELY
NERVE	NETTLE	NEUROTOMY	NEWSIEST	NICENESS
NERVED	NETTLED	NEUSTON	NEWSINESS	NICENESSES
NERVELESS	NETTLES	NEUSTONS	NEWSINESSES	NICER
NERVELET	NETTLIER	NEUTER	NEWSING	NICEST
NERVELETS	NETTLIEST	NEUTERED	NEWSLESS	NICETIES
NERVER	NETTLING	NEUTERING	NEWSMAN	NICETY
NERVERS	NETTLY	NEUTERS	NEWSMEN	NICHE
NERVES	NETTS	NEUTRAL	NEWSPAPER	NICHED
NERVIER	NETTY	NEUTRALLY	NEWSPAPERS	NICHER
NERVIEST	NETWORK	NEUTRALS	NEWSPEAK	NICHERED
NERVILY	NETWORKED	NEUTRETTO	NEWSPEAKS	NICHERING
NERVINE	NETWORKER	NEUTRETTOS	NEWSPRINT	NICHERS
NERVINES	NETWORKERS	NEUTRINO	NEWSPRINTS	NICHES
NERVINESS	NETWORKING	NEUTRINOS	NEWSREEL	NICHING
NERVINESSES	NETWORKINGS	NEUTRON	NEWSREELS	NICISH
NERVING	NETWORKS	NEUTRONS	NEWSROOM	NICK
NERVOUS	NEUK	NEVE	NEWSROOMS	NICKAR
NERVOUSLY	NEUKS	NEVEL	NEWSTRADE	NICKARS
NERVULAR	NEUM	NEVELLED	NEWSTRADES	NICKED
NERVULE	NEUME	NEVELLING	NEWSWIRE	NICKEL
NERVULES	NEUMES	NEVELS	NEWSWIRES	NICKELED
NERVURE	NEUMS	NEVER	NEWSWOMAN	NICKELIC
NERVURES	NEURAL	NEVERMORE	NEWSWOMEN	NICKELINE
NERVY	NEURALGIA	NEVES	NEWSY	NICKELINES
NESCIENCE	NEURALGIAS	NEVI	NEWT	NICKELING
NESCIENCES	NEURALGIC	NEVUS	NEWTON	NICKELISE
NESCIENT	NEURALLY	NEW	NEWTONS	NICKELISED
NESH	NEURATION	NEWBORN	NEWTS	NICKELISES
NESHER	NEURATIONS	NEWCOME	NEXT	NICKELISING
NESHEST	NEURILITIES	NEWCOMER	NEXTLY	NICKELIZE
NESHNESS	NEURILITY	NEWCOMERS	NEXTNESS	NICKELIZED
NESHNESSES	NEURINE	NEWED	NEXTNESSES	NICKELIZES
NESS	NEURINES	NEWEL	NEXTS	NICKELIZING
NESSES	NEURISM	NEWELL	NEXUS	NICKELLED
NEST	NEURISMS	NEWELLED	NGAIO	NICKELLING
NESTED	NEURITE	NEWELLS	NGAIOS	NICKELOUS
NESTER	NEURITES	NEWELS	NGANA	NICKELS
NESTERS	NEURITIC	NEWER	NGANAS	NICKER

The Chambers Dictionary is the authority for many longer words; see *OSW* Introduction, page xii.

NICKERED	NIED	NIGGLY	NIKAU	NINON
NICKERING	NIEF	NIGH	NIKAUS	NINONS
NICKERS	NIEFS	NIGHED	NIL	NINTH
NICKING	NIELLATED	NIGHEST	NILGAI	NINTHLY
NICKNAME	NIELLI	NIGHING	NILGAIS	NINTHS
NICKNAMED	NIELLIST	NIGHLY	NILGAU	NIOBATE
NICKNAMES	NIELLISTS	NIGHNESS	NILGAUS	NIOBATES
NICKNAMING	NIELLO	NIGHNESSES	NILL	NIOBIC
NICKPOINT	NIELLOED	NIGHS	NILLED	NIOBITE
NICKPOINTS	NIELLOING	NIGHT	NILLING	NIOBITES
NICKS	NIELLOS	NIGHTBIRD	NILLS	NIOBIUM
NICKSTICK	NIES	NIGHTBIRDS	NILS	NIOBIUMS
NICKSTICKS	NIEVE	NIGHTCAP	NIM	NIOBOUS
NICKUM	NIEVEFUL	NIGHTCAPS	NIMB	NIP
NICKUMS	NIEVEFULS	NIGHTCLUB	NIMBED	NIPA
NICOL	NIEVES	NIGHTCLUBS	NIMBI	NIPAS
NICOLS	NIFE	NIGHTED	NIMBLE	NIPCHEESE
NICOMPOOP	NIFES	NIGHTFALL	NIMBLER	NIPCHEESES
NICOMPOOPS	NIFF	NIGHTFALLS	NIMBLESSE	NIPPED
NICOTIAN	NIFFED	NIGHTFIRE	NIMBLESSES	NIPPER
NICOTIANA	NIFFER	NIGHTFIRES	NIMBLEST	NIPPERED
NICOTIANAS	NIFFERED	NIGHTGEAR	NIMBLY	NIPPERING
NICOTIANS	NIFFERING	NIGHTGEARS	NIMBS	NIPPERKIN
NICOTINE	NIFFERS	NIGHTGOWN	NIMBUS	NIPPERKINS
NICOTINED	NIFFIER	NIGHTGOWNS	NIMBUSED	NIPPERS
NICOTINES	NIFFIEST	NIGHTHAWK	NIMBUSES	NIPPIER
NICOTINIC	NIFFING	NIGHTHAWKS	NIMBYISM	NIPPIEST
NICTATE	NIFFNAFF	NIGHTIE	NIMBYISMS	NIPPILY
NICTATED	NIFFNAFFED	NIGHTIES	NIMIETIES	NIPPINESS
NICTATES	NIFFNAFFING	NIGHTJAR	NIMIETY	NIPPINESSES
NICTATING	NIFFNAFFS	NIGHTJARS	NIMIOUS	NIPPING
NICTATION	NIFFS	NIGHTLESS	NIMMED	NIPPINGLY
NICTATIONS	NIFFY	NIGHTLIFE	NIMMER	NIPPLE
NICTITATE	NIFTIER	NIGHTLIFES	NIMMERS	NIPPLED
NICTITATED	NIFTIEST	NIGHTLONG	NIMMING	NIPPLES
NICTITATES	NIFTILY	NIGHTLY	NIMONIC	NIPPLING
NICTITATING	NIFTINESS	NIGHTMARE	NIMS	NIPPY
NID	NIFTINESSES	NIGHTMARES	NINCOM	NIPS
NIDAL	NIFTY	NIGHTMARY	NINCOMS	NIPTER
NIDAMENTA	NIGELLA	NIGHTS	NINCUM	NIPTERS
NIDATION	NIGELLAS	NIGHTSPOT	NINCUMS	NIRAMIAI
NIDATIONS	NIGER	NIGHTSPOTS	NINE	NIRAMIAIS
NIDDERING	NIGERS	NIGHTWARD	NINEFOLD	NIRL
NIDDERINGS	NIGGARD	NIGHTWEAR	NINEHOLES	NIRLED
NIDE	NIGGARDED	NIGHTWEARS	NINEPENCE	NIRLIE
NIDERING	NIGGARDING	NIGHTY	NINEPENCES	NIRLIER
NIDERINGS	NIGGARDLY	NIGRICANT	NINEPENNIES	NIRLIEST
NIDERLING	NIGGARDS	NIGRIFIED	NINEPENNY	NIRLING
NIDERLINGS	NIGGER	NIGRIFIES	NINEPIN	NIRLIT
NIDES	NIGGERDOM	NIGRIFY	NINEPINS	NIRLS
NIDGET	NIGGERDOMS	NIGRIFYING	NINES	NIRLY
NIDGETS	NIGGERED	NIGRITUDE	NINESCORE	NIRVANA
NIDI	NIGGERING	NIGRITUDES	NINESCORES	NIRVANAS
NIDIFIED	NIGGERISH	NIGROSIN	NINETEEN	NIS
NIDIFIES	NIGGERISM	NIGROSINE	NINETEENS	NISBERRIES
NIDIFY	NIGGERISMS	NIGROSINES	NINETIES	NISBERRY
NIDIFYING	NIGGERS	NIGROSINS	NINETIETH	NISEI
NIDING	NIGGERY	NIHIL	NINETIETHS	NISEIS
NIDINGS	NIGGLE	NIHILISM	NINETY	NISI
NIDOR	NIGGLED	NIHILISMS	NINJA	NISSE
NIDOROUS	NIGGLER	NIHILIST	NINJAS	NISSES
NIDORS	NIGGLERS	NIHILISTS	NINJITSU	NISUS
NIDS	NIGGLES	NIHILITIES	NINJITSUS	NIT
NIDUS	NIGGLIER	NIHILITY	NINJUTSU	NITE
NIE	NIGGLIEST	NIHILS	NINJUTSUS	NITER
NIECE	NIGGLING	NIHONGA	NINNIES	NITERIE
NIECES	NIGGLINGS	NIHONGAS	NINNY	NITERIES

The Chambers Dictionary is the authority for many longer words; see *OSW* Introduction, page xii.

NITERS	NOBBLE	NODALISED	NOISE	NOMISMS
NITERY	NOBBLED	NODALISES	NOISED	NOMISTIC
NITES	NOBBLER	NODALISING	NOISEFUL	NOMOCRACIES
NITHING	NOBBLERS	NODALITIES	NOISELESS	NOMOCRACY
NITHINGS	NOBBLES	NODALITY	NOISES	NOMOGENIES
NITID	NOBBLING	NODALIZE	NOISETTE	NOMOGENY
NITON	NOBBUT	NODALIZED	NOISETTES	NOMOGRAM
NITONS	NOBBY	NODALIZES	NOISIER	NOMOGRAMS
NITRATE	NOBELIUM	NODALIZING	NOISIEST	NOMOGRAPH
NITRATED	NOBELIUMS	NODALLY	NOISILY	NOMOGRAPHS
NITRATES	NOBILESSE	NODATED	NOISINESS	NOMOI
NITRATINE	NOBILESSES	NODATION	NOISINESSES	NOMOLOGIES
NITRATINES	NOBILIARY	NODATIONS	NOISING	NOMOLOGY
NITRATING	NOBILITIES	NODDED	NOISOME	NOMOS
NITRATION	NOBILITY	NODDER	NOISOMELY	NOMOTHETE
NITRATIONS	NOBLE	NODDERS	NOISY	NOMOTHETES
NITRE	NOBLEMAN	NODDIES	NOLE	NOMS
NITRES	NOBLEMEN	NODDING	NOLES	NON
NITRIC	NOBLENESS	NODDINGLY	NOLITION	NONAGE
NITRIDE	NOBLENESSES	NODDINGS	NOLITIONS	NONAGED
NITRIDED	NOBLER	NODDLE	NOLL	NONAGES
NITRIDES	NOBLES	NODDLED	NOLLS	NONAGON
NITRIDING	NOBLESSE	NODDLES	NOM	NONAGONAL
NITRIDINGS	NOBLESSES	NODDLING	NOMA	NONAGONS
NITRIFIED	NOBLEST	NODDY	NOMAD	NONANE
NITRIFIES	NOBLY	NODE	NOMADE	NONANES
NITRIFY	NOBODIES	NODES	NOMADES	NONARY
NITRIFYING	NOBODY	NODI	NOMADIC	NONCE
NITRILE	NOBS	NODICAL	NOMADIES	NONCES
NITRILES	NOCAKE	NODOSE	NOMADISE	NONE
NITRITE	NOCAKES	NODOSITIES	NOMADISED	NONENTITIES
NITRITES	NOCENT	NODOSITY	NOMADISES	NONENTITY
NITROGEN	NOCENTLY	NODOUS	NOMADISING	NONES
NITROGENS	NOCENTS	NODS	NOMADISM	NONESUCH
NITROSO	NOCHEL	NODULAR	NOMADISMS	NONESUCHES
NITROSYL	NOCHELLED	NODULATED	NOMADIZE	NONET
NITROUS	NOCHELLING	NODULE	NOMADIZED	NONETS
NITROXYL	NOCHELS	NODULED	NOMADIZES	NONETTE
NITROXYLS	NOCK	NODULES	NOMADIZING	NONETTES
NITRY	NOCKED	NODULOSE	NOMADS	NONETTI
NITRYL	NOCKET	NODULOUS	NOMADY	NONETTO
NITRYLS	NOCKETS	NODUS	NOMARCH	NONETTOS
NITS	NOCKING	NOEL	NOMARCHIES	NONG
NITTIER	NOCKS	NOELS	NOMARCHS	NONGS
NITTIEST	NOCTILIO	NOES	NOMARCHY	NONILLION
NITTY	NOCTILIOS	NOESES	NOMAS	NONILLIONS
NITWIT	NOCTILUCA	NOESIS	NOMBLES	NONJURING
NITWITS	NOCTILUCAE	NOETIC	NOMBRIL	NONJUROR
NITWITTED	NOCTUA	NOG	NOMBRILS	NONJURORS
NIVAL	NOCTUARIES	NOGAKU	NOME	NONNIES
NIVEOUS	NOCTUARY	NOGG	NOMEN	NONNY
NIX	NOCTUAS	NOGGED	NOMES	NONPAREIL
NIXED	NOCTUID	NOGGIN	NOMIC	NONPAREILS
NIXES	NOCTUIDS	NOGGING	NOMINA	NONPAROUS
NIXIE	NOCTULE	NOGGINGS	NOMINABLE	NONPLUS
NIXIES	NOCTULES	NOGGINS	NOMINAL	NONPLUSED
NIXING	NOCTURN	NOGGS	NOMINALLY	NONPLUSES
NIXY	NOCTURNAL	NOGS	NOMINALS	NONPLUSING
NIZAM	NOCTURNALS	NOH	NOMINATE	NONPLUSSED
NIZAMS	NOCTURNE	NOHOW	NOMINATED	NONPLUSSES
NO	NOCTURNES	NOHOWISH	NOMINATES	NONPLUSSING
NOB	NOCTURNS	NOIL	NOMINATING	NONPOLAR
NOBBIER	NOCUOUS	NOILS	NOMINATOR	NONSENSE
NOBBIEST	NOCUOUSLY	NOINT	NOMINATORS	NONSENSES
NOBBILY	NOD	NOINTED	NOMINEE	NONSUCH
NOBBINESS	NODAL	NOINTING	NOMINEES	NONSUCHES
NOBBINESSES	NODALISE	NOINTS	NOMISM	NONSUIT

The Chambers Dictionary is the authority for many longer words; see *OSW* Introduction, page xii.

NONSUITED	NORMALISES	NOSES	NOTCHBACKS	NOULDE
NONSUITING	NORMALISING	NOSEY	NOTCHED	NOULE
NONSUITS	NORMALITIES	NOSEYS	NOTCHEL	NOULES
NONUPLE	NORMALITY	NOSH	NOTCHELLED	NOULS
NONUPLET	NORMALIZE	NOSHED	NOTCHELLING	NOUMENA
NONUPLETS	NORMALIZED	NOSHER	NOTCHELS	NOUMENAL
NOODLE	NORMALIZES	NOSHERIES	NOTCHER	NOUMENON
NOODLED	NORMALIZING	NOSHERS	NOTCHERS	NOUN
NOODLEDOM	NORMALLY	NOSHERY	NOTCHES	NOUNAL
NOODLEDOMS	NORMALS	NOSHES	NOTCHIER	NOUNIER
NOODLES	NORMAN	NOSHING	NOTCHIEST	NOUNIEST
NOODLING	NORMANS	NOSIER	NOTCHING	NOUNS
NOOK	NORMAS	NOSIES	NOTCHINGS	NOUNY
NOOKIE	NORMATIVE	NOSIEST	NOTCHY	NOUP
NOOKIER	NORMS	NOSILY	NOTE	NOUPS
NOOKIES	NORSEL	NOSINESS	NOTEBOOK	NOURICE
NOOKIEST	NORSELLED	NOSINESSES	NOTEBOOKS	NOURICES
NOOKS	NORSELLER	NOSING	NOTECASE	NOURISH
NOOKY	NORSELLERS	NOSINGS	NOTECASES	NOURISHED
NOOLOGIES	NORSELLING	NOSOLOGIES	NOTED	NOURISHER
NOOLOGY	NORSELS	NOSOLOGY	NOTEDLY	NOURISHERS
NOOMETRIES	NORTENA	NOSTALGIA	NOTEDNESS	NOURISHES
NOOMETRY	NORTENAS	NOSTALGIAS	NOTEDNESSES	NOURISHING
NOON	NORTENO	NOSTALGIC	NOTELESS	NOURITURE
NOONDAY	NORTENOS	NOSTOC	NOTELET	NOURITURES
NOONDAYS	NORTH	NOSTOCS	NOTELETS	NOURSLE
NOONED	NORTHED	NOSTOI	NOTEPAPER	NOURSLED
NOONER	NORTHER	NOSTOLOGIES	NOTEPAPERS	NOURSLES
NOONERS	NORTHERED	NOSTOLOGY	NOTER	NOURSLING
NOONING	NORTHERING	NOSTOS	NOTERS	NOUS
NOONINGS	NORTHERLIES	NOSTRIL	NOTES	NOUSELL
NOONS	NORTHERLY	NOSTRILS	NOTHING	NOUSELLED
NOONTIDE	NORTHERN	NOSTRUM	NOTHINGS	NOUSELLING
NOONTIDES	NORTHERNS	NOSTRUMS	NOTICE	NOUSELLS
NOONTIME	NORTHERS	NOSY	NOTICED	NOUSES
NOONTIMES	NORTHING	NOT	NOTICES	NOUSLE
NOOP	NORTHINGS	NOTA	NOTICING	NOUSLED
NOOPS	NORTHLAND	NOTABILIA	NOTIFIED	NOUSLES
NOOSE	NORTHLANDS	NOTABLE	NOTIFIER	NOUSLING
NOOSED	NORTHMOST	NOTABLES	NOTIFIERS	NOUT
NOOSES	NORTHS	NOTABLY	NOTIFIES	NOUVEAU
NOOSING	NORTHWARD	NOTAEUM	NOTIFY	NOUVELLE
NOOSPHERE	NORTHWARDS	NOTAEUMS	NOTIFYING	NOUVELLES
NOOSPHERES	NORWARD	NOTAL	NOTING	NOVA
NOPAL	NORWARDS	NOTANDA	NOTION	NOVAE
NOPALS	NOS	NOTANDUM	NOTIONAL	NOVALIA
NOPE	NOSE	NOTAPHILIES	NOTIONIST	NOVAS
NOR	NOSEAN	NOTAPHILY	NOTIONISTS	NOVATION
NORI	NOSEANS	NOTARIAL	NOTIONS	NOVATIONS
NORIA	NOSEBAG	NOTARIES	NOTITIA	NOVEL
NORIAS	NOSEBAGS	NOTARISE	NOTITIAS	NOVELDOM
NORIMON	NOSEBAND	NOTARISED	NOTOCHORD	NOVELDOMS
NORIMONS	NOSEBANDS	NOTARISES	NOTOCHORDS	NOVELESE
NORIS	NOSEBLEED	NOTARISING	NOTORIETIES	NOVELESES
NORITE	NOSEBLEEDS	NOTARIZE	NOTORIETY	NOVELETTE
NORITES	NOSED	NOTARIZED	NOTORIOUS	NOVELETTES
NORK	NOSEDIVE	NOTARIZES	NOTORNIS	NOVELISE
NORKS	NOSEDIVED	NOTARIZING	NOTORNISES	NOVELISED
NORLAND	NOSEDIVES	NOTARY	NOTOUR	NOVELISER
NORLANDS	NOSEDIVING	NOTATE	NOTT	NOVELISERS
NORM	NOSEGAY	NOTATED	NOTUM	NOVELISES
NORMA	NOSEGAYS	NOTATES	NOUGAT	NOVELISH
NORMAL	NOSELESS	NOTATING	NOUGATS	NOVELISING
NORMALCIES	NOSELITE	NOTATION	NOUGHT	NOVELISM
NORMALCY	NOSELITES	NOTATIONS	NOUGHTS	NOVELISMS
NORMALISE	NOSER	NOTCH	NOUL	NOVELIST
NORMALISED	NOSERS	NOTCHBACK	NOULD	NOVELISTS

The Chambers Dictionary is the authority for many longer words; see *OSW* Introduction, page xii.

NOVELIZE	NOYING	NUCLEUS	NULLIPORE	NUNATAKS
NOVELIZED	NOYOUS	NUCLIDE	NULLIPORES	NUNCHAKU
NOVELIZER	NOYS	NUCLIDES	NULLITIES	NUNCHAKUS
NOVELIZERS	NOYSOME	NUCULE	NULLITY	NUNCHEON
NOVELIZES	NOZZER	NUCULES	NULLNESS	NUNCHEONS
NOVELIZING	NOZZERS	NUDATION	NULLNESSES	NUNCIO
NOVELLA	NOZZLE	NUDATIONS	NULLS	NUNCIOS
NOVELLAE	NOZZLES	NUDE	NUMB	NUNCLE
NOVELLAS	NTH	NUDELY	NUMBAT	NUNCLES
NOVELLE	NU	NUDENESS	NUMBATS	NUNCUPATE
NOVELS	NUANCE	NUDENESSES	NUMBED	NUNCUPATED
NOVELTIES	NUANCED	NUDER	NUMBER	NUNCUPATES
NOVELTY	NUANCES	NUDES	NUMBERED	NUNCUPATING
NOVENA	NUANCING	NUDEST	NUMBERER	NUNDINAL
NOVENARIES	NUB	NUDGE	NUMBERERS	NUNDINE
NOVENARY	NUBBED	NUDGED	NUMBERING	NUNDINES
NOVENAS	NUBBIER	NUDGER	NUMBERS	NUNHOOD
NOVENNIAL	NUBBIEST	NUDGERS	NUMBEST	NUNHOODS
NOVERCAL	NUBBIN	NUDGES	NUMBING	NUNNATION
NOVERINT	NUBBING	NUDGING	NUMBINGLY	NUNNATIONS
NOVERINTS	NUBBINS	NUDICAUL	NUMBLES	NUNNERIES
NOVICE	NUBBLE	NUDIE	NUMBLY	NUNNERY
NOVICES	NUBBLED	NUDIES	NUMBNESS	NUNNISH
NOVICIATE	NUBBLES	NUDISM	NUMBNESSES	NUNS
NOVICIATES	NUBBLIER	NUDISMS	NUMBS	NUNSHIP
NOVITIATE	NUBBLIEST	NUDIST	NUMBSKULL	NUNSHIPS
NOVITIATES	NUBBLING	NUDISTS	NUMBSKULLS	NUPTIAL
NOVITIES	NUBBLY	NUDITIES	NUMDAH	NUPTIALS
NOVITY	NUBBY	NUDITY	NUMDAHS	NUR
NOVODAMUS	NUBECULA	NUDNIK	NUMEN	NURAGHE
NOVODAMUSES	NUBECULAE	NUDNIKS	NUMERABLE	NURAGHI
NOVUM	NUBIA	NUFF	NUMERABLY	NURAGHIC
NOVUMS	NUBIAS	NUFFIN	NUMERACIES	NURD
NOW	NUBIFORM	NUFFINS	NUMERACY	NURDLE
NOWADAYS	NUBILE	NUFFS	NUMERAIRE	NURDLED
NOWAY	NUBILITIES	NUGAE	NUMERAIRES	NURDLES
NOWAYS	NUBILITY	NUGATORY	NUMERAL	NURDLING
NOWED	NUBILOUS	NUGGAR	NUMERALLY	NURDS
NOWHENCE	NUBS	NUGGARS	NUMERALS	NURHAG
NOWHERE	NUCELLAR	NUGGET	NUMERARY	NURHAGS
NOWHERES	NUCELLI	NUGGETS	NUMERATE	NURL
NOWHITHER	NUCELLUS	NUGGETY	NUMERATED	NURLED
NOWISE	NUCHA	NUISANCE	NUMERATES	NURLING
NOWL	NUCHAE	NUISANCER	NUMERATING	NURLS
NOWLS	NUCHAL	NUISANCERS	NUMERATOR	NURR
NOWN	NUCLEAL	NUISANCES	NUMERATORS	NURRS
NOWNESS	NUCLEAR	NUKE	NUMERIC	NURS
NOWNESSES	NUCLEASE	NUKED	NUMERICAL	NURSE
NOWS	NUCLEASES	NUKES	NUMEROUS	NURSED
NOWT	NUCLEATE	NUKING	NUMINA	NURSELIKE
NOWTS	NUCLEATED	NULL	NUMINOUS	NURSELING
NOWY	NUCLEATES	NULLA	NUMINOUSES	NURSELINGS
NOX	NUCLEATING	NULLAH	NUMMARY	NURSEMAID
NOXAL	NUCLEATOR	NULLAHS	NUMMULAR	NURSEMAIDED
NOXES	NUCLEATORS	NULLAS	NUMMULARY	NURSEMAIDING
NOXIOUS	NUCLEI	NULLED	NUMMULINE	NURSEMAIDS
NOXIOUSLY	NUCLEIDE	NULLIFIED	NUMMULITE	NURSER
NOY	NUCLEIDES	NULLIFIER	NUMMULITES	NURSERIES
NOYADE	NUCLEIN	NULLIFIERS	NUMNAH	NURSERS
NOYADES	NUCLEINS	NULLIFIES	NUMNAHS	NURSERY
NOYANCE	NUCLEOLAR	NULLIFY	NUMPTIES	NURSES
NOYANCES	NUCLEOLE	NULLIFYING	NUMPTY	NURSING
NOYAU	NUCLEOLES	NULLING	NUMSKULL	NURSINGS
NOYAUS	NUCLEOLI	NULLINGS	NUMSKULLS	NURSLE
NOYED	NUCLEOLUS	NULLIPARA	NUN	NURSLED
NOYES	NUCLEON	NULLIPARAE	NUNATAK	NURSLES
NOYESES	NUCLEONS	NULLIPARAS	NUNATAKER	NURSLING

The Chambers Dictionary is the authority for many longer words; see *OSW* Introduction, page xii.

NURSLINGS	NUTHATCH	NUTRITIVE	NY	NYMPHAEUM
NURTURAL	NUTHATCHES	NUTRITIVES	NYAFF	NYMPHAEUMS
NURTURANT	NUTHOUSE	NUTS	NYAFFED	NYMPHAL
NURTURE	NUTHOUSES	NUTSHELL	NYAFFING	NYMPHALID
NURTURED	NUTJOBBER	NUTSHELLS	NYAFFS	NYMPHALIDS
NURTURER	NUTJOBBERS	NUTTED	NYALA	NYMPHEAN
NURTURERS	NUTLET	NUTTER	NYALAS	NYMPHET
NURTURES	NUTLETS	NUTTERIES	NYANZA	NYMPHETS
NURTURING	NUTLIKE	NUTTERS	NYANZAS	NYMPHIC
NUS	NUTMEAL	NUTTERY	NYAS	NYMPHICAL
NUT	NUTMEALS	NUTTIER	NYASES	NYMPHISH
NUTANT	NUTMEG	NUTTIEST	NYBBLE	NYMPHLIKE
NUTARIAN	NUTMEGGED	NUTTILY	NYBBLES	NYMPHLY
NUTARIANS	NUTMEGGING	NUTTINESS	NYCTALOPES	NYMPHO
NUTATE	NUTMEGGY	NUTTINESSES	NYCTALOPS	NYMPHOS
NUTATED	NUTMEGS	NUTTING	NYE	NYMPHS
NUTATES	NUTPECKER	NUTTINGS	NYED	NYS
NUTATING	NUTPECKERS	NUTTY	NYES	NYSSA
NUTATION	NUTRIA	NUTWOOD	NYING	NYSSAS
NUTATIONS	NUTRIAS	NUTWOODS	NYLGHAU	NYSTAGMIC
NUTBUTTER	NUTRIENT	NUZZER	NYLGHAUS	NYSTAGMUS
NUTBUTTERS	NUTRIENTS	NUZZERS	NYLON	NYSTAGMUSES
NUTCASE	NUTRIMENT	NUZZLE	NYLONS	NYSTATIN
NUTCASES	NUTRIMENTS	NUZZLED	NYMPH	NYSTATINS
NUTGALL	NUTRITION	NUZZLES	NYMPHAE	
NUTGALLS	NUTRITIONS	NUZZLING	NYMPHAEA	

O

OAF	OBBLIGATOS	OBFUSCATED	OBLIGE	OBSCURITIES
OAFISH	OBCONIC	OBFUSCATES	OBLIGED	OBSCURITY
OAFS	OBCONICAL	OBFUSCATING	OBLIGEE	OBSECRATE
OAK	OBCORDATE	OBI	OBLIGEES	OBSECRATED
OAKEN	OBDURACIES	OBIA	OBLIGES	OBSECRATES
OAKENSHAW	OBDURACY	OBIAS	OBLIGING	OBSECRATING
OAKENSHAWS	OBDURATE	OBIED	OBLIGOR	OBSEQUENT
OAKER	OBDURATED	OBIING	OBLIGORS	OBSEQUIAL
OAKERS	OBDURATES	OBIISM	OBLIQUE	OBSEQUIE
OAKIER	OBDURATING	OBIISMS	OBLIQUED	OBSEQUIES
OAKIEST	OBDURE	OBIIT	OBLIQUELY	OBSEQUY
OAKLEAF	OBDURED	OBIS	OBLIQUER	OBSERVANT
OAKLEAVES	OBDURES	OBIT	OBLIQUES	OBSERVANTS
OAKLING	OBDURING	OBITAL	OBLIQUEST	OBSERVE
OAKLINGS	OBEAH	OBITER	OBLIQUID	OBSERVED
OAKS	OBEAHED	OBITS	OBLIQUING	OBSERVER
OAKUM	OBEAHING	OBITUAL	OBLIQUITIES	OBSERVERS
OAKUMS	OBEAHISM	OBITUARIES	OBLIQUITY	OBSERVES
OAKY	OBEAHISMS	OBITUARY	OBLIVION	OBSERVING
OAR	OBEAHS	OBJECT	OBLIVIONS	OBSESS
OARAGE	OBECHE	OBJECTED	OBLIVIOUS	OBSESSED
OARAGES	OBECHES	OBJECTIFIED	OBLONG	OBSESSES
OARED	OBEDIENCE	OBJECTIFIES	OBLONGS	OBSESSING
OARIER	OBEDIENCES	OBJECTIFY	OBLOQUIES	OBSESSION
OARIEST	OBEDIENT	OBJECTIFYING	OBLOQUY	OBSESSIONS
OARING	OBEISANCE	OBJECTING	OBNOXIOUS	OBSESSIVE
OARLESS	OBEISANCES	OBJECTION	OBO	OBSIDIAN
OARS	OBEISANT	OBJECTIONS	OBOE	OBSIDIANS
OARSMAN	OBEISM	OBJECTIVE	OBOES	OBSIGN
OARSMEN	OBEISMS	OBJECTIVES	OBOIST	OBSIGNATE
OARSWOMAN	OBELI	OBJECTOR	OBOISTS	OBSIGNATED
OARSWOMEN	OBELION	OBJECTORS	OBOL	OBSIGNATES
OARWEED	OBELIONS	OBJECTS	OBOLARY	OBSIGNATING
OARWEEDS	OBELISCAL	OBJET	OBOLI	OBSIGNED
OARY	OBELISE	OBJETS	OBOLS	OBSIGNING
OASES	OBELISED	OBJURE	OBOLUS	OBSIGNS
OASIS	OBELISES	OBJURED	OBOS	OBSOLESCE
OAST	OBELISING	OBJURES	OBOVATE	OBSOLESCED
OASTS	OBELISK	OBJURGATE	OBOVATELY	OBSOLESCES
OAT	OBELISKS	OBJURGATED	OBOVOID	OBSOLESCING
OATCAKE	OBELIZE	OBJURGATES	OBREPTION	OBSOLETE
OATCAKES	OBELIZED	OBJURGATING	OBREPTIONS	OBSTACLE
OATEN	OBELIZES	OBJURING	OBS	OBSTACLES
OATER	OBELIZING	OBLAST	OBSCENE	OBSTETRIC
OATERS	OBELUS	OBLASTS	OBSCENELY	OBSTETRICS
OATH	OBESE	OBLATE	OBSCENER	OBSTINACIES
OATHABLE	OBESENESS	OBLATES	OBSCENEST	OBSTINACY
OATHS	OBESENESSES	OBLATION	OBSCENITIES	OBSTINATE
OATMEAL	OBESER	OBLATIONS	OBSCENITY	OBSTRUCT
OATMEALS	OBESEST	OBLATORY	OBSCURANT	OBSTRUCTED
OATS	OBESITIES	OBLIGANT	OBSCURANTS	OBSTRUCTING
OAVES	OBESITY	OBLIGANTS	OBSCURE	OBSTRUCTS
OB	OBEY	OBLIGATE	OBSCURED	OBSTRUENT
OBA	OBEYED	OBLIGATED	OBSCURELY	OBSTRUENTS
OBANG	OBEYER	OBLIGATES	OBSCURER	OBTAIN
OBANGS	OBEYERS	OBLIGATI	OBSCURERS	OBTAINED
OBAS	OBEYING	OBLIGATING	OBSCURES	OBTAINER
OBBLIGATI	OBEYS	OBLIGATO	OBSCUREST	OBTAINERS
OBBLIGATO	OBFUSCATE	OBLIGATOS	OBSCURING	OBTAINING

The Chambers Dictionary is the authority for many longer words; see *OSW* Introduction, page xii.

OBTAINS	OBVIOUSLY	OCCURS	OCTANES	OCULATED
OBTECT	OBVOLUTE	OCEAN	OCTANT	OCULI
OBTECTED	OBVOLUTED	OCEANAUT	OCTANTAL	OCULIST
OBTEMPER	OBVOLVENT	OCEANAUTS	OCTANTS	OCULISTS
OBTEMPERED	OCA	OCEANIC	OCTAPLA	OCULUS
OBTEMPERING	OCARINA	OCEANID	OCTAPLAS	OD
OBTEMPERS	OCARINAS	OCEANIDES	OCTAPLOID	ODA
OBTEND	OCAS	OCEANIDS	OCTAPLOIDS	ODAL
OBTENDED	OCCAM	OCEANS	OCTAPODIC	ODALIQUE
OBTENDING	OCCAMIES	OCELLAR	OCTAPODIES	ODALIQUES
OBTENDS	OCCAMS	OCELLATE	OCTAPODY	ODALISK
OBTENTION	OCCAMY	OCELLATED	OCTAROON	ODALISKS
OBTENTIONS	OCCASION	OCELLI	OCTAROONS	ODALISQUE
OBTEST	OCCASIONED	OCELLUS	OCTAS	ODALISQUES
OBTESTED	OCCASIONING	OCELOID	OCTASTICH	ODALLER
OBTESTING	OCCASIONS	OCELOT	OCTASTICHS	ODALLERS
OBTESTS	OCCIDENT	OCELOTS	OCTASTYLE	ODALS
OBTRUDE	OCCIDENTS	OCH	OCTASTYLES	ODAS
OBTRUDED	OCCIPITAL	OCHE	OCTAVAL	ODD
OBTRUDER	OCCIPITALS	OCHER	OCTAVE	ODDBALL
OBTRUDERS	OCCIPUT	OCHERED	OCTAVES	ODDBALLS
OBTRUDES	OCCIPUTS	OCHERING	OCTAVO	ODDER
OBTRUDING	OCCLUDE	OCHEROUS	OCTAVOS	ODDEST
OBTRUDINGS	OCCLUDED	OCHERS	OCTENNIAL	ODDISH
OBTRUSION	OCCLUDENT	OCHERY	OCTET	ODDITIES
OBTRUSIONS	OCCLUDENTS	OCHES	OCTETS	ODDITY
OBTRUSIVE	OCCLUDER	OCHIDORE	OCTETT	ODDLY
OBTUND	OCCLUDERS	OCHIDORES	OCTETTE	ODDMENT
OBTUNDED	OCCLUDES	OCHLOCRAT	OCTETTES	ODDMENTS
OBTUNDENT	OCCLUDING	OCHLOCRATS	OCTETTS	ODDNESS
OBTUNDENTS	OCCLUSAL	OCHONE	OCTILLION	ODDNESSES
OBTUNDING	OCCLUSION	OCHRE	OCTILLIONS	ODDS
OBTUNDS	OCCLUSIONS	OCHREA	OCTOFID	ODDSMAN
OBTURATE	OCCLUSIVE	OCHREAE	OCTOHEDRA	ODDSMEN
OBTURATED	OCCLUSIVES	OCHREATE	OCTONARIES	ODE
OBTURATES	OCCLUSOR	OCHRED	OCTONARII	ODEA
OBTURATING	OCCLUSORS	OCHREOUS	OCTONARY	ODEON
OBTURATOR	OCCULT	OCHRES	OCTOPI	ODEONS
OBTURATORS	OCCULTED	OCHREY	OCTOPLOID	ODES
OBTUSE	OCCULTING	OCHRING	OCTOPLOIDS	ODEUM
OBTUSELY	OCCULTISM	OCHROID	OCTOPOD	ODEUMS
OBTUSER	OCCULTISMS	OCHROUS	OCTOPODES	ODIC
OBTUSEST	OCCULTIST	OCHRY	OCTOPODS	ODIOUS
OBTUSITIES	OCCULTISTS	OCKER	OCTOPUS	ODIOUSLY
OBTUSITY	OCCULTLY	OCKERISM	OCTOPUSES	ODISM
OBUMBRATE	OCCULTS	OCKERISMS	OCTOPUSH	ODISMS
OBUMBRATED	OCCUPANCE	OCKERS	OCTOPUSHES	ODIST
OBUMBRATES	OCCUPANCES	OCOTILLO	OCTOROON	ODISTS
OBUMBRATING	OCCUPANCIES	OCOTILLOS	OCTOROONS	ODIUM
OBVENTION	OCCUPANCY	OCREA	OCTOSTYLE	ODIUMS
OBVENTIONS	OCCUPANT	OCREAE	OCTOSTYLES	ODOGRAPH
OBVERSE	OCCUPANTS	OCREATE	OCTROI	ODOGRAPHS
OBVERSELY	OCCUPATE	OCTA	OCTROIS	ODOMETER
OBVERSES	OCCUPATED	OCTACHORD	OCTUOR	ODOMETERS
OBVERSION	OCCUPATES	OCTACHORDS	OCTUORS	ODOMETRIES
OBVERSIONS	OCCUPATING	OCTAD	OCTUPLE	ODOMETRY
OBVERT	OCCUPIED	OCTADIC	OCTUPLED	ODONATIST
OBVERTED	OCCUPIER	OCTADS	OCTUPLES	ODONATISTS
OBVERTING	OCCUPIERS	OCTAGON	OCTUPLET	ODONTALGIES
OBVERTS	OCCUPIES	OCTAGONAL	OCTUPLETS	ODONTALGY
OBVIATE	OCCUPY	OCTAGONS	OCTUPLING	ODONTIC
OBVIATED	OCCUPYING	OCTAHEDRA	OCULAR	ODONTIST
OBVIATES	OCCUR	OCTAL	OCULARIST	ODONTISTS
OBVIATING	OCCURRED	OCTALS	OCULARISTS	ODONTOID
OBVIATION	OCCURRENT	OCTAMETER	OCULARLY	ODONTOMA
OBVIATIONS	OCCURRENTS	OCTAMETERS	OCULARS	ODONTOMAS
OBVIOUS	OCCURRING	OCTANE	OCULATE	ODONTOMATA

The Chambers Dictionary is the authority for many longer words; see *OSW* Introduction, page xii.

ODOR	OF	OFFS	OHMMETERS	OKRAS
ODORANT	OFAY	OFFSADDLE	OHMS	OKTA
ODORANTS	OFAYS	OFFSADDLED	OHO	OKTAS
ODORATE	OFF	OFFSADDLES	OHONE	OLD
ODOROUS	OFFAL	OFFSADDLING	OHOS	OLDEN
ODOROUSLY	OFFALS	OFFSCUM	OI	OLDENED
ODORS	OFFBEAT	OFFSCUMS	OIDIA	OLDENING
ODOUR	OFFBEATS	OFFSEASON	OIDIUM	OLDENS
ODOURED	OFFCUT	OFFSEASONS	OIK	OLDER
ODOURLESS	OFFCUTS	OFFSET	OIKIST	OLDEST
ODOURS	OFFED	OFFSETS	OIKISTS	OLDIE
ODS	OFFENCE	OFFSETTING	OIKS	OLDIES
ODSO	OFFENCES	OFFSHOOT	OIL	OLDISH
ODSOS	OFFEND	OFFSHOOTS	OILCAN	OLDNESS
ODYL	OFFENDED	OFFSHORE	OILCANS	OLDNESSES
ODYLE	OFFENDER	OFFSIDE	OILCLOTH	OLDS
ODYLES	OFFENDERS	OFFSIDER	OILCLOTHS	OLDSQUAW
ODYLISM	OFFENDING	OFFSIDERS	OILED	OLDSQUAWS
ODYLISMS	OFFENDS	OFFSIDES	OILER	OLDSTER
ODYLS	OFFENSE	OFFSPRING	OILERIES	OLDSTERS
ODYSSEY	OFFENSES	OFFSPRINGS	OILERS	OLDY
ODYSSEYS	OFFENSIVE	OFFTAKE	OILERY	OLE
ODZOOKS	OFFENSIVES	OFFTAKES	OILFIELD	OLEACEOUS
OE	OFFER	OFLAG	OILFIELDS	OLEANDER
OECIST	OFFERABLE	OFLAGS	OILIER	OLEANDERS
OECISTS	OFFERED	OFT	OILIEST	OLEARIA
OECOLOGIES	OFFEREE	OFTEN	OILILY	OLEARIAS
OECOLOGY	OFFEREES	OFTENER	OILINESS	OLEASTER
OECUMENIC	OFFERER	OFTENEST	OILINESSES	OLEASTERS
OEDEMA	OFFERERS	OFTENNESS	OILING	OLEATE
OEDEMAS	OFFERING	OFTENNESSES	OILLET	OLEATES
OEDEMATA	OFFERINGS	OFTTIMES	OILLETS	OLECRANAL
OEILLADE	OFFEROR	OGAM	OILMAN	OLECRANON
OEILLADES	OFFERORS	OGAMIC	OILMEN	OLECRANONS
OENANTHIC	OFFERS	OGAMS	OILNUT	OLEFIANT
OENOLOGIES	OFFERTORIES	OGDOAD	OILNUTS	OLEFIN
OENOLOGY	OFFERTORY	OGDOADS	OILS	OLEFINE
OENOMANCIES	OFFHAND	OGEE	OILSKIN	OLEFINES
OENOMANCY	OFFHANDED	OGEES	OILSKINS	OLEFINS
OENOMANIA	OFFICE	OGGIN	OILSTONE	OLEIC
OENOMANIAS	OFFICER	OGGINS	OILSTONES	OLEIN
OENOMEL	OFFICERED	OGHAM	OILY	OLEINS
OENOMELS	OFFICERING	OGHAMIC	OINK	OLENT
OENOMETER	OFFICERS	OGHAMS	OINKED	OLEO
OENOMETERS	OFFICES	OGIVAL	OINKING	OLEOGRAPH
OENOPHIL	OFFICIAL	OGIVE	OINKS	OLEOGRAPHS
OENOPHILE	OFFICIALS	OGIVES	OINT	OLEOS
OENOPHILES	OFFICIANT	OGLE	OINTED	OLEUM
OENOPHILIES	OFFICIANTS	OGLED	OINTING	OLEUMS
OENOPHILS	OFFICIATE	OGLER	OINTMENT	OLFACT
OENOPHILY	OFFICIATED	OGLERS	OINTMENTS	OLFACTED
OERLIKON	OFFICIATES	OGLES	OINTS	OLFACTING
OERLIKONS	OFFICIATING	OGLING	OITICICA	OLFACTION
OERSTED	OFFICINAL	OGLINGS	OITICICAS	OLFACTIONS
OERSTEDS	OFFICIOUS	OGMIC	OJIME	OLFACTIVE
OES	OFFING	OGRE	OJIMES	OLFACTORY
OESOPHAGI	OFFINGS	OGREISH	OKAPI	OLFACTS
OESTRAL	OFFISH	OGRES	OKAPIS	OLIBANUM
OESTROGEN	OFFLOAD	OGRESS	OKAY	OLIBANUMS
OESTROGENS	OFFLOADED	OGRESSES	OKAYED	OLID
OESTROUS	OFFLOADING	OGRISH	OKAYING	OLIGAEMIA
OESTRUM	OFFLOADS	OH	OKAYS	OLIGAEMIAS
OESTRUMS	OFFPEAK	OHM	OKE	OLIGARCH
OESTRUS	OFFPRINT	OHMAGE	OKES	OLIGARCHIES
OESTRUSES	OFFPRINTS	OHMAGES	OKIMONO	OLIGARCHS
OEUVRE	OFFPUT	OHMIC	OKIMONOS	OLIGARCHY
OEUVRES	OFFPUTS	OHMMETER	OKRA	OLIGIST

The Chambers Dictionary is the authority for many longer words; see *OSW* Introduction, page xii.

OLIGISTS
OLIGOPOLIES
OLIGOPOLY
OLIGURIA
OLIGURIAS
OLIO
OLIOS
OLIPHANT
OLIPHANTS
OLITORIES
OLITORY
OLIVARY
OLIVE
OLIVENITE
OLIVENITES
OLIVER
OLIVERS
OLIVES
OLIVET
OLIVETS
OLIVINE
OLIVINES
OLLA
OLLAMH
OLLAMHS
OLLAS
OLLAV
OLLAVS
OLM
OLMS
OLOGIES
OLOGY
OLOROSO
OLOROSOS
OLPAE
OLPE
OLPES
OLYCOOK
OLYCOOKS
OLYKOEK
OLYKOEKS
OLYMPIAD
OLYMPIADS
OLYMPICS
OM
OMADHAUN
OMADHAUNS
OMASA
OMASAL
OMASUM
OMBRE
OMBRELLA
OMBRELLAS
OMBRES
OMBROPHIL
OMBROPHILS
OMBU
OMBUDSMAN
OMBUDSMEN
OMBUS
OMEGA
OMEGAS
OMELET
OMELETS
OMELETTE
OMELETTES
OMEN

OMENED
OMENING
OMENS
OMENTA
OMENTAL
OMENTUM
OMER
OMERS
OMERTA
OMERTAS
OMICRON
OMICRONS
OMINOUS
OMINOUSLY
OMISSIBLE
OMISSION
OMISSIONS
OMISSIVE
OMIT
OMITS
OMITTANCE
OMITTANCES
OMITTED
OMITTER
OMITTERS
OMITTING
OMLAH
OMLAHS
OMMATEA
OMMATEUM
OMMATIDIA
OMNEITIES
OMNEITY
OMNIANA
OMNIBUS
OMNIBUSES
OMNIETIES
OMNIETY
OMNIFIC
OMNIFIED
OMNIFIES
OMNIFORM
OMNIFY
OMNIFYING
OMNIUM
OMNIUMS
OMNIVORE
OMNIVORES
OMNIVORIES
OMNIVORY
OMOHYOID
OMOHYOIDS
OMOPHAGIA
OMOPHAGIAS
OMOPHAGIC
OMOPHAGIES
OMOPHAGY
OMOPHORIA
OMOPLATE
OMOPLATES
OMPHACITE
OMPHACITES
OMPHALIC
OMPHALOID
OMPHALOS
OMPHALOSES
OMRAH

OMRAHS
OMS
ON
ONAGER
ONAGERS
ONANISM
ONANISMS
ONANIST
ONANISTIC
ONANISTS
ONBOARD
ONCE
ONCER
ONCERS
ONCES
ONCIDIUM
ONCIDIUMS
ONCOGEN
ONCOGENE
ONCOGENES
ONCOGENIC
ONCOGENS
ONCOLOGIES
ONCOLOGY
ONCOLYSES
ONCOLYSIS
ONCOLYTIC
ONCOLYTICS
ONCOME
ONCOMES
ONCOMETER
ONCOMETERS
ONCOMICE
ONCOMING
ONCOMINGS
ONCOMOUSE
ONCOST
ONCOSTMAN
ONCOSTMEN
ONCOSTS
ONCOTOMIES
ONCOTOMY
ONCUS
ONDATRA
ONDATRAS
ONDINE
ONDINES
ONDING
ONDINGS
ONE
ONEFOLD
ONEIRIC
ONELY
ONENESS
ONENESSES
ONER
ONEROUS
ONEROUSLY
ONERS
ONES
ONESELF
ONEYER
ONEYERS
ONEYRE
ONEYRES
ONFALL
ONFALLS

ONFLOW
ONFLOWS
ONGOING
ONGOINGS
ONION
ONIONED
ONIONING
ONIONS
ONIONY
ONIRIC
ONISCOID
ONKUS
ONLIEST
ONLOOKER
ONLOOKERS
ONLOOKING
ONLY
ONNED
ONNING
ONOMASTIC
ONOMASTICS
ONRUSH
ONRUSHES
ONS
ONSET
ONSETS
ONSETTER
ONSETTERS
ONSETTING
ONSETTINGS
ONSHORE
ONSIDE
ONSIDES
ONSLAUGHT
ONSLAUGHTS
ONST
ONSTEAD
ONSTEADS
ONTO
ONTOGENIC
ONTOGENIES
ONTOGENY
ONTOLOGIC
ONTOLOGIES
ONTOLOGY
ONUS
ONUSES
ONWARD
ONWARDLY
ONWARDS
ONYCHA
ONYCHAS
ONYCHIA
ONYCHIAS
ONYCHITE
ONYCHITES
ONYCHITIS
ONYCHITISES
ONYCHIUM
ONYCHIUMS
ONYMOUS
ONYX
ONYXES
OO
OOBIT
OOBITS
OOCYTE

OOCYTES
OODLES
OODLINS
OOF
OOFS
OOFTISH
OOFTISHES
OOGAMIES
OOGAMOUS
OOGAMY
OOGENESES
OOGENESIS
OOGENETIC
OOGENIES
OOGENY
OOGONIA
OOGONIAL
OOGONIUM
OOH
OOHED
OOHING
OOHS
OOIDAL
OOLAKAN
OOLAKANS
OOLITE
OOLITES
OOLITIC
OOLOGIES
OOLOGIST
OOLOGISTS
OOLOGY
OOLONG
OOLONGS
OOM
OOMIAC
OOMIACK
OOMIACKS
OOMIACS
OOMIAK
OOMIAKS
OOMPAH
OOMPAHED
OOMPAHING
OOMPAHS
OOMPH
OOMPHS
OOMS
OON
OONS
OONT
OONTS
OOP
OOPED
OOPHORON
OOPHORONS
OOPHYTE
OOPHYTES
OOPING
OOPS
OOR
OORIAL
OORIALS
OORIE
OORIER
OORIEST
OOS

The Chambers Dictionary is the authority for many longer words; see *OSW* Introduction, page xii.

OOSE	OPERATES	OPORICES	OPTIME	ORANGEADE
OOSES	OPERATIC	OPOSSUM	OPTIMES	ORANGEADES
OOSIER	OPERATING	OPOSSUMS	OPTIMISE	ORANGER
OOSIEST	OPERATION	OPPIDAN	OPTIMISED	ORANGERIES
OOSPHERE	OPERATIONS	OPPIDANS	OPTIMISES	ORANGERY
OOSPHERES	OPERATIVE	OPPILATE	OPTIMISING	ORANGES
OOSPORE	OPERATIVES	OPPILATED	OPTIMISM	ORANGEST
OOSPORES	OPERATOR	OPPILATES	OPTIMISMS	ORANGEY
OOSY	OPERATORS	OPPILATING	OPTIMIST	ORANGS
OOZE	OPERCULA	OPPONENCIES	OPTIMISTS	ORANT
OOZED	OPERCULAR	OPPONENCY	OPTIMIZE	ORANTS
OOZES	OPERCULUM	OPPONENT	OPTIMIZED	ORARIA
OOZIER	OPERETTA	OPPONENTS	OPTIMIZES	ORARIAN
OOZIEST	OPERETTAS	OPPORTUNE	OPTIMIZING	ORARIANS
OOZILY	OPERON	OPPOSABLE	OPTIMUM	ORARION
OOZINESS	OPERONS	OPPOSE	OPTING	ORARIONS
OOZINESSES	OPEROSE	OPPOSED	OPTION	ORARIUM
OOZING	OPEROSELY	OPPOSER	OPTIONAL	ORARIUMS
OOZY	OPEROSITIES	OPPOSERS	OPTIONS	ORATE
OPACITIES	OPEROSITY	OPPOSES	OPTOLOGIES	ORATED
OPACITY	OPES	OPPOSING	OPTOLOGY	ORATES
OPACOUS	OPHIDIAN	OPPOSITE	OPTOMETER	ORATING
OPAH	OPHIDIANS	OPPOSITES	OPTOMETERS	ORATION
OPAHS	OPHIOLITE	OPPRESS	OPTOMETRIES	ORATIONS
OPAL	OPHIOLITES	OPPRESSED	OPTOMETRY	ORATOR
OPALED	OPHIOLOGIES	OPPRESSES	OPTOPHONE	ORATORIAL
OPALINE	OPHIOLOGY	OPPRESSING	OPTOPHONES	ORATORIAN
OPALINES	OPHITE	OPPRESSOR	OPTRONICS	ORATORIANS
OPALISED	OPHITES	OPPRESSORS	OPTS	ORATORIES
OPALIZED	OPHITIC	OPPUGN	OPULENCE	ORATORIO
OPALS	OPHIURA	OPPUGNANT	OPULENCES	ORATORIOS
OPAQUE	OPHIURAN	OPPUGNANTS	OPULENT	ORATORS
OPAQUED	OPHIURANS	OPPUGNED	OPULENTLY	ORATORY
OPAQUELY	OPHIURAS	OPPUGNER	OPULUS	ORATRESS
OPAQUER	OPHIURID	OPPUGNERS	OPULUSES	ORATRESSES
OPAQUES	OPHIURIDS	OPPUGNING	OPUNTIA	ORATRIX
OPAQUEST	OPHIUROID	OPPUGNS	OPUNTIAS	ORATRIXES
OPAQUING	OPHIUROIDS	OPSIMATH	OPUS	ORB
OPCODE	OPIATE	OPSIMATHIES	OPUSCLE	ORBED
OPCODES	OPIATED	OPSIMATHS	OPUSCLES	ORBICULAR
OPE	OPIATES	OPSIMATHY	OPUSCULA	ORBIER
OPED	OPIATING	OPSOMANIA	OPUSCULE	ORBIEST
OPEN	OPIFICER	OPSOMANIAS	OPUSCULES	ORBING
OPENABLE	OPIFICERS	OPSONIC	OPUSCULUM	ORBIT
OPENED	OPINABLE	OPSONIN	OPUSES	ORBITA
OPENER	OPINE	OPSONINS	OR	ORBITAL
OPENERS	OPINED	OPSONIUM	ORACH	ORBITALS
OPENEST	OPINES	OPSONIUMS	ORACHE	ORBITAS
OPENING	OPING	OPT	ORACHES	ORBITED
OPENINGS	OPINICUS	OPTANT	ORACIES	ORBITER
OPENLY	OPINICUSES	OPTANTS	ORACLE	ORBITERS
OPENNESS	OPINING	OPTATIVE	ORACLED	ORBITIES
OPENNESSES	OPINION	OPTATIVES	ORACLES	ORBITING
OPENS	OPINIONED	OPTED	ORACLING	ORBITS
OPENWORK	OPINIONS	OPTER	ORACULAR	ORBITY
OPENWORKS	OPIOID	OPTERS	ORACULOUS	ORBS
OPEPE	OPIUM	OPTIC	ORACY	ORBY
OPEPES	OPIUMISM	OPTICAL	ORAGIOUS	ORC
OPERA	OPIUMISMS	OPTICALLY	ORAL	ORCA
OPERABLE	OPIUMS	OPTICIAN	ORALISM	ORCAS
OPERAND	OPOBALSAM	OPTICIANS	ORALISMS	ORCEIN
OPERANDS	OPOBALSAMS	OPTICS	ORALITIES	ORCEINS
OPERANT	OPODELDOC	OPTIMA	ORALITY	ORCHARD
OPERANTS	OPODELDOCS	OPTIMAL	ORALLY	ORCHARDS
OPERAS	OPOPANAX	OPTIMALLY	ORALS	ORCHAT
OPERATE	OPOPANAXES	OPTIMATE	ORANG	ORCHATS
OPERATED	OPORICE	OPTIMATES	ORANGE	ORCHEL

The Chambers Dictionary is the authority for many longer words; see *OSW* Introduction, page xii.

ORCHELLA
ORCHELLAS
ORCHELS
ORCHESES
ORCHESIS
ORCHESTIC
ORCHESTICS
ORCHESTRA
ORCHESTRAS
ORCHID
ORCHIDIST
ORCHIDISTS
ORCHIDS
ORCHIL
ORCHILLA
ORCHILLAS
ORCHILS
ORCHIS
ORCHISES
ORCHITIC
ORCHITIS
ORCHITISES
ORCIN
ORCINE
ORCINES
ORCINOL
ORCINOLS
ORCINS
ORCS
ORD
ORDAIN
ORDAINED
ORDAINER
ORDAINERS
ORDAINING
ORDAINS
ORDALIAN
ORDALIUM
ORDALIUMS
ORDEAL
ORDEALS
ORDER
ORDERED
ORDERER
ORDERERS
ORDERING
ORDERINGS
ORDERLESS
ORDERLIES
ORDERLY
ORDERS
ORDINAIRE
ORDINAIRES
ORDINAL
ORDINALS
ORDINANCE
ORDINANCES
ORDINAND
ORDINANDS
ORDINANT
ORDINANTS
ORDINAR
ORDINARIES
ORDINARS
ORDINARY
ORDINATE
ORDINATED

ORDINATES
ORDINATING
ORDINEE
ORDINEES
ORDNANCE
ORDNANCES
ORDS
ORDURE
ORDURES
ORDUROUS
ORE
OREAD
OREADES
OREADS
ORECROWE
ORECROWED
ORECROWES
ORECROWING
ORECTIC
OREGANO
OREGANOS
OREIDE
OREIDES
OREOLOGIES
OREOLOGY
OREPEARCH
OREPEARCHED
OREPEARCHES
OREPEARCHING
ORES
ORESTUNCK
OREWEED
OREWEEDS
OREXIS
OREXISES
ORF
ORFE
ORFES
ORFS
ORGAN
ORGANA
ORGANDIE
ORGANDIES
ORGANELLE
ORGANELLES
ORGANIC
ORGANICAL
ORGANISE
ORGANISED
ORGANISER
ORGANISERS
ORGANISES
ORGANISING
ORGANISM
ORGANISMS
ORGANIST
ORGANISTS
ORGANITIES
ORGANITY
ORGANIZE
ORGANIZED
ORGANIZER
ORGANIZERS
ORGANIZES
ORGANIZING
ORGANON
ORGANS

ORGANUM
ORGANZA
ORGANZAS
ORGANZINE
ORGANZINES
ORGASM
ORGASMED
ORGASMIC
ORGASMING
ORGASMS
ORGASTIC
ORGEAT
ORGEATS
ORGIA
ORGIAS
ORGIAST
ORGIASTIC
ORGIASTS
ORGIC
ORGIES
ORGILLOUS
ORGONE
ORGONES
ORGUE
ORGUES
ORGULOUS
ORGY
ORIBI
ORIBIS
ORICALCHE
ORICALCHES
ORICHALC
ORICHALCS
ORIEL
ORIELLED
ORIELS
ORIENCIES
ORIENCY
ORIENT
ORIENTAL
ORIENTALS
ORIENTATE
ORIENTATED
ORIENTATES
ORIENTATING
ORIENTED
ORIENTEER
ORIENTEERED
ORIENTEERING
ORIENTEERINGS
ORIENTEERS
ORIENTING
ORIENTS
ORIFEX
ORIFEXES
ORIFICE
ORIFICES
ORIFICIAL
ORIFLAMME
ORIFLAMMES
ORIGAMI
ORIGAMIS
ORIGAN
ORIGANE
ORIGANES
ORIGANS
ORIGANUM

ORIGANUMS
ORIGIN
ORIGINAL
ORIGINALS
ORIGINATE
ORIGINATED
ORIGINATES
ORIGINATING
ORIGINS
ORILLION
ORILLIONS
ORIOLE
ORIOLES
ORISON
ORISONS
ORLE
ORLEANS
ORLEANSES
ORLES
ORLOP
ORLOPS
ORMER
ORMERS
ORMOLU
ORMOLUS
ORNAMENT
ORNAMENTED
ORNAMENTING
ORNAMENTS
ORNATE
ORNATELY
ORNATER
ORNATEST
ORNERY
ORNIS
ORNISES
ORNITHIC
ORNITHOID
OROGEN
OROGENIC
OROGENIES
OROGENS
OROGENY
OROGRAPHIES
OROGRAPHY
OROIDE
OROIDES
OROLOGIES
OROLOGIST
OROLOGISTS
OROLOGY
OROPESA
OROPESAS
OROROTUND
OROTUND
ORPHAN
ORPHANAGE
ORPHANAGES
ORPHANED
ORPHANING
ORPHANISM
ORPHANISMS
ORPHANS
ORPHARION
ORPHARIONS
ORPHREY
ORPHREYS

ORPIMENT
ORPIMENTS
ORPIN
ORPINE
ORPINES
ORPINS
ORRA
ORRERIES
ORRERY
ORRIS
ORRISES
ORS
ORSEILLE
ORSEILLES
ORSELLIC
ORT
ORTANIQUE
ORTANIQUES
ORTHIAN
ORTHICON
ORTHICONS
ORTHO
ORTHOAXES
ORTHOAXIS
ORTHODOX
ORTHODOXIES
ORTHODOXY
ORTHOEPIC
ORTHOEPIES
ORTHOEPY
ORTHOPEDIES
ORTHOPEDY
ORTHOPOD
ORTHOPODS
ORTHOPTIC
ORTHOPTICS
ORTHOS
ORTHOSES
ORTHOSIS
ORTHOTIC
ORTHOTICS
ORTHOTIST
ORTHOTISTS
ORTHOTONE
ORTHROS
ORTHROSES
ORTOLAN
ORTOLANS
ORTS
ORVAL
ORVALS
ORYX
ORYXES
OS
OSCHEAL
OSCILLATE
OSCILLATED
OSCILLATES
OSCILLATING
OSCINE
OSCININE
OSCITANCIES
OSCITANCY
OSCITANT
OSCITATE
OSCITATED
OSCITATES

The Chambers Dictionary is the authority for many longer words; see *OSW* Introduction, page xii.

OSCITATING	OSSIFY	OTALGIAS	OUGLIED	OUTBACKERS
OSCULA	OSSIFYING	OTALGIES	OUGLIEING	OUTBACKS
OSCULANT	OSSUARIES	OTALGY	OUGLIES	OUTBAR
OSCULAR	OSSUARY	OTARIES	OUIJA	OUTBARRED
OSCULATE	OSTEAL	OTARINE	OUIJAS	OUTBARRING
OSCULATED	OSTEITIS	OTARY	OUISTITI	OUTBARS
OSCULATES	OSTEITISES	OTHER	OUISTITIS	OUTBID
OSCULATING	OSTENSIVE	OTHERNESS	OUK	OUTBIDDING
OSCULE	OSTENSORIES	OTHERNESSES	OUKS	OUTBIDS
OSCULES	OSTENSORY	OTHERS	OULACHON	OUTBOARD
OSCULUM	OSTENT	OTHERWISE	OULACHONS	OUTBOUND
OSHAC	OSTENTS	OTIC	OULAKAN	OUTBOUNDS
OSHACS	OSTEODERM	OTIOSE	OULAKANS	OUTBOX
OSIER	OSTEODERMS	OTIOSITIES	OULD	OUTBOXED
OSIERED	OSTEOGEN	OTIOSITY	OULDER	OUTBOXES
OSIERIES	OSTEOGENIES	OTITIS	OULDEST	OUTBOXING
OSIERS	OSTEOGENS	OTITISES	OULK	OUTBRAG
OSIERY	OSTEOGENY	OTOCYST	OULKS	OUTBRAGGED
OSMATE	OSTEOID	OTOCYSTS	OULONG	OUTBRAGGING
OSMATES	OSTEOLOGIES	OTOLITH	OULONGS	OUTBRAGS
OSMETERIA	OSTEOLOGY	OTOLITHS	OUNCE	OUTBRAVE
OSMIATE	OSTEOMA	OTOLOGIES	OUNCES	OUTBRAVED
OSMIATES	OSTEOMAS	OTOLOGIST	OUNDY	OUTBRAVES
OSMIC	OSTEOMATA	OTOLOGISTS	OUP	OUTBRAVING
OSMIOUS	OSTEOPATH	OTOLOGY	OUPED	OUTBREAK
OSMIUM	OSTEOPATHS	OTORRHOEA	OUPH	OUTBREAKING
OSMIUMS	OSTEOTOME	OTORRHOEAS	OUPHE	OUTBREAKS
OSMOMETER	OSTEOTOMES	OTOSCOPE	OUPHES	OUTBRED
OSMOMETERS	OSTEOTOMIES	OTOSCOPES	OUPHS	OUTBREED
OSMOMETRIES	OSTEOTOMY	OTTAR	OUPING	OUTBREEDING
OSMOMETRY	OSTIA	OTTARS	OUPS	OUTBREEDINGS
OSMOSE	OSTIAL	OTTAVA	OUR	OUTBREEDS
OSMOSED	OSTIARIES	OTTAVAS	OURALI	OUTBROKE
OSMOSES	OSTIARY	OTTAVINO	OURALIS	OUTBROKEN
OSMOSING	OSTIATE	OTTAVINOS	OURARI	OUTBURN
OSMOSIS	OSTINATO	OTTER	OURARIS	OUTBURNED
OSMOTIC	OSTINATOS	OTTERED	OUREBI	OUTBURNING
OSMOUS	OSTIOLATE	OTTERING	OUREBIS	OUTBURNS
OSMUND	OSTIOLE	OTTERS	OURIE	OUTBURNT
OSMUNDA	OSTIOLES	OTTO	OURIER	OUTBURST
OSMUNDAS	OSTIUM	OTTOMAN	OURIEST	OUTBURSTING
OSMUNDS	OSTLER	OTTOMANS	OURN	OUTBURSTS
OSNABURG	OSTLERESS	OTTOS	OUROBOROS	OUTBY
OSNABURGS	OSTLERESSES	OTTRELITE	OUROBOROSES	OUTBYE
OSPREY	OSTLERS	OTTRELITES	OUROLOGIES	OUTCAST
OSPREYS	OSTRACA	OU	OUROLOGY	OUTCASTE
OSSA	OSTRACEAN	OUABAIN	OUROSCOPIES	OUTCASTED
OSSARIUM	OSTRACISE	OUABAINS	OUROSCOPY	OUTCASTES
OSSARIUMS	OSTRACISED	OUAKARI	OURS	OUTCASTING
OSSEIN	OSTRACISES	OUAKARIS	OURSELF	OUTCASTS
OSSEINS	OSTRACISING	OUBIT	OURSELVES	OUTCLASS
OSSELET	OSTRACISM	OUBITS	OUSEL	OUTCLASSED
OSSELETS	OSTRACISMS	OUBLIETTE	OUSELS	OUTCLASSES
OSSEOUS	OSTRACIZE	OUBLIETTES	OUST	OUTCLASSING
OSSETER	OSTRACIZED	OUCH	OUSTED	OUTCOME
OSSETERS	OSTRACIZES	OUCHES	OUSTER	OUTCOMES
OSSIA	OSTRACIZING	OUCHT	OUSTERS	OUTCRAFTIED
OSSICLE	OSTRACOD	OUCHTS	OUSTING	OUTCRAFTIES
OSSICLES	OSTRACODS	OUGHLIED	OUSTITI	OUTCRAFTY
OSSICULAR	OSTRACON	OUGHLIES	OUSTITIS	OUTCRAFTYING
OSSIFIC	OSTRAKA	OUGHLY	OUSTS	OUTCRIED
OSSIFIED	OSTRAKON	OUGHLYING	OUT	OUTCRIES
OSSIFIES	OSTREGER	OUGHT	OUTAGE	OUTCROP
OSSIFRAGA	OSTREGERS	OUGHTNESS	OUTAGES	OUTCROPPED
OSSIFRAGAS	OSTRICH	OUGHTNESSES	OUTATE	OUTCROPPING
OSSIFRAGE	OSTRICHES	OUGHTS	OUTBACK	OUTCROPS
OSSIFRAGES	OTALGIA	OUGLIE	OUTBACKER	OUTCROSS

The Chambers Dictionary is the authority for many longer words; see *OSW* Introduction, page xii.

OUTCROSSED	OUTFIGHTS	OUTGOINGS	OUTLAUNCE	OUTMATCHED
OUTCROSSES	OUTFIT	OUTGONE	OUTLAUNCED	OUTMATCHES
OUTCROSSING	OUTFITS	OUTGREW	OUTLAUNCES	OUTMATCHING
OUTCROSSINGS	OUTFITTED	OUTGROW	OUTLAUNCH	OUTMODE
OUTCRY	OUTFITTER	OUTGROWING	OUTLAUNCHED	OUTMODED
OUTCRYING	OUTFITTERS	OUTGROWN	OUTLAUNCHES	OUTMODES
OUTDANCE	OUTFITTING	OUTGROWS	OUTLAUNCHING	OUTMODING
OUTDANCED	OUTFITTINGS	OUTGROWTH	OUTLAUNCING	OUTMOST
OUTDANCES	OUTFLANK	OUTGROWTHS	OUTLAW	OUTMOVE
OUTDANCING	OUTFLANKED	OUTGUARD	OUTLAWED	OUTMOVED
OUTDARE	OUTFLANKING	OUTGUARDS	OUTLAWING	OUTMOVES
OUTDARED	OUTFLANKS	OUTGUN	OUTLAWRIES	OUTMOVING
OUTDARES	OUTFLASH	OUTGUNNED	OUTLAWRY	OUTNAME
OUTDARING	OUTFLASHED	OUTGUNNING	OUTLAWS	OUTNAMED
OUTDATE	OUTFLASHES	OUTGUNS	OUTLAY	OUTNAMES
OUTDATED	OUTFLASHING	OUTGUSH	OUTLAYING	OUTNAMING
OUTDATES	OUTFLEW	OUTGUSHED	OUTLAYS	OUTNESS
OUTDATING	OUTFLIES	OUTGUSHES	OUTLEAP	OUTNESSES
OUTDID	OUTFLING	OUTGUSHING	OUTLEAPED	OUTNIGHT
OUTDO	OUTFLINGS	OUTHAUL	OUTLEAPING	OUTNIGHTED
OUTDOES	OUTFLOW	OUTHAULER	OUTLEAPS	OUTNIGHTING
OUTDOING	OUTFLOWED	OUTHAULERS	OUTLEAPT	OUTNIGHTS
OUTDONE	OUTFLOWING	OUTHAULS	OUTLEARN	OUTNUMBER
OUTDOOR	OUTFLOWINGS	OUTHER	OUTLEARNED	OUTNUMBERED
OUTDOORS	OUTFLOWN	OUTHIRE	OUTLEARNING	OUTNUMBERING
OUTDOORSY	OUTFLOWS	OUTHIRED	OUTLEARNS	OUTNUMBERS
OUTDRANK	OUTFLUSH	OUTHIRES	OUTLEARNT	OUTPACE
OUTDRINK	OUTFLUSHED	OUTHIRING	OUTLER	OUTPACED
OUTDRINKING	OUTFLUSHES	OUTHIT	OUTLERS	OUTPACES
OUTDRINKS	OUTFLUSHING	OUTHITS	OUTLET	OUTPACING
OUTDRIVE	OUTFLY	OUTHITTING	OUTLETS	OUTPART
OUTDRIVEN	OUTFLYING	OUTHOUSE	OUTLIE	OUTPARTS
OUTDRIVES	OUTFOOT	OUTHOUSES	OUTLIED	OUTPEEP
OUTDRIVING	OUTFOOTED	OUTHYRE	OUTLIER	OUTPEEPED
OUTDROVE	OUTFOOTING	OUTHYRED	OUTLIERS	OUTPEEPING
OUTDRUNK	OUTFOOTS	OUTHYRES	OUTLIES	OUTPEEPS
OUTDURE	OUTFOUGHT	OUTHYRING	OUTLINE	OUTPEER
OUTDURED	OUTFOX	OUTING	OUTLINEAR	OUTPEERED
OUTDURES	OUTFOXED	OUTINGS	OUTLINED	OUTPEERING
OUTDURING	OUTFOXES	OUTJEST	OUTLINES	OUTPEERS
OUTDWELL	OUTFOXING	OUTJESTED	OUTLINING	OUTPLAY
OUTDWELLED	OUTFROWN	OUTJESTING	OUTLIVE	OUTPLAYED
OUTDWELLING	OUTFROWNED	OUTJESTS	OUTLIVED	OUTPLAYING
OUTDWELLS	OUTFROWNING	OUTJET	OUTLIVES	OUTPLAYS
OUTDWELT	OUTFROWNS	OUTJETS	OUTLIVING	OUTPOINT
OUTEAT	OUTGAS	OUTJOCKEY	OUTLOOK	OUTPOINTED
OUTEATEN	OUTGASSED	OUTJOCKEYED	OUTLOOKED	OUTPOINTING
OUTEATING	OUTGASSES	OUTJOCKEYING	OUTLOOKING	OUTPOINTS
OUTEATS	OUTGASSING	OUTJOCKEYS	OUTLOOKS	OUTPORT
OUTED	OUTGASSINGS	OUTJUMP	OUTLUSTRE	OUTPORTS
OUTEDGE	OUTGATE	OUTJUMPED	OUTLUSTRED	OUTPOST
OUTEDGES	OUTGATES	OUTJUMPING	OUTLUSTRES	OUTPOSTS
OUTER	OUTGAVE	OUTJUMPS	OUTLUSTRING	OUTPOUR
OUTERMOST	OUTGIVE	OUTJUT	OUTLYING	OUTPOURED
OUTERS	OUTGIVEN	OUTJUTS	OUTMAN	OUTPOURER
OUTERWEAR	OUTGIVES	OUTLAID	OUTMANNED	OUTPOURERS
OUTERWEARS	OUTGIVING	OUTLAIN	OUTMANNING	OUTPOURING
OUTFACE	OUTGIVINGS	OUTLAND	OUTMANS	OUTPOURINGS
OUTFACED	OUTGLARE	OUTLANDER	OUTMANTLE	OUTPOURS
OUTFACES	OUTGLARED	OUTLANDERS	OUTMANTLED	OUTPOWER
OUTFACING	OUTGLARES	OUTLANDS	OUTMANTLES	OUTPOWERED
OUTFALL	OUTGLARING	OUTLASH	OUTMANTLING	OUTPOWERING
OUTFALLS	OUTGO	OUTLASHES	OUTMARCH	OUTPOWERS
OUTFIELD	OUTGOER	OUTLAST	OUTMARCHED	OUTPRAY
OUTFIELDS	OUTGOERS	OUTLASTED	OUTMARCHES	OUTPRAYED
OUTFIGHT	OUTGOES	OUTLASTING	OUTMARCHING	OUTPRAYING
OUTFIGHTING	OUTGOING	OUTLASTS	OUTMATCH	OUTPRAYS

The Chambers Dictionary is the authority for many longer words; see *OSW* Introduction, page xii.

OUTPRICE	OUTRIVALS	OUTSKIRTS	OUTSTRIPS	OUTVOICE
OUTPRICED	OUTROAR	OUTSLEEP	OUTSTRUCK	OUTVOICED
OUTPRICES	OUTROARED	OUTSLEEPING	OUTSUM	OUTVOICES
OUTPRICING	OUTROARING	OUTSLEEPS	OUTSUMMED	OUTVOICING
OUTPRIZE	OUTROARS	OUTSLEPT	OUTSUMMING	OUTVOTE
OUTPRIZED	OUTRODE	OUTSMART	OUTSUMS	OUTVOTED
OUTPRIZES	OUTROOP	OUTSMARTED	OUTSWAM	OUTVOTER
OUTPRIZING	OUTROOPER	OUTSMARTING	OUTSWEAR	OUTVOTERS
OUTPUT	OUTROOPERS	OUTSMARTS	OUTSWEARING	OUTVOTES
OUTPUTS	OUTROOPS	OUTSOAR	OUTSWEARS	OUTVOTING
OUTPUTTING	OUTROOT	OUTSOARED	OUTSWELL	OUTVYING
OUTRACE	OUTROOTED	OUTSOARING	OUTSWELLED	OUTWALK
OUTRACED	OUTROOTING	OUTSOARS	OUTSWELLING	OUTWALKED
OUTRACES	OUTROOTS	OUTSOLD	OUTSWELLS	OUTWALKING
OUTRACING	OUTROPE	OUTSOLE	OUTSWIM	OUTWALKS
OUTRAGE	OUTROPER	OUTSOLES	OUTSWIMMING	OUTWARD
OUTRAGED	OUTROPERS	OUTSPAN	OUTSWIMS	OUTWARDLY
OUTRAGES	OUTROPES	OUTSPANNED	OUTSWING	OUTWARDS
OUTRAGING	OUTRUN	OUTSPANNING	OUTSWINGS	OUTWASH
OUTRAIGNE	OUTRUNNER	OUTSPANS	OUTSWOLLEN	OUTWASHES
OUTRAIGNED	OUTRUNNERS	OUTSPEAK	OUTSWORE	OUTWATCH
OUTRAIGNES	OUTRUNNING	OUTSPEAKING	OUTSWORN	OUTWATCHED
OUTRAIGNING	OUTRUNS	OUTSPEAKS	OUTSWUM	OUTWATCHES
OUTRAN	OUTRUSH	OUTSPEND	OUTTAKE	OUTWATCHING
OUTRANCE	OUTRUSHED	OUTSPENDING	OUTTAKEN	OUTWEAR
OUTRANCES	OUTRUSHES	OUTSPENDS	OUTTAKES	OUTWEARIED
OUTRANK	OUTRUSHING	OUTSPENT	OUTTAKING	OUTWEARIES
OUTRANKED	OUTS	OUTSPOKE	OUTTALK	OUTWEARING
OUTRANKING	OUTSAIL	OUTSPOKEN	OUTTALKED	OUTWEARS
OUTRANKS	OUTSAILED	OUTSPORT	OUTTALKING	OUTWEARY
OUTRATE	OUTSAILING	OUTSPORTED	OUTTALKS	OUTWEARYING
OUTRATED	OUTSAILS	OUTSPORTING	OUTTELL	OUTWEED
OUTRATES	OUTSAT	OUTSPORTS	OUTTELLING	OUTWEEDED
OUTRATING	OUTSCOLD	OUTSPRANG	OUTTELLS	OUTWEEDING
OUTRE	OUTSCOLDED	OUTSPREAD	OUTTHINK	OUTWEEDS
OUTREACH	OUTSCOLDING	OUTSPREADING	OUTTHINKING	OUTWEEP
OUTREACHED	OUTSCOLDS	OUTSPREADS	OUTTHINKS	OUTWEEPING
OUTREACHES	OUTSCORN	OUTSPRING	OUTTHOUGHT	OUTWEEPS
OUTREACHING	OUTSCORNED	OUTSPRINGING	OUTTOLD	OUTWEIGH
OUTRED	OUTSCORNING	OUTSPRINGS	OUTTONGUE	OUTWEIGHED
OUTREDDED	OUTSCORNS	OUTSPRUNG	OUTTONGUED	OUTWEIGHING
OUTREDDEN	OUTSELL	OUTSTAND	OUTTONGUES	OUTWEIGHS
OUTREDDENED	OUTSELLING	OUTSTANDING	OUTTONGUING	OUTWELL
OUTREDDENING	OUTSELLS	OUTSTANDS	OUTTOOK	OUTWELLED
OUTREDDENS	OUTSET	OUTSTARE	OUTTOP	OUTWELLING
OUTREDDING	OUTSETS	OUTSTARED	OUTTOPPED	OUTWELLS
OUTREDS	OUTSHINE	OUTSTARES	OUTTOPPING	OUTWENT
OUTREIGN	OUTSHINES	OUTSTARING	OUTTOPS	OUTWEPT
OUTREIGNED	OUTSHINING	OUTSTAY	OUTTRAVEL	OUTWICK
OUTREIGNING	OUTSHONE	OUTSTAYED	OUTTRAVELED	OUTWICKED
OUTREIGNS	OUTSHOOT	OUTSTAYING	OUTTRAVELING	OUTWICKING
OUTRELIEF	OUTSHOOTING	OUTSTAYS	OUTTRAVELLED	OUTWICKS
OUTRELIEFS	OUTSHOOTS	OUTSTEP	OUTTRAVELLING	OUTWIN
OUTREMER	OUTSHOT	OUTSTEPPED	OUTTRAVELS	OUTWIND
OUTREMERS	OUTSHOTS	OUTSTEPPING	OUTTURN	OUTWINDING
OUTRIDDEN	OUTSIDE	OUTSTEPS	OUTTURNS	OUTWINDS
OUTRIDE	OUTSIDER	OUTSTOOD	OUTVALUE	OUTWING
OUTRIDER	OUTSIDERS	OUTSTRAIN	OUTVALUED	OUTWINGED
OUTRIDERS	OUTSIDES	OUTSTRAINED	OUTVALUES	OUTWINGING
OUTRIDES	OUTSIGHT	OUTSTRAINING	OUTVALUING	OUTWINGS
OUTRIDING	OUTSIGHTS	OUTSTRAINS	OUTVENOM	OUTWINNING
OUTRIGGER	OUTSIT	OUTSTRIKE	OUTVENOMED	OUTWINS
OUTRIGGERS	OUTSITS	OUTSTRIKES	OUTVENOMING	OUTWIT
OUTRIGHT	OUTSITTING	OUTSTRIKING	OUTVENOMS	OUTWITH
OUTRIVAL	OUTSIZE	OUTSTRIP	OUTVIE	OUTWITS
OUTRIVALLED	OUTSIZED	OUTSTRIPPED	OUTVIED	OUTWITTED
OUTRIVALLING	OUTSIZES	OUTSTRIPPING	OUTVIES	OUTWITTING

The Chambers Dictionary is the authority for many longer words; see *OSW* Introduction, page xii.

OUTWON	OVERALLS	OVERBUSIED	OVERCROWED	OVERFILLING
OUTWORE	OVERARCH	OVERBUSIES	OVERCROWING	OVERFILLS
OUTWORK	OVERARCHED	OVERBUSY	OVERCROWS	OVERFINE
OUTWORKER	OVERARCHES	OVERBUSYING	OVERDATED	OVERFISH
OUTWORKERS	OVERARCHING	OVERBUY	OVERDID	OVERFISHED
OUTWORKING	OVERARM	OVERBUYING	OVERDIGHT	OVERFISHES
OUTWORKS	OVERATE	OVERBUYS	OVERDO	OVERFISHING
OUTWORN	OVERAWE	OVERBY	OVERDOER	OVERFLEW
OUTWORTH	OVERAWED	OVERCALL	OVERDOERS	OVERFLIES
OUTWORTHED	OVERAWES	OVERCALLED	OVERDOES	OVERFLOW
OUTWORTHING	OVERAWING	OVERCALLING	OVERDOING	OVERFLOWED
OUTWORTHS	OVERBEAR	OVERCALLS	OVERDONE	OVERFLOWING
OUTWOUND	OVERBEARING	OVERCAME	OVERDOSE	OVERFLOWINGS
OUTWREST	OVERBEARS	OVERCARRIED	OVERDOSED	OVERFLOWN
OUTWRESTED	OVERBEAT	OVERCARRIES	OVERDOSES	OVERFLOWS
OUTWRESTING	OVERBEATEN	OVERCARRY	OVERDOSING	OVERFLUSH
OUTWRESTS	OVERBEATING	OVERCARRYING	OVERDRAFT	OVERFLUSHES
OUTWROUGHT	OVERBEATS	OVERCAST	OVERDRAFTS	OVERFLY
OUVERT	OVERBID	OVERCASTING	OVERDRAW	OVERFLYING
OUVERTE	OVERBIDDING	OVERCASTINGS	OVERDRAWING	OVERFOLD
OUVRAGE	OVERBIDDINGS	OVERCASTS	OVERDRAWN	OVERFOLDED
OUVRAGES	OVERBIDS	OVERCATCH	OVERDRAWS	OVERFOLDING
OUVRIER	OVERBITE	OVERCATCHES	OVERDRESS	OVERFOLDS
OUVRIERE	OVERBITES	OVERCATCHING	OVERDRESSED	OVERFOND
OUVRIERES	OVERBLEW	OVERCAUGHT	OVERDRESSES	OVERFREE
OUVRIERS	OVERBLOW	OVERCHECK	OVERDRESSING	OVERFULL
OUZEL	OVERBLOWING	OVERCHECKS	OVERDREW	OVERFUND
OUZELS	OVERBLOWN	OVERCLAD	OVERDRIVE	OVERFUNDED
OUZO	OVERBLOWS	OVERCLOUD	OVERDRIVEN	OVERFUNDING
OUZOS	OVERBOARD	OVERCLOUDED	OVERDRIVES	OVERFUNDINGS
OVA	OVERBOIL	OVERCLOUDING	OVERDRIVING	OVERFUNDS
OVAL	OVERBOILED	OVERCLOUDS	OVERDROVE	OVERGALL
OVALBUMIN	OVERBOILING	OVERCLOY	OVERDUE	OVERGALLED
OVALBUMINS	OVERBOILS	OVERCLOYED	OVERDUST	OVERGALLING
OVALLY	OVERBOLD	OVERCLOYING	OVERDUSTED	OVERGALLS
OVALS	OVERBOOK	OVERCLOYS	OVERDUSTING	OVERGANG
OVARIAN	OVERBOOKED	OVERCOAT	OVERDUSTS	OVERGANGING
OVARIES	OVERBOOKING	OVERCOATS	OVERDYE	OVERGANGS
OVARIOLE	OVERBOOKS	OVERCOME	OVERDYED	OVERGAVE
OVARIOLES	OVERBORE	OVERCOMES	OVERDYEING	OVERGET
OVARIOUS	OVERBORNE	OVERCOMING	OVERDYES	OVERGETS
OVARITIS	OVERBOUGHT	OVERCOOK	OVEREAT	OVERGETTING
OVARITISES	OVERBOUND	OVERCOOKED	OVEREATEN	OVERGIVE
OVARY	OVERBOUNDED	OVERCOOKING	OVEREATING	OVERGIVEN
OVATE	OVERBOUNDING	OVERCOOKS	OVEREATS	OVERGIVES
OVATED	OVERBOUNDS	OVERCOUNT	OVERED	OVERGIVING
OVATES	OVERBRIM	OVERCOUNTED	OVEREXERT	OVERGLAZE
OVATING	OVERBRIMMED	OVERCOUNTING	OVEREXERTED	OVERGLAZED
OVATION	OVERBRIMMING	OVERCOUNTS	OVEREXERTING	OVERGLAZES
OVATIONS	OVERBRIMS	OVERCOVER	OVEREXERTS	OVERGLAZING
OVATOR	OVERBROW	OVERCOVERED	OVEREYE	OVERGLOOM
OVATORS	OVERBROWED	OVERCOVERING	OVEREYED	OVERGLOOMED
OVEN	OVERBROWING	OVERCOVERS	OVEREYEING	OVERGLOOMING
OVENS	OVERBROWS	OVERCRAW	OVEREYES	OVERGLOOMS
OVENWARE	OVERBUILD	OVERCRAWED	OVEREYING	OVERGO
OVENWARES	OVERBUILDING	OVERCRAWING	OVERFALL	OVERGOES
OVENWOOD	OVERBUILDS	OVERCRAWS	OVERFALLEN	OVERGOING
OVENWOODS	OVERBUILT	OVERCROP	OVERFALLING	OVERGOINGS
OVER	OVERBULK	OVERCROPPED	OVERFALLS	OVERGONE
OVERACT	OVERBULKED	OVERCROPPING	OVERFAR	OVERGORGE
OVERACTED	OVERBULKING	OVERCROPS	OVERFED	OVERGORGED
OVERACTING	OVERBULKS	OVERCROW	OVERFEED	OVERGORGES
OVERACTS	OVERBURN	OVERCROWD	OVERFEEDING	OVERGORGING
OVERAGE	OVERBURNED	OVERCROWDED	OVERFEEDS	OVERGOT
OVERAGES	OVERBURNING	OVERCROWDING	OVERFELL	OVERGRAIN
OVERALL	OVERBURNS	OVERCROWDINGS	OVERFILL	OVERGRAINED
OVERALLED	OVERBURNT	OVERCROWDS	OVERFILLED	OVERGRAINING

The Chambers Dictionary is the authority for many longer words; see *OSW* Introduction, page xii.

OVERGRAINS
OVERGRASS
OVERGRASSED
OVERGRASSES
OVERGRASSING
OVERGRAZE
OVERGRAZED
OVERGRAZES
OVERGRAZING
OVERGRAZINGS
OVERGREAT
OVERGREEN
OVERGREENED
OVERGREENING
OVERGREENS
OVERGREW
OVERGROW
OVERGROWING
OVERGROWN
OVERGROWS
OVERHAILE
OVERHAILED
OVERHAILES
OVERHAILING
OVERHAIR
OVERHAIRS
OVERHALE
OVERHALED
OVERHALES
OVERHALING
OVERHAND
OVERHANDED
OVERHANDING
OVERHANDS
OVERHANG
OVERHANGING
OVERHANGS
OVERHAPPY
OVERHASTE
OVERHASTES
OVERHASTY
OVERHAUL
OVERHAULED
OVERHAULING
OVERHAULS
OVERHEAD
OVERHEADS
OVERHEAR
OVERHEARD
OVERHEARING
OVERHEARS
OVERHEAT
OVERHEATED
OVERHEATING
OVERHEATINGS
OVERHEATS
OVERHELD
OVERHENT
OVERHENTING
OVERHENTS
OVERHIT
OVERHITS
OVERHITTING
OVERHOLD
OVERHOLDING
OVERHOLDS
OVERHUNG

OVERHYPE
OVERHYPED
OVERHYPES
OVERHYPING
OVERING
OVERINKED
OVERISSUE
OVERISSUED
OVERISSUES
OVERISSUING
OVERJOY
OVERJOYED
OVERJOYING
OVERJOYS
OVERJUMP
OVERJUMPED
OVERJUMPING
OVERJUMPS
OVERKEEP
OVERKEEPING
OVERKEEPS
OVERKEPT
OVERKEST
OVERKILL
OVERKILLS
OVERKIND
OVERKING
OVERKINGS
OVERKNEE
OVERLADE
OVERLADED
OVERLADEN
OVERLADES
OVERLADING
OVERLAID
OVERLAIN
OVERLAND
OVERLANDED
OVERLANDING
OVERLANDS
OVERLAP
OVERLAPPED
OVERLAPPING
OVERLAPS
OVERLARD
OVERLARDED
OVERLARDING
OVERLARDS
OVERLAY
OVERLAYING
OVERLAYINGS
OVERLAYS
OVERLEAF
OVERLEAP
OVERLEAPED
OVERLEAPING
OVERLEAPS
OVERLEAPT
OVERLEND
OVERLENDING
OVERLENDS
OVERLENT
OVERLIE
OVERLIER
OVERLIERS
OVERLIES
OVERLIVE

OVERLIVED
OVERLIVES
OVERLIVING
OVERLOAD
OVERLOADED
OVERLOADING
OVERLOADS
OVERLOCK
OVERLOCKED
OVERLOCKING
OVERLOCKINGS
OVERLOCKS
OVERLONG
OVERLOOK
OVERLOOKED
OVERLOOKING
OVERLOOKS
OVERLORD
OVERLORDED
OVERLORDING
OVERLORDS
OVERLOUD
OVERLUSTY
OVERLY
OVERLYING
OVERMAN
OVERMANNED
OVERMANNING
OVERMANS
OVERMAST
OVERMASTED
OVERMASTING
OVERMASTS
OVERMATCH
OVERMATCHED
OVERMATCHES
OVERMATCHING
OVERMEN
OVERMERRY
OVERMOUNT
OVERMOUNTED
OVERMOUNTING
OVERMOUNTS
OVERMUCH
OVERNAME
OVERNAMED
OVERNAMES
OVERNAMING
OVERNEAT
OVERNET
OVERNETS
OVERNETTED
OVERNETTING
OVERNICE
OVERNIGHT
OVERNIGHTS
OVERPAGE
OVERPAID
OVERPAINT
OVERPAINTED
OVERPAINTING
OVERPAINTS
OVERPART
OVERPARTED
OVERPARTING
OVERPARTS
OVERPASS

OVERPASSED
OVERPASSES
OVERPASSING
OVERPAST
OVERPAY
OVERPAYING
OVERPAYS
OVERPEDAL
OVERPEDALED
OVERPEDALING
OVERPEDALLED
OVERPEDALLING
OVERPEDALS
OVERPEER
OVERPEERED
OVERPEERING
OVERPEERS
OVERPERCH
OVERPERCHED
OVERPERCHES
OVERPERCHING
OVERPITCH
OVERPITCHED
OVERPITCHES
OVERPITCHING
OVERPLAST
OVERPLAY
OVERPLAYED
OVERPLAYING
OVERPLAYS
OVERPLIED
OVERPLIES
OVERPLUS
OVERPLUSES
OVERPLUSSES
OVERPLY
OVERPLYING
OVERPOISE
OVERPOISED
OVERPOISES
OVERPOISING
OVERPOST
OVERPOSTED
OVERPOSTING
OVERPOSTS
OVERPOWER
OVERPOWERED
OVERPOWERING
OVERPOWERS
OVERPRESS
OVERPRESSED
OVERPRESSES
OVERPRESSING
OVERPRICE
OVERPRICED
OVERPRICES
OVERPRICING
OVERPRINT
OVERPRINTED
OVERPRINTING
OVERPRINTS
OVERPRIZE
OVERPRIZED
OVERPRIZES
OVERPRIZING
OVERPROOF
OVERPROUD

OVERRACK
OVERRACKED
OVERRACKING
OVERRACKS
OVERRAKE
OVERRAKED
OVERRAKES
OVERRAKING
OVERRAN
OVERRANK
OVERRASH
OVERRATE
OVERRATED
OVERRATES
OVERRATING
OVERRAUGHT
OVERREACH
OVERREACHED
OVERREACHES
OVERREACHING
OVERREACT
OVERREACTED
OVERREACTING
OVERREACTS
OVERREAD
OVERREADING
OVERREADS
OVERRED
OVERREDDED
OVERREDDING
OVERREDS
OVERREN
OVERRENNING
OVERRENS
OVERRIDDEN
OVERRIDE
OVERRIDER
OVERRIDERS
OVERRIDES
OVERRIDING
OVERRIPE
OVERRIPEN
OVERRIPENED
OVERRIPENING
OVERRIPENS
OVERROAST
OVERROASTED
OVERROASTING
OVERROASTS
OVERRODE
OVERRUFF
OVERRUFFED
OVERRUFFING
OVERRUFFS
OVERRULE
OVERRULED
OVERRULER
OVERRULERS
OVERRULES
OVERRULING
OVERRULINGS
OVERRUN
OVERRUNNING
OVERRUNS
OVERS
OVERSAIL
OVERSAILED

The Chambers Dictionary is the authority for many longer words; see *OSW* Introduction, page xii.

OVERSAILING	OVERSOUL	OVERSTUFFS	OVERTOPPING	OVERWEIGHS
OVERSAILS	OVERSOULS	OVERSTUNK	OVERTOPS	OVERWENT
OVERSAW	OVERSOW	OVERSWAM	OVERTOWER	OVERWHELM
OVERSCORE	OVERSOWED	OVERSWAY	OVERTOWERED	OVERWHELMED
OVERSCORED	OVERSOWING	OVERSWAYED	OVERTOWERING	OVERWHELMING
OVERSCORES	OVERSOWN	OVERSWAYING	OVERTOWERS	OVERWHELMINGS
OVERSCORING	OVERSOWS	OVERSWAYS	OVERTRAIN	OVERWHELMS
OVERSEA	OVERSPEND	OVERSWEAR	OVERTRAINED	OVERWIND
OVERSEAS	OVERSPENDING	OVERSWEARING	OVERTRAINING	OVERWINDING
OVERSEE	OVERSPENDS	OVERSWEARS	OVERTRAINS	OVERWINDS
OVERSEEING	OVERSPENT	OVERSWELL	OVERTRICK	OVERWING
OVERSEEN	OVERSPILL	OVERSWELLED	OVERTRICKS	OVERWINGED
OVERSEER	OVERSPILLS	OVERSWELLING	OVERTRIP	OVERWINGING
OVERSEERS	OVERSPIN	OVERSWELLS	OVERTRIPPED	OVERWINGS
OVERSEES	OVERSPINS	OVERSWIM	OVERTRIPPING	OVERWISE
OVERSELL	OVERSTAFF	OVERSWIMMING	OVERTRIPS	OVERWORD
OVERSELLING	OVERSTAFFED	OVERSWIMS	OVERTRUMP	OVERWORDS
OVERSELLS	OVERSTAFFING	OVERSWOLLEN	OVERTRUMPED	OVERWORE
OVERSET	OVERSTAFFS	OVERSWORE	OVERTRUMPING	OVERWORK
OVERSETS	OVERSTAIN	OVERSWORN	OVERTRUMPS	OVERWORKED
OVERSETTING	OVERSTAINED	OVERSWUM	OVERTRUST	OVERWORKING
OVERSEW	OVERSTAINING	OVERT	OVERTRUSTED	OVERWORKS
OVERSEWED	OVERSTAINS	OVERTAKE	OVERTRUSTING	OVERWORN
OVERSEWING	OVERSTAND	OVERTAKEN	OVERTRUSTS	OVERWOUND
OVERSEWN	OVERSTANDING	OVERTAKES	OVERTURE	OVERWREST
OVERSEWS	OVERSTANDS	OVERTAKING	OVERTURED	OVERWRESTED
OVERSEXED	OVERSTANK	OVERTALK	OVERTURES	OVERWRESTING
OVERSHADE	OVERSTARE	OVERTALKED	OVERTURING	OVERWRESTS
OVERSHADED	OVERSTARED	OVERTALKING	OVERTURN	OVERWRITE
OVERSHADES	OVERSTARES	OVERTALKS	OVERTURNED	OVERWRITES
OVERSHADING	OVERSTARING	OVERTASK	OVERTURNING	OVERWRITING
OVERSHINE	OVERSTATE	OVERTASKED	OVERTURNS	OVERWRITTEN
OVERSHINES	OVERSTATED	OVERTASKING	OVERUSE	OVERWROTE
OVERSHINING	OVERSTATES	OVERTASKS	OVERUSED	OVERWROUGHT
OVERSHIRT	OVERSTATING	OVERTAX	OVERUSES	OVERYEAR
OVERSHIRTS	OVERSTAY	OVERTAXED	OVERUSING	OVERYEARED
OVERSHOE	OVERSTAYED	OVERTAXES	OVERVALUE	OVERYEARING
OVERSHOES	OVERSTAYING	OVERTAXING	OVERVALUED	OVERYEARS
OVERSHONE	OVERSTAYS	OVERTEEM	OVERVALUES	OVIBOS
OVERSHOOT	OVERSTEER	OVERTEEMED	OVERVALUING	OVIBOSES
OVERSHOOTING	OVERSTEERED	OVERTEEMING	OVERVEIL	OVIBOVINE
OVERSHOOTS	OVERSTEERING	OVERTEEMS	OVERVEILED	OVICIDE
OVERSHOT	OVERSTEERS	OVERTHREW	OVERVEILING	OVICIDES
OVERSIDE	OVERSTEP	OVERTHROW	OVERVEILS	OVIDUCAL
OVERSIGHT	OVERSTEPPED	OVERTHROWING	OVERVIEW	OVIDUCT
OVERSIGHTS	OVERSTEPPING	OVERTHROWN	OVERVIEWS	OVIDUCTAL
OVERSIZE	OVERSTEPS	OVERTHROWS	OVERWASH	OVIDUCTS
OVERSIZED	OVERSTINK	OVERTIME	OVERWASHES	OVIFEROUS
OVERSIZES	OVERSTINKING	OVERTIMED	OVERWATCH	OVIFORM
OVERSIZING	OVERSTINKS	OVERTIMER	OVERWATCHED	OVIGEROUS
OVERSKIP	OVERSTOCK	OVERTIMERS	OVERWATCHES	OVINE
OVERSKIPPED	OVERSTOCKED	OVERTIMES	OVERWATCHING	OVIPARITIES
OVERSKIPPING	OVERSTOCKING	OVERTIMING	OVERWEAR	OVIPARITY
OVERSKIPS	OVERSTOCKS	OVERTIRE	OVERWEARIED	OVIPAROUS
OVERSKIRT	OVERSTOOD	OVERTIRED	OVERWEARIES	OVIPOSIT
OVERSKIRTS	OVERSTREW	OVERTIRES	OVERWEARING	OVIPOSITED
OVERSLEEP	OVERSTREWED	OVERTIRING	OVERWEARS	OVIPOSITING
OVERSLEEPING	OVERSTREWING	OVERTLY	OVERWEARY	OVIPOSITS
OVERSLEEPS	OVERSTREWN	OVERTOIL	OVERWEARYING	OVISAC
OVERSLEPT	OVERSTREWS	OVERTOILED	OVERWEEN	OVISACS
OVERSLIP	OVERSTUDIED	OVERTOILING	OVERWEENED	OVIST
OVERSLIPPED	OVERSTUDIES	OVERTOILS	OVERWEENING	OVISTS
OVERSLIPPING	OVERSTUDY	OVERTONE	OVERWEENINGS	OVOID
OVERSLIPS	OVERSTUDYING	OVERTONES	OVERWEENS	OVOIDAL
OVERSMAN	OVERSTUFF	OVERTOOK	OVERWEIGH	OVOIDS
OVERSMEN	OVERSTUFFED	OVERTOP	OVERWEIGHED	OVOLI
OVERSOLD	OVERSTUFFING	OVERTOPPED	OVERWEIGHING	OVOLO

The Chambers Dictionary is the authority for many longer words; see *OSW* Introduction, page xii.

OVOTESTES	OWLING	OXER	OXLAND	OXYTONES
OVOTESTIS	OWLISH	OXERS	OXLANDS	OY
OVULAR	OWLS	OXFORD	OXLIP	OYE
OVULATE	OWLY	OXFORDS	OXLIPS	OYER
OVULATED	OWN	OXGANG	OXONIUM	OYERS
OVULATES	OWNED	OXGANGS	OXONIUMS	OYES
OVULATING	OWNER	OXGATE	OXSLIP	OYESES
OVULATION	OWNERLESS	OXGATES	OXSLIPS	OYEZ
OVULATIONS	OWNERS	OXHEAD	OXTAIL	OYEZES
OVULE	OWNERSHIP	OXHEADS	OXTAILS	OYS
OVULES	OWNERSHIPS	OXIDANT	OXTER	OYSTER
OVUM	OWNING	OXIDANTS	OXTERED	OYSTERS
OW	OWNS	OXIDASE	OXTERING	OYSTRIGE
OWCHE	OWRE	OXIDASES	OXTERS	OYSTRIGES
OWCHES	OWRECOME	OXIDATE	OXYGEN	OZAENA
OWE	OWRECOMES	OXIDATED	OXYGENATE	OZAENAS
OWED	OWRELAY	OXIDATES	OXYGENATED	OZEKI
OWELTIES	OWRELAYS	OXIDATING	OXYGENATES	OZEKIS
OWELTY	OWRES	OXIDATION	OXYGENATING	OZOCERITE
OWER	OWREWORD	OXIDATIONS	OXYGENISE	OZOCERITES
OWERBY	OWREWORDS	OXIDE	OXYGENISED	OZOKERITE
OWERLOUP	OWRIE	OXIDES	OXYGENISES	OZOKERITES
OWERLOUPEN	OWRIER	OXIDISE	OXYGENISING	OZONATION
OWERLOUPING	OWRIEST	OXIDISED	OXYGENIZE	OZONATIONS
OWERLOUPIT	OWSEN	OXIDISER	OXYGENIZED	OZONE
OWERLOUPS	OWT	OXIDISERS	OXYGENIZES	OZONES
OWES	OWTS	OXIDISES	OXYGENIZING	OZONISE
OWING	OX	OXIDISING	OXYGENOUS	OZONISED
OWL	OXALATE	OXIDIZE	OXYGENS	OZONISER
OWLED	OXALATES	OXIDIZED	OXYMEL	OZONISERS
OWLER	OXALIC	OXIDIZER	OXYMELS	OZONISES
OWLERIES	OXALIS	OXIDIZERS	OXYMORON	OZONISING
OWLERS	OXALISES	OXIDIZES	OXYMORONS	OZONIZE
OWLERY	OXAZINE	OXIDIZING	OXYTOCIC	OZONIZED
OWLET	OXAZINES	OXIME	OXYTOCICS	OZONIZER
OWLETS	OXBLOOD	OXIMES	OXYTOCIN	OZONIZERS
OWLIER	OXBLOODS	OXIMETER	OXYTOCINS	OZONIZES
OWLIEST	OXEN	OXIMETERS	OXYTONE	OZONIZING

The Chambers Dictionary is the authority for many longer words; see *OSW* Introduction, page xii.

P

PA	PACKETED	PADLES	PAGED	PAINLESS
PABOUCHE	PACKETING	PADLOCK	PAGEHOOD	PAINS
PABOUCHES	PACKETS	PADLOCKED	PAGEHOODS	PAINT
PABULAR	PACKFONG	PADLOCKING	PAGER	PAINTABLE
PABULOUS	PACKFONGS	PADLOCKS	PAGERS	PAINTBALL
PABULUM	PACKING	PADMA	PAGES	PAINTBALLS
PABULUMS	PACKINGS	PADMAS	PAGINAL	PAINTED
PACA	PACKMAN	PADOUK	PAGINATE	PAINTER
PACABLE	PACKMEN	PADOUKS	PAGINATED	PAINTERLY
PACAS	PACKS	PADRE	PAGINATES	PAINTERS
PACATION	PACKSHEET	PADRES	PAGINATING	PAINTIER
PACATIONS	PACKSHEETS	PADRONE	PAGING	PAINTIEST
PACE	PACKSTAFF	PADRONI	PAGINGS	PAINTING
PACED	PACKSTAFFS	PADS	PAGLE	PAINTINGS
PACEMAKER	PACKWAY	PADSAW	PAGLES	PAINTRESS
PACEMAKERS	PACKWAYS	PADSAWS	PAGOD	PAINTRESSES
PACER	PACO	PADUASOY	PAGODA	PAINTS
PACERS	PACOS	PADUASOYS	PAGODAS	PAINTURE
PACES	PACT	PADYMELON	PAGODS	PAINTURES
PACEY	PACTA	PADYMELONS	PAGRI	PAINTY
PACHA	PACTION	PAEAN	PAGRIS	PAIOCK
PACHAK	PACTIONAL	PAEANS	PAGURIAN	PAIOCKE
PACHAKS	PACTIONED	PAEDERAST	PAGURIANS	PAIOCKES
PACHALIC	PACTIONING	PAEDERASTS	PAGURID	PAIOCKS
PACHALICS	PACTIONS	PAEDEUTIC	PAGURIDS	PAIR
PACHAS	PACTS	PAEDEUTICS	PAH	PAIRE
PACHINKO	PACTUM	PAEDIATRIES	PAHOEHOE	PAIRED
PACHINKOS	PACY	PAEDIATRY	PAHOEHOES	PAIRES
PACHISI	PAD	PAEDOLOGIES	PAHS	PAIRIAL
PACHISIS	PADANG	PAEDOLOGY	PAID	PAIRIALS
PACHYDERM	PADANGS	PAELLA	PAIDEUTIC	PAIRING
PACHYDERMS	PADAUK	PAELLAS	PAIDEUTICS	PAIRINGS
PACIER	PADAUKS	PAENULA	PAIDLE	PAIRS
PACIEST	PADDED	PAENULAE	PAIDLES	PAIRWISE
PACIFIC	PADDER	PAENULAS	PAIGLE	PAIS
PACIFICAL	PADDERS	PAEON	PAIGLES	PAISA
PACIFIED	PADDIES	PAEONIC	PAIK	PAISANO
PACIFIER	PADDING	PAEONICS	PAIKED	PAISANOS
PACIFIERS	PADDINGS	PAEONIES	PAIKING	PAISAS
PACIFIES	PADDLE	PAEONS	PAIKS	PAISE
PACIFISM	PADDLED	PAEONY	PAIL	PAISLEY
PACIFISMS	PADDLER	PAGAN	PAILFUL	PAISLEYS
PACIFIST	PADDLERS	PAGANISE	PAILFULS	PAITRICK
PACIFISTS	PADDLES	PAGANISED	PAILLASSE	PAITRICKS
PACIFY	PADDLING	PAGANISES	PAILLASSES	PAJAMAS
PACIFYING	PADDLINGS	PAGANISH	PAILLETTE	PAJOCK
PACING	PADDOCK	PAGANISING	PAILLETTES	PAJOCKE
PACK	PADDOCKS	PAGANISM	PAILLON	PAJOCKES
PACKAGE	PADDY	PAGANISMS	PAILLONS	PAJOCKS
PACKAGED	PADELLA	PAGANIZE	PAILS	PAKAPOO
PACKAGER	PADELLAS	PAGANIZED	PAIN	PAKAPOOS
PACKAGERS	PADEMELON	PAGANIZES	PAINED	PAKEHA
PACKAGES	PADEMELONS	PAGANIZING	PAINFUL	PAKEHAS
PACKAGING	PADERERO	PAGANS	PAINFULLER	PAKFONG
PACKAGINGS	PADEREROES	PAGE	PAINFULLEST	PAKFONGS
PACKED	PADEREROS	PAGEANT	PAINFULLY	PAKKA
PACKER	PADISHAH	PAGEANTRIES	PAINIM	PAKORA
PACKERS	PADISHAHS	PAGEANTRY	PAINIMS	PAKORAS
PACKET	PADLE	PAGEANTS	PAINING	PAKTONG

The Chambers Dictionary is the authority for many longer words; see *OSW* Introduction, page xii.

PAKTONGS	PALESTRAS	PALLIATED	PALOMINO	PAMPERING
PAL	PALET	PALLIATES	PALOMINOS	PAMPERO
PALABRA	PALETOT	PALLIATING	PALOOKA	PAMPEROS
PALABRAS	PALETOTS	PALLID	PALOOKAS	PAMPERS
PALACE	PALETS	PALLIDER	PALP	PAMPHLET
PALACES	PALETTE	PALLIDEST	PALPABLE	PAMPHLETS
PALADIN	PALETTES	PALLIDITIES	PALPABLY	PAMS
PALADINS	PALEWISE	PALLIDITY	PALPAL	PAN
PALAESTRA	PALFREY	PALLIDLY	PALPATE	PANACEA
PALAESTRAE	PALFREYED	PALLIER	PALPATED	PANACEAN
PALAESTRAS	PALFREYS	PALLIEST	PALPATES	PANACEAS
PALAFITTE	PALIER	PALLING	PALPATING	PANACHAEA
PALAFITTES	PALIEST	PALLIUM	PALPATION	PANACHAEAS
PALAGI	PALIFORM	PALLONE	PALPATIONS	PANACHE
PALAGIS	PALILALIA	PALLONES	PALPEBRAL	PANACHES
PALAMA	PALILALIAS	PALLOR	PALPED	PANADA
PALAMAE	PALILLOGIES	PALLORS	PALPI	PANADAS
PALAMATE	PALILLOGY	PALLS	PALPING	PANAMA
PALAMINO	PALIMONIES	PALLY	PALPITANT	PANAMAS
PALAMINOS	PALIMONY	PALM	PALPITATE	PANARIES
PALAMPORE	PALING	PALMAR	PALPITATED	PANARY
PALAMPORES	PALINGS	PALMARIAN	PALPITATES	PANATELLA
PALANKEEN	PALINODE	PALMARY	PALPITATING	PANATELLAS
PALANKEENS	PALINODES	PALMATE	PALPS	PANAX
PALANQUIN	PALINODIES	PALMATED	PALPUS	PANAXES
PALANQUINS	PALINODY	PALMATELY	PALS	PANCAKE
PALAS	PALISADE	PALMATION	PALSGRAVE	PANCAKED
PALASES	PALISADED	PALMATIONS	PALSGRAVES	PANCAKES
PALATABLE	PALISADES	PALMED	PALSIED	PANCAKING
PALATABLY	PALISADING	PALMER	PALSIER	PANCE
PALATAL	PALISADO	PALMERS	PALSIES	PANCES
PALATALS	PALISADOED	PALMETTE	PALSIEST	PANCHAX
PALATE	PALISADOES	PALMETTES	PALSTAFF	PANCHAXES
PALATED	PALISADOING	PALMETTO	PALSTAFFS	PANCHAYAT
PALATES	PALISH	PALMETTOES	PALSTAVE	PANCHAYATS
PALATIAL	PALKEE	PALMETTOS	PALSTAVES	PANCHEON
PALATINE	PALKEES	PALMFUL	PALSY	PANCHEONS
PALATINES	PALKI	PALMFULS	PALSYING	PANCHION
PALATING	PALKIS	PALMHOUSE	PALTER	PANCHIONS
PALAVER	PALL	PALMHOUSES	PALTERED	PANCOSMIC
PALAVERED	PALLA	PALMIE	PALTERER	PANCRATIC
PALAVERER	PALLADIC	PALMIER	PALTERERS	PANCREAS
PALAVERERS	PALLADIUM	PALMIES	PALTERING	PANCREASES
PALAVERING	PALLADIUMS	PALMIEST	PALTERS	PAND
PALAVERS	PALLADOUS	PALMIET	PALTRIER	PANDA
PALAY	PALLAE	PALMIETS	PALTRIEST	PANDAR
PALAYS	PALLAH	PALMING	PALTRILY	PANDARED
PALAZZI	PALLAHS	PALMIPED	PALTRY	PANDARING
PALAZZO	PALLED	PALMIPEDE	PALUDAL	PANDARS
PALE	PALLET	PALMIPEDES	PALUDIC	PANDAS
PALEA	PALLETED	PALMIPEDS	PALUDINAL	PANDATION
PALEAE	PALLETISE	PALMIST	PALUDINE	PANDATIONS
PALEBUCK	PALLETISED	PALMISTRIES	PALUDISM	PANDECT
PALEBUCKS	PALLETISES	PALMISTRY	PALUDISMS	PANDECTS
PALED	PALLETISING	PALMISTS	PALUDOSE	PANDEMIA
PALEFACE	PALLETIZE	PALMITATE	PALUDOUS	PANDEMIAN
PALEFACES	PALLETIZED	PALMITATES	PALUSTRAL	PANDEMIAS
PALELY	PALLETIZES	PALMITIN	PALY	PANDEMIC
PALEMPORE	PALLETIZING	PALMITINS	PAM	PANDEMICS
PALEMPORES	PALLETS	PALMS	PAMPA	PANDER
PALENESS	PALLIA	PALMTOP	PAMPAS	PANDERED
PALENESSES	PALLIAL	PALMTOPS	PAMPASES	PANDERESS
PALER	PALLIARD	PALMY	PAMPEAN	PANDERESSES
PALES	PALLIARDS	PALMYRA	PAMPER	PANDERING
PALEST	PALLIASSE	PALMYRAS	PAMPERED	PANDERISM
PALESTRA	PALLIASSES	PALOLO	PAMPERER	PANDERISMS
PALESTRAE	PALLIATE	PALOLOS	PAMPERERS	PANDERLY

The Chambers Dictionary is the authority for many longer words; see *OSW* Introduction, page xii.

PANDEROUS	PANICK	PANSPERMY	PAPACIES	PAPISM
PANDERS	PANICKED	PANSY	PAPACY	PAPISMS
PANDIED	PANICKING	PANT	PAPAIN	PAPIST
PANDIES	PANICKS	PANTABLE	PAPAINS	PAPISTIC
PANDIT	PANICKY	PANTABLES	PAPAL	PAPISTRIES
PANDITS	PANICLE	PANTAGAMIES	PAPALISE	PAPISTRY
PANDOOR	PANICLED	PANTAGAMY	PAPALISED	PAPISTS
PANDOORS	PANICLES	PANTALEON	PAPALISES	PAPOOSE
PANDORA	PANICS	PANTALEONS	PAPALISING	PAPOOSES
PANDORAS	PANIM	PANTALETS	PAPALISM	PAPPADOM
PANDORE	PANIMS	PANTALON	PAPALISMS	PAPPADOMS
PANDORES	PANING	PANTALONS	PAPALIST	PAPPED
PANDOUR	PANISC	PANTALOON	PAPALISTS	PAPPIER
PANDOURS	PANISCS	PANTALOONS	PAPALIZE	PAPPIES
PANDOWDIES	PANISK	PANTED	PAPALIZED	PAPPIEST
PANDOWDY	PANISKS	PANTER	PAPALIZES	PAPPING
PANDS	PANISLAM	PANTERS	PAPALIZING	PAPPOOSE
PANDURA	PANISLAMS	PANTHEISM	PAPALLY	PAPPOOSES
PANDURAS	PANLOGISM	PANTHEISMS	PAPARAZZI	PAPPOSE
PANDURATE	PANLOGISMS	PANTHEIST	PAPARAZZO	PAPPOUS
PANDY	PANMICTIC	PANTHEISTS	PAPAS	PAPPUS
PANDYING	PANMIXIA	PANTHENOL	PAPAW	PAPPUSES
PANE	PANMIXIAS	PANTHENOLS	PAPAWS	PAPPY
PANED	PANMIXIS	PANTHER	PAPAYA	PAPRIKA
PANEGOISM	PANMIXISES	PANTHERS	PAPAYAS	PAPRIKAS
PANEGOISMS	PANNAGE	PANTIES	PAPE	PAPS
PANEGYRIC	PANNAGES	PANTIHOSE	PAPER	PAPULA
PANEGYRICS	PANNE	PANTILE	PAPERBACK	PAPULAE
PANEGYRIES	PANNED	PANTILED	PAPERBACKED	PAPULAR
PANEGYRY	PANNELLED	PANTILES	PAPERBACKING	PAPULE
PANEITIES	PANNES	PANTILING	PAPERBACKS	PAPULES
PANEITY	PANNICK	PANTILINGS	PAPERED	PAPULOSE
PANEL	PANNICKS	PANTINE	PAPERER	PAPULOUS
PANELLED	PANNICLE	PANTINES	PAPERERS	PAPYRI
PANELLING	PANNICLES	PANTING	PAPERING	PAPYRUS
PANELLINGS	PANNIER	PANTINGLY	PAPERINGS	PAR
PANELLIST	PANNIERED	PANTINGS	PAPERLESS	PARA
PANELLISTS	PANNIERS	PANTLER	PAPERS	PARABASES
PANELS	PANNIKEL	PANTLERS	PAPERWARE	PARABASIS
PANES	PANNIKELL	PANTO	PAPERWARES	PARABEMA
PANETTONE	PANNIKELLS	PANTOFFLE	PAPERWORK	PARABEMATA
PANETTONI	PANNIKELS	PANTOFFLES	PAPERWORKS	PARABLE
PANFUL	PANNIKIN	PANTOFLE	PAPERY	PARABLED
PANFULS	PANNIKINS	PANTOFLES	PAPES	PARABLES
PANG	PANNING	PANTOMIME	PAPETERIE	PARABLING
PANGA	PANNINGS	PANTOMIMES	PAPETERIES	PARABOLA
PANGAMIC	PANNOSE	PANTON	PAPILIO	PARABOLAS
PANGAMIES	PANNUS	PANTONS	PAPILIOS	PARABOLE
PANGAMY	PANNUSES	PANTOS	PAPILLA	PARABOLES
PANGAS	PANOCHA	PANTOUFLE	PAPILLAE	PARABOLIC
PANGED	PANOCHAS	PANTOUFLES	PAPILLAR	PARABRAKE
PANGEN	PANOISTIC	PANTOUM	PAPILLARY	PARABRAKES
PANGENE	PANOPLIED	PANTOUMS	PAPILLATE	PARACHUTE
PANGENES	PANOPLIES	PANTRIES	PAPILLOMA	PARACHUTED
PANGENS	PANOPLY	PANTRY	PAPILLOMAS	PARACHUTES
PANGING	PANOPTIC	PANTRYMAN	PAPILLON	PARACHUTING
PANGLESS	PANORAMA	PANTRYMEN	PAPILLONS	PARACLETE
PANGOLIN	PANORAMAS	PANTS	PAPILLOSE	PARACLETES
PANGOLINS	PANORAMIC	PANTUN	PAPILLOTE	PARACME
PANGRAM	PANS	PANTUNS	PAPILLOTES	PARACMES
PANGRAMS	PANSEXUAL	PANZER	PAPILLOUS	PARACUSES
PANGS	PANSIED	PANZERS	PAPILLULE	PARACUSIS
PANHANDLE	PANSIES	PAOLI	PAPILLULES	PARADE
PANHANDLED	PANSOPHIC	PAOLO	PAPISH	PARADED
PANHANDLES	PANSOPHIES	PAP	PAPISHER	PARADES
PANHANDLING	PANSOPHY	PAPA	PAPISHERS	PARADIGM
PANIC	PANSPERMIES	PAPABLE	PAPISHES	PARADIGMS

The Chambers Dictionary is the authority for many longer words; see *OSW* Introduction, page xii.

PARADING	PARALYSE	PARAS	PARDINE	PARHELIA
PARADISAL	PARALYSED	PARASANG	PARDNER	PARHELIC
PARADISE	PARALYSER	PARASANGS	PARDNERS	PARHELION
PARADISES	PARALYSERS	PARASCEVE	PARDON	PARHYPATE
PARADISIC	PARALYSES	PARASCEVES	PARDONED	PARHYPATES
PARADOR	PARALYSING	PARASITE	PARDONER	PARIAH
PARADORES	PARALYSIS	PARASITES	PARDONERS	PARIAHS
PARADOS	PARALYTIC	PARASITIC	PARDONING	PARIAL
PARADOSES	PARALYTICS	PARASOL	PARDONINGS	PARIALS
PARADOX	PARALYZE	PARASOLS	PARDONS	PARIETAL
PARADOXAL	PARALYZED	PARATAXES	PARDS	PARIETALS
PARADOXER	PARALYZER	PARATAXIS	PARDY	PARING
PARADOXERS	PARALYZERS	PARATHA	PARE	PARINGS
PARADOXES	PARALYZES	PARATHAS	PARECIOUS	PARISCHAN
PARADOXIES	PARALYZING	PARATONIC	PARED	PARISCHANS
PARADOXY	PARAMATTA	PARAVAIL	PAREGORIC	PARISH
PARADROP	PARAMATTAS	PARAVANE	PAREGORICS	PARISHEN
PARADROPS	PARAMECIA	PARAVANES	PAREIRA	PARISHENS
PARAFFIN	PARAMEDIC	PARAVANT	PAREIRAS	PARISHES
PARAFFINE	PARAMEDICS	PARAVAUNT	PARELLA	PARISON
PARAFFINED	PARAMENT	PARAZOA	PARELLAS	PARISONS
PARAFFINES	PARAMENTS	PARAZOAN	PARELLE	PARITIES
PARAFFINING	PARAMESE	PARAZOANS	PARELLES	PARITOR
PARAFFINS	PARAMESES	PARAZOON	PARENESES	PARITORS
PARAFFINY	PARAMETER	PARBOIL	PARENESIS	PARITY
PARAFFLE	PARAMETERS	PARBOILED	PARENT	PARK
PARAFFLES	PARAMO	PARBOILING	PARENTAGE	PARKA
PARAFLE	PARAMORPH	PARBOILS	PARENTAGES	PARKAS
PARAFLES	PARAMORPHS	PARBREAK	PARENTAL	PARKED
PARAFOIL	PARAMOS	PARBREAKED	PARENTED	PARKEE
PARAFOILS	PARAMOUNT	PARBREAKING	PARENTING	PARKEES
PARAGE	PARAMOUNTS	PARBREAKS	PARENTINGS	PARKER
PARAGES	PARAMOUR	PARBUCKLE	PARENTS	PARKERS
PARAGOGE	PARAMOURS	PARBUCKLED	PAREO	PARKI
PARAGOGES	PARANETE	PARBUCKLES	PAREOS	PARKIE
PARAGOGIC	PARANETES	PARBUCKLING	PARER	PARKIER
PARAGOGUE	PARANG	PARCEL	PARERGA	PARKIES
PARAGOGUES	PARANGS	PARCELLED	PARERGON	PARKIEST
PARAGON	PARANOEA	PARCELLING	PARERS	PARKIN
PARAGONED	PARANOEAS	PARCELS	PARES	PARKING
PARAGONING	PARANOEIC	PARCENARIES	PARESES	PARKINGS
PARAGONS	PARANOEICS	PARCENARY	PARESIS	PARKINS
PARAGRAM	PARANOIA	PARCENER	PARETIC	PARKIS
PARAGRAMS	PARANOIAC	PARCENERS	PAREU	PARKISH
PARAGRAPH	PARANOIACS	PARCH	PAREUS	PARKLAND
PARAGRAPHED	PARANOIAS	PARCHED	PARFAIT	PARKLANDS
PARAGRAPHING	PARANOIC	PARCHEDLY	PARFAITS	PARKLIKE
PARAGRAPHS	PARANOICS	PARCHES	PARFLECHE	PARKLY
PARAKEET	PARANOID	PARCHESI	PARFLECHES	PARKS
PARAKEETS	PARANYM	PARCHESIS	PARGANA	PARKWARD
PARALALIA	PARANYMPH	PARCHING	PARGANAS	PARKWARDS
PARALALIAS	PARANYMPHS	PARCHMENT	PARGASITE	PARKWAY
PARALEGAL	PARANYMS	PARCHMENTS	PARGASITES	PARKWAYS
PARALEGALS	PARAPET	PARCIMONIES	PARGE	PARKY
PARALEXIA	PARAPETED	PARCIMONY	PARGED	PARLANCE
PARALEXIAS	PARAPETS	PARCLOSE	PARGES	PARLANCES
PARALLAX	PARAPH	PARCLOSES	PARGET	PARLANDO
PARALLAXES	PARAPHED	PARD	PARGETED	PARLAY
PARALLEL	PARAPHING	PARDAL	PARGETER	PARLAYED
PARALLELED	PARAPHS	PARDALE	PARGETERS	PARLAYING
PARALLELING	PARAPODIA	PARDALES	PARGETING	PARLAYS
PARALLELINGS	PARAQUAT	PARDALIS	PARGETINGS	PARLE
PARALLELS	PARAQUATS	PARDALISES	PARGETS	PARLED
PARALOGIA	PARAQUITO	PARDALS	PARGETTED	PARLES
PARALOGIAS	PARAQUITOS	PARDED	PARGETTING	PARLEY
PARALOGIES	PARARHYME	PARDI	PARGETTINGS	PARLEYED
PARALOGY	PARARHYMES	PARDIE	PARGING	PARLEYING

The Chambers Dictionary is the authority for many longer words; see *OSW* Introduction, page xii.

PARLEYS
PARLEYVOO
PARLEYVOOED
PARLEYVOOING
PARLEYVOOS
PARLIES
PARLING
PARLOR
PARLORS
PARLOUR
PARLOURS
PARLOUS
PARLY
PAROCHIAL
PAROCHIN
PAROCHINE
PAROCHINES
PAROCHINS
PARODIC
PARODICAL
PARODIED
PARODIES
PARODIST
PARODISTS
PARODY
PARODYING
PAROEMIA
PAROEMIAC
PAROEMIACS
PAROEMIAL
PAROEMIAS
PAROICOUS
PAROL
PAROLE
PAROLED
PAROLEE
PAROLEES
PAROLES
PAROLING
PARONYM
PARONYMIES
PARONYMS
PARONYMY
PAROQUET
PAROQUETS
PAROTIC
PAROTID
PAROTIDS
PAROTIS
PAROTISES
PAROTITIS
PAROTITISES
PAROUSIA
PAROUSIAS
PAROXYSM
PAROXYSMS
PARP
PARPANE
PARPANES
PARPED
PARPEN
PARPEND
PARPENDS
PARPENS
PARPENT
PARPENTS
PARPING

PARPOINT
PARPOINTS
PARPS
PARQUET
PARQUETED
PARQUETING
PARQUETRIES
PARQUETRY
PARQUETS
PARQUETTED
PARQUETTING
PARR
PARRAKEET
PARRAKEETS
PARRAL
PARRALS
PARREL
PARRELS
PARRHESIA
PARRHESIAS
PARRICIDE
PARRICIDES
PARRIED
PARRIES
PARRITCH
PARRITCHES
PARROCK
PARROCKED
PARROCKING
PARROCKS
PARROQUET
PARROQUETS
PARROT
PARROTED
PARROTER
PARROTERS
PARROTING
PARROTRIES
PARROTRY
PARROTS
PARROTY
PARRS
PARRY
PARRYING
PARS
PARSE
PARSEC
PARSECS
PARSED
PARSER
PARSERS
PARSES
PARSIMONIES
PARSIMONY
PARSING
PARSINGS
PARSLEY
PARSLEYS
PARSNEP
PARSNEPS
PARSNIP
PARSNIPS
PARSON
PARSONAGE
PARSONAGES
PARSONIC
PARSONISH

PARSONS
PART
PARTAKE
PARTAKEN
PARTAKER
PARTAKERS
PARTAKES
PARTAKING
PARTAKINGS
PARTAN
PARTANS
PARTED
PARTER
PARTERRE
PARTERRES
PARTERS
PARTI
PARTIAL
PARTIALLY
PARTIALS
PARTIBLE
PARTICLE
PARTICLES
PARTIED
PARTIES
PARTIM
PARTING
PARTINGS
PARTIS
PARTISAN
PARTISANS
PARTITA
PARTITAS
PARTITE
PARTITION
PARTITIONED
PARTITIONING
PARTITIONS
PARTITIVE
PARTITIVES
PARTITURA
PARTITURAS
PARTIZAN
PARTIZANS
PARTLET
PARTLETS
PARTLY
PARTNER
PARTNERED
PARTNERING
PARTNERS
PARTON
PARTONS
PARTOOK
PARTRIDGE
PARTRIDGES
PARTS
PARTURE
PARTURES
PARTWORK
PARTWORKS
PARTY
PARTYING
PARTYISM
PARTYISMS
PARULIS
PARULISES

PARURE
PARURES
PARVENU
PARVENUS
PARVIS
PARVISE
PARVISES
PAS
PASCAL
PASCALS
PASCHAL
PASCUAL
PASEAR
PASEARED
PASEARING
PASEARS
PASEO
PASEOS
PASH
PASHA
PASHALIK
PASHALIKS
PASHAS
PASHED
PASHES
PASHIM
PASHIMS
PASHING
PASHM
PASHMINA
PASHMINAS
PASHMS
PASPALUM
PASPALUMS
PASPIES
PASPY
PASQUILER
PASQUILERS
PASS
PASSABLE
PASSABLY
PASSADE
PASSADES
PASSADO
PASSADOES
PASSADOS
PASSAGE
PASSAGED
PASSAGES
PASSAGING
PASSAMENT
PASSAMENTED
PASSAMENTING
PASSAMENTS
PASSANT
PASSE
PASSED
PASSEE
PASSEMENT
PASSEMENTED
PASSEMENTING
PASSEMENTS
PASSENGER
PASSENGERS
PASSEPIED
PASSEPIEDS
PASSER

PASSERINE
PASSERINES
PASSERS
PASSES
PASSIBLE
PASSIBLY
PASSIM
PASSING
PASSINGS
PASSION
PASSIONAL
PASSIONALS
PASSIONED
PASSIONING
PASSIONS
PASSIVATE
PASSIVATED
PASSIVATES
PASSIVATING
PASSIVE
PASSIVELY
PASSIVES
PASSIVISM
PASSIVISMS
PASSIVIST
PASSIVISTS
PASSIVITIES
PASSIVITY
PASSKEY
PASSKEYS
PASSLESS
PASSMAN
PASSMEN
PASSMENT
PASSMENTED
PASSMENTING
PASSMENTS
PASSOUT
PASSOUTS
PASSPORT
PASSPORTS
PASSUS
PASSUSES
PASSWORD
PASSWORDS
PAST
PASTA
PASTANCE
PASTANCES
PASTAS
PASTE
PASTED
PASTEL
PASTELS
PASTER
PASTERN
PASTERNS
PASTERS
PASTES
PASTICCI
PASTICCIO
PASTICHE
PASTICHES
PASTIER
PASTIES
PASTIEST
PASTIL

The Chambers Dictionary is the authority for many longer words; see *OSW* Introduction, page xii.

PASTILLE	PATELLA	PATIOS	PATTEE	PAUSER
PASTILLES	PATELLAE	PATLY	PATTEN	PAUSERS
PASTILS	PATELLAR	PATNESS	PATTENED	PAUSES
PASTIME	PATELLAS	PATNESSES	PATTENING	PAUSING
PASTIMES	PATELLATE	PATOIS	PATTENS	PAUSINGLY
PASTINESS	PATEN	PATONCE	PATTER	PAUSINGS
PASTINESSES	PATENCIES	PATRIAL	PATTERED	PAVAGE
PASTING	PATENCY	PATRIALS	PATTERER	PAVAGES
PASTINGS	PATENS	PATRIARCH	PATTERERS	PAVAN
PASTIS	PATENT	PATRIARCHS	PATTERING	PAVANE
PASTISES	PATENTED	PATRIATE	PATTERN	PAVANES
PASTOR	PATENTEE	PATRIATED	PATTERNED	PAVANS
PASTORAL	PATENTEES	PATRIATES	PATTERNING	PAVE
PASTORALE	PATENTING	PATRIATING	PATTERNS	PAVED
PASTORALES	PATENTLY	PATRICIAN	PATTERS	PAVEMENT
PASTORALS	PATENTOR	PATRICIANS	PATTES	PAVEMENTED
PASTORATE	PATENTORS	PATRICIDE	PATTIES	PAVEMENTING
PASTORATES	PATENTS	PATRICIDES	PATTING	PAVEMENTS
PASTORLY	PATER	PATRICK	PATTLE	PAVEN
PASTORS	PATERA	PATRICKS	PATTLES	PAVENS
PASTRAMI	PATERAE	PATRICO	PATTY	PAVER
PASTRAMIS	PATERCOVE	PATRICOES	PATULIN	PAVERS
PASTRIES	PATERCOVES	PATRILINIES	PATULINS	PAVES
PASTRY	PATERERO	PATRILINY	PATULOUS	PAVID
PASTS	PATEREROES	PATRIMONIES	PATZER	PAVILION
PASTURAGE	PATEREROS	PATRIMONY	PATZERS	PAVILIONED
PASTURAGES	PATERNAL	PATRIOT	PAUA	PAVILIONING
PASTURAL	PATERNITIES	PATRIOTIC	PAUAS	PAVILIONS
PASTURE	PATERNITY	PATRIOTS	PAUCITIES	PAVIN
PASTURED	PATERS	PATRISTIC	PAUCITY	PAVING
PASTURES	PATES	PATRISTICS	PAUGHTIER	PAVINGS
PASTURING	PATH	PATROL	PAUGHTIEST	PAVINS
PASTY	PATHED	PATROLLED	PAUGHTY	PAVIOR
PAT	PATHETIC	PATROLLER	PAUL	PAVIORS
PATACA	PATHETICS	PATROLLERS	PAULDRON	PAVIOUR
PATACAS	PATHIC	PATROLLING	PAULDRONS	PAVIOURS
PATAGIA	PATHICS	PATROLMAN	PAULOWNIA	PAVIS
PATAGIAL	PATHING	PATROLMEN	PAULOWNIAS	PAVISE
PATAGIUM	PATHLESS	PATROLOGIES	PAULS	PAVISES
PATAMAR	PATHOGEN	PATROLOGY	PAUNCE	PAVLOVA
PATAMARS	PATHOGENIES	PATROLS	PAUNCES	PAVLOVAS
PATBALL	PATHOGENS	PATRON	PAUNCH	PAVONAZZO
PATBALLS	PATHOGENY	PATRONAGE	PAUNCHED	PAVONAZZOS
PATCH	PATHOLOGIES	PATRONAGED	PAUNCHES	PAVONE
PATCHABLE	PATHOLOGY	PATRONAGES	PAUNCHIER	PAVONES
PATCHIED	PATHOS	PATRONAGING	PAUNCHIEST	PAVONIAN
PATCHER	PATHOSES	PATRONAL	PAUNCHING	PAVONINE
PATCHERIES	PATHS	PATRONESS	PAUNCHY	PAW
PATCHERS	PATHWAY	PATRONESSES	PAUPER	PAWA
PATCHERY	PATHWAYS	PATRONISE	PAUPERESS	PAWAS
PATCHES	PATIBLE	PATRONISED	PAUPERESSES	PAWAW
PATCHIER	PATIENCE	PATRONISES	PAUPERISE	PAWAWED
PATCHIEST	PATIENCES	PATRONISING	PAUPERISED	PAWAWING
PATCHILY	PATIENT	PATRONIZE	PAUPERISES	PAWAWS
PATCHING	PATIENTED	PATRONIZED	PAUPERISING	PAWED
PATCHINGS	PATIENTING	PATRONIZES	PAUPERISM	PAWING
PATCHOCKE	PATIENTLY	PATRONIZING	PAUPERISMS	PAWK
PATCHOCKES	PATIENTS	PATRONNE	PAUPERIZE	PAWKIER
PATCHOULI	PATIN	PATRONNES	PAUPERIZED	PAWKIEST
PATCHOULIES	PATINA	PATRONS	PAUPERIZES	PAWKILY
PATCHOULIS	PATINAS	PATROON	PAUPERIZING	PAWKINESS
PATCHOULY	PATINATED	PATROONS	PAUPERS	PAWKINESSES
PATCHWORK	PATINE	PATS	PAUSAL	PAWKS
PATCHWORKS	PATINED	PATSIES	PAUSE	PAWKY
PATCHY	PATINES	PATSY	PAUSED	PAWL
PATE	PATINS	PATTE	PAUSEFUL	PAWLS
PATED	PATIO	PATTED	PAUSELESS	PAWN

The Chambers Dictionary is the authority for many longer words; see *OSW* Introduction, page xii.

PAWNCE	PEACETIME	PEARLWORTS	PECCARY	PEDALLER
PAWNCES	PEACETIMES	PEARLY	PECCAVI	PEDALLERS
PAWNED	PEACH	PEARMAIN	PECCAVIS	PEDALLING
PAWNEE	PEACHED	PEARMAINS	PECH	PEDALLINGS
PAWNEES	PEACHER	PEARS	PECHED	PEDALO
PAWNER	PEACHERS	PEARST	PECHING	PEDALOES
PAWNERS	PEACHES	PEART	PECHS	PEDALOS
PAWNING	PEACHIER	PEARTLY	PECK	PEDALS
PAWNS	PEACHIEST	PEAS	PECKE	PEDANT
PAWNSHOP	PEACHING	PEASANT	PECKED	PEDANTIC
PAWNSHOPS	PEACHY	PEASANTRIES	PECKER	PEDANTISE
PAWPAW	PEACING	PEASANTRY	PECKERS	PEDANTISED
PAWPAWS	PEACOCK	PEASANTS	PECKES	PEDANTISES
PAWS	PEACOCKED	PEASANTY	PECKING	PEDANTISING
PAX	PEACOCKING	PEASCOD	PECKINGS	PEDANTISM
PAXES	PEACOCKS	PEASCODS	PECKISH	PEDANTISMS
PAXIUBA	PEACOCKY	PEASE	PECKS	PEDANTIZE
PAXIUBAS	PEACOD	PEASECOD	PECS	PEDANTIZED
PAXWAX	PEACODS	PEASECODS	PECTEN	PEDANTIZES
PAXWAXES	PEAFOWL	PEASED	PECTIC	PEDANTIZING
PAY	PEAFOWLS	PEASES	PECTIN	PEDANTRIES
PAYABLE	PEAG	PEASEWEEP	PECTINAL	PEDANTRY
PAYBACK	PEAGS	PEASEWEEPS	PECTINATE	PEDANTS
PAYBACKS	PEAK	PEASING	PECTINEAL	PEDATE
PAYED	PEAKED	PEASON	PECTINES	PEDATELY
PAYEE	PEAKIER	PEAT	PECTINS	PEDATIFID
PAYEES	PEAKIEST	PEATARIES	PECTISE	PEDDER
PAYER	PEAKING	PEATARY	PECTISED	PEDDERS
PAYERS	PEAKS	PEATERIES	PECTISES	PEDDLE
PAYFONE	PEAKY	PEATERY	PECTISING	PEDDLED
PAYFONES	PEAL	PEATIER	PECTIZE	PEDDLER
PAYING	PEALED	PEATIEST	PECTIZED	PEDDLERS
PAYINGS	PEALING	PEATMAN	PECTIZES	PEDDLES
PAYMASTER	PEALS	PEATMEN	PECTIZING	PEDDLING
PAYMASTERS	PEAN	PEATS	PECTOLITE	PEDDLINGS
PAYMENT	PEANED	PEATSHIP	PECTOLITES	PEDERAST
PAYMENTS	PEANING	PEATSHIPS	PECTORAL	PEDERASTIES
PAYNIM	PEANS	PEATY	PECTORALS	PEDERASTS
PAYNIMRIES	PEANUT	PEAVEY	PECTOSE	PEDERASTY
PAYNIMRY	PEANUTS	PEAVEYS	PECTOSES	PEDERERO
PAYNIMS	PEAPOD	PEAVIES	PECULATE	PEDEREROES
PAYOLA	PEAPODS	PEAVY	PECULATED	PEDEREROS
PAYOLAS	PEAR	PEAZE	PECULATES	PEDESES
PAYROLL	PEARCE	PEAZED	PECULATING	PEDESIS
PAYROLLS	PEARCED	PEAZES	PECULATOR	PEDESTAL
PAYS	PEARCES	PEAZING	PECULATORS	PEDESTALLED
PAYSAGE	PEARCING	PEBA	PECULIA	PEDESTALLING
PAYSAGES	PEARE	PEBAS	PECULIAR	PEDESTALS
PAYSAGIST	PEARES	PEBBLE	PECULIARS	PEDETIC
PAYSAGISTS	PEARL	PEBBLED	PECULIUM	PEDICAB
PAYSD	PEARLED	PEBBLES	PECUNIARY	PEDICABS
PAYSLIP	PEARLER	PEBBLIER	PECUNIOUS	PEDICEL
PAYSLIPS	PEARLERS	PEBBLIEST	PED	PEDICELS
PAZAZZ	PEARLIER	PEBBLING	PEDAGOGIC	PEDICLE
PAZAZZES	PEARLIES	PEBBLINGS	PEDAGOGICS	PEDICLED
PEA	PEARLIEST	PEBBLY	PEDAGOGIES	PEDICLES
PEABERRIES	PEARLIN	PEBRINE	PEDAGOGUE	PEDICULAR
PEABERRY	PEARLING	PEBRINES	PEDAGOGUED	PEDICULI
PEACE	PEARLINGS	PEC	PEDAGOGUES	PEDICULUS
PEACEABLE	PEARLINS	PECAN	PEDAGOGUING	PEDICURE
PEACEABLY	PEARLISED	PECANS	PEDAGOGY	PEDICURED
PEACED	PEARLITE	PECCABLE	PEDAL	PEDICURES
PEACEFUL	PEARLITES	PECCANCIES	PEDALED	PEDICURING
PEACELESS	PEARLITIC	PECCANCY	PEDALIER	PEDIGREE
PEACENIK	PEARLIZED	PECCANT	PEDALIERS	PEDIGREED
PEACENIKS	PEARLS	PECCANTLY	PEDALING	PEDIGREES
PEACES	PEARLWORT	PECCARIES	PEDALLED	PEDIMENT

The Chambers Dictionary is the authority for many longer words; see *OSW* Introduction, page xii.

PEDIMENTS
PEDIPALP
PEDIPALPI
PEDIPALPS
PEDLAR
PEDLARIES
PEDLARS
PEDLARY
PEDOLOGIES
PEDOLOGY
PEDOMETER
PEDOMETERS
PEDRAIL
PEDRAILS
PEDRERO
PEDREROES
PEDREROS
PEDRO
PEDROS
PEDS
PEDUNCLE
PEDUNCLES
PEE
PEECE
PEECES
PEED
PEEING
PEEK
PEEKABO
PEEKABOO
PEEKABOOS
PEEKABOS
PEEKED
PEEKING
PEEKS
PEEL
PEELED
PEELER
PEELERS
PEELING
PEELINGS
PEELS
PEEN
PEENED
PEENGE
PEENGED
PEENGEING
PEENGES
PEENGING
PEENING
PEENS
PEEOY
PEEOYS
PEEP
PEEPE
PEEPED
PEEPER
PEEPERS
PEEPES
PEEPING
PEEPS
PEEPUL
PEEPULS
PEER
PEERAGE
PEERAGES
PEERED

PEERESS
PEERESSES
PEERIE
PEERIER
PEERIES
PEERIEST
PEERING
PEERLESS
PEERS
PEERY
PEES
PEESWEEP
PEESWEEPS
PEETWEET
PEETWEETS
PEEVE
PEEVED
PEEVER
PEEVERS
PEEVES
PEEVING
PEEVISH
PEEVISHLY
PEEWEE
PEEWEES
PEEWIT
PEEWITS
PEG
PEGASUS
PEGASUSES
PEGBOARD
PEGBOARDS
PEGGED
PEGGIES
PEGGING
PEGGINGS
PEGGY
PEGH
PEGHED
PEGHING
PEGHS
PEGMATITE
PEGMATITES
PEGS
PEIGNOIR
PEIGNOIRS
PEIN
PEINCT
PEINCTED
PEINCTING
PEINCTS
PEINED
PEINING
PEINS
PEIRASTIC
PEISE
PEISED
PEISES
PEISHWA
PEISHWAH
PEISHWAHS
PEISHWAS
PEISING
PEIZE
PEIZED
PEIZES
PEIZING

PEJORATE
PEJORATED
PEJORATES
PEJORATING
PEKAN
PEKANS
PEKE
PEKES
PEKOE
PEKOES
PELA
PELAGE
PELAGES
PELAGIAN
PELAGIANS
PELAGIC
PELAS
PELE
PELERINE
PELERINES
PELES
PELF
PELFS
PELHAM
PELHAMS
PELICAN
PELICANS
PELISSE
PELISSES
PELITE
PELITES
PELITIC
PELL
PELLACH
PELLACHS
PELLACK
PELLACKS
PELLAGRA
PELLAGRAS
PELLAGRIN
PELLAGRINS
PELLET
PELLETED
PELLETIFIED
PELLETIFIES
PELLETIFY
PELLETIFYING
PELLETING
PELLETISE
PELLETISED
PELLETISES
PELLETISING
PELLETIZE
PELLETIZED
PELLETIZES
PELLETIZING
PELLETS
PELLICLE
PELLICLES
PELLITORIES
PELLITORY
PELLOCK
PELLOCKS
PELLS
PELLUCID
PELMA
PELMANISM

PELMANISMS
PELMAS
PELMATIC
PELMET
PELMETS
PELOID
PELOIDS
PELOLOGIES
PELOLOGY
PELORIA
PELORIAS
PELORIC
PELORIES
PELORISED
PELORISM
PELORISMS
PELORIZED
PELORUS
PELORUSES
PELORY
PELOTA
PELOTAS
PELT
PELTA
PELTAE
PELTAS
PELTAST
PELTASTS
PELTATE
PELTED
PELTER
PELTERED
PELTERING
PELTERS
PELTING
PELTINGLY
PELTINGS
PELTRIES
PELTRY
PELTS
PELVES
PELVIC
PELVIFORM
PELVIS
PELVISES
PEMBROKE
PEMBROKES
PEMICAN
PEMICANS
PEMMICAN
PEMMICANS
PEMOLINE
PEMOLINES
PEMPHIGUS
PEMPHIGUSES
PEN
PENAL
PENALISE
PENALISED
PENALISES
PENALISING
PENALIZE
PENALIZED
PENALIZES
PENALIZING
PENALLY
PENALTIES

PENALTY
PENANCE
PENANCED
PENANCES
PENANCING
PENATES
PENCE
PENCEL
PENCELS
PENCES
PENCHANT
PENCHANTS
PENCIL
PENCILLED
PENCILLER
PENCILLERS
PENCILLING
PENCILLINGS
PENCILS
PENCRAFT
PENCRAFTS
PEND
PENDANT
PENDANTS
PENDED
PENDENCIES
PENDENCY
PENDENT
PENDENTLY
PENDENTS
PENDICLE
PENDICLER
PENDICLERS
PENDICLES
PENDING
PENDRAGON
PENDRAGONS
PENDS
PENDULAR
PENDULATE
PENDULATED
PENDULATES
PENDULATING
PENDULINE
PENDULOUS
PENDULUM
PENDULUMS
PENE
PENED
PENEPLAIN
PENEPLAINS
PENEPLANE
PENEPLANES
PENES
PENETRANT
PENETRANTS
PENETRATE
PENETRATED
PENETRATES
PENETRATING
PENFOLD
PENFOLDS
PENFUL
PENFULS
PENGUIN
PENGUINRIES
PENGUINRY

The Chambers Dictionary is the authority for many longer words; see *OSW* Introduction, page xii.

PENGUINS	PENNYFEE	PENTHOUSE	PEPINOS	PERAI
PENHOLDER	PENNYFEES	PENTHOUSED	PEPLA	PERAIS
PENHOLDERS	PENNYLAND	PENTHOUSES	PEPLOS	PERCALE
PENI	PENNYLANDS	PENTHOUSING	PEPLOSES	PERCALES
PENIAL	PENOLOGIES	PENTICE	PEPLUM	PERCALINE
PENIE	PENOLOGY	PENTICED	PEPLUMS	PERCALINES
PENIES	PENONCEL	PENTICES	PEPLUS	PERCASE
PENILE	PENONCELS	PENTICING	PEPLUSES	PERCE
PENILLION	PENS	PENTISE	PEPO	PERCEABLE
PENING	PENSEE	PENTISED	PEPOS	PERCEANT
PENINSULA	PENSEES	PENTISES	PEPPED	PERCED
PENINSULAS	PENSEL	PENTISING	PEPPER	PERCEIVE
PENIS	PENSELS	PENTODE	PEPPERED	PERCEIVED
PENISES	PENSIL	PENTODES	PEPPERER	PERCEIVER
PENISTONE	PENSILE	PENTOMIC	PEPPERERS	PERCEIVERS
PENISTONES	PENSILITIES	PENTOSAN	PEPPERING	PERCEIVES
PENITENCE	PENSILITY	PENTOSANE	PEPPERINGS	PERCEIVING
PENITENCES	PENSILS	PENTOSANES	PEPPERONI	PERCEIVINGS
PENITENCIES	PENSION	PENTOSANS	PEPPERONIS	PERCEN
PENITENCY	PENSIONED	PENTOSE	PEPPERS	PERCENTAL
PENITENT	PENSIONER	PENTOSES	PEPPERY	PERCEPT
PENITENTS	PENSIONERS	PENTOXIDE	PEPPIER	PERCEPTS
PENK	PENSIONING	PENTOXIDES	PEPPIEST	PERCES
PENKNIFE	PENSIONS	PENTROOF	PEPPING	PERCH
PENKNIVES	PENSIVE	PENTROOFS	PEPPY	PERCHANCE
PENKS	PENSIVELY	PENTS	PEPS	PERCHED
PENLIGHT	PENSTEMON	PENTYLENE	PEPSIN	PERCHER
PENLIGHTS	PENSTEMONS	PENTYLENES	PEPSINATE	PERCHERON
PENMAN	PENSTOCK	PENUCHE	PEPSINATED	PERCHERONS
PENMEN	PENSTOCKS	PENUCHES	PEPSINATES	PERCHERS
PENNA	PENSUM	PENUCHI	PEPSINATING	PERCHERY
PENNAE	PENSUMS	PENUCHIS	PEPSINE	PERCHES
PENNAL	PENT	PENUCHLE	PEPSINES	PERCHING
PENNALISM	PENTACLE	PENUCHLES	PEPSINS	PERCHINGS
PENNALISMS	PENTACLES	PENULT	PEPTIC	PERCIFORM
PENNALS	PENTACT	PENULTIMA	PEPTICITIES	PERCINE
PENNANT	PENTACTS	PENULTIMAS	PEPTICITY	PERCING
PENNANTS	PENTAD	PENULTS	PEPTICS	PERCOCT
PENNATE	PENTADIC	PENUMBRA	PEPTIDASE	PERCOID
PENNATULA	PENTADS	PENUMBRAL	PEPTIDASES	PERCOLATE
PENNATULAE	PENTAGON	PENUMBRAS	PEPTIDE	PERCOLATED
PENNATULAS	PENTAGONS	PENURIES	PEPTIDES	PERCOLATES
PENNE	PENTAGRAM	PENURIOUS	PEPTISE	PERCOLATING
PENNED	PENTAGRAMS	PENURY	PEPTISED	PERCOLIN
PENNEECH	PENTALOGIES	PENWOMAN	PEPTISES	PERCOLINS
PENNEECHS	PENTALOGY	PENWOMEN	PEPTISING	PERCUSS
PENNEECK	PENTALPHA	PEON	PEPTIZE	PERCUSSED
PENNEECKS	PENTALPHAS	PEONAGE	PEPTIZED	PERCUSSES
PENNER	PENTAMERIES	PEONAGES	PEPTIZES	PERCUSSING
PENNERS	PENTAMERY	PEONIES	PEPTIZING	PERCUSSOR
PENNES	PENTANE	PEONISM	PEPTONE	PERCUSSORS
PENNIED	PENTANES	PEONISMS	PEPTONES	PERDENDO
PENNIES	PENTANGLE	PEONS	PEPTONISE	PERDIE
PENNIFORM	PENTANGLES	PEONY	PEPTONISED	PERDITION
PENNILESS	PENTAPODIES	PEOPLE	PEPTONISES	PERDITIONS
PENNILL	PENTAPODY	PEOPLED	PEPTONISING	PERDU
PENNINE	PENTARCH	PEOPLES	PEPTONIZE	PERDUE
PENNINES	PENTARCHIES	PEOPLING	PEPTONIZED	PERDUES
PENNING	PENTARCHS	PEP	PEPTONIZES	PERDURE
PENNINITE	PENTARCHY	PEPERINO	PEPTONIZING	PERDURED
PENNINITES	PENTATHLA	PEPERINOS	PER	PERDURES
PENNON	PENTEL®	PEPEROMIA	PERACUTE	PERDURING
PENNONCEL	PENTELS	PEPEROMIAS	PERAEA	PERDUS
PENNONCELS	PENTENE	PEPERONI	PERAEON	PERDY
PENNONED	PENTENES	PEPERONIS	PERAEONS	PERE
PENNONS	PENTHIA	PEPFUL	PERAEOPOD	PEREGAL
PENNY	PENTHIAS	PEPINO	PERAEOPODS	PEREGALS

The Chambers Dictionary is the authority for many longer words; see *OSW* Introduction, page xii.

PEREGRINE	PERFUSES	PERIKARYA	PERISPERMS	PERMUTED
PEREGRINES	PERFUSING	PERIL	PERISTOME	PERMUTES
PEREIA	PERFUSION	PERILLED	PERISTOMES	PERMUTING
PEREION	PERFUSIONS	PERILLING	PERISTYLE	PERN
PEREIOPOD	PERFUSIVE	PERILOUS	PERISTYLES	PERNANCIES
PEREIOPODS	PERGOLA	PERILS	PERITI	PERNANCY
PEREIRA	PERGOLAS	PERILUNE	PERITRICH	PERNS
PEREIRAS	PERGUNNAH	PERILUNES	PERITRICHA	PERONE
PERENNATE	PERGUNNAHS	PERILYMPH	PERITUS	PERONEAL
PERENNATED	PERHAPS	PERILYMPHS	PERIWIG	PERONES
PERENNATES	PERI	PERIMETER	PERIWIGGED	PERONEUS
PERENNATING	PERIAGUA	PERIMETERS	PERIWIGGING	PERONEUSES
PERENNIAL	PERIAGUAS	PERIMETRIES	PERIWIGS	PERORATE
PERENNIALS	PERIAKTOI	PERIMETRY	PERJINK	PERORATED
PERENNITIES	PERIAKTOS	PERIMORPH	PERJURE	PERORATES
PERENNITY	PERIANTH	PERIMORPHS	PERJURED	PERORATING
PERES	PERIANTHS	PERINAEUM	PERJURER	PEROVSKIA
PERFAY	PERIAPT	PERINAEUMS	PERJURERS	PEROVSKIAS
PERFECT	PERIAPTS	PERINATAL	PERJURES	PEROXIDE
PERFECTA	PERIBLAST	PERINEA	PERJURIES	PEROXIDED
PERFECTAS	PERIBLASTS	PERINEAL	PERJURING	PEROXIDES
PERFECTED	PERIBLEM	PERINEUM	PERJUROUS	PEROXIDING
PERFECTER	PERIBLEMS	PERINEUMS	PERJURY	PERPEND
PERFECTERS	PERIBOLI	PERIOD	PERK	PERPENDED
PERFECTEST	PERIBOLOI	PERIODATE	PERKED	PERPENDING
PERFECTI	PERIBOLOS	PERIODATES	PERKIER	PERPENDS
PERFECTING	PERIBOLUS	PERIODED	PERKIEST	PERPENT
PERFECTLY	PERICARP	PERIODIC	PERKILY	PERPENTS
PERFECTO	PERICARPS	PERIODING	PERKIN	PERPETUAL
PERFECTOR	PERICLASE	PERIODS	PERKINESS	PERPETUALS
PERFECTORS	PERICLASES	PERIOST	PERKINESSES	PERPLEX
PERFECTOS	PERICLINE	PERIOSTEA	PERKING	PERPLEXED
PERFECTS	PERICLINES	PERIOSTS	PERKINS	PERPLEXES
PERFERVID	PERICON	PERIOTIC	PERKS	PERPLEXING
PERFERVOR	PERICONES	PERIOTICS	PERKY	PERRADIAL
PERFERVORS	PERICOPE	PERIPATUS	PERLITE	PERRADII
PERFET	PERICOPES	PERIPATUSES	PERLITES	PERRADIUS
PERFIDIES	PERICRANIES	PERIPETIA	PERLITIC	PERRIER
PERFIDY	PERICRANY	PERIPETIAS	PERLOUS	PERRIERS
PERFORANS	PERICYCLE	PERIPETIES	PERM	PERRIES
PERFORANSES	PERICYCLES	PERIPETY	PERMALLOY	PERRON
PERFORANT	PERIDERM	PERIPHERIES	PERMALLOYS	PERRONS
PERFORATE	PERIDERMS	PERIPHERY	PERMANENT	PERRUQUE
PERFORATED	PERIDIA	PERIPLAST	PERMEABLE	PERRUQUES
PERFORATES	PERIDIAL	PERIPLASTS	PERMEABLY	PERRY
PERFORATING	PERIDINIA	PERIPLUS	PERMEANCE	PERSANT
PERFORCE	PERIDIUM	PERIPLUSES	PERMEANCES	PERSAUNT
PERFORM	PERIDIUMS	PERIPROCT	PERMEASE	PERSE
PERFORMED	PERIDOT	PERIPROCTS	PERMEASES	PERSECUTE
PERFORMER	PERIDOTE	PERIPTERIES	PERMEATE	PERSECUTED
PERFORMERS	PERIDOTES	PERIPTERY	PERMEATED	PERSECUTES
PERFORMING	PERIDOTIC	PERIQUE	PERMEATES	PERSECUTING
PERFORMINGS	PERIDOTS	PERIQUES	PERMEATING	PERSEITIES
PERFORMS	PERIDROME	PERIS	PERMED	PERSEITY
PERFUME	PERIDROMES	PERISARC	PERMING	PERSELINE
PERFUMED	PERIGEAL	PERISARCS	PERMIT	PERSELINES
PERFUMER	PERIGEAN	PERISCIAN	PERMITS	PERSES
PERFUMERIES	PERIGEE	PERISCIANS	PERMITTED	PERSEVERE
PERFUMERS	PERIGEES	PERISCOPE	PERMITTER	PERSEVERED
PERFUMERY	PERIGON	PERISCOPES	PERMITTERS	PERSEVERES
PERFUMES	PERIGONE	PERISH	PERMITTING	PERSEVERING
PERFUMING	PERIGONES	PERISHED	PERMS	PERSICO
PERFUMY	PERIGONIA	PERISHER	PERMUTATE	PERSICOS
PERFUSATE	PERIGONS	PERISHERS	PERMUTATED	PERSICOT
PERFUSATES	PERIGYNIES	PERISHES	PERMUTATES	PERSICOTS
PERFUSE	PERIGYNY	PERISHING	PERMUTATING	PERSIENNE
PERFUSED	PERIHELIA	PERISPERM	PERMUTE	PERSIENNES

The Chambers Dictionary is the authority for many longer words; see *OSW* Introduction, page xii.

PERSIMMON	PERTINENT	PESAUNTS	PETASUSES	PETROSAL
PERSIMMONS	PERTINENTS	PESETA	PETAURINE	PETROSALS
PERSING	PERTLY	PESETAS	PETAURIST	PETROUS
PERSIST	PERTNESS	PESEWA	PETAURISTS	PETS
PERSISTED	PERTNESSES	PESEWAS	PETCHARIES	PETTED
PERSISTING	PERTOOK	PESHWA	PETCHARY	PETTEDLY
PERSISTS	PERTS	PESHWAS	PETCOCK	PETTER
PERSON	PERTURB	PESKIER	PETCOCKS	PETTERS
PERSONA	PERTURBED	PESKIEST	PETECHIA	PETTICOAT
PERSONAE	PERTURBER	PESKILY	PETECHIAE	PETTICOATS
PERSONAGE	PERTURBERS	PESKY	PETECHIAL	PETTIER
PERSONAGES	PERTURBING	PESO	PETER	PETTIES
PERSONAL	PERTURBS	PESOS	PETERED	PETTIEST
PERSONAS	PERTUSATE	PESSARIES	PETERING	PETTIFOG
PERSONATE	PERTUSE	PESSARY	PETERMAN	PETTIFOGGED
PERSONATED	PERTUSED	PESSIMA	PETERMEN	PETTIFOGGING
PERSONATES	PERTUSION	PESSIMAL	PETERS	PETTIFOGGINGS
PERSONATING	PERTUSIONS	PESSIMISM	PETERSHAM	PETTIFOGS
PERSONATINGS	PERTUSSAL	PESSIMISMS	PETERSHAMS	PETTILY
PERSONIFIED	PERTUSSIS	PESSIMIST	PETHER	PETTINESS
PERSONIFIES	PERTUSSISES	PESSIMISTS	PETHERS	PETTINESSES
PERSONIFY	PERUKE	PESSIMUM	PETHIDINE	PETTING
PERSONIFYING	PERUKED	PEST	PETHIDINES	PETTINGS
PERSONISE	PERUKES	PESTER	PETILLANT	PETTISH
PERSONISED	PERUSAL	PESTERED	PETIOLAR	PETTISHLY
PERSONISES	PERUSALS	PESTERER	PETIOLATE	PETTITOES
PERSONISING	PERUSE	PESTERERS	PETIOLE	PETTLE
PERSONIZE	PERUSED	PESTERING	PETIOLED	PETTLED
PERSONIZED	PERUSER	PESTEROUS	PETIOLES	PETTLES
PERSONIZES	PERUSERS	PESTERS	PETIOLULE	PETTLING
PERSONIZING	PERUSES	PESTFUL	PETIOLULES	PETTY
PERSONNEL	PERUSING	PESTHOUSE	PETIT	PETULANCE
PERSONNELS	PERV	PESTHOUSES	PETITE	PETULANCES
PERSONS	PERVADE	PESTICIDE	PETITION	PETULANCIES
PERSPIRE	PERVADED	PESTICIDES	PETITIONED	PETULANCY
PERSPIRED	PERVADES	PESTILENT	PETITIONING	PETULANT
PERSPIRES	PERVADING	PESTLE	PETITIONINGS	PETUNIA
PERSPIRING	PERVASION	PESTLED	PETITIONS	PETUNIAS
PERST	PERVASIONS	PESTLES	PETITORY	PETUNTSE
PERSUADE	PERVASIVE	PESTLING	PETRARIES	PETUNTSES
PERSUADED	PERVE	PESTO	PETRARY	PETUNTZE
PERSUADER	PERVED	PESTOLOGIES	PETRE	PETUNTZES
PERSUADERS	PERVERSE	PESTOLOGY	PETREL	PEW
PERSUADES	PERVERSER	PESTOS	PETRELS	PEWIT
PERSUADING	PERVERSEST	PESTS	PETRES	PEWITS
PERSUE	PERVERT	PET	PETRIFIC	PEWS
PERSUED	PERVERTED	PETAL	PETRIFIED	PEWTER
PERSUES	PERVERTER	PETALINE	PETRIFIES	PEWTERER
PERSUING	PERVERTERS	PETALISM	PETRIFY	PEWTERERS
PERSWADE	PERVERTING	PETALISMS	PETRIFYING	PEWTERS
PERSWADED	PERVERTS	PETALLED	PETROGRAM	PEYOTE
PERSWADES	PERVES	PETALODIES	PETROGRAMS	PEYOTES
PERSWADING	PERVIATE	PETALODY	PETROL	PEYOTISM
PERT	PERVIATED	PETALOID	PETROLAGE	PEYOTISMS
PERTAIN	PERVIATES	PETALOUS	PETROLAGES	PEYOTIST
PERTAINED	PERVIATING	PETALS	PETROLEUM	PEYOTISTS
PERTAINING	PERVICACIES	PETANQUE	PETROLEUMS	PEYSE
PERTAINS	PERVICACY	PETANQUES	PETROLEUR	PEYSED
PERTAKE	PERVING	PETAR	PETROLEURS	PEYSES
PERTAKEN	PERVIOUS	PETARA	PETROLIC	PEYSING
PERTAKES	PERVS	PETARAS	PETROLLED	PEZANT
PERTAKING	PESADE	PETARD	PETROLLING	PEZANTS
PERTER	PESADES	PETARDS	PETROLOGIES	PEZIZOID
PERTEST	PESANT	PETARIES	PETROLOGY	PFENNIG
PERTHITE	PESANTE	PETARS	PETROLS	PFENNIGE
PERTHITES	PESANTS	PETARY	PETRONEL	PFENNIGS
PERTHITIC	PESAUNT	PETASUS	PETRONELS	PFENNING

The Chambers Dictionary is the authority for many longer words; see *OSW* Introduction, page xii.

PFENNINGS
PH
PHACELIA
PHACELIAS
PHACOID
PHACOIDAL
PHACOLITE
PHACOLITES
PHACOLITH
PHACOLITHS
PHAEIC
PHAEISM
PHAEISMS
PHAENOGAM
PHAENOGAMS
PHAETON
PHAETONS
PHAGE
PHAGEDENA
PHAGEDENAS
PHAGES
PHAGOCYTE
PHAGOCYTES
PHALANGAL
PHALANGE
PHALANGER
PHALANGERS
PHALANGES
PHALANGID
PHALANGIDS
PHALANX
PHALANXES
PHALAROPE
PHALAROPES
PHALLI
PHALLIC
PHALLIN
PHALLINS
PHALLISM
PHALLISMS
PHALLOID
PHALLUS
PHALLUSES
PHANG
PHANGED
PHANGING
PHANGS
PHANSIGAR
PHANSIGARS
PHANTASIED
PHANTASIES
PHANTASIM
PHANTASIMS
PHANTASM
PHANTASMA
PHANTASMATA
PHANTASMS
PHANTASY
PHANTASYING
PHANTOM
PHANTOMS
PHANTOMY
PHANTOSME
PHANTOSMES
PHARAONIC
PHARE
PHARES

PHARISAIC
PHARMACIES
PHARMACY
PHAROS
PHAROSES
PHARYNGAL
PHARYNGES
PHARYNX
PHARYNXES
PHASE
PHASED
PHASELESS
PHASEOLIN
PHASEOLINS
PHASES
PHASIC
PHASING
PHASIS
PHASMID
PHASMIDS
PHATIC
PHEASANT
PHEASANTS
PHEAZAR
PHEAZARS
PHEER
PHEERE
PHEERES
PHEERS
PHEESE
PHEESED
PHEESES
PHEESING
PHEEZE
PHEEZED
PHEEZES
PHEEZING
PHELLEM
PHELLEMS
PHELLOGEN
PHELLOGENS
PHELLOID
PHELONION
PHELONIONS
PHENACITE
PHENACITES
PHENAKISM
PHENAKISMS
PHENAKITE
PHENAKITES
PHENATE
PHENATES
PHENE
PHENES
PHENETIC
PHENETICS
PHENGITE
PHENGITES
PHENIC
PHENOGAM
PHENOGAMS
PHENOL
PHENOLATE
PHENOLATES
PHENOLIC
PHENOLOGIES
PHENOLOGY

PHENOLS
PHENOM
PHENOMENA
PHENOMS
PHENOTYPE
PHENOTYPED
PHENOTYPES
PHENOTYPING
PHENYL
PHENYLIC
PHENYLS
PHEON
PHEONS
PHEROMONE
PHEROMONES
PHESE
PHESED
PHESES
PHESING
PHEW
PHI
PHIAL
PHIALLED
PHIALLING
PHIALS
PHILABEG
PHILABEGS
PHILAMOT
PHILAMOTS
PHILANDER
PHILANDERED
PHILANDERING
PHILANDERS
PHILATELIES
PHILATELY
PHILHORSE
PHILHORSES
PHILIBEG
PHILIBEGS
PHILIPPIC
PHILIPPICS
PHILLABEG
PHILLABEGS
PHILLIBEG
PHILLIBEGS
PHILOGYNIES
PHILOGYNY
PHILOLOGIES
PHILOLOGY
PHILOMATH
PHILOMATHS
PHILOMOT
PHILOMOTS
PHILOPENA
PHILOPENAS
PHILTER
PHILTERS
PHILTRE
PHILTRES
PHIMOSES
PHIMOSIS
PHINNOCK
PHINNOCKS
PHIS
PHISNOMIES
PHISNOMY
PHIZ

PHIZOG
PHIZOGS
PHIZZES
PHLEBITIS
PHLEBITISES
PHLEGM
PHLEGMIER
PHLEGMIEST
PHLEGMON
PHLEGMONS
PHLEGMS
PHLEGMY
PHLOEM
PHLOEMS
PHLOMIS
PHLOMISES
PHLOX
PHLOXES
PHLYCTENA
PHLYCTENAE
PHO
PHOBIA
PHOBIAS
PHOBIC
PHOBICS
PHOBISM
PHOBISMS
PHOBIST
PHOBISTS
PHOCA
PHOCAE
PHOCAS
PHOCINE
PHOEBE
PHOEBES
PHOENIX
PHOENIXES
PHOH
PHOHS
PHOLADES
PHOLAS
PHON
PHONAL
PHONATE
PHONATED
PHONATES
PHONATING
PHONATION
PHONATIONS
PHONATORY
PHONE
PHONECARD
PHONECARDS
PHONED
PHONEME
PHONEMES
PHONEMIC
PHONEMICS
PHONER
PHONERS
PHONES
PHONETIC
PHONETICS
PHONETISE
PHONETISED
PHONETISES
PHONETISING

PHONETISM
PHONETISMS
PHONETIST
PHONETISTS
PHONETIZE
PHONETIZED
PHONETIZES
PHONETIZING
PHONEY
PHONEYED
PHONEYING
PHONEYS
PHONIC
PHONICS
PHONIED
PHONIER
PHONIES
PHONIEST
PHONINESS
PHONINESSES
PHONING
PHONMETER
PHONMETERS
PHONOGRAM
PHONOGRAMS
PHONOLITE
PHONOLITES
PHONOLOGIES
PHONOLOGY
PHONON
PHONONS
PHONOPORE
PHONOPORES
PHONOTYPE
PHONOTYPED
PHONOTYPES
PHONOTYPIES
PHONOTYPING
PHONOTYPY
PHONS
PHONY
PHONYING
PHOOEY
PHORMINGES
PHORMINX
PHORMIUM
PHORMIUMS
PHOS
PHOSGENE
PHOSGENES
PHOSPHATE
PHOSPHATED
PHOSPHATES
PHOSPHATING
PHOSPHENE
PHOSPHENES
PHOSPHIDE
PHOSPHIDES
PHOSPHINE
PHOSPHINES
PHOSPHITE
PHOSPHITES
PHOSPHOR
PHOSPHORS
PHOT
PHOTIC
PHOTICS

The Chambers Dictionary is the authority for many longer words; see *OSW* Introduction, page xii.

PHOTINIA	PHRENETICS	PHYSICALS	PICA	PICKLER
PHOTINIAS	PHRENIC	PHYSICIAN	PICADOR	PICKLERS
PHOTISM	PHRENISM	PHYSICIANS	PICADORS	PICKLES
PHOTISMS	PHRENISMS	PHYSICISM	PICAMAR	PICKLING
PHOTO	PHRENITIC	PHYSICISMS	PICAMARS	PICKLOCK
PHOTOCELL	PHRENITIS	PHYSICIST	PICARIAN	PICKLOCKS
PHOTOCELLS	PHRENITISES	PHYSICISTS	PICARIANS	PICKMAW
PHOTOCOPIED	PHRENSIED	PHYSICKED	PICAROON	PICKMAWS
PHOTOCOPIES	PHRENSIES	PHYSICKING	PICAROONS	PICKS
PHOTOCOPY	PHRENSY	PHYSICKY	PICAS	PICKY
PHOTOCOPYING	PHRENSYING	PHYSICS	PICAYUNE	PICNIC
PHOTOCOPYINGS	PHRENTICK	PHYSIO	PICAYUNES	PICNICKED
PHOTOED	PHS	PHYSIOS	PICCADELL	PICNICKER
PHOTOFIT	PHTHALATE	PHYSIQUE	PICCADELLS	PICNICKERS
PHOTOFITS	PHTHALATES	PHYSIQUES	PICCADILL	PICNICKING
PHOTOGEN	PHTHALEIN	PHYTOGENIES	PICCADILLS	PICNICKY
PHOTOGENE	PHTHALEINS	PHYTOGENY	PICCANIN	PICNICS
PHOTOGENES	PHTHALIC	PHYTOLOGIES	PICCANINS	PICOCURIE
PHOTOGENIES	PHTHALIN	PHYTOLOGY	PICCIES	PICOCURIES
PHOTOGENS	PHTHALINS	PHYTON	PICCOLO	PICOT
PHOTOGENY	PHTHISES	PHYTONS	PICCOLOS	PICOTE
PHOTOGRAM	PHTHISIC	PHYTOSES	PICCY	PICOTED
PHOTOGRAMS	PHTHISICS	PHYTOSIS	PICE	PICOTEE
PHOTOING	PHTHISIS	PHYTOTOMIES	PICENE	PICOTEES
PHOTOLYSE	PHUT	PHYTOTOMY	PICENES	PICOTING
PHOTOLYSED	PHUTS	PHYTOTRON	PICEOUS	PICOTITE
PHOTOLYSES	PHUTTED	PHYTOTRONS	PICHURIM	PICOTITES
PHOTOLYSING	PHUTTING	PI	PICHURIMS	PICOTS
PHOTON	PHYCOCYAN	PIA	PICINE	PICQUET
PHOTONICS	PHYCOCYANS	PIACEVOLE	PICK	PICQUETED
PHOTONS	PHYCOLOGIES	PIACULAR	PICKABACK	PICQUETING
PHOTOPHIL	PHYCOLOGY	PIAFFE	PICKABACKS	PICQUETS
PHOTOPHILS	PHYLA	PIAFFED	PICKADELL	PICRA
PHOTOPIA	PHYLAE	PIAFFER	PICKADELLS	PICRAS
PHOTOPIAS	PHYLARCH	PIAFFERS	PICKADILL	PICRATE
PHOTOPIC	PHYLARCHIES	PIAFFES	PICKADILLS	PICRATES
PHOTOPSIA	PHYLARCHS	PIAFFING	PICKAPACK	PICRIC
PHOTOPSIAS	PHYLARCHY	PIANETTE	PICKAPACKS	PICRITE
PHOTOPSIES	PHYLE	PIANETTES	PICKAXE	PICRITES
PHOTOPSY	PHYLES	PIANINO	PICKAXES	PICS
PHOTOS	PHYLETIC	PIANINOS	PICKBACK	PICTARNIE
PHOTOTYPE	PHYLLARIES	PIANISM	PICKBACKS	PICTARNIES
PHOTOTYPED	PHYLLARY	PIANISMS	PICKED	PICTOGRAM
PHOTOTYPES	PHYLLITE	PIANIST	PICKEER	PICTOGRAMS
PHOTOTYPIES	PHYLLITES	PIANISTE	PICKEERED	PICTORIAL
PHOTOTYPING	PHYLLO	PIANISTES	PICKEERER	PICTORIALS
PHOTOTYPY	PHYLLODE	PIANISTIC	PICKEERERS	PICTURAL
PHOTS	PHYLLODES	PIANISTS	PICKEERING	PICTURALS
PHRASAL	PHYLLODIES	PIANO	PICKEERS	PICTURE
PHRASE	PHYLLODY	PIANOLIST	PICKER	PICTURED
PHRASED	PHYLLOID	PIANOLISTS	PICKEREL	PICTURES
PHRASEMAN	PHYLLOME	PIANOS	PICKERELS	PICTURING
PHRASEMEN	PHYLLOMES	PIARIST	PICKERIES	PICUL
PHRASER	PHYLLOPOD	PIARISTS	PICKERS	PICULS
PHRASERS	PHYLLOPODS	PIAS	PICKERY	PIDDLE
PHRASES	PHYLLOS	PIASSABA	PICKET	PIDDLED
PHRASIER	PHYLOGENIES	PIASSABAS	PICKETED	PIDDLER
PHRASIEST	PHYLOGENY	PIASSAVA	PICKETER	PIDDLERS
PHRASING	PHYLUM	PIASSAVAS	PICKETERS	PIDDLES
PHRASINGS	PHYSALIA	PIASTRE	PICKETING	PIDDLING
PHRASY	PHYSALIAS	PIASTRES	PICKETS	PIDDOCK
PHRATRIES	PHYSALIS	PIAZZA	PICKIER	PIDDOCKS
PHRATRY	PHYSALISES	PIAZZAS	PICKIEST	PIDGEON
PHREATIC	PHYSETER	PIAZZIAN	PICKING	PIDGEONS
PHRENESES	PHYSETERS	PIBROCH	PICKINGS	PIDGIN
PHRENESIS	PHYSIC	PIBROCHS	PICKLE	PIDGINS
PHRENETIC	PHYSICAL	PIC	PICKLED	PIE

The Chambers Dictionary is the authority for many longer words; see *OSW* Introduction, page xii.

PIEBALD	PIFFERARI	PIGNUT	PILERS	PILLORYING
PIEBALDS	PIFFERARO	PIGNUTS	PILES	PILLOW
PIECE	PIFFERO	PIGPEN	PILEUM	PILLOWED
PIECED	PIFFEROS	PIGPENS	PILEUS	PILLOWING
PIECELESS	PIFFLE	PIGS	PILEWORK	PILLOWS
PIECEMEAL	PIFFLED	PIGSCONCE	PILEWORKS	PILLOWY
PIECEMEALED	PIFFLER	PIGSCONCES	PILEWORT	PILLS
PIECEMEALING	PIFFLERS	PIGSKIN	PILEWORTS	PILLWORM
PIECEMEALS	PIFFLES	PIGSKINS	PILFER	PILLWORMS
PIECEN	PIFFLING	PIGSNEY	PILFERAGE	PILLWORT
PIECENED	PIG	PIGSNEYS	PILFERAGES	PILLWORTS
PIECENER	PIGBOAT	PIGSNIE	PILFERED	PILOSE
PIECENERS	PIGBOATS	PIGSNIES	PILFERER	PILOSITIES
PIECENING	PIGEON	PIGSNY	PILFERERS	PILOSITY
PIECENS	PIGEONED	PIGSTIES	PILFERIES	PILOT
PIECER	PIGEONING	PIGSTY	PILFERING	PILOTAGE
PIECERS	PIGEONRIES	PIGSWILL	PILFERINGS	PILOTAGES
PIECES	PIGEONRY	PIGSWILLS	PILFERS	PILOTED
PIECING	PIGEONS	PIGTAIL	PILFERY	PILOTING
PIECRUST	PIGFEED	PIGTAILS	PILGRIM	PILOTIS
PIECRUSTS	PIGFEEDS	PIGWASH	PILGRIMER	PILOTLESS
PIED	PIGGED	PIGWASHES	PILGRIMERS	PILOTMAN
PIEDISH	PIGGERIES	PIGWEED	PILGRIMS	PILOTMEN
PIEDISHES	PIGGERY	PIGWEEDS	PILHORSE	PILOTS
PIEDMONT	PIGGIE	PIKA	PILHORSES	PILOUS
PIEDMONTS	PIGGIER	PIKAS	PILI	PILOW
PIEDNESS	PIGGIES	PIKE	PILIFORM	PILOWS
PIEDNESSES	PIGGIEST	PIKED	PILING	PILSENER
PIEING	PIGGIN	PIKELET	PILINGS	PILSENERS
PIEMAN	PIGGING	PIKELETS	PILIS	PILSNER
PIEMEN	PIGGINGS	PIKEMAN	PILL	PILSNERS
PIEND	PIGGINS	PIKEMEN	PILLAGE	PILULA
PIENDS	PIGGISH	PIKER	PILLAGED	PILULAR
PIEPOWDER	PIGGISHLY	PIKERS	PILLAGER	PILULAS
PIEPOWDERS	PIGGY	PIKES	PILLAGERS	PILULE
PIER	PIGGYBACK	PIKESTAFF	PILLAGES	PILULES
PIERAGE	PIGGYBACKS	PIKESTAFFS	PILLAGING	PILUM
PIERAGES	PIGHEADED	PIKING	PILLAR	PILUS
PIERCE	PIGHT	PIKUL	PILLARIST	PIMENT
PIERCED	PIGHTED	PIKULS	PILLARISTS	PIMENTO
PIERCER	PIGHTING	PILA	PILLARS	PIMENTOS
PIERCERS	PIGHTLE	PILAFF	PILLAU	PIMENTS
PIERCES	PIGHTLES	PILAFFS	PILLAUS	PIMIENTO
PIERCING	PIGHTS	PILASTER	PILLED	PIMIENTOS
PIERID	PIGLET	PILASTERS	PILLHEAD	PIMP
PIERIDINE	PIGLETS	PILAU	PILLHEADS	PIMPED
PIERIDS	PIGLING	PILAUS	PILLICOCK	PIMPERNEL
PIERRETTE	PIGLINGS	PILAW	PILLICOCKS	PIMPERNELS
PIERRETTES	PIGMAEAN	PILAWS	PILLING	PIMPING
PIERROT	PIGMEAN	PILCH	PILLINGS	PIMPLE
PIERROTS	PIGMEAT	PILCHARD	PILLION	PIMPLED
PIERS	PIGMEATS	PILCHARDS	PILLIONED	PIMPLES
PIERST	PIGMENT	PILCHER	PILLIONING	PIMPLIER
PIERT	PIGMENTAL	PILCHERS	PILLIONS	PIMPLIEST
PIES	PIGMENTED	PILCHES	PILLOCK	PIMPLY
PIET	PIGMENTS	PILCORN	PILLOCKS	PIMPS
PIETA	PIGMIES	PILCORNS	PILLORIED	PIN
PIETAS	PIGMOID	PILCROW	PILLORIES	PINA
PIETIES	PIGMY	PILCROWS	PILLORISE	PINACOID
PIETISM	PIGNERATE	PILE	PILLORISED	PINACOIDS
PIETISMS	PIGNERATED	PILEA	PILLORISES	PINAFORE
PIETIST	PIGNERATES	PILEATE	PILLORISING	PINAFORED
PIETISTIC	PIGNERATING	PILEATED	PILLORIZE	PINAFORES
PIETISTS	PIGNORATE	PILED	PILLORIZED	PINAKOID
PIETS	PIGNORATED	PILEI	PILLORIZES	PINAKOIDS
PIETY	PIGNORATES	PILEOUS	PILLORIZING	PINAS
PIEZO	PIGNORATING	PILER	PILLORY	PINASTER

The Chambers Dictionary is the authority for many longer words; see *OSW* Introduction, page xii.

PINASTERS	PINGS	PINNINGS	PIOY	PIQUANCIES
PINATA	PINGUEFIED	PINNIPED	PIOYE	PIQUANCY
PINATAS	PINGUEFIES	PINNIPEDE	PIOYES	PIQUANT
PINBALL	PINGUEFY	PINNIPEDES	PIOYS	PIQUANTLY
PINBALLS	PINGUEFYING	PINNIPEDS	PIP	PIQUE
PINCASE	PINGUID	PINNOCK	PIPA	PIQUED
PINCASES	PINGUIN	PINNOCKS	PIPAGE	PIQUES
PINCER	PINGUINS	PINNOED	PIPAGES	PIQUET
PINCERED	PINHEAD	PINNULA	PIPAL	PIQUETED
PINCERING	PINHEADS	PINNULAS	PIPALS	PIQUETING
PINCERS	PINHOLE	PINNULATE	PIPAS	PIQUETS
PINCH	PINHOLES	PINNULE	PIPE	PIQUING
PINCHBECK	PINHOOKER	PINNULES	PIPECLAY	PIR
PINCHBECKS	PINHOOKERS	PINNY	PIPECLAYED	PIRACIES
PINCHCOCK	PINIER	PINOCHLE	PIPECLAYING	PIRACY
PINCHCOCKS	PINIES	PINOCHLES	PIPECLAYS	PIRAGUA
PINCHED	PINIEST	PINOCLE	PIPED	PIRAGUAS
PINCHER	PINING	PINOCLES	PIPEFISH	PIRAI
PINCHERS	PINION	PINOLE	PIPEFISHES	PIRAIS
PINCHES	PINIONED	PINOLES	PIPEFUL	PIRANA
PINCHFIST	PINIONING	PINON	PIPEFULS	PIRANAS
PINCHFISTS	PINIONS	PINONS	PIPELESS	PIRANHA
PINCHGUT	PINITE	PINOT	PIPELIKE	PIRANHAS
PINCHGUTS	PINITES	PINOTS	PIPELINE	PIRARUCU
PINCHING	PINK	PINPOINT	PIPELINES	PIRARUCUS
PINCHINGS	PINKED	PINPOINTED	PIPER	PIRATE
PINDAREE	PINKER	PINPOINTING	PIPERIC	PIRATED
PINDAREES	PINKERTON	PINPOINTS	PIPERINE	PIRATES
PINDARI	PINKERTONS	PINS	PIPERINES	PIRATIC
PINDARIS	PINKEST	PINT	PIPERONAL	PIRATICAL
PINDER	PINKIE	PINTA	PIPERONALS	PIRATING
PINDERS	PINKIER	PINTABLE	PIPERS	PIRAYA
PINDOWN	PINKIES	PINTABLES	PIPES	PIRAYAS
PINDOWNS	PINKIEST	PINTADO	PIPESTONE	PIRL
PINE	PINKINESS	PINTADOS	PIPESTONES	PIRLICUE
PINEAL	PINKINESSES	PINTAIL	PIPETTE	PIRLICUED
PINEAPPLE	PINKING	PINTAILED	PIPETTED	PIRLICUES
PINEAPPLES	PINKINGS	PINTAILS	PIPETTES	PIRLICUING
PINED	PINKISH	PINTAS	PIPETTING	PIRLS
PINERIES	PINKNESS	PINTLE	PIPEWORK	PIRN
PINERY	PINKNESSES	PINTLES	PIPEWORKS	PIRNIE
PINES	PINKO	PINTO	PIPEWORT	PIRNIES
PINETA	PINKOES	PINTOS	PIPEWORTS	PIRNIT
PINETUM	PINKOS	PINTS	PIPI	PIRNS
PINEWOOD	PINKROOT	PINXIT	PIPIER	PIROGUE
PINEWOODS	PINKROOTS	PINY	PIPIEST	PIROGUES
PINEY	PINKS	PIOLET	PIPING	PIROSHKI
PINFISH	PINKY	PIOLETS	PIPINGS	PIROUETTE
PINFISHES	PINNA	PION	PIPIS	PIROUETTED
PINFOLD	PINNACE	PIONED	PIPIT	PIROUETTES
PINFOLDED	PINNACES	PIONEER	PIPITS	PIROUETTING
PINFOLDING	PINNACLE	PIONEERED	PIPKIN	PIROZHKI
PINFOLDS	PINNACLED	PIONEERING	PIPKINS	PIRS
PING	PINNACLES	PIONEERS	PIPLESS	PIS
PINGED	PINNACLING	PIONER	PIPPED	PISCARIES
PINGER	PINNAE	PIONERS	PIPPIER	PISCARY
PINGERS	PINNATE	PIONEY	PIPPIEST	PISCATOR
PINGING	PINNATED	PIONEYS	PIPPIN	PISCATORS
PINGLE	PINNATELY	PIONIC	PIPPING	PISCATORY
PINGLED	PINNED	PIONIES	PIPPINS	PISCATRIX
PINGLER	PINNER	PIONING	PIPPY	PISCATRIXES
PINGLERS	PINNERS	PIONINGS	PIPS	PISCIFORM
PINGLES	PINNET	PIONS	PIPSQUEAK	PISCINA
PINGLING	PINNETS	PIONY	PIPSQUEAKS	PISCINAE
PINGO	PINNIE	PIOTED	PIPUL	PISCINAS
PINGOES	PINNIES	PIOUS	PIPULS	PISCINE
PINGOS	PINNING	PIOUSLY	PIPY	PISCINES

The Chambers Dictionary is the authority for many longer words; see *OSW* Introduction, page xii.

PISE
PISES
PISH
PISHED
PISHES
PISHING
PISHOGUE
PISHOGUES
PISIFORM
PISIFORMS
PISKIES
PISKY
PISMIRE
PISMIRES
PISOLITE
PISOLITES
PISOLITIC
PISS
PISSED
PISSES
PISSHEAD
PISSHEADS
PISSING
PISSOIR
PISSOIRS
PISTACHIO
PISTACHIOS
PISTAREEN
PISTAREENS
PISTE
PISTES
PISTIL
PISTILS
PISTOL
PISTOLE
PISTOLEER
PISTOLEERS
PISTOLES
PISTOLET
PISTOLETS
PISTOLLED
PISTOLLING
PISTOLS
PISTON
PISTONS
PIT
PITA
PITAPAT
PITAPATS
PITAPATTED
PITAPATTING
PITARA
PITARAH
PITARAHS
PITARAS
PITAS
PITCH
PITCHED
PITCHER
PITCHERS
PITCHES
PITCHFORK
PITCHFORKED
PITCHFORKING
PITCHFORKS
PITCHIER
PITCHIEST

PITCHING
PITCHINGS
PITCHMAN
PITCHMEN
PITCHPINE
PITCHPINES
PITCHPIPE
PITCHPIPES
PITCHY
PITEOUS
PITEOUSLY
PITFALL
PITFALLS
PITH
PITHBALL
PITHBALLS
PITHEAD
PITHEADS
PITHECOID
PITHED
PITHFUL
PITHIER
PITHIEST
PITHILY
PITHINESS
PITHINESSES
PITHING
PITHLESS
PITHLIKE
PITHOI
PITHOS
PITHS
PITHY
PITIABLE
PITIABLY
PITIED
PITIER
PITIERS
PITIES
PITIFUL
PITIFULLY
PITILESS
PITMAN
PITMEN
PITON
PITONS
PITPROP
PITPROPS
PITS
PITTA
PITTANCE
PITTANCES
PITTAS
PITTED
PITTEN
PITTER
PITTERED
PITTERING
PITTERS
PITTING
PITTINGS
PITTITE
PITTITES
PITUITA
PITUITARY
PITUITAS
PITUITE

PITUITES
PITUITRIN
PITUITRINS
PITURI
PITURIS
PITY
PITYING
PITYINGLY
PITYROID
PIU
PIUM
PIUMS
PIUPIU
PIUPIUS
PIVOT
PIVOTAL
PIVOTALLY
PIVOTED
PIVOTER
PIVOTERS
PIVOTING
PIVOTINGS
PIVOTS
PIX
PIXEL
PIXELS
PIXES
PIXIE
PIXIES
PIXILATED
PIXY
PIZAZZ
PIZAZZES
PIZE
PIZES
PIZZA
PIZZAIOLA
PIZZAS
PIZZERIA
PIZZERIAS
PIZZICATO
PIZZICATOS
PIZZLE
PIZZLES
PLACABLE
PLACABLY
PLACARD
PLACARDED
PLACARDING
PLACARDS
PLACATE
PLACATED
PLACATES
PLACATING
PLACATION
PLACATIONS
PLACATORY
PLACCAT
PLACCATE
PLACCATES
PLACCATS
PLACE
PLACEBO
PLACEBOS
PLACED
PLACELESS
PLACEMAN

PLACEMEN
PLACEMENT
PLACEMENTS
PLACENTA
PLACENTAE
PLACENTAL
PLACENTALS
PLACENTAS
PLACER
PLACERS
PLACES
PLACET
PLACETS
PLACID
PLACIDER
PLACIDEST
PLACIDITIES
PLACIDITY
PLACIDLY
PLACING
PLACINGS
PLACIT
PLACITA
PLACITORY
PLACITS
PLACITUM
PLACK
PLACKET
PLACKETS
PLACKLESS
PLACKS
PLACODERM
PLACODERMS
PLACOID
PLAFOND
PLAFONDS
PLAGAL
PLAGE
PLAGES
PLAGIARIES
PLAGIARY
PLAGIUM
PLAGIUMS
PLAGUE
PLAGUED
PLAGUES
PLAGUEY
PLAGUIER
PLAGUIEST
PLAGUILY
PLAGUING
PLAGUY
PLAICE
PLAICES
PLAID
PLAIDED
PLAIDING
PLAIDINGS
PLAIDMAN
PLAIDMEN
PLAIDS
PLAIN
PLAINANT
PLAINANTS
PLAINED
PLAINER
PLAINEST

PLAINFUL
PLAINING
PLAININGS
PLAINISH
PLAINLY
PLAINNESS
PLAINNESSES
PLAINS
PLAINSMAN
PLAINSMEN
PLAINSONG
PLAINSONGS
PLAINT
PLAINTFUL
PLAINTIFF
PLAINTIFFS
PLAINTIVE
PLAINTS
PLAINWORK
PLAINWORKS
PLAISTER
PLAISTERS
PLAIT
PLAITED
PLAITER
PLAITERS
PLAITING
PLAITINGS
PLAITS
PLAN
PLANAR
PLANARIAN
PLANARIANS
PLANATION
PLANATIONS
PLANCH
PLANCHED
PLANCHES
PLANCHET
PLANCHETS
PLANCHING
PLANE
PLANED
PLANER
PLANERS
PLANES
PLANET
PLANETARY
PLANETIC
PLANETOID
PLANETOIDS
PLANETS
PLANGENCIES
PLANGENCY
PLANGENT
PLANING
PLANISH
PLANISHED
PLANISHER
PLANISHERS
PLANISHES
PLANISHING
PLANK
PLANKED
PLANKING
PLANKINGS
PLANKS

The Chambers Dictionary is the authority for many longer words; see *OSW* Introduction, page xii.

PLANKTON	PLASMIN	PLATINIC	PLAYMATES	PLEBIFY
PLANKTONS	PLASMINS	PLATINISE	PLAYPEN	PLEBIFYING
PLANLESS	PLASMODIA	PLATINISED	PLAYPENS	PLEBS
PLANNED	PLASMS	PLATINISES	PLAYROOM	PLECTRA
PLANNER	PLAST	PLATINISING	PLAYROOMS	PLECTRE
PLANNERS	PLASTE	PLATINIZE	PLAYS	PLECTRES
PLANNING	PLASTER	PLATINIZED	PLAYSOME	PLECTRON
PLANS	PLASTERED	PLATINIZES	PLAYSUIT	PLECTRONS
PLANT	PLASTERER	PLATINIZING	PLAYSUITS	PLECTRUM
PLANTA	PLASTERERS	PLATINOID	PLAYTHING	PLECTRUMS
PLANTABLE	PLASTERING	PLATINOIDS	PLAYTHINGS	PLED
PLANTAGE	PLASTERINGS	PLATINOUS	PLAYTIME	PLEDGE
PLANTAGES	PLASTERS	PLATINUM	PLAYTIMES	PLEDGED
PLANTAIN	PLASTERY	PLATINUMS	PLAZA	PLEDGEE
PLANTAINS	PLASTIC	PLATITUDE	PLAZAS	PLEDGEES
PLANTAR	PLASTICS	PLATITUDES	PLEA	PLEDGEOR
PLANTAS	PLASTID	PLATONIC	PLEACH	PLEDGEORS
PLANTED	PLASTIDS	PLATONICS	PLEACHED	PLEDGER
PLANTER	PLASTIQUE	PLATOON	PLEACHES	PLEDGERS
PLANTERS	PLASTIQUES	PLATOONS	PLEACHING	PLEDGES
PLANTING	PLASTISOL	PLATS	PLEAD	PLEDGET
PLANTINGS	PLASTISOLS	PLATTED	PLEADABLE	PLEDGETS
PLANTLESS	PLASTRAL	PLATTER	PLEADED	PLEDGING
PLANTLET	PLASTRON	PLATTERS	PLEADER	PLEDGOR
PLANTLETS	PLASTRONS	PLATTING	PLEADERS	PLEDGORS
PLANTLING	PLAT	PLATTINGS	PLEADING	PLEIOMERIES
PLANTLINGS	PLATAN	PLATY	PLEADINGS	PLEIOMERY
PLANTS	PLATANE	PLATYPUS	PLEADS	PLENA
PLANTSMAN	PLATANES	PLATYPUSES	PLEAED	PLENARILY
PLANTSMEN	PLATANNA	PLATYSMA	PLEAING	PLENARTIES
PLANTULE	PLATANNAS	PLATYSMAS	PLEAS	PLENARTY
PLANTULES	PLATANS	PLAUDIT	PLEASANCE	PLENARY
PLANULA	PLATBAND	PLAUDITE	PLEASANCES	PLENILUNE
PLANULAE	PLATBANDS	PLAUDITS	PLEASANT	PLENILUNES
PLANULAR	PLATE	PLAUSIBLE	PLEASANTER	PLENIPO
PLANULOID	PLATEASM	PLAUSIBLY	PLEASANTEST	PLENIPOES
PLANURIA	PLATEASMS	PLAUSIVE	PLEASE	PLENIPOS
PLANURIAS	PLATEAU	PLAUSTRAL	PLEASED	PLENISH
PLANURIES	PLATEAUED	PLAY	PLEASEMAN	PLENISHED
PLANURY	PLATEAUING	PLAYA	PLEASEMEN	PLENISHES
PLANXTIES	PLATEAUS	PLAYABLE	PLEASER	PLENISHING
PLANXTY	PLATEAUX	PLAYAS	PLEASERS	PLENISHINGS
PLAP	PLATED	PLAYBACK	PLEASES	PLENIST
PLAPPED	PLATEFUL	PLAYBACKS	PLEASETH	PLENISTS
PLAPPING	PLATEFULS	PLAYBILL	PLEASING	PLENITUDE
PLAPS	PLATELET	PLAYBILLS	PLEASINGS	PLENITUDES
PLAQUE	PLATELETS	PLAYBOOK	PLEASURE	PLENTEOUS
PLAQUES	PLATEMAN	PLAYBOOKS	PLEASURED	PLENTIES
PLAQUETTE	PLATEMARK	PLAYBOY	PLEASURER	PLENTIFUL
PLAQUETTES	PLATEMARKS	PLAYBOYS	PLEASURERS	PLENTY
PLASH	PLATEMEN	PLAYBUS	PLEASURES	PLENUM
PLASHED	PLATEN	PLAYBUSES	PLEASURING	PLENUMS
PLASHES	PLATENS	PLAYED	PLEAT	PLEON
PLASHET	PLATER	PLAYER	PLEATED	PLEONASM
PLASHETS	PLATERS	PLAYERS	PLEATER	PLEONASMS
PLASHIER	PLATES	PLAYFUL	PLEATERS	PLEONAST
PLASHIEST	PLATFORM	PLAYFULLY	PLEATING	PLEONASTE
PLASHING	PLATFORMED	PLAYGIRL	PLEATS	PLEONASTES
PLASHINGS	PLATFORMING	PLAYGIRLS	PLEB	PLEONASTS
PLASHY	PLATFORMINGS	PLAYGROUP	PLEBBIER	PLEONEXIA
PLASM	PLATFORMS	PLAYGROUPS	PLEBBIEST	PLEONEXIAS
PLASMA	PLATIER	PLAYHOUSE	PLEBBY	PLEONS
PLASMAS	PLATIEST	PLAYHOUSES	PLEBEAN	PLEOPOD
PLASMATIC	PLATINA	PLAYING	PLEBEIAN	PLEOPODS
PLASMIC	PLATINAS	PLAYLET	PLEBEIANS	PLEROMA
PLASMID	PLATING	PLAYLETS	PLEBIFIED	PLEROMAS
PLASMIDS	PLATINGS	PLAYMATE	PLEBIFIES	PLEROME

The Chambers Dictionary is the authority for many longer words; see *OSW* Introduction, page xii.

PLEROMES	PLING	PLOTTING	PLUMBAGOS	PLUMULAE
PLESH	PLINGS	PLOTTINGS	PLUMBATE	PLUMULAR
PLESHES	PLINK	PLOTTY	PLUMBATES	PLUMULATE
PLESSOR	PLINKED	PLOUGH	PLUMBED	PLUMULE
PLESSORS	PLINKING	PLOUGHBOY	PLUMBEOUS	PLUMULES
PLETHORA	PLINKS	PLOUGHBOYS	PLUMBER	PLUMULOSE
PLETHORAS	PLINTH	PLOUGHED	PLUMBERIES	PLUMY
PLETHORIC	PLINTHS	PLOUGHER	PLUMBERS	PLUNDER
PLEUCH	PLIOSAUR	PLOUGHERS	PLUMBERY	PLUNDERED
PLEUCHS	PLIOSAURS	PLOUGHING	PLUMBIC	PLUNDERER
PLEUGH	PLISKIE	PLOUGHINGS	PLUMBING	PLUNDERERS
PLEUGHS	PLISKIES	PLOUGHMAN	PLUMBINGS	PLUNDERING
PLEURA	PLISSE	PLOUGHMEN	PLUMBISM	PLUNDERS
PLEURAE	PLOAT	PLOUGHS	PLUMBISMS	PLUNGE
PLEURAL	PLOATED	PLOUK	PLUMBITE	PLUNGED
PLEURISIES	PLOATING	PLOUKIE	PLUMBITES	PLUNGER
PLEURISY	PLOATS	PLOUKIER	PLUMBLESS	PLUNGERS
PLEURITIC	PLOD	PLOUKIEST	PLUMBOUS	PLUNGES
PLEURITICS	PLODDED	PLOUKS	PLUMBS	PLUNGING
PLEURITIS	PLODDER	PLOUTER	PLUMBUM	PLUNGINGS
PLEURITISES	PLODDERS	PLOUTERED	PLUMBUMS	PLUNK
PLEURON	PLODDING	PLOUTERING	PLUMCOT	PLUNKED
PLEXIFORM	PLODDINGS	PLOUTERS	PLUMCOTS	PLUNKER
PLEXOR	PLODS	PLOVER	PLUMDAMAS	PLUNKERS
PLEXORS	PLOIDIES	PLOVERS	PLUMDAMASES	PLUNKING
PLEXURE	PLOIDY	PLOVERY	PLUME	PLUNKS
PLEXURES	PLONG	PLOW	PLUMED	PLURAL
PLEXUS	PLONGD	PLOWED	PLUMELESS	PLURALISE
PLEXUSES	PLONGE	PLOWING	PLUMELET	PLURALISED
PLIABLE	PLONGED	PLOWS	PLUMELETS	PLURALISES
PLIABLY	PLONGES	PLOWTER	PLUMERIES	PLURALISING
PLIANCIES	PLONGING	PLOWTERED	PLUMERY	PLURALISM
PLIANCY	PLONGS	PLOWTERING	PLUMES	PLURALISMS
PLIANT	PLONK	PLOWTERS	PLUMIER	PLURALIST
PLIANTLY	PLONKED	PLOY	PLUMIEST	PLURALISTS
PLICA	PLONKER	PLOYS	PLUMING	PLURALITIES
PLICAE	PLONKERS	PLUCK	PLUMIPED	PLURALITY
PLICAL	PLONKIER	PLUCKED	PLUMIST	PLURALIZE
PLICATE	PLONKIEST	PLUCKER	PLUMISTS	PLURALIZED
PLICATED	PLONKING	PLUCKERS	PLUMMET	PLURALIZES
PLICATELY	PLONKINGS	PLUCKIER	PLUMMETED	PLURALIZING
PLICATES	PLONKS	PLUCKIEST	PLUMMETING	PLURALLY
PLICATING	PLONKY	PLUCKILY	PLUMMETS	PLURALS
PLICATION	PLOOK	PLUCKING	PLUMMIER	PLURIPARA
PLICATIONS	PLOOKIE	PLUCKS	PLUMMIEST	PLURIPARAE
PLICATURE	PLOOKIER	PLUCKY	PLUMMY	PLURIPARAS
PLICATURES	PLOOKIEST	PLUFF	PLUMOSE	PLURISIE
PLIE	PLOOKS	PLUFFED	PLUMOUS	PLURISIES
PLIED	PLOP	PLUFFIER	PLUMP	PLUS
PLIER	PLOPPED	PLUFFIEST	PLUMPED	PLUSAGE
PLIERS	PLOPPING	PLUFFING	PLUMPEN	PLUSAGES
PLIES	PLOPS	PLUFFS	PLUMPENED	PLUSED
PLIGHT	PLOSION	PLUFFY	PLUMPENING	PLUSES
PLIGHTED	PLOSIONS	PLUG	PLUMPENS	PLUSH
PLIGHTER	PLOSIVE	PLUGGED	PLUMPER	PLUSHER
PLIGHTERS	PLOSIVES	PLUGGER	PLUMPERS	PLUSHES
PLIGHTFUL	PLOT	PLUGGERS	PLUMPEST	PLUSHEST
PLIGHTING	PLOTFUL	PLUGGING	PLUMPIE	PLUSHIER
PLIGHTS	PLOTLESS	PLUGGINGS	PLUMPING	PLUSHIEST
PLIM	PLOTS	PLUGS	PLUMPISH	PLUSHY
PLIMMED	PLOTTED	PLUM	PLUMPLY	PLUSING
PLIMMING	PLOTTER	PLUMAGE	PLUMPNESS	PLUSSAGE
PLIMS	PLOTTERED	PLUMAGED	PLUMPNESSES	PLUSSAGES
PLIMSOLE	PLOTTERING	PLUMAGES	PLUMPS	PLUSSED
PLIMSOLES	PLOTTERS	PLUMATE	PLUMPY	PLUSSES
PLIMSOLL	PLOTTIE	PLUMB	PLUMS	PLUSSING
PLIMSOLLS	PLOTTIES	PLUMBAGO	PLUMULA	PLUTEAL

The Chambers Dictionary is the authority for many longer words; see *OSW* Introduction, page xii.

PLUTEUS
PLUTEUSES
PLUTOCRAT
PLUTOCRATS
PLUTOLOGIES
PLUTOLOGY
PLUTON
PLUTONIC
PLUTONIUM
PLUTONIUMS
PLUTONOMIES
PLUTONOMY
PLUTONS
PLUVIAL
PLUVIALS
PLUVIOSE
PLUVIOUS
PLY
PLYING
PLYWOOD
PLYWOODS
PNEUMA
PNEUMAS
PNEUMATIC
PNEUMATICS
PNEUMONIA
PNEUMONIAS
PNEUMONIC
PNEUMONICS
PO
POA
POACEOUS
POACH
POACHED
POACHER
POACHERS
POACHES
POACHIER
POACHIEST
POACHING
POACHINGS
POACHY
POAKA
POAKAS
POAKE
POAKES
POAS
POCHARD
POCHARDS
POCHAY
POCHAYS
POCHETTE
POCHETTES
POCHOIR
POCHOIRS
POCK
POCKARD
POCKARDS
POCKED
POCKET
POCKETED
POCKETFUL
POCKETFULS
POCKETING
POCKETS
POCKIER
POCKIEST

POCKMANKIES
POCKMANKY
POCKMARK
POCKMARKS
POCKPIT
POCKPITS
POCKS
POCKY
POCO
POD
PODAGRA
PODAGRAL
PODAGRAS
PODAGRIC
PODAGROUS
PODAL
PODALIC
PODARGUS
PODARGUSES
PODDED
PODDIER
PODDIES
PODDIEST
PODDING
PODDY
PODESTA
PODESTAS
PODEX
PODEXES
PODGE
PODGES
PODGIER
PODGIEST
PODGINESS
PODGINESSES
PODGY
PODIA
PODIAL
PODIATRIES
PODIATRY
PODITE
PODITES
PODIUM
PODLEY
PODLEYS
PODOCARP
PODOCARPS
PODOLOGIES
PODOLOGY
PODS
PODSOL
PODSOLIC
PODSOLS
PODZOL
PODZOLS
POEM
POEMATIC
POEMS
POENOLOGIES
POENOLOGY
POESIED
POESIES
POESY
POESYING
POET
POETASTER
POETASTERS

POETASTRIES
POETASTRY
POETESS
POETESSES
POETIC
POETICAL
POETICALS
POETICISE
POETICISED
POETICISES
POETICISING
POETICISM
POETICISMS
POETICIZE
POETICIZED
POETICIZES
POETICIZING
POETICS
POETICULE
POETICULES
POETISE
POETISED
POETISES
POETISING
POETIZE
POETIZED
POETIZES
POETIZING
POETRESSE
POETRESSES
POETRIES
POETRY
POETS
POETSHIP
POETSHIPS
POFFLE
POFFLES
POGGE
POGGES
POGO
POGOED
POGOING
POGOS
POGROM
POGROMS
POH
POI
POIGNADO
POIGNADOES
POIGNANCIES
POIGNANCY
POIGNANT
POILU
POILUS
POINADO
POINADOES
POINCIANA
POINCIANAS
POIND
POINDED
POINDER
POINDERS
POINDING
POINDINGS
POINDS
POINT
POINTE

POINTED
POINTEDLY
POINTEL
POINTELS
POINTER
POINTERS
POINTES
POINTIER
POINTIEST
POINTILLE
POINTING
POINTINGS
POINTLESS
POINTS
POINTSMAN
POINTSMEN
POINTY
POIS
POISE
POISED
POISER
POISERS
POISES
POISING
POISON
POISONED
POISONER
POISONERS
POISONING
POISONOUS
POISONS
POISSON
POISSONS
POITREL
POITRELS
POKAL
POKALS
POKE
POKEBERRIES
POKEBERRY
POKED
POKEFUL
POKEFULS
POKER
POKERISH
POKERS
POKES
POKEWEED
POKEWEEDS
POKEY
POKEYS
POKIER
POKIES
POKIEST
POKING
POKY
POLACCA
POLACCAS
POLACRE
POLACRES
POLAR
POLARISE
POLARISED
POLARISER
POLARISERS
POLARISES
POLARISING

POLARITIES
POLARITY
POLARIZE
POLARIZED
POLARIZER
POLARIZERS
POLARIZES
POLARIZING
POLARON
POLARONS
POLARS
POLDER
POLDERED
POLDERING
POLDERS
POLE
POLECAT
POLECATS
POLED
POLEMARCH
POLEMARCHS
POLEMIC
POLEMICAL
POLEMICS
POLEMISE
POLEMISED
POLEMISES
POLEMISING
POLEMIST
POLEMISTS
POLEMIZE
POLEMIZED
POLEMIZES
POLEMIZING
POLENTA
POLENTAS
POLER
POLERS
POLES
POLEY
POLEYN
POLEYNS
POLEYS
POLIANITE
POLIANITES
POLICE
POLICED
POLICEMAN
POLICEMEN
POLICES
POLICIES
POLICING
POLICY
POLING
POLINGS
POLIO
POLIOS
POLISH
POLISHED
POLISHER
POLISHERS
POLISHES
POLISHING
POLISHINGS
POLITE
POLITELY
POLITER

POLITESSE	POLLSTER	POLYAXONS	POLYPHASE	POMANDERS
POLITESSES	POLLSTERS	POLYBASIC	POLYPHON	POMATO
POLITEST	POLLUSION	POLYCONIC	POLYPHONE	POMATOES
POLITIC	POLLUSIONS	POLYESTER	POLYPHONES	POMATUM
POLITICAL	POLLUTANT	POLYESTERS	POLYPHONIES	POMATUMS
POLITICK	POLLUTANTS	POLYGALA	POLYPHONS	POMBE
POLITICKED	POLLUTE	POLYGALAS	POLYPHONY	POMBES
POLITICKING	POLLUTED	POLYGAM	POLYPI	POME
POLITICKINGS	POLLUTER	POLYGAMIC	POLYPIDE	POMELO
POLITICKS	POLLUTERS	POLYGAMIES	POLYPIDES	POMELOS
POLITICLY	POLLUTES	POLYGAMS	POLYPIDOM	POMEROY
POLITICO	POLLUTING	POLYGAMY	POLYPIDOMS	POMEROYS
POLITICOES	POLLUTION	POLYGENE	POLYPINE	POMES
POLITICOS	POLLUTIONS	POLYGENES	POLYPITE	POMFRET
POLITICS	POLLUTIVE	POLYGENIC	POLYPITES	POMFRETS
POLITIES	POLLY	POLYGENIES	POLYPLOID	POMMEL
POLITIQUE	POLLYANNA	POLYGENY	POLYPOD	POMMELE
POLITIQUES	POLLYANNAS	POLYGLOT	POLYPODIES	POMMELLED
POLITY	POLLYWIG	POLYGLOTS	POLYPODS	POMMELLING
POLK	POLLYWIGS	POLYGLOTT	POLYPODY	POMMELS
POLKA	POLLYWOG	POLYGLOTTS	POLYPOID	POMMETTY
POLKAS	POLLYWOGS	POLYGON	POLYPOSES	POMMIES
POLKED	POLO	POLYGONAL	POLYPOSIS	POMMY
POLKING	POLOIDAL	POLYGONIES	POLYPOUS	POMOERIUM
POLKS	POLOIST	POLYGONS	POLYPS	POMOERIUMS
POLL	POLOISTS	POLYGONUM	POLYPTYCH	POMOLOGIES
POLLACK	POLONAISE	POLYGONUMS	POLYPTYCHS	POMOLOGY
POLLACKS	POLONAISES	POLYGONY	POLYPUS	POMP
POLLAN	POLONIE	POLYGRAPH	POLYS	POMPADOUR
POLLANS	POLONIES	POLYGRAPHS	POLYSEME	POMPADOURS
POLLARD	POLONISE	POLYGYNIES	POLYSEMES	POMPANO
POLLARDED	POLONISED	POLYGYNY	POLYSEMIES	POMPANOS
POLLARDING	POLONISES	POLYHEDRA	POLYSEMY	POMPELO
POLLARDS	POLONISING	POLYLEMMA	POLYSOME	POMPELOS
POLLED	POLONISM	POLYLEMMAS	POLYSOMES	POMPEY
POLLEN	POLONISMS	POLYMASTIES	POLYSOMIES	POMPEYED
POLLENED	POLONIUM	POLYMASTY	POLYSOMY	POMPEYING
POLLENING	POLONIUMS	POLYMATH	POLYSTYLE	POMPEYS
POLLENS	POLONIZE	POLYMATHIES	POLYTENE	POMPHOLYX
POLLENT	POLONIZED	POLYMATHS	POLYTHENE	POMPHOLYXES
POLLER	POLONIZES	POLYMATHY	POLYTHENES	POMPIER
POLLERS	POLONIZING	POLYMER	POLYTONAL	POMPION
POLLEX	POLONY	POLYMERIC	POLYTYPIC	POMPIONS
POLLICAL	POLOS	POLYMERIES	POLYURIA	POMPOM
POLLICES	POLT	POLYMERS	POLYURIAS	POMPOMS
POLLICIE	POLTED	POLYMERY	POLYVINYL	POMPON
POLLICIES	POLTFEET	POLYMORPH	POLYVINYLS	POMPONS
POLLICY	POLTFOOT	POLYMORPHS	POLYWATER	POMPOON
POLLIES	POLTING	POLYNIA	POLYWATERS	POMPOONS
POLLINATE	POLTROON	POLYNIAS	POLYZOA	POMPOSITIES
POLLINATED	POLTROONS	POLYNYA	POLYZOAN	POMPOSITY
POLLINATES	POLTS	POLYNYAS	POLYZOANS	POMPOUS
POLLINATING	POLVERINE	POLYOMA	POLYZOARIES	POMPOUSLY
POLLING	POLVERINES	POLYOMAS	POLYZOARY	POMPS
POLLINGS	POLY	POLYOMINO	POLYZOIC	POMROY
POLLINIA	POLYACID	POLYOMINOS	POLYZONAL	POMROYS
POLLINIC	POLYACT	POLYONYM	POLYZOOID	POMS
POLLINIUM	POLYAMIDE	POLYONYMIES	POLYZOON	POMWATER
POLLIWIG	POLYAMIDES	POLYONYMS	POM	POMWATERS
POLLIWIGS	POLYANDRIES	POLYONYMY	POMACE	PONCE
POLLIWOG	POLYANDRY	POLYP	POMACEOUS	PONCEAU
POLLIWOGS	POLYARCH	POLYPARIES	POMACES	PONCEAUS
POLLMAN	POLYARCHIES	POLYPARY	POMADE	PONCEAUX
POLLMEN	POLYARCHY	POLYPE	POMADED	PONCED
POLLOCK	POLYAXIAL	POLYPES	POMADES	PONCES
POLLOCKS	POLYAXIALS	POLYPHAGIES	POMADING	PONCEY
POLLS	POLYAXON	POLYPHAGY	POMANDER	PONCHO

The Chambers Dictionary is the authority for many longer words; see *OSW* Introduction, page xii.

PONCHOS	PONTIANACS	POOJAHS	POPEHOOD	POPULATED
PONCIER	PONTIANAK	POOJAS	POPEHOODS	POPULATES
PONCIEST	PONTIANAKS	POOK	POPELING	POPULATING
PONCING	PONTIC	POOKA	POPELINGS	POPULISM
PONCY	PONTIE	POOKAS	POPERIES	POPULISMS
POND	PONTIES	POOKING	POPERIN	POPULIST
PONDAGE	PONTIFEX	POOKIT	POPERINS	POPULISTS
PONDAGES	PONTIFF	POOKS	POPERY	POPULOUS
PONDED	PONTIFFS	POOL	POPES	PORAL
PONDER	PONTIFIC	POOLED	POPESHIP	PORBEAGLE
PONDERAL	PONTIFICE	POOLING	POPESHIPS	PORBEAGLES
PONDERATE	PONTIFICES	POOLS	POPINJAY	PORCELAIN
PONDERATED	PONTIFIED	POOLSIDE	POPINJAYS	PORCELAINS
PONDERATES	PONTIFIES	POOLSIDES	POPISH	PORCH
PONDERATING	PONTIFY	POON	POPISHLY	PORCHES
PONDERED	PONTIFYING	POONAC	POPJOY	PORCINE
PONDERER	PONTIL	POONACS	POPJOYED	PORCPISCE
PONDERERS	PONTILE	POONCE	POPJOYING	PORCPISCES
PONDERING	PONTILES	POONCES	POPJOYS	PORCUPINE
PONDEROUS	PONTILS	POONS	POPLAR	PORCUPINES
PONDERS	PONTLEVIS	POONTANG	POPLARS	PORE
PONDING	PONTLEVISES	POONTANGS	POPLIN	PORED
PONDOK	PONTON	POOP	POPLINS	PORER
PONDOKKIE	PONTONEER	POOPED	POPLITEAL	PORERS
PONDOKKIES	PONTONEERS	POOPING	POPLITIC	PORES
PONDOKS	PONTONIER	POOPS	POPOVER	PORGE
PONDS	PONTONIERS	POOR	POPOVERS	PORGED
PONDWEED	PONTONS	POORER	POPPA	PORGES
PONDWEEDS	PONTOON	POOREST	POPPADUM	PORGIE
PONE	PONTOONED	POORHOUSE	POPPADUMS	PORGIES
PONENT	PONTOONER	POORHOUSES	POPPAS	PORGING
PONES	PONTOONERS	POORI	POPPED	PORGY
PONEY	PONTOONING	POORIS	POPPER	PORIER
PONEYS	PONTOONS	POORISH	POPPERING	PORIEST
PONG	PONTS	POORLIER	POPPERINGS	PORIFER
PONGA	PONTY	POORLIEST	POPPERS	PORIFERAL
PONGAS	PONY	POORLY	POPPET	PORIFERAN
PONGED	PONYING	POORNESS	POPPETS	PORIFERS
PONGEE	PONYSKIN	POORNESSES	POPPIED	PORINESS
PONGEES	PONYSKINS	POORT	POPPIER	PORINESSES
PONGID	PONYTAIL	POORTITH	POPPIES	PORING
PONGIDS	PONYTAILS	POORTITHS	POPPIEST	PORISM
PONGIER	POO	POORTS	POPPING	PORISMS
PONGIEST	POOCH	POORWILL	POPPISH	PORISTIC
PONGING	POOCHES	POORWILLS	POPPIT	PORK
PONGO	POOD	POOS	POPPITS	PORKER
PONGOES	POODLE	POOT	POPPLE	PORKERS
PONGOS	POODLES	POOTED	POPPLED	PORKIER
PONGS	POODS	POOTER	POPPLES	PORKIES
PONGY	POOED	POOTERS	POPPLIER	PORKIEST
PONIARD	POOF	POOTING	POPPLIEST	PORKLING
PONIARDED	POOFIER	POOTS	POPPLING	PORKLINGS
PONIARDING	POOFIEST	POOVE	POPPLY	PORKS
PONIARDS	POOFS	POOVERIES	POPPY	PORKY
PONIED	POOFTAH	POOVERY	POPPYCOCK	PORN
PONIES	POOFTAHS	POOVES	POPPYCOCKS	PORNO
PONK	POOFTER	POOVIER	POPRIN	PORNOMAG
PONKED	POOFTERS	POOVIEST	POPRINS	PORNOMAGS
PONKING	POOFY	POOVY	POPS	PORNOS
PONKS	POOGYE	POP	POPSIES	PORNS
PONS	POOGYEE	POPADUM	POPSY	POROGAMIC
PONT	POOGYEES	POPADUMS	POPULACE	POROGAMIES
PONTAGE	POOGYES	POPCORN	POPULACES	POROGAMY
PONTAGES	POOH	POPCORNS	POPULAR	POROMERIC
PONTAL	POOING	POPE	POPULARLY	POROSCOPE
PONTES	POOJA	POPEDOM	POPULARS	POROSCOPES
PONTIANAC	POOJAH	POPEDOMS	POPULATE	POROSCOPIES

The Chambers Dictionary is the authority for many longer words; see *OSW* Introduction, page xii.

POROSCOPY	PORTERLY	PORTULACA	POSSESSED	POSTHORSES
POROSE	PORTERS	PORTULACAS	POSSESSES	POSTHOUSE
POROSES	PORTESS	PORTULAN	POSSESSING	POSTHOUSES
POROSIS	PORTESSE	PORTULANS	POSSESSOR	POSTICHE
POROSITIES	PORTESSES	PORTY	POSSESSORS	POSTICHES
POROSITY	PORTFOLIO	PORWIGGLE	POSSET	POSTICOUS
POROUS	PORTFOLIOS	PORWIGGLES	POSSETED	POSTIE
PORPESS	PORTHOLE	PORY	POSSETING	POSTIES
PORPESSE	PORTHOLES	POS	POSSETS	POSTIL
PORPESSES	PORTHORS	POSADA	POSSIBLE	POSTILION
PORPHYRIA	PORTHORSES	POSADAS	POSSIBLES	POSTILIONS
PORPHYRIAS	PORTHOS	POSAUNE	POSSIBLY	POSTILLED
PORPHYRIES	PORTHOSES	POSAUNES	POSSIE	POSTILLER
PORPHYRIN	PORTHOUSE	POSE	POSSIES	POSTILLERS
PORPHYRINS	PORTHOUSES	POSEABLE	POSSING	POSTILLING
PORPHYRIO	PORTICO	POSED	POSSUM	POSTILS
PORPHYRIOS	PORTICOED	POSER	POSSUMED	POSTING
PORPHYRY	PORTICOES	POSERS	POSSUMING	POSTINGS
PORPOISE	PORTICOS	POSES	POSSUMS	POSTLUDE
PORPOISED	PORTIER	POSEUR	POST	POSTLUDES
PORPOISES	PORTIERE	POSEURS	POSTAGE	POSTMAN
PORPOISING	PORTIERES	POSEUSE	POSTAGES	POSTMARK
PORPORATE	PORTIEST	POSEUSES	POSTAL	POSTMARKS
PORRECT	PORTIGUE	POSEY	POSTALLY	POSTMEN
PORRECTED	PORTIGUES	POSH	POSTALS	POSTNASAL
PORRECTING	PORTING	POSHED	POSTBAG	POSTNATAL
PORRECTS	PORTION	POSHER	POSTBAGS	POSTNATI
PORRENGER	PORTIONED	POSHES	POSTBOX	POSTORAL
PORRENGERS	PORTIONER	POSHEST	POSTBOXES	POSTPONE
PORRIDGE	PORTIONERS	POSHING	POSTBUS	POSTPONED
PORRIDGES	PORTIONING	POSHLY	POSTBUSES	POSTPONER
PORRIGO	PORTIONS	POSHNESS	POSTCARD	POSTPONERS
PORRIGOS	PORTLAND	POSHNESSES	POSTCARDED	POSTPONES
PORRINGER	PORTLANDS	POSHTEEN	POSTCARDING	POSTPONING
PORRINGERS	PORTLAST	POSHTEENS	POSTCARDS	POSTPOSE
PORT	PORTLASTS	POSIER	POSTCAVA	POSTPOSED
PORTA	PORTLIER	POSIES	POSTCAVAE	POSTPOSES
PORTABLE	PORTLIEST	POSIEST	POSTCODE	POSTPOSING
PORTABLES	PORTLY	POSIGRADE	POSTCODED	POSTRIDER
PORTAGE	PORTMAN	POSING	POSTCODES	POSTRIDERS
PORTAGES	PORTMEN	POSINGLY	POSTCODING	POSTS
PORTAGUE	PORTOISE	POSINGS	POSTDATE	POSTULANT
PORTAGUES	PORTOISES	POSIT	POSTDATED	POSTULANTS
PORTAL	PORTOLAN	POSITED	POSTDATES	POSTULATA
PORTALS	PORTOLANI	POSITING	POSTDATING	POSTULATE
PORTANCE	PORTOLANO	POSITION	POSTED	POSTULATED
PORTANCES	PORTOLANOS	POSITIONED	POSTEEN	POSTULATES
PORTAS	PORTOLANS	POSITIONING	POSTEENS	POSTULATING
PORTASES	PORTOUS	POSITIONS	POSTER	POSTURAL
PORTATE	PORTOUSES	POSITIVE	POSTERED	POSTURE
PORTATILE	PORTRAIT	POSITIVES	POSTERING	POSTURED
PORTATIVE	PORTRAITED	POSITON	POSTERIOR	POSTURER
PORTATIVES	PORTRAITING	POSITONS	POSTERIORS	POSTURERS
PORTED	PORTRAITS	POSITRON	POSTERITIES	POSTURES
PORTEND	PORTRAY	POSITRONS	POSTERITY	POSTURING
PORTENDED	PORTRAYAL	POSITS	POSTERN	POSTURIST
PORTENDING	PORTRAYALS	POSNET	POSTERNS	POSTURISTS
PORTENDS	PORTRAYED	POSNETS	POSTERS	POSTWAR
PORTENT	PORTRAYER	POSOLOGIES	POSTFACE	POSTWOMAN
PORTENTS	PORTRAYERS	POSOLOGY	POSTFACES	POSTWOMEN
PORTEOUS	PORTRAYING	POSS	POSTFIX	POSY
PORTEOUSES	PORTRAYS	POSSE	POSTFIXED	POT
PORTER	PORTREEVE	POSSED	POSTFIXES	POTABLE
PORTERAGE	PORTREEVES	POSSER	POSTFIXING	POTABLES
PORTERAGES	PORTRESS	POSSERS	POSTHASTE	POTAGE
PORTERESS	PORTRESSES	POSSES	POSTHASTES	POTAGER
PORTERESSES	PORTS	POSSESS	POSTHORSE	POTAGERS

The Chambers Dictionary is the authority for many longer words; see *OSW* Introduction, page xii.

POTAGES	POTHOLERS	POTTO	POUNCES	POUTHERED
POTAMIC	POTHOLES	POTTOS	POUNCET	POUTHERING
POTASH	POTHOLING	POTTS	POUNCETS	POUTHERS
POTASHED	POTHOLINGS	POTTY	POUNCHING	POUTIER
POTASHES	POTHOOK	POUCH	POUNCING	POUTIEST
POTASHING	POTHOOKS	POUCHED	POUND	POUTING
POTASS	POTHOUSE	POUCHES	POUNDAGE	POUTINGLY
POTASSA	POTHOUSES	POUCHFUL	POUNDAGES	POUTINGS
POTASSAS	POTICARIES	POUCHFULS	POUNDAL	POUTS
POTASSES	POTICARY	POUCHIER	POUNDALS	POUTY
POTASSIC	POTICHE	POUCHIEST	POUNDED	POVERTIES
POTASSIUM	POTICHES	POUCHING	POUNDER	POVERTY
POTASSIUMS	POTIN	POUCHY	POUNDERS	POW
POTATION	POTING	POUDER	POUNDING	POWAN
POTATIONS	POTINS	POUDERS	POUNDS	POWANS
POTATO	POTION	POUDRE	POUPE	POWDER
POTATOES	POTIONS	POUDRES	POUPED	POWDERED
POTATORY	POTLACH	POUF	POUPES	POWDERIER
POTBOY	POTLACHES	POUFED	POUPING	POWDERIEST
POTBOYS	POTLATCH	POUFFE	POUPT	POWDERING
POTCH	POTLATCHES	POUFFED	POUR	POWDERS
POTCHE	POTMAN	POUFFES	POURABLE	POWDERY
POTCHED	POTMEN	POUFFING	POURBOIRE	POWELLISE
POTCHER	POTOMETER	POUFING	POURBOIRES	POWELLISED
POTCHERS	POTOMETERS	POUFS	POURED	POWELLISES
POTCHES	POTOO	POUFTAH	POURER	POWELLISING
POTCHING	POTOOS	POUFTAHS	POURERS	POWELLITE
POTE	POTOROO	POUFTER	POURIE	POWELLITES
POTED	POTOROOS	POUFTERS	POURIES	POWELLIZE
POTEEN	POTPOURRI	POUK	POURING	POWELLIZED
POTEENS	POTPOURRIS	POUKE	POURINGS	POWELLIZES
POTENCE	POTS	POUKES	POURPOINT	POWELLIZING
POTENCES	POTSHARD	POUKING	POURPOINTS	POWER
POTENCIES	POTSHARDS	POUKIT	POURS	POWERBOAT
POTENCY	POTSHARE	POUKS	POURSEW	POWERBOATS
POTENT	POTSHARES	POULAINE	POURSEWED	POWERED
POTENTATE	POTSHERD	POULAINES	POURSEWING	POWERFUL
POTENTATES	POTSHERDS	POULARD	POURSEWS	POWERING
POTENTIAL	POTSHOP	POULARDS	POURSUE	POWERLESS
POTENTIALS	POTSHOPS	POULDER	POURSUED	POWERPLAY
POTENTISE	POTSTONE	POULDERS	POURSUES	POWERPLAYS
POTENTISED	POTSTONES	POULDRE	POURSUING	POWERS
POTENTISES	POTT	POULDRES	POURSUIT	POWIN
POTENTISING	POTTAGE	POULDRON	POURSUITS	POWINS
POTENTIZE	POTTAGES	POULDRONS	POURSUITT	POWN
POTENTIZED	POTTED	POULE	POURSUITTS	POWND
POTENTIZES	POTTER	POULES	POURTRAHED	POWNDED
POTENTIZING	POTTERED	POULP	POURTRAY	POWNDING
POTENTLY	POTTERER	POULPE	POURTRAYD	POWNDS
POTENTS	POTTERERS	POULPES	POURTRAYED	POWNEY
POTES	POTTERIES	POULPS	POURTRAYING	POWNEYS
POTFUL	POTTERING	POULT	POURTRAYS	POWNIE
POTFULS	POTTERINGS	POULTER	POUSOWDIE	POWNIES
POTGUN	POTTERS	POULTERER	POUSOWDIES	POWNS
POTGUNS	POTTERY	POULTERERS	POUSSE	POWNY
POTHECARIES	POTTIER	POULTERS	POUSSES	POWRE
POTHECARY	POTTIES	POULTFEET	POUSSETTE	POWRED
POTHEEN	POTTIEST	POULTFOOT	POUSSETTED	POWRES
POTHEENS	POTTINESS	POULTICE	POUSSETTES	POWRING
POTHER	POTTINESSES	POULTICED	POUSSETTING	POWS
POTHERED	POTTING	POULTICES	POUSSIN	POWSOWDIES
POTHERING	POTTINGAR	POULTICING	POUSSINS	POWSOWDY
POTHERS	POTTINGARS	POULTRIES	POUT	POWTER
POTHERY	POTTINGER	POULTRY	POUTED	POWTERED
POTHOLE	POTTINGERS	POULTS	POUTER	POWTERING
POTHOLED	POTTLE	POUNCE	POUTERS	POWTERS
POTHOLER	POTTLES	POUNCED	POUTHER	POWWAW

The Chambers Dictionary is the authority for many longer words; see *OSW* Introduction, page xii.

POWWOW	PRAEDIALS	PRANKSOME	PREACH	PRECIS
POWWOWED	PRAEFECT	PRANKSTER	PREACHED	PRECISE
POWWOWING	PRAEFECTS	PRANKSTERS	PREACHER	PRECISED
POWWOWS	PRAELUDIA	PRANKY	PREACHERS	PRECISELY
POX	PRAENOMEN	PRASE	PREACHES	PRECISER
POXED	PRAENOMENS	PRASES	PREACHIER	PRECISES
POXES	PRAENOMINA	PRAT	PREACHIEST	PRECISEST
POXIER	PRAESES	PRATE	PREACHIFIED	PRECISIAN
POXIEST	PRAESIDIA	PRATED	PREACHIFIES	PRECISIANS
POXING	PRAETOR	PRATER	PREACHIFY	PRECISING
POXVIRUS	PRAETORS	PRATERS	PREACHIFYING	PRECISION
POXVIRUSES	PRAGMATIC	PRATES	PREACHILY	PRECISIONS
POXY	PRAGMATICS	PRATFALL	PREACHING	PRECISIVE
POYNANT	PRAHU	PRATFALLEN	PREACHINGS	PRECLUDE
POYNT	PRAHUS	PRATFALLING	PREACHY	PRECLUDED
POYNTED	PRAIRIE	PRATFALLS	PREACING	PRECLUDES
POYNTING	PRAIRIED	PRATFELL	PREAMBLE	PRECLUDING
POYNTS	PRAIRIES	PRATIE	PREAMBLED	PRECOCIAL
POYSE	PRAISE	PRATIES	PREAMBLES	PRECOCITIES
POYSED	PRAISEACH	PRATING	PREAMBLING	PRECOCITY
POYSES	PRAISEACHS	PRATINGLY	PREAMP	PRECOITAL
POYSING	PRAISED	PRATINGS	PREAMPS	PRECONISE
POYSON	PRAISEFUL	PRATIQUE	PREASE	PRECONISED
POYSONED	PRAISER	PRATIQUES	PREASED	PRECONISES
POYSONING	PRAISERS	PRATS	PREASES	PRECONISING
POYSONS	PRAISES	PRATT	PREASING	PRECONIZE
POZ	PRAISING	PRATTED	PREASSE	PRECONIZED
POZZ	PRAISINGS	PRATTING	PREASSED	PRECONIZES
POZZIES	PRALINE	PRATTLE	PREASSES	PRECONIZING
POZZOLANA	PRALINES	PRATTLED	PREASSING	PRECOOK
POZZOLANAS	PRAM	PRATTLER	PREBEND	PRECOOKED
POZZY	PRAMS	PRATTLERS	PREBENDAL	PRECOOKING
PRAAM	PRANA	PRATTLES	PREBENDS	PRECOOKS
PRAAMS	PRANAS	PRATTLING	PREBIOTIC	PRECOOL
PRABBLE	PRANAYAMA	PRATTS	PREBORN	PRECOOLED
PRABBLES	PRANAYAMAS	PRATY	PRECAST	PRECOOLING
PRACTIC	PRANCE	PRAU	PRECATIVE	PRECOOLS
PRACTICAL	PRANCED	PRAUNCE	PRECATORY	PRECURRER
PRACTICALS	PRANCER	PRAUNCED	PRECAVA	PRECURRERS
PRACTICE	PRANCERS	PRAUNCES	PRECAVAE	PRECURSE
PRACTICED	PRANCES	PRAUNCING	PRECEDE	PRECURSES
PRACTICING	PRANCING	PRAUS	PRECEDED	PRECURSOR
PRACTICING	PRANCINGS	PRAVITIES	PRECEDENT	PRECURSORS
PRACTICK	PRANCK	PRAVITY	PRECEDENTS	PRECUT
PRACTICKS	PRANCKE	PRAWLE	PRECEDES	PRECUTS
PRACTICS	PRANCKED	PRAWLES	PRECEDING	PRECUTTING
PRACTICUM	PRANCKES	PRAWLIN	PRECEESE	PREDACITIES
PRACTICUMS	PRANCKING	PRAWLINS	PRECENTOR	PREDACITY
PRACTIQUE	PRANCKS	PRAWN	PRECENTORS	PREDATE
PRACTIQUES	PRANDIAL	PRAWNED	PRECEPIT	PREDATED
PRACTISE	PRANG	PRAWNING	PRECEPITS	PREDATES
PRACTISED	PRANGED	PRAWNS	PRECEPT	PREDATING
PRACTISER	PRANGING	PRAXES	PRECEPTOR	PREDATION
PRACTISERS	PRANGS	PRAXIS	PRECEPTORS	PREDATIONS
PRACTISES	PRANK	PRAY	PRECEPTS	PREDATIVE
PRACTISING	PRANKED	PRAYED	PRECESS	PREDATOR
PRACTIVE	PRANKFUL	PRAYER	PRECESSED	PREDATORS
PRACTOLOL	PRANKIER	PRAYERFUL	PRECESSES	PREDATORY
PRACTOLOLS	PRANKIEST	PRAYERS	PRECESSING	PREDAWN
PRAD	PRANKING	PRAYING	PRECIEUSE	PREDAWNS
PRADS	PRANKINGS	PRAYINGLY	PRECIEUSES	PREDEFINE
PRAEAMBLE	PRANKISH	PRAYINGS	PRECINCT	PREDEFINED
PRAEAMBLES	PRANKLE	PRAYS	PRECINCTS	PREDEFINES
PRAECAVA	PRANKLED	PRE	PRECIOUS	PREDEFINING
PRAECAVAE	PRANKLES	PREACE	PRECIOUSES	PREDELLA
PRAECOCES	PRANKLING	PREACED	PRECIPICE	PREDELLAS
PRAEDIAL	PRANKS	PREACES	PRECIPICES	PREDESIGN

The Chambers Dictionary is the authority for many longer words; see *OSW* Introduction, page xii.

PREDESIGNED
PREDESIGNING
PREDESIGNS
PREDEVOTE
PREDIAL
PREDIALS
PREDICANT
PREDICANTS
PREDICATE
PREDICATED
PREDICATES
PREDICATING
PREDICT
PREDICTED
PREDICTER
PREDICTERS
PREDICTING
PREDICTOR
PREDICTORS
PREDICTS
PREDIED
PREDIES
PREDIGEST
PREDIGESTED
PREDIGESTING
PREDIGESTS
PREDIKANT
PREDIKANTS
PREDILECT
PREDOOM
PREDOOMED
PREDOOMING
PREDOOMS
PREDY
PREDYING
PREE
PREED
PREEING
PREEMIE
PREEMIES
PREEN
PREENED
PREENING
PREENS
PREES
PREEVE
PREEVED
PREEVES
PREEVING
PREFAB
PREFABS
PREFACE
PREFACED
PREFACES
PREFACIAL
PREFACING
PREFADE
PREFADED
PREFADES
PREFADING
PREFARD
PREFATORY
PREFECT
PREFECTS
PREFER
PREFERRED
PREFERRER

PREFERRERS
PREFERRING
PREFERS
PREFIGURE
PREFIGURED
PREFIGURES
PREFIGURING
PREFIX
PREFIXED
PREFIXES
PREFIXING
PREFIXION
PREFIXIONS
PREFLIGHT
PREFORM
PREFORMED
PREFORMING
PREFORMS
PREGGERS
PREGNABLE
PREGNANCE
PREGNANCES
PREGNANCIES
PREGNANCY
PREGNANT
PREHALLUCES
PREHALLUX
PREHEAT
PREHEATED
PREHEATING
PREHEATS
PREHEND
PREHENDED
PREHENDING
PREHENDS
PREHENSOR
PREHENSORS
PREHNITE
PREHNITES
PREHUMAN
PREIF
PREIFE
PREIFES
PREIFS
PREJINK
PREJUDGE
PREJUDGED
PREJUDGES
PREJUDGING
PREJUDICE
PREJUDICED
PREJUDICES
PREJUDICING
PREJUDIZE
PREJUDIZES
PRELACIES
PRELACY
PRELATE
PRELATES
PRELATESS
PRELATESSES
PRELATIAL
PRELATIC
PRELATIES
PRELATION
PRELATIONS
PRELATISE

PRELATISED
PRELATISES
PRELATISH
PRELATISING
PRELATISM
PRELATISMS
PRELATIST
PRELATISTS
PRELATIZE
PRELATIZED
PRELATIZES
PRELATIZING
PRELATURE
PRELATURES
PRELATY
PRELECT
PRELECTED
PRELECTING
PRELECTOR
PRELECTORS
PRELECTS
PRELIM
PRELIMS
PRELUDE
PRELUDED
PRELUDES
PRELUDI
PRELUDIAL
PRELUDING
PRELUDIO
PRELUSIVE
PRELUSORY
PREMATURE
PREMED
PREMEDIC
PREMEDICS
PREMEDS
PREMIA
PREMIE
PREMIER
PREMIERE
PREMIERED
PREMIERES
PREMIERING
PREMIERS
PREMIES
PREMISE
PREMISED
PREMISES
PREMISING
PREMISS
PREMISSES
PREMIUM
PREMIUMS
PREMIX
PREMIXED
PREMIXES
PREMIXING
PREMOLAR
PREMOLARS
PREMONISH
PREMONISHED
PREMONISHES
PREMONISHING
PREMORSE
PREMOSAIC
PREMOTION

PREMOTIONS
PREMOVE
PREMOVED
PREMOVES
PREMOVING
PREMY
PRENASAL
PRENASALS
PRENATAL
PRENOTIFIED
PRENOTIFIES
PRENOTIFY
PRENOTIFYING
PRENOTION
PRENOTIONS
PRENT
PRENTED
PRENTICE
PRENTICED
PRENTICES
PRENTICING
PRENTING
PRENTS
PRENUBILE
PRENZIE
PREOCCUPIED
PREOCCUPIES
PREOCCUPY
PREOCCUPYING
PREOCULAR
PREOPTION
PREOPTIONS
PREORAL
PREORDAIN
PREORDAINED
PREORDAINING
PREORDAINS
PREORDER
PREORDERED
PREORDERING
PREORDERS
PREP
PREPACK
PREPACKED
PREPACKING
PREPACKS
PREPAID
PREPARE
PREPARED
PREPARER
PREPARERS
PREPARES
PREPARING
PREPAY
PREPAYING
PREPAYS
PREPENSE
PREPENSED
PREPENSES
PREPENSING
PREPOLLEX
PREPOLLICES
PREPONE
PREPONED
PREPONES
PREPONING
PREPOSE

PREPOSED
PREPOSES
PREPOSING
PREPOSTOR
PREPOSTORS
PREPOTENT
PREPPED
PREPPIER
PREPPIES
PREPPIEST
PREPPILY
PREPPING
PREPPY
PREPS
PREPUCE
PREPUCES
PREPUTIAL
PREQUEL
PREQUELS
PRERECORD
PRERECORDED
PRERECORDING
PRERECORDS
PREROSION
PREROSIONS
PRERUPT
PRESA
PRESAGE
PRESAGED
PRESAGER
PRESAGERS
PRESAGES
PRESAGING
PRESBYOPE
PRESBYOPES
PRESBYOPIES
PRESBYOPY
PRESBYTE
PRESBYTER
PRESBYTERS
PRESBYTES
PRESBYTIC
PRESCHOOL
PRESCHOOLS
PRESCIENT
PRESCIND
PRESCINDED
PRESCINDING
PRESCINDS
PRESCIOUS
PRESCRIBE
PRESCRIBED
PRESCRIBES
PRESCRIBING
PRESCRIPT
PRESCRIPTS
PRESCUTA
PRESCUTUM
PRESE
PRESELECT
PRESELECTED
PRESELECTING
PRESELECTS
PRESENCE
PRESENCES
PRESENT
PRESENTED

The Chambers Dictionary is the authority for many longer words; see *OSW* Introduction, page xii.

PRESENTEE	PRESUMED	PREVERB	PRICKETS	PRIMALLY
PRESENTEES	PRESUMER	PREVERBAL	PRICKING	PRIMARIES
PRESENTER	PRESUMERS	PREVERBS	PRICKINGS	PRIMARILY
PRESENTERS	PRESUMES	PREVES	PRICKLE	PRIMARY
PRESENTING	PRESUMING	PREVIEW	PRICKLED	PRIMATAL
PRESENTLY	PRETENCE	PREVIEWED	PRICKLES	PRIMATE
PRESENTS	PRETENCES	PREVIEWING	PRICKLIER	PRIMATES
PRESERVE	PRETEND	PREVIEWS	PRICKLIEST	PRIMATIAL
PRESERVED	PRETENDED	PREVING	PRICKLING	PRIMATIC
PRESERVER	PRETENDER	PREVIOUS	PRICKLINGS	PRIME
PRESERVERS	PRETENDERS	PREVISE	PRICKLY	PRIMED
PRESERVES	PRETENDING	PREVISED	PRICKS	PRIMELY
PRESERVING	PRETENDS	PREVISES	PRICKWOOD	PRIMENESS
PRESES	PRETENSE	PREVISING	PRICKWOODS	PRIMENESSES
PRESET	PRETENSES	PREVISION	PRICY	PRIMER
PRESETS	PRETERIST	PREVISIONED	PRIDE	PRIMERO
PRESETTING	PRETERISTS	PREVISIONING	PRIDED	PRIMEROS
PRESIDE	PRETERIT	PREVISIONS	PRIDEFUL	PRIMERS
PRESIDED	PRETERITE	PREVUE	PRIDELESS	PRIMES
PRESIDENT	PRETERITES	PREVUED	PRIDES	PRIMEUR
PRESIDENTS	PRETERITS	PREVUES	PRIDIAN	PRIMEURS
PRESIDES	PRETERM	PREVUING	PRIDING	PRIMEVAL
PRESIDIA	PRETERMIT	PREWARM	PRIED	PRIMINE
PRESIDIAL	PRETERMITS	PREWARMED	PRIEF	PRIMINES
PRESIDING	PRETERMITTED	PREWARMING	PRIEFE	PRIMING
PRESIDIO	PRETERMITTING	PREWARMS	PRIEFES	PRIMINGS
PRESIDIOS	PRETEST	PREWARN	PRIEFS	PRIMIPARA
PRESIDIUM	PRETESTED	PREWARNED	PRIER	PRIMIPARAE
PRESIDIUMS	PRETESTING	PREWARNING	PRIERS	PRIMIPARAS
PRESS	PRETESTS	PREWARNS	PRIES	PRIMITIAE
PRESSED	PRETEXT	PREWYN	PRIEST	PRIMITIAL
PRESSER	PRETEXTS	PREWYNS	PRIESTED	PRIMITIAS
PRESSERS	PRETOR	PREX	PRIESTESS	PRIMITIVE
PRESSES	PRETORS	PREXES	PRIESTESSES	PRIMITIVES
PRESSFAT	PRETTIED	PREXIES	PRIESTING	PRIMLY
PRESSFATS	PRETTIER	PREXY	PRIESTLY	PRIMMED
PRESSFUL	PRETTIES	PREY	PRIESTS	PRIMMER
PRESSFULS	PRETTIEST	PREYED	PRIEVE	PRIMMERS
PRESSIE	PRETTIFIED	PREYFUL	PRIEVED	PRIMMEST
PRESSIES	PRETTIFIES	PREYING	PRIEVES	PRIMMING
PRESSING	PRETTIFY	PREYS	PRIEVING	PRIMNESS
PRESSINGS	PRETTIFYING	PREZZIE	PRIG	PRIMNESSES
PRESSION	PRETTILY	PREZZIES	PRIGGED	PRIMO
PRESSIONS	PRETTY	PRIAL	PRIGGER	PRIMORDIA
PRESSMAN	PRETTYING	PRIALS	PRIGGERIES	PRIMOS
PRESSMARK	PRETTYISH	PRIAPIC	PRIGGERS	PRIMP
PRESSMARKS	PRETTYISM	PRIAPISM	PRIGGERY	PRIMPED
PRESSMEN	PRETTYISMS	PRIAPISMS	PRIGGING	PRIMPING
PRESSOR	PRETZEL	PRIBBLE	PRIGGINGS	PRIMPS
PRESSROOM	PRETZELS	PRIBBLES	PRIGGISH	PRIMROSE
PRESSROOMS	PREVAIL	PRICE	PRIGGISM	PRIMROSED
PRESSURE	PREVAILED	PRICED	PRIGGISMS	PRIMROSES
PRESSURED	PREVAILING	PRICELESS	PRIGS	PRIMROSING
PRESSURES	PREVAILS	PRICER	PRILL	PRIMROSY
PRESSURING	PREVALENT	PRICERS	PRILLED	PRIMS
PRESSWORK	PREVE	PRICES	PRILLING	PRIMSIE
PRESSWORKS	PREVED	PRICEY	PRILLS	PRIMULA
PREST	PREVENE	PRICIER	PRIM	PRIMULAS
PRESTED	PREVENED	PRICIEST	PRIMA	PRIMULINE
PRESTERNA	PREVENES	PRICINESS	PRIMACIES	PRIMULINES
PRESTIGE	PREVENING	PRICINESSES	PRIMACY	PRIMUS
PRESTIGES	PREVENT	PRICING	PRIMAEVAL	PRIMUSES
PRESTING	PREVENTED	PRICK	PRIMAGE	PRIMY
PRESTO	PREVENTER	PRICKED	PRIMAGES	PRINCE
PRESTOS	PREVENTERS	PRICKER	PRIMAL	PRINCED
PRESTS	PREVENTING	PRICKERS	PRIMALITIES	PRINCEDOM
PRESUME	PREVENTS	PRICKET	PRIMALITY	PRINCEDOMS

The Chambers Dictionary is the authority for many longer words; see *OSW* Introduction, page xii.

PRINCEKIN
PRINCEKINS
PRINCELET
PRINCELETS
PRINCELIER
PRINCELIEST
PRINCELY
PRINCES
PRINCESS
PRINCESSE
PRINCESSES
PRINCING
PRINCIPAL
PRINCIPALS
PRINCIPIA
PRINCIPLE
PRINCIPLED
PRINCIPLES
PRINCIPLING
PRINCOCK
PRINCOCKS
PRINCOX
PRINCOXES
PRINK
PRINKED
PRINKING
PRINKS
PRINT
PRINTABLE
PRINTED
PRINTER
PRINTERS
PRINTHEAD
PRINTHEADS
PRINTING
PRINTINGS
PRINTLESS
PRINTS
PRION
PRIONS
PRIOR
PRIORATE
PRIORATES
PRIORESS
PRIORESSES
PRIORIES
PRIORITIES
PRIORITY
PRIORS
PRIORSHIP
PRIORSHIPS
PRIORY
PRISAGE
PRISAGES
PRISE
PRISED
PRISER
PRISERS
PRISES
PRISING
PRISM
PRISMATIC
PRISMOID
PRISMOIDS
PRISMS
PRISMY
PRISON

PRISONED
PRISONER
PRISONERS
PRISONING
PRISONOUS
PRISONS
PRISSIER
PRISSIEST
PRISSY
PRISTANE
PRISTANES
PRISTINE
PRITHEE
PRIVACIES
PRIVACY
PRIVADO
PRIVADOES
PRIVADOS
PRIVATE
PRIVATEER
PRIVATEERED
PRIVATEERING
PRIVATEERINGS
PRIVATEERS
PRIVATELY
PRIVATES
PRIVATION
PRIVATIONS
PRIVATISE
PRIVATISED
PRIVATISES
PRIVATISING
PRIVATIVE
PRIVATIVES
PRIVATIZE
PRIVATIZED
PRIVATIZES
PRIVATIZING
PRIVET
PRIVETS
PRIVIER
PRIVIES
PRIVIEST
PRIVILEGE
PRIVILEGED
PRIVILEGES
PRIVILEGING
PRIVILY
PRIVITIES
PRIVITY
PRIVY
PRIZABLE
PRIZE
PRIZED
PRIZEMAN
PRIZEMEN
PRIZER
PRIZERS
PRIZES
PRIZING
PRO
PROA
PROACTIVE
PROAS
PROB
PROBABLE
PROBABLES

PROBABLY
PROBALL
PROBAND
PROBANDS
PROBANG
PROBANGS
PROBATE
PROBATED
PROBATES
PROBATING
PROBATION
PROBATIONS
PROBATIVE
PROBATORY
PROBE
PROBEABLE
PROBED
PROBER
PROBERS
PROBES
PROBING
PROBIT
PROBITIES
PROBITS
PROBITY
PROBLEM
PROBLEMS
PROBOSCIDES
PROBOSCIS
PROBOSCISES
PROBS
PROCACITIES
PROCACITY
PROCAINE
PROCAINES
PROCARYON
PROCARYONS
PROCEDURE
PROCEDURES
PROCEED
PROCEEDED
PROCEEDER
PROCEEDERS
PROCEEDING
PROCEEDINGS
PROCEEDS
PROCERITIES
PROCERITY
PROCESS
PROCESSED
PROCESSES
PROCESSING
PROCESSOR
PROCESSORS
PROCIDENT
PROCINCT
PROCINCTS
PROCLAIM
PROCLAIMED
PROCLAIMING
PROCLAIMS
PROCLISES
PROCLISIS
PROCLITIC
PROCLITICS
PROCLIVE
PROCONSUL

PROCONSULS
PROCREANT
PROCREANTS
PROCREATE
PROCREATED
PROCREATES
PROCREATING
PROCTAL
PROCTITIS
PROCTITISES
PROCTOR
PROCTORS
PROCURACIES
PROCURACY
PROCURE
PROCURED
PROCURER
PROCURERS
PROCURES
PROCURESS
PROCURESSES
PROCUREUR
PROCUREURS
PROCURING
PROD
PRODDED
PRODDING
PRODIGAL
PRODIGALS
PRODIGIES
PRODIGY
PRODITOR
PRODITORS
PRODITORY
PRODNOSE
PRODNOSED
PRODNOSES
PRODNOSING
PRODROMAL
PRODROME
PRODROMES
PRODROMI
PRODROMIC
PRODROMUS
PRODS
PRODUCE
PRODUCED
PRODUCER
PRODUCERS
PRODUCES
PRODUCING
PRODUCT
PRODUCTS
PROEM
PROEMBRYO
PROEMBRYOS
PROEMIAL
PROEMS
PROENZYME
PROENZYMES
PROF
PROFACE
PROFANE
PROFANED
PROFANELY
PROFANER
PROFANERS

PROFANES
PROFANING
PROFANITIES
PROFANITY
PROFESS
PROFESSED
PROFESSES
PROFESSING
PROFESSOR
PROFESSORS
PROFFER
PROFFERED
PROFFERER
PROFFERERS
PROFFERING
PROFFERS
PROFILE
PROFILED
PROFILER
PROFILERS
PROFILES
PROFILING
PROFILIST
PROFILISTS
PROFIT
PROFITED
PROFITEER
PROFITEERED
PROFITEERING
PROFITEERINGS
PROFITEERS
PROFITER
PROFITERS
PROFITING
PROFITINGS
PROFITS
PROFLUENT
PROFORMA
PROFORMAS
PROFOUND
PROFOUNDER
PROFOUNDEST
PROFOUNDS
PROFS
PROFUSE
PROFUSELY
PROFUSER
PROFUSERS
PROFUSION
PROFUSIONS
PROG
PROGENIES
PROGENY
PROGERIA
PROGERIAS
PROGESTIN
PROGESTINS
PROGGED
PROGGING
PROGGINS
PROGGINSES
PROGNOSES
PROGNOSIS
PROGRADE
PROGRADED
PROGRADES
PROGRADING

The Chambers Dictionary is the authority for many longer words; see *OSW* Introduction, page xii.

PROGRAM	PROLEPSES	PROMISSOR	PRONKS	PROPERDINS
PROGRAMME	PROLEPSIS	PROMISSORS	PRONOTA	PROPERLY
PROGRAMMED	PROLEPTIC	PROMMER	PRONOTAL	PROPERS
PROGRAMMES	PROLER	PROMMERS	PRONOTUM	PROPERTIED
PROGRAMMING	PROLERS	PROMO	PRONOUN	PROPERTIES
PROGRAMMINGS	PROLES	PROMOS	PRONOUNCE	PROPERTY
PROGRAMS	PROLETARIES	PROMOTE	PRONOUNCED	PROPERTYING
PROGRESS	PROLETARY	PROMOTED	PRONOUNCES	PROPHAGE
PROGRESSED	PROLICIDE	PROMOTER	PRONOUNCING	PROPHAGES
PROGRESSES	PROLICIDES	PROMOTERS	PRONOUNCINGS	PROPHASE
PROGRESSING	PROLIFIC	PROMOTES	PRONOUNS	PROPHASES
PROGS	PROLINE	PROMOTING	PRONTO	PROPHECIES
PROHIBIT	PROLINES	PROMOTION	PRONUCLEI	PROPHECY
PROHIBITED	PROLING	PROMOTIONS	PRONUNCIO	PROPHESIED
PROHIBITING	PROLIX	PROMOTIVE	PRONUNCIOS	PROPHESIES
PROHIBITS	PROLIXITIES	PROMOTOR	PROO	PROPHESY
PROIGN	PROLIXITY	PROMOTORS	PROOEMION	PROPHESYING
PROIGNED	PROLIXLY	PROMPT	PROOEMIONS	PROPHESYINGS
PROIGNING	PROLL	PROMPTED	PROOEMIUM	PROPHET
PROIGNS	PROLLED	PROMPTER	PROOEMIUMS	PROPHETIC
PROIN	PROLLER	PROMPTERS	PROOF	PROPHETS
PROINE	PROLLERS	PROMPTEST	PROOFED	PROPHYLL
PROINED	PROLLING	PROMPTING	PROOFING	PROPHYLLS
PROINES	PROLLS	PROMPTINGS	PROOFINGS	PROPINE
PROINING	PROLOGISE	PROMPTLY	PROOFLESS	PROPINED
PROINS	PROLOGISED	PROMPTS	PROOFREAD	PROPINES
PROJECT	PROLOGISES	PROMPTURE	PROOFREADING	PROPINING
PROJECTED	PROLOGISING	PROMPTURES	PROOFREADINGS	PROPODEON
PROJECTING	PROLOGIZE	PROMS	PROOFREADS	PROPODEONS
PROJECTINGS	PROLOGIZED	PROMULGE	PROOFS	PROPODEUM
PROJECTOR	PROLOGIZES	PROMULGED	PROOTIC	PROPODEUMS
PROJECTORS	PROLOGIZING	PROMULGES	PROOTICS	PROPOLIS
PROJECTS	PROLOGUE	PROMULGING	PROP	PROPOLISES
PROKARYON	PROLOGUED	PROMUSCES	PROPAGATE	PROPONE
PROKARYONS	PROLOGUES	PROMUSCIDES	PROPAGATED	PROPONED
PROKARYOT	PROLOGUING	PROMUSCIS	PROPAGATES	PROPONENT
PROKARYOTS	PROLONG	PROMUSCISES	PROPAGATING	PROPONENTS
PROKE	PROLONGE	PRONAOI	PROPAGE	PROPONES
PROKED	PROLONGED	PRONAOS	PROPAGED	PROPONING
PROKER	PROLONGER	PRONATE	PROPAGES	PROPOSAL
PROKERS	PROLONGERS	PRONATED	PROPAGING	PROPOSALS
PROKES	PROLONGES	PRONATES	PROPAGULA	PROPOSE
PROKING	PROLONGING	PRONATING	PROPAGULE	PROPOSED
PROLACTIN	PROLONGS	PRONATION	PROPAGULES	PROPOSER
PROLACTINS	PROLUSION	PRONATIONS	PROPALE	PROPOSERS
PROLAMIN	PROLUSIONS	PRONATOR	PROPALED	PROPOSES
PROLAMINE	PROLUSORY	PRONATORS	PROPALES	PROPOSING
PROLAMINES	PROM	PRONE	PROPALING	PROPOUND
PROLAMINS	PROMACHOS	PRONELY	PROPANE	PROPOUNDED
PROLAPSE	PROMACHOSES	PRONENESS	PROPANES	PROPOUNDING
PROLAPSED	PROMENADE	PRONENESSES	PROPANOL	PROPOUNDS
PROLAPSES	PROMENADED	PRONER	PROPANOLS	PROPPANT
PROLAPSING	PROMENADES	PRONES	PROPEL	PROPPANTS
PROLAPSUS	PROMENADING	PRONEST	PROPELLED	PROPPED
PROLAPSUSES	PROMETAL	PRONEUR	PROPELLER	PROPPING
PROLATE	PROMETALS	PRONEURS	PROPELLERS	PROPRIETIES
PROLATED	PROMINENT	PRONG	PROPELLING	PROPRIETY
PROLATELY	PROMISE	PRONGBUCK	PROPELS	PROPS
PROLATES	PROMISED	PRONGBUCKS	PROPEND	PROPTOSES
PROLATING	PROMISEE	PRONGED	PROPENDED	PROPTOSIS
PROLATION	PROMISEES	PRONGHORN	PROPENDING	PROPULSOR
PROLATIONS	PROMISER	PRONGHORNS	PROPENDS	PROPULSORS
PROLATIVE	PROMISERS	PRONGING	PROPENE	PROPYL
PROLE	PROMISES	PRONGS	PROPENES	PROPYLA
PROLED	PROMISING	PRONK	PROPENSE	PROPYLAEA
PROLEG	PROMISOR	PRONKED	PROPER	PROPYLENE
PROLEGS	PROMISORS	PRONKING	PROPERDIN	PROPYLENES

The Chambers Dictionary is the authority for many longer words; see *OSW* Introduction, page xii.

PROPYLIC	PROSINESS	PROTENDING	PROTRUDE	PROVING
PROPYLITE	PROSINESSES	PROTENDS	PROTRUDED	PROVINGS
PROPYLITES	PROSING	PROTENSE	PROTRUDES	PROVINING
PROPYLON	PROSINGS	PROTENSES	PROTRUDING	PROVIRAL
PROPYLS	PROSIT	PROTEOSE	PROTYL	PROVIRUS
PRORATE	PROSO	PROTEOSES	PROTYLE	PROVIRUSES
PRORATED	PROSODIAL	PROTEST	PROTYLES	PROVISION
PRORATES	PROSODIAN	PROTESTED	PROTYLS	PROVISIONED
PRORATING	PROSODIANS	PROTESTER	PROUD	PROVISIONING
PRORATION	PROSODIC	PROTESTERS	PROUDER	PROVISIONS
PRORATIONS	PROSODIES	PROTESTING	PROUDEST	PROVISO
PRORE	PROSODIST	PROTESTOR	PROUDFUL	PROVISOES
PRORECTOR	PROSODISTS	PROTESTORS	PROUDISH	PROVISOR
PRORECTORS	PROSODY	PROTESTS	PROUDLY	PROVISORS
PRORES	PROSOPON	PROTEUS	PROUDNESS	PROVISORY
PROROGATE	PROSOPONS	PROTEUSES	PROUDNESSES	PROVISOS
PROROGATED	PROSOS	PROTHALLI	PROUL	PROVOCANT
PROROGATES	PROSPECT	PROTHESES	PROULED	PROVOCANTS
PROROGATING	PROSPECTED	PROTHESIS	PROULER	PROVOKE
PROROGUE	PROSPECTING	PROTHETIC	PROULERS	PROVOKED
PROROGUED	PROSPECTINGS	PROTHORACES	PROULING	PROVOKER
PROROGUES	PROSPECTS	PROTHORAX	PROULS	PROVOKERS
PROROGUING	PROSPER	PROTHORAXES	PROUSTITE	PROVOKES
PROS	PROSPERED	PROTHYL	PROUSTITES	PROVOKING
PROSAIC	PROSPERING	PROTHYLE	PROVABLE	PROVOST
PROSAICAL	PROSPERS	PROTHYLES	PROVABLY	PROVOSTRIES
PROSAISM	PROSTATE	PROTHYLS	PROVAND	PROVOSTRY
PROSAISMS	PROSTATES	PROTIST	PROVANDS	PROVOSTS
PROSAIST	PROSTATIC	PROTISTIC	PROVANT	PROW
PROSAISTS	PROSTRATE	PROTISTS	PROVE	PROWESS
PROSATEUR	PROSTRATED	PROTIUM	PROVEABLE	PROWESSED
PROSATEURS	PROSTRATES	PROTIUMS	PROVEABLY	PROWESSES
PROSCRIBE	PROSTRATING	PROTOAVIS	PROVED	PROWL
PROSCRIBED	PROSTYLE	PROTOAVISES	PROVEDOR	PROWLED
PROSCRIBES	PROSTYLES	PROTOCOL	PROVEDORE	PROWLER
PROSCRIBING	PROSY	PROTOCOLLED	PROVEDORES	PROWLERS
PROSCRIPT	PROTAMINE	PROTOCOLLING	PROVEDORS	PROWLING
PROSCRIPTS	PROTAMINES	PROTOCOLS	PROVEN	PROWLINGS
PROSE	PROTANDRIES	PROTOGINE	PROVEND	PROWLS
PROSECTOR	PROTANDRY	PROTOGINES	PROVENDER	PROWS
PROSECTORS	PROTANOPE	PROTOGYNIES	PROVENDERED	PROXIES
PROSECUTE	PROTANOPES	PROTOGYNY	PROVENDERING	PROXIMAL
PROSECUTED	PROTASES	PROTON	PROVENDERS	PROXIMATE
PROSECUTES	PROTASIS	PROTONEMA	PROVENDS	PROXIMITIES
PROSECUTING	PROTATIC	PROTONEMATA	PROVER	PROXIMITY
PROSED	PROTEA	PROTONIC	PROVERB	PROXIMO
PROSELYTE	PROTEAN	PROTONS	PROVERBED	PROXY
PROSELYTED	PROTEAS	PROTORE	PROVERBING	PROYN
PROSELYTES	PROTEASE	PROTORES	PROVERBS	PROYNE
PROSELYTING	PROTEASES	PROTOSTAR	PROVERS	PROYNED
PROSEMAN	PROTECT	PROTOSTARS	PROVES	PROYNES
PROSEMEN	PROTECTED	PROTOTYPE	PROVIANT	PROYNING
PROSER	PROTECTING	PROTOTYPED	PROVIANTS	PROYNS
PROSERS	PROTECTOR	PROTOTYPES	PROVIDE	PROZYMITE
PROSES	PROTECTORS	PROTOTYPING	PROVIDED	PROZYMITES
PROSEUCHA	PROTECTS	PROTOXIDE	PROVIDENT	PRUDE
PROSEUCHAE	PROTEGE	PROTOXIDES	PROVIDER	PRUDENCE
PROSEUCHE	PROTEGEE	PROTOZOA	PROVIDERS	PRUDENCES
PROSIER	PROTEGEES	PROTOZOAL	PROVIDES	PRUDENT
PROSIEST	PROTEGES	PROTOZOAN	PROVIDING	PRUDENTLY
PROSIFIED	PROTEID	PROTOZOANS	PROVIDOR	PRUDERIES
PROSIFIES	PROTEIDS	PROTOZOIC	PROVIDORS	PRUDERY
PROSIFY	PROTEIN	PROTOZOON	PROVINCE	PRUDES
PROSIFYING	PROTEINIC	PROTRACT	PROVINCES	PRUDISH
PROSILY	PROTEINS	PROTRACTED	PROVINE	PRUDISHLY
PROSIMIAN	PROTEND	PROTRACTING	PROVINED	PRUH
PROSIMIANS	PROTENDED	PROTRACTS	PROVINES	PRUINA

The Chambers Dictionary is the authority for many longer words; see *OSW* Introduction, page xii.

PRUINAS	PSAMMITE	PSYCHOGASES	PUBIC	PUDDLIEST
PRUINE	PSAMMITES	PSYCHOID	PUBIS	PUDDLING
PRUINES	PSAMMITIC	PSYCHOIDS	PUBISES	PUDDLINGS
PRUINOSE	PSCHENT	PSYCHOS	PUBLIC	PUDDLY
PRUNE	PSCHENTS	PSYCHOSES	PUBLICAN	PUDDOCK
PRUNED	PSELLISM	PSYCHOSIS	PUBLICANS	PUDDOCKS
PRUNELLA	PSELLISMS	PSYCHOTIC	PUBLICISE	PUDDY
PRUNELLAS	PSEPHISM	PSYCHOTICS	PUBLICISED	PUDENCIES
PRUNELLE	PSEPHISMS	PSYCHS	PUBLICISES	PUDENCY
PRUNELLES	PSEPHITE	PSYLLA	PUBLICISING	PUDENDA
PRUNELLO	PSEPHITES	PSYLLAS	PUBLICIST	PUDENDAL
PRUNELLOS	PSEPHITIC	PSYLLID	PUBLICISTS	PUDENDOUS
PRUNER	PSEUD	PSYLLIDS	PUBLICITIES	PUDENDUM
PRUNERS	PSEUDAXES	PSYOP	PUBLICITY	PUDENT
PRUNES	PSEUDAXIS	PSYOPS	PUBLICIZE	PUDGE
PRUNING	PSEUDERIES	PSYWAR	PUBLICIZED	PUDGES
PRUNINGS	PSEUDERY	PSYWARS	PUBLICIZES	PUDGIER
PRUNT	PSEUDISH	PTARMIC	PUBLICIZING	PUDGIEST
PRUNTED	PSEUDO	PTARMICS	PUBLICLY	PUDGINESS
PRUNTS	PSEUDONYM	PTARMIGAN	PUBLICS	PUDGINESSES
PRUNUS	PSEUDONYMS	PTARMIGANS	PUBLISH	PUDGY
PRUNUSES	PSEUDOPOD	PTERIA	PUBLISHED	PUDIBUND
PRURIENCE	PSEUDOPODS	PTERIN	PUBLISHER	PUDIC
PRURIENCES	PSEUDS	PTERINS	PUBLISHERS	PUDICITIES
PRURIENCIES	PSHAW	PTERION	PUBLISHES	PUDICITY
PRURIENCY	PSHAWED	PTEROPOD	PUBLISHING	PUDOR
PRURIENT	PSHAWING	PTEROPODS	PUBS	PUDORS
PRURIGO	PSHAWS	PTEROSAUR	PUCCOON	PUDS
PRURIGOS	PSI	PTEROSAURS	PUCCOONS	PUDSEY
PRURITIC	PSILOCIN	PTERYGIA	PUCE	PUDSIER
PRURITUS	PSILOCINS	PTERYGIAL	PUCELAGE	PUDSIEST
PRURITUSES	PSILOSES	PTERYGIALS	PUCELAGES	PUDSY
PRUSIK	PSILOSIS	PTERYGIUM	PUCELLE	PUDU
PRUSIKED	PSILOTIC	PTERYGOID	PUCELLES	PUDUS
PRUSIKING	PSION	PTERYGOIDS	PUCES	PUEBLO
PRUSIKS	PSIONIC	PTERYLA	PUCK	PUEBLOS
PRUSSIATE	PSIONICS	PTERYLAE	PUCKA	PUER
PRUSSIATES	PSIONS	PTILOSES	PUCKER	PUERED
PRUSSIC	PSIS	PTILOSIS	PUCKERED	PUERILE
PRY	PSOAS	PTISAN	PUCKERING	PUERILISM
PRYER	PSOASES	PTISANS	PUCKERS	PUERILISMS
PRYERS	PSOCID	PTOMAINE	PUCKERY	PUERILITIES
PRYING	PSOCIDS	PTOMAINES	PUCKFIST	PUERILITY
PRYINGLY	PSORA	PTOSES	PUCKFISTS	PUERING
PRYINGS	PSORALEN	PTOSIS	PUCKISH	PUERPERAL
PRYS	PSORALENS	PTYALIN	PUCKLE	PUERS
PRYSE	PSORAS	PTYALINS	PUCKLES	PUFF
PRYSED	PSORIASES	PTYALISE	PUCKS	PUFFBALL
PRYSES	PSORIASIS	PTYALISED	PUD	PUFFBALLS
PRYSING	PSORIATIC	PTYALISES	PUDDEN	PUFFBIRD
PRYTANEA	PSORIC	PTYALISING	PUDDENING	PUFFBIRDS
PRYTANEUM	PSST	PTYALISM	PUDDENINGS	PUFFED
PRYTHEE	PST	PTYALISMS	PUDDENS	PUFFER
PSALM	PSYCH	PTYALIZE	PUDDER	PUFFERIES
PSALMIST	PSYCHE	PTYALIZED	PUDDERED	PUFFERS
PSALMISTS	PSYCHED	PTYALIZES	PUDDERING	PUFFERY
PSALMODIC	PSYCHES	PTYALIZING	PUDDERS	PUFFIER
PSALMODIES	PSYCHIC	PTYXES	PUDDIES	PUFFIEST
PSALMODY	PSYCHICAL	PTYXIS	PUDDING	PUFFILY
PSALMS	PSYCHICS	PTYXISES	PUDDINGS	PUFFIN
PSALTER	PSYCHING	PUB	PUDDINGY	PUFFINESS
PSALTERIA	PSYCHISM	PUBERAL	PUDDLE	PUFFINESSES
PSALTERIES	PSYCHISMS	PUBERTAL	PUDDLED	PUFFING
PSALTERS	PSYCHIST	PUBERTIES	PUDDLER	PUFFINGLY
PSALTERY	PSYCHISTS	PUBERTY	PUDDLERS	PUFFINGS
PSALTRESS	PSYCHO	PUBES	PUDDLES	PUFFINS
PSALTRESSES	PSYCHOGAS	PUBESCENT	PUDDLIER	PUFFS

The Chambers Dictionary is the authority for many longer words; see *OSW* Introduction, page xii.

PUFFY	PULICIDES	PULPSTONES	PULVILLIO	PUNCTA
PUFTALOON	PULIER	PULPWOOD	PULVILLIOS	PUNCTATE
PUFTALOONS	PULIEST	PULPWOODS	PULVILLUS	PUNCTATED
PUG	PULING	PULPY	PULVILS	PUNCTATOR
PUGGAREE	PULINGLY	PULQUE	PULVINAR	PUNCTATORS
PUGGAREES	PULINGS	PULQUES	PULVINARS	PUNCTILIO
PUGGED	PULK	PULSAR	PULVINATE	PUNCTILIOS
PUGGERIES	PULKA	PULSARS	PULVINI	PUNCTO
PUGGERY	PULKAS	PULSATE	PULVINULE	PUNCTOS
PUGGIE	PULKHA	PULSATED	PULVINULES	PUNCTUAL
PUGGIER	PULKHAS	PULSATES	PULVINUS	PUNCTUATE
PUGGIES	PULKS	PULSATILE	PULWAR	PUNCTUATED
PUGGIEST	PULL	PULSATING	PULWARS	PUNCTUATES
PUGGING	PULLED	PULSATION	PULY	PUNCTUATING
PUGGINGS	PULLER	PULSATIONS	PUMA	PUNCTULE
PUGGISH	PULLERS	PULSATIVE	PUMAS	PUNCTULES
PUGGLE	PULLET	PULSATOR	PUMELO	PUNCTUM
PUGGLED	PULLETS	PULSATORS	PUMELOS	PUNCTURE
PUGGLES	PULLEY	PULSATORY	PUMICATE	PUNCTURED
PUGGLING	PULLEYS	PULSE	PUMICATED	PUNCTURER
PUGGREE	PULLING	PULSED	PUMICATES	PUNCTURERS
PUGGREES	PULLOVER	PULSEJET	PUMICATING	PUNCTURES
PUGGY	PULLOVERS	PULSEJETS	PUMICE	PUNCTURING
PUGH	PULLS	PULSELESS	PUMICED	PUNDIT
PUGIL	PULLULATE	PULSES	PUMICEOUS	PUNDITRIES
PUGILISM	PULLULATED	PULSIDGE	PUMICES	PUNDITRY
PUGILISMS	PULLULATES	PULSIDGES	PUMICING	PUNDITS
PUGILIST	PULLULATING	PULSIFIC	PUMIE	PUNDONOR
PUGILISTS	PULMO	PULSING	PUMIES	PUNDONORES
PUGILS	PULMONARY	PULSOJET	PUMMEL	PUNGA
PUGNACITIES	PULMONATE	PULSOJETS	PUMMELLED	PUNGAS
PUGNACITY	PULMONATES	PULTAN	PUMMELLING	PUNGENCE
PUGS	PULMONES	PULTANS	PUMMELS	PUNGENCES
PUH	PULMONIC	PULTON	PUMP	PUNGENCIES
PUIR	PULMONICS	PULTONS	PUMPED	PUNGENCY
PUIRER	PULP	PULTOON	PUMPER	PUNGENT
PUIREST	PULPBOARD	PULTOONS	PUMPERS	PUNGENTLY
PUISNE	PULPBOARDS	PULTUN	PUMPHOOD	PUNIER
PUISNES	PULPED	PULTUNS	PUMPHOODS	PUNIEST
PUISNY	PULPER	PULTURE	PUMPING	PUNILY
PUISSANCE	PULPERS	PULTURES	PUMPION	PUNINESS
PUISSANCES	PULPIER	PULU	PUMPIONS	PUNINESSES
PUISSANT	PULPIEST	PULUS	PUMPKIN	PUNISH
PUISSAUNT	PULPIFIED	PULVER	PUMPKINS	PUNISHED
PUJA	PULPIFIES	PULVERED	PUMPS	PUNISHER
PUJAS	PULPIFY	PULVERINE	PUMY	PUNISHERS
PUKE	PULPIFYING	PULVERINES	PUN	PUNISHES
PUKED	PULPILY	PULVERING	PUNA	PUNISHING
PUKEKO	PULPINESS	PULVERISE	PUNALUA	PUNITION
PUKEKOS	PULPINESSES	PULVERISED	PUNALUAN	PUNITIONS
PUKER	PULPING	PULVERISES	PUNALUAS	PUNITIVE
PUKERS	PULPIT	PULVERISING	PUNAS	PUNITORY
PUKES	PULPITED	PULVERIZE	PUNCE	PUNK
PUKING	PULPITEER	PULVERIZED	PUNCED	PUNKA
PUKKA	PULPITEERS	PULVERIZES	PUNCES	PUNKAH
PUKU	PULPITER	PULVERIZING	PUNCH	PUNKAHS
PUKUS	PULPITERS	PULVEROUS	PUNCHED	PUNKAS
PULA	PULPITRIES	PULVERS	PUNCHEON	PUNKINESS
PULAS	PULPITRY	PULVIL	PUNCHEONS	PUNKINESSES
PULDRON	PULPITS	PULVILIO	PUNCHER	PUNKS
PULDRONS	PULPITUM	PULVILIOS	PUNCHERS	PUNNED
PULE	PULPITUMS	PULVILLAR	PUNCHES	PUNNER
PULED	PULPMILL	PULVILLE	PUNCHIER	PUNNERS
PULER	PULPMILLS	PULVILLED	PUNCHIEST	PUNNET
PULERS	PULPOUS	PULVILLES	PUNCHING	PUNNETS
PULES	PULPS	PULVILLI	PUNCHY	PUNNING
PULICIDE	PULPSTONE	PULVILLING	PUNCING	PUNNINGLY

The Chambers Dictionary is the authority for many longer words; see *OSW* Introduction, page xii.

PUNNINGS
PUNS
PUNSTER
PUNSTERS
PUNT
PUNTED
PUNTEE
PUNTEES
PUNTER
PUNTERS
PUNTIES
PUNTING
PUNTO
PUNTOS
PUNTS
PUNTSMAN
PUNTSMEN
PUNTY
PUNY
PUP
PUPA
PUPAE
PUPAL
PUPARIA
PUPARIAL
PUPARIUM
PUPAS
PUPATE
PUPATED
PUPATES
PUPATING
PUPATION
PUPATIONS
PUPFISH
PUPFISHES
PUPIL
PUPILAGE
PUPILAGES
PUPILAR
PUPILARY
PUPILLAGE
PUPILLAGES
PUPILLAR
PUPILLARY
PUPILLATE
PUPILS
PUPILSHIP
PUPILSHIPS
PUPPED
PUPPET
PUPPETEER
PUPPETEERS
PUPPETRIES
PUPPETRY
PUPPETS
PUPPIED
PUPPIES
PUPPING
PUPPODUM
PUPPODUMS
PUPPY
PUPPYDOM
PUPPYDOMS
PUPPYHOOD
PUPPYHOODS
PUPPYING
PUPPYISH

PUPPYISM
PUPPYISMS
PUPS
PUPUNHA
PUPUNHAS
PUR
PURBLIND
PURCHASE
PURCHASED
PURCHASER
PURCHASERS
PURCHASES
PURCHASING
PURDAH
PURDAHED
PURDAHS
PURDONIUM
PURDONIUMS
PURE
PURED
PUREE
PUREED
PUREEING
PUREES
PURELY
PURENESS
PURENESSES
PURER
PURES
PUREST
PURFLE
PURFLED
PURFLES
PURFLING
PURFLINGS
PURFLY
PURGATION
PURGATIONS
PURGATIVE
PURGATIVES
PURGATORIES
PURGATORY
PURGE
PURGED
PURGER
PURGERS
PURGES
PURGING
PURGINGS
PURI
PURIFIED
PURIFIER
PURIFIERS
PURIFIES
PURIFY
PURIFYING
PURIM
PURIMS
PURIN
PURINE
PURINES
PURING
PURINS
PURIS
PURISM
PURISMS
PURIST

PURISTIC
PURISTS
PURITAN
PURITANIC
PURITANS
PURITIES
PURITY
PURL
PURLED
PURLER
PURLERS
PURLICUE
PURLICUED
PURLICUES
PURLICUING
PURLIEU
PURLIEUS
PURLIN
PURLINE
PURLINES
PURLING
PURLINGS
PURLINS
PURLOIN
PURLOINED
PURLOINER
PURLOINERS
PURLOINING
PURLOINS
PURLS
PURPIE
PURPIES
PURPLE
PURPLED
PURPLER
PURPLES
PURPLEST
PURPLING
PURPLISH
PURPLY
PURPORT
PURPORTED
PURPORTING
PURPORTS
PURPOSE
PURPOSED
PURPOSELY
PURPOSES
PURPOSING
PURPOSIVE
PURPURA
PURPURAS
PURPURE
PURPUREAL
PURPURES
PURPURIC
PURPURIN
PURPURINS
PURPY
PURR
PURRED
PURRING
PURRINGLY
PURRINGS
PURRS
PURS
PURSE

PURSED
PURSEFUL
PURSEFULS
PURSER
PURSERS
PURSES
PURSEW
PURSEWED
PURSEWING
PURSEWS
PURSIER
PURSIEST
PURSINESS
PURSINESSES
PURSING
PURSLAIN
PURSLAINS
PURSLANE
PURSLANES
PURSUABLE
PURSUAL
PURSUALS
PURSUANCE
PURSUANCES
PURSUANT
PURSUE
PURSUED
PURSUER
PURSUERS
PURSUES
PURSUING
PURSUINGS
PURSUIT
PURSUITS
PURSY
PURTIER
PURTIEST
PURTRAID
PURTRAYD
PURTY
PURULENCE
PURULENCES
PURULENCIES
PURULENCY
PURULENT
PURVEY
PURVEYED
PURVEYING
PURVEYOR
PURVEYORS
PURVEYS
PURVIEW
PURVIEWS
PUS
PUSES
PUSH
PUSHED
PUSHER
PUSHERS
PUSHES
PUSHFUL
PUSHFULLY
PUSHIER
PUSHIEST
PUSHINESS
PUSHINESSES
PUSHING

PUSHINGLY
PUSHROD
PUSHRODS
PUSHY
PUSLE
PUSLED
PUSLES
PUSLING
PUSS
PUSSEL
PUSSELS
PUSSER
PUSSERS
PUSSES
PUSSIES
PUSSY
PUSSYFOOT
PUSSYFOOTED
PUSSYFOOTING
PUSSYFOOTS
PUSTULANT
PUSTULANTS
PUSTULAR
PUSTULATE
PUSTULATED
PUSTULATES
PUSTULATING
PUSTULE
PUSTULES
PUSTULOUS
PUT
PUTAMEN
PUTAMINA
PUTATIVE
PUTCHEON
PUTCHEONS
PUTCHER
PUTCHERS
PUTCHOCK
PUTCHOCKS
PUTCHUK
PUTCHUKS
PUTEAL
PUTEALS
PUTELI
PUTELIS
PUTID
PUTLOCK
PUTLOCKS
PUTLOG
PUTLOGS
PUTOIS
PUTREFIED
PUTREFIES
PUTREFY
PUTREFYING
PUTRID
PUTRIDER
PUTRIDEST
PUTRIDITIES
PUTRIDITY
PUTRIDLY
PUTS
PUTSCH
PUTSCHES
PUTSCHIST
PUTSCHISTS

The Chambers Dictionary is the authority for many longer words; see *OSW* Introduction, page xii.

PUTT	PYCNIDIA	PYNE	PYRIDINE	PYROPHONES
PUTTED	PYCNIDIUM	PYNED	PYRIDINES	PYROPUS
PUTTEE	PYCNITE	PYNES	PYRIDOXIN	PYROPUSES
PUTTEES	PYCNITES	PYNING	PYRIDOXINS	PYROS
PUTTEN	PYCNON	PYOGENIC	PYRIFORM	PYROSCOPE
PUTTER	PYCNONS	PYOID	PYRITE	PYROSCOPES
PUTTERED	PYCNOSES	PYONER	PYRITES	PYROSES
PUTTERING	PYCNOSIS	PYONERS	PYRITIC	PYROSIS
PUTTERS	PYE	PYONINGS	PYRITICAL	PYROSOME
PUTTI	PYEBALD	PYORRHOEA	PYRITISE	PYROSOMES
PUTTIE	PYEBALDS	PYORRHOEAS	PYRITISED	PYROSTAT
PUTTIED	PYEING	PYOT	PYRITISES	PYROSTATS
PUTTIER	PYELITIC	PYOTS	PYRITISING	PYROXENE
PUTTIERS	PYELITIS	PYRACANTH	PYRITIZE	PYROXENES
PUTTIES	PYELITISES	PYRACANTHS	PYRITIZED	PYROXENIC
PUTTING	PYELOGRAM	PYRAL	PYRITIZES	PYROXYLE
PUTTINGS	PYELOGRAMS	PYRALID	PYRITIZING	PYROXYLES
PUTTO	PYEMIA	PYRALIDS	PYRITOUS	PYROXYLIC
PUTTOCK	PYEMIAS	PYRALIS	PYRO	PYROXYLIN
PUTTOCKS	PYENGADU	PYRALISES	PYROCLAST	PYROXYLINS
PUTTS	PYENGADUS	PYRAMID	PYROCLASTS	PYRRHIC
PUTTY	PYES	PYRAMIDAL	PYROGEN	PYRRHICS
PUTTYING	PYET	PYRAMIDED	PYROGENIC	PYRRHOUS
PUTURE	PYETS	PYRAMIDES	PYROGENS	PYRROLE
PUTURES	PYGAL	PYRAMIDIA	PYROLATER	PYRROLES
PUTZ	PYGALS	PYRAMIDIC	PYROLATERS	PYRUVATE
PUTZES	PYGARG	PYRAMIDING	PYROLATRIES	PYRUVATES
PUY	PYGARGS	PYRAMIDON	PYROLATRY	PYTHIUM
PUYS	PYGIDIA	PYRAMIDONS	PYROLYSE	PYTHIUMS
PUZEL	PYGIDIAL	PYRAMIDS	PYROLYSED	PYTHON
PUZELS	PYGIDIUM	PYRAMIS	PYROLYSES	PYTHONESS
PUZZEL	PYGIDIUMS	PYRAMISES	PYROLYSING	PYTHONESSES
PUZZELS	PYGMAEAN	PYRE	PYROLYSIS	PYTHONIC
PUZZLE	PYGMEAN	PYRENE	PYROLYTIC	PYTHONS
PUZZLED	PYGMIES	PYRENEITE	PYROLYZE	PYURIA
PUZZLEDOM	PYGMOID	PYRENEITES	PYROLYZED	PYURIAS
PUZZLEDOMS	PYGMY	PYRENES	PYROLYZES	PYX
PUZZLER	PYGOSTYLE	PYRENOID	PYROLYZING	PYXED
PUZZLERS	PYGOSTYLES	PYRENOIDS	PYROMANCIES	PYXES
PUZZLES	PYJAMAED	PYRES	PYROMANCY	PYXIDES
PUZZLING	PYJAMAS	PYRETHRIN	PYROMANIA	PYXIDIA
PUZZOLANA	PYKNIC	PYRETHRINS	PYROMANIAS	PYXIDIUM
PUZZOLANAS	PYKNOSOME	PYRETHRUM	PYROMETER	PYXING
PYAEMIA	PYKNOSOMES	PYRETHRUMS	PYROMETERS	PYXIS
PYAEMIAS	PYLON	PYRETIC	PYROMETRIES	PZAZZ
PYAEMIC	PYLONS	PYREXIA	PYROMETRY	PZAZZES
PYAT	PYLORIC	PYREXIAL	PYROPE	
PYATS	PYLORUS	PYREXIAS	PYROPES	
PYCNIC	PYLORUSES	PYREXIC	PYROPHONE	

The Chambers Dictionary is the authority for many longer words; see *OSW* Introduction, page xii.

Q

QABALAH	QUADRELLAS	QUAIGHS	QUANTAL	QUARTES
QABALAHS	QUADRIC	QUAIL	QUANTED	QUARTET
QADI	QUADRICS	QUAILED	QUANTIC	QUARTETS
QADIS	QUADRIFID	QUAILING	QUANTICAL	QUARTETT
QAIMAQAM	QUADRIGA	QUAILINGS	QUANTICS	QUARTETTE
QAIMAQAMS	QUADRIGAE	QUAILS	QUANTIFIED	QUARTETTES
QALAMDAN	QUADRILLE	QUAINT	QUANTIFIES	QUARTETTI
QALAMDANS	QUADRILLED	QUAINTER	QUANTIFY	QUARTETTO
QANAT	QUADRILLES	QUAINTEST	QUANTIFYING	QUARTETTS
QANATS	QUADRILLING	QUAINTLY	QUANTING	QUARTIC
QASIDA	QUADROON	QUAIR	QUANTISE	QUARTICS
QASIDAS	QUADROONS	QUAIRS	QUANTISED	QUARTIER
QAT	QUADRUMAN	QUAKE	QUANTISES	QUARTIERS
QATS	QUADRUMANS	QUAKED	QUANTISING	QUARTILE
QI	QUADRUPED	QUAKER	QUANTITIES	QUARTILES
QIBLA	QUADRUPEDS	QUAKERS	QUANTITY	QUARTO
QIBLAS	QUADRUPLE	QUAKES	QUANTIZE	QUARTOS
QIGONG	QUADRUPLED	QUAKIER	QUANTIZED	QUARTS
QIGONGS	QUADRUPLES	QUAKIEST	QUANTIZES	QUARTZ
QINGHAOSU	QUADRUPLIES	QUAKINESS	QUANTIZING	QUARTZES
QINGHAOSUS	QUADRUPLING	QUAKINESSES	QUANTONG	QUARTZIER
QINTAR	QUADRUPLY	QUAKING	QUANTONGS	QUARTZIEST
QINTARS	QUADS	QUAKINGLY	QUANTS	QUARTZITE
QIS	QUAERE	QUAKINGS	QUANTUM	QUARTZITES
QIVIUT	QUAERED	QUAKY	QUARE	QUARTZOSE
QIVIUTS	QUAEREING	QUALE	QUARENDEN	QUARTZY
QOPH	QUAERES	QUALIA	QUARENDENS	QUASAR
QOPHS	QUAERITUR	QUALIFIED	QUARENDER	QUASARS
QUA	QUAESITUM	QUALIFIER	QUARENDERS	QUASH
QUACK	QUAESITUMS	QUALIFIERS	QUARER	QUASHED
QUACKED	QUAESTOR	QUALIFIES	QUAREST	QUASHEE
QUACKER	QUAESTORS	QUALIFY	QUARK	QUASHEES
QUACKERIES	QUAFF	QUALIFYING	QUARKS	QUASHES
QUACKERS	QUAFFED	QUALIFYINGS	QUARREL	QUASHIE
QUACKERY	QUAFFER	QUALITIED	QUARRELLED	QUASHIES
QUACKING	QUAFFERS	QUALITIES	QUARRELLING	QUASHING
QUACKLE	QUAFFING	QUALITY	QUARRELLINGS	QUASI
QUACKLED	QUAFFS	QUALM	QUARRELS	QUASSIA
QUACKLES	QUAG	QUALMIER	QUARRIED	QUASSIAS
QUACKLING	QUAGGA	QUALMIEST	QUARRIER	QUAT
QUACKS	QUAGGAS	QUALMING	QUARRIERS	QUATCH
QUAD	QUAGGIER	QUALMISH	QUARRIES	QUATCHED
QUADDED	QUAGGIEST	QUALMLESS	QUARRY	QUATCHES
QUADDING	QUAGGY	QUALMS	QUARRYING	QUATCHING
QUADRANS	QUAGMIRE	QUALMY	QUARRYMAN	QUATORZE
QUADRANT	QUAGMIRED	QUAMASH	QUARRYMEN	QUATORZES
QUADRANTES	QUAGMIRES	QUAMASHES	QUART	QUATRAIN
QUADRANTS	QUAGMIRIER	QUANDANG	QUARTAN	QUATRAINS
QUADRAT	QUAGMIRIEST	QUANDANGS	QUARTANS	QUATS
QUADRATE	QUAGMIRING	QUANDARIES	QUARTE	QUAVER
QUADRATED	QUAGMIRY	QUANDARY	QUARTER	QUAVERED
QUADRATES	QUAGS	QUANDONG	QUARTERED	QUAVERER
QUADRATIC	QUAHAUG	QUANDONGS	QUARTERING	QUAVERERS
QUADRATICS	QUAHAUGS	QUANGO	QUARTERINGS	QUAVERING
QUADRATING	QUAHOG	QUANGOS	QUARTERLIES	QUAVERINGS
QUADRATS	QUAHOGS	QUANNET	QUARTERLY	QUAVERS
QUADRATUS	QUAICH	QUANNETS	QUARTERN	QUAVERY
QUADRATUSES	QUAICHS	QUANT	QUARTERNS	QUAY
QUADRELLA	QUAIGH	QUANTA	QUARTERS	QUAYAGE

The Chambers Dictionary is the authority for many longer words; see *OSW* Introduction, page xii.

QUAYAGES	QUELCHES	QUETSCH	QUIDDITS	QUILTERS
QUAYD	QUELCHING	QUETSCHES	QUIDDITY	QUILTING
QUAYS	QUELEA	QUETZAL	QUIDDLE	QUILTINGS
QUAYSIDE	QUELEAS	QUETZALES	QUIDDLED	QUILTS
QUAYSIDES	QUELL	QUETZALS	QUIDDLER	QUIM
QUEACH	QUELLED	QUEUE	QUIDDLERS	QUIMS
QUEACHES	QUELLER	QUEUED	QUIDDLES	QUIN
QUEACHIER	QUELLERS	QUEUEING	QUIDDLING	QUINA
QUEACHIEST	QUELLING	QUEUEINGS	QUIDNUNC	QUINARIES
QUEACHY	QUELLS	QUEUES	QUIDNUNCS	QUINARY
QUEAN	QUEME	QUEUING	QUIDS	QUINAS
QUEANS	QUEMED	QUEUINGS	QUIESCE	QUINATE
QUEASIER	QUEMES	QUEY	QUIESCED	QUINCE
QUEASIEST	QUEMING	QUEYN	QUIESCENT	QUINCES
QUEASILY	QUENA	QUEYNIE	QUIESCES	QUINCHE
QUEASY	QUENAS	QUEYNIES	QUIESCING	QUINCHED
QUEAZIER	QUENCH	QUEYNS	QUIET	QUINCHES
QUEAZIEST	QUENCHED	QUEYS	QUIETED	QUINCHING
QUEAZY	QUENCHER	QUIBBLE	QUIETEN	QUINCUNX
QUEBRACHO	QUENCHERS	QUIBBLED	QUIETENED	QUINCUNXES
QUEBRACHOS	QUENCHES	QUIBBLER	QUIETENING	QUINE
QUEECHIER	QUENCHING	QUIBBLERS	QUIETENINGS	QUINELLA
QUEECHIEST	QUENCHINGS	QUIBBLES	QUIETENS	QUINELLAS
QUEECHY	QUENELLE	QUIBBLING	QUIETER	QUINES
QUEEN	QUENELLES	QUIBBLINGS	QUIETERS	QUINIC
QUEENDOM	QUEP	QUIBLIN	QUIETEST	QUINIDINE
QUEENDOMS	QUERCETIN	QUIBLINS	QUIETING	QUINIDINES
QUEENED	QUERCETINS	QUICH	QUIETINGS	QUINIE
QUEENHOOD	QUERCETUM	QUICHE	QUIETISM	QUINIES
QUEENHOODS	QUERCETUMS	QUICHED	QUIETISMS	QUININE
QUEENIE	QUERIED	QUICHES	QUIETIST	QUININES
QUEENIER	QUERIES	QUICHING	QUIETISTS	QUINNAT
QUEENIES	QUERIMONIES	QUICK	QUIETIVE	QUINNATS
QUEENIEST	QUERIMONY	QUICKBEAM	QUIETIVES	QUINOA
QUEENING	QUERIST	QUICKBEAMS	QUIETLY	QUINOAS
QUEENINGS	QUERISTS	QUICKEN	QUIETNESS	QUINOID
QUEENITE	QUERN	QUICKENED	QUIETNESSES	QUINOIDAL
QUEENITES	QUERNS	QUICKENER	QUIETS	QUINOIDS
QUEENLESS	QUERULOUS	QUICKENERS	QUIETSOME	QUINOL
QUEENLET	QUERY	QUICKENING	QUIETUDE	QUINOLINE
QUEENLETS	QUERYING	QUICKENINGS	QUIETUDES	QUINOLINES
QUEENLIER	QUERYINGS	QUICKENS	QUIETUS	QUINOLONE
QUEENLIEST	QUEST	QUICKER	QUIETUSES	QUINOLONES
QUEENLY	QUESTANT	QUICKEST	QUIFF	QUINOLS
QUEENS	QUESTANTS	QUICKIE	QUIFFS	QUINONE
QUEENSHIP	QUESTED	QUICKIES	QUIGHT	QUINONES
QUEENSHIPS	QUESTER	QUICKLIME	QUIGHTED	QUINONOID
QUEENY	QUESTERS	QUICKLIMES	QUIGHTING	QUINQUINA
QUEER	QUESTING	QUICKLY	QUIGHTS	QUINQUINAS
QUEERDOM	QUESTINGS	QUICKNESS	QUILL	QUINS
QUEERDOMS	QUESTION	QUICKNESSES	QUILLAI	QUINSIED
QUEERED	QUESTIONED	QUICKS	QUILLAIS	QUINSIES
QUEERER	QUESTIONING	QUICKSAND	QUILLED	QUINSY
QUEEREST	QUESTIONINGS	QUICKSANDS	QUILLET	QUINT
QUEERING	QUESTIONS	QUICKSET	QUILLETS	QUINTA
QUEERISH	QUESTOR	QUICKSETS	QUILLING	QUINTAIN
QUEERITIES	QUESTORS	QUICKSTEP	QUILLINGS	QUINTAINS
QUEERITY	QUESTRIST	QUICKSTEPPED	QUILLMAN	QUINTAL
QUEERLY	QUESTRISTS	QUICKSTEPPING	QUILLMEN	QUINTALS
QUEERNESS	QUESTS	QUICKSTEPS	QUILLON	QUINTAN
QUEERNESSES	QUETCH	QUID	QUILLONS	QUINTAS
QUEERS	QUETCHED	QUIDAM	QUILLS	QUINTE
QUEEST	QUETCHES	QUIDAMS	QUILLWORT	QUINTES
QUEESTS	QUETCHING	QUIDDANIES	QUILLWORTS	QUINTET
QUEINT	QUETHE	QUIDDANY	QUILT	QUINTETS
QUELCH	QUETHES	QUIDDIT	QUILTED	QUINTETT
QUELCHED	QUETHING	QUIDDITIES	QUILTER	QUINTETTE

The Chambers Dictionary is the authority for many longer words; see *OSW* Introduction, page xii.

QUINTETTES	QUIRKIEST	QUITTERS	QUODLIBET	QUORUM
QUINTETTI	QUIRKILY	QUITTING	QUODLIBETS	QUORUMS
QUINTETTO	QUIRKING	QUITTOR	QUODLIN	QUOTA
QUINTETTS	QUIRKISH	QUITTORS	QUODLINS	QUOTABLE
QUINTIC	QUIRKS	QUIVER	QUODS	QUOTABLY
QUINTILE	QUIRKY	QUIVERED	QUOIF	QUOTAS
QUINTILES	QUIRT	QUIVERFUL	QUOIFED	QUOTATION
QUINTROON	QUIRTED	QUIVERFULS	QUOIFING	QUOTATIONS
QUINTROONS	QUIRTING	QUIVERING	QUOIFS	QUOTATIVE
QUINTS	QUIRTS	QUIVERINGS	QUOIN	QUOTATIVES
QUINTUPLE	QUISLING	QUIVERISH	QUOINED	QUOTE
QUINTUPLED	QUISLINGS	QUIVERS	QUOINING	QUOTED
QUINTUPLES	QUIST	QUIVERY	QUOINS	QUOTER
QUINTUPLING	QUISTS	QUIXOTIC	QUOIST	QUOTERS
QUINZE	QUIT	QUIXOTISM	QUOISTS	QUOTES
QUINZES	QUITCH	QUIXOTISMS	QUOIT	QUOTH
QUIP	QUITCHED	QUIXOTRIES	QUOITED	QUOTHA
QUIPO	QUITCHES	QUIXOTRY	QUOITER	QUOTIDIAN
QUIPOS	QUITCHING	QUIZ	QUOITERS	QUOTIDIANS
QUIPPED	QUITCLAIM	QUIZZED	QUOITING	QUOTIENT
QUIPPING	QUITCLAIMED	QUIZZER	QUOITS	QUOTIENTS
QUIPPISH	QUITCLAIMING	QUIZZERIES	QUOKKA	QUOTING
QUIPS	QUITCLAIMS	QUIZZERS	QUOKKAS	QUOTITION
QUIPSTER	QUITE	QUIZZERY	QUOLL	QUOTITIONS
QUIPSTERS	QUITED	QUIZZES	QUOLLS	QUOTUM
QUIPU	QUITES	QUIZZICAL	QUONDAM	QUOTUMS
QUIPUS	QUITING	QUIZZIFIED	QUONK	QUYTE
QUIRE	QUITS	QUIZZIFIES	QUONKED	QUYTED
QUIRED	QUITTAL	QUIZZIFY	QUONKING	QUYTES
QUIRES	QUITTALS	QUIZZIFYING	QUONKS	QUYTING
QUIRING	QUITTANCE	QUIZZING	QUOOKE	QWERTIES
QUIRISTER	QUITTANCED	QUIZZINGS	QUOP	QWERTY
QUIRISTERS	QUITTANCES	QUOAD	QUOPPED	QWERTYS
QUIRK	QUITTANCING	QUOD	QUOPPING	
QUIRKED	QUITTED	QUODDED	QUOPS	
QUIRKIER	QUITTER	QUODDING	QUORATE	

The Chambers Dictionary is the authority for many longer words; see *OSW* Introduction, page xii.

R

RABANNA	RABIDNESSES	RACHITISES	RADAR	RADICCHIO
RABANNAS	RABIES	RACIAL	RADARS	RADICCHIOS
RABAT	RABIS	RACIALISM	RADDLE	RADICEL
RABATINE	RACA	RACIALISMS	RADDLED	RADICELS
RABATINES	RACAHOUT	RACIALIST	RADDLEMAN	RADICES
RABATMENT	RACAHOUTS	RACIALISTS	RADDLEMEN	RADICLE
RABATMENTS	RACCAHOUT	RACIALLY	RADDLES	RADICLES
RABATO	RACCAHOUTS	RACIATION	RADDLING	RADICULAR
RABATOES	RACCOON	RACIATIONS	RADDOCKE	RADICULE
RABATS	RACCOONS	RACIER	RADDOCKES	RADICULES
RABATTE	RACE	RACIEST	RADE	RADII
RABATTED	RACECARD	RACILY	RADGE	RADIO
RABATTES	RACECARDS	RACINESS	RADGER	RADIOED
RABATTING	RACED	RACINESSES	RADGEST	RADIOGRAM
RABATTINGS	RACEGOER	RACING	RADIAL	RADIOGRAMS
RABBET	RACEGOERS	RACINGS	RADIALE	RADIOING
RABBETED	RACEGOING	RACISM	RADIALIA	RADIOLOGIES
RABBETING	RACEGOINGS	RACISMS	RADIALISE	RADIOLOGY
RABBETS	RACEHORSE	RACIST	RADIALISED	RADIONICS
RABBI	RACEHORSES	RACISTS	RADIALISES	RADIOS
RABBIN	RACEMATE	RACK	RADIALISING	RADIOTHON
RABBINATE	RACEMATES	RACKED	RADIALITIES	RADIOTHONS
RABBINATES	RACEME	RACKER	RADIALITY	RADISH
RABBINIC	RACEMED	RACKERS	RADIALIZE	RADISHES
RABBINISM	RACEMES	RACKET	RADIALIZED	RADIUM
RABBINISMS	RACEMIC	RACKETED	RADIALIZES	RADIUMS
RABBINIST	RACEMISE	RACKETEER	RADIALIZING	RADIUS
RABBINISTS	RACEMISED	RACKETEERED	RADIALLY	RADIUSES
RABBINITE	RACEMISES	RACKETEERING	RADIALS	RADIX
RABBINITES	RACEMISING	RACKETEERINGS	RADIAN	RADOME
RABBINS	RACEMISM	RACKETEERS	RADIANCE	RADOMES
RABBIS	RACEMISMS	RACKETER	RADIANCES	RADON
RABBIT	RACEMIZE	RACKETERS	RADIANCIES	RADONS
RABBITED	RACEMIZED	RACKETING	RADIANCY	RADS
RABBITER	RACEMIZES	RACKETRIES	RADIANS	RADULA
RABBITERS	RACEMIZING	RACKETRY	RADIANT	RADULAE
RABBITING	RACEMOSE	RACKETS	RADIANTLY	RADULAR
RABBITRIES	RACEPATH	RACKETT	RADIANTS	RADULATE
RABBITRY	RACEPATHS	RACKETTS	RADIATA	RADWASTE
RABBITS	RACER	RACKETY	RADIATAS	RADWASTES
RABBITY	RACERS	RACKING	RADIATE	RAFALE
RABBLE	RACES	RACKINGS	RADIATED	RAFALES
RABBLED	RACETRACK	RACKS	RADIATELY	RAFF
RABBLER	RACETRACKS	RACKWORK	RADIATES	RAFFIA
RABBLERS	RACEWAY	RACKWORKS	RADIATING	RAFFIAS
RABBLES	RACEWAYS	RACLETTE	RADIATION	RAFFINATE
RABBLING	RACH	RACLETTES	RADIATIONS	RAFFINATES
RABBLINGS	RACHE	RACLOIR	RADIATIVE	RAFFINOSE
RABBONI	RACHES	RACLOIRS	RADIATOR	RAFFINOSES
RABBONIS	RACHIAL	RACON	RADIATORS	RAFFISH
RABI	RACHIDES	RACONS	RADIATORY	RAFFISHLY
RABIC	RACHIDIAL	RACONTEUR	RADICAL	RAFFLE
RABID	RACHIDIAN	RACONTEURS	RADICALLY	RAFFLED
RABIDER	RACHILLA	RACOON	RADICALS	RAFFLER
RABIDEST	RACHILLAS	RACOONS	RADICANT	RAFFLERS
RABIDITIES	RACHIS	RACQUET	RADICATE	RAFFLES
RABIDITY	RACHISES	RACQUETS	RADICATED	RAFFLING
RABIDLY	RACHITIC	RACY	RADICATES	RAFFS
RABIDNESS	RACHITIS	RAD	RADICATING	RAFT

The Chambers Dictionary is the authority for many longer words; see *OSW* Introduction, page xii.

RAFTED	RAGOUTING	RAILROADS	RAITED	RAMBUTAN
RAFTER	RAGOUTS	RAILS	RAITING	RAMBUTANS
RAFTERED	RAGS	RAILWAY	RAITS	RAMCAT
RAFTERING	RAGSTONE	RAILWAYS	RAIYAT	RAMCATS
RAFTERINGS	RAGSTONES	RAILWOMAN	RAIYATS	RAMEAL
RAFTERS	RAGTAG	RAILWOMEN	RAJ	RAMEE
RAFTING	RAGTAGS	RAIMENT	RAJA	RAMEES
RAFTMAN	RAGTIME	RAIMENTS	RAJAH	RAMEKIN
RAFTMEN	RAGTIMER	RAIN	RAJAHS	RAMEKINS
RAFTS	RAGTIMERS	RAINBAND	RAJAHSHIP	RAMEN
RAFTSMAN	RAGTIMES	RAINBANDS	RAJAHSHIPS	RAMENS
RAFTSMEN	RAGTOP	RAINBOW	RAJAS	RAMENTA
RAG	RAGTOPS	RAINBOWED	RAJASHIP	RAMENTUM
RAGA	RAGULED	RAINBOWS	RAJASHIPS	RAMEOUS
RAGAS	RAGULY	RAINBOWY	RAJES	RAMEQUIN
RAGBAG	RAGWEED	RAINCHECK	RAKE	RAMEQUINS
RAGBAGS	RAGWEEDS	RAINCHECKS	RAKED	RAMFEEZLE
RAGBOLT	RAGWHEEL	RAINCOAT	RAKEE	RAMFEEZLED
RAGBOLTS	RAGWHEELS	RAINCOATS	RAKEES	RAMFEEZLES
RAGDE	RAGWORK	RAINDATE	RAKEHELL	RAMFEEZLING
RAGE	RAGWORKS	RAINDATES	RAKEHELLS	RAMI
RAGED	RAGWORM	RAINDROP	RAKEHELLY	RAMIE
RAGEE	RAGWORMS	RAINDROPS	RAKER	RAMIES
RAGEES	RAGWORT	RAINE	RAKERIES	RAMIFIED
RAGEFUL	RAGWORTS	RAINED	RAKERS	RAMIFIES
RAGER	RAH	RAINES	RAKERY	RAMIFORM
RAGERS	RAHED	RAINFALL	RAKES	RAMIFY
RAGES	RAHING	RAINFALLS	RAKESHAME	RAMIFYING
RAGG	RAHS	RAINIER	RAKESHAMES	RAMIN
RAGGED	RAI	RAINIEST	RAKI	RAMINS
RAGGEDER	RAID	RAININESS	RAKING	RAMIS
RAGGEDEST	RAIDED	RAININESSES	RAKINGS	RAMJET
RAGGEDLY	RAIDER	RAINING	RAKIS	RAMJETS
RAGGEDY	RAIDERS	RAINLESS	RAKISH	RAMMED
RAGGEE	RAIDING	RAINMAKER	RAKISHLY	RAMMER
RAGGEES	RAIDS	RAINMAKERS	RAKSHAS	RAMMERS
RAGGERIES	RAIK	RAINPROOF	RAKSHASA	RAMMIES
RAGGERY	RAIKED	RAINPROOFED	RAKSHASAS	RAMMING
RAGGIER	RAIKING	RAINPROOFING	RAKSHASES	RAMMISH
RAGGIES	RAIKS	RAINPROOFS	RAKU	RAMMY
RAGGIEST	RAIL	RAINS	RAKUS	RAMOSE
RAGGING	RAILBED	RAINSTORM	RALE	RAMOUS
RAGGINGS	RAILBEDS	RAINSTORMS	RALES	RAMP
RAGGLE	RAILBUS	RAINTIGHT	RALLIED	RAMPAGE
RAGGLED	RAILBUSES	RAINWATER	RALLIER	RAMPAGED
RAGGLES	RAILCARD	RAINWATERS	RALLIERS	RAMPAGES
RAGGLING	RAILCARDS	RAINWEAR	RALLIES	RAMPAGING
RAGGS	RAILE	RAINWEARS	RALLINE	RAMPAGINGS
RAGGY	RAILED	RAINY	RALLY	RAMPANCIES
RAGHEAD	RAILER	RAIRD	RALLYE	RAMPANCY
RAGHEADS	RAILERS	RAIRDS	RALLYES	RAMPANT
RAGI	RAILES	RAIS	RALLYING	RAMPANTLY
RAGING	RAILHEAD	RAISABLE	RALLYINGS	RAMPART
RAGINGLY	RAILHEADS	RAISE	RALLYIST	RAMPARTED
RAGINGS	RAILING	RAISEABLE	RALLYISTS	RAMPARTING
RAGINI	RAILINGLY	RAISED	RAM	RAMPARTS
RAGINIS	RAILINGS	RAISER	RAMAKIN	RAMPAUGE
RAGIS	RAILLERIES	RAISERS	RAMAKINS	RAMPAUGED
RAGLAN	RAILLERY	RAISES	RAMAL	RAMPAUGES
RAGLANS	RAILLESS	RAISIN	RAMATE	RAMPAUGING
RAGMAN	RAILLIES	RAISING	RAMBLE	RAMPED
RAGMANS	RAILLY	RAISINGS	RAMBLED	RAMPER
RAGMEN	RAILMAN	RAISINS	RAMBLER	RAMPERS
RAGMENT	RAILMEN	RAISONNE	RAMBLERS	RAMPICK
RAGMENTS	RAILROAD	RAIT	RAMBLES	RAMPICKED
RAGOUT	RAILROADED	RAITA	RAMBLING	RAMPICKS
RAGOUTED	RAILROADING	RAITAS	RAMBLINGS	RAMPIKE

The Chambers Dictionary is the authority for many longer words; see *OSW* Introduction, page xii.

RAMPIKES	RANDED	RANSACKERS	RAPIER	RASCALISM
RAMPING	RANDEM	RANSACKING	RAPIERS	RASCALISMS
RAMPINGS	RANDEMS	RANSACKS	RAPINE	RASCALITIES
RAMPION	RANDIE	RANSEL	RAPINES	RASCALITY
RAMPIONS	RANDIER	RANSELS	RAPING	RASCALLIEST
RAMPIRE	RANDIES	RANSHAKLE	RAPIST	RASCALLY
RAMPIRED	RANDIEST	RANSHAKLED	RAPISTS	RASCALS
RAMPIRES	RANDING	RANSHAKLES	RAPLOCH	RASCASSE
RAMPS	RANDOM	RANSHAKLING	RAPLOCHS	RASCASSES
RAMPSMAN	RANDOMISE	RANSOM	RAPPAREE	RASCHEL
RAMPSMEN	RANDOMISED	RANSOMED	RAPPAREES	RASCHELS
RAMROD	RANDOMISES	RANSOMER	RAPPED	RASE
RAMRODDED	RANDOMISING	RANSOMERS	RAPPEE	RASED
RAMRODDING	RANDOMIZE	RANSOMING	RAPPEES	RASES
RAMRODS	RANDOMIZED	RANSOMS	RAPPEL	RASH
RAMS	RANDOMIZES	RANT	RAPPELLED	RASHED
RAMSON	RANDOMIZING	RANTED	RAPPELLING	RASHER
RAMSONS	RANDOMLY	RANTER	RAPPELLINGS	RASHERS
RAMSTAM	RANDOMS	RANTERISM	RAPPELS	RASHES
RAMULAR	RANDON	RANTERISMS	RAPPER	RASHEST
RAMULI	RANDONS	RANTERS	RAPPERS	RASHING
RAMULOSE	RANDS	RANTING	RAPPING	RASHLY
RAMULOUS	RANDY	RANTINGLY	RAPPINGS	RASHNESS
RAMULUS	RANEE	RANTINGS	RAPPORT	RASHNESSES
RAMUS	RANEES	RANTIPOLE	RAPPORTS	RASING
RAN	RANG	RANTIPOLED	RAPS	RASORIAL
RANA	RANGATIRA	RANTIPOLES	RAPT	RASP
RANARIAN	RANGATIRAS	RANTIPOLING	RAPTLY	RASPATORIES
RANARIUM	RANGE	RANTS	RAPTOR	RASPATORY
RANARIUMS	RANGED	RANULA	RAPTORIAL	RASPBERRIES
RANAS	RANGELAND	RANULAS	RAPTORS	RASPBERRY
RANCE	RANGELANDS	RANUNCULI	RAPTURE	RASPED
RANCED	RANGER	RANZEL	RAPTURED	RASPER
RANCEL	RANGERS	RANZELMAN	RAPTURES	RASPERS
RANCELS	RANGES	RANZELMEN	RAPTURING	RASPIER
RANCES	RANGIER	RANZELS	RAPTURISE	RASPIEST
RANCH	RANGIEST	RAOULIA	RAPTURISED	RASPING
RANCHED	RANGINESS	RAOULIAS	RAPTURISES	RASPINGLY
RANCHER	RANGINESSES	RAP	RAPTURISING	RASPINGS
RANCHERIA	RANGING	RAPACIOUS	RAPTURIST	RASPS
RANCHERIAS	RANGOLI	RAPACITIES	RAPTURISTS	RASPY
RANCHERIE	RANGOLIS	RAPACITY	RAPTURIZE	RASSE
RANCHERIES	RANGY	RAPE	RAPTURIZED	RASSES
RANCHERO	RANI	RAPED	RAPTURIZES	RAST
RANCHEROS	RANIFORM	RAPER	RAPTURIZING	RASTA
RANCHERS	RANINE	RAPERS	RAPTUROUS	RASTAFARI
RANCHES	RANIS	RAPES	RARE	RASTER
RANCHING	RANK	RAPESEED	RAREBIT	RASTERS
RANCHINGS	RANKE	RAPESEEDS	RAREBITS	RASTRUM
RANCHMAN	RANKED	RAPHANIA	RAREFIED	RASTRUMS
RANCHMEN	RANKER	RAPHANIAS	RAREFIES	RASURE
RANCHO	RANKERS	RAPHE	RAREFY	RASURES
RANCHOS	RANKES	RAPHES	RAREFYING	RAT
RANCID	RANKEST	RAPHIA	RARELY	RATA
RANCIDER	RANKING	RAPHIAS	RARENESS	RATABLE
RANCIDEST	RANKINGS	RAPHIDE	RARENESSES	RATABLY
RANCIDITIES	RANKLE	RAPHIDES	RARER	RATAFIA
RANCIDITY	RANKLED	RAPHIS	RAREST	RATAFIAS
RANCING	RANKLES	RAPID	RARING	RATAN
RANCOR	RANKLING	RAPIDER	RARITIES	RATANS
RANCOROUS	RANKLY	RAPIDEST	RARITY	RATAPLAN
RANCORS	RANKNESS	RAPIDITIES	RAS	RATAPLANS
RANCOUR	RANKNESSES	RAPIDITY	RASCAILLE	RATAS
RANCOURS	RANKS	RAPIDLY	RASCAILLES	RATBAG
RAND	RANSACK	RAPIDNESS	RASCAL	RATBAGS
RANDAN	RANSACKED	RAPIDNESSES	RASCALDOM	RATCH
RANDANS	RANSACKER	RAPIDS	RASCALDOMS	RATCHED

The Chambers Dictionary is the authority for many longer words; see *OSW* Introduction, page xii.

RATCHES	RATPROOF	RAVAGER	RAYED	REACTORS
RATCHET	RATS	RAVAGERS	RAYING	REACTS
RATCHETED	RATSBANE	RAVAGES	RAYLE	REACTUATE
RATCHETING	RATSBANES	RAVAGING	RAYLED	REACTUATED
RATCHETS	RATTAN	RAVE	RAYLES	REACTUATES
RATCHING	RATTANS	RAVED	RAYLESS	REACTUATING
RATE	RATTED	RAVEL	RAYLET	READ
RATEABLE	RATTEEN	RAVELIN	RAYLETS	READABLE
RATEABLY	RATTEENS	RAVELINS	RAYLING	READABLY
RATED	RATTEN	RAVELLED	RAYNE	READAPT
RATEL	RATTENED	RAVELLING	RAYNES	READAPTED
RATELS	RATTENING	RAVELLINGS	RAYON	READAPTING
RATEPAYER	RATTENINGS	RAVELMENT	RAYONS	READAPTS
RATEPAYERS	RATTENS	RAVELMENTS	RAYS	READDRESS
RATER	RATTER	RAVELS	RAZE	READDRESSED
RATERS	RATTERIES	RAVEN	RAZED	READDRESSES
RATES	RATTERS	RAVENED	RAZEE	READDRESSING
RATFINK	RATTERY	RAVENER	RAZEED	READER
RATFINKS	RATTIER	RAVENERS	RAZEEING	READERS
RATH	RATTIEST	RAVENING	RAZEES	READIED
RATHE	RATTING	RAVENOUS	RAZES	READIER
RATHER	RATTINGS	RAVENS	RAZING	READIES
RATHEREST	RATTISH	RAVER	RAZMATAZ	READIEST
RATHERIPE	RATTLE	RAVERS	RAZMATAZES	READILY
RATHERIPES	RATTLEBAG	RAVES	RAZOO	READINESS
RATHERISH	RATTLEBAGS	RAVIN	RAZOOS	READINESSES
RATHEST	RATTLED	RAVINE	RAZOR	READING
RATHRIPE	RATTLER	RAVINED	RAZORABLE	READINGS
RATHRIPES	RATTLERS	RAVINES	RAZORS	READJUST
RATHS	RATTLES	RAVING	RAZURE	READJUSTED
RATIFIED	RATTLIER	RAVINGLY	RAZURES	READJUSTING
RATIFIER	RATTLIEST	RAVINGS	RAZZ	READJUSTS
RATIFIERS	RATTLIN	RAVINING	RAZZED	READMIT
RATIFIES	RATTLINE	RAVINS	RAZZES	READMITS
RATIFY	RATTLINES	RAVIOLI	RAZZIA	READMITTED
RATIFYING	RATTLING	RAVIOLIS	RAZZIAS	READMITTING
RATINE	RATTLINGS	RAVISH	RAZZING	READOPT
RATINES	RATTLINS	RAVISHED	RAZZLE	READOPTED
RATING	RATTLY	RAVISHER	RAZZLES	READOPTING
RATINGS	RATTON	RAVISHERS	RE	READOPTS
RATIO	RATTONS	RAVISHES	REABSORB	READS
RATION	RATTY	RAVISHING	REABSORBED	READVANCE
RATIONAL	RATU	RAW	REABSORBING	READVANCED
RATIONALE	RATUS	RAWBONE	REABSORBS	READVANCES
RATIONALES	RAUCID	RAWBONED	REACH	READVANCING
RATIONALS	RAUCLE	RAWER	REACHABLE	READVISE
RATIONED	RAUCLER	RAWEST	REACHED	READVISED
RATIONING	RAUCLEST	RAWHEAD	REACHER	READVISES
RATIONS	RAUCOUS	RAWHEADS	REACHERS	READVISING
RATIOS	RAUCOUSLY	RAWHIDE	REACHES	READY
RATITE	RAUGHT	RAWHIDES	REACHING	READYING
RATLIN	RAUN	RAWING	REACHLESS	REAEDIFIED
RATLINE	RAUNCH	RAWINGS	REACQUIRE	REAEDIFIES
RATLINES	RAUNCHED	RAWISH	REACQUIRED	REAEDIFY
RATLING	RAUNCHES	RAWLY	REACQUIRES	REAEDIFYE
RATLINGS	RAUNCHIER	RAWN	REACQUIRING	REAEDIFYED
RATLINS	RAUNCHIEST	RAWNESS	REACT	REAEDIFYES
RATOO	RAUNCHILY	RAWNESSES	REACTANCE	REAEDIFYING
RATOON	RAUNCHING	RAWNS	REACTANCES	REAFFIRM
RATOONED	RAUNCHY	RAWS	REACTANT	REAFFIRMED
RATOONER	RAUNGE	RAX	REACTANTS	REAFFIRMING
RATOONERS	RAUNGED	RAXED	REACTED	REAFFIRMS
RATOONING	RAUNGES	RAXES	REACTING	REAGENCIES
RATOONS	RAUNGING	RAXING	REACTION	REAGENCY
RATOOS	RAUNS	RAY	REACTIONS	REAGENT
RATPACK	RAVAGE	RAYAH	REACTIVE	REAGENTS
RATPACKS	RAVAGED	RAYAHS	REACTOR	REAK

The Chambers Dictionary is the authority for many longer words; see *OSW* Introduction, page xii.

REAKED	REAMING	REARRANGE	REATTEMPTING	REBINDING
REAKING	REAMS	REARRANGED	REATTEMPTS	REBINDS
REAKS	REAMY	REARRANGES	REAVE	REBIRTH
REAL	REAN	REARRANGING	REAVER	REBIRTHS
REALER	REANIMATE	REARREST	REAVERS	REBIT
REALEST	REANIMATED	REARRESTED	REAVES	REBITE
REALGAR	REANIMATES	REARRESTING	REAVING	REBITES
REALGARS	REANIMATING	REARRESTS	REAWAKE	REBITING
REALIA	REANNEX	REARS	REAWAKED	REBITTEN
REALIGN	REANNEXED	REARWARD	REAWAKEN	REBLOOM
REALIGNED	REANNEXES	REARWARDS	REAWAKENED	REBLOOMED
REALIGNING	REANNEXING	REASCEND	REAWAKENING	REBLOOMING
REALIGNS	REANS	REASCENDED	REAWAKENINGS	REBLOOMS
REALISE	REANSWER	REASCENDING	REAWAKENS	REBLOSSOM
REALISED	REANSWERED	REASCENDS	REAWAKES	REBLOSSOMED
REALISER	REANSWERING	REASCENT	REAWAKING	REBLOSSOMING
REALISERS	REANSWERS	REASCENTS	REAWOKE	REBLOSSOMS
REALISES	REAP	REASON	REAWOKEN	REBOANT
REALISING	REAPED	REASONED	REBACK	REBOATION
REALISM	REAPER	REASONER	REBACKED	REBOATIONS
REALISMS	REAPERS	REASONERS	REBACKING	REBOIL
REALIST	REAPING	REASONING	REBACKS	REBOILED
REALISTIC	REAPPAREL	REASONINGS	REBAPTISE	REBOILING
REALISTS	REAPPARELLED	REASONS	REBAPTISED	REBOILS
REALITIES	REAPPARELLING	REASSERT	REBAPTISES	REBORE
REALITY	REAPPARELS	REASSERTED	REBAPTISING	REBORED
REALIZE	REAPPEAR	REASSERTING	REBAPTISM	REBORES
REALIZED	REAPPEARED	REASSERTS	REBAPTISMS	REBORING
REALIZER	REAPPEARING	REASSESS	REBAPTIZE	REBORN
REALIZERS	REAPPEARS	REASSESSED	REBAPTIZED	REBORROW
REALIZES	REAPPLIED	REASSESSES	REBAPTIZES	REBORROWED
REALIZING	REAPPLIES	REASSESSING	REBAPTIZING	REBORROWING
REALLIE	REAPPLY	REASSIGN	REBATE	REBORROWS
REALLIED	REAPPLYING	REASSIGNED	REBATED	REBOUND
REALLIES	REAPPOINT	REASSIGNING	REBATER	REBOUNDED
REALLOT	REAPPOINTED	REASSIGNS	REBATERS	REBOUNDING
REALLOTS	REAPPOINTING	REASSUME	REBATES	REBOUNDS
REALLOTTED	REAPPOINTS	REASSUMED	REBATING	REBRACE
REALLOTTING	REAPS	REASSUMES	REBATO	REBRACED
REALLY	REAR	REASSUMING	REBATOES	REBRACES
REALLYING	REARED	REASSURE	REBBE	REBRACING
REALM	REARER	REASSURED	REBBES	REBUFF
REALMLESS	REARERS	REASSURER	REBBETZIN	REBUFFED
REALMS	REARGUARD	REASSURERS	REBBETZINS	REBUFFING
REALNESS	REARGUARDS	REASSURES	REBEC	REBUFFS
REALNESSES	REARHORSE	REASSURING	REBECK	REBUILD
REALO	REARHORSES	REAST	REBECKS	REBUILDING
REALOS	REARING	REASTED	REBECS	REBUILDS
REALS	REARISE	REASTIER	REBEL	REBUILT
REALTIE	REARISEN	REASTIEST	REBELDOM	REBUKABLE
REALTIES	REARISES	REASTING	REBELDOMS	REBUKE
REALTIME	REARISING	REASTS	REBELLED	REBUKED
REALTOR	REARLY	REASTY	REBELLER	REBUKEFUL
REALTORS	REARM	REATA	REBELLERS	REBUKER
REALTY	REARMED	REATAS	REBELLING	REBUKERS
REAM	REARMICE	REATE	REBELLION	REBUKES
REAME	REARMING	REATES	REBELLIONS	REBUKING
REAMED	REARMOST	REATTACH	REBELLOW	REBURIAL
REAMEND	REARMOUSE	REATTACHED	REBELLOWED	REBURIALS
REAMENDED	REARMS	REATTACHES	REBELLOWING	REBURIED
REAMENDING	REAROSE	REATTACHING	REBELLOWS	REBURIES
REAMENDS	REAROUSAL	REATTAIN	REBELS	REBURY
REAMER	REAROUSALS	REATTAINED	REBID	REBURYING
REAMERS	REAROUSE	REATTAINING	REBIDDEN	REBUS
REAMES	REAROUSED	REATTAINS	REBIDDING	REBUSES
REAMIER	REAROUSES	REATTEMPT	REBIDS	REBUT
REAMIEST	REAROUSING	REATTEMPTED	REBIND	REBUTMENT

The Chambers Dictionary is the authority for many longer words; see *OSW* Introduction, page xii.

REBUTMENTS
REBUTS
REBUTTAL
REBUTTALS
REBUTTED
REBUTTER
REBUTTERS
REBUTTING
REBUTTON
REBUTTONED
REBUTTONING
REBUTTONS
REC
RECAL
RECALESCE
RECALESCED
RECALESCES
RECALESCING
RECALL
RECALLED
RECALLING
RECALLS
RECALMENT
RECALMENTS
RECALS
RECANT
RECANTED
RECANTER
RECANTERS
RECANTING
RECANTS
RECAP
RECAPPED
RECAPPING
RECAPS
RECAPTION
RECAPTIONS
RECAPTOR
RECAPTORS
RECAPTURE
RECAPTURED
RECAPTURES
RECAPTURING
RECAST
RECASTING
RECASTS
RECATCH
RECATCHES
RECATCHING
RECAUGHT
RECCE
RECCED
RECCEED
RECCEING
RECCES
RECCIED
RECCIES
RECCO
RECCOS
RECCY
RECCYING
RECEDE
RECEDED
RECEDES
RECEDING
RECEIPT
RECEIPTED

RECEIPTING
RECEIPTS
RECEIVAL
RECEIVALS
RECEIVE
RECEIVED
RECEIVER
RECEIVERS
RECEIVES
RECEIVING
RECEIVINGS
RECENCIES
RECENCY
RECENSE
RECENSED
RECENSES
RECENSING
RECENSION
RECENSIONS
RECENT
RECENTER
RECENTEST
RECENTLY
RECENTRE
RECENTRED
RECENTRES
RECENTRING
RECEPT
RECEPTION
RECEPTIONS
RECEPTIVE
RECEPTOR
RECEPTORS
RECEPTS
RECESS
RECESSED
RECESSES
RECESSING
RECESSION
RECESSIONS
RECESSIVE
RECESSIVES
RECHARGE
RECHARGED
RECHARGES
RECHARGING
RECHART
RECHARTED
RECHARTER
RECHARTERED
RECHARTERING
RECHARTERS
RECHARTING
RECHARTS
RECHATE
RECHATES
RECHAUFFE
RECHAUFFES
RECHEAT
RECHEATED
RECHEATING
RECHEATS
RECHECK
RECHECKED
RECHECKING
RECHECKS
RECHERCHE

RECHIE
RECHLESSE
RECIPE
RECIPES
RECIPIENT
RECIPIENTS
RECISION
RECISIONS
RECIT
RECITAL
RECITALS
RECITE
RECITED
RECITER
RECITERS
RECITES
RECITING
RECITS
RECK
RECKAN
RECKED
RECKING
RECKLESS
RECKLING
RECKLINGS
RECKON
RECKONED
RECKONER
RECKONERS
RECKONING
RECKONINGS
RECKONS
RECKS
RECLAIM
RECLAIMED
RECLAIMER
RECLAIMERS
RECLAIMING
RECLAIMS
RECLAME
RECLAMES
RECLIMB
RECLIMBED
RECLIMBING
RECLIMBS
RECLINATE
RECLINE
RECLINED
RECLINER
RECLINERS
RECLINES
RECLINING
RECLOSE
RECLOSED
RECLOSES
RECLOSING
RECLOTHE
RECLOTHED
RECLOTHES
RECLOTHING
RECLUSE
RECLUSELY
RECLUSES
RECLUSION
RECLUSIONS
RECLUSIVE
RECLUSORIES

RECLUSORY
RECODE
RECODED
RECODES
RECODING
RECOGNISE
RECOGNISED
RECOGNISES
RECOGNISING
RECOGNIZE
RECOGNIZED
RECOGNIZES
RECOGNIZING
RECOIL
RECOILED
RECOILER
RECOILERS
RECOILING
RECOILS
RECOIN
RECOINAGE
RECOINAGES
RECOINED
RECOINING
RECOINS
RECOLLECT
RECOLLECTED
RECOLLECTING
RECOLLECTS
RECOLLET
RECOLLETS
RECOMBINE
RECOMBINED
RECOMBINES
RECOMBINING
RECOMFORT
RECOMFORTED
RECOMFORTING
RECOMFORTS
RECOMMEND
RECOMMENDED
RECOMMENDING
RECOMMENDS
RECOMMIT
RECOMMITS
RECOMMITTED
RECOMMITTING
RECOMPACT
RECOMPACTED
RECOMPACTING
RECOMPACTS
RECOMPOSE
RECOMPOSED
RECOMPOSES
RECOMPOSING
RECONCILE
RECONCILED
RECONCILES
RECONCILING
RECONDITE
RECONFIRM
RECONFIRMED
RECONFIRMING
RECONFIRMS
RECONNECT
RECONNECTED
RECONNECTING

RECONNECTS
RECONQUER
RECONQUERED
RECONQUERING
RECONQUERS
RECONVENE
RECONVENED
RECONVENES
RECONVENING
RECONVERT
RECONVERTED
RECONVERTING
RECONVERTS
RECONVEY
RECONVEYED
RECONVEYING
RECONVEYS
RECORD
RECORDED
RECORDER
RECORDERS
RECORDING
RECORDINGS
RECORDIST
RECORDISTS
RECORDS
RECOUNT
RECOUNTAL
RECOUNTALS
RECOUNTED
RECOUNTING
RECOUNTS
RECOUP
RECOUPED
RECOUPING
RECOUPS
RECOURE
RECOURED
RECOURES
RECOURING
RECOURSE
RECOURSED
RECOURSES
RECOURSING
RECOVER
RECOVERED
RECOVEREE
RECOVEREES
RECOVERER
RECOVERERS
RECOVERIES
RECOVERING
RECOVEROR
RECOVERORS
RECOVERS
RECOVERY
RECOWER
RECOWERED
RECOWERING
RECOWERS
RECOYLE
RECOYLED
RECOYLES
RECOYLING
RECREANCE
RECREANCES
RECREANCIES

The Chambers Dictionary is the authority for many longer words; see *OSW* Introduction, page xii.

RECREANCY	RECÙLES	REDD	REDHEAD	REDRAFTED
RECREANT	RECULING	REDDEN	REDHEADS	REDRAFTING
RECREANTS	RECUMBENT	REDDENDA	REDIA	REDRAFTS
RECREATE	RECUR	REDDENDO	REDIAE	REDRAW
RECREATED	RECURE	REDDENDOS	REDIAL	REDRAWING
RECREATES	RECURED	REDDENDUM	REDIALED	REDRAWN
RECREATING	RECURES	REDDENED	REDIALING	REDRAWS
RECREMENT	RECURING	REDDENING	REDIALLED	REDRESS
RECREMENTS	RECURRED	REDDENS	REDIALLING	REDRESSED
RECROSS	RECURRENT	REDDER	REDIALS	REDRESSER
RECROSSED	RECURRING	REDDERS	REDID	REDRESSERS
RECROSSES	RECURS	REDDEST	REDING	REDRESSES
RECROSSING	RECURSION	REDDIER	REDINGOTE	REDRESSING
RECRUIT	RECURSIONS	REDDIEST	REDINGOTES	REDREW
RECRUITAL	RECURSIVE	REDDING	REDIP	REDRIVE
RECRUITALS	RECURVE	REDDINGS	REDIPPED	REDRIVEN
RECRUITED	RECURVED	REDDISH	REDIPPING	REDRIVES
RECRUITER	RECURVES	REDDLE	REDIPS	REDRIVING
RECRUITERS	RECURVING	REDDLED	REDIRECT	REDROOT
RECRUITING	RECUSANCE	REDDLEMAN	REDIRECTED	REDROOTS
RECRUITS	RECUSANCES	REDDLEMEN	REDIRECTING	REDROVE
RECS	RECUSANCIES	REDDLES	REDIRECTS	REDS
RECTA	RECUSANCY	REDDLING	REDISTIL	REDSEAR
RECTAL	RECUSANT	REDDS	REDISTILLED	REDSHANK
RECTALLY	RECUSANTS	REDDY	REDISTILLING	REDSHANKS
RECTANGLE	RECUSE	REDE	REDISTILS	REDSHARE
RECTANGLES	RECUSED	REDEAL	REDIVIDE	REDSHIRE
RECTI	RECUSES	REDEALING	REDIVIDED	REDSHORT
RECTIFIED	RECUSING	REDEALS	REDIVIDES	REDSKIN
RECTIFIER	RECYCLE	REDEALT	REDIVIDING	REDSKINS
RECTIFIERS	RECYCLED	REDECRAFT	REDIVIVUS	REDSTART
RECTIFIES	RECYCLES	REDECRAFTS	REDLEG	REDSTARTS
RECTIFY	RECYCLING	REDEEM	REDLEGS	REDSTREAK
RECTIFYING	RECYCLIST	REDEEMED	REDLY	REDSTREAKS
RECTION	RECYCLISTS	REDEEMER	REDNECK	REDTOP
RECTIONS	RED	REDEEMERS	REDNECKS	REDTOPS
RECTITIC	REDACT	REDEEMING	REDNESS	REDUCE
RECTITIS	REDACTED	REDEEMS	REDNESSES	REDUCED
RECTITISES	REDACTING	REDEFINE	REDO	REDUCER
RECTITUDE	REDACTION	REDEFINED	REDOES	REDUCERS
RECTITUDES	REDACTIONS	REDEFINES	REDOING	REDUCES
RECTO	REDACTOR	REDEFINING	REDOLENCE	REDUCIBLE
RECTOR	REDACTORS	REDELESS	REDOLENCES	REDUCING
RECTORAL	REDACTS	REDELIVER	REDOLENCIES	REDUCTANT
RECTORATE	REDAN	REDELIVERED	REDOLENCY	REDUCTANTS
RECTORATES	REDANS	REDELIVERING	REDOLENT	REDUCTASE
RECTORESS	REDARGUE	REDELIVERS	REDONE	REDUCTASES
RECTORESSES	REDARGUED	REDEPLOY	REDOS	REDUCTION
RECTORIAL	REDARGUES	REDEPLOYED	REDOUBLE	REDUCTIONS
RECTORIALS	REDARGUING	REDEPLOYING	REDOUBLED	REDUCTIVE
RECTORIES	REDATE	REDEPLOYS	REDOUBLES	REDUIT
RECTORS	REDATED	REDES	REDOUBLING	REDUITS
RECTORY	REDATES	REDESCEND	REDOUBT	REDUNDANT
RECTOS	REDATING	REDESCENDED	REDOUBTED	REDUVIID
RECTRESS	REDBACK	REDESCENDING	REDOUBTING	REDUVIIDS
RECTRESSES	REDBACKS	REDESCENDS	REDOUBTS	REDWATER
RECTRICES	REDBELLIES	REDESIGN	REDOUND	REDWATERS
RECTRIX	REDBELLY	REDESIGNED	REDOUNDED	REDWING
RECTUM	REDBREAST	REDESIGNING	REDOUNDING	REDWINGS
RECTUMS	REDBREASTS	REDESIGNS	REDOUNDINGS	REDWOOD
RECTUS	REDBRICK	REDEVELOP	REDOUNDS	REDWOODS
RECUILE	REDBUD	REDEVELOPED	REDOWA	REE
RECUILED	REDBUDS	REDEVELOPING	REDOWAS	REEBOK
RECUILES	REDCAP	REDEVELOPS	REDOX	REEBOKS
RECUILING	REDCAPS	REDFISH	REDPOLL	REECH
RECULE	REDCOAT	REDFISHES	REDPOLLS	REECHED
RECULED	REDCOATS	REDHANDED	REDRAFT	REECHES

The Chambers Dictionary is the authority for many longer words; see *OSW* Introduction, page xii.

REECHIE
REECHIER
REECHIEST
REECHING
REECHY
REED
REEDBED
REEDBEDS
REEDE
REEDED
REEDEN
REEDER
REEDERS
REEDES
REEDIER
REEDIEST
REEDINESS
REEDINESSES
REEDING
REEDINGS
REEDLING
REEDLINGS
REEDMACE
REEDMACES
REEDS
REEDSTOP
REEDSTOPS
REEDY
REEF
REEFED
REEFER
REEFERS
REEFING
REEFINGS
REEFS
REEK
REEKED
REEKIE
REEKIER
REEKIEST
REEKING
REEKS
REEKY
REEL
REELED
REELER
REELERS
REELING
REELINGLY
REELINGS
REELMAN
REELMEN
REELS
REEN
REENS
REES
REEST
REESTED
REESTIER
REESTIEST
REESTING
REESTS
REESTY
REEVE
REEVED
REEVES
REEVING

REF
REFACE
REFACED
REFACES
REFACING
REFASHION
REFASHIONED
REFASHIONING
REFASHIONS
REFECT
REFECTED
REFECTING
REFECTION
REFECTIONS
REFECTORIES
REFECTORY
REFECTS
REFEL
REFELLED
REFELLING
REFELS
REFER
REFERABLE
REFEREE
REFEREED
REFEREEING
REFEREES
REFERENCE
REFERENCED
REFERENCES
REFERENCING
REFERENDA
REFERENT
REFERENTS
REFERRAL
REFERRALS
REFERRED
REFERRING
REFERS
REFFED
REFFING
REFFO
REFFOS
REFIGURE
REFIGURED
REFIGURES
REFIGURING
REFILL
REFILLED
REFILLING
REFILLS
REFINE
REFINED
REFINEDLY
REFINER
REFINERIES
REFINERS
REFINERY
REFINES
REFINING
REFININGS
REFIT
REFITMENT
REFITMENTS
REFITS
REFITTED
REFITTING

REFITTINGS
REFLAG
REFLAGGED
REFLAGGING
REFLAGS
REFLATE
REFLATED
REFLATES
REFLATING
REFLATION
REFLATIONS
REFLECT
REFLECTED
REFLECTER
REFLECTERS
REFLECTING
REFLECTOR
REFLECTORS
REFLECTS
REFLET
REFLETS
REFLEX
REFLEXED
REFLEXES
REFLEXING
REFLEXION
REFLEXIONS
REFLEXIVE
REFLEXLY
REFLOAT
REFLOATED
REFLOATING
REFLOATS
REFLOW
REFLOWED
REFLOWER
REFLOWERED
REFLOWERING
REFLOWERINGS
REFLOWERS
REFLOWING
REFLOWINGS
REFLOWS
REFLUENCE
REFLUENCES
REFLUENT
REFLUX
REFLUXED
REFLUXES
REFLUXING
REFOCUS
REFOCUSED
REFOCUSES
REFOCUSING
REFOCUSSED
REFOCUSSES
REFOCUSSING
REFOOT
REFOOTED
REFOOTING
REFOOTS
REFOREST
REFORESTED
REFORESTING
REFORESTS
REFORM
REFORMADE

REFORMADES
REFORMADO
REFORMADOES
REFORMADOS
REFORMAT
REFORMATS
REFORMATTED
REFORMATTING
REFORMED
REFORMER
REFORMERS
REFORMING
REFORMISM
REFORMISMS
REFORMIST
REFORMISTS
REFORMS
REFORTIFIED
REFORTIFIES
REFORTIFY
REFORTIFYING
REFOUND
REFOUNDED
REFOUNDER
REFOUNDERS
REFOUNDING
REFOUNDS
REFRACT
REFRACTED
REFRACTING
REFRACTOR
REFRACTORS
REFRACTS
REFRAIN
REFRAINED
REFRAINING
REFRAINS
REFRAME
REFRAMED
REFRAMES
REFRAMING
REFREEZE
REFREEZES
REFREEZING
REFRESH
REFRESHED
REFRESHEN
REFRESHENED
REFRESHENING
REFRESHENS
REFRESHER
REFRESHERS
REFRESHES
REFRESHING
REFRINGE
REFRINGED
REFRINGES
REFRINGING
REFROZE
REFROZEN
REFS
REFT
REFUEL
REFUELLED
REFUELLING
REFUELS
REFUGE

REFUGED
REFUGEE
REFUGEES
REFUGES
REFUGIA
REFUGING
REFUGIUM
REFULGENT
REFUND
REFUNDED
REFUNDER
REFUNDERS
REFUNDING
REFUNDS
REFURBISH
REFURBISHED
REFURBISHES
REFURBISHING
REFURNISH
REFURNISHED
REFURNISHES
REFURNISHING
REFUSABLE
REFUSAL
REFUSALS
REFUSE
REFUSED
REFUSENIK
REFUSENIKS
REFUSER
REFUSERS
REFUSES
REFUSING
REFUSION
REFUSIONS
REFUSNIK
REFUSNIKS
REFUTABLE
REFUTABLY
REFUTAL
REFUTALS
REFUTE
REFUTED
REFUTER
REFUTERS
REFUTES
REFUTING
REGAIN
REGAINED
REGAINER
REGAINERS
REGAINING
REGAINS
REGAL
REGALE
REGALED
REGALES
REGALIA
REGALIAN
REGALIAS
REGALING
REGALISM
REGALISMS
REGALIST
REGALISTS
REGALITIES
REGALITY

The Chambers Dictionary is the authority for many longer words; see *OSW* Introduction, page xii.

REGALLY	REGIUS	REGULA	REHOUSES	REINING
REGALS	REGIVE	REGULAE	REHOUSING	REINLESS
REGAR	REGIVEN	REGULAR	REHOUSINGS	REINS
REGARD	REGIVES	REGULARLY	REHS	REINSERT
REGARDANT	REGIVING	REGULARS	REHUNG	REINSERTED
REGARDED	REGLET	REGULATE	REHYDRATE	REINSERTING
REGARDER	REGLETS	REGULATED	REHYDRATED	REINSERTS
REGARDERS	REGMA	REGULATES	REHYDRATES	REINSMAN
REGARDFUL	REGMATA	REGULATING	REHYDRATING	REINSMEN
REGARDING	REGNAL	REGULATOR	REIF	REINSPECT
REGARDS	REGNANT	REGULATORS	REIFIED	REINSPECTED
REGARS	REGO	REGULINE	REIFIES	REINSPECTING
REGATHER	REGOLITH	REGULISE	REIFS	REINSPECTS
REGATHERED	REGOLITHS	REGULISED	REIFY	REINSPIRE
REGATHERING	REGORGE	REGULISES	REIFYING	REINSPIRED
REGATHERS	REGORGED	REGULISING	REIGN	REINSPIRES
REGATTA	REGORGES	REGULIZE	REIGNED	REINSPIRING
REGATTAS	REGORGING	REGULIZED	REIGNING	REINSTALL
REGAVE	REGOS	REGULIZES	REIGNS	REINSTALLED
REGELATE	REGRADE	REGULIZING	REIK	REINSTALLING
REGELATED	REGRADED	REGULO®	REIKS	REINSTALLS
REGELATES	REGRADES	REGULOS	REILLUME	REINSTATE
REGELATING	REGRADING	REGULUS	REILLUMED	REINSTATED
REGENCE	REGRANT	REGULUSES	REILLUMES	REINSTATES
REGENCES	REGRANTED	REGUR	REILLUMING	REINSTATING
REGENCIES	REGRANTING	REGURS	REIMBURSE	REINSURE
REGENCY	REGRANTS	REH	REIMBURSED	REINSURED
REGENT	REGRATE	REHANDLE	REIMBURSES	REINSURER
REGENTS	REGRATED	REHANDLED	REIMBURSING	REINSURERS
REGEST	REGRATER	REHANDLES	REIMPLANT	REINSURES
REGESTS	REGRATERS	REHANDLING	REIMPLANTED	REINSURING
REGGAE	REGRATES	REHANDLINGS	REIMPLANTING	REINTER
REGGAES	REGRATING	REHANG	REIMPLANTS	REINTERRED
REGGO	REGRATINGS	REHANGING	REIMPORT	REINTERRING
REGGOS	REGRATOR	REHANGS	REIMPORTED	REINTERS
REGICIDAL	REGRATORS	REHASH	REIMPORTING	REINVEST
REGICIDE	REGREDE	REHASHED	REIMPORTS	REINVESTED
REGICIDES	REGREDED	REHASHES	REIMPOSE	REINVESTING
REGIE	REGREDES	REHASHING	REIMPOSED	REINVESTS
REGIES	REGREDING	REHEAR	REIMPOSES	REINVOLVE
REGIME	REGREET	REHEARD	REIMPOSING	REINVOLVED
REGIMEN	REGREETED	REHEARING	REIN	REINVOLVES
REGIMENS	REGREETING	REHEARINGS	REINDEER	REINVOLVING
REGIMENT	REGREETS	REHEARS	REINDEERS	REIRD
REGIMENTED	REGRESS	REHEARSAL	REINED	REIRDS
REGIMENTING	REGRESSED	REHEARSALS	REINETTE	REIS
REGIMENTS	REGRESSES	REHEARSE	REINETTES	REISES
REGIMES	REGRESSING	REHEARSED	REINFORCE	REISSUE
REGIMINAL	REGRET	REHEARSER	REINFORCED	REISSUED
REGINA	REGRETFUL	REHEARSERS	REINFORCES	REISSUES
REGINAE	REGRETS	REHEARSES	REINFORCING	REISSUING
REGINAL	REGRETTED	REHEARSING	REINFORM	REIST
REGINAS	REGRETTING	REHEARSINGS	REINFORMED	REISTAFEL
REGION	REGRIND	REHEAT	REINFORMING	REISTAFELS
REGIONAL	REGRINDING	REHEATED	REINFORMS	REISTED
REGIONARY	REGRINDS	REHEATER	REINFUND	REISTING
REGIONS	REGROUND	REHEATERS	REINFUNDED	REISTS
REGISSEUR	REGROUP	REHEATING	REINFUNDING	REITER
REGISSEURS	REGROUPED	REHEATS	REINFUNDS	REITERANT
REGISTER	REGROUPING	REHEEL	REINFUSE	REITERATE
REGISTERED	REGROUPS	REHEELED	REINFUSED	REITERATED
REGISTERING	REGROWTH	REHEELING	REINFUSES	REITERATES
REGISTERS	REGROWTHS	REHEELS	REINFUSING	REITERATING
REGISTRAR	REGUERDON	REHOBOAM	REINHABIT	REITERS
REGISTRARS	REGUERDONED	REHOBOAMS	REINHABITED	REIVE
REGISTRIES	REGUERDONING	REHOUSE	REINHABITING	REIVER
REGISTRY	REGUERDONS	REHOUSED	REINHABITS	REIVERS

The Chambers Dictionary is the authority for many longer words; see *OSW* Introduction, page xii.

REIVES
REIVING
REJECT
REJECTED
REJECTER
REJECTERS
REJECTING
REJECTION
REJECTIONS
REJECTIVE
REJECTOR
REJECTORS
REJECTS
REJIG
REJIGGED
REJIGGER
REJIGGERED
REJIGGERING
REJIGGERS
REJIGGING
REJIGS
REJOICE
REJOICED
REJOICER
REJOICERS
REJOICES
REJOICING
REJOICINGS
REJOIN
REJOINDER
REJOINDERS
REJOINED
REJOINING
REJOINS
REJON
REJONEO
REJONEOS
REJONES
REJOURN
REJOURNED
REJOURNING
REJOURNS
REJUDGE
REJUDGED
REJUDGES
REJUDGING
REKE
REKED
REKES
REKINDLE
REKINDLED
REKINDLES
REKINDLING
REKING
RELACHE
RELACHES
RELAID
RELAPSE
RELAPSED
RELAPSER
RELAPSERS
RELAPSES
RELAPSING
RELATE
RELATED
RELATER
RELATERS

RELATES
RELATING
RELATION
RELATIONS
RELATIVAL
RELATIVE
RELATIVES
RELATOR
RELATORS
RELAUNCH
RELAUNCHED
RELAUNCHES
RELAUNCHING
RELAX
RELAXANT
RELAXANTS
RELAXED
RELAXES
RELAXIN
RELAXING
RELAXINS
RELAY
RELAYED
RELAYING
RELAYS
RELEASE
RELEASED
RELEASEE
RELEASEES
RELEASER
RELEASERS
RELEASES
RELEASING
RELEASOR
RELEASORS
RELEGABLE
RELEGATE
RELEGATED
RELEGATES
RELEGATING
RELENT
RELENTED
RELENTING
RELENTINGS
RELENTS
RELET
RELETS
RELETTING
RELEVANCE
RELEVANCES
RELEVANCIES
RELEVANCY
RELEVANT
RELIABLE
RELIABLY
RELIANCE
RELIANCES
RELIANT
RELIC
RELICS
RELICT
RELICTS
RELIDE
RELIE
RELIED
RELIEF
RELIEFS

RELIER
RELIERS
RELIES
RELIEVE
RELIEVED
RELIEVER
RELIEVERS
RELIEVES
RELIEVING
RELIEVO
RELIEVOS
RELIGHT
RELIGHTED
RELIGHTING
RELIGHTS
RELIGIEUX
RELIGION
RELIGIONS
RELIGIOSE
RELIGIOSO
RELIGIOUS
RELIGIOUSES
RELINE
RELINED
RELINES
RELINING
RELIQUARIES
RELIQUARY
RELIQUE
RELIQUES
RELIQUIAE
RELISH
RELISHED
RELISHES
RELISHING
RELIT
RELIVE
RELIVED
RELIVER
RELIVERED
RELIVERING
RELIVERS
RELIVES
RELIVING
RELLISH
RELLISHED
RELLISHES
RELLISHING
RELOAD
RELOADED
RELOADING
RELOADS
RELOCATE
RELOCATED
RELOCATES
RELOCATING
RELUCENT
RELUCT
RELUCTANT
RELUCTATE
RELUCTATED
RELUCTATES
RELUCTATING
RELUCTED
RELUCTING
RELUCTS
RELUME

RELUMED
RELUMES
RELUMINE
RELUMINED
RELUMINES
RELUMING
RELUMINING
RELY
RELYING
REM
REMADE
REMADES
REMAIN
REMAINDER
REMAINDERED
REMAINDERING
REMAINDERS
REMAINED
REMAINING
REMAINS
REMAKE
REMAKES
REMAKING
REMAN
REMAND
REMANDED
REMANDING
REMANDS
REMANENCE
REMANENCES
REMANENCIES
REMANENCY
REMANENT
REMANENTS
REMANET
REMANETS
REMANIE
REMANIES
REMANNED
REMANNING
REMANS
REMARK
REMARKED
REMARKER
REMARKERS
REMARKING
REMARKS
REMARQUE
REMARQUED
REMARQUES
REMARRIED
REMARRIES
REMARRY
REMARRYING
REMASTER
REMASTERED
REMASTERING
REMASTERS
REMATCH
REMATCHED
REMATCHES
REMATCHING
REMBLAI
REMBLAIS
REMBLE
REMBLED
REMBLES

REMBLING
REMEAD
REMEADED
REMEADING
REMEADS
REMEASURE
REMEASURED
REMEASURES
REMEASURING
REMEDE
REMEDED
REMEDES
REMEDIAL
REMEDIAT
REMEDIATE
REMEDIED
REMEDIES
REMEDING
REMEDY
REMEDYING
REMEID
REMEIDED
REMEIDING
REMEIDS
REMEMBER
REMEMBERED
REMEMBERING
REMEMBERS
REMEN
REMENS
REMERCIED
REMERCIES
REMERCY
REMERCYING
REMERGE
REMERGED
REMERGES
REMERGING
REMEX
REMIGATE
REMIGATED
REMIGATES
REMIGATING
REMIGES
REMIGIAL
REMIGRATE
REMIGRATED
REMIGRATES
REMIGRATING
REMIND
REMINDED
REMINDER
REMINDERS
REMINDFUL
REMINDING
REMINDS
REMINISCE
REMINISCED
REMINISCES
REMINISCING
REMINT
REMINTED
REMINTING
REMINTS
REMISE
REMISED
REMISES

The Chambers Dictionary is the authority for many longer words; see *OSW* Introduction, page xii.

REMISING
REMISS
REMISSION
REMISSIONS
REMISSIVE
REMISSLY
REMISSORY
REMIT
REMITMENT
REMITMENTS
REMITS
REMITTAL
REMITTALS
REMITTED
REMITTEE
REMITTEES
REMITTENT
REMITTER
REMITTERS
REMITTING
REMITTOR
REMITTORS
REMIX
REMIXED
REMIXES
REMIXING
REMNANT
REMNANTS
REMODEL
REMODELED
REMODELING
REMODELLED
REMODELLING
REMODELS
REMODIFIED
REMODIFIES
REMODIFY
REMODIFYING
REMONTANT
REMONTANTS
REMORA
REMORAS
REMORSE
REMORSES
REMOTE
REMOTELY
REMOTER
REMOTES
REMOTEST
REMOTION
REMOTIONS
REMOUD
REMOULADE
REMOULADES
REMOULD
REMOULDED
REMOULDING
REMOULDS
REMOUNT
REMOUNTED
REMOUNTING
REMOUNTS
REMOVABLE
REMOVABLY
REMOVAL
REMOVALS
REMOVE

REMOVED
REMOVER
REMOVERS
REMOVES
REMOVING
REMS
REMUAGE
REMUAGES
REMUDA
REMUDAS
REMUEUR
REMUEURS
REMURMUR
REMURMURED
REMURMURING
REMURMURS
REN
RENAGUE
RENAGUED
RENAGUES
RENAGUING
RENAL
RENAME
RENAMED
RENAMES
RENAMING
RENASCENT
RENAY
RENAYED
RENAYING
RENAYS
RENCONTRE
RENCONTRES
REND
RENDER
RENDERED
RENDERER
RENDERERS
RENDERING
RENDERINGS
RENDERS
RENDING
RENDITION
RENDITIONS
RENDS
RENDZINA
RENDZINAS
RENEGADE
RENEGADED
RENEGADES
RENEGADING
RENEGADO
RENEGADOS
RENEGATE
RENEGATES
RENEGE
RENEGED
RENEGER
RENEGERS
RENEGES
RENEGING
RENEGUE
RENEGUED
RENEGUER
RENEGUERS
RENEGUES
RENEGUING

RENEW
RENEWABLE
RENEWABLES
RENEWAL
RENEWALS
RENEWED
RENEWER
RENEWERS
RENEWING
RENEWINGS
RENEWS
RENEY
RENEYED
RENEYING
RENEYS
RENFIERST
RENFORCE
RENFORCED
RENFORCES
RENFORCING
RENFORST
RENGA
RENGAS
RENIED
RENIES
RENIFORM
RENIG
RENIGGED
RENIGGING
RENIGS
RENIN
RENINS
RENITENCIES
RENITENCY
RENITENT
RENMINBI
RENMINBIS
RENNE
RENNED
RENNES
RENNET
RENNETS
RENNIN
RENNING
RENNINGS
RENNINS
RENOUNCE
RENOUNCED
RENOUNCER
RENOUNCERS
RENOUNCES
RENOUNCING
RENOVATE
RENOVATED
RENOVATES
RENOVATING
RENOVATOR
RENOVATORS
RENOWN
RENOWNED
RENOWNER
RENOWNERS
RENOWNING
RENOWNS
RENS
RENT
RENTABLE

RENTAL
RENTALLER
RENTALLERS
RENTALS
RENTE
RENTED
RENTER
RENTERS
RENTES
RENTIER
RENTIERS
RENTING
RENTS
RENUMBER
RENUMBERED
RENUMBERING
RENUMBERS
RENVERSE
RENVERSED
RENVERSES
RENVERSING
RENVERST
RENVOI
RENVOIS
RENVOY
RENVOYS
RENY
RENYING
REOCCUPIED
REOCCUPIES
REOCCUPY
REOCCUPYING
REOFFEND
REOFFENDED
REOFFENDING
REOFFENDS
REOPEN
REOPENED
REOPENER
REOPENERS
REOPENING
REOPENS
REORDAIN
REORDAINED
REORDAINING
REORDAINS
REORDER
REORDERED
REORDERING
REORDERS
REORIENT
REORIENTED
REORIENTING
REORIENTS
REP
REPACK
REPACKAGE
REPACKAGED
REPACKAGES
REPACKAGING
REPACKED
REPACKING
REPACKS
REPAID
REPAINT
REPAINTED
REPAINTING

REPAINTINGS
REPAINTS
REPAIR
REPAIRED
REPAIRER
REPAIRERS
REPAIRING
REPAIRMAN
REPAIRMEN
REPAIRS
REPAND
REPAPER
REPAPERED
REPAPERING
REPAPERS
REPARABLE
REPARABLY
REPARTEE
REPARTEED
REPARTEEING
REPARTEES
REPASS
REPASSAGE
REPASSAGES
REPASSED
REPASSES
REPASSING
REPAST
REPASTED
REPASTING
REPASTS
REPASTURE
REPASTURES
REPAY
REPAYABLE
REPAYING
REPAYMENT
REPAYMENTS
REPAYS
REPEAL
REPEALED
REPEALER
REPEALERS
REPEALING
REPEALS
REPEAT
REPEATED
REPEATER
REPEATERS
REPEATING
REPEATINGS
REPEATS
REPECHAGE
REPECHAGES
REPEL
REPELLANT
REPELLANTS
REPELLED
REPELLENT
REPELLENTS
REPELLER
REPELLERS
REPELLING
REPELS
REPENT
REPENTANT
REPENTANTS

The Chambers Dictionary is the authority for many longer words; see *OSW* Introduction, page xii.

REPENTED
REPENTER
REPENTERS
REPENTING
REPENTS
REPEOPLE
REPEOPLED
REPEOPLES
REPEOPLING
REPERCUSS
REPERCUSSED
REPERCUSSES
REPERCUSSING
REPERTORIES
REPERTORY
REPERUSAL
REPERUSALS
REPERUSE
REPERUSED
REPERUSES
REPERUSING
REPETEND
REPETENDS
REPHRASE
REPHRASED
REPHRASES
REPHRASING
REPINE
REPINED
REPINER
REPINERS
REPINES
REPINING
REPININGS
REPIQUE
REPIQUED
REPIQUES
REPIQUING
REPLA
REPLACE
REPLACED
REPLACER
REPLACERS
REPLACES
REPLACING
REPLAN
REPLANNED
REPLANNING
REPLANS
REPLANT
REPLANTED
REPLANTING
REPLANTS
REPLAY
REPLAYED
REPLAYING
REPLAYS
REPLENISH
REPLENISHED
REPLENISHES
REPLENISHING
REPLETE
REPLETED
REPLETES
REPLETING
REPLETION
REPLETIONS

REPLEVIED
REPLEVIES
REPLEVIN
REPLEVINED
REPLEVINING
REPLEVINS
REPLEVY
REPLEVYING
REPLICA
REPLICAS
REPLICATE
REPLICATED
REPLICATES
REPLICATING
REPLICON
REPLICONS
REPLIED
REPLIER
REPLIERS
REPLIES
REPLUM
REPLY
REPLYING
REPO
REPOINT
REPOINTED
REPOINTING
REPOINTS
REPOMAN
REPOMEN
REPONE
REPONED
REPONES
REPONING
REPORT
REPORTAGE
REPORTAGES
REPORTED
REPORTER
REPORTERS
REPORTING
REPORTINGS
REPORTS
REPOS
REPOSAL
REPOSALL
REPOSALLS
REPOSALS
REPOSE
REPOSED
REPOSEDLY
REPOSEFUL
REPOSES
REPOSING
REPOSIT
REPOSITED
REPOSITING
REPOSITOR
REPOSITORS
REPOSITS
REPOSSESS
REPOSSESSED
REPOSSESSES
REPOSSESSING
REPOST
REPOSTED
REPOSTING

REPOSTS
REPOSURE
REPOSURES
REPOT
REPOTS
REPOTTED
REPOTTING
REPOTTINGS
REPOUSSE
REPOUSSES
REPP
REPPED
REPPING
REPPINGS
REPPS
REPREEVE
REPREEVED
REPREEVES
REPREEVING
REPREHEND
REPREHENDED
REPREHENDING
REPREHENDS
REPRESENT
REPRESENTED
REPRESENTING
REPRESENTS
REPRESS
REPRESSED
REPRESSES
REPRESSING
REPRESSOR
REPRESSORS
REPRIEFE
REPRIEFES
REPRIEVAL
REPRIEVALS
REPRIEVE
REPRIEVED
REPRIEVES
REPRIEVING
REPRIMAND
REPRIMANDED
REPRIMANDING
REPRIMANDS
REPRIME
REPRIMED
REPRIMES
REPRIMING
REPRINT
REPRINTED
REPRINTING
REPRINTS
REPRISAL
REPRISALS
REPRISE
REPRISED
REPRISES
REPRISING
REPRIVE
REPRIVED
REPRIVES
REPRIVING
REPRIZE
REPRIZED
REPRIZES
REPRIZING

REPRO
REPROACH
REPROACHED
REPROACHES
REPROACHING
REPROBACIES
REPROBACY
REPROBATE
REPROBATED
REPROBATES
REPROBATING
REPROCESS
REPROCESSED
REPROCESSES
REPROCESSING
REPRODUCE
REPRODUCED
REPRODUCES
REPRODUCING
REPROGRAM
REPROGRAMMED
REPROGRAMMING
REPROGRAMS
REPROOF
REPROOFED
REPROOFING
REPROOFS
REPROS
REPROVAL
REPROVALS
REPROVE
REPROVED
REPROVER
REPROVERS
REPROVES
REPROVING
REPROVINGS
REPRYVE
REPRYVED
REPRYVES
REPRYVING
REPS
REPTANT
REPTATION
REPTATIONS
REPTILE
REPTILES
REPTILIAN
REPTILOID
REPUBLIC
REPUBLICS
REPUBLISH
REPUBLISHED
REPUBLISHES
REPUBLISHING
REPUDIATE
REPUDIATED
REPUDIATES
REPUDIATING
REPUGN
REPUGNANT
REPUGNED
REPUGNING
REPUGNS
REPULP
REPULPED
REPULPING

REPULPS
REPULSE
REPULSED
REPULSES
REPULSING
REPULSION
REPULSIONS
REPULSIVE
REPUNIT
REPUNITS
REPURE
REPURED
REPURES
REPURIFIED
REPURIFIES
REPURIFY
REPURIFYING
REPURING
REPUTABLE
REPUTABLY
REPUTE
REPUTED
REPUTEDLY
REPUTES
REPUTING
REPUTINGS
REQUERE
REQUERED
REQUERES
REQUERING
REQUEST
REQUESTED
REQUESTER
REQUESTERS
REQUESTING
REQUESTS
REQUICKEN
REQUICKENED
REQUICKENING
REQUICKENS
REQUIEM
REQUIEMS
REQUIGHT
REQUIGHTED
REQUIGHTING
REQUIGHTS
REQUIRE
REQUIRED
REQUIRER
REQUIRERS
REQUIRES
REQUIRING
REQUIRINGS
REQUISITE
REQUISITES
REQUIT
REQUITAL
REQUITALS
REQUITE
REQUITED
REQUITER
REQUITERS
REQUITES
REQUITING
REQUITS
REQUITTED
REQUITTING

The Chambers Dictionary is the authority for many longer words; see *OSW* Introduction, page xii.

REQUOTE	RESCORED	RESERVING	RESINATAS	RESONANT
REQUOTED	RESCORES	RESERVIST	RESINATE	RESONATE
REQUOTES	RESCORING	RESERVISTS	RESINATES	RESONATED
REQUOTING	RESCRIPT	RESERVOIR	RESINED	RESONATES
REQUOYLE	RESCRIPTED	RESERVOIRED	RESINER	RESONATING
REQUOYLED	RESCRIPTING	RESERVOIRING	RESINERS	RESONATOR
REQUOYLES	RESCRIPTS	RESERVOIRS	RESINIFIED	RESONATORS
REQUOYLING	RESCUABLE	RESES	RESINIFIES	RESORB
RERADIATE	RESCUE	RESET	RESINIFY	RESORBED
RERADIATED	RESCUED	RESETS	RESINIFYING	RESORBENT
RERADIATES	RESCUER	RESETTED	RESINING	RESORBING
RERADIATING	RESCUERS	RESETTER	RESINISE	RESORBS
RERAIL	RESCUES	RESETTERS	RESINISED	RESORCIN
RERAILED	RESCUING	RESETTING	RESINISES	RESORCINS
RERAILING	RESEAL	RESETTLE	RESINISING	RESORT
RERAILS	RESEALED	RESETTLED	RESINIZE	RESORTED
RERAN	RESEALING	RESETTLES	RESINIZED	RESORTER
REREAD	RESEALS	RESETTLING	RESINIZES	RESORTERS
REREADING	RESEARCH	RESHAPE	RESINIZING	RESORTING
REREADS	RESEARCHED	RESHAPED	RESINOID	RESORTS
REREBRACE	RESEARCHES	RESHAPES	RESINOIDS	RESOUND
REREBRACES	RESEARCHING	RESHAPING	RESINOSES	RESOUNDED
REREDORSE	RESEAT	RESHIP	RESINOSIS	RESOUNDING
REREDORSES	RESEATED	RESHIPPED	RESINOUS	RESOUNDS
REREDOS	RESEATING	RESHIPPING	RESINS	RESOURCE
REREDOSES	RESEATS	RESHIPS	RESIST	RESOURCED
REREDOSSE	RESEAU	RESHUFFLE	RESISTANT	RESOURCES
REREDOSSES	RESEAUS	RESHUFFLED	RESISTANTS	RESOURCING
REREMICE	RESEAUX	RESHUFFLES	RESISTED	RESPEAK
REREMOUSE	RESECT	RESHUFFLING	RESISTENT	RESPEAKING
REREVISE	RESECTED	RESIANCE	RESISTENTS	RESPEAKS
REREVISED	RESECTING	RESIANCES	RESISTING	RESPECT
REREVISES	RESECTION	RESIANT	RESISTIVE	RESPECTED
REREVISING	RESECTIONS	RESIANTS	RESISTOR	RESPECTER
REREWARD	RESECTS	RESIDE	RESISTORS	RESPECTERS
REREWARDS	RESEDA	RESIDED	RESISTS	RESPECTING
REROUTE	RESEDAS	RESIDENCE	RESIT	RESPECTS
REROUTED	RESEIZE	RESIDENCES	RESITS	RESPELL
REROUTEING	RESEIZED	RESIDENCIES	RESITTING	RESPELLED
REROUTES	RESEIZES	RESIDENCY	RESKEW	RESPELLING
REROUTING	RESEIZING	RESIDENT	RESKEWED	RESPELLS
RERUN	RESELECT	RESIDENTS	RESKEWING	RESPELT
RERUNNING	RESELECTED	RESIDER	RESKEWS	RESPIRE
RERUNS	RESELECTING	RESIDERS	RESKUE	RESPIRED
RES	RESELECTS	RESIDES	RESKUED	RESPIRES
RESAID	RESELL	RESIDING	RESKUES	RESPIRING
RESALE	RESELLING	RESIDUA	RESKUING	RESPITE
RESALES	RESELLS	RESIDUAL	RESNATRON	RESPITED
RESALGAR	RESEMBLE	RESIDUALS	RESNATRONS	RESPITES
RESALGARS	RESEMBLED	RESIDUARY	RESOLD	RESPITING
RESALUTE	RESEMBLER	RESIDUE	RESOLE	RESPLEND
RESALUTED	RESEMBLERS	RESIDUES	RESOLED	RESPLENDED
RESALUTES	RESEMBLES	RESIDUOUS	RESOLES	RESPLENDING
RESALUTING	RESEMBLING	RESIDUUM	RESOLING	RESPLENDS
RESAT	RESENT	RESIGN	RESOLUBLE	RESPOKE
RESAY	RESENTED	RESIGNED	RESOLUTE	RESPOKEN
RESAYING	RESENTER	RESIGNER	RESOLUTES	RESPOND
RESAYS	RESENTERS	RESIGNERS	RESOLVE	RESPONDED
RESCALE	RESENTFUL	RESIGNING	RESOLVED	RESPONDER
RESCALED	RESENTING	RESIGNS	RESOLVENT	RESPONDERS
RESCALES	RESENTIVE	RESILE	RESOLVENTS	RESPONDING
RESCALING	RESENTS	RESILED	RESOLVER	RESPONDS
RESCIND	RESERPINE	RESILES	RESOLVERS	RESPONSA
RESCINDED	RESERPINES	RESILIENT	RESOLVES	RESPONSE
RESCINDING	RESERVE	RESILING	RESOLVING	RESPONSER
RESCINDS	RESERVED	RESIN	RESONANCE	RESPONSERS
RESCORE	RESERVES	RESINATA	RESONANCES	RESPONSES

The Chambers Dictionary is the authority for many longer words; see *OSW* Introduction, page xii.

RESPONSOR
RESPONSORS
RESPONSUM
RESPONSUMS
RESPRAY
RESPRAYED
RESPRAYING
RESPRAYS
RESSALDAR
RESSALDARS
REST
RESTAFF
RESTAFFED
RESTAFFING
RESTAFFS
RESTAGE
RESTAGED
RESTAGES
RESTAGING
RESTART
RESTARTED
RESTARTER
RESTARTERS
RESTARTING
RESTARTS
RESTATE
RESTATED
RESTATES
RESTATING
RESTED
RESTEM
RESTEMMED
RESTEMMING
RESTEMS
RESTER
RESTERS
RESTFUL
RESTFULLER
RESTFULLEST
RESTFULLY
RESTIER
RESTIEST
RESTIFF
RESTIFORM
RESTING
RESTINGS
RESTITUTE
RESTITUTED
RESTITUTES
RESTITUTING
RESTIVE
RESTIVELY
RESTLESS
RESTOCK
RESTOCKED
RESTOCKING
RESTOCKS
RESTORE
RESTORED
RESTORER
RESTORERS
RESTORES
RESTORING
RESTRAIN
RESTRAINED
RESTRAINING
RESTRAININGS

RESTRAINS
RESTRAINT
RESTRAINTS
RESTRICT
RESTRICTED
RESTRICTING
RESTRICTS
RESTRING
RESTRINGE
RESTRINGED
RESTRINGEING
RESTRINGES
RESTRINGING
RESTRINGS
RESTRUNG
RESTS
RESTY
RESTYLE
RESTYLED
RESTYLES
RESTYLING
RESUBMIT
RESUBMITS
RESUBMITTED
RESUBMITTING
RESULT
RESULTANT
RESULTANTS
RESULTED
RESULTFUL
RESULTING
RESULTS
RESUMABLE
RESUME
RESUMED
RESUMES
RESUMING
RESUPINE
RESURGE
RESURGED
RESURGENT
RESURGES
RESURGING
RESURRECT
RESURRECTED
RESURRECTING
RESURRECTS
RESURVEY
RESURVEYED
RESURVEYING
RESURVEYS
RET
RETABLE
RETABLES
RETAIL
RETAILED
RETAILER
RETAILERS
RETAILING
RETAILS
RETAIN
RETAINED
RETAINER
RETAINERS
RETAINING
RETAINS
RETAKE

RETAKEN
RETAKER
RETAKERS
RETAKES
RETAKING
RETAKINGS
RETALIATE
RETALIATED
RETALIATES
RETALIATING
RETAMA
RETAMAS
RETARD
RETARDANT
RETARDANTS
RETARDATE
RETARDATES
RETARDED
RETARDER
RETARDERS
RETARDING
RETARDS
RETCH
RETCHED
RETCHES
RETCHING
RETCHLESS
RETE
RETELL
RETELLER
RETELLERS
RETELLING
RETELLS
RETENE
RETENES
RETENTION
RETENTIONS
RETENTIVE
RETES
RETEXTURE
RETEXTURED
RETEXTURES
RETEXTURING
RETHINK
RETHINKING
RETHINKS
RETHOUGHT
RETIAL
RETIARII
RETIARIUS
RETIARIUSES
RETIARY
RETICELLA
RETICELLAS
RETICENCE
RETICENCES
RETICENCIES
RETICENCY
RETICENT
RETICLE
RETICLES
RETICULAR
RETICULE
RETICULES
RETICULUM
RETICULUMS
RETIE

RETIED
RETIES
RETIFORM
RETILE
RETILED
RETILES
RETILING
RETIME
RETIMED
RETIMES
RETIMING
RETINA
RETINAE
RETINAL
RETINAS
RETINITE
RETINITES
RETINITIS
RETINITISES
RETINOID
RETINOIDS
RETINOL
RETINOLS
RETINUE
RETINUES
RETINULA
RETINULAE
RETINULAR
RETIRACIES
RETIRACY
RETIRAL
RETIRALS
RETIRE
RETIRED
RETIREDLY
RETIREE
RETIREES
RETIRER
RETIRERS
RETIRES
RETIRING
RETITLE
RETITLED
RETITLES
RETITLING
RETOLD
RETOOK
RETOOL
RETOOLED
RETOOLING
RETOOLS
RETORSION
RETORSIONS
RETORT
RETORTED
RETORTER
RETORTERS
RETORTING
RETORTION
RETORTIONS
RETORTIVE
RETORTS
RETOUCH
RETOUCHED
RETOUCHER
RETOUCHERS
RETOUCHES

RETOUCHING
RETOUR
RETOURED
RETOURING
RETOURS
RETRACE
RETRACED
RETRACES
RETRACING
RETRACT
RETRACTED
RETRACTING
RETRACTOR
RETRACTORS
RETRACTS
RETRAICT
RETRAICTS
RETRAIN
RETRAINED
RETRAINING
RETRAINS
RETRAIT
RETRAITE
RETRAITES
RETRAITS
RETRAITT
RETRAITTS
RETRAL
RETRALLY
RETRATE
RETRATED
RETRATES
RETRATING
RETREAD
RETREADED
RETREADING
RETREADS
RETREAT
RETREATED
RETREATING
RETREATS
RETREE
RETREES
RETRENCH
RETRENCHED
RETRENCHES
RETRENCHING
RETRIAL
RETRIALS
RETRIBUTE
RETRIBUTED
RETRIBUTES
RETRIBUTING
RETRIED
RETRIES
RETRIEVAL
RETRIEVALS
RETRIEVE
RETRIEVED
RETRIEVER
RETRIEVERS
RETRIEVES
RETRIEVING
RETRIEVINGS
RETRIM
RETRIMMED
RETRIMMING

The Chambers Dictionary is the authority for many longer words; see *OSW* Introduction, page xii.

RETRIMS	REUNIONS	REVERBING	REVIEWAL	REVOLVES
RETRO	REUNITE	REVERBS	REVIEWALS	REVOLVING
RETROACT	REUNITED	REVERE	REVIEWED	REVOLVINGS
RETROACTED	REUNITES	REVERED	REVIEWER	REVS
RETROACTING	REUNITING	REVERENCE	REVIEWERS	REVUE
RETROACTS	REURGE	REVERENCED	REVIEWING	REVUES
RETROCEDE	REURGED	REVERENCES	REVIEWS	REVULSION
RETROCEDED	REURGES	REVERENCING	REVILE	REVULSIONS
RETROCEDES	REURGING	REVEREND	REVILED	REVULSIVE
RETROCEDING	REUSABLE	REVERENDS	REVILER	REVVED
RETROD	REUSE	REVERENT	REVILERS	REVVING
RETRODDEN	REUSED	REVERER	REVILES	REVYING
RETROFIT	REUSES	REVERERS	REVILING	REW
RETROFITS	REUSING	REVERES	REVILINGS	REWARD
RETROFITTED	REUTTER	REVERIE	REVISABLE	REWARDED
RETROFITTING	REUTTERED	REVERIES	REVISAL	REWARDER
RETROFITTINGS	REUTTERING	REVERING	REVISALS	REWARDERS
RETROFLEX	REUTTERS	REVERIST	REVISE	REWARDFUL
RETROJECT	REV	REVERISTS	REVISED	REWARDING
RETROJECTED	REVALENTA	REVERS	REVISER	REWARDS
RETROJECTING	REVALENTAS	REVERSAL	REVISERS	REWAREWA
RETROJECTS	REVALUE	REVERSALS	REVISES	REWAREWAS
RETRORSE	REVALUED	REVERSE	REVISING	REWEIGH
RETROS	REVALUES	REVERSED	REVISION	REWEIGHED
RETROUSSE	REVALUING	REVERSELY	REVISIONS	REWEIGHING
RETROVERT	REVAMP	REVERSER	REVISIT	REWEIGHS
RETROVERTED	REVAMPED	REVERSERS	REVISITED	REWIND
RETROVERTING	REVAMPING	REVERSES	REVISITING	REWINDING
RETROVERTS	REVAMPS	REVERSI	REVISITS	REWINDS
RETRY	REVANCHE	REVERSING	REVISOR	REWIRE
RETRYING	REVANCHES	REVERSINGS	REVISORS	REWIRED
RETS	REVEAL	REVERSION	REVISORY	REWIRES
RETSINA	REVEALED	REVERSIONS	REVIVABLE	REWIRING
RETSINAS	REVEALER	REVERSIS	REVIVABLY	REWORD
RETTED	REVEALERS	REVERSISES	REVIVAL	REWORDED
RETTERIES	REVEALING	REVERSO	REVIVALS	REWORDING
RETTERY	REVEALINGS	REVERSOS	REVIVE	REWORDS
RETTING	REVEALS	REVERT	REVIVED	REWORK
RETUND	REVEILLE	REVERTED	REVIVER	REWORKED
RETUNDED	REVEILLES	REVERTING	REVIVERS	REWORKING
RETUNDING	REVEL	REVERTIVE	REVIVES	REWORKS
RETUNDS	REVELATOR	REVERTS	REVIVIFIED	REWOUND
RETUNE	REVELATORS	REVERY	REVIVIFIES	REWRAP
RETUNED	REVELLED	REVEST	REVIVIFY	REWRAPPED
RETUNES	REVELLER	REVESTED	REVIVIFYING	REWRAPPING
RETUNING	REVELLERS	REVESTING	REVIVING	REWRAPS
RETURF	REVELLING	REVESTRIES	REVIVINGS	REWRITE
RETURFED	REVELLINGS	REVESTRY	REVIVOR	REWRITES
RETURFING	REVELRIES	REVESTS	REVIVORS	REWRITING
RETURFS	REVELRY	REVET	REVOCABLE	REWRITTEN
RETURN	REVELS	REVETMENT	REVOCABLY	REWROTE
RETURNED	REVENANT	REVETMENTS	REVOKABLE	REWS
RETURNEE	REVENANTS	REVETS	REVOKE	REWTH
RETURNEES	REVENGE	REVETTED	REVOKED	REWTHS
RETURNER	REVENGED	REVETTING	REVOKES	REX
RETURNERS	REVENGER	REVEUR	REVOKING	REYNARD
RETURNIK	REVENGERS	REVEURS	REVOLT	REYNARDS
RETURNIKS	REVENGES	REVEUSE	REVOLTED	REZ
RETURNING	REVENGING	REVEUSES	REVOLTER	REZONE
RETURNS	REVENGINGS	REVICTUAL	REVOLTERS	REZONED
RETUSE	REVENGIVE	REVICTUALLED	REVOLTING	REZONES
RETYING	REVENUE	REVICTUALLING	REVOLTS	REZONING
REUNIFIED	REVENUED	REVICTUALS	REVOLUTE	REZZES
REUNIFIES	REVENUES	REVIE	REVOLVE	RHABDOID
REUNIFY	REVERABLE	REVIED	REVOLVED	RHABDOIDS
REUNIFYING	REVERB	REVIES	REVOLVER	RHABDOM
REUNION	REVERBED	REVIEW	REVOLVERS	RHABDOMS

The Chambers Dictionary is the authority for many longer words; see *OSW* Introduction, page xii.

RHABDUS	RHEUMS	RHODOPSINS	RHYTHM	RIBLET
RHABDUSES	RHEUMY	RHODORA	RHYTHMAL	RIBLETS
RHACHIDES	RHEXES	RHODORAS	RHYTHMED	RIBLIKE
RHACHIS	RHEXIS	RHODOUS	RHYTHMI	RIBOSE
RHACHISES	RHEXISES	RHODY	RHYTHMIC	RIBOSES
RHACHITIS	RHIES	RHOEADINE	RHYTHMICS	RIBOSOMAL
RHACHITISES	RHIME	RHOEADINES	RHYTHMISE	RIBOSOME
RHAGADES	RHIMES	RHOMB	RHYTHMISED	RIBOSOMES
RHAMPHOID	RHINAL	RHOMBI	RHYTHMISES	RIBOZYME
RHAPHE	RHINE	RHOMBIC	RHYTHMISING	RIBOZYMES
RHAPHES	RHINES	RHOMBOI	RHYTHMIST	RIBS
RHAPHIDE	RHINITIS	RHOMBOID	RHYTHMISTS	RIBSTON
RHAPHIDES	RHINITISES	RHOMBOIDS	RHYTHMIZE	RIBSTONE
RHAPHIS	RHINO	RHOMBOS	RHYTHMIZED	RIBSTONES
RHAPONTIC	RHINOLITH	RHOMBS	RHYTHMIZES	RIBSTONS
RHAPONTICS	RHINOLITHS	RHOMBUS	RHYTHMIZING	RIBWORK
RHAPSODE	RHINOLOGIES	RHOMBUSES	RHYTHMS	RIBWORKS
RHAPSODES	RHINOLOGY	RHONCHAL	RHYTHMUS	RIBWORT
RHAPSODIC	RHINOS	RHONCHI	RHYTHMUSES	RIBWORTS
RHAPSODIES	RHIPIDATE	RHONCHIAL	RHYTINA	RICE
RHAPSODY	RHIPIDION	RHONCHUS	RHYTINAS	RICED
RHATANIES	RHIPIDIONS	RHONE	RHYTON	RICEGRAIN
RHATANY	RHIPIDIUM	RHONES	RIA	RICEGRAINS
RHEA	RHIPIDIUMS	RHOPALIC	RIAL	RICER
RHEAS	RHIZIC	RHOPALISM	RIALS	RICERCAR
RHEMATIC	RHIZINE	RHOPALISMS	RIANCIES	RICERCARE
RHENIUM	RHIZINES	RHOS	RIANCY	RICERCARES
RHENIUMS	RHIZOBIA	RHOTACISE	RIANT	RICERCARS
RHEOCHORD	RHIZOBIUM	RHOTACISED	RIAS	RICERCATA
RHEOCHORDS	RHIZOCARP	RHOTACISES	RIATA	RICERCATAS
RHEOCORD	RHIZOCARPS	RHOTACISING	RIATAS	RICERS
RHEOCORDS	RHIZOCAUL	RHOTACISM	RIB	RICES
RHEOLOGIC	RHIZOCAULS	RHOTACISMS	RIBALD	RICEY
RHEOLOGIES	RHIZOID	RHOTACIZE	RIBALDRIES	RICH
RHEOLOGY	RHIZOIDAL	RHOTACIZED	RIBALDRY	RICHED
RHEOMETER	RHIZOIDS	RHOTACIZES	RIBALDS	RICHEN
RHEOMETERS	RHIZOME	RHOTACIZING	RIBAND	RICHENED
RHEOSTAT	RHIZOMES	RHOTIC	RIBANDS	RICHENING
RHEOSTATS	RHIZOPI	RHUBARB	RIBATTUTA	RICHENS
RHEOTAXES	RHIZOPOD	RHUBARBS	RIBATTUTAS	RICHER
RHEOTAXIS	RHIZOPODS	RHUBARBY	RIBAUD	RICHES
RHEOTOME	RHIZOPUS	RHUMB	RIBAUDRED	RICHESSE
RHEOTOMES	RHIZOPUSES	RHUMBA	RIBAUDRIES	RICHESSES
RHEOTROPE	RHO	RHUMBAED	RIBAUDRY	RICHEST
RHEOTROPES	RHODAMINE	RHUMBAING	RIBAUDS	RICHING
RHESUS	RHODAMINES	RHUMBAS	RIBBAND	RICHLY
RHESUSES	RHODANATE	RHUMBS	RIBBANDS	RICHNESS
RHETOR	RHODANATES	RHUS	RIBBED	RICHNESSES
RHETORIC	RHODANIC	RHUSES	RIBBIER	RICHT
RHETORICS	RHODANISE	RHY	RIBBIEST	RICHTED
RHETORISE	RHODANISED	RHYME	RIBBING	RICHTER
RHETORISED	RHODANISES	RHYMED	RIBBINGS	RICHTEST
RHETORISES	RHODANISING	RHYMELESS	RIBBON	RICHTING
RHETORISING	RHODANIZE	RHYMER	RIBBONED	RICHTS
RHETORIZE	RHODANIZED	RHYMERS	RIBBONING	RICIER
RHETORIZED	RHODANIZES	RHYMES	RIBBONRIES	RICIEST
RHETORIZES	RHODANIZING	RHYMESTER	RIBBONRY	RICIN
RHETORIZING	RHODIC	RHYMESTERS	RIBBONS	RICING
RHETORS	RHODIE	RHYMING	RIBBONY	RICINS
RHEUM	RHODIES	RHYMIST	RIBBY	RICK
RHEUMATIC	RHODIUM	RHYMISTS	RIBCAGE	RICKED
RHEUMATICS	RHODIUMS	RHYNE	RIBCAGES	RICKER
RHEUMATIZ	RHODOLITE	RHYNES	RIBIBE	RICKERS
RHEUMATIZES	RHODOLITES	RHYOLITE	RIBIBES	RICKETILY
RHEUMED	RHODONITE	RHYOLITES	RIBIBLE	RICKETS
RHEUMIER	RHODONITES	RHYOLITIC	RIBIBLES	RICKETTY
RHEUMIEST	RHODOPSIN	RHYTA	RIBLESS	RICKETY

The Chambers Dictionary is the authority for many longer words; see *OSW* Introduction, page xii.

RICKING	RIDGINGS	RIGGERS	RIGOROUS	RINGBONE
RICKLE	RIDGLING	RIGGING	RIGORS	RINGBONES
RICKLES	RIDGLINGS	RIGGINGS	RIGOUR	RINGED
RICKLY	RIDGY	RIGGISH	RIGOURS	RINGENT
RICKS	RIDICULE	RIGGS	RIGS	RINGER
RICKSHA	RIDICULED	RIGHT	RIGWIDDIE	RINGERS
RICKSHAS	RIDICULER	RIGHTABLE	RIGWIDDIES	RINGGIT
RICKSHAW	RIDICULERS	RIGHTED	RIGWOODIE	RINGGITS
RICKSHAWS	RIDICULES	RIGHTEN	RIGWOODIES	RINGHALS
RICKSTAND	RIDICULING	RIGHTENED	RIJSTAFEL	RINGHALSES
RICKSTANDS	RIDING	RIGHTENING	RIJSTAFELS	RINGING
RICKSTICK	RIDINGS	RIGHTENS	RIKISHI	RINGINGLY
RICKSTICKS	RIDOTTO	RIGHTEOUS	RILE	RINGINGS
RICKYARD	RIDOTTOS	RIGHTER	RILED	RINGLESS
RICKYARDS	RIDS	RIGHTERS	RILES	RINGLET
RICOCHET	RIEL	RIGHTEST	RILEY	RINGLETED
RICOCHETED	RIELS	RIGHTFUL	RILIER	RINGLETS
RICOCHETING	RIEM	RIGHTING	RILIEST	RINGMAN
RICOCHETS	RIEMPIE	RIGHTINGS	RILIEVI	RINGMEN
RICOCHETTED	RIEMPIES	RIGHTISH	RILIEVO	RINGS
RICOCHETTING	RIEMS	RIGHTIST	RILING	RINGSIDE
RICOTTA	RIEVE	RIGHTISTS	RILL	RINGSIDER
RICOTTAS	RIEVER	RIGHTLESS	RILLE	RINGSIDERS
RICTAL	RIEVERS	RIGHTLY	RILLED	RINGSIDES
RICTUS	RIEVES	RIGHTNESS	RILLES	RINGSTAND
RICTUSES	RIEVING	RIGHTNESSES	RILLET	RINGSTANDS
RICY	RIFE	RIGHTO	RILLETS	RINGSTER
RID	RIFELY	RIGHTOS	RILLETTES	RINGSTERS
RIDABLE	RIFENESS	RIGHTS	RILLING	RINGTAIL
RIDDANCE	RIFENESSES	RIGHTWARD	RILLMARK	RINGTAILS
RIDDANCES	RIFER	RIGHTWARDS	RILLMARKS	RINGWAY
RIDDED	RIFEST	RIGID	RILLS	RINGWAYS
RIDDEN	RIFF	RIGIDER	RIM	RINGWISE
RIDDER	RIFFLE	RIGIDEST	RIMA	RINGWORK
RIDDERS	RIFFLED	RIGIDIFIED	RIMAE	RINGWORKS
RIDDING	RIFFLER	RIGIDIFIES	RIME	RINGWORM
RIDDLE	RIFFLERS	RIGIDIFY	RIMED	RINGWORMS
RIDDLED	RIFFLES	RIGIDIFYING	RIMER	RINK
RIDDLER	RIFFLING	RIGIDISE	RIMERS	RINKED
RIDDLERS	RIFFS	RIGIDISED	RIMES	RINKHALS
RIDDLES	RIFLE	RIGIDISES	RIMIER	RINKHALSES
RIDDLING	RIFLED	RIGIDISING	RIMIEST	RINKING
RIDDLINGS	RIFLEMAN	RIGIDITIES	RIMING	RINKS
RIDE	RIFLEMEN	RIGIDITY	RIMLESS	RINNING
RIDEABLE	RIFLER	RIGIDIZE	RIMMED	RINS
RIDENT	RIFLERS	RIGIDIZED	RIMMING	RINSABLE
RIDER	RIFLES	RIGIDIZES	RIMMINGS	RINSE
RIDERED	RIFLING	RIGIDIZING	RIMOSE	RINSEABLE
RIDERLESS	RIFLINGS	RIGIDLY	RIMOUS	RINSED
RIDERS	RIFT	RIGIDNESS	RIMS	RINSER
RIDES	RIFTE	RIGIDNESSES	RIMU	RINSERS
RIDGE	RIFTED	RIGIDS	RIMUS	RINSES
RIDGEBACK	RIFTIER	RIGLIN	RIMY	RINSIBLE
RIDGEBACKS	RIFTIEST	RIGLING	RIN	RINSING
RIDGED	RIFTING	RIGLINGS	RIND	RINSINGS
RIDGEL	RIFTLESS	RIGLINS	RINDED	RIOT
RIDGELS	RIFTS	RIGMAROLE	RINDIER	RIOTED
RIDGER	RIFTY	RIGMAROLES	RINDIEST	RIOTER
RIDGERS	RIG	RIGOL	RINDING	RIOTERS
RIDGES	RIGADOON	RIGOLL	RINDLESS	RIOTING
RIDGEWAY	RIGADOONS	RIGOLLS	RINDS	RIOTINGS
RIDGEWAYS	RIGATONI	RIGOLS	RINDY	RIOTISE
RIDGIER	RIGG	RIGOR	RINE	RIOTISES
RIDGIEST	RIGGALD	RIGORISM	RINES	RIOTIZE
RIDGIL	RIGGALDS	RIGORISMS	RING	RIOTIZES
RIDGILS	RIGGED	RIGORIST	RINGBIT	RIOTOUS
RIDGING	RIGGER	RIGORISTS	RINGBITS	RIOTOUSLY

The Chambers Dictionary is the authority for many longer words; see *OSW* Introduction, page xii.

RIOTRIES	RISHI	RITZIEST	RIVIERE	ROAMINGS
RIOTRY	RISHIS	RITZY	RIVIERES	ROAMS
RIOTS	RISIBLE	RIVA	RIVING	ROAN
RIP	RISING	RIVAGE	RIVLIN	ROANS
RIPARIAL	RISINGS	RIVAGES	RIVLINS	ROAR
RIPARIAN	RISK	RIVAL	RIVO	ROARED
RIPARIANS	RISKED	RIVALESS	RIVOS	ROARER
RIPE	RISKER	RIVALESSES	RIVULET	ROARERS
RIPECK	RISKERS	RIVALISE	RIVULETS	ROARIE
RIPECKS	RISKFUL	RIVALISED	RIYAL	ROARIER
RIPED	RISKIER	RIVALISES	RIYALS	ROARIEST
RIPELY	RISKIEST	RIVALISING	RIZ	ROARING
RIPEN	RISKILY	RIVALITIES	RIZA	ROARINGLY
RIPENED	RISKINESS	RIVALITY	RIZARD	ROARINGS
RIPENESS	RISKINESSES	RIVALIZE	RIZARDS	ROARS
RIPENESSES	RISKING	RIVALIZED	RIZAS	ROARY
RIPENING	RISKS	RIVALIZES	RIZZAR	ROAST
RIPENS	RISKY	RIVALIZING	RIZZARED	ROASTED
RIPER	RISOLUTO	RIVALLED	RIZZARING	ROASTER
RIPERS	RISOTTO	RIVALLESS	RIZZARS	ROASTERS
RIPES	RISOTTOS	RIVALLING	RIZZART	ROASTING
RIPEST	RISP	RIVALRIES	RIZZARTS	ROASTINGS
RIPIENI	RISPED	RIVALRY	RIZZER	ROASTS
RIPIENIST	RISPETTI	RIVALS	RIZZERED	ROATE
RIPIENISTS	RISPETTO	RIVALSHIP	RIZZERING	ROATED
RIPIENO	RISPING	RIVALSHIPS	RIZZERS	ROATES
RIPIENOS	RISPINGS	RIVAS	RIZZOR	ROATING
RIPING	RISPS	RIVE	RIZZORED	ROB
RIPOSTE	RISQUE	RIVED	RIZZORING	ROBALO
RIPOSTED	RISQUES	RIVEL	RIZZORS	ROBALOS
RIPOSTES	RISSOLE	RIVELLED	ROACH	ROBBED
RIPOSTING	RISSOLES	RIVELLING	ROACHED	ROBBER
RIPP	RISUS	RIVELS	ROACHES	ROBBERIES
RIPPED	RISUSES	RIVEN	ROACHING	ROBBERS
RIPPER	RIT	RIVER	ROAD	ROBBERY
RIPPERS	RITE	RIVERAIN	ROADBLOCK	ROBBING
RIPPIER	RITELESS	RIVERAINS	ROADBLOCKS	ROBE
RIPPIERS	RITENUTO	RIVERBANK	ROADCRAFT	ROBED
RIPPING	RITENUTOS	RIVERBANKS	ROADCRAFTS	ROBES
RIPPINGLY	RITES	RIVERED	ROADHOUSE	ROBIN
RIPPLE	RITORNEL	RIVERET	ROADHOUSES	ROBING
RIPPLED	RITORNELL	RIVERETS	ROADIE	RODINGS
RIPPLER	RITORNELLS	RIVERINE	ROADIES	ROBINIA
RIPPLERS	RITORNELS	RIVERLESS	ROADING	ROBINIAS
RIPPLES	RITS	RIVERLIKE	ROADINGS	ROBINS
RIPPLET	RITT	RIVERMAN	ROADLESS	ROBLE
RIPPLETS	RITTED	RIVERMEN	ROADMAN	ROBLES
RIPPLIER	RITTER	RIVERS	ROADMEN	ROBORANT
RIPPLIEST	RITTERS	RIVERSIDE	ROADS	ROBORANTS
RIPPLING	RITTING	RIVERSIDES	ROADSHOW	ROBOT
RIPPLINGS	RITTS	RIVERWAY	ROADSHOWS	ROBOTIC
RIPPLY	RITUAL	RIVERWAYS	ROADSIDE	ROBOTICS
RIPPS	RITUALISE	RIVERWEED	ROADSIDES	ROBOTISE
RIPRAP	RITUALISED	RIVERWEEDS	ROADSMAN	ROBOTISED
RIPRAPS	RITUALISES	RIVERY	ROADSMEN	ROBOTISES
RIPS	RITUALISING	RIVES	ROADSTEAD	ROBOTISING
RIPSTOP	RITUALISM	RIVET	ROADSTEADS	ROBOTIZE
RIPT	RITUALISMS	RIVETED	ROADSTER	ROBOTIZED
RIPTIDE	RITUALIST	RIVETER	ROADSTERS	ROBOTIZES
RIPTIDES	RITUALISTS	RIVETERS	ROADWAY	ROBOTIZING
RISALDAR	RITUALIZE	RIVETING	ROADWAYS	ROBOTS
RISALDARS	RITUALIZED	RIVETINGS	ROADWORKS	ROBS
RISE	RITUALIZES	RIVETS	ROAM	ROBURITE
RISEN	RITUALIZING	RIVETTED	ROAMED	ROBURITES
RISER	RITUALLY	RIVETTING	ROAMER	ROBUST
RISERS	RITUALS	RIVIERA	ROAMERS	ROBUSTA
RISES	RITZIER	RIVIERAS	ROAMING	ROBUSTAS

The Chambers Dictionary is the authority for many longer words; see *OSW* Introduction, page xii.

ROBUSTER
ROBUSTEST
ROBUSTLY
ROC
ROCAILLE
ROCAILLES
ROCAMBOLE
ROCAMBOLES
ROCH
ROCHES
ROCHET
ROCHETS
ROCK
ROCKAWAY
ROCKAWAYS
ROCKCRESS
ROCKCRESSES
ROCKED
ROCKER
ROCKERIES
ROCKERS
ROCKERY
ROCKET
ROCKETED
ROCKETEER
ROCKETEERS
ROCKETER
ROCKETERS
ROCKETING
ROCKETRIES
ROCKETRY
ROCKETS
ROCKFISH
ROCKFISHES
ROCKIER
ROCKIERS
ROCKIEST
ROCKILY
ROCKINESS
ROCKINESSES
ROCKING
ROCKINGS
ROCKLAY
ROCKLAYS
ROCKLING
ROCKLINGS
ROCKS
ROCKWATER
ROCKWATERS
ROCKWEED
ROCKWEEDS
ROCKWORK
ROCKWORKS
ROCKY
ROCOCO
ROCOCOS
ROCQUET
ROCQUETS
ROCS
ROD
RODDED
RODDING
RODDINGS
RODE
RODED
RODENT
RODENTS

RODEO
RODEOS
RODES
RODEWAY
RODEWAYS
RODFISHER
RODFISHERS
RODGERSIA
RODGERSIAS
RODING
RODINGS
RODLESS
RODLIKE
RODMAN
RODMEN
RODS
RODSMAN
RODSMEN
RODSTER
RODSTERS
ROE
ROEBUCK
ROEBUCKS
ROED
ROEMER
ROEMERS
ROENTGEN
ROENTGENS
ROES
ROESTONE
ROESTONES
ROGATION
ROGATIONS
ROGATORY
ROGER
ROGERED
ROGERING
ROGERINGS
ROGERS
ROGUE
ROGUED
ROGUERIES
ROGUERY
ROGUES
ROGUESHIP
ROGUESHIPS
ROGUING
ROGUISH
ROGUISHLY
ROGUY
ROIL
ROILED
ROILIER
ROILIEST
ROILING
ROILS
ROILY
ROIN
ROINED
ROINING
ROINISH
ROINS
ROIST
ROISTED
ROISTER
ROISTERED
ROISTERER

ROISTERERS
ROISTERING
ROISTERINGS
ROISTERS
ROISTING
ROISTS
ROJI
ROJIS
ROK
ROKE
ROKED
ROKELAY
ROKELAYS
ROKER
ROKERS
ROKES
ROKIER
ROKIEST
ROKING
ROKKAKU
ROKS
ROKY
ROLAG
ROLAGS
ROLE
ROLES
ROLFER
ROLFERS
ROLFING
ROLFINGS
ROLL
ROLLABLE
ROLLED
ROLLER
ROLLERS
ROLLICK
ROLLICKED
ROLLICKING
ROLLICKINGS
ROLLICKS
ROLLING
ROLLINGS
ROLLMOP
ROLLMOPS
ROLLOCK
ROLLOCKS
ROLLOUT
ROLLOUTS
ROLLS
ROM
ROMA
ROMAGE
ROMAGES
ROMAIKA
ROMAIKAS
ROMAL
ROMALS
ROMAN
ROMANCE
ROMANCED
ROMANCER
ROMANCERS
ROMANCES
ROMANCING
ROMANCINGS
ROMANS
ROMANTIC

ROMANTICS
ROMAS
ROMAUNT
ROMAUNTS
ROMNEYA
ROMNEYAS
ROMP
ROMPED
ROMPER
ROMPERS
ROMPING
ROMPINGLY
ROMPISH
ROMPISHLY
ROMPS
RONCADOR
RONCADORS
RONDACHE
RONDACHES
RONDAVEL
RONDAVELS
RONDE
RONDEAU
RONDEAUX
RONDEL
RONDELS
RONDES
RONDINO
RONDINOS
RONDO
RONDOS
RONDURE
RONDURES
RONE
RONEO
RONEOED
RONEOING
RONEOS
RONES
RONG
RONGGENG
RONGGENGS
RONNE
RONNING
RONT
RONTE
RONTES
RONTGEN
RONTGENS
RONTS
RONYON
RONYONS
ROO
ROOD
ROODS
ROOF
ROOFED
ROOFER
ROOFERS
ROOFIER
ROOFIEST
ROOFING
ROOFINGS
ROOFLESS
ROOFLIKE
ROOFS
ROOFSCAPE

ROOFSCAPES
ROOFTOP
ROOFTOPS
ROOFTREE
ROOFTREES
ROOFY
ROOINEK
ROOINEKS
ROOK
ROOKED
ROOKERIES
ROOKERY
ROOKIE
ROOKIES
ROOKING
ROOKISH
ROOKS
ROOKY
ROOM
ROOMED
ROOMER
ROOMERS
ROOMETTE
ROOMETTES
ROOMFUL
ROOMFULS
ROOMIE
ROOMIER
ROOMIES
ROOMIEST
ROOMILY
ROOMINESS
ROOMINESSES
ROOMING
ROOMS
ROOMSOME
ROOMY
ROON
ROONS
ROOP
ROOPED
ROOPIER
ROOPIEST
ROOPING
ROOPIT
ROOPS
ROOPY
ROOS
ROOSA
ROOSAS
ROOSE
ROOSED
ROOSES
ROOSING
ROOST
ROOSTED
ROOSTER
ROOSTERS
ROOSTING
ROOSTS
ROOT
ROOTAGE
ROOTAGES
ROOTED
ROOTEDLY
ROOTER
ROOTERS

The Chambers Dictionary is the authority for many longer words; see *OSW* Introduction, page xii.

ROOTHOLD	RORTIEST	ROSIERE	ROTATOR	ROTUNDED
ROOTHOLDS	RORTING	ROSIERES	ROTATORS	ROTUNDER
ROOTIER	RORTS	ROSIERS	ROTATORY	ROTUNDEST
ROOTIES	RORTY	ROSIES	ROTAVATE	ROTUNDING
ROOTIEST	RORY	ROSIEST	ROTAVATED	ROTUNDITIES
ROOTING	ROSACE	ROSILY	ROTAVATES	ROTUNDITY
ROOTINGS	ROSACEA	ROSIN	ROTAVATING	ROTUNDLY
ROOTLE	ROSACEAS	ROSINATE	ROTAVATOR	ROTUNDS
ROOTLED	ROSACEOUS	ROSINATES	ROTAVATORS	ROTURIER
ROOTLES	ROSACES	ROSINED	ROTAVIRUS	ROTURIERS
ROOTLESS	ROSAKER	ROSINESS	ROTAVIRUSES	ROUBLE
ROOTLET	ROSAKERS	ROSINESSES	ROTCH	ROUBLES
ROOTLETS	ROSALIA	ROSING	ROTCHE	ROUCOU
ROOTLIKE	ROSALIAS	ROSINING	ROTCHES	ROUCOUS
ROOTLING	ROSARIAN	ROSINS	ROTCHIE	ROUE
ROOTS	ROSARIANS	ROSINY	ROTCHIES	ROUES
ROOTSIER	ROSARIES	ROSIT	ROTE	ROUGE
ROOTSIEST	ROSARIUM	ROSITED	ROTED	ROUGED
ROOTSTOCK	ROSARIUMS	ROSITING	ROTENONE	ROUGES
ROOTSTOCKS	ROSARY	ROSITS	ROTENONES	ROUGH
ROOTSY	ROSCID	ROSMARINE	ROTES	ROUGHAGE
ROOTY	ROSE	ROSMARINES	ROTGRASS	ROUGHAGES
ROPABLE	ROSEAL	ROSOGLIO	ROTGRASSES	ROUGHCAST
ROPE	ROSEATE	ROSOGLIOS	ROTGUT	ROUGHCASTED
ROPEABLE	ROSEBAY	ROSOLIO	ROTGUTS	ROUGHCASTING
ROPED	ROSEBAYS	ROSOLIOS	ROTHER	ROUGHCASTS
ROPER	ROSEBOWL	ROSSER	ROTHERS	ROUGHED
ROPERIES	ROSEBOWLS	ROSSERS	ROTI	ROUGHEN
ROPERS	ROSEBUD	ROST	ROTIFER	ROUGHENED
ROPERY	ROSEBUDS	ROSTED	ROTIFERAL	ROUGHENING
ROPES	ROSEBUSH	ROSTELLAR	ROTIFERS	ROUGHENS
ROPEWAY	ROSEBUSHES	ROSTELLUM	ROTING	ROUGHER
ROPEWAYS	ROSED	ROSTELLUMS	ROTIS	ROUGHERS
ROPEWORK	ROSEFINCH	ROSTER	ROTL	ROUGHEST
ROPEWORKS	ROSEFINCHES	ROSTERED	ROTLS	ROUGHIE
ROPEY	ROSEFISH	ROSTERING	ROTOGRAPH	ROUGHIES
ROPIER	ROSEFISHES	ROSTERINGS	ROTOGRAPHED	ROUGHING
ROPIEST	ROSEHIP	ROSTERS	ROTOGRAPHING	ROUGHISH
ROPILY	ROSEHIPS	ROSTING	ROTOGRAPHS	ROUGHLY
ROPINESS	ROSELESS	ROSTRA	ROTOLO	ROUGHNECK
ROPINESSES	ROSELIKE	ROSTRAL	ROTOLOS	ROUGHNECKED
ROPING	ROSELLA	ROSTRATE	ROTOR	ROUGHNECKING
ROPINGS	ROSELLAS	ROSTRATED	ROTORS	ROUGHNECKS
ROPY	ROSELLE	ROSTRUM	ROTOVATE	ROUGHNESS
ROQUE	ROSELLES	ROSTRUMS	ROTOVATED	ROUGHNESSES
ROQUES	ROSEMARIES	ROSTS	ROTOVATES	ROUGHS
ROQUET	ROSEMARY	ROSULA	ROTOVATING	ROUGHSHOD
ROQUETED	ROSEOLA	ROSULAS	ROTOVATOR	ROUGHT
ROQUETING	ROSEOLAS	ROSULATE	ROTOVATORS	ROUGHY
ROQUETS	ROSERIES	ROSY	ROTS	ROUGING
ROQUETTE	ROSERY	ROSYING	ROTTAN	ROUILLE
ROQUETTES	ROSES	ROT	ROTTANS	ROUILLES
RORAL	ROSET	ROTA	ROTTED	ROUL
RORE	ROSETED	ROTAL	ROTTEN	ROULADE
RORES	ROSETING	ROTAPLANE	ROTTENER	ROULADES
RORIC	ROSETS	ROTAPLANES	ROTTENEST	ROULE
RORID	ROSETTE	ROTARIES	ROTTENLY	ROULEAU
RORIE	ROSETTED	ROTARY	ROTTENS	ROULEAUS
RORIER	ROSETTES	ROTAS	ROTTER	ROULEAUX
RORIEST	ROSETTY	ROTATABLE	ROTTERS	ROULES
RORQUAL	ROSETY	ROTATE	ROTTING	ROULETTE
RORQUALS	ROSEWATER	ROTATED	ROTULA	ROULETTES
RORT	ROSEWATERS	ROTATES	ROTULAS	ROULS
RORTED	ROSEWOOD	ROTATING	ROTUND	ROUM
RORTER	ROSEWOODS	ROTATION	ROTUNDA	ROUMING
RORTERS	ROSIED	ROTATIONS	ROTUNDAS	ROUMINGS
RORTIER	ROSIER	ROTATIVE	ROTUNDATE	ROUMS

The Chambers Dictionary is the authority for many longer words; see *OSW* Introduction, page xii.

ROUNCE	ROUTER	ROWERS	ROZZERS	RUBIEST
ROUNCES	ROUTERS	ROWING	RUANA	RUBIFIED
ROUNCEVAL	ROUTES	ROWINGS	RUANAS	RUBIFIES
ROUNCEVALS	ROUTH	ROWLOCK	RUB	RUBIFY
ROUNCIES	ROUTHIE	ROWLOCKS	RUBAI	RUBIFYING
ROUNCY	ROUTHIER	ROWME	RUBAIYAT	RUBIN
ROUND	ROUTHIEST	ROWMES	RUBATI	RUBINE
ROUNDARCH	ROUTHS	ROWND	RUBATO	RUBINEOUS
ROUNDED	ROUTINE	ROWNDED	RUBATOS	RUBINES
ROUNDEL	ROUTINEER	ROWNDELL	RUBBED	RUBINS
ROUNDELAY	ROUTINEERS	ROWNDELLS	RUBBER	RUBIOUS
ROUNDELAYS	ROUTINELY	ROWNDING	RUBBERED	RUBLE
ROUNDELS	ROUTINES	ROWNDS	RUBBERING	RUBLES
ROUNDER	ROUTING	ROWS	RUBBERISE	RUBOUT
ROUNDERS	ROUTINGS	ROWT	RUBBERISED	RUBOUTS
ROUNDEST	ROUTINISE	ROWTED	RUBBERISES	RUBRIC
ROUNDHAND	ROUTINISED	ROWTH	RUBBERISING	RUBRICAL
ROUNDHANDS	ROUTINISES	ROWTHS	RUBBERIZE	RUBRICATE
ROUNDING	ROUTINISING	ROWTING	RUBBERIZED	RUBRICATED
ROUNDINGS	ROUTINISM	ROWTS	RUBBERIZES	RUBRICATES
ROUNDISH	ROUTINISMS	ROYAL	RUBBERIZING	RUBRICATING
ROUNDLE	ROUTINIST	ROYALET	RUBBERS	RUBRICIAN
ROUNDLES	ROUTINISTS	ROYALETS	RUBBERY	RUBRICIANS
ROUNDLET	ROUTINIZE	ROYALISE	RUBBET	RUBRICS
ROUNDLETS	ROUTINIZED	ROYALISED	RUBBING	RUBS
ROUNDLY	ROUTINIZES	ROYALISES	RUBBINGS	RUBSTONE
ROUNDNESS	ROUTINIZING	ROYALISING	RUBBISH	RUBSTONES
ROUNDNESSES	ROUTOUS	ROYALISM	RUBBISHED	RUBY
ROUNDS	ROUTOUSLY	ROYALISMS	RUBBISHES	RUBYING
ROUNDSMAN	ROUTS	ROYALIST	RUBBISHING	RUC
ROUNDSMEN	ROUX	ROYALISTS	RUBBISHLY	RUCHE
ROUNDURE	ROVE	ROYALIZE	RUBBISHY	RUCHED
ROUNDURES	ROVED	ROYALIZED	RUBBIT	RUCHES
ROUNDWORM	ROVER	ROYALIZES	RUBBLE	RUCHING
ROUNDWORMS	ROVERS	ROYALIZING	RUBBLES	RUCHINGS
ROUP	ROVES	ROYALLER	RUBBLIER	RUCK
ROUPED	ROVING	ROYALLEST	RUBBLIEST	RUCKED
ROUPIER	ROVINGLY	ROYALLY	RUBBLY	RUCKING
ROUPIEST	ROVINGS	ROYALS	RUBDOWN	RUCKLE
ROUPING	ROW	ROYALTIES	RUBDOWNS	RUCKLED
ROUPIT	ROWABLE	ROYALTY	RUBE	RUCKLES
ROUPS	ROWAN	ROYNE	RUBEFIED	RUCKLING
ROUPY	ROWANS	ROYNED	RUBEFIES	RUCKS
ROUSANT	ROWBOAT	ROYNES	RUBEFY	RUCKSACK
ROUSE	ROWBOATS	ROYNING	RUBEFYING	RUCKSACKS
ROUSED	ROWDEDOW	ROYNISH	RUBELLA	RUCKSEAT
ROUSEMENT	ROWDEDOWS	ROYST	RUBELLAN	RUCKSEATS
ROUSEMENTS	ROWDIER	ROYSTED	RUBELLANS	RUCKUS
ROUSER	ROWDIES	ROYSTER	RUBELLAS	RUCKUSES
ROUSERS	ROWDIEST	ROYSTERED	RUBELLITE	RUCOLA
ROUSES	ROWDILY	ROYSTERER	RUBELLITES	RUCOLAS
ROUSING	ROWDINESS	ROYSTERERS	RUBEOLA	RUCS
ROUSINGLY	ROWDINESSES	ROYSTERING	RUBEOLAS	RUCTATION
ROUSSETTE	ROWDY	ROYSTERS	RUBES	RUCTATIONS
ROUSSETTES	ROWDYDOW	ROYSTING	RUBESCENT	RUCTION
ROUST	ROWDYDOWS	ROYSTS	RUBICELLE	RUCTIONS
ROUSTED	ROWDYISH	ROZELLE	RUBICELLES	RUD
ROUSTER	ROWDYISM	ROZELLES	RUBICON	RUDAS
ROUSTERS	ROWDYISMS	ROZET	RUBICONED	RUDASES
ROUSTING	ROWED	ROZETED	RUBICONING	RUDBECKIA
ROUSTS	ROWEL	ROZETING	RUBICONS	RUDBECKIAS
ROUT	ROWELLED	ROZETS	RUBICUND	RUDD
ROUTE	ROWELLING	ROZIT	RUBIDIUM	RUDDED
ROUTED	ROWELS	ROZITED	RUBIDIUMS	RUDDER
ROUTEING	ROWEN	ROZITING	RUBIED	RUDDERS
ROUTEMAN	ROWENS	ROZITS	RUBIER	RUDDIED
ROUTEMEN	ROWER	ROZZER	RUBIES	RUDDIER

The Chambers Dictionary is the authority for many longer words; see *OSW* Introduction, page xii.

RUDDIES	RUFFS	RULESSE	RUMORING	RUNNER
RUDDIEST	RUFIYAA	RULIER	RUMOROUS	RUNNERS
RUDDILY	RUFIYAAS	RULIEST	RUMORS	RUNNET
RUDDINESS	RUFOUS	RULING	RUMOUR	RUNNETS
RUDDINESSES	RUG	RULINGS	RUMOURED	RUNNIER
RUDDING	RUGATE	RULLION	RUMOURER	RUNNIEST
RUDDLE	RUGBIES	RULLIONS	RUMOURERS	RUNNING
RUDDLED	RUGBY	RULLOCK	RUMOURING	RUNNINGLY
RUDDLEMAN	RUGELACH	RULLOCKS	RUMOURS	RUNNINGS
RUDDLEMEN	RUGGED	RULY	RUMP	RUNNION
RUDDLES	RUGGEDER	RUM	RUMPED	RUNNIONS
RUDDLING	RUGGEDEST	RUMAL	RUMPIES	RUNNY
RUDDOCK	RUGGEDISE	RUMALS	RUMPING	RUNRIG
RUDDOCKS	RUGGEDISED	RUMBA	RUMPLE	RUNRIGS
RUDDS	RUGGEDISES	RUMBAED	RUMPLED	RUNS
RUDDY	RUGGEDISING	RUMBAING	RUMPLES	RUNT
RUDDYING	RUGGEDIZE	RUMBAS	RUMPLESS	RUNTED
RUDE	RUGGEDIZED	RUMBELOW	RUMPLING	RUNTIER
RUDELY	RUGGEDIZES	RUMBELOWS	RUMPS	RUNTIEST
RUDENESS	RUGGEDIZING	RUMBLE	RUMPUS	RUNTISH
RUDENESSES	RUGGEDLY	RUMBLED	RUMPUSES	RUNTS
RUDER	RUGGELACH	RUMBLER	RUMPY	RUNTY
RUDERAL	RUGGER	RUMBLERS	RUMS	RUNWAY
RUDERALS	RUGGERS	RUMBLES	RUN	RUNWAYS
RUDERIES	RUGGIER	RUMBLIER	RUNABOUT	RUPEE
RUDERY	RUGGIEST	RUMBLIEST	RUNABOUTS	RUPEES
RUDES	RUGGING	RUMBLING	RUNAGATE	RUPIA
RUDESBIES	RUGGINGS	RUMBLINGS	RUNAGATES	RUPIAH
RUDESBY	RUGGY	RUMBLY	RUNAROUND	RUPIAHS
RUDEST	RUGOSE	RUMBO	RUNAROUNDS	RUPIAS
RUDIE	RUGOSELY	RUMBOS	RUNAWAY	RUPTURE
RUDIES	RUGOSITIES	RUME	RUNAWAYS	RUPTURED
RUDIMENT	RUGOSITY	RUMEN	RUNBACK	RUPTURES
RUDIMENTS	RUGOUS	RUMES	RUNBACKS	RUPTURING
RUDISH	RUGS	RUMINA	RUNCH	RURAL
RUDS	RUGULOSE	RUMINANT	RUNCHES	RURALISE
RUE	RUIN	RUMINANTS	RUNCIBLE	RURALISED
RUED	RUINABLE	RUMINATE	RUNCINATE	RURALISES
RUEFUL	RUINATE	RUMINATED	RUND	RURALISING
RUEFULLY	RUINATED	RUMINATES	RUNDALE	RURALISM
RUEING	RUINATES	RUMINATING	RUNDALES	RURALISMS
RUEINGS	RUINATING	RUMINATOR	RUNDLE	RURALIST
RUELLE	RUINATION	RUMINATORS	RUNDLED	RURALISTS
RUELLES	RUINATIONS	RUMKIN	RUNDLES	RURALITIES
RUELLIA	RUINED	RUMKINS	RUNDLET	RURALITY
RUELLIAS	RUINER	RUMLY	RUNDLETS	RURALIZE
RUES	RUINERS	RUMMAGE	RUNDOWN	RURALIZED
RUFESCENT	RUING	RUMMAGED	RUNDOWNS	RURALIZES
RUFF	RUINGS	RUMMAGER	RUNDS	RURALIZING
RUFFE	RUINING	RUMMAGERS	RUNE	RURALLY
RUFFED	RUININGS	RUMMAGES	RUNECRAFT	RURALNESS
RUFFES	RUINOUS	RUMMAGING	RUNECRAFTS	RURALNESSES
RUFFIAN	RUINOUSLY	RUMMER	RUNED	RURALS
RUFFIANED	RUINS	RUMMERS	RUNES	RURP
RUFFIANING	RUKH	RUMMEST	RUNFLAT	RURPS
RUFFIANLY	RUKHS	RUMMIER	RUNG	RURU
RUFFIANS	RULABLE	RUMMIES	RUNGS	RURUS
RUFFIN	RULE	RUMMIEST	RUNIC	RUSA
RUFFING	RULED	RUMMILY	RUNKLE	RUSALKA
RUFFINS	RULELESS	RUMMINESS	RUNKLED	RUSALKAS
RUFFLE	RULER	RUMMINESSES	RUNKLES	RUSAS
RUFFLED	RULERED	RUMMISH	RUNKLING	RUSCUS
RUFFLER	RULERING	RUMMY	RUNLET	RUSCUSES
RUFFLERS	RULERS	RUMNESS	RUNLETS	RUSE
RUFFLES	RULERSHIP	RUMNESSES	RUNNABLE	RUSES
RUFFLING	RULERSHIPS	RUMOR	RUNNEL	RUSH
RUFFLINGS	RULES	RUMORED	RUNNELS	RUSHED

The Chambers Dictionary is the authority for many longer words; see *OSW* Introduction, page xii.

RUSHEE	RUSSIA	RUSTINESS	RUTHS	RYEBREAD
RUSHEES	RUSSIAS	RUSTINESSES	RUTILANT	RYEBREADS
RUSHEN	RUST	RUSTING	RUTILATED	RYEFLOUR
RUSHER	RUSTED	RUSTINGS	RUTILE	RYEFLOURS
RUSHERS	RUSTIC	RUSTLE	RUTILES	RYEPECK
RUSHES	RUSTICAL	RUSTLED	RUTIN	RYEPECKS
RUSHIER	RUSTICALS	RUSTLER	RUTINS	RYES
RUSHIEST	RUSTICATE	RUSTLERS	RUTS	RYFE
RUSHINESS	RUSTICATED	RUSTLES	RUTTED	RYKE
RUSHINESSES	RUSTICATES	RUSTLESS	RUTTER	RYKED
RUSHING	RUSTICATING	RUSTLING	RUTTERS	RYKES
RUSHLIGHT	RUSTICIAL	RUSTLINGS	RUTTIER	RYKING
RUSHLIGHTS	RUSTICISE	RUSTRE	RUTTIEST	RYMME
RUSHLIKE	RUSTICISED	RUSTRED	RUTTING	RYMMED
RUSHY	RUSTICISES	RUSTRES	RUTTINGS	RYMMES
RUSINE	RUSTICISING	RUSTS	RUTTISH	RYMMING
RUSK	RUSTICISM	RUSTY	RUTTY	RYND
RUSKS	RUSTICISMS	RUT	RYA	RYNDS
RUSMA	RUSTICITIES	RUTABAGA	RYAL	RYOKAN
RUSMAS	RUSTICITY	RUTABAGAS	RYALS	RYOKANS
RUSSEL	RUSTICIZE	RUTACEOUS	RYAS	RYOT
RUSSELS	RUSTICIZED	RUTH	RYBAT	RYOTS
RUSSET	RUSTICIZES	RUTHENIC	RYBATS	RYOTWARI
RUSSETED	RUSTICIZING	RUTHENIUM	RYBAUDRYE	RYOTWARIS
RUSSETING	RUSTICS	RUTHENIUMS	RYBAUDRYES	RYPE
RUSSETINGS	RUSTIER	RUTHFUL	RYBAULD	RYPECK
RUSSETS	RUSTIEST	RUTHFULLY	RYBAULDS	RYPECKS
RUSSETY	RUSTILY	RUTHLESS	RYE	RYPER

S

SAB	SABULOUS	SACRALISE	SADE	SAFROLES
SABADILLA	SABURRA	SACRALISED	SADES	SAFRONAL
SABADILLAS	SABURRAL	SACRALISES	SADHE	SAFRONALS
SABATON	SABURRAS	SACRALISING	SADHES	SAG
SABATONS	SAC	SACRALIZE	SADHU	SAGA
SABBAT	SACATON	SACRALIZED	SADHUS	SAGACIOUS
SABBATIC	SACATONS	SACRALIZES	SADIRON	SAGACITIES
SABBATICS	SACCADE	SACRALIZING	SADIRONS	SAGACITY
SABBATINE	SACCADES	SACRAMENT	SADISM	SAGAMAN
SABBATISE	SACCADIC	SACRAMENTED	SADISMS	SAGAMEN
SABBATISED	SACCATE	SACRAMENTING	SADIST	SAGAMORE
SABBATISES	SACCHARIC	SACRAMENTS	SADISTIC	SAGAMORES
SABBATISING	SACCHARIN	SACRARIA	SADISTS	SAGAPENUM
SABBATISM	SACCHARINS	SACRARIUM	SADLY	SAGAPENUMS
SABBATISMS	SACCHARUM	SACRED	SADNESS	SAGAS
SABBATIZE	SACCHARUMS	SACREDLY	SADNESSES	SAGATHIES
SABBATIZED	SACCIFORM	SACRIFICE	SADZA	SAGATHY
SABBATIZES	SACCOI	SACRIFICED	SADZAS	SAGE
SABBATIZING	SACCOS	SACRIFICES	SAE	SAGEBRUSH
SABBATS	SACCOSES	SACRIFICING	SAECULUM	SAGEBRUSHES
SABELLA	SACCULAR	SACRIFIDE	SAECULUMS	SAGELY
SABELLAS	SACCULATE	SACRIFIED	SAETER	SAGENE
SABER	SACCULE	SACRIFIES	SAETERS	SAGENES
SABERED	SACCULES	SACRIFY	SAFARI	SAGENESS
SABERING	SACCULI	SACRIFYING	SAFARIED	SAGENESSES
SABERS	SACCULUS	SACRILEGE	SAFARIING	SAGENITE
SABIN	SACELLA	SACRILEGES	SAFARIS	SAGENITES
SABINS	SACELLUM	SACRING	SAFARIST	SAGENITIC
SABKHA	SACHEM	SACRINGS	SAFARISTS	SAGER
SABKHAH	SACHEMDOM	SACRIST	SAFE	SAGES
SABKHAHS	SACHEMDOMS	SACRISTAN	SAFED	SAGEST
SABKHAS	SACHEMIC	SACRISTANS	SAFEGUARD	SAGGAR
SABKHAT	SACHEMS	SACRISTIES	SAFEGUARDED	SAGGARD
SABKHATS	SACHET	SACRISTS	SAFEGUARDING	SAGGARDS
SABLE	SACHETS	SACRISTY	SAFEGUARDS	SAGGARS
SABLED	SACK	SACRUM	SAFELY	SAGGED
SABLES	SACKAGE	SACS	SAFENESS	SAGGER
SABLING	SACKAGES	SAD	SAFENESSES	SAGGERS
SABOT	SACKBUT	SADDEN	SAFER	SAGGIER
SABOTAGE	SACKBUTS	SADDENED	SAFES	SAGGIEST
SABOTAGED	SACKCLOTH	SADDENING	SAFEST	SAGGING
SABOTAGES	SACKCLOTHS	SADDENS	SAFETIES	SAGGINGS
SABOTAGING	SACKED	SADDER	SAFETY	SAGGY
SABOTEUR	SACKER	SADDEST	SAFETYMAN	SAGIER
SABOTEURS	SACKERS	SADDHU	SAFETYMEN	SAGIEST
SABOTIER	SACKFUL	SADDHUS	SAFFIAN	SAGINATE
SABOTIERS	SACKFULS	SADDISH	SAFFIANS	SAGINATED
SABOTS	SACKING	SADDLE	SAFFLOWER	SAGINATES
SABRA	SACKINGS	SADDLEBAG	SAFFLOWERS	SAGINATING
SABRAS	SACKLESS	SADDLEBAGS	SAFFRON	SAGITTA
SABRE	SACKS	SADDLEBOW	SAFFRONED	SAGITTAL
SABRED	SACLESS	SADDLEBOWS	SAFFRONS	SAGITTARIES
SABRES	SACLIKE	SADDLED	SAFFRONY	SAGITTARY
SABREUR	SACQUE	SADDLER	SAFING	SAGITTAS
SABREURS	SACQUES	SADDLERIES	SAFRANIN	SAGITTATE
SABRING	SACRA	SADDLERS	SAFRANINE	SAGO
SABS	SACRAL	SADDLERY	SAFRANINES	SAGOIN
SABULINE	SACRALGIA	SADDLES	SAFRANINS	SAGOINS
SABULOSE	SACRALGIAS	SADDLING	SAFROLE	SAGOS

The Chambers Dictionary is the authority for many longer words; see *OSW* Introduction, page xii.

SAGOUIN	SAINFOINS	SALABLY	SALIENCE	SALOONS
SAGOUINS	SAINING	SALACIOUS	SALIENCES	SALOOP
SAGS	SAINS	SALACITIES	SALIENCIES	SALOOPS
SAGUARO	SAINT	SALACITY	SALIENCY	SALOP
SAGUAROS	SAINTDOM	SALAD	SALIENT	SALOPIAN
SAGUIN	SAINTDOMS	SALADE	SALIENTLY	SALOPS
SAGUINS	SAINTED	SALADES	SALIENTS	SALP
SAGUM	SAINTESS	SALADING	SALIFIED	SALPA
SAGY	SAINTESSES	SALADINGS	SALIFIES	SALPAE
SAHIB	SAINTFOIN	SALADS	SALIFY	SALPAS
SAHIBA	SAINTFOINS	SALAL	SALIFYING	SALPIAN
SAHIBAH	SAINTHOOD	SALALS	SALIGOT	SALPIANS
SAHIBAHS	SAINTHOODS	SALAMI	SALIGOTS	SALPICON
SAHIBAS	SAINTING	SALAMIS	SALIMETER	SALPICONS
SAHIBS	SAINTISH	SALAMON	SALIMETERS	SALPIFORM
SAI	SAINTISM	SALAMONS	SALINA	SALPINGES
SAIBLING	SAINTISMS	SALANGANE	SALINAS	SALPINX
SAIBLINGS	SAINTLIER	SALANGANES	SALINE	SALPINXES
SAIC	SAINTLIEST	SALARIAT	SALINES	SALPS
SAICE	SAINTLIKE	SALARIATS	SALINITIES	SALS
SAICES	SAINTLING	SALARIED	SALINITY	SALSA
SAICK	SAINTLINGS	SALARIES	SALIVA	SALSAED
SAICKS	SAINTLY	SALARY	SALIVAL	SALSAING
SAICS	SAINTS	SALARYING	SALIVARY	SALSAS
SAID	SAINTSHIP	SALARYMAN	SALIVAS	SALSE
SAIDEST	SAINTSHIPS	SALARYMEN	SALIVATE	SALSES
SAIDS	SAIQUE	SALBAND	SALIVATED	SALSIFIES
SAIDST	SAIQUES	SALBANDS	SALIVATES	SALSIFY
SAIGA	SAIR	SALCHOW	SALIVATING	SALT
SAIGAS	SAIRED	SALCHOWS	SALIX	SALTANDO
SAIKEI	SAIRER	SALE	SALLAD	SALTANT
SAIKEIS	SAIREST	SALEABLE	SALLADS	SALTANTS
SAIKLESS	SAIRING	SALEABLY	SALLAL	SALTATE
SAIL	SAIRS	SALEP	SALLALS	SALTATED
SAILABLE	SAIS	SALEPS	SALLE	SALTATES
SAILBOARD	SAIST	SALERATUS	SALLEE	SALTATING
SAILBOARDS	SAITH	SALERATUSES	SALLEES	SALTATION
SAILCLOTH	SAITHE	SALERING	SALLES	SALTATIONS
SAILCLOTHS	SAITHES	SALERINGS	SALLET	SALTATO
SAILED	SAITHS	SALEROOM	SALLETS	SALTATORY
SAILER	SAJOU	SALEROOMS	SALLIED	SALTBOX
SAILERS	SAJOUS	SALES	SALLIES	SALTBOXES
SAILFISH	SAKE	SALESMAN	SALLOW	SALTBUSH
SAILFISHES	SAKER	SALESMEN	SALLOWED	SALTBUSHES
SAILING	SAKERET	SALESROOM	SALLOWER	SALTCAT
SAILINGS	SAKERETS	SALESROOMS	SALLOWEST	SALTCATS
SAILLESS	SAKERS	SALET	SALLOWING	SALTCHUCK
SAILOR	SAKES	SALETS	SALLOWISH	SALTCHUCKS
SAILORING	SAKI	SALEWD	SALLOWS	SALTED
SAILORINGS	SAKIA	SALEYARD	SALLOWY	SALTER
SAILORLY	SAKIAS	SALEYARDS	SALLY	SALTERN
SAILORS	SAKIEH	SALFERN	SALLYING	SALTERNS
SAILPLANE	SAKIEHS	SALFERNS	SALLYPORT	SALTERS
SAILPLANED	SAKIS	SALIAUNCE	SALLYPORTS	SALTEST
SAILPLANES	SAKIYEH	SALIAUNCES	SALMI	SALTFISH
SAILPLANING	SAKIYEHS	SALIC	SALMIS	SALTFISHES
SAILROOM	SAKKOI	SALICES	SALMON	SALTIER
SAILROOMS	SAKKOS	SALICET	SALMONET	SALTIERS
SAILS	SAKKOSES	SALICETA	SALMONETS	SALTIEST
SAIM	SAKSAUL	SALICETS	SALMONID	SALTILY
SAIMIRI	SAKSAULS	SALICETUM	SALMONIDS	SALTINESS
SAIMIRIS	SAL	SALICETUMS	SALMONOID	SALTINESSES
SAIMS	SALAAM	SALICIN	SALMONOIDS	SALTING
SAIN	SALAAMED	SALICINE	SALMONS	SALTINGS
SAINE	SALAAMING	SALICINES	SALON	SALTIRE
SAINED	SALAAMS	SALICINS	SALONS	SALTIRES
SAINFOIN	SALABLE	SALICYLIC	SALOON	SALTISH

The Chambers Dictionary is the authority for many longer words; see *OSW* Introduction, page xii.

SALTISHLY	SAMAANS	SAMPIRES	SANDBOYS	SANGFROIDS
SALTLESS	SAMADHI	SAMPIS	SANDED	SANGLIER
SALTLY	SAMADHIS	SAMPLE	SANDER	SANGLIERS
SALTNESS	SAMAN	SAMPLED	SANDERS	SANGOMA
SALTNESSES	SAMANS	SAMPLER	SANDERSES	SANGOMAS
SALTO	SAMARA	SAMPLERIES	SANDFLIES	SANGRIA
SALTOED	SAMARAS	SAMPLERS	SANDFLY	SANGRIAS
SALTOING	SAMARIUM	SAMPLERY	SANDGLASS	SANGS
SALTOS	SAMARIUMS	SAMPLES	SANDGLASSES	SANGUIFIED
SALTPETER	SAMAS	SAMPLING	SANDHEAP	SANGUIFIES
SALTPETERS	SAMBA	SAMPLINGS	SANDHEAPS	SANGUIFY
SALTPETRE	SAMBAED	SAMPS	SANDHI	SANGUIFYING
SALTPETRES	SAMBAING	SAMSARA	SANDHILL	SANGUINE
SALTS	SAMBAL	SAMSARAS	SANDHILLS	SANGUINED
SALTUS	SAMBALS	SAMSHOO	SANDHIS	SANGUINES
SALTUSES	SAMBAR	SAMSHOOS	SANDIER	SANGUINING
SALTWATER	SAMBARS	SAMSHU	SANDIEST	SANICLE
SALTWORKS	SAMBAS	SAMSHUS	SANDINESS	SANICLES
SALTWORT	SAMBO	SAMURAI	SANDINESSES	SANIDINE
SALTWORTS	SAMBOS	SAN	SANDING	SANIDINES
SALTY	SAMBUCA	SANATIVE	SANDINGS	SANIES
SALUBRITIES	SAMBUCAS	SANATORIA	SANDIVER	SANIFIED
SALUBRITY	SAMBUR	SANATORY	SANDIVERS	SANIFIES
SALUE	SAMBURS	SANBENITO	SANDLING	SANIFY
SALUED	SAME	SANBENITOS	SANDLINGS	SANIFYING
SALUES	SAMEKH	SANCAI	SANDMAN	SANIOUS
SALUING	SAMEKHS	SANCAIS	SANDMEN	SANITARIA
SALUKI	SAMEL	SANCHO	SANDPAPER	SANITARY
SALUKIS	SAMELY	SANCHOS	SANDPAPERED	SANITATE
SALUTARY	SAMEN	SANCTA	SANDPAPERING	SANITATED
SALUTE	SAMENESS	SANCTIFIED	SANDPAPERS	SANITATES
SALUTED	SAMENESSES	SANCTIFIES	SANDPIPER	SANITATING
SALUTER	SAMES	SANCTIFY	SANDPIPERS	SANITIES
SALUTERS	SAMEY	SANCTIFYING	SANDPIT	SANITISE
SALUTES	SAMFOO	SANCTIFYINGS	SANDPITS	SANITISED
SALUTING	SAMFOOS	SANCTION	SANDPUMP	SANITISES
SALVABLE	SAMFU	SANCTIONED	SANDPUMPS	SANITISING
SALVAGE	SAMFUS	SANCTIONING	SANDS	SANITIZE
SALVAGED	SAMIEL	SANCTIONS	SANDSHOE	SANITIZED
SALVAGES	SAMIELS	SANCTITIES	SANDSHOES	SANITIZES
SALVAGING	SAMIER	SANCTITY	SANDSPOUT	SANITIZING
SALVARSAN	SAMIEST	SANCTUARIES	SANDSPOUTS	SANITY
SALVARSANS	SAMISEN	SANCTUARY	SANDSTONE	SANJAK
SALVATION	SAMISENS	SANCTUM	SANDSTONES	SANJAKS
SALVATIONS	SAMITE	SANCTUMS	SANDSTORM	SANK
SALVATORIES	SAMITES	SAND	SANDSTORMS	SANKO
SALVATORY	SAMITI	SANDAL	SANDWICH	SANKOS
SALVE	SAMITIS	SANDALLED	SANDWICHED	SANNIE
SALVED	SAMIZDAT	SANDALS	SANDWICHES	SANNIES
SALVER	SAMIZDATS	SANDARAC	SANDWICHING	SANNUP
SALVERS	SAMLET	SANDARACH	SANDWORM	SANNUPS
SALVES	SAMLETS	SANDARACHS	SANDWORMS	SANNYASI
SALVETE	SAMLOR	SANDARACS	SANDWORT	SANNYASIN
SALVETES	SAMLORS	SANDBAG	SANDWORTS	SANNYASINS
SALVIA	SAMNITIS	SANDBAGGED	SANDY	SANNYASIS
SALVIAS	SAMNITISES	SANDBAGGING	SANE	SANPAN
SALVIFIC	SAMOSA	SANDBAGS	SANELY	SANPANS
SALVING	SAMOSAS	SANDBANK	SANENESS	SANS
SALVINGS	SAMOVAR	SANDBANKS	SANENESSES	SANSA
SALVO	SAMOVARS	SANDBLAST	SANER	SANSAS
SALVOES	SAMP	SANDBLASTED	SANEST	SANSEI
SALVOR	SAMPAN	SANDBLASTING	SANG	SANSEIS
SALVORS	SAMPANS	SANDBLASTINGS	SANGAR	SANSERIF
SALVOS	SAMPHIRE	SANDBLASTS	SANGAREE	SANSERIFS
SAM	SAMPHIRES	SANDBOX	SANGAREES	SANT
SAMA	SAMPI	SANDBOXES	SANGARS	SANTAL
SAMAAN	SAMPIRE	SANDBOY	SANGFROID	SANTALIN

The Chambers Dictionary is the authority for many longer words; see *OSW* Introduction, page xii.

SANTALINS	SAPOTA	SARCODIC	SAROS	SATANG
SANTALS	SAPOTAS	SARCOID	SAROSES	SATANIC
SANTIR	SAPPAN	SARCOIDS	SARPANCH	SATANICAL
SANTIRS	SAPPANS	SARCOLOGIES	SARPANCHES	SATANISM
SANTOLINA	SAPPED	SARCOLOGY	SARRASIN	SATANISMS
SANTOLINAS	SAPPER	SARCOMA	SARRASINS	SATANITIES
SANTON	SAPPERS	SARCOMAS	SARRAZIN	SATANITY
SANTONICA	SAPPHIC	SARCOMATA	SARRAZINS	SATARA
SANTONICAS	SAPPHICS	SARCOMERE	SARS	SATARAS
SANTONIN	SAPPHIRE	SARCOMERES	SARSDEN	SATAY
SANTONINS	SAPPHIRED	SARCOPTIC	SARSDENS	SATAYS
SANTONS	SAPPHIRES	SARCOUS	SARSEN	SATCHEL
SANTOUR	SAPPHISM	SARD	SARSENET	SATCHELS
SANTOURS	SAPPHISMS	SARDANA	SARSENETS	SATE
SANTS	SAPPHIST	SARDANAS	SARSENS	SATED
SANTUR	SAPPHISTS	SARDEL	SARSNET	SATEDNESS
SANTURS	SAPPIER	SARDELLE	SARSNETS	SATEDNESSES
SAOUARI	SAPPIEST	SARDELLES	SARTOR	SATEEN
SAOUARIS	SAPPINESS	SARDELS	SARTORIAL	SATEENS
SAP	SAPPINESSES	SARDINE	SARTORIAN	SATELESS
SAPAJOU	SAPPING	SARDINES	SARTORII	SATELLES
SAPAJOUS	SAPPLE	SARDIUS	SARTORIUS	SATELLITE
SAPAN	SAPPLED	SARDIUSES	SARTORIUSES	SATELLITED
SAPANS	SAPPLES	SARDONIAN	SARTORS	SATELLITES
SAPANWOOD	SAPPLING	SARDONIC	SARUS	SATELLITING
SAPANWOODS	SAPPY	SARDONYX	SARUSES	SATES
SAPEGO	SAPRAEMIA	SARDONYXES	SASARARA	SATI
SAPEGOES	SAPRAEMIAS	SARDS	SASARARAS	SATIABLE
SAPELE	SAPRAEMIC	SARED	SASH	SATIATE
SAPELES	SAPROBE	SAREE	SASHAY	SATIATED
SAPFUL	SAPROBES	SAREES	SASHAYED	SATIATES
SAPHEAD	SAPROLITE	SARGASSO	SASHAYING	SATIATING
SAPHEADED	SAPROLITES	SARGASSOS	SASHAYS	SATIATION
SAPHEADS	SAPROPEL	SARGASSUM	SASHED	SATIATIONS
SAPHENA	SAPROPELS	SARGASSUMS	SASHES	SATIETIES
SAPHENAS	SAPROZOIC	SARGE	SASHIMI	SATIETY
SAPHENOUS	SAPS	SARGES	SASHIMIS	SATIN
SAPID	SAPSAGO	SARGO	SASHING	SATINED
SAPIDITIES	SAPSAGOS	SARGOS	SASIN	SATINET
SAPIDITY	SAPSUCKER	SARGOSES	SASINE	SATINETS
SAPIDLESS	SAPSUCKERS	SARGUS	SASINES	SATINETTA
SAPIDNESS	SAPUCAIA	SARGUSES	SASINS	SATINETTAS
SAPIDNESSES	SAPUCAIAS	SARI	SASKATOON	SATINETTE
SAPIENCE	SAPWOOD	SARIN	SASKATOONS	SATINETTES
SAPIENCES	SAPWOODS	SARING	SASQUATCH	SATING
SAPIENT	SAR	SARINS	SASQUATCHES	SATINING
SAPIENTLY	SARABAND	SARIS	SASS	SATINS
SAPLESS	SARABANDE	SARK	SASSABIES	SATINWOOD
SAPLING	SARABANDES	SARKIER	SASSABY	SATINWOODS
SAPLINGS	SARABANDS	SARKIEST	SASSAFRAS	SATINY
SAPODILLA	SARAFAN	SARKING	SASSAFRASES	SATIRE
SAPODILLAS	SARAFANS	SARKINGS	SASSARARA	SATIRES
SAPOGENIN	SARANGI	SARKS	SASSARARAS	SATIRIC
SAPOGENINS	SARANGIS	SARKY	SASSE	SATIRICAL
SAPONARIA	SARAPE	SARMENT	SASSED	SATIRISE
SAPONARIAS	SARAPES	SARMENTA	SASSES	SATIRISED
SAPONIFIED	SARBACANE	SARMENTS	SASSIER	SATIRISES
SAPONIFIES	SARBACANES	SARMENTUM	SASSIEST	SATIRISING
SAPONIFY	SARCASM	SARNEY	SASSING	SATIRIST
SAPONIFYING	SARCASMS	SARNEYS	SASSOLIN	SATIRISTS
SAPONIN	SARCASTIC	SARNIE	SASSOLINS	SATIRIZE
SAPONINS	SARCENET	SARNIES	SASSOLITE	SATIRIZED
SAPONITE	SARCENETS	SAROD	SASSOLITES	SATIRIZES
SAPONITES	SARCOCARP	SARODS	SASSY	SATIRIZING
SAPOR	SARCOCARPS	SARONG	SASTRUGA	SATIS
SAPOROUS	SARCODE	SARONGS	SASTRUGI	SATISFICE
SAPORS	SARCODES	SARONIC	SAT	SATISFICED

The Chambers Dictionary is the authority for many longer words; see *OSW* Introduction, page xii.

SATISFICES	SAUCILY	SAVAGERY	SAW	SAYING
SATISFICING	SAUCINESS	SAVAGES	SAWAH	SAYINGS
SATISFICINGS	SAUCINESSES	SAVAGEST	SAWAHS	SAYNE
SATISFIED	SAUCING	SAVAGING	SAWBILL	SAYON
SATISFIER	SAUCISSE	SAVAGISM	SAWBILLS	SAYONARA
SATISFIERS	SAUCISSES	SAVAGISMS	SAWBLADE	SAYONARAS
SATISFIES	SAUCISSON	SAVANNA	SAWBLADES	SAYONS
SATISFY	SAUCISSONS	SAVANNAH	SAWBONES	SAYS
SATISFYING	SAUCY	SAVANNAHS	SAWBUCK	SAYST
SATIVE	SAUFGARD	SAVANNAS	SAWBUCKS	SAYYID
SATORI	SAUFGARDS	SAVANT	SAWDER	SAYYIDS
SATORIS	SAUGER	SAVANTS	SAWDERED	SAZ
SATRAP	SAUGERS	SAVARIN	SAWDERING	SAZERAC®
SATRAPAL	SAUGH	SAVARINS	SAWDERS	SAZERACS
SATRAPIES	SAUGHS	SAVATE	SAWDUST	SAZES
SATRAPS	SAUL	SAVATES	SAWDUSTED	SAZHEN
SATRAPY	SAULGE	SAVE	SAWDUSTING	SAZHENS
SATSUMA	SAULGES	SAVED	SAWDUSTS	SAZZES
SATSUMAS	SAULIE	SAVEGARD	SAWDUSTY	SBIRRI
SATURABLE	SAULIES	SAVEGARDED	SAWED	SBIRRO
SATURANT	SAULS	SAVEGARDING	SAWER	SCAB
SATURANTS	SAULT	SAVEGARDS	SAWERS	SCABBARD
SATURATE	SAULTS	SAVELOY	SAWFISH	SCABBARDED
SATURATED	SAUNA	SAVELOYS	SAWFISHES	SCABBARDING
SATURATES	SAUNAS	SAVER	SAWHORSE	SCABBARDS
SATURATING	SAUNT	SAVERS	SAWHORSES	SCABBED
SATURATOR	SAUNTED	SAVES	SAWING	SCABBIER
SATURATORS	SAUNTER	SAVEY	SAWINGS	SCABBIEST
SATURNIC	SAUNTERED	SAVEYED	SAWMILL	SCABBING
SATURNIID	SAUNTERER	SAVEYING	SAWMILLS	SCABBLE
SATURNIIDS	SAUNTERERS	SAVEYS	SAWN	SCABBLED
SATURNINE	SAUNTERING	SAVIN	SAWNEY	SCABBLES
SATURNISM	SAUNTERINGS	SAVINE	SAWNEYS	SCABBLING
SATURNISMS	SAUNTERS	SAVINES	SAWPIT	SCABBY
SATURNIST	SAUNTING	SAVING	SAWPITS	SCABIES
SATURNISTS	SAUNTS	SAVINGLY	SAWS	SCABIOUS
SATYR	SAUREL	SAVINGS	SAWSHARK	SCABIOUSES
SATYRA	SAURELS	SAVINS	SAWSHARKS	SCABLANDS
SATYRAL	SAURIAN	SAVIOUR	SAWTEETH	SCABRID
SATYRALS	SAURIANS	SAVIOURS	SAWTOOTH	SCABROUS
SATYRAS	SAURIES	SAVOR	SAWYER	SCABS
SATYRESS	SAUROID	SAVORED	SAWYERS	SCAD
SATYRESSES	SAUROPOD	SAVORIES	SAX	SCADS
SATYRIC	SAUROPODS	SAVORING	SAXATILE	SCAFF
SATYRICAL	SAURY	SAVOROUS	SAXAUL	SCAFFIE
SATYRID	SAUSAGE	SAVORS	SAXAULS	SCAFFIES
SATYRIDS	SAUSAGES	SAVORY	SAXES	SCAFFOLD
SATYRISK	SAUT	SAVOUR	SAXHORN	SCAFFOLDED
SATYRISKS	SAUTE	SAVOURED	SAXHORNS	SCAFFOLDING
SATYRS	SAUTED	SAVOURIES	SAXIFRAGE	SCAFFOLDINGS
SAUBA	SAUTEED	SAVOURILY	SAXIFRAGES	SCAFFOLDS
SAUBAS	SAUTEEING	SAVOURING	SAXITOXIN	SCAFFS
SAUCE	SAUTEES	SAVOURLY	SAXITOXINS	SCAG
SAUCEBOX	SAUTEING	SAVOURS	SAXONIES	SCAGLIA
SAUCEBOXES	SAUTES	SAVOURY	SAXONITE	SCAGLIAS
SAUCED	SAUTING	SAVOY	SAXONITES	SCAGLIOLA
SAUCEPAN	SAUTOIR	SAVOYARD	SAXONY	SCAGLIOLAS
SAUCEPANS	SAUTOIRS	SAVOYARDS	SAXOPHONE	SCAGS
SAUCER	SAUTS	SAVOYS	SAXOPHONES	SCAIL
SAUCERFUL	SAVABLE	SAVVEY	SAY	SCAILED
SAUCERFULS	SAVAGE	SAVVEYED	SAYABLE	SCAILING
SAUCERS	SAVAGED	SAVVEYING	SAYED	SCAILS
SAUCES	SAVAGEDOM	SAVVEYS	SAYER	SCAITH
SAUCH	SAVAGEDOMS	SAVVIED	SAYERS	SCAITHED
SAUCHS	SAVAGELY	SAVVIES	SAYEST	SCAITHING
SAUCIER	SAVAGER	SAVVY	SAYID	SCAITHS
SAUCIEST	SAVAGERIES	SAVVYING	SAYIDS	SCALA

The Chambers Dictionary is the authority for many longer words; see *OSW* Introduction, page xii.

SCALABLE
SCALADE
SCALADES
SCALADO
SCALADOS
SCALAE
SCALAR
SCALARS
SCALAWAG
SCALAWAGS
SCALD
SCALDED
SCALDER
SCALDERS
SCALDFISH
SCALDFISHES
SCALDHEAD
SCALDHEADS
SCALDIC
SCALDING
SCALDINGS
SCALDINI
SCALDINO
SCALDS
SCALDSHIP
SCALDSHIPS
SCALE
SCALED
SCALELESS
SCALELIKE
SCALENE
SCALENI
SCALENUS
SCALER
SCALERS
SCALES
SCALEWORK
SCALEWORKS
SCALIER
SCALIEST
SCALINESS
SCALINESSES
SCALING
SCALINGS
SCALL
SCALLAWAG
SCALLAWAGS
SCALLED
SCALLION
SCALLIONS
SCALLOP
SCALLOPED
SCALLOPING
SCALLOPS
SCALLS
SCALLYWAG
SCALLYWAGS
SCALP
SCALPED
SCALPEL
SCALPELS
SCALPER
SCALPERS
SCALPING
SCALPINGS
SCALPINS
SCALPLESS

SCALPRUM
SCALPRUMS
SCALPS
SCALY
SCAM
SCAMBLE
SCAMBLED
SCAMBLER
SCAMBLERS
SCAMBLES
SCAMBLING
SCAMBLINGS
SCAMEL
SCAMELS
SCAMMONIES
SCAMMONY
SCAMP
SCAMPED
SCAMPER
SCAMPERED
SCAMPERING
SCAMPERS
SCAMPI
SCAMPING
SCAMPINGS
SCAMPIS
SCAMPISH
SCAMPS
SCAMS
SCAN
SCAND
SCANDAL
SCANDALLED
SCANDALLING
SCANDALS
SCANDENT
SCANDIUM
SCANDIUMS
SCANNED
SCANNER
SCANNERS
SCANNING
SCANNINGS
SCANS
SCANSION
SCANSIONS
SCANT
SCANTED
SCANTER
SCANTEST
SCANTIER
SCANTIES
SCANTIEST
SCANTILY
SCANTING
SCANTITIES
SCANTITY
SCANTLE
SCANTLED
SCANTLES
SCANTLING
SCANTLINGS
SCANTLY
SCANTNESS
SCANTNESSES
SCANTS
SCANTY

SCAPA
SCAPAED
SCAPAING
SCAPAS
SCAPE
SCAPED
SCAPEGOAT
SCAPEGOATED
SCAPEGOATING
SCAPEGOATINGS
SCAPEGOATS
SCAPELESS
SCAPEMENT
SCAPEMENTS
SCAPES
SCAPHOID
SCAPHOIDS
SCAPHOPOD
SCAPHOPODS
SCAPI
SCAPING
SCAPOLITE
SCAPOLITES
SCAPPLE
SCAPPLED
SCAPPLES
SCAPPLING
SCAPULA
SCAPULAE
SCAPULAR
SCAPULARIES
SCAPULARS
SCAPULARY
SCAPULAS
SCAPUS
SCAR
SCARAB
SCARABAEI
SCARABEE
SCARABEES
SCARABOID
SCARABOIDS
SCARABS
SCARCE
SCARCELY
SCARCER
SCARCEST
SCARCITIES
SCARCITY
SCARE
SCARECROW
SCARECROWS
SCARED
SCAREDER
SCAREDEST
SCARER
SCARERS
SCARES
SCAREY
SCARF
SCARFED
SCARFING
SCARFINGS
SCARFISH
SCARFISHES
SCARFS
SCARFSKIN

SCARFSKINS
SCARFWISE
SCARIER
SCARIEST
SCARIFIED
SCARIFIER
SCARIFIERS
SCARIFIES
SCARIFY
SCARIFYING
SCARING
SCARIOUS
SCARLESS
SCARLET
SCARLETED
SCARLETING
SCARLETS
SCARMOGE
SCARMOGES
SCARP
SCARPA
SCARPAED
SCARPAING
SCARPAS
SCARPED
SCARPER
SCARPERED
SCARPERING
SCARPERS
SCARPETTI
SCARPETTO
SCARPH
SCARPHED
SCARPHING
SCARPHS
SCARPINES
SCARPING
SCARPINGS
SCARPS
SCARRE
SCARRED
SCARRES
SCARRIER
SCARRIEST
SCARRING
SCARRINGS
SCARRY
SCARS
SCART
SCARTED
SCARTH
SCARTHS
SCARTING
SCARTS
SCARVES
SCARY
SCAT
SCATCH
SCATCHES
SCATH
SCATHE
SCATHED
SCATHEFUL
SCATHES
SCATHING
SCATHS
SCATOLE

SCATOLES
SCATOLOGIES
SCATOLOGY
SCATS
SCATT
SCATTED
SCATTER
SCATTERED
SCATTERER
SCATTERERS
SCATTERING
SCATTERINGS
SCATTERS
SCATTERY
SCATTIER
SCATTIEST
SCATTING
SCATTINGS
SCATTS
SCATTY
SCAUD
SCAUDED
SCAUDING
SCAUDS
SCAUP
SCAUPED
SCAUPER
SCAUPERS
SCAUPING
SCAUPS
SCAUR
SCAURED
SCAURIES
SCAURING
SCAURS
SCAURY
SCAVAGE
SCAVAGER
SCAVAGERS
SCAVAGES
SCAVENGE
SCAVENGED
SCAVENGER
SCAVENGERED
SCAVENGERING
SCAVENGERINGS
SCAVENGERS
SCAVENGES
SCAVENGING
SCAVENGINGS
SCAW
SCAWS
SCAWTITE
SCAWTITES
SCAZON
SCAZONS
SCAZONTES
SCAZONTIC
SCAZONTICS
SCEAT
SCEATT
SCEATTAS
SCEDULE
SCEDULED
SCEDULES
SCEDULING
SCELERAT

The Chambers Dictionary is the authority for many longer words; see *OSW* Introduction, page xii.

SCELERATE
SCELERATES
SCELERATS
SCENA
SCENARIES
SCENARIO
SCENARIOS
SCENARISE
SCENARISED
SCENARISES
SCENARISING
SCENARIST
SCENARISTS
SCENARIZE
SCENARIZED
SCENARIZES
SCENARIZING
SCENARY
SCEND
SCENDED
SCENDING
SCENDS
SCENE
SCENED
SCENEMAN
SCENEMEN
SCENERIES
SCENERY
SCENES
SCENIC
SCENICAL
SCENING
SCENT
SCENTED
SCENTFUL
SCENTING
SCENTINGS
SCENTLESS
SCENTS
SCEPSIS
SCEPSISES
SCEPTER
SCEPTERED
SCEPTERS
SCEPTIC
SCEPTICAL
SCEPTICS
SCEPTRAL
SCEPTRE
SCEPTRED
SCEPTRES
SCEPTRY
SCERNE
SCERNED
SCERNES
SCERNING
SCHANSE
SCHANSES
SCHANTZE
SCHANTZES
SCHANZE
SCHANZES
SCHAPPE
SCHAPPED
SCHAPPEING
SCHAPPES
SCHAPSKA

SCHAPSKAS
SCHECHITA
SCHECHITAS
SCHEDULE
SCHEDULED
SCHEDULER
SCHEDULERS
SCHEDULES
SCHEDULING
SCHEELITE
SCHEELITES
SCHELLUM
SCHELLUMS
SCHELM
SCHELMS
SCHEMA
SCHEMATA
SCHEMATIC
SCHEME
SCHEMED
SCHEMER
SCHEMERS
SCHEMES
SCHEMING
SCHEMINGS
SCHERZI
SCHERZO
SCHERZOS
SCHIAVONE
SCHIAVONES
SCHIEDAM
SCHIEDAMS
SCHILLER
SCHILLERS
SCHILLING
SCHILLINGS
SCHIMMEL
SCHIMMELS
SCHISM
SCHISMA
SCHISMAS
SCHISMS
SCHIST
SCHISTOSE
SCHISTOUS
SCHISTS
SCHIZO
SCHIZOID
SCHIZOIDS
SCHIZONT
SCHIZONTS
SCHIZOPOD
SCHIZOPODS
SCHIZOS
SCHLAGER
SCHLAGERS
SCHLEMIEL
SCHLEMIELS
SCHLEMIHL
SCHLEMIHLS
SCHLEP
SCHLEPP
SCHLEPPED
SCHLEPPER
SCHLEPPERS
SCHLEPPIER
SCHLEPPIEST

SCHLEPPING
SCHLEPPS
SCHLEPPY
SCHLEPS
SCHLICH
SCHLICHS
SCHLIEREN
SCHLOCK
SCHLOCKER
SCHLOCKERS
SCHLOCKIER
SCHLOCKIEST
SCHLOCKS
SCHLOCKY
SCHLOSS
SCHLOSSES
SCHMALTZ
SCHMALTZES
SCHMALTZIER
SCHMALTZIEST
SCHMALTZY
SCHMECK
SCHMECKS
SCHMELZ
SCHMELZES
SCHMO
SCHMOCK
SCHMOCKS
SCHMOES
SCHMOOZ
SCHMOOZE
SCHMOOZED
SCHMOOZES
SCHMOOZING
SCHMUCK
SCHMUCKS
SCHMUTTER
SCHMUTTERS
SCHNAPPER
SCHNAPPERS
SCHNAPPS
SCHNAPPSES
SCHNAPS
SCHNAPSES
SCHNAUZER
SCHNAUZERS
SCHNECKE
SCHNECKEN
SCHNELL
SCHNITZEL
SCHNITZELS
SCHNOOK
SCHNOOKS
SCHNORKEL
SCHNORKELS
SCHNORR
SCHNORRED
SCHNORRER
SCHNORRERS
SCHNORRING
SCHNORRS
SCHNOZZLE
SCHNOZZLES
SCHOLAR
SCHOLARCH
SCHOLARCHS
SCHOLARLY

SCHOLARS
SCHOLIA
SCHOLIAST
SCHOLIASTS
SCHOLION
SCHOLIUM
SCHOOL
SCHOOLBAG
SCHOOLBAGS
SCHOOLBOY
SCHOOLBOYS
SCHOOLDAY
SCHOOLDAYS
SCHOOLE
SCHOOLED
SCHOOLERIES
SCHOOLERY
SCHOOLES
SCHOOLING
SCHOOLINGS
SCHOOLMAN
SCHOOLMEN
SCHOOLS
SCHOONER
SCHOONERS
SCHORL
SCHORLS
SCHOUT
SCHOUTS
SCHTICK
SCHTICKS
SCHTIK
SCHTIKS
SCHTOOK
SCHTOOKS
SCHTOOM
SCHTUCK
SCHTUCKS
SCHUIT
SCHUITS
SCHUSS
SCHUSSED
SCHUSSES
SCHUSSING
SCHUYT
SCHUYTS
SCHWA
SCHWAS
SCIAENID
SCIAENIDS
SCIAENOID
SCIAENOIDS
SCIAMACHIES
SCIAMACHY
SCIARID
SCIARIDS
SCIATIC
SCIATICA
SCIATICAL
SCIATICAS
SCIENCE
SCIENCED
SCIENCES
SCIENT
SCIENTER
SCIENTIAL
SCIENTISE

SCIENTISED
SCIENTISES
SCIENTISING
SCIENTISM
SCIENTISMS
SCIENTIST
SCIENTISTS
SCIENTIZE
SCIENTIZED
SCIENTIZES
SCIENTIZING
SCILICET
SCILLA
SCILLAS
SCIMITAR
SCIMITARS
SCINCOID
SCINCOIDS
SCINTILLA
SCINTILLAS
SCIOLISM
SCIOLISMS
SCIOLIST
SCIOLISTS
SCIOLOUS
SCIOLTO
SCION
SCIONS
SCIOSOPHIES
SCIOSOPHY
SCIROC
SCIROCCO
SCIROCCOS
SCIROCS
SCIRRHOID
SCIRRHOUS
SCIRRHUS
SCIRRHUSES
SCISSEL
SCISSELS
SCISSIL
SCISSILE
SCISSILS
SCISSION
SCISSIONS
SCISSOR
SCISSORED
SCISSORER
SCISSORERS
SCISSORING
SCISSORS
SCISSURE
SCISSURES
SCIURINE
SCIURINES
SCIUROID
SCLAFF
SCLAFFED
SCLAFFING
SCLAFFS
SCLATE
SCLATED
SCLATES
SCLATING
SCLAUNDER
SCLAUNDERS
SCLAVE

The Chambers Dictionary is the authority for many longer words; see *OSW* Introduction, page xii.

SCLAVES	SCOLECOID	SCOPING	SCOTOMAS	SCOWLS
SCLERA	SCOLEX	SCOPULA	SCOTOMATA	SCOWP
SCLERAL	SCOLIA	SCOPULAS	SCOTOMIA	SCOWPED
SCLERAS	SCOLICES	SCOPULATE	SCOTOMIAS	SCOWPING
SCLERE	SCOLIOMA	SCORBUTIC	SCOTOMIES	SCOWPS
SCLEREID	SCOLIOMAS	SCORCH	SCOTOMY	SCOWRER
SCLEREIDE	SCOLION	SCORCHED	SCOTOPIA	SCOWRERS
SCLEREIDES	SCOLIOSES	SCORCHER	SCOTOPIAS	SCOWRIE
SCLEREIDS	SCOLIOSIS	SCORCHERS	SCOTOPIC	SCOWRIES
SCLEREMA	SCOLIOTIC	SCORCHES	SCOTS	SCOWS
SCLEREMAS	SCOLLOP	SCORCHING	SCOUG	SCOWTH
SCLERES	SCOLLOPED	SCORCHINGS	SCOUGED	SCOWTHER
SCLERITE	SCOLLOPING	SCORDATO	SCOUGING	SCOWTHERED
SCLERITES	SCOLLOPS	SCORE	SCOUGS	SCOWTHERING
SCLERITIS	SCOLYTID	SCORECARD	SCOUNDREL	SCOWTHERS
SCLERITISES	SCOLYTIDS	SCORECARDS	SCOUNDRELS	SCOWTHS
SCLEROID	SCOLYTOID	SCORED	SCOUP	SCRAB
SCLEROMA	SCOLYTOIDS	SCORELINE	SCOUPED	SCRABBED
SCLEROMAS	SCOMBRID	SCORELINES	SCOUPING	SCRABBING
SCLEROMATA	SCOMBRIDS	SCORER	SCOUPS	SCRABBLE
SCLEROSAL	SCOMBROID	SCORERS	SCOUR	SCRABBLED
SCLEROSE	SCOMBROIDS	SCORES	SCOURED	SCRABBLER
SCLEROSED	SCOMFISH	SCORIA	SCOURER	SCRABBLERS
SCLEROSES	SCOMFISHED	SCORIAC	SCOURERS	SCRABBLES
SCLEROSING	SCOMFISHES	SCORIAE	SCOURGE	SCRABBLING
SCLEROSIS	SCOMFISHING	SCORIFIED	SCOURGED	SCRABS
SCLEROTAL	SCONCE	SCORIFIER	SCOURGER	SCRAE
SCLEROTALS	SCONCED	SCORIFIERS	SCOURGERS	SCRAES
SCLEROTIA	SCONCES	SCORIFIES	SCOURGES	SCRAG
SCLEROTIC	SCONCHEON	SCORIFY	SCOURGING	SCRAGGED
SCLEROTICS	SCONCHEONS	SCORIFYING	SCOURIE	SCRAGGIER
SCLEROTIN	SCONCING	SCORING	SCOURIES	SCRAGGIEST
SCLEROTINS	SCONE	SCORINGS	SCOURING	SCRAGGING
SCLEROUS	SCONES	SCORIOUS	SCOURINGS	SCRAGGLIER
SCLIFF	SCONTION	SCORN	SCOURS	SCRAGGLIEST
SCLIFFS	SCONTIONS	SCORNED	SCOURSE	SCRAGGLY
SCLIM	SCOOG	SCORNER	SCOURSED	SCRAGGY
SCLIMMED	SCOOGED	SCORNERS	SCOURSES	SCRAGS
SCLIMMING	SCOOGING	SCORNFUL	SCOURSING	SCRAICH
SCLIMS	SCOOGS	SCORNING	SCOUSE	SCRAICHED
SCOFF	SCOOP	SCORNINGS	SCOUSER	SCRAICHING
SCOFFED	SCOOPED	SCORNS	SCOUSERS	SCRAICHS
SCOFFER	SCOOPER	SCORODITE	SCOUSES	SCRAIGH
SCOFFERS	SCOOPERS	SCORODITES	SCOUT	SCRAIGHED
SCOFFING	SCOOPFUL	SCORPER	SCOUTED	SCRAIGHING
SCOFFINGS	SCOOPFULS	SCORPERS	SCOUTER	SCRAIGHS
SCOFFLAW	SCOOPING	SCORPIOID	SCOUTERS	SCRAM
SCOFFLAWS	SCOOPINGS	SCORPIOIDS	SCOUTH	SCRAMB
SCOFFS	SCOOPS	SCORPION	SCOUTHER	SCRAMBED
SCOG	SCOOT	SCORPIONS	SCOUTHERED	SCRAMBING
SCOGGED	SCOOTED	SCORRENDO	SCOUTHERING	SCRAMBLE
SCOGGING	SCOOTER	SCORSE	SCOUTHERINGS	SCRAMBLED
SCOGS	SCOOTERS	SCORSED	SCOUTHERS	SCRAMBLER
SCOINSON	SCOOTING	SCORSER	SCOUTHERY	SCRAMBLERS
SCOINSONS	SCOOTS	SCORSERS	SCOUTHS	SCRAMBLES
SCOLD	SCOP	SCORSES	SCOUTING	SCRAMBLING
SCOLDED	SCOPA	SCORSING	SCOUTINGS	SCRAMBLINGS
SCOLDER	SCOPAE	SCOT	SCOUTS	SCRAMBS
SCOLDERS	SCOPAS	SCOTCH	SCOW	SCRAMJET
SCOLDING	SCOPATE	SCOTCHED	SCOWDER	SCRAMJETS
SCOLDINGS	SCOPE	SCOTCHES	SCOWDERED	SCRAMMED
SCOLDS	SCOPED	SCOTCHING	SCOWDERING	SCRAMMING
SCOLECES	SCOPELID	SCOTER	SCOWDERINGS	SCRAMS
SCOLECID	SCOPELIDS	SCOTERS	SCOWDERS	SCRAN
SCOLECIDS	SCOPELOID	SCOTIA	SCOWL	SCRANCH
SCOLECITE	SCOPELOIDS	SCOTIAS	SCOWLED	SCRANCHED
SCOLECITES	SCOPES	SCOTOMA	SCOWLING	

The Chambers Dictionary is the authority for many longer words; see *OSW* Introduction, page xii.

SCRANCHES
SCRANCHING
SCRANNEL
SCRANNIER
SCRANNIEST
SCRANNY
SCRANS
SCRAP
SCRAPBOOK
SCRAPBOOKS
SCRAPE
SCRAPED
SCRAPEGUT
SCRAPEGUTS
SCRAPER
SCRAPERS
SCRAPES
SCRAPHEAP
SCRAPHEAPS
SCRAPIE
SCRAPIES
SCRAPING
SCRAPINGS
SCRAPPED
SCRAPPIER
SCRAPPIEST
SCRAPPILY
SCRAPPING
SCRAPPLE
SCRAPPLES
SCRAPPY
SCRAPS
SCRAPYARD
SCRAPYARDS
SCRAT
SCRATCH
SCRATCHED
SCRATCHER
SCRATCHERS
SCRATCHES
SCRATCHIER
SCRATCHIEST
SCRATCHING
SCRATCHINGS
SCRATCHY
SCRATS
SCRATTED
SCRATTING
SCRATTLE
SCRATTLED
SCRATTLES
SCRATTLING
SCRAUCH
SCRAUCHED
SCRAUCHING
SCRAUCHS
SCRAUGH
SCRAUGHED
SCRAUGHING
SCRAUGHS
SCRAW
SCRAWL
SCRAWLED
SCRAWLER
SCRAWLERS
SCRAWLIER
SCRAWLIEST

SCRAWLING
SCRAWLINGS
SCRAWLS
SCRAWLY
SCRAWM
SCRAWMED
SCRAWMING
SCRAWMS
SCRAWNIER
SCRAWNIEST
SCRAWNY
SCRAWS
SCRAY
SCRAYE
SCRAYES
SCRAYS
SCREAK
SCREAKED
SCREAKIER
SCREAKIEST
SCREAKING
SCREAKS
SCREAKY
SCREAM
SCREAMED
SCREAMER
SCREAMERS
SCREAMING
SCREAMS
SCREE
SCREECH
SCREECHED
SCREECHER
SCREECHERS
SCREECHES
SCREECHIER
SCREECHIEST
SCREECHING
SCREECHY
SCREED
SCREEDED
SCREEDER
SCREEDERS
SCREEDING
SCREEDINGS
SCREEDS
SCREEN
SCREENED
SCREENER
SCREENERS
SCREENING
SCREENINGS
SCREENS
SCREES
SCREEVE
SCREEVED
SCREEVER
SCREEVERS
SCREEVES
SCREEVING
SCREEVINGS
SCREICH
SCREICHED
SCREICHING
SCREICHS
SCREIGH
SCREIGHED

SCREIGHING
SCREIGHS
SCREW
SCREWBALL
SCREWBALLS
SCREWED
SCREWER
SCREWERS
SCREWIER
SCREWIEST
SCREWING
SCREWINGS
SCREWS
SCREWTOP
SCREWTOPS
SCREWY
SCRIBABLE
SCRIBAL
SCRIBBLE
SCRIBBLED
SCRIBBLER
SCRIBBLERS
SCRIBBLES
SCRIBBLIER
SCRIBBLIEST
SCRIBBLING
SCRIBBLINGS
SCRIBBLY
SCRIBE
SCRIBED
SCRIBER
SCRIBERS
SCRIBES
SCRIBING
SCRIBINGS
SCRIBISM
SCRIBISMS
SCRIECH
SCRIECHED
SCRIECHING
SCRIECHS
SCRIED
SCRIENE
SCRIENES
SCRIES
SCRIEVE
SCRIEVED
SCRIEVES
SCRIEVING
SCRIGGLE
SCRIGGLED
SCRIGGLES
SCRIGGLIER
SCRIGGLIEST
SCRIGGLING
SCRIGGLY
SCRIKE
SCRIKED
SCRIKES
SCRIKING
SCRIM
SCRIMMAGE
SCRIMMAGED
SCRIMMAGES
SCRIMMAGING
SCRIMP
SCRIMPED

SCRIMPIER
SCRIMPIEST
SCRIMPILY
SCRIMPING
SCRIMPLY
SCRIMPS
SCRIMPY
SCRIMS
SCRIMSHAW
SCRIMSHAWED
SCRIMSHAWING
SCRIMSHAWS
SCRIMURE
SCRIMURES
SCRINE
SCRINES
SCRIP
SCRIPPAGE
SCRIPPAGES
SCRIPS
SCRIPT
SCRIPTED
SCRIPTING
SCRIPTORY
SCRIPTS
SCRIPTURE
SCRIPTURES
SCRITCH
SCRITCHED
SCRITCHES
SCRITCHING
SCRIVE
SCRIVED
SCRIVENER
SCRIVENERS
SCRIVES
SCRIVING
SCROBE
SCROBES
SCROD
SCRODDLED
SCRODS
SCROFULA
SCROFULAS
SCROG
SCROGGIE
SCROGGIER
SCROGGIEST
SCROGGY
SCROGS
SCROLL
SCROLLED
SCROLLING
SCROLLS
SCROOGE
SCROOGED
SCROOGES
SCROOGING
SCROOP
SCROOPED
SCROOPING
SCROOPS
SCROTA
SCROTAL
SCROTUM
SCROTUMS
SCROUGE

SCROUGED
SCROUGER
SCROUGERS
SCROUGES
SCROUGING
SCROUNGE
SCROUNGED
SCROUNGER
SCROUNGERS
SCROUNGES
SCROUNGING
SCROUNGINGS
SCROW
SCROWDGE
SCROWDGED
SCROWDGES
SCROWDGING
SCROWL
SCROWLE
SCROWLED
SCROWLES
SCROWLING
SCROWLS
SCROWS
SCROYLE
SCROYLES
SCRUB
SCRUBBED
SCRUBBER
SCRUBBERS
SCRUBBIER
SCRUBBIEST
SCRUBBING
SCRUBBINGS
SCRUBBY
SCRUBLAND
SCRUBLANDS
SCRUBS
SCRUFF
SCRUFFIER
SCRUFFIEST
SCRUFFS
SCRUFFY
SCRUM
SCRUMDOWN
SCRUMDOWNS
SCRUMMAGE
SCRUMMAGED
SCRUMMAGES
SCRUMMAGING
SCRUMMED
SCRUMMIER
SCRUMMIEST
SCRUMMING
SCRUMMY
SCRUMP
SCRUMPED
SCRUMPIES
SCRUMPING
SCRUMPOX
SCRUMPOXES
SCRUMPS
SCRUMPY
SCRUMS
SCRUNCH
SCRUNCHED
SCRUNCHES

The Chambers Dictionary is the authority for many longer words; see *OSW* Introduction, page xii.

SCRUNCHIER	SCUFFS	SCUMMY	SCUTELLA	SEABIRDS
SCRUNCHIEST	SCUFT	SCUMS	SCUTELLAR	SEABLITE
SCRUNCHING	SCUFTS	SCUNCHEON	SCUTELLUM	SEABLITES
SCRUNCHY	SCUG	SCUNCHEONS	SCUTES	SEABOARD
SCRUNT	SCUGGED	SCUNGE	SCUTIFORM	SEABOARDS
SCRUNTIER	SCUGGING	SCUNGED	SCUTIGER	SEABORNE
SCRUNTIEST	SCUGS	SCUNGES	SCUTIGERS	SEABOTTLE
SCRUNTS	SCUL	SCUNGIER	SCUTS	SEABOTTLES
SCRUNTY	SCULK	SCUNGIEST	SCUTTER	SEACOAST
SCRUPLE	SCULKED	SCUNGING	SCUTTERED	SEACOASTS
SCRUPLED	SCULKING	SCUNGY	SCUTTERING	SEACOCK
SCRUPLER	SCULKS	SCUNNER	SCUTTERS	SEACOCKS
SCRUPLERS	SCULL	SCUNNERED	SCUTTLE	SEACRAFT
SCRUPLES	SCULLE	SCUNNERING	SCUTTLED	SEACRAFTS
SCRUPLING	SCULLED	SCUNNERS	SCUTTLER	SEACUNNIES
SCRUTABLE	SCULLER	SCUP	SCUTTLERS	SEACUNNY
SCRUTATOR	SCULLERIES	SCUPPAUG	SCUTTLES	SEADROME
SCRUTATORS	SCULLERS	SCUPPAUGS	SCUTTLING	SEADROMES
SCRUTINIES	SCULLERY	SCUPPER	SCUTUM	SEAFARER
SCRUTINY	SCULLES	SCUPPERED	SCUZZ	SEAFARERS
SCRUTO	SCULLING	SCUPPERING	SCUZZBALL	SEAFARING
SCRUTOIRE	SCULLINGS	SCUPPERS	SCUZZBALLS	SEAFARINGS
SCRUTOIRES	SCULLION	SCUPS	SCUZZES	SEAFOLK
SCRUTOS	SCULLIONS	SCUR	SCUZZIER	SEAFOLKS
SCRUZE	SCULLS	SCURF	SCUZZIEST	SEAFOOD
SCRUZED	SCULP	SCURFIER	SCUZZY	SEAFOODS
SCRUZES	SCULPED	SCURFIEST	SCYBALA	SEAFOWL
SCRUZING	SCULPIN	SCURFS	SCYBALOUS	SEAFOWLS
SCRY	SCULPING	SCURFY	SCYBALUM	SEAFRONT
SCRYDE	SCULPINS	SCURRED	SCYE	SEAFRONTS
SCRYER	SCULPS	SCURRIED	SCYES	SEAGULL
SCRYERS	SCULPSIT	SCURRIER	SCYPHI	SEAGULLS
SCRYING	SCULPT	SCURRIERS	SCYPHUS	SEAHAWK
SCRYINGS	SCULPTED	SCURRIES	SCYTALE	SEAHAWKS
SCRYNE	SCULPTING	SCURRIL	SCYTALES	SEAHOG
SCRYNES	SCULPTOR	SCURRILE	SCYTHE	SEAHOGS
SCUBA	SCULPTORS	SCURRING	SCYTHED	SEAHORSE
SCUBAS	SCULPTS	SCURRIOUR	SCYTHEMAN	SEAHORSES
SCUCHIN	SCULPTURE	SCURRIOURS	SCYTHEMEN	SEAHOUND
SCUCHINS	SCULPTURED	SCURRY	SCYTHER	SEAHOUNDS
SCUCHION	SCULPTURES	SCURRYING	SCYTHERS	SEAKALE
SCUCHIONS	SCULPTURING	SCURS	SCYTHES	SEAKALES
SCUD	SCULPTURINGS	SCURVIER	SCYTHING	SEAL
SCUDDALER	SCULS	SCURVIES	SDAINE	SEALANT
SCUDDALERS	SCUM	SCURVIEST	SDAINED	SEALANTS
SCUDDED	SCUMBAG	SCURVILY	SDAINES	SEALCH
SCUDDER	SCUMBAGS	SCURVY	SDAINING	SEALCHS
SCUDDERS	SCUMBER	SCUSE	SDAYN	SEALED
SCUDDING	SCUMBERED	SCUSED	SDAYNED	SEALER
SCUDDLE	SCUMBERING	SCUSES	SDAYNING	SEALERIES
SCUDDLED	SCUMBERS	SCUSING	SDAYNS	SEALERS
SCUDDLES	SCUMBLE	SCUT	SDEIGN	SEALERY
SCUDDLING	SCUMBLED	SCUTA	SDEIGNE	SEALGH
SCUDI	SCUMBLES	SCUTAGE	SDEIGNED	SEALGHS
SCUDLER	SCUMBLING	SCUTAGES	SDEIGNES	SEALINE
SCUDLERS	SCUMBLINGS	SCUTAL	SDEIGNING	SEALINES
SCUDO	SCUMFISH	SCUTATE	SDEIGNS	SEALING
SCUDS	SCUMFISHED	SCUTCH	SDEIN	SEALINGS
SCUFF	SCUMFISHES	SCUTCHED	SDEINED	SEALPOINT
SCUFFED	SCUMFISHING	SCUTCHEON	SDEINING	SEALPOINTS
SCUFFING	SCUMMED	SCUTCHEONS	SDEINS	SEALS
SCUFFLE	SCUMMER	SCUTCHER	SEA	SEALSKIN
SCUFFLED	SCUMMERS	SCUTCHERS	SEABANK	SEALSKINS
SCUFFLER	SCUMMIER	SCUTCHES	SEABANKS	SEALWAX
SCUFFLERS	SCUMMIEST	SCUTCHING	SEABED	SEALWAXES
SCUFFLES	SCUMMING	SCUTCHINGS	SEABEDS	SEALYHAM
SCUFFLING	SCUMMINGS	SCUTE	SEABIRD	SEALYHAMS

The Chambers Dictionary is the authority for many longer words; see *OSW* Introduction, page xii.

SEAM	SEASE	SECANT	SECRETION	SEDATED
SEAMAID	SEASED	SECANTLY	SECRETIONS	SEDATELY
SEAMAIDS	SEASES	SECANTS	SECRETIVE	SEDATER
SEAMAN	SEASHELL	SECATEURS	SECRETLY	SEDATES
SEAMANLY	SEASHELLS	SECCO	SECRETORY	SEDATEST
SEAMARK	SEASHORE	SECCOS	SECRETS	SEDATING
SEAMARKS	SEASHORES	SECEDE	SECS	SEDATION
SEAME	SEASICK	SECEDED	SECT	SEDATIONS
SEAMED	SEASICKER	SECEDER	SECTARIAL	SEDATIVE
SEAMEN	SEASICKEST	SECEDERS	SECTARIAN	SEDATIVES
SEAMER	SEASIDE	SECEDES	SECTARIANS	SEDENT
SEAMERS	SEASIDES	SECEDING	SECTARIES	SEDENTARY
SEAMES	SEASING	SECERN	SECTARY	SEDERUNT
SEAMIER	SEASON	SECERNED	SECTATOR	SEDERUNTS
SEAMIEST	SEASONAL	SECERNENT	SECTATORS	SEDES
SEAMINESS	SEASONED	SECERNENTS	SECTILE	SEDGE
SEAMINESSES	SEASONER	SECERNING	SECTILITIES	SEDGED
SEAMING	SEASONERS	SECERNS	SECTILITY	SEDGELAND
SEAMLESS	SEASONING	SECESH	SECTION	SEDGELANDS
SEAMOUNT	SEASONINGS	SECESHER	SECTIONAL	SEDGES
SEAMOUNTS	SEASONS	SECESHERS	SECTIONED	SEDGIER
SEAMS	SEASPEAK	SECESHES	SECTIONING	SEDGIEST
SEAMSET	SEASPEAKS	SECESSION	SECTIONS	SEDGY
SEAMSETS	SEASURE	SECESSIONS	SECTOR	SEDILE
SEAMSTER	SEASURES	SECKEL	SECTORAL	SEDILIA
SEAMSTERS	SEAT	SECKELS	SECTORED	SEDIMENT
SEAMY	SEATED	SECKLE	SECTORIAL	SEDIMENTED
SEAN	SEATER	SECKLES	SECTORIALS	SEDIMENTING
SEANCE	SEATERS	SECLUDE	SECTORING	SEDIMENTS
SEANCES	SEATING	SECLUDED	SECTORISE	SEDITION
SEANED	SEATINGS	SECLUDES	SECTORISED	SEDITIONS
SEANING	SEATLESS	SECLUDING	SECTORISES	SEDITIOUS
SEANNACHIES	SEATS	SECLUSION	SECTORISING	SEDUCE
SEANNACHY	SEAWARD	SECLUSIONS	SECTORIZE	SEDUCED
SEANS	SEAWARDLY	SECLUSIVE	SECTORIZED	SEDUCER
SEAPLANE	SEAWARDS	SECO	SECTORIZES	SEDUCERS
SEAPLANES	SEAWARE	SECODONT	SECTORIZING	SEDUCES
SEAPORT	SEAWARES	SECODONTS	SECTORS	SEDUCING
SEAPORTS	SEAWATER	SECOND	SECTS	SEDUCINGS
SEAQUAKE	SEAWATERS	SECONDARIES	SECULAR	SEDUCTION
SEAQUAKES	SEAWAY	SECONDARY	SECULARLY	SEDUCTIONS
SEAQUARIA	SEAWAYS	SECONDE	SECULARS	SEDUCTIVE
SEAR	SEAWEED	SECONDED	SECULUM	SEDUCTOR
SEARAT	SEAWEEDS	SECONDEE	SECULUMS	SEDUCTORS
SEARATS	SEAWIFE	SECONDEES	SECUND	SEDULITIES
SEARCE	SEAWIVES	SECONDER	SECUNDINE	SEDULITY
SEARCED	SEAWOMAN	SECONDERS	SECUNDINES	SEDULOUS
SEARCES	SEAWOMEN	SECONDES	SECUNDUM	SEDUM
SEARCH	SEAWORM	SECONDI	SECURABLE	SEDUMS
SEARCHED	SEAWORMS	SECONDING	SECURANCE	SEE
SEARCHER	SEAWORTHY	SECONDLY	SECURANCES	SEEABLE
SEARCHERS	SEAZE	SECONDO	SECURE	SEECATCH
SEARCHES	SEAZED	SECONDS	SECURED	SEECATCHIE
SEARCHING	SEAZES	SECRECIES	SECURELY	SEED
SEARCING	SEAZING	SECRECY	SECURER	SEEDBED
SEARE	SEBACEOUS	SECRET	SECURERS	SEEDBEDS
SEARED	SEBACIC	SECRETA	SECURES	SEEDBOX
SEARER	SEBATE	SECRETAGE	SECUREST	SEEDBOXES
SEAREST	SEBATES	SECRETAGES	SECURING	SEEDCAKE
SEARING	SEBESTEN	SECRETARIES	SECURITAN	SEEDCAKES
SEARINGS	SEBESTENS	SECRETARY	SECURITANS	SEEDCASE
SEARNESS	SEBIFIC	SECRETE	SECURITIES	SEEDCASES
SEARNESSES	SEBUM	SECRETED	SECURITY	SEEDED
SEARS	SEBUMS	SECRETES	SED	SEEDER
SEAS	SEBUNDIES	SECRETIN	SEDAN	SEEDERS
SEASCAPE	SEBUNDY	SECRETING	SEDANS	SEEDIER
SEASCAPES	SEC	SECRETINS	SEDATE	SEEDIEST

The Chambers Dictionary is the authority for many longer words; see *OSW* Introduction, page xii.

SEEDILY	SEESAWS	SEINERS	SELENATES	SEMANTEMES
SEEDINESS	SEETHE	SEINES	SELENIAN	SEMANTIC
SEEDINESSES	SEETHED	SEINING	SELENIC	SEMANTICS
SEEDING	SEETHER	SEININGS	SELENIDE	SEMANTIDE
SEEDINGS	SEETHERS	SEIR	SELENIDES	SEMANTIDES
SEEDLESS	SEETHES	SEIRS	SELENIOUS	SEMANTRA
SEEDLIKE	SEETHING	SEIS	SELENITE	SEMANTRON
SEEDLING	SEETHINGS	SEISE	SELENITES	SEMAPHORE
SEEDLINGS	SEEWING	SEISED	SELENITIC	SEMAPHORED
SEEDLIP	SEG	SEISES	SELENIUM	SEMAPHORES
SEEDLIPS	SEGAR	SEISIN	SELENIUMS	SEMAPHORING
SEEDNESS	SEGARS	SEISING	SELENOUS	SEMATIC
SEEDNESSES	SEGGAR	SEISINS	SELES	SEMBLABLE
SEEDS	SEGGARS	SEISM	SELF	SEMBLABLES
SEEDSMAN	SEGHOL	SEISMAL	SELFED	SEMBLABLY
SEEDSMEN	SEGHOLATE	SEISMIC	SELFHEAL	SEMBLANCE
SEEDY	SEGHOLATES	SEISMICAL	SELFHEALS	SEMBLANCES
SEEING	SEGHOLS	SEISMISM	SELFHOOD	SEMBLANT
SEEINGS	SEGMENT	SEISMISMS	SELFHOODS	SEMBLANTS
SEEK	SEGMENTAL	SEISMS	SELFING	SEMBLE
SEEKER	SEGMENTED	SEITEN	SELFINGS	SEMBLED
SEEKERS	SEGMENTING	SEITENS	SELFISH	SEMBLES
SEEKING	SEGMENTS	SEITIES	SELFISHLY	SEMBLING
SEEKS	SEGNO	SEITY	SELFISM	SEME
SEEL	SEGNOS	SEIZABLE	SELFISMS	SEMEE
SEELD	SEGO	SEIZE	SELFIST	SEMEED
SEELED	SEGOL	SEIZED	SELFISTS	SEMEIA
SEELIER	SEGOLATE	SEIZER	SELFLESS	SEMEION
SEELIEST	SEGOLATES	SEIZERS	SELFNESS	SEMEIOTIC
SEELING	SEGOLS	SEIZES	SELFNESSES	SEMEIOTICS
SEELINGS	SEGOS	SEIZIN	SELFS	SEMEME
SEELS	SEGREANT	SEIZING	SELICTAR	SEMEMES
SEELY	SEGREGATE	SEIZINGS	SELICTARS	SEMEN
SEEM	SEGREGATED	SEIZINS	SELKIE	SEMENS
SEEMED	SEGREGATES	SEIZURE	SELKIES	SEMESTER
SEEMER	SEGREGATING	SEIZURES	SELL	SEMESTERS
SEEMERS	SEGS	SEJANT	SELLA	SEMESTRAL
SEEMING	SEGUE	SEJEANT	SELLABLE	SEMI
SEEMINGLY	SEGUED	SEKOS	SELLAE	SEMIANGLE
SEEMINGS	SEGUEING	SEKOSES	SELLAS	SEMIANGLES
SEEMLESS	SEGUES	SEKT	SELLE	SEMIBOLD
SEEMLIER	SEI	SEKTS	SELLER	SEMIBOLDS
SEEMLIEST	SEICENTO	SEL	SELLERS	SEMIBREVE
SEEMLIHED	SEICENTOS	SELACHIAN	SELLES	SEMIBREVES
SEEMLIHEDS	SEICHE	SELACHIANS	SELLING	SEMIBULL
SEEMLY	SEICHES	SELADANG	SELLOTAPE	SEMIBULLS
SEEMLYHED	SEIF	SELADANGS	SELLOTAPED	SEMICOLON
SEEMLYHEDS	SEIFS	SELAH	SELLOTAPES	SEMICOLONS
SEEMS	SEIGNEUR	SELAHS	SELLOTAPING	SEMICOMA
SEEN	SEIGNEURS	SELCOUTH	SELLS	SEMICOMAS
SEEP	SEIGNIOR	SELD	SELS	SEMIE
SEEPAGE	SEIGNIORIES	SELDOM	SELTZER	SEMIES
SEEPAGES	SEIGNIORS	SELDSEEN	SELTZERS	SEMIFINAL
SEEPED	SEIGNIORY	SELDSHOWN	SELVA	SEMIFINALS
SEEPIER	SEIGNORAL	SELE	SELVAGE	SEMIFLUID
SEEPIEST	SEIGNORIES	SELECT	SELVAGED	SEMIFLUIDS
SEEPING	SEIGNORY	SELECTED	SELVAGEE	SEMILUNAR
SEEPS	SEIK	SELECTEE	SELVAGEES	SEMILUNE
SEEPY	SEIKER	SELECTEES	SELVAGES	SEMILUNES
SEER	SEIKEST	SELECTING	SELVAGING	SEMINAL
SEERESS	SEIL	SELECTION	SELVAS	SEMINALLY
SEERESSES	SEILED	SELECTIONS	SELVEDGE	SEMINAR
SEERS	SEILING	SELECTIVE	SELVEDGED	SEMINARIES
SEES	SEILS	SELECTOR	SELVEDGES	SEMINARS
SEESAW	SEINE	SELECTORS	SELVEDGING	SEMINARY
SEESAWED	SEINED	SELECTS	SELVES	SEMINATE
SEESAWING	SEINER	SELENATE	SEMANTEME	SEMINATED

The Chambers Dictionary is the authority for many longer words; see *OSW* Introduction, page xii.

SEMINATES
SEMINATING
SEMIOLOGIES
SEMIOLOGY
SEMIOTIC
SEMIOTICS
SEMIPED
SEMIPEDS
SEMIPLUME
SEMIPLUMES
SEMIS
SEMISES
SEMISOLID
SEMISOLIDS
SEMITAR
SEMITARS
SEMITAUR
SEMITAURS
SEMITONE
SEMITONES
SEMITONIC
SEMIVOWEL
SEMIVOWELS
SEMMIT
SEMMITS
SEMOLINA
SEMOLINAS
SEMPER
SEMPLE
SEMPLER
SEMPLEST
SEMPLICE
SEMPRE
SEMPSTER
SEMPSTERS
SEMSEM
SEMSEMS
SEMUNCIA
SEMUNCIAE
SEMUNCIAL
SEMUNCIAS
SEN
SENA
SENARIES
SENARII
SENARIUS
SENARY
SENAS
SENATE
SENATES
SENATOR
SENATORS
SEND
SENDAL
SENDALS
SENDED
SENDER
SENDERS
SENDING
SENDINGS
SENDS
SENECIO
SENECIOS
SENEGA
SENEGAS
SENESCENT
SENESCHAL

SENESCHALS
SENGREEN
SENGREENS
SENILE
SENILELY
SENILITIES
SENILITY
SENIOR
SENIORITIES
SENIORITY
SENIORS
SENNA
SENNACHIE
SENNACHIES
SENNAS
SENNET
SENNETS
SENNIGHT
SENNIGHTS
SENNIT
SENNITS
SENS
SENSA
SENSATE
SENSATION
SENSATIONS
SENSE
SENSED
SENSEFUL
SENSELESS
SENSES
SENSIBLE
SENSIBLER
SENSIBLES
SENSIBLEST
SENSIBLY
SENSILE
SENSILLA
SENSILLUM
SENSING
SENSINGS
SENSISM
SENSISMS
SENSIST
SENSISTS
SENSITISE
SENSITISED
SENSITISES
SENSITISING
SENSITIVE
SENSITIVES
SENSITIZE
SENSITIZED
SENSITIZES
SENSITIZING
SENSOR
SENSORIA
SENSORIAL
SENSORILY
SENSORIUM
SENSORIUMS
SENSORS
SENSORY
SENSUAL
SENSUALLY
SENSUM
SENSUOUS

SENT
SENTED
SENTENCE
SENTENCED
SENTENCER
SENTENCERS
SENTENCES
SENTENCING
SENTIENCE
SENTIENCES
SENTIENCIES
SENTIENCY
SENTIENT
SENTIENTS
SENTIMENT
SENTIMENTS
SENTINEL
SENTINELLED
SENTINELLING
SENTINELS
SENTING
SENTRIES
SENTRY
SENTS
SENVIES
SENVY
SENZA
SEPAD
SEPADDED
SEPADDING
SEPADS
SEPAL
SEPALINE
SEPALODIES
SEPALODY
SEPALOID
SEPALOUS
SEPALS
SEPARABLE
SEPARABLY
SEPARATA
SEPARATE
SEPARATED
SEPARATES
SEPARATING
SEPARATOR
SEPARATORS
SEPARATUM
SEPARATUMS
SEPHEN
SEPHENS
SEPIA
SEPIAS
SEPIMENT
SEPIMENTS
SEPIOLITE
SEPIOLITES
SEPIOST
SEPIOSTS
SEPIUM
SEPIUMS
SEPMAG
SEPOY
SEPOYS
SEPPUKU
SEPPUKUS
SEPS

SEPSES
SEPSIS
SEPT
SEPTA
SEPTAL
SEPTARIA
SEPTARIAN
SEPTARIUM
SEPTATE
SEPTATION
SEPTATIONS
SEPTEMFID
SEPTEMVIR
SEPTEMVIRI
SEPTEMVIRS
SEPTENARIES
SEPTENARY
SEPTENNIA
SEPTET
SEPTETS
SEPTETTE
SEPTETTES
SEPTIC
SEPTICITIES
SEPTICITY
SEPTIFORM
SEPTIMAL
SEPTIME
SEPTIMES
SEPTIMOLE
SEPTIMOLES
SEPTLEVA
SEPTLEVAS
SEPTS
SEPTUM
SEPTUOR
SEPTUORS
SEPTUPLE
SEPTUPLED
SEPTUPLES
SEPTUPLET
SEPTUPLETS
SEPTUPLING
SEPULCHER
SEPULCHERED
SEPULCHERING
SEPULCHERS
SEPULCHRE
SEPULCHRED
SEPULCHRES
SEPULCHRING
SEPULTURE
SEPULTURED
SEPULTURES
SEPULTURING
SEQUACITIES
SEQUACITY
SEQUEL
SEQUELA
SEQUELAE
SEQUELS
SEQUENCE
SEQUENCED
SEQUENCER
SEQUENCERS
SEQUENCES
SEQUENCING

SEQUENCINGS
SEQUENT
SEQUENTS
SEQUESTER
SEQUESTERED
SEQUESTERING
SEQUESTERS
SEQUESTRA
SEQUIN
SEQUINED
SEQUINNED
SEQUINS
SEQUOIA
SEQUOIAS
SERA
SERAC
SERACS
SERAFILE
SERAFILES
SERAFIN
SERAFINS
SERAGLIO
SERAGLIOS
SERAI
SERAIL
SERAILS
SERAIS
SERAL
SERANG
SERANGS
SERAPE
SERAPES
SERAPH
SERAPHIC
SERAPHIM
SERAPHIMS
SERAPHIN
SERAPHINE
SERAPHINES
SERAPHINS
SERAPHS
SERASKIER
SERASKIERS
SERDAB
SERDABS
SERE
SERED
SEREIN
SEREINS
SERENADE
SERENADED
SERENADER
SERENADERS
SERENADES
SERENADING
SERENATA
SERENATAS
SERENATE
SERENATES
SERENE
SERENED
SERENELY
SERENER
SERENES
SERENEST
SERENING
SERENITIES

The Chambers Dictionary is the authority for many longer words; see *OSW* Introduction, page xii.

SERENITY	SERINETTES	SERPENTRY	SERVEWING	SETON
SERER	SERING	SERPENTS	SERVICE	SETONS
SERES	SERINGA	SERPIGINES	SERVICED	SETOSE
SEREST	SERINGAS	SERPIGO	SERVICES	SETS
SERF	SERINS	SERPIGOES	SERVICING	SETSCREW
SERFAGE	SERIOUS	SERPULA	SERVIENT	SETSCREWS
SERFAGES	SERIOUSLY	SERPULAE	SERVIETTE	SETT
SERFDOM	SERIPH	SERPULITE	SERVIETTES	SETTEE
SERFDOMS	SERIPHS	SERPULITES	SERVILE	SETTEES
SERFHOOD	SERJEANCIES	SERR	SERVILELY	SETTER
SERFHOODS	SERJEANCY	SERRA	SERVILES	SETTERED
SERFISH	SERJEANT	SERRAE	SERVILISM	SETTERING
SERFLIKE	SERJEANTIES	SERRAN	SERVILISMS	SETTERS
SERFS	SERJEANTS	SERRANID	SERVILITIES	SETTING
SERFSHIP	SERJEANTY	SERRANIDS	SERVILITY	SETTINGS
SERFSHIPS	SERK	SERRANOID	SERVING	SETTLE
SERGE	SERKALI	SERRANOIDS	SERVINGS	SETTLED
SERGEANCIES	SERKALIS	SERRANS	SERVITOR	SETTLER
SERGEANCY	SERKS	SERRAS	SERVITORS	SETTLERS
SERGEANT	SERMON	SERRATE	SERVITUDE	SETTLES
SERGEANTS	SERMONED	SERRATED	SERVITUDES	SETTLING
SERGES	SERMONEER	SERRATES	SERVO	SETTLINGS
SERIAL	SERMONEERS	SERRATI	SESAME	SETTLOR
SERIALISE	SERMONER	SERRATING	SESAMES	SETTLORS
SERIALISED	SERMONERS	SERRATION	SESAMOID	SETTS
SERIALISES	SERMONET	SERRATIONS	SESAMOIDS	SETUALE
SERIALISING	SERMONETS	SERRATURE	SESE	SETUALES
SERIALISM	SERMONIC	SERRATURES	SESELI	SETULE
SERIALISMS	SERMONING	SERRATUS	SESELIS	SETULES
SERIALIST	SERMONINGS	SERRATUSES	SESEY	SETULOSE
SERIALISTS	SERMONISE	SERRE	SESS	SETULOUS
SERIALITIES	SERMONISED	SERRED	SESSA	SETWALL
SERIALITY	SERMONISES	SERREFILE	SESSES	SETWALLS
SERIALIZE	SERMONISING	SERREFILES	SESSILE	SEVEN
SERIALIZED	SERMONIZE	SERRES	SESSION	SEVENFOLD
SERIALIZES	SERMONIZED	SERRICORN	SESSIONAL	SEVENS
SERIALIZING	SERMONIZES	SERRIED	SESSIONS	SEVENTEEN
SERIALLY	SERMONIZING	SERRIES	SESSPOOL	SEVENTEENS
SERIALS	SERMONS	SERRING	SESSPOOLS	SEVENTH
SERIATE	SEROLOGIES	SERRS	SESTERCE	SEVENTHLY
SERIATED	SEROLOGY	SERRULATE	SESTERCES	SEVENTHS
SERIATELY	SERON	SERRY	SESTERTIA	SEVENTIES
SERIATES	SERONS	SERRYING	SESTET	SEVENTY
SERIATIM	SEROON	SERUEWE	SESTETS	SEVER
SERIATING	SEROONS	SERUEWED	SESTETT	SEVERABLE
SERIATION	SEROPUS	SERUEWES	SESTETTE	SEVERAL
SERIATIONS	SEROPUSES	SERUEWING	SESTETTES	SEVERALLY
SERIC	SEROSA	SERUM	SESTETTO	SEVERALS
SERICEOUS	SEROSAE	SERUMS	SESTETTOS	SEVERALTIES
SERICIN	SEROSAS	SERVAL	SESTETTS	SEVERALTY
SERICINS	SEROSITIES	SERVALS	SESTINA	SEVERANCE
SERICITE	SEROSITY	SERVANT	SESTINAS	SEVERANCES
SERICITES	SEROTINAL	SERVANTED	SESTINE	SEVERE
SERICITIC	SEROTINE	SERVANTING	SESTINES	SEVERED
SERICON	SEROTINES	SERVANTRIES	SESTON	SEVERELY
SERICONS	SEROTONIN	SERVANTRY	SESTONS	SEVERER
SERIEMA	SEROTONINS	SERVANTS	SET	SEVEREST
SERIEMAS	SEROTYPE	SERVE	SETA	SEVERIES
SERIES	SEROTYPED	SERVED	SETACEOUS	SEVERING
SERIF	SEROTYPES	SERVER	SETAE	SEVERITIES
SERIFS	SEROTYPING	SERVERIES	SETBACK	SEVERITY
SERIGRAPH	SEROTYPINGS	SERVERS	SETBACKS	SEVERS
SERIGRAPHS	SEROUS	SERVERY	SETIFORM	SEVERY
SERIN	SEROW	SERVES	SETLINE	SEVRUGA
SERINE	SEROWS	SERVEWE	SETLINES	SEVRUGAS
SERINES	SERPENT	SERVEWED	SETNESS	SEW
SERINETTE	SERPENTRIES	SERVEWES	SETNESSES	SEWAGE

The Chambers Dictionary is the authority for many longer words; see *OSW* Introduction, page xii.

SEWAGES	SEXTS	SHADBLOWS	SHAKEN	SHAMBLE
SEWED	SEXTUOR	SHADBUSH	SHAKER	SHAMBLED
SEWEL	SEXTUORS	SHADBUSHES	SHAKERS	SHAMBLES
SEWELLEL	SEXTUPLE	SHADDOCK	SHAKES	SHAMBLIER
SEWELLELS	SEXTUPLED	SHADDOCKS	SHAKIER	SHAMBLIEST
SEWELS	SEXTUPLES	SHADE	SHAKIEST	SHAMBLING
SEWEN	SEXTUPLET	SHADED	SHAKILY	SHAMBLINGS
SEWENS	SEXTUPLETS	SHADELESS	SHAKINESS	SHAMBLY
SEWER	SEXTUPLING	SHADES	SHAKINESSES	SHAMBOLIC
SEWERAGE	SEXUAL	SHADIER	SHAKING	SHAME
SEWERAGES	SEXUALISE	SHADIEST	SHAKINGS	SHAMEABLE
SEWERED	SEXUALISED	SHADILY	SHAKO	SHAMED
SEWERING	SEXUALISES	SHADINESS	SHAKOES	SHAMEFAST
SEWERINGS	SEXUALISING	SHADINESSES	SHAKOS	SHAMEFUL
SEWERS	SEXUALISM	SHADING	SHAKT	SHAMELESS
SEWIN	SEXUALISMS	SHADINGS	SHAKUDO	SHAMER
SEWING	SEXUALIST	SHADOOF	SHAKUDOS	SHAMERS
SEWINGS	SEXUALISTS	SHADOOFS	SHAKY	SHAMES
SEWINS	SEXUALITIES	SHADOW	SHALE	SHAMIANA
SEWN	SEXUALITY	SHADOWED	SHALED	SHAMIANAH
SEWS	SEXUALIZE	SHADOWER	SHALES	SHAMIANAHS
SEX	SEXUALIZED	SHADOWERS	SHALIER	SHAMIANAS
SEXED	SEXUALIZES	SHADOWIER	SHALIEST	SHAMING
SEXENNIAL	SEXUALIZING	SHADOWIEST	SHALING	SHAMISEN
SEXER	SEXUALLY	SHADOWING	SHALL	SHAMISENS
SEXERS	SEXVALENT	SHADOWINGS	SHALLI	SHAMMASH
SEXES	SEXY	SHADOWS	SHALLIS	SHAMMASHIM
SEXFID	SEY	SHADOWY	SHALLON	SHAMMED
SEXFOIL	SEYEN	SHADS	SHALLONS	SHAMMER
SEXFOILS	SEYENS	SHADUF	SHALLOON	SHAMMERS
SEXIER	SEYS	SHADUFS	SHALLOONS	SHAMMES
SEXIEST	SEYSURE	SHADY	SHALLOP	SHAMMIES
SEXINESS	SEYSURES	SHAFT	SHALLOPS	SHAMMING
SEXINESSES	SEZ	SHAFTED	SHALLOT	SHAMMOSIM
SEXING	SFERICS	SHAFTER	SHALLOTS	SHAMMY
SEXISM	SFORZANDI	SHAFTERS	SHALLOW	SHAMOY
SEXISMS	SFORZANDO	SHAFTING	SHALLOWED	SHAMOYED
SEXIST	SFORZANDOS	SHAFTINGS	SHALLOWER	SHAMOYING
SEXISTS	SFORZATI	SHAFTLESS	SHALLOWEST	SHAMOYS
SEXLESS	SFORZATO	SHAFTS	SHALLOWING	SHAMPOO
SEXOLOGIES	SFORZATOS	SHAG	SHALLOWINGS	SHAMPOOED
SEXOLOGY	SFUMATO	SHAGGED	SHALLOWLY	SHAMPOOER
SEXPERT	SFUMATOS	SHAGGIER	SHALLOWS	SHAMPOOERS
SEXPERTS	SGRAFFITI	SHAGGIEST	SHALM	SHAMPOOING
SEXPOT	SGRAFFITO	SHAGGILY	SHALMS	SHAMPOOS
SEXPOTS	SH	SHAGGING	SHALOM	SHAMROCK
SEXT	SHABBIER	SHAGGY	SHALOT	SHAMROCKS
SEXTAN	SHABBIEST	SHAGPILE	SHALOTS	SHAMS
SEXTANS	SHABBILY	SHAGREEN	SHALT	SHAMUS
SEXTANSES	SHABBLE	SHAGREENS	SHALWAR	SHAMUSES
SEXTANT	SHABBLES	SHAGROON	SHALWARS	SHAN
SEXTANTAL	SHABBY	SHAGROONS	SHALY	SHANACHIE
SEXTANTS	SHABRACK	SHAGS	SHAM	SHANACHIES
SEXTET	SHABRACKS	SHAH	SHAMA	SHAND
SEXTETS	SHACK	SHAHS	SHAMABLE	SHANDIES
SEXTETT	SHACKLE	SHAIKH	SHAMAN	SHANDRIES
SEXTETTE	SHACKLED	SHAIKHS	SHAMANIC	SHANDRY
SEXTETTES	SHACKLES	SHAIRN	SHAMANISM	SHANDS
SEXTETTS	SHACKLING	SHAIRNS	SHAMANISMS	SHANDY
SEXTILE	SHACKO	SHAITAN	SHAMANIST	SHANGHAI
SEXTILES	SHACKOES	SHAITANS	SHAMANISTS	SHANGHAIED
SEXTOLET	SHACKOS	SHAKABLE	SHAMANS	SHANGHAIING
SEXTOLETS	SHACKS	SHAKE	SHAMAS	SHANGHAIS
SEXTON	SHAD	SHAKEABLE	SHAMATEUR	SHANK
SEXTONESS	SHADBERRIES	SHAKED	SHAMATEURS	SHANKBONE
SEXTONESSES	SHADBERRY	SHAKEDOWN	SHAMBA	SHANKBONES
SEXTONS	SHADBLOW	SHAKEDOWNS	SHAMBAS	SHANKED

The Chambers Dictionary is the authority for many longer words; see *OSW* Introduction, page xii.

SHANKING	SHARNY	SHAWLLESS	SHECHITAH	SHEIKHS
SHANKS	SHARP	SHAWLS	SHECHITAHS	SHEIKS
SHANNIES	SHARPED	SHAWM	SHECHITAS	SHEILA
SHANNY	SHARPEN	SHAWMS	SHED	SHEILAS
SHANS	SHARPENED	SHAWS	SHEDDER	SHEILING
SHANTEY	SHARPENER	SHAY	SHEDDERS	SHEILINGS
SHANTEYS	SHARPENERS	SHAYA	SHEDDING	SHEKEL
SHANTIES	SHARPENING	SHAYAS	SHEDDINGS	SHEKELS
SHANTUNG	SHARPENS	SHAYS	SHEDS	SHELDDUCK
SHANTUNGS	SHARPER	SHCHI	SHEEL	SHELDDUCKS
SHANTY	SHARPERS	SHCHIS	SHEELED	SHELDRAKE
SHANTYMAN	SHARPEST	SHE	SHEELING	SHELDRAKES
SHANTYMEN	SHARPIE	SHEA	SHEELS	SHELDUCK
SHAPABLE	SHARPIES	SHEADING	SHEEN	SHELDUCKS
SHAPE	SHARPING	SHEADINGS	SHEENED	SHELF
SHAPEABLE	SHARPINGS	SHEAF	SHEENIER	SHELFED
SHAPED	SHARPISH	SHEAFED	SHEENIES	SHELFIER
SHAPELESS	SHARPLY	SHEAFIER	SHEENIEST	SHELFIEST
SHAPELIER	SHARPNESS	SHEAFIEST	SHEENING	SHELFING
SHAPELIEST	SHARPNESSES	SHEAFING	SHEENS	SHELFLIKE
SHAPELY	SHARPS	SHEAFS	SHEENY	SHELFROOM
SHAPEN	SHASH	SHEAFY	SHEEP	SHELFROOMS
SHAPER	SHASHED	SHEAL	SHEEPCOTE	SHELFS
SHAPERS	SHASHES	SHEALED	SHEEPCOTES	SHELFY
SHAPES	SHASHING	SHEALING	SHEEPDOG	SHELL
SHAPING	SHASHLICK	SHEALINGS	SHEEPDOGS	SHELLAC
SHAPINGS	SHASHLICKS	SHEALS	SHEEPFOLD	SHELLACKED
SHAPS	SHASHLIK	SHEAR	SHEEPFOLDS	SHELLACKING
SHARD	SHASHLIKS	SHEARED	SHEEPIER	SHELLACKINGS
SHARDED	SHASTER	SHEARER	SHEEPIEST	SHELLACS
SHARDS	SHASTERS	SHEARERS	SHEEPISH	SHELLBACK
SHARE	SHASTRA	SHEARING	SHEEPO	SHELLBACKS
SHARECROP	SHASTRAS	SHEARINGS	SHEEPOS	SHELLBARK
SHARECROPPED	SHAT	SHEARLEG	SHEEPSKIN	SHELLBARKS
SHARECROPPING	SHATTER	SHEARLEGS	SHEEPSKINS	SHELLDUCK
SHARECROPS	SHATTERED	SHEARLING	SHEEPWALK	SHELLDUCKS
SHARED	SHATTERING	SHEARLINGS	SHEEPWALKS	SHELLED
SHAREMAN	SHATTERS	SHEARMAN	SHEEPY	SHELLER
SHAREMEN	SHATTERY	SHEARMEN	SHEER	SHELLERS
SHARER	SHAUCHLE	SHEARS	SHEERED	SHELLFIRE
SHARERS	SHAUCHLED	SHEAS	SHEERER	SHELLFIRES
SHARES	SHAUCHLES	SHEATFISH	SHEEREST	SHELLFISH
SHARESMAN	SHAUCHLIER	SHEATFISHES	SHEERING	SHELLFISHES
SHARESMEN	SHAUCHLIEST	SHEATH	SHEERLEG	SHELLFUL
SHAREWARE	SHAUCHLING	SHEATHE	SHEERLEGS	SHELLFULS
SHAREWARES	SHAUCHLY	SHEATHED	SHEERLY	SHELLIER
SHARIA	SHAVE	SHEATHES	SHEERS	SHELLIEST
SHARIAS	SHAVED	SHEATHIER	SHEET	SHELLING
SHARIAT	SHAVELING	SHEATHIEST	SHEETED	SHELLINGS
SHARIATS	SHAVELINGS	SHEATHING	SHEETIER	SHELLS
SHARIF	SHAVEN	SHEATHINGS	SHEETIEST	SHELLWORK
SHARIFS	SHAVER	SHEATHS	SHEETING	SHELLWORKS
SHARING	SHAVERS	SHEATHY	SHEETINGS	SHELLY
SHARINGS	SHAVES	SHEAVE	SHEETS	SHELTER
SHARK	SHAVIE	SHEAVED	SHEETY	SHELTERED
SHARKED	SHAVIES	SHEAVES	SHEHITA	SHELTERER
SHARKER	SHAVING	SHEAVING	SHEHITAH	SHELTERERS
SHARKERS	SHAVINGS	SHEBANG	SHEHITAHS	SHELTERING
SHARKING	SHAW	SHEBANGS	SHEHITAS	SHELTERINGS
SHARKINGS	SHAWL	SHEBEEN	SHEIK	SHELTERS
SHARKS	SHAWLED	SHEBEENED	SHEIKDOM	SHELTERY
SHARKSKIN	SHAWLEY	SHEBEENER	SHEIKDOMS	SHELTIE
SHARKSKINS	SHAWLEYS	SHEBEENERS	SHEIKH	SHELTIES
SHARN	SHAWLIE	SHEBEENING	SHEIKHA	SHELTY
SHARNIER	SHAWLIES	SHEBEENINGS	SHEIKHAS	SHELVE
SHARNIEST	SHAWLING	SHEBEENS	SHEIKHDOM	SHELVED
SHARNS	SHAWLINGS	SHECHITA	SHEIKHDOMS	SHELVES

The Chambers Dictionary is the authority for many longer words; see *OSW* Introduction, page xii.

SHELVIER
SHELVIEST
SHELVING
SHELVINGS
SHELVY
SHEMOZZLE
SHEMOZZLED
SHEMOZZLES
SHEMOZZLING
SHEND
SHENDING
SHENDS
SHENT
SHEOL
SHEOLS
SHEPHERD
SHEPHERDED
SHEPHERDING
SHEPHERDS
SHERBET
SHERBETS
SHERD
SHERDS
SHERE
SHEREEF
SHEREEFS
SHERIA
SHERIAS
SHERIAT
SHERIATS
SHERIF
SHERIFF
SHERIFFS
SHERIFIAN
SHERIFS
SHERLOCK
SHERLOCKS
SHERPA
SHERPAS
SHERRIES
SHERRIS
SHERRISES
SHERRY
SHERWANI
SHERWANIS
SHES
SHET
SHETLAND
SHETS
SHETTING
SHEUCH
SHEUCHED
SHEUCHING
SHEUCHS
SHEUGH
SHEUGHED
SHEUGHING
SHEUGHS
SHEVA
SHEVAS
SHEW
SHEWBREAD
SHEWBREADS
SHEWED
SHEWEL
SHEWELS
SHEWING

SHEWN
SHEWS
SHIATSU
SHIATSUS
SHIATZU
SHIATZUS
SHIBAH
SHIBAHS
SHIBUICHI
SHIBUICHIS
SHICKER
SHICKERED
SHICKERS
SHICKSA
SHICKSAS
SHIDDER
SHIDDERS
SHIED
SHIEL
SHIELD
SHIELDED
SHIELDER
SHIELDERS
SHIELDING
SHIELDINGS
SHIELDS
SHIELDUCK
SHIELDUCKS
SHIELED
SHIELING
SHIELINGS
SHIELS
SHIER
SHIERS
SHIES
SHIEST
SHIFT
SHIFTED
SHIFTER
SHIFTERS
SHIFTIER
SHIFTIEST
SHIFTILY
SHIFTING
SHIFTINGS
SHIFTLESS
SHIFTS
SHIFTY
SHIGELLA
SHIGELLAS
SHIITAKE
SHIKAR
SHIKAREE
SHIKAREES
SHIKARI
SHIKARIS
SHIKARS
SHIKSA
SHIKSAS
SHIKSE
SHIKSES
SHILL
SHILLABER
SHILLABERS
SHILLALAH
SHILLALAHS
SHILLED

SHILLING
SHILLINGS
SHILLS
SHILPIT
SHILY
SHIM
SHIMAAL
SHIMAALS
SHIMMED
SHIMMER
SHIMMERED
SHIMMERING
SHIMMERINGS
SHIMMERS
SHIMMERY
SHIMMEY
SHIMMEYS
SHIMMIED
SHIMMIES
SHIMMING
SHIMMY
SHIMMYING
SHIMOZZLE
SHIMOZZLES
SHIMS
SHIN
SHINBONE
SHINBONES
SHINDIES
SHINDIG
SHINDIGS
SHINDY
SHINE
SHINED
SHINELESS
SHINER
SHINERS
SHINES
SHINESS
SHINESSES
SHINGLE
SHINGLED
SHINGLER
SHINGLERS
SHINGLES
SHINGLIER
SHINGLIEST
SHINGLING
SHINGLINGS
SHINGLY
SHINIER
SHINIES
SHINIEST
SHININESS
SHININESSES
SHINING
SHININGLY
SHINNE
SHINNED
SHINNES
SHINNIED
SHINNIES
SHINNING
SHINNY
SHINNYING
SHINS
SHINTIES

SHINTY
SHINY
SHIP
SHIPBOARD
SHIPBOARDS
SHIPFUL
SHIPFULS
SHIPLAP
SHIPLAPPED
SHIPLAPPING
SHIPLAPS
SHIPLESS
SHIPLOAD
SHIPLOADS
SHIPMAN
SHIPMATE
SHIPMATES
SHIPMEN
SHIPMENT
SHIPMENTS
SHIPPED
SHIPPEN
SHIPPENS
SHIPPER
SHIPPERS
SHIPPING
SHIPPINGS
SHIPPO
SHIPPON
SHIPPONS
SHIPPOS
SHIPPOUND
SHIPPOUNDS
SHIPS
SHIPSHAPE
SHIPWAY
SHIPWAYS
SHIPWORM
SHIPWORMS
SHIPWRECK
SHIPWRECKED
SHIPWRECKING
SHIPWRECKS
SHIPYARD
SHIPYARDS
SHIR
SHIRALEE
SHIRALEES
SHIRE
SHIREMAN
SHIREMEN
SHIRES
SHIRK
SHIRKED
SHIRKER
SHIRKERS
SHIRKING
SHIRKS
SHIRR
SHIRRA
SHIRRALEE
SHIRRALEES
SHIRRAS
SHIRRED
SHIRRING
SHIRRINGS
SHIRRS

SHIRS
SHIRT
SHIRTBAND
SHIRTBANDS
SHIRTED
SHIRTIER
SHIRTIEST
SHIRTILY
SHIRTING
SHIRTINGS
SHIRTLESS
SHIRTS
SHIRTY
SHIT
SHITE
SHITED
SHITES
SHITHEAD
SHITHEADS
SHITHOLE
SHITHOLES
SHITING
SHITS
SHITTAH
SHITTAHS
SHITTED
SHITTIER
SHITTIEST
SHITTIM
SHITTIMS
SHITTING
SHITTY
SHIV
SHIVAH
SHIVAHS
SHIVAREE
SHIVAREES
SHIVE
SHIVER
SHIVERED
SHIVERER
SHIVERERS
SHIVERING
SHIVERINGS
SHIVERS
SHIVERY
SHIVES
SHIVOO
SHIVOOS
SHIVS
SHIVVED
SHIVVING
SHLEMIEL
SHLEMIELS
SHLEP
SHLEPPED
SHLEPPER
SHLEPPERS
SHLEPPING
SHLEPS
SHLIMAZEL
SHLIMAZELS
SHLOCK
SHLOCKS
SHMALTZ
SHMALTZES
SHMALTZIER

The Chambers Dictionary is the authority for many longer words; see *OSW* Introduction, page xii.

SHMALTZIEST
SHMALTZY
SHMEK
SHMEKS
SHMO
SHMOCK
SHMOCKS
SHMOE
SHMOES
SHMOOSE
SHMOOSED
SHMOOSES
SHMOOSING
SHMOOZE
SHMOOZED
SHMOOZES
SHMOOZING
SHMUCK
SHMUCKS
SHOAL
SHOALED
SHOALER
SHOALEST
SHOALIER
SHOALIEST
SHOALING
SHOALINGS
SHOALNESS
SHOALNESSES
SHOALS
SHOALWISE
SHOALY
SHOAT
SHOATS
SHOCHET
SHOCHETIM
SHOCK
SHOCKABLE
SHOCKED
SHOCKER
SHOCKERS
SHOCKING
SHOCKS
SHOD
SHODDIER
SHODDIES
SHODDIEST
SHODDILY
SHODDY
SHODER
SHODERS
SHOE
SHOEBILL
SHOEBILLS
SHOEBLACK
SHOEBLACKS
SHOED
SHOEHORN
SHOEHORNED
SHOEHORNING
SHOEHORNS
SHOEING
SHOEINGS
SHOELACE
SHOELACES
SHOELESS
SHOEMAKER

SHOEMAKERS
SHOER
SHOERS
SHOES
SHOESHINE
SHOESHINES
SHOETREE
SHOETREES
SHOFAR
SHOFARS
SHOFROTH
SHOG
SHOGGED
SHOGGING
SHOGGLE
SHOGGLED
SHOGGLES
SHOGGLIER
SHOGGLIEST
SHOGGLING
SHOGGLY
SHOGI
SHOGIS
SHOGS
SHOGUN
SHOGUNAL
SHOGUNATE
SHOGUNATES
SHOGUNS
SHOJI
SHOJIS
SHOLA
SHOLAS
SHOLOM
SHONE
SHONEEN
SHONEENS
SHONKIER
SHONKIEST
SHONKY
SHOO
SHOOED
SHOOFLIES
SHOOFLY
SHOOGIE
SHOOGIED
SHOOGIEING
SHOOGIES
SHOOGLE
SHOOGLED
SHOOGLES
SHOOGLIER
SHOOGLIEST
SHOOGLING
SHOOGLY
SHOOING
SHOOK
SHOOKS
SHOOL
SHOOLE
SHOOLED
SHOOLES
SHOOLING
SHOOLS
SHOON
SHOOS
SHOOT

SHOOTABLE
SHOOTER
SHOOTERS
SHOOTING
SHOOTINGS
SHOOTIST
SHOOTISTS
SHOOTS
SHOP
SHOPBOARD
SHOPBOARDS
SHOPE
SHOPFRONT
SHOPFRONTS
SHOPFUL
SHOPFULS
SHOPHAR
SHOPHARS
SHOPHROTH
SHOPMAN
SHOPMEN
SHOPPED
SHOPPER
SHOPPERS
SHOPPIER
SHOPPIEST
SHOPPING
SHOPPINGS
SHOPPY
SHOPS
SHOPWORN
SHORAN
SHORANS
SHORE
SHOREBIRD
SHOREBIRDS
SHORED
SHORELESS
SHORELINE
SHORELINES
SHOREMAN
SHOREMEN
SHORER
SHORERS
SHORES
SHORESMAN
SHORESMEN
SHOREWARD
SHOREWARDS
SHOREWEED
SHOREWEEDS
SHORING
SHORINGS
SHORN
SHORT
SHORTAGE
SHORTAGES
SHORTARM
SHORTCAKE
SHORTCAKES
SHORTED
SHORTEN
SHORTENED
SHORTENER
SHORTENERS
SHORTENING
SHORTENINGS

SHORTENS
SHORTER
SHORTEST
SHORTFALL
SHORTFALLS
SHORTGOWN
SHORTGOWNS
SHORTHAND
SHORTHANDS
SHORTHOLD
SHORTHORN
SHORTHORNS
SHORTIE
SHORTIES
SHORTING
SHORTISH
SHORTLY
SHORTNESS
SHORTNESSES
SHORTS
SHORTSTOP
SHORTSTOPS
SHORTY
SHOT
SHOTE
SHOTES
SHOTFIRER
SHOTFIRERS
SHOTGUN
SHOTGUNS
SHOTHOLE
SHOTHOLES
SHOTMAKER
SHOTMAKERS
SHOTPROOF
SHOTPUT
SHOTPUTS
SHOTS
SHOTT
SHOTTE
SHOTTED
SHOTTEN
SHOTTES
SHOTTING
SHOTTLE
SHOTTLES
SHOTTS
SHOUGH
SHOUGHS
SHOULD
SHOULDER
SHOULDERED
SHOULDERING
SHOULDERINGS
SHOULDERS
SHOULDEST
SHOULDST
SHOUT
SHOUTED
SHOUTER
SHOUTERS
SHOUTHER
SHOUTHERED
SHOUTHERING
SHOUTHERS
SHOUTING
SHOUTINGS

SHOUTLINE
SHOUTLINES
SHOUTS
SHOVE
SHOVED
SHOVEL
SHOVELER
SHOVELERS
SHOVELFUL
SHOVELFULS
SHOVELLED
SHOVELLER
SHOVELLERS
SHOVELLING
SHOVELS
SHOVER
SHOVERS
SHOVES
SHOVING
SHOW
SHOWBIZ
SHOWBIZZES
SHOWBIZZY
SHOWBOAT
SHOWBOATED
SHOWBOATING
SHOWBOATS
SHOWBOX
SHOWBOXES
SHOWBREAD
SHOWBREADS
SHOWCASE
SHOWCASED
SHOWCASES
SHOWCASING
SHOWDOWN
SHOWDOWNS
SHOWED
SHOWER
SHOWERED
SHOWERFUL
SHOWERIER
SHOWERIEST
SHOWERING
SHOWERINGS
SHOWERS
SHOWERY
SHOWGHE
SHOWGHES
SHOWGIRL
SHOWGIRLS
SHOWIER
SHOWIEST
SHOWILY
SHOWINESS
SHOWINESSES
SHOWING
SHOWINGS
SHOWMAN
SHOWMANLY
SHOWMEN
SHOWN
SHOWPIECE
SHOWPIECES
SHOWPLACE
SHOWPLACES
SHOWROOM

The Chambers Dictionary is the authority for many longer words; see *OSW* Introduction, page xii.

SHOWROOMS	SHRILL	SHROVING	SHUFTIES	SIALOLITHS
SHOWS	SHRILLED	SHROW	SHUFTIS	SIALON
SHOWY	SHRILLER	SHROWD	SHUFTY	SIALONS
SHOWYARD	SHRILLEST	SHROWED	SHUL	SIALS
SHOWYARDS	SHRILLIER	SHROWING	SHULE	SIAMANG
SHOYU	SHRILLIEST	SHROWS	SHULED	SIAMANGS
SHOYUS	SHRILLING	SHRUB	SHULES	SIAMESE
SHRADDHA	SHRILLINGS	SHRUBBED	SHULING	SIAMESED
SHRADDHAS	SHRILLS	SHRUBBERIES	SHULN	SIAMESES
SHRANK	SHRILLY	SHRUBBERY	SHULS	SIAMESING
SHRAPNEL	SHRIMP	SHRUBBIER	SHUN	SIAMEZE
SHRAPNELS	SHRIMPED	SHRUBBIEST	SHUNLESS	SIAMEZED
SHRED	SHRIMPER	SHRUBBING	SHUNNABLE	SIAMEZES
SHREDDED	SHRIMPERS	SHRUBBY	SHUNNED	SIAMEZING
SHREDDER	SHRIMPIER	SHRUBLESS	SHUNNER	SIB
SHREDDERS	SHRIMPIEST	SHRUBLIKE	SHUNNERS	SIBB
SHREDDIER	SHRIMPING	SHRUBS	SHUNNING	SIBBS
SHREDDIEST	SHRIMPINGS	SHRUG	SHUNS	SIBILANCE
SHREDDING	SHRIMPS	SHRUGGED	SHUNT	SIBILANCES
SHREDDINGS	SHRIMPY	SHRUGGING	SHUNTED	SIBILANCIES
SHREDDY	SHRINAL	SHRUGS	SHUNTER	SIBILANCY
SHREDLESS	SHRINE	SHRUNK	SHUNTERS	SIBILANT
SHREDS	SHRINED	SHRUNKEN	SHUNTING	SIBILANTS
SHREEK	SHRINES	SHTCHI	SHUNTINGS	SIBILATE
SHREEKED	SHRINING	SHTCHIS	SHUNTS	SIBILATED
SHREEKING	SHRINK	SHTETEL	SHURA	SIBILATES
SHREEKS	SHRINKAGE	SHTETELACH	SHURAS	SIBILATING
SHREIK	SHRINKAGES	SHTETELS	SHUSH	SIBILATOR
SHREIKED	SHRINKER	SHTETL	SHUSHED	SIBILATORS
SHREIKING	SHRINKERS	SHTETLACH	SHUSHES	SIBILOUS
SHREIKS	SHRINKING	SHTETLS	SHUSHING	SIBLING
SHREW	SHRINKS	SHTICK	SHUT	SIBLINGS
SHREWD	SHRITCH	SHTICKS	SHUTDOWN	SIBS
SHREWDER	SHRITCHED	SHTOOK	SHUTDOWNS	SIBSHIP
SHREWDEST	SHRITCHES	SHTOOKS	SHUTE	SIBSHIPS
SHREWDIE	SHRITCHING	SHTOOM	SHUTES	SIBYL
SHREWDIES	SHRIVE	SHTUCK	SHUTS	SIBYLIC
SHREWDLY	SHRIVED	SHTUCKS	SHUTTER	SIBYLLIC
SHREWED	SHRIVEL	SHTUM	SHUTTERED	SIBYLLINE
SHREWING	SHRIVELED	SHTUMM	SHUTTERING	SIBYLS
SHREWISH	SHRIVELING	SHTUP	SHUTTERINGS	SIC
SHREWMICE	SHRIVELLED	SHTUPPED	SHUTTERS	SICCAN
SHREWS	SHRIVELLING	SHTUPPING	SHUTTING	SICCAR
SHRIECH	SHRIVELS	SHTUPS	SHUTTLE	SICCATIVE
SHRIECHED	SHRIVEN	SHUBUNKIN	SHUTTLED	SICCATIVES
SHRIECHES	SHRIVER	SHUBUNKINS	SHUTTLES	SICCED
SHRIECHING	SHRIVERS	SHUCK	SHUTTLING	SICCING
SHRIEK	SHRIVES	SHUCKED	SHWA	SICCITIES
SHRIEKED	SHRIVING	SHUCKER	SHWAS	SICCITY
SHRIEKER	SHRIVINGS	SHUCKERS	SHY	SICE
SHRIEKERS	SHROFF	SHUCKING	SHYER	SICES
SHRIEKING	SHROFFAGE	SHUCKINGS	SHYERS	SICH
SHRIEKINGS	SHROFFAGES	SHUCKS	SHYEST	SICILIANA
SHRIEKS	SHROFFED	SHUDDER	SHYING	SICILIANE
SHRIEVAL	SHROFFING	SHUDDERED	SHYISH	SICILIANO
SHRIEVE	SHROFFS	SHUDDERING	SHYLY	SICILIANOS
SHRIEVED	SHROUD	SHUDDERINGS	SHYNESS	SICK
SHRIEVES	SHROUDED	SHUDDERS	SHYNESSES	SICKBED
SHRIEVING	SHROUDIER	SHUDDERY	SHYSTER	SICKBEDS
SHRIFT	SHROUDIEST	SHUFFLE	SHYSTERS	SICKED
SHRIFTS	SHROUDING	SHUFFLED	SI	SICKEN
SHRIGHT	SHROUDINGS	SHUFFLER	SIAL	SICKENED
SHRIGHTS	SHROUDS	SHUFFLERS	SIALIC	SICKENER
SHRIKE	SHROUDY	SHUFFLES	SIALOGRAM	SICKENERS
SHRIKED	SHROVE	SHUFFLING	SIALOGRAMS	SICKENING
SHRIKES	SHROVED	SHUFFLINGS	SIALOID	SICKENINGS
SHRIKING	SHROVES	SHUFTI	SIALOLITH	SICKENS

The Chambers Dictionary is the authority for many longer words; see *OSW* Introduction, page xii.

SICKER
SICKERLY
SICKEST
SICKIE
SICKIES
SICKING
SICKISH
SICKISHLY
SICKLE
SICKLED
SICKLEMAN
SICKLEMEN
SICKLEMIA
SICKLEMIAS
SICKLES
SICKLIED
SICKLIER
SICKLIES
SICKLIEST
SICKLILY
SICKLY
SICKLYING
SICKNESS
SICKNESSES
SICKNURSE
SICKNURSES
SICKO
SICKOS
SICKROOM
SICKROOMS
SICKS
SICLIKE
SICS
SIDA
SIDALCEA
SIDALCEAS
SIDAS
SIDDHA
SIDDHAS
SIDDHI
SIDDHIS
SIDDUR
SIDDURIM
SIDE
SIDEARM
SIDEARMS
SIDEBAND
SIDEBANDS
SIDEBAR
SIDEBARS
SIDEBOARD
SIDEBOARDS
SIDEBONES
SIDEBURNS
SIDECAR
SIDECARS
SIDED
SIDEKICK
SIDEKICKS
SIDELIGHT
SIDELIGHTS
SIDELINE
SIDELINED
SIDELINES
SIDELING
SIDELINING
SIDELOCK

SIDELOCKS
SIDELONG
SIDEMAN
SIDEMEN
SIDENOTE
SIDENOTES
SIDEPATH
SIDEPATHS
SIDER
SIDERAL
SIDERATE
SIDERATED
SIDERATES
SIDERATING
SIDEREAL
SIDERITE
SIDERITES
SIDERITIC
SIDEROAD
SIDEROADS
SIDEROSES
SIDEROSIS
SIDERS
SIDES
SIDESHOOT
SIDESHOOTS
SIDESHOW
SIDESHOWS
SIDESLIP
SIDESLIPPED
SIDESLIPPING
SIDESLIPS
SIDESMAN
SIDESMEN
SIDESTEP
SIDESTEPPED
SIDESTEPPING
SIDESTEPS
SIDESWIPE
SIDESWIPED
SIDESWIPES
SIDESWIPING
SIDETRACK
SIDETRACKED
SIDETRACKING
SIDETRACKS
SIDEWALK
SIDEWALKS
SIDEWALL
SIDEWALLS
SIDEWARD
SIDEWARDS
SIDEWAYS
SIDEWISE
SIDHA
SIDHAS
SIDING
SIDINGS
SIDLE
SIDLED
SIDLES
SIDLING
SIEGE
SIEGED
SIEGER
SIEGERS
SIEGES

SIEGING
SIELD
SIEMENS
SIEN
SIENNA
SIENNAS
SIENS
SIENT
SIENTS
SIERRA
SIERRAN
SIERRAS
SIESTA
SIESTAS
SIETH
SIETHS
SIEVE
SIEVED
SIEVERT
SIEVERTS
SIEVES
SIEVING
SIFAKA
SIFAKAS
SIFFLE
SIFFLED
SIFFLES
SIFFLEUR
SIFFLEURS
SIFFLEUSE
SIFFLEUSES
SIFFLING
SIFT
SIFTED
SIFTER
SIFTERS
SIFTING
SIFTINGLY
SIFTINGS
SIFTS
SIGH
SIGHED
SIGHER
SIGHERS
SIGHFUL
SIGHING
SIGHINGLY
SIGHS
SIGHT
SIGHTABLE
SIGHTED
SIGHTER
SIGHTERS
SIGHTING
SIGHTINGS
SIGHTLESS
SIGHTLIER
SIGHTLIEST
SIGHTLINE
SIGHTLINES
SIGHTLY
SIGHTS
SIGHTSAW
SIGHTSEE
SIGHTSEEING
SIGHTSEEINGS
SIGHTSEEN

SIGHTSEER
SIGHTSEERS
SIGHTSEES
SIGHTSMAN
SIGHTSMEN
SIGIL
SIGILLARY
SIGILLATE
SIGILS
SIGISBEI
SIGISBEO
SIGLA
SIGMA
SIGMAS
SIGMATE
SIGMATED
SIGMATES
SIGMATIC
SIGMATING
SIGMATION
SIGMATIONS
SIGMATISM
SIGMATISMS
SIGMATRON
SIGMATRONS
SIGMOID
SIGMOIDAL
SIGN
SIGNAGE
SIGNAGES
SIGNAL
SIGNALED
SIGNALER
SIGNALERS
SIGNALING
SIGNALINGS
SIGNALISE
SIGNALISED
SIGNALISES
SIGNALISING
SIGNALIZE
SIGNALIZED
SIGNALIZES
SIGNALIZING
SIGNALLED
SIGNALLER
SIGNALLERS
SIGNALLING
SIGNALLINGS
SIGNALLY
SIGNALMAN
SIGNALMEN
SIGNALS
SIGNARIES
SIGNARY
SIGNATORIES
SIGNATORY
SIGNATURE
SIGNATURES
SIGNBOARD
SIGNBOARDS
SIGNED
SIGNER
SIGNERS
SIGNET
SIGNETED
SIGNETING

SIGNETS
SIGNEUR
SIGNEURIE
SIGNEURIES
SIGNIEUR
SIGNIEURS
SIGNIFICS
SIGNIFIED
SIGNIFIER
SIGNIFIERS
SIGNIFIES
SIGNIFY
SIGNIFYING
SIGNING
SIGNINGS
SIGNIOR
SIGNIORS
SIGNLESS
SIGNOR
SIGNORA
SIGNORE
SIGNORES
SIGNORI
SIGNORIA
SIGNORIAL
SIGNORIAS
SIGNORIES
SIGNORINA
SIGNORINE
SIGNORINI
SIGNORINO
SIGNORS
SIGNORY
SIGNPOST
SIGNPOSTED
SIGNPOSTING
SIGNPOSTS
SIGNS
SIJO
SIJOS
SIKA
SIKAS
SIKE
SIKES
SIKORSKIES
SIKORSKY
SILAGE
SILAGED
SILAGEING
SILAGES
SILAGING
SILANE
SILANES
SILASTIC
SILASTICS
SILD
SILDS
SILE
SILED
SILEN
SILENCE
SILENCED
SILENCER
SILENCERS
SILENCES
SILENCING
SILENE

SILENES	SILKS	SILVERIZING	SIMPERER	SINCIPITA
SILENI	SILKTAIL	SILVERLY	SIMPERERS	SINCIPUT
SILENS	SILKTAILS	SILVERN	SIMPERING	SINCIPUTS
SILENT	SILKWEED	SILVERS	SIMPERS	SIND
SILENTER	SILKWEEDS	SILVERY	SIMPKIN	SINDED
SILENTEST	SILKWORM	SIM	SIMPKINS	SINDING
SILENTLY	SILKWORMS	SIMA	SIMPLE	SINDINGS
SILENTS	SILKY	SIMAR	SIMPLED	SINDON
SILENUS	SILL	SIMAROUBA	SIMPLER	SINDONS
SILER	SILLABUB	SIMAROUBAS	SIMPLERS	SINDS
SILERS	SILLABUBS	SIMARRE	SIMPLES	SINE
SILES	SILLADAR	SIMARRES	SIMPLESSE	SINECURE
SILESIA	SILLADARS	SIMARS	SIMPLESSES	SINECURES
SILESIAS	SILLER	SIMARUBA	SIMPLEST	SINED
SILEX	SILLERS	SIMARUBAS	SIMPLETON	SINES
SILEXES	SILLIER	SIMAS	SIMPLETONS	SINEW
SILICA	SILLIES	SIMAZINE	SIMPLEX	SINEWED
SILICAS	SILLIEST	SIMAZINES	SIMPLICES	SINEWING
SILICATE	SILLILY	SIMI	SIMPLIFIED	SINEWLESS
SILICATED	SILLINESS	SIMIAL	SIMPLIFIES	SINEWS
SILICATES	SILLINESSES	SIMIAN	SIMPLIFY	SINEWY
SILICATING	SILLOCK	SIMIANS	SIMPLIFYING	SINFONIA
SILICEOUS	SILLOCKS	SIMILAR	SIMPLING	SINFONIAS
SILICIC	SILLS	SIMILARLY	SIMPLINGS	SINFUL
SILICIDE	SILLY	SIMILE	SIMPLISM	SINFULLY
SILICIDES	SILO	SIMILES	SIMPLISMS	SING
SILICIFIED	SILOED	SIMILISE	SIMPLIST	SINGABLE
SILICIFIES	SILOING	SIMILISED	SIMPLISTE	SINGALONG
SILICIFY	SILOS	SIMILISES	SIMPLISTS	SINGALONGS
SILICIFYING	SILPHIA	SIMILISING	SIMPLY	SINGE
SILICIOUS	SILPHIUM	SIMILIZE	SIMPS	SINGED
SILICIUM	SILPHIUMS	SIMILIZED	SIMS	SINGEING
SILICIUMS	SILT	SIMILIZES	SIMUL	SINGER
SILICLE	SILTATION	SIMILIZING	SIMULACRA	SINGERS
SILICLES	SILTATIONS	SIMILOR	SIMULACRE	SINGES
SILICON	SILTED	SIMILORS	SIMULACRES	SINGING
SILICONE	SILTIER	SIMIOUS	SIMULANT	SINGINGLY
SILICONES	SILTIEST	SIMIS	SIMULANTS	SINGINGS
SILICONS	SILTING	SIMITAR	SIMULAR	SINGLE
SILICOSES	SILTS	SIMITARS	SIMULARS	SINGLED
SILICOSIS	SILTSTONE	SIMKIN	SIMULATE	SINGLES
SILICOTIC	SILTSTONES	SIMKINS	SIMULATED	SINGLET
SILICOTICS	SILTY	SIMMER	SIMULATES	SINGLETON
SILICULA	SILURID	SIMMERED	SIMULATING	SINGLETONS
SILICULAS	SILURIDS	SIMMERING	SIMULATOR	SINGLETS
SILICULE	SILURIST	SIMMERS	SIMULATORS	SINGLING
SILICULES	SILURISTS	SIMNEL	SIMULCAST	SINGLINGS
SILING	SILUROID	SIMNELS	SIMULCASTED	SINGLY
SILIQUA	SILVA	SIMONIAC	SIMULCASTING	SINGS
SILIQUAS	SILVAE	SIMONIACS	SIMULCASTS	SINGSONG
SILIQUE	SILVAN	SIMONIES	SIMULIUM	SINGSONGED
SILIQUES	SILVANS	SIMONIOUS	SIMULIUMS	SINGSONGING
SILIQUOSE	SILVAS	SIMONIST	SIMULS	SINGSONGS
SILK	SILVATIC	SIMONISTS	SIMURG	SINGSPIEL
SILKED	SILVER	SIMONY	SIMURGH	SINGSPIELS
SILKEN	SILVERED	SIMOOM	SIMURGHS	SINGULAR
SILKENED	SILVERIER	SIMOOMS	SIMURGS	SINGULARS
SILKENING	SILVERIEST	SIMOON	SIN	SINGULT
SILKENS	SILVERING	SIMOONS	SINAPISM	SINGULTS
SILKIE	SILVERINGS	SIMORG	SINAPISMS	SINGULTUS
SILKIER	SILVERISE	SIMORGS	SINCE	SINGULTUSES
SILKIES	SILVERISED	SIMP	SINCERE	SINICAL
SILKIEST	SILVERISES	SIMPAI	SINCERELY	SINICISE
SILKILY	SILVERISING	SIMPAIS	SINCERER	SINICISED
SILKINESS	SILVERIZE	SIMPATICO	SINCEREST	SINICISES
SILKINESSES	SILVERIZED	SIMPER	SINCERITIES	SINICISING
SILKING	SILVERIZES	SIMPERED	SINCERITY	SINICIZE

The Chambers Dictionary is the authority for many longer words; see *OSW* Introduction, page xii.

SINICIZED
SINICIZES
SINICIZING
SINING
SINISTER
SINISTRAL
SINISTRALS
SINK
SINKAGE
SINKAGES
SINKER
SINKERS
SINKHOLE
SINKHOLES
SINKIER
SINKIEST
SINKING
SINKINGS
SINKS
SINKY
SINLESS
SINLESSLY
SINNED
SINNER
SINNERED
SINNERING
SINNERS
SINNET
SINNETS
SINNING
SINNINGIA
SINNINGIAS
SINOPIA
SINOPIAS
SINOPIS
SINOPISES
SINOPITE
SINOPITES
SINS
SINSYNE
SINTER
SINTERED
SINTERING
SINTERS
SINTERY
SINUATE
SINUATED
SINUATELY
SINUATION
SINUATIONS
SINUITIS
SINUITISES
SINUOSE
SINUOSITIES
SINUOSITY
SINUOUS
SINUOUSLY
SINUS
SINUSES
SINUSITIS
SINUSITISES
SINUSOID
SINUSOIDS
SIP
SIPE
SIPED
SIPES

SIPHON
SIPHONAGE
SIPHONAGES
SIPHONAL
SIPHONATE
SIPHONED
SIPHONET
SIPHONETS
SIPHONIC
SIPHONING
SIPHONS
SIPHUNCLE
SIPHUNCLES
SIPING
SIPPED
SIPPER
SIPPERS
SIPPET
SIPPETS
SIPPING
SIPPLE
SIPPLED
SIPPLES
SIPPLING
SIPS
SIR
SIRCAR
SIRCARS
SIRDAR
SIRDARS
SIRE
SIRED
SIREN
SIRENIAN
SIRENIANS
SIRENIC
SIRENISE
SIRENISED
SIRENISES
SIRENISING
SIRENIZE
SIRENIZED
SIRENIZES
SIRENIZING
SIRENS
SIRES
SIRGANG
SIRGANGS
SIRI
SIRIASES
SIRIASIS
SIRIH
SIRIHS
SIRING
SIRIS
SIRKAR
SIRKARS
SIRLOIN
SIRLOINS
SIRNAME
SIRNAMED
SIRNAMES
SIRNAMING
SIROC
SIROCCO
SIROCCOS
SIROCS

SIRRAH
SIRRAHS
SIRRED
SIRREE
SIRREES
SIRRING
SIRS
SIRUP
SIRUPED
SIRUPING
SIRUPS
SIRVENTE
SIRVENTES
SIS
SISAL
SISALS
SISERARIES
SISERARY
SISES
SISKIN
SISKINS
SISS
SISSERARIES
SISSERARY
SISSES
SISSIER
SISSIES
SISSIEST
SISSIFIED
SISSOO
SISSOOS
SISSY
SIST
SISTED
SISTER
SISTERED
SISTERING
SISTERLY
SISTERS
SISTING
SISTRA
SISTRUM
SISTS
SIT
SITAR
SITARS
SITATUNGA
SITATUNGAS
SITCOM
SITCOMS
SITE
SITED
SITES
SITFAST
SITFASTS
SITH
SITHE
SITHED
SITHEN
SITHENCE
SITHENS
SITHES
SITHING
SITING
SITIOLOGIES
SITIOLOGY
SITOLOGIES

SITOLOGY
SITREP
SITREPS
SITS
SITTAR
SITTARS
SITTER
SITTERS
SITTINE
SITTING
SITTINGS
SITUATE
SITUATED
SITUATES
SITUATING
SITUATION
SITUATIONS
SITULA
SITULAE
SITUS
SITUTUNGA
SITUTUNGAS
SITZKRIEG
SITZKRIEGS
SIVER
SIVERS
SIWASH
SIWASHES
SIX
SIXAIN
SIXAINE
SIXAINES
SIXAINS
SIXER
SIXERS
SIXES
SIXFOLD
SIXPENCE
SIXPENCES
SIXPENNIES
SIXPENNY
SIXSCORE
SIXSCORES
SIXTE
SIXTEEN
SIXTEENER
SIXTEENERS
SIXTEENMO
SIXTEENMOS
SIXTEENS
SIXTEENTH
SIXTEENTHS
SIXTES
SIXTH
SIXTHLY
SIXTHS
SIXTIES
SIXTIETH
SIXTIETHS
SIXTY
SIZABLE
SIZAR
SIZARS
SIZARSHIP
SIZARSHIPS
SIZE
SIZEABLE

SIZED
SIZEISM
SIZEISMS
SIZEIST
SIZEISTS
SIZEL
SIZELS
SIZER
SIZERS
SIZES
SIZIER
SIZIEST
SIZINESS
SIZINESSES
SIZING
SIZINGS
SIZISM
SIZISMS
SIZIST
SIZISTS
SIZY
SIZZLE
SIZZLED
SIZZLER
SIZZLERS
SIZZLES
SIZZLING
SIZZLINGS
SJAMBOK
SJAMBOKKED
SJAMBOKKING
SJAMBOKS
SKA
SKAG
SKAGS
SKAIL
SKAILED
SKAILING
SKAILS
SKAITH
SKAITHED
SKAITHING
SKAITHS
SKALD
SKALDIC
SKALDS
SKALDSHIP
SKALDSHIPS
SKANK
SKANKED
SKANKING
SKANKINGS
SKANKS
SKART
SKARTH
SKARTHS
SKARTS
SKAS
SKAT
SKATE
SKATED
SKATEPARK
SKATEPARKS
SKATER
SKATERS
SKATES
SKATING

SKATINGS	SKELLOCHS	SKI	SKIMMIAS	SKIRMISHES
SKATOLE	SKELLS	SKIABLE	SKIMMING	SKIRMISHING
SKATOLES	SKELLUM	SKIAGRAM	SKIMMINGS	SKIRMISHINGS
SKATS	SKELLUMS	SKIAGRAMS	SKIMP	SKIRR
SKATT	SKELLY	SKIAGRAPH	SKIMPED	SKIRRED
SKATTS	SKELLYING	SKIAGRAPHS	SKIMPIER	SKIRRET
SKAW	SKELM	SKIAMACHIES	SKIMPIEST	SKIRRETS
SKAWS	SKELMS	SKIAMACHY	SKIMPILY	SKIRRING
SKEAN	SKELP	SKIASCOPIES	SKIMPING	SKIRRS
SKEANS	SKELPED	SKIASCOPY	SKIMPS	SKIRT
SKEAR	SKELPING	SKIATRON	SKIMPY	SKIRTED
SKEARED	SKELPINGS	SKIATRONS	SKIMS	SKIRTER
SKEARIER	SKELPS	SKIBOB	SKIN	SKIRTERS
SKEARIEST	SKELTER	SKIBOBBED	SKINFLICK	SKIRTING
SKEARING	SKELTERED	SKIBOBBING	SKINFLICKS	SKIRTINGS
SKEARS	SKELTERING	SKIBOBBINGS	SKINFLINT	SKIRTLESS
SKEARY	SKELTERS	SKIBOBS	SKINFLINTS	SKIRTS
SKEDADDLE	SKELUM	SKID	SKINFOOD	SKIS
SKEDADDLED	SKELUMS	SKIDDED	SKINFOODS	SKIT
SKEDADDLES	SKENE	SKIDDER	SKINFUL	SKITE
SKEDADDLING	SKENES	SKIDDERS	SKINFULS	SKITED
SKEECHAN	SKEO	SKIDDING	SKINHEAD	SKITES
SKEECHANS	SKEOS	SKIDOO	SKINHEADS	SKITING
SKEELIER	SKEP	SKIDOOS	SKINK	SKITS
SKEELIEST	SKEPFUL	SKIDPAN	SKINKED	SKITTER
SKEELY	SKEPFULS	SKIDPANS	SKINKER	SKITTERED
SKEER	SKEPPED	SKIDPROOF	SKINKERS	SKITTERING
SKEERED	SKEPPING	SKIDS	SKINKING	SKITTERS
SKEERIER	SKEPS	SKIED	SKINKS	SKITTISH
SKEERIEST	SKEPSIS	SKIER	SKINLESS	SKITTLE
SKEERING	SKEPSISES	SKIERS	SKINNED	SKITTLED
SKEERS	SKEPTIC	SKIES	SKINNER	SKITTLES
SKEERY	SKEPTICAL	SKIEY	SKINNERS	SKITTLING
SKEESICKS	SKEPTICS	SKIEYER	SKINNIER	SKIVE
SKEET	SKER	SKIEYEST	SKINNIEST	SKIVED
SKEETER	SKERRED	SKIFF	SKINNING	SKIVER
SKEETERS	SKERRICK	SKIFFED	SKINNY	SKIVERED
SKEETS	SKERRICKS	SKIFFING	SKINS	SKIVERING
SKEG	SKERRIES	SKIFFLE	SKINT	SKIVERS
SKEGG	SKERRING	SKIFFLES	SKINTER	SKIVES
SKEGGER	SKERRY	SKIFFS	SKINTEST	SKIVIE
SKEGGERS	SKERS	SKIING	SKIO	SKIVIER
SKEGGS	SKETCH	SKIINGS	SKIOS	SKIVIEST
SKEGS	SKETCHED	SKIJORING	SKIP	SKIVING
SKEIGH	SKETCHER	SKIJORINGS	SKIPJACK	SKIVINGS
SKEIGHER	SKETCHERS	SKILFUL	SKIPJACKS	SKIVVIED
SKEIGHEST	SKETCHES	SKILFULLY	SKIPPED	SKIVVIES
SKEIN	SKETCHIER	SKILL	SKIPPER	SKIVVY
SKEINS	SKETCHIEST	SKILLED	SKIPPERED	SKIVVYING
SKELDER	SKETCHILY	SKILLESS	SKIPPERING	SKIVY
SKELDERED	SKETCHING	SKILLET	SKIPPERINGS	SKLATE
SKELDERING	SKETCHY	SKILLETS	SKIPPERS	SKLATED
SKELDERS	SKEW	SKILLFUL	SKIPPET	SKLATES
SKELETAL	SKEWBACK	SKILLIER	SKIPPETS	SKLATING
SKELETON	SKEWBACKS	SKILLIES	SKIPPIER	SKLENT
SKELETONS	SKEWBALD	SKILLIEST	SKIPPIEST	SKLENTED
SKELF	SKEWBALDS	SKILLING	SKIPPING	SKLENTING
SKELFS	SKEWED	SKILLINGS	SKIPPINGS	SKLENTS
SKELL	SKEWER	SKILLION	SKIPPY	SKLIFF
SKELLIE	SKEWERED	SKILLIONS	SKIPS	SKLIFFS
SKELLIED	SKEWERING	SKILLS	SKIRL	SKLIM
SKELLIER	SKEWERS	SKILLY	SKIRLED	SKLIMMED
SKELLIES	SKEWEST	SKIM	SKIRLING	SKLIMMING
SKELLIEST	SKEWING	SKIMMED	SKIRLINGS	SKLIMS
SKELLOCH	SKEWNESS	SKIMMER	SKIRLS	SKOAL
SKELLOCHED	SKEWNESSES	SKIMMERS	SKIRMISH	SKOFF
SKELLOCHING	SKEWS	SKIMMIA	SKIRMISHED	SKOFFED

The Chambers Dictionary is the authority for many longer words; see *OSW* Introduction, page xii.

SKOFFING
SKOFFS
SKOKIAAN
SKOKIAANS
SKOL
SKOLIA
SKOLION
SKOLLIE
SKOLLIES
SKOLLY
SKOOSH
SKOOSHED
SKOOSHES
SKOOSHING
SKRAN
SKRANS
SKREEN
SKREENS
SKREIGH
SKREIGHED
SKREIGHING
SKREIGHS
SKRIECH
SKRIECHED
SKRIECHING
SKRIECHS
SKRIED
SKRIEGH
SKRIEGHED
SKRIEGHING
SKRIEGHS
SKRIES
SKRIK
SKRIKS
SKRIMMAGE
SKRIMMAGED
SKRIMMAGES
SKRIMMAGING
SKRIMP
SKRIMPED
SKRIMPING
SKRIMPS
SKRUMP
SKRUMPED
SKRUMPING
SKRUMPS
SKRY
SKRYER
SKRYERS
SKRYING
SKUA
SKUAS
SKUDLER
SKUDLERS
SKUG
SKUGGED
SKUGGING
SKUGS
SKULK
SKULKED
SKULKER
SKULKERS
SKULKING
SKULKINGS
SKULKS
SKULL
SKULLCAP

SKULLCAPS
SKULLS
SKULPIN
SKULPINS
SKUMMER
SKUMMERED
SKUMMERING
SKUMMERS
SKUNK
SKUNKBIRD
SKUNKBIRDS
SKUNKED
SKUNKING
SKUNKS
SKURRIED
SKURRIES
SKURRY
SKURRYING
SKUTTLE
SKUTTLED
SKUTTLES
SKUTTLING
SKY
SKYBORN
SKYCLAD
SKYDIVER
SKYDIVERS
SKYER
SKYERS
SKYEY
SKYHOOK
SKYHOOKS
SKYIER
SKYIEST
SKYING
SKYISH
SKYJACK
SKYJACKED
SKYJACKER
SKYJACKERS
SKYJACKING
SKYJACKINGS
SKYJACKS
SKYLAB
SKYLABS
SKYLARK
SKYLARKED
SKYLARKER
SKYLARKERS
SKYLARKING
SKYLARKINGS
SKYLARKS
SKYLIGHT
SKYLIGHTS
SKYLINE
SKYLINES
SKYMAN
SKYMEN
SKYR
SKYRE
SKYRED
SKYRES
SKYRING
SKYROCKET
SKYROCKETED
SKYROCKETING
SKYROCKETS

SKYRS
SKYSAIL
SKYSAILS
SKYSCAPE
SKYSCAPES
SKYTE
SKYTED
SKYTES
SKYTING
SKYWARD
SKYWARDS
SKYWAY
SKYWAYS
SLAB
SLABBED
SLABBER
SLABBERED
SLABBERER
SLABBERERS
SLABBERING
SLABBERS
SLABBERY
SLABBIER
SLABBIEST
SLABBING
SLABBY
SLABS
SLABSTONE
SLABSTONES
SLACK
SLACKED
SLACKEN
SLACKENED
SLACKENING
SLACKENINGS
SLACKENS
SLACKER
SLACKERS
SLACKEST
SLACKING
SLACKLY
SLACKNESS
SLACKNESSES
SLACKS
SLADANG
SLADANGS
SLADE
SLADES
SLAE
SLAES
SLAG
SLAGGED
SLAGGIER
SLAGGIEST
SLAGGING
SLAGGY
SLAGS
SLAID
SLAIN
SLAINTE
SLAIRG
SLAIRGED
SLAIRGING
SLAIRGS
SLAISTER
SLAISTERED
SLAISTERIES

SLAISTERING
SLAISTERS
SLAISTERY
SLAKE
SLAKED
SLAKELESS
SLAKES
SLAKING
SLALOM
SLALOMED
SLALOMING
SLALOMS
SLAM
SLAMMAKIN
SLAMMAKINS
SLAMMED
SLAMMER
SLAMMERS
SLAMMING
SLAMMINGS
SLAMS
SLANDER
SLANDERED
SLANDERER
SLANDERERS
SLANDERING
SLANDERS
SLANE
SLANES
SLANG
SLANGED
SLANGER
SLANGERS
SLANGIER
SLANGIEST
SLANGILY
SLANGING
SLANGINGS
SLANGISH
SLANGS
SLANGULAR
SLANGY
SLANT
SLANTED
SLANTING
SLANTLY
SLANTS
SLANTWAYS
SLANTWISE
SLAP
SLAPJACK
SLAPJACKS
SLAPPED
SLAPPER
SLAPPERS
SLAPPING
SLAPS
SLAPSHOT
SLAPSHOTS
SLAPSTICK
SLAPSTICKS
SLASH
SLASHED
SLASHER
SLASHERS
SLASHES
SLASHING

SLASHINGS
SLAT
SLATCH
SLATCHES
SLATE
SLATED
SLATER
SLATERS
SLATES
SLATHER
SLATHERED
SLATHERING
SLATHERS
SLATIER
SLATIEST
SLATINESS
SLATINESSES
SLATING
SLATINGS
SLATS
SLATTED
SLATTER
SLATTERED
SLATTERING
SLATTERN
SLATTERNS
SLATTERS
SLATTERY
SLATTING
SLATY
SLAUGHTER
SLAUGHTERED
SLAUGHTERING
SLAUGHTERS
SLAVE
SLAVED
SLAVER
SLAVERED
SLAVERER
SLAVERERS
SLAVERIES
SLAVERING
SLAVERS
SLAVERY
SLAVES
SLAVEY
SLAVEYS
SLAVING
SLAVISH
SLAVISHLY
SLAVOCRAT
SLAVOCRATS
SLAW
SLAWS
SLAY
SLAYED
SLAYER
SLAYERS
SLAYING
SLAYS
SLEAVE
SLEAVED
SLEAVES
SLEAVING
SLEAZE
SLEAZEBAG
SLEAZEBAGS

The Chambers Dictionary is the authority for many longer words; see *OSW* Introduction, page xii.

SLEAZES	SLEEVE	SLIDDERS	SLINKWEED	SLIVOWITZ
SLEAZIER	SLEEVED	SLIDDERY	SLINKWEEDS	SLIVOWITZES
SLEAZIEST	SLEEVEEN	SLIDE	SLINKY	SLOAN
SLEAZILY	SLEEVEENS	SLIDED	SLINTER	SLOANS
SLEAZY	SLEEVER	SLIDER	SLINTERS	SLOB
SLED	SLEEVERS	SLIDERS	SLIP	SLOBBER
SLEDDED	SLEEVES	SLIDES	SLIPCASE	SLOBBERED
SLEDDING	SLEEVING	SLIDING	SLIPCASES	SLOBBERING
SLEDDINGS	SLEEVINGS	SLIDINGLY	SLIPE	SLOBBERS
SLEDED	SLEEZIER	SLIDINGS	SLIPES	SLOBBERY
SLEDGE	SLEEZIEST	SLIER	SLIPFORM	SLOBBIER
SLEDGED	SLEEZY	SLIEST	SLIPKNOT	SLOBBIEST
SLEDGER	SLEIDED	SLIGHT	SLIPKNOTS	SLOBBISH
SLEDGERS	SLEIGH	SLIGHTED	SLIPPAGE	SLOBBY
SLEDGES	SLEIGHED	SLIGHTER	SLIPPAGES	SLOBLAND
SLEDGING	SLEIGHER	SLIGHTEST	SLIPPED	SLOBLANDS
SLEDGINGS	SLEIGHERS	SLIGHTING	SLIPPER	SLOBS
SLEDS	SLEIGHING	SLIGHTISH	SLIPPERED	SLOCKEN
SLEE	SLEIGHINGS	SLIGHTLY	SLIPPERIER	SLOCKENED
SLEECH	SLEIGHS	SLIGHTS	SLIPPERIEST	SLOCKENING
SLEECHES	SLEIGHT	SLILY	SLIPPERING	SLOCKENS
SLEECHIER	SLEIGHTS	SLIM	SLIPPERS	SLOE
SLEECHIEST	SLENDER	SLIME	SLIPPERY	SLOEBUSH
SLEECHY	SLENDERER	SLIMEBALL	SLIPPIER	SLOEBUSHES
SLEEK	SLENDEREST	SLIMEBALLS	SLIPPIEST	SLOES
SLEEKED	SLENDERLY	SLIMED	SLIPPING	SLOETHORN
SLEEKEN	SLENTER	SLIMES	SLIPPY	SLOETHORNS
SLEEKENED	SLENTERS	SLIMIER	SLIPRAIL	SLOETREE
SLEEKENING	SLEPT	SLIMIEST	SLIPRAILS	SLOETREES
SLEEKENS	SLEUTH	SLIMILY	SLIPS	SLOG
SLEEKER	SLEUTHED	SLIMINESS	SLIPSHOD	SLOGAN
SLEEKERS	SLEUTHING	SLIMINESSES	SLIPSLOP	SLOGANEER
SLEEKEST	SLEUTHS	SLIMING	SLIPSLOPS	SLOGANEERED
SLEEKIER	SLEW	SLIMLINE	SLIPT	SLOGANEERING
SLEEKIEST	SLEWED	SLIMLY	SLIPWARE	SLOGANEERINGS
SLEEKING	SLEWING	SLIMMED	SLIPWARES	SLOGANEERS
SLEEKINGS	SLEWS	SLIMMER	SLIPWAY	SLOGANISE
SLEEKIT	SLEY	SLIMMERS	SLIPWAYS	SLOGANISED
SLEEKLY	SLEYS	SLIMMEST	SLISH	SLOGANISES
SLEEKNESS	SLICE	SLIMMING	SLISHES	SLOGANISINGS
SLEEKNESSES	SLICED	SLIMMINGS	SLIT	SLOGANISINGS
SLEEKS	SLICER	SLIMMISH	SLITHER	SLOGANIZE
SLEEKY	SLICERS	SLIMNESS	SLITHERED	SLOGANIZED
SLEEP	SLICES	SLIMNESSES	SLITHERIER	SLOGANIZES
SLEEPER	SLICING	SLIMS	SLITHERIEST	SLOGANIZING
SLEEPERS	SLICINGS	SLIMSIER	SLITHERING	SLOGANIZINGS
SLEEPERY	SLICK	SLIMSIEST	SLITHERS	SLOGANS
SLEEPIER	SLICKED	SLIMSY	SLITHERY	SLOGGED
SLEEPIEST	SLICKEN	SLIMY	SLITS	SLOGGER
SLEEPILY	SLICKENED	SLING	SLITTER	SLOGGERS
SLEEPING	SLICKENING	SLINGBACK	SLITTERS	SLOGGING
SLEEPINGS	SLICKENS	SLINGBACKS	SLITTING	SLOGS
SLEEPLESS	SLICKER	SLINGER	SLIVE	SLOID
SLEEPRY	SLICKERED	SLINGERS	SLIVED	SLOIDS
SLEEPS	SLICKERS	SLINGING	SLIVEN	SLOKEN
SLEEPSUIT	SLICKEST	SLINGS	SLIVER	SLOKENED
SLEEPSUITS	SLICKING	SLINGSHOT	SLIVERED	SLOKENING
SLEEPY	SLICKINGS	SLINGSHOTS	SLIVERING	SLOKENS
SLEER	SLICKLY	SLINK	SLIVERS	SLOOM
SLEEST	SLICKNESS	SLINKER	SLIVES	SLOOMED
SLEET	SLICKNESSES	SLINKERS	SLIVING	SLOOMIER
SLEETED	SLICKS	SLINKIER	SLIVOVIC	SLOOMIEST
SLEETIER	SLID	SLINKIEST	SLIVOVICA	SLOOMING
SLEETIEST	SLIDDEN	SLINKING	SLIVOVICAS	SLOOMS
SLEETING	SLIDDER	SLINKS	SLIVOVICS	SLOOMY
SLEETS	SLIDDERED	SLINKSKIN	SLIVOVITZ	SLOOP
SLEETY	SLIDDERING	SLINKSKINS	SLIVOVITZES	SLOOPS

The Chambers Dictionary is the authority for many longer words; see *OSW* Introduction, page xii.

SLOOSH	SLOVENS	SLUICIEST	SLUTTERY	SMARTENED
SLOOSHED	SLOW	SLUICING	SLUTTISH	SMARTENING
SLOOSHES	SLOWBACK	SLUICY	SLY	SMARTENS
SLOOSHING	SLOWBACKS	SLUING	SLYBOOTS	SMARTER
SLOOT	SLOWCOACH	SLUIT ·	SLYER	SMARTEST
SLOOTS	SLOWCOACHES	SLUITS	SLYEST	SMARTIE
SLOP	SLOWED	SLUM	SLYISH	SMARTIES
SLOPE	SLOWER	SLUMBER	SLYLY	SMARTING
SLOPED	SLOWEST	SLUMBERED	SLYNESS	SMARTISH
SLOPES	SLOWING	SLUMBERER	SLYNESSES	SMARTLY
SLOPEWISE	SLOWINGS	SLUMBERERS	SLYPE	SMARTNESS
SLOPIER	SLOWISH	SLUMBERING	SLYPES	SMARTNESSES
SLOPIEST	SLOWLY	SLUMBERINGS	SMA	SMARTS
SLOPING	SLOWNESS	SLUMBERS	SMACK	SMARTWEED
SLOPINGLY	SLOWNESSES	SLUMBERY	SMACKED	SMARTWEEDS
SLOPPED	SLOWPOKE	SLUMBROUS	SMACKER	SMARTY
SLOPPIER	SLOWPOKES	SLUMBRY	SMACKERS	SMASH
SLOPPIEST	SLOWS	SLUMLORD	SMACKING	SMASHED
SLOPPILY	SLOWWORM	SLUMLORDS	SMACKINGS	SMASHER
SLOPPING	SLOWWORMS	SLUMMED	SMACKS	SMASHEROO
SLOPPY	SLOYD	SLUMMER	SMAIK	SMASHEROOS
SLOPS	SLOYDS	SLUMMERS	SMAIKS	SMASHERS
SLOPWORK	SLUB	SLUMMIER	SMALL	SMASHES
SLOPWORKS	SLUBB	SLUMMIEST	SMALLAGE	SMASHING
SLOPY	SLUBBED	SLUMMING	SMALLAGES	SMASHINGS
SLOSH	SLUBBER	SLUMMINGS	SMALLED	SMATCH
SLOSHED	SLUBBERED	SLUMMOCK	SMALLER	SMATCHED
SLOSHES	SLUBBERING	SLUMMOCKED	SMALLEST	SMATCHES
SLOSHIER	SLUBBERINGS	SLUMMOCKING	SMALLING	SMATCHING
SLOSHIEST	SLUBBERS	SLUMMOCKS	SMALLISH	SMATTER
SLOSHING	SLUBBIER	SLUMMY	SMALLNESS	SMATTERED
SLOSHINGS	SLUBBIEST	SLUMP	SMALLNESSES	SMATTERER
SLOSHY	SLUBBING	SLUMPED	SMALLPOX	SMATTERERS
SLOT	SLUBBINGS	SLUMPIER	SMALLPOXES	SMATTERING
SLOTH	SLUBBS	SLUMPIEST	SMALLS	SMATTERINGS
SLOTHED	SLUBBY	SLUMPING	SMALLSAT	SMATTERS
SLOTHFUL	SLUBS	SLUMPS	SMALLSATS	SMEAR
SLOTHING	SLUDGE	SLUMPY	SMALM	SMEARED
SLOTHS	SLUDGES	SLUMS	SMALMED	SMEARIER
SLOTS	SLUDGIER	SLUNG	SMALMILY	SMEARIEST
SLOTTED	SLUDGIEST	SLUNK	SMALMING	SMEARILY
SLOTTER	SLUDGY	SLUR	SMALMS	SMEARING
SLOTTERS	SLUE	SLURB	SMALMY	SMEARS
SLOTTING	SLUED	SLURBS	SMALT	SMEARY
SLOUCH	SLUEING	SLURP	SMALTI	SMEATH
SLOUCHED	SLUES	SLURPED	SMALTITE	SMEATHS
SLOUCHER	SLUG	SLURPER	SMALTITES	SMECTIC
SLOUCHERS	SLUGFEST	SLURPERS	SMALTO	SMECTITE
SLOUCHES	SLUGFESTS	SLURPING	SMALTOS	SMECTITES
SLOUCHIER	SLUGGABED	SLURPS	SMALTS	SMEDDUM
SLOUCHIEST	SLUGGABEDS	SLURRED	SMARAGD	SMEDDUMS
SLOUCHING	SLUGGARD	SLURRIES	SMARAGDS	SMEE
SLOUCHY	SLUGGARDS	SLURRING	SMARM	SMEECH
SLOUGH	SLUGGED	SLURRY	SMARMED	SMEECHED
SLOUGHED	SLUGGER	SLURS	SMARMIER	SMEECHES
SLOUGHIER	SLUGGERS	SLUSE	SMARMIEST	SMEECHING
SLOUGHIEST	SLUGGING	SLUSES	SMARMILY	SMEEK
SLOUGHING	SLUGGISH	SLUSH	SMARMING	SMEEKED
SLOUGHS	SLUGHORN	SLUSHED	SMARMS	SMEEKING
SLOUGHY	SLUGHORNE	SLUSHES	SMARMY	SMEEKS
SLOVE	SLUGHORNES	SLUSHIER	SMART	SMEES
SLOVEN	SLUGHORNS	SLUSHIEST	SMARTARSE	SMEETH
SLOVENLIER	SLUGS	SLUSHING	SMARTARSES	SMEETHS
SLOVENLIEST	SLUICE	SLUSHY	SMARTASS	SMEGMA
SLOVENLY	SLUICED	SLUT	SMARTASSES	SMEGMAS
SLOVENRIES	SLUICES	SLUTS	SMARTED	SMELL
SLOVENRY	SLUICIER	SLUTTERIES	SMARTEN	SMELLED

The Chambers Dictionary is the authority for many longer words; see *OSW* Introduction, page xii.

SMELLER	SMIRKING	SMOKINGS	SMOUSER	SNACK
SMELLERS	SMIRKS	SMOKO	SMOUSERS	SNACKED
SMELLIER	SMIRKY	SMOKOS	SMOUSES	SNACKING
SMELLIEST	SMIRR	SMOKY	SMOUSING	SNACKS
SMELLING	SMIRRED	SMOLDER	SMOUT	SNAFFLE
SMELLINGS	SMIRRIER	SMOLDERED	SMOUTED	SNAFFLED
SMELLS	SMIRRIEST	SMOLDERING	SMOUTING	SNAFFLES
SMELLY	SMIRRING	SMOLDERS	SMOUTS	SNAFFLING
SMELT	SMIRRS	SMOLT	SMOWT	SNAFU
SMELTED	SMIRRY	SMOLTS	SMOWTS	SNAFUS
SMELTER	SMIRS	SMOOCH	SMOYLE	SNAG
SMELTERIES	SMIT	SMOOCHED	SMOYLED	SNAGGED
SMELTERS	SMITE	SMOOCHES	SMOYLES	SNAGGIER
SMELTERY	SMITER	SMOOCHING	SMOYLING	SNAGGIEST
SMELTING	SMITERS	SMOOR	SMUDGE	SNAGGING
SMELTINGS	SMITES	SMOORED	SMUDGED	SNAGGY
SMELTS	SMITH	SMOORING	SMUDGER	SNAGS
SMEUSE	SMITHED	SMOORS	SMUDGERS	SNAIL
SMEUSES	SMITHERIES	SMOOT	SMUDGES	SNAILED
SMEW	SMITHERS	SMOOTED	SMUDGIER	SNAILERIES
SMEWS	SMITHERY	SMOOTH	SMUDGIEST	SNAILERY
SMICKER	SMITHIED	SMOOTHED	SMUDGILY	SNAILIER
SMICKERED	SMITHIES	SMOOTHEN	SMUDGING	SNAILIEST
SMICKERING	SMITHING	SMOOTHENED	SMUDGY	SNAILING
SMICKERINGS	SMITHS	SMOOTHENING	SMUG	SNAILS
SMICKERS	SMITHY	SMOOTHENS	SMUGGED	SNAILY
SMICKET	SMITHYING	SMOOTHER	SMUGGER	SNAKE
SMICKETS	SMITING	SMOOTHERS	SMUGGEST	SNAKEBIRD
SMICKLY	SMITS	SMOOTHEST	SMUGGING	SNAKEBIRDS
SMIDDIED	SMITTED	SMOOTHIE	SMUGGLE	SNAKEBITE
SMIDDIES	SMITTEN	SMOOTHIES	SMUGGLED	SNAKEBITES
SMIDDY	SMITTING	SMOOTHING	SMUGGLER	SNAKED
SMIDDYING	SMITTLE	SMOOTHINGS	SMUGGLERS	SNAKELIKE
SMIDGEN	SMOCK	SMOOTHISH	SMUGGLES	SNAKEROOT
SMIDGENS	SMOCKED	SMOOTHLY	SMUGGLING	SNAKEROOTS
SMIDGEON	SMOCKING	SMOOTHS	SMUGGLINGS	SNAKES
SMIDGEONS	SMOCKINGS	SMOOTING	SMUGLY	SNAKESKIN
SMIDGIN	SMOCKS	SMOOTS	SMUGNESS	SNAKESKINS
SMIDGINS	SMOG	SMORBROD	SMUGNESSES	SNAKEWEED
SMIGHT	SMOGGIER	SMORBRODS	SMUGS	SNAKEWEEDS
SMIGHTING	SMOGGIEST	SMORE	SMUR	SNAKEWISE
SMIGHTS	SMOGGY	SMORED	SMURRED	SNAKEWOOD
SMILAX	SMOGS	SMORES	SMURRIER	SNAKEWOODS
SMILAXES	SMOILE	SMORING	SMURRIEST	SNAKIER
SMILE	SMOILED	SMORZANDO	SMURRING	SNAKIEST
SMILED	SMOILES	SMORZATO	SMURRY	SNAKILY
SMILEFUL	SMOILING	SMOTE	SMURS	SNAKINESS
SMILELESS	SMOKABLE	SMOTHER	SMUT	SNAKINESSES
SMILER	SMOKE	SMOTHERED	SMUTCH	SNAKING
SMILERS	SMOKEBUSH	SMOTHERER	SMUTCHED	SNAKISH
SMILES	SMOKEBUSHES	SMOTHERERS	SMUTCHES	SNAKY
SMILET	SMOKED	SMOTHERING	SMUTCHING	SNAP
SMILETS	SMOKEHOOD	SMOTHERINGS	SMUTS	SNAPHANCE
SMILING	SMOKEHOODS	SMOTHERS	SMUTTED	SNAPHANCES
SMILINGLY	SMOKELESS	SMOTHERY	SMUTTIER	SNAPPED
SMILINGS	SMOKER	SMOUCH	SMUTTIEST	SNAPPER
SMILODON	SMOKERS	SMOUCHED	SMUTTILY	SNAPPERED
SMILODONS	SMOKES	SMOUCHES	SMUTTING	SNAPPERING
SMIR	SMOKETREE	SMOUCHING	SMUTTY	SNAPPERS
SMIRCH	SMOKETREES	SMOULDER	SMYTRIE	SNAPPIER
SMIRCHED	SMOKIER	SMOULDERED	SMYTRIES	SNAPPIEST
SMIRCHES	SMOKIES	SMOULDERING	SNAB	SNAPPILY
SMIRCHING	SMOKIEST	SMOULDERINGS	SNABBLE	SNAPPING
SMIRK	SMOKILY	SMOULDERS	SNABBLED	SNAPPINGS
SMIRKED	SMOKINESS	SMOULDRY	SNABBLES	SNAPPISH
SMIRKIER	SMOKINESSES	SMOUSE	SNABBLING	SNAPPY
SMIRKIEST	SMOKING	SMOUSED	SNABS	SNAPS

The Chambers Dictionary is the authority for many longer words; see *OSW* Introduction, page xii.

SNAPSHOT	SNEAKY	SNICKERED	SNIPERS	SNOOD
SNAPSHOTS	SNEAP	SNICKERING	SNIPES	SNOODED
SNAR	SNEAPED	SNICKERS	SNIPIER	SNOODING
SNARE	SNEAPING	SNICKET	SNIPIEST	SNOODS
SNARED	SNEAPS	SNICKETS	SNIPING	SNOOK
SNARER	SNEATH	SNICKING	SNIPINGS	SNOOKED
SNARERS	SNEATHS	SNICKS	SNIPPED	SNOOKER
SNARES	SNEB	SNIDE	SNIPPER	SNOOKERED
SNARIER	SNEBBE	SNIDELY	SNIPPERS	SNOOKERING
SNARIEST	SNEBBED	SNIDENESS	SNIPPET	SNOOKERS
SNARING	SNEBBES	SNIDENESSES	SNIPPETS	SNOOKING
SNARINGS	SNEBBING	SNIDER	SNIPPETY	SNOOKS
SNARK	SNEBS	SNIDES	SNIPPIER	SNOOL
SNARKS	SNECK	SNIDEST	SNIPPIEST	SNOOLED
SNARL	SNECKED	SNIES	SNIPPING	SNOOLING
SNARLED	SNECKING	SNIFF	SNIPPINGS	SNOOLS
SNARLER	SNECKS	SNIFFED	SNIPPY	SNOOP
SNARLERS	SNED	SNIFFER	SNIPS	SNOOPED
SNARLIER	SNEDDED	SNIFFERS	SNIPY	SNOOPER
SNARLIEST	SNEDDING	SNIFFIER	SNIRT	SNOOPERS
SNARLING	SNEDS	SNIFFIEST	SNIRTLE	SNOOPIER
SNARLINGS	SNEE	SNIFFILY	SNIRTLED	SNOOPIEST
SNARLS	SNEED	SNIFFING	SNIRTLES	SNOOPING
SNARLY	SNEEING	SNIFFINGS	SNIRTLING	SNOOPS
SNARRED	SNEER	SNIFFLE	SNIRTS	SNOOPY
SNARRING	SNEERED	SNIFFLED	SNITCH	SNOOT
SNARS	SNEERER	SNIFFLER	SNITCHED	SNOOTED
SNARY	SNEERERS	SNIFFLERS	SNITCHER	SNOOTFUL
SNASH	SNEERIER	SNIFFLES	SNITCHERS	SNOOTFULS
SNASHED	SNEERIEST	SNIFFLING	SNITCHES	SNOOTIER
SNASHES	SNEERING	SNIFFS	SNITCHING	SNOOTIEST
SNASHING	SNEERINGS	SNIFFY	SNIVEL	SNOOTILY
SNASTE	SNEERS	SNIFT	SNIVELLED	SNOOTING
SNASTES	SNEERY	SNIFTED	SNIVELLER	SNOOTS
SNATCH	SNEES	SNIFTER	SNIVELLERS	SNOOTY
SNATCHED	SNEESH	SNIFTERED	SNIVELLING	SNOOZE
SNATCHER	SNEESHAN	SNIFTERING	SNIVELLY	SNOOZED
SNATCHERS	SNEESHANS	SNIFTERS	SNIVELS	SNOOZER
SNATCHES	SNEESHES	SNIFTIER	SNOB	SNOOZERS
SNATCHIER	SNEESHIN	SNIFTIEST	SNOBBERIES	SNOOZES
SNATCHIEST	SNEESHING	SNIFTING	SNOBBERY	SNOOZIER
SNATCHILY	SNEESHINGS	SNIFTS	SNOBBIER	SNOOZIEST
SNATCHING	SNEESHINS	SNIFTY	SNOBBIEST	SNOOZING
SNATCHY	SNEEZE	SNIG	SNOBBISH	SNOOZLE
SNATH	SNEEZED	SNIGGED	SNOBBISM	SNOOZLED
SNATHE	SNEEZER	SNIGGER	SNOBBISMS	SNOOZLES
SNATHES	SNEEZERS	SNIGGERED	SNOBBY	SNOOZLING
SNATHS	SNEEZES	SNIGGERER	SNOBLING	SNOOZY
SNAZZIER	SNEEZIER	SNIGGERERS	SNOBLINGS	SNORE
SNAZZIEST	SNEEZIEST	SNIGGERING	SNOBS	SNORED
SNAZZY	SNEEZING	SNIGGERINGS	SNOD	SNORER
SNEAD	SNEEZINGS	SNIGGERS	SNODDED	SNORERS
SNEADS	SNEEZY	SNIGGING	SNODDER	SNORES
SNEAK	SNELL	SNIGGLE	SNODDEST	SNORING
SNEAKED	SNELLED	SNIGGLED	SNODDING	SNORINGS
SNEAKER	SNELLER	SNIGGLER	SNODDIT	SNORKEL
SNEAKERS	SNELLEST	SNIGGLERS	SNODS	SNORKELER
SNEAKEUP	SNELLING	SNIGGLES	SNOEK	SNORKELERS
SNEAKEUPS	SNELLS	SNIGGLING	SNOEKS	SNORKELS
SNEAKIER	SNELLY	SNIGGLINGS	SNOG	SNORT
SNEAKIEST	SNIB	SNIGS	SNOGGED	SNORTED
SNEAKILY	SNIBBED	SNIP	SNOGGING	SNORTER
SNEAKING	SNIBBING	SNIPE	SNOGS	SNORTERS
SNEAKISH	SNIBS	SNIPED	SNOKE	SNORTIER
SNEAKS	SNICK	SNIPEFISH	SNOKED	SNORTIEST
SNEAKSBIES	SNICKED	SNIPEFISHES	SNOKES	SNORTING
SNEAKSBY	SNICKER	SNIPER	SNOKING	SNORTINGS

The Chambers Dictionary is the authority for many longer words; see *OSW* Introduction, page xii.

SNORTS	SNOWK	SNUGGEST	SOARE	SOCIALIZED
SNORTY	SNOWKED	SNUGGING	SOARED	SOCIALIZES
SNOT	SNOWKING	SNUGGLE	SOARER	SOCIALIZING
SNOTS	SNOWKS	SNUGGLED	SOARERS	SOCIALLY
SNOTTED	SNOWLESS	SNUGGLES	SOARES	SOCIALS
SNOTTER	SNOWLIKE	SNUGGLING	SOARING	SOCIATE
SNOTTERED	SNOWLINE	SNUGLY	SOARINGLY	SOCIATES
SNOTTERIES	SNOWLINES	SNUGNESS	SOARINGS	SOCIATION
SNOTTERING	SNOWMAN	SNUGNESSES	SOARS	SOCIATIONS
SNOTTERS	SNOWMEN	SNUGS	SOB	SOCIATIVE
SNOTTERY	SNOWS	SNUSH	SOBBED	SOCIETAL
SNOTTIE	SNOWSCAPE	SNUSHED	SOBBING	SOCIETIES
SNOTTIER	SNOWSCAPES	SNUSHES	SOBBINGLY	SOCIETY
SNOTTIES	SNOWSHOE	SNUSHING	SOBBINGS	SOCIOGRAM
SNOTTIEST	SNOWSHOED	SNUZZLE	SOBEIT	SOCIOGRAMS
SNOTTILY	SNOWSHOEING	SNUZZLED	SOBER	SOCIOLECT
SNOTTING	SNOWSHOES	SNUZZLES	SOBERED	SOCIOLECTS
SNOTTY	SNOWSLIP	SNUZZLING	SOBERER	SOCIOLOGIES
SNOUT	SNOWSLIPS	SNY	SOBEREST	SOCIOLOGY
SNOUTED	SNOWSTORM	SNYE	SOBERING	SOCIOPATH
SNOUTIER	SNOWSTORMS	SNYES	SOBERISE	SOCIOPATHS
SNOUTIEST	SNOWY	SO	SOBERISED	SOCK
SNOUTING	SNUB	SOAK	SOBERISES	SOCKED
SNOUTS	SNUBBE	SOAKAGE	SOBERISING	SOCKET
SNOUTY	SNUBBED	SOAKAGES	SOBERIZE	SOCKETED
SNOW	SNUBBER	SOAKAWAY	SOBERIZED	SOCKETING
SNOWBALL	SNUBBERS	SOAKAWAYS	SOBERIZES	SOCKETS
SNOWBALLED	SNUBBES	SOAKED	SOBERIZING	SOCKETTE
SNOWBALLING	SNUBBIER	SOAKEN	SOBERLY	SOCKETTES
SNOWBALLS	SNUBBIEST	SOAKER	SOBERNESS	SOCKEYE
SNOWBERRIES	SNUBBING	SOAKERS	SOBERNESSES	SOCKEYES
SNOWBERRY	SNUBBINGS	SOAKING	SOBERS	SOCKING
SNOWBIRD	SNUBBISH	SOAKINGLY	SOBOLE	SOCKO
SNOWBIRDS	SNUBBY	SOAKINGS	SOBOLES	SOCKS
SNOWBLINK	SNUBS	SOAKS	SOBRIETIES	SOCLE
SNOWBLINKS	SNUCK	SOAP	SOBRIETY	SOCLES
SNOWBOARD	SNUDGE	SOAPBARK	SOBRIQUET	SOCMAN
SNOWBOARDS	SNUDGED	SOAPBARKS	SOBRIQUETS	SOCMEN
SNOWBOOT	SNUDGES	SOAPBERRIES	SOBS	SOCS
SNOWBOOTS	SNUDGING	SOAPBERRY	SOC	SOD
SNOWBOUND	SNUFF	SOAPBOX	SOCA	SODA
SNOWBUSH	SNUFFBOX	SOAPBOXES	SOCAGE	SODAIC
SNOWBUSHES	SNUFFBOXES	SOAPED	SOCAGER	SODAIN
SNOWCAP	SNUFFED	SOAPER	SOCAGERS	SODAINE
SNOWCAPS	SNUFFER	SOAPERS	SOCAGES	SODALITE
SNOWDRIFT	SNUFFERS	SOAPIE	SOCAS	SODALITES
SNOWDRIFTS	SNUFFIER	SOAPIER	SOCCAGE	SODALITIES
SNOWDROP	SNUFFIEST	SOAPIES	SOCCAGES	SODALITY
SNOWDROPS	SNUFFING	SOAPIEST	SOCCER	SODAMIDE
SNOWED	SNUFFINGS	SOAPILY	SOCCERS	SODAMIDES
SNOWFALL	SNUFFLE	SOAPINESS	SOCIABLE	SODAS
SNOWFALLS	SNUFFLED	SOAPINESSES	SOCIABLES	SODBUSTER
SNOWFIELD	SNUFFLER	SOAPING	SOCIABLY	SODBUSTERS
SNOWFIELDS	SNUFFLERS	SOAPLAND	SOCIAL	SODDED
SNOWFLAKE	SNUFFLES	SOAPLANDS	SOCIALISE	SODDEN
SNOWFLAKES	SNUFFLIER	SOAPLESS	SOCIALISED	SODDENED
SNOWFLECK	SNUFFLIEST	SOAPROOT	SOCIALISES	SODDENING
SNOWFLECKS	SNUFFLING	SOAPROOTS	SOCIALISING	SODDENS
SNOWFLICK	SNUFFLINGS	SOAPS	SOCIALISM	SODDIER
SNOWFLICKS	SNUFFLY	SOAPSTONE	SOCIALISMS	SODDIEST
SNOWIER	SNUFFS	SOAPSTONES	SOCIALIST	SODDING
SNOWIEST	SNUFFY	SOAPSUDS	SOCIALISTS	SODDY
SNOWILY	SNUG	SOAPWORT	SOCIALITE	SODGER
SNOWINESS	SNUGGED	SOAPWORTS	SOCIALITES	SODGERS
SNOWINESSES	SNUGGER	SOAPY	SOCIALITIES	SODIC
SNOWING	SNUGGERIES	SOAR	SOCIALITY	SODIUM
SNOWISH	SNUGGERY	SOARAWAY	SOCIALIZE	SODIUMS

The Chambers Dictionary is the authority for many longer words; see *OSW* Introduction, page xii.

SODOMIES	SOGGINESSES	SOLARISE	SOLEMNIFIES	SOLIDIFYING
SODOMISE	SOGGING	SOLARISED	SOLEMNIFY	SOLIDISH
SODOMISED	SOGGINGS	SOLARISES	SOLEMNIFYING	SOLIDISM
SODOMISES	SOGGY	SOLARISING	SOLEMNISE	SOLIDISMS
SODOMISING	SOGS	SOLARISM	SOLEMNISED	SOLIDIST
SODOMITE	SOH	SOLARISMS	SOLEMNISES	SOLIDISTS
SODOMITES	SOHO	SOLARIST	SOLEMNISING	SOLIDITIES
SODOMITIC	SOHS	SOLARISTS	SOLEMNITIES	SOLIDITY
SODOMIZE	SOIGNE	SOLARIUM	SOLEMNITY	SOLIDLY
SODOMIZED	SOIGNEE	SOLARIUMS	SOLEMNIZE	SOLIDNESS
SODOMIZES	SOIL	SOLARIZE	SOLEMNIZED	SOLIDNESSES
SODOMIZING	SOILAGE	SOLARIZED	SOLEMNIZES	SOLIDS
SODOMY	SOILAGES	SOLARIZES	SOLEMNIZING	SOLIDUM
SODS	SOILED	SOLARIZING	SOLEMNLY	SOLIDUMS
SOEVER	SOILIER	SOLARS	SOLENESS	SOLIDUS
SOFA	SOILIEST	SOLAS	SOLENESSES	SOLILOQUIES
SOFAR	SOILINESS	SOLATIA	SOLENETTE	SOLILOQUY
SOFARS	SOILINESSES	SOLATION	SOLENETTES	SOLING
SOFAS	SOILING	SOLATIONS	SOLENODON	SOLION
SOFFIONI	SOILINGS	SOLATIUM	SOLENODONS	SOLIONS
SOFFIT	SOILLESS	SOLD	SOLENOID	SOLIPED
SOFFITS	SOILS	SOLDADO	SOLENOIDS	SOLIPEDS
SOFT	SOILURE	SOLDADOS	SOLEPLATE	SOLIPSISM
SOFTA	SOILURES	SOLDAN	SOLEPLATES	SOLIPSISMS
SOFTAS	SOILY	SOLDANS	SOLER	SOLIPSIST
SOFTBACK	SOIREE	SOLDE	SOLERA	SOLIPSISTS
SOFTBACKS	SOIREES	SOLDER	SOLERAS	SOLITAIRE
SOFTBALL	SOJA	SOLDERED	SOLERS	SOLITAIRES
SOFTBALLS	SOJAS	SOLDERER	SOLES	SOLITARIES
SOFTCOVER	SOJOURN	SOLDERERS	SOLEUS	SOLITARY
SOFTCOVERS	SOJOURNED	SOLDERING	SOLEUSES	SOLITO
SOFTED	SOJOURNER	SOLDERINGS	SOLFATARA	SOLITON
SOFTEN	SOJOURNERS	SOLDERS	SOLFATARAS	SOLITONS
SOFTENED	SOJOURNING	SOLDES	SOLFEGE	SOLITUDE
SOFTENER	SOJOURNINGS	SOLDI	SOLFEGES	SOLITUDES
SOFTENERS	SOJOURNS	SOLDIER	SOLFEGGI	SOLIVE
SOFTENING	SOKAH	SOLDIERED	SOLFEGGIO	SOLIVES
SOFTENINGS	SOKAHS	SOLDIERIES	SOLFEGGIOS	SOLLAR
SOFTENS	SOKE	SOLDIERING	SOLFERINO	SOLLARS
SOFTER	SOKEMAN	SOLDIERINGS	SOLFERINOS	SOLLER
SOFTEST	SOKEMANRIES	SOLDIERLY	SOLGEL	SOLLERET
SOFTHEAD	SOKEMANRY	SOLDIERS	SOLI	SOLLERETS
SOFTHEADS	SOKEMEN	SOLDIERY	SOLICIT	SOLLERS
SOFTIE	SOKEN	SOLDO	SOLICITED	SOLO
SOFTIES	SOKENS	SOLDS	SOLICITIES	SOLOED
SOFTING	SOKES	SOLE	SOLICITING	SOLOING
SOFTISH	SOL	SOLECISE	SOLICITINGS	SOLOIST
SOFTLING	SOLA	SOLECISED	SOLICITOR	SOLOISTS
SOFTLINGS	SOLACE	SOLECISES	SOLICITORS	SOLONCHAK
SOFTLY	SOLACED	SOLECISING	SOLICITS	SOLONCHAKS
SOFTNESS	SOLACES	SOLECISM	SOLICITY	SOLONETS
SOFTNESSES	SOLACING	SOLECISMS	SOLID	SOLONETSES
SOFTPASTE	SOLACIOUS	SOLECIST	SOLIDAGO	SOLONETZ
SOFTS	SOLAH	SOLECISTS	SOLIDAGOS	SOLONETZES
SOFTWARE	SOLAHS	SOLECIZE	SOLIDARE	SOLOS
SOFTWARES	SOLAN	SOLECIZED	SOLIDARES	SOLPUGID
SOFTWOOD	SOLANDER	SOLECIZES	SOLIDARY	SOLPUGIDS
SOFTWOODS	SOLANDERS	SOLECIZING	SOLIDATE	SOLS
SOFTY	SOLANINE	SOLED	SOLIDATED	SOLSTICE
SOG	SOLANINES	SOLEIN	SOLIDATES	SOLSTICES
SOGER	SOLANO	SOLELY	SOLIDATING	SOLUBLE
SOGERS	SOLANOS	SOLEMN	SOLIDER	SOLUM
SOGGED	SOLANS	SOLEMNER	SOLIDEST	SOLUMS
SOGGIER	SOLANUM	SOLEMNESS	SOLIDI	SOLUS
SOGGIEST	SOLANUMS	SOLEMNESSES	SOLIDIFIED	SOLUTE
SOGGILY	SOLAR	SOLEMNEST	SOLIDIFIES	SOLUTES
SOGGINESS	SOLARIA	SOLEMNIFIED	SOLIDIFY	SOLUTION

The Chambers Dictionary is the authority for many longer words; see *OSW* Introduction, page xii.

SOLUTIONED	SOMETIMES	SONGSTER	SOON	SOPOR
SOLUTIONING	SOMEWAY	SONGSTERS	SOONER	SOPORIFIC
SOLUTIONS	SOMEWAYS	SONIC	SOONEST	SOPORIFICS
SOLUTIVE	SOMEWHAT	SONICS	SOOP	SOPOROSE
SOLVABLE	SOMEWHATS	SONLESS	SOOPED	SOPOROUS
SOLVATE	SOMEWHEN	SONNE	SOOPING	SOPORS
SOLVATED	SOMEWHERE	SONNES	SOOPINGS	SOPPED
SOLVATES	SOMEWHILE	SONNET	SOOPS	SOPPIER
SOLVATING	SOMEWHILES	SONNETARY	SOOPSTAKE	SOPPIEST
SOLVATION	SOMEWHY	SONNETED	SOOT	SOPPILY
SOLVATIONS	SOMEWISE	SONNETEER	SOOTE	SOPPINESS
SOLVE	SOMITAL	SONNETEERS	SOOTED	SOPPINESSES
SOLVED	SOMITE	SONNETING	SOOTERKIN	SOPPING
SOLVENCIES	SOMITES	SONNETISE	SOOTERKINS	SOPPINGS
SOLVENCY	SOMITIC	SONNETISED	SOOTES	SOPPY
SOLVENT	SOMMELIER	SONNETISES	SOOTFLAKE	SOPRA
SOLVENTS	SOMMELIERS	SONNETISING	SOOTFLAKES	SOPRANI
SOLVER	SOMNIAL	SONNETIZE	SOOTH	SOPRANINI
SOLVERS	SOMNIATE	SONNETIZED	SOOTHE	SOPRANINO
SOLVES	SOMNIATED	SONNETIZES	SOOTHED	SOPRANINOS
SOLVING	SOMNIATES	SONNETIZING	SOOTHER	SOPRANIST
SOMA	SOMNIATING	SONNETS	SOOTHERED	SOPRANISTS
SOMAN	SOMNIFIC	SONNIES	SOOTHERING	SOPRANO
SOMANS	SOMNOLENT	SONNY	SOOTHERS	SOPRANOS
SOMAS	SON	SONOBUOY	SOOTHES	SOPS
SOMASCOPE	SONANCE	SONOBUOYS	SOOTHEST	SORA
SOMASCOPES	SONANCES	SONOGRAM	SOOTHFAST	SORAGE
SOMATA	SONANCIES	SONOGRAMS	SOOTHFUL	SORAGES
SOMATIC	SONANCY	SONOGRAPH	SOOTHING	SORAL
SOMATISM	SONANT	SONOGRAPHS	SOOTHINGS	SORAS
SOMATISMS	SONANTS	SONORANT	SOOTHLICH	SORB
SOMATIST	SONAR	SONORANTS	SOOTHLY	SORBARIA
SOMATISTS	SONARS	SONORITIES	SOOTHS	SORBARIAS
SOMBER	SONATA	SONORITY	SOOTHSAID	SORBATE
SOMBERED	SONATAS	SONOROUS	SOOTHSAY	SORBATES
SOMBERER	SONATINA	SONS	SOOTHSAYING	SORBED
SOMBEREST	SONATINAS	SONSE	SOOTHSAYINGS	SORBENT
SOMBERING	SONCE	SONSES	SOOTHSAYS	SORBENTS
SOMBERS	SONCES	SONSHIP	SOOTIER	SORBET
SOMBRE	SONDAGE	SONSHIPS	SOOTIEST	SORBETS
SOMBRED	SONDAGES	SONSIE	SOOTILY	SORBING
SOMBRELY	SONDE	SONSIER	SOOTINESS	SORBITE
SOMBRER	SONDELI	SONSIEST	SOOTINESSES	SORBITES
SOMBRERO	SONDELIS	SONSY	SOOTING	SORBITIC
SOMBREROS	SONDES	SONTAG	SOOTLESS	SORBITISE
SOMBRES	SONE	SONTAGS	SOOTS	SORBITISED
SOMBREST	SONERI	SONTIES	SOOTY	SORBITISES
SOMBRING	SONERIS	SOOGEE	SOP	SORBITISING
SOMBROUS	SONES	SOOGEED	SOPH	SORBITIZE
SOME	SONG	SOOGEEING	SOPHERIC	SORBITIZED
SOMEBODIES	SONGBIRD	SOOGEES	SOPHERIM	SORBITIZES
SOMEBODY	SONGBIRDS	SOOGIE	SOPHISM	SORBITIZING
SOMEDAY	SONGBOOK	SOOGIED	SOPHISMS	SORBITOL
SOMEDEAL	SONGBOOKS	SOOGIEING	SOPHIST	SORBITOLS
SOMEDELE	SONGCRAFT	SOOGIES	SOPHISTER	SORBS
SOMEGATE	SONGCRAFTS	SOOJEY	SOPHISTERS	SORBUS
SOMEHOW	SONGFEST	SOOJEYS	SOPHISTIC	SORBUSES
SOMEONE	SONGFESTS	SOOK	SOPHISTRIES	SORCERER
SOMEONES	SONGFUL	SOOKS	SOPHISTRY	SORCERERS
SOMEPLACE	SONGFULLY	SOOLE	SOPHISTS	SORCERESS
SOMERSET	SONGLESS	SOOLED	SOPHOMORE	SORCERESSES
SOMERSETS	SONGLIKE	SOOLES	SOPHOMORES	SORCERIES
SOMERSETTED	SONGMAN	SOOLING	SOPHS	SORCEROUS
SOMERSETTING	SONGMEN	SOOM	SOPITE	SORCERY
SOMETHING	SONGS	SOOMED	SOPITED	SORD
SOMETHINGS	SONGSMITH	SOOMING	SOPITES	SORDA
SOMETIME	SONGSMITHS	SOOMS	SOPITING	SORDID

The Chambers Dictionary is the authority for many longer words; see *OSW* Introduction, page xii.

SORDIDER
SORDIDEST
SORDIDLY
SORDINI
SORDINO
SORDO
SORDS
SORE
SORED
SOREDIA
SOREDIAL
SOREDIATE
SOREDIUM
SOREE
SOREES
SOREHEAD
SOREHEADS
SOREHON
SOREHONS
SOREL
SORELL
SORELLS
SORELS
SORELY
SORENESS
SORENESSES
SORER
SORES
SOREST
SOREX
SOREXES
SORGHO
SORGHOS
SORGHUM
SORGHUMS
SORGO
SORGOS
SORI
SORICINE
SORICOID
SORING
SORITES
SORITIC
SORITICAL
SORN
SORNED
SORNER
SORNERS
SORNING
SORNINGS
SORNS
SOROBAN
SOROBANS
SOROCHE
SOROCHES
SORORAL
SORORATE
SORORATES
SORORIAL
SORORISE
SORORISED
SORORISES
SORORISING
SORORITIES
SORORITY
SORORIZE
SORORIZED

SORORIZES
SORORIZING
SOROSES
SOROSIS
SOROSISES
SORPTION
SORPTIONS
SORRA
SORRAS
SORREL
SORRELS
SORRIER
SORRIEST
SORRILY
SORRINESS
SORRINESSES
SORROW
SORROWED
SORROWER
SORROWERS
SORROWFUL
SORROWING
SORROWINGS
SORROWS
SORRY
SORRYISH
SORT
SORTABLE
SORTANCE
SORTANCES
SORTATION
SORTATIONS
SORTED
SORTER
SORTERS
SORTES
SORTIE
SORTIED
SORTIEING
SORTIES
SORTILEGE
SORTILEGES
SORTILEGIES
SORTILEGY
SORTING
SORTINGS
SORTITION
SORTITIONS
SORTMENT
SORTMENTS
SORTS
SORUS
SOS
SOSS
SOSSED
SOSSES
SOSSING
SOSSINGS
SOSTENUTO
SOT
SOTERIAL
SOTS
SOTTED
SOTTING
SOTTINGS
SOTTISH
SOTTISHLY

SOTTISIER
SOTTISIERS
SOU
SOUARI
SOUARIS
SOUBISE
SOUBISES
SOUBRETTE
SOUBRETTES
SOUCE
SOUCED
SOUCES
SOUCHONG
SOUCHONGS
SOUCING
SOUCT
SOUFFLE
SOUFFLES
SOUGH
SOUGHED
SOUGHING
SOUGHS
SOUGHT
SOUK
SOUKOUS
SOUKOUSES
SOUKS
SOUL
SOULDAN
SOULDANS
SOULDIER
SOULDIERED
SOULDIERING
SOULDIERS
SOULED
SOULFUL
SOULFULLY
SOULLESS
SOULS
SOUM
SOUMED
SOUMING
SOUMINGS
SOUMS
SOUND
SOUNDBITE
SOUNDBITES
SOUNDED
SOUNDER
SOUNDERS
SOUNDEST
SOUNDING
SOUNDINGS
SOUNDLESS
SOUNDLY
SOUNDMAN
SOUNDMEN
SOUNDNESS
SOUNDNESSES
SOUNDS
SOUP
SOUPCON
SOUPCONS
SOUPER
SOUPERS
SOUPIER
SOUPIEST

SOUPLE
SOUPLED
SOUPLES
SOUPLING
SOUPS
SOUPSPOON
SOUPSPOONS
SOUPY
SOUR
SOURCE
SOURCED
SOURCES
SOURCING
SOURCINGS
SOURDINE
SOURDINES
SOURDOUGH
SOURDOUGHS
SOURED
SOURER
SOUREST
SOURING
SOURINGS
SOURISH
SOURISHLY
SOURLY
SOURNESS
SOURNESSES
SOUROCK
SOUROCKS
SOURPUSS
SOURPUSSES
SOURS
SOURSE
SOURSES
SOURSOP
SOURSOPS
SOUS
SOUSE
SOUSED
SOUSES
SOUSING
SOUSINGS
SOUSLIK
SOUSLIKS
SOUT
SOUTACHE
SOUTACHES
SOUTANE
SOUTANES
SOUTAR
SOUTARS
SOUTENEUR
SOUTENEURS
SOUTER
SOUTERLY
SOUTERS
SOUTH
SOUTHED
SOUTHER
SOUTHERED
SOUTHERING
SOUTHERLY
SOUTHERN
SOUTHERNS
SOUTHERS
SOUTHING

SOUTHINGS
SOUTHLAND
SOUTHLANDS
SOUTHMOST
SOUTHPAW
SOUTHPAWS
SOUTHRON
SOUTHRONS
SOUTHS
SOUTHSAID
SOUTHSAY
SOUTHSAYING
SOUTHSAYS
SOUTHWARD
SOUTHWARDS
SOUTS
SOUVENIR
SOUVENIRED
SOUVENIRING
SOUVENIRS
SOUVLAKI
SOUVLAKIA
SOV
SOVENANCE
SOVENANCES
SOVEREIGN
SOVEREIGNS
SOVIET
SOVIETIC
SOVIETISE
SOVIETISED
SOVIETISES
SOVIETISING
SOVIETISM
SOVIETISMS
SOVIETIZE
SOVIETIZED
SOVIETIZES
SOVIETIZING
SOVIETS
SOVRAN
SOVRANLY
SOVRANS
SOVRANTIES
SOVRANTY
SOVS
SOW
SOWANS
SOWAR
SOWARREE
SOWARREES
SOWARRIES
SOWARRY
SOWARS
SOWBACK
SOWBACKS
SOWBREAD
SOWBREADS
SOWCE
SOWCED
SOWCES
SOWCING
SOWED
SOWENS
SOWER
SOWERS
SOWF

The Chambers Dictionary is the authority for many longer words; see *OSW* Introduction, page xii.

SOWFED	SPACESHIPS	SPAGS	SPANGLERS	SPARKLED
SOWFF	SPACESUIT	SPAGYRIC	SPANGLES	SPARKLER
SOWFFED	SPACESUITS	SPAGYRICS	SPANGLET	SPARKLERS
SOWFFING	SPACEY	SPAGYRIST	SPANGLETS	SPARKLES
SOWFFS	SPACIAL	SPAGYRISTS	SPANGLIER	SPARKLESS
SOWFING	SPACIER	SPAHEE	SPANGLIEST	SPARKLET
SOWFS	SPACIEST	SPAHEES	SPANGLING	SPARKLETS
SOWING	SPACING	SPAHI	SPANGLINGS	SPARKLIER
SOWINGS	SPACINGS	SPAHIS	SPANGLY	SPARKLIES
SOWL	SPACIOUS	SPAIN	SPANGS	SPARKLIEST
SOWLE	SPACY	SPAINED	SPANIEL	SPARKLING
SOWLED	SPADASSIN	SPAING	SPANIELLED	SPARKLINGS
SOWLES	SPADASSINS	SPAINGS	SPANIELLING	SPARKLY
SOWLING	SPADE	SPAINING	SPANIELS	SPARKS
SOWLS	SPADED	SPAINS	SPANING	SPARKY
SOWM	SPADEFISH	SPAIRGE	SPANK	SPARLING
SOWMED	SPADEFISHES	SPAIRGED	SPANKED	SPARLINGS
SOWMING	SPADEFUL	SPAIRGES	SPANKER	SPAROID
SOWMS	SPADEFULS	SPAIRGING	SPANKERS	SPAROIDS
SOWN	SPADELIKE	SPAKE	SPANKING	SPARRE
SOWND	SPADEMAN	SPALD	SPANKINGS	SPARRED
SOWNDED	SPADEMEN	SPALDS	SPANKS	SPARRER
SOWNDING	SPADER	SPALE	SPANLESS	SPARRERS
SOWNDS	SPADERS	SPALES	SPANNED	SPARRES
SOWNE	SPADES	SPALL	SPANNER	SPARRIER
SOWNES	SPADESMAN	SPALLE	SPANNERS	SPARRIEST
SOWP	SPADESMEN	SPALLED	SPANNING	SPARRING
SOWPS	SPADEWORK	SPALLES	SPANS	SPARRINGS
SOWS	SPADEWORKS	SPALLING	SPANSULE	SPARROW
SOWSE	SPADGER	SPALLINGS	SPANSULES	SPARROWS
SOWSED	SPADGERS	SPALLS	SPAR	SPARRY
SOWSES	SPADICES	SPALPEEN	SPARABLE	SPARS
SOWSING	SPADILLE	SPALPEENS	SPARABLES	SPARSE
SOWSSE	SPADILLES	SPALT	SPARAXIS	SPARSEDLY
SOWSSED	SPADILLIO	SPALTED	SPARAXISES	SPARSELY
SOWSSES	SPADILLIOS	SPALTING	SPARD	SPARSER
SOWSSING	SPADILLO	SPALTS	SPARE	SPARSEST
SOWTER	SPADILLOS	SPAMMIER	SPARED	SPARSITIES
SOWTERS	SPADING	SPAMMIEST	SPARELESS	SPARSITY
SOWTH	SPADIX	SPAMMY	SPARELY	SPART
SOWTHED	SPADO	SPAN	SPARENESS	SPARTAN
SOWTHING	SPADOES	SPANAEMIA	SPARENESSES	SPARTANS
SOWTHS	SPADONES	SPANAEMIAS	SPARER	SPARTEINE
SOX	SPADOS	SPANAEMIC	SPARERS	SPARTEINES
SOY	SPADROON	SPANCEL	SPARES	SPARTERIE
SOYA	SPADROONS	SPANCELLED	SPAREST	SPARTERIES
SOYAS	SPAE	SPANCELLING	SPARGE	SPARTH
SOYLE	SPAED	SPANCELS	SPARGED	SPARTHE
SOYLES	SPAEING	SPANDEX	SPARGER	SPARTHES
SOYS	SPAEMAN	SPANDEXES	SPARGERS	SPARTHS
SOZZLE	SPAEMEN	SPANDREL	SPARGES	SPARTS
SOZZLED	SPAER	SPANDRELS	SPARGING	SPAS
SOZZLES	SPAERS	SPANDRIL	SPARID	SPASM
SOZZLIER	SPAES	SPANDRILS	SPARIDS	SPASMATIC
SOZZLIEST	SPAEWIFE	SPANE	SPARING	SPASMED
SOZZLING	SPAEWIVES	SPANED	SPARINGLY	SPASMIC
SOZZLY	SPAG	SPANES	SPARK	SPASMING
SPA	SPAGERIC	SPANG	SPARKE	SPASMODIC
SPACE	SPAGERICS	SPANGED	SPARKED	SPASMS
SPACED	SPAGERIST	SPANGHEW	SPARKES	SPASTIC
SPACELESS	SPAGERISTS	SPANGHEWED	SPARKIE	SPASTICS
SPACEMAN	SPAGHETTI	SPANGHEWING	SPARKIER	SPAT
SPACEMEN	SPAGHETTIS	SPANGHEWS	SPARKIES	SPATE
SPACER	SPAGIRIC	SPANGING	SPARKIEST	SPATES
SPACERS	SPAGIRICS	SPANGLE	SPARKING	SPATFALL
SPACES	SPAGIRIST	SPANGLED	SPARKISH	SPATFALLS
SPACESHIP	SPAGIRISTS	SPANGLER	SPARKLE	SPATHE

The Chambers Dictionary is the authority for many longer words; see *OSW* Introduction, page xii.

SPATHED	SPEAKS	SPECTATED	SPEIRING	SPERLING
SPATHES	SPEAL	SPECTATES	SPEIRINGS	SPERLINGS
SPATHIC	SPEALS	SPECTATING	SPEIRS	SPERM
SPATHOSE	SPEAN	SPECTATOR	SPEISS	SPERMARIA
SPATIAL	SPEANED	SPECTATORS	SPEISSES	SPERMARIES
SPATIALLY	SPEANING	SPECTER	SPEK	SPERMARY
SPATLESE	SPEANS	SPECTERS	SPEKBOOM	SPERMATIA
SPATLESEN	SPEAR	SPECTRA	SPEKBOOMS	SPERMATIC
SPATLESES	SPEARED	SPECTRAL	SPEKS	SPERMATICS
SPATS	SPEARFISH	SPECTRE	SPELAEAN	SPERMATID
SPATTED	SPEARFISHES	SPECTRES	SPELD	SPERMATIDS
SPATTEE	SPEARHEAD	SPECTRUM	SPELDED	SPERMIC
SPATTEES	SPEARHEADED	SPECULA	SPELDER	SPERMOUS
SPATTER	SPEARHEADING	SPECULAR	SPELDERED	SPERMS
SPATTERED	SPEARHEADS	SPECULATE	SPELDERING	SPERRE
SPATTERING	SPEARIER	SPECULATED	SPELDERS	SPERRED
SPATTERS	SPEARIEST	SPECULATES	SPELDIN	SPERRES
SPATTING	SPEARING	SPECULATING	SPELDING	SPERRING
SPATULA	SPEARMAN	SPECULUM	SPELDINGS	SPERSE
SPATULAR	SPEARMEN	SPED	SPELDINS	SPERSED
SPATULAS	SPEARMINT	SPEECH	SPELDRIN	SPERSES
SPATULATE	SPEARMINTS	SPEECHED	SPELDRING	SPERSING
SPATULE	SPEARS	SPEECHES	SPELDRINGS	SPERST
SPATULES	SPEARWORT	SPEECHFUL	SPELDRINS	SPERTHE
SPAUL	SPEARWORTS	SPEECHIFIED	SPELDS	SPERTHES
SPAULD	SPEARY	SPEECHIFIES	SPELEAN	SPET
SPAULDS	SPEAT	SPEECHIFY	SPELK	SPETCH
SPAULS	SPEATS	SPEECHIFYING	SPELKS	SPETCHES
SPAVIE	SPEC	SPEECHING	SPELL	SPETS
SPAVIES	SPECCIES	SPEED	SPELLABLE	SPETSNAZ
SPAVIN	SPECCY	SPEEDBALL	SPELLBIND	SPETSNAZES
SPAVINED	SPECIAL	SPEEDBALLS	SPELLBINDING	SPETTING
SPAVINS	SPECIALLY	SPEEDBOAT	SPELLBINDS	SPETZNAZ
SPAW	SPECIALS	SPEEDBOATS	SPELLBOUND	SPETZNAZES
SPAWL	SPECIALTIES	SPEEDED	SPELLDOWN	SPEW
SPAWLED	SPECIALTY	SPEEDER	SPELLDOWNS	SPEWED
SPAWLING	SPECIATE	SPEEDERS	SPELLED	SPEWER
SPAWLS	SPECIATED	SPEEDFUL	SPELLER	SPEWERS
SPAWN	SPECIATES	SPEEDIER	SPELLERS	SPEWIER
SPAWNED	SPECIATING	SPEEDIEST	SPELLFUL	SPEWIEST
SPAWNER	SPECIE	SPEEDILY	SPELLICAN	SPEWINESS
SPAWNERS	SPECIES	SPEEDING	SPELLICANS	SPEWINESSES
SPAWNIER	SPECIFIC	SPEEDINGS	SPELLING	SPEWING
SPAWNIEST	SPECIFICS	SPEEDLESS	SPELLINGS	SPEWS
SPAWNING	SPECIFIED	SPEEDO	SPELLS	SPEWY
SPAWNINGS	SPECIFIES	SPEEDOS	SPELT	SPHACELUS
SPAWNS	SPECIFY	SPEEDS	SPELTER	SPHACELUSES
SPAWNY	SPECIFYING	SPEEDSTER	SPELTERS	SPHAER
SPAWS	SPECIMEN	SPEEDSTERS	SPELTS	SPHAERE
SPAY	SPECIMENS	SPEEDWAY	SPELUNKER	SPHAERES
SPAYAD	SPECIOUS	SPEEDWAYS	SPELUNKERS	SPHAERITE
SPAYADS	SPECK	SPEEDWELL	SPENCE	SPHAERITES
SPAYD	SPECKED	SPEEDWELLS	SPENCER	SPHAERS
SPAYDS	SPECKIER	SPEEDY	SPENCERS	SPHAGNOUS
SPAYED	SPECKIEST	SPEEL	SPENCES	SPHAGNUM
SPAYING	SPECKING	SPEELED	SPEND	SPHAGNUMS
SPAYS	SPECKLE	SPEELER	SPENDABLE	SPHEAR
SPEAK	SPECKLED	SPEELERS	SPENDALL	SPHEARE
SPEAKABLE	SPECKLES	SPEELING	SPENDALLS	SPHEARES
SPEAKEASIES	SPECKLESS	SPEELS	SPENDER	SPHEARS
SPEAKEASY	SPECKLING	SPEER	SPENDERS	SPHENDONE
SPEAKER	SPECKS	SPEERED	SPENDING	SPHENDONES
SPEAKERS	SPECKY	SPEERING	SPENDINGS	SPHENE
SPEAKING	SPECS	SPEERINGS	SPENDS	SPHENES
SPEAKINGS	SPECTACLE	SPEERS	SPENT	SPHENIC
SPEAKOUT	SPECTACLES	SPEIR	SPEOS	SPHENODON
SPEAKOUTS	SPECTATE	SPEIRED	SPEOSES	SPHENODONS

The Chambers Dictionary is the authority for many longer words; see *OSW* Introduction, page xii.

SPHENOID	SPICULE	SPILLED	SPINNETS	SPIRITED
SPHENOIDS	SPICULES	SPILLER	SPINNEY	SPIRITFUL
SPHERAL	SPICULUM	SPILLERS	SPINNEYS	SPIRITING
SPHERE	SPICY	SPILLIKIN	SPINNIES	SPIRITINGS
SPHERED	SPIDE	SPILLIKINS	SPINNING	SPIRITISM
SPHERES	SPIDER	SPILLING	SPINNINGS	SPIRITISMS
SPHERIC	SPIDERIER	SPILLINGS	SPINNY	SPIRITIST
SPHERICAL	SPIDERIEST	SPILLOVER	SPINODE	SPIRITISTS
SPHERICS	SPIDERMAN	SPILLOVERS	SPINODES	SPIRITOSO
SPHERIER	SPIDERMEN	SPILLS	SPINOSE	SPIRITOUS
SPHERIEST	SPIDERS	SPILLWAY	SPINOSITIES	SPIRITS
SPHERING	SPIDERY	SPILLWAYS	SPINOSITY	SPIRITUAL
SPHEROID	SPIE	SPILOSITE	SPINOUS	SPIRITUALS
SPHEROIDS	SPIED	SPILOSITES	SPINOUT	SPIRITUEL
SPHERULAR	SPIEL	SPILT	SPINOUTS	SPIRITUS
SPHERULE	SPIELED	SPILTH	SPINS	SPIRITUSES
SPHERULES	SPIELER	SPILTHS	SPINSTER	SPIRITY
SPHERY	SPIELERS	SPIN	SPINSTERS	SPIRLING
SPHINCTER	SPIELING	SPINA	SPINTEXT	SPIRLINGS
SPHINCTERS	SPIELS	SPINACENE	SPINTEXTS	SPIROGRAM
SPHINGES	SPIES	SPINACENES	SPINULATE	SPIROGRAMS
SPHINGID	SPIFF	SPINACH	SPINULE	SPIROGYRA
SPHINGIDS	SPIFFIER	SPINACHES	SPINULES	SPIROGYRAS
SPHINX	SPIFFIEST	SPINAE	SPINULOSE	SPIROID
SPHINXES	SPIFFING	SPINAL	SPINULOUS	SPIRT
SPHYGMIC	SPIFFY	SPINAR	SPINY	SPIRTED
SPHYGMOID	SPIGHT	SPINARS	SPIRACLE	SPIRTING
SPHYGMUS	SPIGHTED	SPINAS	SPIRACLES	SPIRTLE
SPHYGMUSES	SPIGHTING	SPINATE	SPIRACULA	SPIRTLES
SPIAL	SPIGHTS	SPINDLE	SPIRAEA	SPIRTS
SPIALS	SPIGNEL	SPINDLED	SPIRAEAS	SPIRY
SPIC	SPIGNELS	SPINDLES	SPIRAL	SPIT
SPICA	SPIGOT	SPINDLIER	SPIRALISM	SPITAL
SPICAE	SPIGOTS	SPINDLIEST	SPIRALISMS	SPITALS
SPICAS	SPIK	SPINDLING	SPIRALIST	SPITCHER
SPICATE	SPIKE	SPINDLINGS	SPIRALISTS	SPITE
SPICATED	SPIKED	SPINDLY	SPIRALITIES	SPITED
SPICCATO	SPIKEFISH	SPINDRIFT	SPIRALITY	SPITEFUL
SPICCATOS	SPIKEFISHES	SPINDRIFTS	SPIRALLED	SPITEFULLER
SPICE	SPIKELET	SPINE	SPIRALLING	SPITEFULLEST
SPICEBUSH	SPIKELETS	SPINED	SPIRALLY	SPITES
SPICEBUSHES	SPIKENARD	SPINEL	SPIRALS	SPITFIRE
SPICED	SPIKENARDS	SPINELESS	SPIRANT	SPITFIRES
SPICER	SPIKERIES	SPINELS	SPIRANTS	SPITING
SPICERIES	SPIKERY	SPINES	SPIRASTER	SPITS
SPICERS	SPIKES	SPINET	SPIRASTERS	SPITTED
SPICERY	SPIKIER	SPINETS	SPIRATED	SPITTEN
SPICES	SPIKIEST	SPINETTE	SPIRATION	SPITTER
SPICIER	SPIKILY	SPINETTES	SPIRATIONS	SPITTERS
SPICIEST	SPIKINESS	SPINIER	SPIRE	SPITTING
SPICILEGE	SPIKINESSES	SPINIEST	SPIREA	SPITTINGS
SPICILEGES	SPIKING	SPINIFEX	SPIREAS	SPITTLE
SPICILY	SPIKS	SPINIFEXES	SPIRED	SPITTLES
SPICINESS	SPIKY	SPINIFORM	SPIRELESS	SPITTOON
SPICINESSES	SPILE	SPININESS	SPIREME	SPITTOONS
SPICING	SPILED	SPININESSES	SPIREMES	SPITZ
SPICK	SPILES	SPINK	SPIRES	SPITZES
SPICKER	SPILIKIN	SPINKS	SPIREWISE	SPIV
SPICKEST	SPILIKINS	SPINNAKER	SPIRIC	SPIVS
SPICKNEL	SPILING	SPINNAKERS	SPIRICS	SPIVVERIES
SPICKNELS	SPILINGS	SPINNER	SPIRIER	SPIVVERY
SPICKS	SPILITE	SPINNERET	SPIRIEST	SPIVVIER
SPICS	SPILITES	SPINNERETS	SPIRILLA	SPIVVIEST
SPICULA	SPILITIC	SPINNERIES	SPIRILLAR	SPIVVY
SPICULAR	SPILL	SPINNERS	SPIRILLUM	SPLASH
SPICULAS	SPILLAGE	SPINNERY	SPIRING	SPLASHED
SPICULATE	SPILLAGES	SPINNET	SPIRIT	SPLASHER

The Chambers Dictionary is the authority for many longer words; see *OSW* Introduction, page xii.

SPLASHERS	SPLINTERS	SPOILT	SPOOKING	SPORTANCE
SPLASHES	SPLINTERY	SPOKE	SPOOKISH	SPORTANCES
SPLASHIER	SPLINTING	SPOKEN	SPOOKS	SPORTED
SPLASHIEST	SPLINTS	SPOKES	SPOOKY	SPORTER
SPLASHILY	SPLIT	SPOKESMAN	SPOOL	SPORTERS
SPLASHING	SPLITS	SPOKESMEN	SPOOLED	SPORTFUL
SPLASHINGS	SPLITTED	SPOKEWISE	SPOOLER	SPORTIER
SPLASHY	SPLITTER	SPOLIATE	SPOOLERS	SPORTIEST
SPLAT	SPLITTERS	SPOLIATED	SPOOLING	SPORTILY
SPLATCH	SPLITTING	SPOLIATES	SPOOLS	SPORTING
SPLATCHED	SPLODGE	SPOLIATING	SPOOM	SPORTIVE
SPLATCHES	SPLODGED	SPOLIATOR	SPOOMED	SPORTLESS
SPLATCHING	SPLODGES	SPOLIATORS	SPOOMING	SPORTS
SPLATS	SPLODGIER	SPONDAIC	SPOOMS	SPORTSMAN
SPLATTED	SPLODGIEST	SPONDEE	SPOON	SPORTSMEN
SPLATTER	SPLODGILY	SPONDEES	SPOONBAIT	SPORTY
SPLATTERED	SPLODGING	SPONDULIX	SPOONBAITS	SPORULAR
SPLATTERING	SPLODGY	SPONDYL	SPOONBILL	SPORULATE
SPLATTERS	SPLORE	SPONDYLS	SPOONBILLS	SPORULATED
SPLATTING	SPLORES	SPONGE	SPOONED	SPORULATES
SPLATTINGS	SPLOSH	SPONGEBAG	SPOONEY	SPORULATING
SPLAY	SPLOSHED	SPONGEBAGS	SPOONEYS	SPORULE
SPLAYED	SPLOSHES	SPONGED	SPOONFED	SPORULES
SPLAYING	SPLOSHING	SPONGEOUS	SPOONFUL	SPOSH
SPLAYS	SPLOTCH	SPONGER	SPOONFULS	SPOSHES
SPLEEN	SPLOTCHED	SPONGERS	SPOONHOOK	SPOSHIER
SPLEENFUL	SPLOTCHES	SPONGES	SPOONHOOKS	SPOSHIEST
SPLEENISH	SPLOTCHIER	SPONGIER	SPOONIER	SPOSHY
SPLEENS	SPLOTCHIEST	SPONGIEST	SPOONIES	SPOT
SPLEENY	SPLOTCHING	SPONGILY	SPOONIEST	SPOTLESS
SPLENDENT	SPLOTCHY	SPONGIN	SPOONILY	SPOTLIGHT
SPLENDID	SPLURGE	SPONGING	SPOONING	SPOTLIGHTED
SPLENDOR	SPLURGED	SPONGINS	SPOONS	SPOTLIGHTING
SPLENDORS	SPLURGES	SPONGIOSE	SPOONWAYS	SPOTLIGHTS
SPLENDOUR	SPLURGIER	SPONGIOUS	SPOONWISE	SPOTLIT
SPLENDOURS	SPLURGIEST	SPONGOID	SPOONY	SPOTS
SPLENETIC	SPLURGING	SPONGY	SPOOR	SPOTTED
SPLENETICS	SPLURGY	SPONSAL	SPOORED	SPOTTER
SPLENIA	SPLUTTER	SPONSALIA	SPOORER	SPOTTERS
SPLENIAL	SPLUTTERED	SPONSIBLE	SPOORERS	SPOTTIER
SPLENIC	SPLUTTERING	SPONSING	SPOORING	SPOTTIEST
SPLENII	SPLUTTERINGS	SPONSINGS	SPOORS	SPOTTILY`
SPLENITIS	SPLUTTERS	SPONSION	SPOOT	SPOTTING
SPLENITISES	SPLUTTERY	SPONSIONS	SPOOTS	SPOTTINGS
SPLENIUM	SPODE	SPONSON	SPORADIC	SPOTTY
SPLENIUMS	SPODES	SPONSONS	SPORANGIA	SPOUSAGE
SPLENIUS	SPODIUM	SPONSOR	SPORE	SPOUSAGES
SPLENIUSES	SPODIUMS	SPONSORED	SPORES	SPOUSAL
SPLEUCHAN	SPODOGRAM	SPONSORING	SPORIDESM	SPOUSALS
SPLEUCHANS	SPODOGRAMS	SPONSORS	SPORIDESMS	SPOUSE
SPLICE	SPODUMENE	SPONTOON	SPORIDIA	SPOUSED
SPLICED	SPODUMENES	SPONTOONS	SPORIDIAL	SPOUSES
SPLICER	SPOFFISH	SPOOF	SPORIDIUM	SPOUSING
SPLICERS	SPOFFY	SPOOFED	SPOROCARP	SPOUT
SPLICES	SPOIL	SPOOFER	SPOROCARPS	SPOUTED
SPLICING	SPOILAGE	SPOOFERIES	SPOROCYST	SPOUTER
SPLIFF	SPOILAGES	SPOOFERS	SPOROCYSTS	SPOUTERS
SPLIFFS	SPOILED	SPOOFERY	SPOROGENIES	SPOUTIER
SPLINE	SPOILER	SPOOFING	SPOROGENY	SPOUTIEST
SPLINED	SPOILERS	SPOOFS	SPOROPHYL	SPOUTING
SPLINES	SPOILFIVE	SPOOK	SPOROPHYLS	SPOUTINGS
SPLINING	SPOILFIVES	SPOOKED	SPOROZOAN	SPOUTLESS
SPLINT	SPOILFUL	SPOOKERIES	SPOROZOANS	SPOUTS
SPLINTED	SPOILING	SPOOKERY	SPORRAN	SPOUTY
SPLINTER	SPOILS	SPOOKIER	SPORRANS	SPRACK
SPLINTERED	SPOILSMAN	SPOOKIEST	SPORT	SPRACKLE
SPLINTERING	SPOILSMEN	SPOOKILY	SPORTABLE	SPRACKLED

The Chambers Dictionary is the authority for many longer words; see *OSW* Introduction, page xii.

SPRACKLES	SPREAZED	SPRINKLED	SPUDDED	SPURNER
SPRACKLING	SPREAZES	SPRINKLER	SPUDDIER	SPURNERS
SPRAD	SPREAZING	SPRINKLERS	SPUDDIEST	SPURNES
SPRAG	SPRECHERIES	SPRINKLES	SPUDDING	SPURNING
SPRAGGED	SPRECHERY	SPRINKLING	SPUDDINGS	SPURNINGS
SPRAGGING	SPRECKLED	SPRINKLINGS	SPUDDY	SPURNS
SPRAGS	SPRED	SPRINT	SPUDS	SPURRED
SPRAICKLE	SPREDD	SPRINTED	SPUE	SPURRER
SPRAICKLED	SPREDDE	SPRINTER	SPUED	SPURRERS
SPRAICKLES	SPREDDEN	SPRINTERS	SPUEING	SPURREY
SPRAICKLING	SPREDDES	SPRINTING	SPUES	SPURREYS
SPRAID	SPREDDING	SPRINTINGS	SPUILZIE	SPURRIER
SPRAIN	SPREDDS	SPRINTS	SPUILZIED	SPURRIERS
SPRAINED	SPREDS	SPRIT	SPUILZIEING	SPURRIES
SPRAINING	SPREE	SPRITE	SPUILZIES	SPURRIEST
SPRAINS	SPREED	SPRITELY	SPUING	SPURRING
SPRAINT	SPREEING	SPRITES	SPULE	SPURRINGS
SPRAINTS	SPREES	SPRITS	SPULEBANE	SPURRY
SPRANG	SPREETHE	SPRITSAIL	SPULEBANES	SPURS
SPRANGLE	SPREETHED	SPRITSAILS	SPULEBONE	SPURT
SPRANGLED	SPREETHES	SPRITZER	SPULEBONES	SPURTED
SPRANGLES	SPREETHING	SPRITZERS	SPULES	SPURTING
SPRANGLING	SPREEZE	SPRITZIG	SPULYE	SPURTLE
SPRAT	SPREEZED	SPRITZIGS	SPULYED	SPURTLES
SPRATS	SPREEZES	SPROCKET	SPULYEING	SPURTS
SPRATTLE	SPREEZING	SPROCKETS	SPULYES	SPURWAY
SPRATTLED	SPRENT	SPROD	SPULYIE	SPURWAYS
SPRATTLES	SPREW	SPRODS	SPULYIED	SPUTA
SPRATTLING	SPREWS	SPROG	SPULYIEING	SPUTNIK
SPRAUCHLE	SPRIG	SPROGS	SPULYIES	SPUTNIKS
SPRAUCHLED	SPRIGGED	SPRONG	SPULZIE	SPUTTER
SPRAUCHLES	SPRIGGIER	SPROUT	SPULZIED	SPUTTERED
SPRAUCHLING	SPRIGGIEST	SPROUTED	SPULZIEING	SPUTTERER
SPRAUNCIER	SPRIGGING	SPROUTING	SPULZIES	SPUTTERERS
SPRAUNCIEST	SPRIGGY	SPROUTINGS	SPUME	SPUTTERING
SPRAUNCY	SPRIGHT	SPROUTS	SPUMED	SPUTTERINGS
SPRAWL	SPRIGHTED	SPRUCE	SPUMES	SPUTTERS
SPRAWLED	SPRIGHTING	SPRUCED	SPUMIER	SPUTTERY
SPRAWLER	SPRIGHTLIER	SPRUCELY	SPUMIEST	SPUTUM
SPRAWLERS	SPRIGHTLIEST	SPRUCER	SPUMING	SPY
SPRAWLIER	SPRIGHTLY	SPRUCES	SPUMOUS	SPYAL
SPRAWLIEST	SPRIGHTS	SPRUCEST	SPUMY	SPYALS
SPRAWLING	SPRIGS	SPRUCING	SPUN	SPYGLASS
SPRAWLS	SPRING	SPRUE	SPUNGE	SPYGLASSES
SPRAWLY	SPRINGAL	SPRUES	SPUNGES	SPYHOLE
SPRAY	SPRINGALD	SPRUG	SPUNK	SPYHOLES
SPRAYED	SPRINGALDS	SPRUGS	SPUNKED	SPYING
SPRAYER	SPRINGALS	SPRUIK	SPUNKIE	SPYINGS
SPRAYERS	SPRINGBOK	SPRUIKED	SPUNKIER	SPYMASTER
SPRAYEY	SPRINGBOKS	SPRUIKER	SPUNKIES	SPYMASTERS
SPRAYIER	SPRINGE	SPRUIKERS	SPUNKIEST	SPYPLANE
SPRAYIEST	SPRINGED	SPRUIKING	SPUNKING	SPYPLANES
SPRAYING	SPRINGER	SPRUIKS	SPUNKS	SPYRE
SPRAYS	SPRINGERS	SPRUIT	SPUNKY	SPYRES
SPREAD	SPRINGES	SPRUITS	SPUNYARN	SQUAB
SPREADER	SPRINGIER	SPRUNG	SPUNYARNS	SQUABASH
SPREADERS	SPRINGIEST	SPRUSH	SPUR	SQUABASHED
SPREADING	SPRINGILY	SPRUSHED	SPURGE	SQUABASHES
SPREADINGS	SPRINGING	SPRUSHES	SPURGES	SQUABASHING
SPREADS	SPRINGINGS	SPRUSHING	SPURIAE	SQUABBED
SPREAGH	SPRINGLE	SPRY	SPURIOUS	SQUABBER
SPREAGHS	SPRINGLES	SPRYER	SPURLESS	SQUABBEST
SPREATHE	SPRINGLET	SPRYEST	SPURLING	SQUABBIER
SPREATHED	SPRINGLETS	SPRYLY	SPURLINGS	SQUABBIEST
SPREATHES	SPRINGS	SPRYNESS	SPURN	SQUABBING
SPREATHING	SPRINGY	SPRYNESSES	SPURNE	SQUABBISH
SPREAZE	SPRINKLE	SPUD	SPURNED	SQUABBLE

The Chambers Dictionary is the authority for many longer words; see *OSW* Introduction, page xii.

SQUABBLED	SQUARED	SQUEAKS	SQUIGGLES	SQUIRRS
SQUABBLER	SQUARELY	SQUEAKY	SQUIGGLIER	SQUIRT
SQUABBLERS	SQUARER	SQUEAL	SQUIGGLIEST	SQUIRTED
SQUABBLES	SQUARERS	SQUEALED	SQUIGGLING	SQUIRTER
SQUABBLING	SQUARES	SQUEALER	SQUIGGLY	SQUIRTERS
SQUABBY	SQUAREST	SQUEALERS	SQUILGEE	SQUIRTING
SQUABS	SQUARIAL	SQUEALING	SQUILGEED	SQUIRTINGS
SQUACCO	SQUARIALS	SQUEALINGS	SQUILGEEING	SQUIRTS
SQUACCOS	SQUARING	SQUEALS	SQUILGEES	SQUISH
SQUAD	SQUARINGS	SQUEAMISH	SQUILL	SQUISHED
SQUADDIE	SQUARISH	SQUEEGEE	SQUILLA	SQUISHES
SQUADDIES	SQUARROSE	SQUEEGEED	SQUILLAS	SQUISHIER
SQUADDY	SQUARSON	SQUEEGEEING	SQUILLS	SQUISHIEST
SQUADRON	SQUARSONS	SQUEEGEES	SQUINANCIES	SQUISHING
SQUADRONE	SQUASH	SQUEEZE	SQUINANCY	SQUISHY
SQUADRONED	SQUASHED	SQUEEZED	SQUINCH	SQUIT
SQUADRONES	SQUASHER	SQUEEZER	SQUINCHES	SQUITCH
SQUADRONING	SQUASHERS	SQUEEZERS	SQUINIED	SQUITCHES
SQUADRONS	SQUASHES	SQUEEZES	SQUINIES	SQUITS
SQUADS	SQUASHIER	SQUEEZIER	SQUINNIED	SQUIZ
SQUAIL	SQUASHIEST	SQUEEZIEST	SQUINNIES	SQUIZZES
SQUAILED	SQUASHILY	SQUEEZING	SQUINNY	SRADDHA
SQUAILER	SQUASHING	SQUEEZINGS	SQUINNYING	SRADDHAS
SQUAILERS	SQUASHY	SQUEEZY	SQUINT	ST
SQUAILING	SQUAT	SQUEG	SQUINTED	STAB
SQUAILINGS	SQUATNESS	SQUEGGED	SQUINTER	STABBED
SQUAILS	SQUATNESSES	SQUEGGER	SQUINTERS	STABBER
SQUALENE	SQUATS	SQUEGGERS	SQUINTEST	STABBERS
SQUALENES	SQUATTED	SQUEGGING	SQUINTING	STABBING
SQUALID	SQUATTER	SQUEGGINGS	SQUINTINGS	STABBINGS
SQUALIDER	SQUATTERED	SQUEGS	SQUINTS	STABILATE
SQUALIDEST	SQUATTERING	SQUELCH	SQUINY	STABILATES
SQUALIDLY	SQUATTERS	SQUELCHED	SQUINYING	STABILE
SQUALL	SQUATTEST	SQUELCHER	SQUIRAGE	STABILES
SQUALLED	SQUATTIER	SQUELCHERS	SQUIRAGES	STABILISE
SQUALLER	SQUATTIEST	SQUELCHES	SQUIRALTIES	STABILISED
SQUALLERS	SQUATTING	SQUELCHIER	SQUIRALTY	STABILISES
SQUALLIER	SQUATTLE	SQUELCHIEST	SQUIRARCH	STABILISING
SQUALLIEST	SQUATTLED	SQUELCHING	SQUIRARCHS	STABILITIES
SQUALLING	SQUATTLES	SQUELCHINGS	SQUIRE	STABILITY
SQUALLINGS	SQUATTLING	SQUELCHY	SQUIREAGE	STABILIZE
SQUALLS	SQUATTY	SQUIB	SQUIREAGES	STABILIZED
SQUALLY	SQUAW	SQUIBBED	SQUIRED	STABILIZES
SQUALOID	SQUAWK	SQUIBBING	SQUIREDOM	STABILIZING
SQUALOR	SQUAWKED	SQUIBBINGS	SQUIREDOMS	STABLE
SQUALORS	SQUAWKER	SQUIBS	SQUIREEN	STABLEBOY
SQUAMA	SQUAWKERS	SQUID	SQUIREENS	STABLEBOYS
SQUAMAE	SQUAWKIER	SQUIDDED	SQUIRELY	STABLED
SQUAMATE	SQUAWKIEST	SQUIDDING	SQUIRES	STABLEMAN
SQUAME	SQUAWKING	SQUIDGE	SQUIRESS	STABLEMEN
SQUAMELLA	SQUAWKINGS	SQUIDGED	SQUIRESSES	STABLER
SQUAMELLAS	SQUAWKS	SQUIDGES	SQUIRING	STABLERS
SQUAMES	SQUAWKY	SQUIDGIER	SQUIRM	STABLES
SQUAMOSAL	SQUAWMAN	SQUIDGIEST	SQUIRMED	STABLEST
SQUAMOSALS	SQUAWMEN	SQUIDGING	SQUIRMIER	STABLING
SQUAMOSE	SQUAWS	SQUIDGY	SQUIRMIEST	STABLINGS
SQUAMOUS	SQUEAK	SQUIDS	SQUIRMING	STABLISH
SQUAMULA	SQUEAKED	SQUIER	SQUIRMS	STABLISHED
SQUAMULAS	SQUEAKER	SQUIERS	SQUIRMY	STABLISHES
SQUAMULE	SQUEAKERIES	SQUIFF	SQUIRR	STABLISHING
SQUAMULES	SQUEAKERS	SQUIFFER	SQUIRRED	STABLY
SQUANDER	SQUEAKERY	SQUIFFERS	SQUIRREL	STABS
SQUANDERED	SQUEAKIER	SQUIFFIER	SQUIRRELLED	STACCATO
SQUANDERING	SQUEAKIEST	SQUIFFIEST	SQUIRRELLING	STACCATOS
SQUANDERINGS	SQUEAKILY	SQUIFFY	SQUIRRELS	STACHYS
SQUANDERS	SQUEAKING	SQUIGGLE	SQUIRRELY	STACHYSES
SQUARE	SQUEAKINGS	SQUIGGLED	SQUIRRING	STACK

The Chambers Dictionary is the authority for many longer words; see *OSW* Introduction, page xii.

STACKED	STAGNANT	STALING	STANCES	STANZAIC
STACKER	STAGNATE	STALK	STANCH	STANZAS
STACKERS	STAGNATED	STALKED	STANCHED	STANZE
STACKET	STAGNATES	STALKER	STANCHEL	STANZES
STACKETS	STAGNATING	STALKERS	STANCHELLED	STANZO
STACKING	STAGS	STALKIER	STANCHELLING	STANZOES
STACKINGS	STAGY	STALKIEST	STANCHELS	STANZOS
STACKROOM	STAID	STALKING	STANCHER	STAP
STACKROOMS	STAIDER	STALKINGS	STANCHERED	STAPEDES
STACKS	STAIDEST	STALKLESS	STANCHERING	STAPEDIAL
STACKYARD	STAIDLY	STALKO	STANCHERS	STAPEDII
STACKYARDS	STAIDNESS	STALKOES	STANCHES	STAPEDIUS
STACTE	STAIDNESSES	STALKS	STANCHEST	STAPEDIUSES
STACTES	STAIG	STALKY	STANCHING	STAPELIA
STADDA	STAIGS	STALL	STANCHINGS	STAPELIAS
STADDAS	STAIN	STALLAGE	STANCHION	STAPES
STADDLE	STAINED	STALLAGES	STANCHIONED	STAPH
STADDLES	STAINER	STALLED	STANCHIONING	STAPHS
STADE	STAINERS	STALLING	STANCHIONS	STAPLE
STADES	STAINING	STALLINGS	STANCK	STAPLED
STADIA	STAININGS	STALLION	STAND	STAPLER
STADIAL	STAINLESS	STALLIONS	STANDARD	STAPLERS
STADIALS	STAINS	STALLMAN	STANDARDS	STAPLES
STADIAS	STAIR	STALLMEN	STANDEE	STAPLING
STADIUM	STAIRCASE	STALLS	STANDEES	STAPPED
STADIUMS	STAIRCASED	STALWART	STANDEN	STAPPING
STAFF	STAIRCASES	STALWARTS	STANDER	STAPPLE
STAFFAGE	STAIRCASING	STALWORTH	STANDERS	STAPPLES
STAFFAGES	STAIRCASINGS	STALWORTHS	STANDGALE	STAPS
STAFFED	STAIRED	STAMEN	STANDGALES	STAR
STAFFER	STAIRFOOT	STAMENED	STANDING	STARAGEN
STAFFERS	STAIRFOOTS	STAMENS	STANDINGS	STARAGENS
STAFFING	STAIRHEAD	STAMINA	STANDISH	STARBOARD
STAFFROOM	STAIRHEADS	STAMINAS	STANDISHES	STARBOARDED
STAFFROOMS	STAIRLIFT	STAMINATE	STANDOFF	STARBOARDING
STAFFS	STAIRLIFTS	STAMINODE	STANDPIPE	STARBOARDS
STAG	STAIRS	STAMINODES	STANDPIPES	STARCH
STAGE	STAIRWAY	STAMINODIES	STANDS	STARCHED
STAGED	STAIRWAYS	STAMINODY	STANE	STARCHER
STAGER	STAIRWELL	STAMINOID	STANED	STARCHERS
STAGERIES	STAIRWELLS	STAMMEL	STANES	STARCHES
STAGERS	STAIRWISE	STAMMELS	STANG	STARCHIER
STAGERY	STAIRWORK	STAMMER	STANGED	STARCHIEST
STAGES	STAIRWORKS	STAMMERED	STANGING	STARCHILY
STAGEY	STAITH	STAMMERER	STANGS	STARCHING
STAGGARD	STAITHE	STAMMERERS	STANHOPE	STARCHY
STAGGARDS	STAITHES	STAMMERING	STANHOPES	STARDOM
STAGGED	STAITHS	STAMMERINGS	STANIEL	STARDOMS
STAGGER	STAKE	STAMMERS	STANIELS	STARDRIFT
STAGGERED	STAKED	STAMNOI	STANING	STARDRIFTS
STAGGERER	STAKES	STAMNOS	STANK	STARDUST
STAGGERERS	STAKING	STAMP	STANKS	STARDUSTS
STAGGERING	STALACTIC	STAMPED	STANNARIES	STARE
STAGGERINGS	STALAG	STAMPEDE	STANNARY	STARED
STAGGERS	STALAGS	STAMPEDED	STANNATE	STARER
STAGGING	STALE	STAMPEDES	STANNATES	STARERS
STAGHOUND	STALED	STAMPEDING	STANNATOR	STARES
STAGHOUNDS	STALELY	STAMPEDO	STANNATORS	STARETS
STAGIER	STALEMATE	STAMPEDOED	STANNEL	STARETSES
STAGIEST	STALEMATED	STAMPEDOING	STANNELS	STARETZ
STAGILY	STALEMATES	STAMPEDOS	STANNIC	STARETZES
STAGINESS	STALEMATING	STAMPER	STANNITE	STARFISH
STAGINESSES	STALENESS	STAMPERS	STANNITES	STARFISHES
STAGING	STALENESSES	STAMPING	STANNOUS	STARGAZER
STAGINGS	STALER	STAMPINGS	STANYEL	STARGAZERS
STAGNANCIES	STALES	STAMPS	STANYELS	STARING
STAGNANCY	STALEST	STANCE	STANZA	STARINGLY

The Chambers Dictionary is the authority for many longer words; see *OSW* Introduction, page xii.

STARINGS	STARTS	STATOLITH	STEADING	STEARSMAN
STARK	STARVE	STATOLITHS	STEADINGS	STEARSMEN
STARKED	STARVED	STATOR	STEADS	STEATITE
STARKEN	STARVES	STATORS	STEADY	STEATITES
STARKENED	STARVING	STATUA	STEADYING	STEATITIC
STARKENING	STARVINGS	STATUARIES	STEAK	STEATOMA
STARKENS	STARWORT	STATUARY	STEAKS	STEATOMAS
STARKER	STARWORTS	STATUAS	STEAL	STEATOSES
STARKERS	STASES	STATUE	STEALE	STEATOSIS
STARKEST	STASH	STATUED	STEALED	STED
STARKING	STASHED	STATUES	STEALER	STEDD
STARKLY	STASHES	STATUETTE	STEALERS	STEDDE
STARKNESS	STASHIE	STATUETTES	STEALES	STEDDED
STARKNESSES	STASHIES	STATURE	STEALING	STEDDES
STARKS	STASHING	STATURED	STEALINGS	STEDDIED
STARLESS	STASIDION	STATURES	STEALS	STEDDIES
STARLET	STASIDIONS	STATUS	STEALT	STEDDING
STARLETS	STASIMA	STATUSES	STEALTH	STEDDS
STARLIGHT	STASIMON	STATUTE	STEALTHED	STEDDY
STARLIGHTS	STASIS	STATUTES	STEALTHIER	STEDDYING
STARLIKE	STATABLE	STATUTORY	STEALTHIEST	STEDE
STARLING	STATAL	STAUNCH	STEALTHING	STEDED
STARLINGS	STATANT	STAUNCHED	STEALTHINGS	STEDES
STARLIT	STATE	STAUNCHER	STEALTHS	STEDFAST
STARN	STATED	STAUNCHERS	STEALTHY	STEDING
STARNED	STATEDLY	STAUNCHES	STEAM	STEDS
STARNIE	STATEHOOD	STAUNCHEST	STEAMBOAT	STEED
STARNIES	STATEHOODS	STAUNCHING	STEAMBOATS	STEEDED
STARNING	STATELESS	STAUNCHINGS	STEAMED	STEEDIED
STARNS	STATELIER	STAUNCHLY	STEAMER	STEEDIES
STAROSTA	STATELIEST	STAVE	STEAMERS	STEEDING
STAROSTAS	STATELILY	STAVED	STEAMIE	STEEDS
STAROSTIES	STATELY	STAVES	STEAMIER	STEEDY
STAROSTY	STATEMENT	STAVING	STEAMIES	STEEDYING
STARR	STATEMENTS	STAW	STEAMIEST	STEEK
STARRED	STATER	STAWED	STEAMILY	STEEKING
STARRIER	STATEROOM	STAWING	STEAMING	STEEKIT
STARRIEST	STATEROOMS	STAWS	STEAMINGS	STEEKS
STARRILY	STATERS	STAY	STEAMS	STEEL
STARRING	STATES	STAYAWAY	STEAMSHIP	STEELBOW
STARRINGS	STATESIDE	STAYAWAYS	STEAMSHIPS	STEELBOWS
STARRS	STATESMAN	STAYED	STEAMY	STEELD
STARRY	STATESMEN	STAYER	STEAN	STEELED
STARS	STATEWIDE	STAYERS	STEANE	STEELIER
STARSHINE	STATIC	STAYING	STEANED	STEELIEST
STARSHINES	STATICAL	STAYLESS	STEANES	STEELING
STARSPOT	STATICE	STAYMAKER	STEANING	STEELINGS
STARSPOTS	STATICES	STAYMAKERS	STEANINGS	STEELMAN
STARSTONE	STATICS	STAYNE	STEANS	STEELMEN
STARSTONES	STATIM	STAYNED	STEAPSIN	STEELS
START	STATING	STAYNES	STEAPSINS	STEELWORK
STARTED	STATION	STAYNING	STEAR	STEELWORKS
STARTER	STATIONAL	STAYRE	STEARAGE	STEELY
STARTERS	STATIONED	STAYRES	STEARAGES	STEELYARD
STARTFUL	STATIONER	STAYS	STEARATE	STEELYARDS
STARTING	STATIONERS	STAYSAIL	STEARATES	STEEM
STARTINGS	STATIONING	STAYSAILS	STEARD	STEEMED
STARTISH	STATIONS	STEAD	STEARE	STEEMING
STARTLE	STATISM	STEADED	STEARED	STEEMS
STARTLED	STATISMS	STEADFAST	STEARES	STEEN
STARTLER	STATIST	STEADICAM	STEARIC	STEENBOK
STARTLERS	STATISTIC	STEADICAMS	STEARIN	STEENBOKS
STARTLES	STATISTICS	STEADIED	STEARINE	STEENBRAS
STARTLING	STATISTS	STEADIER	STEARINES	STEENBRASES
STARTLINGS	STATIVE	STEADIES	STEARING	STEENED
STARTLISH	STATOCYST	STEADIEST	STEARINS	STEENING
STARTLY	STATOCYSTS	STEADILY	STEARS	STEENINGS

The Chambers Dictionary is the authority for many longer words; see *OSW* Introduction, page xii.

STEENKIRK
STEENKIRKS
STEENS
STEEP
STEEPED
STEEPEN
STEEPENED
STEEPENING
STEEPENS
STEEPER
STEEPERS
STEEPEST
STEEPIER
STEEPIEST
STEEPING
STEEPISH
STEEPLE
STEEPLED
STEEPLES
STEEPLY
STEEPNESS
STEEPNESSES
STEEPS
STEEPY
STEER
STEERABLE
STEERAGE
STEERAGES
STEERED
STEERER
STEERERS
STEERIES
STEERING
STEERINGS
STEERLING
STEERLINGS
STEERS
STEERSMAN
STEERSMEN
STEERY
STEEVE
STEEVED
STEEVELY
STEEVER
STEEVES
STEEVEST
STEEVING
STEEVINGS
STEGNOSES
STEGNOSIS
STEGNOTIC
STEGODON
STEGODONS
STEGODONT
STEGODONTS
STEGOSAUR
STEGOSAURS
STEIL
STEILS
STEIN
STEINBOCK
STEINBOCKS
STEINED
STEINING
STEININGS
STEINKIRK
STEINKIRKS

STEINS
STELA
STELAE
STELAR
STELE
STELENE
STELES
STELL
STELLAR
STELLATE
STELLATED
STELLED
STELLERID
STELLERIDS
STELLIFIED
STELLIFIES
STELLIFY
STELLIFYING
STELLIFYINGS
STELLING
STELLION
STELLIONS
STELLS
STELLULAR
STEM
STEMBOK
STEMBOKS
STEMBUCK
STEMBUCKS
STEME
STEMED
STEMES
STEMING
STEMLESS
STEMLET
STEMLETS
STEMMA
STEMMATA
STEMME
STEMMED
STEMMER
STEMMERS
STEMMES
STEMMING
STEMMINGS
STEMPEL
STEMPELS
STEMPLE
STEMPLES
STEMS
STEMSON
STEMSONS
STEN
STENCH
STENCHED
STENCHES
STENCHIER
STENCHIEST
STENCHING
STENCHY
STENCIL
STENCILED
STENCILING
STENCILLED
STENCILLING
STENCILLINGS
STENCILS

STEND
STENDED
STENDING
STENDS
STENGAH
STENGAHS
STENLOCK
STENLOCKS
STENNED
STENNING
STENOPAIC
STENOSED
STENOSES
STENOSIS
STENOTIC
STENOTYPIES
STENOTYPY
STENS
STENT
STENTED
STENTING
STENTOR
STENTORS
STENTOUR
STENTOURS
STENTS
STEP
STEPBAIRN
STEPBAIRNS
STEPCHILD
STEPCHILDREN
STEPDAME
STEPDAMES
STEPHANE
STEPHANES
STEPNEY
STEPNEYS
STEPPE
STEPPED
STEPPER
STEPPERS
STEPPES
STEPPING
STEPS
STEPSON
STEPSONS
STEPT
STEPWISE
STERADIAN
STERADIANS
STERCORAL
STERCULIA
STERCULIAS
STERE
STEREO
STEREOME
STEREOMES
STEREOS
STERES
STERIC
STERIGMA
STERIGMATA
STERILANT
STERILANTS
STERILE
STERILISE
STERILISED

STERILISES
STERILISING
STERILITIES
STERILITY
STERILIZE
STERILIZED
STERILIZES
STERILIZING
STERLET
STERLETS
STERLING
STERLINGS
STERN
STERNA
STERNAGE
STERNAGES
STERNAL
STERNEBRA
STERNEBRAE
STERNED
STERNER
STERNEST
STERNFAST
STERNFASTS
STERNING
STERNITE
STERNITES
STERNITIC
STERNLY
STERNMOST
STERNNESS
STERNNESSES
STERNPORT
STERNPORTS
STERNPOST
STERNPOSTS
STERNS
STERNSON
STERNSONS
STERNUM
STERNUMS
STERNWARD
STERNWARDS
STERNWAY
STERNWAYS
STEROID
STEROIDS
STEROL
STEROLS
STERVE
STERVED
STERVES
STERVING
STET
STETS
STETTED
STETTING
STEVEDORE
STEVEDORED
STEVEDORES
STEVEDORING
STEVEN
STEVENS
STEW
STEWARD
STEWARDRIES
STEWARDRY

STEWARDS
STEWARTRIES
STEWARTRY
STEWED
STEWER
STEWERS
STEWIER
STEWIEST
STEWING
STEWINGS
STEWPAN
STEWPANS
STEWPOND
STEWPONDS
STEWPOT
STEWPOTS
STEWS
STEWY
STEY
STEYER
STEYEST
STHENIC
STIBBLE
STIBBLER
STIBBLERS
STIBBLES
STIBIAL
STIBINE
STIBINES
STIBIUM
STIBIUMS
STIBNITE
STIBNITES
STICCADO
STICCADOES
STICCADOS
STICCATO
STICCATOES
STICCATOS
STICH
STICHERON
STICHERONS
STICHIC
STICHIDIA
STICHOI
STICHOS
STICHS
STICK
STICKED
STICKER
STICKERED
STICKERING
STICKERS
STICKFUL
STICKFULS
STICKIED
STICKIER
STICKIES
STICKIEST
STICKILY
STICKING
STICKINGS
STICKIT
STICKJAW
STICKJAWS
STICKLE
STICKLED

The Chambers Dictionary is the authority for many longer words; see *OSW* Introduction, page xii.

STICKLER
STICKLERS
STICKLES
STICKLING
STICKS
STICKWORK
STICKWORKS
STICKY
STICKYING
STICTION
STICTIONS
STIDDIE
STIDDIED
STIDDIEING
STIDDIES
STIDDYING
STIE
STIED
STIES
STIEVE
STIEVELY
STIEVER
STIEVEST
STIFF
STIFFED
STIFFEN
STIFFENED
STIFFENER
STIFFENERS
STIFFENING
STIFFENINGS
STIFFENS
STIFFER
STIFFEST
STIFFING
STIFFISH
STIFFLY
STIFFNESS
STIFFNESSES
STIFFS
STIFFWARE
STIFFWARES
STIFLE
STIFLED
STIFLER
STIFLERS
STIFLES
STIFLING
STIFLINGS
STIGMA
STIGMAS
STIGMATA
STIGMATIC
STIGMATICS
STIGME
STIGMES
STILB
STILBENE
STILBENES
STILBITE
STILBITES
STILBS
STILE
STILED
STILES
STILET
STILETS

STILETTO
STILETTOED
STILETTOING
STILETTOS
STILING
STILL
STILLAGE
STILLAGES
STILLBORN
STILLED
STILLER
STILLERS
STILLEST
STILLIER
STILLIEST
STILLING
STILLINGS
STILLION
STILLIONS
STILLNESS
STILLNESSES
STILLROOM
STILLROOMS
STILLS
STILLY
STILT
STILTBIRD
STILTBIRDS
STILTED
STILTEDLY
STILTER
STILTERS
STILTIER
STILTIEST
STILTING
STILTINGS
STILTISH
STILTS
STILTY
STIME
STIMED
STIMES
STIMIE
STIMIED
STIMIES
STIMING
STIMULANT
STIMULANTS
STIMULATE
STIMULATED
STIMULATES
STIMULATING
STIMULI
STIMULUS
STIMY
STIMYING
STING
STINGAREE
STINGAREES
STINGBULL
STINGBULLS
STINGED
STINGER
STINGERS
STINGFISH
STINGFISHES
STINGIER

STINGIEST
STINGILY
STINGING
STINGINGS
STINGLESS
STINGO
STINGOS
STINGS
STINGY
STINK
STINKARD
STINKARDS
STINKER
STINKERS
STINKHORN
STINKHORNS
STINKING
STINKINGS
STINKO
STINKS
STINKWOOD
STINKWOODS
STINT
STINTED
STINTEDLY
STINTER
STINTERS
STINTIER
STINTIEST
STINTING
STINTINGS
STINTLESS
STINTS
STINTY
STIPA
STIPAS
STIPE
STIPEL
STIPELS
STIPEND
STIPENDS
STIPES
STIPITATE
STIPITES
STIPPLE
STIPPLED
STIPPLER
STIPPLERS
STIPPLES
STIPPLING
STIPPLINGS
STIPULAR
STIPULARY
STIPULATE
STIPULATED
STIPULATES
STIPULATING
STIPULE
STIPULED
STIPULES
STIR
STIRABOUT
STIRABOUTS
STIRE
STIRED
STIRES
STIRING

STIRK
STIRKS
STIRLESS
STIRP
STIRPES
STIRPS
STIRRA
STIRRAH
STIRRAHS
STIRRAS
STIRRE
STIRRED
STIRRER
STIRRERS
STIRRES
STIRRING
STIRRINGS
STIRRUP
STIRRUPS
STIRS
STISHIE
STISHIES
STITCH
STITCHED
STITCHER
STITCHERIES
STITCHERS
STITCHERY
STITCHES
STITCHING
STITCHINGS
STITHIED
STITHIES
STITHY
STITHYING
STIVE
STIVED
STIVER
STIVERS
STIVES
STIVIER
STIVIEST
STIVING
STIVY
STOA
STOAE
STOAI
STOAS
STOAT
STOATS
STOB
STOBS
STOCCADO
STOCCADOS
STOCCATA
STOCCATAS
STOCIOUS
STOCK
STOCKADE
STOCKADED
STOCKADES
STOCKADING
STOCKED
STOCKER
STOCKERS
STOCKFISH
STOCKFISHES

STOCKHORN
STOCKHORNS
STOCKIER
STOCKIEST
STOCKILY
STOCKINET
STOCKINETS
STOCKING
STOCKINGS
STOCKIST
STOCKISTS
STOCKLESS
STOCKLIST
STOCKLISTS
STOCKMAN
STOCKMEN
STOCKPILE
STOCKPILED
STOCKPILES
STOCKPILING
STOCKPILINGS
STOCKPOT
STOCKPOTS
STOCKROOM
STOCKROOMS
STOCKS
STOCKTAKE
STOCKTAKEN
STOCKTAKES
STOCKTAKING
STOCKTAKINGS
STOCKTOOK
STOCKWORK
STOCKWORKS
STOCKY
STOCKYARD
STOCKYARDS
STODGE
STODGED
STODGER
STODGERS
STODGES
STODGIER
STODGIEST
STODGILY
STODGING
STODGY
STOEP
STOEPS
STOGEY
STOGEYS
STOGIE
STOGIES
STOGY
STOIC
STOICAL
STOICALLY
STOICISM
STOICISMS
STOICS
STOIT
STOITED
STOITER
STOITERED
STOITERING
STOITERS
STOITING

The Chambers Dictionary is the authority for many longer words; see *OSW* Introduction, page xii.

STOITS	STONER	STOOPE	STORIES	STOUTHRIE
STOKE	STONERAG	STOOPED	STORIETTE	STOUTHRIES
STOKED	STONERAGS	STOOPER	STORIETTES	STOUTHS
STOKEHOLD	STONERAW	STOOPERS	STORING	STOUTISH
STOKEHOLDS	STONERAWS	STOOPES	STORK	STOUTLY
STOKEHOLE	STONERN	STOOPING	STORKS	STOUTNESS
STOKEHOLES	STONERS	STOOPS	STORM	STOUTNESSES
STOKER	STONES	STOOR	STORMBIRD	STOUTS
STOKERS	STONESHOT	STOORS	STORMBIRDS	STOVAINE
STOKES	STONESHOTS	STOOSHIE	STORMED	STOVAINES
STOKING	STONEWALL	STOOSHIES	STORMFUL	STOVE
STOLE	STONEWALLED	STOP	STORMIER	STOVED
STOLED	STONEWALLING	STOPBANK	STORMIEST	STOVEPIPE
STOLEN	STONEWALLINGS	STOPBANKS	STORMILY	STOVEPIPES
STOLES	STONEWALLS	STOPCOCK	STORMING	STOVER
STOLID	STONEWARE	STOPCOCKS	STORMINGS	STOVERS
STOLIDER	STONEWARES	STOPE	STORMLESS	STOVES
STOLIDEST	STONEWORK	STOPED	STORMS	STOVIES
STOLIDITIES	STONEWORKS	STOPES	STORMY	STOVING
STOLIDITY	STONEWORT	STOPGAP	STORNELLI	STOVINGS
STOLIDLY	STONEWORTS	STOPGAPS	STORNELLO	STOW
STOLLEN	STONG	STOPING	STORY	STOWAGE
STOLLENS	STONIED	STOPINGS	STORYBOOK	STOWAGES
STOLN	STONIER	STOPLESS	STORYBOOKS	STOWAWAY
STOLON	STONIES	STOPLIGHT	STORYETTE	STOWAWAYS
STOLONS	STONIEST	STOPLIGHTS	STORYETTES	STOWDOWN
STOMA	STONILY	STOPOFF	STORYING	STOWDOWNS
STOMACH	STONINESS	STOPOFFS	STORYINGS	STOWED
STOMACHAL	STONINESSES	STOPOVER	STORYLINE	STOWER
STOMACHED	STONING	STOPOVERS	STORYLINES	STOWERS
STOMACHER	STONINGS	STOPPAGE	STOSS	STOWING
STOMACHERS	STONK	STOPPAGES	STOSSES	STOWINGS
STOMACHIC	STONKER	STOPPED	STOT	STOWLINS
STOMACHICS	STONKERED	STOPPER	STOTINKA	STOWN
STOMACHING	STONKERING	STOPPERED	STOTINKI	STOWND
STOMACHS	STONKERS	STOPPERING	STOTIOUS	STOWNDED
STOMACHY	STONKING	STOPPERS	STOTS	STOWNDING
STOMAL	STONKS	STOPPING	STOTTED	STOWNDS
STOMATA	STONN	STOPPINGS	STOTTER	STOWNLINS
STOMATAL	STONNE	STOPPLE	STOTTERS	STOWRE
STOMATIC	STONNED	STOPPLED	STOTTING	STOWRES
STOMP	STONNES	STOPPLES	STOUN	STOWS
STOMPED	STONNING	STOPPLING	STOUND	STRABISM
STOMPER	STONNS	STOPS	STOUNDED	STRABISMS
STOMPERS	STONY	STOPWATCH	STOUNDING	STRAD
STOMPING	STONYING	STOPWATCHES	STOUNDS	STRADDLE
STOMPS	STOOD	STORABLE	STOUNING	STRADDLED
STOND	STOODEN	STORAGE	STOUNS	STRADDLES
STONDS	STOOGE	STORAGES	STOUP	STRADDLING
STONE	STOOGED	STORAX	STOUPS	STRADIOT
STONEBOAT	STOOGES	STORAXES	STOUR	STRADIOTS
STONEBOATS	STOOGING	STORE	STOURIER	STRADS
STONECAST	STOOK	STORED	STOURIEST	STRAE
STONECASTS	STOOKED	STOREMAN	STOURS	STRAES
STONECHAT	STOOKER	STOREMEN	STOURY	STRAFE
STONECHATS	STOOKERS	STORER	STOUSH	STRAFED
STONECROP	STOOKING	STOREROOM	STOUSHED	STRAFES
STONECROPS	STOOKS	STOREROOMS	STOUSHES	STRAFF
STONED	STOOL	STORERS	STOUSHING	STRAFFED
STONEFISH	STOOLBALL	STORES	STOUT	STRAFFING
STONEFISHES	STOOLBALLS	STOREY	STOUTEN	STRAFFS
STONEFLIES	STOOLED	STOREYED	STOUTENED	STRAFING
STONEFLY	STOOLIE	STOREYS	STOUTENING	STRAGGLE
STONEHAND	STOOLIES	STORGE	STOUTENS	STRAGGLED
STONEHANDS	STOOLING	STORGES	STOUTER	STRAGGLER
STONELESS	STOOLS	STORIATED	STOUTEST	STRAGGLERS
STONEN	STOOP	STORIED	STOUTH	STRAGGLES

The Chambers Dictionary is the authority for many longer words; see *OSW* Introduction, page xii.

STRAGGLIER
STRAGGLIEST
STRAGGLING
STRAGGLINGS
STRAGGLY
STRAICHT
STRAICHTER
STRAICHTEST
STRAIGHT
STRAIGHTER
STRAIGHTEST
STRAIGHTS
STRAIK
STRAIKED
STRAIKING
STRAIKS
STRAIN
STRAINED
STRAINER
STRAINERS
STRAINING
STRAININGS
STRAINS
STRAINT
STRAINTS
STRAIT
STRAITED
STRAITEN
STRAITENED
STRAITENING
STRAITENS
STRAITER
STRAITEST
STRAITING
STRAITLY
STRAITS
STRAKE
STRAKES
STRAMACON
STRAMACONS
STRAMASH
STRAMASHED
STRAMASHES
STRAMASHING
STRAMAZON
STRAMAZONS
STRAMMEL
STRAMMELS
STRAMP
STRAMPED
STRAMPING
STRAMPS
STRAND
STRANDED
STRANDING
STRANDS
STRANGE
STRANGELY
STRANGER
STRANGERED
STRANGERING
STRANGERS
STRANGEST
STRANGLE
STRANGLED
STRANGLER
STRANGLERS

STRANGLES
STRANGLING
STRANGURIES
STRANGURY
STRAP
STRAPLESS
STRAPLINE
STRAPLINES
STRAPPADO
STRAPPADOED
STRAPPADOING
STRAPPADOS
STRAPPED
STRAPPER
STRAPPERS
STRAPPIER
STRAPPIEST
STRAPPING
STRAPPINGS
STRAPPY
STRAPS
STRAPWORT
STRAPWORTS
STRASS
STRASSES
STRATA
STRATAGEM
STRATAGEMS
STRATEGIC
STRATEGICS
STRATEGIES
STRATEGY
STRATH
STRATHS
STRATI
STRATIFIED
STRATIFIES
STRATIFY
STRATIFYING
STRATONIC
STRATOSE
STRATOUS
STRATUM
STRATUS
STRAUCHT
STRAUCHTED
STRAUCHTER
STRAUCHTEST
STRAUCHTING
STRAUCHTS
STRAUGHT
STRAUGHTED
STRAUGHTER
STRAUGHTEST
STRAUGHTING
STRAUGHTS
STRAUNGE
STRAVAIG
STRAVAIGED
STRAVAIGING
STRAVAIGS
STRAW
STRAWED
STRAWEN
STRAWIER
STRAWIEST
STRAWING

STRAWLIKE
STRAWN
STRAWS
STRAWWORM
STRAWWORMS
STRAWY
STRAY
STRAYED
STRAYER
STRAYERS
STRAYING
STRAYINGS
STRAYLING
STRAYLINGS
STRAYS
STREAK
STREAKED
STREAKER
STREAKERS
STREAKIER
STREAKIEST
STREAKILY
STREAKING
STREAKINGS
STREAKS
STREAKY
STREAM
STREAMED
STREAMER
STREAMERS
STREAMIER
STREAMIEST
STREAMING
STREAMINGS
STREAMLET
STREAMLETS
STREAMS
STREAMY
STREEK
STREEKED
STREEKING
STREEKS
STREEL
STREELED
STREELING
STREELS
STREET
STREETAGE
STREETAGES
STREETBOY
STREETBOYS
STREETCAR
STREETCARS
STREETED
STREETFUL
STREETFULS
STREETIER
STREETIEST
STREETS
STREETY
STREIGHT
STREIGHTS
STREIGNE
STREIGNED
STREIGNES
STREIGNING
STRELITZ

STRELITZES
STRELITZI
STRENE
STRENES
STRENGTH
STRENGTHS
STRENUITIES
STRENUITY
STRENUOUS
STREP
STREPENT
STREPS
STRESS
STRESSED
STRESSES
STRESSFUL
STRESSING
STRESSOR
STRESSORS
STRETCH
STRETCHED
STRETCHER
STRETCHERED
STRETCHERING
STRETCHERS
STRETCHES
STRETCHIER
STRETCHIEST
STRETCHING
STRETCHY
STRETTA
STRETTE
STRETTI
STRETTO
STREW
STREWAGE
STREWAGES
STREWED
STREWER
STREWERS
STREWING
STREWINGS
STREWMENT
STREWMENTS
STREWN
STREWS
STREWTH
STRIA
STRIAE
STRIATA
STRIATE
STRIATED
STRIATES
STRIATING
STRIATION
STRIATIONS
STRIATUM
STRIATUMS
STRIATURE
STRIATURES
STRICH
STRICHES
STRICKEN
STRICKLE
STRICKLED
STRICKLES
STRICKLING

STRICT
STRICTER
STRICTEST
STRICTISH
STRICTLY
STRICTURE
STRICTURES
STRIDDEN
STRIDDLE
STRIDDLED
STRIDDLES
STRIDDLING
STRIDE
STRIDENCE
STRIDENCES
STRIDENCIES
STRIDENCY
STRIDENT
STRIDES
STRIDING
STRIDLING
STRIDOR
STRIDORS
STRIFE
STRIFEFUL
STRIFES
STRIFT
STRIFTS
STRIG
STRIGA
STRIGAE
STRIGATE
STRIGGED
STRIGGING
STRIGIL
STRIGILS
STRIGINE
STRIGOSE
STRIGS
STRIKE
STRIKEOUT
STRIKEOUTS
STRIKER
STRIKERS
STRIKES
STRIKING
STRIKINGS
STRING
STRINGED
STRINGENT
STRINGER
STRINGERS
STRINGIER
STRINGIEST
STRINGILY
STRINGING
STRINGINGS
STRINGS
STRINGY
STRINKLE
STRINKLED
STRINKLES
STRINKLING
STRINKLINGS
STRIP
STRIPE
STRIPED

The Chambers Dictionary is the authority for many longer words; see *OSW* Introduction, page xii.

STRIPES	STROND	STRUCK	STUCCOERS	STUMM
STRIPEY	STRONDS	STRUCTURE	STUCCOING	STUMMED
STRIPIER	STRONG	STRUCTURED	STUCCOS	STUMMEL
STRIPIEST	STRONGARM	STRUCTURES	STUCK	STUMMELS
STRIPING	STRONGARMED	STRUCTURING	STUCKS	STUMMING
STRIPINGS	STRONGARMING	STRUDEL	STUD	STUMP
STRIPLING	STRONGARMS	STRUDELS	STUDBOOK	STUMPAGE
STRIPLINGS	STRONGBOX	STRUGGLE	STUDBOOKS	STUMPAGES
STRIPPED	STRONGBOXES	STRUGGLED	STUDDED	STUMPED
STRIPPER	STRONGER	STRUGGLER	STUDDEN	STUMPER
STRIPPERS	STRONGEST	STRUGGLERS	STUDDING	STUMPERS
STRIPPING	STRONGISH	STRUGGLES	STUDDINGS	STUMPIER
STRIPPINGS	STRONGLY	STRUGGLING	STUDDLE	STUMPIES
STRIPS	STRONGMAN	STRUGGLINGS	STUDDLES	STUMPIEST
STRIPY	STRONGMEN	STRUM	STUDENT	STUMPILY
STRIVE	STRONGYL	STRUMA	STUDENTRIES	STUMPING
STRIVED	STRONGYLE	STRUMAE	STUDENTRY	STUMPS
STRIVEN	STRONGYLES	STRUMATIC	STUDENTS	STUMPY
STRIVER	STRONGYLS	STRUMITIS	STUDFARM	STUMS
STRIVERS	STRONTIA	STRUMITISES	STUDFARMS	STUN
STRIVES	STRONTIAN	STRUMMED	STUDIED	STUNG
STRIVING	STRONTIANS	STRUMMEL	STUDIEDLY	STUNK
STRIVINGS	STRONTIAS	STRUMMELS	STUDIER	STUNKARD
STROAM	STRONTIUM	STRUMMING	STUDIERS	STUNNED
STROAMED	STRONTIUMS	STRUMOSE	STUDIES	STUNNER
STROAMING	STROOK	STRUMOUS	STUDIO	STUNNERS
STROAMS	STROOKE	STRUMPET	STUDIOS	STUNNING
STROBE	STROOKEN	STRUMPETED	STUDIOUS	STUNNINGS
STROBES	STROOKES	STRUMPETING	STUDS	STUNS
STROBIC	STROP	STRUMPETS	STUDWORK	STUNSAIL
STROBILA	STROPHE	STRUMS	STUDWORKS	STUNSAILS
STROBILAE	STROPHES	STRUNG	STUDY	STUNT
STROBILE	STROPHIC	STRUNT	STUDYING	STUNTED
STROBILES	STROPPED	STRUNTED	STUFF	STUNTING
STROBILI	STROPPIER	STRUNTING	STUFFED	STUNTMAN
STROBILUS	STROPPIEST	STRUNTS	STUFFER	STUNTMEN
STRODDLE	STROPPING	STRUT	STUFFERS	STUNTS
STRODDLED	STROPPY	STRUTS	STUFFIER	STUPA
STRODDLES	STROPS	STRUTTED	STUFFIEST	STUPAS
STRODDLING	STROSSERS	STRUTTER	STUFFILY	STUPE
STRODE	STROUD	STRUTTERS	STUFFING	STUPED
STRODLE	STROUDING	STRUTTING	STUFFINGS	STUPEFIED
STRODLED	STROUDINGS	STRUTTINGS	STUFFS	STUPEFIER
STRODLES	STROUDS	STRYCHNIA	STUFFY	STUPEFIERS
STRODLING	STROUP	STRYCHNIAS	STUGGIER	STUPEFIES
STROKE	STROUPACH	STRYCHNIC	STUGGIEST	STUPEFY
STROKED	STROUPACHS	STUB	STUGGY	STUPEFYING
STROKEN	STROUPAN	STUBBED	STULL	STUPENT
STROKER	STROUPANS	STUBBIER	STULLS	STUPES
STROKERS	STROUPS	STUBBIES	STULM	STUPID
STROKES	STROUT	STUBBIEST	STULMS	STUPIDER
STROKING	STROUTED	STUBBING	STULTIFIED	STUPIDEST
STROKINGS	STROUTING	STUBBLE	STULTIFIES	STUPIDITIES
STROLL	STROUTS	STUBBLED	STULTIFY	STUPIDITY
STROLLED	STROVE	STUBBLES	STULTIFYING	STUPIDLY
STROLLER	STROW	STUBBLIER	STUM	STUPIDS
STROLLERS	STROWED	STUBBLIEST	STUMBLE	STUPING
STROLLING	STROWER	STUBBLY	STUMBLED	STUPOR
STROLLINGS	STROWERS	STUBBORN	STUMBLER	STUPOROUS
STROLLS	STROWING	STUBBORNED	STUMBLERS	STUPORS
STROMA	STROWINGS	STUBBORNING	STUMBLES	STUPRATE
STROMATA	STROWN	STUBBORNS	STUMBLIER	STUPRATED
STROMATIC	STROWS	STUBBY	STUMBLIEST	STUPRATES
STROMB	STROY	STUBS	STUMBLING	STUPRATING
STROMBS	STROYED	STUCCO	STUMBLY	STURDIED
STROMBUS	STROYING	STUCCOED	STUMER	STURDIER
STROMBUSES	STROYS	STUCCOER	STUMERS	STURDIES

The Chambers Dictionary is the authority for many longer words; see *OSW* Introduction, page xii.

STURDIEST	STYLUS	SUBAH	SUBCOSTAL	SUBERS
STURDILY	STYLUSES	SUBAHDAR	SUBCOSTALS	SUBFAMILIES
STURDY	STYME	SUBAHDARIES	SUBCRUST	SUBFAMILY
STURE	STYMED	SUBAHDARS	SUBCRUSTS	SUBFEU
STURGEON	STYMES	SUBAHDARY	SUBDEACON	SUBFEUED
STURGEONS	STYMIE	SUBAHS	SUBDEACONS	SUBFEUING
STURMER	STYMIED	SUBAHSHIP	SUBDEAN	SUBFEUS
STURMERS	STYMIEING	SUBAHSHIPS	SUBDEANS	SUBFIELD
STURNINE	STYMIES	SUBALPINE	SUBDERMAL	SUBFIELDS
STURNOID	STYMING	SUBALTERN	SUBDEW	SUBFLOOR
STURNUS	STYPSIS	SUBALTERNS	SUBDEWED	SUBFLOORS
STURNUSES	STYPSISES	SUBAPICAL	SUBDEWING	SUBFRAME
STURT	STYPTIC	SUBAQUA	SUBDEWS	SUBFRAMES
STURTED	STYPTICAL	SUBARCTIC	SUBDIVIDE	SUBFUSC
STURTING	STYPTICS	SUBAREA	SUBDIVIDED	SUBFUSCS
STURTS	STYRAX	SUBAREAS	SUBDIVIDES	SUBFUSK
STUSHIE	STYRAXES	SUBARID	SUBDIVIDING	SUBFUSKS
STUSHIES	STYRE	SUBASTRAL	SUBDOLOUS	SUBGENERA
STUTTER	STYRED	SUBATOM	SUBDORSAL	SUBGENRE
STUTTERED	STYRENE	SUBATOMIC	SUBDUABLE	SUBGENRES
STUTTERER	STYRENES	SUBATOMICS	SUBDUAL	SUBGENUS
STUTTERERS	STYRES	SUBATOMS	SUBDUALS	SUBGENUSES
STUTTERING	STYRING	SUBAUDIO	SUBDUCE	SUBGOAL
STUTTERINGS	STYROFOAM	SUBAURAL	SUBDUCED	SUBGOALS
STUTTERS	STYROFOAMS	SUBBASAL	SUBDUCES	SUBGRADE
STY	STYTE	SUBBASE	SUBDUCING	SUBGRADES
STYE	STYTED	SUBBASES	SUBDUCT	SUBGROUP
STYED	STYTES	SUBBED	SUBDUCTED	SUBGROUPS
STYES	STYTING	SUBBIE	SUBDUCTING	SUBGUM
STYING	SUABILITIES	SUBBIES	SUBDUCTS	SUBGUMS
STYLAR	SUABILITY	SUBBING	SUBDUE	SUBHEAD
STYLATE	SUABLE	SUBBINGS	SUBDUED	SUBHEADS
STYLE	SUABLY	SUBBRANCH	SUBDUEDLY	SUBHEDRAL
STYLEBOOK	SUASIBLE	SUBBRANCHES	SUBDUER	SUBHUMAN
STYLEBOOKS	SUASION	SUBBREED	SUBDUERS	SUBHUMID
STYLED	SUASIONS	SUBBREEDS	SUBDUES	SUBIMAGINES
STYLELESS	SUASIVE	SUBBUREAU	SUBDUING	SUBIMAGO
STYLES	SUASIVELY	SUBBUREAUS	SUBDUPLE	SUBIMAGOS
STYLET	SUASORY	SUBBUREAUX	SUBDURAL	SUBINCISE
STYLETS	SUAVE	SUBBY	SUBEDAR	SUBINCISED
STYLI	SUAVELY	SUBCANTOR	SUBEDARS	SUBINCISES
STYLIFORM	SUAVER	SUBCANTORS	SUBEDIT	SUBINCISING
STYLING	SUAVEST	SUBCASTE	SUBEDITED	SUBITISE
STYLISE	SUAVITIES	SUBCASTES	SUBEDITING	SUBITISED
STYLISED	SUAVITY	SUBCAUDAL	SUBEDITOR	SUBITISES
STYLISES	SUB	SUBCAVITIES	SUBEDITORS	SUBITISING
STYLISH	SUBABBOT	SUBCAVITY	SUBEDITS	SUBITIZE
STYLISHLY	SUBABBOTS	SUBCELLAR	SUBENTIRE	SUBITIZED
STYLISING	SUBACID	SUBCELLARS	SUBEQUAL	SUBITIZES
STYLIST	SUBACIDLY	SUBCHIEF	SUBER	SUBITIZING
STYLISTIC	SUBACRID	SUBCHIEFS	SUBERATE	SUBITO
STYLISTICS	SUBACT	SUBCHORD	SUBERATES	SUBJACENT
STYLISTS	SUBACTED	SUBCHORDS	SUBERECT	SUBJECT
STYLITE	SUBACTING	SUBCLAIM	SUBEREOUS	SUBJECTED
STYLITES	SUBACTION	SUBCLAIMS	SUBERIC	SUBJECTING
STYLIZE	SUBACTIONS	SUBCLASS	SUBERIN	SUBJECTS
STYLIZED	SUBACTS	SUBCLASSES	SUBERINS	SUBJOIN
STYLIZES	SUBACUTE	SUBCLAUSE	SUBERISE	SUBJOINED
STYLIZING	SUBADAR	SUBCLAUSES	SUBERISED	SUBJOINING
STYLO	SUBADARS	SUBCLIMAX	SUBERISES	SUBJOINS
STYLOBATE	SUBADULT	SUBCLIMAXES	SUBERISING	SUBJUGATE
STYLOBATES	SUBADULTS	SUBCOOL	SUBERIZE	SUBJUGATED
STYLOID	SUBAERIAL	SUBCORTEX	SUBERIZED	SUBJUGATES
STYLOIDS	SUBAGENCIES	SUBCORTEXES	SUBERIZES	SUBJUGATING
STYLOLITE	SUBAGENCY	SUBCORTICES	SUBERIZING	SUBLATE
STYLOLITES	SUBAGENT	SUBCOSTA	SUBEROSE	SUBLATED
STYLOS	SUBAGENTS	SUBCOSTAE	SUBEROUS	SUBLATES

The Chambers Dictionary is the authority for many longer words; see *OSW* Introduction, page xii.

SUBLATING	SUBMISSLY	SUBSEA	SUBSUME	SUBTRUDING
SUBLATION	SUBMIT	SUBSECIVE	SUBSUMED	SUBTYPE
SUBLATIONS	SUBMITS	SUBSELLIA	SUBSUMES	SUBTYPES
SUBLEASE	SUBMITTED	SUBSERE	SUBSUMING	SUBUCULA
SUBLEASED	SUBMITTER	SUBSERES	SUBSYSTEM	SUBUCULAS
SUBLEASES	SUBMITTERS	SUBSERIES	SUBSYSTEMS	SUBULATE
SUBLEASING	SUBMITTING	SUBSERVE	SUBTACK	SUBUNIT
SUBLESSEE	SUBMITTINGS	SUBSERVED	SUBTACKS	SUBUNITS
SUBLESSEES	SUBMUCOSA	SUBSERVES	SUBTEEN	SUBURB
SUBLESSOR	SUBMUCOSAE	SUBSERVING	SUBTEENS	SUBURBAN
SUBLESSORS	SUBMUCOUS	SUBSET	SUBTENANT	SUBURBANS
SUBLET	SUBNEURAL	SUBSETS	SUBTENANTS	SUBURBIA
SUBLETHAL	SUBNIVEAL	SUBSHRUB	SUBTEND	SUBURBIAS
SUBLETS	SUBNIVEAN	SUBSHRUBS	SUBTENDED	SUBURBS
SUBLETTER	SUBNORMAL	SUBSIDE	SUBTENDING	SUBURSINE
SUBLETTERS	SUBNORMALS	SUBSIDED	SUBTENDS	SUBVASSAL
SUBLETTING	SUBOCTAVE	SUBSIDES	SUBTENSE	SUBVASSALS
SUBLETTINGS	SUBOCTAVES	SUBSIDIES	SUBTENSES	SUBVERSAL
SUBLIMATE	SUBOCULAR	SUBSIDING	SUBTENURE	SUBVERSALS
SUBLIMATED	SUBOFFICE	SUBSIDISE	SUBTENURES	SUBVERSE
SUBLIMATES	SUBOFFICES	SUBSIDISED	SUBTEXT	SUBVERSED
SUBLIMATING	SUBORDER	SUBSIDISES	SUBTEXTS	SUBVERSES
SUBLIME	SUBORDERS	SUBSIDISING	SUBTIDAL	SUBVERSING
SUBLIMED	SUBORN	SUBSIDIZE	SUBTIL	SUBVERST
SUBLIMELY	SUBORNED	SUBSIDIZED	SUBTILE	SUBVERT
SUBLIMER	SUBORNER	SUBSIDIZES	SUBTILER	SUBVERTED
SUBLIMES	SUBORNERS	SUBSIDIZING	SUBTILEST	SUBVERTER
SUBLIMEST	SUBORNING	SUBSIDY	SUBTILISE	SUBVERTERS
SUBLIMING	SUBORNS	SUBSIST	SUBTILISED	SUBVERTING
SUBLIMINGS	SUBOVATE	SUBSISTED	SUBTILISES	SUBVERTS
SUBLIMISE	SUBOXIDE	SUBSISTING	SUBTILISING	SUBVIRAL
SUBLIMISED	SUBOXIDES	SUBSISTS	SUBTILIZE	SUBVOCAL
SUBLIMISES	SUBPHYLA	SUBSIZAR	SUBTILIZED	SUBWARDEN
SUBLIMISING	SUBPHYLUM	SUBSIZARS	SUBTILIZES	SUBWARDENS
SUBLIMITIES	SUBPLOT	SUBSOIL	SUBTILIZING	SUBWAY
SUBLIMITY	SUBPLOTS	SUBSOILED	SUBTITLE	SUBWAYS
SUBLIMIZE	SUBPOENA	SUBSOILER	SUBTITLED	SUBZERO
SUBLIMIZED	SUBPOENAED	SUBSOILERS	SUBTITLES	SUBZONAL
SUBLIMIZES	SUBPOENAING	SUBSOILING	SUBTITLING	SUBZONE
SUBLIMIZING	SUBPOENAS	SUBSOILINGS	SUBTLE	SUBZONES
SUBLINEAR	SUBPOLAR	SUBSOILS	SUBTLER	SUCCADE
SUBLUNAR	SUBPOTENT	SUBSOLAR	SUBTLEST	SUCCADES
SUBLUNARY	SUBPRIOR	SUBSONG	SUBTLETIES	SUCCAH
SUBLUNATE	SUBPRIORS	SUBSONGS	SUBTLETY	SUCCAHS
SUBMAN	SUBREGION	SUBSONIC	SUBTLY	SUCCEED
SUBMARINE	SUBREGIONS	SUBSTAGE	SUBTONIC	SUCCEEDED
SUBMARINED	SUBRING	SUBSTAGES	SUBTONICS	SUCCEEDER
SUBMARINES	SUBRINGS	SUBSTANCE	SUBTOPIA	SUCCEEDERS
SUBMARINING	SUBROGATE	SUBSTANCES	SUBTOPIAN	SUCCEEDING
SUBMATRICES	SUBROGATED	SUBSTATE	SUBTOPIAS	SUCCEEDS
SUBMATRIX	SUBROGATES	SUBSTATES	SUBTORRID	SUCCENTOR
SUBMATRIXES	SUBROGATING	SUBSTRACT	SUBTOTAL	SUCCENTORS
SUBMEN	SUBS	SUBSTRACTED	SUBTOTALLED	SUCCES
SUBMENTAL	SUBSACRAL	SUBSTRACTING	SUBTOTALLING	SUCCESS
SUBMENTUM	SUBSAMPLE	SUBSTRACTS	SUBTOTALS	SUCCESSES
SUBMENTUMS	SUBSAMPLED	SUBSTRATA	SUBTRACT	SUCCESSOR
SUBMERGE	SUBSAMPLES	SUBSTRATE	SUBTRACTED	SUCCESSORS
SUBMERGED	SUBSAMPLING	SUBSTRATES	SUBTRACTING	SUCCI
SUBMERGES	SUBSCHEMA	SUBSTRUCT	SUBTRACTS	SUCCINATE
SUBMERGING	SUBSCHEMATA	SUBSTRUCTED	SUBTRIBE	SUCCINATES
SUBMERSE	SUBSCRIBE	SUBSTRUCTING	SUBTRIBES	SUCCINCT
SUBMERSED	SUBSCRIBED	SUBSTRUCTS	SUBTRIST	SUCCINCTER
SUBMERSES	SUBSCRIBES	SUBSTYLAR	SUBTROPIC	SUCCINCTEST
SUBMERSING	SUBSCRIBING	SUBSTYLE	SUBTROPICS	SUCCINIC
SUBMICRON	SUBSCRIBINGS	SUBSTYLES	SUBTRUDE	SUCCINITE
SUBMICRONS	SUBSCRIPT	SUBSULTUS	SUBTRUDED	SUCCINITES
SUBMISS	SUBSCRIPTS	SUBSULTUSES	SUBTRUDES	SUCCINYL

The Chambers Dictionary is the authority for many longer words; see *OSW* Introduction, page xii.

SUCCINYLS	SUCRASES	SUETIER	SUGGESTERS	SULFATE
SUCCISE	SUCRE	SUETIEST	SUGGESTING	SULFATED
SUCCOR	SUCRES	SUETS	SUGGESTS	SULFATES
SUCCORED	SUCRIER	SUETY	SUGGING	SULFATING
SUCCORIES	SUCRIERS	SUFFECT	SUGGINGS	SULFATION
SUCCORING	SUCROSE	SUFFER	SUI	SULFATIONS
SUCCORS	SUCROSES	SUFFERED	SUICIDAL	SULFIDE
SUCCORY	SUCTION	SUFFERER	SUICIDE	SULFIDES
SUCCOSE	SUCTIONS	SUFFERERS	SUICIDES	SULFINYL
SUCCOTASH	SUCTORIAL	SUFFERING	SUID	SULFINYLS
SUCCOTASHES	SUCTORIAN	SUFFERINGS	SUIDIAN	SULFITE
SUCCOUR	SUCTORIANS	SUFFERS	SUIDIANS	SULFITES
SUCCOURED	SUCURUJU	SUFFETE	SUIDS	SULFONATE
SUCCOURER	SUCURUJUS	SUFFETES	SUILLINE	SULFONATED
SUCCOURERS	SUD	SUFFICE	SUING	SULFONATES
SUCCOURING	SUDAMEN	SUFFICED	SUINGS	SULFONATING
SUCCOURS	SUDAMINA	SUFFICER	SUINT	SULFONE
SUCCOUS	SUDAMINAL	SUFFICERS	SUINTS	SULFONES
SUCCUBA	SUDARIA	SUFFICES	SUIT	SULFONIUM
SUCCUBAE	SUDARIES	SUFFICING	SUITABLE	SULFONIUMS
SUCCUBAS	SUDARIUM	SUFFIX	SUITABLY	SULFUR
SUCCUBI	SUDARY	SUFFIXAL	SUITCASE	SULFURATE
SUCCUBINE	SUDATE	SUFFIXED	SUITCASES	SULFURATED
SUCCUBOUS	SUDATED	SUFFIXES	SUITE	SULFURATES
SUCCUBUS	SUDATES	SUFFIXING	SUITED	SULFURATING
SUCCUBUSES	SUDATING	SUFFIXION	SUITES	SULFURED
SUCCULENT	SUDATION	SUFFIXIONS	SUITING	SULFURIC
SUCCULENTS	SUDATIONS	SUFFLATE	SUITINGS	SULFURING
SUCCUMB	SUDATORIA	SUFFLATED	SUITOR	SULFURS
SUCCUMBED	SUDATORIES	SUFFLATES	SUITORED	SULK
SUCCUMBING	SUDATORY	SUFFLATING	SUITORING	SULKED
SUCCUMBS	SUDD	SUFFOCATE	SUITORS	SULKIER
SUCCURSAL	SUDDEN	SUFFOCATED	SUITRESS	SULKIES
SUCCURSALS	SUDDENLY	SUFFOCATES	SUITRESSES	SULKIEST
SUCCUS	SUDDENTIES	SUFFOCATING	SUITS	SULKILY
SUCCUSS	SUDDENTY	SUFFOCATINGS	SUIVANTE	SULKINESS
SUCCUSSED	SUDDER	SUFFRAGAN	SUIVANTES	SULKINESSES
SUCCUSSES	SUDDERS	SUFFRAGANS	SUIVEZ	SULKING
SUCCUSSING	SUDDS	SUFFRAGE	SUJEE	SULKS
SUCH	SUDOR	SUFFRAGES	SUJEES	SULKY
SUCHLIKE	SUDORAL	SUFFUSE	SUK	SULLAGE
SUCHNESS	SUDORIFIC	SUFFUSED	SUKH	SULLAGES
SUCHNESSES	SUDORIFICS	SUFFUSES	SUKHS	SULLEN
SUCHWISE	SUDOROUS	SUFFUSING	SUKIYAKI	SULLENER
SUCK	SUDORS	SUFFUSION	SUKIYAKIS	SULLENEST
SUCKED	SUDS	SUFFUSIONS	SUKKAH	SULLENLY
SUCKEN	SUDSED	SUFFUSIVE	SUKKAHS	SULLIED
SUCKENER	SUDSER	SUGAR	SUKS	SULLIES
SUCKENERS	SUDSERS	SUGARALLIES	SULCAL	SULLY
SUCKENS	SUDSES	SUGARALLY	SULCALISE	SULLYING
SUCKER	SUDSIER	SUGARCANE	SULCALISED	SULPHA
SUCKERED	SUDSIEST	SUGARCANES	SULCALISES	SULPHAS
SUCKERING	SUDSING	SUGARED	SULCALISING	SULPHATE
SUCKERS	SUDSY	SUGARIER	SULCALIZE	SULPHATED
SUCKET	SUE	SUGARIEST	SULCALIZED	SULPHATES
SUCKETS	SUEABLE	SUGARING	SULCALIZES	SULPHATING
SUCKING	SUED	SUGARINGS	SULCALIZING	SULPHIDE
SUCKINGS	SUEDE	SUGARLESS	SULCATE	SULPHIDES
SUCKLE	SUEDED	SUGARLOAF	SULCATED	SULPHINYL
SUCKLED	SUEDES	SUGARLOAVES	SULCATION	SULPHINYLS
SUCKLER	SUEDETTE	SUGARPLUM	SULCATIONS	SULPHITE
SUCKLERS	SUEDETTES	SUGARPLUMS	SULCI	SULPHITES
SUCKLES	SUEDING	SUGARS	SULCUS	SULPHONE
SUCKLING	SUER	SUGARY	SULFA	SULPHONES
SUCKLINGS	SUERS	SUGGEST	SULFAS	SULPHUR
SUCKS	SUES	SUGGESTED	SULFATASE	SULPHURED
SUCRASE	SUET	SUGGESTER	SULFATASES	SULPHURET

The Chambers Dictionary is the authority for many longer words; see *OSW* Introduction, page xii.

SULPHURETED
SULPHURETING
SULPHURETS
SULPHURETTED
SULPHURETTING
SULPHURIC
SULPHURING
SULPHURS
SULPHURY
SULTAN
SULTANA
SULTANAS
SULTANATE
SULTANATES
SULTANESS
SULTANESSES
SULTANIC
SULTANS
SULTRIER
SULTRIEST
SULTRILY
SULTRY
SULU
SULUS
SUM
SUMAC
SUMACH
SUMACHS
SUMACS
SUMATRA
SUMATRAS
SUMLESS
SUMMA
SUMMAE
SUMMAND
SUMMANDS
SUMMAR
SUMMARIES
SUMMARILY
SUMMARISE
SUMMARISED
SUMMARISES
SUMMARISING
SUMMARIST
SUMMARISTS
SUMMARIZE
SUMMARIZED
SUMMARIZES
SUMMARIZING
SUMMARY
SUMMAT
SUMMATE
SUMMATED
SUMMATES
SUMMATING
SUMMATION
SUMMATIONS
SUMMATIVE
SUMMATS
SUMMED
SUMMER
SUMMERED
SUMMERIER
SUMMERIEST
SUMMERING
SUMMERINGS
SUMMERLY

SUMMERS
SUMMERSET
SUMMERSETS
SUMMERSETTED
SUMMERSETTING
SUMMERY
SUMMING
SUMMINGS
SUMMIST
SUMMISTS
SUMMIT
SUMMITAL
SUMMITEER
SUMMITEERS
SUMMITRIES
SUMMITRY
SUMMITS
SUMMON
SUMMONED
SUMMONER
SUMMONERS
SUMMONING
SUMMONS
SUMMONSED
SUMMONSES
SUMMONSING
SUMO
SUMOS
SUMOTORI
SUMOTORIS
SUMP
SUMPH
SUMPHISH
SUMPHS
SUMPIT
SUMPITAN
SUMPITANS
SUMPITS
SUMPS
SUMPSIMUS
SUMPSIMUSES
SUMPTER
SUMPTERS
SUMPTUARY
SUMPTUOUS
SUMS
SUN
SUNBAKE
SUNBAKED
SUNBAKES
SUNBAKING
SUNBATH
SUNBATHE
SUNBATHED
SUNBATHER
SUNBATHERS
SUNBATHES
SUNBATHING
SUNBATHINGS
SUNBATHS
SUNBEAM
SUNBEAMED
SUNBEAMS
SUNBEAMY
SUNBEAT
SUNBEATEN
SUNBED

SUNBEDS
SUNBELT
SUNBELTS
SUNBERRIES
SUNBERRY
SUNBIRD
SUNBIRDS
SUNBLIND
SUNBLINDS
SUNBLOCK
SUNBLOCKS
SUNBOW
SUNBOWS
SUNBRIGHT
SUNBURN
SUNBURNED
SUNBURNING
SUNBURNS
SUNBURNT
SUNBURST
SUNBURSTS
SUNDAE
SUNDAES
SUNDARI
SUNDARIS
SUNDECK
SUNDECKS
SUNDER
SUNDERED
SUNDERER
SUNDERERS
SUNDERING
SUNDERINGS
SUNDERS
SUNDEW
SUNDEWS
SUNDIAL
SUNDIALS
SUNDOG
SUNDOGS
SUNDOWN
SUNDOWNER
SUNDOWNERS
SUNDOWNS
SUNDRA
SUNDRAS
SUNDRESS
SUNDRESSES
SUNDRI
SUNDRIES
SUNDRIS
SUNDROPS
SUNDRY
SUNFAST
SUNFISH
SUNFISHES
SUNFLOWER
SUNFLOWERS
SUNG
SUNGAR
SUNGARS
SUNGLASS
SUNGLASSES
SUNGLOW
SUNGLOWS
SUNHAT
SUNHATS

SUNK
SUNKEN
SUNKET
SUNKETS
SUNKIE
SUNKIES
SUNKS
SUNLAMP
SUNLAMPS
SUNLESS
SUNLIGHT
SUNLIGHTS
SUNLIKE
SUNLIT
SUNN
SUNNED
SUNNIER
SUNNIEST
SUNNILY
SUNNINESS
SUNNINESSES
SUNNING
SUNNS
SUNNY
SUNPROOF
SUNRAY
SUNRAYS
SUNRISE
SUNRISES
SUNRISING
SUNRISINGS
SUNROOF
SUNROOFS
SUNS
SUNSCREEN
SUNSCREENS
SUNSET
SUNSETS
SUNSHADE
SUNSHADES
SUNSHINE
SUNSHINES
SUNSHINY
SUNSPOT
SUNSPOTS
SUNSTONE
SUNSTONES
SUNSTROKE
SUNSTROKES
SUNSTRUCK
SUNSUIT
SUNSUITS
SUNTAN
SUNTANNED
SUNTANS
SUNTRAP
SUNTRAPS
SUNUP
SUNUPS
SUNWARD
SUNWARDS
SUNWISE
SUP
SUPAWN
SUPAWNS
SUPE
SUPER

SUPERABLE
SUPERABLY
SUPERADD
SUPERADDED
SUPERADDING
SUPERADDS
SUPERATE
SUPERATED
SUPERATES
SUPERATING
SUPERB
SUPERBER
SUPERBEST
SUPERBITIES
SUPERBITY
SUPERBLY
SUPERBOLD
SUPERBRAT
SUPERBRATS
SUPERCOIL
SUPERCOILS
SUPERCOLD
SUPERCOOL
SUPERCOOLED
SUPERCOOLING
SUPERCOOLS
SUPEREGO
SUPEREGOS
SUPERETTE
SUPERETTES
SUPERFAST
SUPERFINE
SUPERFLUX
SUPERFLUXES
SUPERFUSE
SUPERFUSED
SUPERFUSES
SUPERFUSING
SUPERGENE
SUPERGENES
SUPERGLUE
SUPERGLUED
SUPERGLUES
SUPERGLUING
SUPERGUN
SUPERGUNS
SUPERHEAT
SUPERHEATED
SUPERHEATING
SUPERHEATS
SUPERHERO
SUPERHEROES
SUPERHIVE
SUPERHIVES
SUPERIOR
SUPERIORS
SUPERJET
SUPERJETS
SUPERLOO
SUPERLOOS
SUPERMAN
SUPERMART
SUPERMARTS
SUPERMEN
SUPERMINI
SUPERMINIS
SUPERNAL

The Chambers Dictionary is the authority for many longer words; see *OSW* Introduction, page xii.

SUPERNOVA SUPPLIALS SURBATE SURFICIAL SURPASSING
SUPERNOVAE SUPPLIANT SURBATED SURFIE SURPLICE
SUPERNOVAS SUPPLIANTS SURBATES SURFIER SURPLICED
SUPERPLUS SUPPLICAT SURBATING SURFIES SURPLICES
SUPERPLUSES SUPPLICATS SURBED SURFIEST SURPLUS
SUPERPOSE SUPPLIED SURBEDDED SURFING SURPLUSES
SUPERPOSED SUPPLIER SURBEDDING SURFINGS SURPRISAL
SUPERPOSES SUPPLIERS SURBEDS SURFMAN SURPRISALS
SUPERPOSING SUPPLIES SURBET SURFMEN SURPRISE
SUPERRICH SUPPLING SURCEASE SURFPERCH SURPRISED
SUPERS SUPPLY SURCEASED SURFPERCHES SURPRISER
SUPERSAFE SUPPLYING SURCEASES SURFS SURPRISERS
SUPERSALT SUPPORT SURCEASING SURFY SURPRISES
SUPERSALTS SUPPORTED SURCHARGE SURGE SURPRISING
SUPERSEDE SUPPORTER SURCHARGED SURGED SURPRISINGS
SUPERSEDED SUPPORTERS SURCHARGES SURGEFUL SURQUEDIES
SUPERSEDES SUPPORTING SURCHARGING SURGELESS SURQUEDRIES
SUPERSEDING SUPPORTINGS SURCINGLE SURGENT SURQUEDRY
SUPERSELL SUPPORTS SURCINGLED SURGEON SURQUEDY
SUPERSELLS SUPPOSAL SURCINGLES SURGEONCIES SURRA
SUPERSOFT SUPPOSALS SURCINGLING SURGEONCY SURRAS
SUPERSPIES SUPPOSE SURCOAT SURGEONS SURREAL
SUPERSPY SUPPOSED SURCOATS SURGERIES SURREBUT
SUPERSTAR SUPPOSER SURCULI SURGERY SURREBUTS
SUPERSTARS SUPPOSERS SURCULOSE SURGES SURREBUTTED
SUPERTAX SUPPOSES SURCULUS SURGICAL SURREBUTTING
SUPERTAXES SUPPOSING SURCULUSES SURGIER SURREINED
SUPERTHIN SUPPOSINGS SURD SURGIEST SURREJOIN
SUPERVENE SUPPRESS SURDITIES SURGING SURREJOINED
SUPERVENED SUPPRESSED SURDITY SURGINGS SURREJOINING
SUPERVENES SUPPRESSES SURDS SURGY SURREJOINS
SUPERVENING SUPPRESSING SURE SURICATE SURRENDER
SUPERVISE SUPPURATE SURED SURICATES SURRENDERED
SUPERVISED SUPPURATED SURELY SURING SURRENDERING
SUPERVISES SUPPURATES SURENESS SURLIER SURRENDERS
SUPERVISING SUPPURATING SURENESSES SURLIEST SURRENDRIES
SUPES SUPREMACIES SURER SURLILY SURRENDRY
SUPINATE SUPREMACY SURES SURLINESS SURREY
SUPINATED SUPREME SUREST SURLINESSES SURREYS
SUPINATES SUPREMELY SURETIED SURLOIN SURROGACIES
SUPINATING SUPREMER SURETIES SURLOINS SURROGACY
SUPINATOR SUPREMES SURETY SURLY SURROGATE
SUPINATORS SUPREMEST SURETYING SURMASTER SURROGATES
SUPINE SUPREMITIES SURF SURMASTERS SURROUND
SUPINELY SUPREMITY SURFACE SURMISAL SURROUNDED
SUPINES SUPREMO SURFACED SURMISALS SURROUNDING
SUPPAWN SUPREMOS SURFACER SURMISE SURROUNDINGS
SUPPAWNS SUPS SURFACERS SURMISED SURROUNDS
SUPPEAGO SUQ SURFACES SURMISER SURROYAL
SUPPEAGOES SUQS SURFACING SURMISERS SURROYALS
SUPPED SUR SURFACINGS SURMISES SURTAX
SUPPER SURA SURFBIRD SURMISING SURTAXED
SUPPERED SURAH SURFBIRDS SURMISINGS SURTAXES
SUPPERING SURAHS SURFBOARD SURMOUNT SURTAXING
SUPPERS SURAL SURFBOARDS SURMOUNTED SURTITLE
SUPPING SURAMIN SURFED SURMOUNTING SURTITLES
SUPPLANT SURAMINS SURFEIT SURMOUNTINGS SURTOUT
SUPPLANTED SURANCE SURFEITED SURMOUNTS SURTOUTS
SUPPLANTING SURANCES SURFEITER SURMULLET SURUCUCU
SUPPLANTS SURAS SURFEITERS SURMULLETS SURUCUCUS
SUPPLE SURAT SURFEITING SURNAME SURVEILLE
SUPPLED SURATS SURFEITINGS SURNAMED SURVEILLED
SUPPLELY SURBAHAR SURFEITS SURNAMES SURVEILLES
SUPPLER SURBAHARS SURFER SURNAMING SURVEILLING
SUPPLES SURBASE SURFERS SURPASS SURVEW
SUPPLEST SURBASED SURFFISH SURPASSED SURVEWE
SUPPLIAL SURBASES SURFFISHES SURPASSES SURVEWED

The Chambers Dictionary is the authority for many longer words; see *OSW* Introduction, page xii.

SURVEWES	SUSSING	SWADDLES	SWANKED	SWARTHIEST
SURVEWING	SUSTAIN	SWADDLING	SWANKER	SWARTHS
SURVEWS	SUSTAINED	SWADDY	SWANKERS	SWARTHY
SURVEY	SUSTAINER	SWADS	SWANKEST	SWARTNESS
SURVEYAL	SUSTAINERS	SWAG	SWANKEY	SWARTNESSES
SURVEYALS	SUSTAINING	SWAGE	SWANKEYS	SWARTY
SURVEYED	SUSTAININGS	SWAGED	SWANKIE	SWARVE
SURVEYING	SUSTAINS	SWAGES	SWANKIER	SWARVED
SURVEYINGS	SUSTINENT	SWAGGED	SWANKIES	SWARVES
SURVEYOR	SUSURRANT	SWAGGER	SWANKIEST	SWARVING
SURVEYORS	SUSURRATE	SWAGGERED	SWANKING	SWASH
SURVEYS	SUSURRATED	SWAGGERER	SWANKPOT	SWASHED
SURVIEW	SUSURRATES	SWAGGERERS	SWANKPOTS	SWASHER
SURVIEWED	SUSURRATING	SWAGGERING	SWANKS	SWASHERS
SURVIEWING	SUSURRUS	SWAGGERINGS	SWANKY	SWASHES
SURVIEWS	SUSURRUSES	SWAGGERS	SWANLIKE	SWASHIER
SURVIVAL	SUTILE	SWAGGIE	SWANNED	SWASHIEST
SURVIVALS	SUTLER	SWAGGIES	SWANNERIES	SWASHING
SURVIVE	SUTLERIES	SWAGGING	SWANNERY	SWASHINGS
SURVIVED	SUTLERS	SWAGING	SWANNIER	SWASHWORK
SURVIVES	SUTLERY	SWAGMAN	SWANNIEST	SWASHWORKS
SURVIVING	SUTOR	SWAGMEN	SWANNING	SWASHY
SURVIVOR	SUTORIAL	SWAGS	SWANNINGS	SWASTIKA
SURVIVORS	SUTORIAN	SWAGSHOP	SWANNY	SWASTIKAS
SUS	SUTORS	SWAGSHOPS	SWANS	SWAT
SUSCEPTOR	SUTRA	SWAGSMAN	SWANSDOWN	SWATCH
SUSCEPTORS	SUTRAS	SWAGSMEN	SWANSDOWNS	SWATCHES
SUSCITATE	SUTTEE	SWAIN	SWANSKIN	SWATH
SUSCITATED	SUTTEEISM	SWAINING	SWANSKINS	SWATHE
SUSCITATES	SUTTEEISMS	SWAININGS	SWAP	SWATHED
SUSCITATING	SUTTEES	SWAINISH	SWAPPED	SWATHES
SUSES	SUTTLE	SWAINS	SWAPPER	SWATHIER
SUSHI	SUTTLED	SWALE	SWAPPERS	SWATHIEST
SUSHIS	SUTTLES	SWALED	SWAPPING	SWATHING
SUSLIK	SUTTLETIE	SWALES	SWAPPINGS	SWATHS
SUSLIKS	SUTTLETIES	SWALIER	SWAPS	SWATHY
SUSPECT	SUTTLING	SWALIEST	SWAPT	SWATS
SUSPECTED	SUTTLY	SWALING	SWAPTION	SWATTED
SUSPECTING	SUTURAL	SWALINGS	SWAPTIONS	SWATTER
SUSPECTS	SUTURALLY	SWALLET	SWARAJ	SWATTERED
SUSPENCE	SUTURE	SWALLETS	SWARAJES	SWATTERING
SUSPEND	SUTURED	SWALLOW	SWARAJISM	SWATTERS
SUSPENDED	SUTURES	SWALLOWED	SWARAJISMS	SWATTING
SUSPENDER	SUTURING	SWALLOWER	SWARAJIST	SWATTINGS
SUSPENDERS	SUVERSED	SWALLOWERS	SWARAJISTS	SWAY
SUSPENDING	SUZERAIN	SWALLOWING	SWARD	SWAYBACK
SUSPENDS	SUZERAINS	SWALLOWS	SWARDED	SWAYBACKS
SUSPENS	SVASTIKA	SWALY	SWARDIER	SWAYED
SUSPENSE	SVASTIKAS	SWAM	SWARDIEST	SWAYER
SUSPENSER	SVELTE	SWAMI	SWARDING	SWAYERS
SUSPENSERS	SVELTER	SWAMIS	SWARDS	SWAYING
SUSPENSES	SVELTEST	SWAMP	SWARDY	SWAYINGS
SUSPENSOR	SWAB	SWAMPED	SWARE	SWAYL
SUSPENSORS	SWABBED	SWAMPER	SWARF	SWAYLED
SUSPICION	SWABBER	SWAMPERS	SWARFED	SWAYLING
SUSPICIONED	SWABBERS	SWAMPIER	SWARFING	SWAYLINGS
SUSPICIONING	SWABBIES	SWAMPIEST	SWARFS	SWAYLS
SUSPICIONS	SWABBING	SWAMPING	SWARM	SWAYS
SUSPIRE	SWABBY	SWAMPLAND	SWARMED	SWAZZLE
SUSPIRED	SWABS	SWAMPLANDS	SWARMER	SWAZZLES
SUSPIRES	SWACK	SWAMPS	SWARMERS	SWEAL
SUSPIRING	SWAD	SWAMPY	SWARMING	SWEALED
SUSS	SWADDIES	SWAN	SWARMINGS	SWEALING
SUSSARARA	SWADDLE	SWANG	SWARMS	SWEALINGS
SUSSARARAS	SWADDLED	SWANHERD	SWART	SWEALS
SUSSED	SWADDLER	SWANHERDS	SWARTH	SWEAR
SUSSES	SWADDLERS	SWANK	SWARTHIER	SWEARD

The Chambers Dictionary is the authority for many longer words; see *OSW* Introduction, page xii.

SWEARDS	SWEETMEAL	SWIFTER	SWINGIEST	SWITHERED
SWEARER	SWEETMEAT	SWIFTERS	SWINGING	SWITHERING
SWEARERS	SWEETMEATS	SWIFTEST	SWINGINGS	SWITHERS
SWEARING	SWEETNESS	SWIFTING	SWINGISM	SWITS
SWEARINGS	SWEETNESSES	SWIFTLET	SWINGISMS	SWITSES
SWEARS	SWEETPEA	SWIFTLETS	SWINGLE	SWIVE
SWEAT	SWEETPEAS	SWIFTLY	SWINGLED	SWIVED
SWEATED	SWEETS	SWIFTNESS	SWINGLES	SWIVEL
SWEATER	SWEETSOP	SWIFTNESSES	SWINGLING	SWIVELLED
SWEATERS	SWEETSOPS	SWIFTS	SWINGLINGS	SWIVELLING
SWEATIER	SWEETWOOD	SWIG	SWINGS	SWIVELS
SWEATIEST	SWEETWOODS	SWIGGED	SWINGTREE	SWIVES
SWEATING	SWEETY	SWIGGER	SWINGTREES	SWIVET
SWEATINGS	SWEIR	SWIGGERS	SWINGY	SWIVETS
SWEATS	SWEIRNESS	SWIGGING	SWINISH	SWIVING
SWEATSUIT	SWEIRNESSES	SWIGS	SWINISHLY	SWIZ
SWEATSUITS	SWEIRT	SWILL	SWINK	SWIZZED
SWEATY	SWELCHIE	SWILLED	SWINKED	SWIZZES
SWEDE	SWELCHIES	SWILLER	SWINKING	SWIZZING
SWEDES	SWELL	SWILLERS	SWINKS	SWIZZLE
SWEE	SWELLDOM	SWILLING	SWIPE	SWIZZLED
SWEED	SWELLDOMS	SWILLINGS	SWIPED	SWIZZLES
SWEEING	SWELLED	SWILLS	SWIPER	SWIZZLING
SWEEL	SWELLER	SWIM	SWIPERS	SWOB
SWEELED	SWELLERS	SWIMMABLE	SWIPES	SWOBBED
SWEELING	SWELLEST	SWIMMER	SWIPEY	SWOBBER
SWEELS	SWELLING	SWIMMERET	SWIPIER	SWOBBERS
SWEENEY	SWELLINGS	SWIMMERETS	SWIPIEST	SWOBBING
SWEENEYS	SWELLISH	SWIMMERS	SWIPING	SWOBS
SWEENIES	SWELLS	SWIMMIER	SWIPPLE	SWOLLEN
SWEENY	SWELT	SWIMMIEST	SWIPPLES	SWOLN
SWEEP	SWELTED	SWIMMING	SWIRE	SWONE
SWEEPBACK	SWELTER	SWIMMINGS	SWIRES	SWONES
SWEEPBACKS	SWELTERED	SWIMMY	SWIRL	SWOON
SWEEPER	SWELTERING	SWIMS	SWIRLED	SWOONED
SWEEPERS	SWELTERINGS	SWIMSUIT	SWIRLIER	SWOONING
SWEEPIER	SWELTERS	SWIMSUITS	SWIRLIEST	SWOONINGS
SWEEPIEST	SWELTING	SWIMWEAR	SWIRLING	SWOONS
SWEEPING	SWELTRIER	SWIMWEARS	SWIRLS	SWOOP
SWEEPINGS	SWELTRIEST	SWINDGE	SWIRLY	SWOOPED
SWEEPS	SWELTRY	SWINDGED	SWISH	SWOOPING
SWEEPY	SWELTS	SWINDGES	SWISHED	SWOOPS
SWEER	SWEPT	SWINDGING	SWISHER	SWOOSH
SWEERED	SWEPTBACK	SWINDLE	SWISHERS	SWOOSHED
SWEERT	SWEPTWING	SWINDLED	SWISHES	SWOOSHES
SWEES	SWERF	SWINDLER	SWISHEST	SWOOSHING
SWEET	SWERFED	SWINDLERS	SWISHIER	SWOP
SWEETCORN	SWERFING	SWINDLES	SWISHIEST	SWOPPED
SWEETCORNS	SWERFS	SWINDLING	SWISHING	SWOPPER
SWEETED	SWERVE	SWINDLINGS	SWISHINGS	SWOPPERS
SWEETEN	SWERVED	SWINE	SWISHY	SWOPPING
SWEETENED	SWERVER	SWINEHERD	SWISSING	SWOPPINGS
SWEETENER	SWERVERS	SWINEHERDS	SWISSINGS	SWOPS
SWEETENERS	SWERVES	SWINEHOOD	SWITCH	SWOPT
SWEETENING	SWERVING	SWINEHOODS	SWITCHED	SWORD
SWEETENINGS	SWERVINGS	SWINERIES	SWITCHEL	SWORDED
SWEETENS	SWEVEN	SWINERY	SWITCHELS	SWORDER
SWEETER	SWEVENS	SWING	SWITCHES	SWORDERS
SWEETEST	SWEY	SWINGBOAT	SWITCHIER	SWORDFISH
SWEETFISH	SWEYED	SWINGBOATS	SWITCHIEST	SWORDFISHES
SWEETFISHES	SWEYING	SWINGE	SWITCHING	SWORDING
SWEETIE	SWEYS	SWINGED	SWITCHINGS	SWORDLESS
SWEETIES	SWIDDEN	SWINGEING	SWITCHMAN	SWORDLIKE
SWEETING	SWIDDENS	SWINGER	SWITCHMEN	SWORDMAN
SWEETINGS	SWIES	SWINGERS	SWITCHY	SWORDMEN
SWEETISH	SWIFT	SWINGES	SWITH	SWORDPLAY
SWEETLY	SWIFTED	SWINGIER	SWITHER	SWORDPLAYS

The Chambers Dictionary is the authority for many longer words; see *OSW* Introduction, page xii.

SWORDS	SYENITES	SYLVIA	SYMPODIUM	SYNCOPTIC
SWORDSMAN	SYENITIC	SYLVIAS	SYMPOSIA	SYNCRETIC
SWORDSMEN	SYENS	SYLVIINE	SYMPOSIAC	SYNCS
SWORE	SYES	SYLVINE	SYMPOSIAL	SYNCYTIA
SWORN	SYKE	SYLVINES	SYMPOSIUM	SYNCYTIAL
SWOT	SYKER	SYLVINITE	SYMPTOM	SYNCYTIUM
SWOTS	SYKES	SYLVINITES	SYMPTOMS	SYND
SWOTTED	SYLLABARIES	SYLVITE	SYMPTOSES	SYNDACTYL
SWOTTER	SYLLABARY	SYLVITES	SYMPTOSIS	SYNDED
SWOTTERS	SYLLABI	SYMAR	SYMPTOTIC	SYNDESES
SWOTTING	SYLLABIC	SYMARS	SYNAGOGAL	SYNDESIS
SWOTTINGS	SYLLABICS	SYMBIONT	SYNAGOGUE	SYNDET
SWOUN	SYLLABIFIED	SYMBIONTS	SYNAGOGUES	SYNDETIC
SWOUND	SYLLABIFIES	SYMBIOSES	SYNANDRIA	SYNDETS
SWOUNDED	SYLLABIFY	SYMBIOSIS	SYNANGIA	SYNDIC
SWOUNDING	SYLLABIFYING	SYMBIOTIC	SYNANGIUM	SYNDICAL
SWOUNDS	SYLLABISE	SYMBOL	SYNANTHIC	SYNDICATE
SWOUNE	SYLLABISED	SYMBOLE	SYNANTHIES	SYNDICATED
SWOUNED	SYLLABISES	SYMBOLES	SYNANTHY	SYNDICATES
SWOUNES	SYLLABISING	SYMBOLIC	SYNAPHEA	SYNDICATING
SWOUNING	SYLLABISM	SYMBOLICS	SYNAPHEAS	SYNDICS
SWOUNS	SYLLABISMS	SYMBOLISE	SYNAPHEIA	SYNDING
SWOWND	SYLLABIZE	SYMBOLISED	SYNAPHEIAS	SYNDINGS
SWOWNDS	SYLLABIZED	SYMBOLISES	SYNAPSE	SYNDROME
SWOWNE	SYLLABIZES	SYMBOLISING	SYNAPSES	SYNDROMES
SWOWNES	SYLLABIZING	SYMBOLISM	SYNAPSIS	SYNDROMIC
SWOZZLE	SYLLABLE	SYMBOLISMS	SYNAPTASE	SYNDS
SWOZZLES	SYLLABLED	SYMBOLIST	SYNAPTASES	SYNE
SWUM	SYLLABLES	SYMBOLISTS	SYNAPTE	SYNECHIA
SWUNG	SYLLABLING	SYMBOLIZE	SYNAPTES	SYNECHIAS
SWY	SYLLABUB	SYMBOLIZED	SYNAPTIC	SYNECTIC
SYBARITE	SYLLABUBS	SYMBOLIZES	SYNARCHIES	SYNECTICS
SYBARITES	SYLLABUS	SYMBOLIZING	SYNARCHY	SYNED
SYBARITIC	SYLLABUSES	SYMBOLLED	SYNASTRIES	SYNEDRIA
SYBBE	SYLLEPSES	SYMBOLLING	SYNASTRY	SYNEDRIAL
SYBBES	SYLLEPSIS	SYMBOLOGIES	SYNAXARIA	SYNEDRION
SYBIL	SYLLEPTIC	SYMBOLOGY	SYNAXES	SYNEDRIUM
SYBILS	SYLLOGISE	SYMBOLS	SYNAXIS	SYNERESES
SYBO	SYLLOGISED	SYMITAR	SYNC	SYNERESIS
SYBOE	SYLLOGISES	SYMITARE	SYNCARP	SYNERGIC
SYBOES	SYLLOGISING	SYMITARES	SYNCARPIES	SYNERGID
SYBOTIC	SYLLOGISM	SYMITARS	SYNCARPS	SYNERGIDS
SYBOTISM	SYLLOGISMS	SYMMETRAL	SYNCARPY	SYNERGIES
SYBOTISMS	SYLLOGIZE	SYMMETRIC	SYNCED	SYNERGISE
SYBOW	SYLLOGIZED	SYMMETRIES	SYNCH	SYNERGISED
SYBOWS	SYLLOGIZES	SYMMETRY	SYNCHED	SYNERGISES
SYCAMINE	SYLLOGIZING	SYMPATHIES	SYNCHING	SYNERGISING
SYCAMINES	SYLPH	SYMPATHIN	SYNCHRO	SYNERGISM
SYCAMORE	SYLPHID	SYMPATHINS	SYNCHRONIES	SYNERGISMS
SYCAMORES	SYLPHIDE	SYMPATHY	SYNCHRONY	SYNERGIST
SYCE	SYLPHIDES	SYMPATRIC	SYNCHROS	SYNERGISTS
SYCEE	SYLPHIDS	SYMPHILE	SYNCHS	SYNERGIZE
SYCEES	SYLPHIER	SYMPHILES	SYNCHYSES	SYNERGIZED
SYCES	SYLPHIEST	SYMPHILIES	SYNCHYSIS	SYNERGIZES
SYCOMORE	SYLPHISH	SYMPHILY	SYNCING	SYNERGIZING
SYCOMORES	SYLPHS	SYMPHONIC	SYNCLINAL	SYNERGY
SYCONIA	SYLPHY	SYMPHONIES	SYNCLINALS	SYNES
SYCONIUM	SYLVA	SYMPHONY	SYNCLINE	SYNESES
SYCOPHANT	SYLVAE	SYMPHYSES	SYNCLINES	SYNESIS
SYCOPHANTS	SYLVAN	SYMPHYSIS	SYNCOPAL	SYNFUEL
SYCOSES	SYLVANER	SYMPHYTIC	SYNCOPATE	SYNFUELS
SYCOSIS	SYLVANERS	SYMPLAST	SYNCOPATED	SYNGAMIC
SYE	SYLVANITE	SYMPLASTS	SYNCOPATES	SYNGAMIES
SYED	SYLVANITES	SYMPLOCE	SYNCOPATING	SYNGAMOUS
SYEING	SYLVANS	SYMPLOCES	SYNCOPE	SYNGAMY
SYEN	SYLVAS	SYMPODIA	SYNCOPES	SYNGAS
SYENITE	SYLVATIC	SYMPODIAL	SYNCOPIC	SYNGASES

The Chambers Dictionary is the authority for many longer words; see *OSW* Introduction, page xii.

SYNGENEIC	SYNONYMS	SYNTEXISES	SYPHILISING	SYRUPS
SYNGRAPH	SYNONYMY	SYNTH	SYPHILIZE	SYRUPY
SYNGRAPHS	SYNOPSES	SYNTHESES	SYPHILIZED	SYSOP
SYNING	SYNOPSIS	SYNTHESIS	SYPHILIZES	SYSOPS
SYNIZESES	SYNOPSISE	SYNTHETIC	SYPHILIZING	SYSSITIA
SYNIZESIS	SYNOPSISED	SYNTHETICS	SYPHILOID	SYSSITIAS
SYNKARYON	SYNOPSISES	SYNTHON	SYPHILOMA	SYSTALTIC
SYNKARYONS	SYNOPSISING	SYNTHONS	SYPHILOMAS	SYSTEM
SYNOD	SYNOPSIZE	SYNTHS	SYPHON	SYSTEMED
SYNODAL	SYNOPSIZED	SYNTONIC	SYPHONED	SYSTEMIC
SYNODALS	SYNOPSIZES	SYNTONIES	SYPHONING	SYSTEMISE
SYNODIC	SYNOPSIZING	SYNTONIN	SYPHONS	SYSTEMISED
SYNODICAL	SYNOPTIC	SYNTONINS	SYPING	SYSTEMISES
SYNODS	SYNOPTIST	SYNTONISE	SYRAH	SYSTEMISING
SYNODSMAN	SYNOPTISTS	SYNTONISED	SYRAHS	SYSTEMIZE
SYNODSMEN	SYNOVIA	SYNTONISES	SYREN	SYSTEMIZED
SYNOECETE	SYNOVIAL	SYNTONISING	SYRENS	SYSTEMIZES
SYNOECETES	SYNOVIAS	SYNTONIZE	SYRINGA	SYSTEMIZING
SYNOECISE	SYNOVITIC	SYNTONIZED	SYRINGAS	SYSTEMS
SYNOECISED	SYNOVITIS	SYNTONIZES	SYRINGE	SYSTOLE
SYNOECISES	SYNOVITISES	SYNTONIZING	SYRINGEAL	SYSTOLES
SYNOECISING	SYNROC	SYNTONOUS	SYRINGED	SYSTOLIC
SYNOECISM	SYNROCS	SYNTONY	SYRINGES	SYSTYLE
SYNOECISMS	SYNTACTIC	SYPE	SYRINGING	SYSTYLES
SYNOECIZE	SYNTAGM	SYPED	SYRINX	SYTHE
SYNOECIZED	SYNTAGMA	SYPES	SYRINXES	SYTHES
SYNOECIZES	SYNTAGMATA	SYPHER	SYRLYE	SYVER
SYNOECIZING	SYNTAGMS	SYPHERED	SYRPHID	SYVERS
SYNOEKETE	SYNTAN	SYPHERING	SYRPHIDS	SYZYGIAL
SYNOEKETES	SYNTANS	SYPHERS	SYRTES	SYZYGIES
SYNOICOUS	SYNTAX	SYPHILIS	SYRTIS	SYZYGY
SYNONYM	SYNTAXES	SYPHILISE	SYRUP	
SYNONYMIC	SYNTECTIC	SYPHILISED	SYRUPED	
SYNONYMIES	SYNTEXIS	SYPHILISES	SYRUPING	

The Chambers Dictionary is the authority for many longer words; see *OSW* Introduction, page xii.

T

TA	TABLETOP	TABUS	TACKLES	TAFFERELS
TAB	TABLETOPS	TACAHOUT	TACKLING	TAFFETA
TABANID	TABLETS	TACAHOUTS	TACKLINGS	TAFFETAS
TABANIDS	TABLEWARE	TACAMAHAC	TACKS	TAFFETASES
TABARD	TABLEWARES	TACAMAHACS	TACKSMAN	TAFFETIES
TABARDS	TABLEWISE	TACAN	TACKSMEN	TAFFETY
TABARET	TABLIER	TACANS	TACKY	TAFFIA
TABARETS	TABLIERS	TACE	TACMAHACK	TAFFIAS
TABASHEER	TABLING	TACES	TACMAHACKS	TAFFIES
TABASHEERS	TABLINGS	TACET	TACO	TAFFRAIL
TABASHIR	TABLOID	TACH	TACONITE	TAFFRAILS
TABASHIRS	TABLOIDS	TACHE	TACONITES	TAFFY
TABBED	TABLOIDY	TACHES	TACOS	TAFIA
TABBIED	TABOGGAN	TACHINID	TACT	TAFIAS
TABBIES	TABOGGANED	TACHINIDS	TACTFUL	TAG
TABBINET	TABOGGANING	TACHISM	TACTFULLY	TAGETES
TABBINETS	TABOGGANS	TACHISME	TACTIC	TAGGED
TABBING	TABOO	TACHISMES	TACTICAL	TAGGEE
TABBOULEH	TABOOED	TACHISMS	TACTICIAN	TAGGEES
TABBOULEHS	TABOOING	TACHIST	TACTICIANS	TAGGER
TABBY	TABOOS	TACHISTE	TACTICITIES	TAGGERS
TABBYHOOD	TABOR	TACHISTES	TACTICITY	TAGGIER
TABBYHOODS	TABORED	TACHISTS	TACTICS	TAGGIEST
TABBYING	TABORER	TACHO	TACTILE	TAGGING
TABEFIED	TABORERS	TACHOGRAM	TACTILIST	TAGGINGS
TABEFIES	TABORET	TACHOGRAMS	TACTILISTS	TAGGY
TABEFY	TABORETS	TACHOS	TACTILITIES	TAGHAIRM
TABEFYING	TABORIN	TACHYLITE	TACTILITY	TAGHAIRMS
TABELLION	TABORING	TACHYLITES	TACTION	TAGLIONI
TABELLIONS	TABORINS	TACHYLYTE	TACTIONS	TAGLIONIS
TABERD	TABORS	TACHYLYTES	TACTISM	TAGMA
TABERDAR	TABOUR	TACHYON	TACTISMS	TAGMATA
TABERDARS	TABOURED	TACHYONS	TACTLESS	TAGMEME
TABERDS	TABOURET	TACHYPNEA	TACTS	TAGMEMES
TABES	TABOURETS	TACHYPNEAS	TACTUAL	TAGMEMIC
TABESCENT	TABOURIN	TACIT	TACTUALLY	TAGMEMICS
TABETIC	TABOURING	TACITLY	TAD	TAGRAG
TABETICS	TABOURINS	TACITNESS	TADDIE	TAGRAGS
TABI	TABOURS	TACITNESSES	TADDIES	TAGS
TABID	TABRERE	TACITURN	TADPOLE	TAGUAN
TABINET	TABRERES	TACK	TADPOLES	TAGUANS
TABINETS	TABRET	TACKED	TADS	TAHA
TABIS	TABRETS	TACKER	TADVANCE	TAHAS
TABLA	TABS	TACKERS	TAE	TAHINA
TABLAS	TABU	TACKET	TAED	TAHINAS
TABLATURE	TABUED	TACKETS	TAEDIUM	TAHINI
TABLATURES	TABUING	TACKETY	TAEDIUMS	TAHINIS
TABLE	TABULA	TACKIER	TAEING	TAHR
TABLEAU	TABULAE	TACKIES	TAEL	TAHRS
TABLEAUX	TABULAR	TACKIEST	TAELS	TAHSIL
TABLED	TABULARLY	TACKILY	TAENIA	TAHSILDAR
TABLEFUL	TABULATE	TACKINESS	TAENIAE	TAHSILDARS
TABLEFULS	TABULATED	TACKINESSES	TAENIAS	TAHSILS
TABLELAND	TABULATES	TACKING	TAENIASES	TAI
TABLELANDS	TABULATING	TACKINGS	TAENIASIS	TAIAHA
TABLES	TABULATOR	TACKLE	TAENIATE	TAIAHAS
TABLET	TABULATORS	TACKLED	TAENIOID	TAIGA
TABLETED	TABUN	TACKLER	TAES	TAIGAS
TABLETING	TABUNS	TACKLERS	TAFFEREL	TAIGLE

The Chambers Dictionary is the authority for many longer words; see *OSW* Introduction, page xii.

TAIGLED	TAIRA	TALAYOTS	TALKS	TAM
TAIGLES	TAIRAS	TALBOT	TALKY	TAMABLE
TAIGLING	TAIS	TALBOTS	TALL	TAMAL
TAIL	TAISCH	TALBOTYPE	TALLAGE	TAMALE
TAILARD	TAISCHES	TALBOTYPES	TALLAGED	TAMALES
TAILARDS	TAISH	TALC	TALLAGES	TAMALS
TAILBACK	TAISHES	TALCED	TALLAGING	TAMANDU
TAILBACKS	TAIT	TALCIER	TALLAT	TAMANDUA
TAILBOARD	TAITS	TALCIEST	TALLATS	TAMANDUAS
TAILBOARDS	TAIVER	TALCING	TALLBOY	TAMANDUS
TAILED	TAIVERED	TALCKED	TALLBOYS	TAMANOIR
TAILERON	TAIVERING	TALCKIER	TALLENT	TAMANOIRS
TAILERONS	TAIVERS	TALCKIEST	TALLENTS	TAMANU
TAILGATE	TAIVERT	TALCKING	TALLER	TAMANUS
TAILGATED	TAJ	TALCKY	TALLEST	TAMARA
TAILGATER	TAJES	TALCOSE	TALLET	TAMARACK
TAILGATERS	TAJINE	TALCOUS	TALLETS	TAMARACKS
TAILGATES	TAJINES	TALCS	TALLIABLE	TAMARAO
TAILGATING	TAK	TALCUM	TALLIATE	TAMARAOS
TAILING	TAKA	TALCUMS	TALLIATED	TAMARAS
TAILINGS	TAKABLE	TALCY	TALLIATES	TAMARAU
TAILLE	TAKAHE	TALE	TALLIATING	TAMARAUS
TAILLES	TAKAHES	TALEA	TALLIED	TAMARI
TAILLESS	TAKAMAKA	TALEAE	TALLIER	TAMARILLO
TAILLEUR	TAKAMAKAS	TALEFUL	TALLIERS	TAMARILLOS
TAILLEURS	TAKAS	TALEGALLA	TALLIES	TAMARIN
TAILLIE	TAKE	TALEGALLAS	TALLISH	TAMARIND
TAILLIES	TAKEABLE	TALENT	TALLITH	TAMARINDS
TAILOR	TAKEAWAY	TALENTED	TALLITHS	TAMARINS
TAILORED	TAKEAWAYS	TALENTS	TALLNESS	TAMARIS
TAILORESS	TAKEN	TALER	TALLNESSES	TAMARISK
TAILORESSES	TAKEOUT	TALERS	TALLOT	TAMARISKS
TAILORING	TAKEOUTS	TALES	TALLOTS	TAMASHA
TAILORINGS	TAKEOVER	TALESMAN	TALLOW	TAMASHAS
TAILORS	TAKEOVERS	TALESMEN	TALLOWED	TAMBAC
TAILPIECE	TAKER	TALI	TALLOWING	TAMBACS
TAILPIECES	TAKERS	TALIGRADE	TALLOWISH	TAMBER
TAILPIPE	TAKES	TALION	TALLOWS	TAMBERS
TAILPIPED	TAKHI	TALIONIC	TALLOWY	TAMBOUR
TAILPIPES	TAKHIS	TALIONS	TALLY	TAMBOURA
TAILPIPING	TAKI	TALIPAT	TALLYING	TAMBOURAS
TAILPLANE	TAKIER	TALIPATS	TALLYMAN	TAMBOURED
TAILPLANES	TAKIEST	TALIPED	TALLYMEN	TAMBOURIN
TAILRACE	TAKIN	TALIPEDS	TALLYSHOP	TAMBOURING
TAILRACES	TAKING	TALIPES	TALLYSHOPS	TAMBOURINS
TAILS	TAKINGLY	TALIPOT	TALMA	TAMBOURS
TAILSKID	TAKINGS	TALIPOTS	TALMAS	TAMBURA
TAILSKIDS	TAKINS	TALISMAN	TALMUD	TAMBURAS
TAILSPIN	TAKIS	TALISMANS	TALMUDS	TAMBURIN
TAILSPINS	TAKS	TALK	TALON	TAMBURINS
TAILSTOCK	TAKY	TALKABLE	TALONED	TAME
TAILSTOCKS	TALA	TALKATHON	TALONS	TAMEABLE
TAILWHEEL	TALAK	TALKATHONS	TALOOKA	TAMED
TAILWHEELS	TALAKS	TALKATIVE	TALOOKAS	TAMELESS
TAILYE	TALANT	TALKBACK	TALPA	TAMELY
TAILYES	TALANTS	TALKBACKS	TALPAE	TAMENESS
TAILZIE	TALAPOIN	TALKED	TALPAS	TAMENESSES
TAILZIES	TALAPOINS	TALKER	TALUK	TAMER
TAINT	TALAQ	TALKERS	TALUKA	TAMERS
TAINTED	TALAQS	TALKFEST	TALUKAS	TAMES
TAINTING	TALAR	TALKFESTS	TALUKDAR	TAMEST
TAINTLESS	TALARIA	TALKIE	TALUKDARS	TAMIN
TAINTS	TALARS	TALKIER	TALUKS	TAMINE
TAINTURE	TALAS	TALKIES	TALUS	TAMINES
TAINTURES	TALAUNT	TALKIEST	TALUSES	TAMING
TAIPAN	TALAUNTS	TALKING	TALWEG	TAMINGS
TAIPANS	TALAYOT	TALKINGS	TALWEGS	TAMINS

The Chambers Dictionary is the authority for many longer words; see *OSW* Introduction, page xii.

TAMIS	TANGERINE	TANNA	TAOISEACH	TAPPET
TAMISE	TANGERINES	TANNABLE	TAOISEACHS	TAPPETS
TAMISES	TANGHIN	TANNAGE	TAP	TAPPICE
TAMMAR	TANGHININ	TANNAGES	TAPA	TAPPICED
TAMMARS	TANGHININS	TANNAH	TAPACOLO	TAPPICES
TAMMIES	TANGHINS	TANNAHS	TAPACOLOS	TAPPICING
TAMMY	TANGI	TANNAS	TAPACULO	TAPPING
TAMOXIFEN	TANGIBLE	TANNATE	TAPACULOS	TAPPINGS
TAMOXIFENS	TANGIBLES	TANNATES	TAPADERA	TAPPIT
TAMP	TANGIBLY	TANNED	TAPADERAS	TAPROOM
TAMPED	TANGIE	TANNER	TAPADERO	TAPROOMS
TAMPER	TANGIER	TANNERIES	TAPADEROS	TAPROOT
TAMPERED	TANGIES	TANNERS	TAPAS	TAPROOTS
TAMPERER	TANGIEST	TANNERY	TAPE	TAPS
TAMPERERS	TANGING	TANNEST	TAPEABLE	TAPSMAN
TAMPERING	TANGIS	TANNIC	TAPED	TAPSMEN
TAMPERINGS	TANGLE	TANNIN	TAPELESS	TAPSTER
TAMPERS	TANGLED	TANNING	TAPELIKE	TAPSTERS
TAMPING	TANGLER	TANNINGS	TAPELINE	TAPSTRY
TAMPINGS	TANGLERS	TANNINS	TAPELINES	TAPU
TAMPION	TANGLES	TANNOY	TAPEN	TAPUED
TAMPIONS	TANGLIER	TANNOYED	TAPENADE	TAPUING
TAMPON	TANGLIEST	TANNOYING	TAPENADES	TAPUS
TAMPONADE	TANGLING	TANNOYS	TAPER	TAR
TAMPONADES	TANGLINGS	TANREC	TAPERED	TARA
TAMPONAGE	TANGLY	TANRECS	TAPERER	TARAKIHI
TAMPONAGES	TANGO	TANS	TAPERERS	TARAKIHIS
TAMPONED	TANGOED	TANSIES	TAPERING	TARAND
TAMPONING	TANGOING	TANSY	TAPERINGS	TARANDS
TAMPONS	TANGOIST	TANTALATE	TAPERNESS	TARANTARA
TAMPS	TANGOISTS	TANTALATES	TAPERNESSES	TARANTARAED
TAMS	TANGOS	TANTALISE	TAPERS	TARANTARAING
TAMWORTH	TANGRAM	TANTALISED	TAPERWISE	TARANTARAS
TAMWORTHS	TANGRAMS	TANTALISES	TAPES	TARANTAS
TAN	TANGS	TANTALISING	TAPESTRIED	TARANTASES
TANA	TANGUN	TANTALISINGS	TAPESTRIES	TARANTASS
TANADAR	TANGUNS	TANTALISM	TAPESTRY	TARANTASSES
TANADARS	TANGY	TANTALISMS	TAPESTRYING	TARANTISM
TANAGER	TANH	TANTALITE	TAPET	TARANTISMS
TANAGERS	TANHS	TANTALITES	TAPETA	TARANTULA
TANAGRA	TANIST	TANTALIZE	TAPETAL	TARANTULAS
TANAGRAS	TANISTRIES	TANTALIZED	TAPETI	TARAS
TANAGRINE	TANISTRY	TANTALIZES	TAPETIS	TARAXACUM
TANAISTE	TANISTS	TANTALIZING	TAPETS	TARAXACUMS
TANAISTES	TANIWHA	TANTALIZINGS	TAPETUM	TARBOGGIN
TANALISED	TANIWHAS	TANTALOUS	TAPEWORM	TARBOGGINED
TANALIZED	TANK	TANTALUM	TAPEWORMS	TARBOGGINING
TANAS	TANKA	TANTALUMS	TAPHONOMIES	TARBOGGINS
TANBARK	TANKAGE	TANTALUS	TAPHONOMY	TARBOOSH
TANBARKS	TANKAGES	TANTALUSES	TAPING	TARBOOSHES
TANDEM	TANKARD	TANTARA	TAPIOCA	TARBOUSH
TANDEMS	TANKARDS	TANTARARA	TAPIOCAS	TARBOUSHES
TANDOOR	TANKAS	TANTARARAS	TAPIR	TARBOY
TANDOORI	TANKED	TANTARAS	TAPIROID	TARBOYS
TANDOORIS	TANKER	TANTI	TAPIRS	TARBUSH
TANDOORS	TANKERS	TANTIVIES	TAPIS	TARBUSHES
TANE	TANKFUL	TANTIVY	TAPISES	TARCEL
TANG	TANKFULS	TANTO	TAPIST	TARCELS
TANGA	TANKIA	TANTONIES	TAPISTS	TARDIED
TANGAS	TANKIAS	TANTONY	TAPLASH	TARDIER
TANGED	TANKIES	TANTRA	TAPLASHES	TARDIES
TANGELO	TANKING	TANTRAS	TAPPA	TARDIEST
TANGELOS	TANKINGS	TANTRIC	TAPPABLE	TARDILY
TANGENCIES	TANKS	TANTRUM	TAPPAS	TARDINESS
TANGENCY	TANKY	TANTRUMS	TAPPED	TARDINESSES
TANGENT	TANLING	TANYARD	TAPPER	TARDIVE
TANGENTS	TANLINGS	TANYARDS	TAPPERS	TARDY

The Chambers Dictionary is the authority for many longer words; see *OSW* Introduction, page xii.

TARDYING	TARRINESS	TARTRATES	TATE	TAUNTERS
TARE	TARRINESSES	TARTS	TATER	TAUNTING
TARED	TARRING	TARTY	TATERS	TAUNTINGS
TARES	TARRINGS	TARWEED	TATES	TAUNTS
TARGE	TARROCK	TARWEEDS	TATH	TAUPE
TARGED	TARROCKS	TARWHINE	TATHED	TAUPES
TARGES	TARROW	TARWHINES	TATHING	TAUPIE
TARGET	TARROWED	TASAR	TATHS	TAUPIES
TARGETED	TARROWING	TASARS	TATIE	TAUREAN
TARGETEER	TARROWS	TASER	TATIES	TAURIC
TARGETEERS	TARRY	TASERED	TATIN	TAURIFORM
TARGETING	TARRYING	TASERING	TATLER	TAURINE
TARGETS	TARS	TASERS	TATLERS	TAURINES
TARGING	TARSAL	TASH	TATOU	TAUS
TARIFF	TARSALGIA	TASHED	TATOUAY	TAUT
TARIFFED	TARSALGIAS	TASHES	TATOUAYS	TAUTED
TARIFFING	TARSALS	TASHING	TATOUS	TAUTEN
TARIFFS	TARSEL	TASIMETER	TATS	TAUTENED
TARING	TARSELS	TASIMETERS	TATT	TAUTENING
TARINGS	TARSI	TASK	TATTED	TAUTENS
TARLATAN	TARSIA	TASKED	TATTER	TAUTER
TARLATANS	TARSIAS	TASKER	TATTERED	TAUTEST
TARMAC	TARSIER	TASKERS	TATTERING	TAUTING
TARMACKED	TARSIERS	TASKING	TATTERS	TAUTIT
TARMACKING	TARSIOID	TASKINGS	TATTERY	TAUTLY
TARMACS	TARSIPED	TASKS	TATTIE	TAUTNESS
TARN	TARSIPEDS	TASLET	TATTIER	TAUTNESSES
TARNAL	TARSUS	TASLETS	TATTIES	TAUTOG
TARNALLY	TART	TASS	TATTIEST	TAUTOGS
TARNATION	TARTAN	TASSE	TATTILY	TAUTOLOGIES
TARNISH	TARTANA	TASSEL	TATTINESS	TAUTOLOGY
TARNISHED	TARTANAS	TASSELED	TATTINESSES	TAUTOMER
TARNISHER	TARTANE	TASSELING	TATTING	TAUTOMERS
TARNISHERS	TARTANED	TASSELL	TATTINGS	TAUTONYM
TARNISHES	TARTANES	TASSELLED	TATTLE	TAUTONYMS
TARNISHING	TARTANRIES	TASSELLING	TATTLED	TAUTS
TARNS	TARTANRY	TASSELLINGS	TATTLER	TAVA
TARO	TARTANS	TASSELLS	TATTLERS	TAVAH
TAROC	TARTAR	TASSELLY	TATTLES	TAVAHS
TAROCS	TARTARE	TASSELS	TATTLING	TAVAS
TAROK	TARTARES	TASSES	TATTLINGS	TAVER
TAROKS	TARTARIC	TASSET	TATTOO	TAVERED
TAROS	TARTARISE	TASSETS	TATTOOED	TAVERING
TAROT	TARTARISED	TASSIE	TATTOOER	TAVERN
TAROTS	TARTARISES	TASSIES	TATTOOERS	TAVERNA
TARP	TARTARISING	TASSWAGE	TATTOOING	TAVERNAS
TARPAN	TARTARIZE	TASTABLE	TATTOOIST	TAVERNER
TARPANS	TARTARIZED	TASTE	TATTOOISTS	TAVERNERS
TARPAULIN	TARTARIZES	TASTED	TATTOOS	TAVERNS
TARPAULINS	TARTARIZING	TASTEFUL	TATTOW	TAVERS
TARPON	TARTARLY	TASTELESS	TATTOWED	TAVERT
TARPONS	TARTARS	TASTER	TATTOWING	TAW
TARPS	TARTER	TASTERS	TATTOWS	TAWA
TARRAGON	TARTEST	TASTES	TATTS	TAWAS
TARRAGONS	TARTIER	TASTEVIN	TATTY	TAWDRIER
TARRAS	TARTIEST	TASTEVINS	TATU	TAWDRIES
TARRASES	TARTINE	TASTIER	TATUED	TAWDRIEST
TARRE	TARTINES	TASTIEST	TATUING	TAWDRILY
TARRED	TARTINESS	TASTILY	TATUS	TAWDRY
TARRES	TARTINESSES	TASTINESS	TAU	TAWED
TARRIANCE	TARTISH	TASTINESSES	TAUBE	TAWER
TARRIANCES	TARTLET	TASTING	TAUBES	TAWERIES
TARRIED	TARTLETS	TASTINGS	TAUGHT	TAWERS
TARRIER	TARTLY	TASTY	TAULD	TAWERY
TARRIERS	TARTNESS	TAT	TAUNT	TAWIE
TARRIES	TARTNESSES	TATAMI	TAUNTED	TAWING
TARRIEST	TARTRATE	TATAMIS	TAUNTER	TAWINGS

The Chambers Dictionary is the authority for many longer words; see *OSW* Introduction, page xii.

TAWNEY
TAWNEYS
TAWNIER
TAWNIES
TAWNIEST
TAWNINESS
TAWNINESSES
TAWNY
TAWPIE
TAWPIES
TAWS
TAWSE
TAWSES
TAWT
TAWTED
TAWTIE
TAWTIER
TAWTIEST
TAWTING
TAWTS
TAX
TAXA
TAXABLE
TAXABLY
TAXACEOUS
TAXAMETER
TAXAMETERS
TAXATION
TAXATIONS
TAXATIVE
TAXED
TAXER
TAXERS
TAXES
TAXI
TAXIARCH
TAXIARCHS
TAXICAB
TAXICABS
TAXIDERMIES
TAXIDERMY
TAXIED
TAXIES
TAXIING
TAXIMAN
TAXIMEN
TAXIMETER
TAXIMETERS
TAXING
TAXINGS
TAXIS
TAXIWAY
TAXIWAYS
TAXLESS
TAXMAN
TAXMEN
TAXOL
TAXOLS
TAXON
TAXONOMER
TAXONOMERS
TAXONOMIC
TAXONOMIES
TAXONOMY
TAXOR
TAXORS
TAXYING

TAY
TAYASSUID
TAYASSUIDS
TAYBERRIES
TAYBERRY
TAYRA
TAYRAS
TAYS
TAZZA
TAZZAS
TAZZE
TCHICK
TCHICKED
TCHICKING
TCHICKS
TE
TEA
TEABERRIES
TEABERRY
TEABOARD
TEABOARDS
TEACH
TEACHABLE
TEACHER
TEACHERLY
TEACHERS
TEACHES
TEACHIE
TEACHING
TEACHINGS
TEACHLESS
TEACUP
TEACUPFUL
TEACUPFULS
TEACUPS
TEAD
TEADE
TEADES
TEADS
TEAED
TEAGLE
TEAGLED
TEAGLES
TEAGLING
TEAING
TEAK
TEAKS
TEAL
TEALS
TEAM
TEAMED
TEAMER
TEAMERS
TEAMING
TEAMINGS
TEAMS
TEAMSTER
TEAMSTERS
TEAMWISE
TEAMWORK
TEAMWORKS
TEAPOT
TEAPOTS
TEAPOY
TEAPOYS
TEAR
TEARABLE

TEARAWAY
TEARAWAYS
TEARER
TEARERS
TEARFUL
TEARFULLY
TEARIER
TEARIEST
TEARING
TEARLESS
TEARS
TEARSHEET
TEARSHEETS
TEARY
TEAS
TEASE
TEASED
TEASEL
TEASELED
TEASELER
TEASELERS
TEASELING
TEASELINGS
TEASELLED
TEASELLER
TEASELLERS
TEASELLING
TEASELLINGS
TEASELS
TEASER
TEASERS
TEASES
TEASING
TEASINGLY
TEASINGS
TEASPOON
TEASPOONS
TEAT
TEATED
TEATIME
TEATIMES
TEATS
TEAZE
TEAZED
TEAZEL
TEAZELED
TEAZELING
TEAZELLED
TEAZELLING
TEAZELS
TEAZES
TEAZING
TEAZLE
TEAZLED
TEAZLES
TEAZLING
TEBBAD
TEBBADS
TECH
TECHIER
TECHIEST
TECHILY
TECHINESS
TECHINESSES
TECHNIC
TECHNICAL
TECHNICS

TECHNIQUE
TECHNIQUES
TECHNO
TECHNOS
TECHS
TECHY
TECKEL
TECKELS
TECTA
TECTIFORM
TECTONIC
TECTONICS
TECTORIAL
TECTRICES
TECTRIX
TECTUM
TED
TEDDED
TEDDER
TEDDERS
TEDDIE
TEDDIES
TEDDING
TEDDY
TEDESCA
TEDESCHE
TEDESCHI
TEDESCO
TEDIER
TEDIEST
TEDIOSITIES
TEDIOSITY
TEDIOUS
TEDIOUSLY
TEDISOME
TEDIUM
TEDIUMS
TEDS
TEDY
TEE
TEED
TEEING
TEEL
TEELS
TEEM
TEEMED
TEEMER
TEEMERS
TEEMFUL
TEEMING
TEEMLESS
TEEMS
TEEN
TEENAGE
TEENAGED
TEENAGER
TEENAGERS
TEEND
TEENDED
TEENDING
TEENDS
TEENE
TEENED
TEENES
TEENIER
TEENIEST
TEENING

TEENS
TEENSIER
TEENSIEST
TEENSY
TEENTIER
TEENTIEST
TEENTSIER
TEENTSIEST
TEENTSY
TEENTY
TEENY
TEEPEE
TEEPEES
TEER
TEERED
TEERING
TEERS
TEES
TEETER
TEETERED
TEETERING
TEETERS
TEETH
TEETHE
TEETHED
TEETHES
TEETHING
TEETHINGS
TEETOTAL
TEETOTALS
TEETOTUM
TEETOTUMS
TEF
TEFF
TEFFS
TEFILLAH
TEFILLIN
TEFS
TEG
TEGG
TEGGS
TEGMEN
TEGMENTA
TEGMENTAL
TEGMENTUM
TEGMINA
TEGS
TEGU
TEGUEXIN
TEGUEXINS
TEGULA
TEGULAE
TEGULAR
TEGULARLY
TEGULATED
TEGUMENT
TEGUMENTS
TEGUS
TEHR
TEHRS
TEIL
TEILS
TEIND
TEINDED
TEINDING
TEINDS
TEKNONYMIES

The Chambers Dictionary is the authority for many longer words; see *OSW* Introduction, page xii.

TEKNONYMY
TEKTITE
TEKTITES
TEL
TELA
TELAE
TELAMON
TELAMONES
TELARY
TELD
TELECAST
TELECASTED
TELECASTING
TELECASTS
TELECHIR
TELECHIRS
TELECINE
TELECINES
TELECOM
TELECOMS
TELEDU
TELEDUS
TELEFAX
TELEFAXED
TELEFAXES
TELEFAXING
TELEFILM
TELEFILMS
TELEGA
TELEGAS
TELEGENIC
TELEGONIC
TELEGONIES
TELEGONY
TELEGRAM
TELEGRAMS
TELEGRAPH
TELEGRAPHED
TELEGRAPHING
TELEGRAPHS
TELEMARK
TELEMARKED
TELEMARKING
TELEMARKS
TELEMATIC
TELEMATICS
TELEMETER
TELEMETERED
TELEMETERING
TELEMETERS
TELEMETRIES
TELEMETRY
TELEOLOGIES
TELEOLOGY
TELEONOMIES
TELEONOMY
TELEOSAUR
TELEOSAURS
TELEOST
TELEOSTS
TELEPATH
TELEPATHED
TELEPATHIES
TELEPATHING
TELEPATHS
TELEPATHY
TELEPHEME

TELEPHEMES
TELEPHONE
TELEPHONED
TELEPHONES
TELEPHONIES
TELEPHONING
TELEPHONY
TELEPHOTO
TELEPLAY
TELEPLAYS
TELEPOINT
TELEPOINTS
TELEPORT
TELEPORTED
TELEPORTING
TELEPORTS
TELERGIC
TELERGIES
TELERGY
TELESALE
TELESALES
TELESCOPE
TELESCOPED
TELESCOPES
TELESCOPIES
TELESCOPING
TELESCOPY
TELESEME
TELESEMES
TELESES
TELESIS
TELESM
TELESMS
TELESTIC
TELESTICH
TELESTICHS
TELETEX
TELETEXES
TELETEXT
TELETEXTS
TELETHON
TELETHONS
TELETRON
TELETRONS
TELEVIEW
TELEVIEWED
TELEVIEWING
TELEVIEWS
TELEVISE
TELEVISED
TELEVISER
TELEVISERS
TELEVISES
TELEVISING
TELEVISOR
TELEVISORS
TELEX
TELEXED
TELEXES
TELEXING
TELFER
TELFERAGE
TELFERAGES
TELFERED
TELFERIC
TELFERING
TELFERS

TELIA
TELIAL
TELIC
TELIUM
TELL
TELLABLE
TELLAR
TELLARED
TELLARING
TELLARS
TELLEN
TELLENS
TELLER
TELLERED
TELLERING
TELLERS
TELLIES
TELLIN
TELLING
TELLINGLY
TELLINGS
TELLINOID
TELLINS
TELLS
TELLTALE
TELLTALES
TELLURAL
TELLURATE
TELLURATES
TELLURIAN
TELLURIANS
TELLURIC
TELLURIDE
TELLURIDES
TELLURION
TELLURIONS
TELLURISE
TELLURISED
TELLURISES
TELLURISING
TELLURITE
TELLURITES
TELLURIUM
TELLURIUMS
TELLURIZE
TELLURIZED
TELLURIZES
TELLURIZING
TELLUROUS
TELLUS
TELLUSES
TELLY
TELOMERE
TELOMERES
TELOPHASE
TELOPHASES
TELOS
TELOSES
TELPHER
TELPHERED
TELPHERIC
TELPHERING
TELPHERS
TELS
TELSON
TELSONS
TELT

TEMAZEPAM
TEMAZEPAMS
TEMBLOR
TEMBLORES
TEMBLORS
TEME
TEMED
TEMENE
TEMENOS
TEMERITIES
TEMERITY
TEMEROUS
TEMES
TEMP
TEMPED
TEMPEH
TEMPEHS
TEMPER
TEMPERA
TEMPERAS
TEMPERATE
TEMPERATED
TEMPERATES
TEMPERATING
TEMPERED
TEMPERER
TEMPERERS
TEMPERING
TEMPERINGS
TEMPERS
TEMPEST
TEMPESTED
TEMPESTING
TEMPESTS
TEMPI
TEMPING
TEMPLAR
TEMPLARS
TEMPLATE
TEMPLATES
TEMPLE
TEMPLED
TEMPLES
TEMPLET
TEMPLETS
TEMPO
TEMPORAL
TEMPORALS
TEMPORARIES
TEMPORARY
TEMPORE
TEMPORISE
TEMPORISED
TEMPORISES
TEMPORISING
TEMPORISINGS
TEMPORIZE
TEMPORIZED
TEMPORIZES
TEMPORIZING
TEMPORIZINGS
TEMPOS
TEMPS
TEMPT
TEMPTABLE
TEMPTED
TEMPTER

TEMPTERS
TEMPTING
TEMPTINGS
TEMPTRESS
TEMPTRESSES
TEMPTS
TEMPURA
TEMPURAS
TEMS
TEMSE
TEMSED
TEMSES
TEMSING
TEMULENCE
TEMULENCES
TEMULENCIES
TEMULENCY
TEMULENT
TEN
TENABLE
TENACE
TENACES
TENACIOUS
TENACITIES
TENACITY
TENACULA
TENACULUM
TENAIL
TENAILLE
TENAILLES
TENAILLON
TENAILLONS
TENAILS
TENANCIES
TENANCY
TENANT
TENANTED
TENANTING
TENANTRIES
TENANTRY
TENANTS
TENCH
TENCHES
TEND
TENDANCE
TENDANCES
TENDED
TENDENCE
TENDENCES
TENDENCIES
TENDENCY
TENDENZ
TENDENZEN
TENDER
TENDERED
TENDERER
TENDERERS
TENDEREST
TENDERING
TENDERINGS
TENDERISE
TENDERISED
TENDERISES
TENDERISING
TENDERIZE
TENDERIZED
TENDERIZES

The Chambers Dictionary is the authority for many longer words; see *OSW* Introduction, page xii.

TENDERIZING	TENOURS	TENTS	TERATISMS	TERMING
TENDERLY	TENPENCE	TENTWISE	TERATOGEN	TERMINI
TENDERS	TENPENCES	TENTY	TERATOGENS	TERMINISM
TENDING	TENPENNY	TENUE	TERATOID	TERMINISMS
TENDINOUS	TENPINS	TENUES	TERATOMA	TERMINIST
TENDON	TENREC	TENUIOUS	TERATOMATA	TERMINISTS
TENDONS	TENRECS	TENUIS	TERBIC	TERMINUS
TENDRE	TENS	TENUITIES	TERBIUM	TERMINUSES
TENDRES	TENSE	TENUITY	TERBIUMS	TERMITARIES
TENDRIL	TENSED	TENUOUS	TERCE	TERMITARY
TENDRILS	TENSELESS	TENUOUSLY	TERCEL	TERMITE
TENDRON	TENSELY	TENURABLE	TERCELET	TERMITES
TENDRONS	TENSENESS	TENURE	TERCELETS	TERMLESS
TENDS	TENSENESSES	TENURED	TERCELS	TERMLIES
TENE	TENSER	TENURES	TERCES	TERMLY
TENEBRAE	TENSES	TENURIAL	TERCET	TERMOR
TENEBRIO	TENSEST	TENUTO	TERCETS	TERMORS
TENEBRIOS	TENSIBLE	TENUTOS	TERCIO	TERMS
TENEBRISM	TENSILE	TENZON	TERCIOS	TERN
TENEBRISMS	TENSILITIES	TENZONS	TEREBENE	TERNAL
TENEBRIST	TENSILITY	TEOCALLI	TEREBENES	TERNARIES
TENEBRISTS	TENSING	TEOCALLIS	TEREBINTII	TERNARY
TENEBRITIES	TENSION	TEOSINTE	TEREBINTHS	TERNATE
TENEBRITY	TENSIONAL	TEOSINTES	TEREBRA	TERNATELY
TENEBROSE	TENSIONED	TEPAL	TEREBRAE	TERNE
TENEBROUS	TENSIONING	TEPALS	TEREBRANT	TERNED
TENEMENT	TENSIONS	TEPEE	TEREBRANTS	TERNES
TENEMENTS	TENSITIES	TEPEES	TEREBRAS	TERNING
TENENDUM	TENSITY	TEPEFIED	TEREBRATE	TERNION
TENENDUMS	TENSIVE	TEPEFIES	TEREBRATED	TERNIONS
TENES	TENSON	TEPEFY	TEREBRATES	TERNS
TENESMUS	TENSONS	TEPEFYING	TEREBRATING	TERPENE
TENESMUSES	TENSOR	TEPHIGRAM	TEREDINES	TERPENES
TENET	TENSORS	TEPHIGRAMS	TEREDO	TERPENOID
TENETS	TENT	TEPHILLAH	TEREDOS	TERPENOIDS
TENFOLD	TENTACLE	TEPHILLIN	TEREFA	TERPINEOL
TENIA	TENTACLED	TEPHRA	TEREFAH	TERPINEOLS
TENIAE	TENTACLES	TEPHRAS	TEREK	TERRA
TENIAS	TENTACULA	TEPHRITE	TEREKS	TERRACE
TENIOID	TENTAGE	TEPHRITES	TERES	TERRACED
TENNE	TENTAGES	TEPHRITIC	TERETE	TERRACES
TENNER	TENTATION	TEPHROITE	TERETES	TERRACING
TENNERS	TENTATIONS	TEPHROITES	TERF	TERRACINGS
TENNES	TENTATIVE	TEPID	TERFE	TERRAE
TENNIES	TENTATIVES	TEPIDARIA	TERFES	TERRAFORM
TENNIS	TENTED	TEPIDER	TERFS	TERRAFORMED
TENNISES	TENTER	TEPIDEST	TERGA	TERRAFORMING
TENNO	TENTERED	TEPIDITIES	TERGAL	TERRAFORMINGS
TENNOS	TENTERING	TEPIDITY	TERGITE	TERRAFORMS
TENNY	TENTERS	TEPIDLY	TERGITES	TERRAIN
TENON	TENTFUL	TEPIDNESS	TERGUM	TERRAINS
TENONED	TENTFULS	TEPIDNESSES	TERIYAKI	TERRAMARA
TENONER	TENTH	TEQUILA	TERIYAKIS	TERRAMARE
TENONERS	TENTHLY	TEQUILAS	TERM	TERRAMARES
TENONING	TENTHS	TEQUILLA	TERMAGANT	TERRANE
TENONS	TENTIE	TEQUILLAS	TERMAGANTS	TERRANES
TENOR	TENTIER	TERAFLOP	TERMED	TERRAPIN
TENORIST	TENTIEST	TERAI	TERMER	TERRAPINS
TENORISTS	TENTIGO	TERAIS	TERMERS	TERRARIA
TENORITE	TENTIGOS	TERAKIHI	TERMINAL	TERRARIUM
TENORITES	TENTING	TERAKIHIS	TERMINALS	TERRARIUMS
TENOROON	TENTINGS	TERAPH	TERMINATE	TERRAS
TENOROONS	TENTLESS	TERAPHIM	TERMINATED	TERRASES
TENORS	TENTORIA	TERAPHIMS	TERMINATES	TERRAZZO
TENOTOMIES	TENTORIAL	TERAS	TERMINATING	TERRAZZOS
TENOTOMY	TENTORIUM	TERATA	TERMINER	TERREEN
TENOUR	TENTORIUMS	TERATISM	TERMINERS	TERREENS

The Chambers Dictionary is the authority for many longer words; see *OSW* Introduction, page xii.

TERRELLA	TERZETTO	TESTONS	TETRODES	THAE
TERRELLAS	TERZETTOS	TESTOON	TETRONAL	THAGI
TERRENE	TES	TESTOONS	TETRONALS	THAGIS
TERRENELY	TESLA	TESTRIL	TETROXIDE	THAIM
TERRENES	TESLAS	TESTRILL	TETROXIDES	THAIRM
TERRET	TESSELLA	TESTRILLS	TETRYL	THAIRMS
TERRETS	TESSELLAE	TESTRILS	TETRYLS	THALAMI
TERRIBLE	TESSELLAR	TESTS	TETTER	THALAMIC
TERRIBLES	TESSERA	TESTUDINES	TETTERED	THALAMUS
TERRIBLY	TESSERACT	TESTUDO	TETTERING	THALASSIC
TERRICOLE	TESSERACTS	TESTUDOS	TETTEROUS	THALER
TERRICOLES	TESSERAE	TESTY	TETTERS	THALERS
TERRIER	TESSERAL	TETANAL	TETTIX	THALIAN
TERRIERS	TESSITURA	TETANIC	TETTIXES	THALLI
TERRIES	TESSITURAS	TETANICS	TEUCH	THALLIC
TERRIFIC	TEST	TETANIES	TEUCHAT	THALLINE
TERRIFIED	TESTA	TETANISE	TEUCHATS	THALLIUM
TERRIFIER	TESTABLE	TETANISED	TEUCHER	THALLIUMS
TERRIFIERS	TESTACIES	TETANISES	TEUCHEST	THALLOID
TERRIFIES	TESTACY	TETANISING	TEUCHTER	THALLOUS
TERRIFY	TESTAE	TETANIZE	TEUCHTERS	THALLUS
TERRIFYING	TESTAMENT	TETANIZED	TEUGH	THALLUSES
TERRINE	TESTAMENTS	TETANIZES	TEUGHER	THALWEG
TERRINES	TESTAMUR	TETANIZING	TEUGHEST	THALWEGS
TERRIT	TESTAMURS	TETANOID	TEW	THAN
TERRITORIES	TESTATE	TETANUS	TEWART	THANA
TERRITORY	TESTATION	TETANUSES	TEWARTS	THANADAR
TERRITS	TESTATIONS	TETANY	TEWED	THANADARS
TERROR	TESTATOR	TETCHIER	TEWEL	THANAGE
TERRORFUL	TESTATORS	TETCHIEST	TEWELS	THANAGES
TERRORISE	TESTATRICES	TETCHILY	TEWHIT	THANAH
TERRORISED	TESTATRIX	TETCHY	TEWHITS	THANAHS
TERRORISES	TESTATRIXES	TETE	TEWING	THANAS
TERRORISING	TESTATUM	TETES	TEWIT	THANATISM
TERRORISM	TESTATUMS	TETHER	TEWITS	THANATISMS
TERRORISMS	TESTE	TETHERED	TEWS	THANATIST
TERRORIST	TESTED	TETHERING	TEXAS	THANATISTS
TERRORISTS	TESTEE	TETHERS	TEXASES	THANATOID
TERRORIZE	TESTEES	TETRA	TEXT	THANE
TERRORIZED	TESTER	TETRACID	TEXTBOOK	THANEDOM
TERRORIZES	TESTERN	TETRACT	TEXTBOOKS	THANEDOMS
TERRORIZING	TESTERNED	TETRACTS	TEXTILE	THANEHOOD
TERRORS	TESTERNING	TETRAD	TEXTILES	THANEHOODS
TERRY	TESTERNS	TETRADIC	TEXTLESS	THANES
TERSE	TESTERS	TETRADITE	TEXTORIAL	THANESHIP
TERSELY	TESTES	TETRADITES	TEXTPHONE	THANESHIPS
TERSENESS	TESTICLE	TETRADS	TEXTPHONES	THANK
TERSENESSES	TESTICLES	TETRAGON	TEXTS	THANKED
TERSER	TESTIER	TETRAGONS	TEXTUAL	THANKEE
TERSEST	TESTIEST	TETRAGRAM	TEXTUALLY	THANKER
TERSION	TESTIFIED	TETRAGRAMS	TEXTUARIES	THANKERS
TERSIONS	TESTIFIER	TETRALOGIES	TEXTUARY	THANKFUL
TERTIA	TESTIFIERS	TETRALOGY	TEXTURAL	THANKING
TERTIAL	TESTIFIES	TETRAPLA	TEXTURE	THANKINGS
TERTIALS	TESTIFY	TETRAPLAS	TEXTURED	THANKLESS
TERTIAN	TESTIFYING	TETRAPOD	TEXTURES	THANKS
TERTIANS	TESTILY	TETRAPODIES	TEXTURING	THANKYOU
TERTIARIES	TESTIMONIED	TETRAPODS	TEXTURISE	THANKYOUS
TERTIARY	TESTIMONIES	TETRAPODY	TEXTURISED	THANNA
TERTIAS	TESTIMONY	TETRARCH	TEXTURISES	THANNAH
TERTIUS	TESTIMONYING	TETRARCHIES	TEXTURISING	THANNAHS
TERTIUSES	TESTINESS	TETRARCHS	TEXTURIZE	THANNAS
TERTS	TESTINESSES	TETRARCHY	TEXTURIZED	THANS
TERVALENT	TESTING	TETRAS	TEXTURIZES	THAR
TERZETTA	TESTINGS	TETRAXON	TEXTURIZING	THARS
TERZETTAS	TESTIS	TETRAXONS	THACK	THAT
TERZETTI	TESTON	TETRODE	THACKS	THATAWAY

The Chambers Dictionary is the authority for many longer words; see *OSW* Introduction, page xii.

THATCH	THEIRS	THEOREMS	THERM	THICK
THATCHED	THEISM	THEORETIC	THERMAE	THICKED
THATCHER	THEISMS	THEORETICS	THERMAL	THICKEN
THATCHERS	THEIST	THEORIC	THERMALLY	THICKENED
THATCHES	THEISTIC	THEORICS	THERMALS	THICKENER
THATCHING	THEISTS	THEORIES	THERMIC	THICKENERS
THATCHINGS	THELEMENT	THEORIQUE	THERMICAL	THICKENING
THATCHT	THELEMENTS	THEORIQUES	THERMIDOR	THICKENINGS
THATNESS	THELF	THEORISE	THERMION	THICKENS
THATNESSES	THELVES	THEORISED	THERMIONS	THICKER
THAUMATIN	THELYTOKIES	THEORISER	THERMITE	THICKEST
THAUMATINS	THELYTOKY	THEORISERS	THERMITES	THICKET
THAW	THEM	THEORISES	THERMOTIC	THICKETED
THAWED	THEMA	THEORISING	THERMOTICS	THICKETS
THAWER	THEMATA	THEORIST	THERMS	THICKETY
THAWERS	THEMATIC	THEORISTS	THEROID	THICKHEAD
THAWIER	THEME	THEORIZE	THEROLOGIES	THICKHEADS
THAWIEST	THEMED	THEORIZED	THEROLOGY	THICKING
THAWING	THEMELESS	THEORIZER	THEROPOD	THICKISH
THAWINGS	THEMES	THEORIZERS	THEROPODS	THICKLY
THAWLESS	THEMING	THEORIZES	THESAURI	THICKNESS
THAWS	THEMSELF	THEORIZING	THESAURUS	THICKNESSES
THAWY	THEMSELVES	THEORY	THESAURUSES	THICKO
THE	THEN	THEOSOPH	THESE	THICKOES
THEACEOUS	THENABOUT	THEOSOPHIES	THESES	THICKOS
THEANDRIC	THENABOUTS	THEOSOPHS	THESIS	THICKS
THEARCHIC	THENAR	THEOSOPHY	THESPIAN	THICKSET
THEARCHIES	THENARS	THEOTOKOI	THESPIANS	THICKSETS
THEARCHY	THENCE	THEOTOKOS	THETA	THICKSKIN
THEATER	THENS	THEOW	THETAS	THICKSKINS
THEATERS	THEOCRACIES	THEOWS	THETCH	THICKY
THEATRAL	THEOCRACY	THERALITE	THETCHED	THIEF
THEATRE	THEOCRASIES	THERALITES	THETCHES	THIEVE
THEATRES	THEOCRASY	THERAPIES	THETCHING	THIEVED
THEATRIC	THEOCRAT	THERAPIST	THETE	THIEVERIES
THEATRICS	THEOCRATS	THERAPISTS	THETES	THIEVERY
THEAVE	THEODICIES	THERAPSID	THETHER	THIEVES
THEAVES	THEODICY	THERAPSIDS	THETIC	THIEVING
THEBAINE	THEOGONIC	THERAPY	THETICAL	THIEVINGS
THEBAINES	THEOGONIES	THERBLIG	THEURGIC	THIEVISH
THECA	THEOGONY	THERBLIGS	THEURGIES	THIG
THECAE	THEOLOGER	THERE	THEURGIST	THIGGER
THECAL	THEOLOGERS	THEREAT	THEURGISTS	THIGGERS
THECATE	THEOLOGIC	THEREAWAY	THEURGY	THIGGING
THECODONT	THEOLOGIES	THEREBY	THEW	THIGGINGS
THECODONTS	THEOLOGUE	THEREFOR	THEWED	THIGGIT
THEE	THEOLOGUES	THEREFORE	THEWES	THIGH
THEED	THEOLOGY	THEREFROM	THEWIER	THIGHBONE
THEEING	THEOMACHIES	THEREIN	THEWIEST	THIGHBONES
THEEK	THEOMACHY	THEREINTO	THEWLESS	THIGHS
THEEKED	THEOMANCIES	THERENESS	THEWS	THIGS
THEEKING	THEOMANCY	THERENESSES	THEWY	THILK
THEEKS	THEOMANIA	THEREOF	THEY	THILL
THEES	THEOMANIAS	THEREON	THIAMIN	THILLER
THEFT	THEONOMIES	THEREOUT	THIAMINE	THILLERS
THEFTBOOT	THEONOMY	THERES	THIAMINES	THILLS
THEFTBOOTS	THEOPATHIES	THERETO	THIAMINS	THIMBLE
THEFTS	THEOPATHY	THEREUNTO	THIASUS	THIMBLED
THEFTUOUS	THEOPHAGIES	THEREUPON	THIASUSES	THIMBLES
THEGITHER	THEOPHAGY	THEREWITH	THIAZIDE	THIMBLING
THEGN	THEOPHANIES	THERIAC	THIAZIDES	THIN
THEGNS	THEOPHANY	THERIACA	THIAZINE	THINE
THEIC	THEORBIST	THERIACAL	THIAZINES	THING
THEICS	THEORBISTS	THERIACAS	THIBET	THINGAMIES
THEINE	THEORBO	THERIACS	THIBETS	THINGAMY
THEINES	THEORBOS	THERIAN	THIBLE	THINGHOOD
THEIR	THEOREM	THERIANS	THIBLES	THINGHOODS

The Chambers Dictionary is the authority for many longer words; see *OSW* Introduction, page xii.

THINGIER	THIRTIETH	THOROUGHEST	THREADY	THRILL
THINGIES	THIRTIETHS	THOROUGHS	THREAP	THRILLANT
THINGIEST	THIRTY	THORP	THREAPING	THRILLED
THINGNESS	THIRTYISH	THORPE	THREAPIT	THRILLER
THINGNESSES	THIS	THORPES	THREAPS	THRILLERS
THINGS	THISNESS	THORPS	THREAT	THRILLIER
THINGUMMIES	THISNESSES	THOSE	THREATED	THRILLIEST
THINGUMMY	THISTLE	THOTHER	THREATEN	THRILLING
THINGY	THISTLES	THOU	THREATENED	THRILLS
THINK	THISTLIER	THOUGH	THREATENING	THRILLY
THINKABLE	THISTLIEST	THOUGHT	THREATENINGS	THRIMSA
THINKER	THISTLY	THOUGHTED	THREATENS	THRIMSAS
THINKERS	THITHER	THOUGHTEN	THREATFUL	THRIPS
THINKING	THIVEL	THOUGHTS	THREATING	THRIPSES
THINKINGS	THIVELS	THOUING	THREATS	THRISSEL
THINKS	THLIPSES	THOUS	THREAVE	THRISSELS
THINLY	THLIPSIS	THOUSAND	THREAVES	THRIST
THINNED	THO	THOUSANDS	THREE	THRISTED
THINNER	THOFT	THOWEL	THREEFOLD	THRISTING
THINNERS	THOFTS	THOWELS	THREENESS	THRISTLE
THINNESS	THOLE	THOWL	THREENESSES	THRISTLES
THINNESSES	THOLED	THOWLESS	THREEP	THRISTS
THINNEST	THOLES	THOWLS	THREEPING	THRISTY
THINNING	THOLI	THRAE	THREEPIT	THRIVE
THINNINGS	THOLING	THRALDOM	THREEPS	THRIVED
THINNISH	THOLOBATE	THRALDOMS	THREES	THRIVEN
THINS	THOLOBATES	THRALL	THREESOME	THRIVER
THIOL	THOLOI	THRALLDOM	THREESOMES	THRIVERS
THIOLS	THOLOS	THRALLDOMS	THRENE	THRIVES
THIOPHEN	THOLUS	THRALLED	THRENES	THRIVING
THIOPHENE	THON	THRALLING	THRENETIC	THRIVINGS
THIOPHENES	THONDER	THRALLS	THRENODE	THRO
THIOPHENS	THONG	THRANG	THRENODES	THROAT
THIOPHIL	THONGED	THRANGED	THRENODIC	THROATED
THIOUREA	THONGS	THRANGING	THRENODIES	THROATIER
THIOUREAS	THORACAL	THRANGS	THRENODY	THROATIEST
THIR	THORACES	THRAPPLE	THRENOS	THROATILY
THIRAM	THORACIC	THRAPPLED	THRENOSES	THROATS
THIRAMS	THORAX	THRAPPLES	THREONINE	THROATY
THIRD	THORAXES	THRAPPLING	THREONINES	THROB
THIRDED	THORIA	THRASH	THRESH	THROBBED
THIRDING	THORIAS	THRASHED	THRESHED	THROBBING
THIRDINGS	THORITE	THRASHER	THRESHEL	THROBBINGS
THIRDLY	THORITES	THRASHERS	THRESHELS	THROBLESS
THIRDS	THORIUM	THRASHES	THRESHER	THROBS
THIRDSMAN	THORIUMS	THRASHING	THRESHERS	THROE
THIRDSMEN	THORN	THRASHINGS	THRESHES	THROED
THIRL	THORNBACK	THRASONIC	THRESHING	THROEING
THIRLAGE	THORNBACKS	THRAVE	THRESHINGS	THROES
THIRLAGES	THORNBILL	THRAVES	THRESHOLD	THROMBI
THIRLED	THORNBILLS	THRAW	THRESHOLDS	THROMBIN
THIRLING	THORNBUSH	THRAWARD	THRETTIES	THROMBINS
THIRLS	THORNBUSHES	THRAWART	THRETTY	THROMBOSE
THIRST	THORNED	THRAWING	THREW	THROMBOSED
THIRSTED	THORNIER	THRAWN	THRICE	THROMBOSES
THIRSTER	THORNIEST	THRAWS	THRID	THROMBOSING
THIRSTERS	THORNING	THREAD	THRIDACE	THROMBUS
THIRSTFUL	THORNLESS	THREADED	THRIDACES	THRONE
THIRSTIER	THORNS	THREADEN	THRIDDED	THRONED
THIRSTIEST	THORNSET	THREADER	THRIDDING	THRONES
THIRSTILY	THORNTREE	THREADERS	THRIDS	THRONG
THIRSTING	THORNTREES	THREADFIN	THRIFT	THRONGED
THIRSTS	THORNY	THREADFINS	THRIFTIER	THRONGFUL
THIRSTY	THORON	THREADIER	THRIFTIEST	THRONGING
THIRTEEN	THORONS	THREADIEST	THRIFTILY	THRONGINGS
THIRTEENS	THOROUGH	THREADING	THRIFTS	THRONGS
THIRTIES	THOROUGHER	THREADS	THRIFTY	THRONING

The Chambers Dictionary is the authority for many longer words; see *OSW* Introduction, page xii.

THROPPLE
THROPPLED
THROPPLES
THROPPLING
THROSTLE
THROSTLES
THROTTLE
THROTTLED
THROTTLER
THROTTLERS
THROTTLES
THROTTLING
THROTTLINGS
THROUGH
THROUGHLY
THROVE
THROW
THROWAWAY
THROWAWAYS
THROWBACK
THROWBACKS
THROWE
THROWER
THROWERS
THROWES
THROWING
THROWINGS
THROWN
THROWS
THROWSTER
THROWSTERS
THRU
THRUM
THRUMMED
THRUMMER
THRUMMERS
THRUMMIER
THRUMMIEST
THRUMMING
THRUMMINGS
THRUMMY
THRUMS
THRUSH
THRUSHES
THRUST
THRUSTED
THRUSTER
THRUSTERS
THRUSTING
THRUSTINGS
THRUSTS
THRUTCH
THRUTCHED
THRUTCHES
THRUTCHING
THRUWAY
THRUWAYS
THRYMSA
THRYMSAS
THUD
THUDDED
THUDDING
THUDS
THUG
THUGGEE
THUGGEES
THUGGERIES

THUGGERY
THUGGISM
THUGGISMS
THUGGO
THUGGOS
THUGS
THUJA
THUJAS
THULIA
THULIAS
THULITE
THULITES
THULIUM
THULIUMS
THUMB
THUMBED
THUMBIER
THUMBIEST
THUMBING
THUMBKINS
THUMBLESS
THUMBLIKE
THUMBLING
THUMBLINGS
THUMBNAIL
THUMBNAILS
THUMBNUT
THUMBNUTS
THUMBPOT
THUMBPOTS
THUMBS
THUMBTACK
THUMBTACKS
THUMBY
THUMP
THUMPED
THUMPER
THUMPERS
THUMPING
THUMPS
THUNDER
THUNDERED
THUNDERER
THUNDERERS
THUNDERING
THUNDERINGS
THUNDERS
THUNDERY
THUNDROUS
THURIBLE
THURIBLES
THURIFER
THURIFERS
THURIFIED
THURIFIES
THURIFY
THURIFYING
THUS
THUSES
THUSNESS
THUSNESSES
THUSWISE
THUYA
THUYAS
THWACK
THWACKED
THWACKER

THWACKERS
THWACKING
THWACKINGS
THWACKS
THWAITE
THWAITES
THWART
THWARTED
THWARTER
THWARTERS
THWARTING
THWARTINGS
THWARTLY
THWARTS
THY
THYINE
THYLACINE
THYLACINES
THYLOSE
THYLOSES
THYLOSIS
THYME
THYMES
THYMI
THYMIC
THYMIDINE
THYMIDINES
THYMIER
THYMIEST
THYMINE
THYMINES
THYMOCYTE
THYMOCYTES
THYMOL
THYMOLS
THYMUS
THYMY
THYRATRON
THYRATRONS
THYREOID
THYREOIDS
THYRISTOR
THYRISTORS
THYROID
THYROIDS
THYROXIN
THYROXINE
THYROXINES
THYROXINS
THYRSE
THYRSES
THYRSI
THYRSOID
THYRSUS
THYSELF
TI
TIAR
TIARA
TIARAED
TIARAS
TIARS
TIBIA
TIBIAE
TIBIAL
TIBIAS
TIC
TICAL

TICALS
TICCA
TICE
TICED
TICES
TICH
TICHES
TICHIER
TICHIEST
TICHY
TICING
TICK
TICKED
TICKEN
TICKENS
TICKER
TICKERS
TICKET
TICKETED
TICKETING
TICKETS
TICKEY
TICKEYS
TICKIES
TICKING
TICKINGS
TICKLE
TICKLED
TICKLER
TICKLERS
TICKLES
TICKLIER
TICKLIEST
TICKLING
TICKLINGS
TICKLISH
TICKLY
TICKS
TICKY
TICS
TID
TIDAL
TIDBIT
TIDBITS
TIDDIER
TIDDIES
TIDDIEST
TIDDLE
TIDDLED
TIDDLER
TIDDLERS
TIDDLES
TIDDLEY
TIDDLEYS
TIDDLIER
TIDDLIES
TIDDLIEST
TIDDLING
TIDDLY
TIDDY
TIDE
TIDED
TIDELAND
TIDELANDS
TIDELESS
TIDEMARK
TIDEMARKS

TIDEMILL
TIDEMILLS
TIDES
TIDESMAN
TIDESMEN
TIDEWATER
TIDEWATERS
TIDEWAVE
TIDEWAVES
TIDEWAY
TIDEWAYS
TIDIED
TIDIER
TIDIES
TIDIEST
TIDILY
TIDINESS
TIDINESSES
TIDING
TIDINGS
TIDIVATE
TIDIVATED
TIDIVATES
TIDIVATING
TIDS
TIDY
TIDYING
TIE
TIEBACK
TIEBACKS
TIED
TIELESS
TIEPIN
TIEPINS
TIER
TIERCE
TIERCED
TIERCEL
TIERCELET
TIERCELETS
TIERCELS
TIERCERON
TIERCERONS
TIERCES
TIERCET
TIERCETS
TIERED
TIERING
TIEROD
TIERODS
TIERS
TIES
TIETAC
TIETACK
TIETACKS
TIETACS
TIFF
TIFFANIES
TIFFANY
TIFFED
TIFFIN
TIFFING
TIFFINGS
TIFFINS
TIFFS
TIFOSI
TIFOSO

The Chambers Dictionary is the authority for many longer words; see *OSW* Introduction, page xii.

TIFT	TILES	TIMERS	TINEAL	TINNIES
TIFTED	TILING	TIMES	TINEAS	TINNIEST
TIFTING	TILINGS	TIMESCALE	TINED	TINNING
TIFTS	TILL	TIMESCALES	TINEID	TINNINGS
TIG	TILLABLE	TIMETABLE	TINEIDS	TINNITUS
TIGE	TILLAGE	TIMETABLED	TINES	TINNITUSES
TIGER	TILLAGES	TIMETABLES	TINFOIL	TINNY
TIGERISH	TILLED	TIMETABLING	TINFOILS	TINPLATE
TIGERISM	TILLER	TIMID	TINFUL	TINPLATED
TIGERISMS	TILLERED	TIMIDER	TINFULS	TINPLATES
TIGERLY	TILLERING	TIMIDEST	TING	TINPLATING
TIGERS	TILLERS	TIMIDITIES	TINGE	TINPOT
TIGERY	TILLIER	TIMIDITY	TINGED	TINPOTS
TIGES	TILLIEST	TIMIDLY	TINGEING	TINS
TIGGED	TILLING	TIMIDNESS	TINGES	TINSEL
TIGGING	TILLINGS	TIMIDNESSES	TINGING	TINSELED
TIGHT	TILLITE	TIMING	TINGLE	TINSELING
TIGHTEN	TILLITES	TIMINGS	TINGLED	TINSELLED
TIGHTENED	TILLS	TIMIST	TINGLER	TINSELLING
TIGHTENER	TILLY	TIMISTS	TINGLERS	TINSELLY
TIGHTENERS	TILS	TIMOCRACIES	TINGLES	TINSELRIES
TIGHTENING	TILT	TIMOCRACY	TINGLIER	TINSELRY
TIGHTENS	TILTABLE	TIMON	TINGLIEST	TINSELS
TIGHTER	TILTED	TIMONEER	TINGLING	TINSEY
TIGHTEST	TILTER	TIMONEERS	TINGLINGS	TINSEYS
TIGHTISH	TILTERS	TIMONS	TINGLISH	TINSMITH
TIGHTLY	TILTH	TIMOROUS	TINGLY	TINSMITHS
TIGHTNESS	TILTHS	TIMORSOME	TINGS	TINSNIPS
TIGHTNESSES	TILTING	TIMOTHIES	TINGUAITE	TINSTONE
TIGHTROPE	TILTINGS	TIMOTHY	TINGUAITES	TINSTONES
TIGHTROPES	TILTS	TIMOUS	TINHORN	TINT
TIGHTS	TIMARAU	TIMOUSLY	TINHORNS	TINTACK
TIGHTWAD	TIMARAUS	TIMPANI	TINIER	TINTACKS
TIGHTWADS	TIMARIOT	TIMPANIST	TINIES	TINTED
TIGLON	TIMARIOTS	TIMPANISTS	TINIEST	TINTER
TIGLONS	TIMBAL	TIMPANO	TINILY	TINTERS
TIGON	TIMBALE	TIMPS	TININESS	TINTIER
TIGONS	TIMBALES	TIN	TININESSES	TINTIEST
TIGRESS	TIMBALS	TINAJA	TINING	TINTINESS
TIGRESSES	TIMBER	TINAJAS	TINK	TINTINESSES
TIGRINE	TIMBERED	TINAMOU	TINKED	TINTING
TIGRISH	TIMBERING	TINAMOUS	TINKER	TINTINGS
TIGRISHLY	TIMBERINGS	TINCAL	TINKERED	TINTLESS
TIGROID	TIMBERS	TINCALS	TINKERER	TINTS
TIGS	TIMBO	TINCHEL	TINKERERS	TINTY
TIKA	TIMBOS	TINCHELS	TINKERING	TINTYPE
TIKAS	TIMBRE	TINCT	TINKERINGS	TINTYPES
TIKE	TIMBREL	TINCTED	TINKERS	TINWARE
TIKES	TIMBRELS	TINCTING	TINKING	TINWARES
TIKI	TIMBRES	TINCTS	TINKLE	TINY
TIKIS	TIME	TINCTURE	TINKLED	TIP
TIKKA	TIMECARD	TINCTURED	TINKLER	TIPCAT
TIL	TIMECARDS	TINCTURES	TINKLERS	TIPCATS
TILAPIA	TIMED	TINCTURING	TINKLES	TIPI
TILAPIAS	TIMEFRAME	TIND	TINKLIER	TIPIS
TILBURIES	TIMEFRAMES	TINDAL	TINKLIEST	TIPPABLE
TILBURY	TIMELESS	TINDALS	TINKLING	TIPPED
TILDE	TIMELIER	TINDED	TINKLINGS	TIPPER
TILDES	TIMELIEST	TINDER	TINKLY	TIPPERS
TILE	TIMELY	TINDERBOX	TINKS	TIPPET
TILED	TIMENOGUY	TINDERBOXES	TINMAN	TIPPETS
TILEFISH	TIMENOGUYS	TINDERS	TINMEN	TIPPIER
TILEFISHES	TIMEOUS	TINDERY	TINNED	TIPPIEST
TILER	TIMEOUSLY	TINDING	TINNER	TIPPING
TILERIES	TIMEPIECE	TINDS	TINNERS	TIPPINGS
TILERS	TIMEPIECES	TINE	TINNIE	TIPPLE
TILERY	TIMER	TINEA	TINNIER	TIPPLED

The Chambers Dictionary is the authority for many longer words; see *OSW* Introduction, page xii.

TIPPLER	TIS	TITLERS	TITUPPING	TOCCATINAS
TIPPLERS	TISANE	TITLES	TITUPS	TOCHER
TIPPLES	TISANES	TITLING	TITUPY	TOCHERED
TIPPLING	TISICK	TITLINGS	TIZWAS	TOCHERING
TIPPY	TISICKS	TITMICE	TIZWASES	TOCHERS
TIPS	TISSUE	TITMOSE	TIZZ	TOCK
TIPSIER	TISSUED	TITMOUSE	TIZZES	TOCKED
TIPSIEST	TISSUES	TITOKI	TIZZIES	TOCKING
TIPSIFIED	TISSUING	TITOKIS	TIZZY	TOCKS
TIPSIFIES	TISWAS	TITRATE	TJANTING	TOCO
TIPSIFY	TISWASES	TITRATED	TJANTINGS	TOCOLOGIES
TIPSIFYING	TIT	TITRATES	TMESES	TOCOLOGY
TIPSILY	TITAN	TITRATING	TMESIS	TOCOS
TIPSINESS	TITANATE	TITRATION	TO	TOCS
TIPSINESSES	TITANATES	TITRATIONS	TOAD	TOCSIN
TIPSTAFF	TITANESS	TITRE	TOADFISH	TOCSINS
TIPSTAFFS	TITANESSES	TITRES	TOADFISHES	TOD
TIPSTAVES	TITANIC	TITS	TOADFLAX	TODAY
TIPSTER	TITANIS	TITTED	TOADFLAXES	TODAYS
TIPSTERS	TITANISES	TITTER	TOADGRASS	TODDE
TIPSY	TITANISM	TITTERED	TOADGRASSES	TODDED
TIPT	TITANISMS	TITTERER	TOADIED	TODDES
TIPTOE	TITANITE	TITTERERS	TOADIES	TODDIES
TIPTOED	TITANITES	TITTERING	TOADRUSH	TODDING
TIPTOEING	TITANIUM	TITTERINGS	TOADRUSHES	TODDLE
TIPTOES	TITANIUMS	TITTERS	TOADS	TODDLED
TIPTOP	TITANOUS	TITTIES	TOADSTONE	TODDLER
TIPTOPS	TITANS	TITTING	TOADSTONES	TODDLERS
TIPULA	TITBIT	TITTISH	TOADSTOOL	TODDLES
TIPULAS	TITBITS	TITTIVATE	TOADSTOOLS	TODDLING
TIRADE	TITCH	TITTIVATED	TOADY	TODDY
TIRADES	TITCHES	TITTIVATES	TOADYING	TODIES
TIRAMISU	TITCHIER	TITTIVATING	TOADYISH	TODS
TIRAMISUS	TITCHIEST	TITTLE	TOADYISM	TODY
TIRASSE	TITCHY	TITTLEBAT	TOADYISMS	TOE
TIRASSES	TITE	TITTLEBATS	TOAST	TOEA
TIRE	TITELY	TITTLED	TOASTED	TOEAS
TIRED	TITER	TITTLES	TOASTER	TOECAP
TIREDER	TITERS	TITTLING	TOASTERS	TOECAPS
TIREDEST	TITFER	TITTUP	TOASTIE	TOECLIP
TIREDLY	TITFERS	TITTUPED	TOASTIES	TOECLIPS
TIREDNESS	TITHABLE	TITTUPING	TOASTING	TOED
TIREDNESSES	TITHE	TITTUPPED	TOASTINGS	TOEHOLD
TIRELESS	TITHED	TITTUPPING	TOASTS	TOEHOLDS
TIRELING	TITHER	TITTUPS	TOASTY	TOEIER
TIRELINGS	TITHERS	TITTUPY	TOAZE	TOEIEST
TIRES	TITHES	TITTY	TOAZED	TOEING
TIRESOME	TITHING	TITUBANCIES	TOAZES	TOELESS
TIRING	TITHINGS	TITUBANCY	TOAZING	TOENAIL
TIRINGS	TITI	TITUBANT	TOBACCO	TOENAILS
TIRL	TITIAN	TITUBATE	TOBACCOES	TOERAG
TIRLED	TITIANS	TITUBATED	TOBACCOS	TOERAGGER
TIRLING	TITILLATE	TITUBATES	TOBIES	TOERAGGERS
TIRLS	TITILLATED	TITUBATING	TOBOGGAN	TOERAGS
TIRO	TITILLATES	TITULAR	TOBOGGANED	TOES
TIROES	TITILLATING	TITULARIES	TOBOGGANING	TOETOE
TIROS	TITIS	TITULARLY	TOBOGGANINGS	TOETOES
TIRR	TITIVATE	TITULARS	TOBOGGANS	TOEY
TIRRED	TITIVATED	TITULARY	TOBOGGIN	TOFF
TIRRING	TITIVATES	TITULE	TOBOGGINED	TOFFEE
TIRRIT	TITIVATING	TITULED	TOBOGGINING	TOFFEES
TIRRITS	TITLARK	TITULES	TOBOGGINS	TOFFIER
TIRRIVEE	TITLARKS	TITULING	TOBY	TOFFIES
TIRRIVEES	TITLE	TITUP	TOC	TOFFIEST
TIRRIVIE	TITLED	TITUPED	TOCCATA	TOFFISH
TIRRIVIES	TITLELESS	TITUPING	TOCCATAS	TOFFS
TIRRS	TITLER	TITUPPED	TOCCATINA	TOFFY

The Chambers Dictionary is the authority for many longer words; see *OSW* Introduction, page xii.

TOFORE	TOKAYS	TOLTS	TOMMY	TONIGHTS
TOFT	TOKE	TOLU	TOMMYING	TONING
TOFTS	TOKED	TOLUATE	TOMOGRAM	TONINGS
TOFU	TOKEN	TOLUATES	TOMOGRAMS	TONISH
TOFUS	TOKENED	TOLUENE	TOMOGRAPH	TONISHLY
TOG	TOKENING	TOLUENES	TOMOGRAPHS	TONITE
TOGA	TOKENISM	TOLUIC	TOMORROW	TONITES
TOGAED	TOKENISMS	TOLUIDINE	TOMORROWS	TONK
TOGAS	TOKENS	TOLUIDINES	TOMPION	TONKED
TOGATE	TOKES	TOLUOL	TOMPIONS	TONKER
TOGATED	TOKING	TOLUOLS	TOMPON	TONKERS
TOGE	TOKO	TOLUS	TOMPONED	TONKING
TOGED	TOKOLOGIES	TOLZEY	TOMPONING	TONKS
TOGES	TOKOLOGY	TOLZEYS	TOMPONS	TONLET
TOGETHER	TOKOLOSHE	TOM	TOMS	TONLETS
TOGGED	TOKOLOSHES	TOMAHAWK	TOMTIT	TONNAG
TOGGERIES	TOKOS	TOMAHAWKED	TOMTITS	TONNAGE
TOGGERY	TOLA	TOMAHAWKING	TON	TONNAGES
TOGGING	TOLAS	TOMAHAWKS	TONAL	TONNAGS
TOGGLE	TOLBOOTH	TOMALLEY	TONALITE	TONNE
TOGGLED	TOLBOOTHS	TOMALLEYS	TONALITES	TONNEAU
TOGGLES	TOLD	TOMAN	TONALITIES	TONNEAUS
TOGGLING	TOLE	TOMANS	TONALITY	TONNEAUX
TOGS	TOLED	TOMATILLO	TONALLY	TONNELL
TOGUE	TOLERABLE	TOMATILLOES	TONANT	TONNELLS
TOGUES	TOLERABLY	TOMATILLOS	TONDI	TONNES
TOHEROA	TOLERANCE	TOMATO	TONDINI	TONNISH
TOHEROAS	TOLERANCES	TOMATOES	TONDINO	TONNISHLY
TOHO	TOLERANT	TOMATOEY	TONDINOS	TONOMETER
TOHOS	TOLERATE	TOMB	TONDO	TONOMETERS
TOHUNGA	TOLERATED	TOMBAC	TONDOS	TONOMETRIES
TOHUNGAS	TOLERATES	TOMBACS	TONE	TONOMETRY
TOIL	TOLERATING	TOMBAK	TONED	TONS
TOILE	TOLERATOR	TOMBAKS	TONELESS	TONSIL
TOILED	TOLERATORS	TOMBED	TONEME	TONSILLAR
TOILER	TOLES	TOMBIC	TONEMES	TONSILS
TOILERS	TOLEWARE	TOMBING	TONEMIC	TONSOR
TOILES	TOLEWARES	TOMBLESS	TONEPAD	TONSORIAL
TOILET	TOLING	TOMBOC	TONEPADS	TONSORS
TOILETED	TOLINGS	TOMBOCS	TONER	TONSURE
TOILETING	TOLL	TOMBOLA	TONERS	TONSURED
TOILETRIES	TOLLABLE	TOMBOLAS	TONES	TONSURES
TOILETRY	TOLLAGE	TOMBOLO	TONETIC	TONSURING
TOILETS	TOLLAGES	TOMBOLOS	TONEY	TONTINE
TOILETTE	TOLLBOOTH	TOMBOY	TONG	TONTINER
TOILETTES	TOLLBOOTHS	TOMBOYISH	TONGA	TONTINERS
TOILFUL	TOLLDISH	TOMBOYS	TONGAS	TONTINES
TOILINET	TOLLDISHES	TOMBS	TONGED	TONUS
TOILINETS	TOLLED	TOMBSTONE	TONGING	TONUSES
TOILING	TOLLER	TOMBSTONES	TONGS	TONY
TOILINGS	TOLLERS	TOMCAT	TONGSTER	TOO
TOILLESS	TOLLHOUSE	TOMCATS	TONGSTERS	TOOART
TOILS	TOLLHOUSES	TOME	TONGUE	TOOARTS
TOILSOME	TOLLING	TOMENTA	TONGUED	TOOK
TOISE	TOLLINGS	TOMENTOSE	TONGUELET	TOOL
TOISEACH	TOLLMAN	TOMENTOUS	TONGUELETS	TOOLBAG
TOISEACHS	TOLLMEN	TOMENTUM	TONGUES	TOOLBAGS
TOISECH	TOLLS	TOMES	TONGUING	TOOLBAR
TOISECHS	TOLSEL	TOMFOOL	TONGUINGS	TOOLBARS
TOISES	TOLSELS	TOMFOOLED	TONIC	TOOLBOX
TOISON	TOLSEY	TOMFOOLING	TONICITIES	TOOLBOXES
TOISONS	TOLSEYS	TOMFOOLS	TONICITY	TOOLED
TOITOI	TOLT	TOMIA	TONICS	TOOLER
TOITOIS	TOLTER	TOMIAL	TONIER	TOOLERS
TOKAMAK	TOLTERED	TOMIUM	TONIES	TOOLHOUSE
TOKAMAKS	TOLTERING	TOMMIED	TONIEST	TOOLHOUSES
TOKAY	TOLTERS	TOMMIES	TONIGHT	TOOLING

The Chambers Dictionary is the authority for many longer words; see *OSW* Introduction, page xii.

TOOLINGS
TOOLKIT
TOOLKITS
TOOLMAKER
TOOLMAKERS
TOOLMAN
TOOLMEN
TOOLROOM
TOOLROOMS
TOOLS
TOOM
TOOMED
TOOMER
TOOMEST
TOOMING
TOOMS
TOON
TOONS
TOORIE
TOORIES
TOOT
TOOTED
TOOTER
TOOTERS
TOOTH
TOOTHACHE
TOOTHACHES
TOOTHCOMB
TOOTHCOMBS
TOOTHED
TOOTHFUL
TOOTHFULS
TOOTHIER
TOOTHIEST
TOOTHILY
TOOTHING
TOOTHLESS
TOOTHLIKE
TOOTHPICK
TOOTHPICKS
TOOTHS
TOOTHSOME
TOOTHWASH
TOOTHWASHES
TOOTHWORT
TOOTHWORTS
TOOTHY
TOOTING
TOOTLE
TOOTLED
TOOTLES
TOOTLING
TOOTS
TOOTSED
TOOTSES
TOOTSIE
TOOTSIES
TOOTSING
TOOTSY
TOP
TOPARCH
TOPARCHIES
TOPARCHS
TOPARCHY
TOPAZ
TOPAZES
TOPAZINE

TOPCOAT
TOPCOATS
TOPE
TOPECTOMIES
TOPECTOMY
TOPED
TOPEE
TOPEES
TOPEK
TOPEKS
TOPER
TOPERS
TOPES
TOPFULL
TOPHI
TOPHUS
TOPI
TOPIARIAN
TOPIARIES
TOPIARIST
TOPIARISTS
TOPIARY
TOPIC
TOPICAL
TOPICALLY
TOPICS
TOPING
TOPIS
TOPKNOT
TOPKNOTS
TOPLESS
TOPLINE
TOPLINED
TOPLINER
TOPLINERS
TOPLINES
TOPLINING
TOPLOFTY
TOPMAKER
TOPMAKERS
TOPMAKING
TOPMAKINGS
TOPMAN
TOPMAST
TOPMASTS
TOPMEN
TOPMINNOW
TOPMINNOWS
TOPMOST
TOPOI
TOPOLOGIC
TOPOLOGIES
TOPOLOGY
TOPONYM
TOPONYMAL
TOPONYMIC
TOPONYMICS
TOPONYMIES
TOPONYMS
TOPONYMY
TOPOS
TOPOTYPE
TOPOTYPES
TOPPED
TOPPER
TOPPERS
TOPPING

TOPPINGLY
TOPPINGS
TOPPLE
TOPPLED
TOPPLES
TOPPLING
TOPS
TOPSAIL
TOPSAILS
TOPSIDE
TOPSIDES
TOPSMAN
TOPSMEN
TOPSOIL
TOPSOILS
TOPSPIN
TOPSPINS
TOQUE
TOQUES
TOQUILLA
TOQUILLAS
TOR
TORAN
TORANA
TORANAS
TORANS
TORBANITE
TORBANITES
TORC
TORCH
TORCHED
TORCHER
TORCHERE
TORCHERES
TORCHERS
TORCHES
TORCHIER
TORCHIERE
TORCHIERES
TORCHIERS
TORCHING
TORCHINGS
TORCHON
TORCHONS
TORCHWOOD
TORCHWOODS
TORCS
TORCULAR
TORCULARS
TORDION
TORDIONS
TORE
TOREADOR
TOREADORS
TORERO
TOREROS
TORES
TOREUTIC
TOREUTICS
TORGOCH
TORGOCHS
TORI
TORIC
TORII
TORMENT
TORMENTA
TORMENTED

TORMENTER
TORMENTERS
TORMENTIL
TORMENTILS
TORMENTING
TORMENTINGS
TORMENTOR
TORMENTORS
TORMENTS
TORMENTUM
TORMENTUMS
TORMINA
TORMINAL
TORMINOUS
TORN
TORNADE
TORNADES
TORNADIC
TORNADO
TORNADOES
TORNADOS
TOROID
TOROIDAL
TOROIDS
TOROSE
TOROUS
TORPEDO
TORPEDOED
TORPEDOER
TORPEDOERS
TORPEDOES
TORPEDOING
TORPEDOS
TORPEFIED
TORPEFIES
TORPEFY
TORPEFYING
TORPID
TORPIDITIES
TORPIDITY
TORPIDLY
TORPIDS
TORPITUDE
TORPITUDES
TORPOR
TORPORS
TORQUATE
TORQUATED
TORQUE
TORQUED
TORQUES
TORR
TORREFIED
TORREFIES
TORREFY
TORREFYING
TORRENT
TORRENTS
TORRET
TORRETS
TORRID
TORRIDER
TORRIDEST
TORRIDITIES
TORRIDITY
TORRIDLY
TORRS

TORS
TORSADE
TORSADES
TORSE
TORSEL
TORSELS
TORSES
TORSI
TORSION
TORSIONAL
TORSIONS
TORSIVE
TORSK
TORSKS
TORSO
TORSOS
TORT
TORTE
TORTEN
TORTES
TORTILE
TORTILITIES
TORTILITY
TORTILLA
TORTILLAS
TORTIOUS
TORTIVE
TORTOISE
TORTOISES
TORTONI
TORTONIS
TORTRICES
TORTRICID
TORTRICIDS
TORTRIX
TORTS
TORTUOUS
TORTURE
TORTURED
TORTURER
TORTURERS
TORTURES
TORTURING
TORTURINGS
TORTUROUS
TORUFFLED
TORULA
TORULAE
TORULI
TORULIN
TORULINS
TORULOSE
TORULOSES
TORULOSIS
TORULUS
TORUS
TOSA
TOSAS
TOSE
TOSED
TOSES
TOSH
TOSHACH
TOSHACHS
TOSHED
TOSHER
TOSHERS

The Chambers Dictionary is the authority for many longer words; see *OSW* Introduction, page xii.

TOSHES	TOTTER	TOUPEE	TOVARISCH	TOWNSCAPING
TOSHIER	TOTTERED	TOUPEES	TOVARISCHES	TOWNSCAPINGS
TOSHIEST	TOTTERER	TOUPET	TOVARISH	TOWNSFOLK
TOSHING	TOTTERERS	TOUPETS	TOVARISHES	TOWNSFOLKS
TOSHY	TOTTERING	TOUR	TOW	TOWNSHIP
TOSING	TOTTERINGS	TOURACO	TOWABLE	TOWNSHIPS
TOSS	TOTTERS	TOURACOS	TOWAGE	TOWNSKIP
TOSSED	TOTTERY	TOURED	TOWAGES	TOWNSKIPS
TOSSEN	TOTTIE	TOURER	TOWARD	TOWNSMAN
TOSSER	TOTTIER	TOURERS	TOWARDLY	TOWNSMEN
TOSSERS	TOTTIES	TOURIE	TOWARDS	TOWNY
TOSSES	TOTTIEST	TOURIES	TOWBAR	TOWPATH
TOSSIER	TOTTING	TOURING	TOWBARS	TOWPATHS
TOSSIEST	TOTTINGS	TOURINGS	TOWBOAT	TOWROPE
TOSSILY	TOTTY	TOURISM	TOWBOATS	TOWROPES
TOSSING	TOUCAN	TOURISMS	TOWED	TOWS
TOSSINGS	TOUCANET	TOURIST	TOWEL	TOWSE
TOSSPOT	TOUCANETS	TOURISTIC	TOWELED	TOWSED
TOSSPOTS	TOUCANS	TOURISTS	TOWELING	TOWSER
TOSSY	TOUCH	TOURISTY	TOWELLED	TOWSERS
TOST	TOUCHABLE	TOURNEDOS	TOWELLING	TOWSES
TOSTADA	TOUCHBACK	TOURNEY	TOWELLINGS	TOWSIER
TOSTADAS	TOUCHBACKS	TOURNEYED	TOWELS	TOWSIEST
TOT	TOUCHDOWN	TOURNEYER	TOWER	TOWSING
TOTAL	TOUCHDOWNS	TOURNEYERS	TOWERED	TOWSY
TOTALISE	TOUCHE	TOURNEYING	TOWERIER	TOWT
TOTALISED	TOUCHED	TOURNEYS	TOWERIEST	TOWTED
TOTALISER	TOUCHER	TOURNURE	TOWERING	TOWTING
TOTALISERS	TOUCHERS	TOURNURES	TOWERLESS	TOWTS
TOTALISES	TOUCHES	TOURS	TOWERS	TOWY
TOTALISING	TOUCHIER	TOUSE	TOWERY	TOWZE
TOTALITIES	TOUCHIEST	TOUSED	TOWHEE	TOWZED
TOTALITY	TOUCHILY	TOUSER	TOWHEES	TOWZES
TOTALIZE	TOUCHING	TOUSERS	TOWIER	TOWZIER
TOTALIZED	TOUCHINGS	TOUSES	TOWIEST	TOWZIEST
TOTALIZER	TOUCHLESS	TOUSIER	TOWING	TOWZING
TOTALIZERS	TOUCHLINE	TOUSIEST	TOWINGS	TOWZY
TOTALIZES	TOUCHLINES	TOUSING	TOWLINE	TOXAEMIA
TOTALIZING	TOUCHMARK	TOUSINGS	TOWLINES	TOXAEMIAS
TOTALLED	TOUCHMARKS	TOUSLE	TOWMON	TOXAEMIC
TOTALLING	TOUCHTONE	TOUSLED	TOWMOND	TOXAPHENE
TOTALLY	TOUCHWOOD	TOUSLES	TOWMONDS	TOXAPHENES
TOTALS	TOUCHWOODS	TOUSLING	TOWMONS	TOXEMIA
TOTANUS	TOUCHY	TOUSTIE	TOWMONT	TOXEMIAS
TOTANUSES	TOUGH	TOUSY	TOWMONTS	TOXEMIC
TOTAQUINE	TOUGHEN	TOUT	TOWN	TOXIC
TOTAQUINES	TOUGHENED	TOUTED	TOWNEE	TOXICAL
TOTARA	TOUGHENER	TOUTER	TOWNEES	TOXICALLY
TOTARAS	TOUGHENERS	TOUTERS	TOWNHOUSE	TOXICANT
TOTE	TOUGHENING	TOUTIE	TOWNHOUSES	TOXICANTS
TOTED	TOUGHENINGS	TOUTIER	TOWNIE	TOXICITIES
TOTEM	TOUGHENS	TOUTIEST	TOWNIER	TOXICITY
TOTEMIC	TOUGHER	TOUTING	TOWNIES	TOXIN
TOTEMISM	TOUGHEST	TOUTS	TOWNIEST	TOXINS
TOTEMISMS	TOUGHIE	TOUZE	TOWNISH	TOXOCARA
TOTEMIST	TOUGHIES	TOUZED	TOWNLAND	TOXOCARAS
TOTEMISTS	TOUGHISH	TOUZES	TOWNLANDS	TOXOID
TOTEMS	TOUGHLY	TOUZIER	TOWNLESS	TOXOIDS
TOTES	TOUGHNESS	TOUZIEST	TOWNLIER	TOXOPHILIES
TOTHER	TOUGHNESSES	TOUZING	TOWNLIEST	TOXOPHILY
TOTIENT	TOUGHS	TOUZLE	TOWNLING	TOY
TOTIENTS	TOUK	TOUZLED	TOWNLINGS	TOYED
TOTING	TOUKED	TOUZLES	TOWNLY	TOYER
TOTITIVE	TOUKING	TOUZLING	TOWNS	TOYERS
TOTITIVES	TOUKS	TOUZY	TOWNSCAPE	TOYING
TOTS	TOUN	TOVARICH	TOWNSCAPED	TOYINGS
TOTTED	TOUNS	TOVARICHES	TOWNSCAPES	TOYISH

The Chambers Dictionary is the authority for many longer words; see *OSW* Introduction, page xii.

TOYISHLY	TRACKMAN	TRAGEDY	TRAMMELS	TRANSECTS
TOYLESOME	TRACKMEN	TRAGELAPH	TRAMMING	TRANSENNA
TOYLESS	TRACKROAD	TRAGELAPHS	TRAMP	TRANSENNAS
TOYLIKE	TRACKROADS	TRAGI	TRAMPED	TRANSEPT
TOYLSOM	TRACKS	TRAGIC	TRAMPER	TRANSEPTS
TOYMAN	TRACKWAY	TRAGICAL	TRAMPERS	TRANSES
TOYMEN	TRACKWAYS	TRAGOPAN	TRAMPET	TRANSEUNT
TOYS	TRACT	TRAGOPANS	TRAMPETS	TRANSFARD
TOYSHOP	TRACTABLE	TRAGULE	TRAMPETTE	TRANSFECT
TOYSHOPS	TRACTABLY	TRAGULES	TRAMPETTES	TRANSFECTED
TOYSOME	TRACTATE	TRAGULINE	TRAMPING	TRANSFECTING
TOYWOMAN	TRACTATES	TRAGUS	TRAMPINGS	TRANSFECTS
TOYWOMEN	TRACTATOR	TRAHISON	TRAMPISH	TRANSFER
TOZE	TRACTATORS	TRAHISONS	TRAMPLE	TRANSFERRED
TOZED	TRACTED	TRAIK	TRAMPLED	TRANSFERRING
TOZES	TRACTILE	TRAIKED	TRAMPLER	TRANSFERS
TOZIE	TRACTING	TRAIKING	TRAMPLERS	TRANSFIX
TOZIES	TRACTION	TRAIKIT	TRAMPLES	TRANSFIXED
TOZING	TRACTIONS	TRAIKS	TRAMPLING	TRANSFIXES
TRABEATE	TRACTIVE	TRAIL	TRAMPLINGS	TRANSFIXING
TRABEATED	TRACTOR	TRAILABLE	TRAMPOLIN	TRANSFORM
TRABECULA	TRACTORS	TRAILED	TRAMPOLINED	TRANSFORMED
TRABECULAE	TRACTRICES	TRAILER	TRAMPOLINING	TRANSFORMING
TRACE	TRACTRIX	TRAILERED	TRAMPOLINS	TRANSFORMINGS
TRACEABLE	TRACTS	TRAILERING	TRAMPS	TRANSFORMS
TRACEABLY	TRACTUS	TRAILERS	TRAMROAD	TRANSFUSE
TRACED	TRACTUSES	TRAILING	TRAMROADS	TRANSFUSED
TRACELESS	TRAD	TRAILS	TRAMS	TRANSFUSES
TRACER	TRADABLE	TRAIN	TRAMWAY	TRANSFUSING
TRACERIED	TRADE	TRAINABLE	TRAMWAYS	TRANSHIP
TRACERIES	TRADEABLE	TRAINBAND	TRANCE	TRANSHIPPED
TRACERS	TRADED	TRAINBANDS	TRANCED	TRANSHIPPING
TRACERY	TRADEFUL	TRAINED	TRANCEDLY	TRANSHIPPINGS
TRACES	TRADELESS	TRAINEE	TRANCES	TRANSHIPS
TRACHEA	TRADEMARK	TRAINEES	TRANCHE	TRANSHUME
TRACHEAE	TRADEMARKS	TRAINER	TRANCHES	TRANSHUMED
TRACHEAL	TRADENAME	TRAINERS	TRANCHET	TRANSHUMES
TRACHEARIES	TRADENAMES	TRAINING	TRANCHETS	TRANSHUMING
TRACHEARY	TRADER	TRAININGS	TRANCING	TRANSIENT
TRACHEATE	TRADERS	TRAINLESS	TRANECT	TRANSIENTS
TRACHEID	TRADES	TRAINS	TRANECTS	TRANSIRE
TRACHEIDE	TRADESMAN	TRAIPSE	TRANGAM	TRANSIRES
TRACHEIDES	TRADESMEN	TRAIPSED	TRANGAMS	TRANSIT
TRACHEIDS	TRADING	TRAIPSES	TRANGLE	TRANSITED
TRACHINUS	TRADINGS	TRAIPSING	TRANGLES	TRANSITING
TRACHINUSES	TRADITION	TRAIPSINGS	TRANKUM	TRANSITS
TRACHITIS	TRADITIONS	TRAIT	TRANKUMS	TRANSLATE
TRACHITISES	TRADITIVE	TRAITOR	TRANNIE	TRANSLATED
TRACHOMA	TRADITOR	TRAITORLY	TRANNIES	TRANSLATES
TRACHOMAS	TRADITORES	TRAITORS	TRANNY	TRANSLATING
TRACHYTE	TRADITORS	TRAITRESS	TRANQUIL	TRANSMEW
TRACHYTES	TRADS	TRAITRESSES	TRANQUILLER	TRANSMEWED
TRACHYTIC	TRADUCE	TRAITS	TRANQUILLEST	TRANSMEWING
TRACING	TRADUCED	TRAJECT	TRANSACT	TRANSMEWS
TRACINGS	TRADUCER	TRAJECTED	TRANSACTED	TRANSMIT
TRACK	TRADUCERS	TRAJECTING	TRANSACTING	TRANSMITS
TRACKABLE	TRADUCES	TRAJECTS	TRANSACTS	TRANSMITTED
TRACKAGE	TRADUCING	TRAM	TRANSAXLE	TRANSMITTING
TRACKAGES	TRADUCINGS	TRAMCAR	TRANSAXLES	TRANSMOVE
TRACKBALL	TRAFFIC	TRAMCARS	TRANSCEND	TRANSMOVED
TRACKBALLS	TRAFFICKED	TRAMLINE	TRANSCENDED	TRANSMOVES
TRACKED	TRAFFICKING	TRAMLINED	TRANSCENDING	TRANSMOVING
TRACKER	TRAFFICKINGS	TRAMLINES	TRANSCENDS	TRANSMUTE
TRACKERS	TRAFFICS	TRAMMED	TRANSE	TRANSMUTED
TRACKING	TRAGEDIAN	TRAMMEL	TRANSECT	TRANSMUTES
TRACKINGS	TRAGEDIANS	TRAMMELLED	TRANSECTED	TRANSMUTING
TRACKLESS	TRAGEDIES	TRAMMELLING	TRANSECTING	TRANSOM

The Chambers Dictionary is the authority for many longer words; see *OSW* Introduction, page xii.

TRANSOMS	TRAPEZOID	TRAVELOG	TREAGUE	TREGETOUR
TRANSONIC	TRAPEZOIDS	TRAVELOGS	TREAGUES	TREGETOURS
TRANSONICS	TRAPING	TRAVELS	TREASON	TREHALA
TRANSPIRE	TRAPLIKE	TRAVERSAL	TREASONS	TREHALAS
TRANSPIRED	TRAPPEAN	TRAVERSALS	TREASURE	TREIF
TRANSPIRES	TRAPPED	TRAVERSE	TREASURED	TREILLAGE
TRANSPIRING	TRAPPER	TRAVERSED	TREASURER	TREILLAGES
TRANSPORT	TRAPPERS	TRAVERSER	TREASURERS	TREILLE
TRANSPORTED	TRAPPIER	TRAVERSERS	TREASURES	TREILLES
TRANSPORTING	TRAPPIEST	TRAVERSES	TREASURIES	TREK
TRANSPORTINGS	TRAPPING	TRAVERSING	TREASURING	TREKKED
TRANSPORTS	TRAPPINGS	TRAVERSINGS	TREASURY	TREKKER
TRANSPOSE	TRAPPY	TRAVERTIN	TREAT	TREKKERS
TRANSPOSED	TRAPROCK	TRAVERTINS	TREATABLE	TREKKING
TRANSPOSES	TRAPROCKS	TRAVES	TREATED	TREKS
TRANSPOSING	TRAPS	TRAVESTIED	TREATER	TRELLIS
TRANSPOSINGS	TRAPUNTO	TRAVESTIES	TREATERS	TRELLISED
TRANSSHIP	TRAPUNTOS	TRAVESTY	TREATIES	TRELLISES
TRANSSHIPPED	TRASH	TRAVESTYING	TREATING	TRELLISING
TRANSSHIPPING	TRASHCAN	TRAVIS	TREATINGS	TREMA
TRANSSHIPPINGS	TRASHCANS	TRAVISES	TREATISE	TREMAS
TRANSSHIPS	TRASHED	TRAVOIS	TREATISES	TREMATIC
TRANSUDE	TRASHERIES	TRAWL	TREATMENT	TREMATODE
TRANSUDED	TRASHERY	TRAWLED	TREATMENTS	TREMATODES
TRANSUDES	TRASHES	TRAWLER	TREATS	TREMATOID
TRANSUDING	TRASHIER	TRAWLERS	TREATY	TREMATOIDS
TRANSUME	TRASHIEST	TRAWLING	TREBLE	TREMBLANT
TRANSUMED	TRASHILY	TRAWLINGS	TREBLED	TREMBLE
TRANSUMES	TRASHING	TRAWLS	TREBLES	TREMBLED
TRANSUMING	TRASHMAN	TRAY	TREBLING	TREMBLER
TRANSUMPT	TRASHMEN	TRAYBIT	TREBLY	TREMBLERS
TRANSUMPTS	TRASHTRIE	TRAYBITS	TREBUCHET	TREMBLES
TRANSVEST	TRASHTRIES	TRAYFUL	TREBUCHETS	TREMBLIER
TRANSVESTED	TRASHY	TRAYFULS	TRECENTO	TREMBLIEST
TRANSVESTING	TRASS	TRAYNE	TRECENTOS	TREMBLING
TRANSVESTS	TRASSES	TRAYNED	TRECK	TREMBLINGS
TRANT	TRAT	TRAYNES	TRECKED	TREMBLY
TRANTED	TRATS	TRAYNING	TRECKING	TREMIE
TRANTER	TRATT	TRAYS	TRECKS	TREMIES
TRANTERS	TRATTORIA	TREACHER	TREDDLE	TREMOLANT
TRANTING	TRATTORIAS	TREACHERIES	TREDDLED	TREMOLANTS
TRANTS	TRATTORIE	TREACHERS	TREDDLES	TREMOLITE
TRAP	TRATTS	TREACHERY	TREDDLING	TREMOLITES
TRAPAN	TRAUCHLE	TREACHOUR	TREDILLE	TREMOLO
TRAPANNED	TRAUCHLED	TREACHOURS	TREDILLES	TREMOLOS
TRAPANNING	TRAUCHLES	TREACLE	TREDRILLE	TREMOR
TRAPANS	TRAUCHLING	TREACLED	TREDRILLES	TREMORED
TRAPDOOR	TRAUMA	TREACLES	TREE	TREMORING
TRAPDOORS	TRAUMAS	TREACLIER	TREED	TREMORS
TRAPE	TRAUMATA	TREACLIEST	TREEING	TREMULANT
TRAPED	TRAUMATIC	TREACLING	TREELESS	TREMULANTS
TRAPES	TRAVAIL	TREACLY	TREEN	TREMULATE
TRAPESED	TRAVAILED	TREAD	TREENAIL	TREMULATED
TRAPESES	TRAVAILING	TREADER	TREENAILS	TREMULATES
TRAPESING	TRAVAILS	TREADERS	TREENS	TREMULATING
TRAPESINGS	TRAVE	TREADING	TREENWARE	TREMULOUS
TRAPEZE	TRAVEL	TREADINGS	TREENWARES	TRENAIL
TRAPEZED	TRAVELED	TREADLE	TREES	TRENAILS
TRAPEZES	TRAVELER	TREADLED	TREESHIP	TRENCH
TRAPEZIA	TRAVELERS	TREADLER	TREESHIPS	TRENCHAND
TRAPEZIAL	TRAVELING	TREADLERS	TREETOP	TRENCHANT
TRAPEZII	TRAVELINGS	TREADLES	TREETOPS	TRENCHARD
TRAPEZING	TRAVELLED	TREADLING	TREF	TRENCHARDS
TRAPEZIUM	TRAVELLER	TREADLINGS	TREFA	TRENCHED
TRAPEZIUMS	TRAVELLERS	TREADMILL	TREFOIL	TRENCHER
TRAPEZIUS	TRAVELLING	TREADMILLS	TREFOILED	TRENCHERS
TRAPEZIUSES	TRAVELLINGS	TREADS	TREFOILS	TRENCHES

The Chambers Dictionary is the authority for many longer words; see *OSW* Introduction, page xii.

TRENCHING	TREVISS	TRIBASIC	TRICKLET	TRIFFER
TREND	TREVISSES	TRIBBLE	TRICKLETS	TRIFFEST
TRENDED	TREW	TRIBBLES	TRICKLIER	TRIFFIC
TRENDIER	TREWS	TRIBE	TRICKLIEST	TRIFFID
TRENDIES	TREWSMAN	TRIBELESS	TRICKLING	TRIFFIDS
TRENDIEST	TREWSMEN	TRIBES	TRICKLINGS	TRIFFIDY
TRENDILY	TREY	TRIBESMAN	TRICKLY	TRIFID
TRENDING	TREYBIT	TRIBESMEN	TRICKS	TRIFLE
TRENDS	TREYBITS	TRIBLET	TRICKSIER	TRIFLED
TRENDY	TREYS	TRIBLETS	TRICKSIEST	TRIFLER
TRENDYISM	TREZ	TRIBOLOGIES	TRICKSOME	TRIFLERS
TRENDYISMS	TREZES	TRIBOLOGY	TRICKSTER	TRIFLES
TRENISE	TRIABLE	TRIBRACH	TRICKSTERS	TRIFLING
TRENISES	TRIACID	TRIBRACHS	TRICKSY	TRIFOCAL
TRENTAL	TRIACT	TRIBUNAL	TRICKY	TRIFOCALS
TRENTALS	TRIACTINE	TRIBUNALS	TRICLINIA	TRIFOLIES
TREPAN	TRIAD	TRIBUNATE	TRICLINIC	TRIFOLIUM
TREPANG	TRIADIC	TRIBUNATES	TRICOLOR	TRIFOLIUMS
TREPANGS	TRIADIST	TRIBUNE	TRICOLORS	TRIFOLY
TREPANNED	TRIADISTS	TRIBUNES	TRICOLOUR	TRIFORIA
TREPANNER	TRIADS	TRIBUTARIES	TRICOLOURS	TRIFORIUM
TREPANNERS	TRIAGE	TRIBUTARY	TRICORN	TRIFORM
TREPANNING	TRIAGES	TRIBUTE	TRICORNE	TRIFORMED
TREPANNINGS	TRIAL	TRIBUTER	TRICORNES	TRIG
TREPANS	TRIALISM	TRIBUTERS	TRICORNS	TRIGAMIES
TREPHINE	TRIALISMS	TRIBUTES	TRICOT	TRIGAMIST
TREPHINED	TRIALIST	TRICAR	TRICOTS	TRIGAMISTS
TREPHINER	TRIALISTS	TRICARS	TRICROTIC	TRIGAMOUS
TREPHINERS	TRIALITIES	TRICE	TRICUSPID	TRIGAMY
TREPHINES	TRIALITY	TRICED	TRICYCLE	TRIGGED
TREPHINING	TRIALLED	TRICEPS	TRICYCLED	TRIGGER
TREPID	TRIALLING	TRICEPSES	TRICYCLER	TRIGGERED
TREPIDANT	TRIALLIST	TRICERION	TRICYCLERS	TRIGGERING
TREPIDER	TRIALLISTS	TRICERIONS	TRICYCLES	TRIGGERS
TREPIDEST	TRIALOGUE	TRICES	TRICYCLIC	TRIGGEST
TREPONEMA	TRIALOGUES	TRICHINA	TRICYCLING	TRIGGING
TREPONEMAS	TRIALS	TRICHINAE	TRICYCLINGS	TRIGLOT
TREPONEMATA	TRIANGLE	TRICHINAS	TRIDACNA	TRIGLOTS
TREPONEME	TRIANGLED	TRICHITE	TRIDACNAS	TRIGLY
TREPONEMES	TRIANGLES	TRICHITES	TRIDACTYL	TRIGLYPH
TRES	TRIAPSAL	TRICHITIC	TRIDARN	TRIGLYPHS
TRESPASS	TRIARCH	TRICHOID	TRIDARNS	TRIGNESS
TRESPASSED	TRIARCHIES	TRICHOME	TRIDE	TRIGNESSES
TRESPASSES	TRIARCHS	TRICHOMES	TRIDENT	TRIGON
TRESPASSING	TRIARCHY	TRICHORD	TRIDENTAL	TRIGONAL
TRESS	TRIATHLON	TRICHORDS	TRIDENTED	TRIGONIC
TRESSED	TRIATHLONS	TRICHOSES	TRIDENTS	TRIGONOUS
TRESSEL	TRIATIC	TRICHOSIS	TRIDUAN	TRIGONS
TRESSELS	TRIATICS	TRICHROIC	TRIDUUM	TRIGRAM
TRESSES	TRIATOMIC	TRICHROME	TRIDUUMS	TRIGRAMS
TRESSIER	TRIAXIAL	TRICING	TRIDYMITE	TRIGRAPH
TRESSIEST	TRIAXIALS	TRICK	TRIDYMITES	TRIGRAPHS
TRESSING	TRIAXON	TRICKED	TRIE	TRIGS
TRESSURE	TRIAXONS	TRICKER	TRIECIOUS	TRIGYNIAN
TRESSURED	TRIBADE	TRICKERIES	TRIED	TRIGYNOUS
TRESSURES	TRIBADES	TRICKERS	TRIENNIAL	TRIHEDRAL
TRESSY	TRIBADIC	TRICKERY	TRIER	TRIHEDRALS
TREST	TRIBADIES	TRICKIER	TRIERARCH	TRIHEDRON
TRESTLE	TRIBADISM	TRICKIEST	TRIERARCHS	TRIHEDRONS
TRESTLES	TRIBADISMS	TRICKILY	TRIERS	TRIHYBRID
TRESTS	TRIBADY	TRICKING	TRIES	TRIHYBRIDS
TRET	TRIBAL	TRICKINGS	TRIETERIC	TRIHYDRIC
TRETS	TRIBALISM	TRICKISH	TRIETHYL	TRIKE
TREVALLIES	TRIBALISMS	TRICKLE	TRIFACIAL	TRIKED
TREVALLY	TRIBALIST	TRICKLED	TRIFECTA	TRIKES
TREVIS	TRIBALISTS	TRICKLES	TRIFECTAS	TRIKING
TREVISES	TRIBALLY	TRICKLESS	TRIFF	TRILBIES

The Chambers Dictionary is the authority for many longer words; see *OSW* Introduction, page xii.

TRILBY	TRINING	TRIPODAL	TRISOMY	TRIVALVES
TRILBYS	TRINITIES	TRIPODIES	TRIST	TRIVET
TRILD	TRINITRIN	TRIPODS	TRISTE	TRIVETS
TRILEMMA	TRINITRINS	TRIPODY	TRISTESSE	TRIVIA
TRILEMMAS	TRINITY	TRIPOLI	TRISTESSES	TRIVIAL
TRILINEAR	TRINKET	TRIPOLIS	TRISTFUL	TRIVIALLY
TRILITH	TRINKETED	TRIPOS	TRISTICH	TRIVIUM
TRILITHIC	TRINKETER	TRIPOSES	TRISTICHS	TRIVIUMS
TRILITHON	TRINKETERS	TRIPPANT	TRISUL	TRIZONAL
TRILITHONS	TRINKETING	TRIPPED	TRISULA	TRIZONE
TRILITHS	TRINKETINGS	TRIPPER	TRISULAS	TRIZONES
TRILL	TRINKETRIES	TRIPPERS	TRISULS	TROAD
TRILLED	TRINKETRY	TRIPPERY	TRITE	TROADE
TRILLING	TRINKETS	TRIPPET	TRITELY	TROADES
TRILLINGS	TRINKUM	TRIPPETS	TRITENESS	TROADS
TRILLION	TRINKUMS	TRIPPING	TRITENESSES	TROAT
TRILLIONS	TRINOMIAL	TRIPPINGS	TRITER	TROATED
TRILLIUM	TRINOMIALS	TRIPPLE	TRITES	TROATING
TRILLIUMS	TRINS	TRIPPLED	TRITEST	TROATS
TRILLO	TRIO	TRIPPLER	TRITHEISM	TROCAR
TRILLOES	TRIODE	TRIPPLERS	TRITHEISMS	TROCARS
TRILLS	TRIODES	TRIPPLES	TRITHEIST	TROCHAIC
TRILOBATE	TRIOLET	TRIPPLING	TRITHEISTS	TROCHAICS
TRILOBE	TRIOLETS	TRIPS	TRITIATE	TROCHAL
TRILOBED	TRIONES	TRIPSES	TRITIATED	TROCHE
TRILOBES	TRIONYM	TRIPSIS	TRITIATES	TROCHEE
TRILOBITE	TRIONYMAL	TRIPTANE	TRITIATING	TROCHEES
TRILOBITES	TRIONYMS	TRIPTANES	TRITICAL	TROCHES
TRILOGIES	TRIOR	TRIPTOTE	TRITICALE	TROCHI
TRILOGY	TRIORS	TRIPTOTES	TRITICALES	TROCHILIC
TRIM	TRIOS	TRIPTYCH	TRITICISM	TROCHILUS
TRIMARAN	TRIOXIDE	TRIPTYCHS	TRITICISMS	TROCHILUSES
TRIMARANS	TRIOXIDES	TRIPTYQUE	TRITIDE	TROCHISK
TRIMER	TRIP	TRIPTYQUES	TRITIDES	TROCHISKS
TRIMERIC	TRIPE	TRIPUDIA	TRITIUM	TROCHITE
TRIMEROUS	TRIPEDAL	TRIPUDIUM	TRITIUMS	TROCHITES
TRIMERS	TRIPEMAN	TRIPUDIUMS	TRITON	TROCHLEA
TRIMESTER	TRIPEMEN	TRIPWIRE	TRITONE	TROCHLEAR
TRIMESTERS	TRIPERIES	TRIPWIRES	TRITONES	TROCHLEAS
TRIMETER	TRIPERY	TRIPY	TRITONIA	TROCHOID
TRIMETERS	TRIPES	TRIQUETRA	TRITONIAS	TROCHOIDS
TRIMETHYL	TRIPEY	TRIQUETRAS	TRITONS	TROCHUS
TRIMETRIC	TRIPHONE	TRIRADIAL	TRITURATE	TROCHUSES
TRIMLY	TRIPHONES	TRIREME	TRITURATED	TROCK
TRIMMED	TRIPIER	TRIREMES	TRITURATES	TROCKED
TRIMMER	TRIPIEST	TRISAGION	TRITURATING	TROCKEN
TRIMMERS	TRIPITAKA	TRISAGIONS	TRIUMPH	TROCKING
TRIMMEST	TRIPITAKAS	TRISECT	TRIUMPHAL	TROCKS
TRIMMING	TRIPLANE	TRISECTED	TRIUMPHALS	TROD
TRIMMINGS	TRIPLANES	TRISECTING	TRIUMPHED	TRODDEN
TRIMNESS	TRIPLE	TRISECTOR	TRIUMPHER	TRODE
TRIMNESSES	TRIPLED	TRISECTORS	TRIUMPHERS	TRODES
TRIMS	TRIPLES	TRISECTS	TRIUMPHING	TRODS
TRIMTAB	TRIPLET	TRISEME	TRIUMPHINGS	TROELIE
TRIMTABS	TRIPLETS	TRISEMES	TRIUMPHS	TROELIES
TRIN	TRIPLEX	TRISEMIC	TRIUMVIR	TROELY
TRINAL	TRIPLEXES	TRISHAW	TRIUMVIRI	TROG
TRINARY	TRIPLIED	TRISHAWS	TRIUMVIRIES	TROGGED
TRINDLE	TRIPLIES	TRISKELE	TRIUMVIRS	TROGGING
TRINDLED	TRIPLING	TRISKELES	TRIUMVIRY	TROGGS
TRINDLES	TRIPLINGS	TRISKELIA	TRIUNE	TROGON
TRINDLING	TRIPLOID	TRISMUS	TRIUNES	TROGONS
TRINE	TRIPLOIDIES	TRISMUSES	TRIUNITIES	TROGS
TRINED	TRIPLOIDY	TRISOME	TRIUNITY	TROIKA
TRINES	TRIPLY	TRISOMES	TRIVALENT	TROIKAS
TRINGLE	TRIPLYING	TRISOMIC	TRIVALVE	TROILISM
TRINGLES	TRIPOD	TRISOMIES	TRIVALVED	TROILISMS

The Chambers Dictionary is the authority for many longer words; see *OSW* Introduction, page xii.

TROILIST	TROPHESY	TROUPING	TRUCKERS	TRUMPINGS
TROILISTS	TROPHI	TROUSE	TRUCKIE	TRUMPS
TROILITE	TROPHIC	TROUSER	TRUCKIES	TRUNCAL
TROILITES	TROPHIED	TROUSERED	TRUCKING	TRUNCATE
TROKE	TROPHIES	TROUSERING	TRUCKINGS	TRUNCATED
TROKED	TROPHY	TROUSERINGS	TRUCKLE	TRUNCATES
TROKES	TROPHYING	TROUSERS	TRUCKLED	TRUNCATING
TROKING	TROPIC	TROUSES	TRUCKLER	TRUNCHEON
TROLL	TROPICAL	TROUSSEAU	TRUCKLERS	TRUNCHEONED
TROLLED	TROPICS	TROUSSEAUS	TRUCKLES	TRUNCHEONING
TROLLER	TROPING	TROUSSEAUX	TRUCKLING	TRUNCHEONS
TROLLERS	TROPISM	TROUT	TRUCKLINGS	TRUNDLE
TROLLEY	TROPISMS	TROUTER	TRUCKMAN	TRUNDLED
TROLLEYED	TROPIST	TROUTERS	TRUCKMEN	TRUNDLER
TROLLEYING	TROPISTIC	TROUTFUL	TRUCKS	TRUNDLERS
TROLLEYS	TROPISTS	TROUTIER	TRUCULENT	TRUNDLES
TROLLIES	TROPOLOGIES	TROUTIEST	TRUDGE	TRUNDLING
TROLLING	TROPOLOGY	TROUTING	TRUDGED	TRUNK
TROLLINGS	TROPPO	TROUTINGS	TRUDGEN	TRUNKED
TROLLIUS	TROSSERS	TROUTLESS	TRUDGENS	TRUNKFISH
TROLLIUSES	TROT	TROUTLET	TRUDGEON	TRUNKFISHES
TROLLOP	TROTH	TROUTLETS	TRUDGEONS	TRUNKFUL
TROLLOPED	TROTHED	TROUTLING	TRUDGER	TRUNKFULS
TROLLOPEE	TROTHFUL	TROUTLINGS	TRUDGERS	TRUNKING
TROLLOPEES	TROTHING	TROUTS	TRUDGES	TRUNKINGS
TROLLOPING	TROTHLESS	TROUTY	TRUDGING	TRUNKS
TROLLOPS	TROTHS	TROUVERE	TRUDGINGS	TRUNNION
TROLLOPY	TROTLINE	TROUVERES	TRUE	TRUNNIONS
TROLLS	TROTLINES	TROUVEUR	TRUED	TRUQUAGE
TROLLY	TROTS	TROUVEURS	TRUEING	TRUQUAGES
TROMBONE	TROTTED	TROVER	TRUEMAN	TRUQUEUR
TROMBONES	TROTTER	TROVERS	TRUEMEN	TRUQUEURS
TROMINO	TROTTERS	TROW	TRUENESS	TRUSS
TROMINOES	TROTTING	TROWED	TRUENESSES	TRUSSED
TROMINOS	TROTTINGS	TROWEL	TRUEPENNIES	TRUSSER
TROMMEL	TROTTOIR	TROWELLED	TRUEPENNY	TRUSSERS
TROMMELS	TROTTOIRS	TROWELLER	TRUER	TRUSSES
TROMP	TROTYL	TROWELLERS	TRUES	TRUSSING
TROMPE	TROTYLS	TROWELLING	TRUEST	TRUSSINGS
TROMPED	TROUBLE	TROWELS	TRUFFLE	TRUST
TROMPES	TROUBLED	TROWING	TRUFFLED	TRUSTED
TROMPING	TROUBLER	TROWS	TRUFFLES	TRUSTEE
TROMPS	TROUBLERS	TROWSERS	TRUFFLING	TRUSTEES
TRON	TROUBLES	TROY	TRUFFLINGS	TRUSTER
TRONA	TROUBLING	TROYS	TRUG	TRUSTERS
TRONAS	TROUBLINGS	TRUANCIES	TRUGS	TRUSTFUL
TRONC	TROUBLOUS	TRUANCY	TRUING	TRUSTIER
TRONCS	TROUGH	TRUANT	TRUISM	TRUSTIES
TRONE	TROUGHS	TRUANTED	TRUISMS	TRUSTIEST
TRONES	TROULE	TRUANTING	TRUISTIC	TRUSTILY
TRONS	TROULED	TRUANTRIES	TRULL	TRUSTING
TROOLIE	TROULES	TRUANTRY	TRULLS	TRUSTLESS
TROOLIES	TROULING	TRUANTS	TRULY	TRUSTS
TROOP	TROUNCE	TRUCAGE	TRUMEAU	TRUSTY
TROOPED	TROUNCED	TRUCAGES	TRUMEAUX	TRUTH
TROOPER	TROUNCER	TRUCE	TRUMP	TRUTHFUL
TROOPERS	TROUNCERS	TRUCELESS	TRUMPED	TRUTHIER
TROOPIAL	TROUNCES	TRUCES	TRUMPERIES	TRUTHIEST
TROOPIALS	TROUNCING	TRUCHMAN	TRUMPERY	TRUTHLESS
TROOPING	TROUNCINGS	TRUCHMANS	TRUMPET	TRUTHLIKE
TROOPS	TROUPE	TRUCHMEN	TRUMPETED	TRUTHS
TROPARIA	TROUPED	TRUCIAL	TRUMPETER	TRUTHY
TROPARION	TROUPER	TRUCK	TRUMPETERS	TRY
TROPE	TROUPERS	TRUCKAGE	TRUMPETING	TRYE
TROPED	TROUPES	TRUCKAGES	TRUMPETINGS	TRYER
TROPES	TROUPIAL	TRUCKED	TRUMPETS	TRYERS
TROPHESIES	TROUPIALS	TRUCKER	TRUMPING	TRYING

The Chambers Dictionary is the authority for many longer words; see *OSW* Introduction, page xii.

TRYINGLY	TUBAE	TUCK	TUILZIED	TUMPIEST
TRYINGS	TUBAGE	TUCKAHOE	TUILZIEING	TUMPING
TRYP	TUBAGES	TUCKAHOES	TUILZIES	TUMPS
TRYPS	TUBAL	TUCKED	TUIS	TUMPY
TRYPSIN	TUBAR	TUCKER	TUISM	TUMS
TRYPSINS	TUBAS	TUCKERBAG	TUISMS	TUMSHIE
TRYPTIC	TUBATE	TUCKERBAGS	TUITION	TUMSHIES
TRYSAIL	TUBBED	TUCKERBOX	TUITIONAL	TUMULAR
TRYSAILS	TUBBER	TUCKERBOXES	TUITIONS	TUMULARY
TRYST	TUBBERS	TUCKERED	TULAREMIA	TUMULI
TRYSTED	TUBBIER	TUCKERING	TULAREMIAS	TUMULT
TRYSTER	TUBBIEST	TUCKERS	TULAREMIC	TUMULTED
TRYSTERS	TUBBINESS	TUCKET	TULBAN	TUMULTING
TRYSTING	TUBBINESSES	TUCKETS	TULBANS	TUMULTS
TRYSTS	TUBBING	TUCKING	TULCHAN	TUMULUS
TSADDIK	TUBBINGS	TUCKS	TULCHANS	TUN
TSADDIKIM	TUBBISH	TUCOTUCO	TULE	TUNA
TSADDIKS	TUBBY	TUCOTUCOS	TULES	TUNABLE
TSADDIQ	TUBE	TUCUTUCO	TULIP	TUNABLY
TSADDIQIM	TUBECTOMIES	TUCUTUCOS	TULIPANT	TUNAS
TSADDIQS	TUBECTOMY	TUFA	TULIPANTS	TUNBELLIES
TSAMBA	TUBED	TUFACEOUS	TULIPS	TUNBELLY
TSAMBAS	TUBEFUL	TUFAS	TULIPWOOD	TUND
TSAR	TUBEFULS	TUFF	TULIPWOODS	TUNDED
TSARDOM	TUBELESS	TUFFE	TULLE	TUNDING
TSARDOMS	TUBELIKE	TUFFES	TULLES	TUNDRA
TSAREVICH	TUBENOSE	TUFFET	TULWAR	TUNDRAS
TSAREVICHES	TUBENOSES	TUFFETS	TULWARS	TUNDS
TSAREVNA	TUBER	TUFFS	TUM	TUNDUN
TSAREVNAS	TUBERCLE	TUFT	TUMBLE	TUNDUNS
TSARINA	TUBERCLED	TUFTED	TUMBLED	TUNE
TSARINAS	TUBERCLES	TUFTER	TUMBLER	TUNEABLE
TSARISM	TUBERCULA	TUFTERS	TUMBLERS	TUNED
TSARISMS	TUBERCULE	TUFTIER	TUMBLES	TUNEFUL
TSARIST	TUBERCULES	TUFTIEST	TUMBLING	TUNEFULLY
TSARISTS	TUBEROSE	TUFTING	TUMBLINGS	TUNELESS
TSARITSA	TUBEROSES	TUFTINGS	TUMBREL	TUNER
TSARITSAS	TUBEROUS	TUFTS	TUMBRELS	TUNERS
TSARS	TUBERS	TUFTY	TUMBRIL	TUNES
TSESSEBE	TUBES	TUG	TUMBRILS	TUNESMITH
TSESSEBES	TUBFAST	TUGBOAT	TUMEFIED	TUNESMITHS
TSETSE	TUBFASTS	TUGBOATS	TUMEFIES	TUNGSTATE
TSETSES	TUBFISH	TUGGED	TUMEFY	TUNGSTATES
TSIGANE	TUBFISHES	TUGGER	TUMEFYING	TUNGSTEN
TSIGANES	TUBFUL	TUGGERS	TUMESCE	TUNGSTENS
TSOTSI	TUBFULS	TUGGING	TUMESCED	TUNIC
TSOTSIS	TUBICOLAR	TUGGINGLY	TUMESCENT	TUNICATE
TSOURIS	TUBICOLE	TUGGINGS	TUMESCES	TUNICATED
TSOURISES	TUBICOLES	TUGHRA	TUMESCING	TUNICATES
TSUBA	TUBIFEX	TUGHRAS	TUMID	TUNICIN
TSUBAS	TUBIFEXES	TUGHRIK	TUMIDITIES	TUNICINS
TSUNAMI	TUBIFORM	TUGHRIKS	TUMIDITY	TUNICKED
TSUNAMIS	TUBING	TUGRA	TUMIDLY	TUNICLE
TSURIS	TUBINGS	TUGRAS	TUMIDNESS	TUNICLES
TSURISES	TUBS	TUGRIK	TUMIDNESSES	TUNICS
TSUTSUMU	TUBULAR	TUGRIKS	TUMMIES	TUNIER
TSUTSUMUS	TUBULATE	TUGS	TUMMY	TUNIEST
TUAN	TUBULATED	TUI	TUMOR	TUNING
TUANS	TUBULATES	TUILLE	TUMOROUS	TUNINGS
TUART	TUBULATING	TUILLES	TUMORS	TUNNAGE
TUARTS	TUBULE	TUILLETTE	TUMOUR	TUNNAGES
TUATARA	TUBULES	TUILLETTES	TUMOURS	TUNNED
TUATARAS	TUBULIN	TUILYIE	TUMP	TUNNEL
TUATH	TUBULINS	TUILYIED	TUMPED	TUNNELED
TUATHS	TUBULOUS	TUILYIEING	TUMPHIES	TUNNELER
TUB	TUCHUN	TUILYIES	TUMPHY	TUNNELERS
TUBA	TUCHUNS	TUILZIE	TUMPIER	TUNNELING

The Chambers Dictionary is the authority for many longer words; see *OSW* Introduction, page xii.

TUNNELLED	TURBONDS	TURNCOAT	TUSHERY	TUTORIAL
TUNNELLER	TURBOPROP	TURNCOATS	TUSHES	TUTORIALS
TUNNELLERS	TURBOPROPS	TURNCOCK	TUSHIE	TUTORING
TUNNELLING	TURBOS	TURNCOCKS	TUSHIES	TUTORINGS
TUNNELLINGS	TURBOT	TURNDUN	TUSHING	TUTORISE
TUNNELS	TURBOTS	TURNDUNS	TUSHKAR	TUTORISED
TUNNIES	TURBULENT	TURNED	TUSHKARS	TUTORISES
TUNNING	TURCOPOLE	TURNER	TUSHKER	TUTORISING
TUNNINGS	TURCOPOLES	TURNERIES	TUSHKERS	TUTORISM
TUNNY	TURD	TURNERS	TUSHY	TUTORISMS
TUNS	TURDINE	TURNERY	TUSK	TUTORIZE
TUNY	TURDION	TURNING	TUSKAR	TUTORIZED
TUP	TURDIONS	TURNINGS	TUSKARS	TUTORIZES
TUPEK	TURDOID	TURNIP	TUSKED	TUTORIZING
TUPEKS	TURDS	TURNIPED	TUSKER	TUTORS
TUPELO	TUREEN	TURNIPING	TUSKERS	TUTORSHIP
TUPELOS	TUREENS	TURNIPS	TUSKIER	TUTORSHIPS
TUPIK	TURF	TURNKEY	TUSKIEST	TUTRESS
TUPIKS	TURFED	TURNKEYS	TUSKING	TUTRESSES
TUPPED	TURFEN	TURNOFF	TUSKINGS	TUTRICES
TUPPENCE	TURFIER	TURNOFFS	TUSKLESS	TUTRIX
TUPPENCES	TURFIEST	TURNOUT	TUSKS	TUTRIXES
TUPPENNIES	TURFINESS	TURNOUTS	TUSKY	TUTS
TUPPENNY	TURFINESSES	TURNOVER	TUSSAH	TUTSAN
TUPPING	TURFING	TURNOVERS	TUSSAHS	TUTSANS
TUPS	TURFINGS	TURNPIKE	TUSSAL	TUTSED
TUPTOWING	TURFITE	TURNPIKES	TUSSEH	TUTSES
TUQUE	TURFITES	TURNROUND	TUSSEHS	TUTSING
TUQUES	TURFMAN	TURNROUNDS	TUSSER	TUTTED
TURACIN	TURFMEN	TURNS	TUSSERS	TUTTI
TURACINS	TURFS	TURNSKIN	TUSSIS	TUTTIES
TURACO	TURFY	TURNSKINS	TUSSISES	TUTTING
TURACOS	TURGENT	TURNSOLE	TUSSIVE	TUTTINGS
TURBAN	TURGENTLY	TURNSOLES	TUSSLE	TUTTIS
TURBAND	TURGID	TURNSPIT	TUSSLED	TUTTY
TURBANDS	TURGIDITIES	TURNSPITS	TUSSLES	TUTU
TURBANED	TURGIDITY	TURNSTILE	TUSSLING	TUTUS
TURBANS	TURGIDLY	TURNSTILES	TUSSOCK	TUTWORK
TURBANT	TURGOR	TURNSTONE	TUSSOCKS	TUTWORKER
TURBANTS	TURGORS	TURNSTONES	TUSSOCKY	TUTWORKERS
TURBARIES	TURION	TURNTABLE	TUSSORE	TUTWORKS
TURBARY	TURIONS	TURNTABLES	TUSSORES	TUX
TURBID	TURKEY	TURPETH	TUT	TUXEDO
TURBIDITE	TURKEYS	TURPETHS	TUTANIA	TUXEDOES
TURBIDITES	TURKIES	TURPITUDE	TUTANIAS	TUXEDOS
TURBIDITIES	TURKIESES	TURPITUDES	TUTEE	TUXES
TURBIDITY	TURKIS	TURPS	TUTEES	TUYERE
TURBIDLY	TURKISES	TURQUOISE	TUTELAGE	TUYERES
TURBINAL	TURLOUGH	TURQUOISES	TUTELAGES	TUZZ
TURBINALS	TURLOUGHS	TURRET	TUTELAR	TUZZES
TURBINATE	TURM	TURRETED	TUTELARIES	TWA
TURBINATES	TURME	TURRETS	TUTELARS	TWADDLE
TURBINE	TURMERIC	TURRIBANT	TUTELARY	TWADDLED
TURBINED	TURMERICS	TURRIBANTS	TUTENAG	TWADDLER
TURBINES	TURMES	TURTLE	TUTENAGS	TWADDLERS
TURBIT	TURMOIL	TURTLED	TUTIORISM	TWADDLES
TURBITH	TURMOILED	TURTLER	TUTIORISMS	TWADDLIER
TURBITHS	TURMOILING	TURTLERS	TUTIORIST	TWADDLIEST
TURBITS	TURMOILS	TURTLES	TUTIORISTS	TWADDLING
TURBO	TURMS	TURTLING	TUTMAN	TWADDLINGS
TURBOCAR	TURN	TURTLINGS	TUTMEN	TWADDLY
TURBOCARS	TURNABOUT	TURVES	TUTOR	TWAE
TURBOFAN	TURNABOUTS	TUSCHE	TUTORAGE	TWAES
TURBOFANS	TURNAGAIN	TUSCHES	TUTORAGES	TWAFALD
TURBOJET	TURNAGAINS	TUSH	TUTORED	TWAIN
TURBOJETS	TURNBACK	TUSHED	TUTORESS	TWAINS
TURBOND	TURNBACKS	TUSHERIES	TUTORESSES	TWAITE

The Chambers Dictionary is the authority for many longer words; see *OSW* Introduction, page xii.

TWAITES	TWEEST	TWILIT	TWIST	TWYERES
TWAL	TWEET	TWILL	TWISTABLE	TWYERS
TWALHOURS	TWEETED	TWILLED	TWISTED	TWYFOLD
TWALPENNIES	TWEETER	TWILLIES	TWISTER	TWYFORKED
TWALPENNY	TWEETERS	TWILLING	TWISTERS	TWYFORMED
TWALS	TWEETING	TWILLS	TWISTIER	TYCHISM
TWANG	TWEETS	TWILLY	TWISTIEST	TYCHISMS
TWANGED	TWEEZE	TWILT	TWISTING	TYCOON
TWANGIER	TWEEZED	TWILTED	TWISTINGS	TYCOONATE
TWANGIEST	TWEEZERS	TWILTING	TWISTOR	TYCOONATES
TWANGING	TWEEZES	TWILTS	TWISTORS	TYCOONERIES
TWANGINGS	TWEEZING	TWIN	TWISTS	TYCOONERY
TWANGLE	TWELFTH	TWINE	TWISTY	TYCOONS
TWANGLED	TWELFTHLY	TWINED	TWIT	TYDE
TWANGLES	TWELFTHS	TWINER	TWITCH	TYE
TWANGLING	TWELVE	TWINERS	TWITCHED	TYED
TWANGLINGS	TWELVEMO	TWINES	TWITCHER	TYEING
TWANGS	TWELVEMOS	TWINGE	TWITCHERS	TYES
TWANGY	TWELVES	TWINGED	TWITCHES	TYG
TWANK	TWENTIES	TWINGES	TWITCHIER	TYGS
TWANKAY	TWENTIETH	TWINGING	TWITCHIEST	TYING
TWANKAYS	TWENTIETHS	TWINIER	TWITCHING	TYKE
TWANKS	TWENTY	TWINIEST	TWITCHINGS	TYKES
TWAS	TWENTYISH	TWINING	TWITCHY	TYKISH
TWASOME	TWERP	TWININGLY	TWITE	TYLECTOMIES
TWASOMES	TWERPS	TWININGS	TWITES	TYLECTOMY
TWAT	TWIBILL	TWINK	TWITS	TYLER
TWATS	TWIBILLS	TWINKED	TWITTED	TYLERS
TWATTLE	TWICE	TWINKING	TWITTEN	TYLOPOD
TWATTLED	TWICER	TWINKLE	TWITTENS	TYLOPODS
TWATTLER	TWICERS	TWINKLED	TWITTER	TYLOSES
TWATTLERS	TWICHILD	TWINKLER	TWITTERED	TYLOSIS
TWATTLES	TWICHILDREN	TWINKLERS	TWITTERER	TYLOTE
TWATTLING	TWIDDLE	TWINKLES	TWITTERERS	TYLOTES
TWATTLINGS	TWIDDLED	TWINKLING	TWITTERING	TYMBAL
TWAY	TWIDDLER	TWINKLINGS	TWITTERINGS	TYMBALS
TWAYS	TWIDDLERS	TWINKS	TWITTERS	TYMP
TWEAK	TWIDDLES	TWINLING	TWITTERY	TYMPAN
TWEAKED	TWIDDLIER	TWINLINGS	TWITTING	TYMPANA
TWEAKING	TWIDDLIEST	TWINNED	TWITTINGS	TYMPANAL
TWEAKINGS	TWIDDLING	TWINNING	TWIZZLE	TYMPANI
TWEAKS	TWIDDLINGS	TWINNINGS	TWIZZLED	TYMPANIC
TWEE	TWIDDLY	TWINS	TWIZZLES	TYMPANICS
TWEED	TWIER	TWINSET	TWIZZLING	TYMPANIES
TWEEDIER	TWIERS	TWINSETS	TWO	TYMPANIST
TWEEDIEST	TWIFOLD	TWINSHIP	TWOCCER	TYMPANISTS
TWEEDLE	TWIFORKED	TWINSHIPS	TWOCCERS	TYMPANO
TWEEDLED	TWIFORMED	TWINTER	TWOCCING	TYMPANS
TWEEDLER	TWIG	TWINTERS	TWOCCINGS	TYMPANUM
TWEEDLERS	TWIGGED	TWINY	TWOER	TYMPANY
TWEEDLES	TWIGGEN	TWIRE	TWOERS	TYMPS
TWEEDLING	TWIGGER	TWIRED	TWOFOLD	TYND
TWEEDS	TWIGGERS	TWIRES	TWONESS	TYNDE
TWEEDY	TWIGGIER	TWIRING	TWONESSES	TYNE
TWEEL	TWIGGIEST	TWIRL	TWOPENCE	TYNED
TWEELED	TWIGGING	TWIRLED	TWOPENCES	TYNES
TWEELING	TWIGGY	TWIRLER	TWOPENNIES	TYNING
TWEELS	TWIGHT	TWIRLERS	TWOPENNY	TYPAL
TWEELY	TWIGHTED	TWIRLIER	TWOS	TYPE
TWEENESS	TWIGHTING	TWIRLIEST	TWOSEATER	TYPECAST
TWEENESSES	TWIGHTS	TWIRLING	TWOSEATERS	TYPECASTING
TWEENIES	TWIGS	TWIRLS	TWOSOME	TYPECASTS
TWEENY	TWIGSOME	TWIRLY	TWOSOMES	TYPED
TWEER	TWILIGHT	TWIRP	TWOSTROKE	TYPES
TWEERED	TWILIGHTED	TWIRPS	TWP	TYPESET
TWEERING	TWILIGHTING	TWISCAR	TWYER	TYPEWRITE
TWEERS	TWILIGHTS	TWISCARS	TWYERE	TYPEWRITES

The Chambers Dictionary is the authority for many longer words; see *OSW* Introduction, page xii.

TYPEWRITING	TYPICALLY	TYRAMINE	TYRANNIZING	TYTHE
TYPEWRITINGS	TYPIFIED	TYRAMINES	TYRANNOUS	TYTHED
TYPEWRITTEN	TYPIFIER	TYRAN	TYRANNY	TYTHES
TYPEWROTE	TYPIFIERS	TYRANED	TYRANS	TYTHING
TYPHLITIC	TYPIFIES	TYRANING	TYRANT	TZADDIK
TYPHLITIS	TYPIFY	TYRANNE	TYRANTED	TZADDIKIM
TYPHLITISES	TYPIFYING	TYRANNED	TYRANTING	TZADDIKS
TYPHOID	TYPING	TYRANNES	TYRANTS	TZADDIQ
TYPHOIDAL	TYPINGS	TYRANNESS	TYRE	TZADDIQIM
TYPHOIDS	TYPIST	TYRANNESSES	TYRED	TZADDIQS
TYPHON	TYPISTS	TYRANNIC	TYRELESS	TZAR
TYPHONIAN	TYPO	TYRANNIES	TYRES	TZARS
TYPHONIC	TYPOLOGIES	TYRANNING	TYRO	TZATZIKI
TYPHONS	TYPOLOGY	TYRANNIS	TYROES	TZATZIKIS
TYPHOON	TYPOMANIA	TYRANNISE	TYRONES	TZETSE
TYPHOONS	TYPOMANIAS	TYRANNISED	TYROS	TZETSES
TYPHOUS	TYPOS	TYRANNISES	TYROSINE	TZIGANIES
TYPHUS	TYPTO	TYRANNISING	TYROSINES	TZIGANY
TYPHUSES	TYPTOED	TYRANNIZE	TYSTIE	TZIMMES
TYPIC	TYPTOING	TYRANNIZED	TYSTIES	
TYPICAL	TYPTOS	TYRANNIZES	TYTE	

The Chambers Dictionary is the authority for many longer words; see *OSW* Introduction, page xii.

U

UAKARI	UHURUS	ULOTRICHY	UMBRACULA	UNADMIRED
UAKARIS	UINTAHITE	ULSTER	UMBRAE	UNADOPTED
UBEROUS	UINTAHITES	ULSTERED	UMBRAGE	UNADORED
UBERTIES	UINTAITE	ULSTERS	UMBRAGED	UNADORNED
UBERTY	UINTAITES	ULTERIOR	UMBRAGES	UNADVISED
UBIETIES	UITLANDER	ULTIMA	UMBRAGING	UNAFRAID
UBIETY	UITLANDERS	ULTIMACIES	UMBRAL	UNAIDABLE
UBIQUE	UJAMAA	ULTIMACY	UMBRAS	UNAIDED
UBIQUITIES	UJAMAAS	ULTIMAS	UMBRATED	UNAIMED
UBIQUITY	UKASE	ULTIMATA	UMBRATIC	UNAIRED
UCKERS	UKASES	ULTIMATE	UMBRATILE	UNAKING
UDAL	UKE	ULTIMATES	UMBRE	UNALIGNED
UDALLER	UKELELE	ULTIMATUM	UMBREL	UNALIKE
UDALLERS	UKELELES	ULTIMO	UMBRELLA	UNALIST
UDALS	UKES	ULTION	UMBRELLAS	UNALISTS
UDDER	UKULELE	ULTIONS	UMBRELLO	UNALIVE
UDDERED	UKULELES	ULTRA	UMBRELLOES	UNALLAYED
UDDERFUL	ULCER	ULTRAISM	UMBRELLOS	UNALLIED
UDDERLESS	ULCERATE	ULTRAISMS	UMBRELS	UNALLOYED
UDDERS	ULCERATED	ULTRAIST	UMBRERE	UNALTERED
UDO	ULCERATES	ULTRAISTS	UMBRERES	UNAMAZED
UDOMETER	ULCERATING	ULTRARED	UMBRES	UNAMENDED
UDOMETERS	ULCERED	ULTRAS	UMBRETTE	UNAMERCED
UDOMETRIC	ULCERING	ULULANT	UMBRETTES	UNAMIABLE
UDOS	ULCEROUS	ULULATE	UMBRIERE	UNAMUSED
UDS	ULCERS	ULULATED	UMBRIERES	UNAMUSING
UEY	ULE	ULULATES	UMBRIL	UNANCHOR
UEYS	ULEMA	ULULATING	UMBRILS	UNANCHORED
UFO	ULEMAS	ULULATION	UMBROSE	UNANCHORING
UFOLOGIES	ULES	ULULATIONS	UMBROUS	UNANCHORS
UFOLOGIST	ULEX	ULVA	UMIAK	UNANELED
UFOLOGISTS	ULEXES	ULVAS	UMIAKS	UNANIMITIES
UFOLOGY	ULICHON	ULYIE	UMLAUT	UNANIMITY
UFOS	ULICHONS	ULYIES	UMLAUTED	UNANIMOUS
UG	ULICON	ULZIE	UMLAUTING	UNANXIOUS
UGGED	ULICONS	ULZIES	UMLAUTS	UNAPPAREL
UGGING	ULIGINOSE	UM	UMPH	UNAPPARELLED
UGH	ULIGINOUS	UMBEL	UMPIRAGE	UNAPPARELLING
UGHS	ULIKON	UMBELLAR	UMPIRAGES	UNAPPARELS
UGLI	ULIKONS	UMBELLATE	UMPIRE	UNAPPLIED
UGLIED	ULITIS	UMBELLULE	UMPIRED	UNAPT
UGLIER	ULITISES	UMBELLULES	UMPIRES	UNAPTLY
UGLIES	ULLAGE	UMBELS	UMPIRING	UNAPTNESS
UGLIEST	ULLAGED	UMBER	UMPTEEN	UNAPTNESSES
UGLIFIED	ULLAGES	UMBERED	UMPTEENTH	UNARGUED
UGLIFIES	ULLAGING	UMBERING	UMPTIETH	UNARISEN
UGLIFY	ULLING	UMBERS	UMPTY	UNARM
UGLIFYING	ULLINGS	UMBERY	UMQUHILE	UNARMED
UGLILY	ULMACEOUS	UMBILICAL	UMWHILE	UNARMING
UGLINESS	ULMIN	UMBILICI	UN	UNARMS
UGLINESSES	ULMINS	UMBILICUS	UNABASHED	UNARTFUL
UGLIS	ULNA	UMBILICUSES	UNABATED	UNASHAMED
UGLY	ULNAE	UMBLES	UNABLE	UNASKED
UGLYING	ULNAR	UMBO	UNACCUSED	UNASSAYED
UGS	ULNARE	UMBONAL	UNACHING	UNASSUMED
UGSOME	ULNARIA	UMBONATE	UNACTABLE	UNASSURED
UHLAN	ULOSES	UMBONES	UNACTED	UNATONED
UHLANS	ULOSIS	UMBOS	UNACTIVE	UNATTIRED
UHURU	ULOTRICHIES	UMBRA	UNADAPTED	UNAU

The Chambers Dictionary is the authority for many longer words; see *OSW* Introduction, page xii.

UNAUS	UNBEING	UNBLOCKING	UNBUCKLE	UNCASES
UNAVENGED	UNBEINGS	UNBLOCKS	UNBUCKLED	UNCASHED
UNAVOIDED	UNBEKNOWN	UNBLOODED	UNBUCKLES	UNCASING
UNAVOWED	UNBELIEF	UNBLOODY	UNBUCKLING	UNCATE
UNAWARE	UNBELIEFS	UNBLOTTED	UNBUDDED	UNCAUGHT
UNAWARES	UNBELIEVE	UNBLOWED	UNBUILD	UNCAUSED
UNAWED	UNBELIEVED	UNBLOWN	UNBUILDING	UNCE
UNBACKED	UNBELIEVES	UNBLUNTED	UNBUILDS	UNCEASING
UNBAFFLED	UNBELIEVING	UNBODIED	UNBUILT	UNCERTAIN
UNBAG	UNBELOVED	UNBODING	UNBUNDLE	UNCES
UNBAGGED	UNBELT	UNBOLT	UNBUNDLED	UNCESSANT
UNBAGGING	UNBELTED	UNBOLTED	UNBUNDLES	UNCHAIN
UNBAGS	UNBELTING	UNBOLTING	UNBUNDLING	UNCHAINED
UNBAITED	UNBELTS	UNBOLTS	UNBUNDLINGS	UNCHAINING
UNBAKED	UNBEND	UNBONE	UNBURDEN	UNCHAINS
UNBALANCE	UNBENDED	UNBONED	UNBURDENED	UNCHANCIER
UNBALANCED	UNBENDING	UNBONES	UNBURDENING	UNCHANCIEST
UNBALANCES	UNBENDINGS	UNBONING	UNBURDENS	UNCHANCY
UNBALANCING	UNBENDS	UNBONNET	UNBURIED	UNCHANGED
UNBANDED	UNBENIGN	UNBONNETED	UNBURIES	UNCHARGE
UNBANKED	UNBENT	UNBONNETING	UNBURNED	UNCHARGED
UNBAPTISE	UNBEREFT	UNBONNETS	UNBURNT	UNCHARGES
UNBAPTISED	UNBERUFEN	UNBOOKED	UNBURROW	UNCHARGING
UNBAPTISES	UNBESEEM	UNBOOKISH	UNBURROWED	UNCHARITIES
UNBAPTISING	UNBESEEMED	UNBOOT	UNBURROWING	UNCHARITY
UNBAPTIZE	UNBESEEMING	UNBOOTED	UNBURROWS	UNCHARM
UNBAPTIZED	UNBESEEMS	UNBOOTING	UNBURTHEN	UNCHARMED
UNBAPTIZES	UNBESPEAK	UNBOOTS	UNBURTHENED	UNCHARMING
UNBAPTIZING	UNBESPEAKING	UNBORE	UNBURTHENING	UNCHARMS
UNBAR	UNBESPEAKS	UNBORN	UNBURTHENS	UNCHARNEL
UNBARBED	UNBESPOKE	UNBORNE	UNBURY	UNCHARNELLED
UNBARE	UNBESPOKEN	UNBOSOM	UNBURYING	UNCHARNELLING
UNBARED	UNBIAS	UNBOSOMED	UNBUSY	UNCHARNELS
UNBARES	UNBIASED	UNBOSOMER	UNBUTTON	UNCHARTED
UNBARING	UNBIASES	UNBOSOMERS	UNBUTTONED	UNCHARY
UNBARK	UNBIASING	UNBOSOMING	UNBUTTONING	UNCHASTE
UNBARKED	UNBIASSED	UNBOSOMS	UNBUTTONS	UNCHECK
UNBARKING	UNBIASSES	UNBOUGHT	UNCAGE	UNCHECKED
UNBARKS	UNBIASSING	UNBOUND	UNCAGED	UNCHECKING
UNBARRED	UNBID	UNBOUNDED	UNCAGES	UNCHECKS
UNBARRING	UNBIDDEN	UNBOWED	UNCAGING	UNCHEERED
UNBARS	UNBIND	UNBOX	UNCALLED	UNCHEWED
UNBASHFUL	UNBINDING	UNBOXED	UNCANDID	UNCHILD
UNBATED	UNBINDINGS	UNBOXES	UNCANDOUR	UNCHILDED
UNBATHED	UNBINDS	UNBOXING	UNCANDOURS	UNCHILDING
UNBE	UNBISHOP	UNBRACE	UNCANNIER	UNCHILDS
UNBEAR	UNBISHOPED	UNBRACED	UNCANNIEST	UNCHOSEN
UNBEARDED	UNBISHOPING	UNBRACES	UNCANNILY	UNCHRISOM
UNBEARING	UNBISHOPS	UNBRACING	UNCANNY	UNCHURCH
UNBEARS	UNBITT	UNBRAIDED	UNCANONIC	UNCHURCHED
UNBEATEN	UNBITTED	UNBRASTE	UNCAP	UNCHURCHES
UNBED	UNBITTING	UNBRED	UNCAPABLE	UNCHURCHING
UNBEDDED	UNBITTS	UNBREECH	UNCAPE	UNCI
UNBEDDING	UNBLAMED	UNBREECHED	UNCAPED	UNCIAL
UNBEDS	UNBLENDED	UNBREECHES	UNCAPES	UNCIALS
UNBEEN	UNBLENT	UNBREECHING	UNCAPING	UNCIFORM
UNBEGET	UNBLESS	UNBRIDGED	UNCAPPED	UNCINATE
UNBEGETS	UNBLESSED	UNBRIDLE	UNCAPPING	UNCINATED
UNBEGETTING	UNBLESSES	UNBRIDLED	UNCAPS	UNCINI
UNBEGGED	UNBLESSING	UNBRIDLES	UNCAREFUL	UNCINUS
UNBEGOT	UNBLEST	UNBRIDLING	UNCARING	UNCIPHER
UNBEGOTTEN	UNBLIND	UNBRIZZED	UNCART	UNCIPHERED
UNBEGUILE	UNBLINDED	UNBROKE	UNCARTED	UNCIPHERING
UNBEGUILED	UNBLINDING	UNBROKEN	UNCARTING	UNCIPHERS
UNBEGUILES	UNBLINDS	UNBRUISED	UNCARTS	UNCITED
UNBEGUILING	UNBLOCK	UNBRUSED	UNCASE	UNCIVIL
UNBEGUN	UNBLOCKED	UNBRUSHED	UNCASED	UNCIVILLY

The Chambers Dictionary is the authority for many longer words; see *OSW* Introduction, page xii.

UNCLAD	UNCOILED	UNCRATES	UNDEAFS	UNDERCLAY
UNCLAIMED	UNCOILING	UNCRATING	UNDEALT	UNDERCLAYS
UNCLASP	UNCOILS	UNCREATE	UNDEAR	UNDERCLUB
UNCLASPED	UNCOINED	UNCREATED	UNDEBASED	UNDERCLUBBED
UNCLASPING	UNCOLT	UNCREATES	UNDECAYED	UNDERCLUBBING
UNCLASPS	UNCOLTED	UNCREATING	UNDECEIVE	UNDERCLUBS
UNCLASSED	UNCOLTING	UNCROPPED	UNDECEIVED	UNDERCOAT
UNCLASSY	UNCOLTS	UNCROSS	UNDECEIVES	UNDERCOATS
UNCLE	UNCOMBED	UNCROSSED	UNDECEIVING	UNDERCOOK
UNCLEAN	UNCOMBINE	UNCROSSES	UNDECENT	UNDERCOOKED
UNCLEANED	UNCOMBINED	UNCROSSING	UNDECIDED	UNDERCOOKING
UNCLEANER	UNCOMBINES	UNCROWDED	UNDECIMAL	UNDERCOOKS
UNCLEANEST	UNCOMBINING	UNCROWN	UNDECK	UNDERCOOL
UNCLEANLY	UNCOMELY	UNCROWNED	UNDECKED	UNDERCOOLED
UNCLEAR	UNCOMMON	UNCROWNING	UNDECKING	UNDERCOOLING
UNCLEARED	UNCOMMONER	UNCROWNS	UNDECKS	UNDERCOOLS
UNCLEARER	UNCOMMONEST	UNCRUDDED	UNDEE	UNDERCUT
UNCLEAREST	UNCONCERN	UNCRUMPLE	UNDEEDED	UNDERCUTS
UNCLEARLY	UNCONCERNS	UNCRUMPLED	UNDEFACED	UNDERCUTTING
UNCLED	UNCONFINE	UNCRUMPLES	UNDEFIDE	UNDERDECK
UNCLENCH	UNCONFINED	UNCRUMPLING	UNDEFIED	UNDERDECKS
UNCLENCHED	UNCONFINES	UNCTION	UNDEFIED	UNDERDID
UNCLENCHES	UNCONFINING	UNCTIONS	UNDEFINED	UNDERDO
UNCLENCHING	UNCONFORM	UNCTUOUS	UNDEIFIED	UNDERDOER
UNCLES	UNCONGEAL	UNCULLED	UNDEIFIES	UNDERDOERS
UNCLESHIP	UNCONGEALED	UNCURABLE	UNDEIFY	UNDERDOES
UNCLESHIPS	UNCONGEALING	UNCURBED	UNDEIFYING	UNDERDOG
UNCLEW	UNCONGEALS	UNCURDLED	UNDELAYED	UNDERDOGS
UNCLEWED	UNCOOKED	UNCURED	UNDELIGHT	UNDERDOING
UNCLEWING	UNCOOL	UNCURIOUS	UNDELIGHTS	UNDERDONE
UNCLEWS	UNCOPE	UNCURL	UNDELUDED	UNDERDRAW
UNCLING	UNCOPED	UNCURLED	UNDER	UNDERDRAWING
UNCLIPPED	UNCOPES	UNCURLING	UNDERACT	UNDERDRAWINGS
UNCLIPT	UNCOPING	UNCURLS	UNDERACTED	UNDERDRAWN
UNCLOAK	UNCORD	UNCURRENT	UNDERACTING	UNDERDRAWS
UNCLOAKED	UNCORDED	UNCURSE	UNDERACTS	UNDERDREW
UNCLOAKING	UNCORDIAL	UNCURSED	UNDERARM	UNDERFED
UNCLOAKS	UNCORDING	UNCURSES	UNDERBEAR	UNDERFEED
UNCLOG	UNCORDS	UNCURSING	UNDERBEARING	UNDERFEEDING
UNCLOGGED	UNCORK	UNCURTAIN	UNDERBEARINGS	UNDERFEEDS
UNCLOGGING	UNCORKED	UNCURTAINED	UNDERBEARS	UNDERFELT
UNCLOGS	UNCORKING	UNCURTAINING	UNDERBID	UNDERFELTS
UNCLOSE	UNCORKS	UNCURTAINS	UNDERBIDDING	UNDERFIRE
UNCLOSED	UNCORRUPT	UNCURVED	UNDERBIDS	UNDERFIRED
UNCLOSES	UNCOS	UNCUS	UNDERBIT	UNDERFIRES
UNCLOSING	UNCOSTLY	UNCUT	UNDERBITE	UNDERFIRING
UNCLOTHE	UNCOUNTED	UNDAM	UNDERBITES	UNDERFISH
UNCLOTHED	UNCOUPLE	UNDAMAGED	UNDERBITING	UNDERFISHED
UNCLOTHES	UNCOUPLED	UNDAMMED	UNDERBITTEN	UNDERFISHES
UNCLOTHING	UNCOUPLES	UNDAMMING	UNDERBORE	UNDERFISHING
UNCLOUD	UNCOUPLING	UNDAMNED	UNDERBORNE	UNDERFLOW
UNCLOUDED	UNCOURTLY	UNDAMPED	UNDERBOUGHT	UNDERFLOWS
UNCLOUDING	UNCOUTH	UNDAMS	UNDERBRED	UNDERFONG
UNCLOUDS	UNCOUTHER	UNDASHED	UNDERBUSH	UNDERFONGED
UNCLOUDY	UNCOUTHEST	UNDATE	UNDERBUSHED	UNDERFONGING
UNCLOVEN	UNCOUTHLY	UNDATED	UNDERBUSHES	UNDERFONGS
UNCLUTCH	UNCOVER	UNDAUNTED	UNDERBUSHING	UNDERFOOT
UNCLUTCHED	UNCOVERED	UNDAWNING	UNDERBUY	UNDERFOOTED
UNCLUTCHES	UNCOVERING	UNDAZZLE	UNDERBUYING	UNDERFOOTING
UNCLUTCHING	UNCOVERS	UNDAZZLED	UNDERBUYS	UNDERFOOTS
UNCO	UNCOWL	UNDAZZLES	UNDERCARD	UNDERFUND
UNCOATED	UNCOWLED	UNDAZZLING	UNDERCARDS	UNDERFUNDED
UNCOCK	UNCOWLING	UNDE	UNDERCART	UNDERFUNDING
UNCOCKED	UNCOWLS	UNDEAD	UNDERCARTS	UNDERFUNDINGS
UNCOCKING	UNCOYNED	UNDEAF	UNDERCAST	UNDERFUNDS
UNCOCKS	UNCRATE	UNDEAFED	UNDERCASTS	UNDERFUR
UNCOIL	UNCRATED	UNDEAFING	UNDERCLAD	UNDERFURS

The Chambers Dictionary is the authority for many longer words; see *OSW* Introduction, page xii.

UNDERGIRD	UNDERPASSES	UNDERTAKEN	UNDOER	UNEATABLE
UNDERGIRDED	UNDERPAY	UNDERTAKES	UNDOERS	UNEATEN
UNDERGIRDING	UNDERPAYING	UNDERTAKING	UNDOES	UNEATH
UNDERGIRDS	UNDERPAYS	UNDERTAKINGS	UNDOING	UNEATHES
UNDERGIRT	UNDERPEEP	UNDERTANE	UNDOINGS	UNEDGE
UNDERGO	UNDERPEEPED	UNDERTIME	UNDONE	UNEDGED
UNDERGOES	UNDERPEEPING	UNDERTIMES	UNDOOMED	UNEDGES
UNDERGOING	UNDERPEEPS	UNDERTINT	UNDOUBLE	UNEDGING
UNDERGONE	UNDERPIN	UNDERTINTS	UNDOUBLED	UNEDITED
UNDERGOWN	UNDERPINNED	UNDERTONE	UNDOUBLES	UNEFFACED
UNDERGOWNS	UNDERPINNING	UNDERTONES	UNDOUBLING	UNELATED
UNDERGRAD	UNDERPINNINGS	UNDERTOOK	UNDOUBTED	UNELECTED
UNDERGRADS	UNDERPINS	UNDERTOW	UNDRAINED	UNEMPTIED
UNDERHAND	UNDERPLAY	UNDERTOWS	UNDRAPED	UNENDING
UNDERHANDS	UNDERPLAYED	UNDERUSE	UNDRAW	UNENDOWED
UNDERHUNG	UNDERPLAYING	UNDERUSED	UNDRAWING	UNENGAGED
UNDERKEEP	UNDERPLAYS	UNDERUSES	UNDRAWN	UNENTERED
UNDERKEEPING	UNDERPLOT	UNDERUSING	UNDRAWS	UNENVIED
UNDERKEEPS	UNDERPLOTS	UNDERVEST	UNDREADED	UNENVIOUS
UNDERKEPT	UNDERPROP	UNDERVESTS	UNDREAMED	UNENVYING
UNDERKING	UNDERPROPPED	UNDERWAY	UNDREAMT	UNEQUABLE
UNDERKINGS	UNDERPROPPING	UNDERWEAR	UNDRESS	UNEQUAL
UNDERLAID	UNDERPROPS	UNDERWEARS	UNDRESSED	UNEQUALLY
UNDERLAIN	UNDERRAN	UNDERWENT	UNDRESSES	UNEQUALS
UNDERLAP	UNDERRATE	UNDERWING	UNDRESSING	UNERRING
UNDERLAPPED	UNDERRATED	UNDERWINGS	UNDRESSINGS	UNESPIED
UNDERLAPPING	UNDERRATES	UNDERWIT	UNDREW	UNESSAYED
UNDERLAPS	UNDERRATING	UNDERWITS	UNDRIED	UNESSENCE
UNDERLAY	UNDERRUN	UNDERWOOD	UNDRILLED	UNESSENCED
UNDERLAYING	UNDERRUNNING	UNDERWOODS	UNDRIVEN	UNESSENCES
UNDERLAYS	UNDERRUNNINGS	UNDERWORK	UNDROSSY	UNESSENCING
UNDERLET	UNDERRUNS	UNDERWORKED	UNDROWNED	UNETH
UNDERLETS	UNDERSAID	UNDERWORKING	UNDRUNK	UNETHICAL
UNDERLETTING	UNDERSAY	UNDERWORKS	UNDUBBED	UNEVEN
UNDERLETTINGS	UNDERSAYE	UNDERWROUGHT	UNDUE	UNEVENER
UNDERLIE	UNDERSAYES	UNDESERT	UNDUG	UNEVENEST
UNDERLIES	UNDERSAYING	UNDESERTS	UNDULANCIES	UNEVENLY
UNDERLINE	UNDERSAYS	UNDESERVE	UNDULANCY	UNEXALTED
UNDERLINED	UNDERSEA	UNDESERVED	UNDULANT	UNEXCITED
UNDERLINES	UNDERSEAL	UNDESERVES	UNDULATE	UNEXPIRED
UNDERLING	UNDERSEALED	UNDESERVING	UNDULATED	UNEXPOSED
UNDERLINGS	UNDERSEALING	UNDESIRED	UNDULATES	UNEXTINCT
UNDERLINING	UNDERSEALINGS	UNDEVOUT	UNDULATING	UNEXTREME
UNDERLIP	UNDERSEALS	UNDID	UNDULLED	UNEYED
UNDERLIPS	UNDERSELF	UNDIES	UNDULOSE	UNFABLED
UNDERLYING	UNDERSELL	UNDIGHT	UNDULOUS	UNFACT
UNDERMAN	UNDERSELLING	UNDIGHTING	UNDULY	UNFACTS
UNDERMANNED	UNDERSELLS	UNDIGHTS	UNDUTEOUS	UNFADABLE
UNDERMANNING	UNDERSELVES	UNDIGNIFIED	UNDUTIFUL	UNFADED
UNDERMANS	UNDERSET	UNDIGNIFIES	UNDYED	UNFADING
UNDERMEN	UNDERSETS	UNDIGNIFY	UNDYING	UNFAILING
UNDERMINE	UNDERSETTING	UNDIGNIFYING	UNDYINGLY	UNFAIR
UNDERMINED	UNDERSHOT	UNDILUTED	UNEARED	UNFAIRED
UNDERMINES	UNDERSIDE	UNDIMMED	UNEARNED	UNFAIRER
UNDERMINING	UNDERSIDES	UNDINE	UNEARTH	UNFAIREST
UNDERMININGS	UNDERSIGN	UNDINES	UNEARTHED	UNFAIRING
UNDERMOST	UNDERSIGNED	UNDINISM	UNEARTHING	UNFAIRLY
UNDERN	UNDERSIGNING	UNDINISMS	UNEARTHLIER	UNFAIRS
UNDERNOTE	UNDERSIGNS	UNDINTED	UNEARTHLIEST	UNFAITH
UNDERNOTED	UNDERSKIES	UNDIPPED	UNEARTHLY	UNFAITHS
UNDERNOTES	UNDERSKY	UNDIVIDED	UNEARTHS	UNFALLEN
UNDERNOTING	UNDERSOIL	UNDIVINE	UNEASE	UNFAMED
UNDERNS	UNDERSOILS	UNDO	UNEASES	UNFANNED
UNDERPAID	UNDERSOLD	UNDOCK	UNEASIER	UNFASTEN
UNDERPART	UNDERSONG	UNDOCKED	UNEASIEST	UNFASTENED
UNDERPARTS	UNDERSONGS	UNDOCKING	UNEASILY	UNFASTENING
UNDERPASS	UNDERTAKE	UNDOCKS	UNEASY	UNFASTENS

The Chambers Dictionary is the authority for many longer words; see *OSW* Introduction, page xii.

UNFAULTY	UNFOOTED	UNGENIAL	UNGUARDING	UNHASPING
UNFAZED	UNFORBID	UNGENTEEL	UNGUARDS	UNHASPS
UNFEARED	UNFORCED	UNGENTLE	UNGUENT	UNHASTING
UNFEARFUL	UNFORGED	UNGENTLY	UNGUENTS	UNHASTY
UNFEARING	UNFORGOT	UNGENUINE	UNGUES	UNHAT
UNFED	UNFORM	UNGERMANE	UNGUESSED	UNHATCHED
UNFEED	UNFORMAL	UNGET	UNGUIDED	UNHATS
UNFEELING	UNFORMED	UNGETS	UNGUIFORM	UNHATTED
UNFEIGNED	UNFORMING	UNGETTING	UNGUILTY	UNHATTING
UNFELLED	UNFORMS	UNGHOSTLY	UNGUIS	UNHATTINGS
UNFELT	UNFORTUNE	UNGIFTED	UNGULA	UNHAUNTED
UNFENCED	UNFORTUNES	UNGILD	UNGULAE	UNHEAD
UNFETTER	UNFOUGHT	UNGILDED	UNGULATE	UNHEADED
UNFETTERED	UNFOUND	UNGILDING	UNGULATES	UNHEADING
UNFETTERING	UNFOUNDED	UNGILDS	UNGULED	UNHEADS
UNFETTERS	UNFRAMED	UNGILT	UNGUM	UNHEAL
UNFEUDAL	UNFRANKED	UNGIRD	UNGUMMED	UNHEALED
UNFEUED	UNFRAUGHT	UNGIRDED	UNGUMMING	UNHEALING
UNFIGURED	UNFRAUGHTED	UNGIRDING	UNGUMS	UNHEALS
UNFILDE	UNFRAUGHTING	UNGIRDS	UNGYVE	UNHEALTH
UNFILED	UNFRAUGHTS	UNGIRT	UNGYVED	UNHEALTHIER
UNFILIAL	UNFREE	UNGIRTH	UNGYVES	UNHEALTHIEST
UNFILLED	UNFREED	UNGIRTHED	UNGYVING	UNHEALTHS
UNFILMED	UNFREEMAN	UNGIRTHING	UNHABLE	UNHEALTHY
UNFINE	UNFREEMEN	UNGIRTHS	UNHACKED	UNHEARD
UNFIRED	UNFREEZE	UNGIVING	UNHAILED	UNHEARSE
UNFIRM	UNFREEZES	UNGLAD	UNHAIR	UNHEARSED
UNFISHED	UNFREEZING	UNGLAZED	UNHAIRED	UNHEARSES
UNFIT	UNFRETTED	UNGLOSSED	UNHAIRING	UNHEARSING
UNFITLY	UNFRIEND	UNGLOVE	UNHAIRS	UNHEART
UNFITNESS	UNFRIENDS	UNGLOVED	UNHALLOW	UNHEARTED
UNFITNESSES	UNFROCK	UNGLOVES	UNHALLOWED	UNHEARTING
UNFITS	UNFROCKED	UNGLOVING	UNHALLOWING	UNHEARTS
UNFITTED	UNFROCKING	UNGLUE	UNHALLOWS	UNHEATED
UNFITTER	UNFROCKS	UNGLUED	UNHALSED	UNHEDGED
UNFITTEST	UNFROZE	UNGLUES	UNHAND	UNHEEDED
UNFITTING	UNFROZEN	UNGLUING	UNHANDED	UNHEEDFUL
UNFIX	UNFUELLED	UNGOD	UNHANDILY	UNHEEDILY
UNFIXED	UNFUMED	UNGODDED	UNHANDING	UNHEEDING
UNFIXES	UNFUNDED	UNGODDING	UNHANDLED	UNHEEDY
UNFIXING	UNFUNNY	UNGODLIER	UNHANDS	UNHELE
UNFIXITIES	UNFURL	UNGODLIEST	UNHANDY	UNHELED
UNFIXITY	UNFURLED	UNGODLIKE	UNHANG	UNHELES
UNFLAWED	UNFURLING	UNGODLILY	UNHANGED	UNHELING
UNFLEDGED	UNFURLS	UNGODLY	UNHANGING	UNHELM
UNFLESH	UNFURNISH	UNGODS	UNHANGS	UNHELMED
UNFLESHED	UNFURNISHED	UNGORD	UNHAPPIED	UNHELMING
UNFLESHES	UNFURNISHES	UNGORED	UNHAPPIER	UNHELMS
UNFLESHING	UNFURNISHING	UNGORGED	UNHAPPIES	UNHELPED
UNFLESHLY	UNFURRED	UNGOT	UNHAPPIEST	UNHELPFUL
UNFLOORED	UNGAG	UNGOTTEN	UNHAPPILY	UNHEPPEN
UNFLUSH	UNGAGGED	UNGOWN	UNHAPPY	UNHEROIC
UNFLUSHED	UNGAGGING	UNGOWNED	UNHAPPYING	UNHERST
UNFLUSHES	UNGAGS	UNGOWNING	UNHARBOUR	UNHEWN
UNFLUSHING	UNGAIN	UNGOWNS	UNHARBOURED	UNHIDDEN
UNFOCUSED	UNGAINFUL	UNGRACED	UNHARBOURING	UNHINGE
UNFOLD	UNGAINLIER	UNGRADED	UNHARBOURS	UNHINGED
UNFOLDED	UNGAINLIEST	UNGRASSED	UNHARDY	UNHINGES
UNFOLDER	UNGAINLY	UNGRAVELY	UNHARMED	UNHINGING
UNFOLDERS	UNGALLANT	UNGRAZED	UNHARMFUL	UNHIP
UNFOLDING	UNGALLED	UNGROOMED	UNHARMING	UNHIRED
UNFOLDINGS	UNGARBLED	UNGROUND	UNHARNESS	UNHITCH
UNFOLDS	UNGAUGED	UNGROWN	UNHARNESSED	UNHITCHED
UNFOOL	UNGEAR	UNGRUDGED	UNHARNESSES	UNHITCHES
UNFOOLED	UNGEARED	UNGUAL	UNHARNESSING	UNHITCHING
UNFOOLING	UNGEARING	UNGUARD	UNHASP	UNHIVE
UNFOOLS	UNGEARS	UNGUARDED	UNHASPED	UNHIVED

The Chambers Dictionary is the authority for many longer words; see *OSW* Introduction, page xii.

UNHIVES
UNHIVING
UNHOARD
UNHOARDED
UNHOARDING
UNHOARDS
UNHOLIER
UNHOLIEST
UNHOLILY
UNHOLPEN
UNHOLY
UNHOMELY
UNHONEST
UNHOOD
UNHOODED
UNHOODING
UNHOODS
UNHOOK
UNHOOKED
UNHOOKING
UNHOOKS
UNHOOP
UNHOOPED
UNHOOPING
UNHOOPS
UNHOPED
UNHOPEFUL
UNHORSE
UNHORSED
UNHORSES
UNHORSING
UNHOUSE
UNHOUSED
UNHOUSES
UNHOUSING
UNHUMAN
UNHUMBLED
UNHUNG
UNHUNTED
UNHURRIED
UNHURT
UNHURTFUL
UNHUSK
UNHUSKED
UNHUSKING
UNHUSKS
UNI
UNIAXIAL
UNICITIES
UNICITY
UNICOLOR
UNICOLOUR
UNICORN
UNICORNS
UNICYCLE
UNICYCLES
UNIDEAL
UNIFIABLE
UNIFIC
UNIFIED
UNIFIER
UNIFIERS
UNIFIES
UNIFILAR
UNIFORM
UNIFORMED
UNIFORMING

UNIFORMLY
UNIFORMS
UNIFY
UNIFYING
UNIFYINGS
UNILLUMED
UNILOBAR
UNILOBED
UNIMBUED
UNIMPEDED
UNIMPOSED
UNINCITED
UNINDEXED
UNINJURED
UNINSURED
UNINURED
UNINVITED
UNION
UNIONISE
UNIONISED
UNIONISES
UNIONISING
UNIONISM
UNIONISMS
UNIONIST
UNIONISTS
UNIONIZE
UNIONIZED
UNIONIZES
UNIONIZING
UNIONS
UNIPAROUS
UNIPED
UNIPEDS
UNIPLANAR
UNIPOD
UNIPODS
UNIPOLAR
UNIQUE
UNIQUELY
UNIQUER
UNIQUES
UNIQUEST
UNIRAMOUS
UNIRONED
UNIS
UNISERIAL
UNISEX
UNISEXUAL
UNISON
UNISONAL
UNISONANT
UNISONOUS
UNISONS
UNIT
UNITAL
UNITARD
UNITARDS
UNITARIAN
UNITARIANS
UNITARY
UNITE
UNITED
UNITEDLY
UNITER
UNITERS
UNITES

UNITIES
UNITING
UNITINGS
UNITION
UNITIONS
UNITISE
UNITISED
UNITISES
UNITISING
UNITIVE
UNITIVELY
UNITIZE
UNITIZED
UNITIZES
UNITIZING
UNITS
UNITY
UNIVALENT
UNIVALENTS
UNIVALVE
UNIVALVES
UNIVERSAL
UNIVERSALS
UNIVERSE
UNIVERSES
UNIVOCAL
UNIVOCALS
UNJADED
UNJEALOUS
UNJOINT
UNJOINTED
UNJOINTING
UNJOINTS
UNJOYFUL
UNJOYOUS
UNJUST
UNJUSTER
UNJUSTEST
UNJUSTLY
UNKED
UNKEMPT
UNKENNED
UNKENNEL
UNKENNELLED
UNKENNELLING
UNKENNELS
UNKENT
UNKEPT
UNKET
UNKID
UNKIND
UNKINDER
UNKINDEST
UNKINDLED
UNKINDLIER
UNKINDLIEST
UNKINDLY
UNKING
UNKINGED
UNKINGING
UNKINGLIER
UNKINGLIEST
UNKINGLY
UNKINGS
UNKISS
UNKISSED
UNKISSES

UNKISSING
UNKNELLED
UNKNIGHT
UNKNIGHTED
UNKNIGHTING
UNKNIGHTS
UNKNIT
UNKNITS
UNKNITTED
UNKNITTING
UNKNOT
UNKNOTS
UNKNOTTED
UNKNOTTING
UNKNOWING
UNKNOWN
UNKNOWNS
UNLACE
UNLACED
UNLACES
UNLACING
UNLADE
UNLADED
UNLADEN
UNLADES
UNLADING
UNLADINGS
UNLAID
UNLASH
UNLASHED
UNLASHES
UNLASHING
UNLAST
UNLASTE
UNLATCH
UNLATCHED
UNLATCHES
UNLATCHING
UNLAW
UNLAWED
UNLAWFUL
UNLAWING
UNLAWS
UNLAY
UNLAYING
UNLAYS
UNLEAD
UNLEADED
UNLEADING
UNLEADS
UNLEAL
UNLEARN
UNLEARNED
UNLEARNING
UNLEARNS
UNLEARNT
UNLEASED
UNLEASH
UNLEASHED
UNLEASHES
UNLEASHING
UNLED
UNLESS
UNLET
UNLICH
UNLICKED
UNLID

UNLIDDED
UNLIDDING
UNLIDS
UNLIGHTED
UNLIKABLE
UNLIKE
UNLIKELIER
UNLIKELIEST
UNLIKELY
UNLIKES
UNLIMBER
UNLIMBERED
UNLIMBERING
UNLIMBERS
UNLIME
UNLIMED
UNLIMES
UNLIMING
UNLIMITED
UNLINE
UNLINEAL
UNLINED
UNLINES
UNLINING
UNLINK
UNLINKED
UNLINKING
UNLINKS
UNLISTED
UNLIT
UNLIVABLE
UNLIVE
UNLIVED
UNLIVELY
UNLIVES
UNLIVING
UNLOAD
UNLOADED
UNLOADER
UNLOADERS
UNLOADING
UNLOADINGS
UNLOADS
UNLOCATED
UNLOCK
UNLOCKED
UNLOCKING
UNLOCKS
UNLOGICAL
UNLOOKED
UNLOOSE
UNLOOSED
UNLOOSEN
UNLOOSENED
UNLOOSENING
UNLOOSENS
UNLOOSES
UNLOOSING
UNLOPPED
UNLORD
UNLORDED
UNLORDING
UNLORDLY
UNLORDS
UNLOSABLE
UNLOST
UNLOVABLE

The Chambers Dictionary is the authority for many longer words; see *OSW* Introduction, page xii.

UNLOVE	UNMINDED	UNNOBLING	UNPENT	UNPLUMED
UNLOVED	UNMINDFUL	UNNOTED	UNPEOPLE	UNPLUMES
UNLOVELY	UNMINGLED	UNNOTICED	UNPEOPLED	UNPLUMING
UNLOVES	UNMIRY	UNOBEYED	UNPEOPLES	UNPOETIC
UNLOVING	UNMISSED	UNOBVIOUS	UNPEOPLING	UNPOINTED
UNLUCKIER	UNMIXED	UNOFFERED	UNPERCH	UNPOISED
UNLUCKIEST	UNMIXEDLY	UNOFTEN	UNPERCHED	UNPOISON
UNLUCKILY	UNMOANED	UNOILED	UNPERCHES	UNPOISONED
UNLUCKY	UNMODISH	UNOPENED	UNPERCHING	UNPOISONING
UNMADE	UNMONEYED	UNOPPOSED	UNPERFECT	UNPOISONS
UNMAILED	UNMONIED	UNORDER	UNPERPLEX	UNPOLICED
UNMAIMED	UNMOOR	UNORDERED	UNPERPLEXED	UNPOLISH
UNMAKABLE	UNMOORED	UNORDERING	UNPERPLEXES	UNPOLISHED
UNMAKE	UNMOORING	UNORDERLY	UNPERPLEXING	UNPOLISHES
UNMAKES	UNMOORS	UNORDERS	UNPERSON	UNPOLISHING
UNMAKING	UNMORAL	UNOWED	UNPERSONED	UNPOLITE
UNMAKINGS	UNMOTIVED	UNOWNED	UNPERSONING	UNPOLITIC
UNMAN	UNMOULD	UNPACED	UNPERSONS	UNPOLLED
UNMANACLE	UNMOULDED	UNPACK	UNPERVERT	UNPOPE
UNMANACLED	UNMOULDING	UNPACKED	UNPERVERTED	UNPOPED
UNMANACLES	UNMOULDS	UNPACKER	UNPERVERTING	UNPOPES
UNMANACLING	UNMOUNT	UNPACKERS	UNPERVERTS	UNPOPING
UNMANAGED	UNMOUNTED	UNPACKING	UNPICK	UNPOPULAR
UNMANLIER	UNMOUNTING	UNPACKINGS	UNPICKED	UNPOSED
UNMANLIEST	UNMOUNTS	UNPACKS	UNPICKING	UNPOSTED
UNMANLIKE	UNMOURNED	UNPAGED	UNPICKS	UNPOTABLE
UNMANLY	UNMOVABLE	UNPAID	UNPIERCED	UNPRAISE
UNMANNED	UNMOVABLY	UNPAINED	UNPILOTED	UNPRAISED
UNMANNING	UNMOVED	UNPAINFUL	UNPIN	UNPRAISES
UNMANS	UNMOVEDLY	UNPAINT	UNPINKED	UNPRAISING
UNMANTLE	UNMOVING	UNPAINTED	UNPINKT	UNPRAY
UNMANTLED	UNMOWN	UNPAINTING	UNPINNED	UNPRAYED
UNMANTLES	UNMUFFLE	UNPAINTS	UNPINNING	UNPRAYING
UNMANTLING	UNMUFFLED	UNPAIRED	UNPINS	UNPRAYS
UNMANURED	UNMUFFLES	UNPALSIED	UNPITIED	UNPREACH
UNMARD	UNMUFFLING	UNPANEL	UNPITIFUL	UNPREACHED
UNMARKED	UNMUSICAL	UNPANELLED	UNPITYING	UNPREACHES
UNMARRED	UNMUZZLE	UNPANELLING	UNPLACE	UNPREACHING
UNMARRIED	UNMUZZLED	UNPANELS	UNPLACED	UNPRECISE
UNMARRIES	UNMUZZLES	UNPANGED	UNPLACES	UNPREDICT
UNMARRY	UNMUZZLING	UNPANNEL	UNPLACING	UNPREDICTED
UNMARRYING	UNMUZZLINGS	UNPANNELLED	UNPLAGUED	UNPREDICTING
UNMASK	UNNAIL	UNPANNELLING	UNPLAINED	UNPREDICTS
UNMASKED	UNNAILED	UNPANNELS	UNPLAIT	UNPREPARE
UNMASKER	UNNAILING	UNPAPER	UNPLAITED	UNPREPARED
UNMASKERS	UNNAILS	UNPAPERED	UNPLAITING	UNPREPARES
UNMASKING	UNNAMABLE	UNPAPERING	UNPLAITS	UNPREPARING
UNMASKINGS	UNNAMED	UNPAPERS	UNPLANKED	UNPRESSED
UNMASKS	UNNANELD	UNPARED	UNPLANNED	UNPRETTY
UNMATCHED	UNNATIVE	UNPARTIAL	UNPLANTED	UNPRICED
UNMATED	UNNATURAL	UNPATHED	UNPLAYED	UNPRIEST
UNMATURED	UNNEATH	UNPAVED	UNPLEASED	UNPRIESTED
UNMEANING	UNNEEDED	UNPAY	UNPLEATED	UNPRIESTING
UNMEANT	UNNEEDFUL	UNPAYABLE	UNPLEDGED	UNPRIESTS
UNMEEK	UNNERVE	UNPAYING	UNPLIABLE	UNPRIMED
UNMEET	UNNERVED	UNPAYS	UNPLIABLY	UNPRINTED
UNMEETLY	UNNERVES	UNPEELED	UNPLIANT	UNPRISON
UNMELTED	UNNERVING	UNPEERED	UNPLUCKED	UNPRISONED
UNMERITED	UNNEST	UNPEG	UNPLUG	UNPRISONING
UNMET	UNNESTED	UNPEGGED	UNPLUGGED	UNPRISONS
UNMETED	UNNESTING	UNPEGGING	UNPLUGGING	UNPRIZED
UNMEW	UNNESTS	UNPEGS	UNPLUGS	UNPROP
UNMEWED	UNNETHES	UNPEN	UNPLUMB	UNPROPER
UNMEWING	UNNETTED	UNPENNED	UNPLUMBED	UNPROPPED
UNMEWS	UNNOBLE	UNPENNIED	UNPLUMBING	UNPROPPING
UNMILKED	UNNOBLED	UNPENNING	UNPLUMBS	UNPROPS
UNMILLED	UNNOBLES	UNPENS	UNPLUME	UNPROVED

The Chambers Dictionary is the authority for many longer words; see *OSW* Introduction, page xii.

UNPROVEN	UNREALIZE	UNRIMED	UNRUMPLED	UNSEATS
UNPROVIDE	UNREALIZED	UNRINGED	UNS	UNSECRET
UNPROVIDED	UNREALIZES	UNRIP	UNSADDLE	UNSECULAR
UNPROVIDES	UNREALIZING	UNRIPE	UNSADDLED	UNSECURED
UNPROVIDING	UNREALLY	UNRIPENED	UNSADDLES	UNSEDUCED
UNPROVOKE	UNREAPED	UNRIPER	UNSADDLING	UNSEEABLE
UNPROVOKED	UNREASON	UNRIPEST	UNSAFE	UNSEEDED
UNPROVOKES	UNREASONS	UNRIPPED	UNSAFELY	UNSEEING
UNPROVOKING	UNREAVE	UNRIPPING	UNSAFER	UNSEEL
UNPRUNED	UNREAVED	UNRIPPINGS	UNSAFEST	UNSEELED
UNPULLED	UNREAVES	UNRIPS	UNSAFETIES	UNSEELING
UNPURGED	UNREAVING	UNRISEN	UNSAFETY	UNSEELS
UNPURSE	UNREBATED	UNRIVEN	UNSAID	UNSEEMING
UNPURSED	UNREBUKED	UNRIVET	UNSAILED	UNSEEMINGS
UNPURSES	UNRECKED	UNRIVETED	UNSAINED	UNSEEMLIER
UNPURSING	UNRED	UNRIVETING	UNSAINT	UNSEEMLIEST
UNPURSUED	UNREDREST	UNRIVETS	UNSAINTED	UNSEEMLY
UNQUALIFIED	UNREDUCED	UNROBE	UNSAINTING	UNSEEN
UNQUALIFIES	UNREDY	UNROBED	UNSAINTLIER	UNSEENS
UNQUALIFY	UNREEL	UNROBES	UNSAINTLIEST	UNSEIZED
UNQUALIFYING	UNREELED	UNROBING	UNSAINTLY	UNSELDOM
UNQUEEN	UNREELING	UNROLL	UNSAINTS	UNSELF
UNQUEENED	UNREELS	UNROLLED	UNSALABLE	UNSELFED
UNQUEENING	UNREEVE	UNROLLING	UNSALTED	UNSELFING
UNQUEENLIER	UNREEVED	UNROLLS	UNSALUTED	UNSELFISH
UNQUEENLIEST	UNREEVES	UNROOF	UNSAPPED	UNSELFS
UNQUEENLY	UNREEVING	UNROOFED	UNSASHED	UNSELVES
UNQUEENS	UNREFINED	UNROOFING	UNSATABLE	UNSENSE
UNQUELLED	UNREFUTED	UNROOFS	UNSATED	UNSENSED
UNQUIET	UNREIN	UNROOST	UNSATIATE	UNSENSES
UNQUIETED	UNREINED	UNROOSTED	UNSATING	UNSENSING
UNQUIETING	UNREINING	UNROOSTING	UNSAVED	UNSENT
UNQUIETLY	UNREINS	UNROOSTS	UNSAVOURY	UNSERIOUS
UNQUIETS	UNRELATED	UNROOT	UNSAY	UNSET
UNQUOTE	UNRELAXED	UNROOTED	UNSAYABLE	UNSETS
UNQUOTED	UNREMOVED	UNROOTING	UNSAYING	UNSETTING
UNQUOTES	UNRENEWED	UNROOTS	UNSAYS	UNSETTLE
UNQUOTING	UNRENT	UNROPE	UNSCALE	UNSETTLED
UNRACED	UNREPAID	UNROPED	UNSCALED	UNSETTLES
UNRACKED	UNREPAIR	UNROPES	UNSCALES	UNSETTLING
UNRAISED	UNREPAIRS	UNROPING	UNSCALING	UNSETTLINGS
UNRAKE	UNRESERVE	UNROSINED	UNSCANNED	UNSEVERED
UNRAKED	UNRESERVES	UNROTTED	UNSCARRED	UNSEW
UNRAKES	UNREST	UNROTTEN	UNSCARY	UNSEWED
UNRAKING	UNRESTFUL	UNROUGED	UNSCATHED	UNSEWING
UNRATED	UNRESTING	UNROUGH	UNSCENTED	UNSEWN
UNRAVEL	UNRESTS	UNROUND	UNSCOURED	UNSEWS
UNRAVELLED	UNREVISED	UNROUNDED	UNSCREW	UNSEX
UNRAVELLING	UNREVOKED	UNROUNDING	UNSCREWED	UNSEXED
UNRAVELLINGS	UNRHYMED	UNROUNDS	UNSCREWING	UNSEXES
UNRAVELS	UNRIBBED	UNROUSED	UNSCREWS	UNSEXING
UNRAZORED	UNRID	UNROVE	UNSCYTHED	UNSEXIST
UNREACHED	UNRIDABLE	UNROYAL	UNSEAL	UNSEXUAL
UNREAD	UNRIDDEN	UNROYALLY	UNSEALED	UNSHACKLE
UNREADIER	UNRIDDLE	UNRUBBED	UNSEALING	UNSHACKLED
UNREADIEST	UNRIDDLED	UNRUDE	UNSEALS	UNSHACKLES
UNREADILY	UNRIDDLER	UNRUFFE	UNSEAM	UNSHACKLING
UNREADY	UNRIDDLERS	UNRUFFLE	UNSEAMED	UNSHADED
UNREAL	UNRIDDLES	UNRUFFLED	UNSEAMING	UNSHADOW
UNREALISE	UNRIDDLING	UNRUFFLES	UNSEAMS	UNSHADOWED
UNREALISED	UNRIFLED	UNRUFFLING	UNSEASON	UNSHADOWING
UNREALISES	UNRIG	UNRULE	UNSEASONED	UNSHADOWS
UNREALISING	UNRIGGED	UNRULED	UNSEASONING	UNSHAKED
UNREALISM	UNRIGGING	UNRULES	UNSEASONS	UNSHAKEN
UNREALISMS	UNRIGHT	UNRULIER	UNSEAT	UNSHALE
UNREALITIES	UNRIGHTS	UNRULIEST	UNSEATED	UNSHALED
UNREALITY	UNRIGS	UNRULY	UNSEATING	UNSHALES

The Chambers Dictionary is the authority for many longer words; see *OSW* Introduction, page xii.

UNSHALING
UNSHAMED
UNSHAPE
UNSHAPED
UNSHAPELIER
UNSHAPELIEST
UNSHAPELY
UNSHAPEN
UNSHAPES
UNSHAPING
UNSHARED
UNSHAVED
UNSHAVEN
UNSHEATHE
UNSHEATHED
UNSHEATHES
UNSHEATHING
UNSHED
UNSHELL
UNSHELLED
UNSHELLING
UNSHELLS
UNSHENT
UNSHEWN
UNSHIP
UNSHIPPED
UNSHIPPING
UNSHIPS
UNSHOCKED
UNSHOD
UNSHOE
UNSHOED
UNSHOEING
UNSHOES
UNSHOOT
UNSHOOTED
UNSHOOTING
UNSHOOTS
UNSHORN
UNSHOT
UNSHOUT
UNSHOUTED
UNSHOUTING
UNSHOUTS
UNSHOWN
UNSHRIVED
UNSHRIVEN
UNSHROUD
UNSHROUDED
UNSHROUDING
UNSHROUDS
UNSHRUBD
UNSHUNNED
UNSHUT
UNSHUTS
UNSHUTTER
UNSHUTTERED
UNSHUTTERING
UNSHUTTERS
UNSHUTTING
UNSICKER
UNSICKLED
UNSIFTED
UNSIGHING
UNSIGHT
UNSIGHTED
UNSIGHTLIER

UNSIGHTLIEST
UNSIGHTLY
UNSIGNED
UNSINEW
UNSINEWED
UNSINEWING
UNSINEWS
UNSISTING
UNSIZABLE
UNSIZED
UNSKILFUL
UNSKILLED
UNSKIMMED
UNSKINNED
UNSLAIN
UNSLAKED
UNSLICED
UNSLING
UNSLINGING
UNSLINGS
UNSLUICE
UNSLUICED
UNSLUICES
UNSLUICING
UNSLUNG
UNSMART
UNSMILING
UNSMITTEN
UNSMOOTH
UNSMOOTHED
UNSMOOTHING
UNSMOOTHS
UNSMOTE
UNSNAP
UNSNAPPED
UNSNAPPING
UNSNAPS
UNSNARL
UNSNARLED
UNSNARLING
UNSNARLS
UNSNECK
UNSNECKED
UNSNECKING
UNSNECKS
UNSNUFFED
UNSOAPED
UNSOCIAL
UNSOCKET
UNSOCKETED
UNSOCKETING
UNSOCKETS
UNSOD
UNSODDEN
UNSOFT
UNSOILED
UNSOLACED
UNSOLD
UNSOLDER
UNSOLDERED
UNSOLDERING
UNSOLDERS
UNSOLEMN
UNSOLID
UNSOLIDLY
UNSOLVED
UNSONSY

UNSOOTE
UNSORTED
UNSOUGHT
UNSOUL
UNSOULED
UNSOULING
UNSOULS
UNSOUND
UNSOUNDED
UNSOUNDER
UNSOUNDEST
UNSOUNDLY
UNSOURCED
UNSOURED
UNSOWN
UNSPAR
UNSPARED
UNSPARING
UNSPARRED
UNSPARRING
UNSPARS
UNSPEAK
UNSPEAKING
UNSPEAKS
UNSPED
UNSPELL
UNSPELLED
UNSPELLING
UNSPELLS
UNSPENT
UNSPHERE
UNSPHERED
UNSPHERES
UNSPHERING
UNSPIDE
UNSPIED
UNSPILLED
UNSPILT
UNSPOILED
UNSPOILT
UNSPOKE
UNSPOKEN
UNSPOTTED
UNSPRUNG
UNSPUN
UNSQUARED
UNSTABLE
UNSTABLER
UNSTABLEST
UNSTACK
UNSTACKED
UNSTACKING
UNSTACKS
UNSTAID
UNSTAINED
UNSTAMPED
UNSTARCH
UNSTARCHED
UNSTARCHES
UNSTARCHING
UNSTATE
UNSTATED
UNSTATES
UNSTATING
UNSTAYED
UNSTAYING
UNSTEADIED

UNSTEADIER
UNSTEADIES
UNSTEADIEST
UNSTEADY
UNSTEADYING
UNSTEEL
UNSTEELED
UNSTEELING
UNSTEELS
UNSTEP
UNSTEPPED
UNSTEPPING
UNSTEPS
UNSTERILE
UNSTICK
UNSTICKING
UNSTICKS
UNSTIFLED
UNSTILLED
UNSTINTED
UNSTIRRED
UNSTITCH
UNSTITCHED
UNSTITCHES
UNSTITCHING
UNSTOCK
UNSTOCKED
UNSTOCKING
UNSTOCKS
UNSTOP
UNSTOPPED
UNSTOPPER
UNSTOPPERED
UNSTOPPERING
UNSTOPPERS
UNSTOPPING
UNSTOPS
UNSTOW
UNSTOWED
UNSTOWING
UNSTOWS
UNSTRAP
UNSTRAPPED
UNSTRAPPING
UNSTRAPS
UNSTRING
UNSTRINGED
UNSTRINGING
UNSTRINGS
UNSTRIP
UNSTRIPED
UNSTRIPPED
UNSTRIPPING
UNSTRIPS
UNSTRUCK
UNSTRUNG
UNSTUCK
UNSTUDIED
UNSTUFFED
UNSTUFFY
UNSTUFT
UNSUBDUED
UNSUBJECT
UNSUBTLE
UNSUCCESS
UNSUCCESSES
UNSUCKED

UNSUIT
UNSUITED
UNSUITING
UNSUITS
UNSULLIED
UNSUMMED
UNSUNG
UNSUNNED
UNSUNNY
UNSUPPLE
UNSURE
UNSURED
UNSURER
UNSUREST
UNSUSPECT
UNSWADDLE
UNSWADDLED
UNSWADDLES
UNSWADDLING
UNSWATHE
UNSWATHED
UNSWATHES
UNSWATHING
UNSWAYED
UNSWEAR
UNSWEARING
UNSWEARINGS
UNSWEARS
UNSWEET
UNSWEPT
UNSWORE
UNSWORN
UNTACK
UNTACKED
UNTACKING
UNTACKLE
UNTACKLED
UNTACKLES
UNTACKLING
UNTACKS
UNTAILED
UNTAINTED
UNTAKEN
UNTAMABLE
UNTAMABLY
UNTAME
UNTAMED
UNTAMES
UNTAMING
UNTANGLE
UNTANGLED
UNTANGLES
UNTANGLING
UNTANNED
UNTAPPED
UNTARRED
UNTASTED
UNTAUGHT
UNTAX
UNTAXED
UNTAXES
UNTAXING
UNTEACH
UNTEACHES
UNTEACHING
UNTEAM
UNTEAMED

The Chambers Dictionary is the authority for many longer words; see *OSW* Introduction, page xii.

UNTEAMING	UNTIMEOUS	UNTUNED	UNVIZARDED	UNWIELDIEST
UNTEAMS	UNTIN	UNTUNEFUL	UNVIZARDING	UNWIELDY
UNTEMPER	UNTINGED	UNTUNES	UNVIZARDS	UNWIFELIER
UNTEMPERED	UNTINNED	UNTUNING	UNVOCAL	UNWIFELIEST
UNTEMPERING	UNTINNING	UNTURBID	UNVOICE	UNWIFELY
UNTEMPERS	UNTINS	UNTURF	UNVOICED	UNWIGGED
UNTEMPTED	UNTIRABLE	UNTURFED	UNVOICES	UNWILFUL
UNTENABLE	UNTIRED	UNTURFING	UNVOICING	UNWILL
UNTENANT	UNTIRING	UNTURFS	UNVOICINGS	UNWILLED
UNTENANTED	UNTITLED	UNTURN	UNVULGAR	UNWILLING
UNTENANTING	UNTO	UNTURNED	UNWAGED	UNWILLS
UNTENANTS	UNTOILING	UNTURNING	UNWAKED	UNWIND
UNTENDED	UNTOLD	UNTURNS	UNWAKENED	UNWINDING
UNTENDER	UNTOMB	UNTUTORED	UNWALLED	UNWINDINGS
UNTENT	UNTOMBED	UNTWINE	UNWANTED	UNWINDS
UNTENTED	UNTOMBING	UNTWINED	UNWARDED	UNWINGED
UNTENTING	UNTOMBS	UNTWINES	UNWARE	UNWINKING
UNTENTS	UNTONED	UNTWINING	UNWARELY	UNWIPED
UNTENTY	UNTORN	UNTWIST	UNWARES	UNWIRE
UNTESTED	UNTOUCHED	UNTWISTED	UNWARIE	UNWIRED
UNTETHER	UNTOWARD	UNTWISTING	UNWARIER	UNWIRES
UNTETHERED	UNTRACE	UNTWISTINGS	UNWARIEST	UNWIRING
UNTETHERING	UNTRACED	UNTWISTS	UNWARILY	UNWISDOM
UNTETHERS	UNTRACES	UNTYING	UNWARLIKE	UNWISDOMS
UNTHANKED	UNTRACING	UNTYINGS	UNWARMED	UNWISE
UNTHATCH	UNTRACKED	UNTYPABLE	UNWARNED	UNWISELY
UNTHATCHED	UNTRADED	UNTYPICAL	UNWARPED	UNWISER
UNTHATCHES	UNTRAINED	UNURGED	UNWARY	UNWISEST
UNTHATCHING	UNTREAD	UNUSABLE	UNWASHED	UNWISH
UNTHAW	UNTREADING	UNUSABLY	UNWASHEN	UNWISHED
UNTHAWED	UNTREADS	UNUSED	UNWASTED	UNWISHES
UNTHAWING	UNTREATED	UNUSEFUL	UNWASTING	UNWISHFUL
UNTHAWS	UNTRESSED	UNUSHERED	UNWATCHED	UNWISHING
UNTHINK	UNTRIDE	UNUSUAL	UNWATER	UNWIST
UNTHINKING	UNTRIED	UNUSUALLY	UNWATERED	UNWIT
UNTHINKS	UNTRIM	UNUTTERED	UNWATERING	UNWITCH
UNTHOUGHT	UNTRIMMED	UNVAIL	UNWATERS	UNWITCHED
UNTHREAD	UNTRIMMING	UNVAILE	UNWATERY	UNWITCHES
UNTHREADED	UNTRIMS	UNVAILED	UNWAYED	UNWITCHING
UNTHREADING	UNTROD	UNVAILES	UNWEAL	UNWITS
UNTHREADS	UNTRODDEN	UNVAILING	UNWEALS	UNWITTED
UNTHRIFT	UNTRUE	UNVAILS	UNWEANED	UNWITTILY
UNTHRIFTS	UNTRUER	UNVALUED	UNWEAPON	UNWITTING
UNTHRIFTY	UNTRUEST	UNVARIED	UNWEAPONED	UNWITTY
UNTHRONE	UNTRUISM	UNVARYING	UNWEAPONING	UNWIVE
UNTHRONED	UNTRUISMS	UNVEIL	UNWEAPONS	UNWIVED
UNTHRONES	UNTRULY	UNVEILED	UNWEARIED	UNWIVES
UNTHRONING	UNTRUSS	UNVEILER	UNWEARY	UNWIVING
UNTIDIED	UNTRUSSED	UNVEILERS	UNWEAVE	UNWOMAN
UNTIDIER	UNTRUSSER	UNVEILING	UNWEAVES	UNWOMANED
UNTIDIES	UNTRUSSERS	UNVEILINGS	UNWEAVING	UNWOMANING
UNTIDIEST	UNTRUSSES	UNVEILS	UNWEBBED	UNWOMANLIER
UNTIDILY	UNTRUSSING	UNVENTED	UNWED	UNWOMANLIEST
UNTIDY	UNTRUSSINGS	UNVERSED	UNWEDDED	UNWOMANLY
UNTIDYING	UNTRUST	UNVETTED	UNWEEDED	UNWOMANS
UNTIE	UNTRUSTS	UNVEXED	UNWEENED	UNWON
UNTIED	UNTRUSTY	UNVIABLE	UNWEETING	UNWONT
UNTIES	UNTRUTH	UNVIEWED	UNWEIGHED	UNWONTED
UNTIL	UNTRUTHS	UNVIRTUE	UNWELCOME	UNWOODED
UNTILE	UNTUCK	UNVIRTUES	UNWELDY	UNWOOED
UNTILED	UNTUCKED	UNVISITED	UNWELL	UNWORDED
UNTILES	UNTUCKING	UNVISOR	UNWEPT	UNWORK
UNTILING	UNTUCKS	UNVISORED	UNWET	UNWORKED
UNTILLED	UNTUMBLED	UNVISORING	UNWETTED	UNWORKING
UNTIMELIER	UNTUNABLE	UNVISORS	UNWHIPPED	UNWORKS
UNTIMELIEST	UNTUNABLY	UNVITAL	UNWHIPT	UNWORLDLIER
UNTIMELY	UNTUNE	UNVIZARD	UNWIELDIER	UNWORLDLIEST

The Chambers Dictionary is the authority for many longer words; see *OSW* Introduction, page xii.

UNWORLDLY	UPBOUND	UPCURL	UPGROWS	UPKNITTED
UNWORMED	UPBOUNDEN	UPCURLED	UPGROWTH	UPKNITTING
UNWORN	UPBRAID	UPCURLING	UPGROWTHS	UPLAID
UNWORRIED	UPBRAIDED	UPCURLS	UPGUSH	UPLAND
UNWORTH	UPBRAIDER	UPCURVED	UPGUSHED	UPLANDER
UNWORTHIER	UPBRAIDERS	UPDATE	UPGUSHES	UPLANDERS
UNWORTHIEST	UPBRAIDING	UPDATED	UPGUSHING	UPLANDISH
UNWORTHS	UPBRAIDINGS	UPDATES	UPHAND	UPLANDS
UNWORTHY	UPBRAIDS	UPDATING	UPHANG	UPLAY
UNWOUND	UPBRAST	UPDRAG	UPHANGING	UPLAYING
UNWOUNDED	UPBRAY	UPDRAGGED	UPHANGS	UPLAYS
UNWOVE	UPBRAYED	UPDRAGGING	UPHAUD	UPLEAD
UNWOVEN	UPBRAYING	UPDRAGS	UPHAUDING	UPLEADING
UNWRAP	UPBRAYS	UPDRAW	UPHAUDS	UPLEADS
UNWRAPPED	UPBREAK	UPDRAWING	UPHEAP	UPLEAN
UNWRAPPING	UPBREAKING	UPDRAWN	UPHEAPED	UPLEANED
UNWRAPS	UPBREAKS	UPDRAWS	UPHEAPING	UPLEANING
UNWREAKED	UPBRING	UPDREW	UPHEAPINGS	UPLEANS
UNWREATHE	UPBRINGING	UPEND	UPHEAPS	UPLEANT
UNWREATHED	UPBRINGINGS	UPENDED	UPHEAVAL	UPLEAP
UNWREATHES	UPBRINGS	UPENDING	UPHEAVALS	UPLEAPED
UNWREATHING	UPBROKE	UPENDS	UPHEAVE	UPLEAPING
UNWRINKLE	UPBROKEN	UPFILL	UPHEAVED	UPLEAPS
UNWRINKLED	UPBROUGHT	UPFILLED	UPHEAVES	UPLEAPT
UNWRINKLES	UPBUILD	UPFILLING	UPHEAVING	UPLED
UNWRINKLING	UPBUILDING	UPFILLINGS	UPHELD	UPLIFT
UNWRITE	UPBUILDINGS	UPFILLS	UPHILD	UPLIFTED
UNWRITES	UPBUILDS	UPFLOW	UPHILL	UPLIFTER
UNWRITING	UPBUILT	UPFLOWED	UPHILLS	UPLIFTERS
UNWRITTEN	UPBURNING	UPFLOWING	UPHOARD	UPLIFTING
UNWROTE	UPBURST	UPFLOWS	UPHOARDED	UPLIFTINGS
UNWROUGHT	UPBURSTING	UPFLUNG	UPHOARDING	UPLIFTS
UNWRUNG	UPBURSTS	UPFOLLOW	UPHOARDS	UPLIGHTED
UNYEANED	UPBY	UPFOLLOWED	UPHOIST	UPLIGHTER
UNYOKE	UPBYE	UPFOLLOWING	UPHOISTED	UPLIGHTERS
UNYOKED	UPCAST	UPFOLLOWS	UPHOISTING	UPLINK
UNYOKES	UPCASTING	UPFRONT	UPHOISTS	UPLINKING
UNYOKING	UPCASTS	UPFURL	UPHOLD	UPLINKINGS
UNZEALOUS	UPCATCH	UPFURLED	UPHOLDER	UPLINKS
UNZIP	UPCATCHES	UPFURLING	UPHOLDERS	UPLOCK
UNZIPPED	UPCATCHING	UPFURLS	UPHOLDING	UPLOCKED
UNZIPPING	UPCAUGHT	UPGANG	UPHOLDINGS	UPLOCKING
UNZIPS	UPCHEARD	UPGANGS	UPHOLDS	UPLOCKS
UNZONED	UPCHEER	UPGATHER	UPHOLSTER	UPLOOK
UP	UPCHEERED	UPGATHERED	UPHOLSTERED	UPLOOKED
UPADAISY	UPCHEERING	UPGATHERING	UPHOLSTERING	UPLOOKING
UPAITHRIC	UPCHEERS	UPGATHERS	UPHOLSTERS	UPLOOKS
UPAS	UPCHUCK	UPGAZE	UPHOORD	UPLYING
UPASES	UPCHUCKED	UPGAZED	UPHOORDED	UPMAKE
UPBEAR	UPCHUCKING	UPGAZES	UPHOORDING	UPMAKER
UPBEARING	UPCHUCKS	UPGAZING	UPHOORDS	UPMAKERS
UPBEARS	UPCLIMB	UPGO	UPHROE	UPMAKES
UPBEAT	UPCLIMBED	UPGOES	UPHROES	UPMAKING
UPBIND	UPCLIMBING	UPGOING	UPHUDDEN	UPMAKINGS
UPBINDING	UPCLIMBS	UPGOINGS	UPHUNG	UPMANSHIP
UPBINDS	UPCLOSE	UPGONE	UPHURL	UPMANSHIPS
UPBLEW	UPCLOSED	UPGRADE	UPHURLED	UPMOST
UPBLOW	UPCLOSES	UPGRADED	UPHURLING	UPON
UPBLOWING	UPCLOSING	UPGRADER	UPHURLS	UPPED
UPBLOWN	UPCOAST	UPGRADERS	UPJET	UPPER
UPBLOWS	UPCOIL	UPGRADES	UPJETS	UPPERCUT
UPBOIL	UPCOILED	UPGRADING	UPJETTED	UPPERCUTS
UPBOILED	UPCOILING	UPGREW	UPJETTING	UPPERMOST
UPBOILING	UPCOILS	UPGROW	UPKEEP	UPPERS
UPBOILS	UPCOME	UPGROWING	UPKEEPS	UPPILED
UPBORE	UPCOMES	UPGROWINGS	UPKNIT	UPPING
UPBORNE	UPCOMING	UPGROWN	UPKNITS	UPPINGS

The Chambers Dictionary is the authority for many longer words; see *OSW* Introduction, page xii.

UPPISH	UPSEND	UPSTROKES	UPTRENDS	URANINITES
UPPISHLY	UPSENDING	UPSURGE	UPTRILLED	URANINS
UPPITY	UPSENDS	UPSURGED	UPTURN	URANISCI
UPRAISE	UPSENT	UPSURGES	UPTURNED	URANISCUS
UPRAISED	UPSET	UPSURGING	UPTURNING	URANISM
UPRAISES	UPSETS	UPSWARM	UPTURNINGS	URANISMS
UPRAISING	UPSETTER	UPSWARMED	UPTURNS	URANITE
UPRAN	UPSETTERS	UPSWARMING	UPTYING	URANITES
UPRATE	UPSETTING	UPSWARMS	UPVALUE	URANITIC
UPRATED	UPSETTINGS	UPSWAY	UPVALUED	URANIUM
UPRATES	UPSEY	UPSWAYED	UPVALUES	URANIUMS
UPRATING	UPSEYS	UPSWAYING	UPVALUING	URANOLOGIES
UPREAR	UPSHOOT	UPSWAYS	UPWAFT	URANOLOGY
UPREARED	UPSHOOTING	UPSWEEP	UPWAFTED	URANOUS
UPREARING	UPSHOOTS	UPSWEEPS	UPWAFTING	URANYL
UPREARS	UPSHOT	UPSWELL	UPWAFTS	URANYLIC
UPREST	UPSHOTS	UPSWELLED	UPWARD	URANYLS
UPRESTS	UPSIDE	UPSWELLING	UPWARDLY	URAO
UPRIGHT	UPSIDES	UPSWELLS	UPWARDS	URAOS
UPRIGHTED	UPSIES	UPSWEPT	UPWELL	URARI
UPRIGHTING	UPSILON	UPSWING	UPWELLED	URARIS
UPRIGHTLY	UPSILONS	UPSWINGS	UPWELLING	URATE
UPRIGHTS	UPSITTING	UPSWOLLEN	UPWELLINGS	URATES
UPRISAL	UPSITTINGS	UPSY	UPWELLS	URBAN
UPRISALS	UPSPAKE	UPTAK	UPWENT	URBANE
UPRISE	UPSPEAK	UPTAKE	UPWHIRL	URBANELY
UPRISEN	UPSPEAKING	UPTAKEN	UPWHIRLED	URBANER
UPRISES	UPSPEAKS	UPTAKES	UPWHIRLING	URBANEST
UPRISING	UPSPEAR	UPTAKING	UPWHIRLS	URBANISE
UPRISINGS	UPSPEARED	UPTAKS	UPWIND	URBANISED
UPRIST	UPSPEARING	UPTEAR	UPWINDING	URBANISES
UPRISTS	UPSPEARS	UPTEARING	UPWINDS	URBANISING
UPRIVER	UPSPOKE	UPTEARS	UPWOUND	URBANITE
UPROAR	UPSPOKEN	UPTHREW	UPWRAP	URBANITES
UPROARED	UPSPRANG	UPTHROW	UPWRAPS	URBANITIES
UPROARING	UPSPRING	UPTHROWING	UPWROUGHT	URBANITY
UPROARS	UPSPRINGING	UPTHROWN	UR	URBANIZE
UPROLL	UPSPRINGS	UPTHROWS	URACHI	URBANIZED
UPROLLED	UPSPRUNG	UPTHRUST	URACHUS	URBANIZES
UPROLLING	UPSTAGE	UPTHRUSTING	URACHUSES	URBANIZING
UPROLLS	UPSTAGED	UPTHRUSTS	URACIL	URCEOLATE
UPROOT	UPSTAGES	UPTHUNDER	URACILS	URCEOLI
UPROOTAL	UPSTAGING	UPTHUNDERED	URAEI	URCEOLUS
UPROOTALS	UPSTAIR	UPTHUNDERING	URAEMIA	URCEOLUSES
UPROOTED	UPSTAIRS	UPTHUNDERS	URAEMIAS	URCHIN
UPROOTER	UPSTAND	UPTIE	URAEMIC	URCHINS
UPROOTERS	UPSTANDING	UPTIED	URAEUS	URD
UPROOTING	UPSTANDS	UPTIES	URAEUSES	URDE
UPROOTINGS	UPSTARE	UPTIGHT	URALI	URDEE
UPROOTS	UPSTARED	UPTIGHTER	URALIS	URDS
UPROSE	UPSTARES	UPTIGHTEST	URALITE	URDY
UPROUSE	UPSTARING	UPTILT	URALITES	URE
UPROUSED	UPSTART	UPTILTED	URALITIC	UREA
UPROUSES	UPSTARTED	UPTILTING	URALITISE	UREAL
UPROUSING	UPSTARTING	UPTILTS	URALITISED	UREAS
UPRUN	UPSTARTS	UPTOOK	URALITISES	UREDIA
UPRUNNING	UPSTATE	UPTORE	URALITISING	UREDINE
UPRUNS	UPSTAY	UPTORN	URALITIZE	UREDINES
UPRUSH	UPSTAYED	UPTOWN	URALITIZED	UREDINIA
UPRUSHED	UPSTAYING	UPTOWNER	URALITIZES	UREDINIAL
UPRUSHES	UPSTAYS	UPTOWNERS	URALITIZING	UREDINIUM
UPRUSHING	UPSTOOD	UPTOWNS	URANIAN	UREDINOUS
UPRYST	UPSTREAM	UPTRAIN	URANIC	UREDIUM
UPS	UPSTREAMED	UPTRAINED	URANIDE	UREDO
UPSCALE	UPSTREAMING	UPTRAINING	URANIDES	UREDOSORI
UPSEE	UPSTREAMS	UPTRAINS	URANIN	UREIC
UPSEES	UPSTROKE	UPTREND	URANINITE	UREIDE

The Chambers Dictionary is the authority for many longer words; see *OSW* Introduction, page xii.

UREIDES	URINOLOGY	URSINE	USUCAPIONS	UTMOST
UREMIA	URINOSE	URSON	USUCAPT	UTMOSTS
UREMIAS	URINOUS	URSONS	USUCAPTED	UTOPIA
UREMIC	URITE	URTEXT	USUCAPTING	UTOPIAN
URENA	URITES	URTEXTS	USUCAPTS	UTOPIANS
URENAS	URMAN	URTICA	USUFRUCT	UTOPIAS
URENT	URMANS	URTICANT	USUFRUCTED	UTOPIAST
URES	URN	URTICARIA	USUFRUCTING	UTOPIASTS
URESES	URNAL	URTICARIAS	USUFRUCTS	UTOPISM
URESIS	URNED	URTICAS	USURE	UTOPISMS
URETER	URNFIELD	URTICATE	USURED	UTOPIST
URETERAL	URNFIELDS	URTICATED	USURER	UTOPISTS
URETERIC	URNFUL	URTICATES	USURERS	UTRICLE
URETERS	URNFULS	URTICATING	USURES	UTRICLES
URETHAN	URNING	URUBU	USURESS	UTRICULAR
URETHANE	URNINGS	URUBUS	USURESSES	UTRICULI
URETHANES	URNS	URUS	USURIES	UTRICULUS
URETHANS	UROCHORD	URUSES	USURING	UTS
URETHRA	UROCHORDS	URVA	USURIOUS	UTTER
URETHRAE	UROCHROME	URVAS	USUROUS	UTTERABLE
URETHRAL	UROCHROMES	US	USURP	UTTERANCE
URETHRAS	URODELAN	USABILITIES	USURPED	UTTERANCES
URETIC	URODELANS	USABILITY	USURPEDLY	UTTERED
URGE	URODELE	USABLE	USURPER	UTTERER
URGED	URODELES	USABLY	USURPERS	UTTERERS
URGENCE	URODELOUS	USAGE	USURPING	UTTEREST
URGENCES	UROGENOUS	USAGER	USURPINGS	UTTERING
URGENCIES	UROGRAPHIES	USAGERS	USURPS	UTTERINGS
URGENCY	UROGRAPHY	USAGES	USURY	UTTERLESS
URGENT	UROKINASE	USANCE	USWARD	UTTERLY
URGENTLY	UROKINASES	USANCES	USWARDS	UTTERMOST
URGER	UROLAGNIA	USE	UT	UTTERMOSTS
URGERS	UROLAGNIAS	USED	UTAS	UTTERNESS
URGES	UROLITH	USEFUL	UTASES	UTTERNESSES
URGING	UROLITHIC	USEFULLY	UTE	UTTERS
URGINGS	UROLITHS	USELESS	UTENSIL	UTU
URIAL	UROLOGIC	USELESSLY	UTENSILS	UTUS
URIALS	UROLOGIES	USER	UTERI	UVA
URIC	UROLOGIST	USERS	UTERINE	UVAE
URICASE	UROLOGISTS	USES	UTERITIS	UVAROVITE
URICASES	UROLOGY	USHER	UTERITISES	UVAROVITES
URIDINE	UROMERE	USHERED	UTEROTOMIES	UVAS
URIDINES	UROMERES	USHERESS	UTEROTOMY	UVEA
URINAL	UROPOD	USHERESSES	UTERUS	UVEAL
URINALS	UROPODS	USHERETTE	UTES	UVEAS
URINANT	UROPYGIA	USHERETTES	UTILE	UVEITIC
URINARIES	UROPYGIAL	USHERING	UTILISE	UVEITIS
URINARY	UROPYGIUM	USHERINGS	UTILISED	UVEITISES
URINATE	UROPYGIUMS	USHERS	UTILISER	UVEOUS
URINATED	UROSCOPIC	USHERSHIP	UTILISERS	UVULA
URINATES	UROSCOPIES	USHERSHIPS	UTILISES	UVULAE
URINATING	UROSCOPY	USING	UTILISING	UVULAR
URINATION	UROSES	USNEA	UTILITIES	UVULARLY
URINATIONS	UROSIS	USNEAS	UTILITY	UVULAS
URINATIVE	UROSOME	USTION	UTILIZE	UVULITIS
URINATOR	UROSOMES	USTIONS	UTILIZED	UVULITISES
URINATORS	UROSTEGE	USUAL	UTILIZER	UXORIAL
URINE	UROSTEGES	USUALLY	UTILIZERS	UXORIALLY
URINED	UROSTOMIES	USUALNESS	UTILIZES	UXORICIDE
URINES	UROSTOMY	USUALNESSES	UTILIZING	UXORICIDES
URINING	UROSTYLE	USUALS	UTIS	UXORIOUS
URINOLOGIES	UROSTYLES	USUCAPION	UTISES	

V

VAC
VACANCE
VACANCES
VACANCIES
VACANCY
VACANT
VACANTLY
VACATE
VACATED
VACATES
VACATING
VACATION
VACATIONED
VACATIONING
VACATIONS
VACATUR
VACATURS
VACCINAL
VACCINATE
VACCINATED
VACCINATES
VACCINATING
VACCINE
VACCINES
VACCINIA
VACCINIAL
VACCINIAS
VACCINIUM
VACCINIUMS
VACHERIN
VACHERINS
VACILLANT
VACILLATE
VACILLATED
VACILLATES
VACILLATING
VACKED
VACKING
VACS
VACUA
VACUATE
VACUATED
VACUATES
VACUATING
VACUATION
VACUATIONS
VACUIST
VACUISTS
VACUITIES
VACUITY
VACUOLAR
VACUOLATE
VACUOLE
VACUOLES
VACUOUS
VACUOUSLY
VACUUM
VACUUMED
VACUUMING

VACUUMS
VADE
VADED
VADES
VADING
VADOSE
VAE
VAES
VAGABOND
VAGABONDED
VAGABONDING
VAGABONDS
VAGAL
VAGARIES
VAGARIOUS
VAGARISH
VAGARY
VAGI
VAGILE
VAGILITIES
VAGILITY
VAGINA
VAGINAE
VAGINAL
VAGINALLY
VAGINANT
VAGINAS
VAGINATE
VAGINATED
VAGINITIS
VAGINITISES
VAGINULA
VAGINULAE
VAGINULE
VAGINULES
VAGITUS
VAGITUSES
VAGRANCIES
VAGRANCY
VAGRANT
VAGRANTS
VAGROM
VAGUE
VAGUED
VAGUELY
VAGUENESS
VAGUENESSES
VAGUER
VAGUES
VAGUEST
VAGUING
VAGUS
VAHINE
VAHINES
VAIL
VAILED
VAILING
VAILS
VAIN

VAINER
VAINESSE
VAINESSES
VAINEST
VAINGLORIED
VAINGLORIES
VAINGLORY
VAINGLORYING
VAINLY
VAINNESS
VAINNESSES
VAIR
VAIRE
VAIRIER
VAIRIEST
VAIRS
VAIRY
VAIVODE
VAIVODES
VAKASS
VAKASSES
VAKEEL
VAKEELS
VAKIL
VAKILS
VALANCE
VALANCED
VALANCES
VALE
VALENCE
VALENCES
VALENCIES
VALENCY
VALENTINE
VALENTINES
VALERIAN
VALERIANS
VALES
VALET
VALETA
VALETAS
VALETE
VALETED
VALETES
VALETING
VALETINGS
VALETS
VALGOUS
VALGUS
VALGUSES
VALI
VALIANCE
VALIANCES
VALIANCIES
VALIANCY
VALIANT
VALIANTLY
VALIANTS
VALID

VALIDATE
VALIDATED
VALIDATES
VALIDATING
VALIDER
VALIDEST
VALIDITIES
VALIDITY
VALIDLY
VALIDNESS
VALIDNESSES
VALINE
VALINES
VALIS
VALISE
VALISES
VALLAR
VALLARY
VALLECULA
VALLECULAE
VALLEY
VALLEYS
VALLONIA
VALLONIAS
VALLUM
VALLUMS
VALONEA
VALONEAS
VALONIA
VALONIAS
VALOR
VALORISE
VALORISED
VALORISES
VALORISING
VALORIZE
VALORIZED
VALORIZES
VALORIZING
VALOROUS
VALORS
VALOUR
VALOURS
VALSE
VALSED
VALSES
VALSING
VALUABLE
VALUABLES
VALUABLY
VALUATE
VALUATED
VALUATES
VALUATING
VALUATION
VALUATIONS
VALUATOR
VALUATORS
VALUE

VALUED
VALUELESS
VALUER
VALUERS
VALUES
VALUING
VALUTA
VALUTAS
VALVAL
VALVAR
VALVASSOR
VALVASSORS
VALVATE
VALVE
VALVED
VALVELESS
VALVELET
VALVELETS
VALVES
VALVING
VALVULA
VALVULAE
VALVULAR
VALVULE
VALVULES
VAMBRACE
VAMBRACED
VAMBRACES
VAMOOSE
VAMOOSED
VAMOOSES
VAMOOSING
VAMOSE
VAMOSED
VAMOSES
VAMOSING
VAMP
VAMPED
VAMPER
VAMPERS
VAMPING
VAMPINGS
VAMPIRE
VAMPIRED
VAMPIRES
VAMPIRIC
VAMPIRING
VAMPIRISE
VAMPIRISED
VAMPIRISES
VAMPIRISING
VAMPIRISM
VAMPIRISMS
VAMPIRIZE
VAMPIRIZED
VAMPIRIZES
VAMPIRIZING
VAMPISH
VAMPLATE

The Chambers Dictionary is the authority for many longer words; see *OSW* Introduction, page xii.

VAMPLATES	VANTBRACE	VARGUENO	VARMINT	VASTNESSES
VAMPS	VANTBRACES	VARGUENOS	VARMINTS	VASTS
VAN	VANTS	VARIABLE	VARNA	VASTY
VANADATE	VANWARD	VARIABLES	VARNAS	VAT
VANADATES	VAPID	VARIABLY	VARNISH	VATABLE
VANADIC	VAPIDER	VARIANCE	VARNISHED	VATFUL
VANADIUM	VAPIDEST	VARIANCES	VARNISHER	VATFULS
VANADIUMS	VAPIDITIES	VARIANT	VARNISHERS	VATIC
VANADOUS	VAPIDITY	VARIANTS	VARNISHES	VATICIDE
VANDAL	VAPIDLY	VARIATE	VARNISHING	VATICIDES
VANDALISE	VAPIDNESS	VARIATED	VARNISHINGS	VATICINAL
VANDALISED	VAPIDNESSES	VARIATES	VARROA	VATMAN
VANDALISES	VAPOR	VARIATING	VARROAS	VATMEN
VANDALISING	VAPORABLE	VARIATION	VARSAL	VATS
VANDALISM	VAPORED	VARIATIONS	VARSITIES	VATTED
VANDALISMS	VAPORETTI	VARIATIVE	VARSITY	VATTER
VANDALIZE	VAPORETTO	VARICELLA	VARTABED	VATTERS
VANDALIZED	VAPORETTOS	VARICELLAS	VARTABEDS	VATTING
VANDALIZES	VAPORIFIC	VARICES	VARUS	VATU
VANDALIZING	VAPORING	VARICOSE	VARUSES	VATUS
VANDALS	VAPORISE	VARIED	VARVE	VAU
VANDYKE	VAPORISED	VARIEDLY	VARVED	VAUDOO
VANDYKED	VAPORISER	VARIEGATE	VARVEL	VAUDOOS
VANDYKES	VAPORISERS	VARIEGATED	VARVELLED	VAUDOUX
VANDYKING	VAPORISES	VARIEGATES	VARVELS	VAULT
VANE	VAPORISING	VARIEGATING	VARVES	VAULTAGE
VANED	VAPORIZE	VARIER	VARY	VAULTAGES
VANELESS	VAPORIZED	VARIERS	VARYING	VAULTED
VANES	VAPORIZER	VARIES	VARYINGS	VAULTER
VANESSA	VAPORIZERS	VARIETAL	VAS	VAULTERS
VANESSAS	VAPORIZES	VARIETALS	VASA	VAULTING
VANG	VAPORIZING	VARIETIES	VASAL	VAULTINGS
VANGS	VAPOROUS	VARIETY	VASCULA	VAULTS
VANGUARD	VAPORS	VARIFORM	VASCULAR	VAULTY
VANGUARDS	VAPORWARE	VARIOLA	VASCULUM	VAUNCE
VANILLA	VAPORWARES	VARIOLAR	VASCULUMS	VAUNCED
VANILLAS	VAPOUR	VARIOLAS	VASE	VAUNCES
VANILLIN	VAPOURED	VARIOLATE	VASECTOMIES	VAUNCING
VANILLINS	VAPOURER	VARIOLATED	VASECTOMY	VAUNT
VANISH	VAPOURERS	VARIOLATES	VASES	VAUNTAGE
VANISHED	VAPOURING	VARIOLATING	VASIFORM	VAUNTAGES
VANISHER	VAPOURINGS	VARIOLE	VASOMOTOR	VAUNTED
VANISHERS	VAPOURISH	VARIOLES	VASSAIL	VAUNTER
VANISHES	VAPOURS	VARIOLITE	VASSAILS	VAUNTERIES
VANISHING	VAPOURY	VARIOLITES	VASSAL	VAUNTERS
VANISHINGS	VAPULATE	VARIOLOID	VASSALAGE	VAUNTERY
VANITAS	VAPULATED	VARIOLOIDS	VASSALAGES	VAUNTFUL
VANITASES	VAPULATES	VARIOLOUS	VASSALESS	VAUNTIER
VANITIES	VAPULATING	VARIORUM	VASSALESSES	VAUNTIEST
VANITORIES	VAQUERO	VARIORUMS	VASSALLED	VAUNTING
VANITORY	VAQUEROS	VARIOUS	VASSALLING	VAUNTINGS
VANITY	VARA	VARIOUSLY	VASSALRIES	VAUNTS
VANNED	VARACTOR	VARISCITE	VASSALRY	VAUNTY
VANNER	VARACTORS	VARISCITES	VASSALS	VAURIEN
VANNERS	VARAN	VARISTOR	VAST	VAURIENS
VANNING	VARANS	VARISTORS	VASTER	VAUS
VANNINGS	VARAS	VARIX	VASTEST	VAUT
VANQUISH	VARDIES	VARLET	VASTIDITIES	VAUTE
VANQUISHED	VARDY	VARLETESS	VASTIDITY	VAUTED
VANQUISHES	VARE	VARLETESSES	VASTIER	VAUTES
VANQUISHING	VAREC	VARLETRIES	VASTIEST	VAUTING
VANS	VARECH	VARLETRY	VASTITIES	VAUTS
VANT	VARECHS	VARLETS	VASTITUDE	VAVASORIES
VANTAGE	VARECS	VARLETTO	VASTITUDES	VAVASORY
VANTAGED	VARES	VARLETTOS	VASTITY	VAVASOUR
VANTAGES	VAREUSE	VARMENT	VASTLY	VAVASOURS
VANTAGING	VAREUSES	VARMENTS	VASTNESS	VAWARD

The Chambers Dictionary is the authority for many longer words; see *OSW* Introduction, page xii.

VAWARDS	VEGETATES	VELATURAS	VENATOR	VENGED
VAWTE	VEGETATING	VELD	VENATORS	VENGEFUL
VAWTED	VEGETATINGS	VELDS	VEND	VENGEMENT
VAWTES	VEGETE	VELDSKOEN	VENDACE	VENGEMENTS
VAWTING	VEGETIVE	VELDSKOENS	VENDACES	VENGER
VEAL	VEGETIVES	VELDT	VENDAGE	VENGERS
VEALE	VEGGIE	VELDTS	VENDAGES	VENGES
VEALER	VEGGIES	VELE	VENDANGE	VENGING
VEALERS	VEGIE	VELES	VENDANGES	VENIAL
VEALES	VEGIES	VELETA	VENDED	VENIALITIES
VEALIER	VEHEMENCE	VELETAS	VENDEE	VENIALITY
VEALIEST	VEHEMENCES	VELIGER	VENDEES	VENIALLY
VEALS	VEHEMENCIES	VELIGERS	VENDER	VENIDIUM
VEALY	VEHEMENCY	VELL	VENDERS	VENIDIUMS
VECTOR	VEHEMENT	VELLEITIES	VENDETTA	VENIN
VECTORED	VEHICLE	VELLEITY	VENDETTAS	VENINS
VECTORIAL	VEHICLES	VELLENAGE	VENDEUSE	VENIRE
VECTORING	VEHICULAR	VELLENAGES	VENDEUSES	VENIREMAN
VECTORINGS	VEHM	VELLET	VENDIBLE	VENIREMEN
VECTORISE	VEHME	VELLETS	VENDIBLES	VENIRES
VECTORISED	VEHMIC	VELLICATE	VENDIBLY	VENISON
VECTORISES	VEHMIQUE	VELLICATED	VENDING	VENISONS
VECTORISING	VEIL	VELLICATES	VENDIS	VENITE
VECTORIZE	VEILED	VELLICATING	VENDISES	VENITES
VECTORIZED	VEILIER	VELLON	VENDISS	VENNEL
VECTORIZES	VEILIEST	VELLONS	VENDISSES	VENNELS
VECTORIZING	VEILING	VELLS	VENDITION	VENOM
VECTORS	VEILINGS	VELLUM	VENDITIONS	VENOMED
VEDALIA	VEILLESS	VELLUMS	VENDOR	VENOMING
VEDALIAS	VEILLEUSE	VELOCE	VENDORS	VENOMOUS
VEDETTE	VEILLEUSES	VELOCITIES	VENDS	VENOMS
VEDETTES	VEILS	VELOCITY	VENDUE	VENOSE
VEDUTA	VEILY	VELODROME	VENDUES	VENOSITIES
VEDUTE	VEIN	VELODROMES	VENEER	VENOSITY
VEDUTISTA	VEINED	VELOUR	VENEERED	VENOUS
VEDUTISTI	VEINIER	VELOURS	VENEERER	VENT
VEE	VEINIEST	VELOUTE	VENEERERS	VENTAGE
VEENA	VEINING	VELOUTES	VENEERING	VENTAGES
VEENAS	VEININGS	VELOUTINE	VENEERINGS	VENTAIL
VEEP	VEINLET	VELOUTINES	VENEERS	VENTAILE
VEEPS	VEINLETS	VELSKOEN	VENEFIC	VENTAILES
VEER	VEINOUS	VELSKOENS	VENEFICAL	VENTAILS
VEERED	VEINS	VELUM	VENERABLE	VENTANA
VEERIES	VEINSTONE	VELURE	VENERABLY	VENTANAS
VEERING	VEINSTONES	VELURED	VENERATE	VENTAYLE
VEERINGLY	VEINSTUFF	VELURES	VENERATED	VENTAYLES
VEERINGS	VEINSTUFFS	VELURING	VENERATES	VENTED
VEERS	VEINY	VELVERET	VENERATING	VENTER
VEERY	VELA	VELVERETS	VENERATOR	VENTERS
VEES	VELAMEN	VELVET	VENERATORS	VENTIDUCT
VEG	VELAMINA	VELVETED	VENEREAL	VENTIDUCTS
VEGA	VELAR	VELVETEEN	VENEREAN	VENTIFACT
VEGAN	VELARIA	VELVETEENS	VENEREANS	VENTIFACTS
VEGANIC	VELARIC	VELVETING	VENEREOUS	VENTIGE
VEGANISM	VELARISE	VELVETINGS	VENERER	VENTIGES
VEGANISMS	VELARISED	VELVETS	VENERERS	VENTIL
VEGANS	VELARISES	VELVETY	VENERIES	VENTILATE
VEGAS	VELARISING	VENA	VENERY	VENTILATED
VEGES	VELARIUM	VENAE	VENEWE	VENTILATES
VEGETABLE	VELARIZE	VENAL	VENEWES	VENTILATING
VEGETABLES	VELARIZED	VENALITIES	VENEY	VENTILS
VEGETABLY	VELARIZES	VENALITY	VENEYS	VENTING
VEGETAL	VELARIZING	VENALLY	VENGE	VENTINGS
VEGETALS	VELARS	VENATIC	VENGEABLE	VENTOSE
VEGETANT	VELATE	VENATICAL	VENGEABLY	VENTOSITIES
VEGETATE	VELATED	VENATION	VENGEANCE	VENTOSITY
VEGETATED	VELATURA	VENATIONS	VENGEANCES	VENTRAL

The Chambers Dictionary is the authority for many longer words; see *OSW* Introduction, page xii.

VENTRALLY	VERBERATE	VERIDICAL	VERMIS	VERSINE
VENTRALS	VERBERATED	VERIER	VERMOUTH	VERSINES
VENTRE	VERBERATES	VERIEST	VERMOUTHS	VERSING
VENTRED	VERBERATING	VERIFIED	VERNAL	VERSINGS
VENTRES	VERBIAGE	VERIFIER	VERNALISE	VERSINS
VENTRICLE	VERBIAGES	VERIFIERS	VERNALISED	VERSION
VENTRICLES	VERBICIDE	VERIFIES	VERNALISES	VERSIONAL
VENTRING	VERBICIDES	VERIFY	VERNALISING	VERSIONER
VENTRINGS	VERBID	VERIFYING	VERNALITIES	VERSIONERS
VENTROUS	VERBIDS	VERILY	VERNALITY	VERSIONS
VENTS	VERBIFIED	VERISM	VERNALIZE	VERSO
VENTURE	VERBIFIES	VERISMO	VERNALIZED	VERSOS
VENTURED	VERBIFY	VERISMOS	VERNALIZES	VERST
VENTURER	VERBIFYING	VERISMS	VERNALIZING	VERSTS
VENTURERS	VERBLESS	VERIST	VERNALLY	VERSUS
VENTURES	VERBOSE	VERISTIC	VERNANT	VERSUTE
VENTURI	VERBOSELY	VERISTS	VERNATION	VERT
VENTURING	VERBOSER	VERITABLE	VERNATIONS	VERTEBRA
VENTURINGS	VERBOSEST	VERITABLY	VERNICLE	VERTEBRAE
VENTURIS	VERBOSITIES	VERITIES	VERNICLES	VERTEBRAL
VENTUROUS	VERBOSITY	VERITY	VERNIER	VERTED
VENUE	VERBOTEN	VERJUICE	VERNIERS	VERTEX
VENUES	VERBS	VERJUICED	VERONAL	VERTEXES
VENULE	VERDANCIES	VERJUICES	VERONALS	VERTICAL
VENULES	VERDANCY	VERKRAMP	VERONICA	VERTICALS
VENUS	VERDANT	VERLIG	VERONICAS	VERTICES
VENUSES	VERDANTLY	VERLIGTE	VERONIQUE	VERTICIL
VENVILLE	VERDELHO	VERLIGTES	VERQUERE	VERTICILS
VENVILLES	VERDELHOS	VERMAL	VERQUERES	VERTICITIES
VERACIOUS	VERDERER	VERMEIL	VERQUIRE	VERTICITY
VERACITIES	VERDERERS	VERMEILED	VERQUIRES	VERTIGINES
VERACITY	VERDEROR	VERMEILING	VERREL	VERTIGO
VERANDA	VERDERORS	VERMEILLE	VERRELS	VERTIGOES
VERANDAH	VERDET	VERMEILLED	VERREY	VERTIGOS
VERANDAHS	VERDETS	VERMEILLES	VERRUCA	VERTING
VERANDAS	VERDICT	VERMEILLING	VERRUCAE	VERTIPORT
VERATRIN	VERDICTS	VERMEILS	VERRUCAS	VERTIPORTS
VERATRINE	VERDIGRIS	VERMELL	VERRUCOSE	VERTS
VERATRINES	VERDIGRISED	VERMELLS	VERRUCOUS	VERTU
VERATRINS	VERDIGRISES	VERMES	VERRUGA	VERTUE
VERATRUM	VERDIGRISING	VERMIAN	VERRUGAS	VERTUES
VERATRUMS	VERDIN	VERMICIDE	VERRY	VERTUOUS
VERB	VERDINS	VERMICIDES	VERS	VERTUS
VERBAL	VERDIT	VERMICULE	VERSAL	VERVAIN
VERBALISE	VERDITE	VERMICULES	VERSALS	VERVAINS
VERBALISED	VERDITER	VERMIFORM	VERSANT	VERVE
VERBALISES	VERDITERS	VERMIFUGE	VERSANTS	VERVEL
VERBALISING	VERDITES	VERMIFUGES	VERSATILE	VERVELLED
VERBALISM	VERDITS	VERMIL	VERSE	VERVELS
VERBALISMS	VERDOY	VERMILIES	VERSED	VERVEN
VERBALIST	VERDURE	VERMILION	VERSELET	VERVENS
VERBALISTS	VERDURED	VERMILIONED	VERSELETS	VERVES
VERBALITIES	VERDURES	VERMILIONING	VERSER	VERVET
VERBALITY	VERDUROUS	VERMILIONS	VERSERS	VERVETS
VERBALIZE	VERECUND	VERMILLED	VERSES	VERY
VERBALIZED	VERGE	VERMILLING	VERSET	VESICA
VERBALIZES	VERGED	VERMILS	VERSETS	VESICAE
VERBALIZING	VERGENCE	VERMILY	VERSICLE	VESICAL
VERBALLED	VERGENCES	VERMIN	VERSICLES	VESICANT
VERBALLING	VERGENCIES	VERMINATE	VERSIFIED	VESICANTS
VERBALLY	VERGENCY	VERMINATED	VERSIFIER	VESICATE
VERBALS	VERGER	VERMINATES	VERSIFIERS	VESICATED
VERBARIAN	VERGERS	VERMINATING	VERSIFIES	VESICATES
VERBARIANS	VERGES	VERMINED	VERSIFORM	VESICATING
VERBATIM	VERGING	VERMINOUS	VERSIFY	VESICLE
VERBENA	VERGLAS	VERMINS	VERSIFYING	VESICLES
VERBENAS	VERGLASES	VERMINY	VERSIN	VESICULA

The Chambers Dictionary is the authority for many longer words; see *OSW* Introduction, page xii.

VESICULAE	VETIVERS	VIBRAHARPS	VICIOSITIES	VIDS
VESICULAR	VETKOEK	VIBRANCIES	VICIOSITY	VIDUAGE
VESPA	VETKOEKS	VIBRANCY	VICIOUS	VIDUAGES
VESPAS	VETO	VIBRANT	VICIOUSLY	VIDUAL
VESPER	VETOED	VIBRANTLY	VICOMTE	VIDUITIES
VESPERAL	VETOES	VIBRATE	VICOMTES	VIDUITY
VESPERS	VETOING	VIBRATED	VICTIM	VIDUOUS
VESPIARIES	VETS	VIBRATES	VICTIMISE	VIE
VESPIARY	VETTED	VIBRATILE	VICTIMISED	VIED
VESPINE	VETTING	VIBRATING	VICTIMISES	VIELLE
VESPOID	VETTURA	VIBRATION	VICTIMISING	VIELLES
VESSAIL	VETTURAS	VIBRATIONS	VICTIMIZE	VIER
VESSAILS	VETTURINI	VIBRATIVE	VICTIMIZED	VIERS
VESSEL	VETTURINO	VIBRATO	VICTIMIZES	VIES
VESSELS	VEX	VIBRATOR	VICTIMIZING	VIEW
VEST	VEXATION	VIBRATORS	VICTIMS	VIEWABLE
VESTA	VEXATIONS	VIBRATORY	VICTOR	VIEWDATA
VESTAL	VEXATIOUS	VIBRATOS	VICTORESS	VIEWDATAS
VESTALS	VEXATORY	VIBRIO	VICTORESSES	VIEWED
VESTAS	VEXED	VIBRIOS	VICTORIA	VIEWER
VESTED	VEXEDLY	VIBRIOSES	VICTORIAS	VIEWERS
VESTIARIES	VEXEDNESS	VIBRIOSIS	VICTORIES	VIEWIER
VESTIARY	VEXEDNESSES	VIBRISSA	VICTORINE	VIEWIEST
VESTIBULA	VEXER	VIBRISSAE	VICTORINES	VIEWINESS
VESTIBULE	VEXERS	VIBRONIC	VICTORS	VIEWINESSES
VESTIBULED	VEXES	VIBS	VICTORY	VIEWING
VESTIBULES	VEXILLA	VIBURNUM	VICTRESS	VIEWINGS
VESTIBULING	VEXILLARIES	VIBURNUMS	VICTRESSES	VIEWLESS
VESTIGE	VEXILLARY	VICAR	VICTRIX	VIEWLY
VESTIGES	VEXILLUM	VICARAGE	VICTRIXES	VIEWPHONE
VESTIGIA	VEXING	VICARAGES	VICTROLLA	VIEWPHONES
VESTIGIAL	VEXINGLY	VICARATE	VICTROLLAS	VIEWPOINT
VESTIGIUM	VEXINGS	VICARATES	VICTUAL	VIEWPOINTS
VESTIMENT	VEXT	VICARESS	VICTUALLED	VIEWS
VESTIMENTS	VEZIR	VICARESSES	VICTUALLING	VIEWY
VESTING	VEZIRS	VICARIAL	VICTUALS	VIFDA
VESTINGS	VIA	VICARIATE	VICUNA	VIFDAS
VESTITURE	VIABILITIES	VICARIATES	VICUNAS	VIGESIMAL
VESTITURES	VIABILITY	VICARIES	VID	VIGIA
VESTMENT	VIABLE	VICARIOUS	VIDAME	VIGIAS
VESTMENTS	VIADUCT	VICARS	VIDAMES	VIGIL
VESTRAL	VIADUCTS	VICARSHIP	VIDE	VIGILANCE
VESTRIES	VIAE	VICARSHIPS	VIDELICET	VIGILANCES
VESTRY	VIAL	VICARY	VIDENDA	VIGILANT
VESTRYMAN	VIALFUL	VICE	VIDENDUM	VIGILANTE
VESTRYMEN	VIALFULS	VICED	VIDEO	VIGILANTES
VESTS	VIALLED	VICELESS	VIDEODISC	VIGILS
VESTURAL	VIALS	VICENARY	VIDEODISCS	VIGNERON
VESTURE	VIAMETER	VICENNIAL	VIDEOED	VIGNERONS
VESTURED	VIAMETERS	VICEREINE	VIDEOFIT	VIGNETTE
VESTURER	VIAND	VICEREINES	VIDEOFITS	VIGNETTED
VESTURERS	VIANDS	VICEROY	VIDEOGRAM	VIGNETTER
VESTURES	VIAS	VICEROYS	VIDEOGRAMS	VIGNETTERS
VESTURING	VIATICA	VICES	VIDEOING	VIGNETTES
VESUVIAN	VIATICALS	VICESIMAL	VIDEOS	VIGNETTING
VESUVIANS	VIATICUM	VICHIES	VIDEOTAPE	VIGOR
VET	VIATICUMS	VICHY	VIDEOTAPED	VIGORISH
VETCH	VIATOR	VICIATE	VIDEOTAPES	VIGORISHES
VETCHES	VIATORIAL	VICIATED	VIDEOTAPING	VIGORO
VETCHIER	VIATORS	VICIATES	VIDEOTEX	VIGOROS
VETCHIEST	VIBES	VICIATING	VIDEOTEXES	VIGOROUS
VETCHLING	VIBEX	VICINAGE	VIDEOTEXT	VIGORS
VETCHLINGS	VIBICES	VICINAGES	VIDEOTEXTS	VIGOUR
VETCHY	VIBIST	VICINAL	VIDETTE	VIGOURS
VETERAN	VIBISTS	VICING	VIDETTES	VIHARA
VETERANS	VIBRACULA	VICINITIES	VIDIMUS	VIHARAS
VETIVER	VIBRAHARP	VICINITY	VIDIMUSES	VIHUELA

The Chambers Dictionary is the authority for many longer words; see *OSW* Introduction, page xii.

VIHUELAS	VILLI	VINTAGED	VIRANDAS	VIROIDS
VIKING	VILLIAGO	VINTAGER	VIRANDO	VIROLOGIES
VIKINGISM	VILLIAGOES	VINTAGERS	VIRANDOS	VIROLOGY
VIKINGISMS	VILLIAGOS	VINTAGES	VIRE	VIROSE
VIKINGS	VILLIFORM	VINTAGING	VIRED	VIROSES
VILAYET	VILLOSE	VINTAGINGS	VIRELAY	VIROSIS
VILAYETS	VILLOSITIES	VINTED	VIRELAYS	VIROUS
VILD	VILLOSITY	VINTING	VIREMENT	VIRTU
VILDE	VILLOUS	VINTNER	VIREMENTS	VIRTUAL
VILDLY	VILLS	VINTNERS	VIRENT	VIRTUALLY
VILDNESS	VILLUS	VINTRIES	VIREO	VIRTUE
VILDNESSES	VIM	VINTRY	VIREOS	VIRTUES
VILE	VIMANA	VINTS	VIRES	VIRTUOSA
VILELY	VIMANAS	VINY	VIRESCENT	VIRTUOSE
VILENESS	VIMINEOUS	VINYL	VIRETOT	VIRTUOSI
VILENESSES	VIMS	VINYLS	VIRETOTS	VIRTUOSIC
VILER	VIN	VIOL	VIRGA	VIRTUOSO
VILEST	VINA	VIOLA	VIRGAS	VIRTUOSOS
VILIACO	VINACEOUS	VIOLABLE	VIRGATE	VIRTUOUS
VILIACOES	VINAL	VIOLABLY	VIRGATES	VIRTUS
VILIACOS	VINAS	VIOLAS	VIRGE	VIRUCIDAL
VILIAGO	VINASSE	VIOLATE	VIRGER	VIRUCIDE
VILIAGOES	VINASSES	VIOLATED	VIRGERS	VIRUCIDES
VILIAGOS	VINCA	VIOLATER	VIRGES	VIRULENCE
VILIFIED	VINCAS	VIOLATERS	VIRGIN	VIRULENCES
VILIFIER	VINCIBLE	VIOLATES	VIRGINAL	VIRULENCIES
VILIFIERS	VINCULA	VIOLATING	VIRGINALLED	VIRULENCY
VILIFIES	VINCULUM	VIOLATION	VIRGINALLING	VIRULENT
VILIFY	VINDALOO	VIOLATIONS	VIRGINALS	VIRUS
VILIFYING	VINDALOOS	VIOLATIVE	VIRGINED	VIRUSES
VILIPEND	VINDEMIAL	VIOLATOR	VIRGINING	VIS
VILIPENDED	VINDICATE	VIOLATORS	VIRGINITIES	VISA
VILIPENDING	VINDICATED	VIOLD	VIRGINITY	VISAED
VILIPENDS	VINDICATES	VIOLENCE	VIRGINIUM	VISAGE
VILL	VINDICATING	VIOLENCES	VIRGINIUMS	VISAGED
VILLA	VINE	VIOLENT	VIRGINLY	VISAGES
VILLADOM	VINED	VIOLENTED	VIRGINS	VISAGIST
VILLADOMS	VINEGAR	VIOLENTING	VIRGULATE	VISAGISTE
VILLAGE	VINEGARED	VIOLENTLY	VIRGULE	VISAGISTES
VILLAGER	VINEGARING	VIOLENTS	VIRGULES	VISAGISTS
VILLAGERIES	VINEGARS	VIOLER	VIRICIDAL	VISAING
VILLAGERS	VINEGARY	VIOLERS	VIRICIDE	VISAS
VILLAGERY	VINER	VIOLET	VIRICIDES	VISCACHA
VILLAGES	VINERIES	VIOLETS	VIRID	VISCACHAS
VILLAGIO	VINERS	VIOLIN	VIRIDIAN	VISCERA
VILLAGIOES	VINERY	VIOLINIST	VIRIDIANS	VISCERAL
VILLAGIOS	VINES	VIOLINISTS	VIRIDITE	VISCERATE
VILLAGREE	VINEW	VIOLINS	VIRIDITES	VISCERATED
VILLAGREES	VINEWED	VIOLIST	VIRIDITIES	VISCERATES
VILLAIN	VINEWING	VIOLISTS	VIRIDITY	VISCERATING
VILLAINIES	VINEWS	VIOLONE	VIRILE	VISCID
VILLAINS	VINEYARD	VIOLONES	VIRILISED	VISCIDITIES
VILLAINY	VINEYARDS	VIOLS	VIRILISM	VISCIDITY
VILLAN	VINIER	VIPER	VIRILISMS	VISCIN
VILLANAGE	VINIEST	VIPERINE	VIRILITIES	VISCINS
VILLANAGES	VINING	VIPERISH	VIRILITY	VISCOSE
VILLANIES	VINO	VIPEROUS	VIRILIZED	VISCOSES
VILLANOUS	VINOLENT	VIPERS	VIRING	VISCOSITIES
VILLANS	VINOLOGIES	VIRAEMIA	VIRINO	VISCOSITY
VILLANY	VINOLOGY	VIRAEMIAS	VIRINOS	VISCOUNT
VILLAR	VINOS	VIRAEMIC	VIRION	VISCOUNTIES
VILLAS	VINOSITIES	VIRAGO	VIRIONS	VISCOUNTS
VILLATIC	VINOSITY	VIRAGOES	VIRL	VISCOUNTY
VILLEIN	VINOUS	VIRAGOISH	VIRLS	VISCOUS
VILLEINS	VINS	VIRAGOS	VIROGENE	VISCUM
VILLENAGE	VINT	VIRAL	VIROGENES	VISCUMS
VILLENAGES	VINTAGE	VIRANDA	VIROID	VISCUS

The Chambers Dictionary is the authority for many longer words; see *OSW* Introduction, page xii.

VISE	VISTO	VITICETA	VIVIANITE	VOAR
VISED	VISTOS	VITICETUM	VIVIANITES	VOARS
VISEED	VISUAL	VITICETUMS	VIVID	VOCAB
VISEING	VISUALISE	VITICIDE	VIVIDER	VOCABLE
VISES	VISUALISED	VITICIDES	VIVIDEST	VOCABLES
VISIBLE	VISUALISES	VITILIGO	VIVIDITIES	VOCABS
VISIBLES	VISUALISING	VITILIGOS	VIVIDITY	VOCABULAR
VISIBLY	VISUALIST	VITIOSITIES	VIVIDLY	VOCAL
VISIE	VISUALISTS	VITIOSITY	VIVIDNESS	VOCALESE
VISIED	VISUALITIES	VITRAGE	VIVIDNESSES	VOCALESES
VISIEING	VISUALITY	VITRAGES	VIVIFIC	VOCALIC
VISIER	VISUALIZE	VITRAIL	VIVIFIED	VOCALION
VISIERS	VISUALIZED	VITRAIN	VIVIFIER	VOCALIONS
VISIES	VISUALIZES	VITRAINS	VIVIFIERS	VOCALISE
VISILE	VISUALIZING	VITRAUX	VIVIFIES	VOCALISED
VISILES	VISUALLY	VITREOUS	VIVIFY	VOCALISER
VISING	VISUALS	VITREUM	VIVIFYING	VOCALISERS
VISION	VITA	VITREUMS	VIVIPARIES	VOCALISES
VISIONAL	VITAE	VITRIC	VIVIPARY	VOCALISING
VISIONARIES	VITAL	VITRICS	VIVISECT	VOCALISM
VISIONARY	VITALISE	VITRIFIED	VIVISECTED	VOCALISMS
VISIONED	VITALISED	VITRIFIES	VIVISECTING	VOCALIST
VISIONER	VITALISER	VITRIFORM	VIVISECTS	VOCALISTS
VISIONERS	VITALISERS	VITRIFY	VIVO	VOCALITIES
VISIONING	VITALISES	VITRIFYING	VIVRES	VOCALITY
VISIONINGS	VITALISING	VITRINE	VIXEN	VOCALIZE
VISIONIST	VITALISM	VITRINES	VIXENISH	VOCALIZED
VISIONISTS	VITALISMS	VITRIOL	VIXENLY	VOCALIZER
VISIONS	VITALIST	VITRIOLIC	VIXENS	VOCALIZERS
VISIT	VITALISTS	VITRIOLS	VIZAMENT	VOCALIZES
VISITABLE	VITALITIES	VITTA	VIZAMENTS	VOCALIZING
VISITANT	VITALITY	VITTAE	VIZARD	VOCALLY
VISITANTS	VITALIZE	VITTATE	VIZARDED	VOCALNESS
VISITATOR	VITALIZED	VITTLE	VIZARDING	VOCALNESSES
VISITATORS	VITALIZER	VITTLES	VIZARDS	VOCALS
VISITE	VITALIZERS	VITULAR	VIZCACHA	VOCATION
VISITED	VITALIZES	VITULINE	VIZCACHAS	VOCATIONS
VISITEE	VITALIZING	VIVA	VIZIED	VOCATIVE
VISITEES	VITALLY	VIVACE	VIZIER	VOCATIVES
VISITER	VITALS	VIVACIOUS	VIZIERATE	VOCES
VISITERS	VITAMIN	VIVACITIES	VIZIERATES	VOCODER
VISITES	VITAMINE	VIVACITY	VIZIERIAL	VOCODERS
VISITING	VITAMINES	VIVAED	VIZIERS	VOCULAR
VISITINGS	VITAMINS	VIVAING	VIZIES	VOCULE
VISITOR	VITAS	VIVAMENTE	VIZIR	VOCULES
VISITORS	VITASCOPE	VIVANDIER	VIZIRATE	VODKA
VISITRESS	VITASCOPES	VIVANDIERS	VIZIRATES	VODKAS
VISITRESSES	VITATIVE	VIVARIA	VIZIRIAL	VOE
VISITS	VITE	VIVARIES	VIZIRS	VOES
VISIVE	VITELLARY	VIVARIUM	VIZIRSHIP	VOGIE
VISNE	VITELLI	VIVARIUMS	VIZIRSHIPS	VOGIER
VISNES	VITELLIN	VIVARY	VIZOR	VOGIEST
VISNOMIE	VITELLINE	VIVAS	VIZORED	VOGUE
VISNOMIES	VITELLINES	VIVAT	VIZORING	VOGUED
VISNOMY	VITELLINS	VIVATS	VIZORS	VOGUEING
VISON	VITELLUS	VIVDA	VIZSLA	VOGUEINGS
VISONS	VITEX	VIVDAS	VIZSLAS	VOGUER
VISOR	VITEXES	VIVE	VIZY	VOGUERS
VISORED	VITIABLE	VIVELY	VIZYING	VOGUES
VISORING	VITIATE	VIVENCIES	VIZZIE	VOGUEY
VISORS	VITIATED	VIVENCY	VIZZIED	VOGUIER
VISTA	VITIATES	VIVER	VIZZIEING	VOGUIEST
VISTAED	VITIATING	VIVERRA	VIZZIES	VOGUING
VISTAING	VITIATION	VIVERRAS	VLEI	VOGUINGS
VISTAL	VITIATIONS	VIVERRINE	VLEIS	VOGUISH
VISTALESS	VITIATOR	VIVERS	VLIES	VOICE
VISTAS	VITIATORS	VIVES	VLY	VOICED

The Chambers Dictionary is the authority for many longer words; see *OSW* Introduction, page xii.

VOICEFUL	VOLERY	VOLUNTEERING	VORTICISM	VOWELLESS
VOICELESS	VOLES	VOLUNTEERS	VORTICISMS	VOWELLING
VOICER	VOLET	VOLUSPA	VORTICIST	VOWELLY
VOICERS	VOLETS	VOLUSPAS	VORTICISTS	VOWELS
VOICES	VOLING	VOLUTE	VORTICITIES	VOWER
VOICING	VOLITANT	VOLUTED	VORTICITY	VOWERS
VOICINGS	VOLITATE	VOLUTES	VORTICOSE	VOWESS
VOID	VOLITATED	VOLUTIN	VOTARESS	VOWESSES
VOIDABLE	VOLITATES	VOLUTINS	VOTARESSES	VOWING
VOIDANCE	VOLITATING	VOLUTION	VOTARIES	VOWS
VOIDANCES	VOLITIENT	VOLUTIONS	VOTARIST	VOX
VOIDED	VOLITION	VOLUTOID	VOTARISTS	VOYAGE
VOIDEE	VOLITIONS	VOLVA	VOTARY	VOYAGED
VOIDEES	VOLITIVE	VOLVAS	VOTE	VOYAGER
VOIDER	VOLITIVES	VOLVATE	VOTED	VOYAGERS
VOIDERS	VOLK	VOLVE	VOTEEN	VOYAGES
VOIDING	VOLKS	VOLVED	VOTEENS	VOYAGEUR
VOIDINGS	VOLKSRAAD	VOLVES	VOTELESS	VOYAGEURS
VOIDNESS	VOLKSRAADS	VOLVING	VOTER	VOYAGING
VOIDNESSES	VOLLEY	VOLVOX	VOTERS	VOYEUR
VOIDS	VOLLEYED	VOLVOXES	VOTES	VOYEURISM
VOILA	VOLLEYER	VOLVULI	VOTING	VOYEURISMS
VOILE	VOLLEYERS	VOLVULUS	VOTIVE	VOYEURS
VOILES	VOLLEYING	VOLVULUSES	VOTRESS	VOZHD
VOISINAGE	VOLLEYS	VOMER	VOTRESSES	VOZHDS
VOISINAGES	VOLOST	VOMERINE	VOUCH	VRAIC
VOITURE	VOLOSTS	VOMERS	VOUCHED	VRAICKER
VOITURES	VOLPINO	VOMICA	VOUCHEE	VRAICKERS
VOITURIER	VOLPINOS	VOMICAE	VOUCHEES	VRAICKING
VOITURIERS	VOLPLANE	VOMICAS	VOUCHER	VRAICKINGS
VOIVODE	VOLPLANED	VOMIT	VOUCHERS	VRAICS
VOIVODES	VOLPLANES	VOMITED	VOUCHES	VRIL
VOL	VOLPLANING	VOMITING	VOUCHING	VRILS
VOLA	VOLS	VOMITINGS	VOUCHSAFE	VROOM
VOLABLE	VOLT	VOMITIVE	VOUCHSAFED	VROOMED
VOLAE	VOLTA	VOMITIVES	VOUCHSAFES	VROOMING
VOLAGE	VOLTAGE	VOMITO	VOUCHSAFING	VROOMS
VOLAGEOUS	VOLTAGES	VOMITORIA	VOUCHSAFINGS	VROUW
VOLANT	VOLTAIC	VOMITORIES	VOUDOU	VROUWS
VOLANTE	VOLTAISM	VOMITORY	VOUDOUED	VROW
VOLANTES	VOLTAISMS	VOMITOS	VOUDOUING	VROWS
VOLAR	VOLTE	VOMITS	VOUDOUS	VUG
VOLARIES	VOLTES	VOMITUS	VOUGE	VUGGIER
VOLARY	VOLTIGEUR	VOMITUSES	VOUGES	VUGGIEST
VOLATIC	VOLTIGEURS	VOODOO	VOULGE	VUGGY
VOLATILE	VOLTINISM	VOODOOED	VOULGES	VUGS
VOLATILES	VOLTINISMS	VOODOOING	VOULU	VULCAN
VOLCANIAN	VOLTMETER	VOODOOISM	VOUSSOIR	VULCANIAN
VOLCANIC	VOLTMETERS	VOODOOISMS	VOUSSOIRED	VULCANIC
VOLCANISE	VOLTS	VOODOOIST	VOUSSOIRING	VULCANISE
VOLCANISED	VOLUBIL	VOODOOISTS	VOUSSOIRS	VULCANISED
VOLCANISES	VOLUBLE	VOODOOS	VOUTSAFE	VULCANISES
VOLCANISING	VOLUBLY	VOR	VOUTSAFED	VULCANISING
VOLCANISM	VOLUCRINE	VORACIOUS	VOUTSAFES	VULCANISM
VOLCANISMS	VOLUME	VORACITIES	VOUTSAFING	VULCANISMS
VOLCANIST	VOLUMED	VORACITY	VOW	VULCANIST
VOLCANISTS	VOLUMES	VORAGO	VOWED	VULCANISTS
VOLCANIZE	VOLUMETER	VORAGOES	VOWEL	VULCANITE
VOLCANIZED	VOLUMETERS	VORANT	VOWELISE	VULCANITES
VOLCANIZES	VOLUMINAL	VORPAL	VOWELISED	VULCANIZE
VOLCANIZING	VOLUMING	VORRED	VOWELISES	VULCANIZED
VOLCANO	VOLUMIST	VORRING	VOWELISING	VULCANIZES
VOLCANOES	VOLUMISTS	VORS	VOWELIZE	VULCANIZING
VOLE	VOLUNTARIES	VORTEX	VOWELIZED	VULCANS
VOLED	VOLUNTARY	VORTEXES	VOWELIZES	VULGAR
VOLENS	VOLUNTEER	VORTICAL	VOWELIZING	VULGARER
VOLERIES	VOLUNTEERED	VORTICES	VOWELLED	VULGAREST

The Chambers Dictionary is the authority for many longer words; see *OSW* Introduction, page xii.

VULGARIAN	VULGARIZING	VULNERATED	VULSELLAE	VULVAL
VULGARIANS	VULGARLY	VULNERATES	VULSELLUM	VULVAR
VULGARISE	VULGARS	VULNERATING	VULTURE	VULVAS
VULGARISED	VULGATE	VULNING	VULTURES	VULVATE
VULGARISES	VULGATES	VULNS	VULTURINE	VULVIFORM
VULGARISING	VULGO	VULPICIDE	VULTURISH	VULVITIS
VULGARISM	VULGUS	VULPICIDES	VULTURISM	VULVITISES
VULGARISMS	VULGUSES	VULPINE	VULTURISMS	VUM
VULGARITIES	VULN	VULPINISM	VULTURN	VUMMED
VULGARITY	VULNED	VULPINISMS	VULTURNS	VUMMING
VULGARIZE	VULNERARIES	VULPINITE	VULTUROUS	VUMS
VULGARIZED	VULNERARY	VULPINITES	VULVA	VYING
VULGARIZES	VULNERATE	VULSELLA	VULVAE	VYINGLY

W

WABAIN	WADMOLS	WAGERERS	WAILER	WAIVODES
WABAINS	WADS	WAGERING	WAILERS	WAIWODE
WABBIT	WADSET	WAGERS	WAILFUL	WAIWODES
WABBLE	WADSETS	WAGES	WAILING	WAKA
WABBLED	WADSETT	WAGGED	WAILINGLY	WAKANE
WABBLER	WADSETTED	WAGGERIES	WAILINGS	WAKANES
WABBLERS	WADSETTER	WAGGERY	WAILS	WAKAS
WABBLES	WADSETTERS	WAGGING	WAIN	WAKE
WABBLING	WADSETTING	WAGGISH	WAINAGE	WAKED
WABOOM	WADSETTS	WAGGISHLY	WAINAGES	WAKEFUL
WABOOMS	WADT	WAGGLE	WAINED	WAKEFULLY
WABSTER	WADTS	WAGGLED	WAINING	WAKELESS
WABSTERS	WADY	WAGGLES	WAINS	WAKEMAN
WACK	WAE	WAGGLIER	WAINSCOT	WAKEMEN
WACKE	WAEFUL	WAGGLIEST	WAINSCOTED	WAKEN
WACKER	WAENESS	WAGGLING	WAINSCOTING	WAKENED
WACKERS	WAENESSES	WAGGLY	WAINSCOTINGS	WAKENER
WACKES	WAES	WAGGON	WAINSCOTS	WAKENERS
WACKIER	WAESOME	WAGGONED	WAINSCOTTED	WAKENING
WACKIEST	WAESUCKS	WAGGONER	WAINSCOTTING	WAKENINGS
WACKINESS	WAFER	WAGGONERS	WAINSCOTTINGS	WAKENS
WACKINESSES	WAFERED	WAGGONING	WAIST	WAKER
WACKO	WAFERING	WAGGONS	WAISTBAND	WAKERIFE
WACKS	WAFERS	WAGHALTER	WAISTBANDS	WAKERS
WACKY	WAFERY	WAGHALTERS	WAISTBELT	WAKES
WAD	WAFF	WAGING	WAISTBELTS	WAKF
WADD	WAFFED	WAGMOIRE	WAISTBOAT	WAKFS
WADDED	WAFFING	WAGMOIRES	WAISTBOATS	WAKIKI
WADDIE	WAFFLE	WAGON	WAISTCOAT	WAKIKIS
WADDIED	WAFFLED	WAGONAGE	WAISTCOATS	WAKING
WADDIES	WAFFLER	WAGONAGES	WAISTED	WAKINGS
WADDING	WAFFLERS	WAGONED	WAISTER	WALD
WADDINGS	WAFFLES	WAGONER	WAISTERS	WALDFLUTE
WADDLE	WAFFLIER	WAGONERS	WAISTLINE	WALDFLUTES
WADDLED	WAFFLIEST	WAGONETTE	WAISTLINES	WALDGRAVE
WADDLER	WAFFLING	WAGONETTES	WAISTS	WALDGRAVES
WADDLERS	WAFFLINGS	WAGONFUL	WAIT	WALDHORN
WADDLES	WAFFLY	WAGONFULS	WAITE	WALDHORNS
WADDLING	WAFFS	WAGONING	WAITED	WALDRAPP
WADDS	WAFT	WAGONLOAD	WAITER	WALDRAPPS
WADDY	WAFTAGE	WAGONLOADS	WAITERAGE	WALDS
WADDYING	WAFTAGES	WAGONS	WAITERAGES	WALE
WADE	WAFTED	WAGS	WAITERING	WALED
WADED	WAFTER	WAGTAIL	WAITERINGS	WALER
WADER	WAFTERS	WAGTAILS	WAITERS	WALERS
WADERS	WAFTING	WAHINE	WAITES	WALES
WADES	WAFTINGS	WAHINES	WAITING	WALI
WADI	WAFTS	WAHOO	WAITINGLY	WALIER
WADIES	WAFTURE	WAHOOS	WAITINGS	WALIES
WADING	WAFTURES	WAID	WAITRESS	WALIEST
WADINGS	WAG	WAIDE	WAITRESSES	WALING
WADIS	WAGE	WAIF	WAITS	WALIS
WADMAAL	WAGED	WAIFED	WAIVE	WALISE
WADMAALS	WAGELESS	WAIFING	WAIVED	WALISES
WADMAL	WAGENBOOM	WAIFS	WAIVER	WALK
WADMALS	WAGENBOOMS	WAIFT	WAIVERS	WALKABLE
WADMOL	WAGER	WAIFTS	WAIVES	WALKABOUT
WADMOLL	WAGERED	WAIL	WAIVING	WALKABOUTS
WADMOLLS	WAGERER	WAILED	WAIVODE	WALKATHON

The Chambers Dictionary is the authority for many longer words; see *OSW* Introduction, page xii.

WALKATHONS	WALTY	WANGLINGS	WANWORTH	WARDROP
WALKED	WALTZ	WANGS	WANWORTHS	WARDROPS
WALKER	WALTZED	WANGUN	WANY	WARDS
WALKERS	WALTZER	WANGUNS	WANZE	WARDSHIP
WALKING	WALTZERS	WANHOPE	WANZED	WARDSHIPS
WALKINGS	WALTZES	WANHOPES	WANZES	WARE
WALKMILL	WALTZING	WANIER	WANZING	WARED
WALKMILLS	WALTZINGS	WANIEST	WAP	WAREHOUSE
WALKS	WALY	WANIGAN	WAPENSHAW	WAREHOUSED
WALKWAY	WAMBENGER	WANIGANS	WAPENSHAWS	WAREHOUSES
WALKWAYS	WAMBENGERS	WANING	WAPENTAKE	WAREHOUSING
WALL	WAMBLE	WANINGS	WAPENTAKES	WAREHOUSINGS
WALLA	WAMBLED	WANK	WAPINSHAW	WARELESS
WALLABA	WAMBLES	WANKED	WAPINSHAWS	WARES
WALLABAS	WAMBLIER	WANKER	WAPITI	WARFARE
WALLABIES	WAMBLIEST	WANKERS	WAPITIS	WARFARED
WALLABY	WAMBLING	WANKIER	WAPPED	WARFARER
WALLAH	WAMBLINGS	WANKIEST	WAPPEND	WARFARERS
WALLAHS	WAMBLY	WANKING	WAPPER	WARFARES
WALLAROO	WAME	WANKLE	WAPPERED	WARFARIN
WALLAROOS	WAMED	WANKS	WAPPERING	WARFARING
WALLAS	WAMEFUL	WANKY	WAPPERS	WARFARINGS
WALLBOARD	WAMEFULS	WANLE	WAPPING	WARFARINS
WALLBOARDS	WAMES	WANLY	WAPS	WARHABLE
WALLED	WAMMUS	WANNA	WAQF	WARHEAD
WALLER	WAMMUSES	WANNABE	WAQFS	WARHEADS
WALLERS	WAMPEE	WANNABEE	WAR	WARHORSE
WALLET	WAMPEES	WANNABEES	WARATAH	WARHORSES
WALLETS	WAMPISH	WANNABES	WARATAHS	WARIBASHI
WALLFISH	WAMPISHED	WANNED	WARBIER	WARIBASHIS
WALLFISHES	WAMPISHES	WANNEL	WARBIEST	WARIER
WALLIE	WAMPISHING	WANNER	WARBLE	WARIEST
WALLIER	WAMPUM	WANNESS	WARBLED	WARILY
WALLIES	WAMPUMS	WANNESSES	WARBLER	WARIMENT
WALLIEST	WAMPUS	WANNEST	WARBLERS	WARIMENTS
WALLING	WAMPUSES	WANNING	WARBLES	WARINESS
WALLINGS	WAMUS	WANNISH	WARBLING	WARINESSES
WALLOP	WAMUSES	WANS	WARBLINGS	WARING
WALLOPED	WAN	WANT	WARBY	WARISON
WALLOPER	WANCHANCY	WANTAGE	WARD	WARISONS
WALLOPERS	WAND	WANTAGES	WARDCORN	WARK
WALLOPING	WANDER	WANTED	WARDCORNS	WARKS
WALLOPINGS	WANDERED	WANTER	WARDED	WARLIKE
WALLOPS	WANDERER	WANTERS	WARDEN	WARLING
WALLOW	WANDERERS	WANTHILL	WARDENED	WARLINGS
WALLOWED	WANDERING	WANTHILLS	WARDENING	WARLOCK
WALLOWER	WANDERINGS	WANTIES	WARDENRIES	WARLOCKRIES
WALLOWERS	WANDEROO	WANTING	WARDENRY	WARLOCKRY
WALLOWING	WANDEROOS	WANTINGS	WARDENS	WARLOCKS
WALLOWINGS	WANDERS	WANTON	WARDER	WARLORD
WALLOWS	WANDLE	WANTONED	WARDERED	WARLORDS
WALLPAPER	WANDOO	WANTONER	WARDERING	WARM
WALLPAPERS	WANDOOS	WANTONEST	WARDERS	WARMAN
WALLS	WANDS	WANTONING	WARDING	WARMBLOOD
WALLSEND	WANE	WANTONISE	WARDINGS	WARMBLOODS
WALLSENDS	WANED	WANTONISED	WARDMOTE	WARMED
WALLWORT	WANES	WANTONISES	WARDMOTES	WARMEN
WALLWORTS	WANEY	WANTONISING	WARDOG	WARMER
WALLY	WANG	WANTONIZE	WARDOGS	WARMERS
WALLYDRAG	WANGAN	WANTONIZED	WARDRESS	WARMEST
WALLYDRAGS	WANGANS	WANTONIZES	WARDRESSES	WARMING
WALNUT	WANGLE	WANTONIZING	WARDROBE	WARMINGS
WALNUTS	WANGLED	WANTONLY	WARDROBER	WARMISH
WALRUS	WANGLER	WANTONS	WARDROBERS	WARMLY
WALRUSES	WANGLERS	WANTS	WARDROBES	WARMNESS
WALTIER	WANGLES	WANTY	WARDROOM	WARMNESSES
WALTIEST	WANGLING	WANWORDY	WARDROOMS	WARMONGER

The Chambers Dictionary is the authority for many longer words; see *OSW* Introduction, page xii.

WARMONGERS	WARRIOR	WASHING	WASTES	WATERMARKS
WARMS	WARRIORS	WASHINGS	WASTFULL	WATERMEN
WARMTH	WARRISON	WASHLAND	WASTING	WATERPOX
WARMTHS	WARRISONS	WASHLANDS	WASTINGS	WATERPOXES
WARN	WARS	WASHOUT	WASTNESS	WATERS
WARNED	WARSHIP	WASHOUTS	WASTNESSES	WATERSHED
WARNER	WARSHIPS	WASHPOT	WASTREL	WATERSHEDS
WARNERS	WARSLE	WASHPOTS	WASTRELS	WATERSIDE
WARNING	WARSLED	WASHRAG	WASTRIES	WATERSIDES
WARNINGLY	WARSLES	WASHRAGS	WASTRIFE	WATERWAY
WARNINGS	WARSLING	WASHROOM	WASTRIFES	WATERWAYS
WARNS	WARST	WASHROOMS	WASTRY	WATERWEED
WARP	WART	WASHSTAND	WASTS	WATERWEEDS
WARPATH	WARTED	WASHSTANDS	WAT	WATERWORK
WARPATHS	WARTHOG	WASHTUB	WATAP	WATERWORKS
WARPED	WARTHOGS	WASHTUBS	WATAPS	WATERY
WARPER	WARTIER	WASHWIPE	WATCH	WATS
WARPERS	WARTIEST	WASHWIPES	WATCHABLE	WATT
WARPING	WARTIME	WASHY	WATCHBOX	WATTAGE
WARPINGS	WARTIMES	WASM	WATCHBOXES	WATTAGES
WARPLANE	WARTLESS	WASMS	WATCHCASE	WATTER
WARPLANES	WARTLIKE	WASP	WATCHCASES	WATTEST
WARPS	WARTS	WASPIE	WATCHDOG	WATTLE
WARRAGAL	WARTWEED	WASPIER	WATCHDOGS	WATTLED
WARRAGALS	WARTWEEDS	WASPIES	WATCHED	WATTLES
WARRAGLE	WARTWORT	WASPIEST	WATCHER	WATTLING
WARRAGLES	WARTWORTS	WASPISH	WATCHERS	WATTLINGS
WARRAGUL	WARTY	WASPISHLY	WATCHES	WATTMETER
WARRAGULS	WARWOLF	WASPNEST	WATCHET	WATTMETERS
WARRAN	WARWOLVES	WASPNESTS	WATCHETS	WATTS
WARRAND	WARY	WASPS	WATCHFUL	WAUCHT
WARRANDED	WAS	WASPY	WATCHING	WAUCHTED
WARRANDING	WASE	WASSAIL	WATCHMAN	WAUCHTING
WARRANDS	WASEGOOSE	WASSAILED	WATCHMEN	WAUCHTS
WARRANED	WASEGOOSES	WASSAILER	WATCHWORD	WAUFF
WARRANING	WASES	WASSAILERS	WATCHWORDS	WAUFFED
WARRANS	WASH	WASSAILING	WATE	WAUFFING
WARRANT	WASHABLE	WASSAILINGS	WATER	WAUFFS
WARRANTED	WASHBALL	WASSAILRIES	WATERAGE	WAUGH
WARRANTEE	WASHBALLS	WASSAILRY	WATERAGES	WAUGHED
WARRANTEES	WASHBASIN	WASSAILS	WATERED	WAUGHING
WARRANTER	WASHBASINS	WASSERMAN	WATERER	WAUGHS
WARRANTERS	WASHBOARD	WASSERMEN	WATERERS	WAUGHT
WARRANTIES	WASHBOARDS	WAST	WATERFALL	WAUGHTED
WARRANTING	WASHBOWL	WASTABLE	WATERFALLS	WAUGHTING
WARRANTINGS	WASHBOWLS	WASTAGE	WATERFOWL	WAUGHTS
WARRANTOR	WASHCLOTH	WASTAGES	WATERFOWLS	WAUK
WARRANTORS	WASHCLOTHS	WASTE	WATERHEN	WAUKED
WARRANTS	WASHDAY	WASTED	WATERHENS	WAUKER
WARRANTY	WASHDAYS	WASTEFUL	WATERIER	WAUKERS
WARRAY	WASHED	WASTEL	WATERIEST	WAUKING
WARRAYED	WASHEN	WASTELAND	WATERING	WAUKMILL
WARRAYING	WASHER	WASTELANDS	WATERINGS	WAUKMILLS
WARRAYS	WASHERED	WASTELOT	WATERISH	WAUKRIFE
WARRE	WASHERIES	WASTELOTS	WATERLESS	WAUKS
WARRED	WASHERING	WASTELS	WATERLILIES	WAUL
WARREN	WASHERMAN	WASTENESS	WATERLILY	WAULED
WARRENER	WASHERMEN	WASTENESSES	WATERLINE	WAULING
WARRENERS	WASHERS	WASTER	WATERLINES	WAULINGS
WARRENS	WASHERY	WASTERED	WATERLOG	WAULK
WARREY	WASHES	WASTERFUL	WATERLOGGED	WAULKED
WARREYED	WASHHOUSE	WASTERIES	WATERLOGGING	WAULKER
WARREYING	WASHHOUSES	WASTERIFE	WATERLOGS	WAULKERS
WARREYS	WASHIER	WASTERIFES	WATERMAN	WAULKING
WARRIGAL	WASHIEST	WASTERING	WATERMARK	WAULKMILL
WARRIGALS	WASHINESS	WASTERS	WATERMARKED	WAULKMILLS
WARRING	WASHINESSES	WASTERY	WATERMARKING	WAULKS

The Chambers Dictionary is the authority for many longer words; see *OSW* Introduction, page xii.

WAULS	WAXER	WAZIR	WEARISH	WEDELNED
WAUR	WAXERS	WAZIRS	WEARISOME	WEDELNING
WAURED	WAXES	WE	WEARS	WEDELNS
WAURING	WAXIER	WEAK	WEARY	WEDGE
WAURS	WAXIEST	WEAKEN	WEARYING	WEDGED
WAURST	WAXILY	WEAKENED	WEASAND	WEDGES
WAVE	WAXINESS	WEAKENER	WEASANDS	WEDGEWISE
WAVEBAND	WAXINESSES	WEAKENERS	WEASEL	WEDGIE
WAVEBANDS	WAXING	WEAKENING	WEASELED	WEDGIER
WAVED	WAXINGS	WEAKENS	WEASELER	WEDGIES
WAVEFORM	WAXWING	WEAKER	WEASELERS	WEDGIEST
WAVEFORMS	WAXWINGS	WEAKEST	WEASELING	WEDGING
WAVEFRONT	WAXWORK	WEAKFISH	WEASELLED	WEDGINGS
WAVEFRONTS	WAXWORKER	WEAKFISHES	WEASELLER	WEDGY
WAVEGUIDE	WAXWORKERS	WEAKLIER	WEASELLERS	WEDLOCK
WAVEGUIDES	WAXWORKS	WEAKLIEST	WEASELLING	WEDLOCKS
WAVELESS	WAXY	WEAKLING	WEASELLY	WEDS
WAVELET	WAY	WEAKLINGS	WEASELS	WEE
WAVELETS	WAYBILL	WEAKLY	WEATHER	WEED
WAVELIKE	WAYBILLS	WEAKNESS	WEATHERED	WEEDED
WAVELLITE	WAYBOARD	WEAKNESSES	WEATHERING	WEEDER
WAVELLITES	WAYBOARDS	WEAL	WEATHERINGS	WEEDERIES
WAVEMETER	WAYBREAD	WEALD	WEATHERLY	WEEDERS
WAVEMETERS	WAYBREADS	WEALDS	WEATHERS	WEEDERY
WAVER	WAYED	WEALS	WEAVE	WEEDICIDE
WAVERED	WAYFARE	WEALSMAN	WEAVED	WEEDICIDES
WAVERER	WAYFARED	WEALSMEN	WEAVER	WEEDIER
WAVERERS	WAYFARER	WEALTH	WEAVERS	WEEDIEST
WAVERING	WAYFARERS	WEALTHIER	WEAVES	WEEDINESS
WAVERINGS	WAYFARES	WEALTHIEST	WEAVING	WEEDINESSES
WAVEROUS	WAYFARING	WEALTHILY	WEAVINGS	WEEDING
WAVERS	WAYFARINGS	WEALTHS	WEAZAND	WEEDINGS
WAVERY	WAYGONE	WEALTHY	WEAZANDS	WEEDLESS
WAVES	WAYGOOSE	WEAMB	WEAZEN	WEEDS
WAVESHAPE	WAYGOOSES	WEAMBS	WEAZENED	WEEDY
WAVESHAPES	WAYING	WEAN	WEAZENING	WEEING
WAVESON	WAYLAID	WEANED	WEAZENS	WEEK
WAVESONS	WAYLAY	WEANEL	WEB	WEEKDAY
WAVEY	WAYLAYER	WEANELS	WEBBED	WEEKDAYS
WAVEYS	WAYLAYERS	WEANER	WEBBIER	WEEKE
WAVIER	WAYLAYING	WEANERS	WEBBIEST	WEEKEND
WAVIES	WAYLAYS	WEANING	WEBBING	WEEKENDED
WAVIEST	WAYLEAVE	WEANLING	WEBBINGS	WEEKENDER
WAVILY	WAYLEAVES	WEANLINGS	WEBBY	WEEKENDERS
WAVINESS	WAYLESS	WEANS	WEBER	WEEKENDING
WAVINESSES	WAYMARK	WEAPON	WEBERS	WEEKENDINGS
WAVING	WAYMARKED	WEAPONED	WEBFEET	WEEKENDS
WAVINGS	WAYMARKING	WEAPONRIES	WEBFOOT	WEEKES
WAVY	WAYMARKS	WEAPONRY	WEBFOOTED	WEEKLIES
WAW	WAYMENT	WEAPONS	WEBS	WEEKLY
WAWE	WAYMENTED	WEAR	WEBSTER	WEEKNIGHT
WAWES	WAYMENTING	WEARABLE	WEBSTERS	WEEKNIGHTS
WAWL	WAYMENTS	WEARED	WEBWHEEL	WEEKS
WAWLED	WAYPOST	WEARER	WEBWHEELS	WEEL
WAWLING	WAYPOSTS	WEARERS	WEBWORM	WEELS
WAWLINGS	WAYS	WEARIED	WEBWORMS	WEEM
WAWLS	WAYSIDE	WEARIER	WECHT	WEEMS
WAWS	WAYSIDES	WEARIES	WECHTS	WEEN
WAX	WAYWARD	WEARIEST	WED	WEENED
WAXBERRIES	WAYWARDLY	WEARIFUL	WEDDED	WEENIER
WAXBERRY	WAYWISER	WEARILESS	WEDDER	WEENIES
WAXBILL	WAYWISERS	WEARILY	WEDDERED	WEENIEST
WAXBILLS	WAYWODE	WEARINESS	WEDDERING	WEENING
WAXCLOTH	WAYWODES	WEARINESSES	WEDDERS	WEENS
WAXCLOTHS	WAYWORN	WEARING	WEDDING	WEENY
WAXED	WAYZGOOSE	WEARINGLY	WEDDINGS	WEEP
WAXEN	WAYZGOOSES	WEARINGS	WEDELN	WEEPER

The Chambers Dictionary is the authority for many longer words; see *OSW* Introduction, page xii.

WEEPERS	WEIRD	WELKS	WERNERITE	WHACKERS
WEEPHOLE	WEIRDED	WELKT	WERNERITES	WHACKIER
WEEPHOLES	WEIRDER	WELL	WERSH	WHACKIEST
WEEPIE	WEIRDEST	WELLADAY	WERSHER	WHACKING
WEEPIER	WEIRDIE	WELLANEAR	WERSHEST	WHACKINGS
WEEPIES	WEIRDIES	WELLAWAY	WERT	WHACKO
WEEPIEST	WEIRDING	WELLBEING	WERWOLF	WHACKOES
WEEPING	WEIRDLY	WELLBEINGS	WERWOLVES	WHACKOS
WEEPINGLY	WEIRDNESS	WELLED	WESAND	WHACKS
WEEPINGS	WEIRDNESSES	WELLHEAD	WESANDS	WHACKY
WEEPS	WEIRDO	WELLHEADS	WEST	WHAISLE
WEEPY	WEIRDOS	WELLHOUSE	WESTBOUND	WHAISLED
WEER	WEIRDS	WELLHOUSES	WESTED	WHAISLES
WEES	WEIRED	WELLIE	WESTER	WHAISLING
WEEST	WEIRING	WELLIES	WESTERED	WHAIZLE
WEET	WEIRS	WELLING	WESTERING	WHAIZLED
WEETE	WEISE	WELLINGS	WESTERINGS	WHAIZLES
WEETED	WEISED	WELLNESS	WESTERLIES	WHAIZLING
WEETEN	WEISES	WELLNESSES	WESTERLY	WHALE
WEETER	WEISING	WELLS	WESTERN	WHALEBACK
WEETEST	WEIZE	WELLY	WESTERNER	WHALEBACKS
WEETING	WEIZED	WELSH	WESTERNERS	WHALEBOAT
WEETINGLY	WEIZES	WELSHED	WESTERNS	WHALEBOATS
WEETLESS	WEIZING	WELSHER	WESTERS	WHALEBONE
WEETS	WEKA	WELSHERS	WESTING	WHALEBONES
WEEVER	WEKAS	WELSHES	WESTINGS	WHALED
WEEVERS	WELAWAY	WELSHING	WESTLIN	WHALEMAN
WEEVIL	WELCH	WELT	WESTLINS	WHALEMEN
WEEVILED	WELCHED	WELTED	WESTMOST	WHALER
WEEVILLED	WELCHER	WELTER	WESTS	WHALERIES
WEEVILLY	WELCHERS	WELTERED	WESTWARD	WHALERS
WEEVILS	WELCHES	WELTERING	WESTWARDS	WHALERY
WEEVILY	WELCHING	WELTERS	WET	WHALES
WEFT	WELCOME	WELTING	WETA	WHALING
WEFTAGE	WELCOMED	WELTS	WETAS	WHALINGS
WEFTAGES	WELCOMER	WEM	WETBACK	WHALLY
WEFTE	WELCOMERS	WEMB	WETBACKS	WHAM
WEFTED	WELCOMES	WEMBS	WETHER	WHAMMED
WEFTES	WELCOMING	WEMS	WETHERS	WHAMMIES
WEFTING	WELD	WEN	WETLAND	WHAMMING
WEFTS	WELDABLE	WENCH	WETLANDS	WHAMMO
WEID	WELDED	WENCHED	WETLY	WHAMMOS
WEIDS	WELDER	WENCHER	WETNESS	WHAMMY
WEIGELA	WELDERS	WENCHERS	WETNESSES	WHAMPLE
WEIGELAS	WELDING	WENCHES	WETS	WHAMPLES
WEIGH	WELDINGS	WENCHING	WETTED	WHAMS
WEIGHABLE	WELDLESS	WEND	WETTER	WHANG
WEIGHAGE	WELDMENT	WENDED	WETTEST	WHANGAM
WEIGHAGES	WELDMENTS	WENDIGO	WETTING	WHANGAMS
WEIGHED	WELDMESH\tm	WENDIGOS	WETTISH	WHANGED
WEIGHER	WELDMESHES	WENDING	WETWARE	WHANGEE
WEIGHERS	WELDOR	WENDS	WETWARES	WHANGEES
WEIGHING	WELDORS	WENNIER	WEX	WHANGING
WEIGHINGS	WELDS	WENNIEST	WEXE	WHANGS
WEIGHS	WELFARE	WENNISH	WEXED	WHAP
WEIGHT	WELFARES	WENNY	WEXES	WHAPPED
WEIGHTED	WELFARISM	WENS	WEXING	WHAPPING
WEIGHTIER	WELFARISMS	WENT	WEY	WHAPS
WEIGHTIEST	WELFARIST	WENTS	WEYARD	WHARE
WEIGHTILY	WELFARISTS	WEPT	WEYS	WHARES
WEIGHTING	WELK	WERE	WEYWARD	WHARF
WEIGHTINGS	WELKE	WEREGILD	WEZAND	WHARFAGE
WEIGHTS	WELKED	WEREGILDS	WEZANDS	WHARFAGES
WEIGHTY	WELKES	WEREWOLF	WHA	WHARFED
WEIL	WELKIN	WEREWOLVES	WHACK	WHARFING
WEILS	WELKING	WERGILD	WHACKED	WHARFINGS
WEIR	WELKINS	WERGILDS	WHACKER	WHARFS

The Chambers Dictionary is the authority for many longer words; see *OSW* Introduction, page xii.

WHARVE	WHEENGES	WHEREOF	WHIFFINGS	WHINCHAT
WHARVES	WHEENGING	WHEREON	WHIFFLE	WHINCHATS
WHAT	WHEENS	WHEREOUT	WHIFFLED	WHINE
WHATEN	WHEEPLE	WHERES	WHIFFLER	WHINED
WHATEVER	WHEEPLED	WHERESO	WHIFFLERIES	WHINER
WHATNA	WHEEPLES	WHERETO	WHIFFLERS	WHINERS
WHATNESS	WHEEPLING	WHEREUNTO	WHIFFLERY	WHINES
WHATNESSES	WHEESH	WHEREUPON	WHIFFLES	WHINGE
WHATNOT	WHEESHED	WHEREVER	WHIFFLING	WHINGED
WHATNOTS	WHEESHES	WHEREWITH	WHIFFLINGS	WHINGEING
WHATS	WHEESHING	WHEREWITHS	WHIFFS	WHINGEINGS
WHATSIS	WHEESHT	WHERRET	WHIFFY	WHINGER
WHATSISES	WHEESHTED	WHERRETED	WHIFT	WHINGERS
WHATSIT	WHEESHTING	WHERRETING	WHIFTS	WHINGES
WHATSITS	WHEESHTS	WHERRETS	WHIG	WHINIARD
WHATSO	WHEEZE	WHERRIES	WHIGGED	WHINIARDS
WHATTEN	WHEEZED	WHERRY	WHIGGING	WHINIER
WHAUP	WHEEZES	WHERRYMAN	WHIGS	WHINIEST
WHAUPS	WHEEZIER	WHERRYMEN	WHILE	WHININESS
WHAUR	WHEEZIEST	WHET	WHILED	WHININESSES
WHAURS	WHEEZILY	WHETHER	WHILERE	WHINING
WHEAL	WHEEZING	WHETS	WHILES	WHININGLY
WHEALS	WHEEZINGS	WHETSTONE	WHILING	WHININGS
WHEAR	WHEEZLE	WHETSTONES	WHILK	WHINNIED
WHEARE	WHEEZLED	WHETTED	WHILLIED	WHINNIER
WHEAT	WHEEZLES	WHETTER	WHILLIES	WHINNIES
WHEATEAR	WHEEZLING	WHETTERS	WHILLY	WHINNIEST
WHEATEARS	WHEEZY	WHETTING	WHILLYING	WHINNY
WHEATEN	WHEFT	WHEUGH	WHILLYWHA	WHINNYING
WHEATMEAL	WHEFTS	WHEUGHED	WHILLYWHAED	WHINS
WHEATMEALS	WHELK	WHEUGHING	WHILLYWHAING	WHINSTONE
WHEATS	WHELKED	WHEUGHS	WHILLYWHAS	WHINSTONES
WHEATWORM	WHELKIER	WHEW	WHILOM	WHINY
WHEATWORMS	WHELKIEST	WHEWED	WHILST	WHINYARD
WHEE	WHELKS	WHEWING	WHIM	WHINYARDS
WHEECH	WHELKY	WHEWS	WHIMBERRIES	WHIP
WHEECHED	WHELM	WHEY	WHIMBERRY	WHIPBIRD
WHEECHING	WHELMED	WHEYEY	WHIMBREL	WHIPBIRDS
WHEECHS	WHELMING	WHEYIER	WHIMBRELS	WHIPCAT
WHEEDLE	WHELMS	WHEYIEST	WHIMMED	WHIPCATS
WHEEDLED	WHELP	WHEYISH	WHIMMIER	WHIPCORD
WHEEDLER	WHELPED	WHEYS	WHIMMIEST	WHIPCORDS
WHEEDLERS	WHELPING	WHICH	WHIMMING	WHIPCORDY
WHEEDLES	WHELPS	WHICHEVER	WHIMMY	WHIPJACK
WHEEDLING	WHEMMLE	WHICKER	WHIMPER	WHIPJACKS
WHEEDLINGS	WHEMMLED	WHICKERED	WHIMPERED	WHIPLASH
WHEEL	WHEMMLES	WHICKERING	WHIMPERER	WHIPLASHED
WHEELBASE	WHEMMLING	WHICKERS	WHIMPERERS	WHIPLASHES
WHEELBASES	WHEN	WHID	WHIMPERING	WHIPLASHING
WHEELED	WHENAS	WHIDAH	WHIMPERINGS	WHIPLIKE
WHEELER	WHENCE	WHIDAHS	WHIMPERS	WHIPPED
WHEELERS	WHENCES	WHIDDED	WHIMPLE	WHIPPER
WHEELIE	WHENCEVER	WHIDDER	WHIMPLED	WHIPPERS
WHEELIER	WHENEVER	WHIDDERED	WHIMPLES	WHIPPET
WHEELIES	WHENS	WHIDDERING	WHIMPLING	WHIPPETS
WHEELIEST	WHERE	WHIDDERS	WHIMS	WHIPPIER
WHEELING	WHEREAS	WHIDDING	WHIMSEY	WHIPPIEST
WHEELINGS	WHEREAT	WHIDS	WHIMSEYS	WHIPPING
WHEELMAN	WHEREBY	WHIFF	WHIMSICAL	WHIPPINGS
WHEELMEN	WHEREFOR	WHIFFED	WHIMSIER	WHIPPY
WHEELS	WHEREFORE	WHIFFER	WHIMSIES	WHIPS
WHEELWORK	WHEREFORES	WHIFFERS	WHIMSIEST	WHIPSAW
WHEELWORKS	WHEREFROM	WHIFFET	WHIMSILY	WHIPSAWED
WHEELY	WHEREIN	WHIFFETS	WHIMSY	WHIPSAWING
WHEEN	WHEREINTO	WHIFFIER	WHIN	WHIPSAWS
WHEENGE	WHERENESS	WHIFFIEST	WHINBERRIES	WHIPSTAFF
WHEENGED	WHERENESSES	WHIFFING	WHINBERRY	WHIPSTAFFS

The Chambers Dictionary is the authority for many longer words; see *OSW* Introduction, page xii.

WHIPSTALL	WHISKS	WHITEWOOD	WHOLESOMER	WHOT
WHIPSTALLED	WHISKY	WHITEWOODS	WHOLESOMEST	WHOW
WHIPSTALLING	WHISPER	WHITEY	WHOLISM	WHUMMLE
WHIPSTALLS	WHISPERED	WHITEYS	WHOLISMS	WHUMMLED
WHIPSTER	WHISPERER	WHITHER	WHOLIST	WHUMMLES
WHIPSTERS	WHISPERERS	WHITHERED	WHOLISTIC	WHUMMLING
WHIPSTOCK	WHISPERING	WHITHERING	WHOLISTS	WHUNSTANE
WHIPSTOCKS	WHISPERINGS	WHITHERS	WHOLLY	WHUNSTANES
WHIPT	WHISPERS	WHITIER	WHOM	WHY
WHIPTAIL	WHISPERY	WHITIES	WHOMBLE	WHYDAH
WHIPWORM	WHISS	WHITIEST	WHOMBLED	WHYDAHS
WHIPWORMS	WHISSED	WHITING	WHOMBLES	WHYEVER
WHIR	WHISSES	WHITINGS	WHOMBLING	WICCA
WHIRL	WHISSING	WHITISH	WHOMEVER	WICCAN
WHIRLBAT	WHIST	WHITLING	WHOMMLE	WICCANS
WHIRLBATS	WHISTED	WHITLINGS	WHOMMLED	WICCAS
WHIRLED	WHISTING	WHITLOW	WHOMMLES	WICE
WHIRLER	WHISTLE	WHITLOWS	WHOMMLING	WICH
WHIRLERS	WHISTLED	WHITRET	WHOOBUB	WICHES
WHIRLIER	WHISTLER	WHITRETS	WHOOBUBS	WICK
WHIRLIEST	WHISTLERS	WHITS	WHOOP	WICKED
WHIRLIGIG	WHISTLES	WHITSTER	WHOOPED	WICKEDER
WHIRLIGIGS	WHISTLING	WHITSTERS	WHOOPEE	WICKEDEST
WHIRLING	WHISTLINGS	WHITTAW	WHOOPEES	WICKEDLY
WHIRLINGS	WHISTS	WHITTAWER	WHOOPER	WICKEDS
WHIRLPOOL	WHIT	WHITTAWERS	WHOOPERS	WICKEN
WHIRLPOOLS	WHITE	WHITTAWS	WHOOPING	WICKENS
WHIRLS	WHITEBAIT	WHITTER	WHOOPINGS	WICKER
WHIRLWIND	WHITEBAITS	WHITTERED	WHOOPS	WICKERED
WHIRLWINDS	WHITEBASS	WHITTERING	WHOOPSIE	WICKERS
WHIRLY	WHITEBASSES	WHITTERS	WHOOPSIES	WICKET
WHIRR	WHITEBEAM	WHITTLE	WHOOSH	WICKETS
WHIRRED	WHITEBEAMS	WHITTLED	WHOOSHED	WICKIES
WHIRRET	WHITECAP	WHITTLER	WHOOSHES	WICKING
WHIRRETED	WHITECAPS	WHITTLERS	WHOOSHING	WICKIUP
WHIRRETING	WHITECOAT	WHITTLES	WHOOT	WICKIUPS
WHIRRETS	WHITECOATS	WHITTLING	WHOOTED	WICKS
WHIRRIED	WHITED	WHITTLINGS	WHOOTING	WICKY
WHIRRIES	WHITEFLIES	WHITTRET	WHOOTS	WIDDIES
WHIRRING	WHITEFLY	WHITTRETS	WHOP	WIDDLE
WHIRRINGS	WHITEHEAD	WHITY	WHOPPED	WIDDLED
WHIRRS	WHITEHEADS	WHIZ	WHOPPER	WIDDLES
WHIRRY	WHITELY	WHIZBANG	WHOPPERS	WIDDLING
WHIRRYING	WHITEN	WHIZBANGS	WHOPPING	WIDDY
WHIRS	WHITENED	WHIZZ	WHOPPINGS	WIDE
WHIRTLE	WHITENER	WHIZZED	WHOPS	WIDEAWAKE
WHIRTLES	WHITENERS	WHIZZER	WHORE	WIDEAWAKES
WHISH	WHITENESS	WHIZZERS	WHORED	WIDEBODY
WHISHED	WHITENESSES	WHIZZES	WHOREDOM	WIDELY
WHISHES	WHITENING	WHIZZING	WHOREDOMS	WIDEN
WHISHING	WHITENINGS	WHIZZINGS	WHORES	WIDENED
WHISHT	WHITENS	WHO	WHORESON	WIDENER
WHISHTED	WHITEPOT	WHOA	WHORESONS	WIDENERS
WHISHTING	WHITEPOTS	WHODUNNIT	WHORING	WIDENESS
WHISHTS	WHITER	WHODUNNITS	WHORISH	WIDENESSES
WHISK	WHITES	WHOEVER	WHORISHLY	WIDENING
WHISKED	WHITEST	WHOLE	WHORL	WIDENS
WHISKER	WHITEWALL	WHOLEFOOD	WHORLBAT	WIDER
WHISKERED	WHITEWALLS	WHOLEFOODS	WHORLBATS	WIDES
WHISKERS	WHITEWARE	WHOLEMEAL	WHORLED	WIDEST
WHISKERY	WHITEWARES	WHOLEMEALS	WHORLS	WIDGEON
WHISKET	WHITEWASH	WHOLENESS	WHORT	WIDGEONS
WHISKETS	WHITEWASHED	WHOLENESSES	WHORTS	WIDGET
WHISKEY	WHITEWASHES	WHOLES	WHOSE	WIDGETS
WHISKEYS	WHITEWASHING	WHOLESALE	WHOSEVER	WIDGIE
WHISKIES	WHITEWING	WHOLESALES	WHOSO	WIDGIES
WHISKING	WHITEWINGS	WHOLESOME	WHOSOEVER	WIDISH

The Chambers Dictionary is the authority for many longer words; see *OSW* Introduction, page xii.

WIDOW
WIDOWED
WIDOWER
WIDOWERS
WIDOWHOOD
WIDOWHOODS
WIDOWING
WIDOWMAN
WIDOWMEN
WIDOWS
WIDTH
WIDTHS
WIDTHWAYS
WIDTHWISE
WIEL
WIELD
WIELDABLE
WIELDED
WIELDER
WIELDERS
WIELDIER
WIELDIEST
WIELDING
WIELDLESS
WIELDS
WIELDY
WIELS
WIENIE
WIENIES
WIFE
WIFEHOOD
WIFEHOODS
WIFELESS
WIFELIER
WIFELIEST
WIFELIKE
WIFELY
WIFIE
WIFIES
WIG
WIGAN
WIGANS
WIGEON
WIGEONS
WIGGED
WIGGERIES
WIGGERY
WIGGING
WIGGINGS
WIGGLE
WIGGLED
WIGGLER
WIGGLERS
WIGGLES
WIGGLIER
WIGGLIEST
WIGGLING
WIGGLY
WIGHT
WIGHTED
WIGHTING
WIGHTLY
WIGHTS
WIGLESS
WIGLIKE
WIGS
WIGWAG

WIGWAGGED
WIGWAGGING
WIGWAGS
WIGWAM
WIGWAMS
WILD
WILDCAT
WILDCATS
WILDCATTED
WILDCATTING
WILDED
WILDER
WILDERED
WILDERING
WILDERS
WILDEST
WILDFIRE
WILDFIRES
WILDFOWL
WILDFOWLS
WILDGRAVE
WILDGRAVES
WILDING
WILDINGS
WILDISH
WILDLAND
WILDLANDS
WILDLIFE
WILDLIFES
WILDLY
WILDNESS
WILDNESSES
WILDS
WILDWOOD
WILDWOODS
WILE
WILED
WILEFUL
WILES
WILFUL
WILFULLY
WILGA
WILGAS
WILI
WILIER
WILIEST
WILILY
WILINESS
WILINESSES
WILING
WILIS
WILJA
WILJAS
WILL
WILLABLE
WILLED
WILLEMITE
WILLEMITES
WILLER
WILLERS
WILLEST
WILLET
WILLETS
WILLEY
WILLEYED
WILLEYING
WILLEYS

WILLFUL
WILLIE
WILLIED
WILLIES
WILLING
WILLINGLY
WILLIWAW
WILLIWAWS
WILLOW
WILLOWED
WILLOWING
WILLOWISH
WILLOWS
WILLOWY
WILLPOWER
WILLPOWERS
WILLS
WILLY
WILLYARD
WILLYART
WILLYING
WILT
WILTED
WILTING
WILTJA
WILTJAS
WILTS
WILY
WIMBLE
WIMBLED
WIMBLES
WIMBLING
WIMBREL
WIMBRELS
WIMP
WIMPIER
WIMPIEST
WIMPISH
WIMPISHLY
WIMPLE
WIMPLED
WIMPLES
WIMPLING
WIMPS
WIMPY
WIN
WINCE
WINCED
WINCER
WINCERS
WINCES
WINCEY
WINCEYS
WINCH
WINCHED.
WINCHES
WINCHING
WINCHMAN
WINCHMEN
WINCING
WINCINGS
WINCOPIPE
WINCOPIPES
WIND
WINDAC
WINDACS
WINDAGE

WINDAGES
WINDAS
WINDASES
WINDBAG
WINDBAGS
WINDBLOW
WINDBLOWN
WINDBLOWS
WINDBORNE
WINDBOUND
WINDBREAK
WINDBREAKS
WINDBURN
WINDBURNS
WINDED
WINDER
WINDERS
WINDFALL
WINDFALLS
WINDGALL
WINDGALLS
WINDGUN
WINDGUNS
WINDHOVER
WINDHOVERS
WINDIER
WINDIEST
WINDIGO
WINDIGOS
WINDILY
WINDINESS
WINDINESSES
WINDING
WINDINGLY
WINDINGS
WINDLASS
WINDLASSED
WINDLASSES
WINDLASSING
WINDLE
WINDLES
WINDLESS
WINDMILL
WINDMILLED
WINDMILLING
WINDMILLS
WINDOCK
WINDOCKS
WINDORE
WINDORES
WINDOW
WINDOWED
WINDOWING
WINDOWINGS
WINDOWS
WINDPIPE
WINDPIPES
WINDPROOF
WINDRING
WINDROSE
WINDROSES
WINDROW
WINDROWED
WINDROWING
WINDROWS
WINDS
WINDSAIL

WINDSAILS
WINDSES
WINDSHAKE
WINDSHAKES
WINDSHIP
WINDSHIPS
WINDSOCK
WINDSOCKS
WINDSTORM
WINDSTORMS
WINDSURF
WINDSURFED
WINDSURFING
WINDSURFINGS
WINDSURFS
WINDSWEPT
WINDTHROW
WINDTHROWS
WINDTIGHT
WINDWARD
WINDWARDS
WINDY
WINE
WINEBERRIES
WINEBERRY
WINED
WINEGLASS
WINEGLASSES
WINEPRESS
WINEPRESSES
WINERIES
WINERY
WINES
WINESKIN
WINESKINS
WINEY
WING
WINGBEAT
WINGBEATS
WINGDING
WINGDINGS
WINGE
WINGED
WINGEDLY
WINGEING
WINGER
WINGERS
WINGES
WINGIER
WINGIEST
WINGING
WINGLESS
WINGLET
WINGLETS
WINGS
WINGSPAN
WINGSPANS
WINGY
WINIER
WINIEST
WINING
WINK
WINKED
WINKER
WINKERS
WINKING
WINKINGLY

The Chambers Dictionary is the authority for many longer words; see *OSW* Introduction, page xii.

WINKINGS	WIPER	WISER	WITGAT	WITTINESSES
WINKLE	WIPERS	WISES	WITGATS	WITTING
WINKLED	WIPES	WISEST	WITH	WITTINGLY
WINKLER	WIPING	WISH	WITHAL	WITTINGS
WINKLERS	WIPINGS	WISHBONE	WITHDRAW	WITTOL
WINKLES	WIPPEN	WISHBONES	WITHDRAWING	WITTOLLY
WINKLING	WIPPENS	WISHED	WITHDRAWN	WITTOLS
WINKS	WIRE	WISHER	WITHDRAWS	WITTY
WINN	WIRED	WISHERS	WITHDREW	WITWALL
WINNA	WIREDRAW	WISHES	WITHE	WITWALLS
WINNABLE	WIREDRAWING	WISHFUL	WITHED	WITWANTON
WINNER	WIREDRAWINGS	WISHFULLY	WITHER	WITWANTONED
WINNERS	WIREDRAWN	WISHING	WITHERED	WITWANTONING
WINNING	WIREDRAWS	WISHINGS	WITHERING	WITWANTONS
WINNINGLY	WIREDREW	WISING	WITHERINGS	WIVE
WINNINGS	WIRELESS	WISKET	WITHERITE	WIVED
WINNLE	WIRELESSED	WISKETS	WITHERITES	WIVEHOOD
WINNLES	WIRELESSES	WISP	WITHERS	WIVEHOODS
WINNOCK	WIRELESSING	WISPED	WITHES	WIVERN
WINNOCKS	WIREMAN	WISPIER	WITHHAULT	WIVERNS
WINNOW	WIREMEN	WISPIEST	WITHHELD	WIVES
WINNOWED	WIREPHOTO	WISPING	WITHHOLD	WIVING
WINNOWER	WIREPHOTOS	WISPS	WITHHOLDEN	WIZARD
WINNOWERS	WIRER	WISPY	WITHHOLDING	WIZARDLY
WINNOWING	WIRERS	WISSED	WITHHOLDS	WIZARDRIES
WINNOWINGS	WIRES	WISSES	WITHIER	WIZARDRY
WINNOWS	WIRETAP	WISSING	WITHIES	WIZARDS
WINNS	WIRETAPPED	WIST	WITHIEST	WIZEN
WINO	WIRETAPPING	WISTARIA	WITHIN	WIZENED
WINOS	WIRETAPS	WISTARIAS	WITHING	WIZENING
WINS	WIREWAY	WISTED	WITHOUT	WIZENS
WINSEY	WIREWAYS	WISTERIA	WITHOUTEN	WIZIER
WINSEYS	WIREWORK	WISTERIAS	WITHS	WIZIERS
WINSOME	WIREWORKS	WISTFUL	WITHSTAND	WO
WINSOMELY	WIREWORM	WISTFULLY	WITHSTANDING	WOAD
WINSOMER	WIREWORMS	WISTING	WITHSTANDS	WOADED
WINSOMEST	WIREWOVE	WISTITI	WITHSTOOD	WOADS
WINTER	WIRIER	WISTITIS	WITHWIND	WOBBEGONG
WINTERED	WIRIEST	WISTLY	WITHWINDS	WOBBEGONGS
WINTERIER	WIRILY	WISTS	WITHY	WOBBLE
WINTERIEST	WIRINESS	WIT	WITHYWIND	WOBBLED
WINTERING	WIRINESSES	WITAN	WITHYWINDS	WOBBLER
WINTERISE	WIRING	WITBLITS	WITING	WOBBLERS
WINTERISED	WIRINGS	WITBLITSES	WITLESS	WOBBLES
WINTERISES	WIRRICOW	WITCH	WITLESSLY	WOBBLIER
WINTERISING	WIRRICOWS	WITCHED	WITLING	WOBBLIES
WINTERIZE	WIRY	WITCHEN	WITLINGS	WOBBLIEST
WINTERIZED	WIS	WITCHENS	WITLOOF	WOBBLING
WINTERIZES	WISARD	WITCHERIES	WITLOOFS	WOBBLINGS
WINTERIZING	WISARDS	WITCHERY	WITNESS	WOBBLY
WINTERLY	WISDOM	WITCHES	WITNESSED	WOBEGONE
WINTERS	WISDOMS	WITCHETTIES	WITNESSER	WOCK
WINTERY	WISE	WITCHETTY	WITNESSERS	WOCKS
WINTLE	WISEACRE	WITCHIER	WITNESSES	WODGE
WINTLED	WISEACRES	WITCHIEST	WITNESSING	WODGES
WINTLES	WISECRACK	WITCHING	WITS	WOE
WINTLING	WISECRACKED	WITCHINGS	WITTED	WOEBEGONE
WINTRIER	WISECRACKING	WITCHKNOT	WITTER	WOEFUL
WINTRIEST	WISECRACKS	WITCHKNOTS	WITTERED	WOEFULLER
WINTRY	WISED	WITCHLIKE	WITTERING	WOEFULLEST
WINY	WISELING	WITCHMEAL	WITTERS	WOEFULLY
WINZE	WISELINGS	WITCHMEALS	WITTICISM	WOES
WINZES	WISELY	WITCHY	WITTICISMS	WOESOME
WIPE	WISENESS	WITE	WITTIER	WOFUL
WIPED	WISENESSES	WITED	WITTIEST	WOFULLY
WIPEOUT	WISENT	WITELESS	WITTILY	WOFULNESS
WIPEOUTS	WISENTS	WITES	WITTINESS	WOFULNESSES

The Chambers Dictionary is the authority for many longer words; see *OSW* Introduction, page xii.

WOG	WOMANIZING	WOODCHATS	WOODSIAS	WOOLLIEST
WOGGLE	WOMANKIND	WOODCHIP	WOODSIER	WOOLLY
WOGGLES	WOMANKINDS	WOODCHIPS	WOODSIEST	WOOLMAN
WOGS	WOMANLESS	WOODCHUCK	WOODSKIN	WOOLMEN
WOIWODE	WOMANLIER	WOODCHUCKS	WOODSKINS	WOOLPACK
WOIWODES	WOMANLIEST	WOODCOCK	WOODSMAN	WOOLPACKS
WOK	WOMANLIKE	WOODCOCKS	WOODSMEN	WOOLS
WOKE	WOMANLY	WOODCRAFT	WOODSPITE	WOOLSACK
WOKEN	WOMANS	WOODCRAFTS	WOODSPITES	WOOLSACKS
WOKS	WOMB	WOODCUT	WOODSTONE	WOOLSEY
WOLD	WOMBAT	WOODCUTS	WOODSTONES	WOOLSEYS
WOLDS	WOMBATS	WOODED	WOODSY	WOOLSHED
WOLF	WOMBED	WOODEN	WOODWALE	WOOLSHEDS
WOLFBERRIES	WOMBING	WOODENER	WOODWALES	WOOLWARD
WOLFBERRY	WOMBLIKE	WOODENEST	WOODWARD	WOOLWORK
WOLFED	WOMBS	WOODENLY	WOODWARDS	WOOLWORKS
WOLFER	WOMBY	WOODENTOP	WOODWAX	WOOMERA
WOLFERS	WOMEN	WOODENTOPS	WOODWAXEN	WOOMERANG
WOLFHOUND	WOMENFOLK	WOODHOLE	WOODWAXENS	WOOMERANGS
WOLFHOUNDS	WOMENFOLKS	WOODHOLES	WOODWAXES	WOOMERAS
WOLFING	WOMENKIND	WOODHORSE	WOODWIND	WOON
WOLFINGS	WOMENKINDS	WOODHORSES	WOODWINDS	WOONED
WOLFISH	WOMERA	WOODHOUSE	WOODWORK	WOONING
WOLFISHLY	WOMERAS	WOODHOUSES	WOODWORKS	WOONS
WOLFKIN	WON	WOODIE	WOODWORM	WOORALI
WOLFKINS	WONDER	WOODIER	WOODWORMS	WOORALIS
WOLFLING	WONDERED	WOODIES	WOODWOSE	WOORARA
WOLFLINGS	WONDERER	WOODIEST	WOODWOSES	WOORARAS
WOLFRAM	WONDERERS	WOODINESS	WOODY	WOOS
WOLFRAMS	WONDERFUL	WOODINESSES	WOODYARD	WOOSEL
WOLFS	WONDERING	WOODING	WOODYARDS	WOOSELL
WOLFSBANE	WONDERINGS	WOODLAND	WOOED	WOOSELLS
WOLFSBANES	WONDEROUS	WOODLANDS	WOOER	WOOSELS
WOLFSKIN	WONDERS	WOODLARK	WOOERS	WOOSH
WOLFSKINS	WONDRED	WOODLARKS	WOOF	WOOSHED
WOLLIES	WONDROUS	WOODLESS	WOOFED	WOOSHES
WOLLY	WONGA	WOODLICE	WOOFER	WOOSHING
WOLVE	WONGAS	WOODLOUSE	WOOFERS	WOOT
WOLVED	WONGI	WOODMAN	WOOFIER	WOOTZ
WOLVER	WONGIED	WOODMEAL	WOOFIEST	WOOTZES
WOLVERENE	WONGIING	WOODMEALS	WOOFING	WOOZIER
WOLVERENES	WONGIS	WOODMEN	WOOFS	WOOZIEST
WOLVERINE	WONING	WOODMICE	WOOFTER	WOOZILY
WOLVERINES	WONINGS	WOODMOUSE	WOOFTERS	WOOZINESS
WOLVERS	WONKIER	WOODNESS	WOOFY	WOOZINESSES
WOLVES	WONKIEST	WOODNESSES	WOOING	WOOZY
WOLVING	WONKY	WOODNOTE	WOOINGLY	WOP
WOLVINGS	WONNED	WOODNOTES	WOOINGS	WOPPED
WOLVISH	WONNING	WOODPILE	WOOL	WOPPING
WOLVISHLY	WONNINGS	WOODPILES	WOOLD	WOPS
WOMAN	WONS	WOODREEVE	WOOLDED	WORCESTER
WOMANED	WONT	WOODREEVES	WOOLDER	WORCESTERS
WOMANHOOD	WONTED	WOODROOF	WOOLDERS	WORD
WOMANHOODS	WONTING	WOODROOFS	WOOLDING	WORDAGE
WOMANING	WONTLESS	WOODRUFF	WOOLDINGS	WORDAGES
WOMANISE	WONTS	WOODRUFFS	WOOLDS	WORDBOOK
WOMANISED	WOO	WOODRUSH	WOOLEN	WORDBOOKS
WOMANISER	WOOBUT	WOODRUSHES	WOOLENS	WORDBOUND
WOMANISERS	WOOBUTS	WOODS	WOOLFAT	WORDBREAK
WOMANISES	WOOD	WOODSCREW	WOOLFATS	WORDBREAKS
WOMANISH	WOODBIND	WOODSCREWS	WOOLFELL	WORDED
WOMANISING	WOODBINDS	WOODSHED	WOOLFELLS	WORDGAME
WOMANIZE	WOODBINE	WOODSHEDDED	WOOLLED	WORDGAMES
WOMANIZED	WOODBINES	WOODSHEDDING	WOOLLEN	WORDIER
WOMANIZER	WOODBLOCK	WOODSHEDDINGS	WOOLLENS	WORDIEST
WOMANIZERS	WOODBLOCKS	WOODSHEDS	WOOLLIER	WORDILY
WOMANIZES	WOODCHAT	WOODSIA	WOOLLIES	WORDINESS

The Chambers Dictionary is the authority for many longer words; see *OSW* Introduction, page xii.

WORDINESSES	WORKSHOP	WORRYINGS	WOUNDWORTS	WRAWLING
WORDING	WORKSHOPS	WORRYWART	WOUNDY	WRAWLS
WORDINGS	WORKSHY	WORRYWARTS	WOURALI	WRAXLE
WORDISH	WORKSOME	WORSE	WOURALIS	WRAXLED
WORDLESS	WORKTABLE	WORSED	WOVE	WRAXLES
WORDLORE	WORKTABLES	WORSEN	WOVEN	WRAXLING
WORDLORES	WORKTOP	WORSENED	WOW	WRAXLINGS
WORDPLAY	WORKTOPS	WORSENESS	WOWED	WREAK
WORDPLAYS	WORKWEAR	WORSENESSES	WOWEE	WREAKED
WORDS	WORKWEARS	WORSENING	WOWF	WREAKER
WORDSMITH	WORKWEEK	WORSENS	WOWFER	WREAKERS
WORDSMITHS	WORKWEEKS	WORSER	WOWFEST	WREAKFUL
WORDY	WORKWOMAN	WORSES	WOWING	WREAKING
WORE	WORKWOMEN	WORSHIP	WOWS	WREAKLESS
WORK	WORLD	WORSHIPPED	WOWSER	WREAKS
WORKABLE	WORLDED	WORSHIPPING	WOWSERS	WREATH
WORKADAY	WORLDLIER	WORSHIPS	WOX	WREATHE
WORKADAYS	WORLDLIEST	WORSING	WOXEN	WREATHED
WORKBAG	WORLDLING	WORST	WRACK	WREATHEN
WORKBAGS	WORLDLINGS	WORSTED	WRACKED	WREATHER
WORKBENCH	WORLDLY	WORSTEDS	WRACKFUL	WREATHERS
WORKBENCHES	WORLDS	WORSTING	WRACKING	WREATHES
WORKBOAT	WORLDWIDE	WORSTS	WRACKS	WREATHIER
WORKBOATS	WORM	WORT	WRAITH	WREATHIEST
WORKBOOK	WORMCAST	WORTH	WRAITHS	WREATHING
WORKBOOKS	WORMCASTS	WORTHED	WRANGLE	WREATHS
WORKBOX	WORMED	WORTHFUL	WRANGLED	WREATHY
WORKBOXES	WORMER	WORTHIED	WRANGLER	WRECK
WORKDAY	WORMERIES	WORTHIER	WRANGLERS	WRECKAGE
WORKDAYS	WORMERS	WORTHIES	WRANGLES	WRECKAGES
WORKED	WORMERY	WORTHIEST	WRANGLING	WRECKED
WORKER	WORMHOLE	WORTHILY	WRANGLINGS	WRECKER
WORKERIST	WORMHOLED	WORTHING	WRAP	WRECKERS
WORKERISTS	WORMHOLES	WORTHLESS	WRAPOVER	WRECKFISH
WORKERS	WORMIER	WORTHS	WRAPOVERS	WRECKFISHES
WORKFARE	WORMIEST	WORTHY	WRAPPAGE	WRECKFUL
WORKFARES	WORMING	WORTHYING	WRAPPAGES	WRECKING
WORKFOLK	WORMS	WORTLE	WRAPPED	WRECKINGS
WORKFOLKS	WORMSEED	WORTLES	WRAPPER	WRECKS
WORKFORCE	WORMSEEDS	WORTS	WRAPPERED	WREN
WORKFORCES	WORMWOOD	WOS	WRAPPERING	WRENCH
WORKFUL	WORMWOODS	WOSBIRD	WRAPPERS	WRENCHED
WORKGIRL	WORMY	WOSBIRDS	WRAPPING	WRENCHES
WORKGIRLS	WORN	WOST	WRAPPINGS	WRENCHING
WORKHORSE	WORRAL	WOT	WRAPROUND	WRENCHINGS
WORKHORSES	WORRALS	WOTCHER	WRAPROUNDS	WRENS
WORKHOUSE	WORREL	WOTS	WRAPS	WREST
WORKHOUSES	WORRELS	WOTTED	WRAPT	WRESTED
WORKING	WORRICOW	WOTTEST	WRASSE	WRESTER
WORKINGS	WORRICOWS	WOTTETH	WRASSES	WRESTERS
WORKLESS	WORRIED	WOTTING	WRAST	WRESTING
WORKLOAD	WORRIEDLY	WOUBIT	WRASTED	WRESTLE
WORKLOADS	WORRIER	WOUBITS	WRASTING	WRESTLED
WORKMAN	WORRIERS	WOULD	WRASTS	WRESTLER
WORKMANLY	WORRIES	WOULDS	WRATE	WRESTLERS
WORKMATE	WORRIMENT	WOULDST	WRATH	WRESTLES
WORKMATES	WORRIMENTS	WOUND	WRATHED	WRESTLING
WORKMEN	WORRISOME	WOUNDABLE	WRATHFUL	WRESTLINGS
WORKPIECE	WORRIT	WOUNDED	WRATHIER	WRESTS
WORKPIECES	WORRITED	WOUNDER	WRATHIEST	WRETCH
WORKPLACE	WORRITING	WOUNDERS	WRATHILY	WRETCHED
WORKPLACES	WORRITS	WOUNDILY	WRATHING	WRETCHES
WORKROOM	WORRY	WOUNDING	WRATHLESS	WRETHE
WORKROOMS	WORRYCOW	WOUNDINGS	WRATHS	WRETHED
WORKS	WORRYCOWS	WOUNDLESS	WRATHY	WRETHES
WORKSHEET	WORRYGUTS	WOUNDS	WRAWL	WRETHING
WORKSHEETS	WORRYING	WOUNDWORT	WRAWLED	WRICK

The Chambers Dictionary is the authority for many longer words; see *OSW* Introduction, page xii.

WRICKED
WRICKING
WRICKS
WRIED
WRIER
WRIES
WRIEST
WRIGGLE
WRIGGLED
WRIGGLER
WRIGGLERS
WRIGGLES
WRIGGLIER
WRIGGLIEST
WRIGGLING
WRIGGLINGS
WRIGGLY
WRIGHT
WRIGHTS
WRING
WRINGED
WRINGER
WRINGERS
WRINGING
WRINGINGS
WRINGS
WRINKLE
WRINKLED
WRINKLES
WRINKLIER
WRINKLIES
WRINKLIEST

WRINKLING
WRINKLY
WRIST
WRISTBAND
WRISTBANDS
WRISTIER
WRISTIEST
WRISTLET
WRISTLETS
WRISTS
WRISTY
WRIT
WRITABLE
WRITATIVE
WRITE
WRITER
WRITERESS
WRITERESSES
WRITERLY
WRITERS
WRITES
WRITHE
WRITHED
WRITHEN
WRITHES
WRITHING
WRITHINGS
WRITHLED
WRITING
WRITINGS
WRITS
WRITTEN

WRIZLED
WROATH
WROATHS
WROKE
WROKEN
WRONG
WRONGDOER
WRONGDOERS
WRONGED
WRONGER
WRONGERS
WRONGEST
WRONGFUL
WRONGING
WRONGLY
WRONGNESS
WRONGNESSES
WRONGOUS
WRONGS
WROOT
WROOTED
WROOTING
WROOTS
WROTE
WROTH
WROUGHT
WRUNG
WRY
WRYBILL
WRYBILLS
WRYER
WRYEST

WRYING
WRYLY
WRYNECK
WRYNECKS
WRYNESS
WRYNESSES
WRYTHEN
WUD
WUDDED
WUDDING
WUDS
WULFENITE
WULFENITES
WULL
WULLED
WULLING
WULLS
WUNNER
WUNNERS
WURLEY
WURLEYS
WURLIES
WURST
WURSTS
WURTZITE
WURTZITES
WUS
WUSES
WUSHU
WUSHUS
WUSS
WUSSES

WUTHER
WUTHERED
WUTHERING
WUTHERS
WUZZLE
WUZZLED
WUZZLES
WUZZLING
WYANDOTTE
WYANDOTTES
WYCH
WYCHES
WYE
WYES
WYLIECOAT
WYLIECOATS
WYN
WYND
WYNDS
WYNN
WYNNS
WYNS
WYSIWYG
WYTE
WYTED
WYTES
WYTING
WYVERN
WYVERNS

X

XANTHAM	XENOGAMIES	XERARCH	XIPHOPAGI	XYLOMA
XANTHAMS	XENOGAMY	XERASIA	XIS	XYLOMAS
XANTHAN	XENOGRAFT	XERASIAS	XOANA	XYLOMATA
XANTHANS	XENOGRAFTS	XERIC	XOANON	XYLOMETER
XANTHATE	XENOLITH	XEROCHASIES	XU	XYLOMETERS
XANTHATES	XENOLITHS	XEROCHASY	XYLEM	XYLONIC
XANTHEIN	XENOMANIA	XERODERMA	XYLEMS	XYLONITE
XANTHEINS	XENOMANIAS	XERODERMAS	XYLENE	XYLONITES
XANTHENE	XENOMENIA	XEROMA	XYLENES	XYLOPHAGE
XANTHENES	XENOMENIAS	XEROMAS	XYLENOL	XYLOPHAGES
XANTHIC	XENON	XEROMATA	XYLENOLS	XYLOPHONE
XANTHIN	XENONS	XEROMORPH	XYLIC	XYLOPHONES
XANTHINE	XENOPHILE	XEROMORPHS	XYLITOL	XYLORIMBA
XANTHINES	XENOPHILES	XEROPHAGIES	XYLITOLS	XYLORIMBAS
XANTHINS	XENOPHOBE	XEROPHAGY	XYLOCARP	XYLOSE
XANTHOMA	XENOPHOBES	XEROPHILIES	XYLOCARPS	XYLOSES
XANTHOMAS	XENOPHOBIES	XEROPHILY	XYLOGEN	XYLYL
XANTHOMATA	XENOPHOBY	XEROPHYTE	XYLOGENS	XYLYLS
XANTHOUS	XENOPHYA	XEROPHYTES	XYLOGRAPH	XYST
XANTHOXYL	XENOTIME	XEROSES	XYLOGRAPHS	XYSTER
XANTHOXYLS	XENOTIMES	XEROSIS	XYLOID	XYSTERS
XEBEC	XENURINE	XEROSTOMA	XYLOIDIN	XYSTI
XEBECS	XERAFIN	XEROSTOMAS	XYLOIDINE	XYSTOI
XENIA	XERAFINS	XEROSTOMATA	XYLOIDINES	XYSTOS
XENIAL	XERANSES	XEROTES	XYLOIDINS	XYSTS
XENIAS	XERANSIS	XEROTIC	XYLOL	XYSTUS
XENIUM	XERANTIC	XI	XYLOLOGIES	
XENOCRYST	XERAPHIM	XIPHOID	XYLOLOGY	
XENOCRYSTS	XERAPHIMS	XIPHOIDAL	XYLOLS	

Y

YABBER
YABBERED
YABBERING
YABBERS
YABBIE
YABBIES
YABBY
YACCA
YACCAS
YACHT
YACHTED
YACHTER
YACHTERS
YACHTIE
YACHTIES
YACHTING
YACHTINGS
YACHTS
YACHTSMAN
YACHTSMEN
YACK
YACKED
YACKER
YACKERS
YACKING
YACKS
YAFF
YAFFED
YAFFING
YAFFLE
YAFFLES
YAFFS
YAGER
YAGERS
YAGGER
YAGGERS
YAH
YAHOO
YAHOOS
YAHS
YAK
YAKHDAN
YAKHDANS
YAKIMONA
YAKIMONAS
YAKITORI
YAKITORIS
YAKKA
YAKKAS
YAKKED
YAKKER
YAKKERS
YAKKING
YAKOW
YAKOWS
YAKS
YAKUZA
YALD
YALE

YALES
YAM
YAMEN
YAMENS
YAMMER
YAMMERED
YAMMERING
YAMMERINGS
YAMMERS
YAMS
YAMULKA
YAMULKAS
YANG
YANGS
YANK
YANKED
YANKER
YANKERS
YANKIE
YANKIES
YANKING
YANKS
YANQUI
YAOURT
YAOURTS
YAP
YAPOCK
YAPOCKS
YAPOK
YAPOKS
YAPON
YAPONS
YAPP
YAPPED
YAPPER
YAPPERS
YAPPIE
YAPPIER
YAPPIES
YAPPIEST
YAPPING
YAPPS
YAPPY
YAPS
YAPSTER
YAPSTERS
YAQONA
YAQONAS
YARD
YARDAGE
YARDAGES
YARDANG
YARDANGS
YARDBIRD
YARDBIRDS
YARDED
YARDING
YARDLAND

YARDLANDS
YARDMAN
YARDMEN
YARDS
YARDSTICK
YARDSTICKS
YARDWAND
YARDWANDS
YARE
YARELY
YARER
YAREST
YARFA
YARFAS
YARMULKA
YARMULKAS
YARMULKE
YARMULKES
YARN
YARNED
YARNING
YARNS
YARPHA
YARPHAS
YARR
YARRAMAN
YARRAMANS
YARROW
YARROWS
YARRS
YARTA
YARTAS
YARTO
YARTOS
YASHMAK
YASHMAKS
YATAGAN
YATAGANS
YATAGHAN
YATAGHANS
YATE
YATES
YATTER
YATTERED
YATTERING
YATTERINGS
YATTERS
YAUD
YAUDS
YAULD
YAUP
YAUPON
YAUPONS
YAW
YAWED
YAWEY
YAWING
YAWL
YAWLED

YAWLING
YAWLS
YAWN
YAWNED
YAWNIER
YAWNIEST
YAWNING
YAWNINGLY
YAWNINGS
YAWNS
YAWNY
YAWP
YAWPED
YAWPER
YAWPERS
YAWPING
YAWPS
YAWS
YAWY
YBET
YBLENT
YBORE
YBOUND
YBOUNDEN
YBRENT
YCLAD
YCLED
YCLEEPE
YCLEEPED
YCLEEPES
YCLEEPING
YCLEPED
YCLEPT
YCOND
YDRAD
YDRED
YE
YEA
YEAD
YEADING
YEADS
YEAH
YEALDON
YEALDONS
YEALM
YEALMED
YEALMING
YEALMS
YEAN
YEANED
YEANING
YEANLING
YEANLINGS
YEANS
YEAR
YEARBOOK
YEARBOOKS
YEARD
YEARDED

YEARDING
YEARDS
YEARLIES
YEARLING
YEARLINGS
YEARLONG
YEARLY
YEARN
YEARNED
YEARNER
YEARNERS
YEARNING
YEARNINGS
YEARNS
YEARS
YEAS
YEAST
YEASTED
YEASTIER
YEASTIEST
YEASTING
YEASTLIKE
YEASTS
YEASTY
YECH
YEDE
YEDES
YEDING
YEED
YEEDING
YEEDS
YEGG
YEGGMAN
YEGGMEN
YEGGS
YELD
YELDRING
YELDRINGS
YELDROCK
YELDROCKS
YELK
YELKS
YELL
YELLED
YELLING
YELLINGS
YELLOCH
YELLOCHED
YELLOCHING
YELLOCHS
YELLOW
YELLOWED
YELLOWER
YELLOWEST
YELLOWING
YELLOWISH
YELLOWS
YELLOWY
YELLS

The Chambers Dictionary is the authority for many longer words; see *OSW* Introduction, page xii.

YELM	YEUK	YMOLT	YOJANA	YOUNGEST
YELMED	YEUKED	YMOLTEN	YOJANAS	YOUNGISH
YELMING	YEUKING	YMPE	YOJANS	YOUNGLING
YELMS	YEUKS	YMPES	YOK	YOUNGLINGS
YELP	YEVE	YMPING	YOKE	YOUNGLY
YELPED	YEVEN	YMPT	YOKED	YOUNGNESS
YELPER	YEVES	YNAMBU	YOKEL	YOUNGNESSES
YELPERS	YEVING	YNAMBUS	YOKELISH	YOUNGS
YELPING	YEW	YO	YOKELS	YOUNGSTER
YELPINGS	YEWEN	YOB	YOKES	YOUNGSTERS
YELPS	YEWS	YOBBERIES	YOKING	YOUNGTH
YELT	YEX	YOBBERY	YOKINGS	YOUNGTHLY
YELTS	YEXED	YOBBISH	YOKKED	YOUNGTHS
YEN	YEXES	YOBBISHLY	YOKKING	YOUNKER
YENNED	YEXING	YOBBISM	YOKOZUNA	YOUNKERS
YENNING	YFERE	YOBBISMS	YOKOZUNAS	YOUR
YENS	YGLAUNST	YOBBO	YOKS	YOURN
YENTA	YGO	YOBBOES	YOKUL	YOURS
YENTAS	YGOE	YOBBOS	YOLD	YOURSELF
YEOMAN	YIBBLES	YOBS	YOLDRING	YOURSELVES
YEOMANLY	YICKER	YOCK	YOLDRINGS	YOURT
YEOMANRIES	YICKERED	YOCKED	YOLK	YOURTS
YEOMANRY	YICKERING	YOCKING	YOLKED	YOUTH
YEOMEN	YICKERS	YOCKS	YOLKIER	YOUTHFUL
YEP	YIELD	YOD	YOLKIEST	YOUTHHEAD
YEPS	YIELDABLE	YODE	YOLKS	YOUTHHEADS
YERBA	YIELDED	YODEL	YOLKY	YOUTHHOOD
YERBAS	YIELDER	YODELLED	YOMP	YOUTHHOODS
YERD	YIELDERS	YODELLER	YOMPED	YOUTHIER
YERDED	YIELDING	YODELLERS	YOMPING	YOUTHIEST
YERDING	YIELDINGS	YODELLING	YOMPS	YOUTHLY
YERDS	YIELDS	YODELS	YON	YOUTHS
YERK	YIKE	YODLE	YOND	YOUTHSOME
YERKED	YIKES	YODLED	YONDER	YOUTHY
YERKING	YIKKER	YODLER	YONDERLY	YOW
YERKS	YIKKERED	YODLERS	YONDERS	YOWE
YERSINIA	YIKKERING	YODLES	YONGTHLY	YOWES
YERSINIAE	YIKKERS	YODLING	YONI	YOWIE
YERSINIAS	YILL	YOGA	YONIS	YOWIES
YES	YILLS	YOGAS	YONKER	YOWL
YESES	YIN	YOGH	YONKERS	YOWLED
YESHIVA	YINCE	YOGHOURT	YONKS	YOWLEY
YESHIVAH	YINS	YOGHOURTS	YONT	YOWLEYS
YESHIVAHS	YIP	YOGHS	YOOF	YOWLING
YESHIVAS	YIPPED	YOGHURT	YOOFS	YOWLINGS
YESHIVOT	YIPPEE	YOGHURTS	YOOP	YOWLS
YESHIVOTH	YIPPER	YOGI	YOOPS	YOWS
YESK	YIPPERS	YOGIC	YOPPER	YPIGHT
YESKED	YIPPIES	YOGIN	YOPPERS	YPLAST
YESKING	YIPPING	YOGINI	YORE	YPLIGHT
YESKS	YIPPY	YOGINIS	YORES	YPSILOID
YESSES	YIPS	YOGINS	YORK	YPSILON
YEST	YIRD	YOGIS	YORKED	YPSILONS
YESTER	YIRDED	YOGISM	YORKER	YRAPT
YESTERDAY	YIRDING	YOGISMS	YORKERS	YRAVISHED
YESTERDAYS	YIRDS	YOGURT	YORKIE	YRENT
YESTEREVE	YIRK	YOGURTS	YORKIES	YRIVD
YESTEREVES	YIRKED	YOHIMBINE	YORKING	YRNEH
YESTERN	YIRKING	YOHIMBINES	YORKS	YRNEHS
YESTREEN	YIRKS	YOICK	YOS	YSAME
YESTS	YITE	YOICKED	YOU	YSHEND
YESTY	YITES	YOICKING	YOUK	YSHENDING
YET	YLEM	YOICKS	YOUKED	YSHENDS
YETI	YLEMS	YOICKSED	YOUKING	YSHENT
YETIS	YLIKE	YOICKSES	YOUKS	YSLAKED
YETT	YLKE	YOICKSING	YOUNG	YTOST
YETTS	YLKES	YOJAN	YOUNGER	YTTERBIA

The Chambers Dictionary is the authority for many longer words; see *OSW* Introduction, page xii.

YTTERBIAS
YTTERBIUM
YTTERBIUMS
YTTRIA
YTTRIAS
YTTRIC
YTTRIOUS
YTTRIUM
YTTRIUMS
YU
YUAN
YUCA
YUCAS
YUCCA
YUCCAS
YUCK
YUCKED

YUCKER
YUCKERS
YUCKIER
YUCKIEST
YUCKING
YUCKS
YUCKY
YUFT
YUFTS
YUG
YUGA
YUGAS
YUGS
YUK
YUKATA
YUKATAS
YUKE

YUKED
YUKES
YUKIER
YUKIEST
YUKING
YUKKIER
YUKKIEST
YUKKY
YUKO
YUKOS
YUKS
YUKY
YULAN
YULANS
YULE
YULES
YULETIDE

YULETIDES
YUMMIER
YUMMIEST
YUMMY
YUMP
YUMPED
YUMPIE
YUMPIES
YUMPING
YUMPS
YUNX
YUNXES
YUP
YUPON
YUPONS
YUPPIE
YUPPIEDOM

YUPPIEDOMS
YUPPIES
YUPPIFIED
YUPPIFIES
YUPPIFY
YUPPIFYING
YUPPY
YUPS
YURT
YURTS
YUS
YWIS
YWROKE

Z

ZABAIONE	ZANDERS	ZASTRUGA	ZEK	ZESTING
ZABAIONES	ZANELLA	ZASTRUGI	ZEKS	ZESTS
ZABETA	ZANELLAS	ZATI	ZEL	ZESTY
ZABETAS	ZANIED	ZATIS	ZELANT	ZETA
ZABRA	ZANIER	ZAX	ZELANTS	ZETAS
ZABRAS	ZANIES	ZAXES	ZELATOR	ZETETIC
ZABTIEH	ZANIEST	ZEA	ZELATORS	ZETETICS
ZABTIEHS	ZANINESS	ZEAL	ZELATRICE	ZEUGMA
ZACK	ZANINESSES	ZEALANT	ZELATRICES	ZEUGMAS
ZACKS	ZANJA	ZEALANTS	ZELATRIX	ZEUGMATIC
ZADDIK	ZANJAS	ZEALFUL	ZELATRIXES	ZEUXITE
ZADDIKIM	ZANJERO	ZEALLESS	ZELOSO	ZEUXITES
ZADDIKS	ZANJEROS	ZEALOT	ZELOTYPIA	ZEX
ZAFFER	ZANTE	ZEALOTISM	ZELOTYPIAS	ZEXES
ZAFFERS	ZANTES	ZEALOTISMS	ZELS	ZEZE
ZAFFRE	ZANTHOXYL	ZEALOTRIES	ZEMINDAR	ZEZES
ZAFFRES	ZANTHOXYLS	ZEALOTRY	ZEMINDARI	ZHO
ZAG	ZANY	ZEALOTS	ZEMINDARIES	ZHOMO
ZAGGED	ZANYING	ZEALOUS	ZEMINDARIS	ZHOMOS
ZAGGING	ZANYISM	ZEALOUSLY	ZEMINDARS	ZHOS
ZAGS	ZANYISMS	ZEALS	ZEMINDARY	ZIBELINE
ZAIRE	ZANZE	ZEAS	ZEMSTVA	ZIBELINES
ZAKAT	ZANZES	ZEBEC	ZEMSTVO	ZIBELLINE
ZAKATS	ZAP	ZEBECK	ZEMSTVOS	ZIBELLINES
ZAKUSKA	ZAPATA	ZEBECKS	ZENANA	ZIBET
ZAKUSKI	ZAPATEADO	ZEBECS	ZENANAS	ZIBETS
ZAMAN	ZAPATEADOS	ZEBRA	ZENDIK	ZIFF
ZAMANG	ZAPOTILLA	ZEBRAS	ZENDIKS	ZIFFIUS
ZAMANGS	ZAPOTILLAS	ZEBRASS	ZENITH	ZIFFIUSES
ZAMANS	ZAPPED	ZEBRASSES	ZENITHAL	ZIFFS
ZAMARRA	ZAPPER	ZEBRINA	ZENITHS	ZIG
ZAMARRAS	ZAPPERS	ZEBRINAS	ZEOLITE	ZIGAN
ZAMARRO	ZAPPIER	ZEBRINE	ZEOLITES	ZIGANKA
ZAMARROS	ZAPPIEST	ZEBRINNIES	ZEOLITIC	ZIGANKAS
ZAMBO	ZAPPING	ZEBRINNY	ZEPHYR	ZIGANS
ZAMBOMBA	ZAPPY	ZEBROID	ZEPHYRS	ZIGGED
ZAMBOMBAS	ZAPS	ZEBRULA	ZEPPELIN	ZIGGING
ZAMBOORAK	ZAPTIAH	ZEBRULAS	ZEPPELINS	ZIGGURAT
ZAMBOORAKS	ZAPTIAHS	ZEBRULE	ZERDA	ZIGGURATS
ZAMBOS	ZAPTIEH	ZEBRULES	ZERDAS	ZIGS
ZAMBUCK	ZAPTIEHS	ZEBU	ZEREBA	ZIGZAG
ZAMBUCKS	ZARAPE	ZEBUB	ZEREBAS	ZIGZAGGED
ZAMBUK	ZARAPES	ZEBUBS	ZERIBA	ZIGZAGGING
ZAMBUKS	ZARATITE	ZEBUS	ZERIBAS	ZIGZAGGY
ZAMIA	ZARATITES	ZECCHINE	ZERO	ZIGZAGS
ZAMIAS	ZAREBA	ZECCHINES	ZEROED	ZIKKURAT
ZAMINDAR	ZAREBAS	ZECCHINI	ZEROING	ZIKKURATS
ZAMINDARI	ZAREEBA	ZECCHINO	ZEROS	ZILA
ZAMINDARIES	ZAREEBAS	ZECCHINOS	ZEROTH	ZILAS
ZAMINDARIS	ZARF	ZED	ZERUMBET	ZILCH
ZAMINDARS	ZARFS	ZEDOARIES	ZERUMBETS	ZILCHES
ZAMINDARY	ZARIBA	ZEDOARY	ZEST	ZILLAH
ZAMOUSE	ZARIBAS	ZEDS	ZESTED	ZILLAHS
ZAMOUSES	ZARNEC	ZEE	ZESTER	ZILLION
ZAMPOGNA	ZARNECS	ZEES	ZESTERS	ZILLIONS
ZAMPOGNAS	ZARNICH	ZEIN	ZESTFUL	ZILLIONTH
ZAMPONE	ZARNICHS	ZEINS	ZESTFULLY	ZILLIONTHS
ZAMPONI	ZARZUELA	ZEITGEIST	ZESTIER	ZIMB
ZANDER	ZARZUELAS	ZEITGEISTS	ZESTIEST	ZIMBI

The Chambers Dictionary is the authority for many longer words; see *OSW* Introduction, page xii.

ZIMBIS	ZIPLOCK	ZOETROPES	ZOOEAL	ZOONOMIES
ZIMBS	ZIPPED	ZOETROPIC	ZOOEAS	ZOONOMIST
ZIMMER	ZIPPER	ZOIATRIA	ZOOECIA	ZOONOMISTS
ZIMMERS	ZIPPERED	ZOIATRIAS	ZOOECIUM	ZOONOMY
ZIMOCCA	ZIPPERS	ZOIATRICS	ZOOGAMETE	ZOONOSES
ZIMOCCAS	ZIPPIER	ZOIC	ZOOGAMETES	ZOONOSIS
ZINC	ZIPPIEST	ZOISITE	ZOOGAMIES	ZOONOTIC
ZINCED	ZIPPING	ZOISITES	ZOOGAMOUS	ZOONS
ZINCIER	ZIPPO	ZOISM	ZOOGAMY	ZOOPATHIES
ZINCIEST	ZIPPOS	ZOISMS	ZOOGENIC	ZOOPATHY
ZINCIFIED	ZIPPY	ZOIST	ZOOGENIES	ZOOPERAL
ZINCIFIES	ZIPS	ZOISTS	ZOOGENOUS	ZOOPERIES
ZINCIFY	ZIPTOP	ZOMBI	ZOOGENY	ZOOPERIST
ZINCIFYING	ZIRCALOY	ZOMBIE	ZOOGLOEA	ZOOPERISTS
ZINCING	ZIRCALOYS	ZOMBIES	ZOOGLOEAE	ZOOPERY
ZINCITE	ZIRCON	ZOMBIFIED	ZOOGLOEAS	ZOOPHAGAN
ZINCITES	ZIRCONIA	ZOMBIFIES	ZOOGLOEIC	ZOOPHAGANS
ZINCKED	ZIRCONIAS	ZOMBIFY	ZOOGONIES	ZOOPHAGIES
ZINCKIER	ZIRCONIC	ZOMBIFYING	ZOOGONOUS	ZOOPHAGY
ZINCKIEST	ZIRCONIUM	ZOMBIISM	ZOOGONY	ZOOPHILE
ZINCKIFIED	ZIRCONIUMS	ZOMBIISMS	ZOOGRAFT	ZOOPHILES
ZINCKIFIES	ZIRCONS	ZOMBIS	ZOOGRAFTS	ZOOPHILIA
ZINCKIFY	ZIT,	ZOMBORUK	ZOOGRAPHIES	ZOOPHILIAS
ZINCKIFYING	ZITE	ZOMBORUKS	ZOOGRAPHY	ZOOPHILIES
ZINCKING	ZITHER	ZONA	ZOOID	ZOOPHILY
ZINCKY	ZITHERN	ZONAE	ZOOIDAL	ZOOPHOBIA
ZINCO	ZITHERNS	ZONAL	ZOOIDS	ZOOPHOBIAS
ZINCODE	ZITHERS	ZONARY	ZOOKS	ZOOPHORI
ZINCODES	ZITI	ZONATE	ZOOLATER	ZOOPHORIC
ZINCOID	ZITS	ZONATED	ZOOLATERS	ZOOPHORUS
ZINCOS	ZIZ	ZONATION	ZOOLATRIA	ZOOPHYTE
ZINCOUS	ZIZANIA	ZONATIONS	ZOOLATRIAS	ZOOPHYTES
ZINCS	ZIZANIAS	ZONDA	ZOOLATRIES	ZOOPHYTIC
ZINCY	ZIZEL	ZONDAS	ZOOLATRY	ZOOPLASTIES
ZINEB	ZIZELS	ZONE	ZOOLITE	ZOOPLASTY
ZINEBS	ZIZYPHUS	ZONED	ZOOLITES	ZOOS
ZINFANDEL	ZIZYPHUSES	ZONELESS	ZOOLITH	ZOOSCOPIC
ZINFANDELS	ZIZZ	ZONES	ZOOLITHIC	ZOOSCOPIES
ZING	ZIZZED	ZONING	ZOOLITHS	ZOOSCOPY
ZINGED	ZIZZES	ZONINGS	ZOOLITIC	ZOOSPERM
ZINGEL	ZIZZING	ZONK	ZOOLOGIES	ZOOSPERMS
ZINGELS	ZLOTY	ZONKED	ZOOLOGIST	ZOOSPORE
ZINGER	ZLOTYS	ZONKING	ZOOLOGISTS	ZOOSPORES
ZINGERS	ZO	ZONKS	ZOOLOGY	ZOOSPORIC
ZINGIBER	ZOA	ZONOID	ZOOM	ZOOTAXIES
ZINGIBERS	ZOARIA	ZONULA	ZOOMANCIES	ZOOTAXY
ZINGIER	ZOARIUM	ZONULAE	ZOOMANCY	ZOOTECHNIES
ZINGIEST	ZOBO	ZONULAR	ZOOMANTIC	ZOOTECHNY
ZINGING	ZOBOS	ZONULAS	ZOOMED	ZOOTHECIA
ZINGS	ZOBU	ZONULE	ZOOMETRIC	ZOOTHEISM
ZINGY	ZOBUS	ZONULES	ZOOMETRIES	ZOOTHEISMS
ZINKE	ZOCCO	ZONULET	ZOOMETRY	ZOOTHOME
ZINKED	ZOCCOLO	ZONULETS	ZOOMING	ZOOTHOMES
ZINKENITE	ZOCCOLOS	ZONURE	ZOOMORPH	ZOOTOMIC
ZINKENITES	ZOCCOS	ZONURES	ZOOMORPHIES	ZOOTOMIES
ZINKES	ZODIAC	ZOO	ZOOMORPHS	ZOOTOMIST
ZINKIER	ZODIACAL	ZOOBIOTIC	ZOOMORPHY	ZOOTOMISTS
ZINKIEST	ZODIACS	ZOOBLAST	ZOOMS	ZOOTOMY
ZINKIFIED	ZOEA	ZOOBLASTS	ZOON	ZOOTOXIN
ZINKIFIES	ZOEAE	ZOOCHORE	ZOONAL	ZOOTOXINS
ZINKIFY	ZOEAL	ZOOCHORES	ZOONIC	ZOOTROPE
ZINKIFYING	ZOEAS	ZOOCHORIES	ZOONITE	ZOOTROPES
ZINKING	ZOECHROME	ZOOCHORY	ZOONITES	ZOOTROPHIES
ZINKY	ZOECHROMES	ZOOCYTIA	ZOONITIC	ZOOTROPHY
ZINNIA	ZOEFORM	ZOOCYTIUM	ZOONOMIA	ZOOTYPE
ZINNIAS	ZOETIC	ZOOEA	ZOONOMIAS	ZOOTYPES
ZIP	ZOETROPE	ZOOEAE	ZOONOMIC	ZOOTYPIC

The Chambers Dictionary is the authority for many longer words; see *OSW* Introduction, page xii.

ZOOZOO
ZOOZOOS
ZOPILOTE
ZOPILOTES
ZOPP
ZOPPO
ZORGITE
ZORGITES
ZORIL
ZORILLE
ZORILLES
ZORILLO
ZORILLOS
ZORILS
ZORINO
ZORINOS
ZORRO
ZORROS
ZOS
ZOSTER
ZOSTERS
ZOUK

ZOUKS
ZOUNDS
ZOWIE
ZUCCHETTO
ZUCCHETTOS
ZUCCHINI
ZUCCHINIS
ZUCHETTA
ZUCHETTAS
ZUCHETTO
ZUCHETTOS
ZUFFOLI
ZUFFOLO
ZUFOLI
ZUFOLO
ZUGZWANG
ZUGZWANGS
ZULU
ZULUS
ZUMBOORUK
ZUMBOORUKS
ZUPA

ZUPAN
ZUPANS
ZUPAS
ZURF
ZURFS
ZUZ
ZUZIM
ZYGA
ZYGAENID
ZYGAENINE
ZYGAENOID
ZYGAL
ZYGANTRA
ZYGANTRUM
ZYGANTRUMS
ZYGOCACTI
ZYGODONT
ZYGOMA
ZYGOMAS
ZYGOMATA
ZYGOMATIC
ZYGON

ZYGOPHYTE
ZYGOPHYTES
ZYGOSE
ZYGOSES
ZYGOSIS
ZYGOSPERM
ZYGOSPERMS
ZYGOSPORE
ZYGOSPORES
ZYGOTE
ZYGOTES
ZYGOTIC
ZYLONITE
ZYLONITES
ZYMASE
ZYMASES
ZYME
ZYMES
ZYMIC
ZYMITE
ZYMITES
ZYMOGEN

ZYMOGENIC
ZYMOGENS
ZYMOID
ZYMOLOGIC
ZYMOLOGIES
ZYMOLOGY
ZYMOLYSES
ZYMOLYSIS
ZYMOLYTIC
ZYMOME
ZYMOMES
ZYMOMETER
ZYMOMETERS
ZYMOSES
ZYMOSIS
ZYMOTIC
ZYMOTICS
ZYMURGIES
ZYMURGY
ZYTHUM
ZYTHUMS

APPENDIX

DICTIONARY OF
2- AND 3-LETTER WORDS
ALLOWABLE FOR
SCRABBLE®

Note that, although these are complete lists of all the 2- and 3-letter words allowable for Scrabble, the meanings are not necessarily comprehensive; the full range can be found in *The Chambers Dictionary*.

The definitions have been selected to help players to remember the words, and at the same time to act as guides to possible derivatives. For example, CUE is defined both as 'a signal to begin a speech, etc' (the plural CUES being implied), and as 'to give such a signal' (implying the forms CUES (again), CUEING, and CUED). Remember however that this dictionary is intended only as an aide-mémoire. *Official Scrabble*® *Words*, in conjunction with *The Chambers Dictionary*, is the final authority.

Different parts of speech are separated by ' ▌ ', and different meanings of the same word by ';'.

Bold type is used when reference is being made to other words. Often these words are defined in the lists; when, however, the reference is to longer words, definitions have been given for those that are felt to be less familiar.

AA a type of lava

AD colloquial for **advertisement**

AE Scots word for **one** (adjective)

AH interjection expressing surprise, joy, etc ▌ to make such an interjection

AI the three-toed sloth; same as **ayu**

AM present tense of **be**

AN the indefinite article used before a vowel

AR the letter 'R'

AS in whatever way ▌ so ▌ a mythological Norse god

AT preposition denoting position in space or time

AW interjection expressing disappointment, sympathy, etc

AX US form of **axe**

AY always ▌ yes ▌ an affirmative vote or voter

BA in ancient Egyptian religion, the soul

BE to exist or live

BI colloquial short form of **bisexual**, (a person who is) attracted sexually to both sexes

BO interjection intended to startle ▌ in US slang, a term of address to a man

BY beside; near; through ▌ same as **bye**

CH obsolete dialect pronoun meaning **I**

DA a Burmese knife; a dialect form of **dad**, a father

DI a plural of **deus**, Latin word for **god**

DO to perform ▌ a celebration; same as **doh**

EA dialect word meaning **river**

EE Scots word for **eye** (noun)

EF the letter 'F'

EH interjection expressing inquiry ▌ to say 'eh'

EL the letter 'L', or anything of that shape; an elevated railway

EM the letter 'M'; a unit of measurement in printing

EN the letter 'N'; in printing, half of an **em**

ER interjection expressing hesitation

ES the letter 'S', or anything of that shape

EX the letter 'X'; someone no longer in a previous relationship

FA a musical note (in sol-fa)

FY same as **fie**

GI same as **gie**, a judo or karate costume

GO to pass from one place to another ▌ energy or activity; a Japanese board game

GU same as **gue**

HA interjection expressing a wide range of emotions or responses

HE pronoun used in referring to a male person or thing ▌ a male

HI interjection calling attention

HO interjection calling attention, expressing surprise, etc ▌ stopping, cessation ▌ obsolete word meaning to stop

ID a fish of the carp family; part of the human personality

IF on condition that; whether ▌ a condition

IN not out ▌ someone or something that is in ▌ to take in

IO interjection expressing joy, triumph or grief ▌ a cry of 'io'

IS present tense of **be**

IT pronoun referring to an inanimate thing ▌ an indefinable quality; Italian vermouth

JO Scots word for a loved one

KA the spirit or soul; a god; same as **kae**, a jackdaw

KO a Maori digging-stick

KY same as **kye**

LA a musical note (in sol-fa)

	‖ interjection with various meanings		acidity or alkalinity
LI	a Chinese unit of distance	PI	a letter in the Greek alphabet
LO	interjection meaning see, look or behold		‖ pious or sanctimonious
		PO	short form of **chamberpot**
		QI	an individual's life force
MA	childish or familiar word for **mother** (noun)		
ME	pronoun representing oneself	RE	a musical note (in sol-fa) ‖ about
MI	a musical note (in sol-fa)		
MO	old word for **more**	SH	interjection requesting silence
MU	a letter in the Greek alphabet	SI	an earlier form of **ti**, a musical note
MY	of or belonging to me	SO	in such a way ‖ same as **sol**, a musical note
NA	Scots word for **no**, not at all	ST	interjection requesting silence
NE	obsolete word meaning not		
NÉ	(of a man) born	TA	interjection expressing thanks
NO	a word of negation; not at all ‖ a negative vote or voter	TE	same as **ti**, a musical note
		TI	a musical note (in sol-fa); a small Pacific tree
NU	a letter in the Greek alphabet		
NY	obsolete spelling of **nigh** (adjective and verb)	TO	in the direction of, towards
OB	an objection	UG	to loathe
OD	a hypothetical force; old word for **god**, often used as a mild oath	UM	interjection expressing doubt or hesitation
OE	same as **oy**	UN	dialect word for **one** (noun)
OF	belonging to	UP	in a higher place ‖ a rise; a spell of prosperity ‖ to move up
OH	interjection expressing surprise, interest, pain, etc	UR	interjection expressing hesitation
OI	interjection used to attract attention	US	pronoun used in referring to oneself and others
OM	an intoned Hindu sacred symbol	UT	a syllable representing **doh**
ON	not off; available ‖ in cricket, the on-side ‖ to go on		
OO	Scots form of **wool** ‖ Scots form of **we**	WE	pronoun used in referring to oneself and others
OR	in heraldry, the tincture gold or yellow ‖ a word expressing alternatives	WO	variant of **woe**
OS	a bone	XI	a letter in the Greek alphabet
OU	Scots interjection expressing concession	XU	a Vietnamese coin
OW	interjection expressing pain; same as **ou**	YE	old word for **you**; old spelling of **the**
OX	a general name for a bovine animal	YO	interjection calling for effort or attention
OY	Scots word for **grandchild**	YU	precious jade
PA	childish or familiar word for **father**; a Maori fort		
PH	a number used to express degree of	ZO	same as **zho**

AAS plural of **aa**

ABA an outer garment worn by some Arab women

ABB a textile yarn

ABY to pay (as) a penalty

ACE a winning serve in tennis ▌outstanding ▌to play an ace

ACH same as **och**

ACT to do in a specified way ▌something done

ADD to make an addition

ADO bustle or fuss

ADS plural of **ad**

ADZ US form of **adze**, a cutting tool

AFT behind; near the stern of a vessel, etc

AGA a Turkish commander or chief officer

AGE the time during which a person has existed ▌to grow old

AGO past; since

AHA interjection expressing exultation, pleasure, surprise, etc

AHS present tense of **ah**

AIA an Indian or South African nursemaid

AID to help or assist ▌help; something that helps

AIL to be indisposed ▌a trouble

AIM to point or direct ▌a purpose

AIN Scots word for **own** (adjective)

AIR the mixture of gases breathed by people and animals; an appearance or manner ▌to make known publicly

AIS plural of **ai**

AIT a small island

AKE old spelling of **ache** (verb)

ALA an outgrowth on a fruit

ALB a priest's long white vestment

ALE a kind of beer

ALL comprising the whole amount, extent, etc of ▌the whole; everybody or everything

ALP a high mountain; a mountain pasture

ALS obsolete form of **also**, or **as** (adverb)

ALT a high tone; a halt or rest

AMI French word for **friend**

AMP short form of **ampere** and **amplifier**

ANA in equal quantities (in recipes and prescriptions)

AND also; indicating addition ▌something added

ANE Scots word for **one**

ANI a tropical American bird

ANN old Scots word for a payment to a parish minister's widow

ANT a small industrious insect

ANY some; whichever, no matter which

APE a monkey ▌to imitate

APT suitable ▌obsolete word meaning to adapt

ARB short form of **arbitrageur**, a person who profits by judicious dealing in stocks and shares

ARC a part of the circumference of a circle ▌to form an arc

ARD a primitive type of plough

ARE present tense of **be** ▌a unit of metric land measure

ARK a floating vessel ▌obsolete word meaning to put in an ark

ARM a limb; a weapon ▌to provide with weapons

ARS plural of **ar**

ART the creation of works of beauty; a human skill

ARY dialect word for **any**

ASH a kind of tree; the remains of anything burnt

ASK to request, inquire, or invite ▌dialect word for **newt**

ASP a venomous snake

ASS a long-eared animal like a small horse; a stupid person

ATE past tense of **eat**

AUF obsolete word for an elf's child

AUK a heavy black-and-white seabird

AVA Scots word meaning **at all**

AVE a recitation of the address or prayer to the Virgin Mary

AWA Scots word for **away**

AWE fear or dread ▌to strike with awe

AWL a pointed instrument for boring

AWN the beard of barley, etc ▌to shelter with an awning

AXE a tool for chopping ▌to chop or cut down

AYE ever; yes ▌an affirmative vote or voter

AYS plural of **ay**

AYU a small edible Japanese fruit

BAA the cry of a sheep ▌to bleat

BAD evil; wicked; faulty ▌something evil, wicked, etc

BAG a receptacle for containing

something ▌ to put into a bag

BAH interjection expressing disgust or contempt

BAM a hoax ▌ to hoax or cheat

BAN a prohibition ▌ to forbid or prohibit

BAP a large, flat breakfast roll

BAR a block of a solid substance; an obstruction ▌ to obstruct or prevent

BAS plural of **ba**

BAT a flying mammal; an implement for striking a ball ▌ to strike with a bat

BAY an inlet of the sea; the barking (of hounds) ▌ to bark or howl

BED a place to sleep on ▌ to put to bed

BEE an insect that makes honey; the letter 'B'

BEG to ask for ▌ another word for **bey**

BEL a measure of noise

BEN Scots or Irish word for **mountain**

BET a sum of money, etc, gambled ▌ to gamble (money, etc)

BEY a Turkish governor

BEZ the second tine of a deer's horn

BIB a protective piece of material fastened under a child's chin ▌ to tipple

BID an offer ▌ to make an offer

BIG large; very important ▌ Scots word for **build**

BIN a container for rubbish; a case for wine ▌ to put into a bin

BIO short form of **biography**

BIS twice

BIT a small piece; a curb or restraint ▌ to curb or restrain

BIZ slang word for **business**

BOA a large constricting snake

BOB to move quickly up and down ▌ a curtsy

BOD a person

BOG a marsh ▌ to sink

BOH same as **bo** (interjection)

BOK South African word for a goat or an antelope

BON French word for **good**

BOO a sound expressing disapproval or contempt ▌ to make such a sound

BOP short for **bebop**, a variety of jazz music ▌ to dance to pop music

BOR East Anglian form of address meaning **neighbour**

BOS plural of **bo**

BOT the maggot of a botfly ▌ Australian word meaning to cadge

BOW a bending of the neck or body in greeting ▌ to bend or incline downwards

BOX a case or receptacle for holding anything; a blow with the hand or fists ▌ to put into a box; to strike with the hand or fists

BOY a male child ▌ Shakespearean word meaning to play (a female part) as a boy

BRA short for **brassière**, an undergarment worn to support a woman's breasts

BRO a place for which one feels a strong affinity

BUB old word for a strong drink

BUD a flower not yet opened ▌ to produce buds

BUG a kind of insect ▌ to pester or irritate

BUM a tramp or sponger ▌ to sponge or live dissolutely

BUN a kind of sweet roll or cake

BUR a prickly seed-case; a throaty sound of 'r' ▌ to whisper hoarsely

BUS a road vehicle for passengers ▌ to transport by bus

BUT except; nevertheless ▌ an objection ▌ to put forward as an objection

BUY to purchase ▌ something purchased

BYE a pass to the next round (of a competition, etc)

BYS plural of **by**

CAB a taxi-cab

CAD a dishonourable man

CAM a projection on a revolving shaft; a whitening stone ▌ to whiten with a cam

CAN a container of tin-plate ▌ to store in such a container

CAP a covering for the head, a chimney, etc ▌ to put a cap on or cover the top of

CAR a self-propelled wheeled vehicle

CAT a small, furry domestic animal ▌ to vomit

CAW to cry as a crow ▌ the cry of a crow

CAY a low islet

CEE the letter 'C', or anything of that shape

CEL short form of **celluloid**, a strong, often transparent, plastic material

CEP a kind of edible mushroom

CHA tea

CHE dialect form of **I**, used by Shakespeare

CHI feminine of **chal**, a fellow or person

CID a chief, captain or hero

CIG short for **cigarette**

CIT contemptuous term for someone who is not a gentleman
CLY old word meaning to seize or steal
COB a male swan; a wicker basket ▌ to strike
COD a kind of fish; a hoax ▌ to hoax or make fun of
COG a projection on a toothed wheel ▌ to furnish with cogs
COL a pass in a mountain range
CON a trick or swindle ▌ to trick; to persuade by dishonest means
COO to make a sound like a dove ▌ the sound made by a dove
COP to capture ▌ a policeman; a capture or arrest
COR interjection expressing surprise ▌ a Hebrew measure
COS a crisp, long-leaved lettuce
COT a small bed for a young child
COW the female of bovine and some other animals ▌ to subdue
COX short for **coxswain**, (to act as) a person who steers a boat
COY bashful or modest
COZ short for **cousin**
CRU French word meaning **vineyard** or **vintage**
CRY to utter a sound of pain or grief, or loudly ▌ such a sound
CUB the young of some animals, eg a fox ▌ to produce cubs
CUD food chewed again by a ruminating animal
CUE a signal to begin a speech, etc ▌ to give such a signal
CUM combined with; with the addition of
CUP a small round drinking-vessel ▌ to form into a cup shape
CUR a worthless mongrel dog
CUT to make an incision in; to reduce ▌ an incision or reduction
CUZ obsolete form of **coz**
CWM Welsh word for **valley**

DAB to touch or press gently ▌ a gentle touch or wipe; an expert ▌ expert
DAD a father; a thump ▌ to thump
DAE Scots form of **do** (verb)
DAG a dirty tuft of wool on a sheep ▌ to cut off dags
DAH same as **da**, a Burmese knife
DAK in India, the mail or post; a letter
DAL a kind of Indian edible pea
DAM an embankment to restrain water ▌ to restrain (water) with an embankment or bank
DAN a level of efficiency (in Japanese combative sports)

DAP to dip bait gently into the water (in fishing) ▌ bait so dipped
DAS plural of **da**
DAW a jackdaw ▌ to dawn
DAY the time when it is light; 24 hours
DEB colloquial form of **débutante**, a young woman making her first formal appearance in society
DEE the letter 'D', or anything of that shape ▌ euphemism for **damn**
DEF excellent, brilliant
DEI a plural of **deus**, Latin word for **god**
DEL another word for **nabla**, a mathematical symbol
DEN the lair of a wild animal; a private place ▌ to retire to a den
DEW moisture deposited from the air on cooling ▌ to moisten (as) with dew
DEY formerly, the pasha of Algiers
DIB to fish by dapping ▌ a small bone in a sheep's leg
DID past tense of **do**
DIE to lose life ▌ a small cube, a dice
DIG to use a spade; to excavate ▌ an act of digging
DIM not bright ▌ to make dim
DIN a loud jarring noise ▌ to annoy with such a noise
DIP to immerse briefly; to lower ▌ an act or period of dipping
DIT named or reputed (French) ▌ Scots word meaning to block
DIV an evil spirit of Persian mythology
DOB to inform on or betray
DOC contraction of **doctor** (noun)
DOD dialect word meaning to cut the hair of ▌ Scots word for a rounded hill
DOE the female of a deer, rabbit, and some other animals
DOG one of a family of four-legged animals, often the domestic variety ▌ to follow like a dog
DOH a musical note (in sol-fa)
DON a university lecturer, etc ▌ to put on (clothes, etc)
DOO Scots word for **dove**, a pigeon
DOP a kind of brandy ▌ obsolete word meaning to dip
DOR a dung-beetle ▌ obsolete word meaning to mock
DOS plural of **do**, a musical note
DOT a very small spot ▌ to make such a spot
DOW same as **dhow**, an Arab sailing vessel ▌ obsolete and Scots word meaning to be able
DRY without liquid ▌ to make or become dry
DSO same as **zho**

DUB to add sound effects, etc, to ‖ Scots word for **puddle**

DUD something or someone ineffectual ‖ ineffective; useless

DUE something owed ‖ Shakespearean word meaning to endue

DUG past tense of **dig** ‖ a nipple of an animal

DUN greyish brown ‖ a greyish-brown horse ‖ to press for payment

DUO two people considered a pair for a specific reason

DUP Shakespearean word meaning to undo

DUX a leader

DYE to stain ‖ a colour produced by dyeing

DZO same as **zho**

EAN Shakespearean word meaning to give birth to

EAR the organ of hearing; the part of corn, etc, containing the seeds ‖ to produce (corn) ears; obsolete word meaning to plough

EAS plural of **ea**

EAT to take in food ‖ an archaic word for **food**

EAU French word for **water**; same as **ea**

EBB to move back from the land (of the tide) ‖ such a movement of the tide

ECH Shakespearean word meaning to eke out

ECO concerned with habitat and environment

ECU a European unit of currency

EDH same as **eth**

EEK interjection expressing fright

EEL a long, smooth cylindrical fish

EEN plural of **ee**

EFF euphemism for **fuck**

EFS plural of **ef**

EFT a newt

EGG an oval or round body from which young are hatched ‖ to add eggs to (in cooking, etc)

EGO the 'I' or self

EHS present tense of **eh**

EIK Scots form of **eke**

EKE to add ‖ an addition

ELD old word for age or old age

ELF a diminutive, mischievous supernatural being ‖ a Shakespearean word meaning to entangle (hair)

ELK a kind of large deer

ELL a measure of length

ELM a tree with serrated leaves

ELS plural of **el**

ELT dialect word for a young sow

EME obsolete word for **uncle**

EMS plural of **em**

EMU a flightless, fast-running bird

END the last point; termination or close ‖ to finish or close

ENE obsolete, dialect or poetic word for **even**

ENG a phonetic symbol

ENS plural of **en**; being or existence

EON same as **aeon**, an eternity

ERA a series of years; an age

ERE before ‖ same as **ear**, to plough

ERF South African word for a garden plot

ERG a unit of work

ERK slang word for **aircraftsman**

ERN old spelling of **earn**

ERR to make a mistake

ERS the bitter vetch

ESS same as **es**

EST a programme designed to develop human potential

ETA a letter in the Greek alphabet

ETH a letter used in Old English

EUK dialect word meaning to itch ‖ an itching

EVE poetic word for **evening**

EWE a female sheep

EWK same as **euk**

EWT old form of **newt**, a tailed amphibious animal

EYE the organ of sight ‖ to look at carefully

FAB marvellous

FAD an interest intensely but briefly pursued; a craze

FAG a cigarette; drudgery ‖ to work, or be worked, hard

FAH same as **fa**

FAN an instrument used for cooling ‖ to cool, (as) with a fan

FAP Shakespearean word meaning fuddled or drunk

FAR remote or distant ‖ dialect word meaning to remove to a distance

FAS plural of **fa**

FAT plump; obese ‖ solid vegetable or animal oil ‖ to make or grow fat

FAW a gypsy

FAX a machine that scans electronically ‖ to send messages by such a machine

FAY poetic word for a fairy ‖ dialect word meaning to clean out (eg a ditch)

FED past tense of **feed** ‖ US slang for a Federal agent

FEE the price paid for services ‖ to pay

a fee to
FEN low marshy land
FET obsolete form of **fetch** (verb)
FEU a Scottish form of land tenure ▌ to grant or hold land in feu
FEW not many
FEY whimsical; foreseeing the future ▌ same as **fay** (verb)
FEZ a red brimless cap of wool or felt
FIB a little lie ▌ to tell such a lie
FID a conical pin of hard wood
FIE old interjection expressing disapproval
FIG a kind of tropical fruit packed with seeds ▌ Shakespearean word meaning to make an insulting gesture at
FIL Shakespearean word for the shaft of a vehicle
FIN a steering, swimming, or balancing organ on an aquatic animal
FIR a kind of conifer
FIT healthy; suitable ▌ something that fits ▌ to make suitable
FIX to make firm; to arrange ▌ a difficulty; something fraudulently arranged
FIZ to make a hissing or sputtering sound ▌ such a sound; a fizzy drink
FLU short form of **influenza**
FLY to move through the air ▌ a kind of flying insect ▌ surreptitious or sly
FOB a small watch pocket ▌ obsolete word meaning to pocket
FOE an enemy
FOG a thick mist ▌ to be affected by fog
FOH an expression of disgust or contempt
FON obsolete word for a fool ▌ to play the fool
FOP an affected dandy
FOR in the place of; in favour of; towards
FOU Scots word for **drunk** (adjective)
FOX a wild animal related to the dog ▌ to act cunningly, to cheat
FOY Spenserian word meaning **allegiance**, loyalty
FRA Italian word meaning **brother** or **friar**
FRO obsolete word for **from**
FRY to cook in oil or fat ▌ a dish so cooked; a number of young fish
FUB old word meaning to put off
FUD Scots word for a rabbit's or hare's tail
FUG a very hot, close atmosphere ▌ to cause a fug in

FUM same word as **fung**, a fabulous Chinese bird
FUN pleasure, enjoyment, merriment ▌ to play
FUR the thick, soft, fine hair of some animals; a crust formed by hard water ▌ to cover or coat with fur

GAB to chatter ▌ idle talk
GAD to wander about idly ▌ a miner's chisel
GAE Scots word for **go** (verb)
GAG to silence ▌ something that gags the mouth
GAL dialect word for **girl**
GAM a school of whales ▌ to join up in a gam
GAN past tense of the old verb **gin**, to begin
GAP an opening ▌ to make a gap in
GAR Scots word meaning to compel ▌ a garfish
GAS a substance which is neither solid nor liquid ▌ to poison with gas
GAT slang word for a gun
GAU under the Nazi regime, a German political district
GAY lively ▌ a homosexual
GED dialect word for **pike** (fish)
GEE the letter 'G' ▌ of horses, to move on
GEL a jelly-like solution ▌ to form a gel
GEM a precious stone ▌ old word meaning to adorn with gems
GEN general information
GEO a gully or creek
GET to obtain ▌ a stupid person
GEY Scots word meaning **fairly** ▌ Scots word meaning **considerable**
GHI clarified butter
GIB a wedge-shaped piece of metal ▌ to fasten with a gib
GID a sheep disease
GIE Scots word for **give** (verb) ▌ a judo costume
GIF old word meaning **if**
GIG a band or pop group's engagement ▌ to play a gig
GIN an alcoholic spirit ▌ to snare in a gin trap
GIO same as **geo**
GIP same as **gyp** (noun)
GIS plural of **gis**
GIT a stupid person
GJU same as **gue**
GNU an African antelope
GOA a Tibetan gazelle
GOB slang word for the mouth ▌ to spit

GOD an object of worship ▮ to deify

GOE older form of **geo** ▮ old form of **go** (verb)

GON a geometrical grade

GOO a sticky substance

GOS plural of **go**

GOT past tense of **get**

GOV short form of **governor**

GOY a Gentile

GUB Australian word for a white man

GUE a kind of violin formerly used in Shetland

GUM a sticky substance ▮ to smear, coat, etc with gum

GUN a weapon for discharging explosive projectiles, etc ▮ to discharge such projectiles, etc

GUP slang word for gossip or prattle

GUR an unrefined cane sugar

GUS plural of **gu**

GUT the intestine ▮ to take the guts out of (fish, etc)

GUV same as **gov**

GUY colloquial term for a person generally ▮ to make fun of

GYM short form of **gymnasium**, **gymnastics**, etc

GYP slang word for a cheat ▮ to swindle

HAD past tense of **have**

HAE Scots form of **have**

HAG an ugly old woman ▮ Scots word meaning to hack or hew

HAH an interjection expressing various emotions, such as surprise, exultation, dismay

HAJ a Muslim pilgrimage to Mecca

HAM salted and smoked flesh from the leg of a pig; a bad actor ▮ to overact, exaggerate

HAN Spenserian plural form of **have** (verb)

HAP chance, fortune ▮ to happen by chance

HAS present tense of **have**

HAT a covering for the head ▮ to provide or cover with a hat

HAW the fruit of the hawthorn ▮ to make indecisive noises

HAY cut grass, used for fodder ▮ to make hay

HEM an edge or border ▮ to form a hem on

HEN a female domestic fowl ▮ to challenge to a daring act

HEP slang word meaning knowing, abreast of knowledge and taste ▮ a rosehip

HER pronoun representing a female person or thing ▮ of or belonging to such a person or thing

HES plural of **he**

HET slang word for **heterosexual**

HEW to cut with blows ▮ Spenserian form of **hue**

HEX something that brings misfortune ▮ to bring misfortune

HEY interjection calling attention, etc ▮ a winding country-dance ▮ to dance this dance

HIC interjection representing a hiccup

HID past tense of **hide**

HIE to turn (a horse) to the left ▮ a cry requesting such a turn

HIM pronoun representing a male person or thing

HIN a Hebrew liquid measure

HIP part of the thigh ▮ to carry on the hip

HIS of or belonging to a male person or thing

HIT to strike ▮ an act of striking

HOA interjection expressing exultation, surprise, etc ▮ cessation ▮ obsolete word meaning to stop

HOB a flat surface on a cooker

HOC Latin word for **this**

HOD a trough for carrying bricks ▮ Scottish word meaning to bob or jog

HOE a tool for loosening the earth ▮ to use a hoe

HOG a kind of pig ▮ to use selfishly

HOH same as **ho**

HOI interjection used to attract attention

HON short for **honey**, as a term of endearment

HOO Shakespearean interjection expressing boisterous emotion

HOP to leap on one leg ▮ a leap on one leg

HOS plural of **ho**

HOT very warm ▮ to heat

HOW in what way ▮ a manner or means

HOX Shakespearean word meaning to hock or hamstring

HOY a large one-decked boat ▮ interjection requesting someone or something to stop ▮ to incite

HUB the centre of a wheel

HUE a colour or tint

HUG to embrace ▮ an embrace

HUH interjection expressing disgust

HUI a Maori gathering; a social gathering

HUM to make a sound like bees ▮ the noise of bees

HUP to turn (a horse) to the right ▮ a cry requesting such a turn

HUT a small house or shelter ▮ to settle in a hut

HYE obsolete form of **hie** or **high**

HYP old word for **hypochondria**, excessive worry about one's health ■ to offend

ICE frozen water ■ to cool with ice
ICH Shakespearean word meaning to eke or augment ■ dialect word for **I**
ICY covered with ice; frosty
IDE same as **id**, a fish
IDS plural of **id**
IFF conjunction used in logic to express 'if and only if'
IFS plural of **if**
ILK a type or kind
ILL unwell ■ harm; misfortune
IMP a mischievous child; a wicked spirit ■ to engraft (a hawk) with new feathers
INK a coloured liquid used in writing ■ to colour with ink
INN a small hotel ■ old word meaning to lodge
INS plural of **in**
ION an electrically charged particle
IOS plural of **io**
IRE anger
IRK to annoy or weary
ISH Scottish legal word meaning issue or expiry
ISM any distinctive theory or fad
ISO short for **isolated replay**, a TV and film facility
ITA the miriti palm
ITS of or belonging to a something
IVY a climbing evergreen plant

JAB to poke or stab ■ a poke or stab, an injection
JAG a sharp projection ■ to pierce
JAK same as **jack**, an East Indian tree
JAM a conserve made with fruit and sugar; a blockage ■ to block up (eg a street) by crowding
JAP same as **jaup**, a Scots word meaning to splash or a splash
JAR a wide-mouthed container ■ to put in jars
JAW part of the skull holding the teeth ■ to chatter at length
JAY a bird of the crow family
JEE same as **gee**
JET a stream of liquid; a jetplane ■ to spout; to travel by jet
JEU French word for **game**
JEW offensive word meaning to cheat or get the better of
JIB a triangular sail ■ to show objection
JIG a lively dance ■ to dance a jig; to

jump up and down
JIZ same as **gizz**, Scots word for a wig
JOB a piece of work ■ to work at jobs
JOE same as **jo**
JOG to run at a slow, steady pace ■ a spell of jogging
JOR the second movement of a raga
JOT a little bit, an iota ■ to note down
JOW Scots word meaning to toll ■ a stroke of a bell
JOY gladness, delight ■ an obsolete word meaning to rejoice
JUD a mass of coal
JUG a container for liquids ■ to stew (eg hare) in a closed pottery jar
JUS Latin word for a law or a legal right
JUT to project ■ a projection

KAE Scots word for **jackdaw** ■ to serve
KAI in New Zealand, etc, food, a meal
KAM Shakespearean word meaning **awry**, twisted or distorted
KAS plural of **ka**
KAT same as **khat**, an E African shrub; an ancient Egyptian unit of weight
KAW same as **caw**
KAY the letter 'K'
KEA a large New Zealand parrot
KEB Scots word meaning to give birth to a premature or stillborn lamb ■ a ewe giving birth to such a lamb
KED a wingless fly that infests sheep
KEF a drug that produces a dreamy repose; such repose
KEG a small cask
KEN to know ■ a range of knowledge
KEP dialect word meaning to catch ■ a catch
KET Scots word for **carrion**, rotting flesh of an animal
KEX a dry stalk
KEY an instrument for locking, tuning, etc ■ to enter (data) into a computer
KID a young goat; a child ■ to hoax or deceive
KIF same as **kef**
KIN one's relations
KIP a nap ■ to have a nap or sleep
KIR a wine and blackcurrant drink
KIT equipment ■ to provide with equipment
KOA a Hawaiian acacia
KOB an African waterbuck
KON Spenserian word meaning to know
KOP South African word for **hill**
KOS same as **coss**, an Indian measure of distance
KOW same as **cow**, Scots word for a

bunch of twigs

KYE Scots word for **cows**, cattle

KYU in judo, one of the novice grades

LAB contraction of **laboratory**

LAC a dark-red resin

LAD a boy or youth

LAG a delay; insulating material █ to fall behind; to cover (eg pipes) with insulating material

LAH same as **la**, a musical note

LAM to beat █ a hurried flight from the police (US slang)

LAP a circuit of a race-track █ to scoop up with the tongue

LAR the god relating to a house

LAS plural of **la**

LAT short form of **latrine**, a lavatory

LAV short form of **lavatory**

LAW a rule or statute █ obsolete word meaning to take to court

LAX slack, careless, or negligent █ a kind of salmon

LAY to place or set down; to produce eggs █ a lyric or song

LEA meadow or pasture █ fallow

LED past tense of **lead**

LEE shelter; the sheltered side █ Scots word meaning to tell a lie

LEG a limb for walking and standing █ to walk briskly

LEI a garland or wreath; plural of **leu**

LEK the unit of Albanian currency █ of blackcocks, etc, to gather and display

LEP dialect word meaning to leap

LES same as **lez**

LET to allow; to grant use of in return for payment █ a hindrance; an instance of letting for payment

LEU the unit of Romanian currency

LEV the unit of Bulgarian currency

LEW same as **lev** █ tepid

LEX Latin word for **law**

LEY rare form of **leu** █ same as **lea**

LEZ short form of **lesbian**, a female homosexual

LIB short form of **liberation**, setting free, especially from discrimination or prejudice █ dialect word meaning to geld

LID a cover or covering

LIE a false statement █ to tell a lie; to be in a horizontal position

LIG a dialect form of **lie**

LIN Spenserian word meaning to cease █ same as **linn**, a waterfall

LIP one of the folds of flesh round the mouth █ to use or touch with the lips

LIS a fleur-de-lis

LIT past tense of **light**

LOB a ball hit (in tennis) or thrown (in cricket) in a specific way █ to hit or throw a ball in this way

LOG a fallen or cut tree-trunk █ to enter in a record

LOO colloquial form of **lavatory**; a card game █ to subject to a forfeit at loo

LOP to cut off unnecessary parts █ an act of lopping

LOR colloquial form of **lord**, interjection expressing surprise

LOS praise, reputation

LOT a great deal; a set of things offered together for sale █ to allot

LOW not tall or high █ an area where things (eg spirits, health, finances, etc) are low █ to make the noise of cattle

LOX liquid oxygen; a kind of smoked salmon

LOY in Ireland, a long, narrow spade

LUD a form of **lord**, a judge

LUG to pull or drag with difficulty █ dialect word for **ear**

LUM Scots word for **chimney**

LUR same as **lure**, a Bronze Age trumpet

LUV love, a term of endearment

LUX a unit of illumination

LUZ a supposedly indestructible bone, possibly the sacrum

LYE a short branch of a railway; an alkaline solution

LYM Shakespearean for **lyam**, a leash

MAA of a goat, to bleat

MAC contraction of **mackintosh**

MAD insane; angry █ Shakespearean word meaning to drive mad

MAE Scots word for **mo**

MAG short form of **magazine**; an old word for a halfpenny █ dialect word for to tease or to chatter

MAK Scots word meaning to make

MAL French word for **pain**, **sickness**

MAM dialect word for **mother**

MAN an adult human male █ to provide with a (human) operator

MAP a diagram of the surface of the earth, etc █ to make a map of

MAR to spoil or damage

MAS a house or farm in the south of France; plural of **ma**

MAT a floor covering █ to tangle

MAW the stomach of an animal

MAX obsolete word for **gin**, the drink

MAY may blossom █ to gather may blossom

MEG variant form of **mag**, a halfpenny
MEL honey
MEN plural of **man**
MES plural of **me**
MET past tense of **meet** ▌short form of **meteorology**, the study of weather
MEU the plant spignel
MEW (of a cat) to make a thin, high-pitched cry ▌this cry; a gull
MHO a former unit of electrical inductance
MID middle ▌the middle; short for **midshipman**
MIL a unit of wire measurement; a Cyprian coin
MIM Scots and dialect word meaning **prim**
MIR a Russian peasant farming commune; a Muslim ruler
MIS Spenserian word meaning to fail ▌plural of **mi**
MIX to mingle ▌a mixture
MIZ short form of **misery** or **miserable**
MNA same as **mina**, a Greek unit of weight or money
MOA a gigantic extinct bird like an ostrich
MOB a disorderly crowd ▌to form into a mob
MOD a Highland Gaelic festival
MOE obsolete form of **mo**, more ▌obsolete form of **mow**, a wry face ▌to make a wry face
MOG same as **moggy**, a cat
MOI French word meaning **me**, facetiously used in English
MOM US colloquial word for **mother**
MON a Japanese family badge or crest
MOO (of cattle) to low ▌a cow's low
MOP a sponge, etc, on a stick ▌to clean with a mop
MOR a layer of humus
MOT French word meaning **word**
MOU Scots word for a mouth
MOW to cut the grass on ▌a pile of hay; obsolete word for a wry face
MOY Shakespearean word for a coin or a measure
MOZ Australian word meaning a type of curse
MUD wet soft earth ▌to bury or hide in mud
MUG a cup with vertical sides ▌to attack from behind
MUM child's word for **mother** (noun) ▌silent ▌to act in a mime
MUN dialect word for **must** (verb) ▌dialect word for **man** (noun)
MUS plural of **mu**
MUX US and dialect word meaning to spoil, botch ▌a mess

NAB to seize ▌a hilltop
NAE Scots form of **no**, not any, certainly not
NAG a small horse ▌to worry or annoy constantly
NAM same as **naam**, distraint ▌past tense of **nim**
NAN same as **naan**, slightly leavened bread
NAP to take a short sleep ▌a short sleep
NAS form of obsolete **ne has**, has not, and **ne was**, was not
NAT colloquial form of **nationalist**, a person who strives for the unity or independence of a nation
NAY old form of **no** ▌a denial
NEB a beak or bill ▌to put a bill on
NED a young hooligan
NÉE (of a woman) born
NEF obsolete word for a church nave
NEK South African word for **col**
NEP dialect word for **catmint**, a plant attractive to cats
NET an open material, formed into meshes ▌to catch (fish) in a net
NEW recently made, bought, produced, etc ▌something new ▌old word meaning to renew
NIB the writing point of a pen ▌to provide with a nib
NID a pheasant's nest or brood
NIE obsolete spelling of **nigh** (adjective and verb)
NIL nothing; zero
NIM obsolete word meaning to take or steal ▌an old game involving taking objects (usually matches) alternately from heaps
NIP a small quantity of spirits ▌to pinch
NIS in Scandinavian folklore, a brownie or goblin
NIT a young louse; a fool; a unit of information
NIX nothing; ▌to veto or cancel
NOB a person of high social rank
NOD to move the head forward in assent or greeting ▌such a movement of the head
NOG an egg and alcohol drink; a wooden peg or cog ▌to fix with a nog
NOH same as **no**, a traditional style of Japanese drama
NOM French word for **name**
NON Latin word for **not**
NOR and not; neither
NOS plural of **no**
NOT word expressing denial, negation, or refusal

NOW at the present time; immediately ▌ the present time
NOX nitrogen oxide
NOY Spenserian word meaning to hurt or annoy ▌ vexation, hurt or trouble
NTH adjective implying a large number
NUB the point or gist; same as **knub**, a knob ▌ to hang
NUN a female member of a religious order
NUR same as **knur**, a knot on a tree
NUS plural of **nu**
NUT an edible seed in a hard shell ▌ to look for and gather nuts
NYE obsolete spelling of **nigh** (adjective and verb) ▌ another word for **nid**
NYS Spenserian word meaning **is not**

OAF a lout; an idiot
OAK a kind of tree; its wood
OAR a pole with a blade for rowing a boat ▌ to row a boat
OAT a kind of grass, the seeds of which are used as food
OBA in West Africa, a chief or ruler
OBI West Indian, etc witchcraft; a fetish or charm ▌ to bewitch
OBO a vessel for carrying oil and bulk ore
OBS plural of **ob**
OCA a South American wood-sorrel
OCH Scottish or Irish interjection expressing impatience or regret
ODA a room in a harem
ODD strange; unpaired, left over ▌ in golf, an additional or allowed stroke
ODE an elaborate lyric addressed to someone or something
ODS plural of **od**
OES plural of **oe**
OFF not on; away; not available ▌ in cricket, the off-side ▌ to go off
OFT often
OHM a unit of electrical resistance
OHO an expression of triumph and surprise or gratification
OIK an inferior person; a lout
OIL a greasy, flammable liquid ▌ to smear or lubricate with oil
OKE a Turkish weight
OLD advanced in years; worn out ▌ times past, olden times
OLE Spanish interjection expressing approval or support
OLM a blind salamander
OMS plural of **om**
ONE single; undivided; only ▌ an individual thing or person; the

number or figure 1; a symbol representing it
ONS plural of **on**
OOF slang word for money
OOH an expression of pleasure, surprise, etc ▌ to make such an expression
OOM South African word for **uncle**
OON Scots word for **oven**
OOP same as **oup**
OOR Scots word for **our**
OOS plural of **oo**, Scots word for **wool**
OPE poetic word meaning to open
OPT to decide or choose
ORB a circle or sphere ▌ to form into an orb
ORC an orca, a killer whale
ORD obsolete word meaning a point, eg of a weapon
ORE a solid mineral aggregate
ORF a viral infection of sheep
ORS plural of **or**
ORT dialect word for a leftover from a meal
OUK Scots word for **week**
OUP Scots word meaning to bind with thread or to join
OUR of or belonging to us
OUT not in; excluded ▌ someone or something that is out ▌ to put or throw out; to make public
OVA plural of **ovum**
OWE to be in debt for
OWL a nocturnal predacious bird; a wiseacre ▌ to behave like an owl
OWN to possess ▌ belonging to oneself
OWT dialect word for **anything**
OYE same as **oy**
OYS plural of **oy**

PAD a wad of soft material used to cushion, protect, fill out, etc ▌ to cover or fill with soft material
PAH same as **pa**, a Maori fort or settlement
PAL colloquial word for **friend** ▌ to associate as a pal
PAM the knave of clubs
PAN a broad, shallow container ▌ to wash earth for gold
PAP soft food for infants ▌ to feed with such food
PAR a state of equality; same as **parr**, a young fish, especially a young salmon
PAS French word for **step**; plural of **pa**
PAT a gentle stroke with the palm of the hand ▌ to stroke gently
PAW a clawed foot ▌ to scrape with a paw

3-LETTER WORDS

PAX the kiss of peace; Latin word for **peace**

PAY to hand over money; to be profitable ▌ salary or wages

PEA a vegetable, the rounded seed of a climbing plant

PEC colloquial short form for a pectoral muscle

PED short for **pedestrian**, a person who travels on foot

PEE the letter 'P' ▌ to urinate

PEG a pin or fixture ▌ to fasten with a peg

PEN an implement for writing ▌ to write down on paper

PEP vigour or spirit ▌ to put pep into

PER for each; by

PET a tame animal; a favourite ▌ to treat as a pet

PEW a bench in a church

PHI a letter in the Greek alphabet

PHO same as **foh**

PHS plural of **ph**

PIA a tropical plant

PIC colloquial word for **picture** (noun)

PIE meat, fruit, etc baked in a pastry; confusion ▌ to reduce to confusion

PIG a farm animal bred for food ▌ slang word meaning to eat greedily

PIN a piece of wood or metal used for fastening ▌ to fasten with a pin

PIP a small hard seed in a fruit; offence or disgust ▌ to offend or disgust

PIR a Muslim title of honour, given to a holy man

PIS plural of **pi**

PIT a hole in the earth ▌ to put in a pit

PIU Italian word for **more**

PIX same as **pyx**

PLY a fold ▌ to bend or fold

POA a meadow-grass plant

POD the shell of leguminous plants ▌ to shell (eg peas)

POH interjection expressing impatient contempt

POI a Hawaiian dish, fermented taro

POM colloquial word for a Pomeranian dog

POO slang word for **faeces**, excrement ▌ to defecate

POP a mild explosive sound ▌ to make a pop

POS plural of **po**

POT a utensil for cooking or storing ▌ to cook or put in a pot

POW Scots word for **head** (noun)

POX any of several viral diseases with pustules ▌ obsolete word meaning to infect with pox

POZ old short form of **positive** (adjective)

PRE colloquial word meaning **before**

PRO in favour ▌ someone who is in favour; colloquial short form of **professional** and **prostitute** (nouns)

PRY to examine things with curiosity ▌ an act of prying

PSI a letter in the Greek alphabet

PST interjection used to attract attention

PUB a public house

PUD colloquial word for **pudding**

PUG a small dog with a wrinkled face; clay, ground with water ▌ to grind with water

PUH Shakespearean spelling of **pooh**, interjection expressing disgust, etc

PUN to play on words ▌ a play on words

PUP a young dog ▌ to give birth to pups

PUR obsolete spelling of **purr**, (of a cat) to make a contented sound ▌ the sound made

PUS thick yellowish fluid formed by suppuration

PUT to place; to throw ▌ a push; a throw

PUY a small volcanic cone

PYE same as **pie**, confusion ▌ to reduce to confusion

PYX a box in which coins are kept for testing ▌ to test

QAT same as **kat**, an E African shrub

QIS plural of **qi**

QUA in the capacity of

RAD a unit of radiation dosage

RAG a worn scrap of cloth ▌ to tease or ridicule

RAH an expression of approbation or joy ▌ to make such an expression

RAI a modern, North African form of popular music

RAJ rule, government, or sovereignty

RAM a male sheep ▌ to push or cram down hard

RAN past tense of **run**

RAP a sharp blow ▌ to strike sharply

RAS a headland; an Ethiopian prince

RAT a rodent like a large mouse ▌ to hunt rats

RAW uncooked

RAX dialect word meaning to stretch ▌ a stretch

RAY a beam of light ▌ to radiate
REC a recreation ground
RED of a colour like blood ▌ the colour of blood; something that is red ▌ Scots word meaning to tidy
REE Scots word for an enclosure (for sheep, etc)
REF short form of **referee**, (to act as) an umpire or judge
REH an efflorescence of salts on soil in India, etc
REM a unit of radiation dosage
REN old spelling of **run**
REP a commercial representative ▌ to work or act as a rep
RES short form of (North American Indian) **reservation**
RET to expose to moisture; to soak
REV a revolution in an internal-combustion engine ▌ to increase the speed of revolution
REW Spenserian spelling of **row** (noun)
REX obsolete plural word meaning tricks or pranks
REZ same as **res**
RHO a letter in the Greek alphabet
RHY Spenserian spelling of **rye**, the grass
RIA a drowned valley
RIB a bone curving forward from the backbone ▌ to tease
RID to free or clear
RIG to fit with sails; to equip or clothe ▌ an arrangement of sails and masts; an outfit
RIM an edge or border ▌ to provide with a rim
RIN Scots form of **run**
RIP to tear open or apart ▌ a rent or tear
RIT Scots word meaning to slit ▌ a slit
RIZ US past tense of **rise**
ROB to steal ▌ a fruit syrup
ROC an enormous bird in Arabian legend
ROD a slender stick or bar ▌ to push a rod through
ROE a mass of fish eggs; a small species of deer
ROK same as **roc**
ROM a gypsy man
ROO short form of **kangaroo**
ROT to decay ▌ decay or corruption
ROW a line or rank; a noisy squabble ▌ to quarrel ▌ to propel through water with oars
RUB to apply friction ▌ an impediment or difficulty
RUC same as **roc**
RUD archaic or dialect word meaning redness or complexion

▌ Spenserian word meaning to redden
RUE a strong smelling plant; regret ▌ to regret
RUG a heavy floor-mat ▌ Scots word meaning to pull roughly
RUM a spirit distilled from sugar cane ▌ odd, droll
RUN to move quickly ▌ an act or instance of running
RUT a furrow made by wheels ▌ to make such a furrow
RYA a type of Scandinavian rug
RYE a cereal grass; its grain

SAB a saboteur
SAC in biology, a baglike structure
SAD unhappy, sorrowful
SAE Scots form of **so**, in this way, accordingly, etc
SAG to bend or hang down ▌ an act or instance of sagging
SAI the capuchin monkey
SAL a large North Indian tree; a salt
SAM Spenserian word meaning **together**
SAN old short form of **sanatorium**, a kind of hospital; a Japanese form of address
SAP a liquid circulating through plants ▌ to drain
SAR Scots form of **savour**, (to) taste; a sea bream
SAT past tense of **sit**
SAW a cutting tool with a toothed blade ▌ to use a saw; past tense of **see**
SAX short form of **saxophone**, a musical instrument; a chopper for trimming slates
SAY to utter in words, speak ▌ something said or stated
SAZ a stringed instrument of Turkey, North Africa, etc
SEA a great expanse of water
SEC a secant ▌ of wines, dry
SED Miltonic spelling of **said** (verb)
SEE to perceive by the eye ▌ an area under the authority of a bishop
SEG a stud in the sole of a shoe
SEI a whale, a kind of rorqual
SEL Scots form of **self**
SEN a monetary unit (in Japan, etc) of various values ; a coin of these values
SET to put or place in position ▌ a group; a complete series
SEW to work on with a needle and thread
SEX the quality of being male or female ▌ to identify the sex of

SEY   Scots word for a part of a carcase of beef

SEZ   slang spelling of **says** (verb)

SHE   pronoun used in referring to a female person or thing ▊ a female

SHY   embarrassed; bashful ▊ to jump aside; to recoil

SIB   a blood relation, a kinsman

SIC   thus ▊ Scots word for **such** ▊ to incite (a dog to attack)

SIM   short for **Simeonite**, an evangelical

SIN   moral offence ▊ to commit sin

SIP   to drink in small mouthfuls ▊ a quantity sipped

SIR   a word used in addressing a man ▊ to address as 'sir'

SIS   contracted form of **sister**

SIT   to rest on the buttocks ▊ a spell of sitting

SIX   the number after five

SKA   Jamaican music similar to reggae

SKI   a narrow strip attached to a boot for gliding over snow ▊ to move on skis

SKY   the space visible above the earth ▊ to hit high into the air

SLY   cunning, wily; surreptitious

SMA   Scots word for **small**

SNY   same as **snye**, a side channel of a river

SOB   to cry uncontrollably, taking intermittent breaths ▊ the sound of a breath so taken

SOC   historically, the right of holding a local court

SOD   an obnoxious person; a piece of cut turf ▊ to cover with sods

SOG   dialect word for a soft, wet place ▊ to soak

SOH   same as **sol**, a musical note

SOL   a musical note (in sol-fa); a colloidal suspension in a liquid

SON   a male offspring

SOP   bread, etc soaked in liquid ▊ to soak

SOS   plural of **so**, a musical note

SOT   a habitual drunkard ▊ to act as a sot

SOU   an old small French coin

SOV   short form of **sovereign**, a gold coin

SOW   a female pig ▊ to scatter seed on the ground

SOX   slang spelling of **socks** (plural noun)

SOY   dark, salty sauce made from fermented beans

SPA   a resort with a mineral spring ▊ to stay at a spa

SPY   a secret agent employed to watch ▊ to watch secretly

STY   a pen for pigs ▊ to keep in a sty

SUB   colloquial shortening of **subscription**, **subeditor**, and many other words ▊ to subscribe, subedit, etc

SUD   rare singular form of **suds**, froth of soapy water

SUE   to prosecute at law

SUI   Latin word meaning of himself, herself, itself

SUK   same as **souk**, a market-place

SUM   the total, whole amount ▊ to add, make up the total of

SUN   the star that is the source of light ▊ to expose to the sun's rays

SUP   to take (liquid) into the mouth ▊ a small mouthful

SUQ   same as **souk**, a market-place

SUR   French word for **on**, **above**

SUS   a suspect ▊ to arrest for suspicious behaviour

SWY   an Australian game, two-up

SYE   dialect word meaning to strain ▊ a sieve

TAB   a small tag, flap, or other attachment ▊ to fix a tab to

TAD   a small amount

TAE   Scots form of **toe**, **too**, and **to**

TAG   a tab or label ▊ to put a tag on

TAI   a Japanese sea bream

TAJ   a crown; a dervish's conical cap

TAK   Scots form of **take**

TAM   a cap with a broad circular flat top

TAN   brown colour of the skin after exposure to the sun's rays ▊ to become brown in the sun

TAP   a gentle knock or its sound ▊ to knock gently

TAR   a black bituminous substance ▊ to coat with tar

TAT   shabby articles ▊ to touch up

TAU   a letter in the Greek alphabet

TAW   to prepare skins for white leather ▊ a thong

TAX   a contribution levied towards a country's revenue ▊ to impose a tax on

TAY   dialect, especially Irish, word for **tea**

TEA   a drink made from the dried leaves of a shrub ▊ to take tea

TED   a Teddy boy or girl ▊ to spread out (cut grass) for drying

TEE   a support for a golf ball ▊ to place on a tee

TEF   an Ethiopian cereal grass

TEG   a sheep in its second year

TEL   in Arab countries, a hill or mound

TEN   the number after nine

TES   plural of **te**

TEW to hustle ▌ excitement
THE the definite article
THO Spenserian word for **those** or **then**
THY of thee
TIC an involuntary twitching of muscles
TID Scots word meaning **mood**, a temporary state of mind
TIE to bind, fasten or knot ▌ something for tying
TIG a touch; a game involving touching ▌ to touch
TIL sesame
TIN a silvery-white metal ▌ to coat with tin
TIP a gratuity; a helpful piece of advice ▌ to give a tip
TIS plural of **ti**
TIT a nipple; a small bird; a tug ▌ to tug
TOC telecommunications code for signalling the letter 'T'
TOD an old wool weight ▌ to yield a tod
TOE a digit at the end of a foot ▌ to kick or touch with the toes
TOG a unit of measurement of thermal insulation ▌ to dress
TOM a male cat
TON a unit of weight
TOO also
TOP the highest point, part or level ▌ to cover the top; to surpass
TOR a hill
TOT a small child or drink ▌ to add or total
TOW to pull along (behind) ▌ an act of towing ▌ prepared fibres of flax or hemp
TOY an object for playing with ▌ to play idly with
TRY to attempt; to make an effort ▌ an effort
TUB a small carton; a bath ▌ to bath in a tub
TUG to pull forcibly ▌ a forcible pull, a jerk
TUI a New Zealand bird, a honey-guide
TUM colloquial word for **stomach**
TUN a large cask ▌ to put in a tun
TUP a ram ▌ of a ram, to copulate
TUT interjection expressing rebuke or disapproval ▌ to say 'tut'
TUX short for **tuxedo**, a dinner-jacket
TWA Scots form of **two**
TWO the number after one
TWP dim-witted, stupid (Welsh)
TYE a trough for washing ore ▌ to wash in a tye
TYG an old drinking-cup with two or more handles

UDO a Japanese species of Aralia
UDS old interjection meaning **God's** or **God save**
UEY a U-turn
UFO an unidentified flying object
UGH interjection expressing repugnance ▌ an old representation of a cough or grunt
UGS present tense of **ug**
UKE a ukulele
ULE a Central American rubber tree
UNI colloquial for **university**
UNS plural of **un**
UPS plural and present tense of **up**
URD an Indian bean
URE an extinct wild ox
URN a type of vase ▌ to put in an urn
USE to put to some purpose ▌ the purpose for which something is used
UTE Australian short form of **utility**, a small truck
UTS plural of **ut**
UTU settlement of a debt (Maori)
UVA a grape or grape-like berry

VAC vacation; a vacuum-cleaner ▌ to clean with a vac
VAE same as **voe**
VAN a light transport vehicle ▌ to go or send in a van
VAS a duct carrying liquid
VAT a large vessel or tank ▌ to put or treat in a vat
VAU an obsolete letter in the Greek alphabet
VEE the letter 'V', or anything of that shape or angle
VEG short for **vegetable(s)**
VET a veterinary surgeon ▌ to treat an animal medically; to examine
VEX to distress or annoy ▌ Scots word meaning **grief**
VIA Latin word for **way** or **road** ▌ by way of, through
VID short form of **video**
VIE to contend in rivalry ▌ obsolete word meaning a bid
VIM energy, vigour
VIN French word for **wine**
VIS Latin word for **force**
VLY low-lying wet ground, a swamp
VOE in Orkney and Shetland, a bay or creek
VOL in heraldry, two wings displayed and conjoined
VOR Shakespearean word meaning to warn
VOW a solemn promise ▌ to make a vow or vows
VOX voice

VUG Cornish word for a cavity in a rock
VUM US word meaning to vow

WAD a pad or mass of loose material
▮ to form into a wad
WAE Scots word for **woe**
WAG to move from side to side ▮ an act
of wagging; a habitual joker
WAN lacking colour, pale ▮ to make or
become wan
WAP to throw or pull quickly ▮ a sharp
blow
WAR a state of conflict ▮ to make war
WAS past tense of **be**
WAT a Thai Buddhist temple or
monastery
WAW a Spenserian or Scott word
meaning a wave
WAX a fatty substance ▮ to treat with
wax; to grow larger
WAY a route or passage ▮ Spenserian
word meaning to journey
WEB a fine structure spun by a spider
▮ to envelop with a web
WED to marry ▮ a pledge, security
WEE small ▮ a short distance ▮ to
urinate
WEM old word for **wame**, the womb or
belly
WEN a sebaceous cyst; former name for
wyn
WET containing, or soaked or covered
with, liquid ▮ to make wet
WEX obsolete form of **wax**
WEY a measure for dry goods
WHA Scots form of **who**
WHO pronoun used in referring to a
person or people
WHY for what reason; because of which
▮ a reason
WIG an artificial covering of hair ▮ to
scold
WIN to gain; to be successful ▮ a gain
or victory
WIS sham archaic word meaning to
know
WIT humour; intelligence ▮ archaic
word meaning to know
WOE misery
WOG offensive word for a non-white
foreigner
WOK a pan used in Chinese cookery
WON past tense of win ▮ the monetary
unit of Korea
WOO to court; to seek the support of
WOP offensive word for someone of a
Mediterranean or Latin race
WOS plural of **wo**, woe
WOT facetious spelling of **what**
▮ another form of **wit**, to know

WOW interjection expressing wonder
▮ to impress ▮ anything thrillingly
impressive
WOX obsolete past tense of **wax**
WRY twisted to one side; sardonic ▮ to
give a twist to
WUD Scots form of **wood**
WUS a term used in addressing a
companion (Welsh)
WYE the letter 'Y', or anything shaped
like it
WYN a rune, having the value of modern
English 'w'

XIS plural of **xi**

YAH variant of **yea** ▮ interjection
expressing derision, etc
YAK a species of ox; persistent talk ▮ to
talk persistently
YAM a sweet potato
YAP to bark sharply or constantly ▮ a
yelp
YAW to deviate from course ▮ such a
deviation
YEA yes ▮ an affirmative vote or voter
YEN a Japanese coin; an intense desire
▮ to desire or yearn
YEP variant of **yes**
YES a word of affirmation ▮ an
affirmative vote or voter
YET in addition, besides; nevertheless
YEW a type of evergreen tree
YEX Scots word for **hiccup**
YGO Spenserian past participle of **go**
YIN one of the two opposing principles
of Chinese philosophy
YIP to give a short, sudden cry ▮ such
a cry
YOB a lout
YOD past tense of Spenserian **yead**, to go
YOK a laugh ▮ to laugh
YON that, the thing known ▮ yonder
YOS plural of **yo**
YOU pronoun referring to the person
being spoken or written to
YOW variant of **ewe**
YUG same as **yuga**, one of the four
Hindu ages of the world
YUK something unpleasantly messy,
disgusting or sickly
YUP same as **yep**
YUS plural of **yu**

ZAG a change of direction on a zigzag
course ▮ to change direction on
such a course
ZAP to destroy ▮ vitality or force
ZAX variant of **sax**, a chopper for
trimming slates

ZEA part of a cereal plant, once used as a diuretic

ZED the letter 'Z'; a bar of metal of this shape

ZEE US form of **zed**

ZEK in the former USSR, an inmate of a prison or labour camp

ZEL an Oriental cymbal

ZEX variant of **zax**

ZHO in the Himalayas, an animal that is a cross between a yak and a cow

ZIG same as **zag**

ZIP energy, vitality ▌ to be full of or act with energy

ZIT a pimple

ZIZ a nap or sleep ▌ to take a nap

ZOA plural of **zoon**, a unified individual creature

ZOO a garden or park where animals are kept

ZOS plural of **zo**

ZUZ an ancient Palestinian coin